THE WILD BLUE YONDER :
Songs of the Air Force

Volume II

Stag Bar Edition

C.W. "Bill" Getz – Editor

Keith Ferris – Art

Brig. Gen. Robin Olds – Introduction

The Redwood Press   **Burlingame, California**

A division of Syntax Associates

FIRST EDITION

© 1986 by: THE REDWOOD PRESS
                    P. O. Box 412
              Burlingame, CA 94011-0412

Pen & Ink Aircraft Drawings By Keith Ferris:
© 1985 Keith Ferris

Reproduction in any manner, in whole or in part is
prohibited. All rights are reserved.

LIBRARY OF CONGRESS Catalog Card Number: 81-52998
                Volume II of two volumes

ISBN: 0-941196-49-6

COVER PHOTO: Courtesy of TRW, Inc.
                  Westinghouse Electric Corp.

GRAPHICS: Walter W. Zawojski

Printed in the United States of America

WARNING

This is a word of warning--a warning to those readers whose tender sensibilities may--or more accurately will --be offended by the language of some of the ballads in this volume. But it is no apology to them. For these are songs that are sung by flying officers and men throughout the English speaking world. They reflect the manners of men at war, the morals of pilots who drink to forget for an evening the combat mission they must fly at dawn. Many of these lyrics were adopted to the Korean and Vietnam "situations" after becoming popular among the same warriors during World Wars I and II, and at least one or two were sung around the campfires on the eve of Gettysburg.

It follows, therefore, that they are not the product of a particular degenerate generation. They are instead, as they always have been, an integral part of military life in the field, no more and no less than a cold tent, bathing in a helmit, dehydrated potatoes and dysentery.

You must accept or ignore them as we accept or ignore the conditions that inspired their authors to write them and us to sing them.

* * * * *

Adapted and updated from "Songs My Mother Never Taught Me," song book of the 18th Fighter-Bomber Wing -- Korea 1956

DEDICATION

TO THE HEROES OF VIETNAM

The United States of America entered the Southeast Asian conflict with a noble purpose -- to protect a nation and its people from communist oppressors. When the dust settles, and time has placed those times in the proper perspective of history, the Vietnam War will not be remembered as the war we lost, but rather as the war we did not want to win.

Despite this extra burden to carry, while fighting the most difficult war in our history, the American fighting man displayed unusual valor and dedication. He was never defeated on the battlefield by the enemy, but by some members of Congress who did not support the American military or South Vietnam; by some irresponsible members of the news media who undermined the determination of the public; by some civilian leaders who lacked the courage and moral turpitude to prosecute the war, and interfered with battlefield decisions; and by American traitors who gave aid and comfort to the enemy--in some cases broadcasting from Hanoi for the enemy while American prisoners were being tortured. These traitors will be forever remembered along with the other Benedict Arnolds of history.

Vietnam Veterans have much to be proud of. They served in the highest traditions of the United States military, and for the highest ideals of mankind. They did not fail. The Nation failed them.

With humility at the inadequacy of words, and with pride in what they did, this book is dedicated to the American **Heroes of Vietnam**.

INTRODUCTION

INTO THE WILD BLUE WITH BRIGADIER GENERAL ROBIN OLDS . . . .

O.K., he couldn't read a note of music and played piano in only one key. His friend, Tooey Spaatz, either accompanied or led (no one was sure which), and certainly didn't pluck on a twelve stringed classical guitar. But they sang, that pursuit pilot father of mine and his dashing, flamboyant friends from World War I days. They sang with a gusto, spirit, and enthusiasm that matched their approach to life itself. They sang with the confident pride of men who had every reason to respect one another and who shared a common bond of love for that vault of heaven, *the wild blue yonder*. Saturday nights the strains of **Dinah, 'Ole Virginny, Tipperary** and **Beside A Belgian Water Tank**, wafted in sweet, if uncertain harmony to the top of the stairs where this little boy sat entranced. I was thrilled to eavesdrop and longed for the day when I would be a pilot and sing like that. I didn't have to know why, but I knew it was fun and sharing and part of what my dad and his friends stood for. I wanted to belong and sing about the water tank, the **Mademoiselle From Arementieres**, and those objects of scorn, **The Kiwis** and members of **The SOS**, whoever and whatever they were.

Then one day it happened! As we marched to our first class in primary flight training, someone struck up, *I've got sixpence, jolly, jolly sixpence . . .* We bawled it out lustily in cadence to our steps and in tune with all that was happening that summer of 1942. We suddenly felt ourselves a part of the big picture, and we were one with our heroes of the Battle of Britain and Guadalcanal. Today, the PT-19, tomorrow the WORLD! Look out Tojo and Hitler, we were on our way. That one song did more for us that any traditional, *Benny Havens* or *Tom Sawyerish* football claptrap at West Point had ever done. It gave us identification, and a sense of sharing and belonging. Just that one song.

Not until we reached England in May of 1944 did I realize my Battle of Britain heroes probably never sang anything so blatantly goodie-two-shoes as *sixpence*. Their songs were down-to-earth, direct and live-for-today. They voiced a warrior's ritual of definance: screw you, world, screw what you're doing to me, and screw the horse you rode in on. And their songs separated them from the reality of another empty chair in the mess. To Hell with tomorrow!

Ribald and bawdy, RAF voices rose in exalted deification of mankind's bodily functions (*or more particularly and specifically, of woman's*). There were derisive songs about certain aircraft and those who built them, sung mostly by those who had survived flying the things. There were songs about the bumbling asses in higher headquarters who, . . . *run and they shout, talking of things they know nothing about!*, in contrast to the . . . *boys that fly high in the sky, bosom buddies while boozing.* And sometimes, not often, there were sad songs, late in the evening, when defiance had abated, and a measure of lonely hopelessness crept in; . . . *Stand to your glasses steady, Here's a toast to the dead already, Hoorah for the next man to die!*

The origins of nearly all of these songs lie deep in the mists of time, certainly in expression if not in exact form. You can't tell me Rameses' victorious troops didn't sing marching back to Egypt; or Alexander's adventurers didn't invent derisively bawdy songs about Darius the Great and his concubines. Down through the ages came these expressions of the warrior's reaction to his profession, words and music suitable to the era, the sentiment fitting all the ages.

In 1942, as America's young fighting men spread around the globe, these songs percolated into their mess tents in New Guinea by way of Australia. They became a part of squadron life in the deserts of North Africa by way of the RAF's Desert Air Force. They were learned in British pubs and on contact with the men of the RAF. They were a delightful addition to America's own milder creations, and helped infuse an entirely new gusto in our appreciation of ourselves in the crucible of combat. The **Belgian Water Tank** magically moved to New Guinea and became a **Waterfall**. The bowel movements of **Adelaide Schmidt** were of direct and delighted concern to all from Moresby to Benghazi. **Mary Ann Burns'** fundamental orifice was known, admired, and sung about from sea to shining sea. *Sally's* flatulence rocked fliers in every bar from Sydney to Southhampton. And that granddaddy of them all, **The Bloody Great Wheel**, ground out its function to the delight of thousands around the world, including, I suspect, some of those wearing the uniform of the Luftwaffe.

The vast force reduction at the end of World War II left a small number of squadrons scattered in the Zone of the Interior (continental U.S.) and overseas. These were manned by the relatively few combat veterans remaining on active duty. These men came from all theaters of operation, and from all manner of squadrons. They brought with them not only a global background of combat expertise, but also a global repertoire of warrior's songs. In effect, this small handful of pilots had become an important reservoir of professionalism and of future ribald enlightenment.

Then came Korea. The old heads returned to combat to be joined by a new group of fledglings. The physical and emotional demands of that unpleasantness brought forth an explosion of creative musical talent. The songs of yore were still howled at the rafters, while completely new, lyrical expressions of contempt, defiance, humor, and sadness were happily and widely adopted. The results were unique in that the old ballads, while never supplanted, were matched by songs of strictly American origin.

In the years between Korea and Southeast Asia, singing became a normal and eagerly accepted ritual at U. S. fighter bases at home and abroad. The *Dining-In* (not originated by General Hap Arnold as tradition has it), was accepted as a part of military life; the *Stag Bar* was recognized (albeit not universally) as a necessary fixture. Both provided an eminently suitable environment for comrade, joshing, fun-loving steam-blowing, and song.

The drawn out war (yes, Virginia, it was a war) in Southeast Asia evoked perhaps even deeper passions than had WW II and Korea. For one thing, it lasted longer. For another, it had its own brand of horror and its own type of heroes.

More than even before, diverse units worked in close cooperation with one another, leading to a broad understanding and a mutuality of respect among the men involved. No song in memory matches the emotional depth of respect and gratitude expressed by the jocks at Ubon Airbase singing, *Jolly Green, Jolly Green, prettiest sight I've ever seen.* Anyone who ever flew over Laos and the Vietnams, remembers the call sign *Jolly Green*, representing the chopper crews who were there, *That others may live*, and were your sole source of rescue should you, too, go down in that jungle Hell. And we'll always remember a rendition of Dick Jonas', a haunting melody questioning whether . . . *the sun will rise tomorrow, or whether there will be any time left to borrow.* Not that this was sung at the bar, but it was certainly listened to on all the brand new tape machines in the quiet of the hooches, a sure indication of the nature of the other side of the emotional coin.

Never mind the sad and the sentimental, the new songs of SEA were overwhelmingly of the bawdy and rigid-middle-digit genre'. They would have delighted the hearts of true warriors throughout the ages. Old and new, they are all now being sung just as lustily from Kunsan to Bitburg, and from Myrtle Beach to Luke. It doesn't end. You want to know why? I'll tell you a secret. *Wars change. The men who fight them don't.*

We owe a debt of gratitude to Bill Getz for this compilation. All of us have old, mimeographed squadron song books stashed away in footlockers. Most of today's units have their own updated versions. But I doubt that anyone in recent times has had the interest and courage to put it all down between hard covers. Lord help the candy-asses or the little old ladies who might pick up a copy. But then, if they don't understand, they might learn something. If they don't learn anything, they shouldn't have picked up the book in the first place.

I still wonder if my dad ever sang, **The Balls of O'Leary** or **Ring Dang Doo**. I cannot believe that he didn't. How could those men of steel in wings of fabric have survived otherwise? Surely, a generation that revels in bathtub gin, bra-less flappers, rolled-silk stockings, and the **Black Bottom**; that gave us the giants of aerial knighthood, who made a joke of national prudery; who brought to fruition their dream of air power--surely they knew and sang, *Fuck 'Em All!*

Check Six!

Robin Olds
Brigadier General
USAF (Retired)

ROBIN OLDS

Born on an Army post in Honolulu in 1922, *the first sounds I remember were the cough of Liberty engines warming up at dawn, and the slap of the rope in the night wind against the flagpole in the parade ground.* In this way, General Robin Olds recalls his childhood as an *Army Brat*. His father was Major General Robert Olds, a flight instructor in France during World War I, and aide to Billy Mitchell, and a pioneer in heavy bombers in the mid-1930s. Robin grew up at Langley Field, Virginia, and Army posts throughout the world. Class president for three consecutive years in high school, he entered West Point in the summer of 1940, where he was captain of the football team and an All-American tackle. He went into combat crew training immediately upon graduation in 1943, and was assigned to the Eighth Air Force in England.

Olds first saw action in the summer of 1944 flying the P-38 with the 434th Squadron, 479th Fighter Group. Although a latecomer to the war, he learned quickly, downing two aircraft on 14 August and three more on 25 August 1944. More success followed, and his two victories on 14 February 1945, brought his total to nine, and made him the Eighth's top-scoring P-38 pilot of the war. His unit then converted to the P-51 Mustang, and Olds added three more aerial victories, ending the war with 107 combat missions and an impressive total of twelve air-to-air victories and eleven aircraft destroyed on the ground. He won the British and American Distinguished Flying Crosses for his wartime exploits, and had been promoted to the rank of major at the age of twenty-two.

After the war, Robin Olds continued to meet challenges head on. He was a co-founder and team member of the Air Force's first jet aerobatic team. Flying the P-80, he placed second in the Thompson Trophy race in Cleveland in 1946. On 12 June 1946, he participated in the first round trip transcontinental flight completed in one day. He became the first American to command a regular Royal Air Force squadron when he took the helm of the famous No. 1 Squadron at Tangmere, England in 1948, flying the RAF's first operational jet fighter, the Gloster Meteor.

In the early '50s, Olds was assigned to an Air Defense unit, and then staff and command positions in the United States, Germany and Libya. These were followed by command of the 81st Tactical Fighter Wing in England. In 1963 he graduated from the National War College, and later, in 1966, assumed command of the 8th Tactical Fighter Wing, the *Wolfpack*, at Ubon, Thailand.

Robin Olds' achievements as commander of the *Wolfpack* are legendary. He led the famous **Operation Bolo** MIG sweep mission on 2 January 1967, in which he shot down his first jet aircraft, almost twenty-two years after his last victory in Europe (see the Keith Ferris painting of this event on the dust jacket of Volume I). He scored a total of four MIG kills in 117 missions over North Vietnam, bringing his career victory tally to sixteen. He was subsequently promoted to Brigadier General and returned to the United States as Commandant of Cadets at the Air Force Academy, followed by an assignment as the Air Force's Director of Aerospace Safety. He currently resides in Steamboat Springs, Colorado.

FLIGHT OF THE EGO . . . .

England - 1944

C. W. "Bill" Getz is a writer, publisher, educator, and general "busybody". Retired from the Air Force in 1962, he was gainfully employed in industry and government in the fields of computers and tele-communications until his venture into the mad, mad, literary world.

Bill was one of the youngest 4-engine crew commanders in the Air Force (19 years old)—maybe the youngest. He flew his first tour with the 491st Bomb Group (B-24) 8th U.S. Air Force. His second tour in P-51s was with the 2nd Air Division Scouting Force. Bill completed his second tour and was a captain before he could legally drink|

The next 17 years were an exciting mixture of flying, the H-Bomb program, and the Air Force's ballistic missile and space program.

Between 1962 and 1980, Bill was with an aerospace firm; Assistant Controller of the Atomic Energy Commission; Vice President of a national credit reporting company; Vice President of an international credit card company; and Regional Commissioner for Automated Data & Telecommunications for the General Services Administration in San Francisco. That ended his indentured career.

He lists two major accomplishments: (1) the privilege of being married to two great women, Jo and Vicki—not at the same time, of course. And (2) being blessed with three wonderful children.

Since 1980, Bill has worked full-time as a publisher and writer. He publishes nonfiction and writes fiction adventure novels. He does not plan to retire, and expects to live forever.

California - 1986

PREFLIGHT

THERE I WAS . . . .

> *. . . over Berlin, flat on my back, four engines feathered and hanging by my throat mike . . . That was the good news. The bad news was that I forgot to mail my monthly life insurance premium!*

This rather corny joke illustrates something about the songs in Volume II. The *There I was* is one of hundreds of a series of puns to come out of the second world war. They even evolved into well-known cartoons by Bob Stevens that continue today (1986) in **Air Force** magazine. The second part of the pun--the *good news, bad news* is instantly recognizable as a more recent craze in story-telling. Combining the two marries the old with the new. And that is what Air Force songsters have done--married the old songs of the Air Corps with the new Air Force. And, yes, some of the songs are also pretty corny.

But time does march on, and several new elements entered the Air Force scene that have influenced the songs Airmen sing. Even the term *Airmen*, as applied to both male and female members of the Air Force raises a few hackles here and there. It isn't only the gender influence. The number of mature (translate *old*) members of the AF family--the retired ranks--has dramatically increased in recent years. It may be difficult for some to realize that it has been over a decade since the United States withdrew from Southeast Asia. And the World War II types are celebrating as many as 45 year reunions; and there are song books and songs written just for reunions (See Class 40A songs in this volume).

A third element is slowly creeping into Air Force song compositions--technology change. Sure, AF songs have always reflected changes in type of aircraft--**Give Me Operations** is a fine example. But the influence of missiles is starting to enter the scene. General Russ Dougherty, former Strategic Air Command Commander (SAC), and now (1986) Executive Director of the Air Force Association, suggested to the Editor that Volume II include songs of SAC and missile units. The quest was dismal until just before publication of this volume. Air Force Major Scott McElvain sent a tape of songs and lyrics to the Editor that had them all; eleven songs about missile crewmen, and six hilarious songs of SAC airmen. The Editor was able to trace the composer of ten of the missile-related songs to Vandenberg AFB--what more appropriate spot. He is Major Rollie Stoneman, who was kind enough to provide a recording and the lyrics to his songs. In addition to these terrific songs, several other missile-related goodies are in Volume II. One is a hilarious, non-song, that the Editor has named an *Epistle* (**Missile Combat Crew Lament**). There is one Air Force Missile Test Center song, one Army song about missiles the Editor just had to include (you'll see why), and a real scoop--an original song, both lyrics and music, titled, *The Air Force*, by Marvin Liblick, A.S.C.A.P. This is a march that brings the Air Force right up-to-date with lyrics that include astronauts, rockets and space.

Los Angeles Times' Paul Dean said in an article about the Editor and Volume I (Los Angeles Times, June 26, 1985), *It seems that two guys staring at a red button in a concrete bunker just don't stir sentimental juices.* Could be, but they are certainly inspired to write some hilarious antedotes about the life of our missile crews. Thanks to Majors McElvain and Stoneman, the Air Force is off into *The Wild Space Yonder* -- at least in song.

A HISTORICAL NOTE OR TWO . . .

There are some wonderful tidbits of Air Force history in song in Volume II as in Volume I. As an example, through the efforts of Lieutenant General Truman Spangrud, three songs have been added to the collection that are priceless treasures of Air Force memorabilia from the Vietnam War. It seems that the Pentagon Powers of the time devised a scheme for conducting the day-to-day airwar that was very unpopular with just about everybody that had to do the fighting. This idiot brain child was given the name, *Rapid Roger*. The story will be found with the song, *On The Day That Rapid Roger Died* (Song 0023). The other two *Rapid Roger* songs are, *Gotta Travel On* (GG06) and *Olds And The Eighth Wolf Pack* (0017).

The ballads in Volume II, again, like Volume I, cover the period from World War I through the Vietnam War, but, unlike Volume I, there are songs published as recently as 1980 by Air Force songsters. Special events in Air Force history have not been forgotten by the Bards in Blue. The Berlin Airlift was a big event for the Air Force and the world, and *The Airlift Song* (AA12), captures that historical moment in time that broke the Russian blockade.

Even the Iranian Hostage crisis did not escape the attention of Air Force balladeers. The *Ayatollah Song* (AA25) must be the result of a very fired-up Blue-suiter who reads the *riot act* to the Ayatollah in verse.

For a more comprehensive discussion about Air Force songs and their history, see the **Preflight** section in Volume I.

THE AVIATION ART OF KEITH FERRIS . . .

The Editor's collaborator on this book, the great American artist, **Keith Ferris**, deserves a special note of recognition for his many years of contribution to the United States Air Force. The Volume I dust jacket contains two reproductions of oil paintings by Keith. Volume II contains 21 original pen and ink sketches he created especially for this book. The aircraft subjects of these sketches, like the songs in the books, span the history of the Air Force--and there are missiles, too.

Keith grew up in the Air Force. His father, Carlisle I. (Lisle) Ferris, served in the Air Force from 1926 to 1956, and trained many of the early pilots. Keith was told by his parents that he began drawing airplanes when he was four years old. His early ambition for an Air Force flying career was dashed by an allergy problem, but that did not stop his interest. Today, he is recognized as one of the finest aviation artists in the world. His 75′ by 25′ mural of B-17s in the Smithsonian Air & Space Museum has been seen by millions. His paintings hang in private collections and in the halls of the Pentagon. The Air Force still flies him all over the world as part of the Air Force Art Program. Keith has flown in many of the latest and oldest of Air Force aircraft. He said in his book, *The Aviation Art of Keith Ferris*, *And perhaps by documenting flight, I have found a way to serve my country after all.* Keith, you have and **are** serving it well.

CAN YOU BELIEVE 1000 AIR FORCE SONGS? . . .

O. K., 997 songs and 11 poems to be exact. That's the number in Volumes I and II. There are 336 songs or variations, 5 poems, 7 toasts, and several miscellaneous items in Volume II. About half of the ballads fall into the bawdry category--some spell it *bawdy*. We used to say, *dirty*, but that seems so *unliterary*. Other songs are new to the collection, and date from World War I to the latest, a song book for the 1985 reunion of the Flying School Class 40-A. The tradition goes on. The latest Air Force unit song book is dated 1980 (from the 95th Fighter Interceptor Squadron).

The coarse, obscene--or bawdry--songs are mostly English in origin; probably from the famous music halls of London that flourished years ago. But it is war itself that seems to bring out the *worst and the best* in men (and women, it should be added). As one dirty song sage remarked;

> *Oh, it is in war the bawdy ballad thrives: up to the waist in urine or blood or even rain, men begin to sing, and richly. I must say I have never well understood why it is that those who order and control such fine wars are so prudish about the cultural harvest that is reaped from a really sopping trench or freezing billet.*

Regardless of one's feelings about the X-rated songs, they are a part of the heritage of war, and thus, a part of the heritage of the Air Force. Every bawdry--all right, bawdy if you prefer--song in this collection came from an Air Force unit song book, one or more of those listed in the **Tech Orders** section, as did all of the songs in Volume I. There are some minor exceptions: those individual songs submitted by a few of the many kind contributors to this collection. They are listed in the **Tech Orders** section.

HOW TO FIND THE SONGS . . .

As in Volume I, songs and their variants have been grouped together in the text so that the reader can compare different versions of the same song, often representing different wars, as with the 16 parodies of the old American folk-song, *The Dying Hobo*, represented in this Volume by two songs, *Beside An Oahu Waterfall*, from World War II; and *Laotian Karst*, from the Vietnam War. Sometimes the differences between songs represents differences between aircraft as well as the wars. The previously mentioned, *Give Me Operations* is probably the classic in this regard, and there are new, great verses in this volume to add to the many in Volume I.

In the **Checklist** (table of contents) songs are listed alphabetically, not including the word, *The* when it is the first word of the title. Song titles beginning with an *A*, like *A Doggie Pilot's Lament,* are listed under "A." Since many songs have more than one title, all songs and their variants are listed together in the **Checklist**, and grouped together in the **Flight Section** (text) regardless of the alphabetical order of their titles. The alphabetical sections are named with a double alphabetical character, i.e., *AA* or *BB*, in Volume II to differentiate from those in Volume I. This is only important when references are made to songs in a particular Volume. You got all that?

AND THE MELODY LINGERS ON . . .

For those of you who want to know the melodies to the songs, the tune has been indicated in the text with the song title when the tune is known. Some of the titles to the tunes may be strange and unknown. That's the nature of parodies. They are often based upon very old folksongs or songs popular in earlier centuries. You either know the tune or you don't--or you can see if the words will fit to a melody you do know. The Editor did this to several in this book, as you will note. If you really get stuck, and must know the tune, call the Editor and he'll try to struggle through it with you. No collect calls or calls after 9:00 P.M. West Coast time! The Editor needs his beauty sleep. But seriously, in some cases the Editor does have the musical score and would be pleased to share these with serious (sober) researchers.

A FEW MEA CULPAS . . .

Apologies that is, for a few errors or omissions in Volume I that have come to light. A number of renditions of songs were not 100% correct as presented in Volume I, and the Editor is indebted to those who brought errors to his attention. You will find clearly marked, corrected lyrics in Volume II. But not all are errors. The Editor also included the tune to many Volume I songs that were not known at the time of its publication.

A few additional tidbits of information about Volume I songs were received from Ed Cray, author of *The Erotic Muse* (see Tech Orders section). Ed says the song *In The Middle Of Salisbury Plain* (Volume I, song I13), is a version of *Paddy Works On The Erie*, which can be found in Carl Sandburg's *American Songbag*, page 356. This is an interesting reversal for a Royal Air Corps song to be a parody of an American song. Many U. S. Air Force songs are taken from the British. Maybe this has something to do with Lend-Lease (in WW I?).

Ed also says that the Volume I song, *Northrup's Folly* (N12) is sung to the tune, *She's Too Fat For Me*. *Beer Hall Chant*, song B16, is a variant of *Samuel Hall*, versions of which will be found in both Volumes I and II. Thanks Ed.

According to Jack Havener, the song, *Dirty Lil* (Song D7, Volume I), is sung to a fractured version of *Little Brown Jug*.

AND ONE FINAL WORD . . .

As Four Star General Jimmy Doolittle said in the Introduction to Volume I (he got his fourth star since publication of Volume I--probably because of the stirring introduction he wrote! What? You don't believe that!), *The history of the Air Force is captured in melody in this unique collection of songs sung by airmen.* General Doolittle is correct. Songs of the Air Force are but expressions of the times, the events, the sorrows, the joys, the frustrations, the hopes; all of the emotions of the people who fight the wars and keep the peace. This Volume was proudly dedicated to the **Heroes of Vietnam**, but in truth, the songs of the Air Force are a tribute to all of the men and women who wear or have worn Air Force blue--or khaki. So, buckle up, and here we go . . .

Off Into The Wild Blue Yonder -- and beyond!

MUSIC TRIVIA:

The music of **For He's A Jolly Good Fellow** *was written by Ludwig von Beethoven. So was the music of* **My Country 'Tis of Thee,** *also known as* **God Save The Queen (or King).** *Both were passages from Beethoven's* **Wellington's Victory**. *The music to the great military classic,* **Stand To Your Glasses** *was written by Mozart, and titled,* **Away With Melancholy.**

TRUE MUSIC

(by an unknown author of World War I)

These boys have won to glory
In battle everywhere,
Tremendous is their story
And yet the bard's despair;
For though their deeds astounding
Thrill all your heart and brain,
They'd jeer the minstrel sounding
A fine heroic strain.

They speak of war's endeavor
When men are mowed like wheat,
Of things that live forever,
In slang of field and street;
Seek you for tales of duties
Where trenches run with blood,
They grin and talk of *cooties*
Of *Army chow* and mud.

What though their fame hereafter
Shall gleam in living fire?
The singer courts their laughter
Unless he strikes his lyre
In accents syncopated
And makes the cat-gut thrum
To simple music, freighted
With tunes that they can hum.

So, if their songs lack splendor
Of deeds that echo far
It is because they render
Our soldiers as they are,
But if you care to hear it
The faith they will not own--
The true heroic spirit
Is in the undertone.

TECH ORDERS

AND CHECKLISTS

TECH ORDERS
(SOURCES AND CREDITS)

SONGBOOKS OF MILITARY ORGANIZATIONS

1. **Air Force Songs And Verses,** songbook of the Royal Air Force (London: Aeronautics, Ltd., 1927).
2. **Amarillo Field Airs,** Amarillo Army Air Field, Texas, undated, probably 1942-44 period, Brigadier General Arthur Easterbrook, Commander.
3. **Army Song Book,** War Department, 1918.
4. **Army Song Book,** The Adjutant General's Office, 1941.
5. **Beeliners Sing,** Song Book of the 21st Troop Carrier Squadron.
6. **Kun Songs By The Sea,** Kunsan Air Base, Korea.
7. **Lowry Field Song Book,** Lowry Army Air Field, undated, probably 1942-44.
8. **More Kunsongs By The Sea,** compiled by "Slither" (?), Kunsan Air Base, Korea, 16 May 1977.
9. **Nuthampstead Hit Tunes,** 398th Bomb Group, 8th Air Force, England.
10 **Official Hymnal of the 421st Tactical Fighter Squadron**
11. **Songbook - 18th Fighter Bomber Wing,** Kadena Air Base, Okinawa, 1957 (originally the songbook of the 18th Pursuit Group of pre-WW II days. See #12, below.
12. **Songs My Mother Never Taught Me,** 18th Pursuit Group, Pre-World War II.
13. **Songs My Mother Never Taught Me,** Royal Australian Air Force, Japan/Korea, 1950-51.
14. **Songs Of Nellis Air Force Base,** date unknown.
15. **Songs Of SEA And Other Places, Other Things** (no other identification).
16. **Songs Of Squadron Officers Course,** 1953.
17. **Songs Of The Army Fliers,** (Order Of The Daedalians: 1937).
18. **Songs Of The Friendly 8th,** 8th Bomb Squadron, 3rd Bomb Wing, Korea.
19. **Songs Of The 8th Fighter Wing,** attributed to three persons (probably three different editions); Capt. George S. Thomas, Lt. "Rosie" Rosencrans and Capt. William F. "Romeo" McCrystal, 1952.
20. **Songs Of The 11th Fighter Interceptor Squadron,** Korea.
21. **Songs Of The 49th Fighter-Bomber Wing,** compiled in 1952 by Willy Williams.
22. **Songs Of The 325th Fighter Interceptor Squadron,** Hamilton Air Force Base, CA, 1954.
23. **Songs Of The 327th Fighter Interceptor Squadron,** compiled by Mr. Penn Bowers, North American Aviation, Korea.
24. **Songs That Kearnsmen Sing,** Camp Kearns 5th B.T.C., Utah, 1942-44
25. **Songs To Drink By,** 355th Tactical Fighter Wing, Takhli, RTAFB, Thailand ("Yankee Air Pirates").
26. **Souvenir Song Book** 45th Reunion Flying School Class 40-A, 1985.
27. **Stag Bar Supplement To Songs Of SEA, And Other Places, Other Things** (Item 2)
28. **Stovepipe Serenade,** 2nd Edition, 1956, compiled at the Worldwide Rocketry Meet, Vincent Air Force Base, Arizona. The First Edition was published in 1954.
29. **We're Here For Fun,** (unidentified song book - may be Kirtland AFB songbook, 1950s vintage.
30. **Women's Army Corps (WAC) Song Book,** War Department, 1941.
31. **8th Tactical Fighter Wing Stag Bar** (see Item 7 above). Kunsan Air Base, Korea.
32. **15th Fighter Interceptor Squadron Songsheet,** no other identification).
33. **92nd Tactical Fighter Squadron** Song Book.
34. **95th Tactical Fighter Interceptor Training Squadron** Song Book.
35. **339th Fighter Interceptor Squadron Songbook,** Johnson Air Base, Japan.
36. **405th Green Dragon Squadron Songsheet,** 38th Bomb Group (B-25).
37. **437th Fighter Interceptor Squadron Songbook** (no other identification).
38. **445th Fighter Interceptor Squadron Songbook** (no other identification) 1954.
39. **523rd Tactical Fighter Squadron Fighter Pilot's Songbook,** 2nd Edition (no other identification)

BOOKS

1. *Air Force Airs*, Army Air Forces Aid Society, 1943.
2. *Air Force Airs*, William Walrich, ed., (New York: Duell, Sloan and Pierce) 1957.
3. *Airman's Song Book*, C. H. Ward-Jackson, ed., Royal Air Force (Edinburgh & London: William Blackwood & Sons, Ltd.) 1970.
4. *The American Songbag*, Carl Sandberg, ed., (New York: Harcourt, Brace & Company) 1927.
5. *The Book of Navy Songs*, The Trident Society (New York: Doubleday, Doran & Co.) 1942.
6. *Buddy Ballads*, Songs of the A.E.F., Berton Bradley (New York: George H. Doran Company) 1919.
7. *The Erotic Muse*, Ed Cray (New York: Pyramid Communinications, Inc.) 1972.
8. *G.I. Songs*, Edgar A. Palmer, ed., (New York: Sheridan House) 1944.
9. *Popular Songs Of The A.E.F.*, American Expeditionary Force Y.M.C.A., Paris, 1918.
10. *The Saga of the Seventh* (not certain this is a book or chapter), page 149.
11. *The Second Army Air Service History*, 1st Lt. Hugo Law, ed., (Nancy, France: Berger-Levrault) 1919.
12 *Singing Soldiers*, John J. Niles (New York: Charles Scribner's Sons) 1927.
13. *So Little Time*, John P. Marquand, (Boston: Little, Brown & Co.) 1943.
14. *Songs & Music of the Redcoats*, Lewis Winstock (London: Leo Cooper, Ltd.) 1970.
15. *Songs For Swinging Housemothers*, James Leisy (San Francisco: Fearon Publishers, Inc.) 1961.
16. *Songs From The Front & Rear*, Anthony Hopkins (Edmonton: Hurtig Publishers) 1979.
17. *Songs My Mother Never Taught Me* (New York: The Macaulay Co.) 1929.
18. *Songs The Soldiers And Sailors Sing* (New York: Leo Feist, Inc.) 1918.
19. *Sound Off*, Edward Arthur Dolph (New York: Farrar & Rhinehart).
20. *The Three Hats*, The Drunken Press (privately published by Dick Boutelle, former President of Fairchild Aircraft Corp.), undated, but post WW II, probably pre-Korea.
21. *The Three Hats - Volume II*, The Drunken Press (see #9), post WW II, undated, post Korea.
22. *Weep Some More My Lady*, Sigmund Spaeth, (Garden City, NY: Doubleday, Page & Co.) 1927.
23. *Ye A. E. F. Hymnal*, (Nancy, France: Berger- Levrault, Publishers) 1918.

MISCELLANEOUS SOURCES

1. *Advance To Memory*, 390th Strategic Missile Wing publication, 1970.
2. *Air Force* magazine, "Air Mail" section, December, 1982.
3. *Folklore Forum*, "Folksongs of the American Fighter Pilot in S.E.A. 1967-68", Joseph Tuso, Folklore Forum Society, Folklore Institute, Bloomington, IN.
4. *Ladycom* magazine, "Daughter's Letters," Patti O'Donoghue, August, 1983.
5. *Western Aerospace Museum Newsletter*, Oakland, CA, 1983.

CONTRIBUTORS

SPECIAL ACKNOWLEDGEMENTS: There are a few people and companies that deserve special recognition for their contribution to this collection and the production of this book. The Editor has tried to include everyone, but should someone have been inadvertently left out, profuse apologies are extended.

Thanks to **Robin Olds** for a truly outstanding and appropriate introduction to Volume II. When the Editor first asked General Olds to take on this task, his response was immediate and positive. He said he had been looking for an opportunity to express some deep and long-held feelings, which he has eloquently done. His introduction was not edited. With his gift of writing--Robin could write some great stories. And he should.

And *thanks* to **Dr. Reuben Mettler**, Chairman and C.E.O. of TRW Inc. The cover photograph was originally used in a joint advertisement by TRW/ Westinghouse in *Air Force* magazine. The Editor knew that was the picture for the cover. He also knew that he would soon see Rube Mettler at the 30th Anniversary meeting of the **Schoolhouse Gang**, the Air Force missile pioneers (they started in 1954 in an abandoned schoolhouse in Inglewood, California). At the reunion, the Editor told Rube he wanted to *con* him out of something. Rube was no stranger to the Editor's cunning, but this brilliant scientist/executive was overcome by the awesome charm and persuasive powers of the Editor, and had his able staff, Dr. Gerry Morton and Valerie Clark, provide a color transparency.

INDIVIDUALS - KNOWN: A special *thanks* is extended to those persons who sent collections and individual songs. Unfortunately, this list is not complete and only includes recent contributors and not the many helpful people over the past years whose contributions are deeply appreciated, if unacknowledged (ranks indicated if they were given):

Mickey Balsam
Jim W. Baugh
Captain Jeffrey Brown
George F. Coen
John R. Cooley
Colonel William A. Donnelly, Jr.
Kaye *Ramrod* Downing
Glenn R. Fitzgerald
Captain Marc *Mongo* Frith
G. P. Harry
Jack K. Havener
George Hocutt
Lt. Col. William F. *Toby* Hughes
Mathew J. Johnson
Captain Jon C. Kahl
John E. Kennard
Lt. Colonel Horace S. Levy
Marvin Liblitz, ASCAP

Julian MarDuck, M.D.
Major Scott McElvain
Allen T. "Red" Miller
Robert H. Murray
Captain Michael P. Nishimut
Lt. Col. John Piowaty
Milt Rasmussen
Bill Richards
Peter Seeger
Lt. Colonel Russ Shaw
William W. Siler
Lt. General Truman Spangrud
Major E. W. Spiller
Major Carlton A. Stidsen
Howard Stillwell
Major Rollie Stoneman
Joseph F. Tuso
Lt. Colonel George L. Weiss

COPYRIGHT GRANTORS - KNOWN: To the Editor's knowledge, there is only one copyrighted song in Volume II. The sources for most of the songs in the collection are published Air Force unit song books, and seldom do these indicate copyrights. Sometimes The Editor *goofs* as he did in Volume I. After publication, the Editor received a letter from Mickey Balsam that said he was the composer and copyright holder of that great song, **Lilly From Piccadilly** (Volume I, song L9). After reviewing Volume I, Mickey kindly gave us his blessing. In another case, the Editor discovered in a round-about way that Lt. Colonel Toby Hughes is the composer of the lyrics to three songs from Volume I, (1) *Armed Recce* (A33), (2) *One-Hundred Sixty VC In The Open* (O30), and *Tchepone* (T04). Toby pointed out some changes in the Volume I versions of his songs from the originals. The changes may have been made by another AF jock to fit the song to his own situation--a common source of parodies. So, the Editor is pleased to reprint two of Toby's songs in Volume II; *Armed Recce* and *Tchepone*. The Editor is also delighted to acknowledge the creative contributions of Mickey and Tobey.

COPYRIGHT OWNERS - UNKNOWN: Finally, to any holders of copyrights (or composers) that the Editor missed, his appreciation for your wonderful songs, and his apologies for not having obtained your permission to use the words of your songs. Ignorance is his plea.

And another thanks to Vicki . . . . whose help, understanding and encouragement were the most important contributions made to the production of Volumes I & II. And she continues to be a daily joy and inspiration to the Editor.

A thanks to Peggy . . . . who keeps the brushes steady, busy, unfettered--and the brush-holder, Keith Ferris, happy.

And to Jo . . . . on a different plane of existence at a different place in time, but never forgotten.

POINT TO PONDER . . . .

> *I hope that the United States of America has not yet passed the peak of honor and beauty, and that our people can still sustain certain simple philosophies at which some miserable souls feel it incumbent to sneer. I refer to some of the Psalms, and the Gettysburg Address, and the Scout Oath. I refer to the Lord's Prayer, and to that other oath which a man must take when he stands with hand uplifted, and swears that he will defend his country.*

General Curtis E. LeMay

PILOT'S PSALM

(by Chaplain E. R. Jones)

The Lord is my pilot; I shall not crash. He maketh me fly in clear skies; he leadeth me down to smooth landings, he keepeth my chart. He guideth me through the pathless ways of the skies for His Name's sake. . . . Yea, though I fly through the storms and tempests of life, I shall dread no danger; for thou are near me; Thy love and Thy care, they protect me . . . . Thou preparest an airport before me in the homeland of eternity; Thou emblazoneth the skies with thy beauty; my plane flies gracefully. Surely sunlight and starlight shall favor me on the flight I take, and I will abide in the presence of my God forever.

Republic F-105

CHECKLIST AA
(*Table of Contents*)

KEYS			KEYS	
(s)	= similar to		(K)	= Korean War
(i)	= identical to		(V)	= Vietnam War
(I)	= World War I		(U)	= Unknown
(II)	= World War II		(N)	= No war association

==

TITLE	WAR	PAGE
01. A BABBLING BROOK...	K	AA1
(i) *Bubbling Brook*		
02. ABDUL ABULBUL EMIR (*Also see Vol. I*)......................	II	AA1
(i) *Abdul*		
(i) *Abdul A Bul Bul Ameer*		
(i) *Ivan Skavinski Skavar*		
03. ADELINE SCHMIDT...	V	AA2
(i) *Blinded By Shit*		
(s) *Brown, Brown*		
(i) *Madeline Schmidt*		
04. A DOGGIE PILOT'S LAMENT (*See TT17*)........................	POST V	TT10
05 AERIAL ADVENTURE..	I	AA3
06. AEROPLANE COMMANDER, THE....................................	PRE-II	AA3
07. AGGRESSORS TDY SONG, THE....................................	V	AA4
08. AH, SWEET MYSTERY OF LIFE...................................	K	AA4
(i) *Nellie*		
(i) *Nell(y)ie Darling*		
09. AIR FORCE, THE..	POST V	AA4
10. AIR FORCE LAMENT (*S.E.A. Version. Also see Vol. I, A19*)....	V	AA5
(s) *Air Corps Lament*		
(s) *The Air Force Has Gone To Hell*		
(S) *Glory Flying Regulation*		
11. AIR FORCE SONG (*Variant of official song. See Vol.I, U8*)...	V	AA5
12. AIRLIFT SONG, THE...	POST II	AA6
00. AIRMAN'S LAMENT or THE BIG WHEEL (*See BB24*)...............	K	BB16
00. AI, YI, YI, YI (*See SS17*)................................	V	SS7
13. ALCOHOLIC BABY..	POST K	AA6
14. ALICE BLUE GOWN...	K	AA6
00. ALPHABET SONG (*See AA17*)..................................	K	AA7
00. AN ENGINEER'S SONG (*See BB24*).............................	V	BB16
00. ANGELES POM-POM SONG (*See MM03*)...........................	K	MM2
15. A NIGHT IN KUNSAN KOREA.....................................	K	AA7
(i) *A Night In Town*		
(i) *A Soldier Dreams of An AWAS*		
16. ANOTHER GREETING FROM WESTERN UNION (*Also see SS16*)........	V	SS7
17. ANTHONY ROLY...	II	AA7
(i) *Alphabet Song*		

	TITLE	WAR	PAGE
18.	A POOR AVIATOR LAY DYING (S.E.A.) *Also see Vol. I, A30*.....	V	AA8
19.	A PROHIBITION SONG...	POST V	AA9
20.	ARCHIE..	I	AA9
00.	ARMED RECCE (*Also see Vol. I, A33*)........................	V	AA10
00.	A SHAU CANYON BRAWL, THE (*See BB02*).......................	V	BB1
21.	ASHAU VALLEY..	V	AA11
00.	A SOLDIER DREAMS OF AN AWAS (*See AA15*)....................	K	AA7
22.	ASS HOLES ARE CHEAP TODAY...................................	II	AA11
23.	A TISKET-A TASKET (*Air Force version*).....................	POST V	AA12
00.	A TWO-TON TITTY (*See TT13*)................................	POST V	TT7
00.	A VERY FINE SONG (*See SS17*)...............................	K	SS7
24.	AXTATER'S FLIGHT..	PRE-II	AA12
25.	AYATOLLAH SONG..	POST V	AA12

CHECKLIST BB

	TITLE	WAR	PAGE
00.	BAD MOUTH (*See Vol. 1, C20*)...............................	V	C6
01.	BALLAD OF AFMTC...	N	BB1
02.	BALLAD OF BERNIE FISCHER....................................	V	BB1
	(i) *A Shau Canyon Brawl*		
	(i) *Hobo 51*		
03.	BALLAD OF THE C-130...	V	BB2
04.	BALLAD OF FUNAFUTI, THE.....................................	II	BB3
05.	BALLAD OF MACHETE TWO, THE (*See HH6*)......................	V	HH5
06	BALLAD OF MEAN GENE...	POST V	BB3
07.	BALLAD OF THE GREEN BRASSIERE...............................	V	BB4
00.	BALLAD OF THE MIG-21 PILOT (*See Vol. I, W37*)..............	V	W14
08.	BALLAD OF THE P.I.O...	V	BB4
09.	BALLAD OF THE VARK..	V	BB5
10.	BALL AT KERRIMURE, THE......................................	V	BB6
	(i) *The Ball of Ballynoor*		
	(i) *The Ball of Kerrymoor*		
	(i) *Balls to Your Partner*		
	(i) *The Great Bloody Ball*		
	(i) *Scotch Wedding*		
11.	BALL OF YARN...	K	BB8
	(s) *That Little Ball Of Yarn*		
12.	BALLS OF O'LEARY, THE.......................................	II	BB9
00.	BALLS TO YOUR PARTNER (*See BB10*)..........................	POST V	BB6
13.	BANG, BANG LULU (*similar to BB14, below*)..................	K	BB9
14.	BANG IT INTO LULU (*similar to BB13, above*)................	K	BB9
15.	BARNACLE BILL...	POST V	BB10
	(s) *Barnacle Bill The Pilot-I* (See Vol. I, B13)		
16	BARNACLE BILL THE PILOT - II................................	POST V	BB10
17.	BASTARD KING OF ENGLAND, THE................................	II	BB12
18.	BATTLE OF DOUMER BRIDGE.....................................	V	BB12

TITLE		WAR	PAGE
19.	BATTLE HYMN..	K	BB13
	(i) *Battle Hymn of the Thud (or Phantom, Jug, etc.)*		
	(i) *Fighter Pilot's Hymn (not same as in Vol.I)*		
	(i) *The Thud (or Phantom, Jug, Sabre, etc.;)*		
00.	BATTLE HYMN OF THE THUD (*or Phantom, Jug, etc. See BB19*)...	K	BB13
20.	BEELINER SONG...	POST K	BB13
21.	BESIDE AN OAHU WATERFALL (*Also see Volume I*)................	PRE-II	BB14
	(All versions below in Volume I except as noted)		
	(s) *Beneath A Bridge In Sicily*		
	(s) *Beside A Belgian Staminet*		
	(s) *Beside A Belgian Watertank*		
	(s) *Beside A Brewery At St. Mihiel*		
	(s) *Beside A (New) Guinea Waterfall*		
	(s) *Beside A Korean Waterfall*		
	(s) *Beside A Minnesota Waterfall*		
	(s) *Beside A Tucson Waterfall*		
	(s) *Laotian Karst (Volume II)*		
	(s) *Laotian Waterfall*		
	(s) *The Passing Pilot - I*		
	(s) *The Passing Pilot - II*		
	(s) *Ting-A-Ling*		
	(s) *To Cadets Who Failed At Kelly*		
	(s) *Under A Korean Sun*		
	(s) *U. S. Air Force Heaven*		
	(s) *The Warthog Driver (Volume II)*		
	(s) *The Young Pursuiter*		
22.	BIG BALLS..	V	BB15
00.	BIG GREY RAT, THE (*See Vol. I, G12*)........................	POST K	BB16
00.	BIG WHEEL, THE (*See BB24*)..................................	II	BB16
00.	BIRD, THE (*See Vol. I, L12*)................................	V	L16
23.	BLESSED ARE WOMEN..	K	TT16
00.	BLESS 'EM ALL (*See Vol. I, B33 & Vol. II, TT24*)............	II	BB16
00.	BLINDED BY SHIT (*See AA03*).................................	II	AA2
24.	BLOODY GREAT WHEEL, THE......................................	K	BB16
	(i) *Airman's Lament*		
	(i) *Engineer's Song*		
	(i) *The Big Wheel*		
	(i) *The Great Fucking Wheel*		
	(i) *Sweet Violets*		
	(i) *The Wheel*		
25.	BLUE HEAVEN...	K	BB16
	(i) *Little Red Light*		
	(i) *My Red Haven*		
26.	BLUES IN A FIGHT...	II	BB17
27.	BLUE STAR, THE (*Also see Vol. I, M23*)......................	V	BB17
28.	BMTS BLUES (*not necessarily correct title*)................	POST V	BB17
29.	BOMBER PILOT'S LAMENT..	II	BB18
00.	BOOM TODAY (*Also see Vol. I, B47*)..........................	K	BB18

TITLE	WAR	PAGE
30. BORN LOSER, THE (M)...................................	POST V	BB18
31. BOSOM BUDDIES - II (*Also see Vol. I, A14*).................	POST V	BB18
(i) *Bosom Buddies - I*		
(i) *Boozin' Buddies*		
(i) *Stand To Your Glasses*		
00. BRIDGE, THE (*Also see Vol.I, W37*)......................	V	W14
00. BRING BACK MY C-54 (*See Vol. I, B53*)...................	POST K	BB19
32. BRITISH GRENADIERS...................................	K	BB19
33. BROWN ANCHOR....................................	K	BB19
34. BROWN, BROWN (*See AA03*)...........................	K	AA2
00. BUBBLING BROOK (*See AA01*).........................	K	AA1
35. BUGGARED..	K	BB20
36. BUMMING AROUND TOWN..............................	K	BB21
37. BYE, BYE CHERRY..................................	U	BB21
38. BYE, BYE USAF...................................	U	BB22
39. BY THE LIGHT....................................	POST V	BB22
(i) *Flickering Match*		
00. B-18 SONG.......................................	PRE-II	BB22

CHECKLIST CC

TITLE	WAR	PAGE
00. CAFOOZALEM (*See KK01*)...........................	K	KK1
01. CALL OUT THE ARMY AND THE NAVY	II	CC1
(s) *Fleet Air Wing - Alma Mater (See Vol. I, F23)*		
(i) *Gor Blimey*		
(s) *I Don't Want To Be A Soldier*		
(i) *I Don't Want To Be A 'Ero*		
(i) *I Don't Want To Join The Army (Air Force)*		
(i) *Piccadilly*		
(s) *Sidney Special*		
02. CANDLER'S BOY, THE...............................	K	CC2
03. CANDLE SONG, THE.................................	K	CC2
04. CAROLINA, THE COWPUNCHER'S WHORE.....................	POST V	CC2
(s) *Charlot The Harlot*		
05. CASE OF THE ILL-STARRED LOVERS......................	K	CC3
06. CATS ON THE ROOFTOP..............................	K	CC3
(i) *You Revel In The Joys of Copulation*		
00. CHARLOT THE HARLOT (*See CC04*).....................	K	CC2
07. CLASS OF FORTY-A.................................	POST V	CC4
08. CLEAN SONG, THE.................................	K	CC5
09. CLEAR THE PATTERN................................	POST V	CC6
10. COLONEL TARA'S BAND (*Also see Vol. I, E20*).............	POST K	CC6
(s) *Early Abort*		
11. COLUMBO..	II	CC6
(i) *Columbus*		
12. COMIN' BACK TO YOU (M)............................	POST V	CC7

TITLE		WAR	PAGE
13.	COMING AROUND THE MOUNTAIN (*not what you think it is*)......	V	CC8
14.	COMMERCIAL ADVERTISING...................................	K	CC8
15.	COOL..	K	CC9
00.	COPILOT'S LAMENT, THE (*Also see Vol. I, C27*).............	II	CC9
16.	CRAWLING & CREEPING......................................	K	CC9
	(i) *Creeping & Crawling*		
17.	CREW THAT NEVER RETURNED - I (M), THE....................	POST V	CC10
18.	CREW THAT NEVER RETURNED - II, THE.......................	POST V	CC10

CHECKLIST DE

01.	DANGEROUS DAN MCGREW.....................................	II	DE1
	(i) *The Grooving of Dan McGrew*		
02.	DARK AND DREAMY EYES.....................................	II	DE1
	(s) *Old Soldiers Never Die - II (Also See Vol. I, 024)*		
03.	DAY OF THE EAGLE, THE....................................	V	DE3
04.	DEAR MOM...	V	DE3
	(i) *The FAC Song*		
05.	DEL RIO HOMESICK BLUES...................................	POST V	DE4
06.	DILL DO, THE...	U	DE5
07.	DON'T BURN THE SHIT-HOUSE DOWN...........................	K?	DE5
	(i) *Our Outhouse*		
	(i) *Outhouse Song*		
	(i) *Please Don't Burn The Shit-house Down*		
08.	DON'T CRY LADY...	V	DE5
09.	DOWN IN THE VALLEY.......................................	K	DE5
10.	DO YOU KEN (Know) MY SISTER TILLY?.......................	II	DE6
	(s) *My Family*		
11.	DO YOUR BALLS HANG LOW?..................................	K	DE6
12.	DUCHESS, THE...	U	DE7
	(i) *Highland Tinker*		
	(i) *Tinker, The*		
	(s) *Thinker, The*		
13.	EIGHTH TACTICAL FIGHTER WING.............................	V	DE7

CHECKLIST FF

00.	FAC SONG, THE (*See DE04*)...............................	POST V	DE3
00.	FIGHTER PILOT (*See Vol. I, YZ4*)........................	II	YZ2
00.	FIGHTER PILOTS EAT PUSSY (*See SS17*)....................	K	SS7
00.	FIGHTER PILOT'S HYMN (*See BB19*)........................	K	BB13
00.	FIGHTER PILOT'S TOAST (*See TT22*).......................	V	TT15
01.	FIGHTING HOOTERS...	POST V	FF1

TITLE	WAR	PAGE
02. FINICULE, FINICULA..	U	FF1
(i) *Funiculi, Funicula*		
(s) *Last Night*		
(i) *Last Night I Stayed Up*		
03. FIRST WITH THE 21ST......................................	POST K	FF2
04. FLEETING GLANCES..	II	FF3
00. FLICKERING MATCH (*See BB39*)............................	V	BB22
05. FLYING COLONEL, THE......................................	II	FF3
(i) *Recce To Berlin (Vol. I, R6)*		
(i) *Recce To Pyongyang (Vol. I, R6)*		
06. FORESKIN FUGITIVES......................................	K	FF4
07. FORTY-A HOO-RAY..	POST V	FF4
08. FORTY-A IS HERE...	POST V	FF4
09. FORTY-A IS THE WAY......................................	POST V	FF5
10. FOUR-NINETY-SECOND......................................	V	FF5
11. FORTY-EIGHTH BEER CALL..................................	V	FF5
00. FOUR BASTARDS, THE (*Also see Vol. I, F20*)...............	II	FF5
00. FRIAR OF GREAT RENOWN (*See MM10*).......................	V	MM7
12. FRIGGIN' IN THE RIGGIN'.................................	K	FF5
(i) *The Good Ship Venus*		
13. FUTURES (THE PILOT).....................................	I	FF7
14. F-4K SONG, THE..	V	FF8

CHECKLIST GG

TITLE	WAR	PAGE
00. GABE 01 (*See HH06*).....................................	V	HH4
01. GANG BANG SONG, THE.....................................	POST V	GG1
(i) *Gang Bang*		
02. GAY CABALERO, THE.......................................	K	GG2
(s) *I Once Was A Gay Cabalero*		
03. GHOST FUCKERS IN THE SKY (*Also see Vol. I, G1*).........	K	GG2
(s) *Ghost Flyers In The Sky*		
04. GIVE ME OPERATIONS (*S.E.A. version. Also See Vol. I, G4*)...	V	GG3
(s) *I'd Rather Fly A Warthog*		
(s) *Just Give Me Operations (See Vol. I, G4)*		
05. GLORIOUS..	U	GG6
00. GONNA TIE MY PECKER TO A TREE (*See TT21*)...............	POST V	TT14
00. GOOD SHIP VENUS, THE (*See FF12*)........................	K	FF5
00. GOR BLIMEY (*See CC01*)..................................	K?	CC1
06. GOTTA TRAVEL ON...	V	GG7
00. GREAT BLOODY BALL (*See BB10*)...........................	U	BB6
00. GREAT FUCKING WHEEL (*BB24*).............................	K	BB16
07. GREECY HOG, THE...	POST V	GG7
00. GROOVING OF DAN MCGREW (*See DE01*)......................	II	DE1
08. GRUNT SONG, THE...	V	GG8
09. GUNNER'S BOY..	POST V	GG8
10. GYPSY 93RD, THE...	II	GG9

TITLE	WAR	PAGE

CHECKLIST HH

01	HAIL TO THE AIR GUARD OF VIRGINIA.......................	POST V	HH1
00.	HAIRS ON HER DIKI-DI-DOO (See MM01).......................	V	MM1
02.	HALLELUJAH - III (S.E.A.) See TT17.......................	V	TT11
03.	HAMBURG ZOO, THE.......................	II	HH2
	(s) *The Wild West Show - I*		
	(s) *The Wild West Show - II*		
04.	HANG DOWN YOUR BOOM, ROSS COOLEY.......................	POST V	HH3
	(i) *KC-135 Boom Operator*		
00.	HARLOT OF JERUSALEM, THE (See KK01).......................	K	KK1
05.	HAVE YOU TRIED YESSUP?.......................	K	HH4
06.	HELLO, CAM RANH TOWER.......................	V	HH4
	(s) *Air Force 801 (Vol. I, A17)*		
	(s) *The Ballad of Machete Two (Vol. II)*		
	(i) *Gabe 01 (Vol. II)*		
	(s) *Itazuke Tower (Vol. I, A17)*		
07.	HERE'S TO BROTHER	POST V	HH6
08.	HIGH FLIGHT (A Poem).......................	II	HH7
00.	HIGHLAND BALL (See BB010).......................	II	BB6
00.	HIGHLAND TINKER (See DE12).......................	POST V	DE7
09.	HINKY DI (S.E.A.) Also See Vol. I, H23.......................	V	HH7
10.	HI ZIGGIE ZIGGIE.......................	V	HH8
00.	HOBO 51 (See BB02).......................	V	BB1
11.	HOLIDAY ON WINGS (*not original title*).......................	II	HH8
12.	HOME IN THE HOLE (M).......................	POST V	HH9
13.	HOME ON THE PAD.......................	POST V	HH9
14.	THE HORSESHIT SONG (See MM10).......................	K	MM7
15.	HUMORESQUE.......................	K	HH10
	(s) *Sherman's Horse (Vol. I, S26)*		
	(s) *Was It You Who Did The Push'n? (Vol. II)*		

CHECKLIST II

01.	I AM EAGLE.......................	V	II1
00.	I DON'T WANT TO BE A 'ERO (See CC01).......................	II	CC1
00.	I DON'T WANT TO BE A SOLDIER (See CC01).......................	II	CC1
00.	I DON'T WANT TO JOIN THE AIR FORCE (ARMY) See CC01.........	POST V	CC1
02.	I'D RATHER FLY A WARTHOG (See GG04).......................	POST V	GG4
00.	IF ALL LITTLE GIRLS (See RR08).......................	K	RR5
00.	IF ALL THE YOUNG MAIDENS (See RR08).......................	POST V	RR5
03.	I FLY THE LINE.......................	V	II1
04.	IF YOU FLY (*Also see Vol. I, B47*).......................	POST V	II2
	(s) *Boom Today*		
	(s) *Will You Go Boom Today?*		
00.	I HEADED DOWN THE RUNWAY (See TT17).......................	POST II	TT9

TITLE	WAR	PAGE

05.   I KNOW A GIRL FROM ARKANSAS.................................. POST V   II2
06.   I'LL SEE YOU IN MY DREAMS (*not commercial version*)......... II   II3
07.   I LOVE MY BEAR... V   II3
08.   I LOVE MY GIRL .... U   II3
    (i) *I Love My Wife*
09.   I'M AN ASSHOLE... V   II4
10.   I'M DREAMING OF A WHITE MISTRESS............................. K   II4
11.   I'M LOOKING UNDER.. K   II4
00.   I'M YOUR MAILMAN (*See MM02*)................................ K   MM1
12.   IN AN OLD KENTUCKY TOWN...................................... U   II4
13.   IN BOHUNKAS TENNESEE... II   II4
    (s) *Hail You Fighter Pilots (See Vol. I, H3)*
14.   IN MOBILE.. K   II5
15.   IN THE SPRINGTIME.. K   II6
16.   IN THE TALL GRASS.. K   II6
    (i) *Tall Grass*
17.   INTO THE AIR JUNIOR BIRDMAN (*Also see Vol. I, S53*)......... II   II6
    (s) *Into The Air Army Air Corps*
    (s) *Into The Air 69ers*
    (s) *Official Song of Randolph Field*
    (s) *Spirit Of The Air Corps*
    (i) *Up In The Air Junior Birdman*
18.   I SAW HER SNATCH... K   II7
19.   I SMELL KIMSHEE.. K   II7
20.   IT DON'T HURT ANYMORE.. V   II7
21.   IT'S A LIE (*Also see Vol. I, Y4*).......................... K   II7
    (s) *You Can Tell A Fighter Pilot*
22.   IT WAS ROUGH IN OLD MANILA................................... POST II   II8
00.   IVAN SKAVINSKI SKAVAR (*See AA02*)........................... U   AA1
23.   I WANT A SPAD.. I   II8
24.   I WANT(ed) TO PLAY PIANO IN A WHOREHOUSE..................... K   II8

CHECKLIST KK

01.   KATHUSELEM... K   KK1
    (i) *Cafoozalem*
    (i) *The Harlot of Jerusalem*
    (i) *Methuselem: An Ancient Love Song*
00.   KC-135 BOOM OPERATOR (*See HH03*)............................ POST V   KK2
02.   KHARTOUM... II   KK2
03.   KIMPO BLUES.. K   KK2
04.   KIMPO SONATA (*Also see Vol. I, P13*)....................... K   KK3
    (s) *Perrin to Youngstown*
05.   KI YI YIPPIE... K   KK3
06.   KOTEX SONG... K   KK4
    (i) *You Can Tell by the Smell*

TITLE	WAR	PAGE

CHECKLIST LL

01.	LANCASTER LEAVING THE RUHR (*See TT24*)...........	II	TT17
02.	LAOTIAN KARST (*See BB21*).........................	V	BB14
03.	LAST NIGHT (*See FF02*)............................	K	FF1
00.	LAST NIGHT I STAYED UP (*See FF02*)...............	POST V	FF1
04.	LEE'S HOOCHIE.....................................	K	LL1
05.	LET 'OLE MOTHER NATURE HAVE HER WAY...............	K	LL2
06.	LIFE PRESENTS A DISMAL PICTURE....................	K	LL3
07.	LIQUOR AND LONGEVITY..............................	K	LL3
08.	LISTEN HOOTERS....................................	POST V	LL3
09.	LITTLE ANGELINE...................................	K	LL4
	(i) *Poor Little Angeline*		
10.	LITTLE BOXES (M)..................................	POST V	LL5
00.	LITTLE RED LIGHT (*See BB25*)......................	K	BB16
10.	LITTLE TOWN OF HO CHI MINH........................	V	LL5
11.	LUPEE NUMBER ONE..................................	II	LL6
12.	LUPEE NUMBER TWO..................................	II	LL6
00.	LYMERICKS (*See SS17*).............................	V	SS7

CHECKLIST MM

00.	MADELINE SCHMIDT (*See AA03*)......................	V	AA2
01.	MAID OF THE MOUNTAIN..............................	K	MM1
	(i) *The Mayor of Bayswater*		
	(i) *The Hairs on Her Diki-Di-Doo*		
02.	MAILMAN'S SONG, THE...............................	POST V	MM1
	(i) *I'm Your Mailman*		
03.	MANILA POM-POM SONG...............................	II	MM2
	(i) *Angeles Pom Pom Song*		
	(i) *Rum & Coca Cola*		
00.	MAN IN THE MOON (*See RR08*).......................	K	RR5
04.	MARAUDER'S SONG, THE..............................	II	MM2
05.	MARRYING KIND, THE................................	K	MM3
06.	MARY ANN BURNS (*also Byrnes and Barnes*).........	II	MM4
00.	MAYOR OF BAYSWATER, THE (*See MM01*)..............	K	MM1
07.	MEDARIS, VON BRAUN AND ME.........................	POST K	MM4
00.	METHUSELEM: AN ANCIENT LOVE SONG (*See KK01*).....	V	KK1
08.	MISSILE COMBAT CREW LAMENT (An Epistle)...........	POST V	MM5
09.	MOM'S IN BED......................................	K	MM6
10.	MONK, THE...	K	MM7
	(i) *The Friar of Great Renown*		
	(i) *The Friar's Song*		
	(s) *The Horseshit Song*		
	(i) *On A Stump*		
11.	MOTHER HUMPER'S BALL..............................	K	MM8

TITLE	WAR	PAGE

12. MRS. MURPHY..	U	MM8
13. MU GIA..	V	MM8
14. MUSTANG PILOT'S SONG..	II	TT17
15. MY FAMILY (*See DE10*)......................................	II	DE6
16. MY GAL'S A CORKER..	K	MM8
17. MY GIRL..	U	MM9
18. MY GRANDFATHER'S COCK......................................	U	MM9
19. MY HUSBAND'S A COLONEL.....................................	U	MM9
00. MY RED HAVEN (*See BB25*)..................................	K	BB16
20. MY WARTHOG FLIES OVER THE OCEAN............................	POST V	MM10

CHECKLIST NN

00. NAIL FAC SONG, THE (*See Vol. I, D1*)......................	V	DE1
01. NAUGHTY LITTLE DOG...	K	NN1
00. NELLIE DARLING (*Also Nelly*) *See AA08*...................	K	AA4
00. NINETY-FOURTH'S SQUAWK (*Same as Vol. I, B50*).............	V	B18
02. NINETY-THIRD LAMENT..	II	NN2
03. NO BALLS AT ALL - I..	K	NN2
04. NO BALLS AT ALL - II.......................................	K	NN3
05. NOMCOMBATANT ASSHOLES......................................	V	NN3
06. NOVEMBER (M)...	POST V	NN4

CHECKLIST OO

01. ODE TO A BOMBARDIER (*A Poem*).............................	II	OO1
02. ODE TO A GREAT FUCKIN' SAR EFFORT..........................	V	OO2
03. ODE TO A SYDNEY LEAVE......................................	II	OO3
04. ODE TO THE FOUR-LETTER WORDS (*A Poem*)....................	N	OO5
05. ODE TO THE RETIRED WEATHERMEN..............................	POST II	OO6
00. OFFICIAL SONG OF RANDOLPH FIELD (*See Vol.I, S53*).........	PRE-II	S18
06. OFF WE GO - II (*Also see Vol. I,O8*)......................	V	OO7
07. OF THE MISERY OF LIVING IN SIN.............................	II	OO7
08. OH, BEAUTIFUL..	POST V	OO8
09. OH, MY DARLING "54"..	POST K	OO8
10. OH MY GOD..	K	OO8
11. OH, NOW I AM A KAYDET (*Revised. Also see Vol. I, O11*).....	PRE-II	OO8
12. OH, RIP THE FEATHERS AWAY..................................	K	OO9
13. OH, RUBY...	POST V	OO9
14. OLD BAZAAR IN CAIRO, THE...................................	V	OO9
15. OLD GREY BUSTLE..	K	OO10
16. OLD KING COLE..	K	OO10
00. OLD KUNSAN (*See Vol. I, K23*).............................	K	OO11
17. OLDS AND THE EIGHTH WOLF PACK..............................	V	OO11

TITLE	WAR	PAGE
18. OLD SMOKEY (*Also see Vol. I, 036 through 043*)............	V	0012
(s) *On Top Of Old Baldy*		
(s) *On Top Of Old Fuji*		
(s) *On Top Of Old Hanoi*		
(s) *On Top Of Old Pyongyang*		
(s) *On Top Of Old Ranier*		
(s) *On Top Of Old Smokey-Air Version (Vol. II & Vol. I)*		
(s) *On Top Of Old Pop-Up*		
19. OLD SOLDIERS NEVER DIE - II (*See DE02: Also see Vol. I, 024*)	II	0013
20. OLD 95TH GANG..	POST V	0013
21. O'LEARY'S BALLS......................................	V	0013
00. ON A STUMP (*See MM10*)...............................	K	MM7
00. ONE-EYED RILEY, THE (*See 0027*)......................	II	0016
22. ONE-EYED TROUSER SNAKE, THE...........................	V	0014
23. ON THE DAY THAT RAPID ROGER DIED......................	V	0014
24. ON THE LINE (M).......................................	POST V	0015
25. ON TOP OF OLD SMOKEY (*See 0018*).....................	POST V	0012
26. OPERATIONS AND WEATHER................................	POST K	0015
27. O'REILLY'S DAUGHTER...................................	K	0016
(i) *The One-Eyed Riley*		
28. OUR LEADERS...	V	0016
00. OUR OUTHOUSE (*See DE07*).............................	K	DE5
00. OUTHOUSE SONG (*See DE07*)............................	K	DE5

CHECKLIST PP

	WAR	PAGE
01. PHANTOM (*A Poem*)....................................	V	PP1
02. PHANTOMS IN THE SKY...................................	V	PP1
00. PICCADILLY (*See CC01*)...............................	II	CC1
00. PILOTS ALWAYS EAT PUSSY (*See SS17*)..................	POST V	SS7
00. PILOT'S LAMENT (*Also see Vol. I, P17*)...............	II	PP1
03. PILOT'S MATING CALL...................................	V	PP1
00. PILOT'S TOAST (*See TT22*)............................	N	TT15
00. PIMPING THE AIR FORCE (*See CC01*)....................	POST V	CC1
04. PIPER LAURIE..	K	PP2
05. PISS ON THE (*Unit Name*).............................	K	PP2
06. PLAINS (M), THE.......................................	POST V	PP2
00. PLEASE DON'T BURN THE SHITHOUSE DOWN (*See DE07*)......	K	DE5
07. PLEASE DON'T PUT YOUR PANTS ON........................	K	PP3
00. POOR LITTLE ANGELINE (*See LL09*).....................	K	LL4
08. PORTIONS OF A WOMAN, THE..............................	K	PP3
09. PUBIC HAIRS...	U	PP4
10. PUFF, THE TRAGIC WAGON................................	V	PP4
11. PULL YOUR SHADES DOWN MARYANN.........................	II	PP4
12. P-39 TALE, THE..	II	PP4

TITLE	WAR	PAGE

CHECKLIST RR

TITLE	WAR	PAGE
01. RANGY LIL...	U	RR1
00. RECCE TO BERLIN (*Also see Vol. I, R6*).....................	II	RR2
02. RED RIVER VALLEY - III (*Also See Vol. I, P23*).............	V	RR2
(i) *Po River Valley*		
03. REMEMBER...	K	RR3
04. REPUBLIC BATTLE HYMN, THE................................	POST V	RR3
(i) *One Little Teensy-Weensy Bomb*		
(i) *Tons and Tons of Ammunition*		
(i) *The B-17 (B-29, B-36, B-52, F-94, etc.)*		
05. RETURN, THE (*A Poem*).....................................	II	RR3
06. RICKEY DAN DO (*Also see RR7, below*)......................	K	RR4
07. RING DANG DO (*Also see RR6, above*).......................	K	RR4
08. ROLL YOUR LEG OVER - I...................................	K	RR5
(i) *If All Little Girls*		
(i) *If All The Young Maidens*		
(i) *The Man In The Moon*		
09. ROLL YOUR LEG OVER - II..................................	K	RR6
10. ROMANTIC NEW GUINEA......................................	II	RR7
11. RO-TIDDLE-EE-O...	U	RR8
00. RUM AND COCA COLA (*See MM03*)............................	II	MM2

CHECKLIST SS

TITLE	WAR	PAGE
01. SAC LAMENT, THE..	POST V	SS1
02. SALLEY IN THE ALLEY......................................	K	SS1
(i) *Sally*		
03. SALOME...	K	SS1
04. SAMMY SMALL - II (*Also see Vol. I, S10*)..................	V	SS2
(i) *Samari Sall (Korean Version)*		
(s) *Sam Hall*		
(s) *Samuel Hall*		
(s) *Sammy Small - I*		
05. SAMMY SMALL - III (*Also see SS04 above*).................	V	SS3
06. SAT TROOP LULLABY (M)....................................	POST V	SS3
07. SAVE A FIGHTER PILOTS ASS (*See TT17 and Vol. I, F13*)......	II	TT12
00. SCOTCH WEDDING (*See BB10*)...............................	K	BB6
08. SCROTUM..	POST V	SS4
09. SEXIATUS MANIA...	K	SS4
10. SHEEPHERDER LAY, THE.....................................	K	SS4
(i) *The Sheepherder*		
11. SHE JUMPED INTO BED......................................	K	SS5

TITLE	WAR	PAGE
12. SHE WAS POOR BUT SHE WAS HONEST (*Also see Vol. I, P21*).....	K	SS5
(s) *Poor But Honest*		
(s) *Twenty-Seventh Lament*		
13. SHIT HOT FROM KARAT...................................	V	SS5
00. SHITHOUSE, THE (*See DE07*)............................	POST V	DE5
14. SIDE BY SIDE..	POST K	SS6
15. SILVER THREADS AMONG THE GOLD.........................	II	SS7
16. SINGING TELEGRAM, THE.................................	V	SS7
(s) *Another Greeting From Western Union*		
17. SING US ANOTHER ONE DO................................	K	SS7
(s) *A Very Fine Song*		
(s) *Ai, Yi, Yi, Yi*		
(s) *Fighter Pilots Eat Pussy*		
(s) *Lymericks*		
(s) *Pilots Always Eat Pussy*		
(s) *Tell Us Another*		
(s) *There Was A Young Man*		
(s) *Waltz Me Around Again, Willy*		
00. SIX POUNDS OF BOOBIES (*See TT13*).....................	K	TT7
18. SIXTEEN TIMES...	K	SS12
19. SOLIDARITY SONG (U.S. TACAIR EASTER)..................	POST V	SS12
20. SONG OF THE FORTY-NINERS..............................	II	SS13
21. SOUTH OF THE NAVEL....................................	K	SS13
22. SPANISH GUITARS.......................................	V	SS14
23. SPRINGTIME AT DUCHI...................................	V	SS14
24. SQUADRONS ALL...	II	SS14
25. SQUADRON D..	II	SS15
26. STOP KICKING MY FUF AROUND............................	K	SS16
27. STRAFE THE TOWN - I...................................	V	SS16
28. STRAFE THE TOWN - II..................................	V	SS16
29. STRAFING IN A MOUNTAIN PASS...........................	K	SS17
30. STUDENT AVIATOR, THE..................................	I	SS17
31. SUPER HOG RECALL......................................	POST V	SS18
32. SUPER HOG REFRAIN.....................................	POST V	SS18
33. SWEETHEART OF ? (*not original title*)................	II	SS19

CHECKLIST TT

TITLE	WAR	PAGE
01. TAEGU GIRLS..	K	TT1
02. TALKING BLUES..	II	TT1
00. TALL GRASS (*See II16*)..............................	U	II6
03. TCHEPONE (*Also see Volume I, T04*)..................	V	TT2
00. TELL US ANOTHER (*See SS17*).........................	K	SS7
04. TEN DAYS OF TET (*See TT26*).........................	V	TT18
05. THEM DOODLE DASHERS (*Also see TT07 and TT08*).......	U	TT2
00. THAT LITTLE BALL OF YARN (*See BB11*)................	K	BB8

TITLE	WAR	PAGE
06. THAT MAY BE SO (*Also See Vol. I, T14*)........................	U	TT3
07. THEM MOOSE GOOSERS (*Also see TT05 and TT08*).................	U	TT4
08. THEM TOAD SUCKERS (*Also see TT05 and TT07*).................	U	TT4
09. THERE ARE NO FIGHTER PILOTS DOWN IN HELL (*Also see TT10/11*)	V	TT4
(s) *Fighter Pilots (Vol. I, F9)*		
(s) *Fighter Pilots's Lament (Vol. I, F9)*		
(s) *No Fighter Pilots Down In Hell (Vol. I, F9)*		
10. THERE ARE NO MISSILEMEN DOWN IN HELL (M) *Also see TT09/11*..	POST V	TT5
11. THERE ARE NO SAC CREWMEN DOWN IN HELL		
(*Also see TT09 and TT10*)................................	POST V	TT6
00. THERE WAS A YOUNG MAN (*See SS17*)...........................	II	SS7
12. THESE FOOLISH THINGS..	K	TT7
(i) *Those Foolish Things*		
13. THESE THINGS REMIND ME OF YOU.............................	U	TT7
(i) *A Two-Ton Titty*		
(i) *Six Pounds of Boobies*		
14. THEY CALLED THE BASTARD STEPHENS........................	K	TT8
00. THINKER, THE (*Also Tinker*) *See DE12*......................	U	DE7
00, THOSE FOOLISH THINGS (*See TT12*).........................	POST V	TT7
15. THREE OLD MAIDS (*Also See Vol. I, T31*)...................	II	TT8
(s) *Three Old Maids*		
(s) *Three Old Maids In A Lavatory*		
16. THREE OLD MAIDS FROM BOSTON.............................	K	TT8
00. THREE OLD WHORES (*See TT16*).............................	POST V	TT8
00. THREE WHORES OF CANADA JUNCTION (*See TT16*).............	K	TT8
17. THROW A NICKEL ON THE GRASS (*Also see Vol. I, F9*).........	V	TT9
(a) *A Doggie Pilot's Lament (Vol. II)*		
(b) *Cruising Down The Yalu*		
(c) *Cruising Over Hanoi*		
(d) *Fighter Pilot's Hymn*		
(e) *Hallelujah - I*		
(f) *Hallelujah - II*		
(g) *Hallelujah - III (Vol. II)*		
(h) *I Was Headed Down The Runway*		
(i) *Mayday! Mayday! Mayday!*		
(j) *Rollin' Down The Runway*		
(k) *The Sabre Song*		
(l) *Save A Fighter Pilot's Ass (Vol. II)*		
(m) *Save A Fighter Pilot's Life*		
00. THUD, THE (*Also Phantom, Jug, etc. See BB19*)...............	K	BB13
18. THUD DRIVERS THEME, THE....................................	V	TT13
19. THUNDERBOLT SONG..	II	TT13
20. TIDDLY..	POST V	TT14
21. TIE MY PECKER AROUND [TO] A TREE..........................	U	TT14
(i) *Gonna Tie My Pecker To A Tree*		
(i) *Tie My Root Around A Tree*		
00. TIE MY ROOT AROUND A TREE (*See TT21*)..................	U	TT14

TITLE	WAR	PAGE
22. TOASTS TO ROAST..	K	TT15
(s) *Fighter Pilot's Toast*		
(s) *Pilots Toast*		
Five other unnamed toasts		
23. TOGETHER...	U	TT16
24. TROOP SHIP LEAVING BOMBAY (*Also see Vol. I, B33*)...........	II	TT16
(i) *Bless 'Em All*		
(s) *Fortress Leaving Calais (Vol. I, B36)*		
(s) *Lancaster Leaving The Ruhr (Vol. II)*		
(s) *Love They Neighbors (Vol. I, B36)*		
(s) *Mustang Pilot's Song (Vol. II)*		
(s) *Prang 'Em All (Vol. I, B33)*		
(s) *Tip Tanks & Tailpipes (Vol. I, B36)*		
25. TROOP TRANSPORT SONG.....................................	II	TT17
00. TWAS A COLD WINTER EVENING (*See Vol. I, C16*)..............	II	C6
00. TWELVE DAYS OF CHRISTMAS (*See TT27 & also see Vol. I, T50*).	K	TT18
26. TWELVE DAYS OF TET..	V	TT18
(s) *Ten Days of TET Plus Two*		
(i) *Twelve Days of Christmas*		
(s) *Twelve Nights of Bonehead*		
27. TWELVE NIGHTS OF BONEHEAD (*See TT26*).....................	POST V	TT18

CHECKLIST UV

00. UP IN THE AIR JUNIOR BIRDMAN (*See II17*)...................	II	II6
01. VICTOR ALERT SONG, THE....................................	K	UV1
02. VITAL DIFFERENCE, THE (*original title unknown*)............	II	UV1
03. VIT MEIN HAND ON MEIN SELF................................	K	UV2

CHECKLIST WW

00. WALTZ ME AROUND AGAIN, WILLY (*See SS17*)...................	U	SS7
01. WAND'RIN' MAN...	V	WW1
02. WARTHOG DRIVER, THE (*See BB21*)..........................	V	BB15
03. WAS IT YOU WHO DID THE PUSH'N? (*See HH15*)...............	V	HH10
04. WASP NATIONAL ANTHEM, THE................................	II	WW2
05. WEASEL-BEARS' PICNIC, THE.................................	V	WW2
06. WEATHER MEN'S LAMENT, THE (*not original title*)............	POST-II	WW3
07. WE WERE THERE..	II	WW3
08. WE'VE BEEN WORKING ON THE RAILROAD (*S.E.A. version*)........	V	WW4
00. WHEEL, THE (*See BB24*)...................................	II	BB16
09. WHEN YOU ARE OLD..	K	WW4
10. WHERE'D THEY ALL COME FROM?...............................	K	WW4
11. WHISPERING DEATH - I......................................	V	WW5
12. WHISPERING DEATH - II.....................................	V	WW5

TITLE	WAR	PAGE

13.	WHOREHOUSE QUARTET, THE..............................	POST V	WW6
14.	WHY DO THE DRUMS GO BOOM?............................	K	WW7
15.	WILD WEST SHOW - I, THE (See HH03)..................	V	HH2
16.	WILD WEST SHOW - II, THE (See HH03).................	V	HH3
17.	WINNEPEG WHORE.......................................	K	WW8
18.	WIRRAWAYS DON'T BOTHER ME............................	II	WW8
19.	WOMEN, WOMEN, WOMEN..................................	II	WW9
20.	WOODPECKER SONG, THE.................................	K	WW9
21.	WRECK OF THE OLD 97 - II, THE (Also see Vol. I, 020).......	POST V	WW10

CHECKLIST YY

01.	YELLOW TAILS...	POST V	YY1
02.	YOU CAN TELL BY THE SMELL............................	POST V	YY1
	(i) *You Can Tell*		
03.	YOU CAN'T SAY SHIT HOT...............................	V	YY1
00.	YOU REVEL IN THE JOYS OF COPULATION (See CC06).............	II	CC3
04.	YUKON PETE...	POST V	YY2

GLOSSARY OF TERMS.(*Begins after Page YY-2*).....................	POST V	

INDEX TO KEITH FERRIS PEN AND INK SKETCHES

Before the Wars   Page No.

1.	1909 Wright Flyer Type A	Checklist 17
2.	Curtiss Pusher	DE8

Aircraft of World War I

3.	Fokker E-III	LL8
4.	DeHavilland DH-2	0017
5.	Fokker D-VII	AA14
6.	Spad 13	SS20

Aircraft of World War II

7.	Seversky P-35	GG10
8.	Curtis P-40B Warhawk	BB11
9.	Mitsubishi Zero	0018

Aircraft of World War II(*continued*)

10.   Messerschmitt Bf-109G LL8
11.   Consolidated B-24D CC12
12.   Supermarine Spitfire FF8
13.   Boeing B-17G SS9

Aircraft of the Korean War

14.   North American F-86 Sabrejet AA13
15.   Mikoyan-Gurevich MiG-15 ....   RR8
16.   Douglas A1-H Skyraider SS19

Aircraft of the Southeast Asia War

17.   McDonnelll F-4E Phantom II UV2
18.   Republic F-105D Thunderchief .... Sources & Credits 6
19.   Cessna L-19 Bird Dog LL7
20.   Boeing B-52 Stratofortress KK4

Missiles

21.   Atlas ICBM MM10
22.   Minuteman ICBM MM10

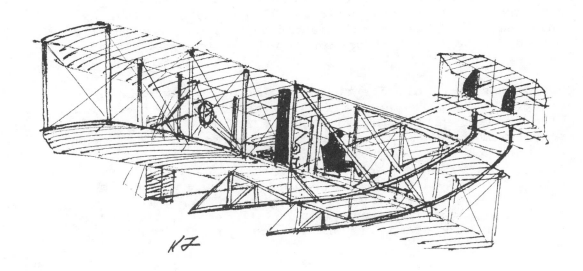

1909 Wright A Flyer

THE FIGHTER PILOT -- A TRIBUTE*

*Dedicated to the members of the Red River Valley Fighter
Pilot's Association*

Say what you will about him--arrogant, cocky, boisterous, and
a fun-loving fool to boot. He has earned his place in the
sun. Across the span of fifty years he has given this
country some of its proudest moments and most cherished
military traditions. But fame is short-lived and little the
world remembers.

Almost forgotten are the 1400 fighter pilots who stood alone
against the might of Hitler's Germany during the dark summer
of 1940, and in the words of Sir Winston Churchill, gave
England, *Its finest hour*. Gone from the hardstands of
Duxford are the 51s with their checkerboard noses (78th
Fighter Group) that terrorized the finest fighter squadrons
the Luftwaffe had.

Dimly remembered--the 4th Fighter Group that gave Americans
some of their few proud moments in the skies over Korea (and
over Europe in WW-II). And many a fighter jock from WW-II
had to do it all over again in Korea. It is almost a forgotten war; the one between World War II and Vietnam. That was
when the United States still fought aggression. But it also
marked the beginning of *no-win* policies that would dramatically weaken the free world.

How fresh in recall are the Air Commandos who valiantly
struck the VC with their aging *Skyraiders* in the rain and
blood-soaked valley called *A Shau*. And how long will be
remembered the *Phantoms* and the *Thuds* over Route Pack Six and
the flak-filled skies above Hanoi?

Barrel roll, steel tiger, and tally ho; so here's a *Nickle On
The Grass* to you, my friend, for your spirit, enthusiasm,
sacrifice, and courage--but most of all to your friendship.
Yours is a dying breed, and when you are gone, the world will
be a lessor place.

---

* Adapted with modifications from the *Aggressors Song Book*.

FLIGHT SECTION AA

(01) A BABBLING BROOK
(Tune: *A Sleepy Lagoon*)

Alternate Titles and Variations:

(a) *A Bubbling Brook*

NOTE: *The first song in the book has the distinction (it is?) of extolling a theme that posters and the chaplain used to warn us about. This same message will be found in many songs throughout this literary masterpiece.*

A BABBLING BROOK

A babbling brook, a shady nook, a girl
    dressed in yellow.
Two snow white tits, two ruby lips,
    oh, you lucky fellow.
Between the hours of two and four when
    he began to linger,
She said, "Young man, if you are
    through, I'll finish with my finger."
So he got up and took a piss, and she
    got up and farted.

Nine days went by, he heaved a sigh, a
    sigh of pain and sorrow.
The pimples pink were on his dink, but
    there'll be more tomorrow.
Nine months went by and she heaved a sigh,
    a sigh of pain and sorrow.
Two little mutts were in her guts, but
    they'll be out tomorrow.

(02) ABDUL A BUL BUL AMEER
        (Tune: *Original*)

Alternate Titles and Variations:

(a) *Abdul*
(b) *Abdul Abulbul Emir*
(c) *Ivan Skavinski Skavar*

NOTE: *There are several variations of this song, including those in Volume I. The version below comes from the song-book of 77 Squadron, Royal Australian Air Force in Korea, 1950-51. The editor has substituted some verses from other songbooks to create a version representative of all.*

F-111 AARDVARK

ABDUL A BUL BUL AMEER

In the harems of Egypt, close guarded
    and secret,
The women are fairest of fair,
The fairest was Greek she was owned by
    a sheik,
Known as Abdul A Bul Bul Ameer.

A travelling brothel that came to the
    town,
Owned by a Russian who came from afar,
He offered a challenge to all who could
    shag,
As Ivan Skavinsky Skavar.

(*continued on next page*)

How Abdul rode up with his snatch at his
    side,
His eyes flamed with a burning desire,
And he wagered ten thousand that he
    could out-shag,
This Ivan Skavinsky Skavar.

They came on the track with their tools
    hanging slack,
The starter's gun punctured the air,
They were quick to the rise, and all
    gaped at the size,
Of Abdul A Bul Bul Ameer.

Although Abdul was quick at flicking his
    flick,
And the action was learnt by the Czar,
He couldn't compete with the long steady
    beat,
Of Count Ivan Skavinsky Skavar.

Now Ivan had won and was polishing his
    gun,
And bent over to polish his pair,
When he felt something pass up his great
    hairy arse,
It was Abdul A Bul Bul Ameer.

The harlots turned green, the men
    shouted, "Queen,"
They were ordered apart by the Czar,
But Abdul, fuck his luck, had got him-
    self stuck,
In the arse of Skavinsky Skavar.

Now the cream of the joke, when at last
    they were broke,
Was laughed at for years by the Czar,
For Abdul, the fool, had left half of
    his tool,
In the arse of Skavinsky Skavar.

(03) ADELINE SCHMIDT
(Tune: *Sweet Betsy From Pike*)

Alternate Titles and Variations:

    (a) *Blinded By Shit*
    (b) *Brown, Brown*
    (c) *Madeline Schmidt*

There once was a maiden named Adeline
    Schmidt,
Who went to the doctor cause she
    couldn't shit.
He gave her some medicine all wrapped up
    in glass,
And up went the window and out went her
    ass.

CHORUS (*repeat after each verse*)

    It was brown, brown, shit falling
        down.
    Brown, brown, shit all around.
    It was brown, brown, shit falling
        down.
    The whole world was covered with
        shit, shit, shit, shit.

A handsome young copper was walking his
    beat.
He happened to be on that side of the
    street.
He looked up so bashful, he looked up so
    shy,
When a big piece of shit hit him right
    in the eye.

That handsome young copper, he cursed
    and he swore.
He called that young maiden a diry old
    whore,
And on London Bridge you can still see
    him sit,
With a sign 'round his neck saying,
    "Blinded by shit."

BROWN, BROWN
(Tune: *Sweet Betsy From Pike*)

There once was a maiden named Adeline
    Guff,
Said, "Faith and begorra, I must have a
    'stuff.'
I can't lay here farting and just
    passing gas."
So she ups the window and hoists out her
    ass.

(*continued on next page*)

CHORUS

    It was brown, brown stuff falling
      down.
    Brown, brown stuff all around.
    It was brown, brown stuff falling
      down.
    His life was ruined by stuff, stuff,
      stuff stuff!

A certain young copper was pounding his
    beat.
You could tell it was him by the sound
    of his feet.
When all of a sudden he looks up in the
    sky,
And a dirty brown clod hit him right in
    the eye.

This certain young copper, he cursed and
    he swore,
And he called Adeline a dirty old whore.
By London Bridge you can still see him
    sit,
With a sign hanging over him, "Blinded
    by stuff."

(04) A DOGGIE PILOT'S LAMENT (*See TT17*)

(05) AERIAL ADVENTURES
    (Tune: *Unavailable*)

<u>NOTE</u>: *This is the first of three songs
and poems in this Volume from World War
I that have not seen print since 1919,
when they were published in a book
called,* **Buddy Ballads.** *All authors are
unknown, unfortunately; nor did the book
indicate which were ballads and which
were songs, although in some cases it
was obvious. As the Editor says in
several places throughout Volume II (as
reminders), What is a song but a poem
set to music? This particular piece is
a good companion to the well-known
painting by Jack Pardue of the* **Knight of
the Skies** *that appeared on the December
1981 cover of* **Air Force** *magazine. The
poem/song should give inspiration to all
present and past Air Force members.*

AERIAL ADVENTURES

Out of the past they roust,
Spirit of times that knew
Tourney and reckless joust;
They are the chosen few
Living the old romance
Playing the knightly game,
Wielding for flashing lance,
Bullets that flare and flame.

Cuirasseurs of the air
Riding their winged steeds,
Forth to the clouds they fare
Heroes of breathless deeds.
Field of the Cloth of Gold
Never knew such emprise;
Knights on their chragers bold
Swooping across the skies.

High in the vault above
Driving a combat Spad,
We shall find splendor of
Arthur and Galahad;
Sheepskin for shirt of mail,
Yammering gun for lance;
Ranging the eagle's trail
Knights of the old Romance.

(06) THE AEROPLANE COMMANDER
(Tune: *Rambling Wreck From Georgia Tech*)

If you ever see a guy,
With lots of age and rank,
Who's just about as useful
As an empty belly tank;
Who hardly ever flys at all,
Who's quiet as a lamb --
It's an aeroplane commander,
And he isn't worth a damn.

For up in Washington they found,
The Air Corps had a lot
Of broken down old pilots,
Who weren't very hot;
So they gave a fancy rating
To each decrepit lout;
Thus we got Command Pilots,
You can see them all about.

(*continued on next page*)

When he gets inside a ship,
We help him to his seat.
We tell him to be careful
Not to get beneath our feet.
We let him hold the maps when he
Would like to bear a hand,
But as aeroplane commander
He can't take her off or land.

When the autopilot's on
And everything is sweet,
We sometimes let him come and take
The young copilot's seat.
He thinks the plane is guided by
A pair of leather reins,
For he's got three thousand hours - but,
He ain't got no brains!

He doesn't take command at all,
He's always fast asleep,
And when we ask for his advice,
He doesn't give a peep.
But when we roll her in a ball,
With lots of noise and flame,
It's the aeroplane commander
Who always takes the blame.

He's lost what flying skill he's had,
He's old and broken down.
Young pilots all feel sorry for
This poor enfeebled clown.
Instead of feeling sorry
They should all be pretty glum.
They'll be aeroplane commanders, too,
In the years to come.

(07) THE AGGRESSORS TDY SONG
(Tune: *Unavailable*)

The aggressors are in the bar tonight,
A little bit pissed and a little bit
   tight.
Doctor says it will be alright.

Second verse, same as the first
A lttle bit louder,
And a little bit worse.

(Make each succeeding verse a little
bit louder until the bar is being
shaken apart)

(08) AH, SWEET MYSTERY OF LIFE
(Tune: *Ah, Sweet Mystery Of Life*)

Alternate Titles and Variations:

   (a) *Nellie*
   (b) *Nelly(ie) Darling*

Oh, your ass is like a stovepipe, Nelly
   Darling,
And the nipples on your tits are turning
   green.
There's a yard of lint protruding from
   your navel.
You're the ugliest fucking bitch I've
   ever seen.

There's an odor of blue ointment 'round
   your pussy.
When you piss you piss a stream as green
   as grass.
There's enough wax in your ears to make
   a candle,
So why not make one, dear, and shove it
   up your ass.

(09) THE AIR FORCE
(*Words & music by Marvin Liblick, ASCAP*)

© 1979 by Marvin Liblick
   Used by permission

NOTE: *This is the only song in the collection dedicated to or about Air Force Astronauts, and thus fills a unique place in the annals of Air Force history in song. The song was originally dedicated to Lt. General James P. Mullins upon the occassion of his retirement. It is also the only known copyrighted song in Volume II, and a late comer to the collection. But when the Editor saw the words, and listened to the tape that Mr. Liblick provided, it was clearly a musical composition worthy of the esteem of all Air Force enthusiasts. This composition, in March tempo, was performed by the March Air Force Base music department for the tape. Mr. Liblick also composed a song*

(*continued on next page*)

called, **Three Cheers For America** which
is a great, patriotic and stirring song.
It is good to know that in 1985, there
are still hearts that swell with pride
and proud emotion at the Stars and
Stripes, and can put that feeling into
music in the tradition of Irving Berlin
and George M. Cohan.

THE AIR FORCE

The Astronauts will ride through the
  air,
In roaring rockets of fiery flare--
And when the countdown is near,
Then all the nations will cheer,
'Cause the Air Force will do it again.

The Astronauts will ride in space,
And visit planets all over the place--
And then they'll shuttle and roam,
And then they'll travel back home,
And then the Air Force will do it again

  So we'll rocket right out for man's
    advance and then,
  The Air Force will do it again, and
    again,
  The Air Force will do it again.

The Astronauts will do it again.
We've got the knowledge, the finest of
  men,
And they may reach for the sars,
And visit Venus and Mars,
And the Air Force will do it again.

There's just one thing we want you to
  know,
We'll back our Forces wherever they go,
And now that NASA's so proud,
The crew is singing out loud,
Because the Air Force will do it again.

  So we'll rocket right out for man's
    advance and then,
  The Air Force will do it again, and
    again,
  The Air Force will do it again.

(10) AIR FORCE LAMENT (*S.E.A. Version*)
    (Tune: *Battle Hymn of the Republic*)

Alternate Titles and Variations:

  (a) *Air Corps Lament*
  (b) *Air Force Has Gone To Hell*
  (c) *Glory Flying Regulation*

NOTE: *These are additional verses only
to the original song found in Volume I,
song A16. These new verses are from the*
Aggressors' *Song Book (527th TFTAS)
contributed by Captain Jeffrey Brown.*

AIR FORCE LAMENT

Once they flew B-26s through a living
    Hell of flak,
And bloody dying pilots gave their all
    to bring them back,
But now they play pingpong in the
    operations shack,
The Force is shot to Hell!

The Sabre's in Korea drove the MIGS out
    of the sky,
The pilots then were fearless men and
    not afraid to die,
But now the regs are written, you can
    kiss your ass goodbye,
The Force is shot to Hell!

(11) AIR FORCE SONG (*A parody*)
    (Tune: *The Air Force Song*)

Off we go, on a one-hour test hop,
Over the land, not over the sea.
And for this feat, we get a ten day
    furlough,
A raise in pay, a DFC.
We're heros all, if you can tell by the
    medals,
We get a lot, and more as we go.
We're out..to kill..ourselves..we will,
For nothing can stop the U.S. Air Force
(From getting a medal)
Nothing can stop the U.S. Air Force!
(Those raving assholes)
Nothing can stop the U.S. Air Force!

(12) THE AIRLIFT SONG
(Tune: *The Whiffenpoof Song*)

NOTE: *This wonderful ballad from the Berlin Airlift almost didn't make it into Volume II, being a very late entrant. But the Editor is pleased that Lt. Colonel Russ Shaw squeaked it in. Another moment of Air Force history captured in melody. It was because of the Berlin Airlift that the Editor was pulled from his desk in Tokyo and began flying C-54s again (1948). See the* Note *with* **Beeliner Song,** *BB19.*

THE AIRLIFT SONG

From the airlift task force bases,
To the place where Lucius dwells;[1]
To that dear old Templehof[2] we know so
    well.
Have the vittlers all assembled,
With their cargo raised on high,
And the magic of their tonnage casts a
    spell.

Yes the magic of their tonnage,
Through the weather known so well,
It's two-hundred and a quarter of a mile
We will make a pass at Berlin,
Through fog as thick as Hell,
Hoping GCA will bring us down in style.

REFRAIN

We are poor little pilots
Who have lost our way,
Bahhh, Bahhh, Bahhh.
We are homeward bound,
And we've gone astray,
Bahhh, Bahhh, Bahhh.

Corridor jockeys off on a spree,
Beacon to Beacon repeatedly,
Gunpost [3] guides us, we cannot see,
I --- F --- R ---.

Darmstadt, Fritzlar, Staden[4], too,
Thorugh Russians, Navy or Lord knows
    who;
General Turner's[5] crews came through,
T --- D --- Y ---.

[1] *General Lucius Clay commanded U. S. forces during the Berlin Airlift, and his headquarters was in Berlin.*

[2] *Templehof was the main air terminal in Berlin that received air supplies.*

[3] *Gunpost was the call sign for the enroute air traffic controller.*

[4] *Darmstadt, Fritzlar and Staden were radio beacons at the edges of the Berlin corridor through which aircraft had to approach the city.*

[5] *General Turner commanded the Air Transport Command (ATC).*

(00) AIRMAN'S LAMENT or THE BIG WHEEL
(*See BB24*)

(00) AI, YI, YI, YI (*See SS17*)

(13) ALCOHOLIC BABY
(Tune: *Melancholy Baby*)

Come to me my alcoholic baby.
Cuddle up and have a few.
All your tears are dropping in my
    whiskey,
You know dear that I'm as drunk as you.
Every stomach needs a cast iron lining,
Wait until the gin seeps through,
Smile my honey dear, and have another
    beer,
And then I will be alcoholic too.

(14) ALICE BLUE GOWN)
(Tune: *Alice Blue Gown*)

In her sweet little Alice blue gown.
The first time she lay on the ground.
She was bashful and shy,
When she opened my fly,
And the first time she saw it,

(*continued on next page*)

I thought she would die.
It went up and wouldn't go down,
Until I finally had her on the ground.
I shoved it and shoved it,
My God, how she loved it,
Underneath her Alice blue gown.

(00) ALPHABET SONG (*See AA17*)

(00) AN ENGINEER'S SONG (*See BB24*)

(00) ANGELES POM-POM SONG (*See MM03*)

(15) A NIGHT IN KUNSAN KOREA
      (Tune: *Unavailable*)

Alternate Titles and Variations:

   (a) *A Night In Town*
   (b) *A Soldier Dreams Of An AWAS*

NOTE: *The Editor took the liberty of combining two versions into this one.*

A little maiden passing by,
A little twinkling of the eye,
A little smile, a little date,
To meet when the hour is late.
A little promise not to tell,
A little room in some hotel.
A little fussing in some chair,
A little messing of the hair.

A little drink, a fond caress.
A little question, the answer, "yes."
A little shirt waist shed aside,
A little breast that tried to hide.
A little hand that went stealing inside,
A little pleased with funny feeling.
A little coaxing, a little teasing,
A form revealed that is most pleasing.

A pair of panties mostly lace,
A little blush upon the face.
A little shading of the light,
A little bed with sheets so white;
A little sigh, a quiet room,
A little loving in the gloom;
A pair of lips, so warm and wet,
A little whisper, "Please not yet."

A little pillow for the head,
Slipped beneath the hips instead.
A little effort to begin,
A little help to get it in;
A little arm that grips me tight,
And when I ask, "Does it feel all
      right?"
She smiles and says, "It feels so good"
And I reply, "I thought it would."

Two little legs around me wind,
Two slanted eyes look into mine;
A little movement to and fro,
A little "ah", a little "oh."
Two little hearts beat as one,
Two little lovers having fun;
A little hunch, a little sigh,
A little question, "You come yet, G.I.?"

A bigger surge of something hot,
A little whisper, "Please, all you've
      got."
A little effort to repeat,
A little spot upon the sheet;
A little shower when you're through,
A little drink, maybe two.
Finally, a little sleep and then,
A little breakfast at half-past ten;

A little bill, a little tip,
A porter wishing a pleasant trip.
Like little children after play,
A little weariness the next day.
A little wish that you and I,
May have some more another day.
Then you arise and put on your hat,
Look back and say, "Did I fuck that?"

(16) ANOTHER GREETING FROM WESTERN UNION
      (*See SS16*)

(17) ANTHONY ROLY
(Tune: *The Froggie He Would A'Wooing Go*)

Alternate Titles and Variations:

   (a) *The Alphabet Song*

(*continued on next page*)

NOTE: *The tune is an old English drinking song. If you want to know the melody, ask any English or Australian vet, and chances are he will know it.*

ANTHONY ROLY

"A" is for arseholes, all covered with shit

CHORUS #1 (*repeat after every other line*)

   Heigh Ho said Roly.

And "B" is for bugger who revels in it.

CHORUS #2 (*repeat after every other line*)

   With a Roly Poly, gammon and spinach,
   Heigh Ho for Anthony Roly.

"C's" for cunt, all dripping in piss,

CHORUS #1

And "D" for the drunkard who gave it a
   kiss.

CHORUS #2 (*repeat choruses as indicated*)

"E's" for the eunuch with only one ball,
And "F" for the fucker with no balls at
   all.

"G" is for goiter, gonorrhea and gout,
And "H" is for harlot who dishes it out.

"I" is for injection for syphilis and
   itch, (or "pox and itch")
And "J" is for jump of a dog on a bitch.

"K" is for king who shot on the floor,

Alternate K:

"K" is the king who thought fucking a
   bore,
And "L" is for lousy, licentious whore.

Alternate L:

And "L" is the lesbian who came back for
   more,

"M" is for maidenhead, tattered and torn

And "N" is for Nancy whose arshole is
   worn.

Alternate "N":

And "N" is for Noble who died with a
   horn,

"O" is for orifice, already revealed,
And "P" is for penis ready unpeeled.

Alternate P:

And "P" is for penis all pranged up and
   peeled,

"Q" is for quaker who shot in his hat,
And "R" is for Rodger who rodgered the
   cat.

"S" is for shit-pot full to the brim,
And "T" is the turd that is floating
   therein.

"U" is the usher who taught in the
   school,
And "V" is the virgin who played with
   his tool.

"W" is for the whore who thinks fuckings
   a farce,
And "X", "Y" and "Z" you can stick up
   your arse!

(18) A POOR AVIATOR LAY DYING
(Tune: *My Bonnie Lies Over The Ocean*)

NOTE: *This is a parody of a parody. The words are a parody of the song of the same name in Volume I, song A30. But the melody is quite different. The words below are from one of the most enduring of Air Force songs, dating from World War I. This version is from the VMFA 312 (Checkerboards) song book (S.E.A.). After all, if we include some British songs, we must include some Marine & Navy songs. They are Allies too! And this is a great update of an old song.*

(continued on next page)

A POOR AVIATOR LAY DYING

A poor aviator lay dying,
At the end of a cold winter day.
His comrades had gathered around him,
To carry his fragments away.

The airplane was piled on his breastbone
The gyro was wrapped 'round his head.
He wore a wing tank on each elbow,
'Twas plain he would shortly be dead.

He spit out a valve and a gasket,
And stirred in the oil where he lay.
To mechanics who 'round him came sighing
These brave parting words he did say.

Take the landing gear out of my stomach,
And the drogue chute off of my neck.
Extract from my liver the throttles,
There's lots of good parts in this wreck
There's a hydraulic pump in my larynx,
And a good SPC in my brain.
Take the impingement valve from my
    kidneys,
And assemble the damn plane again!

(19) A PROHIBITION SONG
   (Tune: *Unavailable*)

NOTE: *Another song of British Navy origin, but the 95th FITS song book (1979), fails to give the tune. This is another one of those songs for which you can get help from a British friend. The title in the 95th's book has* **for Capt. Dick** *after it. So, Captain, here it is.*

Ohhh, we don't eat fruit cakes because
    it has rum . . .
And one little bite turns a man to a bum
Cannnn you imagine the utter disgrace...
Of a bum in the gutter with crumbs on
    his face.

CHORUS (*repeat after each verse*)

   Away, away with rum by gum
   With rum by golly with rum by gum
   Away, away with rum by gum
   Say we of the Temperance Union.

Ohhh, we don't eat bread because it has
    yeast . . .
And one little bite turns a man to a
    beast.
Cannnn you imagine the total disgrace...
Of a bum in the gutter with crumbs on
    his face.

(20) ARCHIE (ANTI-AIRCRAFT GUN)
   (Tune: *Unavailable*)

NOTE: *This is the second of four songs/ poems from the rare 1919 book,* **Buddy Ballads.** *It is doubtful that many WW II, Korean or Vietnam bomber vets can share the cavalier attitude of the WW I fighter pilot towards what in later wars was called* **flak** *(a German word meaning, anti-aircraft fire). However, the attitude may have been partly shared by some WW II fighter jocks, such as the Editor. After flying bombers, the Editor's fighter tour was quite a relief from the heavy flak directed towards bombers.* **Archie** *is a terrific military parody, and the Editor is happy to rescue it from the back closets of history.*

ARCHIE

Archie sits on the ground below
Pointing his nose in air.
Archie's trying his best to throw
Shells that'll get me fair.
He tosses his shoots and spins and
    curves
Up where my Nieuport flits;
But he isn't hard on a fellow's nerves
For Archibald seldom hits.

I'm sneakingly fond of Archie,
Except when he comes too near.
He adds to the zest of travel
'Round in the ozone here.
I look down and grin at Archie
Straffing the atmosphere.

(*continued on next page*)

Archie scatters his puffy shells
Freely along my trail,
Filling my path with bumps and swells,
Up where he sees me sail;
And if I stand on my tail and stall
I oftentimes hear his bark;
But it's hardly ever he bites at all,
So dodging him is a lark!

A hopeful old dear is Archie;
He misses ten thousand tries;
But patiently goes on shooting
At every old thing that flies,
Making the birds unhappy
Here in the pleasant skies.

Archie's brothers quite frequently
Join in his air barrage,
Seeking to make a hit on me
Right in the fuselage.
So I split-tail 'round and I spin and
   dive,
And thus, when the party's through,
I'm perfectly safe and much alive
And--Archibald's healthy, too.

So here's to your fortune, Archie,
You plodding old patient Hun.
May you never lack shells to scatter
Wherever the aircraft run.
May you hopefully go on straffing,
And never hit anyone!

(OO) ARMED RECCE
(Tune: *The Fastest Gun Around* from the
 Marty Robbin's albums, *Gunfighter
 Ballads and Trail Songs*)
Lyrics: *Lt. Colonel W. F. Toby Hughes*

NOTE: **Armed Recce** *is one of the all-
time greats of combat story telling in
song. The version of this song in
Volume I is a variant of the original.
The composer of the song, Toby Hughes,
provided the correct lyrics, below.
Also see his song* **Tchepone** *in this
volume. The 527th TFTAS song book uses
an entirely different melody:* **Ghost
Riders In The Sky.** *It fits well. Just
shows how these ballads do get around--
and changed! See the Glossary for an
explanaion of terms.*

ARMED RECCE

In the skies of Southeast Asia
Where the fighter pilots dwell,
There's a mission that you'll fly a lot;
You'll get to know it well.

They call it Armed Reconnaissance;
You fly it fast and low
In the southern part of Package One
That's known as Tally-Ho.

   You're briefed on the defenses
   All along the route you'll fly.
   You're scared, but still you've got
      to go,
   And so you take the sky.

   You get pre-strike refueling
   And you take your flight on down;
   Cross the coast at Butterfly
   And start to move around.

You're headed north up Route 1-A,
The road looks clean and bare,
But a truck is mighty hard to see
From one mile in the air.

You know you've got to take it down
Though your heart is in your mouth.
Now dead ahead's the Ferry,
That's the point you'll turn back south.

   Then suddenly your heart stops
   As you see the thing you dread.
   Triple-A is coming up
   And it fills the sky ahead.

   You fake a turn to left
   And then you break hard up and right,
   Then your wingman's in with CBU
   And that's a pretty sight.

And now you're heading south again
And really movin' 'round
To make a tougher target
For the gunners on the ground.

And it's then you see the convoy
Sittin' still beside the road.
Arm up all your switches
And prepare to dump your load.

(*continued on next page*)

Touch off afterburner
And pop up into the sun,
But keep the convoy in your sight
And start to make your run.

Then the gunners start to shoot again
You see the flak ahead.
Then it's bursting all around you
And the sky is filled with lead.

You can't go left; you can't go right
The flak is all around,
So keep the convoy in your sight
And keep on boring down.

Pickle off your bomb load
And then pull and trust to luck
That the tripe-A will miss you
And your bombs will hit the truck.

But the flak is coming closer
And your eyes are filled with tears,
And before you reach the coastline
You have aged a hundred years.

Then suddenly you're out of it,
The water's down below.
Breathe easy now, but don't relax,
'Cause sure as Hell you know

That tomorrow is another day,
And once again you'll go
To the southern part of Package One
And recce Tally-Ho.

(00) THE A SHAU CANYON BRAWL (*See BB02*)

(21) ASHAU VALLEY
(Tune: *See Note*)

NOTE: *It is doubtful this little verse is actually a song--but it's pure fighter pilot!*

Oh! Who'll carry the mail through the
    Ashau Valley?
REPLY: I'll carry the mail through the
    Ashau Valley.

But there's lions in the Ashau Valley.
REPLY: Fuck the lions.

You'd fuck a lion?
REPLY: I'd fuck a lion's mother!

YOU LION MOTHER FUCKER

But there's Indians in the Ashau Valley.
REPLY: Fuck the Indians!

You'd fuck an Indian?
REPLY: I'd fuck an Eskimo!

YOU COOL MOTHER FUCKER

(00) A SOLDIER DREAMS OF AN AWAS
    (*See AA15*)

(22) ASS HOLES ARE CHEAP TODAY
    (Tune: *See Note*)

NOTE: *With a little effort, this ditty can be fitted to the tune,* **Tra La La Boom De A** *(or however it is spelled). The Editor added a few words in parenthesis to help make it work.*

ASS HOLES ARE CHEAP TODAY

Ass holes are cheap today,
Cheaper than yesterday.
Little boys cost half a crown,
Standing up or lying down.
Larger boys cost seven and six,
'Cause they take bigger pricks.
Ass holes are cheap (today)
(Ass holes) Are cheap today.

(23) A TISKET A TASKET
(Tune: *A Tisket A Tasket*)

A tisket, a tasket, a single-engined
    basket,
They wrote a letter to my mum
And told her that I crashed it.
I crashed it, I crashed it,
That single-engined basket,
I turned on finals, yanked the stick,
Son of a bitch, I snapped it,
That single-engined basket,
A two-turn spin, I torque-stalled in,
Oh, Jesus, how I smashed it!

(00) A TWO-TON TITTY (*See TT13*)

(00) A VERY FINE SONG (*See SS17*)

(24) AXTATER'S FLIGHT
(Tune: *Abdul A Bul Bul Ameer*)

NOTE: *This is a real pre-WW II gem that
came from the Flying School Class 40-A
song book published for their 1985
reunion. It is reminiscent of another
pre-WW II song,* **The Wreck Of The Old 97**
(See Volume I, song 020).

AXTATER'S FLIGHT

T'was a warm summer's night,
All the stars shone so bright,
And the south wind came flowing up the
    blue.
With his map in his hand,
Of the trip he had planned,
Axtater went to his BC-One.

There was a tear in his eye
As he took to the sky,
For his way he knew he'd never find,
And the thought of the noise,
That he'd hear from the boys,
Haunted his poor troubled mind.

Oh, the dude hummed a song,
As he flew her along,
The engine just purred through the
    stacks.
He whispered a prayer,

Way up there in the air,
Praying he'd find railroad tracks.

Oh, his young heart stood still,
As he buzzed o'er a hill,
For Hondo lay right in his face.
He was bound for Seguin,
So t'was easily seen,
Somehow he was not in his place.

Then he picked up his phone,
And his brave heart was stone,
He hollered for Kelly Field tower.
"Sirs, I can't find my way,
Guess I'll call it a day,
Get me back where I ought to be."

They directed him home,
From the course he had flown,
And he wound up landing down tee.
And in case you ain't heard,
How he's getting the bird,
Axtater ne'er did find Sequin.

(25) AYOTOLLAH SONG
(Tune: *Sweet Betsy From Pike*)

NOTE: *A fascinating ditty from the
period of American hostages in Iran.
This is evidence, together with other
songs found in this volume, that the
song writing talents of the people of
the Air Force has not diminished. The
songs continue to record Air Force
history in melody.*

AYOTOLLAH SONG

We see the plot thicken,
We know what's in store.
Your students know nothing,
They're asking for more.
Your people are waiting for grace from
    Islam,
But the Air Force will bring in the
    first load of bombs.

(continued on next page)

CHORUS (*sing after each verse*)

   Oh it's rags, rags, rags on your head
   Rags, rags, rags on your head.
   Oh it's rags, rags, rags on your head
   Tomorrow you'll wake up and find
     yourself dead.

Iranian people
We'll bring you some food,
Coat hangars and goat meat,
It will be so good.
So make up some Kebobs and wish for the
  best,
We'll bring the Napalm and cook the
  rest.

You bearded old fagot,
You can't get it up.
So lift up your veil
And take a big suck.
You important bastard, you'll be on the
  run,
When we roll in STRAFFING, and
  STRAFFING FOR FUN!

Oh, Mr. Khomeini
You are an asshole.
Your laws are from Islam,
Your students are dumb.
You may think you're shit-hot, but we
  know the score,
Your father's a goat and your mother's
  a whore!

North American F86

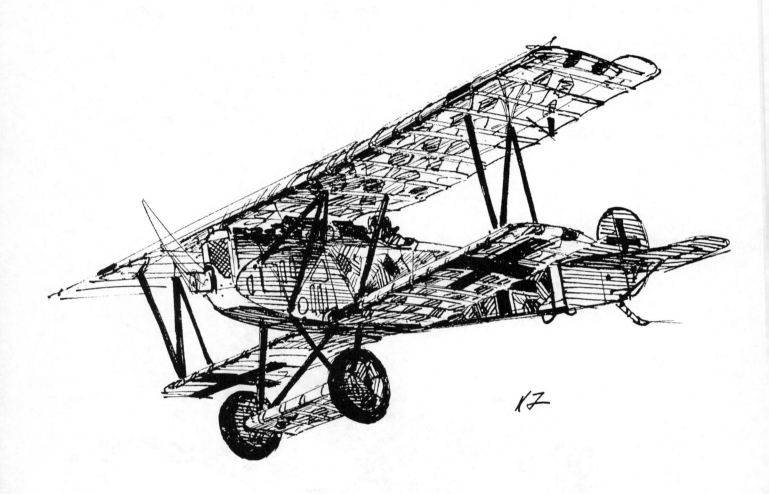

Fokker D-VII

FLIGHT SECTION BB

(00) BAD MOUTH (*See Volume I, song C20*)

(01) THE BALLAD OF AFMTC
(Tune: *Whiffenpoof Song*)
Lyrics: Col. L. T. Taylor
Maj. A. L. Taylor
Maj. R. F. Swantz
Maj. Ted McGrath

NOTE: **AFMTC** *is the Air Force Missile Test Center at Patrick Air Force Base, Cape Canaveral, Florida. This is a great song that captures the mood of the organization in the tradition of military parodies. The Editor was a member of the* **BMD** *(Ballistic Missiles Division of the Air Research and Development Command), originally the Western Development Division, the people responsible for the Nation's first ballistic missiles and space vehicles.*

THE BALLAD OF AFMTC

At a cape we call Canaveral, where the
    missile men all dwell,
And their gleaming badges shine on
    every chest.
They live in concrete houses, with the
    gantries raised on high,
And they always say they've had a
    perfect test.

REFRAIN

We are poor missile men who have gone
    aloft,
COUNT.....COUNT.....COUNT.
We are bold astronauts who have now
    gone soft,
HOLD.....HOLD.....HOLD.
Missile men blasted off on a spree;
Damned from THE Cape to Station
    Three.

Yates.....have mercy on such as we.
SCRUB.....SCRUB.....SCRUB.

From the blockhouse at Canaveral, to the
    bleak Ascension shore,
Fly the missiles with their nose cones
    flaming bright.
So the operations squadron, with its
    red-eyed scanners bold,
Can recover and be home before the night

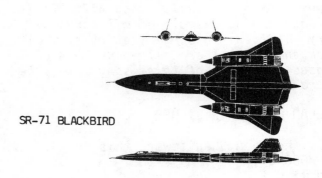

SR-71 BLACKBIRD

REFRAIN

We learned to count at M...I...T..,
ONE......TWO......THREE.
But here we count to a new decree,
THREE.....TWO.....ONE.
Martin and Convair all agree, they'll
    live and die on BMD,
Range Safety.....don't pull the chain
    on me,
GO.....GO.....GO.

(02) BALLAD OF BERNIE FISHER
(Tune: *Wabash Cannonball*)

Alternate Titles and Variations:

(a) *A Shau Canyon Brawl*
(b) *HOBO 51*

(*continued on next page*)

NOTE: *This song is one of the most stirring ballads to come out of the war in Southeast Asia. It is near and dear to the hearts of every aircrew member, no matter what type of aircraft he flew or what mission he performed. This ballad was written about Major Bernie Fisher, an A-1 pilot flying combat missions out of Qui Nhon, a small airbase on the northeast coast of Vietnam. On this fateful day, Major Fisher--whose call sign was* **HOBO 51**--*for his heroic deeds in a rescue of a downed A-1 pilot in the A Shau Valley, was awarded the highest honor ever to be bestowed upon a military man, the Congresional Medal of Honor. (From the 95th FITS Hymn Book). There is a definite genealogy between this song and the Korean War favorite,* **Air Force 801** *also known as,* **Itazuke Tower.** *See Volume I, song A17. It is an outstanding example of military history written in song--what this whole book and Vol. I are all about. A condensed version of this song will be found in Volume I, song B3.*

BALLAD OF BERNIE FISHER

Well, hello A Shau tower, this is
   HOBO 51,
I'd like to use your runway,
Although it's overrun.
A friend of mine is down there,
He's hiding in a ditch;
I'd like to make a passenger stop,
And save that son-of-a-bitch.

CHORUS (*sing after each verse*)

   Well, listen to the small arms,
   Hear the 20MM roar,
   Those A-1Es are bouncing off
   The A Shau Valley floor.
   With a mighty roar of vengence,
   Hear the lonesome HOBOB call,
   We'll get you home to mother,
   When the work's all done this fall.

Well, he scrambled out of Qui Nhon,
To try to save that camp.
They got him in their gunsights,
And now his shorts are damp.

The engine was on fire,
It gave a final wheeze;
He's hiding in the bushes now.
Altimeter setting, please.

Now the VC are descending
Upon his hiding place.
We'll, have him meet the aircraft,
I'm turning on my base.
I see him over yonder,
He's running awfully fast.
With the VC right behind him
With a rifle up his ass.

Now our wingman sees a VC,
Oh, strafe him if you can;
You'll have to get him quickly
To save that dear old man.
I've got him in the cockpit,
He's standing on his head,
You better let us take off,
Or soon we'll both be dead.

Now the takeoff, it was frightful,
They shot him full of holes.
It looks just like a sieve,
But still that A-1 rolls.
Johnny looks at Bernie,
And Bernie breathes a sigh.
Goodbye, dear old A Shau,
Lord, I thought we'd die.

(03) BALLAD OF THE C-130
(Tune: *Ghost Riders In The Sky*)

A trash hauler flew overhead,
One dark and windy day,
He passed above our runway,
As he flew upon his way.
When all at once our flight of four
Gave him an awful fright.
We flew within a hundred feet
And pitched out on his right.

CHORUS (*repeat after each verse*)

   Yippee aye aay, yippee aye o-oh
   Trash haulers in the sky.

We called out on the radio,
He hit a power dive,

(*continued on next page*)

And prayed to God and Orville Wright
That he'd remain alive.
He cut down through our pattern,
And pulled about two Gs,
When he gained control again,
He barely cleared the trees!

We told him on the radio,
We said to him, "My son,"
We said, "My boy, if you want to live
You'd damn well better run,
So push those frappin' throttles up
And head across the sky,
And never venture near again
Where fighter pilots fly!"

(04) THE BALLAD OF FUNAFUTI
(Tune: Abdul A Bul Bul Ameer)

NOTE: *The author of the book,* One Damned Island After Another *says this song was written by a B-24 pilot, veteran of Gilbert Island strikes. It was supposedly written during R&R in Hawaii. The author neglected to include the tune. The Editor supplied the tune, above, as it seems to fit. The Editor is not certain why the title of the song says* Funafuti *when the song says* Funafu.

THE BALLAD OF FUNAFUTI

Draw close as I tell
My tale of Hell--
I swear to you it's true.
Let me take you back
To the night attack
On the Island of Funafu.

It had rained just enough
To dampen the ruff
Of the foilage, and dimple the sea,
Then the moon came out
And I heard a shout,
"Take cover!" My God, they meant me.

I found my tin hat,
And gas mask at that.
"Put out the goddamned light!"
Most every soul
Had found him a hole,
But others weren't sure they were right.

Then came the drone
Of engines, a tone
I could hear while still in my tent.
The siren's shrill wail
Cut the air like a nail
Driven rustily into cement.

There was firing at first,
A regular burst,
From the guns manned by game Marines

(05) THE BALLAD OF MACHETE TWO
(See HH5)

(06) THE BALLAD OF MEAN GENE (M)
(Tune: *Combination of Mountain Dew and White Lightning*
Lyrics: *Rollie Stoneman*)

NOTE: *This is the first of ten songs by Rollie Stoneman about missilemen and places. If you get stuck trying to fit the lyrics with the music, the Editor has a recording by Rollie and his Air Force group (called* The Groobers) *that can help you.*

THE BALLAD OF MEAN GENE

They call us the good old Capsule Crew.
And men of our courage are few.
We live like a mole way down in the
    hole.
That good old Capsule Crew.

Well, at Hotel Flight way out in the
    sticks,
Lived a crew commander named Mean Gene
    Hicks.
He'd watch his missiles 'till the sun
    went down,
Then he'd sing right out with a joyful
    sound.

REFRAIN

    Missile duty's pleasin',
    I never will be leavin',
    Ooo, I love it.

(continued on next page)

'Twas the third of June, that fateful
   day,
Gene went on alert so far away.
Then the fuel shortage hit, it still
   hasn't passed,
Now he'll never be relieved 'cause there
   isn't any gas.

REPEAT REFRAIN

Well, I asked mean Gene why he called
   his crew.
The "Tight Twosome" 'stead of one-O-two.
When he kissed his deputy it all came
   clear.
Missile duty made Mean Gene a queer.

REPEAT REFRAIN

(*Bridge*)

   Sky Cops, OSI, CIA
   They're all chasin' Mean Gene trying
      to put him away.
   They're lookin', tryin' to book him,
   But Mean Gene kept on truckin'.
   Ooo, I love it.

REPEAT FIRST VERSE

(07) BALLAD OF THE GREEN BRASSIERE
(Tune: *Ballad Of The Green Berets*)

NOTE: *How are such songs born? Here's
how this one was written. "During the
early part of the war, the Special
Forces club near Bien Hoa burned during
a spirited party. The only item saved
was an olive-drab brassiere that had
hung over the bar. The G.I. issue bra
was escorted to the Air Force club bar,
and with a properly noisy ceremony,
installed there, 'on loan.' It seemed
appropriate that a song commemorate the
occasion, and in a few days---." Thus
was this song introduced in* **Air Force**
magazine in September 1971.

BALLAD OF THE GREEN BRASSIERE

Put silver wings upon her stone
To let her know she's not alone.
We love the maid who's buried here,
The girl who wore...
   The Green Brassiere.

Now let me tell you about this girl,
She's a true Vietnam pearl.
She wore a flower above her ear,
And on her chest...
   The Green Brassiere.

A VC shell came from above,
Only left one thing to remind us of
This little girl we love so dear--
A slightly tattered...
   Green Brassiere.

Put silver wings upon her stone
To let her know she's not alone.
We love the girl who's buried here,
The girl who wore...
   The Green Brassiere.

(00) BALLAD OF THE MIG-21 PILOT
(*See Volume I, song W37*)

(08) BALLAD OF THE PIO
(Tune: *Ballad Of The Green Berets*)

There he goes, the PIO,
Last to know, the first to go;
One hundred times he flies the Huey's,
Flown by publicity-seeking looey's.

Out to battle he must go,
Sent by those in the know;
He may take a sniper's round,
And be left upon the ground.

Fighting men may pass him by,
And when they ask, "Who was that guy?"
"I dunno, it's hard to say.
What the Hell, just let him lay."

And when he gets to the golden gate,
St. Peter says, "You've goofed up, mate!
So go to Hell in all your glory;
When you get back you can do your story"

(09) THE BALLAD OF THE 'VARK
(Tune: *Battle Hymn Of The Republic*)
Lyrics: *Colonel Ron Barker*

NOTE: *This song originated at Korat, Thailand, in 1974, when the composer, Colonel Barker, commanded the 429th Tactical Fighter Squadron. The 429th was known as the* **Black Falcons,** *but John Piowaty, contributor of this song, said that the insignia looked more like a* **Black Crow.** *John probably had* **Old Crow** *in mind. Korat is about 100 miles NNE of Bangkok, and was an F-105 base. The last fighter-bomber mission in Southeast Asia was flown from Korat, and by none other than Lt. Colonel John Piowaty. His call sign on that historic flight was* **COACH 1.**

THE BALLAD OF THE 'VARK

The orders from headquarters meant my
    fighter days were through,
They said, "Report to Nellis to
    Commander 442,"
To learn to fly the Aardvark, there was
    nothing I could do,
I ain't a fighter pilot no more.

CHORUS

    Glory, glory what a helluva way to
        fly,
    Flogging that swing-wing bomber
        through the fighter pilot's sky.
    I'll button my top button, sir, and
        never question why,
    I ain't a fighter pilot no more.

Oh, the F-one-eleven is a McNamara
    scheme,
It's everything to everyone, a
    politician's dream,
But if they ground it one more time, I
    think that I will scream,
I ain't a fighter pilot no more.

CHORUS

    Glory, glory what a helluva way to
        fly,
    The Navy and the British both decided
        not to buy,

But it never entered our dumb heads
    to ask the bastards why,
I ain't a fighter pilot no more.

They sent us off to FTD, the sergeants
    were in charge,
They fed us enough worthless crap to
    sink a friggn' barge.
They should stuff their stupid tinker
    toys in the general's garage,
I ain't a fighter pilot no more.

CHORUS

    Glory, glory what a helluva way to
        fly,
    I read so many goddamned books, I
        thought that I would die,
    You can keep your academics, sir, my
        classroom is the sky,
    I ain't a fighter pilot no more.

Though academics bored me, the
    simulator's worse,
That box is made for idiots and nothing
    in it works,
I think the damned thing was designed to
    check out drugstore clerks,
I ain't a fighter pilot no more.

CHORUS

    Glory, glory what a helluva way to go
    So many things to study and so many
        things to know.
    But will someone please explain, what
        is a WSO?
    I ain't a fighter pilot no more.

I never thought I'd see the day I'd
    welcome company,
But there are so many switches, that I
    think I must agree,
That he can have them all if he'll just
    leave the pole for me,
I ain't a fighter pilot no more.

CHORUS

    Glory, glory fighter gator
    Though the fighter jocks will think
    That I'm a traitor,

(*continued on next page*)

In the Aardvark you're a super
  aviator,
But you ain't a fighter pilot (and
  don't you forget it, Buster!)

After five weeks the day arrived they
  finally let me fly,
I leaped into my Aardvark and I grabbed
  a piece of sky,
And I'll say this that from now on I'll
  make no alibi,
I'll be a fighter pilot ever more.

CHORUS

  Glory, glory oh the Aardvark is the
    thing.
  It's systems are fantastic and I love
    that swinging wing,
  And if you don't like my Switchblade
    you're a flippin' ding-a-ling,
  I'll be a fighter pilot ever more.

NOTE: *At this point, the last verse and
chorus were struck out as if they did
not belong. The verse seems to follow
the song, but the Chorus appears to be a
left-over from another time. The Editor
has included them for posterity (whoever
that is!). For you pre-Vietnam jocks,*
Sierra Hotel *is phonetic alphabet for* **S**
and **H** *(no more* **Sugar How**, *fellows), and
are the initials for* **Shit Hot**, *which in
current jock lingo means THE best! Got
that?*

Then they sent me off to Heyford to join
  this swinging wing,
We flew one stinking sortie, then they
  grounded the damned thing.
They said the chutes were faulty, but
  that ain't no big thing,

CHORUS

  Glory, glory oh, we mustn't be too
    rude,
  But inspectors who tried to have us
    were found standing in the nude.
  Because of guys like Ken and Fred and
    old smooth-talking Jude,
  Yes, the 20th is Sierra Hotel.

(10) THE BALL OF KERRIMUIR
    (Tune: *Unavailable*)

Alternate Titles and Variations:

  (a) *The Ball Of Kerrymoor*
  (b) *Balls To Your Partner*
  (c) *The Great Bloody Ball*
  (d) *Scotch Wedding*

NOTE: *The tune is probably a Scottish
Highland ballad--the Editor has the
score. This is one of the most popular
of the bawdy songs, and appears in many
of the Air Force unit songbooks under
various names. The Editor has combined
the several versions, leading off with
20 of the original verses (note some of
the strange words of Scottish origin),
and followed by Air Force(?) variations.*

THE BALL OF KERRIMUIR

'Twas at the gathering of the Clans,
And all the Scots were there,
'A feelin' up the lassies
Among the pubic hair.

CHORUS (*repeat after each verse*)

  Singin' balls to your partner
  Arse against the wall,
  If you can't get fucked this Saturday
    night,
  You'll never get fucked at all.

There was fucking in the haystacks,
Fucking in the ricks,
You couldn't hear the music
For the swishin' of the pricks.

The Undertaker he was there,
Dressed in a long black shroud,
Swingin' from a chandelier,
And pissin' on the crowd.

The village cripple he was there,
But didn't shag too much,
His old John Thomas had fallen off,
So he fucked 'em with his crutch.

(*continued on next page*)

The local sweepy he was there,
A really filthy brute,
And every time he farted,
He covered 'em all with soot.

The village idiot he was there,
Up to his favorite trick,
Bouncin' on his testicles,
And whistlin' through his prick.

The district nurse was there as well,
She had us all in fits,
Jumping off the mantelpiece,
And landin' on her tits.

The village cooper he was there,
He had a mighty tool,
He pulled his foreskin o'er his head,
And yodeled through the hole.

The country postman he was there,
He had a dose of pox,
As he couldn't fuck the lassies,
So he shagged the letter box.

The old fishmonger he was there,
A dirty stinkin' sod
He never got a stand that night,
So he fucked 'em with a cod.

There was buggery in the parlour,
Sodomy on the stairs,
You couldn't see the dancin' floor,
For the mass of pubic hairs.

There was Dr. Jameson,
The one that fought the Boers,
He leaped up on the table,
And shouted for the whores.

Jock the blacksmith he was there,
He couldn't play the game,
He fucked a lassie seven times,
And wouldn't see her hame (hame???).

NOTE: *It is possible this was a typo in the source document, and should have been* name. *However, even that change doesn't make sense. Oh, well.*

The village elders they were there,
And they were shocked to see,
Four and twenty maidenheads
A hangin' from a tree.

The old schoolmaster he was there,
He fucked by rule of thumb;
By logarithms he worked out
The time that he would come.

Four and twenty virgins,
Came down from Cuiremore,
Only two got back again,
And they were double bore.

In the morning early,
The farmer nearly shat,
For twenty acres of his corn
Were fairly fuckin' flat

And when the ball was over,
The maidens all confessed,
Although they liked the music
The fucking was the best.

ADDITIONAL VERSES

Sandy McPhereson he came along,
It was a bloody shame,
He fucked a lassie forty times,
And wouldn't take her home.

CHORUS #2

Singin', "Who'll do me this time?
Who'll do me now?
The one who did me last time,
Must've used a plough."

The parson's daughter she was there,
The cunning little runt,
With poison up her arse,
And thistle up her cunt.

Four and twenty virgins
Came down from Inverness,
But after the ball was over,
There were four and twenty less.

The bride was in the kitchen,
Explaining to the groom,

(continued on next page)

That the vagina, not the rectum,
Was the entrance to the womb.

The village smithy he was there,
Sitting by the fire
Doing abortions by the score,
With a lump of red-hot wire.

Now farmer Giles he was there,
His sickle in his hand,
And every time he swung around,
He circumcised the band.

The vicar's wife she was there,
Back against the wall.
"Put your money on the table,
I'm fit to do you all."

The village doctor he was there,
He had his bag of tricks,
And in between the dances,
He was sterilizing pricks.

There was fucking on the couches,
There was fucking on the cots,
And lined up against the wall,
Were rows of grinning twots.

Oh the village blacksmith he was there,
His hammer and his awes,
Talking to the queen,
And showing off his balls.

The butcher's wife, oh, she was there,
She wasna' weel,
For she had to go and piddle,
After every little feel.

Little Willie, he was there,
He was only eight.
He could not fuck the women,
So he had to masturbate.

NOTE: *There are more verses, but we have to stop this ball sometime!*

(11) BALL OF YARN
(Tune: *Available*)

Alternate Titles and Variations:

   (a) *That Little Ball Of Yarn*

'Twas a sunny day in June,
All the flowers were in bloom.
The birds were singing gaily on the
   farm,
When I spied a maiden fair
And I said unto her there,
"Let me wind up your little ball of
   yarn."

She said, "Sir, can't you see
You're a stranger to me,
But follow me out behind the barn.
There's a shady little nook
Beside the babbling brook,
Where you can wind up my little ball of
   yarn.

Now young man take my advice,
Never stay out late at night,
And you'll never lose your cherry or
   your charm.
Be like the bluebird and the robin;
Keep your little "P" from bobbin',
And you'll never wind up that little
   ball of yarn.

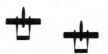

(00) THAT LITTLE BALL OF YARN
(Tune: *Available*)

Oh, it was a day in June
And the flowers were in bloom,
And the birds were singing sweetly in
   the trees.
I saw a pretty miss
And I simply asked her this,
"Could I wind up your little ball of
   yarn?"

She gave me her consent
And behind the fence we went,
Never thinking I would do her any harm.
I layed her on the ground
And I ruffled up her gown,
And I wound up her little ball of yarn.

Nine months later after that,
In a poolroom that I sat,

(*continued on next page*)

Never thinking I had done her any harm.
'Long came a man in blue
Saying, "Boy, I'm looking for you.
You're the father of a nine pound ball
    of yarn."

Now in jail as I sit
With my fingers in my shit,
And the birdbugs playing ping pong with
        my balls,
All the ladies as they pass,
Throw peanuts at my ass,
All for winding up that little ball of
    yarn.

(12) THE BALLS OF O'LEARY
(Tune: *The Bells Of St. Mary's*)

The balls of O'Leary
Are wrinkled and hairy.
They're shapely and stately,
Like the dome of St. Paul.
The women all muster
To see that great cluster.
They stand and they stare
At that hairy great pair
Of O'Leary's balls.

(13) BANG, BANG LULU
(Tune: *Unavailable*)

Alternate Titles or Variations:

(a) *Bang It Into Lulu*

Some girls work in ice cream parlors,
Some girls work in shows,
But Lulu works in a big hotel
With a dozen other whores.

CHORUS (*repeat after each verse*)

    Bang, bang Lulu
    Banging away all day.
    What'll we do for banging
    When Lulu goes away?

Rich girls wear a ring of gold;
The poor a ring of brass;
But the only ring that Lulu wears,
Is the ring around her ass.

Rich girls ride in Cadillacs;
A poor girl rides in a Ford.
But Lulu rides the bedsprings,
To pay her room and board.

A rich girl uses Vaseline,
A poor girl uses lard.
But Lulu uses axle grease,
And it goes in twice as hard.

Rich girls wear a Kotex,
Poor girls wear a rag.
But Lulu's box is so damn big
She wears a burlap bag.

The rich girl wears a coat of mink,
The poor girl wears a fox.
But the only fur that Lulu wears,
Is the fur around her box.

(14) BANG IT INTO LULU
(Tune: *Unavailable*)

Some girls work in factories,
Some girls work in stores.
My girl worked in a knockin' shop
With forty other whores.

CHORUS (*repeat after each verse*)

    Bang it into Lulu,
    Bang it good and strong.
    What'll we do for banging
    When Lulu's dead and gone?

Wish I was a pisspot
Under Lulu's bed.
Every time she stooped to pee,
I'd see her maidenhead.

Wish I was a finger,
On Lulu's little hand.
Every time she wiped her ass,
I'd see the promised land.

Lulu had a baby,
She had it on a rock.
She couldn't call it Lulu,
'Cause the bastard had a cock.

(*continued on next page*)

Lulu had a baby,
She named it Sonny Jim.
She threw it in the pisspot
To teach it how to swim.

Last time I saw Lulu,
I haven't seen her since,
She was suckin' off a tiger
Through a barbed wire fence.

(15) BARNACLE BILL
(Tune: *Barnacle Bill The Sailor*)

Alternate Titles and Variations:

(a) *Barnacle Bill The Pilot - I*
    (See Volume I, song B13)
(b) *Barnacle Bill The Pilot - II*

NOTE: *This is just one version of an old sea-faring song, but it is from the song book of the 92nd TFS, the first A-10 squadron in the USAF.*

BARNACLE BILL

"Who's that knocking at my door?
Who's that knocking at my door?
Who's that knocking at my door?"
Asked the fair young maiden.

"Open the door, you dirty old whore,"
Said Barnacle Bill the sailor.
"Open the door, you dirty old whore,"
Said Barnacle Bill the sailor.

NOTE: *Continue the same repetition of lines, injecting the lines as to whom is speaking as in the verses above.*

"Would you care to have some tea?"
"To Hell with the brew, and on with the screw!"

"Would you care to have a dance?"
"To Hell with the dance, and off with your pants!"

"What's that hanging 'tween your legs?"
"That's the pole I'll stick in your hole!"

"What's this running down my leg?"
"That's the shot that missed the spot!"

"What if I should do to jail?"
"We'll pick the lock with my salty old cock!"

"What if ma and pa should see?"
"We'll shoot your pa and fuck your ma!"

"What if I should have a child?"
"We'll dig a ditch and bury the bitch!"

"When will I see you again?"
"Never more you dirty old whore!"

(16) BARNACLE BILL THE PILOT - II
(Tune: *Barnacle Bill The Sailor*)

NOTE: *With minor changes in words, this version of the ditty is much the same as the one above, and was found in the 95th FITS* **Hymn Book,** *a post-Vietnam publication (1979). Only the new verses are presented below, and their proper positioning in the song are obvious.*

BARNACLE BILL THE PILOT - II

"Who's that standing in my door?"
"Close the door and lie on the floor,"
    said Barnacle Bill the pilot."

* * * *

"What's that grass around your pole?"
"That's the grass to tickle your ass,"

* * * *

"What if we should go to jail?"
"We'll rack their balls and tear down the walls,"

"What if we should get the chair?"
"We'll cut a fart and blow it apart,"

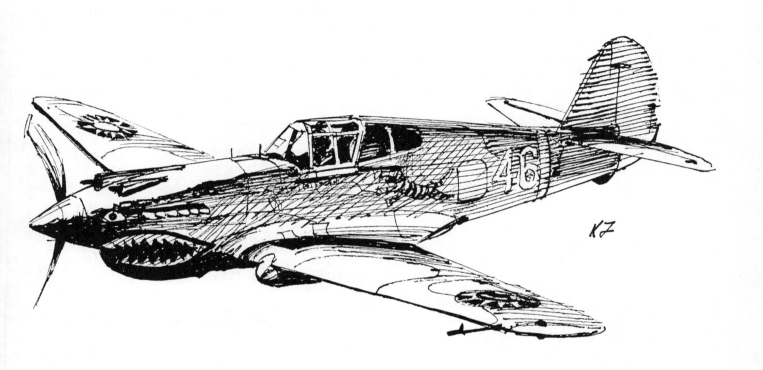

Curtiss P-40

(17) THE BASTARD KING OF ENGLAND
(Tune: *Available*)

The minstrels sing of a bastard king
Of a thousand years ago,
Who ruled this land with an iron hand,
Though his mind was mean and low.

He was very fond of hunting
And roving the royal wood.
He was also fond of apple jack,
And pulling the royal pud.

He was forty, fat, and full o' fleas,
The royal nob hung next his knees
Twelve inches long and a two-inch span,
As King he made a dirty old man.

Now the Queen of Spain was an amorous
  dame,
And a sprightly wench was she;
She longed to fool with the royal tool
Of the King across the sea.

So she sent a secret message
By a lean ambassador,
To ask the King if he would spend
A month in bed with her.

Now Phillip of France when he heard
  this chance,
Within his royal court,
He swore, "By God, she loves his nob,
Because my tool is short."

So he sent the rotten Duc d'Alsace
To give the Queen a dose of clap,
To ruin the length and burn the sap
Of the Bastard King of England.

When news of this foul deed was heard,
Within fair London's walls,
The King he swore by the royal whore
He'd have King Phillip's balls.

And he issued a proclamation
That a tuft of the Queen's cunt hair
He'd give to the sod who brought him the
  rod,
And the nuts of Philip the fair.

The brave young Duke of Buckingham
Went instantly to France,
And lay that night with the royal
  catamite
And when he downed his pants.

He fastened a thong to Fair Philip's
  dong,
Jumped on a horse and galloped along,
Over the cliffs and under the seas,
And brought them both to the Bastard's
  knees.

Now all the whores in silken drawers
Sat on the castle walls,
When the Duke sang "King, I got his
  thing!"
They merely answered, "Balls."

But the King threw up his breakfast,
And grovelled on the floor,
For in the ride, the French King's pride
Had stretched a yard or more.

And Philip alone usurped his throne,
His sceptre was his royal bone,
He fucked each member of the realm
And the Bastard King went down to Hell.

(18) BATTLE OF DOUMER BRIDGE
(Tune: *Joshua Fought The Battle Of Jericho*)

NOTE: *December 18, 1967 went down in many a squadron's history as the day they fought the* **Battle of Doumer Bridge** *a Vietnam War classic. Bob White led this raid, according to Colonel George Weiss.*

BATTLE OF DOUMER BRIDGE

CHORUS (*repeat after each verse*)

  We fought the Battle of Doumer Bridge
  Doumer Bridge, Doumer Bridge.
  We fought the Battle of Doumer Bridge
  And the bridge went tumblin' down.

(*continued on next page*)

Eighteen December, sixty-seven--
It seemed like a thunderclap.
We dropped Doumer Bridge on down.
Into Ho Chi Minh's red lap.

Now you talk about your River Kwai
    Bridge,
And the one at Thanh Hoa, too.
We got ten seconds over that bridge,
Then into the mountain dew.

Uncle Ho holds all the cards, boys,
And he plays them with great joy.
Wonder how he liked that game of bridge
Up at old Hanoi?

Now we lost some friends up yonder
Died to SAMs and MIGs and flak,
But if Ho puts that damn bridge up,
Well, we'll all be going back.

For those who've gone before us,
For those who've left our shore,
I know we're not forgetting them
So let's sing it just once more.
(Chorus twice)

(19) BATTLE HYMN
(Tune: *Battle Hymn Of The Republic*)

Alternate Titles and Variations:

    (a) *Battle Hymn of the Thud*
        (or Phantom, Sabre, Jug, etc.)
    (b) *Fighter Pilot's Hymn (not same as*
        in Volume I, F13)
    (c) *The Thud (or Phantom, Jug, Sabre)*

We fly our fucking Thuds at 10,000 fucking
    feet.
We fly our fucking Thuds through the rain
    and through the sleet,
And though we think we're flying south
We're flying fucking north,
And we make our fucking landfall on the
    Firth of fucking Forth.

CHORUS (*repeat after each verse*)

    Glory, glory what a helluva way to die.
    Glory, glory what a helluva way to die.
    Glory, glory what a helluva way to die.
    Glory, glory what a helluva way to die,
    (*INSERT LAST LINE OF EACH VERSE*)

We fly those fucking Phantoms at fuck all
    thousand feet.
We fly those fucking Phantoms through the
    trees and corn and wheat.
And though we think we fly with skill
We fly with fucking luck,
But we don't give a fucking damn or care
    a fucking fuck.

We fly those fucking Phantoms at 10,000
    fucking feet.
We fly those fucking Phantoms through rain
    and snow and sleet.
And though we think we're flying up,
We're flying fucking down,
And we bust our fucking asses when we hit
    the fucking ground.

(20) BEELINER SONG
(Tune: *Whiffenpoof Song*)

NOTE: *This song comes from the song book*
of the 21st Squadron (The Beeliners),
374th Troop Carrier Wing. The Editor
was a TDY member of this wing for four
months in 1948-49 on Guam, during the
Berlin Airlift. It was called a group
at that time. As an ex-C-54 pilot (1945-
46), the Editor was pulled from his desk
in Tokyo (Thank you, Lord) and placed
TDY to replace the aircrews sent to
Europe. The 21st Squadron song book
came later. This is also an example of
how a good parody is made from the orig-
inal words and music of a song.

BEELINER SONG

From the boys up in the barracks,
To the guys down on the line,
To the wild blue yonder that we'll
    always love,
Stand the Red Cap Squad assembled,

(*continued on next page*)

With their glasses raised on high,
And the magic of their singing casts
    a spell.
Yes, the magic of their singing
Of the songs we love so well,
Jolly Sixpence, Wild Blue Yonder and
    the rest.
We will serenade Division
While life and voice shall last,
Then we'll pass and be forgotten with
    the rest.

REFRAIN

    We are poor little Bees
    Who have found the Way,
    Bzzz, Bzzzzzz, Bzzzz.
    We are good little Bees
    Who have gone astray,
    Bzzz, Bzzzzzz, Bzzzz.
    Beeliner Squadron off on a spree,
    Fly from here to eternity,
    God have mercy on such as we,
    Bzzz, Bzzzzzz, Bzzzz.

(21) BESIDE AN OAHU WATERFALL
    (Tune: *The Dying Hobo*)

Alternate Titles and Variations:
(*All in Volume I except* **h** *below*)

    (a) *Beneath A Bridge In Sicily*
    (b) *Beside A Belgian Staminet*
    (c) *Beside A Belgian Watertank*
    (d) *Beside A Brewery At St. Mihiel*
    (d) *Beside A (New) Guinea Waterfall*
    (e) *Beside A Korean Waterfall*
    (f) *Beside A Minnesota Waterfall*
    (g) *Beside A Tucson Waterfall*
    (h) *Laotian Karst (see below)*
    (i) *Laotian Waterfall*
    (j) *The Passing Pilot - I*
    (k) *The Passing Pilot - II*
    (l) *Ting-A-Ling*
    (m) *To Cadets Who Failed At Kelly*
    (n) *Under A Korean Sun*
    (o) *U. S. Air Force Heaven*
    (p) *The Warthog Driver (below)*
    (q) *The Young Pursuiter*

NOTE: *Parodies based upon the 19th
Century railroad song,* **The Dying Hobo,**
*are legend in the Air Force, and date
from World War I. This first version
below dates from pre-World War II days,
and is a welcome addition to the collection, courtesy of the Flying Class of
40-A. It is interesting that the last
verse, a wish expressed over 45 years
ago--the part about* women--*could well be
true in today's Air Force. The second
rendition is from a small (4" X 5") song
book of the 347th Tactical Fighter Wing,
undated, courtesy of that great balladeer, John Piowaty. The third addition
to the collection comes from the song
book of the 92nd Tactical Fighter Squadron, the first A-10 squadron in the Air
Force. And fellows of the 92nd, you
don't have to go to Heaven to have
female crew chiefs!*

BESIDE AN OAHU WATERFALL

Beside an Oahu Waterfall
One bright and sunny day,
Beside his shattered Kittyhawk
The young peashooter lay.

His parachute hung from a nearby tree,
He was not yet quite dead,
Oh, listen to the very last words,
The young peashooter said.

"I'm going to a better land
Where everything is bright,
Where whiskey flows from telephone poles
Play poker every night.

You never have to work at all
Just sit around and sing;
And all your crew are women--
Oh--death--where--is--thy--sting?"

(OO) LAOTIAN KARST
(Tune: *The Dying Hobo*)

NOTE: *The Websters Collegiate Dictionary says a* **karst** *is an irregular limestone region with sinks, underground
streams and caverns. Whatever. The
Second Edtion of Webster's Unabridged
didn't even have the word. Golly!*

(continued on next page)

LAOTIAN KARST

Beside a Laotian chunk of Karst,
One dark and windy night,
Inside their shattered capsule,
What a fucking plight.

The parachute hung from a nearby tree,
They were not yet quite dead.
So listen to the very last words,
These young pursuiters said.

"I'm going to a better land,
Where everything is right.
Where whiskey flows from telegraph
  poles,
There's poker every night.

"There's not a fucking thing to do,
But sit around and sing.
Where all the girls are women;
Oh, death, where is they sting?"

Oh, death, where is thy stingalingaling?
Oh, death, where is they sting?
The bells of Hell will ringalingaling,
For you but not for me.

Sooo, tingalingalingling, blow it out
  your ass!
Tingalingalingling, blow it out your
  ass.
Tingalingalingling, blow it out your
  ass.
Better days are coming by and by.

(00) THE WARTHOG DRIVER
(Tune: *The Dying Hobo*)

Beside the German Autobahn,
The Warthog pilot lay.
His armored bathtub was all gone,
His rudder shot away.
His A-10 burned by a nearby tree,
But he was not yet quite dead.
So listen to the story,
That the Warthog driver said.

He said, "I'm going to a better land,
Where everything's all right,
Where whiskey flows from telegraph poles
Play poker every night.
And all there is to do all day

Is sit around and sing.
The crew chiefs are all women,
Oh, Death, where is they sting?

Oh, Death, where is thy sting? Ding-
  a-ling.
Oh, Death, where is thy sting? Ding-
  a-ling.
The bells of Hell may ring-a-ling-
  a-ling
For you but not for me. . .

Oh . . . ring-a-ding a-ding-ding, blow
  it out your ass.
Ring-a-ding a-ding-ding, blow it out
  your ass (and singin').
Ring-a-ding a-ding-ding, blow it out
  your ass.
Better days are coming by and by . . .
BULL...SHIT!

(22) BIG BALLS
(Tune: *Unavailable*)

There was a man, Sir Anthony Clair,
A nobleman beyond compare,
And he was famous everywhere,
As a man who could play with his balls.

CHORUS (*repeat after each verse*)

  For they were big balls,
  Big and heavy as lead,
  With a flick and a twist
  Of his muscular wrist,
  He could throw them right over his
    head.

As he was walking down the street,
A fair young maid he chanced to meet,
Who tho't would be a helluva treat,
To watch a man play with his balls.

As he was twirling 'em 'round and 'round
Down they came with a Hell of a bound,
Right on the head of a faithful hound,
Who was watching him play with his balls

They hauled him in 'fore the magistrate,
Who put him in a cell of state,
And left him there to cogitate,
And play with his beautiful balls.
(*continued on next page*)

His trial was held without delay,
In fact 'twas that very same day.
The magistrate said I see no reason why,
A man can't play with his balls.

(00) THE BIG GREY RAT
(*See Volume I, song G12*)

(00) THE BIG WHEEL (*See BB24*)

(00) THE BIRD (*See Volume I, L12*)

(23) BLESSED ARE WOMEN
        (Tune: *Unavailable*)

Blessed are women,
Those creatures divine;
Blossom every month,
Bear every nine.

They're the only creatures
In either heaven or Hell,
Who can get juice out of a nut,
Without cracking the shell!

(00) BLESS 'EM ALL (*See TT 24*)

(00) BLINDED BY SHIT (*See AA03*)

(24) THE BLOODY GREAT WHEEL
(Tune: *Oh Master, Let Me Walk With Thee*)

Alternate Titles and Variations:

   (a) *Airman's Lament*
   (b) *The Big Wheel*
   (c) *Engineer's Song*
   (d) *The Great Fucking Wheel*
   (e) *Sweet Violets*
   (f) *The Wheel*

NOTE: One of the most popular of the
bawdy songs. This Air Force parody
sticks   very   close   to   the   original
British Navy song dating waaay back.

THE BLOODY GREAT WHEEL

An airman told me before he died,
And I don't think that the bastard lied,
That he had a wife with a cunt so wide,
That she could never be satisfied.

So he invented a prick of steel,
Driven by a bloody great wheel--
Two brass balls all filled with cream
And the whole fucking issue was driven
        by steam.

'Round and 'round went the bloody great
        wheel,
In and out went the prick of steel--
Until at last the maiden cried,
"Enough, enough, I'm satisfied."

But now we come to the bitter bit,
There was no way of stopping it.
She was split from ass to tit,
And the whole fucking issue was covered
        in shit.

CHORUS

   Sweet violets
   Sweeter than all the roses.
   Covered all over from ass to tit,
   Covered all over with--
   Sweet violets...

(25) BLUE HEAVEN
(Tune: *My Blue Heaven*)

Alternative Titles or Variations:

   (a) *Little Red Light*
   (b) *My Red Haven*

A turn to the right,
A little red light,
Will lead you to my blue heaven.

You'll see a smiling face on a pillow
        case,
A form divine.
She's just a whore, she's been had
        before,
But now she's mine.

(*continued on next page*)

Just Molly and me,
There'll never be three.
We're careful in my blue heaven.

(26) BLUES IN A FIGHT
(Tune: *Blues In The Night*)

From Bremen to Munster,
From Munster to Berlin,
Wherever the heavies go.
I've been in some big fights,
I've seen me some big flak,
And there is one thing I know;
A JU's a two-place,
A worriesome thing
That will lead you to sing
The blues in a fight.

See the flak a-blowing,
Watch the Forts a-going, blooey.
Hear the lonesome gunner,
Riding by the rudder, whooey.
To whooey, to whooey,
Oh, flickety flak, comes
Echoing back,
The blues in a fight.

(27) THE BLUE STAR
(Tune: *My Bonnie Lies Over The Ocean*)

NOTE: *This song dates back to World War I, and this version was used by both the Air Force and the Marines in Korea. Also see Volume I, song M23.*

Take the blue star out of the window,
   Mother,
Replace it with one made of gold;
Your son was a damn good wingman,
But he died in a whore house in Seoul,
   tough shit!

CHORUS (*repeat after each verse*)

   Tough shit, tough shit,
   He died in a whore house in Seoul,
      tough shit!
   Tough shit, tough shit,
   He died in a whore house in Seoul,
      tough shit!

Take the blue star out of the window,
   Mother,
Replace it with a gold one instead,
Your son just got hit with a mortar,
It blew off his whole fucking head,
   tough shit!

Take the blue star out of the window,
   Mother,
Replace it with one made of brass,
Your son was an F4B driver,
Who yesterday busted his ass,
   tough shit!

Take the blue star out of the window,
   Mother,
Your son hasn't got any nerve,
He says he's defending his country,
And he's just a Goddamn reserve,
   HORSE SHIT!!!!

(28) BMTS BLUES (*original title unknown*)
(Tune: *The Twelve Days Of Christmas*)

NOTE: *This song originated in Basic Military Training School at Lackland AFB, and it came from a series of letters from Air Force Nurse, Lt. Sharon Cooper, to her mother. The Lieutenant's version did not include the words, in a pear tree--which the editor supplied-- but there had to be something there to make it work. Sorry, Mam, if that wasn't right. The Editor hasn't the foggiest about some of the terms. The ballad is similar to* **Twelve Days of Christmas** *(and* **TET** *and* **Bonehead***) all found in* Flight Section TT *of this volume. Also see Volume I, songs T50 and T51.*

BMTS BLUES

On the first day of basic my TI gave to
   me,
1 set of green fatigues, in a pear tree.

On the second day of basic my TI gave to
   me,
2 glasses of water, in a pear tree.

(*continued on next page*)

REPEAT THE LINES WITH THE NEXT DAY:

3   41s
4   hospital corners
5   name tags
6   inch T-shirts
7   drill movements
8   minute showers
9   hour briefings
10 airmen rushing
11 miles of marching
12 duty hours

(29) BOMBER PILOT'S LAMENT
(Tune: *When You Wore A Tulip*)

When I flew a bomber,
A big heavy bomber,
And you flew a thirty nine.
While you were playing,
I would be praying,
You were always out of line.

There was a snafu,
You missed a rendevous,
Up where the M.E.s whine.
You shot my navigator,
In my old Liberator,
When you flew a thirty nine.

(00) BOOM TODAY (*See Vol. I, B17*)

NOTE: *The correct tune for this ditty
from the Korean War is,* **Tra La La Boom
Toolray.** *There is some question about
the spelling of the last word in the
title, but you got the drift!*

(30) THE BORN LOSER (M)
(Tune: *Teenager In Love*)
 Lyrics: *Rollie Stoneman*

They sent me out on backup, I didn't
    want to go.
And then to make things worse, you know,
    I told them so.

Now every night I ask my attorney with-
    out fail,
"Why must I be a crew member in jail?"

The IG came to Delta, I was asleep in
    bed.
My deputy was shakey, but he may soon
    be dead.
He didn't wear his gun when he opened up
    the door.
The elevator woke me up when I began
    to snore.

REFRAIN

    I cry a tear, for nobody but me.
    I'd be so happy now if I could just
        be free.

We didn't make our keyturn, our keys
    were in the safe.
We lost a crypto book, couldn't find it
    any place.
My pistol fired when I tripped upon the
    rail.
No one ever asked my side, they just
    threw me in jail.

REPEAT REFRAIN

The wing commander loves me, says I'm
    still number one.
Of course, he is my father, and I'm his
    only son.
But even so he won't pay my bail,
So I'll remain a crew member in jail.

(31) BOSOM BUDDIES - II
(Tune: Verses - *Stand To Your Glasses*
       Chorus - *Wrap Me Up In My
               Tarpaulin Jack*)

Altenate Titles and Variations:
       (*Volume I, A14*)

    (a) *Bosom Buddies*
    (b) *Boozin' Buddies*
    (c) *Stand To Your Glasses*

NOTE: *This is another combined song,
similar to those of the same name in*

(*continued on next page*)

Volume I (See Bosom Buddies and Boozin Buddies under song A14). This one comes from the 92nd Fighter Squadron song book, and it combines the Boozin song with the classic, Stand To Your Glasses. Now just what melody they are using for the verses and chorus had to be guessed. The Editor did a little editing on the verses to correct them to the original song and melody (that's what editors are suppose to do!).

BOSOM BUDDIES - II

We stand 'neath silent rafters,
The walls around us are bare.
They echo back our laughter,
It seems like the dead are all there.

So, stand to your glasses steady,
And ne'er let a tear fill your eye.
Here's a toast to the dead already,
And hoorah for the next man to die.

CHORUS

> For we are the boys who fly high in
>   the sky.
> Bosom buddies while boozin' are we.
> Yes, we are the boys who they send up
>   to die,
> Bosom buddies while boozin' are we.

Up at headquarters they scream and they
  shout,
About lots of things they know nothing
  about,
But we are the boys who they send up
  to die,
Bosom buddies while boozin' are we.

We climb in the purple twilight,
We loop in the silvery dawn.
Black smoke trails behind us,
To show where our comrades have gone.

REPEAT CHORUS

(00) THE BRIDGE *(See Volume I, song W37)*

(00) BRING BACK MY C-54
(See Volume I, song B53)

NOTE: *This song is similar to Bring Back My C-82, in Volume I, song B53, except for the name of the aircraft, the manufacturer's name and the city. Any aircraft substitutions can be made to make a new parody.*

(32) BRITISH GRENADIERS
   (Tune: *See Note*)

NOTE: *Although no tune was provided in the source song book, with some effort on the last two lines, this song seems to fit the original British Grenadiers.*

BRITISH GRENADIERS

Some die of diabetes, and some die of
      diarrhea,
Some die of drinking whiskey, and some
      of drinking beer;
But of all the world's diseases, there's
      none that can compare
With the drip, drip, drip, from the end
      of your prick,
Of the British Gonorrhea.

(33) BROWN ANCHOR
(Tune: Oh, Susannah)

NOTE: **Brown Anchor** *is the name of the airborne refueling tankers so vital to the figher jock on long-range missions in 'Nam. The Editor is not familiar with all the jargon used in this great song from the S.E.A. fracas--which dates the Editor! However, he does know that the initials B.D.A. means Bomb Damage Assessment, a term used more frequently after WW II.*

BROWN ANCHOR

The phone did ring at half past four,
For briefing I wasn't there.
"Get your ass here right away.
You've been elected spare."

(continued on next page)

CHORUS #1 (*repeat after each verse*)

   Oh, Brown Anchor,
   With my two hour ass.
   A Fabnestock Clip upon my dick;
   Oh, Leader go home fast!

I was sitting by the runway,
And feeling mighty low.
"Bear four, you've got a hydraulic leak.
I guess I'll have to go."

I guess I told a little lie,
It probably wasn't fair.
It was my only chance to say,
"Bear spare is in the air."

It was raining out when we took off,
Night weather we did fly.
We rendezvoused at nineteen thou,
My tanks were nearly dry.

As we climbed out I had to fart,
My belly it did swell.
I had to put my mask back on,
I couldn't stand the smell.

They're 12 o'clock at 5 miles.
You're cleared refueling freq.
"Tally-ho" our flight leader cried,
And head-on we did meet.

We hung out at 14 thou,
The burner going strong.
The flak came flying by my bow,
We can't hang out here long.

Oh, I pulled off the target,
And for B.D.A. looked back.
I couldn't see the bomb burst,
For the son-of-a-bitchen' flak!

Finally got my hundred flown,
To the States I'm flying back.
Six more hours on my ass,
And then into the sack.

CHORUS #2 (*repeat after each verse*)

   No more Brown Anchor,
   For my two hour ass.
   Get that clip right off my dick,
   And jump in bed right fast.

I opened my hold baggage,
My wife she sure did flip.
I hope that she will understand,
I just adopted "Nip".

I rolled over with a sigh,
Bed springs were sagging low.
Put a mark upon the wall,
Only 99 to go.

Though I had a Bravo frag
As I jumped into bed,
It was a real tight target,
So I marked it up in red.

REPEAT CHORUS #2 TWICE

(34) BROWN, BROWN (*See AA03*)

(00) BUBBLING BROOK (*See AA01*)

(35) BUGGARED
(Tune: *Botany Bay*)

NOTE: *This is one song that will hit home with many of the older vets--and we're not talking about the Spanish American War, fellows! The only thing good about growing old is ---- I'll be damned if I know! There are one or two British terms in this ditty that you can figure out for yourself.*

BUGGARED

For forty years I've been buggared
With horrible aches and pains.
I've had every ailment I reckon,
From rupture to varicose veins.

CHORUS (*repeat after each verse*)

   Singing too-ra-li-oo-ra-li-addity,
   Too-ra-li-oo-ra-li-aa
   Singing too-ra-li-oo-ra-li-addity,
   Too-ra-li-oo-ra-li-aa

(*continued on next page*)

Neuritis with me is a hobby.
I've bunions and corns on my feet,
And I seem to breed stones in my bladder
Like fuckin' great lumps of concrete.

I've spent a small fortune on chemists,
I've lain months in hospital beds,
And the stuff I've taken to shift me,
Has torn my poor stomach to shreds.

And in spite of the cures I'm taking,
There's hardly a day I feel fit;
And it takes a full pound of gunpowder,
Before I can bloody-well shit.

I've a stricture in the tube of my penis
And I don't mind telling you this,
I've to whistle "The Last Rose of
   Summer,"
To coax my poor doodle to piss.

And as for a first class erection,
The idea is simply absurd;
For my cock's like an undersized maggot,
And as soft as a night commode turd.

So my time's all spent in the shithouse,
Or moaning or groaning in bed;
While my friends they all murmur when
   passing,
"It's time the poor bastard was dead."

(36) BUMMING AROUND TOWN
(Tune: *The Strawberry Roan*)

NOTE: *The story of an extraordinary whore who posed a challenge to some macho guy, is standard fare for the balladeer. This song, along with* **Lupee 2, Rangy Lil, Yukon Pete,** *and* **Kathuselem** *are some of the songs in this volume with this same macho-male (sometimes macho-female) theme.*

BUMMING AROUND TOWN

I was bumming around town, not spending
   a dime,
So steps in a whorehouse, to have a good
   time.
Up steps an old bitch, who says I
   suppose,
That your a good cunt-man, by the cut of
   your clothes.

I'm a young airman a'building my fame.
Do you happen to have any old whore to
   tame?
Yes, I am one that you cannot fuck;
At throwing good riders, I've had lots
   of luck.
So I lays an old ten spot right down on
   the line,
And she steps in the bedroom and pulls
   down the blind.

She lay on the bed with a horrible groan
The hair on her ass was strawberry roan;
She commenced her wild movement, and I
   made my pass,
And landed my donneker right square in
   her ass.

Now, I'm telling you boys that old gal
   could step,
And I was an airman a'building my rep.
With a hell of a lunge and a god-awful
   cry,
She left me a'sitting way up in the sky.

I turned over twice 'ere I came back to
   earth,
And I lay there a'cussing the day of her
   birth;
Now I'm telling you boys, there's no
   pilot alive,
That can ride that old bitch when she
   makes that high dive.

(37) BYE, BYE CHERRY
(Tune: *Bye, Bye Blackbirds*)

Back your ass against the wall,
Here I come, balls and all.
Bye, bye, cherry.

(*continued on next page*)

I ain't got a helluva lot,
But what I got will fill your twat.
Bye, bye, cherry.

CHORUS

  Wrap your legs around me tighter.
  Make my load become a little lighter.
  Shake your ass and wiggle your tits,
  'Till my big John Henry spits.
  Bye, bye, cherry.

ALTERNATE CHORUS

  I took her to my cottage in the wild
    woods,
  And there I took advantage of her
    childhood.
  I came once, she came twice;
  Oh, my god, it was nice.
  Cherrr--iiees, bye bye.

(38) BYE, BYE, USAF
(Tune: *Bye, Bye, Blackbirds*)

NOTE: *It will not come as a surprise to
realize that not all members of the Air
Force were happy in their work. Writing
and singing songs was (and is) one way
the airman had of vexing his/her feelings, as in this poignant polemic--
whatever that means!*

BYE, BYE, USAF

When we get back home again
We're not going Air Force then;
Bye, bye, USAF.

This rotation plan is great;
Never more than two years late.
Bye, bye, USAF.

No one in this outfit understands me.
Look at all the shit they always hand
  me.
Silver wings, bars of brass,
You can shove them up your ass!
Air Force, bye, bye.

Look at all the shit they threw,
To get my ass up in the blue.
Bye, bye, USAF.

Sexy parties, girls galore,
But we wind up with a whore.
Bye, bye, USAF.

Some one in this outfit sure seduced me,
With a purple shaft they really goosed
  me.
Silver wings, bars of brass,
You can shove them up your ass.
Air Force, bye, bye.

They called us in and threw us out.
That's why we all shout,
Bye, bye, USAF.

We're all here, yes we are,
But the Hudson High Boys get the star.
Bye, bye, USAF.

When they threw me out that's fine,
They can kiss my ass next time.
Air Force, bye, bye.

(39) BY THE LIGHT
(Tune: *By The Light Of The Silvery Moon*)

Alternate Titles and Variations:

  (a) *Flickering Match*

NOTE: "-- --" stands for "choo-choo"

By the light -- -- of the flickering
    match -- --
I saw her snatch -- --
In the watermelon patch--ooh, ooh.

By the light -- -- of the flickering
    match -- --
I saw her gleam,
I heard her scream,
You are burning my snatch -- -- with
    your goddamn match! -- --

(00) THE B-18 SONG

NOTE: *This song is nearly identical to
the song,* **The B-17, We Love You,** *which
can be found in Volume I, song B59, By
substituting the word* **Digby** *(as the B-18
was called) for* **B-17,** *the songs are the
same, give or take a word or two.*

FLIGHT SECTION CC

(00) CAFOOZALEM (*See KK01*)

(01) CALL OUT THE ARMY AND THE NAVY
   (Tune: *Unavailable*)

Alternate Titles and Variations:

   (a) *Fleet Air Wing - Alma Mater
       (See Volume I, F23)*
   (b) *Gor Blimey*
   (c) *I Don't Want To Be A Soldier*
   (d) *I Don't Want To Be A 'Ero*
   (e) *I Don't Want To Join The Army
       (or Air Force)*
   (f) *Piccadilly*
   (g) *Sidney Special*

NOTE: *There are several variations of
this favorite British song, but most of
them involve minor word differences or
arrangements. The version below is
representative of most, and is actually
a composite of several.*

CALL OUT THE ARMY AND THE NAVY

Monday I touched her on the ankle,
Tuesday I touched her on the knee,
Wednesday with success,
I lifted up her dress,
Thursday, her chemise, Gor Blimey.
Friday, I put my hand upon it,
Saturday night she gave me balls a
   tweak,
And Sunday after supper,
I rammed the old boy up her,
And now I'm paying seven bob a week,
Gor Blimey.

CHORUS

   I don't want to join the Air Farce,
   I don't want to go to war.
   I just want to hang around

The Picadilly Underground,
Living off the earnings of a high-
   born "lady".
Don't want a bullet up my arse-hole.
Don't want my buttocks shot away.
I'd rather be in England,
In jolly, jolly England,
And fornicate me bloody life away.

C-46 COMMANDO

Call out the Army and the Navy.
Call out the rank and file.
Call out the royal territorials,
They face danger with a smile.
Call out the boys of the old brigade,
That made Old England free.
You can call out me mother,
Me sister and me brother,
But for God's sake,
Don't call me!
Gor Blimey.

(02) THE CANDLER'S BOY
(Tune: *The Thing*)

Oh, the boy went into the candler's
 shop,
Some candles for to buy.
He hunted all over the candler's shop,
The candler to espy.
He hunted, he hollered, he screamed, he
 bawled,
When he suddenly heard a tap, tap,tap,
 right above his head.
Yes, he suddenly heard a tap, tap, tap,
 right above his head.

Now, this little boy was very sly,
He started to climb the stairs.
So as not to disturb the hairs.
And there on the bed lay the candler's boy,
Between a lady's thighs,
And they were having a tap, tap, tap,
 right before his eyes.
Yes, they were having a tap, tap, tap,
 right before his eyes.

Now, when the game was over,
The lady raised her head,
And she was very surprised to see
The boy beside her bed.
Said she, "Young man, if my secret
 you'll keep,
To you I will be kind,
And you'll be having a tap, tap, tap
 whenever you're so inlcined.
Yes, you'll be having a tap, tap, tap,
 whenever you're so inclined."

Now, all you men who do have wives,
Whenever you go to town,
Make sure you either lock 'em up,
Or else you tie 'em down.
For if they're like the candler's wife
And true to the ways of their kind,
Why they'll be having a tap, tap, tap
 whenever they're so inclined.
Yes, they'll be having a tap, tap, tap,
 whenever they're so inclined.

Now, this is the end of my story,
And if you nod your head,
We'll just turn out the lights right
 here,
And slowly climb to bed.
For if you're like the candler's wife,

And maybe you're so inclined,
Well, we'll be having a tap, tap, tap,
 when you make up your mind.
Yes, we'll be having a tap, tap, tap,
 when you make up your mind.

(03) THE CANDLE SONG
(Tune: *Unavailable*)

All the nice girls love a candle,
'Cause a candle has a wick,
And there's something about a candle,
That reminds them of a prick.
Nice and greasy, slips in easy.
It's the maidens pride and joy.
You can hear them sing and shout
"Ship ahoy! Ship ahoy!"

(04) CAROLINA, THE COWPUNCHER'S WHORE
(Tune: *Unavailable*)

Alternate Title and Variations:

 (a) *Charlot The Harlot*

NOTE: *By substituting* **Charlot** *for*
Carolina, *and* **Texas** *for* **Alabama**, *you
have the parody* **Charlot The Harlot**
*However, an authority said (the only
person sober at the bar), that the
second sentence of the first verse describes Texas better than Alabama.*

CAROLINA, THE COWPUNCHER'S WHORE

Way down in Alabama,
Where the bullshit lies thick,
Where the girls are so pretty,
Their babies come quick.
There lived Carolina,
The queen of them all,
Carolina, Carolina, the cowpuncher's
 whore.

She's handy, she's dandy,
She shits in the street.
Wherever you see her,
She's always in heat.
You have your fly open,
She's after your meat,

(*continued on next page*)

The smell of her cunt,
Knocks you right off your feet.
One night I was riding,
Way down by the falls.
One hand on my pistol,
The other on my balls.
I saw Carolina
A'using a stick,
Instead of the end
Of a cowpuncher's dick.

I caressed her, I undressed her,
I laid her down there,
And parted the tresses
Of her pubic hair.
Inserted the thickness
Of my sturdy horse,
And then there began
A strange intercourse.

Faster and faster
Went my trusty steed,
Until Carolina rejoiced
At the speed.
When all of a sudden
My horse did backfire,
And shot Carolina
Right into the fire.

I found Carolina,
All covered with muck;
She said, "Oh, my dear,
What a glorious fuck!"
Then her sexual organ
Fell out on the floor,
And that was the end
Of the cowpuncher's whore.

(05) CASE OF THE ILL-STARRED LOVERS
(Tune: *Unavailable*)

They were married but not to each other;
(Now I might as well make this explicit)
They could never cut loose from their
    marital noose,
And they were forced to a passion elicit

With no hope for a happy finale,
With a future that led to a bleak end;
They agreed to enact a sad suicide pact,
In a riotous fling on the weekend.

In a riotous fling on the weekend,
In a tourist motel by a rock's side,
Without any regrets they turned on the
    jets,
And awaited the carbon monoxide.

They awaited the carbon monoxide,
(They preferred it to shootin' or
    stabbin'),
And they were going, but quick, but
    were saved in time's nick,
By their spouses who shared the next
cabin.

(06) CATS ON THE ROOF TOPS
(Tune: *John Peel*)

Alternate Titles and Variations:

    (a) *You Revel In The Joys Of
        Copulation*

NOTE: *The version below of this British
ditty is a composite from several songbooks.   The last three verses, however,
do not appear to fit the meter of the
other verses, and may actually come from
a different, but similar song.*

CATS ON THE ROOF TOP

The hippopotamus, so it seems,
Seldom if ever has wet dreams.
But when he does, he comes in streams,
As he revels in the joys of copulation.

CHORUS (*repeat after each verse*)

    Cats on the roof tops, cats on the
      tiles.
    Cats with the syphillis, cats with
      the piles.
    Cats with their assholes wreathed in
      smiles,
    As we revel in the joys of copulation

Down in the Pampas, down in the grass,
Mama armadillo has an iron-bound ass.
But papa armadillo has a prick of brass,
As they revel in the joys of copulation.

(*continued on next page*)

Way down south where the alligators
   roar,
There isn't such a thing as an alligator
   whore.
'Cause all the alligators are too sore,
As they revel in the joys of copulation.

Oh, the elephant is a solitary bloke,
Who seldom ever gets a poke,
But when he does, he lets it soak,
As he revels in the joys of copulation.

Oh, the Ostrich is a funny old dick,
It isn't very often that he dips his
   wick,
But when he does he dips it quick,
As he revels in the joys of copulation.

Poor old bovine, poor old bull,
Very seldom gets a pull,
But when he does, the cow is full,
As they revel in the joys of copulation.

Poor little tortoise in his shell,
Doesn't manage very well,
But when he does he comes like Hell,
As he revels in the joys of copulation.

Bow-legged women shit like goats.
Bald-headed men all fuck like goats.
While the congregation sits and gloats,
And revels in the joys of copulation.

Now, I met a girl and she was a dear,
But she gave me a dose of gonorrhea.
Fools rush in where angels fear
To revel in the joys of copulation.

Do you ken John Peel with his coat so
   gay.
He's a dirty old sod so all men say,
For he can't toss off in the normal way,
So his hounds lick his horn in the
   morning.

When you wake up in the morning and
   you're feeling full of joy,
And your wife isn't willing and your
   daughter isn't coy,
Then you've got to use the arsehole of
   your eldest boy,
As you revel in the joys of copulation.

When you wake up in the morning with a
   ten-inch stand,
And there isn't any woman in the whole
   of the land,
Then there's nothing for it but to use
   your hand,
As you revel in the joys of copulation.

(00) CHARLOT THE HARLOT (*See CC04*)

(07) CLASS OF FORTY-A
(Tune: *Throw A Nickel On The Drum*)
   Lyrics:: *Wilson T. Jones - Class 40-A*

<u>NOTE</u>: *This and other songs of Class 40-A found in this volume represent some of the best examples of history in song, the military parody. In this particular ballad, the history of a pre-World War II flying class is cleverly captured in melody, and comes from the Class 40-A song book prepared especially for their 45th anniversary reunion held in Colorado Springs, September 5-8, 1985.*

CLASS OF FORTY-A

We came from ev'ry U.S. state
Mid "Nineteen Thirty-Nine."
Three hundred ninety-nine of us,
To take up Air Corps fly'n
At nine civilian flying schools.
The washout rate was high,
For those of us that made it through,
Our limit was the sky.

CHORUS (*repeat after each verse*)

   Sing hallelujah, hallelujah
   We're the Class of Forty-A,
   Though our hair has turned to gray.
   Sing hallelujah, hallelujah,
   Forty-A had left its mark on history.

We were the first expanded class,
A fact we all did hail,
Because the class before us,
With ours did not dovetail.

(*continued on next page*)

So if we're somewhat mav-er-ick
Compared to other groups,
It could be 'cause no upper class,
Shook us in our boots.

Then on to basic training,
To fly in BT-Nines,
At Randolph Field in San Antone,
We taxied the flight lines.
We walked the ramp to Luper's beat,
And to Hank Amen's too,
We took our gigs, hung in there tough,
And took off in the blue.

And then on to Kelly for advanced,
In BC-Ones we flew.
Two hundred and twenty of us
Got wings when March winds blew.
For A. Adams to "Pee Wee" Zins,
The glorious Forty-A
Joined the ranks of Air Corps groups
Worldwide, and drew flight pay.

In every theater we flew
The planes of World War Two;
From Pearl Harbor to Berlin,
Distinguished service grew.
The cross was won by Thompson, Smith,
McCallum, Thomas, Collins,
Leverette, Mahoney, Church.
Brav'ry was their callin'.

An Air Force Base was named for Dow,
For Royall, Postal Stations.
A road took on Burhanna's name.
Five aces blessed our Nation,
Hedman, Leverette, and Thyng,
(Thyng was a double ace)
Mahoney, Bechtel each downed five.
Four and forty downs took place.

The stars came out in Forty-A,
Of them we brag a lot.
One star: Wallace, Thyng, Briggs, Frost
Hamrick, Thompson, Scott.
Two stars: McCutcheon, Sands, Two Browns
Campbell, Gibbons--six in all,
Three stars: McGehee, LeBailey,
Four stars: Estes, Burchinal.

"Incredible," a word that best
Describes Class Forty-A.
Indominatable flying men,
Who fought to save our way.

Our "e'sprit de corps" is always such
It leads to victory.
Here's to what each of us did
To guard our liberty.

Now everyone in Forty-A
Deserves so many lines,
Their sagas, caterpillar tales
Fill volumes of grapevines.
A digest version can be found,
Frank Schirmer wrote it down.
For now let's toast each other's fame,
And have another round.

(08) THE CLEAN SONG
(Tune: *Unavailable*)

There once was a sailor,
He looked through the glass,
And spied a fair maiden,
With scales on her
Island where seagulls fly over the nest.
She combed the long hair that hung over
    her
Shoulders and caused it to tickle and
    itch;
The sailor cried out there's a
    beautiful
Mermaid out sitting there on the rocks.
The crew came a'running a'grabbing their
Glasses, all eager to share in this fine
    piece of news
That the captain soon heard from the
Watch. He put on his pants which he
    kept by the door
In case he might someday encounter a
Mermaid. He knew he must use all of
    his wits,
Crying, "Throw out a line, we'll lasso
    her
Flippers, feeling free just after the
    farce,
She splashed in the waves and fell flat
    on her
After coming with spleen.
This song may seem dull, but it's
    certainly
Clean!

(09) CLEAR THE PATTERN
(Tune: *Wake The Town And Tell The People*)

Clear the pattern, call the crash crew,
_____ leads the group.
They were lost, fuel exhausted,
They'll be landing from a loop.
Yes, he led us into weather,
Lightning flashes all around.
_____ says, "I'll fly the gauges,"
But we came out upside down.

REPEAT THE FIRST FOUR LINES

(10) COLONEL TARA'S BAND
(Tune: *McNamara's Band*)

Alternate Titles and Variations:

(a) *Early Abort*

NOTE: *There are five versions of this song in Volume I (E20) under the title,* **Early Abort.** *What makes this song especially interesting is that it must be personalized with some commander's name, and tailors the song to a military unit. In the case of the version below, it is the 21st Troop Carrier Squadron, 374th Troop Carrier Wing--and as the Editor said elsewhere, his old TDY alma matter from 1948-49.*

COLONEL TARA'S BAND

My name is Colonel Tara,
I'm the leader of the group.
I get up every morning,
Just to give the boys the poop.
I tell' em 'bout the mission that
We're gonna have to hack.
The first one off the runay,
Is the first one in the sack.

CHORUS #1

Early abort, avoid the rush.
Early abort, avoid the rush.
Early abort, avoid the rush,
Oh, the first one off the runway
Is the first one in the sack.

We fly our ships to Pusan and
We fly them to Taegu.
We fly them in foul weather and
Mostly nighttime too.
When the sun is shining
We are sitting on the ground
But when the weather's stinking,
We'll be flying all around.

CHORUS #2

Beacon approach, and GCA,
Beacon approach, and GCA,
Beacon approach, and GCA,
Oh, when the weather's stinking,
We'll be flying all around

We are stationed at Old Tachi and
We're happy as can be,
But why we should be happy
Is a mystery to me.
From Tachi to Korea nearly
Every day we roam;
Tachi's just like stateside,
We are O.J.T. for home.

CHORUS #1

(11) COLUMBO
(Tune: *Unavailable*)

Alternate Titles and Variations:

(a) *Columbus*

NOTE: *This song is another example of how words and verses interchange between songs. The third verse, as an example, is the same as the fifth verse in the long ditty,* **Friggin' In The Riggin'** *(FF11).*

COLUMBO

In Fourteen Hundred and Ninety-two,
A Dago from Italy,
Walked the streets of old Madrid,
And pissed in every alley.
All night long, from midnight on.

(*continued on next page*)

He walked up to the Queen of Spain,
And asked for ships and cargo.
He said, "I'll be a son-of-a-bitch
If I don't bring back Chicago."
All night long, from midnight on.

CHORUS (*repeat after every other verse*)

>   He thought the world was round-o,
>   His balls hung to the ground-o,
>   That navigatin' masturbatin'
>   Son-of-a-bitch, Columbo

Columbo had a cabin boy,
The dirty little dipper.
He lines his ass with broken glass,
And circumcised the skipper.
All night long, from midnight on.

Columbo had a second mate,
He loved him like a brother.
They went down below the deck,
And corn-holed one another.
All night long, from midnight on.

For forty days and forty nights,
They sailed the blue Atlantic.
They spied a whore upon the shore,
And the whole damn crew went frantic.
All night long, from midnight on.

They screwed her once,
They screwed her twice.
They screwed her once too often.
They broke the main spring in her ass,
And now she's in her coffin,
All night long, from midnight on.

(12) COMIN' BACK TO YOU (M)
(*Maintenance Lament*)
Music & Lyrics by Rollie Stoneman

NOTE: *Of the ten songs in Volume II that were written by Major Rollie Stoneman, this is the only one that is not a parody but an original composition. It is a story that will tug at the heart of all members of the Air Force family--the stress and strain of separation from the family, whether it be from an unaccompanied overseas tour, or duty out at Kilo One, as in this song. Despite the hardships, there is a note of unabashed patriotism, similar to the expression in Dick Jonas' great song, Blue Four (Volume I, B40). The Editor has a recording of this Rollie Stoneman song (and the other Rollie songs), and can attest that he ranks with the best of Air Force songsters. The tradition lives on.*

COMIN' BACK TO YOU

Drivin' down this lonesome road thinkin'
   back to you.
Why I left tonight I'll never know.
Wind is whistlin' by my ear, I shiver
   with the cold.
I wish I was back home again, I need
   your hand to hold.

When morning comes you'll find my note,
   please try to understand.
You know I didn't want to leave this
   way.
Give little Jenny a great big hug; Tell
   her don't be sad.
Tell her happy birthday from her dad.

REFRAIN

>   'Cause I got the call, I've got to go
>   These birds of war can't wait.
>   I know it's hard for you to under-
>   stand.
>   But something deep inside me makes me
>   proud to do my share.
>   And I'm comin' back to you soon as I
>   can.

I know I promised that I'd have this
   special day at home.
You've heard those words so many times
   before.
Now, I guess I'll spend her birthday out
   at Kilo One.
It's just a day, not special any more.

REFRAIN

>   But my little girl won't understand
>   why daddy isn't there.
>   It's hard to understand when you're
>   just two.

(*continued on next page*)

There's something deep inside me
   makes me proud to do my share.
And I'm comin' back to you as soon
   as I can.

Come the spring, we'll be leavin', leave
   this place behind.
We're gonna be a family again.
We'll visit the zoo, take a walk or two,
   we'll wrestle on the floor.
I won't be chasin' missiles anymore.

REPEAT FIRST REFRAIN

(13) COMING AROUND THE MOUNTAIN
(Tune: *She'll Be Comin' 'Round The
      Mountain When She Comes*

Oh, they call them Skoshi Tigers when
   they come,
And they come in freedom fighters when
   they come;
If an F-5 flys on Sunday,
They must change the engines Monday,
But they'll all get airborne someday
   when they come.

Oh, they all will bring a camera if
   they come,
And they'll be on cinerama if they come;
And we all have a suspicion
They may use real ammunition,
Making color war-time movies with their
   gun.

Oh, their planes go supersonic when they
   go.
They're transistor-electronic if they go
The F-5' sophisticated,
And it's also over-rated,
For it will not fly in slush or sleet
   or snow.

By themselves the GE engines will not
   start.
The F-5 can't go without a power cart.
When it goes, it goes, I think,
Far as any kitchen sink,
Though it may go farther if the crews
   will fart.

Oh, their bomb load may consist of only
   four,
But their teenie weenie wing will hold
   no more.
If they had a bigger wing,
On that silly fucking thing,
They could find a better use for that
   old whore.

Oh, they lunber down the runway when
   they roll,
And the pilot feeds it just a little
   coal.
It took off from the grass,
They would surely bust their ass
McNamara's paper tiger's in a hole.

But we're glad to have the F-5 here at
   war,
Though the pilots may be rotten to the
   core.
They may drink and they may swear,
Hit the road without a care--but,
They'll be here aborting aircraft by the
   score.

Now we call them Skoshi Pussy when they
   fly,
For they can't quite get their ass up in
   the sky;
They may huff and puff their back up
If they ever have a crack up,
There'll be bloody Skoshi Pussy where
   they lie.

NOTE: *Unfortunately, the remainder of
the song is missing from the material
sent to the Editor. Maybe some kind
soul will send the complete rendition.*

(14) COMMERCIAL ADVERTISING
   (Tune: *Unavailable*)

Chinese couple going wild,
Want to have a pure white child.
But find no way of having one,
They watch TV and while they sit,
They find a way of having it.
On the job without delay,
Sideways is the Chinese way.
Baby born with great delight,

(*continued on next page*)

Little fellow pure and white.
Father proud and full of glee,
Tells what he learnt on TV.
"Hooley Dooley, he no fooley,
He put Persil on his tooley.
Wifey, wifey, very canny,
Use Blue Omo on her fanny."
Wonder where the yellow went?
Brushed his balls with Pepsodent.

(15) COOL
(Tune: *The Beverly Hillbillies*)

NOTE: *The words remind the Editor of the West Point plebe's answer to the question from an upperclassman, How cold is it in Maine?*

COOL

Cool as the tip of an eskimo's tool,
Cool as a fish in a frozen pond,
Cool as a pane of frosty glass,
Cool as the ring around a polar bear's
    ass.

CHORUS (*repeat after each verse*)

    Cool, cool, cool, cool, cool, cool,
    cool, cool.

Cooler than the nipple on a witch's tit,
Cooler than a bucket of penguin shit,
Cooler than the frost on a champagne
    glass,
Cooler than the fringe around a polar
    bear's ass.

Cool as the lines on an arctic chart,
Cool as the breeze from a fur seal's
    fart,
Cool as the feathers on an arctic duck,
Cool as the end of an Eskimo fuck.

(00) THE COPILOT'S LAMENT
(*See Volume I, Song C10*)

NOTE: *Since publication of Volume I, the Editor learned that the correct tune for this great parody is,* **Sweet Betsy From Pike**. *Volume I has the lyrics.*

(16) CRAWLING AND CREEPING
(Tune: *Unavailable*)

Alternate Title and Variations:

    (a) *Creepin' and Crawlin'*

NOTE: *The chorus in this song is the same as that in the ditty,* **Roll Your Leg Over** *(RR08).*

One night while I was a-crawling and
    a-creeping,
One night while I was a-crawling and
    a-creeping,
One night while I was a-crawling and
    a-creeping,
I spied a young maiden so peacefully
    sleeping.

CHORUS (*repeat after each verse*)

    Oh, roll your leg over, roll your leg
    over once more.

I said to her, "Can I come to bed ya?"
(*repeat twice more*)
And then she replied, "You're not hand-
    cuffed or tied."

Her drawers were tight and I could not
    get in them,
(*repeat twice more*)
And then she replied, "There's a knife
    on the window."

That knife was sharp and her drawers
    split asunder,
(*repeat twice more*)
And then we were banging away like
    lightning and thunder.

In about three months lay the poor maid
    a-weeping,
(*repeat twice more*)
And then she remembered the crawling and
    creeping.

In about nine months lay the poor maid
    asunder,
(*repeat twice more*)
And then she remembered the lightning
    and thunder.

(17) THE CREW THAT NEVER RETURNED - I(M)
(Tune: *MTA*)
  Lyrics: *Rollie Stoneman*

NOTE: *Another case of SAC missile crew members not wanting to be outdone by the SAC flyboys. The missile crew's version of the song about those guys who went on duty and were never seen again. See the song immediately following for the air-crew's version (CC18).*

THE CREW THAT NEVER RETURNED - I

Let me tell you all about a crew
    commander named Charlie
In the merry, merry month of May.
He grabbed his Tech Data, kissed his
    wife and family,
And went on alert that day.

REFRAIN

    But, did they ever return?
    No, they never returned.
    And their fate may be unlearned.
    They may drive forever on the plains
        of Nebraska,
    The crew that never returned.

The deputy was driving toward western
    Nebraska
At a speed of a hundred and two.
When a state patrolman waved that crew
    van over sayin',
"He, buddy, I want YOU."

So from the jail Charlie called the
    command post,
And told them of his plight.
The controller said, "Hold on! I've
    got to call Omaha.
For now you've just gotta sit tight.

REPEAT REFRAIN

Charlie broke from the jail and headed
    for the capsule,
Down into the LCC.
He slammed the blast door, turned around
    and shuddered,
For waiting there was DOV.

Now seven major errors is a poor
    performance
As all of you surely know.
The Standboard crew waved a finger at
    Charlie,
Said, "Charlie, you've got to go."

REPEAT REFRAIN

Charlie called the command post and told
    them what had happened.
He asked to be relieved in the field.
The controller said, "NO! I can't let
    you go."
He was firm and would not yield.

REFRAIN 2

    He said, "Don't ever return. Don't
        ever return.
    Your fate has now been learned.
    You will stay forever 'neath the
        plains of Nebraska
    To Warren don't ever return.
    I say again, to Warren don't ever
        return."

(18) THE CREW THAT NEVER RETURNED - II
(Tune: *MTA*)

NOTE: *It doesn't pay to screw up in SAC if you are to believe this ditty from the pen of a SAC songster (no, there is no MOS for that skill). This is closely related to the ditty above, CC17, the missile crew version. You'll love it.*

THE CREW THAT NEVER RETURNED - II

Let me tell you the story of a pilot
    named Chalie,
And his crew so brave and sound.
They went up one day on a normal train-
    ing mission,
So far they've never come down.

They had a bad day of precision bombing,
With a 10,000 foot CPA.
And on the way home, they called SAC
    control,
Control had this to say.

(*continued on next page*)

CHORUS

"Don't you ever return, please don't
  ever return,
Your fate is still unlearned.
You may fly forever in the wild blue
  yonder,
To Sheppard don't ever return.

When Charlie got back for his Sheppard
  penetration,
With a 10,000 pound fuel load,
He got on the horn and called for a
  tanker,
Said, "How about one for the road?"

It happened that day, the last of the
  quarter,
And squares were hard to fill.
And their refueling squadrons were so
  far behind,
So far that they'd never get well.

Now Charlie was no good at air refueling
On the boom he could not stay.
So his Radar helped him out with the
  tracking handle,
And the gunner bailed out of the bombay.

CHORUS

If they ever return, no they never
  returned,
Their fate is still unlearned.
They may fly forever in the wild blue
  yonder,
To Sheppard they never returned.

Charlie kept on going from one tanker to
  the other,
'Til he finished with tanker 28.
Then that man in Omaha said, "Get those
  tankers airborne,
We'll finish SAC 50-8."

Everyday at Base Operations,
Everyday at a quarter past noon,
They load up bread and water into the
  tanker,
That they send Charlie's crew down the
  boom.

After six weeks of flyin', Charlie's
  wife came cryin'
To our colonel one day at noon.
We don't know what she said, but his
  face got mighty red
When he cried, "You can't send *that*
  down the boom."

CHORUS

Did they ever return, no they never
  returned.
Their fate had now been shown.
They may fly forever in the wild blue
  yonder,
As the best square pillars ever known

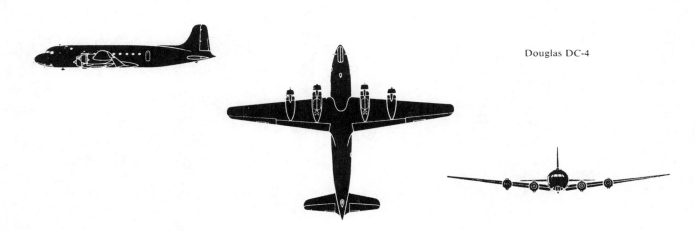

Douglas DC-4

Consolidated B-24D

FLIGHT SECTION DE

(01) DANGEROUS DAN MCGREW
      (Tune: *Unavailable*)

Alternate Titles and Variations:

   (a) *The Grooving of Dan McGrew*

NOTE: *The version of the song printed
below is a compilation from two sources.*

A bunch of the boys were whooping it up
In one of those Yukon halls.
The piano player sat against the wall,
A quietly scratching his balls.

The Fargo Kid had had his hand on the
      box
Of the lady that's known as Lu,
And there on the floor, on top of a
      whore,
Was Dangerous Dan McGrew.

Then out of the night, as black as a
      bitch,
And into the din of the hole,
Came this raunchy old prick, just in
      from the crick,
With a rusty old load in his pole.

His pants were split and covered with
      shit,
And he squatted down on a keg.
His balls hung low and swung to and fro
Whenever he moved his leg.

In his ragged clothes, he stood ready
      to hose,
As the passion within him burned;
Then he pulled out his cock to display
      to the flock,
And every asshole squirmed.

The lights went out, and he dove to the
      floor,
His cries were heard in the dark;

His aim was true, the sparks they flew,
When his joy stick found the mark.

With might and main, and screams of pain
A man's voice filled the room.
Amid sighs and moans, and farts and
      groans,
Came at last a very loud "boom."

The lights came on, and the stranger
      rose
With a satisfied grin on his pan;
And there on the floor, with his asshole
      tore,
Was poor old, cornholed, Dan.

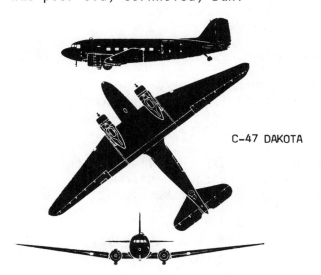

C-47 DAKOTA

(02) DARK AND DREAMY EYES
      (Tune: *Unavailable*)

Alternate Titles and Variations:

   (a) *Old Soldiers Never Die - II*

NOTE: *This ballad is obviously British
in origin, as are many in Volume II.* **NO**

(continued on next page)

conclusion drawn! The first version below is the Air Force rendition of a much older beer hall ballad; and this one comes from our modern-day U.S. Air Force, the 1979 issue of the 95th FITS Hymn Book. The second version, Old Soldiers Never Die - II, comes from the Fighter Pilot's Song Book, of the 523rd Tactical Fighter Squadron, S.E.A.

DARK AND DREAMY EYES

A few old whores of Portsmith town
Were drinking Spanish wine.
The gist of the conversation was,
"Is your cunt bigger than mine?"

Then up there spake the airman's wife,
And she was dressed in beige;
And in one corner of her funny little
    thing,
She had a Handley-Page.
She had a Handley-Page, my boys,
With a joy stick and its knob,
And in the other corner,
Were two airmen on the job.

CHORUS (*repeat when you have a mind to*)

    She had those dark and dreamy eyes,
    And a whizz-bang up her jacksey.
    She was one of the flash-eyed 'hores
    One of the old brigade.

And then up spake the pilot's wife,
And she was dressed in chrome;
And in one corner of her funny little
    thing,
She had the aerodrome.
She had the aerodrome, my boys,
The bombers and the troops,
And in the other corner,
Their Wimpys looping loops.

Then up there spake the ops room girl,
And she was a little WAAF;
And in one corner of her funny little
    thing,
She had the ops room staff.
She had the ops room staff, my boys,
All fucking there like hell,
And in the other corner,
She'd the signals staff as well.

And then up spake the telephone girl,
And she was dressed very strange,
And in one corner of her funny little
    thing,
She had a camp exchange.
She had a camp exchange, my boys,
The wires and all the switches,
And in the other corner,
The C.O.'d left his britches.

(00) OLD SOLDIERS NEVER DIE - II
(Tune: *Unavailable*)

NOTE: *This is not the same song as the one in Volume I, 024, of the same name.*

Then up and spoke a sailors wife,
And she was dressed in green,
And in one corner of her funny little
    thing,
She had a submarine.
She had a submarine, my boys,
With conning tower complete,
And in the other corner,
She had half the fucking fleet.

CHORUS (*repeat after each verse*)

    She had those dark and dreamy eyes,
    With a whiz bang up her nighty.
    Singing, "Hi Jack, come and have a
        skin back;
    Come and have a bang at Liza, singing
    Old soldiers never die, they just
        smell that way."

Then up and spoke the gunner's wife,
And she was full of fun,
And in one corner of her funny little
    thing,
She had a Vickers gun.
She had a Vickers gun, my boys,
With the breach block and the sear,
And in the other corner,
She had provisions for a year.

Then up and spoke the pilot's wife,
And she was chewing gum,
And in one corner of her funny little
    thing,
She had a fifty-one.

(*continued on next page*)

She had a fifty-one, my boys,
Two napalms and six guns,
And in the other corner,
She had rockets by the tons.

Then up and spoke the skipper's wife,
She was dressed in black;
And in one corner of her funny little
    thing,
She had a fishing smack.
She had a fishing smack, my boys,
The oarlocks and the oars,
And in the other corner,
She had bags and bags of sores.

Then up and spoke the jockey's wife,
And she was dressed in red.
And in one corner of her funny little
    thing,
She had a horse's head.
She had a horse's head, my boys,
The bridle and the bit.
And in the other corner,
She had bags and bags of shit.

Then up and spoke the brewer's wife,
And she was dressed in gray,
And in one corner of her funny little
    thing,
She had a brewer's dray.
She had a brewer's dray, my boys,
The barrels and the beer,
And in the other corner,
She had syph and gonorrhea.

(03) THE DAY OF THE EAGLE
(Tune: *On Top Of Old Smokey*)

Now gather 'round closely,
I'll sing this shor song,
'Bout the day of the Eagle,
The day things went wrong.

The takeoff was normal,
No problems in sight.
He went to the circle,
And started to fight.

The battle was bitter,
And fought to the end;
T'was time then to go home,
T'was time to extend.

While cruising on back home,
Just chasing the breeze,
The blow jets went poof, poof,
Snap, crackle, and wheeze.

The silence was deafening,
He called on the freq;
"What does the dash one say
'Bout gliding this thing?"

The driver then pondered,
He thought long and cool,
And finally decided,
Mom ain't raised no fool.

I've survived all my training
It seems, now let's see,
How well they taught me
Survival at sea.

He leaped from his Eagle,
Goodbye, sadly he bade,
Wondering briefly if
His insurance was paid.

The Eagle has landed,
No doubt in my mind;
But seems that he left
His airplane behind.

That's the end of the story,
I'm sorry to say;
And one each F-Fifteen
Lies out in the bay.

(04) DEAR MOM
(Tune: *Unavailable*)

Alternate Titles and Variations:

   (a) *The FAC Song*

NOTE: **FAC** *is Forward Air Controller.
There are two versions of this product
of the Vietnam War in the Editor's collection. They differ in three repects;
(1) the beginning telegram sequence
appears in one version; (2) in one song
the pilot calls the* **DASC** *on his radio (a
control center); in the other, it is a
call sign or a nickname for a control*

(continued on next page)

center, 'Ol Big; and (3) the note on the end of the song to repeat the first verse (and adds a few words), appears in only one version.

DEAR MOM

Knock--knock

Who's there?

It's the Western Union, Ma'am.

Oh, really. Do you have a telegram for me? I've never had a singing telegram before--please.

Ma'am, I'm not sure this is the kind of telegram you should sing.

Please, oh, please sing it!

Well, O.K., here it goes.

Dear Mom, your son is dead,
He bought the farm today.
He crashed his OV-10 on Ho Chi Minh's
   Highway.
It was a rocket pass,
And then he busted his ass.
HMMMMMMMM, HMMMMMMMM, HMMMMMMMM

The FAC, he crossed the fence
To see what he could see,
And there it was as plain as it could be
It was a truck on the road
With a big heavy load.
HMMMMMMMM, HMMMMMMMM, HMMMMMMMM

He got right on the horn
And gave the DASC a call,
"Send me air, I've got a truck that's
   stalled."
The DASC said, "That's all right,
I'll send you Juvat flight."
HMMMMMMMM, HMMMMMMMMM, HMMMMMMMM

The fighters checked right in,
Gunfighters two by two;
Low on gas and tanker overdue.
They asked the FAC to mark
Just where the truck was parked.
HMMMMMMMM, HMMMMMMMMM, HMMMMMMMM

The FAC he rolled tight in
With his smoke to mark
Exactly where that truck was parked.
The rest is in doubt,
'Cause he never pulled out.
HMMMMMMMM, HMMMMMMMM, HMMMMMMMM

IN REVERENCE: Repeat Verse 1 followed by the verse below instead of the HMMMMMMM.

Him, Him, fuck him.
How did he go?
Straight in.
What was he doing?
351.
Hell of a deal! WOOOOOOOO!!

(05) DEL RIO HOMESICK BLUES
(Tune: *Jerry Jeff Walker's* London Homesick Blues)

NOTE: *This song is attributed to Greg Landers of the 86th FITS, Laughlin AFB.*

When you're down on your luck,
And you ain't got a buck,
In Del Rio you're a goner.
Even Acuna Bridge is falling down,
And moved to Arizona,
And I know why.
And I'll substantiate the rumor,
That the Beaner sense of humor
Is drier than the Arab sand.
Well you can put up your Dukes,
And you can bet your boots,
That I'll be leavin' just as fast as
   I can.

CHORUS (*repeat after each verse*)

   I wanna go home with the Armandillo,
   Good country music from Amarillo and
      Abilene.
   The friendliest people and the
   Purtiest women you've ever seen.

Well, it's cold down here and I swear,
I wish they'd turn the heat off!
And where in the world are those Beaner
   girls?

(*continued on next page*)

I promised I'd meet at the Sonic?
Well, I don't know.
And of the whole DAMN lot,
The only friend I've got
Is a Longneck and a cheap cigar.
Well, my mind keeps a'roamin',
And my heart keeps a'longin'
To be far from this Texas bar.

Well, I decided that I'd get my cowboy
    hat,
And go down to Cleo's bar...
'Cause when a flier fancies,
He'll take his chances,
And chances will be taken,
And that's for sure!
And them bloodshot eyes,
They was eyein' the prize,
Some people call manly footwear.
And they said, "You're from down South,
'Cause when you open your mouth,
You always seem to put your 'thing'
    there."

(06) THE DILL DO
(Tune: *Unavailable*)

"What is a Dill Do, Daddy?"
Asked my young daughter, aged 9.
"A Dill Do, my chick,
Is a property prick,
About five times the size of mine."

Your mother got one for Christmas.
It hung on the Christmas tree.
Now she has it away,
About five times a day,
And she don't give a fuck for me.

(07) DON'T BURN THE SHITHOUSE DOWN
    (Tune: *Available*)

Alternate Titles:

    (a) *Our Outhouse*
    (b) *Outhouse Song*
    (c) *Please Don't Burn The Shithouse
        Down*

Please don't burn the shithouse down.
Mother has promised to pay.
Mother is drunk, father's in jail,
Sister's in a family way.
Brother dear is mighty queer.
Times are fucking hard.
So, please don't burn the shithouse down,
Or we'll all have to shit in the yard.

(08) DON'T CRY LADY
(Tune: *Unavailable*)

Don't cry lady,
I'll buy your goddamn pencils.
Don't cry lady,
I'll buy your flowers, too.
Don't cry lady,
Take off those dark brown glasses;
Hello, mother, I knew it was you!

(09) DOWN IN THE VALLEY (Air Version)
    (Tune: *Unavailable*)

The first time I saw her she was all
    dressed in white,
All in white, all in white, my God, her
    cunt was tight.
Down in the valley, where she followed
    me.
The next time I saw her she was all
    dressed in brown,
All in brown, all in brown, I took her
    nickers down.

The next time I saw her, she was all
    dressed in green,
All in green, all in green, I filled her
    soup tureen,
Down in the valley where she followed
    me.
The next time I saw her she was all
    dressed in fawn,
All in fawn, all in fawn, two little
    bastards born,
Down in the valley where she followed
    me.

The next time I saw her she was all
    dressed in red,

(*continued on next page*)

All in red, all in red, two little
    bastards dead,
Down in the valley where she followed
    me.
The next time I saw her she was all
    dressed in black,
All in black, all in black, boards
    nailed across her crack,
Down in the valley where she followed
    me.

(10) DO YOU KEN MY SISTER TILLY?
    (Tune: *John Peel*)

Alternate Titles and Variations:

    (a) *My Family*

NOTE: **Ken** *means* **Know,** *as if you didn't
know. This English masterpiece proves
that family togetherness is still alive
in merry 'ole England.*

DO YOU KEN MY SISTER TILLY?

Do you ken my sister Tilly,
She's a whore on Piccdilly,'
And my mother is the same upon the
    Strand;
And my father sells his asshole
At the Elephant and Castle.
We're the finest whoring family in the
    land.

When you wake up in the morning
With your hands upon your knees,
And the shadow of your penis on the
    wall,
And the hair a-growing thick
Between your asshole and your prick,
And the rats are playing snooker with
    your balls.

(00) MY FAMILY

Have you met my Uncle Hector?
He's a cock and ball inspector,
At a celebrated English public school.
And my brother sells French letters,
And a patent cure for wetters.
We're not the best of families, ain't it
        cruel?

My little sister Lily is a whore in
    Piccadilly,
My mother is another on the Strand.
My father hawks his arse hole,
'Round the Elephant and Castle.
We're the finest fuckin' family in the
    land.
There's a gentlemen's convenience
A short way down the Strand,
And the ladies' is a little further on.
For a penny on deposit, you can sit upon
    the closet,
But a season's ticket costs you half a
    crown.

(11) DO YOUR BALLS HANG LOW?
(Tune: *March Of The Toy Soldiers*)

Do your balls hang low, do they swing to
    and fro,
Can you tie them in a knot, can you tie
    'em in a bow,
Can you throw them o'er your shoulder
    like a European soldier?
Do your balls hang low?

In days of old when knights were bold,
They shit right in their britches,
They wiped their ass with broken glass;
Those tough old sons-of-bitches.

In days of old when knights were bold,
And women wore mere trifles,
They hung their balls upon the walls,
And shot them down with rifles.

In days of old when knights were bold,
And women weren't particular.
They bound them up against the wall,
And fucked them perpendicular.

In days of old when knights were bold,
They wore all leather britches,
They beat their pricks with hickory
    sticks,
And yell'd like sons-of-bitches.

(12) THE DUCHESS
(Tune: *Available*)

Alternate Titles or Variations:

   (a) *Highland Tinker*
   (b) *The Thinker*
   (c) *The Tinker*

The Duchess was a-dressin', a-dressin'
   for the ball,
When out thru the window, she did spy
   him pissin' on the wall.

CHORUS (repeat after each verse)

   With his lily white kidney wiper,
   And balls the size of these,
   And half a yard of foreskin,
   Hangin' below his knees.
   Oh, hanging down!
   Oh, hangin' down!
   With half a yard of foreskin,
   Hangin' down below his knees.

So she wrote to him a letter, and in it
   she did say,
"I'd rather be fucked by you than by my
   husband any day."

So he mounted his white charger and on
   it he did ride,
With his cock slung o'er his shoulder
   and his balls hung by his side.

He rode into the courtyard. He rode
   into the hall.
"My God", cried the butler, "He's come
   to fuck us all."

He fucked the cook in the kitchen, He
   fucked the maid in the hall,
But when he fucked the butler, 'twas the
   dirtiest fuck of all!

Well, he mounted his white charger and
   rode into the street,
With little drops of semen, pitter,
   patter at his feet.

YAK-28   Tu-22   AB212

(00) THE THINKER
(Tune: *Available*)

NOTE: *This version of the song is about the same as* **The Duchess,** *except that it has a delightful last verse:*

Oh, the thinker's dead and buried, I'll
   bet he's gone to Hell.
He said he'd fuck the devil, and I'll
   bet he's done it well.

(13) EIGHTH TACTICAL FIGHTER WING
(Tune: *My Bonnie Lies Over The Ocean*)

NOTE: *This is a protest song of sorts, written in the 1971-72 period after a change of command at Ubon Airbase, Republic of Thailand. Although it names people (necessary for the rhyme), there is no indication these were real names, and false names may have been used to create the rhyme just to make the composer's point. This ditty is an excellent example of the military parody that permits the composer and singers to vent their feelings through song. Songs are escape valves that permit the soldier, the sailor and the airman to vent their frustrations, fears and lonliness. In that spirit, this ballad belongs in the folklore of Air Force parodies. If the gentlemen named are real, don't take the words too personal; they are one of the hazards of command and payment for privilege.*

EIGHTH TACTICAL FIGHTER WING

We got us a new Wing Commander,
His name was Colonel Jim Young,
He came here and made lots of changes,
He can suck out my bloody red bum.

CHORUS (*repeat after each verse*)

   Fuck off, fuck off, fuck off Eighth
   TAC Fighter Wing, fuck off.
   Fuck off, fuck off, fuck off Eighth
   TAC Fighter Wing.

(*continued on next page*)

The Wild Blue Yonder - II

Along came a DO named showers,
He worked for "Old Scarface," you know,
He was known to search by the hours,
Just looking for dead goats to blow.

We had us an ASS-istant DO.
His name was Colonel Van Horn,
He used to eat little babies,
Before those babies were born.

Now Young was replaced by Miller,
A weak dick he was not.
The O Club again has door handles[*],
And the Wolf Pack again is shit hot.

NEW CHORUS

Shit hot, shit hot, shit hot, Eighth
 TAC Fighter Wing, shit hot.
Shit hot, shit hot, shit hot, Eighth
 TAC Fighter Wing.

F-15 EAGLE

*NOTE: *The reference to door handles on the O Club doors refers to the actions of the Wing CO in removing the exterior door handles from the Officer's Club bar doors. This evidently was a source of some contention at the time, requiring everyone to walk around to the front of the building to enter, rather than permitting entry directly into the bar from the street. It never fails, that some leaders of men underestimate the importance of detail to those they lead, assuming superior attitudes and judgements out-of-tune with reality.*

Curtiss Pusher

FLIGHT SECTION FF

(00) THE FAC SONG (*See DE04*)

(00) FIGHTER PILOT
(*See Volume I, song YZ04*)

(00) FIGHTER PILOTS EAT PUSSY (*See SS17*)

(00) FIGHTER PILOT'S HYMN (*See BB19*)

(00) FIGHTER PILOT'S TOAST (*See TT22*)

(01) FIGHTING HOOTERS
(Tune: *Mr. Bojangles*)

I knew a band of Hooters, and they'd
   fight for you in worn out jets.
Sparrows, and heaters, we'll kill for
   you, just place your bets.
We fly so high, fly so high,
Then we gently touch down.

Mac, wake up, we're all signed out, how
   'bout some jets?
Standby, sir!
We got our jets, and poopy suits,
   where's Adashi?*
Now Hooters pissed.
The driver's here, driver's here,
Let's step to our jets.

CHORUS

   Fighting Hooters,
   Fighting Hooters,
   Fighting Hooters, fly. . .

Standing by for time hack check, with
   three and four, But where is two?
His intercom has something wrong, the
   Redball's there, we'll give him a few

We got our checks, got our checks,
Then we fuck'n took off.

Reno Two, they're on the nose for
   twenty miles at eighteen thou'.
Tally Ho, and bandit call, Fox 1's
   away, that's two more down!
It's Miller time, Miller time,
Let's head for the hootch.

CHORUS

* *Korean for* old man, *the driver.*

F-16 FIGHTING FALCON

(02) FINICULE, FINICULA
(Tune: *Finicule, Finicula*)

Alternate Titles or Variations:

   (a) *Funiculi, Funicula*
   (b) *Last Night (below)*
   (c) *Last Night I Stayed Up*

Last night I pulled my put,
I thought I would, to do me good.
Last night I used the long stroke,

(*continued on next page*)

I used the short stroke,
I used my hand, 'twas simply grand.
Smack it, crash it, bash it on the floor;
Heave it, squeeze it, jam it in the door.
Some folks stick to buggery,
And some think fucking is grand,
But for personal enjoyment,
I shall always use my hand.

(00) LAST NIGHT
(Tune: *Finicule, Finicula*)

Last night I stayed up late to
    masturbate.
It felt so good -- I knew it would.
Last night I stayed up late to beat my
    meat.
It felt so nice -- I did it twice.

You should really see me on the short
    strokes   ;
It feels so grand, I use my hand.
You must really catch me on the long
    strokes;
It feels so neat, I use my feet.

Shake it, break it, beat it on the
    floor;
Smash it, bash it thrust it through the
    door   ;
Some people seem to think that fucking's
    grand,
But for all around enjoyment, I prefer
    to use my hand.

(03) FIRST WITH THE 21ST
(Tune: *Battle Hymn Of The Republic*)

NOTE: *Another from the stalwart, former
TDY comrades of the Editor's--the fighting (in the club) 21st Squadron of the
374th Troop Carrier Group--later called
a Wing as inflation hit the organiza
tions of the Air Force. The theme of
this ballad is a popular one among Air
Force songsters--competition between
drivers of different aircraft; in this
case the C-54 versus the C-124. However, rivalry between bomber pilots did
not exist. Pilots of the B-24 and B-17
loved each other and each other's air
craft--what? You don't believe that?*

FIRST WITH THE 21ST

There is a Wing at Tachi,
And they have One Twenty Fours;
On a half a tank of gas, they boast,
We'll fly to Frisco's shores.
Then it never really happens,
'Cause there are C-54s,
And they go flying on.

CHORUS

Glory, glory, see them sailing
    through the air,
Glory, glory, you are sure that
    they'll be there,
Glory, glory when they'er late it's
    very rare,
And they go flying on.

The One Two Four is mighty big
Gigantic to behold;
They look so very pretty,
But can hardly fly I'm told.
If they get into the air at all,
They stagger and they hold,
And then it's once around.

CHORUS

Glory, glory see them stagger through
    the air,
Glory, glory how the hell do they get
    there,
Glory, glory though they fly it's
    very rare,
And then it's once around.

Oh, the Sixth and Twenty-second
They can have the One Two Four,
But the 21st will take the plane
That flies a good deal more;
The great Beeliner Squadron
Is the first on every score,
And they will carry on.

CHORUS

Glory, glory for the good old 21st,
Glory, glory they are proud to be
    the first.
Glory, glory let the others do their
    worst,
But we will carry on.

(04) FLEETING GLANCES
(Tune: *Unavailable*)

NOTE: *If you want to know the tune to this ditty, you will have to get in touch with Jack Havener of Memphis, Tennesee. He says he can sing it (off key), but doesn't remember the name of the tune. So sing along with Jack, ex-Air Force, composer, song publisher, and good guy.*

FLEETING GLANCES

I saw her ass,
She stood upon the platform;
I saw her butt,
A moment in the rain.

I saw her snatch,
A parcel from the window;
As she came to see her brother,
Jack off on the train.

(00) FLICKERING MATCH (*See BB39*)

(05) THE FLYING COLONEL
(Tune: *The Wreck Of Old 97*)

Alternate Titles and Variations:

   (a) *Recce To Berlin*
   (b) *Recce To Pyongyang* (Vol. I, R6)

NOTE: *Although this song is a near-duplicate of* **Recce To Pyongyang** *in Volume I, the version below is from World War II--probably the original. In the* **Flying Colonel** *rendition, the first line of verses 1 and 2 is, . . . from Rangoonie to Shannon. The Editor substituted the lines from,* **Recce To Berlin,** *and used the unit's number and commander's name as in the original song. So, the rendition below is a combination of the two versions. All of this may be very confusing --but at least it makes a good song!*

THE FLYING COLONEL (RECCE TO BERLIN)

It's a long, hard road on a recce to
   Berlin,
And the flak was burstin' high,
And the P-51s and the P-47s,
They were guarding us high in the sky.

We were halfway between Lake Lummer and
   Hamburg
When all Hell broke loose in the blue,
'Cause the Jerries spotted us from five
   o'clock under,
And came up to see what they could do.

Now, the first pass was made on the
   462nd,
  Colonel Shower's was in the lead.
And he pissed and he moaned, and shit
   and he groaned,
For he thought he would surely be dead.

So, the colonel called to his brave
   navigator,
Said, "Give me a headin' home,"
But the brave navigator, with his hand
   on the ripcord,
Said, "Shit, boy, you're goin' home
   alone."

So the colonel he called to his brave
   bombardier,
Said, "Give me a headin' home."
But the brave bombardier had already
   scuttled;
There was silence on the ship's
   interphone.

Well, at 24,000 he chewed on his candy,
And his balls drew up in their sacks;
And he pissed and moaned, and shit and
   groaned,
For he thought he would never get back.

But with four engines feathered, he
   glided into safety
On the runway of his own home base;
And it's with great pride that he tells
   this story,
With a shit-eating grin on his face.

(06) FORESKIN FUGITIVE
(Tune: *Unavailable*)

Eyes right, assholes tight, foreskins to
    the front,
We're the boys who make no noise,
We're always chasing cunt.
We are the fliers of the night,
We'd rather fuck than fight,
We are the foreskin fugitives.

(07) FORTY-A HOO RAY
(*Words and original music by Wilson T.
Jones, Flying School Class of 40-A*)

NOTE: *This is the first of three songs
(two to follow in this section) about
Flying School Class 40-A. It is one of
those rare AF gems where the words AND
music are original. Unfortunately, the
musical score was not included with the
words, but I'll bet you can get them
from Colonel Dave Hassemer in San
Antonio, who together with Wilson Jones,
compiled the souvenir song book for the
Class 40-A 45th anniversay reunion.*

FORTY-A HOO RAY

We've got lots of pa-zazz,
Lots of raz-a-ma-taz,
We are loaded with brass,
'Cause our thinking has class.
We're for having a bash,
To help hold friendships fast.
Could it be 'cause we've no upper,
Be 'cause we've no upper,
Be 'cause we've no upper class?
(Off we go - Forty-A)

CHORUS

    Forty-A, Forty-A, Forty-A it's a
      hooray,
    You're forty five years older today.
    Though your hair has turned to gray,
    And you've lost your flight pay,
    You are still styled in gung-ho array
    (Forty-A Hoo Ray)

At the girls our eyes cast,
Married models enmass.
We've a history at last

To remember our past.
Love for country has dash,
And our loyalty's vast.
Could it be 'cause we've no upper,
Be 'cause we've no upper,
Be 'cause we've no upper class?
(Off we go - Forty-A)

(08) FORTY-A IS HERE --
A Word For The Wives
(Tune: *Send In The Clowns*)
(Words: *Frank Schirmer*)

NOTE: *There is a note of sadness and a
note of pride in this unusual parody.
It is a tribute to those who have had
their day, look back over their careers
and sometimes wonder if the real heroes
were the wives who had little choice in
the difficult careers of their Air Force
men. Wives may be the neglected heroes
of the Air Force--and neglected in song
until Frank Schirmer wrote this--**A Word
For The Wives**. Frank is the Class 40-A
Historian.*

FORTY-A IS HERE

Forty-A's here - don't we have a flair?
We're here at last on the ground, 'stead
    of midair.
Send in the clowns.

We're all retired. Hope you approve.
So used to flying around; now we can't
    move.
Where are the clowns? Send in the
    clowns.

Just when I'd stopped - flying on tours,
Finally knowing the one that I wanted
    was yours.
Making my entrance again - with my usual
    flair,
Sure of myself - way up in the air.

Love the Air Force. My fault I fear,
I thought you'd want what I want,
Sorry - my dear!
But where are the clowns? Send in the
    clowns.
Don't bother, we're here.
(*continued on next page*)

Forty-A is here, be of good cheer,
Gaining our friendships this late in
    our career.
We're all like clowns - we ought to be
    clowns,
Well, maybe next year.

(09) FORTY-A IS THE WAY
(Tune: *Ting-Ting a Ling a Ling Ling*)
(Words: *D. Hassemer and Wilson Jones*)

Nine civilian primary schools
WE TOLD YOU SO (*REPEAT AFTER EACH LINE*)
BT-Nines at Randolph Field
Got our wings at Kelly Field
Forty-A was on its way

Jackson was for some of us
WE TOLD YOU SO (*REPEAT AFTER EACH LINE*)
Benning's dust was really rough
McClellan wore us to a nub
Forty-A now led the way.

Carried the banner 'round the world
WE TOLD YOU SO (*REPEAT AFTER EACH LINE*)
Some gave their lives on the way
Now we're here to sing and say
Forty-A IS THE WAY

(10) FOUR-NINETY-SECOND
    (Tune: *Available*)

Well, then it's goodby Four-ninety-
    fourth and Four-ninety-third,
We are the boys who fly the big blur-
    tailed bird.
We got a mission to fly,
We got a party to throw,
We are the boys who have that go! go!
    go!
Then it's wheels on the runway with the
    ABs to the wall,
Wheels in the well, we'll wax 'em all.
Now we've got 'em by the tail pipe,
Hang right in there Four-ninety-two.

(11) FORTY-EIGHTH BEER CALL
    (Tune: *Unavailable*)

Oh, we're from the 48th, the beer-
    drinking 48th.
Whenever we go out we have a ball.
We take delight in stirring up a fight,
And knocking them in the head, 'til
    they're dead;
Ha, ha, ha, oh, oh, oh, hee, hee, hee!
We have gotten a reporve in written.
We put poison in our C.O.'s Cream of
    Wheat.
We're from the 48th, the beer-drinking
    48th,
And we eat raw meat!
Call the waiter, more beer.

(00) THE FOUR BASTARDS
(*See Volume I, song F29*)

NOTE: *Colonel William Donnelly, Jr., of
North Edgecomb, Maine, offered these
tidbits of information about this very
funny song in Volume I.* "The Four
Bastards *was originally titled,* Three
Prominent Bastards, *or in the more
restrictive language of the 1930s,*
Three Prominent So-and-So's. *It was
written by Ogden Nash, and may have been
published in the New Yorker Magazine.
The first character is alleged to have
been Charles E. Mitchell, Chairman of
the Board of the (then) National City
Bank of New York. The second, I think,
was Charles Van Sweringen of Cleveland
Railroad fame. And the third, suppos
edly, was Senator Huey P. Long of
Louisiana.*"

(00) FRIAR OF GREAT RENOWN (*See MM10*)

(11) FRIGGIN' IN THE RIGGIN'
    (Tune: *Available*)

Alternate Titles and Variations:

    (a) *The Good Ship Venus*

(*continued on next page*)

NOTE: *This is an English sailor's song that was very popular among the airmen from at least WW II on. The last three verses of the original have been deleted. That may seem unusual in a volume of bawdy songs. However, the last three verses go beyond being* dirty, *but are objectionally profane.*

The use of the word ditty *in the 14th verse does not refer to a song but to a* ditty bag. *This was a small, purse-like container that sailors used to store small articles like needle and thread. Otherwise, the Editor uses the word* ditty *throughout the songbook in its usual meaning of a short, simple song. There is some similarity between this song and* **The Ball At Kerrimuir,** *found earlier in this Volume.*

FRIGGIN' IN THE RIGGIN'

'Twas on the good ship Venus,
My God you should have seen us.
The figure head was a whore in bed,
And the mast a rampant penis.

CHORUS (*repeat after each verse*)

    Friggin' in the riggin',
    Friggin' in the riggin',
    Friggin' in the riggin',
    There's fuck all else to do.

The captain of this lugger,
He was a dirty bugger.
He wasn't fit to shovel shit,
From one place to another.

The first mate's name was Morgan,
My God was he a gorgon.
Ten times a day he used to play,
Upon his sexual organ.

The second mates's name was Andy,
He was so young and randy,
They boiled his bun in steaming rum,
For coming in the brandy.

The midshipman's name was Nipper,
He was a dirty ripper.
He filled his ass with broken glass
And circumcised the skipper.

The captain's wife was Mabel,
Whenever she was able,
She'd fornicate with the second mate,
Upon the galley table.

The captain had a daughter,
Who fell into the water,
Delighted squeals revealed the eels,
Has found her sexual quarter.

The crew they were hard cases,
You could see it in their faces.
They took to frigging in the rigging,
For want of better places.

So drunk with exultation,
We reached our China station,
And sunk a junk in a sea of spunk,
'Caused my mutual masterbation.

The quartermaster was Pember,
He had a crashing member.
On nights of frost, himself he tossed,
Before a glowing amber.

The bosun's name was Walker,
He really was a corker.
The filthy sod had been in quod,
For dalliance with a porker.

Once in a drunken frolick,
The bosun lost a bullock.
With foul intent, on Mable bent,
He impaled it on a rowlock.

The ship's dog's name was Rover,
By gad he was in clover.
We ground and ground
That faithful hound,
From Tenereefe to Dover.

The cabin boy was pretty,
It really is a pity,
The things they did
To that poor kid,
Would quite upset his ditty.

They sailed to far Algeria,
To none were they inferior.
The prostitutes
Along the routes,
Grew wearier and wearier.

(*continued on next page*)

They made for the Bahamas,
The harems and zenanas.
They did eschew that poxy crew,
And much preferred bananas.

They sailed to Buenos Aires,
And laid with all the fairies.
They got the syph at Tenerefe,
And clap in the Canaries.

NOTE: *The last three verses have been deleted because they are objectionally profane, i.e., bring religious subjects into obscene circumstances.*

(13) FUTURES (THE PILOT)
(Tune: *Unavailable*)

NOTE: *This is the third great contribution to the collection from the 1919 book,* **Buddy Ballads,** *a rare and truly different collection of WW I poems and ballads. This is one from that book that is more ballad than poem--at least it has a chorus. But again, like so many, no tune is assigned. Nevertheless, the sentiments in this song will bring many a lump to the pilots of yore.*

FUTURES (THE PILOT)

When I get through with this man's war
    and out of this man's army,
The kind of life I'm looking for is one
    that cannot harm me.
No, not for me the speedy plane I used
    to pot the Hun with,
A second-handed little Ford will do to
    have my fun with.
This thing of dodging through the skies
    has made me tense and nervous,
I'll make my tours in Pullman seats
    when I am through the service,
And bump to work in trolley cars like
    other city dwellers,
And thank my stars I'm not behind the
    blast of air propellers.

CHORUS

    That's me when I
    Don't have to fly
    With Army aviators,

    The only time
    I'll ever climb
    Will be in elevators.

When I am through with this man's war
    and out of this man's army,
I'll be a person who'll abhor whatever
    might alarm me;
For after months of split-tail stunts
    and wild and reckless chances,
It's me to play things safe and sane in
    placed circumstances.
I'll take my risks in auction bridge and
    penny-ante poker,
Where there's no German Fokker bus to be
    the little joker.
Let others gamble in the games of danger
    and endurance,
My family'll be old and gray when they
    get my insurance!

CHORUS

    I'll never take
    The jobs that make
    A fellow's frame grow thinner;
    I plan to plod
    Acquire a pod
    And nod each night at dinner.

My bus? It's that one over there. Some
    traveler, that baby.
And when I'm through, well, yes, some-
    times I'll thing about her, maybe,
And dream of shoutin, "Contact, boys,"
    and of her motor roaring,
And taxiing along the field and lifting,
    zooming, soaring.
Just now, what looks the best to me is
    peace and rest and quiet.
I'm planning for the simple life and
    hoping, when I try it,
That I won't find this Spad of mine
    still has the lure to charm me,
And make me dream of this man's war and
    long for this man's army.

(*continued on next page*)

CHORUS

    Say, but she's trim
    And swift and slim
    As through the clouds I weave her.
    And I'll admit
    That when I quit
    I sure will hate to leave her!

(14) THE F-4K SONG
(Tune: *Unavailable*)

<u>NOTE</u>: *Try as he could, the Editor could not figure out the melody to this ditty. It is called a song, so melody it must have--somewhere. If you add another* **PSSSH** *and* **ROAR** *on the last line of each*

respective verse, you can sing this to, **Here We Go 'Round The Mulberry Bush.** *But tune aside, it is easy to see the rivalry between the competing pilots of F-5Es and F-5Ks--the stuff good Air Force parodies are made of.*

THE F-4K SONG

F-5E's are tinker toys,
They are flown by little boys,
And they make a real weak noise---
PSSSH, PSSSH

F-4K's are rocketships,
They are flown by real hot shits,
And they make a mightly roar---
ROAR, ROAR!!!

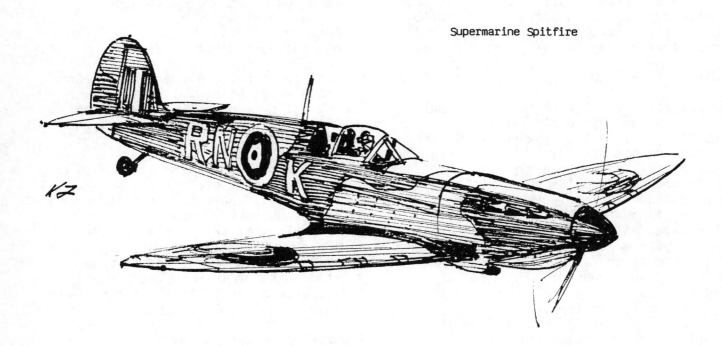

Supermarine Spitfire

FLIGHT SECTION GG

(00) GABE 01 (*See HH06*)

(01) GANG BANG SONG, THE
    (Tune: *Unavailable*)

Alternate Titles and Variations:

  (a) *Gang Bang*

I love to gang bang,
I always will,
Because a gang bang gives me such a
    thrill.
When I was younger, and in my prime,
I used to gang bang all the time;
But now I'm older and turning gray,
I only gang bang once a daa-a-ay.

Knock, knock.
Who's there?
Anita.
Anita who?
I needa a gang bang, I aways will...

Knock, knock.
Who's there?
Eisenhower.
Eisenhower who?
I'se an hour late to a gang bang,
    I always will...

Knock, knock.
Who's there?
Wanda.
Wanda who?
I want ta gang bang, I always will...

Knock, knock.
Who's there?
Eulah.
Eulah who?
You love to gang bang, you always will..

Knock, knock.
Who's there?
Wendy.
Wendy who?
When de moon comes over the mountain,
    I love to...

C5A GALAXY

Knock, knock.
Who's there?
Issac Tenor.
Issac Tenor who?
I sent 10 or 12 girls out to the car,
    and they all wanted to...

Knock, knock.
Who's there?
Bill.
Bill who?
Billet me with a WAF, and I'll never
    need a...

(02) THE GAY CABALLERO (*Air Version*)
(Tune: *The Gay Caballero*)

Alternate Titles and Variations:

   (a) *I Once Was A Gay Caballero*

<u>NOTE</u>: *The word* **gay** *is used in its proper sense to mean* happy, carefree, *and not in the current, perverted use as a name for a homosexual.*

THE GAY CABALLERO

Oh, I'm a gay caballero,
Coming from Rio de Janiero,
Bringing with me my lum bum ba de,
And two of my lum bum ba deros.

I went to see a sweet senorita,
And exceedingly sweet senorita,
Taking with me my lum bum ba de,
And both of my lum bum ba deros.

We went to a soft sofita,
An exceedingly soft sofita,
She wanted to see my lum bum ba de,
And both of my lum bum ba deros.

I got a case of clapetos,
And exceedingly bad case of clapetos,
On the tip of my lum bum ba de,
And one of my lum bum ba deros.

I went to see a medico,
An exceedingly fine medico,
Taking with me my lum bum ba de,
And both of my lum bum ba deros.

The medico drew a stiletto,
And exceedingly sharp stiletto,
And cut off the tip of my lum bum ba de,
And one of my lum bum ba deros.

Now I'm a sad caballero,
Coming from Rio de Janiero,
Taking with me no lum bum ba de,
And only one lum bum ba dero.

(00) I ONCE WAS A GAY CABALLERO
(Tune: *The Gay Caballero*)

I once was a gay caballero,
Who went down to Rio de Janerio.
I took with me my la trabule,
And both of my la trabularos.

I met there a gay senorita.
A very gay senorita.
I asked her to see my la trabule,
And both of my la trabularos.

She said that she hadn't oughta,
For she was her father's daughter,
But she said that she'd see my la trabule,
And one of my la trabularos.

We went to her cabrita,
And sat down on the sophita.
I inserted with glee, my la trabule,
And one of my la trabularos.

Oh fie on that gay senorita.
She gave me a dose of clapita.
She gave it to me in my la trabule,
And one of my la trabularos.

I went to a famous medico.
A very famous medico.
He cut off for me my la trabule,
And one of my la trabularos.

At night when I lay down to sleepa,
I feel down under the sheeta.
I find nothing there, but a handful of hair,
And one of my la trabularos.

(03) GHOST FUCKERS IN THE SKY
(Tune: *Ghost Riders In The Sky*)

Alternate Titles and Variations:
   (*See Volume I, song G1*)

   (a) *Ghost Flyers In The Sky*

An old cowpoke went riding out one dark
     and windy day,
Stopped beneath a shady tree and paused
     to beat his meat.

(*continued on next page*)

When all at once a slant-eyed bitch came
    ridin' down the trail.
He stopped her and asked her, "How about
    a fuck of tail?"

CHORUS (*repeat after each verse*)

    Yipee-yi yeaaaaaa, yipee-yi yoooooo,
    Ghost fuckers in the sky.

Her tits were all a-floppin', her cunt
    ate out with clap.
He socked it to her anyway and gave her
    ass a slap.
She shit, she moaned, she threw him from
    her crack.
He rolled across the desert and broke his
    fuckin' back.

(04) GIVE ME OPERATIONS (*SEA Version*)
(Tune: *Variation of "Bless 'Em All"*)

Alternate Titles and Variations:

    (a) *I'd Rather Fly A Warthog*
    (b) *Just Give Me Operations*

NOTE: *One of the all-time greats of Air
Force songs. As long as they keep
making more AF planes, there will be new
verses. The Editor hasn't come across a
missile verse, yet, but there is probably one out there, somewhere. Most of
the verses to this song are in Volume I,
song G04, but here are a few more that
have been added to the collection. What
is rare about the first offering below
iss that the verses are related--as
opposed to the usual independent verses
about particular aircraft. And it is
full of Southeast Asia jargon, a mystery
to your aged Editor. This gem is from
the 35th Tactical Fighter Wing, Phan
Rang Air Force Base, South Vietnam,
1969. The second version, from the 92nd
Tactical Fighter Squadron (A-10s), is a
highly original, new version of this old
favorite, which brings it up-to-date
with the modern Air Force. The
remaining verses are additional gems
about aircraft types to add to those of
Volume I. Have you heard of a P-43?*

GIVE ME OPERATIONS

Don't give me an old **Phantom II**,
That sports not one pilot, but two;
The guy in the back could just stay in
    the sack,
Don't give me an old Phantom II.

CHORUS (*repeat after each verse*)

    Just give me operations,
    Way out on some lonely atoll,
    For I am too young to die,
    I just want to grow old.

Don't frag me for old **Tiger Hound**[*],
Bad weather, high mountains abound;
They don't five you credit, so screw it,
    forget it,
Don't frag me for old Tiger Hound.

And don't frag me for old **Package 6**[*],
I'll be in one hell of a fix;
The MIGs all come on when my radar is
    gone,
Don't frag me for old Package 6.

And don't frag me for **Silver Dawn West**[*],
Your butt doesn't get any rest;
You think it won't last, your poor
    aching ass,
Don't frag me for Silver Dawn West.

And don't frag me for **Silver Dawn East**[*],
I hear it's one hell of a beast;
Both crew members reek, and you can't
    take a leak,
Don't frag me for Silver Dawn East.

Well, I'll take back that old
    Phantom II,
That sports not one pilot, but two;
The guy in the front seat might just
    sit on his rump,
I'll take back an old Phantom II.

[*] *See* **Glossary** *for an explanation of
    the terms in the song.*

(continued on next page)

(00) I'D RATHER FLY A WARTHOG

CHORUS (*repeat after each verse*)

    Oh, I'd rather fly my Warthog
    On a twenty-five foot strafing run.
    We'll get down in the grass
    And kick Ivan's ass,
    With our 30 mike-mike Gatling gun.

Oh, don't make me an **F-15 jock**,
Those bastards sure know how to talk.
You can't press the attack when your
    engines roll back,
So don't make me an F-15 jock.

Don't give me a **Foxtrot One Six**,
With a handle instead of a stick.
She'll get on your tail, but the engine
    will fail,
Don't give me a Foxtrot One Six.

Don't give me an **A-7D**,
My computer's my manhood to me.
Without my black box I ain't much of a
    jock,
So don't give me an A-7D.

Don't give me a **Foxtrot Four-D**,
With two people where one should be.
They train you a Luke and then give you
    a nuke,
Don't give me a Foxtrot Four-D.

Don't give me an **Aardvark** to fly,
It's a guaranteed sure way to die.
Hands off on the deck and you'll break
    your damn neck.
Don't give me an Aardvark to fly.

Oh, don't give me a **Tango Three Eight**,
It's small and it's sleek and that's
    great.
They'll put you in the pit with your
    hand on your dick.
Don't give me a Tango Three Eight.

Oh, don't fly my **Hog** into a cloud,
Or you'll hear me crying out loud.
They don't pay me the wages to fly on
    the gauges.
Don't fly my hog into a cloud.

Don't give me a **F One-one-one**,
'Cause an autopilot's no fun.
You sit side-by-side just along for
    the ride,
Don't give me an F One-one-one.

Don't give me an **F-104**.
That airplane's a ground-lovin' whore.
She'll cough and she'll wheeze, and
    head straight for the trees,
So, don't give me an F-104.

Oh, don't give me a **Foxtrot Five E**.
And Aggressor I don't want to be.
It's tough to get laid when you're a big
    training aid,
Oh, don't give me a Foxtrot Five E.

An **Alpha Jet's** just not for me,
Though it's fast and it's damn hard to
    see.
No bombs and no gun, but it's sure lots
    of fun,
But, an Alpha Jet's just not for me.

Don't give me an old **Phantom Two**.
It's TAC's two-seat B-52.
Drop your bombs, go around, hope they
    all hit the ground.
Don't give me an old Phantom Two.

Oh, don't give me a **Bongo Five Two**.
With eight engines, a bed, and a loo.
You fly with a crew telling you what to
    do,
Don't give me a Bongo Five Two.

Don't give me a **Foxtrot Fifteen**,
Though everyone thinks that you're keen,
Twice as fast as a MIG and four times as
    big.
Don't give me a Foxtrot Fifteen.

Don't give me an **F-16** jet.
That bastard ain't ops-ready yet.
You can't stay in the fight with the
    stick on the right,
So, don't give me an F-16 jet.

(*continued on next page*)

Don't give me a **star to wear**.
It's obvious they don't really care.
Their minds locked in a room, now our
    flyin's been doomed.
Don't give me a star to wear.

Oh, don't give me an **OH Five Eight**,
'Cause a scout is just Z-S-U bait.
You'll peek through the grass, and he'll
    blow off your ass.
Don't give me an OH Five Eight.

In a **Cobra** out flying around,
You're sure to hit the damn ground.
You'll hose off a TOW and then down you
    will go,
In a Cobra out flying around.

ADDITIONAL VERSES TO BASIC SONG:

Don't give me an old **F4D**,
With a navigator flying with me.
Her dihedral's neat, but she's got a
    back seat,
Don't five me an old F4D.

ORIGINAL CHORUS
(*repeat after each verse*)

> Just give me operations,
> Way out on some lonely atoll.
> For I am too young to die,
> I just wanna go home.

Don't give me a **P-43**,
She scares the Hell out of me;
She'll nose up you see,
And come down right on me,
Don't give me a P-43.

NOTE: *For those who have not heard of a
P-43, it was built in 1940 by Republic
as a follow-on design of the Seversky
P-35. It never made it as a fighter,
and was converted to photo reconnaissance in 1942. Out of the 272 aircraft
built, only 103 sent to China saw
action. So now you know.*

Don't give me a **C-47**,
She's a one-way ticket to heaven;
When she spins to the deck,
I'll be found in the wreck,
Don't give me a C-47.

QUESTION: *Who wants to spin a C-47?*

Don't give me a **P-51**,
She goes when you give her the gun;
She's known for her turn,
But she also will burn,
Don't give me a P-51.

Don't give me a **P-51**,
No airplane to fight with the Hun;
Hydraulics will bubble,
And then you got trouble,
Don't give me a P-51.

NOTE: *The next verse is dedicated to the
Beeliners of the 21st Squadron, 374th
Troop Carrier Wing.*

Don't give me a **C-54**,
Six inches of rug on the floor.
And we'll go fat-cattin'
From here to Manhattan,
Don't give me a C-54.

Don't give me an **F-86**,
She's gone before you get fixed;
She smokes and she blows,
She also digs holes,
Don't give me an F-86.

Don't give me an **F-105**,
'Cause I love being alive.
She's great for attack, she soaks up
    more flak,
Don't give me an F-105.

Don't give me an **F-105**,
I'd much rather remain alive;
I don't want my belly hung with
    gasoline jelly,
Don't give me an F-105.

Don't give me an **Alpha One-E**,
That airplane sure ain't for me;
All it's got is torque, and you're sure
    to get dorked,
Don't give me an Alpha One-E.
(*continued on next page*)

SOUTHEAST ASIA CHORUS
(*repeat after each verse of your choice*)

O, give me Operations,
In lovely old Thailand,
For I am too young to die,
I prefer to live in Siam.

Don't give me an **F One Oh Oh**,
It'sa little too old and too slow;
The Thunderbirds like 'em, but they
    ain't a-fightin',
Don't give me an F One Oh Oh.

Don't give me an **HU-16**,
She's a most awkward machine;
With gear that folds double, your're
    heading for trouble,
Don't give me an HU-16.

Don't give me a **McDonnell's Voodoo**,
There's nothing that she will not do,
She'll really pitch up, she'll make you
    throw up,
Don't give a McDonnell Voodoo.

Don't give me a **One Double Oh**,
To drop bombs all over the foe.
She's trim and she's neat but she's now
    obsolete,
Don't give me a One Double Oh.

Don't give me an **Oscar One** E,
Much too old, too slow for me;
That damned old slow poke is just
    armored with smoke,
Don't give me an Oscar One E.

Don't give me an old **Shooting Star**,
She flys like a Model-T car,
She flew in Korea, she gives diahrrhea,
Don't give me an old Shooting Star.

Don't give me an **F-Shooting Star**,
It'll go but not very far.
It'll rumble and spout,
And soon will flame out,
Don't give me an F-Shooting Star.

(05) GLORIOUS
(Tune: *Unavailable*)

Now the first thing they prayed for
They prayed for their king.
Glorious, glorious, glorious king.
If he has one son, may he also have
    ten.
"May we have a fuckin' army", cried the
    airmen, amen.

CHORUS (*repeat after each verse*)

Now the Squadron Leader and the Wing
    Commander,
And the Group Captain, too,
Hands in their pockets with fuck all
    to do.
Robbing the pay of the poor Acey-Due.
May the Lord shit you sideways
Cried the airmen, "Fuck you".

Now the next thing they prayed for,
They prayed for their queen.
Glorious, glorious, glorious queen.
If she has one daughter, maybe she
    will also have ten.

Now the next thing they prayed for,
They prayed for their beer.
Glorious, glorious, glorious, beer.
If we have one beer, may we also have
    ten,
"May we have the fuckin' brewery," cried
    the airmen. Amen

(00) GONNA TIE MY PECKER TO A TREE
(*See TT21*)

(00) THE GOOD SHIP VENUS (*See FF12*)

(00) GOR BLIMEY (*See CC01*)

(06) GOTTA TRAVEL ON

(Tune: *Gotta Travel On*)
Composed by Major (now Lt. General)
Truman Spangrud

<u>NOTE</u>: *This is one of a trilogy of great songs about an exercise in S.E.A. called* **Rapid Roger**. *For the full story, see the song,* **On The Day Rapid Roger Died,** *song 0022). General Spangrud plays the banjo, so if you want to know the melody, give him a call in the Pentagon.*

GOTTA TRAVEL ON

He's laid around and played around
This old base too long.
Counter's are almost gone, free-bee's
comin' on.
He's laid around and played around
This old base too long,
And he damn well ought to travel on.

The secretary told the colonel
That Roger needed a home.
How about old Ubon?
Com' on you're putting me on.
The secretary told the colonel
That he's comin' to Ubon,
Regardless of the war that's going on.

If we could win the war with numbers,
Old Roger would mean a lot,
That's not any rot.
Old Roger would mean a lot,
If we could win the war with numbers,
Old Roger would mean a lot,
But so far he's minimum shit-hot!

For awhile we thought that Roger
Had found a permanent home,
Never more to roam.
He'd found a permanent home,
But now he's met his maker,
And we'll miss him not a bit,
'Cause so far he's maximum dog-shit!

(00) GREAT BLOODY BALL (*See BB10*)

(00) GREAT FUCKING WHEEL (*See BB24*)

(07) THE GREECY HOG

(Tune: *Sweet Betsy From Pike*)

<u>NOTE</u>: *The clever ditty doodler who wrote this parody created a pun in the title by combining a story of a flight to Greece with the nickname of the F-84. Another great song from the Virginia Air National Guard about the F-84 (also see songs SS29 and SS30). The Editor thinks the last verse is a classic.*

THE GREECY HOG

O don't you remember the F-84,
That crossed the Atlantic with a big
mighty roar,
But we struck right with her through the
wheezes and smoke,
We couldn't punch out 'cause we can't
swim a stroke.

CHORUS

With a cough, wheeze, whistle and
snore,
Sounds like an F-84.
It's a cough, wheeze, whistle and
snore,
Our flying collection of garbage and
junk.

We stopped in Madrid just to rest for
awhile,
The gay Senoritas all begged for a
smile,
But their poor hearts were broken, I'm
sorry to tell,
We stuck with those Superhogs
My God, war is Hell!

Then on to Old Greece where the girls
are so sweet.
We frightened the Russians by sixes
and twelves,
But it seemed most of all we just
frightened ourselves.

(00) GROOVING OF DAN MCGREW (*See DE01*)

(08) THE GRUNT SONG
(Tune: *Unavailable*)

NOTE: **Grunt** *is the term that aircrew members applied to nonflying personnel in Southeast Asia. For you older folks, the term used to be* **groundpounder** *There has always been a rivalry between the two groups, but it has been a friendly rivalry. Both groups are real pros, and cannot exist without the other. The term has been applied to both military and civilian employees of the government and also to contractor personnel--but generally in the same context--nonflying support people.*

THE GRUNT SONG

Well, we came to old Korat in the year
   of '69,
To stay and fight the war upon the front
They told us about the flak and SAMS and
   natives, too;
But they forgot to warn us all about the
   grunt.

CHORUS (*repeat after each verse*)

   I said, "Where in the Hell do you all
     come from?"
   That's something I'd like to know.
   They live around the base and they
     take up all the space.
   I'd like to tell them all just where
     to go.

They beat you to the dining hall, they
   beat you to the bar.
You have to stand in line in the
   latrine.
I don't know if they plan it all or
   leave it all to chance,
But it makes the pilots think its
   mighty mean.

You see them at the swimming pool and
   at coffee all day long,
And a lot of other things that forgot,
I think the devil hired 'em and sent 'em
   everyone,
To really make it Hell in old Korat.

They'll gamble you at poker or they'll
   gamble at dice.
I tell you men I think its getting
   worse.
I asked them for the change to a twenty-
   dollar bill,
And the bastard almost hit me with his
   purse.

(09) GUNNER'S BOYS
(Tune: *Pancho And Lefty*)

NOTE: *This song was written by Rocky Farry of the 497th Tactical Fighter Suadron (*Hooters*) at Taegu Air Base, Republic of Korea, in 1983. Also see the other* **Hooter** *songs:* **Listen Hooters,** *and* **Fighting Hooters.** **Gunner** *was a squadron commander--Lt. Colonel Charles Heltsley. After his departure, the song was sung with* **Hooter** *substituted for* **Gunner.**

GUNNER'S BOYS

Liv'in' in the air we said,
Gonna' make us free and lean.
Now our eyes are hard as iron,
Wings upon our chest do gleam.

Fighting hard and flying low,
Anywhere we're sure to go.
We don't think that we will die.
They say it's our foolish pride.

CHORUS

   Yes, we are all Gunner's boys,
   Jets as fast as polished steel.
   War machines strapped to our backs,
   For all the fuckin' (or Commie) world
     to fear.

Some have met their match, you know,
Bandits, flack and SA-2s.
Nobody heard their dying words,
Ah, but that's the way it goes (ending).

(*continued on next page*)

Poets tell how the Phantom flew,
105's, Linebacker 2,
Jungle's quiet, the wind is cold,
Carries the names of the fallen bold.
They all need your prayers, it's true,
Save some for me and you.
We will do what we have to do,
Before we all grow old.

REPEAT CHORUS

(10) THE GYPSY 93RD
(Tune: *Turkey In The Straw*)

NOTE: *This is the last song to be entered into the collection before publication. And what a ditty! It is about the 93rd Bomb Group, oldest bomb group in the 8th Air Force, and the only wartime organization in the USAF that has not been inactivated since original formation on 1 May 1942. The 93rd is known as* **The Traveling Circus**, *the most traveled group in the 8th. It flew its first mission on 9 October 1942, and its last mission in WW II on 25 April 1945. Two of its better known commanders were General (then Colonel) Edward Timberlake and General (then Lt. Col.) George Brown. General Brown, who later became Chairman of the Joint Chiefs, was Acting Commander for six days. Don't laugh. He did all right. The Editor flew many a B-24 mission along side this great outfit from Hardwick, their airbase in England. The copy of the song received by the Editor came from Don Cramer of Naples, Florida via Dave Hassemer of San Antonio. It is typed on stationery of the Central Hotel, Cloncurry, Central Queensland, Australia, circa May 1942. According to Don, who was with the 19th Bomb Group, some of the members of the 19th were ex-93rd members. Don says that a fellow by the name of McClellan brought this song with him to Australia all the way from the 93rd in England. That's show biz!*

THE GYPSY 93RD

There's a pilot in the cabin,
And a bomber in the nose,
A tail full of gunners and
Off she goes;
To some far off place of
Which we've never heard,
But we don't give a damn
In the gypsy 93rd.

With a belly full of bombs
Cruising 20,000 feet,
The chatter guns are loaded
Engines sounding mighty sweet;
We don't know where we're going
In this big tin bird,
And we don't give a damn
In the gypsy 93rd.

Oh! the navigators lost
And the pilots sleeping sound,
And the Goddamn ship's headed
Towards the ground;
For the copilot's flying
Like a dodo bird,
But we don't give a damn
In the gypsy 93rd.

Oh! the fans are turning backwards,
And the tanks are out of gas,
The wings are kind of sagging
Where they shot away our ass;
And the mills are making noises
Like we never before have heard,
But we don't give a damn
In the gypsy 93rd.

So it's home again
From a job well done,
There isn't any glory;
And it wasn't any fun,
But the flag still flies,
Just as free as a bird,
'Cause they don't give a damn
In the gypsy 93rd.

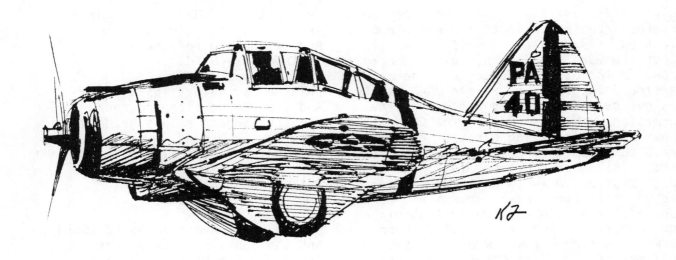

Seversky P-35

FLIGHT SECTION HH

(01) HAIL TO THE AIR GUARD OF VIRGINIA
(Tune: *Battle Hymn of the Republic*)

NOTE: *This is one of several songs in Volume II about the Air National Guard; the first such songs in the collection. They come from the* **Song Book of the Old Dominion Fighter Squadron** *(149th Tactical Fighter Squadron, 192nd Tactical Fighter Group). They call themselves,* The Last of the gentlemen day fighter pilots. *The Editor would like to dedicate this and all the songs from the Virgina guard to all Air Guard members in every State. This ditty is a gem of humor, story-telling, and making fun of fellow fighter pilots and their antics-- in verse and melody.*

HAIL TO THE AIR GUARD OF VIRGINIA

Here's to Charlie Wintzer, he's our
   hero of the year,
Never curses, won't chase women, hardly
   ever touches beer.
Gets his kicks from landing airplanes
   without lowering the gear.
He's the oldest damn lieutenant in the
   Guard.

CHORUS (*repeat after each verse*)

   Hail the Guard of Virginia,
   They will really stick it in ya.
   They'll violate your drawers like a
     happy Santa Claus,
   And you'll keep coming back for more.

Mobile Bill's a sight to see while
   peering through the glass,
Picking his nose with the flaregun with
   his finger up his ass!
He's a lover of reknown who has never
   yet gone down,
Ops! Charlie's on the ground.....boom!
   -- Scrape!

Here's the gory story of 'ole Masa
   Washington,
Jerking off on final when his engine
   ceased to run.
'Tho he didn't dig no ditches, he sure
   filled up his britches
And he won't forget the switches any
   more.

C130 HERCULES

It's half past eight and Ryan's late for
   briefing again we fear,
But with blood-shot eyes and unused dick
   he'll suddenly appear.
It's a 60-second stroll from the couck
   to takeoff roll,
Keeps his head up his asshole for
   inspiration.

Listen and I'll tell you of our legend
   lover, Mal,
In Cape Cod or Savannah he could always
   find a pal.
'Tho we near ran out of gas, keeping
   Mallory in ass,
Occasionally he would pass (as a pilot).

(*continued on next page*)

Oh, great stock collector, mighty
  warrior of the South,
Sixty-seven pounds of horseshit, eighty-
  seven pounds of mouth.
He's our genius in the bud, sticks his
  airline in the mud,
He's the schekie congious dud William
  Burbage.

(00) THE HAIRS ON HER DIKI-DI-DOO)
  (*See MM01*)

(02) HALLELUJAH - III (*S.E.A. See TT17*)

(03) THE HAMBURG ZOO
(Tune: *Unavailable*)

Alternate Titles and Variations:

  (a) *The Wild West Show - I*
  (b) *The Wild West Show - II*

NOTE: *The verses in this song are very
uneven, and without the music, it was
not possible to make corrections or
evaluate which is the proper syntax.*
The Wild West Show - II, *below, appears
to be additional verses to the original
song.* **The Wild West Show - I** *version is
identical to the original.*

THE HAMBURG ZOO

The Alligator:

Over here, ladies and gentlemen, we have
  the al-i-gat-or.
Each year the female al-i-gat-or swims
  upstream, and lays one million eggs.
The male al-i-gat-or follows her upstream and eats 999,999 of those eggs
Why does he eat all those eggs?
Otherwise, we'd be up to our ass in al-
  i-gat-ors.

CHORUS (*repeat after each verse*)

  Oh, we're off to the Hamburg Zoo,
  To see the elephants and the
    kangaroos.
  We'll all be together,
  In fair or stormy weather,
  We're off to the Hamburg Zoo.

The Leopard

Over here we have the Le-o-pard.
The Le-o-pard who has one spot for every
  day of the year.
Lift up the Le-o-pard's tail and show
  the lady the 24th of November.

The Tight-skinned Owl

Here we have the tight-skinned owl,
Whose skin is so tight that everytime he
  blinks, he masturbates himself.
Little boys have been known to jack him
  off by throwing sand in his eyes.

The Orangatang

Here we have the O-rang-a-tang,
The O-rang-a-tang whose balls hang so
  low, that everytime he swings from
    tree to tree,
His balls go O-rang-a-tang.

The Ki Ki Bird

Over here, ladies and gentlemen, we have
  the Ki Ki Bird.
The Ki Ki Bird who flies in ever-
  decreasing circles until he flies up
    his own asshole.
The Ki Ki Bird can be distinguished by
  his inimitable cry, "Ki Ki Ki-rist,
It's dark in here!"

The Lost Tribe Of Africa

Here we have the lost tribes of Africa.
The lost tribe of Africa who wandered
  lost in the jungle for many a year.
The lost tribes' cry would be heard in
  the jungle,
"Fuga we, Fuga we, where the fug are
  we?"

The Horny Bird

The female Horny Bird can be distin-
   guished by her cry,
"Want some, want some, want some";
And the male Horny Bird by his cry,
"Her it tis, Here it tis, Here it tis!"

(00) THE WILD WEST SHOW - II

CHORUS   (*repeat when you have a mind to-
preferably after each verse*)

   Ohhhhh, we're off to see the Wild
      West Show,
   The elephants and the kangaroos.
   No matter what the weather,
   As long as we're together.
   We're off to see the Wild West Show.

Ladies and gentlemen, in this corner we
   have _____.

REFRAIN: Fantastic, incredible, no shit?
            Tell us about it mother fucker.

*REPEAT AS ABOVE USING THE REFRAIN AND
THE VERSES BELOW*

1. The MATHEMATICAL WONDER is a very
   strange girl, indeed.

She is a girl who was 8 before she was 7

2. The WHERETHEFUCKAREWE TRIBE is a very
   strange tribe indeed.

They are a group of natives who are 3
   feet tall,
Walking around in 6-foot jungle grass
   saying,
"Where the fuck are we, tribe? Where
   the fuck are we, tribe?"

3. The OH NO BIRD is a very strange
   bird, indeed.

The OH NO BIRD makes his home on a
   corrugated roof.
And the OH NO BIRD has a 2-foot scrotum
   and 1-foot legs.
And every time he comes in for a landing
   he says, "Ohhhhh-no!"

4. LULU, THE TATOOED LADY is a very
   strange woman, indeed.

LULU, THE TATOOED LADY has tatooed on
   one cheek the letter "M,"
And on the other cheek she has tatooed
   the letter "M;"
And when she bends over she says, "MOM,"
And when she stands on her head, she
   says, "WOW,"
And when she does cartwheels, she says,
   "WOW, MOM, WOW!"

5. LULU, THE TATOOED LADY'S SISTER is a
   very strange woman indeed.

LULU, THE TATOOED LADY'S SISTER, has
   tatooed on one thigh, "Merry Xmas,"
And on the other thigh she has tatooed
   "Happy New Year."
And she tells all her friends to come up
   and see her between the holidays.

(04) HANG DOWN YOUR BOOM, ROSS COOLEY
   (Tune: *Bill Bailey*)

Alternate Titles and Variations:

   (a) *KC-135 Boom Operator*

NOTE: *There are songs in both volumes
about all members of the crew, and this
ditty adds to the list. The* Boom, *the
guy who operates the refueling boom on
tankers, is an important part of the SAC
combat crew team. Many a thirsty pilot
has appreciated the skill of the boom
operator in the tail of the tanker.*

HANG DOWN YOUR BOOM, ROSS COOLEY

His name is 'ole Ross Cooley,
The best damn Boom in SAC.
His father was a gunner,
His mother was a WAC.

Met the crew in Operations,
Said, "Where do we pass gas?"
The pilot scowled at the Boomer,
Said, "Boom, now watch your sass."

(continued on next page)

CHORUS

> And then hang down your boom, Ross
>   Cooley,
> Hang down your boom today.
> Hang down your boom, Ross Cooley,
> Don't call a breakaway.

Boom said, "You're just a chauffer
For the trip aloft.
Now wake me at the IP,
I'll get the JP off.

They rolled out for the take off
The engines they did roar.
The Boomer screamed to the pilot,
"Didn't close the cargo door."

The bomber called in early,
He said, "I'm over Goose.
I've got a fuel shortage.
I'm out of juice."

CHORUS

> Please hang down your boom, Ross
>   Cooley,
> Hang down your boom and fly,
> Hang down your boom Ross Cooley,
> I'll be there by and by.

The bomber came in wobblin',
A-flyin' like a jay.
The Boomer said, "You better watch it,
They call me 'Breakaway.'"

They landed on the runway.
The Boomer got off fast.
He said, "I can't a'hang around,
I'm headed for a blast."

I'll tickle all the girlies,
I'll dance and stomp all night,
And if a Swabbie speaks to me,
There's going to be a fight.

Now listen all you pilots.
The moral of this ode.
A Boomer is a roughneck,
But he lives by the Boomer's code.

He'll fill your hears with joy,
He'll fill your heart with grief,
But come around promotion time,
He'll help you get your leaves.

(00) THE HARLOT OF JERUSALEM (*See KK01*)

(05) HAVE YOU TRIED YESSUP?
(Tune: *Have You Tried Wheaties?*)

Have you tried Yessup,
The best breakfast food in the land?
Have you tried Yessup,
The best breakfast food in the land?
Delicious, nutritious, the whole day through
Jack Hard-on never tires of it, and neither
      will you.
Oh, have you tried Yessup,
The best breakfast food in the land?
Yessup spelled backwards is PUSSY,
Spelled sideways is slurp-slurp.

(06) HELLO, CAM RANH TOWER
(Tune: *The Wabash Cannonball*)

Alternate Titles and Variations:

> (a) *Air Force 801* (See Volume I, A17)
> (b) *The Ballad of Machete Two (below)*
> (b) *Gabe 01*
> (c) *Itazuke Tower* (See Volume I, A17)

NOTE: *The original of this song,* **Air Force 801,** *also known as,* **Itazuke Tower,** *is one of the all-time favorites of fighter jocks. It originated during the Korean War and has become an Air Force classic. In a letter to your Editor, Colonel Don Miller said that Major* **Romeo McCrystal** *and* **Rosie Rosecrans** *(retired Lt. General), collaborated on writing the original song. FF-801 was the field number on Romeo's P-51. The two versions below are from the S.E.A. fracas. The first version is* **Hello, Cam Ranh Tower,** *and the second is,* **The Ballad of Machete Two.** *The original is in Volume I, A17.*

(*continued on next page*)

HELLO, CAM RANH TOWER

Hello, Can Ranh Tower, this is Hammer 41
My BLC light's glowing, I've just lost
    PC-1.
The engine's running roughly, the EGT is
    high,
Please clear me for a straight-in, this
    bird's about to die.

Hammer 41, this is Cam Ranh Tower here,
We'd like to let you in right now, but a
    senator is near.
He's here to please constituents, his
    plane is close at hand.
So please divert to Tuy Hoa, we can't
    clear you to land.

Hello, Cam Ranh Tower, this is Hammer 41
I'm turning into final, hydraulic
    pressure's gone.
The generator's off the line, the RPM
    just fell,
Please send the senator around, and
    tell him, "War is Hell!"

Hammer 41, this Cam Ranh Tower again;
You'll have to keep on circling,
    regardless of your plan.
I'm sorry 'bout your problem, but you
    will have to yield,
We must give the priority to Senator
    _____(name).

Now LISTEN, Cam Ranh Tower, I'll lay it
    on the line,
The situation's fuckin' tense, we're
    running out of time.
My fuel low level light is on, this
    bird's about to quit,
So tell that goddamn senator he doesn't
    count for shit!

Hammer 41, QSY to channel four;
You'll have to clear with Air Patch, I
    can't do any more.
Roger, Cam Ranh Tower, I'm switching
    channels now,
I'm sure Air Patch will clear me to
    land this bird, somehow.

Air Patch, Air Patch, Air Patch, this
    is Hammer 41;
The tower made me check with you to see
    what could be done.
I know you'll understand my plight, I've
    confidence in you,
So clear me onto final, send the senator
    on through.

Sorry 'bout that, 41, your story breaks
    my heart;
If this had happened yesterday, we could
    have done our part;
You will divert to Tuy Hoa, consider
    this a must,
For Senator _____ _____ would
    dislike this fuss.

Roger, roger, Air Patch, I get your
    message clear;
Situation understood; the VIP's too
    near.
We'll nurse this bird to Tuy Hoa, on
    this you can depend,
We'll keep this airplane flying, until
    the very end.

Mayday! Mayday! Crown, this is Hammer 41
Our fate is up to you boys, now, the
    home drome let us down.
We can't make it to Tuy Hoa, we'll have
    to punch out here,
So please alert the Jolly Greens, we
    hope that help is near.

BEEP, BEEP, BEEP, BEEP, BEEP, BEEP

(OO) THE BALLAD OF MACHETE TWO
(Tune: *The Wabash Canonball*)

Hello, Ubon Tower, this here's Machete
    Two,
It's rainin' on the runway,
Oh Lord, what will I do?
My gas tank's getting empty,
And I am puckered tight,
Tell me, Ubon Tower, why must we fly all
    night?

(*continued on next page*)

Hello there, Machete, do you see the
   runway's end?
'Cause if you don't then go around,
And we'll try once again;
Machete Two is on the go,
I need some JP-4
Just let me hit the tanker,
And then we'll try once more.

Lion, I need vectors out to Green Anchor
   Plane,
Please expedite the join up,
I'm flyin' in the rain,
I've got to hit the tanker,
'Cause I sure need some gas,
If he ain't got no JP-4,
Then he can kiss my ass.

Hello there, Machete, Lion here, you're
   three miles out,
I'll have you on Blue Anchor soon,
Of that there is no doubt,
OOPS disregard the last word,
You're fifty miles in trail;
If you will just be patient,
This time I will not fail.

Hello Lion, Machete, you can't mean
   fifty miles,
I'm reading seven hundred pounds
Here on my gas tank dials,
I'm headin' back to Ubon,
I'll try it one more time,
The truth about my chances is that
They ain't worth a dime.

Hello, Ubon Tower, this here's Machete
   Two,
I'm standing by my airplane,
In mud up to my knees,
I don't know just what happened,
I'd like to tell you how,
Won't you send the crew truck,
I'd like to come in now.

Hello there, Machete, this here is Ubon
   Tower,
Just make a left three-sixty,
You'll be down within the hour,
We've got some TAC departures
Lined up on the other end,
Just let me get 'em airborne,
And you can come on in.

Ubon Tower, Machete, you just don't
   understand,
We are no longer flying,
We're settin' in the sand,
Our airplane is inverted
And lyin' on its back,
So come and take us home,
I'm tired and wanna hit the sack.

Machete, Ubon Tower, you say you're on
   the ground?
You know without a clearance
That you can't set her down.
If you have violated regs you know
You'll have to wait;
Machete, do you hear me?
I hear you -- FSH!

The moral of my story is
That if you're low on gas,
Just get it on the runway,
And only make one pass;
On unprepared dirt runways--
Now listen carefully--
You know it is illegal,
To land the F4D!

(07) HERE'S TO BROTHER _____
    (Tune: *Unavailable*)

Here's to Brother _____, Brother
   _____, Brother _____.
Here's to Brother _____, who's
   with us tonight...
   He eats it, he beats it,
   He often mistreats it,
So, here's to Brother _____,
   who's with us tonight...
Drink mother-fucker, drink mother-
   fucker, etc.
Here's to Brother _____, who's
   with us tonight!

No Tune - Just chant

    He ought to be publicly chastised.
    He ought to be publicly shot,
    And tied to a public urinal,
    And left there to fester and rot...

HIM, HIM, FUCK HIM!

(08) HIGHFLIGHT
(*A Poem by J. G. Magee*)

NOTE: *The Editor originally made the decision not to include this poem in Volume I because it is so well-known and available in many publications. He had second thoughts. This poem has become an Air Force classic, and is contained in at least one Air Force unit song book in the Editor's collection. For those of you who might have forgotten the story, John Gillespie Magee, Jr., was a nineteen-year-old American who joined the Royal Canadian Air Force and was killed in his Spitfire in December, 1941. This poem has been carried in the pockets of many a pilot, and even Astronaut Michael Collins took his copy with him aboard Gemini 10 during his forty-six orbit rendezvous and docking flight in September 1965. Although the Editor is not aware that this poem has ever been set to music, it is a good candidate. Maybe the Editor will do it.*

HIGH FLIGHT

Oh! I have slipped the surly bonds of
    Earth,
And danced the skies on laughter-
    silvered wings:
Sunward I've climbed, and joined the
    tumbling mirth
Of sun-split clouds--and done a hundred
    things
You have not dreamed of--wheeled and
    soared and swung
High in the sunlit silence. Hov'ring
    there,
I've chased the shouting wind along, and
    flung
My eager craft through footless halls
    of air.
Up, the long, delirious, burning blue
I've topped the windswept heights with
    easy grace
Where never lark, or even eagle flew
And, while with silent, lifting mind
    I've trod
The high untrespassed sancitity of
    space,
Put out my hand, and touched the face
    of God.

(00) HIGHLAND BALL (*See BB10*)

(00) HIGHLAND TINKER (*See DE12*)

(09) HINKY DI
(Tune: *Unavailable*)

NOTE: *This song originated with the Marines. Volume I contains the Korean War version (song H23), and this is the S.E.A. version. Both versions are from AF song books, which shows interservice cooperation exists on some levels (the barroom floor?). Although the tune was not identified, it may go with,* **Drinking Rum and Coca-Cola.**

HINKY DI

Up in Vietnam midst high rocks and heat
The poor Viet Cong are feeling quite
    beat.
For as the Phantoms roar by overhead,
He knows that his buddies all soon will
    be dead.

CHORUS (*repeat after each verse*)

    Hinky di, hinky hinky di
    Hinki di, dinky dinky di
    (repeat last line of verse)

Ho Chi went way up to old Phu Bai,
His prize Commie Army in action to spy.
He got there a half hour after the U.S.
And all that he found was their hats,
    ass and shoes.

Uncle Ho Chi, your stooges have found,
It just doesn't pay to invade foreign
    ground,
For when they disturbed the serene
    morning calm,
They brought on the rockets, the bombs
    and Napalm.

We fought a Da Nang and at Chu Lai, too,
At Khe Sahn and Ben Hai and Citadel "U";
So here's to our pilots, and here's to
    our crew,
The target, the Nape, and the great
    Phantom II.

(10) HI ZIGGIE ZIGGIE
(Tune: *Unavailable*)

NOTE: *The original song sent to the Editor by John Piowaty, had penciled changes to the type of aircraft, an indication how various Air Force units borrowed songs from each other (and between services and nations). The penciled changes were Aardvark, the swing-wing, F-111. The Editor has no idea what melody this was sung to. Call John Piowaty in Destin, FL--he knows.*

HI ZIGGIE ZIGGIE

Hi ziggie ziggie, twin-engine piggy,
    fuck him!
The Aardvark's a fat whore, needs a bomb
    door, bull shit, rat fink;
Two engines to go - to see Uncle Ho.
And a tanker to feed her when dry, suck,
    suck, suck.
Bomb a little, little, just a little bit
    MIG CAP.
You can never fool the 347th with that
    crap, fuck you.
As your ABs unwind
To save your behind,
Your asshole is gobbling the seat, chomp
    chomp, chomp.
Hey miggie, miggie, I'm a little piggie,
    Aardvark.
With your belly up, you're a sitting
    duck, I missed, oh, shit!
It's back thru the flak, my thumb up
    my crack,
And a seat that is covered with shit,
    shit, shit.
See the missiles come, you're a fuckin'
    bum, Sam site.
We don't want to fight, hope the
    burner's light, knock, knock, rat
    shit.
We ain't dropped a bomb on North Vietnam

We're going home empty tonight, dump,
    dump, dump.
Hi ziggie ziggie, you're a little
    piggie, hot shit.
When you try to drink, you're a dirty
    fink, crumb out, barf, barf.
You can't hold a light, to Thunderchief
    drivers tonight.
We'll drag your ass home to the sty,
    oink, oink, oink.

(00) HOBO 51 (See *BB02*)

(11) HOLIDAY ON WINGS
(Tune: *Holiday For Strings*)

NOTE: *This is another song from Pete Seeger's famous notes from the Marianas, September 16, 1945. This ditty wasn't named, so the Editor provided one. Clever. Thanks Pete.*

HOLIDAY ON WINGS

We will leave the Marianas
Catch the Haps in their pajamas,
Drop our eggs on Fujiyama, Tokahama,
    Yokahama,
Matsuama, Kobe and have a holiday on
    wings.

CHORUS

    We will fly o'er Kito Jima,
    Iwo Jima, Chi Chi Jima.
    Ha-ha-ha-ha-ha-ha Jima, Okinawa is a
      shima.
    We'll have lots of gasolina for our
      holiday on wings.

Guam, Saipan, we love you Tinian.
Don't knocka, you will find,
We'll rocka, block by blocka, in Osaka.

CHORUS

    Matsu-o-ka hear us, you will learn,
    To fear us, here we come,
    What's moya, we'll drink saki in
      Nagoya.

(*continued on next page*)

Retto Jima, Kato Jima,
Iwo Jima, Chi Chi Jima;
My oh my Minami Jima, ha-ha-ha-ha-ha-ha
 Jima.
This I know, that it will seema like a
 holiday on wings.

(12) HOME IN THE HOLE (M)
(Tune: *Home On The Range*)
 Lyrics: *Rollie Stoneman*

NOTE: *This song of the SAC missilemen is*
very similar to the one following, **Home**
On The Pad *(HH13), song of SAC aircrew*
members on alert. Whether one is sit-
ting in a hole, or on a **Pad**, *life can be*
boring, boring, boring.

HOME IN THE HOLE

Oh, give me a home, where the Ops
 weenies roam,
Where the SAT troops and Site Mothers
 stay.
Where seldom is heard, an ungarbled
 word,
And we never see the light of the day.

CHORUS

 Home, home in the hole,
 Where all our SAC missilemen stay.
 Where we do our best, and pass all
  the tests.
 Oh, when do we get alert pay?

We drive to our site, though it takes
 half the night,
Through the wind and the rain and the
 snow.
Our leaders are brave, but at home they
 must stay.
How we'd like to tell them where to go.

CHORUS

 Home, home in the hole.
 Where all our SAC missilemen stay.
 We watch our tin birds, until the
  warble tone's heard,
 But it's only an Olympic Play.

The food tastes just great, like an old
 paper plate,
And the water is not fit to drink.
Television they say will be installed
 on the day,
That Hell freezes over, I think!

CHORUS

 Home, home in the hole,
 Where all our SAC missilemen stay.
 The battles we fight, to stay awake
  through the night,
 Oh, when do we get alert pay?

We read magazines filled with lush
 bedroom scenes.
Frustration does things to our brain.
Champagne is taboo, females are, too,
So for thirty-six hours we abstain.

We feel old men, on alert we have been.
It touches our hearts like a knife.
But to tell you the truth, we regain
 our youth,
The night we're back home with our
 wives.

CHORUS

 Home, home in the hole,
 Where all our SAC missilemen stay.
 Where we do our best, and pass all
  the tests.
 Oh, when do we get alert pay?

(13) HOME ON THE PAD
(Tune: *Home On The Range*)

NOTE: *This is the SAC airmen's version*
of the missilemen's song, **Home In The**
Hole *(HH12), or vice versa.*

HOME ON THE PAD

Oh, give me a home, where the winged
 weenies roam.
Where the guards and the sentry dogs
 stay.
Where always is heard, the ungarbled
 word,
And the Klaxon horn blows everyday.
(*Continued on next page*)

CHORUS

> Home, home on the the pad.
> Where all our SAC crew members stay.
> Where we do our best, and pass all
>   the tests,
> When do we get alert pay?

The food is divine, but we stand in
   line,
And we can watch color TV.
Champagne is taboo, females are too,
Seven days, like eternity.

CHORUS

> Home, home on the pad,
> Where all our SAC crew members stay.
> Where we park our big birds,
> 'Till the Klaxon is heard.
> We're ready for the big fray.

For SAC we are glad, but alert pad,
Our work week of seventy-four hours.
Our training is rough, it has been
   enough,
Twenty years of peace through airpower.

CHORUS

> Home, home on the pad.
> Where all our SAC crew members stay.
> We're ready to go,
> Even E - W - O,
> When do we get alert pay?

We feel like old men, on alert we have
   been.
It touches our hearts like a knife.
But to tell you the truth, we regain our
   youth,
The night we're back home with our wives

CHORUS

> Home, home on the pad.
> Where all our SAC crew members stay.
> Where always is heard, the ungarbled
>   word,
> And when do we get alert pay?

(14) THE HORSESHIT SONG (See MM10)

(15) HUMORESQUE
(Tune: Available)

Alternate Titles and Variations:

   (a) Sherman's Horse (See Vol. I, S26)
   (b) Was It You Who Did The Push'n?

Passengers will please refrain
From flushing the toilets while the
   train
Is standing in the station, I love you.
As we go strolling through the park,
And goosing shadows in the dark,
If Sherman's horse can take it,
Why can't you?

You're the guy that did the pushing,
Put the wet spots on the cushion;
Foot prints on the dash board upside
   down.
Ever since you met my daughter,
She's had trouble passing water.
Wish that you had never come to town.

I'm the guy that did the pushing,
Put the wet spots on the cushion;
Foot prints on the dash board upside
   down.
Since I met your daughter, Venus,
I've had trouble with my penis.
Wish I'd never seen this Goddamn town!

(00) WAS IT YOU WHO DID THE PUSH'N?
(Tune: Available)

Was it you who did the push'n,
Put the stains upon the cush'n,
Footprints on the dashboard upside
   down?
Was it you with sly wood pecker,
Got into my girl, Rebecca?
If it was, you'd better leave this town.

REPLY

Yes, it was I who did the push'n,
Put the stains upon the cush'n,
Footprints on the dashboard upside
   down.
But since I laid your daughter,
I've had trouble pass'n water,
Guess we'll call it even all around.

FLIGHT SECTION II

(01) I AM EAGLE
(Tune: *I Am Woman*)

I am Eagle, hear me roar,
I am too big to ignore.
Paint me little, paint me tiney, paint
   me small.
I can sort and pick and choose,
But somehow I always lose;
I guess it's 'cause I've got no clue at
   all,
But they said in UPT that the Eagle
   was for me;
That my hands were made of gold and
   couldn't fail;
But my radar just went tits,
Oh, my God, ain't this the shits.
I've got Phantoms and Aggressors on my
   tail.

CHORUS (*repeat after each verse*)

   Ye, I am wise but it's feeling from
      the pain,
   Ye, I've paid the price but look at
      what I've gained.
   If I had to, I can do anything.
   I am large, I am invincible, I am
      Eagle,
   Watch me die.

As I fly the speed of light,
Blowing both ways thru the fight,
I know that auto-guns won't let me down
But I've got no tally-ho,
And I don't know which way to go,
So I guess it's time to slow this
   mother down;
But you never really know,
Just which way the flames will go,
When both throttles are placed up
   against the wall,
So I lie here on my back,
With both engines rolling back,
When my GCI controller says - ATOLL!

(00) I DON'T WANT TO BE A 'ERO
(*See CC01*)

(00) I DON'T WANT TO BE A SOLDIER
(*See CC01*)

(00) I DON'T WANT TO JOIN THE AIR FORCE
(or ARMY) *See CC01*

(02) I'D RATHER FLY A WARTHOG (*See GG04*)

(00) IF ALL LITTLE GIRLS (*See RR08*)

(00) IF ALL THE YOUNG MAIDENS (*See RR08*)

UH-1 IROQUOIS

(03) I FLY THE LINE
(Tune: *I Walk The Line*)

I keep a close watch on these lands of
   mine,
I keep my eyes wide open all the time.
Directing air strikes is a specialty of
   mine;
This sector's mine, I fly the line.

(*continued on next page*)

Dawn patrol around An Khe is really
   great,
It's those out-country missions that I
   hate.
I'll fly and fight anywhere and anytime,
Because they're mine, I fly the line.

Small arms and 37s I don't sweat,
Fifty cal and ZPU are what I get;
White puffs far away are a good sign;
This sector's mine, I fly the line.

Armed with rockets and binoculars I go,
Out to see what I can see and hope to
   know.
Where ol' Charlie runs and hides and
   spends his time;
This sector's mine, I fly the line.

When I find Charlie on the ground, I
   call for Air,
Then I roll in to mark when they get
   there;
Hit my smoke and run in on the East-
   West line,
This sector's mine, I fly the line.

I keep a close watch on these lands of
   mine;
I keep my eyes wide open all the time,
Directing air strikes is a specialty
   of mine.
This sector's mine, I fly the line.

(04) IF YOU FLY
      (Tune: *Ta-Ra-Ra Boom De-Ay*)

Alternate Titles and Variations:
   (*In Volume I, song B47*)

   (a) *Boom Today*
   (b) *Will You Go Boom Today?*

..OTE: *You might know that some jock
during a wild party would dream up a
couple X-rated verses to this Air Force
classic. Although they add little to
the literature of the world, they are
still a part of the folklore of war.
The original of this song in Volume I is
much like the great ditty,* **Give Me
Operations***--there are almost as many
verses as there are different aircraft.*

*The two additional verses below are
presented with the chorus. It is suspected the names in the song refer to
real people in the squadron from whose
song book these were taken. If so, they
are now immortalized (or mortified).*

IF YOU FLY

If you fly a 38,
You'll never masturbate,
Ask Pappy and he'll say,
You'll get laid every day.

NEW CHORUS #1 (*repeat after each verse*)

   Did you go BOOM today?
   Did you go BOOM today?
   Two more blew up yesterday,
   G. E. ain't here to stay.

And if you fly a tweet,
You'll have to beat your meat,
And do it several times,
Just go ask Colonel Heinz.

If you fly a 1-2-4,
You will find it quite a bore.
It flies like an old barn door,
And it makes your fanny sore.

NEW CHORUS #2

   Did you go OUCH today?
   Did you go OUCH today?
   Fourteen hours yesterday,
   What a way to earn your pay!

(00) I HEADED DOWN THE RUNWAY (*See TT17*)

(05) I KNOW A GIRL FROM ARKANSAS
      (Tune: *Unavailable*)

I know a girl from Arkansas, honey,
   honey.
I know a girl from Arkansas, babe,
   babe.
I know a girl from Arkansas,
She can take your balls and all, honey,
   oh baby mine.

(*continued on next page*)

Go to your left, your right, your left,
Go to your left, your right, your left.

USE SAME FORMAT ABOVE FOR ALL VERSES:

I know a girl from Kentuck,
She can't cook but she sure can fuck.

I know a girl all dressed in red,
She makes her living in a bed.

I know a girl all dressed in black,
She makes her living on her back.

If I die on the Russian front,
Bury me with a Russian cunt.

If I die on the Cuban rear,
Bury me with a Cuban queer.

I don't know but I've been told,
Eskimo pussy's mighty cold.

I got a girl from Niagara Falls,
She's got a mortgage on my balls.

I know a girl who lives on a hill,
She won't do it, but her sister will.

(06) I'LL SEE YOU IN MY DREAMS
(Tune: *I'll See You In My Dreams*)

I'll see you in my dreams,
Hold you in my arms;
There you lay upon the white bed,
Naked from your toes to your head.

Lips that once were mine,
In rhapsody divine;
When I awoke,
The bed was soaked,

I'll see you in my dreams.

(07) I LOVE MY BEAR
(Tune: *Unavailable*)

NOTE: *This ditty is a derivative of* I Love My Girl, *II08, below. The* bear *is the Electronic Systems Officer of the two-seat fighters of the Vietnam War-- the F-4D (and other models) Phantom II,*

or the F-84F, two-seat version of F-84 Thunderchief, *better known as the* Thud. *Also see* The Weasel-Bears' Picnic, *Volume II, WW05. The F-84F was also given the name* Weasel *or* Wild Weasel *when it was specially equipped to track and destroy enemy SAM sites.*

I LOVE MY BEAR

I love my Bear, yes I do, yes I do.
I love that asshole.
I love the scope that he looks into.
I love his blips, tiddely-ips, tiddely-
  ips, and his little black boxes.
He'll fly until his ass is black and
  blue.

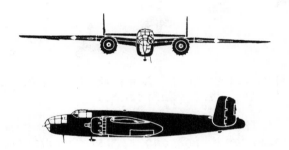

(08) I LOVE MY GIRL
(Tune: *Unavailable*)

Alternate Titles and Variations:

  (a) *I Love My Wife*

NOTE: *There is a second version to this song, but the Editor could not imagine that anyone would be interested in* two *of these! One is bad enough!.*

I LOVE MY GIRL

I love my girl, yes I do, deed I do.
I love her truly.
I love the hole that she pisses through.
I love her ruby red lips and her lily
  white tits
And the hair around her butthole.
I'd eat her stuff, chompety, chomp,
  chompety chomp,
With a rusty spoon.

(09) I'M AN ASSHOLE
(Tune: *Clementine*)

NOTE: *Talk about a ditty (a short song, etc.) this qualifies as a gem. It tells it all, short and sweet (bitter to some).*

I'M AN ASSHOLE

I'm an asshole,
I'm an asshole,
I'm an asshole, yes I am;
But I'd rather be an asshole,
Than to fly the F-15.

(10) I'M DREAMING OF A WHITE MISTRESS
(Tune: *White Christmas*)

NOTE: *In the environment of 1986, some may consider this song racist. However, with easy changes, one can substitute any color one desires. Morality was NOT a big consideration in Volume II; capturing history was.*

I'M DREAMING OF A WHITE MISTRESS

I'm dreaming of a white mistress,
Just like the ones I used to know.
With lips empassioned and charms
    unrationed,
And thighs that glisten like the snow.
I'm dreaming of a white mistress,
The kind that the Arabs do not know;
For though colors may change at night,
Yet, may all my mistresses be white.

I'm dreaming of a white mistress,
Unmarred by wind or dust or sun.
Like a supple willow, with breasts to
    pillow,
My tired head when day is done.
I'm dreaming of a white mistress,
Who's neither yellow, tan, nor black,
But dreaming's not any fun, so,
Knock it off and let's all hit the sack.

(11) I'M LOOKING UNDER
(Tune: *I'm Looking Over*)

I'm looking under a dress and wonder
Why I haven't looked before.
First comes the ankles, then comes the
    knees;
Then comes the panties that sway in the
    breeze.
No use explaining the thing remaining,
Is something we all adore.
I'm looking under a dress and wonder,
Why I haven't looked before.

(00) I'M YOUR MAILMAN (*See MM02*)

(12) IN AN OLD KENTUCKY TOWN
(Tune: *Unavailable*)

NOTE: *Part of this ditty would seem to fit with the tune, **When You Wore A Tulip**, but other parts do not seem to fit. Many songs were created from more than one melody, and this may be one of them.*

IN AN OLD KENTUCKY TOWN

I met her in a whore house,
In an old Kentucky town.
She wore no evening gown,
Her pants were hanging down.
Her lips were red as a roosters ass,
Her eyes were cat-turd brown.
Her tits hung down like a buffalo's cod.
I'll fuck her before the sun goes down.
I wore a tulip, a big yellow tulip,
And she wore a big red rose.
Oh! how it did tickle,
When she squeezed my pickle,
And I whitewashed her big red rose.

(13) IN BOHUNKAS TENNESEE
(Tune: *Unavailable*)

Alternate Titles and Variations:
    (*See Volume I, H3*)

(a) *Hail You Fighter Pilots*

(*continued on next page*)

IN BOHUNKAS TENNESEE

In Bohunkas Tennesee lives a horse's ass
   like me,
And my father shoveled horseshit in the
   street.
And one day when I was young,
They found rubies in my dung,
And they said my boy a flyer you will
   be.

Hail, hail, hail to masturbation.
Raise your thundermugs on high -- hear,
   hear!
And we'll drink another glass to the
   biggest horse's ass,
In the brotherhood of all the men that
   fly.

(14) IN MOBILE
(Tune: *Unavailable*)

NOTE: *This is an adaptation of an English song--those naughty English! The Editor had two problems with this song. First, the sometimes unevenness of the verses such as Verse #2. Unfortunately, the Editor had only one source and could not make a cross-check. The Editor also exercised a little discretion in eliminating one verse that is totally inappropriate as noted below.*

IN MOBILE

There's a shortage of good whores in
   Mobile.
(*repeat twice more*)
But there's keyholes in the doors,
And there's knot-holes in the floors, in
   Mobile.

There's a blockage of bogs in Mobile.
(*repeat twice more*)
It's a habit of the working classes,
When they've finished with their
   glasses,
They just stuff them up their arses, in
   Mobile.

Oh, the old dun cow is dead in Mobile.
(*repeat twice again*)
But the children must be fed,
So we'll milk the bull instead, in
   Mobile.

Oh, the eagles they fly high in Mobile.
(*repeat twice more*)
And they shit right in your eye,
So thank God the cows don't fly, in
   Mobile.

NOTE: *The next verse was eliminated by the Editor because it is racist and totally inappropriate.*

There's no shortage of good beer in
   Mobile.
(*repeat twice more*)
And they give us damn good cheer.
Oh, thank God that we are here, in
   Mobile.

There's a lovely girl called Dinah in
   Mobile.
(*repeat twice more*)
For a fuck there is no finer,
'Cause she's got the best vagina, in
   Mobile.

There's a man called Lanky Danny in
   Mobile.
(*repeat twice more*)
And his instinct is uncanny
When he's fingering a fanny, in Mobile.

There is a tavern in the town in Mobile.
(*repeat twice more*)
Where for half a fucking crown,
You can get a bit of brown, in Mobile.

Oh, the girls all wear tin pants in
   Mobile.
(*repeat twice more*)
But they take them off to dance
Just to give the boys a chance, in
   Mobile.

There's excess of copulation in Mobile.
(*repeat twice more*)
They relax for stimulation
Or mutual masturbation, in Mobile.

(*continued on next page*)

The CO is a bugger in Mobile.
(*repeat twice more*)
And the adjutant he is another,
So they bugger one another, in Mobile.

(15) IN THE SPRINGTIME
    (Tune: *Unavailable*)

NOTE: *This is another of those guessing
songs where you are suppose to supply
the missing words. The Editor had some
difficulty with this, and the words in
parenthesis are his nominees. O.K.?*

IN THE SPRINGTIME

In the springtime, in the springtime,
In the springtime of yore,
I met a young lady who looked like a
      _____ (flower?).

Darling young maiden, as she lay in the grass
And gently rolled over to show me her
      ___ (birthmark?)

Diamonds and bracelets and little pet duck,
And told be she'd teach me a new way to
      ____ (whistle?)

Bring up my children and teach them to knit,
While farmers in barnyards were shoveling
      out ____ (hay?)

Feed for their horses and cattle and sheep,
In the springtime, in the springtime,
In the springtime so sweet.

(16) IN THE TALL GRASS
    (Tune: *Unavailable*)

Alternate Titles and Variations:

    (a) *Tall Grass*

In the tall, tall grass,
Young Mary lay a-sleeping.
When out of the tall grass,
A pilot came a-creeping
With his long dingle dangle, dingling.

Three months have gone by.
Young Mary she grew bolder.

She wished that the pilot
Would come and do it over,
With his long dangle dingle, dangling.

Six months have gone by,
And Mary she grew fatter.
The neighbors did wonder
Just who had been at her,
With his long dingle dangle, dingling.

Nine months have gone by,
And Mary burst asunder,
And out jumped a pilot
With his (unit) number,
With his skoshi dangle dingle, dangling,
Right down to his knees.

(17) INTO THE AIR, JUNIOR BIRDMEN
(Tune: *The Spirit of The Air Corps*)

Alternate Titles and Variations:

    (a) *Into The Air (Army Air Corps)*
        (See Volume I, song S53)
    (b) *Into The Air, 69ers (Vol. I, S53)*
    (c) *Official Song of Randolph Field*
    (d) *Spirit of the Air Corps*
    (e) *Up In The Air, Junior Birdman*

NOTE: *George Hocutt of Newhall, Calif-
fornia says he learned this as an
Aviation Cadet at Goodfellow Air Force
Base (great name for a cadet base).*

INTO THE AIR, JUNIOR BIRDMEN

Into the air, junior birdmen,
Into the air upside down.
Into the air junior birdmen,
Keep your nose up in the brown, up in
   the brown.
And when you hear the Captain shouting,
That you've earned your wings of tin,
You can bet the junior birdmen,
Have sent their box-tops in.

NOTE: *From the* **Up In The Air, Junior
Birdman** *version, add the following to
the last verse:*

(*continued on next page*)

Well, it takes five box tops,
Four bottle bottoms,
Three wrappers,
Two coupons,
AND, one thin dime.
(Now make the sound of a plane diving,
followed by a machine gun firing)

(18) I SAW HER SNATCH
(Tune: *Unavailable*)

I saw her "snatch" her satchel from the
    window.
I held her for a moment in the rain.
I kissed her "as" she hurried to the
    station,
To see her brother "Jack off" the train.

(19) I SMELL KIMSHEE
(Tune: *I Wonder Why*)

I smell Kimshee and there is no one
    there.
I pat her on the bottom and her peaches
    bare.
All night long I search and search for
    hair.
She have-a-no, she have-a-no.

I've been eating Kimshee each day and
    night,
And somehow I've lost my appetite.
Now Josans who spread their pearly
    thighs
To try me out for size.
I have-a-no.

(20) IT DON'T HURT ANYMORE
(Tune: *Unavailable*)

It don't hurt anymore,
'Cause she's had it before.
Her cherry feels no pain,
'Cause you're searching in vain.
Three or four maybe more
Have all made her before.
So if you hear her squeal,
Please don't think it's for real.

The first time she tried,
She moaned and she sighed.

The pain hurt her so much,
But she won't flinch,
It's really a cinch.
She hardly feels the touch,
That's the way it all goes.
Something you ought to know,
You see she's really a whore,
And it don't hurt anymore.

(21) IT'S A LIE
(Tune: *Battle Hymn Of The Republic*)

Alternate Titles and Variations:

(a) *You Can Tell A Fighter Pilot*
    (See Volume I, Y4)

NOTE: *This is one of those songs that
has been put together from others, and
then changed a little to make a new
song. Different parts of this ditty
will be found in both variations listed
above.*

ITS A LIE

By the ring around his eyes,
You can tell a bombardier.
You can tell a bomber pilot
By the spread across his rear.
You can tell a navigator
By his sextants, charts and such.
You can tell a fighter pilot,
But you can't tell him much.

CHORUS (*repeat after each verse*)

It's a lie, it's a lie.
You can tell the silly bastards
It's a lie, it's a lie.
You can tell the silly bastards
It's a silly fucking lie.

First lady forward,
And the second lady back.
Third lady's finger
Up the fourth lady's crack.
Now all gather 'round
To the center of the room.
Will the lady who just farted
Kindly leave the fucking room?

(*continued on next page*)

Flying fucking fighters
Down at forty fucking feet,
Through the fucking snow and
Even through the fucking sleet.
First you're flying fucking up
And then you're flying fucking down,
And you'll be the first to know it
When you hit the fucking ground.

(22) IT WAS ROUGH IN OLD MANILA
(Tune: *Unavailable*)

It was rough in old Manila,
It was rough in Tokyo,
But this Hell in the Marianas
Is the roughest place I know.
You can go to Agana Air Strip
Any hour of any day;
You can watch the Navy aircraft
As they crash in Tumon Bay.
You can take these coral beaches,
You can take this withered grass,
You can take these Marianas,
And to that I'll raise my GLASS.

(00) IVAN SKAVINSKI SKAVAR (*See AA02*)

POINT TO PONDER . . . .

(23) I WANT A SPAD
(Tune: *I Want A Girl*)

I want a Spad, just like the Spad
That buried dear old dad.
It was a Spad, and the only Spad
That daddy ever had.
A good old fashioned plane with lots
     of wing,
It took six guys to crank the damn
     machine.
I want a Spad, just like the Spad
That buried dear old dad.

(24) I WANT(ED) TO PLAY PIANO
IN A WHOREHOUSE
(Tune: *Unavailable*)

I want to play piano in a whorehouse.
That is my one desire.
Some may be bankers or ranchers out in
     Butte.
I just want to play in a house of ill
     repute.
You may laugh at this my humble
     advocation,
But carnal copulation is here to stay.
I don't want fame or riches,
I just want to play for those old
     bitches.
I want to play piano in a whorehouse.

*Societies exist under three forms: (1) without govern-
ment, as among our Indians, (2) under governments wherein
the will of everyone has a just influence, and (3) under
governments of force. It is a problem not clear in my
mind that the first condition is not the best.*

Thomas Jefferson

FLIGHT SECTION KK

(01) KATHUSELEM
(Tune: *Available*)

Alternate Titles and Variations:

    (a) *Cafoozalem*
    (b) *The Harlot of Jeruslalem*
    (c) *Methuselem: An Ancient Love Song*

<u>NOTE</u>: *There is a similarity in story, if not in song, between this dirty ditty and the four devilish dirges,* **Bumming Around Town, Lupee 2, Rangy Lil,** *and* **Yukon Pete,** *all in this volume. Each involves loose women and a jock with a super you-know-what. Some psychiatrists might attribute these songs to male chauvinist, macho fantasies. The Editor knows better. They were probably written by a bunch of dirty old, ex-B-17 (the Hollywood bomber) crew members!*

KATHUSLELEM

In ancient days there lived a maid,
Who used to ply a filthy trade,
A prostitute of ill repute,
The harlot of Jerusalem.

CHORUS (*repeat after each verse*)

    Kathuselem's snatch was bold and bare,
    Upon her gash there grew no hair,
    For hair won't grow on a thorough-fare,
    Like the snatch of old Kathuselem.

Kathuselem's cunt was round and red,
For forty years it had not bled,
It smelled as though it had been dead,
Since the founding of Jerusalem.

Now, Kathuselem was a wily witch,
A goddamn fucking son-of-a-bitch,

And every pecker that had the itch,
Had dangled in Kathuselem.

Next door there lived a giant tall,
His prick of steel could smash a wall,
His balls hung down like basketballs,
The giant of old Jerusalem.

One night returning from a spree,
A quite consistent jubilee,
His balls hung well below his knees,
He chanced to cross Kathuselem.

KAMAN

HH-2/UH-2C

And so he challenged her to fuck,
And wishing her the best of luck,
He led her to shady nook,
And there unfurled his mighty hook.

This giant of old was underslung,
'He missed her cunt and hit her bung,
And with his giant pecker stung,
The pride of all Jerusalem.

Kathuselem she knew her art,
She cocked her ass and blew a fart,
She blew him like a bloody dart,
Through the walls of old Jerusalem.

(*continued on next page*)

And there he lay a broken mass,
His cock all bent with shit and gas,
And Kathuselem got up and wiped her ass,
All over the walls of Jerusalem.

(00) KC-135 BOOM OPERATOR (*See HH04*)

(02) KHARTOUM
(Tune: *Unavailable*)

NOTE: *Not having the tune to this ditty, it was not possible to verify that the irregular verse structure was intended. The song is obviously British in origin, hence the reference to the British air craft carriers* **Somersetshire**, **Rodney** *and* **Hood**. *SPs, of course, are Shore Patrols, the Navy equivalent of MPs, Military Police. Despite this being a British Navy song, American airmen en joyed it during the times of the Second World War and Korea.*

KHARTOUM

There's bags of batchy airmen,
Way down in the sunny Sudan,
Where everyone is batch,
And so's the fucking old man.
There's bags and bags of bullshit,
Saluting on the square,
And when we're not saluting,
We're up in the fucking air.

We're leaving Khartoum
By the light of the moon.
We travel by night and by day.
As we pass Kasfereit,
We'll have fuck all to eat,
'Cause we've thrown all
Our rations away.

Shire, Shire, Somersetshire,,
The skipper looks on her with pride.
He'd have a blue fit,
If he saw any shit,
On the side of the Somersetshire.

This is my story,
This is my song.
I've been in this Air Force
Too fucking long.

So bring on the Rodney,
The Nelson, Renown.
They can't bring the Hood,
'Cause the fuckers gone down.
Tooralay, tooralay,
Oh, we'll fuck all the SPs
Who come down our way.

(03) KIMPO BLUES
(Tune: *A Little Bit Of Heaven*)

NOTE: *From the chorus on, this is not the same song as the first two verses. You will note that the first two verses follow the old Irish melody quite well, but the chorus is from a totally differ- ent melody. The chorus seems to work with the old song,* **Am I Blue?**. *Oh, those wonderful Air Force songwriters!*

KIMPO BLUES

Oh, a little bit of shit fell down
Out of the sky one day.
And it landed in the Chosen,
Oh, so very far away.
And when the Senate saw it,
It looked so fucking bare,
They said, "That's what we're looking
   for;
We'll send our Air Force there.

So they sent their '86's,
Air Base Group and medics too;
And they sent the dreaded 336th,
They knew just what to do.
And now you'll find them languished
In a place that's so remote,
That all you'll hear those bastards
   shouts,
"Where are these fucking boats?"

CHORUS (*repeat after every other verse*)

   I've got those Kimpo Blues,
   Kimchi blues.
   I'm fed up,
   And I'm fucked up,
   And I'm blue.

(*continued on next page*)

We tried to please old Sygman,
But it really was a farce.
The only thing 'twas left to do,
Was shove it up his arse.
Oh, we found our Alma Mater
In a house in Yong Dong Po.
The brass got there before us,
They showed us where to go.

(04) KIMPO SONATA)
(Tune: *Unavailable*)

Alternate Titles and Variations:

   (a) *Perrin To Youngstown*
      (See Volume I, P13)

NOTE: *With a little straining, it is possible to sing this to the first few bars of* **Blues In The Night,** *but the Editor is not certain of the original tune. Air Force song book publishers were not too helpful in printing tune titles.*

KIMPO SONATA

Oh, I was sent to Nellis,
I was sent to train.
I learned how to bomb and strafe,
From an aeroplane.

Oh, I was sent to Kimpo,
To be a killer, too,
But all I got is a bunch of shit
From you and you and you.

I knew a fighter pilot,
No smile upon his face,
And many's the time I heard him say,
I HATE THIS FUCKING PLACE!

(05) KI YI YIPPIE YAY
   (Tune: *Unavailable*)

NOTE: *Another intellectual test of the highest order! Finish the missing words of this song, and you'll win a prize from the* **International Association of Dirty Song Writers at Bucking Hors House, Porno-By-The-Sea, England.** *In the first verse, they are doing some-thing through a barbed-wire fence. In the song,* **Bang It Into Lulu,** *(BB12), Lulu was also doing* something *through a barbed-wire fence. In* **Tie My Pecker Around A Tree,** *later in this volume, she was doing* something *through a barbed-wire fence. What's with the barbed-wire? Hey guys, are we missing* some-thing? *(or just the Editor?). The song is apparently a cowboy classic (?).*

KI YI YIPPIE YAY

The last time I seen her,
And I haven't seen her since,
She was _____ *off a feller,*
Through a barbed wire fence.

CHORUS (repeat after each verse)

   Come a ki yi yippee, yippee yay,
     yippie yay,
   Come a ki yi yippee, yippee yay

I asked her if she would,
And she said she didn't.
So I grabbed her by the ____,
And I swung right on her.

I went down the cellar
To get a jug of cider.
There was a cockroach,
_____ off a spider.

I went upstairs
To get a jug of gin.
Fell in the piss pot,
Up to my chin.

I couldn't swim,
Couldn't float,
A big fat turd
Went sliding down my throat.

I grabbed her by the ____,
And I threw her on the grass,
And I showed her the wiggle
Of a cowboy's ___.

I saw her once again,
A-floating down the stream,
With an ___ full of magots
And a ____ full of cream.
(*continued on next page*)

NOTE: *This next verse does not follow the construction of the others.*

As I was riding down the cow ____ trail,
With my _____ in my hand,
And a pony by the tail.
I met a little girl
And I offered her a quarter,
She said, "Hell, no,
I'm a bootlegger's daughter."

I took her in the woods,
And I layed her on a log,
And I jumped on her,
Like an old bullfrog.

I took her upstairs,
And I layed her on the floor.
The wind from her ___,
Blew the cat out the door.

I took her in the valley,
And layed her on a rock,
And gave her twelve inches,
Of a cowboy's ____.

(06) KOTEX SONG
(Tune: *Field Artillery Song*)

Alternate Titles and Variations:

   (a) *You Can Tell By The Smell*

You can tell by the smell
That she isn't feeling well,
When the end of the month rolls around.

Now she turns, how she squirms,
How she gets a case of worms,
When the end of the month rolls around.

For it's hi, hi, hee,
In the Kotex industry.
Call out your sizes loud and strong.
"Super-Junior-Band Aid;"
For where 'ere you go,
The blood will always flow,
When the end of the month rolls around.

Boeing B-52

FLIGHT SECTION LL

(01) LANCASTER LEAVING THE RUHR
   (*See TT24*)

(02) LAOTIAN KARST (*See BB21*)

(03) LAST NIGHT (*See FF02*)

(00) LAST NIGHT I STAYED UP (*See FF02*)

(04) LEE'S HOOCHIE
(Tune: *On Top Of Old Smokey*)

NOTE: *This song and the one immediately following read like the medic's and chaplain's propaganda against VD (now you all remember what that is!). This is a popular theme in song--the wages of sin--and will be found in many ballads in this volume.*

LEE'S HOOCHIE

I went to Seoul City and met a Miss Lee,
She said for a short time, oh, come
   sleep with me.
We went to Lee's hoochie, a room with
   hot floors.
I left my shoes outside, and slid shut
   the door.

She took off her long johns, and rolled
   out the pad.
I gave her ten thousand, 'twas all that
   I had.
Her breath smells of kimshie, her bosoms
   were flat,
No hair on her pussy, now what about
   that!

I asked to go benjo, she led me outside.
I reached for old smokey, he crawled
   back inside.
I rushed to the medics, cried, "What
   shall I do?"
The Doc was dumbfounded, old smokey was
   blue.

LOCKHEED C-141

Now when you're in Seoul City, on your
   next three day pass,
Don't go to Lee's hoochie, sit flat on
   your ass.
Now your ass may get blistered, and Lee
   may tempt you,
But better the red ass, than old smokey
   blue.

(05) LET 'OLE MOTHER NATURE HAVE HER WAY
(Tune: *Unavailable*)

Boy-san, wipe away them tears,
We're goin' down to the house of
   mirrors,
To let 'ole mother nature have her way.
Goin' to look into them mirrors of
   glass,
And watch myself get a piece of ass.
Lettin' 'ole mother nature have her way.

CHORUS (*repeat after each verse*)

   Closer, come a skoshi bit closer.
   Oh, there ain't no use to dick around
     this way.
   Put your belly close to mine,
   We're gonna go pom-pom four or five
     times,
   To let 'ole mother nature have her
     way.

Mushi, mushi, boy-san make a skoshi
   trip,
Down to the Officer's Club at the strip,
To let 'ole mother nature have her way.
We're goin' down to that glorified pub,
Known as the Allied Officer's Club,
To let 'ole mother nature have her way.

Shrimp cocktails and a great big steak,
Will really put us on the make,
To let 'ole mother nature have her way.
But before we go down to that palace of
   sin,
We better load up with a few thousand
   Yen,
To let' ole mother nature have her way.

Hooray, now here we are at last.
Mama-san parade them jo-sans past,
To let 'ole mother nature have her way..
Now, that 'un's as cute as a pup with
   specks,
Them chi-chi's didn't come from no P.X.
Just let 'ole mother nature have her
   way.

Mama-san, I'll take that one over there,
With the great big chi-chi's and the
   skoshie hair,
To let 'ole mother nature have her way.
Oh, it shorely seems an awful sin,

To pay this jo-san a thousand yen,
To let 'ole mother nature have her way.

Jo-san taihen kawaii aa,
Pom-pom O-mae-ni suki des' ka,
To let 'ole mother nature have her way.
Hai, hai, so desu, suki desho,
Keredomo shakuhachii suki nai yo,
To let 'ole mother nature have her way.

Oh, you wake up in the morning feeling
   like shit,
And nine days later it starts to drip,
To let 'ole mother nature have her way.
You tell Doc Beetlebaum the fix you're
   in.
He fills your ass full of penicillin,
To let 'ole mother nature have her way.

But you will really begin to curse yore
   fate,
When your shankers break out as big as
   pie plates,
To let 'ole mother nature have her way.
Down to Doc Beetlebaum's office again,
To get yore ass full of aureomycin,
To let 'ole mother nature have her way.

Then one fine mornin' you jump out of
   the sack,
To find the little son-of-a-bitch has
   turned coal black,
To let 'ole mother nature have her way.
The doc says stand on your toes and
   cough,
Imagine his surprise when yore balls
   fall off,
To let 'ole mother nature have her way.

Don't worry Doc Beetlebaum tells you the
   score,
They'll never be missed on your next
   60-4,
To let 'ole mother nature have her way.
But you'll sound a little funny trans-
   mittin' for a fix,
(*High voice*) "Hello DF Homer one, two,
   three, four, five, six",
To let 'ole mother nature have her way.

(06) LIFE PRESENTS A DISMAL PICTURE
(Tune: *What A Friend We Have In Jesus*)

NOTE: *You think you got problems! The last verse may surprise some of you male chauvinists. This ditty came to the collection from Captain Mike Krall of the RCAF via John Piowaty, circa 1968.*

LIFE PRESENTS A DISMAL PICTURE

Life presents a dismal picture,
Full of sorrow and or gloom.
Father has an anal stricture,
Mother has a fallen womb.
Brother Percy's been deported,
For a homosexual crime.
Sister Sue has been aborted
For the forty-second time.

Uncle Charlie has a chancre,
Caught from Uncle Henry's wife.
May's in bed with menstration,
Auntie's at the change of life.
Life presents a dismal picture;
No one hardly ever smiles;
Mine's a gloomy occupation,
Crushing ice for Grandpa's piles.

Life presents a dismal picture-
Found a fetus in a case;
Dr. Bowden says it's murder-
Of Sister Anne there is no trace.
Brother Bill's emasculated,
For the safety of the place,
Sister Anne is now frustrated,
No man's safe around our place.

As for me I had a discharge,
With mercury I did annoint,
But it was not worth a cracker:
Now I've got a Charcot's joint.
Gonococcal Salpingitis,
It has blocked my tubes for me;
So you see my dearest doctor,
It's no use to do a D & C.

(07) LIQUOR AND LONGEVITY
(Tune: *Unavailable*)

NOTE: *For all of you guys and gals who have been looking for that ultimate excuse for frequent imbibing--here it is, straight from the ABA--and they ain't lawyers! (American Bartenders Association).*

LIQUOR AND LONGEVITY

The horse and mule live thirty years,
And nothing knows of wines and beers.
The goat and sheep at twenty die,
And never a taste of scotch or rye.
The cow drinks water by the ton,
At eighteen years her life is done.
The dog at fifteen cashes in,
Without the air of rum or gin.
The cat in milk and water soaks,
And then in twelve short years it croaks
The modest sober bone-dry hen,
Lays eggs (for nogs) and dies at ten.
All animals are strictly dry:
They sinless live and quickly die.
But sinful, skinful, rum-soaked men,
Survive for three score years and ten.
And some of them, though very few,
Stay pickled 'till they are ninety-two.

(08) LISTEN HOOTERS
(Tune: *One Tin Soldier Died Today*)

NOTE: *This is one of several songs of the **Hooters**--497th Tactical Fighter Squadron, 51st Tactical Fighter Wing (Korea) submitted to the Editor by Captain Michael P. Nishimuta. Of this song he commented, ". . . reminds us of the days when the **Night Owls** (Hooters) flew continuous night missions in the ground attack role. Now (1984) the Hooters are based in Korea with an air superiority mission as part of the 51st TFW from Osan." This song has become a part of the history and heritage of the 497th Squadron. The Editor does not recognize the suggested tune, but the words do seem to fit, **The Wabash Cannonball**--with a little improvising.*

LISTEN HOOTERS

Listen, Hooters to a story that was
    written long ago,
'Bout the Night Owls up in Thailand,

(continued on next page)

And the missions that they flew.
Fragged to go up North to Hanoi,
In the darkness they did fly,
Drop their napalm on the convoys,
Watch those commies scream and die.

CHORUS

Go ahead and strafe a commie,
Go ahead and waste a red;
Do it in the name of freedom,
You can stack 'em up when they're
    dead.
There won't be any commies breathin'
Come the judgement day;
On the bloody morning after...
One more gomer died today.

Now the Hooters fly from Taegu,
Fighting in their F-4Es;
Lead the Juvats to their targets, up
    above the DMZ;
Armed with Sparrows, heaters ready,
Kim-Il Sung knows we're the best.
If you really doubt us, asshole,
Come on down and press-to-test!

(09) LITTLE ANGELINE
(Tune: *Available*)

Alternate Titles and Variations:

(a) *Poor Little Angeline*

NOTE: *There are several variations to this originally English beer hall song. Since some versions had departed from the right meter of verse, the Editor has taken editorial license to combine the versions into what appears to be the correct story and song. In any case, it was a terrible ordeal for* **Poor Little Angeline**--*until the happy ending.*

LITTLE ANGELINE

She was sweet sixteen, little Angeline,
Always dancing on the village green,
Was a virgin still, never had a thrill,
Poor little Angeline.

Now the village squire was of low desire
Filthiest bastard in the whole damn
    shire
And he'd set his heart on that vital
    part,
Of poor little Angeline

T'was the day of the fair, and the
    squire was there,
Masturbating in the village square,
When he chanced to see, the dainty
    little knee,
Of poor little Angeline.

She had lifted her skirt to avoid the
    dirt,
Skipping o'er the puddles of the
    squire's last squirt.
And his knob grew raw at the sight he
    saw,
Of poor little Angeline.

As he raised his hat, he said " Miss,
    your cat
Has been run over and squashed quite
    flat,
My car's in the square, so I'll take
    you there,
My poor little Angeline."

Now they hadn't gone far, when he
    stopped the car,
Took little Angeline into a bar.
Where he filled her with gin, to tempt
    her to sin.
Poor little Angeline.

When he filled her quite well, he took
    her to a dell,
Where he attemped to give her Hell,
As he tried his luck on a low down fuck,
With poor little Angeline.

Angeline cried, "Rape," as he raised her
    cape,
Unhappy darlin' there was no escape;
T'was time someone came to save the
    name,
Of poor little Angeline.

(*continued on next page*)

Now it can be told, the blacksmith bold,
Had loved little Angeline for years
  untold,
And it must be true, that she loved him,
  too,
Poor little Angeline.

But sad to say, on that self same day,
The blacksmith had been put in the gaol
  to stay
For coming in his pants at the local
  dance,
With poor little Angeline.

Now the window of his cell, overlooked
  the dell
Where the squire was trying to give the
  maiden Hell,
As they reached the grass, he saw the
  ass
Of poor little Angeline.

So with a mighty start, and a hearty
  fart,
He blew the prison bars wide apart.
And he ran like shit, lest the squire
  should split
Poor little Angeline.

When he reached the spot, and he saw
  what's what,
He tied the villain's penis in a grannie
  knot,
And as away he crawls, he got a kick in
  the balls,
From poor little Angeline.

"Oh, dear blacksmith bold, I love you
  true,
I can see by your trousers that you love
  me too!
As I'm undressed, come and try your best
Said poor little Angeline.

Now it won't take long, to end this song
For the blacksmith's tool was two feet
  long,
And his unfailing charm was as strong as
  his arm,
Happy little Angeline.

(10) LITTLE BOXES (M)
(Tune: *Little Boxes*)
  Lyrics: *Rollie Stoneman*

Little boxes in Wyoming, little boxes
  in Montana,
Little boxes in Dakota, little boxes all
  the same.
There are green ones and green ones,
And green ones and green ones.
And they're all made out of ticky-tacky
And they all look just the same.

And the crewmen in the capsules all went
  to the university,
And then into the Air Force where they
  came out all the same.
There are line crews and instructor
  crews,
And Standboard weenie crews.
And they all dress in ticky-tacky
And they all look just the same.

On alert in the capsule at three in the
  morning,
We all watch for Fault lights
But the Fault lights look the same.
And we order from a menu which is very
  diversified . . .
But the food is put in foil packs
And it all tastes just the same.

And the snow comes to Wyoming, Montana
  and Dakota.
We're stuck in the capsule
And each day is the same.
So we scrutinize the pornography
Then glance at our manuals.
But after three days there it all
  looks just the same.

REPEAT FIRST VERSE

(00) LITTLE RED LIGHT (*See BB25*)

(11) LITTLE TOWN OF HO CHI MINH
(Tune: *Oh Little Town Of Bethlehem*)

Oh, little town of Ho Chi Minh,
How safe you think you lie;

(*continued on next page*)

Beneath your ring of SA-2s,
You think our guys won't fly.
Yet through the cloud deck raineth,
A deadly trail of bombs;
Too late for fear, the end is near,
So fuck off Ho Chi Minh.

(12) LUPEE #1
(Tune: *Down In The Valley*)

Down in cunt valley, where red rivers
    flow,
Where cocksuckers flourish and whore-
    mongers grow;
'Twas where I met Lupee, the girl I
    adore...
She's my hot fucking, cocksucking,
    Mexican whore.

CHORUS (*repeat after each verse*)

    She'll roll you, she'll blow you,
        she'll knaw at your nuts;
    She'll wrap her legs 'round you and
        squeeze out your guts.
    She'll wrap her legs 'round you till
        you think you'll die...
    Oh, I'd rather eat Lupee than blue-
        berry pie!

She got her first piece at the young age
    of eight,
While swinging one day on the old garden
    gate;
The crossbar went out and the upright
    went in...
Ever since she has lived in a welter of
    sin.

Now, Lupee, dear Lupee, lies dead in her
    tomb,
The worms crawl out of her decomposed
    womb;
The smile on her face is a mute cry for
    more...
She's my hot fucking, cocksucking,
    Mexican whore.

(13) LUPEE #2
(Tune: *Down In The Valley*)

NOTE: *This is quite a different story,
almost a continuation of the one above,
but definetly a derivative. Lupee must
have been some kind of gal. Another of
the several songs in this volume where a
super stud meets a super slut for the
battle of the sexes. A typical male
fantasy. See* Bumming Around, Kathuselem, Rangy Lil, *and* Yukon Pete.

LUPEE #2

I was down in Laredo, out drinking one
    night,
I was hitting the high spots and doing
    all right.
There I saw a floor show with Lupee as
    the star,
She was fuckin' the major on top of the
    bar.

Her knees were all bloody, he had sores
    on his toes,
Sweat poured from his balls and it
    dripped from his nose.
From Lupee the laughter was pouring in
    peals,
As she clawed him and pounded his ass
    with her heels.

Said Lupee disgusted, "Ain't none of you
    cocks,
That can fuck for ten minutes without
    blowing your rocks?"
She stood there defiant with a gleam in
    her eye,
As a long, lanky Texan unbuttoned his
    fly.

Her gleam didn't wilt when he showed her
    his cock,
It was seventeen inches from bottom to
    top.
Said he, "Stand back, gentlemen, and let
    me on through,
'Cause this is where Lupee meets her
    Waterloo!"

(*continued on next page*)

The bar was of marble and it was well-
   built,
But it shuddered and groaned as he drove
   to the hilt.
"Viva la Mexico!", Lupee she cried,
"Remember the Alamo", the Texan replied.

For three solid hours she begged him for
   more,
They fell off the bar and they fucked on
   the floor.
From the floor to the sidewalk to the
   street they did fuck,
Right into the path of an oncoming
   truck.

The airhorn it bellowed, the trailor
   brakes locked,
But neither Lupee, the Texan, nor truck
   could be stopped.
The bartender said with a gleam in his
   eye,
"I guess in all fairness, we'll call it
   a tie."

Now, down in Laredo a statue is seen,
But most of the tourists, they think
   it's obscene.
Only the few who were there understand,
There's no finer tribute to woman or
   man.

Oh, she'll fuck you, she'll suck you,
   she'll nibble your nuts,
And if you're not careful, she'll suck
   out your guts.
Now that there was Lupee, the girl I
   adore,
She's a hot fucking, cocksucking,
   Mexican whore.

(OO) LYMERICKS (*See SS17*)

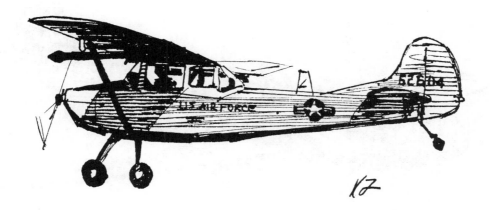

Cessna L-19A "Birddog"

Fokker E-III

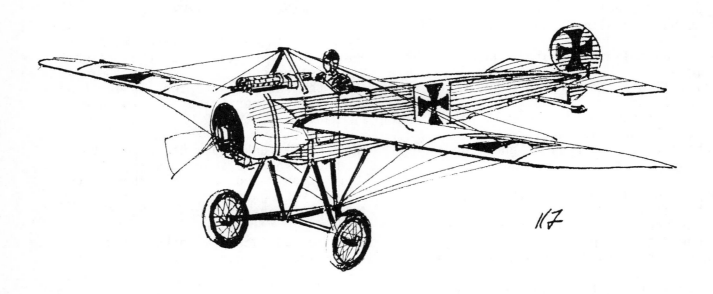

Messerschmitt 109G

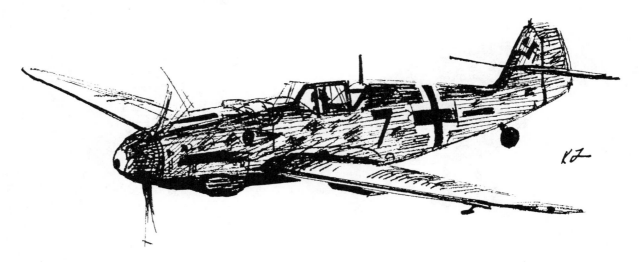

FLIGHT SECTION MM

(00) MADELINE SCHMIDT (*See AA03*)

(01) THE MAID OF THE MOUNTAIN
(Tune: *Unavailable*)

Alternate Titles & Variations:

(a) *The Mayor Of Bayswater*
(b) *The Hairs On Her Diki-Di-Doo*

The maid of the mountain,
She pisses like a little fountain,
'Cause the hairs on her dickie-di-doo
Hang down to her knees.

One black one, one white one,
And one with a little shit on,
'Cause the hairs on her dickie-di-doo
Hang down to her knees.

There's a red one, there's a cherry one,
There's one with a dingle-berry on,
'Cause the hairs on her dickie-di-doo,
Hang down to her knees.

I've been there, I've seen it.
I've been right between it.
'Cause the hairs on her dickie-di-doo,
Hang down to her knees.

I've smelt it, I've felt it,
And it feels just like velvet.
'Cause the hairs on her dickie-di-doo,
Hang down to her knees.

I've tangled, I've dangled,
I've fucking near got strangled,
'Cause the hairs on her dickie-di-doo,
Hang down to her knees.

(02) THE MAILMAN'S SONG
(Tune: *Bye, Bye, Blackbird*)

Alternate Titles and Variations:

(a) *I'm Your Mailman*

I'm so happy, I'm so gay,
Cause I come twice a day,
I'm your mailman.

Lift your knockers, ring your bell,
Makes you think I am swell.
I'm your mailman.

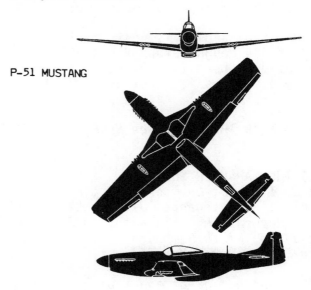

P-51 MUSTANG

CHORUS

I can come in any kind of weather,
That's because my bag is made of
    leather.
I don't mess with keys or locks,
I just slip it in your box.
I'm your mailman.

(03) MANILA POM-POM SONG
(Tune: *Rum and Coca-Cola*)

Alternate Titles and Variations:

(a) *Angeles Pom-Pom Song*
(b) *Rum and Coca-Cola--not commercial*

Have you ever been in the Philippines?
The place is full of pom-pom queens.
The clap is bad but the syph is worse,
So flub your dub for safety first.

CHORUS (*repeat after each verse*)

Singing rum and Coca-Cola
Come down to old Manila.
Both mother and daughter
Working for the GI dollar.

The women with their dirty feet,
Walk up and down Manila Street.
They come up close and whisper low,
"How about a little pom-pom, Joe?"

The Philippine pimp is very smart,
He gets his dough before you start.
The pom-pom there is very nice,
But twenty pesos is a helluva price!

(00) MAN IN THE MOON (*See RR08*)

(04) THE MARAUDER SONG
(Tune: *I've Got No Use For Women*)
Lyrics: *Lieutenants Jim W. Baugh and Lt. Raymond P. Flanagan, 432nd Bomb Squadron, 17th Bomb Group, 1st Tactical Air Force (World War II).*

NOTE: *Another great and typical parody that has many original verses mixed with verses from other songs, notably,* **Liberator Blues** *and* **The Invader** *(Vol. I, L8), both of which are probably adaptations from still other songs. This ballad was written in early 1945 in the 17th Bomb Group's bivouac at Rouvres en Plain, outside Dijon, France. The 17th has an active reunion association.*

THE MARAUDER SONG

When learning to fly a Marauder,
He heard many wonderful things,
But all he could see was the engines.
Oh, where in the hell are the wings!

CHORUS (*repeat after each verse*)

O-O-OH, why did I join the Air Corps,
For mother, dear mother knew best.
Here I lie 'neath the wreckage,
Marauder all over my chest!

Oh, roaring off down the runway,
In his mind was a horrible doubt,
As the co-pilot jerked all the wheels up
Both lousy engines cut out!

While looking down on a roof top,
A pretty young chick he did see,
He dived down to look at her closer,
And clipped off the top of a tree!

Now bussing he did for a pastime,
He roared through the farmer's front
    yard,
He waved at the girl on the doorstep,
And wound up in the silo but hard!

The Marauder's a very good airplane,
Constructed of rivets and tin.
A very good airplane to look at,
But in flak, it's hell to be in!

Now if you fly a pea-shooter,
Or plane of similar ilk,
And if you get into trouble,
Why Hell there's no crew, hit the silk!

When we go out on a mission,
And a 109 makes a pass,
Roll back your seat and start jumping,
To hell with the crew, save your ass.

Now the pilot of a Marauder,
Is a man with plenty of guts,
But after he flies a few missions,
He's either shot down or he's NUTS!

(*continued on next page*)

Though the heavies are very big boxcars,
Compared to Marauders they're toys,
The B-26 is the airplane
That separates the men from the boys.

Once I went on a milk-run,
But whenI got back to the base,
The wheels folded up on the runway,
MARAUDER ALL OVER THE PLACE!!!!

We always knew very early,
Before the briefing begun,
With the rank and "gears" on the
    schedule,
The mission's a milky milk run.

When the Mitchells go in on a target,
They bomb to the Heine's delight,
But after they miss their objective,
The Marauders will do the job right.

They tell of an eager tail gunner,
With hopes of a Jerry or two,
But after one pass by a jet job,
The eager tail gunner was through!

If you've gotten sixty-one missions,
And they haven't sent you on home,
Best you see Doc about rest camp,
Or they'll send you back over Rome.

Take the cylinders out of my backbone,
Connecting rods out of my brain,
From my heart and my lungs take the
    crankshaft,
AND ASSEMBLE THE ENGINE AGAIN!

A Marauder is just like a woman,
She'll trick you and keep you in doubt,
You can't go on living forever,
I'd rather die in one than out.

A Lib is an overgrown junk pile,
Known as the worst of them all,
They scatter their bombs with abandon,
And don't give a damn where they fall!

Now Curtiss causes our troubles,
That prop is a murder machine,
When they both run away on take-off,
Nothing is left to be seen!

The 17th is a hot outfit,
Really the best that there is,
So here's to the pilot that runs it,
On restrictions he's really a whiz!

In Marauders we get few promotions,
Tho' some men will get to the top,
It's easy to see how they get there,
Oh, when will this brown-nosing stop?

(05)THE MARRYING KIND
(Tune: *Unavailable*)

NOTE: *Another of the many, many British
dirty ditties in Volume II. In this
case, it would help to know something
about the game of Rugby -- a game your
Editor knows nothing about!*

THE MARRYING KIND

If I were a marrying maid,
Which thank the Lord I'm not, sir,
The kind of man that I would wed,
Would be a Rugby fullback, sir.
For he'd find touch, and I'd find touch,
We'd both find touch, together.
We'd be all right in the middle of the
    night,
Finding touch together.

*REPEAT THE VERSE PATTERN USING THE
FOLLOWING TEAM POSTIONS . . . . . .*

A wing three-quarter....he'd go fast.
A center three-quarter....he'd go straight.
A stand-off half....he'd go through.
A Rugby scrun half....he'd put it in.
A Rugby loose forward....he'd break fast.
A second row forward....he'd bind tight.
A front row forward....he'd push hard.
A Rugby referee....he'd blow hard.
A Rugby linesman....he'd put it up.

LAST VERSE

A Rugby spectator....
For he'd clap, clap,
And I'd clap, clap.
We'd both clap, clap together.
We'd be alL right in the middle of the
    night,
CLAP, CLAP, CLAP, together.

(06) MARY ANN BURNS
(*Also Byrnes and Barnes*)
Tune: *Unavailable*

Mary Ann Burns is the queen of all the
    acrobats.
She can do tricks that will give a man
    the shits.
Roll green peas up her fundamental
    orifice.
Do a double back flip, catch 'em on her
    tits.
She's a great big son-of-a-bitch twice
    the size of me.
With hair aroung her ass like the
    branches on a tree.
She can shit, fart, fight, fuck, roll a
    barrel, drive a truck;
Mary Ann Burns is the girl for me.

(00) THE MAYOR OF BAYSWATER (*See MM01*)

(07) MEDARIS, VON BRAUN AND ME
    (Tune: *Unavailable*)

NOTE: *So this is an Army song! It comes
from an Air Force source, so it qualifies. And it is about missiles at a
time the politics were running high as
to which service--the Army or the Air
Force--would develop and deploy
intermediate range ballistic missiles
(IRBM). It was the Army's* **Jupiter**
versus the Air Force's **Thor**. *The Editor
was privileged to have met Major General
John Medaris, commander of the* **Redstone
Arsenal** *at the time, and the Editor also
met Werner von Braun. General Medaris
wanted the Editor for a year's TDY to
assist them in establishing a management
control system, but the Editor's boss,
General Bernard A. Schriever, the Air
Force's missile boss, said, "No," but
agreed to three days. The Editor worked
with an Army major by the name of
Frankenstein (honest). In those days,
the services were getting their scientists from anywhere they could find
them--Germany, Transylvania, Oshkosh (?)*

*The Air Force finally won this battle
for the IRBM, ICBM and military space,
but the Army team at Huntsville was one
of the finest, and made great contributions to this Nation's missiles and
space programs. And John Medaris is
one fine gentleman. This fine ballad
captures the dreams and aspirations of
the Army team. It accurately predicted
the future in space--missions assigned
to NASA and the Air Force. The battle
may be heating up again with the* **Stra
tegic Defense Initiative (Star Wars)**
*program. Maybe this time the Army will
win. This ain't football you know!*

MEDARIS, VON BRAUN AND ME

In the missile game, we've won great
    fame,
The world knows our Jupiter C,
And what we've done with Explorer I,
Medaris, von Braun and me.

Now Explorer II went off in the blue,
On its own self-guided spree.
Number III kept in track, and now
    reports back,
To Medaris, von Braun and me.

We'll send up others to join their
    brothers.
Some will orbit, some fall in the sea.
Yet history will toast the men with the
    most,
Medaris, von Braun and me.

Oh, watch our smoke as we go for broke,
To solve the space mystery.
We have a thirst to be there first,
Medaris, von Braun and me.

Our skill we pride, we'll travel wide,
Into space so wild and free.
To the moon, then Mars, then to distant
    stars,
Medaris, von Braun and me.

When finally we've planned a space ship
    that's manned,
And they call for brave men two or three
To try first for the moon in that metal
    balloon,
Call Medaris, von Braun--NOT ME!

(00) METHUSELEM: AN ANCIENT LOVE SONG
(*See KK01*)

(08) MISSILE COMBAT CREW LAMENT
An Epistle by MSgt. J. L. McCoy &
SSgt. F. W. Kerr

NOTE: *Through the kindness of Major Carlton A. Stidsen, USAFR, there is a great epistle--some might say a prose poem--that has been included in this collection. And what are songs but poems put to music. This is what Major Stidsen had to say: "When I was on active duty in the mid-60s at Davis-Monthan AFB (390th Strategic Missile Wing, 571st Squadron), I was an MCCC at the Titan II sites south and west of the city. We never sung anything (SAC, you know, is a dignified bunch. The main bar at Davis-Monthan was dead most nights). I know of only one attempt at humor sanctioned by the Wing while I was there (November 1965 - March 1970), that being the, Missile Combat Crew Lament, as published privately in the commemorative book, Advance To Memory. In order to appreciate this gem, you have to know the terms--strange to old World War II and Korean jocks; maybe even to some of the S.E.A. troops. Major Stidsen was kind and provided some definitions that you will find at the end of the epistle. Pay attention! This is a masterpiece.*

MISSILE COMBAT CREW LAMENT

And so it was that in the thirteenth hour of the sun, in the Land of the Burning Cactus, the heavy-laden lay down their briefcases[1] and lifted their voices in prayer toward the center cubicle, from which all things began.

And as the Pushers of Buttons and the Watchers of Lights assemble in prayer there ariseth great clamor, weeping and lamentation, for they are heavy of eye, sore of fingers, and in need of shaves--for their tails have indeed been great. Surely now the Master shall grant them C^2R[2] (*See Note 2*).

Then there is a great hush, for the hallowed portals of the center cubicle at the Command Post open and the Master and his Disciples cometh forth from their sanctuary and don their white hard hats[3] and rose-colored glasses--for lo, the sun is painful even to them.

And one Disciple steps forth and speaketh unto them of the ORI[4] on the the morrow and calleth on the Pushers of Buttons and Watchers of Lights to give freely and cheerfully of their labours and crew rest; for the ORI surpasseth all earthly things.

Then there is another great hush, for the Master Himself cometh forth to speak; and he sayeth unto them, "Return ye to your labours, and if the ORI be of great success, surely there shall be no back-to-backs[5] during the third week of the half moon; and ye shall have your hour of respite."

And lo, one of the braver of the Pushers of Buttons and Watchers of Lights ariseth and maketh great harangue and speaketh to the Master saying, "Surely Thou has not so soon forgotten Thy promise that on this day Thou wouldst grant us rest?"

Then the Master becometh agape and exceedingly wrathful and speaketh in a thunderous voice; and the Pushers of Buttons and Watchers of Lights whimper and quaketh in their whites[6] and there is sweat in their blue neckbands for their fear is great indeed.

For the Master sayeth: "Be though then accursed, for thine ingratitude is great." And the Pushers of Buttons and Watchers of Lights murmur, "Yea, verily, we are of the accursed."

And the Master speaketh yet again, "Fear my judgment, for ye are the unfortunate. Ye shall henceforth pull twice as many back-to-back tours; we shall brief ye at

(*continued on next page*)

great lengths of weather conditions, parking lot hazards and of many small things; and I shall send the High Yellow Scarves[7] to work mischief among the crews and to harrass and to spy upon thee, and ye shall have no more spare lamp bulbs. And great indeed will be the plaques that I shall visit upon thee. Yea, though I walk through the throngs, I shall be deaf to your pleas, and ye shall come to know the torments of the checklist and of many marble-marbles[8] and giant foxes[9] in the dark of night.

And the Pushers of Buttons and Watchers of Lights rent their whites and sit in the ashes and plea for mercy, but the Master is unforgiving.

Then the Master and his Disciples turn away from the pleas and go thence into the places under which rivers of beer flow; and they abide there during the darker hours.

And the many Pushers of Buttons and Watchers of Lights return to their tasks and they push buttons and watch lights; and if ye listen closely ye can hear their whispers, "Five, four, three, two, one ..."

DEFINTIONS

[1] *BRIEFCASES.* Navigator bags in which missile crews carried personal gear such as slippers, paperback books, snacks, etc., plus checklists, etc.

[2] *C^2R^2.* Combat Crew Rest & Recreation. The 12-hour period following an alert tour that crews coud not be called in for training, standards board or "other harrassment."

[3] *WHITE HARD HATS.* VIPs had white hard hats, crews had blue ones.

[4] *ORI.* Operational Readiness Inspection. An annual test of capability that got a lot of commanders fired or transferred. A real pain in the ass, but necessary.

[5] *BACK-TO-BACK TOURS.* As Major Stidsen describes it; "We usually did eight tours per month. After a 30-hour tour, most people needed two days to recover. A 'back-to-back' sent us out to the sites 24-hours after our last tour -- except on Monday, off Tuesday (C^2R^2 plus 12)--on Wednesday our efficiency would go to Hell after the first 12-hours or so. Still done, so I'm told (1984)."

[6] *WHITES.* The missile crews once used white, one-piece coveralls. About 1968 they changed to two-piece blues.

[7] *HIGH YELLOW SCARVES.* Standboard (now called "Stan/Eval") personnel wore yellow scarves. Instructors wore white. "Line swine, i.e., the guys who did the work and stood the alerts, wore blue scarves."

[8] *MARBLE-MARBLES.* The audible alert signal for incoming messages.

[9] *GIANT FOXES.* Local ORI-type exercises.

(09) MOM'S IN BED
(Tune: *Unavailable*)

Mom's in bed, pop's on top.
Kid's in the cradle say'n, "Shoot it to her, pop."

Mom's in bed, pop's in jail,
Sis is in the corner yellin', "Pussy for sale."

Mom's in the kitchen, pop's locked up,
My hunch-backed brother's got my sister knocked up.

Got a Model T Ford, a tank full of gas,
A mouth full of titty, and a hand full of ass.

Haven't got a nickel, haven't got a dime
A house full of kids, and none of them mine.

(10) THE MONK
(Tune: *Available*)

Alternate Titles and Variations:

(a) *The Friar of Great Renown*
(b) *The Friar's Song*
(c) *The Horseshit Song*
(d) *On A Stump*

There lived a monk of great renown.
There lived a monk of great renown.
There lived a monk of great renown,
And he fucked all the women all over town.

CHORUS (*repeat after each verse*)

The old sod, the old sod
The dirty old bastard,
The bugger deserved to die, fuck!
Let us pray -- glory, glory, halleluja.

One day he met a maiden fair.
(*repeat twice more*)
And he lured her up into his lair.

He took her to his marble halls.
(*repeat twice more*)
And showed her his prick and bloody great
balls.

He took her to his lily white bed.
(*repeat twice more*)
And fucked her till she was dead.

The other monks all cried "For shame".
(*repeat twice more*)
They took up a knife and cut off his fame.

But on that ressurection morn.
(*repeat twice more*)
The dirty old bugger had still got a horn.

And so that monk has gone to Hell.
(*repeat twice more*)
And we've heard that he's fucking the devil
as well.

NOTE: *In one of the several versions of this song (**The Horseshit Song**), "pilot" is substituted for "monk." However, there are other fundamental differences. In the **Horseshit** versions, the last line is repeated after each verse, and then this line is added; " Ha, ha, ha, ho, ho, ho, horse shit!" It is doubtful these two songs could be sung to the same melody. There also may be some relationship between this song and* **In Mobile,** *song II14.*

(00) THE HORSESHIT SONG
(Tune: Unavailable)

There was a pilot of great renown,
There was a pilot of great renown,
There was a pilot of great renown,
Until he fucked a girl from our town--
Fucked a girl from our town--
Ha ha ha, ho ho ho, horseshit.

He laid her in a feather bed,
(*Repeat twice more*)
And then he twisted out her maidenhead,
Twisted out her maidenhead,
Ha ha ha, ho ho ho, horseshit!

He laid her on a winding stair,
(*repeat twice more*)
And then he shoved it in clear up to
there,
Shoved it clear up to there--
Ha ha ha, ho ho ho, horseshit!

He laid her down beside a stump,
(*repeat twice more*)
And then he missed her cunt and split
the stump,
Missed her cunt and split the stump--
Ha ha ha, ho ho ho, horseshit!

He laid her down beside a pond,
(*repeat twice more*)
And then he fucked her with his magic
wand,
Fucked her with his magic wand,
Ha ha ha, ho ho ho, horseshit!

He laid her on the dewey grass,
(*repeat twice more*)
And then he shoved the old boy up her
    ass,
Shoved the old boy up her ass,
Ha ha ha, ho ho ho, horseshit!

He took her to the countryside,
(*repeat twice more*)
And then he fucked the girl until she
    died,
Ha ha ha, ho ho ho, horseshit!

He took her to the burial ground,
(*repeat twice more*)
And then he thought he'd have another
    round,
Though he'd have another round,
Ha ha ha, ho ho ho, HORSESHIT, HORSESHIT

(11) MOTHER HUMPER'S BALL
(Tune: *Darktown Strutter's Ball*)

Alternate Titles and Variations:

   (a) *Mother Fuckers Ball*

Oh, there's gonna be a ball at the
    Mother Humper's Hall.
The witches and the bitches gonna be
    there all.
Now honey don't be late, 'cause they're
    passin' out pussy, 'bout half-past
    eight.

Now, I've humped in France and I've
    humped in Spain,
I've been humpin' on the coast of Maine;
But the best piece I ever saw,
Was when I humped my mother-in-law,
Last Saturday night at the Mother
    Humper's Ball.

(12) MRS. MURPHY
(Tune: *Unavailable*)

Oh, take it in your hand, Mrs. Murphy.
It only weighs a quarter of a pound.
It has hair 'round its neck like a
    turkey,
And it spits when you rub it up and
    down.

(13) MU GIA
(Tune: *Unavailable*)

NOTE: *I'm sure this is clear to every-
one--except the Editor.*

Mu Gia, I just dropped my bombs in
    Mu Gia
I think I hit a truck.
I don't give a fuck.
It counted.....Mu Gia......

(14) MUSTANG PILOT'S SONG (*See TT17*)

(15) MY FAMILY (*See DE10*)

(16) MY GAL'S A CORKER
(Tune: *try She Told Me So*)

NOTE: *This song is obviously incomplete.
The first verse is poorly constructed
for the what the Editor has determined
must be the melody. The second verse
ran together and made no sense
whatsoever; so the Editor separated the
obvious lines, but even this does not
complement the melody. Each verse
requires additional lines, ending with,
"That's where my money goes". The song is
apparently a parody of an old college
fraternity song the author's brother
sang in the thirties at Indiana University. Use a little imagination.*

MY GAL'S A CORKER

My gal's a corker, she's a New Yorker.
I buy her everything to keep her in style.
She wears my coveralls, I stand and freeze
        my balls.
Hey boys, that's where my money goes.

(*continued on next page*)

She's got a pair of legs,
Just like two whiskey kegs.

She's got a pair of hips,
Just like a battleship.

She's got a hairy runt,
Just like an elephant.

She wears silk underwear,
I wear my G.I. pair.

She's got a pair of tits,
Just like two boxing mits.

NOTE: *In case you were wondering how the Indiana University version went - and it will help you fill in the missing lines above - the Editor will insert one verse. He is not certrain about the first line, but is comfortable with the remaining words, although they are written from memory going back about 45 years!*

My girl's a helluva slew*
She hails from old I.U.
She wears her colors true,
Yes'm she do.
And in my future life,
She's gonna be my wife.
How in the Hell did I get that way?
She told me so.

* *A variance of "slough", a swamp in one definition, obviously not a very nice refernece. It is possible the first line should be "My girl's name is Sue", although that fits the melody only with difficulty.*

(17) MY GIRL
(Tune: *Unavailable*)

The nipples on her tits are as big as
    plums.
The wiggle when she walks would make a
    dead man come.
She's a mean mother-fucker, she's a
    great cocksucker.
She's my girl - she fucks!

(18) MY GRANDFATHER'S COCK
(Tune: *Grandfather's Clock*)

My grandfather's cock was too long for
    his slacks,
So it drug ninety years on the floor.
It was longer by half than the old man
    himself,
Though it weighed not a pennyweight
    more.
It was found on the morn of the day that
    he was born,
And was always his pleasure and pride.
But it drooped, wilted, never to rise
    again,
When the old man died.

Ninety years without limbering;
What a cock! What a cock!
His pieces of ass numbering.
What a cock! What a cock!
But it drooped, wilted never to rise again,
When the old man died.

(19) MY HUSBAND'S A COLONEL
      (Tune: *Unavailable*)

My husband's a Coloel, a Colonel, a
    Colonel.
A very fine Colonel is he.
All day he fucks off, he fucks off, he
    fucks off.
At night he comes home and fucks me.

CHORUS (*repeat after each verse*)

    Sing a little bit, fuck a little bit,
    Follow the band, follow the band,
        follow the band.
    Sing a little bit, fuck a little bit,
    Follow the band, follow the happy
        band.

My husband's a Lieutenant Colonel, a
    Lieutenant Colonel, a Lieutenant
    Colonel.
A very fine Lieutenant Colonel is he.
All day he chews ass, chews ass, chews
    ass.
At night he comes home and chews me.

(*continued on next page*)

NOTE: *Repeat verse, but use the follow-ing ranks and words in the appropriate places. The words* **Juvat** *and* **Panther**, *are organization nick names. The last three, designated by (???) are complete mysteries to the Editor, and come from the 527th* **Aggressor's** *song book.*

A Colonel; makes plans; makes me.
A Major; screws up; screws me.
A Captain; kisses ass; kisses me.
A Lieutenant; gets shit on; shits on me.
A Juvat; eats cunt; eats me.
A Panther; paws around; paws me.
A Flight Nurse; pumps blood; pumps me.
A MAC Puke (???); bores holes; bores me.
A Peugot (???); gets tracked; jinks and
   gets assholed; he's Winchester for me
A Fujin (???); beats mud; beats off.

(00) MY RED HAVEN (*See BB25*)

(20) MY WARTHOG FLIES OVER THE OCEAN
(Tune: *My Bonnie Flies Over The Ocean*)

My Warthog flies over the ocean,
It takes the best part of a day.
It took us eight hours to Lajes,
And that's barely half of the way!

CHORUS (*repeat after each verse*)

   Warthog, Warthog, why is it so hard
     to make you go?
   Warthog, Warthog, why are you so

We launched in the darkness from Myrtle.
We joined with the tankers at four.
They had to slow down to stay with us,
My God! you're a slow bloody whore!

We finally made it to Lajes.
Our jet lag had all gone away.
We arrived at the same time we'd started
Except that it was the next day!

I raced with a Cessna 150,
Who thought his was slower than mine.
I looked down to see a Bloke mini,
Leave us in dust trails behind!

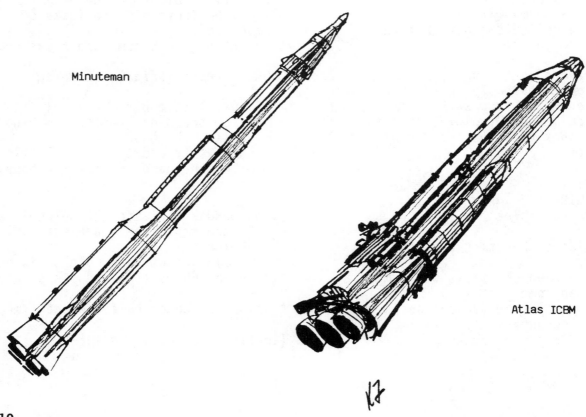

Minuteman

Atlas ICBM

FLIGHT SECTION NN

(00) THE NAIL FAC SONG
    (*See Volume I, D1*)

(01) NAUGHTY LITTLE DOG
    (Tune: *Unavailable*)

NOTE: *Another guessing game for the poets who are reading these classics. How many will find the clues?*

NAUGHTY LITTLE DOG

Once I had a naughty little dog,
A naughty little dog was he.
I loaned him to a lady friend
To keep her company.

Now all around the house that night,
That naughty little dog did hunt.
He'd stick his nose beneath her dress,
And try to smell her ____.

Shame on you, you naughty little dog.
You make my temper rise.
There's only one man in this whole world
Who can sleep between her _____.

Thank the lady for the wine.
I'll drink it for my supper.
Damn the man who's got a girl
And ain't got the guts to _____.

Fumble, fumble all around.
It's time that we should start.
I ate some beans for supper,
And I think I'm going to ____.

Forty dollars I will bid,
And six bits I will pass.
Damn the girl that stole my dice,
And stuck them up her ___.

Ask your partner for her name.
I need it for a list.

Excuse me while I go outside,
And try to take a _____.

Pistol belt around my hips,
And around this town I'll frolic.
Take your partners in the house,
While he plays with his _____.

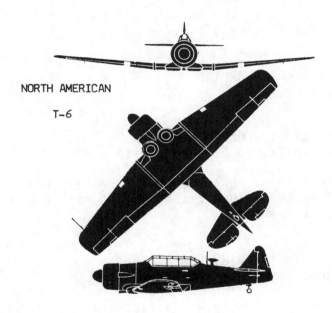

NORTH AMERICAN

T-6

"Ball, play ball", the umpire cried,
Oh, how that man can hit.
Take him to the alley,
'Cause I think he's going to ____.

Shame on you, you naughty little boy.
You know that mule will kick.
And there you stand behind him,
With your hand upon his _____.

Prick the elephant with the prod,
To hear the monster yell.
If he should step upon you,
He would smash you all to ____.

(*continued on next page*)

"Help, help", the sailor cried,
As through the sea he swam.
"Swim or sink," the skipper said,
"'Cause I don't give a _____.

Damn my hide for every little thing.
I'll sing a little more.
Once I sat in a parlor,
With my arms around a _____.

Hold on there my pretty little girl.
What is it that you say?
If you should sit on another man's lap,
You'd get a dose of _____.

Clap, clap, clap your hands.
My song will never last.
If you don't like this song I sing,
You can kiss my bloody -- nose!

(00) NELLIE DARLING
(Also "Nelly" - See AA08)

(00) NINETY-FOURTH'S SQUAWK
(See Volume I, beginning with song B50)

NOTE: *This song is the same as the referenced Volume I song except for the unit's name.*

(02) NINETY-THIRD LAMENT
(Tune: *Turkey In The Straw*)

NOTE: *This ditty was a last-minute contribution from Matt Johnson of Garrison, NY. It is about the 93rd Squadron of the famous 19th Bomb Group at Mindanao, Philippine Islands, 1942, and probably about the B-17, although that is not clear. It could be about the B-10, or perhaps the B-18 in those days. "Them were bad days", but the 93rd still had a singing sense of humor. This song is dedicated to those staunch heroes of the 19th and 93rd who knew about the war before most Americans were aware there was one. Oh, yes, Matt didn't indicate any title, so the Editor gave it a name. Genius!*

NINETY-THIRD LAMENT

There's a pilot in the cabin,
And a bomber in the nose,
A tail full of gunners,
And off she goes
To some far-off place
Of which we've never heard;
But we don't give a damn
In the gypsy ninety-third!

(03) NO BALLS AT ALL - I
(Tune: *Casey Jones - more or less*)

NOTE: *This delicious dirty ditty has been sung from hither to yond, and comes in two different versions.*

NO BALLS AT ALL - I

Gather you rounders and listen to me.
I'll tell you a story that'll fill you
   with glee.
It's about a young maiden so fair and so
   tall,
Who married a man who had no balls at
   all...
WHAT?

CHORUS (*repeat after each verse*)

   No balls at all, no balls at all,
   She married a man who had no balls at
      all.

On their wedding night when she jumped
   into bed,
Her cheeks were all rosey, her lips were
   all red.
She reached for his thing, his thing was
   small.
She reached for his balls, he had no
   balls at all...
WHAT?

Mother, dear mother, I wish I were dead.
I'll go to my grave with my own
   maidenhead.

(*continued on next page*)

My future is slender, my hopes they are
    small,
For I've married a man who has no balls
at all...
WHAT?

Daughter, dear daughter, now don't be so
    sad.
I had the same trouble when I married
    your dad.
But many's the flyer who will answer the
    call,
Of the wife of the man who has no balls
    at all...
WHAT?

Now this young maid took her mother's
    advice,
And found the proceedings excedingly
    nice.
And a bouncing young baby was born in
    the fall,
To the wife of the man who had no balls
    at all...
WHAT?

Now the babe was examined that very same
    night,
By a doctor who swore he examined it
    right.
And the thing that he found most
    peculiar of all,
Was, the babe had a thing, but no balls
    at all. . . . WHAT????

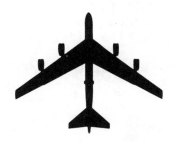

(04) NO BALLS AT ALL - II
(Tune: *Casey Jones - more or less*)

There once was a girl named Sarah McFox,
With hair on her chest and cheese in her
    box.
She married a man named Patrick McCall,
With a very short peter and no balls at
    all.

CHORUS (*repeat after each verse*)

    No balls, no balls
    A very short peter
    And no balls at all.

The very first night that they were wed,
They took off their clothes and went
    straight to bed.
She reached for his pecker, it was very
    small,
She reached for his balls, he had no
    balls at all!

Now mother, dear mother, oh, what shall
    I do?
I've married a man who never can screw.
I reached for his pecker, it was very
    small.
I reached for his balls, he had no balls
    at all.

Oh, daughter, dear daughter, don't you
    be sad.
It was the same trouble I had with your
    dad.
There's many a man who will come to the
    call,
Of the wife of a man who has no balls at
    all.

The daughter went home, took her
    mother's advice,
And found the results exceedingly nice.
A bouncing youg baby was born in the
    fall,
To the wife of the man who had no balls
    at all.

(05) NONCOMBATANT ASSHOLES
(Tune: *Unavailable*)

You are a noncombatant asshole,
You have never killed a Cong.
You just sit around and shoot the shit,
Stand there and play on your dong.

You bought your medals in a pawnshop,
They only cost 2.95.
You were alive in '65 and you'll be
    alive in '90.
You are a noncombatant ASSHOLE!

(06) NOVEMBER (M)
(Tune: *Acres Of Clams*)
Lyrics: *Rollie Stoneman*

<u>NOTE</u>: *This is a terrific example of a military parody. It shows the rivalry between various occupations within the Air Force--in this case, the missilemen versus the pilots. In the past, and even today, there is rivalry between non-flying and flying members of the Air Force, as can be seen in many of the songs in Volume I and II. This song proves that nothing has changed but the weapons. Gripes are an important part of military tradition, and Rollie Stoneman has done a great job in bringing these sentiments to song.*

NOVEMBER

I was driving way out to November,
A trip of a hundred or so.
Fighting the wind and the weather,
The wind and the rain and the snow.

I stayed awake through the briefing,
Though my bloodshot eyes could not see.
I'd heard the same thing for the past
   eight months,
"Let's get ready for the IG."

REFRAIN

   And nothing's too good for the
    missilemen,
   And nothing is just what we get.
   The pilots get all the gravy,
   The missilemen get all the grit.

I picked up my truck at the motor pool,
And drove toward the rising sun.
With luck and a helluva tail wind,
I'll be there before day is done.

I headed way out to the "boonies,"
Where mere mortals dare not tread.
'Cause the missilemen guard the country,
While the pilots are shacked up in bed.

REPEAT REFRAIN

I asked the DO, "Where's November?"
His answer it gave me a fright.
"Just drive to the edge of the world,"
   he said,
"And when you get there, hang a right."

So I drove 'till the gas tank was empty,
I drove 'till I ran out of gas.
To the left or the right not a soul
   could be seen,
So I lay down to die in the grass.

REPEAT REFRAIN

I shinnied the pole up to Heaven.
Oh, listen to what I do tell.
When I saw the SAC fist on the Pearly
   Gates,
I thought I was surely in Hell.

Saint Peter was watching me struggle.
He threw back his head and he laughed.
He said, "everyone else rides the
   elevator,
But missilemen still get the shaft!"

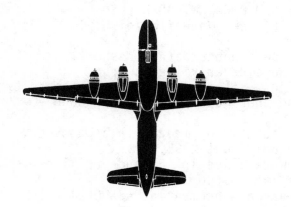

FLIGHT SECTION OO

(01) ODE TO A BOMBARDIER
(A Poem: *Author unknown*)

NOTE: *This poem is from* **The War Chronicle of John** *Hank* **Henry,** *a B-25 driver in WW-II. Hank sent the Editor some very valuable material for Volume-I, and this poem was obtained after publication of the first volume. It is sad that Hank took his last flight not too long afterwards. Any ex-Bombardier that can read this dry-eyed is a fake! The Editor would like to dedicate this poem to his ex-Bombardier from WW-II, Charles* **Chuck** *Voyles of Indianapolis, Indiana; and to Colonel E. C.* **Ned** *Humphreys, who organized the* **Bombardiers** *association. The association held its first reunion in April 1985 at Midland, Texas, where many of them had trained.*

ODE TO A BOMBARDIER

On a lonely road, through a cold, bleak
    night,
A grizzled old man trudged into sight;
And the people all whispered over their
    beers,
There goes the last of the Bombardiers.

What's a Bombardier? There came no
    reply,
The men turned silent--the women sighed;
As death-like silence filled the place,
With the gaunt, gray ghost, of a long,
    lost race.

It's hard to explain, that catch of
    breath,
As they seemed to sense the approach of
    death;
Furtive glances--from ceiling to floor,
'Til something, or someone opened the
    door.

The bravest of hearts turned cold with
    fear,
The thing in the door was a Bombardier;
His hands were boney, his hair white
    and thin,
His back was curved, like an old bent
    pin.

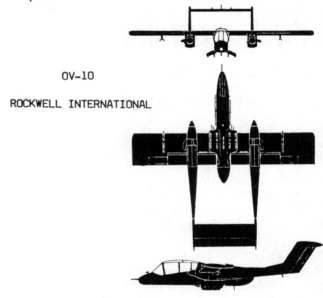

OV-10

ROCKWELL INTERNATIONAL

His eyes were two empty rings of black,
And he vaguely murmured, "Shack, Shack,
    Shack."
This ancient relic of the Second World
    War,
Crept 'cross the room and slouched to
    the bar.

They spoke not a word, but watched in
    the glass,
As the broken old man showed a worn
    bombsight pass;
And hollow tones from his shrunken
    chest,
Demanded a drink and only the best.

(*continued on next page*)

The glass to his lips, they heard him
   say,
"The bomb bay is open--the bombs are
   away;"
With no other word, he slipped through
   the door,
--And the last Bombardier was seen no
   more.

(02) ODE TO A GREAT FUCKIN' SAR EFFORT
(Tune: *The Night Before Xmas - with
apologies from the composer!*)

NOTE *This is a great combat song from
the Vietnam War. It reflects the finest
in story-telling in song and verse,
written by one who knew what he was
writing about--and feeling.*

ODE TO A GREAT FUCKIN' SAR EFFORT

One fine day, just last summer,
('Twas prior to a raid)
The jocks were hung over -
From screwing the maid.

So with canopies open
And heads hung in grief,
Their sorrows were many;
Their crew rest too brief.

The mission commander
By some marvelous feat,
Got them all to the Anchor --
Cycled through, then did meet

With those beautiful Thuds
Spread in "pod" - Quite a force!
The Phantoms moved in
Like the old Trojan Horse.

The MIG's had been scrambled,
Were headed out east,
But the gunners are hosing
Eighty-fives at our beast!

"Why the Hell should they hate *me*,"
I cried in dismay,
"I'm egressing, you bastards,
So play it my way!"

But my cry went unheeded,
As our bird took a hit;
And I knew there and then
Things had just turned to shit!

Tho' my chances were nil,
There was fuck else to do,
But head for the Black
With our whole fuckin' crew.

So in anger, and pissed,
Did we drop the whole load
On the cock-suckin' gunner's
Kids, wife and abode!

There was no goddamn grief
As I cried out with glee,
"Eat your heart out, you bitch,
For you'll never get me!"

So with eighty percent
(That was all we could get)
We headed for North Point
With hopes of a TET.

But 'twas mostly in vain
As we swung past the Red -
I knew that my ass
Was fuckin' near dead.

'Cause Yen Bay came alive,
Like the Fourth of July!
The flak was so thick
That I wanted to cry.

As my two three and four
Broke down, left, then right -
Leaving us solo
In the dwindling light.

"Well, ol' buddy," my number one
GIB says to me,
"It looks like there's just
Gonna be me and thee."

"And with your goddamn luck,
We should punch out at ten -
So the rest of the fall,
We can take with a grin.

(*continued on next page*)

"For I just *know* goddamn well,
As I sit here in fright
That both fuckin' chutes
Were packed wrong last night!

"And I want you to know,"
He hastened to add,
"That in case we don't make it -
Pleae don't get mad!"

"It isn't my fault
That the pod didn't work -
I told you that *twice*,
You dumb, fuckin' jerk!

A tank didn't feed;
The doppler was short;
(You said) "We'll get our counter -
No matter what!"

Well, you've got your first counter -
It may be the last,
Unless this old whore
Can take one more blast!

"Shut your trap, and eject!"
Was the word of the day;
So we punched, not at ten,
But at two, so they say ....

(03) ODE TO A SYDNEY LEAVE
(Tune: *Do Ye Ken John Peel?*)
Composed by those bush-happy buggers:
Larry, Easy, The Mad Russian, and Chief

NOTE: *This is a long and VERY funny song. It has a moral similar to that found in several other songs in Volume II--"She may look clean...BUT!" There is no relationship between this ballad and the song,* **Sidney Leave,** *in Volume I, song B37. This ballad is reminiscent of the popular English song,* **Cats on The Roof Top,** *(CC06) which is sung to the same tune. Both have rhyming words as the last word of each verse. In the case of the* **Cats,** *the same word (copulation). In* **Ode,** *each rhyming word is different. All rhyming words in both versions end in ---*ion. *There is certainly a technical term for that!*

ODE TO A SYDNEY LEAVE

He had been in Guinea fourteen months,
and hadn't had a leave.
The heat, the mud, the diet made his
brain begin to weave.
He finally got to Sydney, and he wasn't
in a peeve,
As he thought of all the joys of
anticipation.

In the Australia Hotel lobby, he leaned
against a post,
Watching the damsels passing by for the
wench he liked the most.
Finally, he saw one and her he did
accost,
While his heart began the throes of
palpitation.

He rented an apartment, the best that
he could find,
Where no matter how he acted, the
landlord wouldn't mind.
He took his light of love in tow, and
said, "Now we will find
All the joys there are to know in
osculation".

He started in quite slowly, asked her
if she'd like a drink.
"Why, yes, my dear", she answered him,
"I'll take mine straight, I think".
And after seven or ten or twelve, they
sure were in the pink
As they revelled in the joys of
assignation.

He started his advances as gently as he
could.
She said she should't do it, though he
was sure she would.
And finally nature took it's course, in
nakedness she stood.
While she suffered all the pangs of
agitation.

He gaped at her in wonder, how Nature'd
been defied,
With pads and paints and powder, My god,
how she had lied.

(continued on next page)

For where her bosom ought to be - two
   cantelopes were tied.
And he goggled there at the arts of
   exaggeration.

Her left eye was a beauty, the best
   Australian glass.
The hair she had upon her head - for
   a floor mop it would pass.
Nine tenths of all her volume was
   encompassed in her ass,
While he marvelled at the peculiar
   allocations.

Her knees were fully yards apart when
   she held her feet together.
Her skin was just the texture of the
   finest pigskin leather.
Her bunions were like tennis balls and
   made him wonder whether
Her blood ever got around in
   circulation.

Her feet were built like snowshoes, her
   arms like cricket bats.
The fuzz upon her pussy had crotch
   crickets large as rats.
And as he found out later, she had had
   eleven brats,
Which to him was quite a bit of
   revelation.

Her teeth were made of china, the finest
   sort of crockery.
And as often stated here before, her
   breasts were a hollow mockery.
And the nipper on her incision made him
   think she'd worked in a factory,
And he raised his hands in horror and
   consternation.

He took her to the bedroom and proudly
   bared his cock.
And all two inches of his meat stood
   sturdy as a rock.
And when she looked upon it, she fainted
   from the shock,
And her eyes popped open wide in
   consternation.

He started to explore her frame to find
   the famous spot
Immortalized in poetry by Shakespeare
   and by Scott.

And he swore that he would find it if
   she offered help or not,
While he muttered nasty words of
   intimidation.

Finally after looking, he found it
   without a hitch,
And wondered how he'd missed it, this
   six foot drainage ditch,
And said, "Get ready, Dearie, for I'm
   about to pitch."
And he started in with the greatest
   application.

Barely had he bridged the gap, when he
   found he'd shot his wad.
Instead of any stiffness, he had a
   soggy prod.
He said, "Be patient, Sweetie, while
   I resuscitate this rod,
I'm always at my best in syncopation."

He beat it on the bed post, he flailed
   it with his fist,
He ran it through a ringer, did everything on the list.
He finally gave up trying and went
   outdoors and pissed,
Calling it all the words he knew in
   defamation.

But after a time it lifted, got its
   second wind,
Proudly raised its bloody head in spite
   of its chagrin.
All ready for another go, it looked at
   her and grinned,
And nodded its head at her in
   supplication.

This time he was successful, he lasted
   all the night.
Across the floor and up the wall, he
   flew her like a kite.
At seven in the morning he still was in
   the fight,
And brought to her a sexual education.

He was lying there in bed with her, and
   not just like a brother,
In walked a woman, said she was the
   wench's mother.

(*continued on next page*)

Then under the bed clothes his head he
   began to smother
While he suffered all the pangs of
   mortification.

He knocked it fourteen times each night,
   he tried to wear it out.
He found the entrance easily, even
   though she was so stout.
And now, with bloody prick in hand, he
   hears the doctor shout,
"Reflect, my boy, the joys of
   moderation.

His pecker, it was shrivelled, his balls
   were hanging low,
And every time he took a stop, they
   swung both to and fro.
But he didn't have ambition enough to
   tie them in a bow,
And he often wished he'd undergone
   castration.

His seven days are over, to Mascot
   Field he goes,
Staggering to the transport, rum-
   blossom for a nose.
She waved him off with honors, and all
   her hopes arose,
As she dwelled upon the thoughts of her
   gestation.

And now he's back in Guinea, his wounds
   are nearly healed.
He'd shot his wad and bankroll, and his
   combat nerves are steeled.
He's praying for another leave, after
   the eagle squealed,
And dreams of love with great
   elaboration.

Suddenly to his dismay, his prick began
   to burn.
Every time he shook his lily, his
   folly he did learn,
And finally in desperation to the doctor
   he did turn,
While suffering all the pangs in
   urination.

The doctor gave him sulpha drugs, said
   "Son, you've got the clap,
You ought to know to take a pro, you
   stupid, silly sap.

Perhaps in future escapades, you'll not
   unbutton your flap,
Nor bother me with woe and
   consultation."

Six months or so have passed, and the
   wench began to swell,
She wrote to him letters every day,
   and gave him holy Hell.
So now he uses rubbers, and hopes that
   all goes well,
And avoids increasing Australian
   population.

Now we've loaned Australians tanks and
   guns, clothing, oil and dyes,
Aeroplanes and gasoline and about a
   million guys.
But the biggest thing we've given them-
   is American pricks, king size.
And at least the women love this lend-
   lease action.

(04) ODE TO THE FOUR-LETTER WORDS
(A Poem by an Unknown Author)

NOTE. *This "unmelodied" Ode is dedicated to those with tender sensibilities
who did not heed the warning at the
beginning of this Volume. Although
there are "blanks" at the end of some
lines, this is not one of those intellectual games that you will find in
various places in this volume. After
all, noone promised you an education!*

ODE TO THE FOUR-LETTER WORDS

Banish the use of the four-letter words,
Whose meanings are never obscure.
The Anglos and Saxons, those bawdy old
   birds,
Were vulgar, obscene, and impure.
But cherish the use of the weaseling
   phrase
That never quite says what you mean;
You'd better be known for your hypocrite
   ways
Than vulgar, impure and obscene.

(continued on next page)

When nature is calling, plain speaking
    is out,
When the ladies, God bless 'em, are
    milling about;
You may wee-wee, make water, or empty
    the glass;
You can powder your nose--even "johnnie"
    may pass.
Shake the dew off the lily, see a man
    'bout a dog,
But please to remember, if you would
    know bliss--
That only in Shakespeare do characters
    ____!

A woman has bosoms, a bust, or a breast.
Those lily-white swellings that bulge
    near her vest.
They are towers of ivory, or sheaves of
    new wheat;
In a moment of passion, ripe apples to
    eat.
You may speak of her nipples as fingers
    of fire,
With hardly a question of raising her
    ire.
But by Rabelais' beard, she will throw
    several fits,
If you speak of them roundly as good
    honest ____!

It's a cavern of joy you are thinking
    of now--
A "warm tender field awaiting the plow."
It's a quivering pigeon, caressing your
    hand,
Or the National Anthem--it makes us all
    stand.
Or perhaps it's a flower, a grotto, a
    wall,
But friend, heed this warning--beware
    the affront
Of aping the Saxons--don't call it a
    ____!

Though a lady repel your advance, she'll
    be kind
As long as you intimate what's on your
    mind;
You may tell her to see how your
    etchings are hung.
You may mention the ashes that need to
    be hauled,

Put the lid on the saucepan--even "lay's
    not too bald.
But the moment you're forthright, get
    ready to duck,
For the girl isn't born who'd stand for,
    "Let's ____!"

So banish the words that Elizabeth used,
When she was a queen on her throne.
The modern maid's virtue is easily
    bruised,
By the four-letter words all alone.
Let your morals be loose as an alder-
    man's vest,
If your language is always obscure.
Today, not the act but the word is the
    test,
Of the vulgar, obscene and impure!

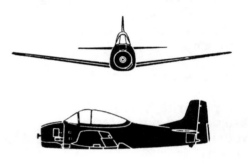

(05) ODE TO THE RETIRED WEATHERMAN
(Tune: *Whiffenpoof Song*)
Composed by Milt Rasmussen

NOTE: *This song, together with those about Flying Class 40-A, elsewhere in this volume, were composed by members of the Air Force whose day is past, whose eyes are a little dimmer, but whose spirits are still as strong as when they sang at the "O" or airmen's club bar or the local pub. And what aircrew member can't remember how many times the unsung weatherman saved their necks (and other parts of the anatomy). The Editor could tell many stories about the great contributions of the Weathermen of the Air Force; but for now, our hats off and glasses raised TO THE WEATHERMEN! What are they drinking?* **Millibar Martinis** *(dry, of course),* **Dew Point Daquiris** *and* **Smog Screwdrivers.**

(continued on next page)

ODE TO THE RETIRED WEATHERMEN

We're retired weatherman, turned in our
    cystral balls,
Milliabar, dew point and smog.
Went to school in Chanute, Texas and NYU
Chicago and Cal Tech too.
Instructors we've had are world renown,
Bjerknes and Byers Namisa, Jerome,
Taught us vorticity, radar, cyclone,
Millibar, dew point and smog.

We've served in Hywcombe, Fuchu, Rhein
    Main,
Offutt, Thule and March.
We've briefed Tooey Spaatz, Hap Arnold,
    Lemay,
Doolittle and Hoyt Vandenburg,
Plotted our own maps did them all on
    acetate.
No help from satellites, computers or
    tapes,
Millibar, dew point and smog.

Oh my we were good, that's how we won
    the war,
Operations, plans and IG
Nicknames have tagged on us, embedded
    and plastered,
Foggy, stormy and you (blip blip).
Shift work on holidays, service with
    a smile,
Grease pencil overlays, prog charts in
    a while,
Forecast calls for clear, but ye gads,
    it's snowing,
Milliabar, Dew Point and smog.

From prognosticating we have graduated,
Operations, plans and IG.
Now we're teaching or selling or in
    real estate,
But our true love for weather will not
    fade,
Here among the dying embers, these in
    the main are my regrets,
When I am right no one seems to remember
When I am wrong, no one forgets.

(00) OFFICIAL SONG OF RANDOLPH FIELD
    (*See Volume I, S53*)

(06) OFF WE GO - II
(*Also see Volume I, 08*)
Tune: *A different tune for each
line. You'll know which one!*

NOTE: *This song was included to promote
interservice cooperation. The Editor
even lifted it from a Marine Corps song
book (from an Air Force source).*

OFF WE GO - II

Off we go into the wild blue yonder---
CRASH!
Anchors aweigh my boys---
SPLASH!
Over hill, over dale, as we hit the
    dusty trail---
COUGH, COUGH, CHOUGH!
From the Halls of Montezuma--
TAKE MY PICTURE!

(07) OF THE MISERY OF LIVING IN SIN
    (Tune: *Unavailable*)

Why I went over on PCS
To live in Morocco is anyone's guess.
To live in Morocco is anyone's guess.
Little did I know that life in Maroc,
Could ruin a red-bellied, healthy
    hot-rock.

CHORUS (*repeat after each verse*)

    Oh, the misery of livin' in sin
    If you keep on flying, you're bound
      to spin in.
    If down Fedela road you travel too
      far
    Black Dragon, you'll meet death at
      the bar.

I went to Fedela one bright sunny day.
There were boucoup Fatimas to take all
    my pay.
I picked out a clean one and gave her
    a go.
Doc Brossi, Doc Brossi, please say it
    ain't so.

(*continued on next page*)

There were small ones and tall ones, and
    fat ones and thin ones.
They washed it, kisssed it and then
    stuffed it in.
They suck you, they fuck you, tie your
    nuts in a knot.
If the vino doesn't kill you, you'll
    die of the rot.

While sittin' on five, you have fuck all
    to do.
No bogies, no strangers to shoot at for
    you.
Don't sit with your thumb up your ass
    where it stinks.
Call Randall for pidgeons direct to the
    Sphinx.

When the cob gets so hard that you can't
    force a pee,
Don't sweat it Black Dragons, just
    listen to me.
Go down to Fedela with three mill on
    hand,
Thirty minutes in heaven will wilt any
    man.

(08) OH BEAUTIFUL . . .
(Tune: *America The Beautiful*)

NOTE: *Attributed to* **Bruggemeyer**, *56th
Tactical Fighter Wing, flying F-4s*

OH beautiful for spreading thigh,
For pubic patch of brown.
For four quart bosom majesty,
Go bouncing up and down.
Oh, Erica, Oh, Erica,
Now spread your legs for me...
I'll bury my head in fury bed,
Between your spreading knees.

(09) OH, MY DARLING "54"
(Tune: *Clementine*)

NOTE: *They've done it again! The
stalwarts of the 21st Troop Carrier
Squadron have written another song about
the great C-54.*

OH, MY DARLING "54"

Oh my darling, oh my darling,
Oh my darling 54.
Put together with one rivet,
Glue and paste and nothing more.

We go rolling down the runway,
Gathering airspeed mighty slow,
Douglas says they'll fly forever,
He designed them he should know.

Other types of transport aircraft,
Just to see them makes me sore.
You can fly them without trouble,
Still I'll take my 54.

Oh the taxpayer gripes at taxes,
I don't think they know the score.
They don't fly 'em they just buy 'em,
Oh my darling 54.

(10) OH MY GOD
(Tune: *Unavailable*)

NOTE: *This could have been aptly named,
"True Confessions of a Fighter Pilot".*

Oh my God, we've all gone wrong.
We've all been drunk for goddamn long,
And we don't give a damn if it rains,
    hails or freezes.
Let the old man say what he goddamn
    pleases.
We're just a bunch of shitsters, a
    bunch of booze histers.
FIGHTER PILOTS ALL!

(11) OH, NOW I AM A KAYDET
(Tune: *Throw A Nickel On The Drum*)

NOTE: *A similar variation of this song
will be found in Volume I under the same
title (Song 011). However, as Colonel
David Hassemer (Class 40-A) pointed out
to the Editor, there is a line missing
in the last verse. Also, Dave provided
some additional material. In the
interest of accuracy, and seeing as how
Dave was "a class or two" ahead of the*

(continued on the next page)

*Editor (Class 43-G), the entire song is presented below and dedicated to the famous Class of 40-A THAT HAD NO UPPER-CLASS! See the song, **Forty-A Hooray** if you want to know why (FF08). This song is closely related to **Fighter Pilot's Hymn**, Volume I, song F13, and to **Throw A Nickel On The Grass**, in this volume.*

OH, NOW I AM A KAYDET

I was lying in the gutter,
All covered up with beer;
With pretzels in my whiskers,
I knew my end was near.
Then came the glorious Army,
And saved me from the hearse,
Now everybody strain a gut,
And sing another verse.

CHORUS

Sing hallelujah, hallelujah,
Throw a nickel on the drum,
Take a quarter on the run.
Sing hallelujah, hallelujah,
Throw a nickel on the drum and you'll
  be saved.

NOTE: *In the next verse, the hyphonated letters are to be spelled out.*

Oh it's G - L - O - R - Y,
I am S - A - V - E - D.
H - A - P - P - Y
To be F - R - double - E,
V - I - C - T - O - R - Y,
From the ways of S - I - N,
Glory, glory hallelujah,
Tra - la - la, amen.

CHORUS

Sing hallelujah, hallelujah,
Throw a nickel on the stump,
Just to save a Ka-det's rump.
Sing hallelujah, hallelujah,
Throw a nickel on the stump,
And you'll be saved.

For now I am a kaydet,
A-learnin' how to fly.
My glorious salvation
Shall lift me to the sky.

The Army is my savior,
From the straight and narrow way.
They pay me seventy-five a month,
And take it all away.

CHORUS

Sing hallelujah, hallelujah,
Throw a nickel on the grass,
Just to save a pilot's ass.
Sing hallelujah, hallelujah,
Throw a nickel on the grass,
And you' - ll - be - saved.

(12) OH, RIP THE FEATHERS AWAY
   (Tune: *Unavailable*)

Oh, rip the feathers away, away,
Oh, rip the feathers away.
Oh, the ass of a duck
Makes a wonderful fuck,
If you rip the feathers away.

(13) OH, RUBY
(Tune: *Oh, Ruby*)

Oh, Ruby I see you've rolled and curled
  your pubic hair.
Ruby, are you contemplating, coming out
  somewhere?
The shadow on the wall tells me your
  pants are coming down.
Oh, Ruuu-bby--don't take your twat to
  town.

CHORUS

I know it's hard to love a man
Whose cock is red and raw--
Oh, Ruuu-bby-you dirty fucking whore.

(14) THE OLD BAZAAR IN CAIRO
   (Tune: *Unavailable*)

Sandbags, windbags, camels with a hump,
Fat girls, thin girls, some a little
  plump.
Slave girls sold here, 50 bob a lump,
In the old bazaar in Cairo.

(continued on next page)
(continued on next page)

CHORUS (*that's what it said!*)

EHYA-AH, EHYA-YA, EH-YA-YA-YA-YA

Rice pud, very good, what's it all about
Made it in a kettle and they couldn't
    get it out.
Everybody took a turn to suck it
    through the spout,
In the old bazaar in Cairo.

CHORUS

    You can buy most anything,
    Sheep eyes, sandpies, watch without a
        spring.
    You can purchase anything you wish,
    A clock, a dish, or something for
        your Auntie Nelly.

Harem, scarem, what do you think of
    that?
Bare knees, striptease, dancing on the
    mat.
Umpa, umpa--that's enough of that,
In the old bazaar in Cairo.

CHORUS

    All your needs they will provide,
    Breakfast, dinner, a little on the
        side.
    Even those who haven't got a clue,
    Will soon find out exactly what they
        have to do.

Yashmacs, pontefracts, what a strange
    affair;
Dark girls, fair girls, some with
    ginger hair.
The rest of this is funny but the censor
    cut it there,
In the old bazaar in Cairo.

(15) OLD GREY BUSTLE
(Tune: *Old Grey Bonnet*)

Put on your old grey bustle
And get out and hustle,
For tomorrow the rent's coming due.
Put your ass in clover,
Let the boys look it over,
If you can't get five, take two.

Put on those old pink panties,
That used to be your aunties,
And we'll go for a tussel in the hay.
Now there's no use duckin',
Cause you're gonna get a fuckin'
In the good old fashioned way.

Put on that old blue ointment
The crabs disappointment,
And we'll kill those bastards where they
    lay.
Though it scratches and it itches,
It will kill those sons of bitches
In the good old fashioned way.

(16) OLD KING COLE
(Tune: *Old King Cole*)

Old King Cole was a merry old soul,
And a merry old soul was he.
He called for his wife in the middle of
    the night,
And he called for his fiddlers three.
Now every fiddler had a very fine fiddle
And a very fine fiddle had he.
"Oh, fiddle like fuck, like fuck," said
    the fiddler,
"What merry men are we.
There's none so fair as can compare with
    the boys of the varsity."

REPEAT SAME VERSE STRUCTURE AS ABOVE
SUBSTITUTING EACH OF THE FOLLOWING (*if
you can't figure it out, call the Editor
--on your nickel*)

"Balls in the air, in the air," said
    the jugglers.
"Throw your balls in the air," said
    the jugglers.
"Pull it out, pull it out," said the
    barmaids.
"Round and round and round," said the
    cyclists.
"Root-diddly-oot-diddly-oot," said the
    flutists.
"Thread it in and out, in and out," said
    the tailors.
"Wop it up and down, up and down," said
    the painters.

(*continued on next page*)

"Ride it up and down, up and down,"
    said the horsemen.
"Bang away, bang away," said the
    carpenters.
"Do you want it in the front or the
    back?" said the coalmen.
'Cut it round the knob, make it throb,"
    said the surgeons.
"Cut it in half, in half," said the
    butchers.
"Mine is six foot long," said the
    fishermen.
"Up with the horn in the morn," said
    the huntsmen.

(00) OLD KUNSAN (*See Volume I, K23*)

NOTE: *Volume I will refer you back to Volume II. No, this isn't a gimmick to sell both volumes. Originally, this version was to be included here; but the difference between the two versions is so minor as not to warrant the inclusion. Soooo, go back to Volume I (and if you haven't got one, go buy it!)*

(17) OLDS AND THE EIGHTH WOLF PACK
    (Tune: *Rum and Coca-Cola*)

NOTE: *As Air Force songs go, this one must qualify as unique and classic. First, it is written about a jock who was an ace in World War II (13 air and 11 1/2 ground), and then was credited with four jets in S.E.A (2 MIG 21s and 2 MIG 17s). He is a fighter pilot's fighter pilot. Secondly, one of the composers of the song, Colonel Chappie James is a legend by himself. He rose to the rank of four stars, the first Black officer to do so. And finally, this is another of three songs in this book that refers to the disliked Air Force exercise called,* **Rapid Roger**. *See* **Gotta Travel On** *(GG06), and* **On The Day Rapid Roger Died** *(OO23).*

OLDS AND THE EIGHTH WOLF PACK

CHORUS

    Olds and the Eighth Wolf Pack
    Killed nine and came back,
    Fighting and drinking in S-E-A
    We've just begun to have our day!

Now we have three squadrons and that's
    just right.
The enemies covered both day and night.
We're flying a craft called the F-4C,
We're headed north you wait and see.

We had two days thus far this year,
Where eighteen guys were buying beer.
They downed nine MIGS with just a few,
The twenty-one force we cut in two.

REPEAT CHORUS

Our job right now is a little slow.
Weather has held us to Talley-Ho.
Rapid Roger is about to die,
Soon the Eighth Wolf Pack will own
    the sky.

Squadron by squadron, plane by plane,
Man by man, we'll make our own claim.
In package three, four, five and six,
Give us a word by frag or Twix.

REPEAT CHORUS

Now the triple nickel is a little
    ahead,
But 'ole Jess Allen ain't goin' to
    bed.
He's pacing the floor, he's a
    constant nag,
He's standing 'round ops, waiting
    for a frag.

The four thirty-third is swinging in
    gear,
Savidge's peakin' 'em and feeding 'em
    beer.
They got four MIGs and a taste of fame,
You can bet your ass, it's not the end
    of the game.

(*continued on next page*)

The four nine seven is doing just right,
Cussing Rapid Roger and flying all night
Halliwell's telling them to toe the mark
But all they seem to get is a trip to
    Clark.

REPEAT CHORUS

(18) OLD SMOKEY
(Tune: *On Top Of Old Smokey*)

Alternate Titles and Variations:
(*In Volume I, beginning with 036
 unless otherwise noted*)

    (a) *On Top Of Old Baldy*
    (b) *On Top Of Old Fuji*
    (s) *On Top Of Old Hanoi*
    (s) *On Top Of Old Pyongyang*
    (s) *On Top Of Old Ranier*
    (s) *On Top Of Old Smokey-Air Version*
       (*Also see below*)
    (s) *On Top Of Old Pop-Up*

NOTE: *This is a close cousin of the ten parodies of* **On Top Of Old Smokey** *that are in Volume I, beginning with song 036. However, this version is different enough to be considered by itself, and comes from the songsters of the 35th Tactical Fighter Wing, Phan Rang Air Force Base, South Vietnam, 1969. It is also only the second song in the collection about* **The Poor Copilot** *(See Vol. I, song C28)--in a fighter jock's song book? This story brings back memories to the Editor of the bomb runs he made over Europe in B-24s.* **Ruummmpff!** *The second version, below,* **On Top Of Old Smokey,** *is more akin to the Vol. I verses, previously mentioned.*

OLD SMOKEY

Flying over old Cam Ranh
En route to the North,
My hands got so shaky
From the thoughts that came forth.

The sun was bright shining,
The sky it was clear,
But my heart it did falter,
I was frozen with fear.

As we crossed the border
I thought I would die,
But my fearless commander,
Oh, how well he did fly.

With this inspiration,
What more could I do?
I screwed up my courage,
And pressed on anew.

We started our bomb run,
The sights I did set,
We rippled our bombs off,
Then wiped off the sweat.

We turned toward the Tonkin,
With the engines full bore;
She really smokin'
Like a two dollar whore.

When once past the coast line,
With a sign of relief,
We'd gotten the job done,
Just as it had been briefed.

This mission accomplished,
So important to me,
They're sure to award us,
Our first DFC.

I'm an outstanding airman,
This story is true,
For I'm a co-pilot
On a B-52.

(00) ON TOP OF OLD SMOKEY
(Tune: *On Top Of Old Smokey*)

NOTE: *Below are some additional verses to the many versions of this song to be found in Volume I, beginning with song 036. The following verses belong to the Korean War variations of the song. Several verses that duplicated those in Volume I were omitted since this version --unlike* **Old Smokey** *--does not read like one, coherent story, but is composed of relatively independent verses. Got that? You can add any of these verses to your favorite version of this long-lasting classic. The "***" indicates where verses were left out.*
(*continued on next page*)

ON TOP OF OLD SMOKEY

On top of old smokey,
All covered with snow,
Lay a Red Beret pilot
And his wingman below.

* * * * * * *

Way down in St. Mildreds
Just rolling in dough,
Played an '86 pilot
And a showgirl named Flo.

The moral of this story
Is easy to see;
Be an eighty-six pilot,
I mean 86-D.

* * * * * * *

He put on an air show,
He did it for me;
With 100% on,
He clobbered a tree.

* * * * * * *

(19) OLD SOLDIERS NEVER DIE - II
(See DE02)

NOTE: *There is no similarity between
this song and the one of the same name
in Volume I, 024.*

(20) OLD 95TH GANG
(Tune: *Ghost Riders In The Sky*)

Old 95th gang went out to fly
One dark and stormy day,
And as they taxied past I heard
'Ole Colonel Roehm did say,
"95th is gonna fly,
It makes me mighty proud,
To know I have one squadron that
Can penetrate a cloud."

CHORUS *(repeat after each verse)*

   Yippee-yi-aye, yippee-yi-oh-h-h-h-h,
   Boneheads in the sky.

Old 95th gang went out to fly,
One bright and sunny day.
And as a 4-ship joined
'Ole Colonel Roehm did say,
"Go Diamond, then go Arrowhead,
'Cause I'm proud to see,
No one can make a join-up look
Nearly as good as we."

Old 95th gang went out to fly,
One cloudy, foggy day,
And as he stepped out of the door
'Ole Colonel Roehm did say,
"To Hell with o'dark thirty briefs,
I'm tired of this ol' grind,
Maybe I'll go to Stan/Eval
And fly at only nine.

Old 95th gang went out to fly,
One clear and sunny day.
And met a new commander,
Colonel Wyman did say,
"95th is gonna fly
And not just as they please."
And he took up a formation, then
Debriefed them to their knees.

(21) O'LEARY'S BALLS
(Tune: *Unavailable*)

NOTE: *Although the tune was not indicated in* **The Aggressor's Song Book,** *the
words seem to fit to the Irish melody*
Molly Malone.

O'LEARY'S BALLS

The balls of O'Leary,
Are wrinkled and hairy,
They're stately and shapely,
Like the domes of St. Paul's.
The women all muster,
To see that great cluster;
They stand and they stare
At the great hairy pair,
Of O'Leary's balls.

(00) ON A STUMP *(See MM10)*

(00) ONE-EYED RILEY, THE *(See 0027)*

(22) THE ONE-EYED TROUSER SNAKE
(Tune: *Unavailable*)

Well, I got this little creature,
I suppose you'd call him a pet.
When something goes wrong with him,
I don't have to call the vet.
He goes everywhere that I do,
Whether sleeping or awake,
Oh God, help me if I ever lose
My little one-eyed trouser snake.

CHORUS (*repeat after each verse*)

    Oh, my one-eyed trouser snake,
    My one-eyed trouser snake.
    God help me if I ever lose
    My little one-eyed trouser snake.

Now one day I took to reading,
In the old sky pilot's book;
About two strarchers bastards
Who make the world go crook.
They said it was the serpent
That made Eve that apple take.
Christ! that was no serpent,
T'was Adam's one-eyed trouser snake.

Now I met this Arty Sheila,
I'd never met before,
When something kind a'told me
That she banged like a shithouse door.
I said come up and see my etchings,
You know they're not a fake,
She said the only thing that's etching
Is your one-eyed trouser snake.

Now come all ye little Sheila's
And listen to this song.
The moral of the trouser snake
Is short as it is long.
Beware of imitations.
Don't lock your bedroom door,
Caus' when the pyjama python bites you,
You'll be screaming out for more. Finis

(00) ONE-HUNDRED SIXTY VC IN THE OPEN
(*See Volume I, 030*)

NOTE: *The tune is not indicated in Volume I. The lyrics are another of Colonel Toby Hughes' creations (See* **Armed Recce** *and* **Tchepone** *in both Vols. I*

and II); and is sung to the melody One-hundred Acres In The Valley *from* Marty Robbins' *albums,* Gunfighter Ballads *and* Trail Songs.

(23) ON THE DAY THAT RAPID ROGER DIED
(Tune: *Paddy Murphy*)
Lyrics: *Colonel George Halliwell,*
(497th CC)
Colonel Bill Savidge
(433rd CC)

NOTE: *One of the three songs about the DOD idea during the Vietnam War (1967), ". . to man aircraft for round-the-clock operation. To do so, we had to limit the flight time of each sortie, and that meant flying in Laos and we got no credit for that--so it was an unpopular program. These were the songs we used when we celebrated the end of the* **Rapid Roger** *program. We built a casket-- filled it with* **Rapid Roger** *computer cards, had a wake and a torch-lit trek to the flight line where we buried* **Rapid Roger**. *Robin Olds drove a silver spike through the heart of the casket before we covered it up. We had a great time."* (Commentary by Lieutenant General Truman Spangrud who contributed the songs). *The other two songs in this Volume are,* **Gotta Travel On,** *and,* **Olds And The Eighth Wolf Pack.** *This is a true military classic, and must be preserved to remind us what can happen when someone tries to run the day-to-day operations of a war from the Pentagon. Since Vietnam, there has been no discernible indication that anyone in power at DOD has learned that lesson--at least as of this writing (1986).*

ON THE DAY THAT RAPID ROGER DIED

On the day that Rapid Roger died,
The Eighth Wing had a riot.
The Four Nine Seven made the grave,
The Four Three Three the casket.
The Five Five Five, the Epitaph,
And Colonel Olds approved it,
On the day that Roger died.86

(continued on next page)

CHORUS (*repeat after each verse*)

That's how we said goodye to Rapid
   Roger;
That's how we showed our courage and
   our pride.
That's how we said goodbye to Rapid
   Roger,
On the night that Roger died.

The night that Rapid Roger died,
I never shall forget.
The squadrons got so friggin' drunk,
That some ain't sober yet.
The only thing they did that night
That filled my heart with fear,
The crew chiefs took the data forms
And threw them on the bier.

The wake was so enjoyable,
You really should have seen it.
We danced a jig,
And had a mug
Of cheer for Rapid Roger.
We were all drunk with happiness,
You better had believe it,
On the day that bastard died.

Now that he's gone,
The Eighth will press
To fly a lot of sorties.
To down more MIGs
And dodge the SAMs
And write some brilliant stories.
Now we can do much better than we've
   ever done before,
Now that dear old Roger's gone.

(24) ON THE LINE (M)
(Tune: *I Walk The Line*)
Lyrics: *Rollie Stoneman*

SAC keeps a close watch on this life of
   mine.
They keep their thumb upon me all the
   time.
They're always looking for mistakes
   sublime.
This ass of mine is on the line.

SAC makes it very, very easy to screw
   up.

They caught me drinking from the wrong
   side of a cup.
And when I try to make a point, they
   say, "Tough luck!"
This ass of mine is on the line.

As sure as night is dark and day is
   light,
They say I'm wrong even when I prove I'm
   right.
And revelation only serves to cloud
   their sight.
This ass of mine is on the line.

My brief career is threatened every day.
I was checked by 3901st and now they
   say,
"You'd best get ready for the IG's on
   his way."
This ass of mine is on the line.

(25) ON TOP OF OLD SMOKEY (*See 0018*)

(26) OPERATIONS AND WEATHER
(Tune-Verses: *The Man On The Flying
                Trapeze*)
(Tune-Chorus: *Cigarettes And Whiskey*)

NOTE: *The song book from whence this
song was taken, listed the tune as*
Cigarettes And Whiskey. *Well, there was
just no way the verses could be sung to
that tune.   But it wasn't difficult to
figure out what the composer of the
parody had in mind--so the Editor has
provided the verse melody, with apologies to Captain W. G. Wall, compiler of
the 21st Troop Carrier Squadron song
book--and a great book it is.   Such a
smart Editor!*

(*continued on next page*)

OPERATIONS AND WEATHER

Once I was happy and had a good wife,
I thought I'd be happy the rest of my
  life.
My orders read Tachi and that's where
  I came,
When my tour is completed, I won't be
  the blame.

CHORUS (*repeat after each verse*)

  Operations and weather and wild, wild
    planning,
  They'll drive you crazy, they'll
    drive you insane.
  Operations and weather and wild, wild
    planning,
  They'll drive you crazy, they'll
    drive you insane.

They set up commitments with block time
  at five,
They wake you at three tho' you're
  barely alive.
You check in with weather, and file
  Item Fox,
'Cause the weather's so foggy it's
  shrinking your socks.

You must clear Atsugi at four thousand
  feet,
'Cause someone is holding at three in
  the sleet.
There's six men for crew, and you like
  it that way,
There's one man for flying, and five
  men to pray.

(27) O'REILLEY'S DAUGHTER (Also O'Riley)
    (Tune: *Available*)

Alternate Titles and Variations:

  (a) *The One-Eyed Riley*
      (original title)

As I was sitting at O"Reilley's Bar,
Listening to tales of blood and
  slaughter,
Came a thought into my mind,
Why not shag O'Reilley's daughter?

CHORUS (*repeat after each verse*)

  Fiddley-I-E, Fiddley-I-O,
  Fiddley-I-E for the one ball
   O'Reilley,
  Rubby dub dub, jig balls and all.
  Rubby dub dub, shag on.

I grabbed the she-bitch by the hair,
Then I threw my left leg over.
Shagged and shagged and shagged some
  more,
Shagged and shagged till the fun was
  over.

There came a knock upon the door,
Who should it be but her one ball
  father.
Two horse pistols by his side,
Looking for the guy who shagged his
  daughter.

I grabbed that bastard by the ball,
Shoved his head in a pail of water.
Shoved those pistols up his ass,
A damn sight farther than I shagged
  his daughter.

Now, as I go walking down the street,
People shout from every corner,
"There goes the dirty son-of-a-bitch,
The one who shagged O'Reilley's
  daughter."

(28) OUR LEADERS
    (Tune: *Manana*)

NOTE: *A terrific parody that, like the song,* **On The Day That Rapid Roger Died,** *berates the Pentagon's running of combat operations as well as the over-regulation of the fighter jock's conduct at the O-club. Although this ditty comes from the clambake in S.E.A., the whole idea of over-regulation has been around the Air Force for a long time. Refer to* **Air Corps Lament,** *Volume I, song A16.*

(*continued on next page*)

OUR LEADERS

At Phillips Range in Kansas,
The jocks all had the knack,
But now that we're in combat,
We've got Colonels on our back.
And every time we say, "Shit-hot,"
Or whistle in the bar,
We have to answer to somebody
Looking for a star.

CHORUS (*repeat after each verse*)

    Our leaders, our leaders,
    Our leaders, is what they always say,
    But it's bullshit, it's bullshit,
    It's bullshit they feed us every day!

Today we had a hot one,
And the jocks were scared as hell,
They ran to meet us with a beer,
And tell us we were swell.
But Recce took the BDA
And said we missed a hair;
Now we'll catch all kinds of Hell
From the wheels at Seventh Air.

They send us out in bunches,
To bomb a bridge and die,

These tactics are for bombers
That our leaders used to fly.
The bastards don't trust our Colonel
Up in Wing, and I guess,
We'll have to leave the thinking to
The wheels in JCS!

The JCS are generals,
But they're not always right,
Sometimes they have to think it over
Well into the night;
When they have a question,
Or something they can't hack,
They have to leave the judgment to
That money-saving Mac!

Now Mac's job is in danger,
For he's on salary, too;
To have the final say-so,
Is something he can't do;
Before we fly a mission,
And everything's O.K.,
Mac had to get permission from
Flight Leader L.B.J.!!

(OO) OUR OUTHOUSE (*See DE07*)

(OO) OUTHOUSE SONG (*See DE07*)

DeHavilland DH-2

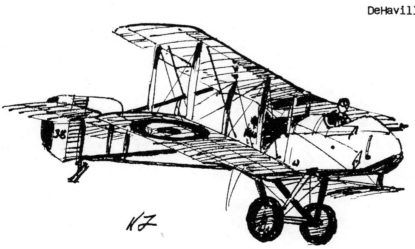

Mitsubishi Zero

FLIGHT SECTION PP

(01) PHANTOM
(*A Poem by Major Paul*)

NOTE: *This brief poem captures the fantasy of flight with the same beauty of the famous poem,* **Highflight** *(HH06). This is a picture painted in words.*

PHANTOM

Yesterday I raced a fleeting shadow,
   swift as light
It hurtled over sunlit fields and lush
   brown hills;
With careless ease it leaped the rivers,
   highlands, woodlands, and the
     scattered towns.
A thing of beauty, sun-born, wild with
   speed
It foiled the clutching fingers of the
   grey mesquite.
I landed--and the Phantom came to rest
   beneath my wings.
I felt that I had killed a thing of life
   and mourned its passing.

(02) PHANTOMS IN THE SKY
(Tune: *The Ballad of the Green Beret*)

Phantoms in the sky,
Charlie Cong prepare to die.
Rolling in with snake and nape,
God creates, but we cremate.

North of Khe Sahn we did go,
Then the FAC said from below,
Hit my smoke and you will find,
The NVA are in a bind.

We rolled in at a 1000 feet,
We saw them bastards beating feet;
But they couldn't run quite half as
   fast,
As my pipper was on their ass.

(00) PICADILLY (*See CC01*)

(00) PILOTS ALWAYS EAT PUSSY (*See SS17*)

(00) PILOT'S LAMENT

NOTE: *The lyrics are in Volume I, P17, but the tune is not given. The Editor has since learned the name of the melody from Colonel George Weiss. Tune:* **If I Had The Wings Of An Angel**.

F4 PHANTOM II

(03) PILOT'S MATING CALL
   (Tune: *Unavailable*)

Let's all gather 'round and give the
   pilot's mating call.
Oh, let's all gather 'round and give
   the pilot's mating call.
Oh, let's all gather 'round and 'round
   and give that Goddamn awful sound.
AAAAAAAAA, AAAA, AAAAAAAA, AAAA, the
   pilot's mating call.

(*continued on next page*)

Oh, fat girls, skinny girls, even girls
    quite tall,
All come a'running when they hear the
    pilot's call.
Oh, let's all gather 'round and 'round
    and give that Goddamn awful sound.
AAAAAAAA, AAAA, AAAAAAAA, AAAA, the
    pilot's mating call.

(00) PILOT'S TOAST (*See TT22*)

(00) PIMPING THE AIR FORCE (*See CC01*)

(04) PIPER LAURIE
(Tune: *Unavailable*)

Salvation Army, Salvation Army.
Standing on the corner in the night,
    night, night.
Beating on your drum with your finger
    up your bung,
Singing mama, hold my pee-pee while
    I pee.

Sergeant Major, Sergeant Major.
Standing in your uniform so bright,
    bright, bright.
Saluting with your hand with your
    bollix in the sand.
Singing Corporal, hold my pee-pee while
    I pee.

General Barcus, General Barcus.
Looking at your stars so big and bright,
    bright, bright.
Coming down the hill singing Colonel
    have a thrill.
Singing Colonel hold my pee-pee while
    I pee.

Piper Laurie, Piper Laurie.
Having skoshie chop-chop at the club,
    club, club.
As I gaze into your eyes and my pee-pee
    starts to rise,
Singing Piper hold my pee-pee while
    I pee.

(05) PISS ON THE _____ (Unit Name)
(Tune: *Here We Go 'Round The Mulberry
    Bush*)

Let's all go down and piss on the _____
Piss on the _____, piss on the _____.
Let's all go down and piss on the _____
Till they float away.
Till they float away.
Till they float away.

Let's all go down and piss on the _____
Piss on the ____, piss on the _____
Let's all go down and piss on the _____
Till they float away.

(06) THE PLAINS (M)
(Tune: *The Seine*)
  Lyrics: *Rollie Stoneman*

One night along 16th Street, the heart
    of old Cheyenne,
I met a lovely lady; that's where it all
    began.
We shared a silent moment beneath a
    starry sky.
I knew we'd soon be lovers, 'twas
    something we could not deny.

REFRAIN (*repeat after each verse*)

    The Plains, the Plains, when will I
      again
    Meet her there, greet her there
    In the Men's Room down at the Plains?

She hooked her arm around me, and led me
    through the door.
I could tell by her clothing, she surely
    was . . . twenty-four.
She was so captivating, I reconciled my
    fate.
My eyes undressed her body, and she was
    nearly eighty-eight.

She led me to the Men's Room, down a
    shadowed stair.
The door swung shut and then she ran her
    fingers through my hair.

(*continued on next page*)

My heart was pounding in my breast, I
   felt so much alive.
"I'll make you feel much better," she
   said, "for only $14.95 ... plus tax."

Our talk was very heady, the evening
   quickly passed.
And lying in her warm embrace, I knew it
   couldn't last.
The night we slept there on the tile, I
   remember, oh too well,
For that night I was arrested in the
   Men's Room of The Plains Hotel.

**(00) PLEASE DON'T BURN THE SHITHOUSE
DOWN** (*See DE07*)

(07) PLEASE DON'T PUT YOUR PANTS ON
   (Tune: *Unavailable*)

Please don't put your pants on,
We haven't said goodnight.
For two or three more hours,
I'm going to try with all my might.
You and your virtue, honey,
I'm not going to hurt you,
Please don't put your pants on,
Because we haven't said goodnight.

(00) POOR LITTLE ANGELINE (*See LL09*)

(08) THE PORTIONS OF A WOMAN
   (Tune: *Unavailable*)

The portions of a woman that appeal to
   man's depravity,
Are fashioned with considerable care,
And what at first appears to be a
   harmless little cavity,
Is really an elaborate affair.
Doctors of distinction have examined
   the abdomena

Of various experimental dames,
And have listed the components of
   these womanly phenomena.
There's the clitoris, the vagina, the
   vulva, perineum,
And the hymen in the case of certain
   brides.
Delightful small devices you would love
   if you could see 'em.
There's a hundred other little things
   besides.
Isn't it a pity then, that when we poor
   men chatter
Upon the things to which I have
   referred,
We use for what is really a most
   complicated matter
Such a short and unattractive little
   word.

THE REPLY

The erudite authorities who study the
   geography
Of these remote but interesting lands,
Are able to indulge their taste for
   intimate topography,
And view the scenic details close at
   hand.

But while we lesser mortals are aware of
   the existence
Of mysteries beneath the pubic knoll,
We're normally contented to survey them
   at a distance,
And treat them, roughy speaking, as a
   (w)hole.

But when we are confronted with some
   morsel of virginity,
We exercise a gentle sense of touch.
We do not cloak the matter in
   meticulous Latinity,
But call the whole affair a such and
   such.

Men have made this useful but inelegant
   commodity,
The subject of inumerable jibes,
And while the name we call it by, is
   something of an oddity,
It seems to fit the subject it
   describes.

(09) PUBIC HAIRS
(Tune: *Baby Face*)

Pubic hairs,
You've got the cutest little pubic
   hairs.
There's not another that can compare,
Pubic hairs,
Penis or vagina, nothing could be finer.
Pubic hairs,
I'm up in heaven when I'm in your
   underwear.
I didn't need a shove to take a mouth-
   full of your pretty,
Pubic hairs.

(10) PUFF, THE TRAGIC WAGON
(Tune: *Puff, The Magic Dragon*)

NOTE: **Puff, the Magic Dragon**, *was the name given to the old reliable C-47s that were mounted with rapid-firing Gatling guns in the waist, and used in the early days of the Vietnam War for ground support. Fifty years after its introduction, the old, reliable "gooney" still flies, earning its way around the world. Old Goonies never die, they just fly away.*

PUFF, THE TRAGIC WAGON

Puff, the tragic wagon,
Came across the sea.
Conceited turds in gooney birds,
They came to kill the VC.

The VC shook in terror,
Whenever they appeared.
The mini ones with miniguns,
A-sticking out their rears.

Puff, the tragic wagon,
At Danang by the sea,
Though Rinkelman is number one,
His waist is 63.

The FC-47 flies all afternoon,
Half a day of boredom
In that silly, fucking goon!

(11) PULL YOUR SHADES DOWN MARY ANN
(Tune: *Hold Your Hand Out, Naughty Boy, as sung by Miss Florrie Forde -- an English music hall number.*)

Pull your shades down, Mary Ann,
Pull your shades down, Mary Ann.
Late last night by the pale moonlight,
I saw you,
I saw you.
You were combing your golden hair,
You were changing your underwear.
If you want to keep your secrets
From your future man,
Pull your shades down, Mary Ann.

(12) THE P-39 TALE
(Tune: *Clementine*)

NOTE: *There is a slight resemblance between this ditty and,* **Oh, My Darling 54**, *song 0009.*

Oh, my darling, oh, my darling
Oh, my darling, thirty-nine.
Tho' you're lost and gone forever,
Fare thee well, my thirty-nine.

In the cockpit of the cobra,
Trying hard to reach the line.
But alas my engine faltered,
Fare thee well, my thirty-nine.

Half a snap roll, all inverted
With a spin not far behind.
How the Hell will I recover,
Fare thee well, my thirty-nine.

Kick the rudder, pull the stick back,
And hope you're just in time.
'Cause the man said that it would tumble
Fare thee well, my thirty-nine.

Where's the Bell man, where's he hiding
With his propaganda line,
For he surely lost his marbles
If he spins the thirty-nine.

All the brass hats and the Congress,
They have signed the dotted line.
They are lucky, they just bought it,
They don't fly the thirty-nine.

FLIGHT SECTION RR

(01) RANGY LIL
(Tune: *Unavailable*)

NOTE: *There is a similarity in story, if not in song, between this gem and* **Kathuselem**, *song KK01. This is one of several songs in this volume whose theme is the macho man matching his sexual prowess against a super-sexy woman--a male's favorite fantasy. See* **Lupee #2**, **Bumming Around**, *and* **Yukon Pete**. *There are some uneven verses, but without the tune or a second source, it is difficult to know the proper verse structure.*

RANGY LIL

Now, don't move over stranger,
That ain't shit on your seat.
I just got in from the West,
And that's mud on my feet.

I just got in from the West
With tales wild, wooly and bold,
And some of those stories, stranger,
Just gotta be told.

Now sit a spell if you will,
And I'll spin you the yarn about
    Rangy Lil.
Now, Lil was a school teacher before
    she came West,
But she gave that up, cause she liked
    fuckin' best.

And when she fucked she fucked for keeps
And piled her victims up in heaps.
It was a standard bet around our town,
That no man alive could fuck Lil down.

Now, out of the bottom of Bare Ass
    Creek,
Came a Barrel Bellied Bastard named
    Piss Pit Pete,

Who boasted 18 pounds of that swinging
    meat.
And when he laid it on Murphy's Bar,
It stretched from Har to Thar;
And stink! My God.

Now, old Lil knew she'd met her fate,
But to call the bet was a little too
    late.
The time and place was set by Lil,
In front of the Shit House on Duffy's
    Hill.

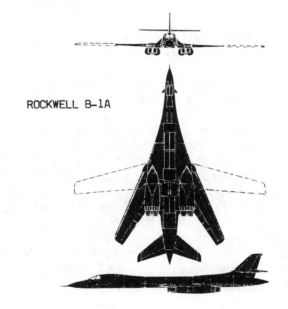

ROCKWELL B-1A

The people gathered from the county
    seat,
To see the half-breed sink his meat.
Old Lil, she tried hops, skips and
    jumps,
And other tricks unknown to common
    cunts.

But alas, she missed a stroke,
And the half-breed pinned her before
    she broke.
(*continued on next page*)

The country side was tore up for miles
  around,
Where old Lil's ass had drug the ground.

They hung her skivvies on the shithouse
  door,
To commemerate the plucky whore.
And when the half-breed left the town,
They all said - "Thars the man that
  fucked Lil down."

(00) RECCE TO BERLIN (*See Volume I, R6*)

NOTE: *This song is identical to, Recce To Pyongyang in Volume I, except for the city (Berlin) and the aircraft (P-51 and P47). Obviously this version came first, but for some reason was not in the collection of unit song books that found their way into Volume I.*

(02) RED RIVER VALLEY - III
   (Tune: *Red River Valley*)

Alternate Titles and Variations:
   (*See Note below*)

NOTE: *This is another version of the very popular parodies of the old cowboy song, and the third military version to carry the same title. This particular version, from S.E.A., combines verses from, The Po River Valley (Volume I, song P23), and Red River Valley - II, (Volume I, song R9). As an Honorary Member of The Red River Valley Fighter Pilot's Association, this song has special appeal to the Editor.*

RED RIVER VALLEY - III

To the Red River Valley we're going,
For to get us some trains and some
  tracks,
But if I had my say-so about it,
I'd still be back home in the sack.

Come and sit by my side at the briefing.
Do not hasten to bid me adieu;
To the Red River Valley we're going,
And I'm flying four in Flight Blue.

NOTE: *See the song, Blue Four, song B40, Volume I.*

We went for to check on the weather,
And they said it was clear as could be.
I lost my wingman 'round the field,
And the rest augered in out at sea.

NOTE: *Technical error by the songwriter. Blue Four was a wingman. He would not have one of his own. In a few verses, the code name changes from Blue Flight to Beak Flight. Too many drinks at the bar!*

S-2 said there's no flak where we're
  going;
S-2 said there's no flak on the way.
There's a dark overcast o'er the target;
I'm beginning to doubt what they say.

To the Valley they say we are going,
And many strange sights will we see,
But the one there that held my attention
Was the SAM that they threw up at me.

To the Valley he said he was flying,
And he never saw the medal that he
  earned.
Many jocks have flown into the Valley,
And a number have never returned.

So I listened as he briefed on the
  mission,
Tonight at the bar BEAK Flight will sing
But we're going to the Red River Valley,
And today you are flying my wing.

Oh, the flak is so thick in the Valley,
That the MIGs and the SAMs we don't
  need,
So fly high and down sun in the Valley,
And guard well the ass of BEAK Lead.

Now things turn to shit in the Valley,
And the Briefing I gave, you don't heed.
They'll be waiting at the Hanoi Hilton,
And it's fish heads and rice for BEAK
  Lead.

We refueled on the way to the Valley.
In the States it had always been fun,
(*continued on next page*)

But with thunder and lightning all
   around us,
T'was the last AAR BEAK One.

When we came to a bridge in the Valley,
He saw a duty that he couldn't shun,
For the first to roll in on the target,
Was my leader, Old BEAK Number One.

Oh, he flew through the flak toward the
   target.
With his bombs and rockets drew a bead,
But he never pulled out of his bomb run,
T'was fatal for another BEAK lead.

So come sit by my side at the briefing,
We will sit there and tickle the beads,
For we're going to the Red River Valley,
And my call sign today is BEAK Lead.

(03) REMEMBER (*not the original!*)
   (Tune: *Remember*)

Remember the night,
When you were tight.
My darling, remember?

When I was on heat,
And said you might,
My darling, remember?

Remember you found a tender spot,
Right in the middle of my twot.

You said you'd withdraw,
Before you shot,
But you forgot, to remember.

(04) THE REPUBLIC BATTLE HYMN
(Tune: *Battle Hymn of the Republic*)

Alternate Titles & Variations:
(*all in Volume I, page 0-10*)

   (a) *One Little Teensy-Weesy Bomb*
   (b) *Tons & Tons of Ammunition*
   (c) *The B-17*
   (d) *The B-29*
   (e) *The B-36*
   (f) *The B-52*
   (g) *The F-94*
   (h) *add your own plane*

We fly our fucking Super Hogs at 20,000
   feet,
We fly our fucking Super Hogs thru rain
   and snow and sleet,
And though we think we're flying south
We're flying fucking north,
And we make our fucking landfall on the
   Firth of Fucking Forth.

CHORUS (*repeat after each verse*)

   Glory, glory, hallelujah,
   Glory, glory, hallelujah,
   Glory, glory, hallelujah,
   (*Insert last line of each verse*)

We fly our fucking Super Hogs at fucking
   all 1000 feet,
We fly those fucking Super Hogs thru
   the trees and corn and wheat,
And tho we think we fly with skill,
We fly with fucking luck,
But we don't give a fucking damn or a
   fucking fuck!

We fly those fucking Super Hogs at
   20,000 fucking feet,
We fly those fucking Super Hogs thru
   the rain and snow and sleet,
And tho we think we're flying up,
We're flying fucking down,
And we bust our fucking asses when we
   hit the fucking ground.

(05) THE RETURN
   (*A Poem*)

NOTE: *This poem was written by a copilot
enroute to his airbase after a minimum
altitude strike against Mapanget in the
Celebes Islands on 21 November 1944.
Unfortunately, no names were provided.
It appeared in the* **The War Chronicle of
John *Hank* Henry,** *September 1940 -
October 1945, An Autobiography. Hank
was a contributor to Volumes I and II
(See* **Ode to a Bombardier,** *0001), but has
since taken his last flight into* **The
Wild Blue Yonder.** *The author expresses*

(continued on next page)

feelings that many of us have felt. Now, for those of you that would like to put this poem to music, there are several melodies that can be fitted. Try **Wabash Cannonball,** *among others.*

THE RETURN

Five minutes from the target,
The auto-pilot set;
The peaceful drone of engines,
Hands clammy, forehead wet.

Our atack was very successful,
We caught them by surprise;
We bombed and heavily strafed them,
Smoke poured up in the sky.

We may have left destruction,
In planes and bodies, too;
But here beyond the target;
There's the quiet of the blue.

The sky's in all it's glory,
Of floating, fluffy clouds;
The large one rears it's cotton head,
The smaller ones it crowds.

And just beneath the water,
A melancholy blue;
It's waves are small, it's flashes
   bright,
As sunlight filters through.

We're at war, we know it well,
The targets just behind
But flying now, in nature's realm;
Her restfulness is kind.

For nature cares not if there's war,
The world is hers to roam;
And now our mission is complete;
It's peaceful going home.

(06) RICKY DAN DO
(Tune: Available*)*

<u>NOTE</u>: *This ditty is related to the one following,* **Ring Rang Doo,** *but is still a different song. A poor relation?*

RICKY DAN DO

As I was walking down the street,
A fair young maid I chanced to meet.
She said, "Hello, how do you do?
Would you like to play with my Ricky
   Dan Do?"
"Your Ricky Dan Do", I said, "What's
   that?"
"It's soft and smooth like a pussy cat.
Hairs all 'round and split in two.
That's what I call my Ricky Dan Do."

She took me to her father's cellar.
She said to me, "You're a very nice
   feller."
She gave me wine and whiskey, too,
And I played all night with her Ricky
   Dan Do.
There came a policeman up to her door.
"Show me your license to be a whore."
"I have no license, tell you what I'll
   do,
I'll let you play with my Ricky Dan Do."

The boys all came and the boys all went.
The price came down to eighteen cents.
From sweet sixteen to eight-two,
All had a bash at her Ricky Dan Do.
There came a guy, a son-of-a-bitch,
Who had the pox and the sailor's itch.
He had blue balls and shankers, too,
And he played all night with her Ricky
   Dan Do.

And the Ricky Dan Do now is badly worn,
The Ricky Dan Do is tattered and torn.
The Ricky Dan Do now is up the kite,
To the Ricky Dan Do we'll say
   "Goodnight."

(07) RING DANG DOO
(Tune: Available*)*

<u>NOTE</u>: *This song is related to the one above. The theme follows that of many songs in this volume,* The wages of sin-- may be catching!

(continued on next page)

RING DANG DOO

When I was young and sweet sixteen,
I met a girl from New Orleans.
Oh, she was young and pretty, too,
She had what you call a ring-dang-doo.

A ring-dang-doo, pray what is that?
It's round and soft like a pussy cat.
It's round and soft and split in two.
That's what you call a ring-dang-doo.

She took me down into the cellar.
She said I was a very fine feller.
She gave me wine and whiskey, too,
And she let me play with her ring-dang-
    doo.

She took me up into her bed.
She placed her tits beneath my head.
And then she took my hickey-floo,
And placed it in her ring-dang-doo.

Now, six months later she began to
    swell,
She swelled and swelled till she looked
    like hell.
She told her ma and her father, too,
That I took a crack at her ring-dang-
    doo.

Her father said, "You filthy whore.
You've gone and lost your maiden's
    lore.
Pack up your bags and your nighty, too,
And make your living from your ring-
    dang-doo."

She went to the city to become a whore.
She hung a sign upon her door.
Five dollars now nothing else will do,
To take a crack at my ring-dang-doo.

And the fellers came and the fellers
    went,
And the price went down to fifteen
    cents.
Fifteen cents and nothing else will do,
To take a crack at my ring-dang-doo.

And then one day, a son-of-a-bitch,
He had the crabs and the jockey itch.

He had the syph and diarrhea, too,
And he took a crack at the ring-dang-
    doo.

They hung her tits in the city hall.
They pickled her ass in alcohol.
Now all you bums and hobos, too,
You've heard my tale of the ring-dang-
    doo.

So they buried her near the city hall,
And they engraved upon the wall,
"She's learned her lesson and you
    should, too,
Just stay away from the ring-dang-doo."

(08) ROLL YOUR LEG OVER - I
    (Tune: *Available*)

Alternative Titles and Variations:

    (a) *If All Little Girls*
    (b) *If All The Young Maidens*
    (c) *The Man In The Moon*

Oh, if all little girls were like fish
    in the ocean,
And I were a whale, I would teach them
    emotion.

CHORUS (*repeat after each verse*)

    Oh, roll your leg over, oh, roll
        your leg over,
    Oh, roll your leg over the man in
        the moon.

Oh, if all little girls were like bells
    in the tower,
And I were a clapper, I'd bang by the
    hour.

Oh, if all little girls were like fish
    in the river,
And I were a sandbar, I'd sure make them
    quiver.

(*continued on next page*)

Oh, if all little girls were like sheep
  in the pasture,
And I were a ram, I'd make them run
  faster.

Oh, if all little girls were like little
  white rabbits,
And I were a hare, I would teach them
  bad habits.

Oh, if all little girls were like little
  red vixens,
And I were a fox, I surely would fix
  them.

Oh, if all little girls were like Hedy
  Lamarr
I'd try twice as hard and get twice as
  far.

NOTE: *With no slight intended, the Editor doubts that many--if any--in today's Air Force will recognize the name of Hedy Lamarr, the beautiful, dark beauty of the movies in the 30s and 40s.*

Oh, if all little girls were like cows
  in the clover,
And I were a bull, I would chase them
  all over.

Oh, if all little girls were like little
  white flowers,
And I was a bee, I would buzz them for
  hours.

Oh, if all little girls were like little
  white chickens,
And I was a rooster, I'd give them the
  dickens.

Oh, if all little girls were like little
  'ole turtles,
And I was a turtle, I'd get in their
  girdles.

Oh, if all little girls were like Gypsy
  Rose Lee,
And I were her G-string, oh, boy, what
  I'd see!

NOTE: *The Editor feels compelled to again identify for the younger generation that Gypsy Rose Lee was a very famous stripper back in the days when daddy (grandaddy?) was young.*

Oh, if all little girls were like
  nurses who would,
And I were a doctor, I would if I could.

NOTE: *At this point, there is a definite change in verse stucture and the chorus--and although from the same song book as the preceeding--leads the Editor to suggest this was originally another version of this popular song. At least one verse was obviously written by an Air Force jock. The Editor has elected to treat this as a separate version. They both come from the song book of the* **Yankee Air Pirates,** *355th Tactical Fighter Wing, Takhli RTAFB, Thailand. During World War II, when the Editor was flying P-51s in a special scouting organization, his unit was assigned for maintenance and support to the 355th Fighter Group, Steeple Morden, England, daddy (grandaddy?) of the 355th Wing.*

(09) ROLL YOUR LEG OVER - II
(Tune: *Available*)

I wish little girls were like statues of
  Venus,
And I were a man with a petrified penis.

CHORUS (*repeat after each verse*)

  Oh, roll your leg over, oh, roll your
    leg over,
  Oh, roll your leg over, it's better
    that way.

I wish all young girls were like bats in
  the steeple,
And I were a bat, there'd be more bats
  than people.

I wish all girls were like mountain road
  passes,
And I were a sports car, I'd buzz all
  their asses.

(*continued on next page*)

I wish all little girls were like
diamonds and rubies,
And I were a jeweler, I'd polish their
    boobies.

I wish all little girls were like B-29s,
And I were a fighter pilot, I'd buzz
    their behinds.

I wish all little girls were like straw-
    berry patches,
And I were a farmer, I'd harvest their
    snatches.

NOTE: *Another change in verse structure,
and probably taken from another version.*

I wish all young girls were like fish in
    a pool,
And I were a shark with a water-proof
    tool.

I wish all young girls were like fish in
    the ocean,
And I were a wave, I'd show them the
    motion.

I wish all young girls were like trees
    in a forest,
And I were a woodsman, I'd split their
    clitoris.

I wish all young girls were like bricks
    in a pile,
And I were a mason, I'd lay them in
    style.

I wish all young girls were like mares
    in a stable,
And I were a groom, I'd mount all I was
    able.

(10) ROMANTIC NEW GUINEA
    (Tune: *Unavailable*)

NOTE: *Here is a song written with the
strong emotions of an airman or soldier
at war, where the enemy is not only the
Japanese, but the jungle, the heat, the
boredom, the lonliness. Being shot at
isn't always the worst thing that can
happen during a war. At least that
holds your attention!*

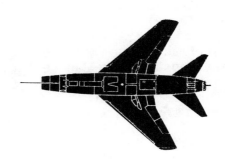

ROMANTIC NEW GUINEA

Down where there are no Ten Commandments
And a man can raise a thirst,
He's the outcast of civilization,
The victim of life at its worst.

Down on this tropical island,
Where men that God forgot,
Battle the ever present fever,
The itch and jungle rot.

Nobody knows they're living,
And nobody gives a damn.
Back home they're soon forgotten,
These soldiers of Uncle Sam.

Living with the dirty natives,
Down in the sweltering zone,
Down by the muddy river,
Many thousand miles from home.

Drenched with sweat in the evening,
They sit on their bunks and dream
Of killing themselves with coconuts,
And making things not quite as they
    seem.

No place to go on payday,
To squander their meager pay.
Nowhere to raise Hell for an evening,
Only work, work, every day.

Vermin at night on their pillows,
Ills that no doctor can cure.
Hell no!, we're not convicts,
Just soldiers on foreign tour.

There's just one small consolation,
Gather 'round and I shall tell,
When we die we'll go to heaven,
For we served our term in HELL!

(11) RO-TIDDLE-EE-O
(Tune: *Unavailable*)

Oh, Mr. Fisherman, home from the sea,
Have you any lobsters you can sell to
    me?

CHORUS (*repeat after each verse*)

    Singing Ro-tiddle-ee-o, shit or bust,
    Never let your bollocks dangle in the
      dust.

"Yes," said the fisherman, I have two,
The biggest of the bastards I will sell
    to you.

I wrapped the lobster up and I took the
    bastards home,
I showed them to the missus, but she was
    on the phone.

I opened up the fridge, but I couldn't
    find a dish,
So I put them in the place where the
    missus has a piss.

Now half-way through the night as you
    must know,
The missus got up to have a so-and-so.

Now the missus gave a squeal, and the
    missus gave a grunt,

When the silly fucking lobster bit her
    on the cunt.

Now I picked up a mop, and the missus
    grabbed a broom,
And we chased that fucking lobster all
    around the room.

Now we hit it on the head and we hit it
    on the side;
We hit that fucking lobster 'till the
    bastard died.

There's a moral to this story, and the
    moral is this,
Always have a shufty* before you have a
    piss.

That's the end of this story, and there
    isn't any more,
There's an apple up my arse-hole, you
    can have the core.

* *In this English song, the Editor assumes that* shufty *means to flush the toilet. When are our English friends going to learn to speak the King's English?*

(00) RUM AND COCA-COLA (*See MM03*)

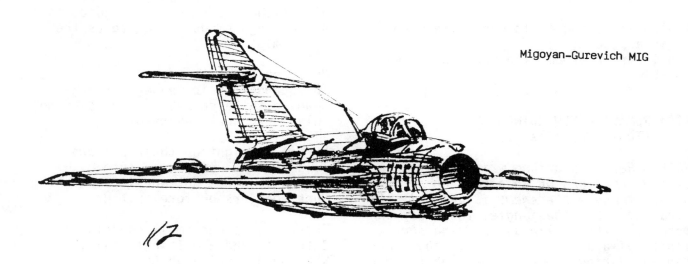

Migoyan-Gurevich MIG

FLIGHT SECTION SS

(01) THE SAC LAMENT
(Tune: *Jamaica Farewell*)

For long, long years, he tried in vain
To win his escape from SAC's domain.
Requests for transfer all come back,
"We cannot spare you," said Saint SAC.

At other bases he'd enlist,
To flee the clutch of SAC's mailed fist.
"We need your skills, Sarge," he was
   told,
And back he went into SAC's fold.

He tried and tried a thousand times,
To free himself of SAC's confine,
But in his heart the hope burned bright,
That ease would come for his sad plight.

At last his hitch on earth was done,
Long lost fredom had been won.
"I'm free," he cried, "My spirit rides.
No more alerts, no more TDYs."

But as he neared the Pearly Gates,
He saw this sign that sealed his fate.
"As of this date, the Promised Land
Becomes part of SAC Command."

(02) SALLY IN THE ALLEY
   (Tune: *Available*)

Alternative Titles and Variations:

   (a) *Sally*

Sally in the alley sifting cinders,
Lifted up her leg and farted like a man,
Wind from her bloomers blew six winders
Cheeks of her ass went
BAM! BAM! BAM!

(03) SALOME
(Tune: *Unavailable*)

Now, down our street we had a crashing
   party,
Everybody there was so gay and hearty;
Talk about a treat, we wolfed up all
   the meat,
Drank all the beer in the boozer down
   the street.

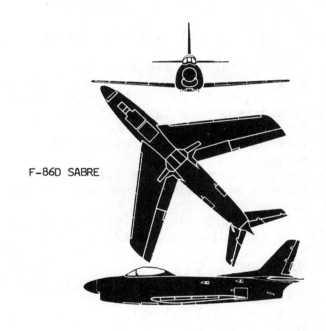

F-86D SABRE

There was old Uncle Joe, fairly fucked
   up,
We put him in the cellar with the bull-
   dog pup,
And little Sonny Jim tryin' to get it
   in,
With his arsehole winkin' at the moon!

(*continued on next page*)

CHORUS

O Salome! Salome!
You should see Salome!
Dancing there
With her tits all bare,
Every little wriggle
Makes the boys all stare.
She swings it,
She flings it,
And the boys all murmur, "Oh,"
Take her around,
Lay her on the ground,
Down where the roses grow!

She's a great big cow, twice the size
of me;
Hairs on her fanny like the branches of
a tree.
She can run, jump, fight, shit, suck
and fuck;
Push a barrow wheel, a truck--that's
my Salome.
On a Monday night I shove it up the
back;
Tuesday night she takes it in the crack;
Every Wednesday she takes a spell.

On Thursday night she fucks like bloody
Hell.
Friday evening up her snout it goes,
In between her fingers, down between her
toes,
And all day long she guzzles on my dong.
All day Saturday and Sunday.

CHORUS

O Salome! Salome!
That's my girl Salome!
Standing there
With her arse all bare,
Waiting with a stare
To shove it right up there,
Slide it,
Glide it
Up her hungry cunt.
Two swollen balls
And a gallon of best spunk,
That's my girl Salome!

(04) SAMMY SMALL - II
(Tune: *Unavailable*)

Alternate Titles and Variations:

    (a) *Samari Sall (Korean Version)*
    (b) *Sam Hall (See Volume I, S10)*
    (c) *Samuel Hall (See Volume I, S10)*
    (d) *Sammy Small - I (See Vol. I, S10)*
    (e) *Sammy Small - III (S.E.A. version)*

Oh, my name is Sammy Small, fuck 'em all
Oh, my name is Sammy Small, fuck 'em all
Oh, my name is Sammy Small, and I only
have one ball,
But it's better than none at all, so
fuck 'em all.

Oh, they say I shot a man, fuck 'em all
Oh, they say I shot a man, fuck 'em all
They say I shot him dead with a piece of
fucking lead,
Now that silly fucker's dead, so fuck
'em all.

Oh, they say I'm going to swing, fuck
'em all.
Oh, they say I'm going to swing, fuck
'em all.
Oh, they say I'm going to swing from a
piece of fucking string,
What a silly fucking thing, so fuck 'em
all.

Oh, the parson he will come, so fuck 'em
all,
Oh, the parson he will come, so fuck 'em
all,
Oh, the parson he will come with his
tales of kingdom come,
He can shove it up his bum, so fuck 'em
all.

Oh, the hangman wore a mask, fuck 'em
all,
Oh, the hangman wore a mask, fuck 'em
all,
Oh, the hangman wore a mask for his
silly fucking task,
What a silly fucking ass, so fuck 'em
all

(*continued on next page*)

Oh, the sheriff will be there, too, fuck
'em all,
Oh, the sheriff will be there, too, fuck
'em all,
Oh, the sheriff will be there, too, with
his silly fucking crew,
They've got fuck all else to do, so fuck
'em all.

I saw Molly in the crowd, fuck 'em all,
I saw Molly in the crowd, fuck 'em all,
I saw Molly in the crowd, and I felt so
fucking proud,
That I shouted right loud, FUCK 'EM ALL!

(05) SAMMY SMALL - III (S.E.A Version)
(Tune: *Unavailable*)

NOTE: *This is the air warrior's version
of this popular song. Variations have
been found in 13 Air Force unit song
books. This particular gem comes from*
More Kunsongs By The SEA, *Kunsan Air
Base, Korea, 16 May 1977.*

SAMMY SMALL - III

O, come 'round us fighter pilots, fuck
'em all,
O, come 'round us fighter pilots, fuck
'em all,
O, we fly the goddamn plane through the
flak and through the rain,
And tomorrow we'll do it again, fuck 'em
all.

O, they tell us not to think, fuck 'em
all,
O, they tell us not to think, fuck 'em
all,
O, they tell us not to think, just to
dive and just to jink,
LBJ's a goddamn fink, so fuck 'em all.

O, we bombed Mu Gia Pass, fuck 'em all,
O, we bombed Mu Gia Pass, fuck 'em all,
O, we bombed Mu Gia Pass, though we only
made one pass,
They really stuck it up our ass, so
fuck 'em all.

O, we're on a JCS, fuck 'em all,
O, we're on a JCS, fuck 'em all,

O, they sent the whole damn wing,
Probably half of us will sing,
What a silly fucking thing, so fuck
'em all.

O, we lost our fucking way, fuck 'em
all,
O, we lost our fucking way, fuck 'em
all,
O, we strafed goddamn Hanoi, killed
every girl and every boy,
What a goddamn fucking joy, so fuck 'em
all.

O, my bird got all shot up, fuck 'em
all,
O, my bird got all shot up, fuck 'em
all,
O, my bird got all shot up, and I'll
probably cry a lot,
But I still think that it's shit-hot,
so fuck 'em all.

While I'm swinging in my chute, fuck
'em all,
While I'm swinging in my chute, fuck
'em all,
While I'm tangled in my chute, come this
silly fucking toot,
Hangs a medal on my root, so FUCK 'EM
ALL!

(06) SAT TROOP LULLABY (M)
(Tune: *Irish Lullaby*)
Lyrics: *Wally Odd*

Over in Nebraska, a day or so ago.
I heard a SAT troop singing, on his
pickup radio.
His song was full of meaning, and his
voice was full of fear.
The echo of his M-16 was ringing in my
ear.

(*continued on next page*)

CHORUS (*repeat after each verse*)

> A tour or two at Tango
> A tour or three at "I"
> The song that I am singing, is a SAT
>   troop lullaby.

As commander, I was worried and my
    deputy stood near.
Together we could see it as the end of
    our career.
We huddled at the console, and turned up
    the radio,
With great anticipation to hear the
    voice of the FSO.

Then within the garble there came a
    blare of hope,
The target of their shooting was the
    pronghorned antelope.

(07) SAVE A FIGHTER PILOT'S ASS
(*See TT17*)

(00) SCOTCH WEDDING (*See BB10*)

(08) SCROTUM
(Tune: *Unavailable*)

NOTE: *The Editor is suspicious of this
song because of the uneven verse structure. Inasmuch as this is another in
the collection that did not indicate the
tune, it is difficult to assess (that is
not the plural of* ass, *fellows!). Since
this ditty was in the* **95th FITS Hymn
Book** *(1980), and covered such an important subject, the Editor decided to
include it.*

SCROTUM

Scrotum, scrotum---S-C-R-O-T-U-M
Mangy, grangy, covered with hair.
What would you do if it wasn't there?
Your scrotum, scrotum, S-C-R-O-T-U-M!

Hangs a little low and a little behind,
Comes in a bag with a fancy design.
Your scrotum, scrotum, S-C-R-O-T-U-M.
Fun to play with every night,

Better watch out if you get in a fight,
Your scrotum, scrotum, S-C-R-O-T-U-M.
Fits just right in the palm of your hand
Only thing that proves that you're
    really a man,
Your scrotum, scrotum, S-C-R-O-T-U-M.

It holds your balls in, S-C-R-O-T-U-M!
It's fun to play with, S-C-R-O-T-U-M!

(09) SEXIATUS MANIA
(Tune: *Unavailable*)

NOTE: *Despite the Editor's four years
of Latin, it is not one of his big
suits. Soooo,* **a fronte praecipitium, a
tergo lupus.** *Got that?*

SEXIATUS MANIA

Sexiatus mania
Frustratatum randium
Sexiatus mania
Frustriatum randium
Prostitutum contraceptum
Hamd et fingum masturbatum
Satisfactor relievium
Satisfactor relievuim

(10) THE SHEEPHERDER LAY
(Tune: *Unavailable*)

Alternate Titles and Variations:

(a) *The Sheepherder*

The sheepherder lay in the tall, tall
    grass,
His favorite dog lay close to his ass.
Through a hole in his worn blue
    coveralls,
A toothless Ewe lay licking his balls.
A Magpie watched from a fence close by,
Gazing at the scene with practiced eye.
His gun went off, the old Ewe quit,
The hound dog yelped, and the Magpie
    shit.

(11) SHE JUMPED INTO BED
    (Tune: *Unavailable*)

She jumped into bed and covered up her
    head,
And said I couldn't find her.
But I knew damn well, she lied like
    Hell,
So I jumped right in beside her.

Oh, I lifted up the sheet, and took a
    little peek,
And saw her sausage grinder.
The white of an egg rolled down her leg
And the rest rolled down behind her.

I fucked her once, I fucked her twice,
I fucked her once too often;
I broke the mainspring in her ass,
And now she's in her coffin.

She lay out there in the moonlit air,
And we opened up her coffin.
The moonlight shone on the nipple of
    her tit,
She looked like a statue on a pile of
    shit.

(12) SHE WAS POOR BUT SHE WAS HONEST
    (Tune: *Unavailable*)

Alternate Titles and Variations:
(*In Volume I, song P21*)

    (a) *Poor But Honest*
    (b) *Twenty-Seventh Lament*

NOTE: *This ballad is similar to the one
in Volume I, song P21, but the Volume I
version is not complete--a situation
discovered only after receiving the song
book containing the version below.   So
here's the whole thing--hopefully.*

SHE WAS POOR BUT SHE WAS HONEST

She was poor but she was honest,
Victim of the Squire's game;
First he loved her, then he left her,
And she lost her honest name.

CHORUS (*repeat after each verse*)

    It's the same the whole world over,
    It's the poor that gets the blame;
    It's the rich that lives in clover,
    Ain't that a bleeding shame?

Then she ran away to London,
For to hide her grief and shame.
There she met another Squire,
And she lost her name again.

In the rich man's arms she flutters,
Like a bird with broken wing;
First he loved her, then he left her,
And she hasn't got a ring.

See him in his splendid mansion,
Entertaining with the best,
While the girl he has ruined,
Entertains a sordid guest.

See him in the House of Commons,
Making laws to put down crime,
While the victim of his passions,
Trails her way thro' mud and slime.

Standing on the bridge at midnight,
She says, "Farewell, blighted love,"
Then a scream, a splash--"Good Heavens,
What is she a-doin' of?"

Then they dragged her from the river,
Water from her clothes they wrang,
For they thought that she was drowned,
But the corpse got up and sang.

*GO DIRECTLY TO LAST VERSE, DO NOT CROSS
THE FINISH LINE--DO NOT COLLECT $200*

It's the same the whole world over,
It's the poor that gets the blame,
It's the rich that lives in clover,
Ain't it all a bloody shame?

(13) SHIT-HOT FROM KORAT
(Tune: *Sweet Betsy From Pike*)

NOTE: *See the* Note *with the song,* **You
Can't Say Shit-Hot,** *YY02, for an explanation of the term,* **shit-hot.** *You will*

(*continued on next page*)

also discover the name of the person who first uttered these immortal words. This is a very educational book.

SHIT-HOT FROM KORAT

When this base opened and all things
    were new,
The jocks had a need for somebody to
    screw;
When up jumped this girl and said, "For
    five baht.
I'm Chum Chim the whore and shit-hot
    from Korat."

CHORUS (*repeat after each verse*)

    It was Chum Chim the whore from Korat
    Chum Chim the jocks screwed a lot.
    It was Chum Chim the whore from Korat
    Chum Chim the whore from Korat that's
        shit-hot!

Standing or sitting she's good anyway,
That's what the jocks at Korat always
    say.
They can't understand why her crotch
    doesn't rot,
Chum Chim the whore and shit-hot from
    Korat.

A very young jock that first opened her
    box,
Became her pimp and later got shot;
But still couldn't tie the marital knot,
To Chum Chim the whore and shit-hot from
    Korat.

She's good in a hammock, but better in
    bed,
That's what the jocks from Kadena have
    said.
Some left their wives, believe it or
    not,
For Chum Chim the whore and shit-hot
    from Korat.

She was a jewel to the pilots from TAC,
When they had the honor to lay in her
    rack.
They never forgot that dirty old twat,
Chum chim the whore and shit-hot from
    Korat.

With F-4C crews she never had trouble,
Once she learned how to take them on
    double.
Though it was daylight, it bothered her
    not,
Chum Chim the whore and shit-hot from
    Korat.

When she met the Weasels she sure had
    the knack,
One in the front and the other in back.
She liked this arrangement, it doubled
    her baht,
Chum Chim the whore and shit-hot from
    Korat.

(00) THE SHITHOUSE (*See DE07*)

(14) SIDE BY SIDE
(Tune: *Side By Side*)

NOTE: *This ditty reminds the Editor of parts of the song,* **Ode To A Sydney Leave** *(0003).*

Oh, we went up to bed for our first
    night.
She undressed in the pale moonlight,
Her teeth and her hair,
She placed on the chair,
Side by side.

Then out came one of her glass eyes,
I took one look and said, "Oh, my."
As with her teeth and her hair,
She placed it there on the chair,
Side by side.

CHORUS

    Then all sorts of movements,
    She started to go through.
    Her arm came off, her leg came off
    As she started to unscrew.

NOTE: *The last verse from the source song book just didn't follow the tune, so the Editor attempted to make a change or two so it would fit. It is still less than satisfactory, but fake it.*

(*continued on next page*)

All her beauty had gone when
She jumped into bed,
I slept over on the chair,
There was more of her there, there on
   the chair
Side by side.

(15) SILVER THREADS AMONG THE GOLD
(Tune: *Silver Threads Among The Gold*)

Darling let me fix your garter,
Just an inch above your knee.
And if I should wander farther,
Please don't blame it all on me.

The hair around your pussy's turning
   silver,
The hair around my cock is turning gold.
So let's put our two things together,
Silver threads among the gold.

So she let me fix her garter,
Just an inch above her knee;
And my hand did wander farther,
And she pissed all over me.

(16) THE SINGING TELEGRAM
(Tune: *Unavailable*)

NOTE: *The next two songs have different
tunes and different words, but they are
still a pair. They originated in a
Marine Air Corps song book. The Editor
converted the song to U. S. Air Force by
changing* Subic Bay, *in the Philippines
--a Navy Base--to Cam Ranh Bay of Vietnam. Also in the last line,* **Air Force**
was substituted for **Navy**. *They both
make a very grim reminder that war is
not fun and games, and clearly illustrates how the fighting man vented his
fears and frustrations in song.*

THE SINGING TELEGRAM

Your son got killed today,
He bought the farm, ha, ha.
He flew his F4B right into Cam Ranh Bay.
While flying high and far,
On his horizon bar,

He went down spinning, tuning,
   descending, way too far.
Upon recovery, quite accidentally,
He had a rendevous with a friendly
   Sparrow III . . . FLY AIR FORCE!

(00) ANOTHER GREETING FROM WESTERN UNION
(Tune: *Camptown Races*)

Your son died in Vietnam, doo dah,
   doo ha.
Your son died in Vietnam, oh, doo dah
   day.
Shot him through the head,
Killed that fucker dead.
Your son died in Vietnam, oh doo dah
   day.

A-7

(17) SING US ANOTHER ONE DO
(Tune: *Unavailable*)

Alternate Titles and Variations:

   (a) *A Very Fine Song*
   (b) *Ai, Yi, Yi Yi*
   (c) *Fighter Pilots Eat Pussy*
   (d) *Lymericks*
   (e) *Pilots Always Eat Pussy*
   (f) *Tell Us Another*
   (g) *There Was A Young Man*
   (h) *Waltz Me Around Again, Willy*

NOTE: *The longest and most popular songs
in the collection, probably due to the
fact that verses are easy to compose
since they do not have to relate to
other verses. These are called* **Limer-
icks**, *which are light verse and have
five chiefly anapestic lines with a
rhyme scheme of* aabba. *Not all of the
poets who wrote the following verses
followed the proper meter. Forgive
their artistic license in light of their
artistic fervor. All of the versions
have been combined into this one, yuk!*

(*continued on next page*)

SING US ANOTHER ONE DO

There was a young man from Boston,
Who traded his car for an Austin;
There was room for his ass,
And a gallon of gas,
But his balls hung out and he lost 'em.
CHORUS (*repeat after each verse if you
have the energy*)

That was a very fine song.
Sing us another one,
Just like the other one.
Sing us another one, do.

ALTERNATE CHORUS (*take your pick*)

I yi, yi, yi, in China they never eat
chili.
That was the worst verse,
Worse than the other verse,
So waltz me around again, Willie.

There was a young man from Dundee,
Who buggered an ape in a tree.
The result was most horrid,
All ass and no forehead,
Three balls and a purple goatee.

There was a young man from Kildair,
Who buggered his girl on the stairs;
The bannister broke,
He doubled his stroke,
And finished her off in mid-air.

There was a queer from Khartoum,
Who took a young lesbian to his room.
They argued all night,
As to who had the right
To do what, with which and to whom.

There was a professor from the Mall,
Who possessed a cylindrical ball.
The cube root of its weight,
Plus his penis plus eight,
Was one-half of two-thirds of fuck all.

There was a young girl from St. Paul,
Who wore a newspaper dress to a ball.
Her dress caught on fire,
And burned her entire
Front page, sports section and all.

There was a young lady from Wheeling,
Who had a peculiar feeling.
She laid on her back,
And tickled her crack,
And pissed all over the ceiling.

There was a young man from Nantucket,
Whose dick was so long he could suck it.
He said with a grin,
As he wiped off his chim,
"If my ear were a cunt I could fuck it!"

There was a young man from Kent,
Whose dick was so long that it bent.
To save himself trouble,
He put it in double,
And instead of coming, he went.

There was a man of class,
Whose balls were made of brass.
When they swung together,
They played Stormy Weather,
And lightening shot out of his ass.

There was a young man from Sparta,
Who was the world's champion farter.
On the strength of one bean,
He played God Save The Queen,
And Beethoven's Moonlight Sonata.

There once was a man from Rangoon,
Who was born by the light of the moon;
He had not the luck,
To be born by a fuck,
But was a wet dream scooped up in a
spoon.

There once was a boy from Baclaridge,
And he was his parent's disparage.
He sucked-off his brother,
And went down on his mother,
And ate up his sister's miscarriage.

There once was a pilot from K-2,
Who buggered a girl down in Taegu.
He said to the doc,
As he handed him his cock,
"Will I lose both my testicles, too?"

(*continued on Page 10*)

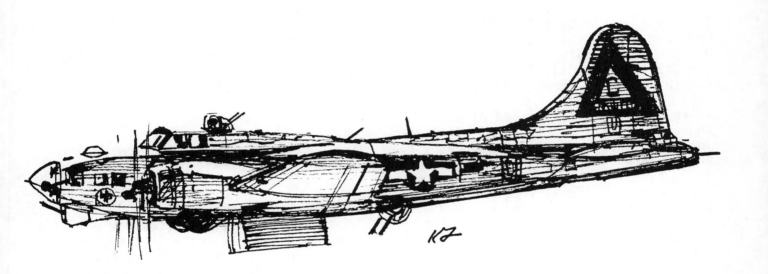

Boeing B-17

There once was a man from Trieste,
Who loved his wife with a zest;
Despite all her howls,
He sucked out her bowels,
And deposited the mess on her breast.

In the garden of Eden sat Adam,
With his hand on the butt of his madam;
He chuckled with mirth,
For he knew on this earth,
There were only two balls and he had
    'em.

There was an old hermit named Dave,
Who kept a dead whore in his cave;
He said I'll admit,
I'm a bit of a shit,
But think of the money I save.

There once was a girl named Alice,
Who used a dynamite stick for a fallice;
They found her vagina in South Carolina,
And a piece of her hymen in Dallas.

There once was a girl from France,
Who boarded a train by chance;
The engineer fucked her and so'd the
    conductor,
And the brakeman went off in his pants.

There once was a man from Bombay,
Who fashioned a cunt out of clay;
The heat of his prick turned the clay
    into brick,
And rubbed all his foreskin away.

There once was a girl name Gail,
Between her tits was the price of her
    tail;
And on her behind for the sake of the
    blind,
Was the same information in braile.

There once was a girl from the Azores,
Whose cunt was all covered with sores;
The dogs in the street would not eat the
    green meat,
That hung in festoons from her drawers.

There was a young girl named Myrtle,
Who was raped on the beach by a turtle;
The results of the fuck were two eggs
    and a duck,

Which proved that the turtle was fertile

There was a young lady from Ransom,
Who had it three times in a hansom;
When she cried for more, a voice from
    the floor
Cried, "My name is Simpson not Sampson."

There was a young man from Nottingham,
Who stood on the bridge at Buckingham,
Just watching the stunts of the cunts
    and the punts,
And the tricks of the pricks that were
    fuckingham.

An Argentine Gaucho named Bruno,
Said fucking is one thing I do know;
All women are fine and sheep are devine,
But llamas are numero uno.

There was a young man from New Brighton,
Who said my dear you've a tight one;
Said she, "'Pon my soul, you have the
    wrong hole,
It's the one up in front that's the
    right one.

There was a man from St. James,
Who played most unusual games;
He lit a match to his grandmother's
    snatch,
And laughed as she pissed through the
    flames.

There once was a man named McGruder,
Who wooed a nude in Bermuda;
Now the nude thought it crude to be
    wooed in the nude,
But McGruder was cruder he screwed her.

There was a young man from Kieth,
Who skinned back pricks with his teeth;
It wasn't for pleasure he adopted this
    measure,
But for the cheese he found underneath.

(continued on next page)

There was a young man from Brock,
Who tied a violin string to his cock;
With just one erection he could play a
    selection,
From Johann Sebastian Bach.

There once was a girl from Cape Cod,
Who thought all babies came from God;
But it wasn't the Almighty who lifted
    her nighty,
It was Roger the lodger, the sod.

There once was a lady named Lil,
Who swallowed an atomic pill;
They found her vagina in North Carolina,
And one of her tits in Brazil.

There once was a pirate named Bates,
Who was learning to rhumba on skates;
He fell on his cutlass which rendered
    him nutless,
And practically useless on dates.

There once was a monk from Mongolia,
Whose life was lonlier and lonlier;
One night just for fun, he took out a
    nun,
And now she's a Mother Superior.

There once was a young man from Florida,
Who liked his friend's wife so he
    borrowed her;
He said in surprise as he spread wide
    her thighs,
It isn't a crotch, it's a corridor.

There was a young lady from Ecuador,
Who was so beautiful men craned their
    necks at her;
One went so far as to wave from his car,
The distinguishing marks of his sex at
    her.

There was a young lady from Nottingham,
Who made some tarts and put snot in
    them;
She added some turds and a couple of
    dead birds,
And scratched off a dog until he shot
    in 'em.

There was a young man from St. Ives,
Who had balls of two different sizes;
One was so small, it was hardly a ball
    at all,
While the other so large that it won
    prizes.

There was a man from Calcutta,
Who was pounding off in the gutter;
But the tropical sun played a trick on
    his gun,
And turned all his milk into butter.

There was a young man named Gore,
Who wanted a piece from a whore;
Said she, "Young man, go get it by hand,
My cunt, you see, is too sore."

There once was a couple named Kelly,
Who were found stuck belly to belly;
It seems in their haste, they used
    library paste
Instead of petroleum jelly.

A lady of doubtful nativity,
Had a rear of such sensitivity,
She could sit on the lap
Of any Nazi or Jap,
And determine Fifth Column activity.

There was a young fellow named Clyde,
Who fell in a shit house and died;
He had a young brother, who fell in
    another,
Now they're "in-turred" side-by-side.

There was a young man from from Bianca,
Who had syph, pox and a shanker;
He got the whole four from the same
    bloody whore,
And he wrote her a postcard to thank her

There was a young man from Austrailia,
Who painted his ass like a dahlia;
The likeness was there, and the color
    was fair,
But the oder was absolute failure.

There once was a hermit named Dave,
Who kept a dead _____,
He said, "I'll admit,
She smells worse than s___,
But look at the money I save.
(continued on next page)

There was a young lady from Dover,
Who lay on her back in the clover.
She said, "I don't give a damn
If I don't have a man,
Here Rover."

There was a young girl from Nantucket,
Who went to hell in a bucket.
But when she got there,
They asked for the fare,
She took out her t__ and said, "Suck it".

NOTE: *The last verse, below, was written by the infamous Air Force balladeer, John Piowaty of Destin, Florida, who made many contributions to the Editor's collection.*

There once was a man named Boris,
Who collected stone clitoris.
He said with a grin,
"I prefer them of flint,
Though sandstone is soft and more
    porous."

(00) SIX POUNDS OF BOOBIES (*See TT13*)

(18) SIXTEEN TIMES
(Tune: *Sixteen Tons*)

NOTES: *This could have been called,* **The 26th Fighter's Lament.** *It is a great fighter pilot's song and a fine example of military parodies. The Editor believes the best military songs are those about specific units and people. You know these are written with first-hand experience and emotion.*

SIXTEEN TIMES

Some people say a man is made out of
    fear,
But a fighter pilot's made out of
    whiskey and beer--
Whiskey and beer, rum and rye,
If you fly the Dot, you're sure to spin
    in.

CHORUS (*repeat after each verse*)

    You fly sixteen times, what'd you
        get?
    Another day older and your weapon
        is bent.
    Colonel Donalson don't you call me,
        I'm weak and lame,
    I lost my ass in a poker game.

I awoke one morning when the sun didn't
    shine,
Got my chute and went down to the line;
Down to the line to fly the "D,"
But it was raining so hard I couldn't
    see.

I scrambled one morning with blood in
    my eye,
I'd had my fill of Overholt Rye--
Shot sixteen holes in a T-33,
They're going to hand my ass from a
    coconut tree.

When you see me comin' better break to
    the right,
'Cause the 26th Fighter had a party
    last night--
My eyeballs are red and I'm mean as a
    bear,
Believe me SAMAP better clear the air.

(19) SOLIDARITY SONG - US TACAIR EASTER
(Tune: *The Ballad of the Green Beret*)

NOTE: *This song post-dates the Vietnam War and is one of numerous songs in Volume II written in a more recent era of the Air Force. Although the background of this song was not available in the source song book, the words suggest it was written during the times of troubles with Iran. Also see* the **Ayatollah Song,** *AA22.*

SOLIDARITY SONG

East Coast flyers in the sky,
Persian pukes, prepare to die.
Marine, TACAIR, Navy too, and U. S. Air
    Force
Have gifts for you.
(*continued on next page*)

Ayatollah, check your six,
TACAIR'S here, and we are pissed.
Our bombs are armed, our missiles too,
With an Easter treat for you.

One minaret is now afire,
See the smoke, it's getting higher.
Rolling in, with snake and nape,
Allah creates, but we cremate.

U. S. TACAIR, we are the best,
See the wings upon our chests.
Swept-winged fighters, through and
    through.
With an Easter gift for you (Everybody
    flip the bird!)

(20) SONG OF THE FORTY-NINERS
(Tune: *Clementine*)
 Lyrics: *Ralph L. Royce*

NOTES: *The Editor realized that some of
you San Francisco fans will be disappointed that this song is NOT about your
team.   Colonel Horace S. Levy, who submitted this song, says, "The 49th
Fighter Group was the first organized
unit to depart the U. S. for combat duty
after Pearl Harbor.   After a brief
training period in Australia, in which
the assigned pilots--bomber trained
originally--were converted to fighter
jocks flying P-40s, the squadrons were
deployed to Darwin, Australia, where
they turned back the Japanese advance.
Some of the top and best known aces of
World War II served with the 49th;*

Major Richard I. Bong (40)
1st Lt. George E. Preddy (25.8)
Lt. Col. Gerald R. Johnson (22)
1st Lt. James Hagerstrom (14.5)
1st Lt. John D. Landers (14.5)
Capt. Robert DeHaven (14)
Capt. James A. Watkins (12)
PLUS 37 other aces, 5-10 victories

*"The 49th Fighter Group was the first to
enter the Phillipines and Japan, and to
continue in Korea and Vietnam.   It is
still on the active list."   The composer, Major General Ralph L. Royce was*
*an Air Corps pioneer, and one of the
early participants in the Pacific air
war.*

SONG OF THE FORTY-NINERS

Uncle Sam, he had an Air Force,
But he had to have some more;
So he formed the FORTY-NINERS,
And he sent them off to war.

Out of 'Frisco sailed the transport,
Wives and sweethearts left behind;
FORTY-NINERS off to battle,
Dreadful sorry, wife o'mine.

In Austrailia, girls were pining,
For their men were overseas;
Then along came the FORTY-NINERS,
And the girls were put at ease.

Over Darwin came the Zeros,
And the bombers formed in Vs;
Then they met the FORTY-NINERS,
Dreadful sorry, Nipponese.

Sick of Darwin, the mosquitoes,
Lack of beer and lousy chow;
Mac, remember, the FORTY-NINERS,
We've been up here too long now.

(21) SOUTH OF THE NAVEL
(Tune: *South of the Border*)

NOTE: *Another unheeded warning from the
       Doc!*

South of the navel, down testicle way;
That's where the battle's won when my
    big gun comes into play.
The doctor's have warned me, that I
    mustn't stray,
South of the navel, down testicle way.

CHORUS

    Now she smiled as she kissed my
      banana,
    Never dreaming that I was farting;
    And I smiled as she kissed my banana,
    For my banana never came.

(*continued on next page*)

South of the navel, down testicle way;
That's where I got the bug, as on the
    rug I had my lay.
No more shall I wander, no more shall I
    stray,
South of the navel, down testicle way.

(22) SPANISH GUITAR
(Tune: *Spanish Guitar*)

Oh, the first port of call it was Aden,
    Aden,
Where the girls wouldn't screw, but we
    made 'em, made 'em.

CHORUS (*repeat after each verse*)

    Three dollars you pay, for a bang up
        each way,
    And a tune on a Spanish Guitar, plink
        plink, plink.
    Singing hi-ziggy-ziggy, fuck a little
        piggy sideways.
    Swish-swish.
    My idea of a woman is a big fat whore
    Shit bang, fuck stick.
    Three dollars you pay, for a bang up
        each way,
    And a tune on a Spanish Guitar, plink
        plink, plink.

Oh, the next port of call was Boston,
    Boston.
Where the girls wouldn't screw, but we
    forced 'em, forced 'em.

Oh, the next port of call it was Malta,
    Malta.
Where the girls wouldn't, but ought'a,
    ought'a.

Oh, the next port of call it was Suwon,
    Suwon.
Where the girls they would do it for two
    won, two won.

(23) SPRINGTIME AT DUCHI
(Tune: *Springtime In The Rockies*)

When it's springtime at Duchi Base,
And the Aggressors come out to play,
And the contrails run in circles,
Fighter pilots earn their pay.
We'll hold our triggers steady,
When our sights are zeroed in;
We'll hold our glasses ready,
When they pass out the rum and gin.

When it's springtime at Duchi Base,
And the napalm is in bloom,
And your Vulcan's do the talking,
And it's just a MIG and you.
Once again you'll hear whisper,
That my fuel is running low;
When it's springtime at Duchi Base,
Then it's time for us to go.

(24) SQUADRONS ALL
(Tune: *Grenadier Guards*)
    Lyrics: *Aviation Cadet J. E. Kennard*

NOTE: *This song and the one following
are products of the Boca Raton, Florida
Army Air Forces Technical Training
Center--World War II. These were submitted by John E. Kennard, who wrote
this song, and who made these interesting comments as a page in Air Corps
history. "At one point in '44 at Lowry
Field, there were about ten thousand (a
guess) disenfranchised cadets--some
wearing wings, even Navy gold wings--who
had completed multi-engine transition,
but to no avail. Their creativity in
composing songs and doggerel personi-
fying their frustrations with the old
Air Corps/Army Air Force's policies as
to who deserved to pilot, navigate and
bombardier the Nation's aircraft--was,
indeed, startling. And they roared
their defiance in fixed cadence, reverb-
erating against the Denver skyline;
deathless prose lost in space."*
(Editor's note: But not lost to poster-
ity--as of now!). *Soooo, the Editor
dedicates the next two songs to those
ex-cadets who were denied the opportuni-*

(continued on next page)

ties to fly as pilots, bombardiers and navigators. The Editor does recommend singing, **I Wanted Wings** *Volume I, song I29). John also submitted other songs including the a tribute to the nonflying members of the Air Force,* **The Vital Difference,** *later in this volume.*

SQUADRONS ALL

Above the gleaming towers
We see the bombers roar,
And we hear the call of bugles
Re-echo down the shore.
With one ideal before us,
And one ideal alone,
We join a mighty chorus,
The men of Boca Raton.

CHORUS

Before the war's great heroes
Have heard the battles roar,
The men who must precede them
Are the Army Air Corps.

To the squadrons of the Air Corps,
We chant our song anew,
To men of fight and daring
We'll keep our pledges true.
To all the men before us,
We raise our voices high,
In never ending chorus
We praise them to the sky.

CHORUS

Of all this war's great heroes
Who've heard the battle roar,
The men who do surpass them
Are the Army Air Corps.

(25) SQUADRON D
(Tune: *McNamara's Band*)

NOTE: *Another product of the Army Air Force's Technical Training Command (see* **Squadrons All,** *above). This ditty is not a direct derivative of* **Boys From Old B Flight** *(Volume I, song B50, and its several variations), but they are closely related. All are sung to the same tune and have similar themes. In*

some respects, the version below can be called a parody of parodies. It also immortalizes a *Major Wise.*

SQUADRON D

Oh, you've heard of all the squadrons'
    boys,
That run from A to Z,
But here's the one that tops them all,
It's good old Squadron D.

Oh, remember too the generals
From Hannibal to Lee,
But here's some boys who'll stop them
    'em all,
The boys from Squadron D.

CHORUS

Oh, the drums go bang, the cymbals
    clang, the horns they blow away,
As Squadron D we'll lead the field
    as we go on our way.
Oh, singing and marching we'll blaze
    a trail that ne'er forgot shall be
A credit to the Air Corps--is good
    old Squadron D.

HUM THE REMAINDER OF THE CHORUS

We're men of wit and men of charm,
And really rugged guys,
But that is only natural,
We're under Major Wise.

We can march and sing to anything,
We really are the best.
We stand alone at Boca Raton,
We'll pass the acid test.

REPEAT CHORUS

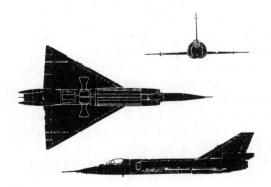

(26) STOP KICKING MY FUF AROUND
(Tune: *Unavailable*)

CHORUS (*repeat after each verse*)

Oh, every time I go to town,
The boys keep kicking my FUF*
   around.
Makes no difference if he is a clown,
They gotta stop kicking my FUF
   around.

He's been up there for a thousand hours,
In VFR and thundershowers,
But he still doesn't know his shit,
Say a little prayer for the guys in his
   pit.

He's changing squawks and cranking mils,
Here we go, "Look out for those hills!"
With his head up his ass and locked up
   tight,
His presence is felt all thru the night.

* NOTE: *Unofficial Air Force acronymn
meaning,* Fellow Up Front, *OR* Fuck-Up
Front. *Of course, the official Air
Force terminology for this position is*
ASO, Airplane Systems Operator (*From* **Kun
Songs By The Sea,** *Kunsan Air Base,
Korea*).

(27) STRAFE THE TOWN - I
(Tune: *Wake Up The Town*)

NOTE: *This is one of the songs from the
Vietnam War unlike most military parodies in the collection. (also see*
Chocolate-Covered Napalm, *Volume I, song
C9; and* **Strafing The Town,** *immediately
following below). It represents a song
of frustration and tragic soul-searching
by a warrior who knows he kills women
and children as well as enemy soldiers--
a condition in every war. Yet, Vietnam
was different, because sometimes those
innocent women and children were used by
the North Vietnamese and Viet Cong as
soldiers to kill Americans. But which
ones? And from the air, who is to know?
This is a song written by an unknown*
warrior who is saying, "Fellows,
fighting wars is not always a heroic
thing, but a dirty business that kills
women and children. We can write our
macho songs about our heroic deeds, but
someone has to write about those poor
people on both sides who died for no
reason at all." Now maybe the composer
of this song didn't have those exact
words in mind, but you can make your own
determination.

STRAFE THE TOWN - I

Strafe the town and kill the people;
Lay your high drags in the square.
Roll in early Sunday morning;
Catch them while they're still at prayer

Drop some candy to the orphans;
Watch them as they gather 'round.
Use your 20 millimeter;
Mow the little bastards down.

See the fat old pregnant women
Running thru the field in fear;
Run your 20 mike mike thru them,
Hope the film comes our real clear.

Strafe the town and kill the people;
Hit them with your poison gas.
See them throwing up their breakfast
As you make your second pass.

(28) STRAFE THE TOWN - II
(Tune: *Wake Up The Town*)

NOTE: *This song is similar to* **Strafe The
Town** *- I, above, but only in sentiment
and tune. The words are different, but
may have been inspired by the other--or
vice versa. They both come from different song books.*

STRAFE THE TOWN - II

Strafe the town and kill the people,
It's the only thing to do.
Set your gunsights residential,
You'll get more kills if you do.

(*continued on next page*)

Drop the naplam in the schoolyard,
See the children run and shout.
Note the mass hysteria,
As they try to put it out.

Drop your snakeyes in the temple;
See the zippers in the blast.
Watch them trample one another,
As they try to save their ass.

Shoot your zunis at the sanpan;
Pull up quick to miss the fire,
BABY WON'T YOU LIGHT MY FIRE!

(29) STRAFING IN A MOUNTAIN PASS
(Tune: *Unavailable*)

Strafing in a mountain pass,
Couldn't make the turn.
Twelve tons of Thunderjet,
Watch that fucker burn.

We've fought the MIGs at Kunuri,
We fought at Sinajee.
They nailed us down at Kyomipo,
And we lost quite a few.

We flew these birds from old K-2,
Six thousand feet they say.
Don't ask a 49er boys,
The fuckers are all dead.

(30) THE STUDENT AVIATOR
(Tune: *Unavailable*)

NOTE: *This is the third of the WW I poems/songs from the 1919 book, **Buddy Ballads**. The story of this student aviator must sound a little familiar to John Kennard who wrote of the trials and tribulations of some WW II Aviation Cadets who went to flying school but never got to fly (See the Notes with song SS22, above). From one war to another, the airman's thoughts were often the same in song. In this case, the life of **The Student Aviator** of WW I was not too different from that of the cadets in early WW II, in that they were taught many Army skills of little use in the air.*

THE STUDENT AVIATOR

They gave me Army tactics,
They filled me full of math.
They taught me how to build a trench,
And march along a path.
I had a course in rifle fire,
(Which isn't used in air)
They drilled me on the bayonet
'Till I had skill to spare.

I learned to take a plane apart
And set it up again;
I studied motor theory
For weeks and weeks, and then
When I looked forward hopefully
To zooming through the sky,
They said I must't flip, because
I hadn't learned to fly.

So it was school at Kelly Field,
And Mineola, too,
And then they shipped me over here
And hope sprung up anew;
But what I got was school again,
They forced me to endure
A three months' course at Issoudum
Which followed one at Tours.

For eighteen months of dreary work,
The same, unending round
They've fitted me to aviate
But kept me on the ground.
I joined to drive a chasse[1] plane
And know war's greatest thrill
But what I got was drill and books
And I am at it still.

It's well enough to ground a man
Completely, at the start,
But wherefore keep him on the ground
Until you break his heart?
I've studied 'till the war is done,
I've hoped and dreamed, but I
Am sure I'll never drive a bus[2]
'Till I'm too old to fly.

[1] **Chasse** *is an almost archaic form for* chase, *but since it is French in origin, and our WW I song writers were in France, it is not unusual to find such words in American songs, as with the next note, below.*

(*continued on next page*)

2 *The term* **bus** *was common in WW I for an aeroplane. It is probably British in origin, and will be found in many of the 36 Royal Air Force WW I songs in Vol. I.*

(31) SUPER HOG RECALL
(Tune: *Battle Hymn of the Republic*)

NOTE: *Air National Guard units have been under-represented in this collection-- that is until the Editor received the* **Song Book of the Old Dominion Fighter Squadron,** *149th Tactical Fighter Squadron, 192nd Tactical Fighter Group, Virginia Air National Guard (thanks to Wally Fey). This ballad, the one to follow, and several others in Volume II, represent the finest in Air Force parodies. This one in particular exposes the some-time feeling by Guardsmen that they may be treated as second-class citizens--at least as far as equipment is concerned.*

SUPER HOG RECALL

Oh, they finally stopped conceding
To Nikita and his boys;
They substituted Super Hogs
For diplomatic poise.
Yes, they called upon the Air Guard
WITH THEIR OBSOLESCENT TOYS --
Send the raggedy-ass militia to the
    fray.

Oh, we'll fly the North Atlantic
Just as Lindbergh did before,
Provided we get airborne
In this ground-lovin' whore.
The water's cold, the cockpit hot,
And our ass so Goddamn sore --
Send the raggedy-ass militia to the
    fray.

Oh, we'll pack a bag, kick the tire,
Give the map a glance;
Just a navigation flight
To an unknown part of France.
When the Paris dollies get the word,
Down will come their pants --
Send the raggedy-ass militia to the
    fray.

Oh, the MIG has got the altitude,
Turning rate and mach,
But nothing can compare with
The Super Hog's fancy clock,
And when you point her nose down,
She falls just like a rock --
Send the raggedy-ass militia to the
    fray.

Oh, the armament on an 84
Is a boon to the infantry troop,
The cameras in the RF
Make it the super snoop;
But what use is a fighter
That flames out in the soup --
Send the raggedy-ass militia to the
    fray.

(32) SUPER HOG REFRAIN
(Tune: *Manana*)

My altitude is falling,
And my pucker string is tight,
The engine fuel pump's busted,
Oh, I'll not be home tonight.

CHORUS

    Republic, Republic, the Super Hog's
    The airplane for me;
    Republic, Republic, Long Island's
    Pig iron foundary.

The Super Hog is great for those
Who've grown too old to fly,
It's the oldest fighter
That leaps off into the sky.

She loves to eat up runway
Ten thousand feet you'll need.
Just pull the gear up early,
To get up flying speed.

REPEAT CHORUS

Draw 'round and hear the story
Of a fighter pilot's plight;
He jumped into a Super Hog,
Checked out on his first flight.

(*continued on next page*)

He flew the traffic pattern
At low airspeed and fell;

He's filling out his flight log now,
With all his friends in Hell.

REPEAT CHORUS

So all you fighter pilots,
Who are blessed with this 'ole whore,
Just never mind and you will find
Experience in store.

She moans and groans and climbs real
   slow,
And truly loves the ground;
But if you want to make her fly,
Just point her nose straight down.

REPEAT CHORUS

(33) SWEETHEART OF ????
(Tune: *The Sweetheart of Sigma Chi*)

NOTE: *This is not the original title of
the song, but none was provided and the*
*Editor had to improvise. According to
Jack Havener, who submitted this song,
"One of our gunners was a college grad
and used to sing this parody." The way
things are today--particularly in the
San Francisco area where the Editor
lives--one doesn't know whether this
song is being sung by a man or woman!
Ah, for the good old days and Viva la
difference!*

SWEETHEART OF ????

I want to be wed
And carried to bed,
In the arms of the man I love.

I want the door to be locked,
And the key to be lost,
And the night to be seven years long.

I want the lights to be dim,
And the clothes to be thin,
If there are any clothes at all.

I want to place in his hands,
All that true love demands,
Oh, my God! How I love my man!

Douglas A-1H

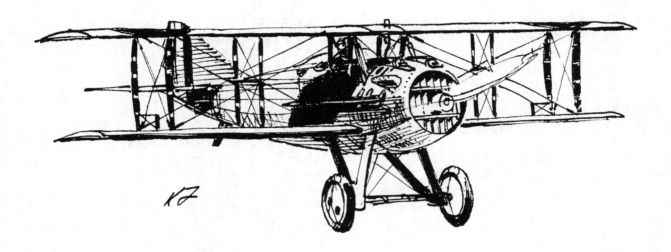

SPAD 13

FLIGHT SECTION TT

(01) TAEGU GIRLS
(Tune: *Unavailable*)

We are from Taegu, Taegu are we.
We don't believe in virginity--oh, horse
  shit!
We don't use candles, we use broom
  handles.
We are the Taegu girls.

And every night at twelve on the clock,
We watch the white man piss on the ROK.
We like the way he handles his cock;
We are the Taegu girls.

And every year at our annual dance,
We go around without any pants.
We like to give those pilots a chance,
We are the Taegu, talk about your Taegu,
  we are the Taegu girls.

(02) TALKING BLUES
(Tune: *Casey Jones*)

NOTE: *This ditty comes from the 11th
Bomb Group (B-17s) in the Solomon
Islands as reported in the book,* **The
Saga of the Seventh** *(Air Force). This
is respectfully dedicated to the veterans of the 11th Bomb Group--even if they
did fly B-17s! (the Editor flew B-24s).
For those copilots who are upset by this
song's last verse, the Editor suggests
that you see Volume I, song C27.*

TALKING BLUES

Back in Oahu in '42,
Eager beavers me and you.
Guadalcanal--'43
Reluctant dragons, you and me.

Espiritu Santo, Fiji and all.
We're behind it--the big 8-ball.

Lizards, flies, mosquitoes, too,
Corned beef hash and G.I. stew.

Eight hundred miles out to sea,
Started to sweat that Number 3;
That goes out, we come down,
Nothing but ocean all around.

F-105 THUNDERCHIEF

Here I sit, tear in my eye,
Tired of living, too young to die,
Going to Auckland pretty soon,
Get me a woman--howl at the moon.

Striking force out to sea,
Sighted transport--him or me?
We make our run, AA got rough,
On the way home, Zeroes got tough.

(*continued on next page*)

Pilots can fly, gunners can gun,
Bombardiers busy during the run.
Navigator's got a gun--he shoots, too.
Damn co-pilot's got nothing to do.

(00) TALL GRASS (See II16)

(03) TCHEPONE
(Tune: *"The Strawberry Roan" from the Marty Robbin's albums, "Gunfighter Ballads and Trail Songs".*
Lyrics: *Lt. Colonel W. F.* Toby *Hughes*

NOTE: *The version below is the original submitted by the composer, Toby Hughes, and corrects the version in Volume I. This ballad, together with Toby's* **Armed Recce**, *also in this Volume, are two of the finest combat stories in song of any war. Toby also wrote the lyrics to* **One Hundred Sixty VC In The Open** *that is in Volume I (030). Of* **Tchepone**, *Toby said, "Years ago, the small village of Tchepone ceased to exist except as a military encampment. . . Strategically located at a major junction astride the Ho Chi Minh Trail, the town had long ago been taken over by the North Vietnamese, who used the village as a barracks, storage, and staging area. There were also quite a a large number of AA guns on the hills around Tchepone . . . if you didn't know it, it took just one mission to learn.* **Tchepone** *is about a fictitious jock sent by a fictitious colonel on a fictitious mission. The part about the ground fire is fact. We who conducted the research can attest to that!" Toby dedicated this song to his friends of the 557th Tactical Fighter Squadron, the* **Sharkbaits**, *of 1967-68.*

TCHEPONE

I was hangin' 'round Ops, just spendin'
  my time,
Off of the schedule, not earnin' a dime.
A colonel comes up and he says, "I
  suppose
You fly a fighter, from the cut of your
  clothes."

He figures me right, "I'm a good one,"
  I say.
"Do you happen to have me a target
  today?"
Says, "Yes," he does, "A real easy one.
No sweat, my boy, it's an old-time milk
  run."

I gets all excited and asks where it's
  at,
He gives me a wink and a tip of his hat.
"It's three-fifty miles to the northwest
  of home,
A small, peaceful hamlet that's known as
  Tchepone."
(Ah, you'll sure love Tchepone.)

I go get my g-suit and strap on my gun,
Helmet and gloves, out the door on the
  run.
Fire up my Phantom and take to the air;
Two's tucked in tight and we haven't a
  care.

In forty-five minutes we're over the
  town;
From twenty-eight thousand we're
  screamin' on down;
Arm up the switches and dial in the
  mills;
Rack up the wings and roll in for the
  kill.

We feel a bit sorry for folks down
  below,
Of destruction that's coming, they
  surely don't know.
But the thought passes quickly, we know
  a war's on,
And on down we scream toward peaceful
  Tchepone.
(Unsuspecting, peaceful, Tchepone.)

Release altitude, and the pipper's not
  right.
I'll press just a little and lay 'em in
  tight.
I pickle those beauties at two-point-
  five grand,
Startin' my pull when it all hits the
  fan.

(*continued on next page*)

A black puff in front and then two off
  the right,
Then six or eight more and I suck it up
  tight.
There's small arms and tracers and heavy
  ack-ack;
It's scattered-to-broken with all kinds
  of flak.

I jink hard to left and head out for the
  blue;
My wingman says, "Lead! They're
  shooting at you!"
"No bull!" I cry as I point it toward
  home;
Still comes the fire from the town of
  Tchepone.
(Dirty, deadly, Tchepone.)

I make it back home with six holes in
  my bird.
With the colonel who sent me, I'd sure
  like a word.
But he's nowhere around, though I look
  near and far;
He's gone back to Seventh to help run
  the war.

I've been 'round this country for many
  a day;
I've seen the things that they're
  throwin' my way.
I know that there's places I don't like
  to go,
Down in the Delta and in Tally-Ho.

But I'll bet all my flight pay the jock
  ain't been born,
Who can keep all his cool when he's
  over Tchepone.
(Oh, don't go to Tchepone.)

(00) TELL US ANOTHER (*See SS17*)

(04) TEN DAYS OF TET PLUS TWO (*See TT26*)

(05) THEM DOODLE DASHERS
  (Tune: *Unavailable*)

NOTE: *This strange ditty is one of three
similar songs (see* **Them Toad Suckers** *and*

Them Moose Goosers) *that came from the
famous 8th Tactical Fighter Wing's Stag
Bar Edition song book.*

THEM DOODLE DASHERS

How about the doodle dashers?
Ain't they jewels?
Jumpin' out of bushes
Wavin' they tools.

Jumpin' out of palm trees,
Jumpin' out of shrubs,
Leapin' out of flower beds,
Wavin' they nubs.

Look at them doodle dashers,
Ain't they queer?
Flaggin' they talleywhacker,
Then disappear.

Them ever-lovin' doodle dashers,
Ain't they pearls?
Wavin' they doodle knobs,
At them girls.

How to be a doodle dasher,
Well, you don't need a ticket;
Get your doodle handy,
Jump from a thicket.

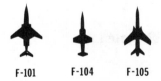

F-101   F-104   F-105

(00) THAT LITTLE BALL OF YARN (*See BB11*)

(06) THAT MAY BE SO
  (Tune: *Available*)

NOTE: *Another one of those little,
strange ditties that pop up from time-
to-time in song books. This is very
similar to the song of the same name in
Volume I, song T14, but with one
different line. As George Coen--the
source of this latest contribution--says
regarding the song in Volume I, "The
true, the blushful Hippocrene is:"*

(continued on next page)

THAT MAY BE SO

It may be so, I don't know,
It sounds so mighty queer.
So tell your jokes, to other folks,
'Cause your bull-shit don't go here.

(06) THEM MOOSE GOOSERS
(Tune: *Unavailable*)

NOTE: *This is the second of the three, related songs mentioned in the note with the song,* **The Doodle Dashers,** *above. Also see,* **Them Toad Suckers** *to follow. These are the classical, nonsensical kind of songs that make complete sense in the O-club, airmen's club, or just the bar, after about five drinks (it only takes a fighter pilot one drink).*

THEM MOOSE GOOSERS

How about them moose goosers?
Ain't they recluse?
Up in them boondocks,
Goosin' them moose.

Goosin' them huge moose,
Goosin' them tiny,
Goosin' them mother goose
In they heine.

Look at them moose goosers.
Ain't they dumb?
Some use an unbrella,
Some use a thumb.

Them obtuse moose goosers,
Sneakin' thru the woods.
Pokin' them snoozy moose
In they goods.

How to be a moose gooser?
It'll turn you puce.
Get your gooser loose,
And rouse a drowsy moose.

(08) THEM TOAD SUCKERS
(Tune: *Unavailable*)

NOTE: *As promised. Here is the third of those crazy, funny, little ditties that* make *about as much sense as an outside loop in a B-52. But who is to argue with the stalwarts of the 8th Tactical Fighter Wing? See* **Them Doodle Dashers** *and* **Them Moose Goosers** *above.*

THEM TOAD SUCKERS

How about them toad suckers,
Ain't they hogs?
Sittin' there sucking
Them green toady frogs.

Suckin' them hop toads,
Suckin' them chunkers,
Suckin' them leafy types.
Suckin' them plunkers.

Look at them toad suckers,
Way down south.
Stickin' them sucky toads
In they mouth.

How to be a toad sucker?
No way to duck it.
Get yourself a toad,
Rare back and suck it.

(09) THERE ARE NO FIGHTER PILOTS DOWN IN HELL
(Tune: *She'll Be Comin' 'Round The Mountain*)

Alternate Titles and Variations:
(*See Volume I, song F9*)

    (a) *Fighter Pilots*
    (b) *Fighter Pilots Lament*
    (c) *No Fighter Pilots Down In Hell*

NOTE: *This is one of the Editor's favorite songs, a sentiment apparently shared by many AF types--judging by the number of song books in which it appears. Volume I contains the basic song, a product of World War II, and the several variations that appeared during the Korean and Vietnam wars. Listed below are two additional verses that appeared in the song book of the 527th Squadron's*

(continued on next page)

Aggressor's Song Book, *a contribution by Captain Jeffrey Jiffy Jeff Jeffries, USAF, and the first post-Vietnam verses in the collection.*

ADDITIONAL VERSES

Oh, there are no fighter pilots up in
    wing,
Oh, there are no fighter pilots up in
    wing,
The place is full of brass,
Sitting 'round on their fat ass,
Oh, there are no fighter pilots up in
    wing.

Oh, there are no fighter pilots in
    F-fifteens,
Oh, there are no fighter pilots in
    F-fifteens,
Drive their Eagles through the blue,
    Just like Bongo-52s,
Oh, there are no fighter pilots in
    F-fifteens.

NOTE: *The next two verses are not new, but in the Volume I versions of these verses, there are prompts where you are suppose to add your unit's number as in, "Oh, look at the (unit number) in the club". The Aggressors went one better, so the Editor included these two verses. The grammatical error in the last line of the second verse was retained as it may have been intentional.*

ADDITIONAL VERSES

Oh, look at the Eagle pilots in the club
Oh, look at the Eagle pilots in the club
They don't party, they don't sing,
The Aggressors do everything,
Oh, look at the Eagle pilots in the club

When an Eagle jock walks into our club,
When an Eagle jock walks into our club,
He don't drink his share of suds,
All he does is flub his dub,
Oh, there is no fighter pilots down in
    Hell.

**(10) THERE ARE NO MISSILEMEN
        DOWN IN HELL (M)**
(Tune: *She'll Be Comin' Round The
        Mountain*)
    Lyrics: *Rollie Stoneman*

NOTE: *One of the all-time greats of Air Force parodies has been updated to the era of the missiles. The next rendition will probably be,* **There Are No Shuttle Crews Down In Hell,** *followed by ???? At any rate, the missilemen did not want to be outsung by the flyboys of SAC, and this is there version of the Air Force classic. Note the SAC flyboy version that follows, song TT11.*

THERE ARE NO MISSILEMEN DOWN IN HELL

There are no missilemen down in Hell.
There are no missilemen down in Hell.
There are hippie agitators,
And a dozen navigators,
But there are no missilemen down in hell

The crew commander's life is just a
    farce.
The crew commander's life is just a
    farce.
The Change-In-Status isn't on,
He's reading Penthouse on the john,
Oh, the crew commander's life is just
    a farce.

The deputy thinks he has lots of class.
The deputy thinks he has lots of class.
On the gravy train he rides,
When there's work to do he hides,
And you'll always find him sitting on
    his . . . chair.

The flight commander thinks he is first
    rate.
The flight commander thinks he is first
    rate.
Oh, he thinks he's bright and perky,
But he's really just a turkey,
But to himself he thinks he is first
    rate.

The site cook really is a dope.
The site cook really is a dope.

(continued on next page)

But never tell him that he's dumb,
If you do you'll have to run,
When you find your dinner tasting just
    like soap.

The SAT troops are the worst by far.
The SAT troops are the worst by far.
They're always driving into town,
Chasing women all around,
And they often make their LF checks
    from bars.

Instructor crews are always in the dark.
Instructor crews are always in the dark.
It's perfection that they seek,
With new procedures every week,
Oh, instructor crews are always in the
    dark.

The Standboard weenies think they are so
    fair.
The Standboard weenies think they are so
    fair.
They say, "That checkride sure was weak,
We'll see you at the formal critique."
You can tell them by their palms all
    covered with hair.

There are no missilemen down in Hell.
There are no missilemen down in Hell.
They just flunked their ORI, and they're
    too damn scared to die,
Oh, there are no missilemen down in Hell

(11) THERE ARE NO SAC CREWMEN
DOWN IN HELL
(Tune: *She'll Be Comin' 'Round
        The Mountain*)

NOTE: *Another case where the flyboys and
missilemen of SAC share a great, old Air
Force parody. Compare with the song
above, TT10.*

THERE ARE NO SAC CREWMEN DOWN IN HELL

There are no SAC crew members down in
    Hell,
There are no SAC crew members down in
    Hell.
Oh, the place has racketeers, and
    civilians drinking beer,
There are no SAC crew members down in
    Hell.

Our Wing Staff thinks that they are just
    the most.
Our Wing Staff thinks that they are just
    the most.
All they do is make up tests, 'till they
    think they are the best,
And the color of their noses looks like
    toast.

A bomber pilot's life is just a farce.
A bomber pilot's life is just a farce.
The automatic pilot's on, he's reading
    novels in the john,
The bomber pilot's life is just a farce.

Our ECM man never does no work.
Our ECM man never does no work.
Goes to sleep in the climb, don't even
    know the time.
He ain't nothin' but a spot-from-Otis
    jerk.

Our Radar thinks he is a VIP.
Our Radar thinks he is a VIP.
On the gravy train he rides, when
    there's work to do he hides,
We always wake him up at the IP.

Our navigator is always in the dark.
Our navigator is always in the dark.
He's suppose to shoot the stars, but
    he always uses VORs,
Our navigator's always in the dark.

Our gunner is the worse one of the bunch
Our gunner is the worse one of the bunch
He is always found in town, chasing
    girlies all around,
And he always has a case of beer for
    lunch.

(*continued on next page*)

There are no SAC crew members down in
   Hell.
There are no SAC crew members down in
   Hell.
They just flunk their ORIs, and they're
   too damn scarred to die.
There are no SAC crew members down in
   Hell.

(00) THERE WAS A YOUNG MAN (*See SS17*)

(12) THESE FOOLISH THINGS
(Tune: *These Foolish Things Remind
      Me of You*)

Alternate Titles and Variations:

   (a) *Those Foolish Things*

<u>NOTE</u>: *There is a close relationship
between this song and the one immediately following,* **These Things Remind Me
of You.** *They are completely different
in words, but the same in theme and
melody.*

THESE FOOLISH THINGS

A book of sex with fifty well-thumbed
   pages,
An old French letter that has been used
   for ages,
Abortions quite a few,
These foolish things, remind me of you.

Remember dear, that we talked of
   marriage,
That was the night you had your first
   miscarriage.
Abortions quite a few,
These foolish things, remind me of you.

CHORUS

   I came, you came, all over me,
   And in our ecstasy we simply knew
      that it had to be.

The newsboys calling out, "Late night
   final,"
The faint aroma of a gents urinal,

Oh, how the memory clings,
These foolish things, remind me of you.

The limp inertness of a used French
   letter,
That I discarded when I knew you better
A bed of creaking springs,
These foolish things, remind me of you.

REPEAT CHORUS

The lumpy sofa that we had our shags on,
The smell that told me that you had your
   rags on;
Oh, how the memory clings,
These foolish things, remind me of you.

(13) THESE THINGS REMIND ME OF YOU
(Tune: *These Foolish Things Remind Me
      of You*)

Alternate Titles and Variations:

   (a) *A Two-Ton Titty*
   (b) *Six Pounds of Boobies*

<u>NOTE</u>: *There is a marked similarity
between this song and the preceeding
song,* **These Foolish Things.**

THESE THINGS REMIND ME OF YOU

Ten pounds of titty in a loose brassiere
A twat that twitches like a moose's ear
Ejaculations in my glass of beer;
These foolish things remind me of you.

A naked photograph of Liberace,
The way you softly whisper, "Suck-a-
   hatchi,"
Syphlytic scars that make your face so
   blotchy;
These foolish things remind me of you.

A pubic hair in my breakfast roll,
The smelly odor of your pungent hole,
The way you wrap your thighs around my
   pole;
These foolish things remind me of you.

(*continued on next page*)

A dirty whore strolling down the street,
A bloody Kotex in the rumbleseat,
I love my poontang but I beat my meat;
These foolish things remind me of you.

(14) THEY CALLED THE BASTARD STEPHENS
(Tune: *They Called The Wind Maria*)

A maid sat in a mountain glen,
Seducing herself with a fountain pen,
The capsule broke, the ink ran wild,
And she gave birth to a blue-black
    child.

And they called the bastard, Stephens,
And they called the bastard, Stephens,
And they called the bastard, Stephens,
'Cause he was a blue-black child.
No matter how nor where nor when,
Use Stephen's Ink in your fountain pen.

(00) THE THINKER (or TINKER) See *DE12*

(00) THOSE FOOLISH THINGS (*See TT12*)

(15) THREE OLD MAIDS
(Tune: *See Note*)

Alternate Titles and Variations:
    (*In Volume I, T31*)

  (a) *Three Old Maids*
  (b) *Three Old Maids In A Lavatory*

NOTE: *The Editor has the musical score to this ditty. It also seems to lend itself to,* **Oh, Dear, What Can The Matter Be?**

THREE OLD MAIDS

CHORUS (*repeat after each verse*)

  Oh, dear, what can the matter be,
  Three old maids were locked in the
    lavatory,
  They were there from Monday to
    Saturday,
  Nobody knew they were there.

This first lady's name was Elizabeth
    Bender,
She was the Bishop of Chichester's
    daughter,
Who went to get rid of some old virgin
    water,
And nobody knew she was there.

The second lady's name was Elizabeth
    Humphery,
Who went for a pee and could not get
    her bum free.
She said, "Oh dear, this is really
    quite comfy,"
Nobody knew she was there.

The third lady's name was Elizabeth
    Bender,
Who went to adjust a broken suspender,
And got it mixed up with her feminine
    gender,
And nobody knew she was there.

ALTERNATE VERSES

The second old maid, her name was Miss
    Porter,
She went in to pass some superflous
    water,
The water got deeper than water should
    orter,
And nobody knew she was there.

The third old maid, her name was Miss
    Powell,
She went in to clear a stopped bowel.
The bowel it cleared in a manner most
    foul,
And everyone knew she was there.

(16) THREE OLD MAIDS FROM BOSTON
        (Tune: *Available*)

Alternate Titles and Variations:

  (a) *Three Old Whores*
  (b) *Three Whores From Canada Junction*

NOTE: *The Editor has taken the liberty of combining three different versions*

(continued on next page)

spanning the time from World War II to post-Vietnam (1980). It is interesting that some songwriters seem to be fascinated with the size of the female vaginal opening as evidenced in this song and in another of similar theme, **Dark And Dreamy Eyes** and referenced briefly in **Bang, Bang Lulu**, both in this Volume.

THREE OLD MAIDS FROM BOSTON

Three old maids from Boston,
Were drunk on cherry wine.
The topic of conversation,
Was, "Yours is no bigger than mine."

NOTE: *You can substitute,* "Three whores walked down from Canada Junction" *in the first line--although this changes the meter, and perhaps the melody?????*

CHORUS (repeat after each verse)

Roly poly tickle my holey,
Slippery, slimy slew.
Rub your nuts across my guts,
I'm one of the whorey crew.

The first old maid, she ups and says,
"Why mine's as big as the air.
Planes fly in, and planes fly out,
And never touch a hair."

The second old maid she ups and says,
"Why mine's as big as the sea.
The ships sail in, the ships sail out,
And never bother me."

The third old maid she ups and says,
"Why mine's as big as the moon.
A pilot went in in January,
And didn't come out 'til June."

ALTERNATE VERSES

The second old whore up and said,
"Mine's as big as a well.
A farm boy slipped on the edge one day,
And never knew he fell."

The third old whore got up and said,
Man, you're all talking balls!
'Cause when I have my periods,
It's like Niagara Falls!

F-4   F-5

(17) THROW A NICKEL ON THE GRASS
(Tune: *Throw A Nickel On The Drum*)

Alternate Titles and Variations
(*from Volume I, beginning page F-6 unless otherwise noted*):

(a) *A Doggie Pilot's Lament (below)*
(b) *Cruising Down The Yalu*
(c) *Cruising Over Hanoi*
(d) *Fighter Pilot's Hymn*
(e) *Hallelujah - I*
(f) *Hallelujah - II (below)*
(g) *I Was Headed Down The Runway*
(h) *Mayday! Mayday! Mayday!*
(i) *Rollin' Down The Runway*
(j) *The Sabre Song*
(k) *Save A Fighter Pilot's Ass (below)*
(l) *Save A Fighter Pilot's Life*

NOTE: *The first version below of this most popular of Air Force songs is almost an identical version to* **Save A Fighter Pilot's Life - II**, *Volume I, page F-9. That is a Korean War version, and the Editor decided to include this Vietnam War version despite its close resemblance. Another great example of how these great songs migrate from war to war. Let's hope the migration is over. I'll buy that! (better not say that at the bar). The second version below,* **A Doggie Pilot's Lament**, *is a post-Vietnam version and a confirmation that the traditions live one. The third rendition is a true, original gem from the S.E.A. air show. And the fourth version, below, is unique;* **Save A Fighter Pilot's Ass**. *Why? Read on.*

THROW A NICKEL ON THE GRASS

It was midnight in old Udon Thani,
All the pilots were asleep,
When up stepped Colonel _____,
And this is what he said;
"Phantoms, gentle Phantoms, Phantoms,
   one and all.

(*continued on next page*)

Pilots, gentle pilots, and all the
   pilot's balls."
When up stepped a young lieutenant,
With a voice as bold as brass,
"You can take those Goddamn Phantoms,
   and shove them up your ass!"

CHORUS (*repeat after each verse*)

   Oh, hallelujah, hallelujah, throw a
      nickel on the grass
   Save a fighter pilot's ass.
   Oh, halleluhjah, hallelujah, throw a
      nickel on the grass and you'll be
      saved.

I was cruising down the Mekong, doing
   six and twenty per,
There came a call from the major, "Oh,
   won't you save me, sir?
My guns ain't got no ammo, my tanks
   ain't got no gas,
Mayday, mayday, mayday, I got six MIGs
   on my ass!"

I shot my traffic pattern, to me it
   looked all right.
The airspeed read 130, my God I racked
   it tight.
The airframe gave a shudder, the engine
   gave a wheez,
"Mayday, mayday, mayday, spin instructions please."

Fouled up my crosswind landing, my left
   wing hit the ground.
There came a call from the tower, "Pull
   up and go around."
I racked that Phantom in the air, a
   dozen feet or more,
The engine quit, I almost shit, the
   gear came through the floor.

I was split-S on my bomb run, and got
   too Goddamm low,
I pressed that bloody button, and I let
   those babies go;
Sucked the stick back fast as blazes
   and hit a high-speed stall,
Now I won't see my mother when the
   works all done next Fall.

They sent me up to Hanoi, the brief
   said no ack-ack.

But by the time I got there, my wings
   were holed by flak.
My aircraft coughed and shuddered, it
   was too cut up to fly,
"Mayday, mayday, mayday, I'm too young
   to die."

I bailed out from my Phantom, my landing
   turned out fine.
With my E and E equipment, I made for
   our front line.
When I opened up my ration, to see what
   was in it,
My God! the Quartermaster had filled the
   thing with shit!

Now in this Commie prison camp, I am
   obliged to sit,
For one cannot go very far on a ration
   of shit.
If I am ever free again, I will no
   longer fly,
But I'll have the Quartermaster's balls
   for breakfast 'till I die.

Tu-20

(OO) A DOGGIE PILOT'S LAMENT
(Tune: *Throw A Nickel On The Grass*)

A'rollin' down the runway, with after-
   burner in,
Looked at my aft fire-warning light,
As yellow as all sin.
I yanked back on the throttle,
I wished I'd gone DNIF.
The runway's almost gone.

CHORUS (*repeat after each verse*)

   Oh, hallelujah, sing hallelujah,
   Throw a sixpence on the grass,
   Save a doggie pilot's ass.
   Oh, hallelujah, sing hallelujah,
   Throw a sixpence on the grass and
      you'll be saved.

(*continued on next page*)

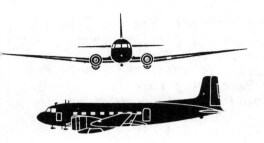

I shoved the throttle forward,
And pulled back on the stick,
And staggered off into the air, as if
    the dog was sick.
The weather closed around me,
No more was the nest seen,
So there I sit, ten tons of shit,
And a five-inch TV screen.

I soon made angels forty,
And leveled off all right.
I looked up all around me,
Not a single thing in sight.
Looked back down at the radar,
And told my friends, "No luck."
Said to myself, this is a Hell-of-a-way
    to make a buck.

They gave me a new vector, one-twenty
    to the right,
And when I rolled out level,
That bogie was in sight.
I squeezed the trigger then and there,
And then I thought, you goon!
You've gone and fired all twenty-four
    of rockets at the moon.

I turned back to the station,
And began to let down.
They'd briefed, "About one thousand
    you'd
Start to see the ground."
My dog's now on the overrun,
With gear up through the wing,
'Cause all the way down GCA,
I never saw a thing!

The moral to this story is very plain
    to see,
The best damn squadron on the base
    belongs to the 95th.
The two FITS are hopeless,
They can't get in the air,
And all the rest have buggered off,
And scattered everywhere.

(OO) HALLELUJAH - III
(Tune: *Throw A Nickel On The Grass*)

<u>NOTE:</u> *Another S.E.A. version of this popular ballad (See Volume I). Also another outstanding example of the military parody that names people, aircraft and actual combat conditions.*

HALLELUJAH - III

It was midnight in Thailand,
All the aircrews were in bed,
When up stepped Colonel Seaver,
And this is what he said.
"Pilots, gentle navs, fighter pilots
    all,
Switchblades, gentle Switchblades,"
And all the pilots shouted, "Balls!"
When up stepped a young PWSO with a
    voice as harsh as brass.
"You can take those Goddamn Aaardvark
    jets,
And shove them up your ass!"

CHORUS (*repeat after each verse*)

    Oh, hallelujah, hallelujah, throw a
        nickel on the grass
    Save a fighter pilot's ass.
    Oh, hallelujah, hallelujah, throw a
        nickel on the grass
    And you'll be saved.

Up and down Mu Gia
I know the route by rote.
The airplane's at two-hundred feet,
My balls are in my throat.
The eighty-fives go flashing by,
They're bursting all around.
Don't make no fucking difference,
I'll probably hit the ground.

I crossed the ridge at Xuan Son,
My airspeed it was high.
I looked out of the window,
A seagull passed me by.
The seagull gave a grunt and shit,
The engine gave a wheeze,
"Mayday, mayday, mayday,
SOF's instructions please."

(*continued on next page*)

I flashed across the target,
My bombs they did not go.
I looked at my right seater,
He said, "Fuck, I don't know!"
I racked her hard up to the left,
And straight ahead we flew.
I cursed General Dynamics,
And fucking Elmer's glue.

We cycled all our switches,
Reset my reference light,
The gator jumped into the scope,
He swore with all his might.
I did a hard one-eighty,
To try and save the mission.
The WSO threw his hands up high,
We don't have a prediction.

I flew my traffic pattern,
To me it looked all right.
My airspeed read one-fifty,
My God I racked it tight.
The airframe gave a shudder,
The engines gave a wheeze,
"Mayday, mayday, mayday,
Spin instructions, please."

I flew my cross-wind landing,
My left wing hit the ground.
I heard a call from mobile,
"Pull up and go around."
I yanked that Switchblade in the air,
A dozen feet or more.
The engines quit, I almost shit,
The gear came through the floor.

We got the bird back to the ramp,
Or what was left of it.
The crew chief took one look at it,
My God I thought he'd shit!
I'll never fly Switchblades again,
This flight will be my last.
I checked tomorrow's schedule,
I'm set to double blast.

(OO) SAVE A FIGHTER PILOT'S ASS
(Tune: *Throw A Nickel On The Drum*)

NOTE: *This is a product of the Korean War, but more important, it can be called an* **Anti-Fighter Pilot Hymn,** *one of the few songs in the collection that takes on the pilots and reminds them*

they wouldn't be off into the wild blue yonder if it wasn't for the ground crew; in this case the Air Base Group. Perhaps the title of this song should have been, **Air Base Group Lament.** *A great song honoring a great bunch of people.*

SAVE A FIGHTER PILOT'S ASS

Pilots, gentle pilots, pilots one and
    all,
Fly boys, flashy fly boys, please listen
    to our call,
Buzz boys, busy buzz boys, this is all
    we ask,
Take those goddamn Sabre Jets and shove
    them up your ass!

CHORUS (*repeat after each verse*)

    Sing hallelujah, sing hallelujah,
    Stick your finger up your ass,
    Join the fighter pilot's class.
    Sing hallelujah, sing hallelujah,
    Stick your finger up your ass
    And flap your wings.

Who feeds the sons of bitches, and
    clothes their scrawny backs?
Who guards their goddamn airplanes, and
    heats their fucking shacks?
Who gives them light and water, not
    Kimpo Power and Gas?
If they don't like the service, they can
    blow it out their ass!

TDY to Tsuiki went the Sabre Dance,
Saw a Sukoshi pilot get in a Josan's
    pants,
It cost him thirty dollars for just a
    little feel,
Along came an Air Base Group man who
    got it for a steal.

Jet jocks are the hot shots, we'll tell
    you one and all,
And when it comes to shooting, they're
    really on the ball.
They had a little contest to prove who
    was the first,
But when the score was counted, they
    ended up the worst.

(*continued on next page*)

You see these flashy jet boys, climb
from their shiny hacks,
With moon suits and silly jock straps
a'hangin' from their backs.
They sing the praise of Sammy Small with
wild and side acclaim,
Just fighter pilots--pilots, without a
fucking brain.

They spin their yarns of the air way, by
pilots brave and fair,
Eighty percent is bullshit, and twenty
more is air.
We hear that they're by far the best and
that we'd better believe,
But where in the Hell would the fly boys
be,
If the Air Base Group should leave?

The squawk box screams of flak holes and
tanks all out of gas,
Of takusan MIGs and bandits a'playin' on
thier ass.
They git their bloomin' balls shot off,
but still they brag of it,
With one accord we'll tell the world,
THEY CAN'T FLY FOR SHIT!

(00) THE THUD (*See BB19*)

(18) THE THUD DRIVER'S THEME
(Tune: *The Whiffenpoof Song*)

Alternate Titles and Variations:

(a) *Whiffenpoof -S.E.A. Version*

NOTE: *This is a terrific parody from the 35th Tactical Fighter Wing's song book, Phan Rang Air Force Base, South Vietnam, 1969. Written by fighter jocks--with feeling.*

THE THUD DRIVERS THEME

From a hootch in Southeast Asia,
To the place where aces dwell,
To the strip club down at 'Zuke
We knew so well;
Sing the fighter jocks assembled,
With their glasses raised on high,
Sing they poorly, not too clearly,
Loud as well.

We will throw our glasses wildly
And throw our bombs as well,
And the finks at Two AD can go to Hell!

REFRAIN

We are poor fighter jocks who have lost
our way,
HELP--HELP--HELP.
We flew to the town of Hanoi today,
HELP--HELP--HELP.
Steely-eyed pilots up in the blue,
Lead got zapped by an SA-2,
Let's haul ass of they'll zap us, too,
A_____ B_____now!!!

NOTE: *An alternate Refrain from the 347th Tactical Fighter Wing goes as follows:*

We are poor Switchblade crews
Who have lost our way,
Help, help, help.
We TFRed in Pack One they say,
Help, help, help.
Steely-eyed jocks, down in the black,
TFR won't let us come back.
Let's haul ass and dodge the flak.
A_____ B_____now!!!

(19) THUNDERBOLT SONG
(Tune: *Yankee Doodle Dandy*)

NOTE: *This WW-II gem was originally contributed by Lt. R. J. Liebfarth, 352nd Fighter Group, and is part of the collection sent to the Editor by G. P. Harry down in Florida. It's a dandy.*

(continued on next page)

THUNDERBOLT SONG

We're the snafu's of the squadron,
Snafus through and through are we.
Real live pilots, by the Grace of God,
Off on a drunken spree.

In our auger 47s,
We're as proud as we can be.
From thirty-thousand to the deck,
Peel off from the our squadron,
We're in compressibility.

(20) TIDDLY
(Tune: *Unavailable*)

NOTE: *Another* intellectual *song that
requires you to provide the missing
words. Should you have difficulty
(usually after the fifth drink), DON'T
call the Editor!*

TIDDLY

Tiddly had a chicken,
Tiddly had a duck,
She put them on the table,
To see if they could ____.

CHORUS (*repeat after the verses with
the missing words*)

  Bang, bang Tiddly,
  Tiddly bang, bang,
  Who's going to bang Tiddly,
  When Johnny goes away?

Tiddly had a boyfriend,
His name was Diamond Dick.
She never got the diamonds,
She always got the ____.

Tiddly had a baby,
His name was Tiny Tim.
She put him in the river,
To see if he could swim.

Timmy burped and gargled,
And headed for the falls.
Tiddly reached and grabbed him,
She grabbed him by the ____.

Rich women use Kotex,
Poor women use rags,
Tiddly's crack is so damn big,
She uses burlap bags.

Rich girls wear rings of gold,
Poor girls wear rings of brass.
The only ring that Tiddly has,
Is the one around her ____.

Rich girls drive a Porsche,
Poor girls drive a truck.
The only time Tiddly rides,
Is when she wants to ____.

(21) TIE MY PECKER AROUND (TO) A TREE
      (Tune: *Chisolm Trail*)

Alternate Title and Variation:

  (a) *Gonna Tie My Pecker To A Tree*
  (b) *Tie My Root Around A Tree*

NOTE: *You will be able to easily date
this immortal ballad by the cost of the
services mentioned in the song. It is
a sad tale (tail?) that warns of the
wages of sin. During WW-II there was a
famous saying,* **A Slip Of The Lips Can
Sink A Ship.** *This ditty and several
others in Volume II suggest another
saying,* **A Slip Of The Zipper Can Sink A
Prick.** *The Editor doesn't believe this
latter saying will soon be engraved in
the stone of posterity (and for you
fighter jocks, that last word does not
refer to your ass!). Stay with the
program!*

TIE MY PECKER AROUND A TREE

Reached in my pocket, pulled out a
  penny,
She said, "Boy, you can't have any."

CHORUS (*repeat after each verse*)

  Come and tie my root around a tree,
   'round a tree,
  Come and tie my root around a tree.

(*continued on next page*)

Reached in my pocket, pulled out a
    nickel,
She said, "For that you don't even get
    a tickle."

Reached in my pocket, pulled out a dime,
She said, "Young man, you're wasting
    your time."

Reached in my pocket, pulled out a
    quarter,
She said, "Young man, I'm a preacher's
    daughter."

Reached in my pocket, pulled out a half,
She said, "Young man, you make me
    laugh."

Reached in my pocket, pulled out six
    bits,
All she did was wriggle her tits.

Reached in my pocket, pulled out a buck,
She said, "Young man, you've bought a
    fuck."

Took her to the kitchen, laid her on the
    sink,
Oh, my God, how her pussy did stink.

Fucked her sittin', fucked her lyin',
If I'd had wings, I'd a fucked her
    flyin'.

I awoke in the morning, and guess what
    I saw,
Fifteen chancers and a big blue ball.

I went to the doctor, 'cause my pecker
    was sore,
"My God," said the doctor, "you've been
    taken by a whore."

And now you can see, I'm a peckerless
    man,
I fuck 'em with my finger and fool 'em
    when I can.

Now the last time I saw her, and I
    haven't seen her since,
She was jacking off a doggie through a
    barbed-wire fence.

(22) TOASTS TO ROAST
(*No Tune*)

NOTE: *These are not songs, although
some clever jock may find a tune to
them. There are seven different toasts.
It is up to you to find the occasion.*

TOAST 1

Here's to the girl in the high-heeled
    shoes.
She'll take your money and drink your
    booze.
She'll hug you and kiss you and say
    she's your lover,
Then she'll go home and sleep with her
    mother.

TOAST 2

Here's to the girl with bright blue eyes
And the patch of hair between her thighs
She's got no dick but that's no sin,
She's got a damn fine place to put one
    in.

TOAST 3

I drink to your health when we're
    together,
I drink to your health when I'm alone.
I drink to your health so Goddamn often,
I'm rapidly loosing my own.

TOAST 4

Here's to you and here's to me.
May we never disagree.
But if we do, fuck you,
And here's to me.

TOAST 5

May all your friends forsake you,
And corns grow on your feet;
And crabs as big as cockroaches
Crawl on your balls and eat.

(*continued on next page*)

And when your old and gray,
And just a syphilated wreck,
I hope your head falls through your ass,
And breaks your fucking neck.

TOAST 6

NOTE: *The Editor is going to give you a more serious toast, one that his mother taught him when he was a young teenager, before joining the Air Force. Now don't go asking why his mother would teach him a toast to a girl at an age when he wasn't even drinking--but then, you didn't know his mother! (a beautiful lady). Anyway, in later years, the Editor found this a very effective line while in the Air Corps (Force et al). Now it joins history, although in some pretty seamy company! This is spoken to a wife or girlfriend, over candlelight and champagne. Try it, she'll like it.*

Here is to you with a face that would stop a clock. *PAUSE (there will be a slow burn rising in her cheeks).* Holding the glass up and looking into her eyes, then say;

You are so fair, that even Time stops to linger there.

WARNING: *Timing is everything. If you pause to long, you may end up with a broken head. No Purple Hearts!*

TOAST 7 (*A Pilot's Toast*)

May all your skies be blue,
And the wind on your tail.

B-1   **B-58A**

(23) TOGETHER
(Tune: *Together*)

We both got drunk, together.
Took off our junk, together.
Lay in a bunk, together,
But it was no joke,
When the rubber broke.

Now we have twins, together.
For we have sinned, together.
Now trade it from me,
Keep good company,
And keep both your legs, together.

(24) TROOP SHIP LEAVING BOMBAY
      (Tune: *Original*)

Alternate Titles & Variations:
(*In Volume I unless indicated otherwise*)

   (a) *Bless 'Em All*
   (b) *Fortress Leaving Calais*
   (c) *Lancaster Leaving The Ruhr (Below)*
   (d) *Love They Neighbor*
   (e) *Mustang Pilot's Song (See below)*
   (f) *Prang 'Em All*
   (g) *Tiptanks & Tailpipes*

NOTE: *This favorite of American and British soldiers in several wars is contained in Volume I (B33) in several versions. However, the Editor discovered that the original version presented in Volume I is not accurate. Therefore, the correct original is presented below. The Editor DOES like accuracy. Two additional variants of this popular song came into the collection and will be found below. The first is from the Royal Canadian Air Force via ex RCAF Bill Siler (and ex-457th and 25th U. S Bomb Groups). The second version below,* **Mustang Pilot's Song,** *is of particular interest to the Editor, an ex-P-51 (and B-24) refugee.*

TROOP SHIP LEAVING BOMBAY

They say there's a troop ship leaving
   Bombay,
Bound for old Blimey's shore.
'Evenly laiden with time-expired men,
Bound for the land they adore.
There's many a man who has served out
   his time,
And many a boot signing on,
But there'll be no promotion,
This side of the ocean,
So cheer up my lads, bless 'em all.

(*continued on next page*)

Bless 'em all, bless 'em all,
The long and the short and the tall,
Bless all the Sergeants and Double-U-Oh
    ones,
Bless all the corporals and their
    blinking sons,
For were saying goodbye to them all,
The long and the short and the tall,
There'll be no promotion,
This side of the ocean,
So cheer up my lads, bless 'em all.

(00) LANCASTER LEAVING THE RUHR
(Tune: *Bless 'Em All*)

They say there's a Lancaster leaving the
    Ruhr,
Bound for old Blighty's shores.
Heavily laden with terrified men,
Shit-scared and prone on the floor.
There's many a flak gun shooting them
    down,
There's many a night fighter, too,
But there'll be no promotions,
This side of the ocean,
So, cheer up my lads, fuck 'em all.

CHORUS

    Fuck 'em all, fuck 'em all
    The long and the short and the tall.
    Fuck all the sergeants and WO-1s
    Fuck all the corporals and their
        bastard sons,
    For we are saying goodbye to them all
    The long and the short and the tall.
    There'll be no promotions
    This side of the ocean,
    So, cheer up my lads, fuck 'em all.

(00) MUSTANG PILOT'S SONG
(Tune: *Bless 'Em All*)

Now they say there's a convoy leaves New
    York tonight,
Bound for Old England they say.
Heavily laden with browned-off young
    men,
Bound for the land they "adore."

Now they all know their Mustangs are
    keen as can be,

To catch a Focke-Wolf in their sights.
They're experts at moaning and bitching
    and groaning,
When everything's going all right.

REFRAIN

Bless 'em all, bless 'em all,
The needle , the airspeed, the ball.
They sent us to solo and left us to die,
And if ever your fighter should stall,
You're in for one helluva fall,
No lillies and violets for dead fighter
    pilots,
So cheer up my lads, bless 'em all.

Bless all the harness that fastens us
    in,
Bless all the radio's ear-splitting din.
So we'll loop and we'll roll and we'll
    dive,
'Til we are more dead than alive,
No future in flying, unless you like
    dying,
So cheer up my lads, bless 'em all.

 F-15   F-111a

(25) TROOP TRANSPORT SONG
(Tune: *Casey Jones*)

NOTE: *Originally contributed to the
source song book by a Captain Edwards,
but to the Editor by G. P. Harry.*

TROOP TRANSPORT SONG

The props are turning, but God knows
    why,
Let's get this baby up in the sky.
The wind's on our tail and the cowling
    is loose,
There's a big green light,
Let's give her the goose.

Off we go, singn' down the runway,
Off we go, shoving her the coal.
Off we go, pull her off at sixty,
We're dragging a fence,
And a telegraph pole.

(*continued on next page*)

Got our nose pointed down the road,
There's a bowl-legged donkey with a
    helluva load.
We don't give a damn for we are hot,
If we bend a prop,
We will wear the pot.

Here we come, following the contours;
Here we come, kicking up the sand.
Here we come, buzzing down the runway,
On our way,
To the Promised Land.

(00) 'TWAS A COLD WINTER EVENING
(See Volume I, song C16)

(26) TWELVE DAYS OF TET
(Tune: *Twelve Days of Christmas*)

Alternate Titles and Variations:
(See Volume I, page T-18)

    (a) *Ten Days of TET Plus Two*
    (b) *Twelve Days of Christmas*
    (c) *Twelve Days of Combat*
    (d) *Twelve Nights of Bonehead (TT24)*

NOTE: *A product of the Vietnam War.
Another version from S.E.A titled,*
Twelve Days of Combat, *will be found in
Volume I, song T51. A Marine Air Corps
rendition from Vietnam (via the Air
Force) is included below,* **Ten Days of
TET Plus Two.**

TWELVE DAYS OF TET

On the first day of "TET,"
My D. O. gave to me,
A gun on a Phantom F-4C.

2nd - 2 CBUs
3rd - 3 rocket launchers
4th - 4 high drags
5th - 5 hand grenades
6th - 6 Side Winders
7th - 7 750s
8th - 8 charging Sparrows
9th - 9 nasty napes
10th - 10 tons of bombs
11th - 11 Lady Fingers
12th - 12 Firecrackers

(00) TEN DAYS OF TET PLUS TWO
(Tune: *Twelve Days of Christmas*)

On the first day of TET my Marine gave
    to me,
A hand job in a CV.

2nd day - 2 brass bars
3rd day - 3 ugly BAMS
4th day - 4 blown tires
5th day - 5 days in hack
6th day - 6 days of duty
7th day - 7 O' dark thirties
8th day - 8 smelly skivies
9th day - 9 gooks a'gunning
10th day - 10 TPQs
11th day - 11 AOMs
12th day - 12 drippy dicks

AB-47G2

(27) TWELVE NIGHTS OF BONEHEAD
(Tune: *Twelve Days of Christmas*)

NOTE: *There is both a clean version of
the* **Twelve Days of Christmas,** *in Vol. I,
song T50, and this x-rated jobbie below,
which also goes under the same name as
well as the* **Bonehead** *title used here.*

TWELVE NIGHTS OF BONEHEAD

On the first day of Christmas,
My true love gave to me;
A hand job in a pear tree.

On the second day of Christmas,
My true love gave to me;
Two brass balls and a hand job in a
    pear tree.

3rd day - Three French ticklers
4th day - Four cocksuckers
5th day - Five mother-fuckers
6th day - Six sacks of shit
7th day - Seven scrotums swinging
8th day - Eight assholes aching
9th day - Nine nymphos nibbling
10th day - Ten tits a-tingling
11th day - Eleven lesbians licking
12th day - Twelve twats a-twitching

FLIGHT SECTION UV

(00) UP IN THE AIR JUNIOR BIRDMEN
(See II17)

(01) THE VICTOR ALERT SONG
(Tune: *A Few of My Favorite Things*)

NOTE: *There is a great deal of cynicism in the lyrics to this song, written in Kunsan, Korea, probably after the conflict in Vietnam.*

THE VICTOR ALERT SONG

Reading our porno, picking our asses,
Checking the forms out, and passing our
   gases,
Silver-sleek B-61 strapped below, nuclear
   war,
And we're ready to go.

OOMPH PA PA ... OOMPH PA PA ...

Departing the orbit, our pits start to
   sweat,
We'll asshole those Ruskies, and that's
   a sure bet.
Killing those fuckers and covering them
   with dirt,
That's why we like sitting Victor Alert.

OOMPH PA PA ... OOMPH PA PA ...

Fagots and Frescos, and Fishbeds and
   Farmers,
Goas and gainfuls, and big Goddamn
   bombers,
Tubrick and Cheesbrick, and Quad 23
Just thinking of it scares the shit out
   of me.

OOMPH PA PA ... OOMPH PA PA ...

When the Colonels ping,
When my Phantom's broke,
When I'm feeling sad,

I think of that glorious white mushroom
   cloud,
And then I don't feel so bad.

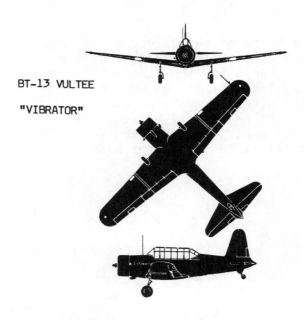

BT-13 VULTEE

"VIBRATOR"

(02) THE VITAL DIFFERENCE
(Tune: *Unavailable*)

NOTE: *This short ditty expresses the same sentiment contained in Bob Crawford's 1943 copyrighted song,* **Mechs of the Air Corps.** *See Volume I (M7). Bob, of course, wrote the official* **Air Corps (Force)** *song. This song originally appeared in the* Airmail *section of the December 1982 edition of* **Air Force** *magazine. John Kennard was responding to an article that had appeared in the October issue, and included the words to this song. He doesn't know the title--nor*

(continued on next page)

the tune--but his letter was headlined by the magazine as, **The Vital Difference,** *alluding to the importance of the ground crews as well as the flying crews in making a success of the Air Force mission. True. So the Editor decided to name the song,* **The Vital Difference** *as a tribute to the non-flying members of the Air Force team. John says this was a song that they used to sing while marching along at the* **Boca Raton Technical Training Center.** *Try singing it to* **The Battle Hymn of the Republic.**

THE VITAL DIFFERENCE

You've heard of the pilots so daring,
As they gracefully soar through the air.
If it weren't for the men in the hangar
They wouldn't be flying up there!
So here's to the men who maintain them,
The Oilers and Grease Monkeys, too--
If a thing has two wings and an engine,
We'll fix it to fly in the blue!

(03) VIT MEIN HAND ON MEIN SELF
(Tune: *Unavailable*)

VIT MEIN HAND ON MEIN SELF

Vit mein hand on mein self,
Vas ist das here?
Das ist mein think-boxer, my momma bear.
Think-boxer, inky, dinky, do.
Dat's vat ve learn in da school!

Vit mein hand on mein self,
Vas ist das here?
Das ist mein ein-blinker, my momma dear.
Ein-blinker, thin-boxer, inky, dinky, do
Dat's vat ve learn in da school!

REPEAT USING:

    Schnatt-locker
    Bull-shitter
    Milk-shaker (high voiced)
    Stink-boxer
    Trouble-maker
    Knee-bender
    Ass-kicker

McDonnell F4J (Navy)

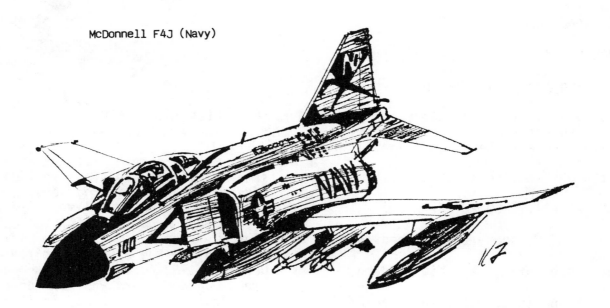

FLIGHT SECTION WW

(00) WALTZ ME AROUND AGAIN, WILLY
   (*See SS17*)

(01) WAND'RIN' MAN
(Tune: *Original music and words by former Air Force Major Joe Tuso*)

NOTE: *Joe Tuso wrote this in Southeast Asia in 1968. Later he was an Associate Professor of History at the Air Force Academy. Under the auspices of the* **Folklore Forum,** *Joe published a song book titled,* **Folksongs of the American Fighter Pilot In Southeast Asia, 1967 - 1968.** *All 33 songs in Joe's book will be found in Volumes I & II. This song is a beautifully told story of the lonliness of the fighting man, and his searching questions about the love he left behind. The story is the same in every war--at least in battle one can fight the enemy, but lonliness for your loved one is the worst enemy of all.*

WAND'RIN' MAN

When I am weary and can't get no rest,
I long for my baby, the one I love best,
She knows what I'm missin', she knows
   what I lack,
She knows I'm a wand'rin' man, but I
   always come back.

It's been such a long time since I've
   seen her smile,
The sights are the same now, I hate
   every mile.
Will I ever find her? Will she wait for
   me?
Can she love a wand'rin' man that fights
   to be free?

The days are too long, that old sun
   doesn't shine,

How is my baby, is she doin' fine?
I'm so lost without her, I must find her
   soon,
Their highways and byways will lead me
   to ruin.

A-10A WARTHOG

There is no moon out, the stars are all
   dim,
Where is my baby, does she dream of him?
Does she think I'm lost now, does she
   think we're through?
Does she need somebody else so she
   won't feel blue?

It's been such a long time since I've
   seen her smile,
The sights are the same now, I hate
   every mile,
Will I ever find her? Will she wait
   for me?
Can she love a wand'rin' man that fights
   to be free?

(00) THE WARTHOG DRIVER (*See BB21*)

(03) WAS IT YOU WHO DID THE PUSH'N?
(*See HH15*)

F-102   A-7

(04) THE WASP NATIONAL ANTHEM
(Tune: *Bell Bottom Trousers*)

Alternate Titles and Variations:
(*Volume I, Page G-12*)

   (a) *G Suits and Parachutes*
   (b) *Zoot Suits and Parachutes*

NOTE: *This is the only song of the* **Women Airforce Service Pilots (WASPs)** *in the collection. However, the original lyrics did not fit the title, so the Editor took some literary license and changed a line or two. You'll never guess. The Editor remembers his first encounter with* **WASPs.** *He was a new, 19-year old second lieutenant that had just checked out in B-24s at Smyrna, Tennesee. He was so* hot *nothing could touch him--flying those big planes. One morning a new, sleek (?) B-24 landed, being ferried to the base. It was a* greased *landing, and a smart taxi to the flight line. The engines were cut, and out pops two very feminine pilots--* **WASPs.** *Now a B-24 is no Sunday driving roadster. It's more like a truck as any B-17 pilot will tell you. But those two lady drivers handled the* big rig *like a roadster. From that day the Editor never had any question about the abilities of the female sex. He also lost a full hat size.*

THE WASP NATIONAL ANTHEM

Before I was a member of the AAFTD,
I used to be a working girl in
   Washington, D.C.
My bosses were unkind to me, they
   worked me night and day.
I always had the time to work, but never
   time to play.

CHORUS (*repeat after each verse*)

   Singing Zoot suits, parachutes and
     wings of silver too,
   She'll ferry planes like her daddy
     used to do.

Along came a pilot a-ferrying a plane,
He asked me to go flying down in Lover's
   Lane.
And I like a silly fool, and thinking it
   no harm,
Jumped into the cockpit to keep the
   pilot warm.

Early in the morning, before the break
   of day,
He handed me a snorter bill*, these
   words to me did say,
"Now take this my darling for all the
   harm I've done;
You may have a daughter, you may have
   a son.
Now if you have a daughter, just teach
   her how to fly,
Put her in the WASPs, and get the
   bastard in the sky.

Now the moral of this story, as you can
   plainly see,
Is never trust a pilot an inch above
   your knee.
He'll kiss you, caress you, and promise
   to be true,
And have a girl on every field as pilots
   always do.

(05) THE WEASEL-BEARS' PICNIC
(Tune: *Unavailable*)

NOTE: **Bear** *is a reference to the Elec-* **tronic Systems Officer** *in a two-seat fighter like the* **Phantom II,** *but in this case, the* F-105F, *two-seat version of the one-seat F-105D* **Thunderchief** *or just plain,* **Thud.** *However, there is some disagreement among the troops. In Vietnam Vet and Academician Joe Tuso's song book,* **Folklore Forum,** *he calls* **bear** *an "affectionate term for an aircraft." However, the Editor is inclined to*

(*continued on next page*)

accept the ESO as being the true bear. In this song, **Weasel** (or **Wild Weasel**) is a reference to the F-105G, also called **Iron Hands** after the program to equip the Thud to detect and hit hostile **SAM** sites. The basic difference between the F-105F and G was the addition of an ECM pod on the lower side of the fuselage, and four **Shrike** or two standard **ARM** anti-radar missiles. The F-105G was affectionately called **Wild Weasel**. Also see the song **Wild Weasel**, Volume I, W30. The term **BUF** in the last stanza means, **Big Ugly Fucker**, the fighter pilot's name for the B-52.

THE WEASEL-BEARS' PICNIC

If you go up into the sky today,
You will go alone.
If you go into a dive today,
No bear will screech or moan;
For every bear that ever there was
Is on the ground for certain because
Today's the day the Weasel-Bears have
    their picnic.
They'll all sit around the pool today
And steadily bitch and moan.

This lack of action in the skys,
They barely can condone.
Assistant fighter pilots are they,
They feel like a horse whose put to hay.
Today's the day the Weasel-Bears' have
    their picnic.

Just put us back into the Thud they say,
And our souls will be content.
Just put us into the skys to play,
A night BUF will pay the rent.
Please leave us no more down on the
    ground,
'Cause in the pool we almost did drown,
Today's the day the Weasel-Bears' have
    their picnic.

(06) THE WEATHERMEN'S LAMENT
    (Tune: *McNamara's Band*)

NOTE: *Don Hyde, who submitted this little ditty, had this to say. "I don't remember all of the words anymore, or whether (weather) there was more than*

one verse, but it was one of the songs we sang marching to class in weather school." The original title is unknown.

THE WEATHERMEN'S LAMENT

I'll never forget the weather was wet,
The general wanted to fly.
He said, "My boy is it O.K. for me to
    go on high?"
When I said, "No," it's going to snow,"
You should have seen him frown.
Say, I'm the only guy whose ever
Kept the general down!

We are the men,
The weather men,
We may be wrong,
Oh, now and then,
But when you see
The planes on high,
Just remember, we're the ones
Who let them fly.

(07) WE WERE THERE
(Tune: *The Marine Hymn*)

NOTE: *For those of you that believe interservice rivalry is something that developed recently, this WW-II era song should give you food for thought. It was all in fun, and just to prove that everyone was and is a friend, the Editor included some songs in Volume II from the song book of VMFA 312,* **The Checkerboard** *squadron of the Marines, Southeast Asia. Fighter pilots all, although the Marines did sing in a slightly higher voice.*

WE WERE THERE

From the shores of Eniwetok,
To the slopes of Tapachau.
We have fought our country's battles,
And we'll fight again right now.
Oh, the Army, Navy, Air Corps,
All were present at the scene.
But the guys that got the credit were,
The United States Marines.

(continued on next page)

From the rockbound coast of Garapan,
To Charon Kanoyas Mill,
The Marines just barely took a beach,
And by God they'd be there still.
But they sent an Air Corps unit in,
To stop those Banzai screams;
For we were the secret weapon of,
The United States Marines!

From the fogs above the channel,
To high o'er the mountain snows.
We have fought our country's battle,
We have shot down all our foes.
If the Army, Navy and Marines,
Ever gain to Heaven's shores,
They will find the angels sleeping there
With the Army's GR-EAT AIR CORPS.

(08) WE'VE BEEN WORKING ON THE RAILROAD
　　　(Southeast Asia Version)
　　　(Tune: *I've Been Working On The
　　　　　Railroad*)

We've been working on the railroad,
Every fucking day.
We've been working on the railroad,
Up Thai Nguyen way.

Uncle Ho ain't got no railroad,
No rolling stock or switches,
But Seventh frags us on the railroad,
Those dirty sons-of-bitches.

SAMs galore, 57s too,
Eighty-fives will scragg your old yazoo!
Fuck, shit, hate, shit-hot too.
So what the Hell is new?

Someone's up a tree on Thud Ridge,
Someone's in the drink I know o-o-o-o,
Someone's in the Karst near Hoa Lac,
Shouting on the radio.

Shouting, fee, fi, fiddly-i-o,
Fee, fi, fiddly-i-oh, oh, oh, oh.
Fee, fi, Jolly Green Oh,
Only 99 more to go.

(00) THE WHEEL (*See BB24*)

(09) WHEN YOU ARE OLD
　　　(Tune: *Tom Lehrer*)

NOTE: *This is a song that will be
enjoyed most by those of the same era as
the Editor (WW-II). Young jocks may not
be thinking about these things these
days--or are they? Vicki hasn't complained. And who in the Hell is Tom
Lehrer?*

WHEN YOU ARE OLD - TOM LEHRER

An awful liability,
Lessened utility,
Loss of mobility,
A strong possibility.
In all probability,
I'll lose my virility,
And you your fertility
And desirability,
And this liability
Of total sterility,
Will lead to hostility
And sense of futility,
So let's act with agility,
While we still have the faculty,
For we'll soon reach senility,
And lose the ability.

(10) WHERE'D THEY ALL COME FROM?
　　　(Tune: *Unavailable*)

I came to old Korat in the year of
　　sixty-seven,
To stay and fight the war about the
　　cliffs.
They told me about the flak and SAMs,
　　and the Navy, too;
But forgot to warn me about the Grunts.

CHORUS (*repeat after each verse*)

　　Where the Hell they all come from?
　　It's something I'd like to know.
　　They mill around the base,
　　And they take up all the space.
　　I'd like to tell them all just where
　　　to go.
(*continued on next page*)

They beat you to the dining hall,
They beat you to the bar.
You have to stand in line at the latrine
I don't know if they plan it all,
Or leave it all to chance;
But it makes a fellow's thinking mighty
    mean.

You feed them in the morning,
They come back all day long,
And a lot of other things I've forgot.
I think the devil hired 'em,
And sent 'em in every one,
To really make it Hell in old Korat.

They gamble you at poker,
Or they'll gamble you at dice.
I tell you boys, I think it's gettin'
    worse.
I ask one for the change of
A twenty dollar bill,
And the bastard almost hit me with his
    purse.

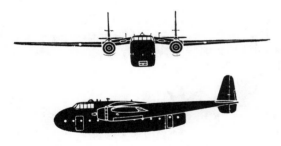

(11) WHISPERING DEATH - I
(Tune: *Ghost Riders In The Sky*)
  Lyrics: *Captain Wilson Briley, 523rd
          Tactical Fighter Squadron, Canon
          Air Force Base, New Mexico.*

NOTE: *Although this ballad was presented
as a poem in the source document, the
Editor noted that the composition
appeared to fit the melody of* **Ghost
Riders In The Sky.** *But whether you read
it as a poem or sing it as a song--makes
no difference. It is a great Air Force
story either way. And after all, a song
is but a poem set to music (that sounds
familiar). Of special interest is the
fact that a second, completely different
song, but with the same name, was found
in another song book. And it too, lends
itself to the same melody.*

WHISPERING DEATH - I

Slipping swiftly thru the dark of night,
Thru storm or blinding snow
A whisper, then a roar,
Then the fears of Hell you'll know.
With our wings swept back, we ride the
    wind,
Our vengeance just begun.
Heed our warning you who tempt the wrath
Of the Foxtrot One-One-One.

Whispering death, and freedom's the
    quest,
The quest of the Foxtrot One-One-One.

Hear me you who put asunder
All the dreams and hopes of men.
Listen closely in the darkness,
For the message we will send.
'Tween the whisper of our coming,
And the roar of the bomb,
Know that you have earned the wrath
Of the Foxtrot One-One-One.

Whispering death, and freedom's the
    quest,
The quest of the Foxtrot One-One-One.

There are those of us who gave their
    all,
And more may do the same.
We do not search for glory,
And we never may know fame.
Crusaders in a steed of steel,
Our task is never done.
Hearts filled with pride, we're proud
    to ride,
The Foxtrot One-One-One.

Whispering death, and freedom's the
    quest,
The quest of the Foxtrot One-One-One.

(12) WHISPERING DEATH - II
(Tune: *Ghost Riders In The Sky*)

NOTE: *The Editor admits a preference for
songs such as this one; the military
parody written by the men that have
tasted combat and write about their*

(continued on next page)

unit, aircraft, commanders and buddies by name. A little slice of Air Force history in melody. It is what Volumes I and II are all about. This is great.

WHISPERING DEATH - II

To the frightful town of Hanoi came a
  stranger one dark night.
To Phuc Yen, Kep, and Haiphong, came
  this stranger to the fight.
She flew low, she moved fast, two-
  hundred feet TF.
To the delta came this stranger known
  as Whispering Death.
Known as Whispering Death.

The war trudged on for many years, then
  one day she got her chance,
To fly and fight for feedom, and the
  cause to help enhance.
Colonel Nelson obliged, he headed way
  out West;
He gathered up his fighters and said,
  "We'll do our best."
He said, "We'll do our best."

She remained a stranger not for long,
  her victories were soon acclaimed.
She'd cut the northeast railroad, and
  SAM sites she had maimed.
She hit hard, she hit true, her deeds
  you won't forget,
Nor the stress and strain of combat, and
  of goin' out feet wet.
Goin' out feet wet.

Now AARDVAARK's not a pretty name, but
  here it earned respect,
And we're sure there are buff drivers
  who'll swear she saved their necks.
We held our heads high knowin' of
  prestige she was to claim;
That sleek and silent fighter with the
  strange and amusing name.
Strange and amusing name.

But the struggle wasn't easy and the
  price we paid was high.
Many friends were lost for freedom, but
  still our hopes were high,
That someday soon we'd see the end and
  know the war would cease.

We'd be proud of Whisperin' Death, and
  how she helped to bring the peace.
Helped to bring the peace.

Her endeavors weren't confined to the
  badlands way up North,
To the PDJ, Saravan, and Takeo she
  burst forth.
The Khmer Rouge, the Pathet Lao were
  soon to meet their fate,
For the might of Whisperin' Death,
  they had realized too late.
Realized too late.

Now my story has no moral for you see
  it has no end.
What the Vark has done for liberty,
  she's prepared to do again.
We pray she'll not be needed, but if
  conflicts do arise,
We'll be proud to fly her through dark
  and perilous skies.
Dark and perilous skies.

Whisperin' Death, Whisperin' Death, to
  the delta came this stranger
Known as Whisperin' Death,
Whisperin' Death.

Mig Mig-21 Mig-19 Mig-23

(13) THE WHOREHOUSE QUARTET
  (Tune: *Unavailable*)

Well..., she burped and she farted, and
  she shit on the floor,
And the gas from her ass blew the knob
  off the door.
And the moon shined bright on the nipple
  of her tit,
As she carved her initials in a bag of
  shit.

CHORUS

  Sung by a whorehouse quartet.
  Do you have a hard-on, not yet.
  Are you going to get one? You bet!
  You fucker, you!

(continued on next page)

Well..., she looked so fair in the mid-
    night air,
As the wind blew up her nighty.
Her tits hung loose like the balls on a
    goose,
And I yelled, "Great glory be to Betsy!"
She jumped in bed and covered up her
    head,
And swore I couldn't find her.
I knew damn well she was lying like Hell
So I jumped right in behind her.
She flipped and we flooped, and I landed
    on her top,
And started my organ grinder.
She wouldn't turn loose so I turned on
    the juice,
And now I got a baby ten pounder.

(14) WHY DO THE DRUMS GO BOOM?
    (Tune: *Unavailable*)

NOTE: *The Editor suspects this started*
out as a typical, bawdy English beer
hall ballad, but was quickly adopted and
adapted by a U. S. Air Force songwriter.

WHY DO THE DRUMS GO BOOM?

I had a little girl down in Baltimore,
But the funk from her drawers knocked me
    flat on the floor.

CHORUS (*repeat after each verse - if you*
    can last that long)

Well...I took her to the church just to
    meet all the people,
But the funk from her drawers knocked the
    cross off the steeple.

Well...I took her to the store just to
    buy some peas,
But the funk from her drawers knocked
    the clerk on his knees.

Well...I took her to the form just to
    get a job,
But the funk from her drawers knocked
    the corn off the cob.

Well...I took her to the movie, but the
    crowd got mad,

The funk from her drawers knocked the
    flick off the screen.

Well...I took her to the beach, man she
    was a dish,
But the funk from her drawers knocked
    the scales off the fish.

Well...I took her to the club for bite
    to eat,
But the funk from her drawers burned a
    hole in the seat.

Well...I took her to Korat just to meet
    the Thais,
But the funk from her drawers brought
    tears to their eyes.

Well...I took her to the field just to
    watch me fly,
But the funk from her drawers knocked my
    Thud from the sky.

Well...I took her to Veenas but they
    started bitchen',
When the funk from her drawers drew the
    flies from the kitchen.

Well...I took her to my hooch 'cause I
    thought I'd score,
But the funk from her drawers burned the
    paint off the door.

Well...I took her to the park just to
    roll in the grass,
But the funk from her drawers curled the
    hairs on my ass.

Well...I took her to my room and I
    started to hunch,
But the funk from her drawers made me
    blow my lunch.

Well...I slipped it up her tubes and I
    tried to coat 'em,
But the funk from her drawers peeled the
    skin off my scrotum.

Well...I fucked her on the floor, man it
    was a feeling,
When the funk from her drawers stuck my
    ass to the ceiling.

(*continued on next page*)

Well...I paid her fifty bucks 'cause it
    was a thrill,
But the funk from her drawers wiped the
    ink off the bill.

Well...they took my little girl to the
    police station,
Said the funk from her drawers was a
    threat to the nation.

Well...they took her to the court for
    speedy trial,
But the funk from her drawers laid the
    judge in the aisle.

Well...they locked her in a jail, but
    she's doin' well,
'Cause the funk from her drawers killed
    the rats in her cell.

Well...I lost my little girl, but I
    didn't mind,
'Cause the funk from her drawers nearly
    made me blind.

Well...the moral of this story, you can
    plainly see,
Before you get a little girl, have her
    do her laun-da-ry.

NOTE: *Last verse courtesy the Editor.
Such Talent!*

(15) THE WILD WEST SHOW - I (*See HHO3*)

(16) THE WILD WEST SHOW - II (*See HHO3*)

(17) WINNEPEG WHORE
(Tune: *Available*)

I took a trip up the Chippesaw river,
Just to view the Canadian shore.
There I met that two-bit bitch,
Commonly known as the Winnepeg Whore.

She said, "Come unto me darling,
Rest your hand upon my knee.
We will do some fancy diddling,
A buck and a half wil be my fee."

She was diddling, I was diddling,
I didn't know what it was all about,
'Till I missed my watch and wallet,
Holy Christ! did I shout out.

Up jumped pimps, whores and bitches,
To see my ass fly out that door.

NOTE: *The Editor does not understand the
two-line verse. It was probably an
error in the source song book, but who
knows? Some of these songs are crazy!*

My last trip up the Chippesaw river,
Ain't never going back no more.
I don't wanta do no more diddling,
With that two-bit bitch, the Winnepeg
    Whore.

Tu-16

(18) WIRRAWAYS DON'T BOTHER ME
    (Tune: *Bless 'Em All*)

Wirraways don't bother me,
Wirraways dont't worry me,
Oil-burning bastards with flaps on their
    wings,
With buggered up pistons and buggered
    up rings.
The bomb load is so fucking small,
Three-fifths of five-eights of fuck all
There's such a commotion, out over the
    ocean,
So cheer up my lads, fuck 'em all.

They say that the Japs have a very fine
    kite,
That we're no longer in doubt,
When there's a Zero way out on your tail
This is the way to get out:
Be cool and collected, be calm and
    serene,
Don't let your British blood boil,
Don't hesitate, shove her right through
    the gate,
And drown the poor bastard in oil!

(19) WOMEN, WOMEN, WOMEN
(Tune: *Trees - more or less*)

NOTE: *The tune was not indicated in the source song book, therefore the Editor took a guess. The problem is that the song appears to have a verse structure that suggests more than one tune was used. This is not unusual with military parodies, but it is difficult to decipher if the tunes are not indicated. In this case, the major break seems to come at a point about three-quarters through the song. It is possible there were two different songs, and the source song book editor mistakenly combined them. It is unfortunate that so many songs in the collection do not have the tune specified. C'est le guerre!*

WOMEN, WOMEN, WOMEN

I think that I will never want,
A thing as tired as a debutante.
A debutante is one who is so tired of it
    all,
One wonders how she'll get her offspring
    sired, if at all.
I could tolerate a girl who got drunk,
    and publically threw away her pants,
But for God's sake, spare me the
    debutantes.

The nicest thing about women is
    anticipation,
And the nicest thing to anticipate is
    indiscretion.
So, when a femme is short on sinuosities
She can get nothing out of me but
    animosities.

If she always wears a girdle,
She'll never get me over the hurdle.
If she never wears a low-cut bodice,
What desire is there to prod us???
But there is one type who gets me in
    toto,
The one that looks like a Hurrell photo.

She may be gross and otherwise feminine,
But if she really wants to do some
    hemmin' in,
She'll soak herself in a heady stench,

And she'll have me where I can't
    retrench.
Leave the beauts on the benches,
What I like is sexy wenches,
And nothing puts me in greater stitch
Than perfume on some little femme
    (bitch?)

NOTE: *Here is where the break in meter appears, and is either a different tune or a different song.*

No one objects--to good clean sex--sooo

Here's a toast to the woman who won't,
For she misses the best in life.
Yet strange to say when we settle down,
We choose that kind for a wife.
Here's a toast to the woman who will,
For she's filled with a passionate fire,
Both good and bad, and gay and sad,
The kind that fills man's desire.
And now a toast to both of them, sooo,
Come and ye glasses fill,
And lift them up to the the woman who
    won't
I'll drink to the woman who will.

It will not last forever,
Nor will the earth and skies;
But he that drinks in season,
Shall live before he dies.

(20) THE WOODPECKER SONG
    (Tune: *Unavailable*)

Oh, I stuck my finger in a Woodpecker
    hole,
And the Woodpecker said, "God bless my
    soul,
Take it out, take it out, take it out,
    remove it."

So, I removed my finger from the
    Woodpecker's hole.
The Woodpecker said, "God bless my soul,
Put it back, put it back, put it back,
    replace it."

(*continued on next page*)

I replaced my finger in the Woodpecker's
   hole,
And the Woodpecker said, "God bless your
   soul,
Turn it around, turn it around, turn it
   around, revolve it.

I revolved my finger in the Woodpecker's
   hole,
And the Woodpecker said, "God bless your
   soul,
In and out, in and out, in and out,
   reciprocate it.

I reciprocated my finger in the
   Woodpecker's hole,
And the Woodpecker said, "God bless my
   soul,
Pull it out, pull it out, pull it out,
   retract it.

I retracted my finger from the
   Woodpecker's hole,
And the Woodpecker said, "God bless
   your soul,
Take a smell, take a smell, take a smell
   REVOLTING!

(21) THE WRECK OF THE OLD 97 - II
   (Tune: *Original Music*)

NOTE: *Another version of that old
favorite based upon a 19th Century
railroad song. See Volume I, song 020,
page O-5. This version brings us right
up-to-date as Air Force song traditions
continue. The narrator for this song,
on a tape the Editor received from Major
Scott McElvain, said this song is based
upon a true incident. But aren't they
all? This one also has a lesson.*

THE WRECK OF THE OLD 97

They gave him his orders in Castle,
   California,
Saying, "Make your take off at night.
You need one more flight before your
   graduation,
Put her over SACTO on time."

He turned around and said, to his hard-
   working crewmen,
"A perfect mission is our goal.
When we cross that Sacramento bomb plot,
Watch old 97 go."

It's a mighty rough runway on One-two-
   zero,
It lies on a downhill grade.
It was on that grade that he lost his
   drag chute,
You see what a difference that made.

He was headed down the runway, making
   ninety knots an hour,
His copilot let out a scream.
"You forgot to drop the flaps, we're
   running out of runway.
You'll never get up enough speed"

At one-hundred-sixty knots the IP shoved
   the throttle,
And yelled, "Abort," to the crew.
The airbrakes went to six, the drag
   chute failed to blossom,
Scratch one B-52.

Now all you pilots, you better take
   warning,
From this time on and on.
Don't forget to use your checklist,
You may leave us and never return.

FLIGHT SECTION YY

(01) YELLOW TAILS
(Tune: *Strawberry Blonde*)

NOTE: *This is a terrific ditty, and a fine example of the military parody that illustrates the rivalry between Air Force fighter units.   In this case, the* **Yellow Tails** *refers to the* 149th TFS, Virginia Air National Guard.

YELLOW TAILS

Now the 141st Yankees they don't show
   me much,
While the Yellow Tails fly.
Their technique is bad and their
   bombing is sad,
While the Yellow Tails fly.

Their guns are corroded, their pilots
   are loaded,
Their cockpits are covered with dust.
They fly for awhile, but they ain't
   got no style,
While the Yellow Tails fly.

(02) YOU CAN TELL BY THE SMELL
(Tune: *The Field Artillery Song*)

Alternate Titles and Variations:

   (a) *You Can Tell*

You can tell by the smell
That she ain't feeling well,
When the end of the month rolls around.
You'd better give up the rump
Or it'll be a bloody stump,
When the end of the month rolls around.

CHORUS

   For it's Hi, Hi, Hee, in the Kotex
      industry,

Shout out your sizes loud and strong
"Small--medium--large, surperduper,
   bale of hay, mattress,"
For where 'ere you go, you will
   always know,
When the end of the month rolls
   around.

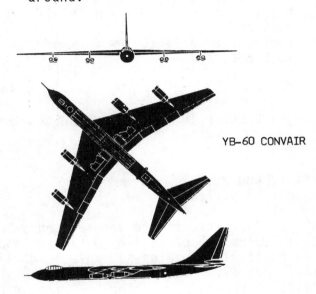

YB-60 CONVAIR

(03) YOU CAN'T SAY SHIT-HOT
   (Tune: *Unavailable*)

NOTE: *The term,* **shit-hot** *is a product of the Vietnam War, and generally means, the best, the sharpest. It seems to be one used mostly by fighter pilots, although it may have been in more common use.   According to former AF balladeer, John Piowaty, a fellow jock by the name of William* Bart *Barthelmas, Jr., popularized the expression,* **Very shit-hot,** *now reduced to the present* **shit-hot.** *This little ditty shows that the young jocks may have had some problems with the older boss jocks who made the rules.*

(continued on next page)

And this may be an indication that it was the Vietnam War where the generation gap between the WW-II retreads and the younger fighter pilots began to appear. There were a few who made the transition between wars and were accepted. Robin Olds was one of those. The youngsters looked up to him. He was **shit-hot**.

YOU CAN'T SAY SHIT-HOT

You can't say, "shit-hot" in the
  officer's club,
You can't say, "Hey, show us your tits."
The bullshit is getting so deep here,
It's up to my fucking armpits.
Fuck off, fuck off, 10 TRW fuck off,
  fuck off.
Fuck off, fuck off, 10 TRW fuck off,
  fuck off.

(OO) YOU REVEL IN THE JOYS OF COPULATION
(See CCO6)

(04) YUKON PETE
(Tune: *Unavailable*)

NOTE: *The last of the several songs in this volume about well-hung males and inexhaustible females--a male fantasy that has lived on through the ages; at least through the history of the Air Force. The Editor suspects the fantasy will persist. Also see* **Bumming Around, Kathuselem, Lupee #2,** *and* **Rangy Lil.** *There is also another version of* **Yukon Pete** *called,* **Yukon Pete - Beetle Version (NACHO Flight),** *but it is a shortened version of the original, and was in the same song book (95th FITS). The Editor elected to include just one.*

YUKON PETE

Here's a story of a little town,
Called Northen Will.
About a mean old whore named
Big-Ass Lil.
Now Lil wasn't just another whore,
She fucked everybody, and fucked some
  more.
Word got around that little town
That nobody could put Big Lil's ass
  down.
But a-way up North
Where the twin-pines meet,
Lives a bald-headed halfbreed
Named Yukon Pete.
Pete wasn't just another stud,
His pride and joy was his 20-inch pud.
Pete rolled into that little town,
With his 18 pounds a hangin' down.
The scene was set, and the night was
  still,
At an old shit house owned by Lil.
Well, they fucked and they fucked,
And they fucked for hours,
Tearin' up the ground, trees, and
  flowers.
Lil came down with a whorehouse squeeze,
That brought that halfbreed to his knees
Pete came back with a barroom grunt,
That spread her legs, and split her
  cunt.
Lil rolled over on her bloody thighs,
Cut two farts and then she died.
What were the last words spoken by Pete?
I'm goin' back to the Yukon
To beat my meat!

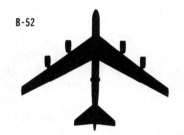

B-52

C-130

DEBRIEFING

WHEN IT'S ALL OVER*

(Author unknown)

When bugles sound their final notes,
And bombs explode no more;
And we return to what we did
Before we went to war.
The sudden shift of status,
Will make some worthy gentlemen
Feel like an awful mess.

Just think of some poor captain
Minus all his silver bars,
Standing up behind some counter,
Selling peanuts and cigars.

And think of all the majors,
With their oak leaves far behind,
And the uniform they're wearing
Is the Western Union kind.

———————————

Shed a tear for some poor colonel,
If he doesn't feel for himself.
Jerking sodas isn't easy
When your eagle's on the shelf.

Tis a bitter pill to swallow,
Tis a matter for despair.
Being messengers and clerks again,
Is a mighty cross to bear.

So, be kind to working people,
Wherever you may go,
For the waiter at your table,
May be your old C.O.

———————————

* World War II

POINT TO PONDER . . . .

Panic !

IT'S GONE ?

PILOT TO COPILOT: *Give me 2400 RPM.*

COPILOT TO PILOT: *Fuck you!   You stick your hand out!*

GLOSSARY

NOTE: This glossary was originally published in the **Folklore Forum** (*See the* **Tech Order** *section at the beginning of the volume*), and has been modified by the Editor. Most of the terms are from the Vietnam era, and are provided for those (*including the Editor*) who find Air Force terminology of that era as incomprehensible as some political speeches--and for those of you not familiar with any Air Force jargon of any era.

AAR -- air-to-air refueling, generally from a KC-135 jet tanker to F-4s, F-105s, or other aircraft with an air-to-air refueling capability.

AB -- afterburner, which provides additional thrust to a jet engine; usually used sparingly because it consumes great amounts of fuel.

AC -- aircraft commander, the pilot in charge of an aircraft.

ace -- means *good*. Also refers to a pilot who has shot down at least five enemy aircraft.

AD -- air division; it consists of several wings of aircraft, usually operating out of different bases.

air patch -- air-to-ground radio relay system for voice communication.

anchor -- an air refueling control point or area where tanker and receiver aircraft rendezvous.

Bac Can -- airfield 65 nautical miles (nm.) north of Hanoi.

Bac Giang -- city 25 nm. north of Hanoi on the Northeast Railroad to China.

Bac 9 -- an arresting cable for stopping aircraft on a runway in emergencies.

Bac Ninh -- city 15 nm. northeast of Hanoi on the Northeast Railroad to China.

Bannana Valley -- pilot-coined name for a geographical spot.

Ban Ban -- city and airfield in Laos, 115 nm. northeast of Vientiane near the eastern end of the Plain of Jarres. Ban Ban was noted for its heavy defensive flak.

bandit call -- radio call warning of the approach or proximity of enemy aircraft (bandits). *Bad Bandit call*, a false alarm.

Barracuda -- an aircraft carrying electronic warfare detection devices to warn other aircraft of hostile missile launches.

Bat Lake -- descriptive name for a lake in North Vietnam, 12 nm. north of the DMZ and 8 nm. from the coast of the Gulf of Tonkin.

BDA -- bomb damage assessment. Probable or actual results of a bombing mission determined from photos or other evidence.

bear -- affectionate term for an aircraft; also *beast*.

beep -- sound made by a downed aircrew member's emergency radio by which rescue aircraft fix his position.

Bingo -- means an aircraft has minimum fuel.

bird -- an aircraft; not as affectionate a term as *bear* or *beast*.

black boxes -- computers, radar equipment, or other electronic gear.

Black River -- a strategically important river running parallel and south of the Red River from the northwest to southeast across North Vietnam.

Black Route -- a reconnaissance route between the North Vietnam 17th and 18th parallels.

BLC -- boundary layer control; air from the engine compressor of the F4 directed over the wings which increases lift at slow speeds; the BLC light comes on to indicate that the air is becoming too hot for continued safe flight.

Blue Route -- similar to Black Route.

boreslide -- a play on the word *boresight*; an aircraft with its weapon release system in boresight has optimum synchronization between its radar, optical sight, and computers; also *bore* meaning to fly, or in this case, *to fly down a slide*, to dive.

bridges, both bridges -- two large bridges near Hanoi.

Brown, or Brown Anchor -- air refueling area in the Gulf of Tonkin.

BUF -- *Big Ugly Fucker*, believed to originally have been a fighter pilot's name for the B-52 bomber. Later, applied generally to other aircraft and *friends*.

bullseye -- nickname for Hanoi.

bust, or bust your ass -- to collide, crash, to *ding*.

call sign -- radio name for an aircraft or flight of aircraft.

Cam Rahn, Cam Ranh Bay -- large U. S. airfield in South Vietnam about 165 nm. northeast of Saigon on the coast.

Cao Bang -- airfield 100 nm. north-northeast of Hanoi, 10 nm. from the Chinese border.

cap, high cap, MIG cap -- fighter aircraft *capping* or flying cover to protect fighter-bombers or other aircraft from hostile planes.

CBU -- cluster bomb unit; has the same effect as dropping many hand grenades.

Channel 97 -- radio navigation aid for friendly aircraft.

combat pay -- $65.00 monthly paid to fliers above their regular pay for flying combat missions.

communism -- the opiate of the asses.

egotist -- a guy who's always **me**-*deep* in conversation.

experience -- the ability to recognize a mistake whenever you make it again.

51 -- Channel 51, the radio navigation aid located at Ubon Royal Thai Air Force Base, Thailand.

falsies -- twin bluffs.

final -- proper aircraft heading, descent rate, airspeed, and altitude during runway approach prior to landing.

Fives -- F-105s

Flight -- 2, 4 or more aircraft flying in formation under the command of a flight leader in number one aircraft.

Flight Leader, or Lead -- commander of a flight of aircraft.

foxtrot -- the letter *F* in the Air Force phonetic alphabet.

frag -- noun and verb; scheduled target and tactics for a specific air combat mission.

frappin' -- euphemism for *fuckin'*.

FSH -- fighter pilot war cry, often uttered in exasperation; may mean *fight!, shit! hate!* which were supposed to be - for some - the only essential functions of the genuine fighter pilot.

funnel -- the end of the air-to-air refueling boom is usually funnel-shaped for better aerodynamic stability.

G -- a unit of measurement which equals one times the force of gravity.

geico -- a prolific Southeast Asian lizard usually three to five inches long; it is found on the walls and ceilings of even the best hotels, and is said to make an obscene sound. Also found and revered in Hawaii, where they eat mosquitoes and other undesirables.

Gia Lam -- an airfield just north of Hanoi.

GIB -- acronym for *Guy In Back*; the pilot or navigator who flys in the back seat of the F-4 Phantom, or generally, any tandem, two-seat aircraft.

Green Anchor -- an air refueling area.

Grunt -- name given to nonflying personnel by aircrew members in Southeast Asia. Identical meaning to the term *groundpounder*, which originated in WW II or earlier. Can also include civilian employees of the government as well as contractor personnel.

guard channel -- a radio channel used primarily for emergency calls.

gun -- an aerial cannon used for air-to-air combat or strafing.

hack -- *to hack*, to perform effectively.

Hammer 41 -- an aircraft radio call sign arbitrarily assigned for an individual mission, e.g. Falcon 3, Blivit 2.

Hanoi Hilton -- a famous, or perhaps infamous, POW camp in North Vietnam.

haul ass -- to leave quickly.

HEI -- high-explosive incendiary.

high drags -- bombs with special fins or other devices to increase the time of fall.

Ho or Uncle Ho -- Ho Chi Minh, former North Vietnamese leader, deceased.

Hoa Binh -- an airfield 30 nm. southwest of Hanoi.

Hoa Loc -- an airfield 20 nm. west of Hanoi.

home drome -- the base where a given aircraft is permanently stationed.

hootch -- a hut or building; fighter pilots both live in and attack hootches.

houseboy -- usually on an 8-to-5 shift, he makes the pilot's bed, shines his shoes, dusts the room, and empties trash.

Huey -- an HU1E; a small, easily maneuverable helicopter.

hundred -- 100 missions over North Vietnam equaled a complete combat tour for a fighter pilot -- after the bombing halt of November 1968, the ususal tour was one year.

Iron bombs -- conventional bombs, contrasted with napalm, CBU's, high drags, or other specialized ordinance.

Iron Hands -- This was the name of the program to equip F-105F, two-seat aircraft to detect and hit hostile SAM sites during the Vietnam War. At times the term was applied to the aircraft itself. The converted aircraft were designated F-105G, and known as *Wild Weasels*. The conversion consisted of an ECM pod mounted on the lower fueslage, and the addition of four Shrike or two Standard ARM anti-radar missiles.

JCS -- U. S. Joint Chiefs of Staff, the highest ranking officers in the U. S. Armed Forces; at the Pentagon, they advise the Secretary of Defense and the President, as well as oversee their respective services.

jinking -- erratic evasive maneuvering of a fighter aircraft after weapon release; makes it difficult for enemy gunners to track and hit the aircraft.

jock -- from *jockey*; a pilot; possibly also from *jockstraps*, since those who wear them are ususally quite athletic, or *macho*, and therefore manly and rugged.

joinup -- airborne maneuver wherby two aircraft join to fly in formation, or for air-to-air refueling.

JP-4 -- aircraft jet fuel.

Kep -- airfield 30 nm. northeast of Hanoi on the Northeast Railroad to China.

Korat -- a U. S. airbase in Northern Thailand, the home of F-4s, F105s, and other aircraft.

ladyfingers -- 500 pound iron bombs.

Lang Son -- an airfield 60 nm. north of Haiphong, about 8 nm. from the Chinese border on the Notheast Railroad out of Hanoi.

launch light -- indicates the launch of enemy missiles against an aircraft; warns the pilot to maneuver and pray, together, or in that order.

Lead -- leader, or flight leader; the number one, or command aircraft in a formation.

Lion -- agency at Ubon that monitored and controled aircraft arrivals and departures by radar and radio communication; also aided or arranged emergency air-to-air refueling.

Luey, or Looie -- slang for lieutenant.

Mac -- Robert S. McNamarra, former Secretary of Defense under Presidents Kennedy and Johnson.

Mark 82 -- a 500 pound iron bomb.

Mayday -- traditional radio distress call; means *emergency*.

MIG -- a Russian-built series of jet fighters.

MIG Ridge -- near Hanoi, the site of many downed enemy aircraft.

mike-mike -- millimeter; e.g., 20 mike-mike refers to 20 millimeter guns.

Nam Dinh -- an airfield 38 nm. southwest of Haiphong.

nape, or napes -- napalm

97 -- Channel 97, a radio naviational aid in friendly territory.

Northeast Railroad -- runs for 85 nm. from Hanoi to the Chinese border; up the road from the border for another 100 nm. is the Chinese town of Nan-Ning.

number one -- the best in a shifting scale of quality from 1-10; a number 10 pilot would be the worst possible. The opposite of a number 10 girl!

o'clock -- relative clock poisiton of another aircraft to yours; one dead ahead would be at twelve o'clock, and so on.

old heads -- experienced fliers, in contrast with FNGs (*fuckin' new guys*).

Olds, Robin -- former commander of the 8th Tactical Fighter Wing, Ubon, Thailand, and foremost fighter jock of the Vietnam War, and fighter ace of World War II.

one hundred, or one hundred missions -- see *hundred*.

outboards -- the racks furthest out on the aircraft's wings; could carry ordinance or auxillary fuel tanks.

Package Six -- for air combat purposes, North Vietnam was divided into six operational areas called Packages One through Six. Package Six was the Hanoi area, an extremely dangerous Package.

pass -- to dive, or to lunge at a hostile aircraft.

pedestrian -- a car owner who has found a parking space.

PC-1 -- aircraft primary hydraulic control system.

Phantom II -- the McDonnell F-4 two-engine jet fighter; the workhorse of the tactical air war over Vietnam.

Phuc Yen -- an airfield 15 nm. northwest of Hanoi.

PIO -- Public Information Officer (or office), a military man who worked between the media and the military; a military news reporter or editor.

pissed, to get -- to become exceedingly angry.

pop up -- to climb rapidly.

punch out -- to eject from an aircraft.

Purple Route -- similar to Black Route.

QSY -- command to change radio channels.

Quang Khe -- a city in North Vietnam 40 nm. north of the DMZ on the coast of the Gulf of Tonkin.

Quang Tri -- a city and airfield in South Vietnam 25 nm. northwest of Hue near the coast, and 15 nm. south of the DMZ.

radar -- used in a fighter to detect other aircraft and in conjunction with ordinance release when practicable.

recce -- air reconnaissance.

Red, Red River, Red River Valley -- a strategically important North Vietnamese river and valley runnning from the northwest to southeast across North Vietnam and through Hanoi.

Red Route -- similar to Black Route.

regs -- regulations.

riding -- the art of keeping a horse between yourself and the ground.

ripple -- to drop off bombs in an almost random pattern.

Robin or Robin Olds -- see *Olds*.

roger -- Air Force jargon meaning, *Yes, I understand and will comply.* Before adoption of the current phonetic alphabet, *roger* was the phonetic name for the letter R, and was also used to mean, *Yes.* The term *wilco* was used with *roger* to indicate *will comply*, as in *roger, wilco.*

round -- a single bullet, artillery shell, or ground-to-ground rocket.

RTB -- return to base.

RTU -- a replacement training unit; a stateside unit which trains aircrew members for Southeast ASia or other operational flying bases throughout the world.

Russian Techs -- Russian techinical advisers to forces of communist bloc nations, or in this case, North Vietnam.

sack -- bed, *to stay in the sack*.

SAM -- a surface-to-air missile directed at opposing aircraft.

SAM break -- evasive action taken to cause a SAM to miss an aircraft.

samlar -- a Thai bicycle cab which holds two people uncomfortably; it is three-wheeled, and the driver (*or samlar*) peddles in front.

Sam Neua -- a city in northeast Laos about 100 nm. southwest of Hanoi and 20 nm. from the North Vietnamese border.

Sandy -- an A1-E, propeller-driven aircraft most frequently used to suppress enemy ground fire during a rescue operation of a downed American flier.

SAT -- Security Alert Team. These hearty souls are responsible for physical security at Missile Launch Control Facilities (LCF), and the individual Launch Facilities (LFs). Theyare required to make a periodic inspection of each LF and radio their findings to the Flight Security Controller (FSO) located at the LCF.

SA-2 -- a Russian made surface-to-air missile.

scanner -- the boom operator who rides on his belly in the tail of a tanker aircraft; he faces aft and "scans" or looks through a large window.

750 -- a 750 pound bomb.

Seventh Air Force -- headquartered at Tan Son Nhut Ari Base near Saigon, it directed all Allied air operations in Southeast Asia.

shit-hot -- as an adjective, it qualifies something as being the very best; as an expletive, it connotes great pleasure or joy on the speaker's part.

Sidewinder -- an air-to-air missile which is especially effective close-in because of its heat-seeking capability; a favored weapon against MIGs by such fighter jocks as Robin Olds.

Silver Dawn West, or East -- air combat operations areas to the extreme west and east in Vietnam; these identifiers were used very early in the air war and were dropped probably in mid-1967.

site -- a SAM site or location.

Site Mother -- is responsible for all the general housekeeping chores at a Launch Control Facility. Usually a Staff or Technical Sergeant.

snivel -- to work one's way into North Vietnam when not originally scheduled to fly there; a fast-talking pilot would often try to talk controlling agencies into letting him use extra ordnance in North Vietnam when it was not needed elsewhere; thus he could convert a mission which didn't count toward ending his tour to one which would (cf, *hundred*).

Son Tay -- a town 20 nm. west-northwest of Hanoi; the site of the attempt to rescue American POWs on 20 November 1970.

Sparrow -- a radar guided air-to-air missile.

TAC departures -- tactical aircraft departing or about to depart on a combat mission.

Takhli -- a U. S. airbase in Thailand.

Tee Lucks -- mistress or girl friend; English corruption of Thai word.

Tet -- Southeast Asian holiday season of the lunar new year in late January.

Thai Binh -- city 20 nm. southwest of Haiphong.

Thai-Nguyen -- airfield 35 nm. north of Hanoi.

three-sixty -- a 360 degree compass turn which delays time and puts an aircraft back on its initial heading. Common pilot expression since WW-II days.

Thud -- pilot's affectionate name for the F-105 Republic Thunderchief, a jet fighter-bomber (*compare to Jug, name given to the P-47 Republic Thunderbolt, propeller-drive fighter-bomber of WW-II*)

Thud Ridge -- west of Hanoi, a ridge where many Thuds crashed.

Thunderchief -- see *Thud*.

Tiger Hound -- a combat air operation area in Laos.

TOC -- tactical operations center of a fighter wing.

Tonkin -- the Gulf west of Vietnam, north of the DMZ.

tour -- a tour of duty in Vietnam for an American flier; prior to November 1968, it was 100 missions over North Vietnam; after that date it was normally one year long (*cf, "hundred," and "snivel"*).

trail -- one behind the other in a straight line; e.g., bombs in trail, aircraft in trail.

Trash Haulers -- C-130 cargo aircraft and their crews; the importance of what they carried was frequently questioned by fun-loving fighter pilots (*and pilots in general who had little good to say about the aircraft flown by other units in friendly competition*).

triple-A -- anti-aircraft artillery.

Tuy Hoa -- American airbase in South Vietnam.

tweat or tweet -- a T-33 jet trainer whose pilots were frequently the object of jokes by fighter pilots.

Two AD -- Second Air Division

Ubon Rarchanthani -- or simply, **Ubon**; an American airbase in southwest Thailand; home of the 8th Tactical Fighter Wing.

up, SAMs or MIGs are -- operationally active, a threat to Americna aircraft.

VC -- Vietcong, military supporters of the National Liberation Front, South Vietnamese militant communists.

Viet Tri -- a hamlet 25 nm. northeast of Hanoi with a strategically important railroad bridge across the Red River.

VIP -- a very important person.

Vulcan -- a highspeed, Gatling-type airborne cannon (the Editor promises not to mention *Star Trek*).

Weasel, or Wild Weasel -- refer to **Iron Hand**.

Wing -- a military unit consisting of several squadrons of approximately 25 aircraft each plus the men and equipment to support them; the Air Force's minimum size unit capable of completely independent operation.

Willie Pete, or Willy Pete -- white phosphorus ordinance used primarily by spotter planes to mark targets for fighter aircraft.

Wolf Pack -- nickname of the 8th Tactical Fighter Wing based at Ubon Airfield, Thailand; under the leadership of then-Colonel Robin Olds, this wing shot down more MIGs over North Vietnam than any other.

Yankee Air Pirate -- North Vietnamese English nickname for American fliers, taken from news releases to the world press; used derogatorily by the North Vietnamese, the label was later worn with pride by American fighter pilots.

Yen Bai -- an airfield 65 nm. northwest of Hanoi.

Zapped -- to get hit by enemy antiaircraft, missile, or ground fire.

'Zuke -- Itazuke Air Force Base, Japan.

W9-CUL-647

THE HUMANITIES
IN WESTERN CULTURE

VOLUME II

THE HUMANITIES IN WESTERN CULTURE

A SEARCH FOR HUMAN VALUES

EDITION IX

ROBERT C. LAMM
ARIZONA STATE UNIVERSITY

NEAL M. CROSS

Book Team

Developmental Editor *Deborah Reinbold*
Production Editor *Debra DeBord*
Designer *Christopher E. Reese*
Art Editor *Miriam J. Hoffman*
Photo Editor *Lori Gockel*
Permissions Editor *Gail Wheatley*
Art Processor *Jodi Wagner*
Visuals/Design Developmental Consultant *Marilyn A. Phelps*

WCB Brown & Benchmark

A Division of Wm. C. Brown Communications, Inc.

Vice President and General Manager *Thomas E. Doran*
Executive Managing Editor *Ed Bartell*
Executive Editor *Edgar J. Laube*
Director of Marketing *Kathy Law Laube*
National Sales Manager *Eric Ziegler*
Marketing Manager *Kathleen Nietzke*
Advertising Manager *Jodi Rymer*
Managing Editor, Production *Colleen A. Yonda*
Manager of Visuals and Design *Faye M. Schilling*

Design Manager *Jac Tilton*
Art Manager *Janice Roerig*
Photo Manager *Shirley Charley*
Production Editorial Manager *Ann Fuerste*
Publishing Services Manager *Karen J. Slaght*
Permissions/Records Manager *Connie Allendorf*

Wm. C. Brown Communications, Inc.

Chairman Emeritus *Wm. C. Brown*
Chairman and Chief Executive Officer *Mark C. Falb*
President and Chief Operating Officer *G. Franklin Lewis*
Corporate Vice President, Operations *Beverly Kolz*
Corporate Vice President, President of WCB Manufacturing *Roger Meyer*

Cover credit: Background (also for part and chapter openers) Tony Stone Worldwide. (Inset) Scala/Art Resource, N.Y.

Copyeditor *Kathy Pruno*

The credits section for this book begins on page 465 and is considered an extension of the copyright page.

Copyright © 1948, 1950, 1960 by Neal M. Cross and Leslie Dae Lindou

Copyright © 1968, 1972, 1977, 1981, 1984, 1988, 1993 by Wm. C. Brown Communications, Inc. All rights reserved

Unless otherwise credited, all photographs © Kathryn S. Lamm or © Robert C. Lamm

Library of Congress Catalog Card Number: 90–85922

ISBN 0–697–10667–5
     0–697–10948–8 (w/cassettes)

No part of this publication may be reproduced, stored in a retrieval system, or transmitted, in any form or by any means, electronic, mechanical, photocopying, recording, or otherwise, without the prior written permission of the publisher.

Printed in the United States of America by Wm. C. Brown Communications, Inc., 2460 Kerper Boulevard, Dubuque, IA 52001

10 9 8 7 6 5 4 3 2 1

Brief Contents

Volume I

Prologue: An Introduction to Integrated Humanities   1

UNIT 1
Ancient River-Valley Civilizations   7

1   Mesopotamia   9
2   Egypt   25

UNIT 2
Greece: Birthplace of Western Civilization   37

3   The Aegean Heritage, ca. 3000–1100 B.C.   39
4   Early Greece: Preparation for the Good Life   48
5   Hellenic Athens: The Fulfillment of the Good Life   70
6   Greece: From Hellenic to Hellenistic World   138
7   The Greek Arts   170

UNIT 3
Rome: The International Culture   205

8   A Thousand Years of Rome   207
9   Roman Art and Music: The Arts of Megalopolis   257

UNIT 4
Judaism and Christianity   277

10   The Star and the Cross   279
11   The Beginnings of Christian Art   293

UNIT 5
The Age of Faith   309

12   Building Medieval Walls   311
13   The Late Middle Ages: Expansion and Synthesis   349
14   The Medieval Synthesis in Art   396
15   Medieval Music: Sacred and Secular   423

Volume II

Prologue: An Introduction to Integrated Humanities   1

UNIT 6
The Renaissance, 1350–1600   7

16 New Ideas and Discoveries Result from a New Way of Looking at the World   9
17 Renaissance Art: A New Golden Age   23
18 Renaissance Music: Court and Church   57
19 Shadow and Substance: Literary Insights into the Renaissance   65

UNIT 7
The Early Modern World, 1600–1789   127

20 Science, Reason, and Absolutism   129
21 Art: Baroque, Rococo, and Neoclassic   181
22 Music: Baroque, Rococo, and Classical   207

UNIT 8
The Middle Modern World, 1789–1914   221

23 Revolution, Romanticism, Realism   223
24 Romanticism in Music   272
25 Nineteenth-Century Art: Conflict and Diversity   286

UNIT 9
The Twentieth Century   311

26 Things Fall Apart: The Center Cannot Hold   313
27 Ideas and Conflicts That Motivate the Twentieth Century   324
28 Art in the Twentieth Century: Shock Waves and Reactions   348
29 Modern Music   388
30 Twentieth-Century Literature   405

Expanded Contents

List of Listening Examples   xiii
Illustrations: Figures/Maps   xiv
Preface/Acknowledgments   xx

Prologue: An Introduction to Integrated Humanities   1
Why Study the Humanities?   2
A Common Basis for Understanding the Arts   5
Summary   6

UNIT 6
The Renaissance, 1350–1600   7

Time Chart for the Renaissance   8

16   **New Ideas and Discoveries Result from a New Way of Looking at the World**   9
The Rise of Humanism   9
Literary Selection

Mirandola, *Oration on the Dignity of Man*   10

Renaissance Science and Technology   11
Exploration and Discovery   12
The Reformation: New Ideas about God and Humankind   14
The Counter-Reformation   16
A Day in Renaissance Florence   17
The Relation of the Individual to the Group   18
Summary   21
Culture and Human Values   21
Renaissance Men and Women: Real and Ideal   21
The Renaissance Problem   22

17   **Renaissance Art: A New Golden Age**   23
The Early Renaissance in Fifteenth-Century Italy   23
The Early Renaissance in the North   33
The High Renaissance in Italy, ca. 1495–1520   39
High and Late Renaissance and Mannerism in Sixteenth-Century Italy   45
Late Renaissance and Mannerism in Italy and Spain   50
High and Late Renaissance in the North, ca. 1500–1600   53
Summary   56
Culture and Human Values   56

18 Renaissance Music: Court and Church 57
    Northern Origins of the Musical Renaissance 57
    The Franco-Flemish Tradition 59
    Developments in Italy 60
    Instrumental Music 63
    English Secular Vocal Music 63
    Summary 64
    Culture and Human Values 64

19 Shadow and Substance: Literary Insights into the Renaissance 65
    Renaissance Authors 65
    Literary Selections

        Petrarch, *Sonnet III* 71
        Petrarch, *Sonnet LXIX* 71
        Petrarch, *Sonnet XLVII* 72
        Petrarch, *Sonnet CCXCII* 72
        Petrarch, *Sonnet CCCXIII* 72
        Erasmus, *Praise of Folly* 72
        Machiavelli, *The Prince* 76
        Michelangelo, *Sonnet XXX* 85
        Michelangelo, *Sonnet XXXII* 85
        Michelangelo, *Sonnet LXI* 86
        Castiglione, *The Book of the Courtier* 86
        Rabelais, *Gargantua and Pantagruel* 90
        More, *Utopia* 92
        Shakespeare, *The Tempest* 97

    Summary 125
    Culture and Human Values 125

UNIT 7
The Early Modern World, 1600–1789   127

        Time Chart for the Early Modern World 128

20 Science, Reason, and Absolutism 129
    The Seventeenth Century 129
    The Eighteenth Century 132
    A Day at Versailles with Louis XIV 133
    Literature, 1600–1789 139
    Literary Selections

        Donne, *Song* 139
        Donne, *The Flea* 139
        Donne, *Holy Sonnet X* 140
        Marvell, *To His Coy Mistress* 140
        Milton, *On the Late Massacre in Piedmont* 141
        Milton, *On His Blindness* 141
        Molière, *Tartuffe* 143
        Pope, *Essay on Man* 164
        Swift, *A Modest Proposal* 168
        Voltaire, *Candide* 172

    Summary 180
    Culture and Human Values 180

21 Art: Baroque, Rococo, and Neoclassic 181
    The Baroque Age, ca. 1580–1700 181
    Rococo Art, ca. 1715–1789 194
    Neoclassic Art 198
    Summary 205
    Culture and Human Values 206

22 Music: Baroque, Rococo, and Classical 207
    Baroque Music, 1600–1750 207
    Keyboard Music 207
    Instrumental 210
    Vocal-Instrumental 211
    Opera 212
    Rococo, 1725–1775 213
    Classicism in Music, 1760–1827 214
    Summary 219
    Culture and Human Values 220

UNIT 8
The Middle Modern World, 1789–1914 221

    Time Chart for the Middle Modern World 222

23 Revolution, Romanticism, Realism 223
    Revolution to Waterloo 223
    The Revolutions of 1830 and 1848 225
    The Industrial Revolution 225
    Development of the Western Nations 226
    Literary Selections

        Tennyson, *The Charge of the Light Brigade* 228
        Lincoln, Second Inaugural Address 229

    The End of an Era 230
    Literary Selections

        Scott, *Breathes There the Man* 232
        Hardy, *Cry of the Homeless* 232

    Romanticism 234
    Literary Selection

        Rousseau, *Émile* 234

    The Romantic Movement 238
    Literary Selections

        Blake, *The Lamb* 238
        Blake, *The Tiger* 239
        Wordsworth, *The World Is Too Much With Us* 239
        Coleridge, *Kubla Khan* 240
        Byron, *When a Man Hath No Freedom to Fight For at Home* 240
        Byron, *Prometheus* 241
        Shelley, *To a Skylark* 242
        Keats, *La Belle Dame sans Merci* 243
        von Goethe, *VIII. Book of Suleika* 244

    Philosophy, Science, and Social Thought 246
    Literary Selections

        Marx and Engels, *Manifesto of the Communist Party* 247
        Darwin, *The Descent of Man* 249

    A Day in Victorian London 251
    Victorian Poets 252
    Literary Selections

        Tennyson, *Ulysses* 252
        Arnold, *Dover Beach* 253
        Hardy, *Neutral Tones* 254
        Hardy, *The Darkling Thrush* 254

    Materialism and Pessimism 254
    Literary Selection

        Dostoevsky, ''The Grand Inquisitor'' from *The Brothers Karamazov* 255

    Romanticism and Realism in America 260

Literary Selections

    Poe, *Annabel Lee* 261
    Emerson, *The Rhodora* 262
    Emerson, *Concord Hymn* 262
    Whitman, *I Hear America Singing* 263
    Whitman, *By the Bivouac's Fitful Flame* 263
    Melville, *The Portent* 264
    Melville, *Shiloh* 264
    Melville, *A Utilitarian View of the Monitor's Fight* 265
    Twain, *The Notorious Jumping Frog of Calaveras County* 265
    Dickinson, *VI: A Service of Song* 268
    Dickinson, *XLVI: Dying* 268
    Dickinson, *XVII* 268
    Dickinson, *X* 268
    Dickinson, *XI* 268
    Dickinson, *XXVII: The Chariot* 268
    Dunbar, *Sympathy* 269
    Crane, Two Poems (Untitled) 269

Summary 270
Culture and Human Values 270

24 **Romanticism in Music** **272**
    German Lieder 273
    Piano Music 274
    The Symphony 276
    Opera 281
    Impressionism in Music 282
    Summary 285
    Culture and Human Values 285

25 **Nineteenth-Century Art: Conflict and Diversity** **286**
    The Romantic Movement and the Neoclassic Style 286
    Realism 293
    Impressionism 297
    Post-Impressionism 303
    Summary 310
    Culture and Human Values 310

UNIT 9
The Twentieth Century 311

    Time Chart for the Twentieth Century 312

26 **Things Fall Apart: The Center Cannot Hold** **313**
    Historical Overview, 1914–1939 313
    The Culture-Epoch Theory and the Twentieth Century 315
    Modern Science 315
    Freud and the Inner World 318
    Literary Selections

        Eliot, *The Love Song of J. Alfred Prufrock* 320
        Owen, *Dulce et Decorum Est* 321
        Yeats, *The Second Coming* 322
        Jeffers, *Shine, Perishing Republic* 322
        Cullen, *Yet Do I Marvel* 323

    Summary 323
    Culture and Human Values 323

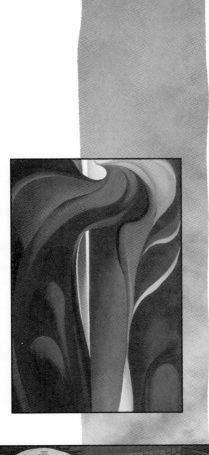

27 Ideas and Conflicts That Motivate the Twentieth Century   324
Historical Overview, 1939–1990s   324
Literary Selection

Eberhart, *The Fury of Aerial Bombardment*   324

The Cold War, ca. 1945–1990   324
Literary Selection

Levertov, *Tenebrae*   325

Philosophy   327
Literary Selection

Camus, *The Myth of Sisyphus*   329

Civil Rights   331
Literary Selections

King, From *Letter from Birmingham Jail*   331
Hughes, *Harlem*   332

The Feminist Movement   333
Literary Selections

Griffin, *I Like to Think of Harriet Tubman*   333
Woolf, *If Shakespeare Had a Sister*   334

Racism   339
Literary Selection

Gordimer, *A Soldier's Embrace*   339

The Information Society and the Global Village   345
Summary   346
Culture and Human Values   347

28 Art in the Twentieth Century: Shock Waves and Reactions   348
Prelude   348
Artistic Styles to 1945   348
Artistic Styles Since 1945   363
Summary   385
Culture and Human Values   387

29 Modern Music   388
Modernism   388
Atonality   389
Neoclassicism, Expressionism, and Neoromanticism   390
Serial Technique and Electronic Music   392
Jazz in America   396
The Styles of Jazz   399
Summary   404
Culture and Human Values   404

30 Twentieth-Century Literature   405
Conventions and Revolts   405
Poetry   408
Literary Selections

cummings, *anyone lived in a pretty how town*   408
Thomas, *When All My Five and Country Senses See*   409

Drama   409
Modern Prose Fiction   411

Literary Selections

   Borges, *The Disinterested Killer Bill Harrigan*   413
   Welty, *The Worn Path*   415
   Ellison, Chapter 1 from *Invisible Man*   418
   Reed, *Naming of Parts*   424
   Berryman, *Life, Friends, Is Boring. We Must Not Say So*   425
   Brooks, *The Bean Eaters*   425
   Brooks, *We Real Cool*   425
   Dickey, *Adultery*   426
   Rich, *Two Songs*   426
   Momaday, "Flight on the Wind" from *House Made of Dawn*   427
   Godwin, *A Sorrowful Woman*   430
   Giovanni, *Nikki-Rosa*   432
   Heller, Chapter 39, "The Eternal City" from *Catch-22*   433

Summary   439
Culture and Human Values   440
Suggested Reading and Viewing   440
The Literature of Moving Images   442

Appendix: Music Listening and Notation   443
Glossary   450
Annotated Bibliography   460
Credits   465
Index   468

Listening Examples

The following listening examples are available on a cassette accompanying this book:

Listening Example 13: Mass movement. Dufay, "Missa Se la face ay pale," 15th century, Kyrie

Listening Example 14: Motet. Josquin des Près, "Ave Maria" (excerpt)

Listening Example 15: Italian Madrigal. Orlando de Lassus, "Matona mia cara," (1550) (excerpt)

Listening Example 16: Mass Movement. Palestrina, "Veni sponsa Christi," (before 1554). Agnus Dei I

Listening Example 17: Motet. G. Gabrieli, "In Ecclesiis" (excerpt)

Listening Example 18: Madrigal. Bennet, "Thyrsis, Sleepest Thou?" (before 1625)

Listening Example 19: Dance Suite. Bach, "French Suite No. 4 in E-Flat Major 6." Gigue, from English or Irish jig. "French Suite No. 4 in E-Flat Major, S. 815" (1722)

Listening Example 20: Violin Concerto. Vivaldi, "Spring," from *The Four Seasons,* Allegro

Listening Example 21: Chorale Prelude. Bach, Schubler Chorale Preludes, S. 645/50 (1746). 5. Sleepers Awake

Listening Example 22: Oratorio Chorus. Handel, "The Messiah" (1742). 44. Hallelujah Chorus

Listening Example 23: Dance Movement for Harpsichord. Couperin, "Le Croc-en-jambe," from Ordre No. 22

Listening Example 24: Symphonic Movement. Mozart, "Symphony No. 35 in D, K. 385, Haffner" (1782). 4. Presto

Listening Example 25: Symphonic Movement. Beethoven, "Symphony No. 5 in C Minor, Op. 67" (1808). 3. Scherzo

Listening Example 26: German Art Song (Lied). Franz Schubert, "Gretchen am Spinnrade" ("Gretchen at the Spinning Wheel"), 1814

Listening Example 27: Étude. Chopin, "Étude in G-Flat Major, Op. 10, No. 5"

Listening Example 28: Symphony in Five Movements. Berlioz, "Symphonie Fantastique" (1830). 4. March to the Scaffold

Listening Example 29: Dance. Tchaikovsky, "Suite from the Ballet 'The Nutcracker,' Op. 71a" (1892). 4. Russian Dance

Listening Example 30: Piano Solo. Debussy, "Preludes for Piano, Book I" (1913). 2. Voiles

Listening Example 31: Ballet Suite. Stravinsky, "The Rite of Spring." Last Scene: Sacrificial Dance

Listening Example 32: Berg, "Violin Concerto." I Andante (excerpt)

Listening Example 33: Ives, "Three Places in New England" (1903–1911). II. Putnam's Camp, Redding, Connecticut (excerpt)

Listening Example 34: Webern, "Three Songs, Op. 18" (1925). 1. Schatzerl Klein (little treasure)

Listening Example 35: Babbitt, "Ensemble for Synthesizer" (excerpt)

Listening Example 36: Lil Hardin Armstrong, "Hotter than That" (1927)

Listening Example 37: Steele, "High Society" (1955)

Listening Example 38: Paul Desmond, "Take Five," with the Dave Brubeck Quartet

Illustrations

Figures

P.1   Bull, ceiling painting   1
16.1   Lucas Cranach the Younger, *Martin Luther and the Wittenberg Reformers*   15
16.2   Quentin Matsys, *The Money Lender and His Wife*   18
17.1   View of Florence across the Arno River   23
17.2   Florentine Cathedral Group (aerial view)   24
17.3   Giotto, Campanile   24
17.4   South Tower, Chartres Cathedral   25
17.5   Brunelleschi, Pazzi Chapel, Cloister of Church of Santa Croce   25
17.6   Interior, Pazzi Chapel   25
17.7   Lorenzo Ghiberti, "Gates of Paradise"   26
17.8   Lorenzo Ghiberti, *Story of Adam and Eve*   26
17.9   Donatello, *Prophet ("Zuccone")*   26
17.10 Donatello, *David*   27
17.11 Donatello, *Equestrian Monument of Gattamelata*   27
17.12 Masaccio, *Tribute Money*   28
17.13 Paolo Uccello, "The Unhorsing of Bernardino della Carda"   29
17.14 Leonbattista Alberti and Bernardo Rossellino, Facade, Palazzo Rucellai   29
17.15 Leonbattista Alberti, Facade, Santa Maria Novella   30
17.16 Andrea del Verrocchio, *David*   30
17.17 Andrea del Verrocchio, *Equestrian Monument of Bartolommeo Colleoni*   31
17.18 Andrea del Verrocchio, *Lorenzo de' Medici*   31
17.19 Sandro Botticelli, *Birth of Venus (Venus Landing on the Shore)*   32
17.20 Domenico del Ghirlandaio, *Old Man with a Child*   32
17.21 Perugino, *The Crucifixion with the Virgin, Saint Jerome, and Saint Mary Magdalene*   33
17.22 The Limbourg Brothers, "February"   34
17.23 Jan van Eyck, *Ghent Altarpiece* (closed)   34
17.24 Jan van Eyck, *Ghent Altarpiece* (open)   35
17.25 Jan van Eyck, *Annunciation*   36
17.26 Jan van Eyck, *Giovanni Arnolfini and His Bride*   36
17.27 Rogier van der Weyden, *Portrait of a Lady*   37
17.28 Hans Memling, *The Presentation in the Temple*   37
17.29 Hieronymus Bosch, *Garden of Delights*   38
17.30 Leonardo da Vinci, *Ginevra de'Benci*   39
17.31 Leonardo da Vinci, *The Last Supper*   40
17.32 Michelangelo, *Pietà*   41
17.33 Michelangelo, *David*   41

17.34 Michelangelo, *Creation of Adam* 42
17.35 Donato Bramante, *Tempietto* 43
17.36 Raphael, *The Alba Madonna* 44
17.37 Raphael, *Baldassare Castiglione* 44
17.38 Raphael, *The School of Athens* 45
17.39 Giorgione, *Adoration of the Shepherds* 46
17.40 Giorgione (and Titian?), *Fête Champêtre* 46
17.41 Michelangelo, *Tomb of Giuliano de' Medici* 47
17.42 Michelangelo, *Tomb of Lorenzo de' Medici* 48
17.43 Michelangelo, *The Last Judgment* 48
17.44 Michelangelo, *Rondanini Pietà* 49
17.45 Michelangelo, Dome of St. Peter's 49
17.46 Parmigianino, *Madonna with the Long Neck* 50
17.47 Titian, *Venus with a Mirror* 50
17.48 Tintoretto, *Christ at the Sea of Galilee* 51
17.49 Tintoretto, *The Last Supper* 51
17.50 Palladio, Villa Rotunda, Vicenza 52
17.51 Paolo Veronese, *The Finding of Moses* 52
17.52 El Greco, *The Penitent St. Peter* 53
17.53 El Greco, *Laokoön* 53
17.54 Albrecht Dürer, *Knight, Death, and the Devil* 54
17.55 Matthias Grünewald, *The Small Crucifixion* 54
17.56 Chateau of Chambord 55
17.57 Pieter Bruegel the Elder, *Landscape with the Fall of Ikaros* 55
17.58 Pieter Bruegel the Elder, *Winter (Return of the Hunters)* 56
18.1 St. Mark's Cathedral 61
18.2 Simplified floor plan of St. Mark's, Venice 61
18.3 Interior, St. Mark's, Venice 62
18.4 *Lady Playing a Dulcimer* 63
19.1 Albrecht Dürer, *Erasmus of Rotterdam* 66
19.2 Hans Holbein the Younger, *Sir Thomas More* 68
20.1 French school after Gianlorenzo Bernini, *Bust of Louis XIV* 132
20.2 Forces acting on the moon to determine its motion 134
20.3 Molière and his troupe of players 142
20.4 Dean Jonathan Swift 169
21.1 G. B. Vignola and G. C. della Porta, Il Gesù, Rome 181
21.2 Interior, Il Gesù 182
21.3 Caravaggio, *The Conversion of St. Paul* 182
21.4 Caravaggio, *Supper at Emmaus* 183
21.5 Artemesia Gentileschi, *Judith Slaying Holofernes* 183
21.6 Gianlorenzo Bernini, *David* 184
21.7 St. Peter's Basilica, Rome 184
21.8 Gianlorenzo Bernini, *Baldacchino* 184
21.9 Gianlorenzo Bernini, *Ecstasy of St. Theresa* 185
21.10 Francesco Borromini, S. Carlo alle Quattro Fontane 185
21.11 Francisco de Zurbarán, *Agnus Dei* 186
21.12 Diego Velasquez, *Maids of Honor (Las Meninas)* 186
21.13 Andrea Pozzo, *Apotheosis of Saint Ignatius* 187
21.14 Peter Paul Rubens, *The Assumption of the Virgin* 188
21.15 Peter Paul Rubens, *Rape of the Daughters of Leucippus* 188
21.16 Anthony van Dyck, *Marchesa Elena Grimaldi* 188
21.17 Nicolas Poussin, *Holy Family on the Steps* 189
21.18 Hyacinthe Rigaud, *Portrait of Louis XIV* 190
21.19 Louis le Vau and Jules Hardouin Mansart, Palace of Versailles 190
21.20 Frans Hals, *Portrait of an Officer* 191
21.21 Judith Leyster, *Self-Portrait* 191
21.22 Rembrandt van Rijn, *The Descent from the Cross* 192
21.23 Rembrandt van Rijn, *The Apostle Bartholomew* 192
21.24 Jan Vermeer, *Woman Holding a Balance* 193
21.25 Jan Vermeer, *The Girl with a Red Hat* 193
21.26 Jacob van Ruisdael, *Wheatfields* 194

21.27 Jean Antoine Watteau, *A Pilgrimage to Cythera*   195
21.28 François Boucher, *Venus Consoling Love*   196
21.29 Jean-Honoré Fragonard, *The Swing*   196
21.30 Étienne Falconet, *Madame de Pompadour as the Venus of the Doves*   197
21.31 Jean-Baptiste-Simeon Chardin, *The Kitchen Maid*   197
21.32 Thomas Gainsborough, *Mrs. Richard Brinsley Sheridan*   197
21.33 Dominikus Zimmermann, Wieskirche, Upper Bavaria   198
21.34 Inigo Jones, Queen's House   198
21.35 Christopher Wren, St. Paul's Cathedral   199
21.36 James Gibbs, St. Martin-in-the-Fields   199
21.37 Drawing Room, No. 1 Crescent Circle, Bath, England   199
21.38 Ange-Jacques Gabriel, Petit Trianon   200
21.39 Jean-Baptiste Greuze, *The Village Bride*   201
21.40 Jacques-Louis David, *The Death of Sokrates*   202
21.41 Circle of David, *Portrait of a Lady*   202
21.42 Constance Marie Charpentier, *Mlle. Charlotte du Val d'Ognes*   203
21.43 Jean Antoine Houdon, *Voltaire*   203
21.44 Antonio Canova, *Pauline Borghese as Venus*   204
21.45 Gilbert Stuart, *Mrs. Richard Yates*   204
21.46 Thomas Jefferson, State Capitol, Richmond Virginia   205
22.1 Harpsichord   208
22.2 Baroque pipe organ   209
22.3 François Cuvilliés, Hall of Mirrors, The Amalienburg, Nymphenburg Palace, Munich   213
23.1 Jacques-Louis David, *Napoleon in His Study*   224
23.2 Eugène Delacroix, *The Massacre at Chios*   227
23.3 Matthew Brady, *Portrait of Lincoln*   229
23.4 Kaspar David Friedrich, *Cloister Graveyard Under Snow*   246
24.1 Arnold Böcklin, *Island of the Dead*   273
24.2 Eugène Delacroix, *Fréderic Chopin*   275
24.3 Typical seating plan of a modern symphony orchestra   276
24.4 A modern symphony orchestra   277
24.5 Felix Mendelssohn   277
24.6 Hector Berlioz   277
24.7 Franz Liszt   279
24.8 Richard Strauss   279
24.9 Peter Ilich Tchaikovsky   281
24.10 Giacomo Puccini   281
24.11 Claude Debussy   284
25.1 Jean François Chalgrin (and others), Arch of Triumph, Place Charles de Gaulle, Paris   286
25.2 Pierre Vignon, *The Madeleine,* Paris   286
25.3 Jean-Auguste-Dominique Ingres, *Grand Odalisque*   287
25.4 Francisco de Goya, *Majas on a Balcony*   287
25.5 Francisco de Goya, *The Third of May, 1808, at Madrid: The Shootings on Principe Pío Mountain*   288
25.6 Francisco de Goya, *Grande hazaña! Con muertos!*   289
25.7 Théodore Géricault, *The Raft of the Medusa*   289
25.8 Eugène Delacroix, *Arabs Skirmishing in the Mountains*   290
25.9 John Constable, *Wivenhoe Park, Essex*   291
25.10 Joseph M. W. Turner, *Keelman Heaving Coals by Moonlight*   291
25.11 Thomas Cole, *Oxbow (The Connecticut River near Northampton)*   292
25.12 George Caleb Bingham, *Fur Traders Descending the Missouri*   292
25.13 Barry and Pugin, The Houses of Parliament, London   292
25.14 Victorian Gothic mansion, Eureka, California   293
25.15 François Millet, *The Sower*   293
25.16 Jean-Baptiste-Camille Corot, *Forest of Fontainebleau*   293
25.17 Honoré Daumier, *Le Ventre Legislatif*   294
25.18 Honoré Daumier, *Third-Class Carriage*   294
25.19 Gustave Courbet, *Burial at Ornans*   295
25.20 Winslow Homer, *Breezing Up*   295

25.21 Thomas Eakins, *Max Schmitt in a Single Scull* 296
25.22 Joseph Paxton, Crystal Palace 296
25.23 Gustave Eiffel, Eiffel Tower 296
25.24 Édouard Manet, *Déjeuner sur l'herbe* 297
25.25 Édouard Manet, *Olympia* 298
25.26 Édouard Manet, *The Dead Toreador* 298
25.27 Claude Monet, *Rouen Cathedral, West Facade Sunlight* 299
25.28 Pierre Auguste Renoir, *Le Moulin de la Galette* 299
25.29 Edgar Degas, *Four Dancers* 300
25.30 Berthe Morisot, *In the Dining Room* 301
25.31 Mary Cassatt, *The Bath* 301
25.32 James McNeill Whistler, *The White Girl: Symphony in White, No. 1* 302
25.33 Auguste Rodin, *The Walking Man* 302
25.34 Auguste Rodin, *The Thinker* 303
25.35 Paul Cézanne, *Le Château Noir* 303
25.36 Kitagawa Utamaro, *Uwaki, Half-Length Portrait* 304
25.37 Vincent van Gogh, *La Mousmé* 304
25.38 Vincent van Gogh, *The Starry Night* 305
25.39 Paul Gauguin, *Vision after the Sermon (Jacob Wrestling with the Angel)* 305
25.40 Paul Gauguin, *Self-Portrait* 306
25.41 Paul Gauguin, *Where Do We Come From? What Are We? Where Are We Going?* 306
25.42 Georges Seurat, *Sunday Afternoon on the Island of La Grande Jatte* 307
25.43 Henri de Toulouse-Lautrec, *Quadrille at the Moulin Rouge* 308
25.44 Henri Rousseau, *The Equatorial Jungle* 309
25.45 Edvard Munch, *The Scream* 309
26.1 Memorial Sculpture, Dachau, Germany 314
26.2 Albert Einstein playing a violin at a chamber music rehearsal in Princeton, N.J. 317
26.3 Sigmund Freud 319
28.1 Henri Matisse, *The Blue Window* 349
28.2 Henri Matisse, *Odalisque with Tambourine: Harmony in Blue* 349
28.3 Georges Rouault, *Christ Mocked by Soldiers* 350
28.4 Ernst Barlach, *Shivering Woman* 350
28.5 Käthe Kollwitz, *The Only Good Thing About It* 350
28.6 George Grosz, *I Am Glad I Came Back* 351
28.7 Wassily Kandinsky, *Panel (3)* 351
28.8 Pablo Picasso, *The Tragedy* 352
28.9 Pablo Picasso, *Family of Saltimbanques* 352
28.10 Pablo Picasso, *Les Demoiselles d'Avignon* 353
28.11 Pablo Picasso, *Still Life* 353
28.12 Pablo Picasso, *Girl Before a Mirror* 353
28.13 Pablo Picasso, *Guernica* 354
28.14 Georgia O'Keeffe, *Jack-in-the-Pulpit, No. 5* 354
28.15 Alfred Stieglitz, *The Terminal* 355
28.16 Stuart Davis, *Radio Tubes* 355
28.17 Piet Mondrian, *Composition in White, Black, and Red* 355
28.18 Piet Mondrian, *Broadway Boogie Woogie* 356
28.19 Constantin Brancusi, *Bird in Space* 356
28.20 Marc Chagall, *I and the Village* 356
28.21 Paul Klee, *Fish Magic* 357
28.22 Giorgio de Chirico, *The Nostalgia of the Infinite* 357
28.23 Marcel Duchamp, *The Bride Stripped Bare by Her Bachelors, Even* 358
28.24 Kurt Schwitters, *Sichtbar* 358
28.25 Joan Miró, *Person Throwing Stone at a Bird* 359
28.26 Salvador Dali, *The Persistence of Memory* 359
28.27 Meret Oppenheim, *Object* 359
28.28 Alberto Giacometti, *The Palace at 4 A.M.* 360
28.29 René Magritte, *The False Mirror* 360
28.30 John Sloan, *Roof Gossips* 360
28.31 Edward Hopper, *House by the Railroad* 361

28.32 Diego Rivera, *The Liberation of the Peon*   361
28.33 José Orozco, *Zapatistas*   361
28.34 David Alfaro Siqueiros, *Echo of a Scream*   362
28.35 Antonio Gaudi, Church of the Holy Family   362
28.36 Walter Gropius, Workshop of the Bauhaus   363
28.37 Le Corbusier, Villa Savoye   363
28.38 Frank Lloyd Wright, Kaufmann House   363
28.39 Jackson Pollock, *Number 1*   364
28.40 Willem de Kooning, *Woman I*   364
28.41 Mark Rothko, *Number 10*   365
28.42 Robert Rauschenberg, *Monogram*   365
28.43 Roy Lichtenstein, *Drowning Girl*   365
28.44 Edward Kienholz, *The State Hospital*   366
28.45 Marisol, *Women and Dog*   366
28.46 Josef Albers, *Homage to the Square: Star Blue*   367
28.47 Helen Frankenthaler, *Interior Landscape*   367
28.48 Louise Nevelson, *Illumination—Dark*   368
28.49 Bridget Riley, *Current*   369
28.50 Jean Dubuffet, *Portrait of Henri Michaux*   369
28.51 Francis Bacon, *Number VII from Eight Studies for a Portrait*   369
28.52 Rufino Tamayo, *Man*   370
28.53 Fritz Scholder, *Waiting Indian No. 4*   370
28.54 Alexander Calder, *Many Pierced Discs*   370
28.55 Mark di Suvero, *Side Frames*   371
28.56 Henry Moore, *Family Group*   371
28.57 Tony DeLap, *Sentaro*   371
28.58 David Smith, *Cubi XV*   372
28.59 Ronald Bladen, *X*   372
28.60 Audrey Flack, *World War II, April 1945*   373
28.61 Otto Duecker, *Russell, Terry, J. T., and a Levi Jacket*   373
28.62 Robert Smithson, *Spiral Jetty*   374
28.63 Christo (Christo Jaracheff), *Running Fence*   375
28.64 Joshua Johnson, *The Westwood Children*   376
28.65 Robert S. Duncanson, *Blue Hole, Flood Waters, Little Miami River*   376
28.66 Horace Pippin, *Victorian Interior*   376
28.67 Jacob Lawrence, *Daybreak—A Time to Rest*   377
28.68 Wallace K. Harrison, Le Corbusier, and others, Secretariat Building of the United Nations   378
28.69 Ludwig Mies van der Rohe, Seagram Building, New York City   379
28.70 Le Corbusier, Notre-Dame-du-Haut   379
28.71 Frank Lloyd Wright, The Solomon R. Guggenheim Museum   379
28.72 Interior, Solomon R. Guggenheim Museum   380
28.73 Eero Saarinen, TWA Terminal   380
28.74 Utzon, Hall, Todd, and Littleton, Sydney Opera House   380
28.75 Ansel Adams, *Moonrise, Hernandez, New Mexico, 1944*   381
28.76 W. Eugene Smith, *Spanish Wake*   381
28.77 Margaret Bourke-White, *Flood Victims, Louisville, Kentucky, 1937*   382
28.78 Dorothea Lange, *Migrant Mother, Nipomo, California, 1936*   382
28.79 Gerhard Richter, *Vase*   383
28.80 Sylvia Mangold, *Schunnemunk Mountain*   383
28.81 Jennifer Bartlett, *Sad and Happy Tidal Wave*   384
28.82 Philip Johnson, AT&T Building (model)   385
28.83 Michael Graves, The Portland Public Services Building   385

Because each major culture merits its own special study, this is an examination of the evolution of Western civilization and its place in North American culture in the United States and Canada. The rapidly changing populations of both nations that now include many immigrants from Asia and other parts of the world strongly reinforces the necessity of studying the cultural heritage of the West. Many immigrants are, after all, attracted to Western civilization because of the educational and vocational opportunities and the high standard of living, all of which have derived from the economic, political and scientific development of Western nations. This does not imply, however, that newer citizens must leave their culture behind: far from it. The subsequent study of other major cultures plus what is currently called "global humanities" is strongly recommended, for global considerations are among the conspicuous realities of the late twentieth century. Given the level of cultural awareness and knowledge of today's average undergraduate, however, the author is convinced that most students, whether native-born or recent arrivals, would derive greater benefits from studying other cultures after they have acquired a better understanding of the Western heritage. Establishing a frame of reference seems the most practical and efficient way of comprehending cultural developments around the globe.

This new edition brings many changes in both content and style; a humanities textbook is, or should be, a living document that adjusts to the ever-changing world. New facts are continually emerging about the past, and today's world changes so rapidly as to leave us grasping for comprehension, not to mention gasping for breath.

In volumes I and II the color illustrations have been quadrupled, from seventy to nearly three hundred, black-and-white figures have been replaced, as necessary, with sharper images, and the number of maps has been doubled. In volume I the chapter on Greek music has been integrated into the chapters on art and philosophy. Added to the art chapters are descriptions and color illustrations of the art and craft of jewelry. The *Lysistrata* by Aristophanes is a long-overdue addition to the study of Greek comedy. An equally past-due satire by Horace has been added to the Roman literature section. Included in the Medieval unit is additional material on Islamic arts plus a selection from Christine de Pizan, a major writer and early feminist. There is, in fact, increased coverage throughout of some notable contributions of women, especially in art and literature.

Additions to volume II include "The Book of Suleika" from *Poetical Works* by Johann von Goethe, "The Grand Inquisitor" section from Dostoevsky's *The Brothers Karamazov,* and an essay on Billy the Kid by Argentine writer Jorge Luis Borges. The material on Karl Marx, Sigmund Freud, contemporary political and cultural events, and modern science has been updated.

What has not changed is the reading level of the text. After abundant input from users, reviewers, editors, and other interested parties, the author has concluded that writing down to the average competence of the current crop of college students benefits no one. No one disputes the lamentable state of literacy even at the college level, but a watered-down text is manifestly unfair to students, teachers, and higher education in general. Textual clarifications have been added as deemed necessary, and the glossary has been revised to better support the meaningful utilization of technical terminology. All of the material has been reorganized with more precise heads and subheads that should contribute to the clarity of the text. Overall, the author has endeavored to compose lucid material that is both accurate and consistently interesting, even entertaining, bearing in mind that the Greeks demanded of their dramas both enlightenment *and* entertainment. It should surprise no one that much of the content is challenging in terms of reading comprehension, abstract concepts, and other complexities of acquiring a college education. What is most important, however, is that this material, whether in this text or another of similar persuasion, represents an essential aspect of what it means to be prepared to live and even flourish in a complex world of ceaseless change.

The basic problem in writing a humanities textbook (or teaching a humanities course) is deciding what must be omitted. A survey of Western culture in twenty volumes is much less daunting than trying to examine the same topics in only two volumes. As it is, some users note that there is too much material—literature in particular—for the standard two-semester humanities course. There is indeed an abundance of resources but better too much rather than too little. The instructor can evaluate each class and react accordingly; what should be abstracted or omitted is up to the individual teacher, which is just the way it should be. Teaching the humanities is, in the final analysis, a very personal endeavor by highly motivated teachers.

Robert C. Lamm

Acknowledgments

This book could not have been written without the expertise and diligence of a reference librarian, photographic associate, and in-house editor, namely, Katy Lamm.

Special thanks also to Al Cohen, director of the Office of Testing and Evaluation Services at the University of Wisconsin—Madison, who has provided valuable assistance in the development of the Test Item File. Dr. Cohen has worked directly with the author to ensure that questions are worded with precision and structured in a consistent manner.

I also wish to thank the following professors whose careful reading of the manuscript proved invaluable for this ninth edition.

Vaughan B. Baker
University of Southwestern Louisiana

Charline L. Burton
Central State University

Camille A. Caruso
West Virginia University–Main Campus

Harvey A. Collins
Olivet Nazarene University

Michael G. Davros
Oakton Community College

Ellen Hofmann
Highline Community College

Stanley J. Kozikowski
Bryant College

David L. Matson
Cedarville College

James V. Mehl
Missouri Western State College

Sharon L. Merrell
Boise State University

Deborah Patterson
Edison Community College

Sister Marie J. Ryan
Aquinas College

Steven C. Schaber
San Diego State University

Darryl R. Sycher
Columbus State Community College

Richard C. Tubbs
Community College of Aurora

Joseph R. Urgo
Bryant College

An Introduction to Integrated Humanities

prologue

Each of the [artistic] masterpieces is a purification of the world, but their common message is that of their existence and the victory of each individual artist over his servitude, spreading like ripples on the sea of time, implementing art's eternal victory over the human situation.

André Malraux

In Spain and in the modest mountains of southwestern France are numerous caves decorated with paintings that date from the late Old Stone (Paleolithic) Age (ca. 20,000–10,000 B.C.). In the caves of Lascaux there is, for example, a giant chamber whose lofty ceiling is covered with paintings of antelope, horses, bulls, and other animals. Too deep and dark for human habitation, this may have been a sanctuary for religious rites or, less likely, a setting for ritualistic magic to insure successful hunting, but no one knows for sure. No one knows the intentions of the people who created these images, but there is no question about what these people were. They were artists. Using intellect and imagination, late Paleolithic people had invented representation, a momentous step in the evolution of culture.

The invention of art symbolized major changes in the lives of people no longer at the mercy of the elements. Working together and planning ahead for seasonal changes, they hunted and gathered at optimum times and stored food for the long winters. Paleontologists believe that they devoted as little as fifteen to twenty hours a week to the necessities of existence. There was time left over to make more efficient weapons and warmer clothing, to carve ivory and wood, to play, and to decorate cave sanctuaries. Late Paleolithic clans had created what every society must have if it is to advance its culture: free and unstructured time.

The creation of art also signified the emergence of individual artists. Lugging materials down through winding cave passages and erecting a scaffolding were undoubtedly communal efforts, but the artwork was done by an individual. That person,

Figure P.1   *Bull, ceiling painting, 18' long, caves of Lascaux near Montignac, France, ca. 13,000 B.C..*

the artist, mounted the platform and painted a bull (figure P.1) in sweeping, confident lines, elegantly capturing a sense of life and communicating the illusion of powerful motion. In today's high-tech, nuclear-threatened world, the art of Lascaux is a poignant reminder of our kinship with Stone Age artists who, along with a multitude of successors, inspire us to recall our humanity, our intellect and imagination, our creative potential for a better life.

Everyone is capable of living a more rewarding life, which is reason enough for studying the humanities. From cave art to the present, the arts and ideas of humans are beacons of hope, truth, and beauty for a world that needs to pay far more attention to the humanities, to the arts that teach us "nothing except the significance of life" (Henry Miller). In our integrated approach to the humanities, we examine literature, painting, music, sculpture, philosophy, and architecture not as separate disciplines but as interrelated manifestations of human creativity. Nor do we study the arts and artists in isolation. Artists are individuals, coping with the stress and strain of everyday life and, perhaps more than other people, influenced by the ideas and values of their society. "Artists are," observed composer Ned Rorem, "like everyone else, only more so."

The main focus of our study of the humanities is the idea that the quality of life can be enhanced and that this enrichment is available to all. Unlike world oil reserves, the reservoir of Western (or any other) culture is limitless; the more we draw from it the more there is to draw on. The only deposits necessary are time and effort. The process amounts to addition or even multiplication; no one has to discard a rock record collection to listen to Beethoven nor does Cowboy Art have to be exchanged for Rembrandt.

This prologue is an introduction to the significance of the artist as an individual, the necessity of art, and the primacy of human values. Fundamental to cultural development are values such as truth, beauty, love, justice, and faith. Our investigation of how other cultures developed their value systems is chronological, a "return to the past" to see how the Egyptians, Greeks, and later civilizations handled their problems: the questions they asked and the solutions they tried. We explore earlier cultures from the vantage point of our own world, studying prior achievements not as museum pieces but as living evidence of enduring responses to the perplexities of life. This priceless legacy becomes a basic part of our attempts to make sense of the world about us and of our own lives. Some will ask if we can really look to the past to prepare for the future. Where else can we look?

Why Study the Humanities?

We explore the humanities not just to acquire facts about past eras but to try to understand those societies: their questions; their answers; what they valued. We can see the qualities they prized in their art and philosophy, and in their social and political institutions. We examine all of these areas to learn what they did; more importantly, we are concerned with *why* and *how* their cultures evolved in certain unique ways. Culture has sometimes been defined as that which remains after a particular society has vanished. What is left behind amounts to much more than artifacts; the creations of other cultures tell us of their visions, their hopes, their dreams.

This is a text for the integrated or interdisciplinary humanities, the interrelationships of the arts, philosophy, and social and political ideas and institutions. Life is itself interdisciplinary. Using the interdisciplinary approach we study the "lives" of other civilizations to see how their values are manifested in just about everything they did, made, or thought. Whatever we learn from other cultures leads inevitably to a fuller understanding of civilization in general and our own culture in particular.

Each of us has the option of accepting value systems from institutions or other persons; or we can generate a personal set of beliefs and values. Working to acquire an informed set of per-

sonal values is, of course, a lifelong project. The acquisition of knowledge and understanding about other cultures and about ourselves is certainly its own reward, but there are additional advantages. If "the unexamined life is not worth living," as Sokrates said, then self-knowledge would seem to be an acquired virtue. The greater our understanding of what is going on in our lives, the more likely we are to be aware of our options and thus of opportunities to improve the quality of life.

We can achieve the freedom to objectively examine alternatives and possibly make better choices. This freedom is not conditioned absolutely by political, social, and economic considerations, although these factors can help or hinder our actions. One can imagine a political prisoner of a totalitarian state whose knowledge and informed personal values allow a free and independent spirit in the most squalid of surroundings. The prisoner's goals, in this case, are not those of going somewhere or of acquiring material things, but of being a particular person. Those who, in Thoreau's phrase, "live lives of quiet desperation" are at the mercy—intellectually and spiritually—of unknown forces over which they have no control; with no knowledge, no understanding, there is no way to determine whether there are one, two, or more viable choices. All of us have to accept the "slings and arrows of outrageous fortune" (Shakespeare) when we have no alternative. The trick is to be so aware of what is going on in our society and in our lives that we can, at least some of the time, select viable options that will help improve the quality of life. It is worth our while—worth our lives in fact—to study cultures of the past and present, and to make conscious cultural choices on an ascending scale from good to better to the best we can do.

Western Civilization

As proclaimed by the title, this book is primarily—but not exclusively—concerned with Western civilization and its monumental contributions to world culture: its art, literature, performing arts, philosophy, science, and technology. Because of its complexity and influence and because it is our very own heritage, Western civilization commands our full attention. With the inherent limitations of a two-volume text, there is no attempt at an integrated "global humanities," for that would water down Western culture while slighting other rich cultures.

All important cultures have ingenuities of their own. They are all marvelous manifestations of the power of the mind. But our own culture—Western civilization—is the most intellectual of all. More than the others, it is the product of systematic thought. The whole world uses its inventions. Its [science and] scientific methods . . . have been adopted by other civilizations and are transforming them.[1]

---

1. Gilbert Highet, *Man's Unconquerable Mind* (New York: Columbia University Press, 1954), p. 14.

That the preeminence of Western culture is the result of systematic thought is only part of the equation. By asking "systematic thought about what?" we can find the key to Western dominance in science.

> Dear Sir
> Development of Western Science is based on two great achievements; the invention of the formal logical system (in Euclidean geometry) by the Greek philosophers, and the discovery of the possibility to find out causal relationship by systematic experiment (Renaissance). In my opinion one has not to be astonished that the Chinese sages have not made these steps. The astonishing thing is that these discoveries were made at all.[2]

Yes, these discoveries are astonishing for they led to the preeminence of the West in empirical science and technological advances, but there is more. The social and political values of the West have also had worldwide influence, ranging from the thought of Solon, Plato, and Aristotle to Cicero, Dante, Voltaire, John Locke, Thomas Jefferson, and Martin Luther King, Jr. Though immigrants from Asia, and Africa, for example, cannot readily perceive Western culture as "theirs," the fact is that their own cultures have adopted much of Western culture, and only partly because of colonialism. The adoption in various degrees of Western technology, science, and political and economic systems by the rest of the world speaks for itself. The further fact that Western civilization was, in general, created by what some have called "dead white men," alters nothing for we cannot rewrite history. The Greeks invented democracy, speculative philosophy, and formal logic, and Renaissance innovators invented and developed the experimental scientific method. The list of Western inventions is virtually endless: the incandescent light bulb, telephone, automobile, airplane, computer, space flight, and, yes, nuclear fission and fusion. The power eventually attained from nuclear-fusion power plants may even save the world from its manifold excesses.

The Culture-Epoch Theory

To understand any culture, one must study its history to determine how that particular civilization developed. Rather than an analysis of previous events, *history is an ongoing discussion about the meaning of the past*. In this book we consider the past in terms of a simplified version of the *culture-epoch theory* of cultural formation. Except for a smattering of political-military history, many of us are neither concerned nor knowledgeable about our cultural heritage. In helping overcome that deficiency, the culture-epoch theory has several virtues: it stresses the critical fact of ceaseless change; cultural and intellectual history are woven into a historic tapestry; and evolutionary process is emphasized as the key to human knowledge. The theory is neither more nor less

---

2. Albert Einstein, letter to J. E. Switzer dated April 23, 1953, in D. J. de S. Price, *Science Since Babylon* (New Haven, Conn.: Yale University Press, 1962), p. 15n.

"true" than other theories of cultural evolution; for our purpose, in an interdisciplinary context, the theory works.

According to the culture-epoch theory, a culture is founded on whatever conception of reality is held by the great majority of people over a considerable period of time. The majority of people may not be aware of any concept of reality or, more probably, take it so much for granted that they don't recognize it as simply a human idea, held on faith. Thus, for most people at the time this is written, a typewriter is real, a physical tree is real, and all things that can be seen, heard, smelled, felt, or tasted are real.

In fact, a number of scientists, philosophers, and theologians have given us different concepts of reality, which have also been widely held. These thinkers have contemplated the millions of forms of life, many of them bearing resemblances to others, yet each one different; they have examined the forms of earth, air, fire, and water; they have wondered about the processes of change by which a tree today may, at some time in the future, disintegrate into earth and reappear in some totally alien form. They have watched such nontangible things as sunlight and air becoming leaf and branch. Pondering these things, they come inevitably to the ultimate question: "What is the nature of reality?"

To reach an answer, they usually focus on a few profound inquiries, some of which may be given here. They might say, for example, "We see change all around us. We see grass eaten and turn into cow. We see cow eaten and turn into human. We see humans disintegrate and become earth. If all these changes can take place, what are the universal elements of which all things are composed?" Or they might say, "We see an individual human, Jane Doe, as baby, as youth, as adult, as frail old woman, as corpse. From one moment to the next, she is never the same; yet she is always the same, Jane Doe, a distinct being. Can it be that nothing is permanent, that reality is a process rather than a thing or group of things? If we have change, then, how does the process take place? And more to the point, we know that we live in a world of constant change, but what force directs the process?"

"Nonsense," retorts another group of thinkers. "Anything in a constant state of flux cannot be real. Only that which is permanent and unchanging can be real. What, then, in the universe is permanent, unchanging in itself, yet is able to transform itself, manifest itself, or produce from itself the countless forms we see around us?" The responses to basic questions such as these are various concepts of reality.

Based on the idea of reality accepted as "true," specialized thinkers build different thought structures that underlie visible institutions. These include a philosophy of justice from which particular forms of law and government spring; a philosophy of education that dictates the nature of schools and the material taught in them; a religious philosophy that becomes apparent in churches and creeds; an economic philosophy that is manifested in the particular ways of producing and distributing goods and services. There are, of course, other philosophies and institutions, but these are some that greatly affect our daily living.

The culture is complete and balanced when the philosophies and institutions agree with the concept of reality, but by the time such a pattern is established, there are forces at work that will undermine it. The wreckers are new critics who note inconsistencies within the idea of reality itself, who question postulates and detect contradictions.

From these innovative thinkers (philosophers, scientists, theologians) emerges a new idea of reality so convincing it cannot be brushed aside. Once the new reality is generally accepted, the whole cultural structure finds itself without foundation. Law and justice of the old culture are no longer appropriate; educational philosophies are unsatisfactory; religious beliefs must be adjusted or even discarded; old ways of making and distributing things no longer suffice. Over a stretch of time, the culture is plunged into a *period of chaos*, the first step in the formation of a new epoch.

Periods of Chaos

A notable example of a chaotic period is the Early Middle Ages (ca. 450–800), once called the Dark Ages. The relative stability of the Graeco-Roman era of 480 B.C. to A.D. 180 began to disintegrate following the reign of Marcus Aurelius. The Greek ideal of the Individual as reality was superseded by the Roman view that reality was the State without seriously disturbing the cultural balance. Both were secular societies with a general respect for law and justice, a stable social order, and reasonably effective governments. The decline of Rome was very gradual as government, the economy, and the rule of law began to unravel. The rise of Christianity and the barbarian invasions helped finish off a weary and decadent civilization, and most of Western Europe soon found itself deep in a period of chaos. Graeco-Roman civilization was not totally destroyed—as demonstrated by the classically inspired Renaissance—but the stage was set for a new idea of reality through which order would be restored.

Period of Adjustment

Out of the turmoil and confusion of chaotic periods of past cultures emerges the *period of adjustment*. At this time innovative artists and thinkers—whether painters, scientists, writers, composers, or philosophers—make important contributions that can suggest innovative lines, shapes, or patterns for a new culture.

No one needs to know all about new ideas of reality. In our own time, for example, artists (in particular) may or may not understand Einstein's theories of relativity. As very sensitive persons, they generally feel the tensions caused by Einstein's work and its implications. Because they are creators, artists feel compelled to explore the impact that theories, ideas, and events have on their society and to examine or invent new experiences and relationships.

Many people experience the tension and turmoil in periods of chaos and adjustment, but artists tend to actively respond to the chaos and confusion. They explore conflicts within their culture and create new structures and designs; they synthesize the elements of dissension and give fresh meaning to experience. Some artworks are so outstanding that they become symbols of the new age. The Parthenon, for example (see figure 7.34), still symbolizes the Golden Age of Athens.

At some point another element of the population—we may call them *intellectuals*—enters the picture. They are people such as ourselves, college students and faculty, government officials, business executives, philosophers, and many others who have been troubled by the tensions and conflicts of the time. Still laboring in the period of adjustment, they become aware of fresh meanings and patterns produced by artists and other innovators. They begin reshaping these designs into new philosophies of government, justice, education, economics, and the like. Through their work, order slowly emerges out of chaos. Based on the idea of the Christian God as the ultimate reality, the period of adjustment of the medieval world saw the expansion of the power of the Church of Rome, the rise of universities and growth of cities (plus other factors) that coalesced in the thirteenth century into the period of balance of the High Middle Ages.

Period of Balance

Order is the hallmark of the *period of balance*. At this point the idea of reality, the philosophies underlying the basic institutions, and the institutions themselves, are all in harmony. Life must be very satisfying. Most everyone must know the reason for getting up every morning and with no problem too big to solve. But, virtually simultaneously, new and challenging ideas are already stirring. It is unlikely that very many people in thirteenth-century Europe perceived their era as a period of balance. No one was aware, at the time, that the balance would be upended by forces leading to stronger national states, the revival of humanism, the rediscovery of Greek philosophy and science, and the Reformation.

But change is perhaps the only constant and it occurs inevitably. At the beginning of this century, for example, physicists were convinced that the monumental discoveries had been made with little left but some tidying up. At the same time Einstein was formulating theories that would supersede previous knowledge in physics. Just when people become certain of virtually everything during a period of balance, new ideas are already fermenting that will dump the apple cart into a new period of chaos.

A word of caution is needed here. This systematic description of an epoch makes it appear that artists function only in a time of chaos or adjustment, or that philosophers quit philosophizing until their proper time comes around. Of course this is not true. Whereas any epoch can be divided roughly into the three periods described above, all functions occur with greater or lesser impact throughout the entire time period.

A Common Basis for Understanding the Arts

In the humanities we take art seriously. As Aristotle observed, "Art is a higher type of knowledge than experience." As previously indicated in the description of a culture-epoch, eminent artists help create patterns for a way of life; "The object of art is to give life a shape" (Jean Anouilh). The Parthenon, Chartres cathedral, Augustine's *The City of God,* Beethoven's Ninth Symphony, Michelangelo's *David* and Sistine Chapel ceiling are only a few examples of artworks that have affected life in the Western world.

One might ask what area of the universe is the darkest, the most unknown. The universe itself? Einstein once said that the most incomprehensible fact about the universe is that it is so comprehensible. No, the most bewildering portion of the universe is yourself. As a member of the human race, you are (or should be) asking yourself such questions as "Who am I?" "What am I?" "Why am I here?" It is the artist (e.g., writer, painter, musician) who persists in reacting to these questions, who seeks answers from within, and who discovers answers that strike responsive chords in the rest of us. As Henry Miller said, "Art teaches nothing, except the significance of life."

A Shakespearean scholar once stated that, in his plays, Shakespeare had made discoveries as important as those of a scientist. Such an assertion seems, at first, to be an overreaction to the dominance of science in today's world. Consider, however, the playwright's treatment of love and hate in *Romeo and Juliet,* good and evil in *King Lear,* and murder and revenge in *Macbeth.* As enacted on stage, these aspects of the human condition constitute artistic truths. This idea of discoveries by Shakespeare or any other artist can provide a basis for a better understanding of the arts. In this respect, as Jean Cocteau observed, "Art is science in the flesh."

The physical world is explored by the sciences; the social sciences make discoveries about the behavior and activities of people in various groups; the arts and humanities probe the inner meaning: humanity's hopes, fears, loves, delights as individuals act and react within a social context. "All art is social," historian James Adams noted, "because it is the result of a relationship between an artist and his time." Art is also exploration, and the discoveries made can be expressed as *concepts* and *percepts.* Concepts are intangible ideas such as friendship, beauty, truth, and justice. What we perceive with our senses are percepts: line, taste, color, aroma, volume, pitch, and so forth. Artists express concepts by the unique manner in which they choose to arrange the percepts, that is, the sense-apparent objects and materials. Obviously this kind of vivid creativity can never be done by committee; "Art is the most intense mode of individualism that the world has known" (Oscar Wilde).

Differences and Similarities

Because of variations in media and modes of expression, the arts differ from one another in a variety of ways. Certainly a *time-art* such as music, which exists only as long as it is heard, differs from a *space-art* such as painting, which uses visual symbols as its means of expression. Both arts are separated from literature, a *word-art* that has a minimum requirement of fully developed literacy. The differences between Beethoven's Fifth Symphony, the *Mona Lisa,* and *Hamlet* are certainly obvious; what is not so obvious are their similarities. "Painting," wrote Emerson, "was called silent poetry, and poetry speaking painting. The laws of each art are convertible into the laws of any other." As early as the fourteenth century Dante called sculpture "visible speech." The common basis of all the arts is the exploration by means of sensory percepts into the emotions, mind, and personality of human beings; their common goal is to speak directly to our inner being. As Emerson also wrote: "Raphael paints wisdom; Handel sings it; Pheidias carves it; Shakespeare writes it."

The artist deals subjectively with all materials as he or she draws on a singular store of personal experience. Artistic production depends as much on the background and personality of the artist as it does on the raw material of experience. It therefore follows that each artist is unique and that the artist's production is necessarily unique. To illustrate, let us examine the treatment two literary artists make of the same theme: the emptiness of the life of a woman who, herself, is virtually a complete blank, but who moves from man to man, living only as a reflection of each man. Read Dorothy Parker's "Big Blonde" and Anton Chekhov's "The Darling," both short stories. Though the experience is very similar in the two stories, the end result is quite dissimilar and the reader's experience is also different. The reader might protest, "But one of them must be right about this woman and one must be wrong." Actually, both Parker and Chekhov are right in this case—both stories have the ring of truth—and any other artist treating the same material with a different insight would also be right. The discovery of multiple truths is a personal matter, and the corollary is that the realm of truth in personality, that prime area where the arts are focused, is inexhaustible. The person who understands any work of art grows with each facet of experience shared with the artist, i.e., our boundaries are constantly expanded as we add the artist's experiences to our own.

Thanks to art, instead of seeing one world,
our own, we see it multiplied and, as many original
artists as there are, so many worlds are at our disposal.

André Malraux

Summary

The humanities include, but are not limited to, the arts of literature, painting, music, sculpture, architecture, and dance, and the discipline of philosophy that permeates all the arts and finally unites them all. The arts, taken together, are a separate field of human knowledge with their own area of exploration and discovery, and with a method of their own. Beginning with the Renaissance, this volume concentrates on some of the most significant artistic production of the major periods of Western civilization. Each unit begins with an overview of the social, scientific, religious, and philosophic climate of the period in which the artists were working, for the artists usually accept the scientific and social world-picture of their time. Following these introductory discussions, attention is focused on the arts themselves, with enough examples of each to reveal new answers to the great questions of humankind, new patterns, structures, and meaning the artists found for life in their time. This procedure will enable the student to trace the development and changes through history of the problems that still plague us so sorely in our own time. Equipped with knowledge of the great answers found in the past that still shape the way we live today, having come to know the exalted expressions of humanity revealed at their fullest, each individual can work to develop an informed set of values and a freedom to be the person he or she would like to be.

In such fashions as those illustrated, artists, whatever their medium—music, painting, literature—have made form the vehicle of idea, have made the raw materials of art acquire significance by arrangement and handling. It is a different kind of meaning from that of scientists, which can be perceived and measured in an objective world, for this sort of meaning can be known only by the individual who can perceive the relationships the artists have formulated, and who can find them valid in their own life. It is not an easy process; just as the effectiveness of the scientist depends on two things—the validity of the discovery and the ability of the beholder to understand or comprehend it—so the effectiveness of the artist depends on the validity of the discovery and the sensitivity of the beholder to comprehend it. "I don't get it" is no refutation of either Einstein or Bach.

Not everyone will derive the same kind or degree of satisfaction from a particular art form, but the educated person is obligated to know that "there is something in it," even if that "something" does not deeply move that individual. And perhaps, with deeper acquaintance and wider knowledge, that "something" will become clearer and of greater value.

We have made the assertion that the artist is an explorer and discoverer in the realm of the human personality. The artist uses the method of intuition and composition. The artist's raw material lies in the human personality and in human experience, with their vast and unknown reaches, their disrupting conflicts. The artist gives form to the component elements of personality and experience and in so doing generates an artistic truth. No matter whether we speak of literature, painting, sculpture, music, or any of the other arts, this concept of creating form out of chaos is the common basis and foundation for all aesthetics.

THE RENAISSANCE,

1350–1600

THE RENAISSANCE

1350–1600

	People and Events	Art and Architecture	Literature and Music	Philosophy, Science, Discovery
1350	**1305–1376** Papacy at Avignon **1348–1350** Black Death **1382** Wiclif's Bible	**Limbourg Brothers fl.** 1385–1416 *Tres Riches Heures de Duc de Berry*	**Petrarch** 1304–1374 sonnets **Boccaccio** 1313–1375 *The Decameron*	
1400	**1415** Jan Hus burned at stake Henry V of England defeats French at Agincourt **1378–1417** Great Schism of Church **1428** Joan of Arc defeats English **1436** Dedication of Florence Cathedral **1419–1467** Philip the Good of Burgundy **1453** Hundred Years' War ends Constantinople falls to Turks **1449–1492** Lorenzo de'Medici **1456** Gutenberg Bible printed **1469–1504** Reign of Ferdinand and Isabella of Spain **1492–1503** Alexander VI (Borgia pope) **1494** Beginning of French and Spanish invasions of Italy **1498** Savonarola burned at stake Petrucci obtains printing monopoly in Venice	**Brunelleschi** 1377–1446 Florence Cathedral dome; Pazzi Chapel **Donatello** 1386–1466 *David* **van Eyck** 1390–1441 Ghent Altarpiece **Uccello** 1397–1475 *Battle of San Romano* **van der Weyden** 1400–1464 *Portrait of a Lady* **Masaccio** 1401–1428? *Tribute Money* **Alberti** 1404–1472 Santa Maria Novella **Verrocchio** 1435–1488 *David* **Memling** 1440–1494 *The Presentation in the Temple* **Bramante** 1444–1514 Tempietto **Botticelli** 1445–1510 *Birth of Venus* **Bosch** 1450–1516 *Garden of Delights* **da Vinci** 1452–1519 *Mona Lisa*	**Dunstable** ca. 1380?–1453 English composer **Dufay** 1400–1474 Burgundian composer **Lorenzo Valla** ca. 1407–1457 proved *Donation of Constantine* a forgery **Isaac** 1450–1517 German composer at Medici court **des Près** 1450–1521 Franco-Flemish composer **Mirandola** 1463–1494 *Oration on the Dignity of Man* **Erasmus** 1466–1536 *Praise of Folly* **Machiavelli** 1469–1527 *The Prince* **Sir Thomas More** 1478–1535 *Utopia* **Castiglione** 1478–1529 *The Book of the Courtier* **1498** *The Witches Hammer* A manual for finding witches	**Prince Henry the Navigator** 1394–1460 improved compass and navigation charts **Ficino** 1433–1499 translated Plato for Platonic Acad. **1462** Cosimo de' Medici founds Platonic Acad. **Copernicus** 1473–1543 heliocentric theory **1486** Diaz sailed down African coast **1492** Columbus discovered America **1497** John Cabot landed in America; North America claimed by British **1497–1499** Vasco de Gama sailed around Africa to India
1500 **1600**	**1503–1513** Julius II (Warrior Pope) **1517** Luther posts 95 theses **1521** Diet of Worms: Luther's formal break with Rome **1509–1547** Henry VIII of England **1515–1547** Francis I of France **1519** Cortés conquered Aztecs in Mexico **1527** Rome sacked by Charles V **1531–1533** Pizarro conquered Incas in Peru **1534** Church of England founded by Henry VIII **1540** Society of Jesus officially sanctioned **1545–1564** Council of Trent; Inquisition renewed **1547** Calvin's Bible **1588** English defeat Spanish Armada **1558–1603** Elizabeth I of England	**Grünewald** 1483?–1528 *The Small Crucifixion* **Dürer** 1471–1528 *Erasmus of Rotterdam* **Giorgione** 1475–1510 *Adoration of the Shepherds* **Michelangelo** 1475–1564 *David, Pieta,* Sistine Chapel **Raphael** 1483–1520 *Alba Madonna* **Titian** 1488–1576 *Venus with a Mirror* **Holbein** 1497–1543 *Sir Thomas More* **Parmigianino** 1503–1540 *Madonna with the Long Neck* **Tintoretto** 1518–1594 *Last Supper* **Palladio** 1518–1580 Villa Rotunda **Bruegel the Elder** 1525–1569 *Winter (Return of the Hunters)* **Veronese** 1528–1588 *The Finding of Moses* **El Greco** 1541–1614 *Laokoön*	**Rabelais** 1490–1553 *Gargantua and Pantagruel* **Vasari** 1511–1574 *Lives of Architects, Painters, Sculptors* **Palestrina** 1524/5–1594 Roman composer **Lassus** 1532–1594 Flemish composer **Montaigne** 1533–1592 *Essays* **Cervantes** 1547–1616 *Don Quixote* **Gabrieli** 1557–1612 Venetian composer **Shakespeare** 1564–1616 *The Tempest* **Farnaby** 1565–1640 English composer **Bennet** 1575–1625 English madrigal composer	**1513** Balboa discovered Pacific **1519–1522** Magellan sailed around world **Tycho Brahe** 1546–1601 astronomer **Francis Bacon** 1561–1626 empirical science **Galileo** 1564–1642 laws of motion **Kepler** 1571–1630 elliptical orbits **Descartes** 1596–1650 dualism

New Ideas and Discoveries Result from a New Way of Looking at the World

chapter *16*

The Renaissance (ca. 1350–1600) was a remarkable period of intellectual energy and artistic creativity that ushered out the Middle Ages and set the stage for the emergence of the modern world. It was also a turbulent time of social unrest, political turmoil, religious conflict, and particularly in Italy, constant warfare. The era was seen by its contemporaries as a "rebirth" of classical civilization, but it was also a period of chaos following the breakdown of the balanced culture of the High Middle Ages. Graeco-Roman civilization had neither died nor been "lost"; rather, it had been both replaced and partly absorbed by a thousand years of what humanists designated as the "Middle Age" between the fall of Rome and the revival of Graeco-Roman culture.

The medieval idea of God as the ultimate reality was gradually superseded by a new reality that viewed men and women as unique human beings who were the noblest creations of God. Everyone had worth and dignity and a free will that enabled them to use their God-given capacities to transform the world. They could and should develop their minds by study and reflection, activities advocated by Cicero as worthy of the "dignity of the human race" (On duties I, 30). Renaissance men and women were often as religious, superstitious, and narrow as their medieval ancestors, but they were also more individualistic, materialistic, and skeptical than most anyone in that vanished world. The enthusiastic revival of their ancient heritage reinforced their pride in being singular individuals who could create a brave new world.

The glorification of the distant past originated in Italy and spread to France, England, and the Low Countries, none of which even possessed a classical heritage though all contained Roman ruins. What Italy and the northern countries had in common was vigorous trade, the expansion of capitalism, expanding craft guilds, burgeoning industries, growing cities, and a widespread spirit of creative endeavor.

The Rise of Humanism

On 8 April 1341 Petrarch (Francesco Petrarca; 1304–1374) was crowned with a laurel wreath as the first poet laureate of modern times. Symbolizing an intellectual movement called *humanism* that had begun in Verona and Padua a century earlier, the ceremony honoring the leading humanist took place, fittingly enough, in Rome. Humanism was the rediscovery of the culture of classical antiquity: literature, history, rhetoric, ethics, and politics. Describing his abandoned law studies at Bologna as "the art of selling justice," Petrarch devoted his life to acquiring what he called the "golden wisdom" of the ancients: the proper conduct of one's private life; the rational governance of the state; the enjoyment of beauty; and the quest for truth. Humanism was a union of love and reason that stressed earthly fulfillment rather than medieval preparations for paradise. The humanists had rediscovered their ancestors, seeing them as real people lending assistance in the restatement of human values. Petrarch wrote letters to Cicero, whom he called his father, and to Virgil, who was, he said, his brother.

There had been earlier stirrings of classical revivals in the ninth-century Carolingian Renaissance and in the twelfth century at the Cathedral School of Chartres and the Court of Eleanor of Aquitaine, but not until the middle of the fourteenth century did the rediscovery of antiquity become a true cultural movement. Petrarch's friend, the writer Giovanni Boccaccio (bo-KOTCH-yo; 1313–1375), was one of the first Westerners to study Greek, but by 1400 nearly all the Greek authors had been recovered and translated into Latin and Italian: Homer, Herodotos, Thucydides, Aiskhylos, Sophokles, Euripides, Aristophanes, and all the dialogues of Plato. For the humanists there were three ages of humankind: ancient, middle, and their own modern era. The middle period, the Middle Ages, was deemed a benighted phase between the fall of Rome and the rebirth of classical cultures. The men and women of the Renaissance were, in effect, discovering themselves as they recovered the past. They were aware that their time was significantly different from the Middle Ages, that they were the spiritual heirs of a distant past that was being reborn through their own efforts. There was no Latin word for rebirth, but Giorgio Vasari (1511-1574; see chapter 17) invented the word *Rinascita (Renaissance)* in his *Lives of the Most Excellent Italian Architects, Painters, and Sculptors from Cimabue to our own Times* (Florence, 1550). Vasari's term was applied to the fine arts that had developed out of early humanism, but the label now describes an era that consciously freed itself from the bondage of medievalism.

Lorenzo Valla (ca. 1407-1457), one of the few Renaissance scholars not associated with Florence, confined his activities mainly to Rome and Naples, where he translated Herodotos and Thucydides into Latin. A dedicated scholar of immense learning, he dared to challenge any authority. He criticized Cicero's supposedly flawless Latin, wrote a philological critique of the New Testament, and most notably, exposed the *Donation of Constantine* as a forgery. This was the document that willed Constantine's entire empire to the Church of Rome and on which Rome based its claims to temporal power.[1] Valla would be called a bookworm today, for he was one of the many scholars who devoted their careers to conserving antiquity by copying and translating ancient documents. Other humanists, such as Boccaccio and Rabelais, preferred writing in the vernacular, whereas still others tried to synthesize the classical past with the Christian present. Marsilio Ficino and Pico della Mirandola were two of the most important of the synthesizers, particularly for the Platonists of Florence.

Platonic Academy

One of the most influential centers of humanistic studies was the Platonic Academy founded at Florence in 1462 by the banker Cosimo de' Medici (1389-1464), the sire of a family that was to dominate Florence throughout most of the Renaissance. The guiding force of the academy, Marsilio Ficino (fi-CHEE-no; 1433-1499), promoted the study of Platonism through his translations into Latin of Plato, Plotinus, and other philosophers. In his major work, the *Theologia Platonica* (1482), Ficino described a universe presided over by a gracious and loving God who sought to bring humankind to Him through Beauty, one of His attributes. The contemplation of the beauty of nature, of beautiful things, of glorious art became a sort of worship of this God. When beauty was arranged in words or paintings (e.g., figure 17.19), these works of art, too, became a part of the circle of love by which people reached beyond themselves to a loving God. Ficino's theory of "Platonic love," a spiritual bond between lovers of beauty, had strong repercussions in later English, French, and Italian literature.

---

1. C. B. Coleman, ed., *The Treatise of Lorenzo Valla on the Donation of Constantine* (New Haven: Yale University Press, 1922).

Pico della Mirandola (PEA-ko della mere-AN-do-luh; 1463-1494) was a colleague of Ficino and a major influence on the Florentine humanists. His broadly based classical education in Greek and Latin was enriched by studies in Hebrew and Arabic that brought him into contact with Jewish and Arabic philosophy. Pico's attack on astrology impressed even the astronomer Johannes Kepler. More importantly, his conception of the dignity of the human race and the ideal of the unity of truth were significant contributions to Renaissance thought. His *Oration on the Dignity of Man* has been called "The Manifesto of Humanism." The following excerpts from Pico's ringing affirmation of the nobility of humankind epitomize the optimistic Renaissance point of view.

Literary Selection

ORATION ON THE DIGNITY OF MAN, 1486
Pico della Mirandola (1463-1494)

I have read in the records of the Arabians, reverend Fathers, that Abdala the Saracen, when questioned as to what on this stage of the world, as it were, could be seen most worthy of wonder, replied: "There is nothing to be seen more wonderful than man." In agreement with this opinion is the saying of Hermes Trismegistus: "A great miracle, Asclepius, is man." But when I weighed the reason for these maxims, the many grounds for the excellence of human nature reported by many men failed to satisfy me—that man is the intermediary between creatures, the intimate of the gods, the king of the lower beings, by the acuteness of his senses, by the discernment of his reason, and by the light of his intelligence the interpreter of nature, the interval between fixed eternity and fleeting time, and (as the Persians say) the bond, nay, rather, the marriage song of the world, on David's testimony but little lower than the angels. Admittedly great though these reasons be, they are not the principal grounds, that is, those which may rightfully claim for themselves the privilege of the highest admiration. For why should we not admire more the angels themselves and the blessed choirs of heaven? At last it seems to me I have come to understand why man is the most fortunate of creatures and consequently worthy of all admiration and what precisely is that rank which is his lot in the universal chain of Being—a rank to be envied not only by brutes but even by the stars and by minds beyond this world. It is a matter past faith and a wondrous one. Why should it not be? For it is on this very account that man is rightly called and judged a great miracle and a wonderful creature indeed.

2. But hear, Fathers, exactly what this rank is and, as friendly auditors, conformably to your kindness, do me this favor. God the Father, the supreme Architect, had already built this cosmic home we behold, the most sacred temple of His godhead, by the laws of His mysterious wisdom. The region above the heavens He had adorned with Intelligences, the heavenly spheres He had quickened with eternal souls, and the excrementary and filthy parts of the lower world He had filled with a multitude of animals of every kind. But, when the work was finished, the Craftsman kept wishing that there were someone to ponder the plan of so great a

---

work, to love its beauty, and to wonder at its vastness. Therefore, when everything was done (as Moses and Timaeus bear witness), He finally took thought concerning the creation of man. But there was not among His archetypes that from which He could fashion a new offspring, nor was there in His treasurehouses anything which He might bestow on His new son as an inheritance, nor was there in the seats of all the world a place where the latter might sit to contemplate the universe. All was now complete; all things had been assigned to the highest, the middle, and the lowest orders. But in its final creation it was not the part of the Father's power to fail as though exhausted. It was not the part of His wisdom to waver in a needful matter through poverty of counsel. It was not the part of His kindly love that he who was to praise God's divine generosity in regard to others should be compelled to condemn it in regard to himself.

3. At last the best of artisans ordained that that creature to whom He had been able to give nothing proper to himself should have joint possession of whatever had been peculiar to each of the different kinds of being. He therefore took man as a creature of indeterminate nature and, assigning him a place in the middle of the world, addressed him thus: "Neither a fixed abode nor a form that is thine alone nor any function peculiar to thyself have we given thee, Adam, to the end that according to thy longing and according to thy judgment thou mayest have and possess what abode, what form, and what functions thou thyself shalt desire. The nature of all other beings is limited and constrained within the bounds of laws prescribed by Us. Thou, constrained by no limits, in accordance with thine own free will, in whose hand We have placed thee, shalt ordain for thyself the limits of thy nature. We have set thee at the world's center that thou mayest from thence more easily observe whatever is in the world. We have made thee neither of heaven nor of earth, neither mortal nor immortal, so that with freedom of choice and with honor, as though the maker and molder of thyself, thou mayest fashion thyself in whatever shape thou shalt prefer. Thou shalt have the power to degenerate into the lower forms of life, which are brutish. Thou shalt have the power, out of thy soul's judgment, to be reborn into the higher forms, which are divine."

4. O supreme generosity of God the Father, O highest and most marvelous felicity of man! To him it is granted to have whatever he chooses, to be whatever he wills. Beasts as soon as they are born (so says Lucilius) bring with them from their mother's womb all they will ever possess. Spiritual beings, either from the beginning or soon thereafter, become what they are to be for ever and ever. On man when he came into life the Father conferred the seeds of all kinds and the germs of every way of life. Whatever seeds each man cultivates will grow to maturity and bear in him their own fruit. If they be vegetative, he will be like a plant. If sensitive, he will become brutish. If rational, he will grow into a heavenly being. If intellectual, he will be an angel and the son of God. And if, happy in the lot of no created thing, he withdraws into the center of his own unity, his spirit, made one with God, in the solitary darkness of God, who is set above all things, shall surpass them all. Who would not admire this our chameleon? Or who could more greatly admire aught else whatever? It is man who Asclepius of Athens, arguing from his mutability of character and from his self-transforming nature, on just grounds says was symbolized by Proteus in the mysteries. Hence those metamorphoses renowned among the Hebrews and the Pythagoreans.

5. For the occult theology of the Hebrews sometimes transforms the holy Enoch into an angel of divinity whom they call "Mal'akh Adonay Shebaoth," and sometimes transforms others into other divinities. The Pythagoreans degrade impious men into brutes and, if one is to believe Empedocles, even into plants. Mohammed, in imitation, often had this saying on his tongue: "They who have deviated from divine law become beasts," and surely he spoke justly. For it is not the bark that makes the plant but its senseless and insentient nature; neither is it the hide that makes the beast of burden but its irrational, sensitive soul; neither is it the orbed form that makes the heavens but its undeviating order; nor is it the sundering from body but his spiritual intelligence that makes the angel. For if you see one abandoned to his appetites crawling on the ground, it is a plant and not a man you see; if you see one blinded by the vain illusions of imagery, as it were of Calypso, and softened by their gnawing allurement, delivered over to his senses, it is a beast and not a man you see. If you see a philosopher determining all things by means of right reason, him you shall reverence: he is a heavenly being and not of this earth. If you see a pure contemplator, one unaware of the body and confined to the inner reaches of the mind, he is neither an earthly nor a heavenly being; he is a more reverend divinity vested with human flesh. . . .

7. Let us disdain earthly things, despise heavenly things, and, finally, esteeming less whatever is of the world, hasten to that court which is beyond the world and nearest to the Godhead. There, as the sacred mysteries relate, Seraphim, Cherubim, and Thrones hold the first places; let us, incapable of yielding to them, and intolerant of a lower place, emulate their dignity and their glory. If we have willed it, we shall be second to them in nothing.

Virtu

These innovative scholars taught that *virtu* was the highest goal of human existence. *Virtu* is not our word *virtue;* it can be loosely defined as "excellence as a person." *Virtu* embraces skill in many fields, exceptional intelligence, physical courage and daring, and above all, *action* that reveals all these characteristics.[2] Aspirations toward *virtu* led to the concept of the "Renaissance man" as exemplified by Leonardo da Vinci.

Renaissance Science and Technology

The Copernican Revolution

The medieval idea of the universe was based on Ptolemy, whose geocentric theory identified the earth as the center of the universe, with the moon, planets, and stars revolving around the earth in more or less fixed spheres. Around the whole lay the crystalline sphere, outside of which was the realm of God. However, many medieval scientists, particularly the Arabic astronomers, had observed movements of stars and planets that did not readily fit into this scheme and that required the addition of more and more spheres. Working within the confines of Ptolemaic assumptions,

---

2. A comparison can be made with the Greek word *arete,* which was such a crucial concept in ancient Greece. *Arete* translates as "diligence in the pursuit of excellence."

these scientists postulated certain backward loops of the heavenly bodies to account for variations in their periods of rotation. By the time of the Renaissance, astronomers had compiled a complicated system of more than seventy spheres surrounding the earth, with each of the heavenly bodies performing an epicycle, or little backward rotation of its own around a central point on its orbit.

The Ptolemaic system was first questioned by the Polish astronomer and mathematician Nicholas Copernicus (1473–1543). Copernicus never advanced the theory that the earth was not the center of the universe; he believed that mathematical calculations would be less complicated if one accepted the sun as a stationary point and based the computations on a heliocentric system. Though he failed to design a simpler system or to eliminate mistaken assumptions about orbits, his contribution was monumental. Copernicus opened the door to modern astronomy.

> Today we honor Copernicus not because he produced the modern view of the solar system (he didn't) or because his system was simpler than Ptolemy's (it wasn't), but because he was the first person in 'modern times' who had the courage and perseverance to carry his idea beyond the realm of philosophical speculation. It was he who pointed out that the emperor's new clothes might be missing, so that after him everyone came to see geocentrism as just an assumption, one that could be challenged like any other.[3]

Paradoxically, other advances in Renaissance science were made by translating the ancient writings of Galen, Arkhimedes, Hippokrates, and other Greek scientists into Latin. Additionally, there were improvements in anatomical and geological studies, but on the whole, Renaissance scientific studies were mainly preparation for the scientific revolution of the seventeenth century.

Technology

Printing was invented in China in 756, gunpowder around 1100, and the magnetic compass a decade or two later. Like many Chinese innovations, these were so rigidly controlled by the imperial government that they had no value for the common people. With no equivalent central authority in Europe the impact of just these three inventions was dramatic. Movable type was invented in the 1440s in the Rhine river valley of Germany, possibly in Mainz by Johannes Gutenberg (1398?–1468). Once the privilege of the few who could afford hand-copied books, learning became available to all. The invention of printing made possible the most rapid expansion of knowledge that we have known prior to the proliferation of computers in our own time. By 1500 there were over a thousand print shops and millions of volumes in print. The printing press was the key to the success of the Protestant Ref-

ormation—Martin Luther's tracts attacking the Church of Rome were rushed into print and spread like wildfire throughout Europe.

The technique of making gunpowder was imported from China and first used during the latter years of the Hundred Years' War (1337–1453) between England and France. Subsequent improvements in firearms and artillery made gunpowder, in effect, a great leveler. One man with a gun was more than a match for a knight on horseback, and even primitive cannons could bombard medieval castles into submission. The feudal age ended abruptly and, one might say, explosively.

Exploration and Discovery

Trade between European cities and those of the Near and Middle East was an important factor in the evolution of the Renaissance, but the conquests of the Ottoman Turks had cut off the traditional Mediterranean routes. Limited navigational aids forced sailing vessels to generally remain within sight of Mediterranean shores, which worked satisfactorily until other routes to the Middle and Far East had to be found. A few intrepid travelers, the most famous of whom was the Venetian Marco Polo (1254?–1324?), made their way along the great land routes to India and China. Marco Polo returned to Venice after spending many years in China (1271–1295), but no one at the time believed any of the wonders that he related.

Not until the fifteenth century would European sailors have the capability to circumnavigate Africa to reach China, and the driving force behind this exploration was Prince Henry the Navigator (1394–1460), son of King John I of Portugal. Apparently without referring to Chinese work, a crude magnetic compass had been invented in the twelfth century. Henry improved this crucial device, had accurate maps and tables drawn, improved the design of ships, and reintroduced the astrolabe, an Arab invention. A ship's latitude (north-south) could be calculated to within about thirty miles by using the astrolabe to determine the angle of the sun above the horizon at noon. This figure was then compared with Henry's tables of the sun's declination at known latitudes for each day of the year.

Navigation could not be made more precise until the marine chronometer was invented in 1760 to determine longitude (east-west). Nevertheless, navigational aids were adequate for voyages of exploration. In 1497, for example, Vasco da Gama (ca. 1469–1524) sailed southwest and then south from Portugal for ninety-seven days before turning east and sailing directly to the known latitude of his African destination, the Cape of Good Hope. He continued around Africa and on to India, returning to Lisbon in 1499 (see map 16.1). Prior to da Gama's successful voyage, India had been the destination of Christopher Columbus (ca. 1451–1506), who sailed west rather than south and discovered instead a New World—new to Europeans, that is, with the exception of earlier Viking voyages. Columbus claimed the land for Spain, which was confirmed when Spain and Portugal drew a vertical line in the Atlantic, with the Americas awarded to Spain and Africa

3. James Trefil, *The Dark Side of the Universe; A Scientist Explores the Cosmos* (New York: Macmillan Publishing Company, 1988), p. 18.

to Portugal. No one knew at the time that the line ran through Brazil until it was accidentally discovered by the Portuguese captain Pedro Cabral (1460–ca. 1526), who was blown off course as he sailed down the African coast. A treaty later confirmed Portugal's ownership of Brazil. It apparently occurred to no one that the Americas and Africa were already inhabited by people who were never consulted by their new owners. European colonialism had begun.

Vasco de Balboa (1475–1517) marched across the Isthmus of Panama in 1513 to discover a Pacific Ocean that residents of the Pacific Basin had always known was there. Ferdinand Magellan (1480–1521), a Portuguese in the service of Spain, sailed west in 1519 with five ships to find a passage, now called the Straits of Magellan, around South America and across the Pacific to Asia. He was killed in the Philippines, but his explorations proved empirically that the world was round.

Spain and Portugal planned on dividing the entire overseas world between them but England and France had other ideas. An Italian mariner whom the English called John Cabot (1450–1498) was dispatched in 1497 to find a "northwest passage" to the Indies. The passage did not exist, of course, but Cabot's landings somewhere around Labrador and Newfoundland provided England with

an opportunity to claim all of North America. The explorations of Jacques Cartier (1494–1553) plus later discoveries by Samuel de Champlain (1567?–1635) gave France competing claims, and the Dutch joined the competition with the explorations of Henry Hudson (?–1611), an Englishman who entered Dutch service in 1609.

Maritime explorers were followed by adventurers such as Hernando Cortés (1485–1547) and Francisco Pizarro (1471–1541) who conquered the only two high civilizations of the New World. Cortés took the Aztec empire of Mexico in 1519 with 600 soldiers, and Pizarro conquered the Inca empire of Peru in 1531–1533 with only 180 soldiers.

There was treasure aplenty in the New World, but Europeans found another in their own minds. Accounts of the voyages of explorers inspired Renaissance imaginations much as space exploration fascinates today's world. Renaissance Europe had opened up new frontiers in art, literature, philosophy, and science, and now there was the lure and challenge of new lands as well. America became, for many Europeans, the literal utopia that Sir Thomas More used as the setting for his fictional *Utopia* (see chapter 19).

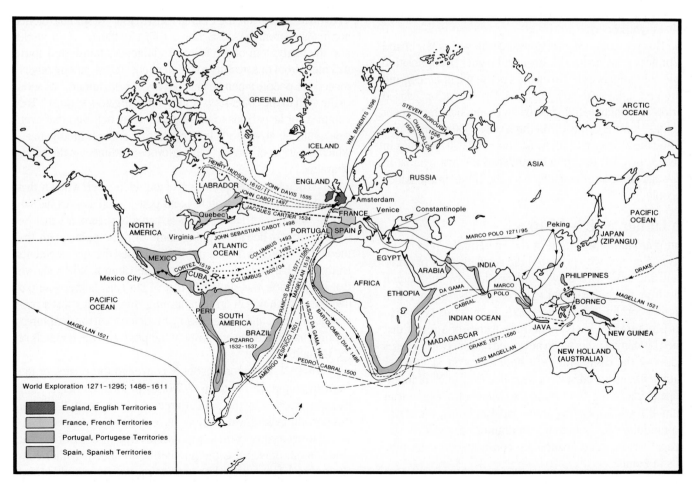

Map 16.1 *World Exploration 1271–1295; 1486–1611.*

The Reformation: New Ideas about God and Humankind

Concepts about the world and the universe changed rapidly during the Renaissance, but it was the Reformation that transformed the face of Europe. It not only divided a once monolithic institution but kindled social, political, economic, and intellectual revolutions. There had been earlier challenges to the authority of the Church of Rome, but the Reformation inaugurated by Martin Luther was the first to succeed on a large scale.

Centuries earlier, in 1170, a French merchant named Peter Waldo (d. 1217) founded a puritan sect known as the Waldenses. Preaching apostolic poverty, they rejected Rome and its papal claims. Though excommunicated in 1184 and persecuted for centuries, the sect survives today as the *Vaudois* in the Alps of Italy and France.

In England, John Wiclif (or Wycliffe; ca. 1320–1384), an Oxford scholar, revived interest in St. Augustine and openly questioned the need for a priestly hierarchy. Contending that God and the Scriptures were the sole sources of spiritual authority, he translated the Vulgate into English and urged everyone to read it for themselves. He was silenced by the Church, but the Wiclif Bible became important after 1534 when Henry VIII, with his Act of Supremacy, broke away from the Church of Rome and confiscated all church property.

Jan Hus (or Huss; 1369–1415) was a follower of Wiclif and a priest/professor at Charles University in Prague. His opposition to the sale of indulgences led to charges of the Wiclif heresy, and he was burned at the stake on 6 July 1415. His martyrdom caused bloody riots in Bohemia, followed by an evangelical movement of the Unitas Fratrum (Unity of Brethren). By 1500 the Brethren (later called the Moravian Church) had over 200,000 members in 400 parishes. In 1501, the church published the first hymnal in the vernacular and placed it, along with the Bible, in the hands of the people.

Martin Luther, 1483–1546

The term *reformation* was used in the late Middle Ages by individuals and groups who protested the secularization of Christianity and the abuses of power and privilege by the church hierarchy, from the popes down to parish priests. An unbroken succession of corrupt Renaissance popes, from Sixtus IV (1471–1484) to Leo X (1513–1521), fueled the flames of a revolt that was ignited by Martin Luther when he posted his ninety-five Theses on the door of the castle church at Wittenberg on 31 October 1517. Luther was incensed at what he called the "sale" of indulgences, particularly the fund-raising activities of a Dominican monk named Tetzel. Operating under papal authority, Tetzel was dealing in indulgences, soliciting contributions to swell the depleted papal treasury and finance the construction of the new St. Peter's in Rome.

Luther intended, at first, a clarification of the teachings of the Church. The *origins* of the Reformation are found primarily in Luther's religion. An Augustinian friar and professor of theology at the University of Wittenberg, Luther had experienced a spiritual crisis. Convinced that he was a lost soul and destined for Hell, Luther took the advice of a confessor and plunged with characteristic fervor into intensive study of the Bible. He rediscovered, in the epistles of Paul, a faith in salvation by grace. The central doctrines of the early church fathers, especially Augustine, confirmed his belief in the authority of the Word of God: faith alone was sufficient for salvation. Church doctrine stipulated that faith *and* good works were necessary, but Luther stood firm in the conviction that he articulated the true faith of the Church. Faith and the Bible were enough for Luther; the break with Rome was inevitable.

Why was Luther so concerned about indulgences? Indulgences were remissions by the Church of temporal punishment either on earth or in purgatory. The Sacrament of Penance of the Church of Rome consists of contrition, confession, absolution, and satisfaction on the part of the penitent. The penitent must feel contrition for his or her sins, confess to the priest, and be absolved of guilt. The sinner must satisfy God's justice by working out the penalties assigned by the priest. Indulgences could be granted for the guilt or punishment in purgatory but, after confession to the priest, the sin remained. According to the doctrine of *Thesaurus Meritorum,* the Church had a treasury of spiritual merits accumulated from the satisfaction of Christ for the sins of the world and the martyrdom of the Saints. Indulgences transferred spiritual merit from this treasury to the penitent. Tetzel, among others, misled the people when he chanted his favorite refrain: "As soon as the coin in the coffer rings A soul from Purgatory springs." Too complex for laypersons to understand, many believed that even sins could be absolved if they could buy enough indulgences, which, as Luther observed, "put a grievous instrument in the hands of avarice."

"Therefore those preachers of indulgences err who say that a papal pardon frees a man from all penalty and assures his salvation" was one of Luther's theses, actually statements that he would publicly debate. Arguing some of these points with the theologian John Eck, Luther publicly admitted that his statements really did challenge the authority of the Church. When shown that his position was similar to that of Jan Hus, Luther asserted that the Church was in error in burning Hus. Jan Hus was a condemned heretic, and Luther, basing his defense on the Scriptures, openly challenged the authority of the pope and the councils of the Church.

In 1521, Emperor Charles V convened the estates of the German empire in the town of Worms to force Luther, already excommunicated by the pope, to retract his writings. "I neither can nor will make any retraction, since it is neither safe nor honorable to act against conscience" was his response. Insisting that "the Church universal is the number of the elect," Luther concluded his defense, according to tradition, with the words, "Here I stand. I cannot do otherwise. God help me. Amen." The Diet declared Luther an outlaw, but the verdict was academic because Luther had many supporters among the German princes (figure 16.1). Corruption in the Church and the formation of a new faith helped promote Luther's church, but a rising tide of nationalism and ending the flow of money to Rome were perhaps even more significant in the rapid spread of the Reformation throughout the Holy Roman Empire, Denmark, Norway, and Sweden (see map 16.2).

The principles of Lutheranism were later formulated by a Lutheran scholar, Melancthon (1497–1560), who stated them as follows:

1. The only final authority either for conduct or belief is in the Scriptures *(Sola Scriptura)*.
2. The one condition of salvation is faith or trust in Divine Love *(Sola Fide)*.
3. Faith itself is a gift of God, not an achievement of man *(Sola Gratia)*.
4. The community of the faithful is the true church whose only head is Christ. The growth of this church is fostered by preaching the gospel and the observance of two sacraments, Baptism and the Lord's Supper.

Figure 16.1 *Lucas Cranach the Younger (1515–1586),* Martin Luther and the Wittenberg Reformers, *ca. 1543. Oil on panel, 27⅝″ × 15⅜″. Luther is at the far left and Ulrich Zwingli at the far right. Looming large in the center is John Frederick the Magnanimous, Elector of Saxony and patron of the reformers and the Lutheran Church. The Toledo Museum of Art. Gift of Edward Drummond Libbey.*

Map 16.2 *Europe about 1520.*

The Lutheran belief stresses individuality; salvation and a knowledge of God is a direct process, needing no church or priestly intercessor.

Calvinism

The Reformation in Germany was closely followed by a notable movement in Switzerland, first led by Ulrich Zwingli (1484–1531; figure 16.1), who even more than Luther believed in the individuality of worship and the authority of the Scriptures. Later, this group was led by John Calvin (1509–1564), a French Protestant who was originally educated for the law as well as theology. Persecuted in France, he fled to Geneva, where he established a theocratic republic, that is, a government ruled by the elders of the church.

Calvin stated the philosophy of his faith in *The Institutes of the Christian Religion* (revised into its final form in 1559). This rests on the unconditional sovereignty of God; whatever transpires is because God wills it so. The assistance of a Saviour is necessary because Calvin believed in humanity's abject helplessness and total depravity. Predestination was rigorous and universal; a few of the elect will be saved through faith in God but many will be forever damned. Finally, he stated that the group of the elect constitutes the Church, the preservation of which is the duty of religious authorities *and* civil authorities. An infraction of divine law therefore requires civil punishment by officials subject to church authorities. This, as one can see, was a very stern belief; Calvin forbade many of the ordinary pleasures of life in Geneva and vigorously persecuted all who did not follow his faith.

Various forms of Calvinism spread throughout Europe. John Knox (1505–1572) founded the Presbyterian church in Scotland and England following the principles laid down by the Swiss leader. The English Puritans were Calvinists who emigrated to America to found their own theocratic colony.

Other Sects

The individual's right to interpret the Scriptures, virtually the cornerstone of churches spawned by the Reformation, quite naturally led to the formation of many sects. Lutheranism and Calvinism attracted converts from the growing middle class, but many of the newer sects, for whatever reason, drew their following from the poorer classes. Among these latter were the Anabaptists, who believed in baptism only when the individual had reached adulthood and was able to make a free choice. This concept of rebirth through baptism continues today as the Reborn Christian movement. From the Anabaptists came such modern denominations as the Friends (Quakers) and Baptists. The Socinians, who took their name from Faustus Socinus (1539–1604), were antitrinitarians who refused to hold serfs or take part in any war. Persecuted in Poland by the Catholic church led by the Jesuits, they were banished in 1658 on pain of death. The Socinians were the single most important source for the Unitarian church. The Arminian church was led by the Dutch theologian Jacobus Arminius (1560–

1609). It was an offshoot of Calvinism but asserted that each person was free to choose his or her own way of living, thus denying the doctrine of predestination. Its theology was, in essence, accepted by John Wesley (1703–1791), ordained in the Church of England, who founded the movement leading to the Methodist church.

The Church of England itself resulted from Henry VIII's quarrel with Rome. The immediate cause of the separation was the pope's refusal to annul Henry's marriage to Catherine of Aragon, but the real reasons were more fundamental; English monarchs were weary of sending money to Rome and coveted the splendid Roman properties. By 1534 the break was completed with the Act of Supremacy, which recognized the king as the official head of the English church. English became, of course, the language of the new church, but there was little difference, at the time, in the theology and liturgy of the English and Roman churches.

The Counter-Reformation

The Catholic Reformation, also called the Counter-Reformation, was the papal response to Luther's revolt. Convened by Pope Paul III (1534–1549), the Council of Trent met from 1545 to 1563 to reaffirm every phase of Catholic doctrine attacked by the reformers: original sin, grace, redemption, the Sacraments, the Sacrifice of the Mass, and Purgatory. Every violation of discipline was denounced, reforms were enacted, and observance was demanded under pain of censure. The music of the Church was reformed, and there was a strong thrust of Counter-Reformation art and architecture (see chapter 21). The Counter-Reformation was given a mighty assist by the Jesuits (Society of Jesus), founded by Ignatius Loyola in 1534 and formally approved by Pope Paul III in 1540. The Jesuits represented the disciplined drive of the movement, but the popes also revived the Inquisition, an old and seasoned mechanism for stamping out heresy. Sitting as medieval courts and employing medieval methods of torture, the Papal and Spanish Inquisitions sentenced convicted heretics to "purification." The operative term was *auto-da-fe* (Portuguese, "act of the faith") meaning that the secular authorities carried out the sentence by burning the victims at the stake. Though these judicial murders failed to stem the Protestant tide, the Spanish Inquisition was not eradicated until 1834.

How can we sum up the influence of the Reformation on the lives of people? First, it encouraged national identity, the strongest single force moving through this entire period. Second, it had a marked influence on education, in many cases divorcing it from ecclesiastical domination. On the other hand, under the strict influence of the Calvinists in particular, the scope of education was limited largely to subjects of immediate utilitarian value. In terms of the rise of individuality, the Reformation encouraged religious independence; if the Bible is the sole basis for religious beliefs, there are any number of possible interpretations. As a result, Protestantism generated a host of sects in which the individual could find virtually any type of religious belief. Fi-

A DAY IN RENAISSANCE FLORENCE

Awakened by the melodious bells of Santa Maria del Fiore, the Florentine citizen rises with the summer dawn, already feeling the humidity that will make the city stifling by midday. Standing on the imported carpet, Giorgio proudly regards his massive bed with its intricate carvings, elaborate canopy, and rich drapes—even in the oppressive summer heat of the Arno River valley. After checking the mulberry twigs under the bed (they attract fleas from the double mattresses), he summons his valet from the cot in the corner of the bedroom. After a cursory washup, his valet assists him into red tights, a bright blue tunic, soft Florentine leather boots, and his simple citizen's cap. After an admiring glance at his colorful wall tapestry (the sure sign of a successful Florentine businessman), he hides on his person the necessary piece of fur (to attract lice from his body), and hurries through the first-floor rooms on the way to his shop on the ground floor.

Passing through his wife Lucia's bedroom, he notes her high platform shoes, used for crossing the few muddy streets left in booming Florence. She is summering in their villa in the *campagna* (countryside) with their children, Lucrezia and Antonio; he misses them. Normally, she would greet him each morning in her full-flowing dress with its tight bodice and high neckline, her eyes shining beneath the high forehead (stylishly plucked) and the frizzy bleached hair (equally stylish).

He descends to his fabric shop to confer with his head clerk. As a member of the Calimala Guild for dyeing and finishing foreign fabrics, Giorgio ships finished fabrics over much of Europe.

His instructions completed, Giorgio heads for the central *piazza*. The city gates had opened at dawn, and already the narrow paved streets are jammed—farmers with donkey carts, construction workers (all Florence seems under construction), merchants, and women on their way to mass. As usual, last night's drunks (rightly fearful of the evening curfew) are stealing home after spending the night in a tavern.

Giorgio passes through the crowded street where similar crafts are clustered together, just as they were in ancient Rome: blacksmiths, jewelers, goldsmiths, cabinet-makers, stonecutters, marble workers, and most importantly, the prosperous bankers of Florence. He pauses at the artists' street to watch a brawny sculptor skillfully wield a hammer and chisel on a block of Carrara marble, wondering idly if this is the Michelangelo people have been talking about. Poor fellow. How much better to be a merchant dealing in beautiful cloth in a tidy shop.

Nearing the Old Market Piazza he hears the familiar street tumult of fishmongers, butchers, and grocers hawking their wares. Aromas of fish, chickens, horses, garbage, sewage, and the people themselves—who seldom bathed—assaulted his nostrils. No matter. These are the sights, sounds, and odors of his beloved Florence.

His arrangements for a consignment of dyed cloth completed, Giorgio hurries home to his mid-morning breakfast. He usually ate in the kitchen, sharing a pewter plate with Lucia, both wiping their hands on the tablecloth. Today, feeling extra lonely, he strokes the cat as he eats his fruit, cheese, bread, and jam. Looking from his comfortable kitchen toward the blocks of dismal houses, Giorgio thanks God for providing him with better fare than the thin soup and coarse bread of the numerous poor.

By late afternoon he can retire to his *loggia,* his delightful roofed gallery on the housetop, to read letters from Lucia and his son Antonio. Lucia writes glowingly about the progress of the children with their tutor, of her domestic duties—spinning, weaving, needlework—and Lucrezia's growing skills in these household arts. Describing the fruitfulness of the garden, especially the strawberries and zucchini, she hopes that he can join them soon for a weekend. Writing in Latin to impress his father, Antonio (age ten) mournfully relates his efforts to read Virgil, concluding his letter with a less than subtle reminder that moves his father to laughter: "I who have written in Latin to give my letters a proper literary tone, have yet to receive that pony you promised me."

At 5:00, Giorgio seats himself in the dining room for the main meal of the day. Lonesome for his family, he consoles himself with a green salad, soup with sausage, bread, and cheese followed by a choice of figs, grapes, pears, melon, and, of course, a fine, mellow cheese. A friend drops by later to play some chess and to discuss politics, a favorite topic, particularly the apparently boundless ambitions of the Medici family.

As he retires for the night, Giorgio reflects on how fortunate he is to live in a civilized city infinitely superior in every respect to those gloomy, backward cities in the North. Settling down into his capacious bed, he contemplates the ways and means to spend a cool weekend with his family in the *campagna*. Surely he is clever enough to devise some way to see his family and also conduct a bit of business. That is, after all, the Florentine way.

---

nally, Protestantism influenced the growth of capitalism, for the ideal Calvinist, Methodist, or Lutheran took the first psalm to heart:

> Blessed is the man that walketh not in the counsel of the ungodly, nor standeth in the way of sinners, nor sitteth in the seat of the scornful. But his delight is in the law of the Lord; and in his law doth he meditate day and night. And he shall be like a tree planted by the rivers of water, that bringeth forth his fruit in his season; his leaf also shall not wither; and whatsoever he doeth shall prosper.

Clearly this psalm tells us that good people shall prosper. In a time when making, saving, and spending money became more and more the surest sign of success, we can conclude that prosperous people were good people. Furthermore, the sober, steady, shoulder-to-the-wheel and nose-to-the-grindstone way of life advocated by most of the new sects was exactly the sort of life that would promote industrious work and prudent spending. And so began the Protestant work ethic, which produces the ideal person for a capitalist system.

The Relation of the Individual to the Group

Capitalism

We who live in a capitalistic society tend to take our institutions for granted, assuming they have always existed. There was considerable mercantile activity in the Middle Ages, especially in the twelfth and thirteenth centuries, but the economic system called mercantile capitalism did not come into full flower until the Renaissance. The growth of capitalism is but one more example of the trend toward individualism that characterized a transitional period busily rebuilding its society to match the new view of reality. Until this time economic affairs had been dominated by political or religious concerns, granted that merchants always keep an eye on the bottom line. Now, just as knowledge of the real world developed into science, so an economic system evolved into a field of human endeavor little encumbered by religious or political considerations.

The old medieval guilds produced solely for human needs with manufacturing and selling an interrelated process. A cobbler, for instance, made shoes to order and only then. If there were no orders, he could close his shop and go on a picnic. His guild regulated the quality of materials and workmanship and set the prices. There was no competition and the business died with the cobbler, unless he had a son who wished to follow in his footsteps.

The development of Renaissance capitalism can be understood by following the fortunes of the Fugger family of Germany. Anton Fugger became a weaver in Augsberg in 1380 and soon began collecting and selling the products of other weavers. His son, Jacob Fugger I, continued a business that was vastly enlarged under Jacob Fugger II, the leading capitalist of the era. Jacob expanded into metals within the Hapsburg empire, dealing in silver and copper in Austria and silver and mercury in Spain. He also lent huge sums of money (at high interest) to the Hapsburg emperors to finance their many wars, receiving in return monopoly rights on the ores he mined. Inevitably, he bought the mines in order to control all his products from raw materials to market. No one supervised the quality of his products, and Fugger set the price at whatever the traffic would bear. Finally, he formed a company that existed outside himself that piled up profits far exceeding the needs of the Fuggers or any other family. Rather than lands or goods, these profits were measured in power fuelled by money. From this example we can explore the essential attributes of capitalism.

Characteristics of Capitalism

Capitalism creates "companies" that exist separately from the people who make them up. The company can conduct business, make contracts, assume debts, distribute and/or reinvest profits, and be subject to litigation. The purpose of the company is to make money with no possibility of making too much money. Using a modern example, we can consider a single family that acquires

Figure 16.2 *Quentin Matsys (1465?–1530),* **The Money Lender and His Wife,** *1514. Oil on wood, 28" × 26¾". Distracted from reading her Bible, the wife is as fascinated as her husband as he lovingly examines his money. The Louvre, Paris.*

more money than it can spend. Family members can buy any number of luxury items but ride in only one chauffeur-driven limousine (or Lear jet) at a time, live in one house at a time, and consume just so much food in a lifetime. There is a physical limit to what can be bought and used but no limit whatever on the amount of money (and power) that can be amassed (see figure 16.2). Capitalism assumes that the acquisition of money is the goal of economic activity, a logical assumption, of course, because no sensible person goes into business to lose money.

A company is a rational organization that must plan and control every step of its operation from raw materials to the marketplace. It must have an accounting system that keeps track of materials, money, and human energies. Capitalism shapes ends to means and the end is making a profit. This is a rational goal with no room for feeling or emotion. The system is pragmatic; whatever works is good and what doesn't is eliminated.

An irrational aspect of early capitalism was the lack of safety standards either within an industry or imposed by a government. Competition between companies could and did exploit the consumer. Moreover, workers were paid as little as possible and worked as long as possible. In the final analysis:

> Profits, no matter how large, can never reach a level sufficiently high to satisfy the economic agent—acquisition therefore becomes unconditional, absolute. Not only does it seize on all phenomena within the economic realm, but it reaches over into other cultural fields and develops a tendency to proclaim the supremacy of business interest over all other values.[4]

4. Edwin R. Seligman, ed., "Capitalism," in *Encyclopedia of the Social Sciences,* vol. 3 (New York: Macmillan, 1937), p. 197.

The Effects of Capitalism

The flourishing of capitalism certainly increased the possibilities of individualism. Those who made it to the top of the economic heap acquired the power to do whatever they wished. The only limits on individuals lay in their own imagination, creativity, and ability to spot and exploit opportunities. A second effect was the marked increase in available goods. Guilds made goods when people wanted them, but capitalists made more of everything and sold the surplus to ever more people. In the ownership of material things capitalism was a whopping success; the rise of the standard of living in sixteenth-century Europe was due almost entirely to the expansion of the economic system.

Not the least of the effects of capitalism was how it changed cities. Before this time stores had not existed except as booths at fairs, if they could indeed be called stores. In the guild system the factory was the store, i.e., the workshop and living quarters for the craftsman, his apprentices, and his family. Capitalists had to get their merchandise before the public, and this required buildings in which goods were "stored." The impact on Renaissance cities of the expanding industry of retail sales was, of course, remarkable.

The Development of the Sovereign Power

Perhaps the most striking development of the Renaissance was the increase of royal power. We saw the beginning of this movement during the latter part of the Middle Ages, when the inadequacies of feudalism—lack of a common currency, trade hampered by feudal tariff barriers, inconsistencies in the administration of justice, and the lack of trained civil servants—revealed themselves, and the kings drove to new power. Royal might was increasingly keyed to the extravagant stream of treasure from the newly discovered lands across the sea. The Spanish monarch, for example, claimed a fifth of all riches brought to Spain by the *conquistadores*. With seemingly unlimited funds, kings created brilliant courts that attracted the nobles from their muddy country estates and made them dependent on the monarch for their livelihood and for their amusement. Most nobles were more than willing to sell out their rural independence for the privilege of participating in the rituals, grand balls, and resplendent festivals of the royal courts in France, England, and Spain.

Not only did the nobles pledge their allegiance to the sovereign, but the common people looked to the throne as the single source of order in a world changing so rapidly they could scarcely keep up. Order had been the rule in the Middle Ages but "future shock" was present in the Renaissance as it is today. Protestantism shattered the monolithic authority of Rome, science demolished the unity of the universe, and capitalism dismembered the old economic order controlled by the guilds. The king was the single stabilizing influence in all this chaos. Wherever we turn, we find references to the centrality of the sovereign. In Shakespeare's play *Hamlet,* Rosencrantz speaks of the monarch's importance thus:

The cease of majesty
Dies not alone, but, like a gulf doth draw
What's near it with it; it is a massy wheel,
Fix'd on the summit of the highest mount,
To whose huge spokes ten thousand lesser things
Are mortis'd and adjoin'd; which, when it falls,
Each small annexment, petty consequence,
Attends the boisterous ruin. Never alone
Did the king sigh, but with a general groan.

Historically, the Renaissance saw the brilliant reigns of the Tudor rulers in England, especially Henry VIII (ruled 1509–1547) and Elizabeth I (ruled 1558–1603). These two monarchs understood the rising importance of trade and commerce and the vital role the middle class played in England's growing prosperity. It was under Elizabeth, also, that the English navy defeated the mighty Spanish Armada in 1588, making England mistress of the seas until well into the twentieth century.

In France, Francis I (ruled 1515–1547) set a pattern for later kings, such as Louis XIV (ruled 1643–1715), by bringing the best artists to a sumptuously furnished court that became a model for all of Europe. Francis I cemented national feeling by a series of wars fought largely by mercenary soldiers in a helpless and divided Italy. France was later bitterly embroiled in a struggle between the Protestant Huguenots, led by the house of Bourbon, and the Catholics, led by the house of Guise. This struggle reached its conclusion in 1598 when Henry of Navarre took the throne as Henry IV, the first Bourbon king (ruled 1598–1610). Henry professed himself a Catholic, but guaranteed certain rights to the Huguenots in selected cities, rights that Louis XIV later cancelled, at which time thousands of Huguenots left the country.

Spain reached its single high point of brilliance at this time, at first under the rule of Ferdinand and Isabella (1474–1504). They and later rulers enjoyed tremendous profits from the Spanish conquests in Central and South America. In fact, the decline of Spain can be attributed to their disinterest in permanent colonies, preferring instead to plunder their holdings. Later, Spain became one of the countries ruled over by the Hapsburgs, for Charles I of Spain (ruled 1519–1556) also held the title of Archduke of Austria. He was, moreover, Charles V, Emperor of the Holy Roman Empire. His holdings included the kingdom of Naples and Sicily, plus the Netherlands. The Spanish Hapsburgs became the leading Catholic monarchs in Europe and had the force of the Church of Rome as a part of their spiritual and secular power.

In 1566 the Netherlands revolted against the Hapsburg kings, a revolt provoked in large part by the importation of the ruthless Inquisition. After a series of bloody wars Holland became an independent nation, but the area known today as Belgium did not free itself until 1713. Portugal also achieved full independence during the Renaissance and, like Spain, achieved a short-lived glory based on the wealth plundered from its hapless possessions.

Germany became the battleground of the Thirty Years' War (1618–1648), which began as a conflict between Catholics and Protestants and ended as a political struggle against the Hapsburgs by Holland, France, Sweden, and other nations. Germany was devastated as the largest armies since Roman days surged over the countryside. Sweden alone had over 200,000 men in the field. The ferocity of the struggle prompted the writing of the *Law of War and Peace* (1625) by the Dutch jurist Hugo Grotius. Though he recognized war as "legitimate," he did distinguish between just and unjust conflicts and laid down principles for "humane" warfare. Drawing on actual events of the war, he condemned such acts as poisoning wells, mutilating prisoners, massacring hostages, raping, and pillaging. In time, the work of Grotius became the basis of the Geneva Conventions. It was this bitter and disastrous war that spurred emigration to America, where there would be a clear separation of church and state and no more religious disagreements fought out on a battlefield.

Italy's fate deserves a special note, for it was in Italy that humanism first appeared, not to mention the inspired creations of artists such as Leonardo da Vinci, Michelangelo, and Raphael (see chapter 17). One of the most important factors in this period was the development of individuals who could exploit the early mercantile capitalism of enterprising Italian cities. As a result, a few powerful families rose in Italy, each controlling one of the important cities. The Visconti family ruled in Milan, a council of rich merchants took over the Venetian republic, and the Sforza family was a power in Lombardy and later in Milan. The most notable of the ruling families was the Medici clan in Florence, whose leading member was the famous Lorenzo the Magnificent (1449–1492)—a banker, ruler, artist, and patron of the arts. Like the Greek city-states of old, however, the rich and powerful cities of Italy could never unite, and they went into decline after 1500, when Italy became a battleground for internal squabbles and rampaging foreign armies that were more efficiently organized under central sovereign powers (see map 16.3).

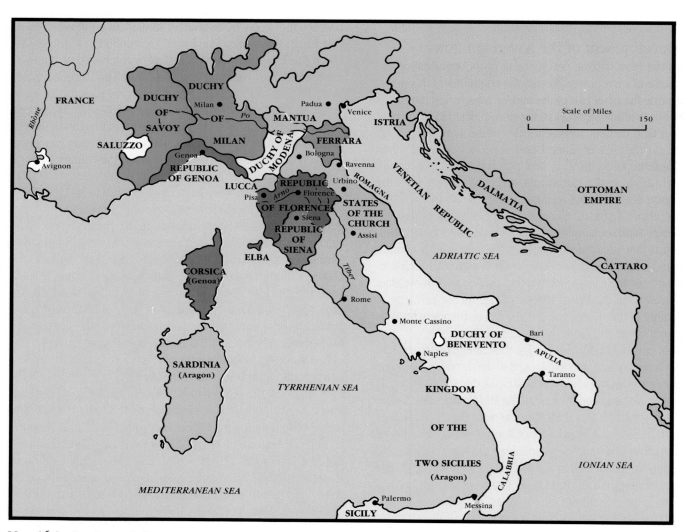

Map 16.3 *Renaissance Italy.*

Summary

There has scarcely been a time, except perhaps our own, when people busied themselves so industriously exploring the dark room of their universe. Wherever they went they turned up new facts that upset any and all old balances and old institutions. Humanism, as one of the manifestations of the secular spirit, stripped the allegory from all manifestations of nature and helped people to see the world as it really was. Humanism also stressed the importance of the individual and the harmonious and complete functioning of the natural person in a rich world guided, the humanists hoped, by moderation and good sense. To a certain extent, humanism was a revolt against the submissive nature of Christian ethics, not only in its turning back to classical sources, but also in its insistence on the reasons for leading the good life; it was not in the hope of eternal bliss in heaven, but because the good life was its own reward. The view of what constituted the real world was shifting from the medieval idea that God was the ultimate reality to the belief that human existence on earth had its own validity. This shift did not necessarily mean that there was widespread denial of Christianity or the Christian message. Rather, growing resentment over corruption in the church hierarchy led people to question whether this powerful bureaucracy provided the best way to the kingdom of heaven. The Great Schism certainly forced many to wonder which of the two or three competing popes was the true keeper of the keys of the kingdom. Amidst all the negative factors, humanism served as a positive bridge from the medieval to the modern world.

The new science, of which the high points were the heliocentric view of the solar system and the mechanistic theory of the universe, completely shifted the base of all human institutions. Before that time God had been the whole purpose and goal of human life, and it was on these teleological assumptions that people had based their lives. That foundation for human aspirations was swept aside, and men and women regarded themselves as inhabitants of a brave new world.

Culture and Human Values

Not only was the theoretical foundation for human values invalidated by scientific discoveries, but the institution that had formerly controlled life's most important functions was questioned and rejected. The keystone of the revolt against the Church of Rome was the dazzling realization that people could live in a direct relation to God with no necessity for an intermediary hierarchy. Those who needed religious authority to direct their lives could turn to the Scriptures and read and interpret for themselves. And those who did not need or want religious authority could live their lives without fear. However, the new churches did institute their own authorities with restrictions sometimes comparable to those of the old Church of Rome. Ultimately, the movement from a monolithic church to a multiplicity of faiths meant that people had a choice.

Vast areas for human endeavor opened at the same time. The idea, as much as the reality, of the New World swept aside musty medieval walls and liberated the European intellect. One tangible reality did come from the New World, and that was money. Wealth poured into the countries who sent their buccaneers forth, and the new riches bought ease and luxury. Capitalism offered another marvelously stimulating outlet for individual enterprise. The sky was the limit for creative, ambitious, and resourceful individuals.

Each of these freedoms brought with it an undercurrent of doubt and pessimism. If the earth and its inhabitants were no longer the center of God's attention, and God no longer the goal and purpose of men and women, then what were we and what was our purpose, if any, here on earth? If the Bible was to be read and interpreted by each person, where was there any certainty? In a world that ran like a machine, where could people find answers about their relationship to each other and to the Creator of that world? Was the new relationship between people only dog eat dog as capitalism suggested? The sole answer the Renaissance could suggest to the necessity for order and stability was that of the absolute monarch. In the seventeenth century these monarchs would claim they were ordained by God to care for his people and would therefore rule by divine right. As perceptive people observed the actions of their rulers, they had abundant reasons to be apprehensive about this new basis for an orderly existence.

Another trend, too small and remote as yet to cause pessimism, but present nevertheless in the intellectual currents of the time, deserves mention. Science had discovered a rational world that appeared to operate like a machine, and capitalism, though it guaranteed near freedom for the captains of commerce and industry, operated "rationally" within the companies that composed it. This meant that the men and women who worked in capitalistic units were not truly free. They had cast off their heavenly bondage and guild regulations, but they had acquired a new bondage: the clock, production quotas, and the account book. The coming industrial revolution would intensify that servitude.

Renaissance Men and Women: Real and Ideal

> What a piece of work is man! how noble in reason! how infinite in faculty! in form in moving how express and admirable! in action how like an Angel! in apprehension, how like a God! the beauty of the world! the paragon of animals! And yet, to me, what is this quintessence of dust? man delights not me. . . .
>
> Hamlet

When contemplating the Renaissance, one can call to mind the glories of exploration and discovery and names such as Michelangelo, Luther, Copernicus, Shakespeare, Cervantes, and Elizabeth I. We picture the era as a time of radiant optimism and expansion of the human spirit. The possible zones of human action were widened, it seems, in every respect: geographically, with the new discoveries; spiritually, with the Reformation; economically, with the growth of capitalism. This, of course, is true but it is only a part of the total picture. Hamlet ends his soliloquy: "What is this quintessence of dust? Man delights not me."

This hints at another aspect of the Renaissance that is as important as the first exuberant picture. Throughout the whole period ran a troubling melancholy strain, a deep-seated pessimism concerning the nature of human beings. What is Hamlet saying? Primarily, that in all appearances, in actions, and in potentialities, men (and women) are great. Yet somehow in reality they fall short of greatness. Such pessimism usually indicates a failure to reach some ideal.

The Renaissance Problem

What was the problem that confronted the thinkers of the time? On the one hand they had opportunity unlimited with beckoning horizons extending in all directions. Human beings, with their awesome achievements, could at last become Godlike creatures.

Yet at the same moment, the very forces that opened these new possibilities undermined the very concept of humans as special among all of God's creations. The matters of the soul, of divinity, and even of human emotions were relegated to a secondary position relative to the physical and quantifiable qualities. Even further, the more purposes and hopes that were held out for humankind, the more did it seem that people's animal nature won ascendancy over their nobler qualities. All too often people seized opportunities savagely and selfishly. Not only did those of low station show themselves unworthy, but even the best and the wisest, the noblest among men and women, saw deeply into their own personalities and found the same base instincts there.

Here, then, is the problem. How can this animal nature of human beings, which now seemed dominant over all other aspects of their character, be dealt with so people could become the noble creatures that, on the surface, they seemed to be? How can the rough, crude, and selfish aspects of human nature be disciplined so that all men and women could achieve fulfillment in the expanding world in which they lived? Philosophers, theologians, artists, psychologists, and men and women in all walks of life have wrestled with the problem, but the question remains.

Exercises

1. Give a definition of Renaissance humanism in your own words. What is a humanist in today's world? How does a humanitarian differ from a humanist?
2. The invention of movable type and gunpowder changed history. Which, in your opinion, had the greater impact? Why?
3. Has the invention of nuclear weapons changed history as much as gunpowder did? More than gunpowder? Why?

chapter 17

Renaissance Art:
A New Golden Age

The Early Renaissance in Fifteenth-Century Italy

Florence (from *Flora*), the city of flowers, dates back to the Bronze Age (3,000 B.C.). Influenced by the Greeks as early as the eighth century B.C., it flourished under Roman rule and continued to prosper during the difficult centuries following the demise of the empire. As early as 1199 it was a city of bankers and wealthy craft guilds, destined to become a leading financial power and the city most closely identified with the Renaissance (figure 17.1). Intended to symbolize Florentine wealth and influence, the great cathedral Santa Maria del Fiore (St. Mary of the Flower) was begun by Arnolfo di Cambio in 1296. Work slowed down after Arnolfo's death in 1302 and stopped altogether during the terrible days of

the Black Death in 1348 and several subsequent years. Like many cities in Europe, Florence was devastated by the plague, its population falling in just a few summer months from about 130,000 to around 65,000. Recovery was relatively swift, however, and in 1368 the cathedral design was finalized and building resumed, though no one had the faintest idea of how to construct the dome.

Filippo Brunelleschi, ca. 1377–1446

In 1417 a special commission announced a competition for the design of the dome, optimistically trusting in Italian genius to solve the problem. The expected genius materialized in the person of Brunelleschi (broo-nuh-LES-key), the greatest architect of the Renaissance. His design was selected in 1420 and triumphantly completed sixteen years later.

Figure 17.1 *View of Florence across the Arno River. Looking from left to right: the Gothic tower of the Palazzo Vecchio, the square white tower of Giotto's Campanile, and the Cathedral of Santa Maria del Fiore with its mighty dome.*

On 25 March 1436 all of Florence was bursting with anticipation. Pope Eugene IV, then residing in the Florentine monastery of Sta. Maria Novella, was to preside over the long-awaited consecration of the cathedral. On the day of the Feast of the Annunciation, the pope, accompanied by thirty-seven bishops, seven cardinals, the ruling Signoria, and envoys of foreign powers, began the solemn procession from the doors of the monastery. Moving along the specially constructed passageway (sumptuously carpeted and decorated with tapestries, damask, silk, and fresh flowers), the notables turned into the Via de' Banchi—most fittingly—where the major banking houses were located. Passing through the eleventh-century Baptistery, the dignitaries entered the spacious nave of the cathedral, where a five-hour service celebrated the completion of what was then the largest church in Christendom. The most famous composer of the time, Guillaume Dufay (doo-FYE; see chapter 18), was present to hear the choir sing his motet *Nuper Rosarum Flores (Flower of Rose),* which was commissioned for the occasion by the Florentine Republic.

Brunelleschi began his artistic career as a sculptor, but after losing the 1401 competition for the north doors of the Baptistery to Ghiberti, he turned his attention to architecture. He subsequently made several trips to Rome in the company of the young sculptor Donatello to study and measure the existing buildings of ancient Rome. His design for the largest dome since the Pantheon consisted of eight massive ribs arching upward from an octagonal drum and held in place by a classically inspired lantern (figure 17.2).

Within the dome a complex web of smaller ribs and horizontal buttresses tied the main ribs firmly together. The design was not only exceptionally stable but also economical; it needed no expensive scaffolding. In addition to designing ribs that could be erected without centering, Brunelleschi invented a hoisting device so practical and simple that city authorities had to issue injunctions forbidding children from riding it to the dome. Averaging 140′ in diameter, the dome was 367′ high, the dominant feature of the Florentine skyline from that day to this.

The 269′ campanile situated at the southwest corner of the 508′–long cathedral was designed by Giotto in 1334 and completed by Talenti in the 1350s (figure 17.3). Though many of the design elements are Gothic, the multicolored marble facing and the lucid proportions of the basically horizontal design reflect Italy's classical heritage. When compared with the dynamic thrust of the South Tower of Chartres Cathedral (figure 17.4), Giotto's Campanile is coolly restrained, poised, and serene.

It was in the Pazzi Chapel (figure 17.5) in the cloister of the Church of Santa Croce that Brunelleschi applied his knowledge of classical designs. A diminutive building measuring only 59′9″ × 35′8″, its Renaissance design is clearly apparent, perhaps because the architect was not preoccupied with complex structural problems. In this beautifully proportioned building the break

Figure 17.2 *Florentine Cathedral Group (aerial view). The Romanesque Baptistery (1060–1150) is at the upper left, partly obscured by Giotto's Campanile (1334–1350s). Cathedral 1296–1436.*

Figure 17.3 *Giotto, Campanile, 1334–1350s, Florence.*

Figure 17.4 *South Tower, Chartres Cathedral, ca. 1280. Ht. 344'.*

Figure 17.6 *Interior, Pazzi Chapel.*

Figure 17.5 *Brunelleschi, Pazzi Chapel, Cloister of Church of Santa Croce, Florence, ca. 1441–1460.*

with the Gothic tradition is total. Gothic pointed arches are re-placed with Corinthian columns and pilasters in even, harmonious spacing. The walls are treated as solid, flat surfaces and, overall, there is a subtle and graceful balance of horizontal and vertical elements. The portico was perhaps designed by Giuliano da Maiano and added after Brunelleschi's death.

Rather than dominating the building, the central dome rests effortlessly on its supporting rim. From within (figure 17.6), it seems to float on the light of the twelve *occuli,* somewhat in the manner of Hagia Sophia (see figure 11.24). The white stucco is articulated by the *pietra serena* (It., "clear stone") pilasters and moldings of clear gray Tuscan limestone and highlighted by the deep blue backgrounds of the terra-cotta reliefs and the Pazzi coat

of arms on the pendentives. The harmonious proportions of the facade are confirmed by an interior space that is also shaped into clear geometric units. The Pazzi Chapel is a prototype of the new Renaissance style, which revived the concept of harmonious proportions on a human scale, a point of view even more germane to the work of Renaissance sculptors and metalworkers.

Lorenzo Ghiberti, 1378–1455

Though initially trained in the International Gothic style, Ghiberti (gee-BEAR-tea) later mastered perspective and classical motifs to emerge as a master metalworker of the Early Renaissance. Winner over Brunelleschi of a competition to design the north doors of the Baptistery in 1401, Ghiberti went on to design the east doors that were quickly pronounced (by Michelangelo) as worthy of the Gates of Paradise. Illustrating ten scenes from the Old Testament, the bronze, gilded doors are a classically inspired landmark of the Early Renaissance style (figure 17.7). Contrary to the International Style, the figures and their settings are perfectly proportioned, creating the illusion that these events are taking place on stage right before our eyes. The *Story of Adam and Eve* (top of the left door; figure 17.8) is designed in three receding planes using the technique of high, middle, and low relief. In the foreground is the creation of Adam and Eve (left and center). The Garden of Eden appears in the middle ground, with the background representing God and his angels as part of a remote past. Bordering the panels are figures and portrait busts representing Hebrew prophets and sibyls of antiquity who had supposedly foretold the coming of Christ.

Figure 17.7 *Lorenzo Ghiberti, "Gates of Paradise," east doors of Baptistery of S. Giovanni of Florence Cathedral. Commissioned 1425, executed 1429–1452. Gilt on bronze, ht. 18'6". Scala/Art Resource.*

Figure 17.8 *Lorenzo Ghiberti,* Story of Adam and Eve, *detail of east doors of Baptistery of S. Giovanni of Florence Cathedral. Gilt on bronze, ht. 31¼" × 31¼". Scala/Art Resource, New York.*

Figure 17.9 *Donatello,* Prophet ("Zuccone"), *ca. 1423–1425. Marble, ht. 6'5". Originally on the campanile, Florence; now in the Museo dell'Opera del Duomo, Florence. Photo: Alinari/Art Resource.*

Donatello (Donato de Niccolò Bardi), 1386?–1466

When Donatello (don-a-TEL-o) completed his statue of a biblical prophet (figure 17.9), he is said to have commanded it to "Speak, speak or the plague take you." The story may be apocryphal, but Renaissance artists did view themselves as creators, not as mere makers of things. With an assurance that the ancient Greeks would have admired, these artists hacked, hewed, painted, and composed as though they partook of the Divine Spirit. Though still regarded by society as craftsmen engaged in manual labor, they repeatedly proclaimed their preeminence as *artists*, an elevated status finally accorded artists such as Leonardo, Raphael, and Michelangelo in the sixteenth century. Created for a niche in Giotto's campanile, Donatello's biblical prophet displays the rude power of a zealot, a man of God fiercely denouncing wickedness and vice. Known in Donatello's time as Zuccone ("pumpkin

head," i.e., baldy), the figure is not a category but a specific individual. Wearing a cloak thrown hurriedly over his body, the prophet is intent on his mission: calling down the wrath of God on the faithless.

Figure 17.10 *Donatello,* David, *ca. 1430–1432 but maybe later. Bronze, ht. 62". Museo Nazionale del Bargello, Florence. Photo: Art Resource.*

Figure 17.11 *Donatello,* Equestrian Monument of Gattamelata, *1443–1453. Bronze, ht. 12'2". Piazza del Santo, Padua. Photo: Art Resource.*

After a prolonged stay in Rome studying Roman art, Donatello returned in the early 1430s to Florence, where he created the *David* (figure 17.10), a favorite image of Republican Florence, which saw itself as a latter-day David, champion of liberty. Representing a second stage in the development of Renaissance art, *David* is more classical than the biblical prophet (figure 17.9), standing in a pose reminiscent of the *Hermes* by Praxiteles (see figure 7.49). Though the gracefully flowing lines and the balance of tension and relaxation is classical, this is the body of an adolescent boy and not that of a Greek athlete or warrior. The Tuscan shepherd's cap and warrior boots emphasize what is possibly the first life-size freestanding nude since antiquity. The agony evident in the face of the slain Goliath offers a strong contrast to the curiously impassive facial expression of the shepherd boy. The Middle Ages interpreted David's triumph as symbolic of Christ's victory over death, but Donatello's intentions remain a tantalizing mystery.

Donatello's colossal equestrian statue of the Venetian condottiere Gattamelata (figure 17.11) was commissioned by the general's family, undoubtedly as authorized by the Venetian Senate. Donatello's ten-year sojourn in Padua in effect exported the Florentine Renaissance to northern Italy, spawning a whole school of painting and sculpture influenced by his powerful personality. The statue itself was possibly influenced by the Roman vigor of the equestrian statue of Marcus Aurelius in Rome (see figure 9.30), then thought to portray Constantine. Donatello's

work, however, exceeded the representation of the Roman emperor in the concentrated power of his figure's commanding presence. Apparently guiding his charger by sheer willpower (note the slack reins and spurs), the general is an idealized image of majestic power. Outfitted with a combination of Roman and Venetian armor, the composition of horse and rider is unified by the vigorous diagonals of the general's baton and long sword. Donatello not only solved the technical problems of large-scale bronze casting, but created a masterpiece in the process.

Though no one knows exactly what Donatello meant by his *David,* the intentions of Early Renaissance painters are quite clear—they were concerned with creating the illusion of the natural world without regard to metaphysical symbols. Artists studied anatomy to determine how the human body was constructed and how it functioned. By using scientific procedures they developed linear and aerial perspectives to create the illusion of actual space. They studied optics, light, and color to add the final touches to the illusion of light and personality. Through keen observation they confidently developed new forms for the new age.

Masaccio (Tommaso di Ser Giovanni), 1401–1428?

Renaissance painting appeared in the 1420s in fully developed form in the work of a single artist. Though only in his midtwenties, Masaccio (ma-SOT-cho) created a fresh repertory of illusionist techniques that were avidly studied by later Renaissance painters, especially Leonardo and Michelangelo. Working with his colleague Masolino, Masaccio painted a series of frescoes in the Brancacci Chapel, of which his *Tribute Money* (figure 17.12) is the acknowledged masterpiece. The subject is based on Matthew 17:24–27, in which the Roman tax collector, wearing the

Figure 17.12 *Masaccio,* Tribute Money, *ca. 1425. Fresco, 8'4" × 19'8". Brancacci, Chapel, Church of Santa Maria del Carmine, Florence. Photo: Scala/Art Resource.*

short tunic, demands his tribute of Peter. Christ instructs Peter to cast a hook and take the first fish caught. In the fish's mouth Peter will find a shekel that he will give to the tax collector "for me and for yourself." Told in continuous narration in the Roman manner (see Trajan's Column, figure 9.25), Peter appears first in the center, fishing at the left, and finally handing the coin to the tax collector at the right. At the time of the painting, Florence was debating a new tax, the *catasto,* based in the modern manner on the ability to pay. Given the outdoor setting of the Arno Valley, rather than the Sea of Galilee, it is possible that the fresco appealed to people to pay their proper earthly taxes, or so the painting was interpreted by a fifteenth-century Florentine archbishop.

Masaccio used three Renaissance illusionist devices in this painting: linear perspective, atmospheric perspective, and chiaroscuro. Apparently developed by Brunelleschi, *linear perspective* is based on the principle of all lines converging on a single vanishing point, located, in this case, at the head of Christ. Perhaps invented in Italy by Masaccio, *atmospheric perspective* is based on the optical fact that colors become dimmer and outlines hazier as they recede into the distance. Flooding the painting from outside the pictorial space, light strikes the figures at an angle, outlining the bodies in a tangible space, a technique also used by the contemporaneous Northern Renaissance painter Jan van Eyck (see figure 17.26). With light sculpting the bodies in gradations of light and dark, called *chiaroscuro* (key-AR-o-SCOOR-o), the illusion communicates weight, substance, and bulk. Van Eyck in Bruges also used atmospheric perspective, indicating that naturalistic painting had become, virtually simultaneously, the goal of a number of widely separated artists.

Paolo Uccello, 1397–1475

For an age already using crossbows, gunpowder, and cannons, Renaissance warfare was paradoxical, a cultivated legacy from the Age of Chivalry. Based on soldiering for pay, the so-called *condottiere* (kon-dot-TYAY-ray; It., "one hired as leader") system followed the tradition of medieval lists: armored knights in formal combat, complete with code of honor and the pageantry of wheeling and charging with trumpets blowing and banners flying. For the Florentines, the relatively minor fray at San Romano epitomized fifteenth-century concepts of honor and, most especially, *virtu.* Immortalized by Uccello (oot-SCHELL-o) in three magnificent panels, the *Battle of San Romano* originally hung in the bedchamber of Lorenzo the Magnificent. The central panel (figure 17.13) portrays the climax of the battle. One more incident in the wars between Siena and Florence, the Sienese were ravaging the Tuscan countryside until challenged on 1 June 1432 by Florence's military hero Niccolò da Tolentino. After an eight-hour battle capped by the unhorsing of their leader, the Sienese were routed. Uccello was obsessed with the problems of scientific linear perspective, and thus more concerned with the patterns of lances, armor, trumpets, and crossbows than with the ferocity of warfare. The result is a stylized composition of a bloodless battle, with horses looking like transplants from a merry-go-round. The work is both a study in perspective and a memorial to military honor, Renaissance style.

Figure 17.13 *Paolo Uccello, "The Unhorsing of Bernardino della Carda,"* Battle of San Romano, *ca. 1455. Tempera on wood, 6' × 10'5". Uffizi Gallery, Florence. Photo: Scala/Art Resource.*

Leonbattista Alberti, 1404–1472

During the first half of the fifteenth century such classical elements of the Roman past as columns, capitals, and arches were examined by Brunelleschi, Donatello, and others. By mid-century the whole of antiquity was scrutinized, led by the remarkable humanist Alberti, who adopted the glorious past as a way of life. The first to study in detail the works of the Roman architect Vitruvius (first century B.C.), Alberti wrote enormously influential scientific treatises on painting, architecture, and sculpture. His design for the facade of a wealthy merchant's townhouse was inspired by Roman architecture but, there being no precedents in an ancient society in which rich men lived in country villas, Alberti invented for the Palazzo Rucellai (figure 17.14) a new architecture based on his classically derived system of ideal proportions. Divided into three even and clearly articulated stories separated by friezes and architraves, the structure is faced with rusticated blocks of identical patterns in each bay, changing to related patterns in the upper two stories. Alberti adapted the articulation of superimposed pilasters from the Colosseum (see figure 9.20), but without the deep spaces of that impressive exterior. He used the Tuscan order for the ground floor and the Corinthian for the top floor. In between he invented his own composite order, a layer of acanthus leaves around a palmette, maintaining that a thorough knowledge of classical designs enabled architects to extend the vocabulary, and then proving his point.

Figure 17.14 *Leonbattista Alberti (design) and Bernardo Rossellino (architect), Facade, Palazzo Rucellai. Begun 1461, Florence. Photo: Art Resource.*

Figure 17.15 *Leonbattista Alberti, Facade, Santa Maria Novella. Completed 1470, Florence.*

Figure 17.16 *Andrea del Verrocchio,* David, *ca. 1465. Bronze, ht. 49⅝". Museo Nazionale del Bargello, Florence. Photo: Art Resource.*

Alberti was responsible for two buildings in Florence, the Palazzo Rucellai and the facade of the Church of Santa Maria Novella, neither of which had any noticeable effect on Florentine artists of the time. Outside of Florence, however, and continuing into the sixteenth century, Alberti's classical designs influenced all Renaissance architects, especially Bramante, Michelangelo, and Palladio. His design for the facade of Santa Maria Novella (figure 17.15) had to cope with the existing Gothic arches on the ground level, which he accomplished brilliantly by topping them with blind arches and matching their green and white marbles with the corner pilasters and the four pilasters on the second story. His masterstroke was the addition of the volutes on both sides of the narrow upper temple, which solved two problems: (1) it supplied needed buttressing for the nave walls and (2) it beautifully filled the space above the side aisles of a basilica-plan church. The harmonious whole of the facade was the result of a rigorous set of proportions. Width and height are identical with a ratio of 1:1. The upper structure can be encased in a square one-fourth the size of the basic square, or a ratio of 1:4. The lower portion is a rectangle of double squares forming a ratio of 1:2. Throughout the facade the proportions can be expressed in whole-number relationships: 1:1, 1:2, 1:3, and so on. Along with Brunelleschi, Alberti was convinced that beauty was inherent in these ratios.

Andrea del Verrocchio, 1435–1488

An overriding characteristic of Renaissance artists was their individuality, their need to be uniquely and unmistakably themselves. In three works by Verrocchio (veh-ROE-key-o) we see distinct manifestations of this drive for individuality when treating the same subject. Verrocchio's *David* (figure 17.16) is totally different from Donatello's conception. Donatello's figure is essen-

tially a composition of sinuous and graceful lines; in his young warrior Verrocchio emphasizes texture, a delicate rendering in gleaming bronze of skin, underlying veins, muscle, and bone. These are qualities that, unfortunately, can be best appreciated only when walking around the actual work. The tactile qualities are enhanced by clothing the figure in a skintight short skirt designed to look like leather. That Verrocchio used his pupil Leonardo da Vinci as a model may or may not be true, but the age is about right and Leonardo may have looked like this.

Donatello's *Equestrian Monument of Gattamelata* (see figure 17.11) is idealized, but Verrocchio's portrayal of Bartolommeo Colleoni (figure 17.17) is strikingly realistic, with the fiercely scowling general readying his mace as he rides boldly into battle. Twisting in his saddle, the powerful figure seems almost too massive for the sprightly horse to carry. The tensions of horse and rider are portrayed in a dynamic moment in time. The battle is clearly at hand. Also naturalistic is Verrocchio's portrait bust of Lorenzo the Magnificent (figure 17.18), banker, poet, patron of the arts, and Florentine autocrat. Any accomplished craftsman can reproduce the crooked ski-slope nose, tight lips, and knitted brow. These are details that assist in the communication of a tangible presence: the overpowering personality of a unique human being. Classical portraiture had been revived and, without question, this is a masterful portrait of one of the dominant figures of the Italian Renaissance.

Figure 17.17 *Andrea del Verrocchio (completed by Leopardi),* Equestrian Monument of Bartolommeo Colleoni, *ca. 1481–1496. Bronze, ht. ca. 13'. Campo SS Giovanni a Paolo, Venice. Photo: Art Resource.*

Figure 17.18 *Andrea del Verrocchio,* Lorenzo de' Medici, *ca. 1480. Terra-cotta, life size. Samuel H. Kress Collection. National Gallery of Art, Washington, D.C.*

Sandro Botticelli, 1445–1510

Three of the leading painters of the last quarter of the century—Botticelli, Ghirlandaio, and Perugino—were all vastly different in temperament and style. Botticelli (bot-tee-CHEL-lee), in fact, stands alone as one of the great masters in the use of line. In his celebrated *Birth of Venus (Venus Landing on the Shore)* (figure 17.19), Botticelli subordinates perspective and "correct" anatomical proportions and details to the elegant and sensual lines that make his style so delightfully unique. Like many of his generation, especially the elite circle of Lorenzo de' Medici and the Platonic Academy, Botticelli was fascinated with themes from classical mythology. According to an ancient myth, Venus was born from the sea, a legend interpreted by Ficino as an allegory of the birth of beauty. What the Florentine Neoplatonists actually did believe is still debated. Much of Plato's work had become available, but there was also a large body of Neoplatonist writings with Christian elements superimposed on Platonic theories. Whether Botticelli's Venus symbolizes non-Christian or Christian ideas, or both, she is certainly lovely. Possibly inspired by a poem by Poliziano, Botticelli has painted her poised lightly on a conch shell as she is blown gently to shore by two Zephyrs as one of the Hours hastens to drape her body with a flowered mantle. This is poetry in motion. The sea is flat, marked by upward thrusting V-shaped lines and bound by a stylized shoreline to form a serene setting for the sinuous lines of the moving figures. Probably inspired by classical statues in the Medici collection, the body of the goddess of spiritual and intellectual beauty is elongated and exquisitely curved, proportionately larger than the scale of the landscape. The gold-line shading on the trees is a further indication that Botticelli intended no realistic representation of the landscape. It was, in fact, this sort of stylized treatment of the background that led to Leonardo's comment that Botticelli created landscapes by throwing a sponge at the canvas.

Domenico del Ghirlandaio, 1449–1494

Botticelli was favored by the intellectual elite of Florence, but the style of Ghirlandaio (gear-lan-DAH-yo) was preferred by the merchants and bankers of the city. Not interested in mythological fantasies, Ghirlandaio was a conservative painter for a commercial clientele and, as might be expected, a very successful artist. His *Old Man with a Child* (figure 17.20), one of his most endearing works, is a compassionate portrayal of an elderly man holding an adoring child who could be his grandson, though the subjects have never been identified. Perhaps influenced by the naturalism of Flemish painting, which was well-known in Italy by this time, the objective treatment of thinning hair and a deformed nose actually adds to the tender scene of familial love. As was customary in Renaissance portraiture, the human subjects totally dominate a composition that is reinforced by the lovely and distant landscape.

Figure 17.19 *Sandro Botticelli,* Birth of Venus (Venus Landing on the Shore), *after 1482. Tempera on canvas, 5'9" × 9'½". Uffizi Gallery, Florence. Photo: Art Resource, New York.*

Figure 17.20 *Domenico del Ghirlandaio,* Old Man with a Child, *ca. 1480 (detail). Panel, 24⅜" × 18". The Louvre, Paris. Cliché des Musées Nationaux, Paris.*

Perugino (Pietro Vanucci), ca. 1445–1523

Until about the middle of the fifteenth century, the Early Renaissance was essentially Florentine; the second half of the century saw the dissemination of Renaissance techniques throughout Italy, notably by artists such as Perugino and Bellini. Though his early training is a mystery, Pietro Vanucci was in Florence by 1472, where he acquired his knowledge of drawing and perspective, possibly from Verrocchio. It was in the Umbrian city of Perugia that he established his reputation and acquired the name by which he is known today: Perugino (pay-roo-GEE-no), the "Perugian." In his *Crucifixion with the Virgin, Saint Jerome, and Saint Mary Magdalene* (figure 17.21), Perugino created a masterful pictorial space that is much more open than Florentine landscapes, with a sky stretching to infinity. As polished and cool as the work of the Flemish painter Hans Memling (see figure 17.28), and probably influenced by his work, the altarpiece shows none of the usual emotions of Florentine crucifixions. Christ is not racked by pain nor do Mary at the left nor John at the right display any grief. In the wings St. Jerome and Mary Magdalene stand serenely in counterbalancing poses. In the vast expanse of the natural setting all is quietude. Whether the absence of emotion reflects Vasari's statement that Perugino was an atheist may be a moot point.

Figure 17.21 *Perugino,* The Crucifixion with the Virgin, Saint Jerome, and Saint Mary Magdalene, *before 1481. Panel, transferred to canvas: center, 40" × 22¼"; wings, 37¼" × 12" each. Andrew W. Mellon Collection. National Gallery of Art, Washington, D.C.*

Though religious convictions were important for many people at that time, Renaissance artists were valued chiefly for their skills, not their spirits.

The Early Renaissance in the North

Limbourg Brothers, ca. 1385–1416

The focus of significant new developments in art and in music (see chapter 18) was the sumptuous court of the Dukes of Burgundy, from which the dukes governed the most prosperous lands in all of Europe (see map 18.1). Philip the Bold and his brother, the Duke of Berry, sponsored leading artists such as the Limbourg Brothers: Paul, Herman, and Jean. Their work in manuscript illumination marked the high point of the International Style (Late

Gothic), while also moving beyond to a new naturalism. Commissioned by the Duke of Berry, they created for him a personal prayer book, a Book of Hours containing passages of Scripture, prayers, and Office Hours, all lavishly decorated and illustrated with paintings. Of particular interest are the twelve illuminated calendar pages; ten include peasants and aristocrats and two are devoted solely to peasant genre scenes. The month of "February" (figure 17.22) has, at the top, a zodiac representing the route of the chariot of the sun and including, in this case, the zodiacal signs of Aquarius and Pisces. The scene is an intensely cold, snowy landscape, the first convincing snow scene in Western art. On the upper level a peasant cuts firewood as another herds a donkey laden with faggots toward a distant village. In the tiny farmyard snow caps the beehives and covers the roof of the sheep pen

Figure 17.22 *The Limbourg Brothers, "February" from the* Très Riches Heures du Duc de Berry, *1413–1416. Illumination. Musée Condé, Chantilly, France. Giraudon/Art Resource, N.Y.*

Figure 17.23 *Jan van Eyck,* Ghent Altarpiece *(closed), ca. 1425–1432. 11'3" × 7'2". St. Bavon, Ghent, Belgium. © A. C. L., Bruxelles.*

except for the unrepaired hole in the roof. At the right a woman blows on her icy hands and stamps her feet to try to restore circulation. With the front wall removed for our benefit, we see a man and a woman seated before the fire with skirts raised high to gather in the welcome warmth. At the doorway, the lady of the house rather more decorously lifts her skirt; the cat is, of course, cozily warm and comfortable. The perspective that gives the illusion of depth is empirical rather than mathematically precise; this is how the artists actually perceived the scene. Marking the beginning of the Northern tradition of naturalistic art, the overriding concern is with the visible world, with loving care devoted to minute details in all their complexity.

The decisive victory of the English king Henry V at Agincourt in 1415 effectively ended, for some forty years, the dominance of the French court and thus royal sponsorship of the courtly International Style. The center for art shifted to the Low Countries, where Philip the Good (ruled 1419–1467) maintained his Burgundian court and negotiated hardheaded trade alliances with England. Artists found in the flourishing cities of Flanders— Bruges, Ghent, Louvain, Brussels—new patrons in the bankers and merchants who were the true arbiters of the wealthiest society in Europe. The society was bourgeois, but cosmopolitan rather than provincial, with powerful banking and trade connections throughout Europe. This solid middle class wanted art that pictured the real world and, by a strange coincidence, there were several artists of genius available to help fulfill the passion for naturalism.

Jan van Eyck, ca. 1390–1441

The leading painter of the early Flemish school, indeed of any age, van Eyck (van Ike) first served the court of John of Bavaria and later at the Burgundian court of Philip the Good. Credited by Vasari with inventing oil painting, it is likely that van Eyck perfected an existing technique. Until the fifteenth century, panel painters worked in tempera, an emulsion of pigment and egg yolk capable of detail and bright color, but limited to a narrow range between light and dark. Too dark colors became dead and very light ones became chalklike. Using a technique still not fully understood, van Eyck probably used a *gesso* coating on his panel, a mixture of plaster and water, followed by successive coats of pigments suspended in linseed oil. Applying alternate layers of opaque and translucent color, van Eyck enhanced the brilliance of his colors from the darkest to the lightest with no loss of intensity. With slow-drying oil paints he made infinitely subtle and smooth gradations between color tones, obtaining a jewellike radiance comparable to medieval stained glass. He undoubtedly learned some of his techniques from manuscript painters such as the Limbourg Brothers, but it also seems likely that van Eyck was influenced, possibly inspired, by Gothic stained glass.

Ghent Altarpiece

The greatest work of early Flemish painting and a monumental accomplishment in any age, the *Ghent Altarpiece* (figure 17.23) is a polyptych, a central painting with two hinged wings measuring 11'3" × 7'2" when closed and 11'3" × 14'5" in the open

Figure 17.24 *Jan van Eyck,* Ghent Altarpiece *(open). 11'3" × 14'5". © A. C. L., Bruxelles.*

position. The twenty different panels of the work range from the Annunciation on the outer panels to the Adoration of the Mystic Lamb within. In the lunettes of figure 17.23, the prophet Zechariah (left) with the Erythraean Sibyl, Cumean Sibyl, and prophet Micah symbolize the coming of Christ. The annunciation figures are placed in a contemporary room containing Romanesque and Gothic elements that probably symbolize the Old and New Testaments. In the center panels below, the simulated sculptural figures of St. John the Baptist and St. John the Evangelist are flanked by the donors Jodoc Vyt and his wife.

In the open altarpiece (figure 17.24), the lower central panel shows the community of saints, come from the four corners of the world to worship at the altar of the Mystic Lamb, from whose heart blood cascades into a chalice. In the foreground the Fountain of Life pours from spigots into an octagonal basin, running toward the observer as the "river of life" (Rev. 22:1). In the left-hand panel, judges and knights ride to the altar; on the right, hermits, pilgrims, and the giant St. Christopher walk to an altar scene backed by the heavenly Jerusalem in the distance. Forming a continuous view of Paradise, the five lower panels are designed with a rising perspective, another of the innovations of the artist. On the upper level, the Lord has Mary as the Queen of Heaven on his right hand and St. John the Baptist on his left. To either side are choirs of angels with St. Cecilia seated at the portative (portable) organ, flanked by Adam and Eve on the outer panels. The first large nudes in Northern panel painting, the figures of Adam and Eve reveal a keen appreciation of the human body and in-

novative painting techniques in perspective and lighting. Once bowed by shame, the figures stand erect as the First Man and First Woman. The placement of the altarpiece puts the feet of the two nudes at eye level, which accounts for the view of the sole of Adam's foot. This bit of naturalism is typical of a visual reality so precise that botanists can identify dozens of flowers and plants in this awesome work.

The *Ghent Altarpiece* was created early in the supremacy of the Duchy of Burgundy but, even as van Eyck worked on his masterpiece, Joan of Arc (ca. 1412–1431) was leading Charles VII and the French army to victory (in 1428) over the English invaders. By 1453 Charles VII had triumphantly ended the Hundred Years' War with England (1338–1453) and absorbed Burgundy, Picardy, and Flanders.

Other van Eyck Paintings

Probably completed while he was working on the *Ghent Altarpiece,* the *Annunciation* (figure 17.25) is a relatively small work that, with its strong control of space, has a monumental quality. Set in an imaginary church whose mixed Romanesque and Gothic details probably symbolize the Old and New Testaments, the scene is dominated by an oversized Virgin, portrayed here as the Queen of Heaven. Heavenly light streams in through an upper window, bearing the Dove of the Holy Spirit, its diagonal thrust balanced at the lower right by the lilies of purity. No detail is extraneous; even the designs of the stained-glass window and floor tiles foretell the Advent of Christ.

Figure 17.26 *Jan van Eyck,* Giovanni Arnolfini and His Bride, *1434. Oil on canvas, 32¼" × 23½". National Gallery, London.*

Figure 17.25 *Jan van Eyck,* Annunciation, *ca. 1430. Oil on panel, 36½" × 14⅜". Andrew W. Mellon Collection. National Gallery of Art, Washington, D.C.*

The meticulous details in a van Eyck painting are fascinating, but the whole of a picture—its unity—is greater than the sum of its parts. In a work commissioned by Giovanni Arnolfini, an Italian merchant, he and his bride, Jeanne Cenami, apparently pose for a wedding portrait as a form of wedding certificate, duly witnessed by the artist (seen in the mirror) and notarized on the back wall: "Jan van Eyck was here" (figure 17.26). The light, space, volume, and the two distinct personalities are all unified, both visually and psychologically. Patron and artist must have been more than acquaintances; two individuals make up this wedding couple, joined in a tender moment without the slightest hint of sentimentality. The texture of cloth, glass, metal, wood, and even the furry little dog are exquisitely detailed. Though unobtrusive, symbols abound. The single lighted candle is, according to custom, the last to be extinguished on the wedding night, but it may also symbolize Christ as the Light of the World. Carved on the post of a bedside chair is the image of St. Margaret, the patron saint of childbirth. The dog represents fidelity (*fides,* "Fido"), and the abandoned slippers are a reminder that the couple is standing on holy ground. Craftsmanship at this level verges on the superhuman; indeed, nothing like this had ever been done before.

Rogier van der Weyden, ca. 1400–1464

Because his paintings were perfect in their own marvelously unique way, van Eyck had many admirers in Northern Europe, Spain, and Italy, but no emulators. There were imitators, of course, but no disciples who could even approach his rare gifts. Adopting

Figure 17.27 *Rogier van der Weyden,* Portrait of a Lady, *ca. 1455–1460. Oil on wood, 14½″ × 10¾″. National Gallery, London.*

Figure 17.28 *Hans Memling,* The Presentation in the Temple, *ca. 1463. Oil on panel, 23½″ × 19″. Samuel H. Kress Collection. National Gallery of Art, Washington, D.C.*

a more expressive and emotional style than that of van Eyck, van der Weyden (van dur VYE-den) was the leading Flemish painter of the next generation, becoming City Painter for Brussels in 1435. When he traveled to Italy for the Holy Year of 1450, he influenced Italian art and was, in turn, impressed by what he saw there. As technically accomplished as van Eyck, his portraits had a psychological depth then unknown in Flemish painting. *Portrait of a Lady* (figure 17.27) is a study of a young woman tentatively identified as Marie de Valengin, the daughter of Philip the Good, Duke of Burgundy. Her forehead and eyebrows are shaved, a fashionable indication of intellectual acumen. Also high fashions, the high-waisted dress and triangular coif focus attention on the exquisite modeling of the face. The portrait is both beautiful and baffling. The impression of an almost ascetic contemplation is contradicted by the sensuality of the full mouth with its ripe underlip. The overall impression is that of an assertive personality, an intelligent, self-confident, and strong-willed young woman. She certainly looks like a princess. Contrasting curiously with the broad facial planes, the thin fingers are almost Gothic in style. Bewitching and beguiling, this is a masterful psychological study by one of the first of a long line of Low Country painters leading directly to Hals and Rembrandt.

Hans Memling, ca. 1440–1494

Memling served his apprenticeship in his native Germany, but then moved to Flanders (then a French province) where he apparently studied with van der Weyden. A contemporary of Ghirlandaio in Italy, his style is similarly genial and rather naive; it appealed to a large clientele of merchants and led ultimately to a considerable fortune. Using extensive studies of earlier Flemish masters, particularly van Eyck, he developed a somewhat melancholy art of extreme refinement. In *The Presentation in the Temple* (figure 17.28) the figures are immobile, frozen in time, or even outside of time. The light falls on people grouped in harmony with their imaginary setting, which appears to be neither inside nor outside a church. The overall feeling is unworldly and slightly sad.

Memling's work was in tune with a general feeling of pessimism, an erosion of confidence in the moral authority of the church, an almost prophetic feeling of the impending Reformation. In Italy the pessimism was fully warranted, for it was in 1494—the year of Memling's death—that the Medicis were expelled from Florence, coinciding with the invasion of the French armies of Charles VIII, which launched a tumultuous era of warfare in Italy.

Hieronymus Bosch, ca. 1450–1516

This pessimistic age found its supreme artist in the person of Bosch (BOS), one of history's most enthralling and enigmatic painters. He lived and worked in present-day southern Holland, but little else is known about either his life or his artistic intentions. Art

Figure 17.29 *Hieronymus Bosch,* Garden of Delights *(center panel of triptych), ca. 1505–1510. Oil on panel, 85⅝″ × 76¾″. Museo del Prado, Madrid. Photo: Scala/Art Resource.*

historians have wondered about his bizarre iconography, but so have psychiatrists. This was an age obsessed with death and with an almost pathological fear of the devil and his demons. Based on his work, it is plain that Bosch had a pessimistic view of human nature—though some would call his vision realistic—and he certainly raged against sinfulness. One of his major and most enigmatic works is the huge triptych entitled *Garden of Delights.* Consisting of three large panels, this incredible work depicts Heaven and Hell in the side panels (not shown), both rendered in an unconventional but fairly consistent manner. The central panel (figure 17.29) is quite another matter. Complex, bizarre, and bewildering, the sparse landscape teems with hundreds of naked men and women and various animals, both real and imaginary—and in all sizes. There are several lakes, a pond, giant strawberries, mussel shells, eggs, and assorted mysterious and grotesque objects. Frail of body and seeming all the same age— about twenty-one—men and women frolic and tease and gambol about the strange arena.

Despite the universal nudity and much pairing off, there is no explicit sexual activity. The general ambience is certainly erotic, but no one displays any sexual desire except, perhaps, by stroking a giant strawberry. Most are busy with silly or foolish activities. One cuddling couple wears an owl for a headdress and someone rides a lion while clutching a giant fish. The foolishness is virtually endless, but apparently harmless. The faces are generally calm and composed; the entire scene appears to resemble a genteel nudist camp.

What does all this mean? In the absence of a universally accepted interpretation, there are several possibilities. Perhaps there are messages hidden behind symbolic acts and objects, a vocabulary taken from non-Christian traditions, Flemish folklore, and medieval bestiaries. Pursuing this version leads one into a quagmire of ambiguities that apparently have no resolution. Too much of the old symbolic vocabularies have been lost over the intervening centuries.

Others take the view that this is a message in code directed to people practicing a secret religion. This kind of activity amounts to heresy and a possible death sentence—hence the code. But can we accept these vapid people as high practitioners of a secret sect? Their actions seem too ridiculous for that. There is, in fact, nothing in this picture that has any religious connotation whatsoever, and this at a time when religion pervaded every nook and cranny of life.

We can never know exactly how Bosch's contemporaries viewed this painting but, in our own time, there are startling flashes of recognition. All too familiar is the aimless pursuit of pleasure, the lack of ambition, direction, or purpose, the games people play. Did Bosch anticipate the twentieth century, or has he perhaps indicted all humankind for persistent foolishness and failure?

When considering Bosch's total output, there is no denying his pessimism; his was perhaps the darkest vision in an age of deep pessimism. This painting seems to be, therefore, a despairing depiction of the human condition in which there is no Christ, no Redemption, no Salvation. Humanity is doomed, not because it is vicious or depraved, but because it is vain, vapid, and silly. The Incarnation is useless because folly was present in the Garden of Eden and remains as the dominant characteristic of the human race.[1] This interpretation leaves us no alternative but to see Bosch as the ultimate pessimist: humankind will move endlessly from folly to damnation with no hope of heaven.

Enormously popular in the sixteenth century, Bosch's paintings typify an age that groveled in a sickening undercurrent of fear of the devil, leading to fierce, misdirected religious zeal. In 1484 Pope Innocent VIII declared witchcraft (possession by the Devil) a prime heresy. During the next two centuries a wave of sadism and misogyny led to the torture, hanging, and burning of some 100,000 to 200,000 women plus many men (and children) who were enveloped in the madness. Two unscrupulous Dominican monks wrote a handbook for self-appointed witch-hunters, *The Witches Hammer,*[2] a best-seller that went to thirty editions, an ironic testimony to the dissemination of printed books.

The career of Hieronymus Bosch marked the end of the Early Northern Renaissance and the beginning of a tormented

---

1. See also Erasmus, *Praise of Folly,* in chapter 19.

2. Heinrich Kramer and James Sprenger, *Malleus Maleficarum,* trans. Montague Summers (London: Pushkin Press, 1928). Approved by the pope, the handbook was originally published in 1490.

period of warfare in Italy, of corrupt and dissolute Renaissance popes, and of spiritually bankrupt religious orders. One year after Bosch's death Martin Luther published his *Ninety-five Theses* to set in motion the irrepressible Reformation.

The High Renaissance in Italy, ca. 1495–1520

The relatively peaceful and prosperous existence of Florence ended in two rough jolts in the fateful years of 1492 and 1494. Lorenzo the Magnificent, a strong, moderating force in the fortunes of Florence, died in 1492, the same year in which Ferdinand and Isabella captured Cordoba, the last Moorish stronghold in Spain. Columbus, using a map drawn in Florence, discovered the New World; in Rome, Rodrigo Borgia was crowned as Pope Alexander VI, the embodiment of a decadent and corrupt Renaissance pontiff and a merciless enemy of the Florentine Republic.

In 1494, concerned about the military support of Lorenzo's dim and feckless son Piero, Ludovico Sforza of Milan encouraged Charles VIII of France to invade Italy. Charles, who was spoiling for a fight, willingly did so. For the next thirty-five years French and Spanish armies, the latter freed by the removal of the Moors, fought the Italian city-states and, for good measure, each other. Always assuming that each invasion was the last, the Italian city-states never banded together to expel their foreign tormentors. Paradoxically, it was against this backdrop of almost constant warfare that High Renaissance art flourished. Exploiting and refining Early Renaissance discoveries in Italy and the North, Leonardo da Vinci, Michelangelo, Raphael, and Bramante created masterworks that crowned the Italian Renaissance.

Leonardo da Vinci, 1452–1519

The illegitimate son of a peasant girl known only as Caterina, and Piero da Vinci, a notary, Leonardo da Vinci (lay-o-NAR-do da VIN-chee) was the acknowledged universal man of the Renaissance, the most astounding genius in an age of giants. Inventor, civil and military engineer, architect, musician, geologist, botanist, physicist, anatomist, sculptor, and painter, Leonardo left untouched only classical scholarship, poetry, and philosophy. Theology was of no interest to him; he was a lifelong skeptic who recognized no authority higher than the eye, which he called the "window of the soul."

As was customary with bastardy during the Renaissance, Leonardo was acknowledged by his father and, at about age fifteen, apprenticed to Verrocchio in Florence. Though little else is known about the first thirty years of his life, records indicate that Leonardo, like Masaccio and Botticelli before him, was admitted to the guild as a craftsman in painting. Unlike Early Renaissance masters, however, Leonardo along with Michelangelo launched a successful campaign to raise the status of artists to the highest level of society.

Figure 17.30 *Leonardo da Vinci*, Ginevra de'Benci, *ca. 1474. Oil and tempera on panel, 15″ × 14½″.* **Ailsa Mellon Bruce Fund. National Gallery of Art, Washington, D.C.**

In 1481 Pope Sixtus IV summoned the "best" Tuscan artists to work in the Vatican, including Botticelli, Ghirlandaio, and Perugino, but not Leonardo. Furious at the slight, Leonardo decided to leave Florence, but not before he had completed a commission for the de'Benci family of wealthy bankers. His portrait of Ginevra de'Benci (figure 17.30), the only Leonardo painting in the United States, is an enchanting study of a lovely but strangely tense and wary young woman. She was known to be a very devout person, ill at ease in the fun-loving exuberance of Florence, and sternly disapproving of Lorenzo de' Medici's long-term affair with her aunt. Framing her golden curls in juniper branches (Ginevra means "juniper"), Leonardo has created a melancholy work; the pallid face is set against a thinly misted background, with details deliberately softened and blurred. Though not invented by Leonardo, this *sfumato* (sfoo-MAH-toh) technique (literally "smoky") was one of that artist's significant contributions to the art of painting. The twilight atmosphere is another innovation, contrasting sharply with the sunlit paintings of other masters. The painting is minus some six inches at the bottom, which may explain why the lady's hands are not shown, as they are in the *Mona Lisa* and two of Leonardo's other portraits.

Figure 17.31 *Leonardo da Vinci,* The Last Supper, *ca. 1495–1498. Mural, oil and tempera on plaster, 14'5" × 28'. Refectory of Sta. Maria della Grazie, Milan. Photo: Scala/Art Resource.*

Seeking a more appreciative patron than the Medicis or the pope, Leonardo wrote to Ludovico Sforza, Duke of Milan, touting his expertise as a military engineer but mentioning, in just two sentences, that he was also a sculptor and a painter. During his stay in Milan (1482–1499) Leonardo produced *The Last Supper* (figure 17.31), a treatment of the familiar theme unlike anything before or since. The High Renaissance begins with this magnificent composition. After suffering the indignities of Leonardo's experimentation with fresco painting, damp walls, Napoleon's troops, and World War II bombing, the painting has been restored, but only to an approximation of its original condition. The moment of the painting is not the traditional one of the Eucharist but Christ's electrifying statement: "One of you shall betray me." Except for Christ, Leonardo used life models for the disciples and had difficulty only in finding a suitable Judas. According to Vasari, when the prior of Sta. Maria complained to Sforza that Leonardo was "lazy" in his execution of the painting, Leonardo remarked that locating a Judas was difficult but that the prior would serve nicely. Leonardo's contemporaries would have looked for Judas where other artists had placed him—across the table from Jesus. Instead, we see Judas as part of the first group of three Apostles to the left of Christ, composed in a tight, dark triangle with no light shining on his face. Clutching a bag of money, Judas is in the group but not a part of it. His dark bulk is in sharp contrast to the lighted profile of Peter and the luminous radiance of John. Each Apostle is an individual psychological study, reacting to Christ's startling statement in a manner consistent with his personality.

The design of *The Last Supper* has a mathematical unity, with divisions of groups of threes and fours that add up to seven (3 + 4) and multiply into twelve (3 × 4). The three windows place Christ's head in the center window as the second person of the Trinity. The shocked Apostles are grouped into four units of three each, divided in the middle by the isolated triangular design of Christ. Echoing the four groups are the wall panels on either side, and on the ceiling there are seven beams running from both front to back and side to side. Leonardo may have had Christian number symbolism in mind (Holy Trinity, Four Gospels, Seven Cardinal Virtues, Twelve Gates of the New Jerusalem, and so on) but three, four, and seven also stand for the Trivium and Quadrivium of the Seven Liberal Arts. Moreover, Pythagorean number symbolism includes the concept of one as unity, three as the most logical number (beginning, middle, end), and four as symbolizing Justice. Given Leonardo's skepticism and explicit anticlerical feelings, something other than Christian symbolism may be a more appropriate interpretation. There is no question, however, about the picture as a whole. Despite the mathematical precision of the perspective, there is no place from which a spectator can view the perspective "correctly"; it exists as a work apart, on an ideal level beyond everyday experience. This is the elevated style of formal design and noble theme that characterizes the Italian High Renaissance.

Leonardo insisted that painters were noble creatures and that painting should be a part of the seven liberal arts. For him, sculptors were craftsmen standing in dust and debris chiseling away at stubborn marble. Michelangelo, on the other hand, claimed that sculpture was as superior to painting as the sun was to the moon.

Figure 17.32 *Michelangelo,* Pietà, *1498–1499/1500. Marble, ht. 68½". St. Peter's, Rome. Photo: Art Resource.*

Figure 17.33 *Michelangelo,* David, *Florence, 1501–1504. Marble, ht. 13'5". Photo: Art Resource.*

Michelangelo Buonarroti, 1475–1564

Perhaps the greatest artistic genius who ever lived, Michelangelo (me-kell-AHN-djay-lo) excelled in sculpture, architecture, painting, and poetry. A towering figure even in his own time, he was the "Divine Michelangelo." Words and more words have been written trying to account for such a man, but there is no accounting for him. Born of a vain and mean-spirited father and a dimly pathetic mother to whom he never referred, he appeared with prodigious gifts at a time and place seemingly destined to make him immortal. He learned painting techniques in Ghirlandaio's studio, sculpting from a pupil of Donatello and from ancient works in the Medici collection. His first masterpiece, the *Pietà* (figure 17.32), is more fifteenth than sixteenth century in style, with elegant lines reminiscent of Botticelli. The triangular composition is fashioned of contradictions. Though Christ is dead, the blood pumps through his veins as if he were asleep. The Virgin is portrayed as younger than her son, her lovely face composed rather than distorted by grief; only her left hand indicates her sorrow. The figure of Christ is life size but that of the Virgin is elongated; her head is the same size as Christ's, but in proportion she would be about seven feet tall if she were standing. The overall visual effect of these distortions is a super authenticity beyond earthbound reality.

The *Pietà* was a youthful work but the *David* (figure 17.33), initiated only a year or so later, was the first monumental statue of the High Renaissance, a product of Michelangelo's already mature genius. Though the Palazzo della Signoria proudly possessed three Davids, two by Donatello (figure 17.10) and one by Verrocchio (figure 17.16), one more hero was not too many for a city battling to maintain its power and independence. After the Medicis were expelled in 1494, the crusading monk Savonarola ruled Florence, having declared Christ the King of Florence. Savonarola then legally banned all acts he considered sinful. By 1498 the powerful but corrupt Borgia pope Alexander VI had excommunicated Savonarola. Incredibly, Savonarola excommunicated the pope; following this he was arrested by the Florentine Signoria and, with two associates, hanged and then burned. While Michelangelo was working on his David, the dangerous Alexander VI died, in 1503, and shortly thereafter the incompetent Piero de' Medici, known as Piero the Unfortunate, drowned while fighting with the French in an attempt to gain reentry to the city. By 1504 Florence was finally at peace and the prime civic concern was where to place Michelangelo's mighty *David*. The commission to select the site included Leonardo, Botticelli, Perugino, and others, attesting to the status the nearly completed work had already acquired. Originally scheduled to be placed high on Florence Cathedral, *David* was triumphantly set in front of the center of government, the Palazzo Vecchio, where it became the symbol of a republic ready to battle all enemies. (During the nineteenth century the statue was replaced by a copy and moved indoors to protect it from the weather.)

Figure 17.34 *Michelangelo,* Creation of Adam, *detail of Sistine Chapel Ceiling, 1511. Fresco. Vatican, Rome. "© Nippon Television Network Corp. Tokyo 1991." Note: This photo was taken after the ceiling was cleaned during the 1980s.*

The Davids of Donatello and Verrocchio were adolescent boys; this is a strapping young man who is standing alert, every muscle vibrant with power. The head might be that of Apollo and the body of Herakles, yet this is the portrait of an ideal, a Platonic ideal as well as David the King. His father was both Hebrew and, collectively, Lorenzo, Ficino, and the Platonic Academy of Florence.

The fame of the *David* was instant, and Michelangelo had more commissions than he could handle, including one to construct a vast tomb for Pope Julius II. The tomb project was never finished as originally planned; instead, somehow, Michelangelo found himself in 1508 standing atop the scaffolding in the Sistine Chapel. How all this came about has never been satisfactorily explained, but one plausible theory concerns the possible machinations of Bramante, the recently appointed architect of the new St. Peter's. He was known to be concerned about funds for his project and was also intensely jealous of Michelangelo. Julius had lavished enormous sums on his tomb project, money that Bramante needed for his mighty basilica. If the pope could be encouraged to put Michelangelo to work painting the Sistine Chapel ceiling, a monumental undertaking Bramante felt not even Michelangelo could bring off, then he would have no further financial or artistic competition. Whatever transpired behind the scenes, Michelangelo was, in fact, the only artist who was capable of tackling the project.

With a 68' high ceiling that is proportionately too high for its 44 × 132' dimensions, the private chapel of the popes was neither intimate nor monumental; Michelangelo's frescoes *made* it monumental. In only four years, 1508–1512, he filled the entire 700 square yards of barrel-vaulted ceiling with over 300 powerful figures. Relating the Genesis story from the Creation through the Flood, Michelangelo fused Judeo-Christian theology with ancient mythology and Neoplatonic philosophy to create one of the truly awesome works of Western art. In just one detail, the *Creation of Adam* (figure 17.34), one can perceive some of the majesty of the total work. Embracing an awestruck Eve and with his left hand resting on the shoulder of the Christ Child, God the Father extends his finger and the spark of life to an inert Adam. Against a background of generations waiting to be born, the twisting, dynamic figure is lovingly paternal, imparting to Adam the soul that will actuate his potential nobility. After protesting for four years that he was a sculptor, not a painter, Michelangelo proved that he was both; all the figures are sculptural forms, conceived in the mind's eye of a sculptor and executed in paint on wet plaster.[3] A recent cleaning of the entire ceiling has brilliantly revealed the original rich, even dazzling colors employed by the sculptor-cum-painter. Totally overwhelming the work of many notable artists on the walls, the ceiling frescoes express the optimism of a supreme artist at the peak of his powers.

The following sonnet[4] embodies Michelangelo's personal and agonizingly physical reaction to four years of standing on a platform and painting over his head:

SONNET V
To Giovanni da Pistoia
"On the Painting of the Sistine Chapel"
(I' ho gia fatto un gozzo)

I've grown a goitre by dwelling in this den—
    As cats from stagnant streams in Lombardy,
    Or in what other land they hap to be—
    Which drives the belly close beneath the chin:
My beard turns up to heaven; my nape falls in,
    Fixed on my spine: my breast-bone visibly
    Grows like a harp: a rich embroidery
    Bedews my face from brush-drops thick and thin.
My loins into my paunch like levers grind:
    My buttock like a crupper bears my weight;
    My feet unguided wander to and fro;
In front my skin grows loose and long; behind,
    By bending it becomes more taut and strait;
    Crosswise I strain me like a Syrian bow:
        Whence false and quaint, I know,
    Must be the fruit of squinting brain and eye;
    For ill can aim the gun that bends awry.
        Come then, Giovanni, try
    To succour my dead pictures and my fame;
    Since foul I fare and painting is my shame.

Donato Bramante, 1444–1514

The dominant political figure and artistic patron of the High Renaissance was Pope Julius II (1503–1513), known as the Warrior Pope. Determined to obliterate the appalling memories of Alexander VI and the Borgia crimes, he refused to even live in the apartment of his decadent predecessor. Julius II restored order to the city of Rome, reconquered papal provinces with the sword,

Figure 17.35 *Donato Bramante,* Tempietto, *1502. Ht. 46' with external diameter of 29'. S. Pietro in Montorio, Rome. Photo: Art Resource.*

and proceeded energetically to rebuild his beloved Rome. A fortuitous quirk of history put a dynamic pope in power at precisely the time when he could utilize the mature talents of Michelangelo, Raphael, and Bramante. Bramante of Urbino, the foremost architect of the High Renaissance and a close friend of the pope, was entrusted with many building projects, the greatest of which was the construction of a new St. Peter's. Julius II decided, in 1505, that the 1100-year-old Basilica of St. Peter's was to be replaced by a Renaissance structure worthy of the imperial splendor of the new Rome, a project that was not completely finished until 1626, some fourteen architects, twenty popes, and one Reformation later.

Though much of Bramante's design can still be seen in St. Peter's, his architectural genius is better illustrated by a circular structure of only modest size but of immense influence in architectural history. Constructed on the spot where St. Peter was supposedly crucified, the *Tempietto* (little temple; figure 17.35) became the prototype of classical domed architecture in Europe and the United States. Placed on a three-step base like a Greek temple, the exquisitely proportioned building was conceived as an articulated work of sculpture in the manner of classical Greek architecture. Influenced by Leonardo's radial designs, the building is distinguished by the severely Doric colonnade, above which are classical triglyphs and metopes topped by a lightly rhythmical balustrade. The overall effect of majestic serenity in a small building may have been the decisive factor in Bramante's selection as the papal architect.

3. On his first paycheck he pointedly wrote, "I, Michelangelo Buonarroti, *sculptor,* have received 500 ducats on account . . . for *painting* the vault of the Sistine chapel." From Peter De Rosa, *Vicars of Christ: The Dark Side of the Papacy.* (New York: Macmillan Publishing Company, 1988).

4. John Addington Symonds, trans., *The Sonnets of Michelangelo Buonarotti and Tommaso Campanella* (London: Smith, Elder & Co., 1878), p. 35. See chapter 19 for other poems by Michelangelo.

Figure 17.36 *Raphael*, The Alba Madonna, *ca. 1510. Transferred from wood to canvas, diameter of 37¼". Andrew W. Mellon Collection. National Gallery of Art, Washington, D.C.*

Raphael (Raffaello Sanzio), 1483–1520

The third artist working in the Vatican, in addition to Bramante and Michelangelo, was Raphael (RAHF-ee-el), one of the greatest painters in Western art. Born in Urbino like Bramante, Raphael studied first with Perugino and then, as so many artists had done before him, moved to Florence. Over the four-year period of 1504–1508, he studied the works of Leonardo and Michelangelo and painted many of his famous Madonnas.

The most reproduced painter of the Renaissance, the work of Raphael, especially the Madonnas, is perhaps too familiar. Raphael was an intellectual painter whose works should be studied for both form and content, but viewers tend to see his Madonnas as pretty and sweet, partly because they were intended as sympathetic portrayals of Mother and Child and because of countless sentimental imitations of Raphael's style. *The Alba Madonna* (figure 17.36) is a tightly controlled triangular composition derived from Leonardo's style, but designed as a *tondo* (circular painting). Unlike Leonardo and other Madonna painters, Raphael used life models, usually in the nude, sketching the basic figure until he had all elements just right. In this work he was concerned with subtly contrasting the humanity of John the Baptist with the divinity of the Christ Child, who is the actual focal point of the painting. The counterbalancing diagonals of the left arm of the Madonna and the back of the kneeling John form the top of the pyramid; the left leg of Christ echoes the reverse diagonal that extends from the Madonna's left forearm and down her leg. Enclosed within the space between the blue-draped leg and the fur-covered back of John, the figure of the Christ Child is essen-

Figure 17.37 *Raphael*, Baldassare Castiglione, *ca. 1515. Oil on canvas, 32¼" × 26½". The Louvre, Paris.*

tially vertical. The one horizontal element in the composition is the right arm of Christ, leading our eye to the slender cross so lightly held. Like so many of Raphael's paintings, this masterpiece suffers perhaps from too much loving care; it has been so vigorously cleaned that the colors are not as vibrant as they undoubtedly once were.

Characterized as Aristotelian in his approach to art, Raphael was a keen observer of nature and of people. His mastery of his craft combined with his perceptive examination of the world about him enabled Raphael to be one of the foremost portrait painters of his age. A member of the circle of Baldassare Castiglione, author of the *Courtier,* a book about courtesy and conduct (see chapter 19), Raphael was described by the writer Aretino as having "every virtue and every grace that is appropriate to a gentleman." It was, in fact, Raphael's social graces and material success that lay at the heart of his cold war with the socially inept Michelangelo. In his portrait of Castiglione (figure 17.37) Raphael depicts his friend in the coolly composed pose of a Renaissance gentleman. The poise and quiet confidence are emphasized by the restrained elegance of his dress, which exemplifies a cultured society reacting against the flamboyant dress of the preceding century.

Raphael was an active member of a philosophical circle dedicated to reconciling the views of Plato and Aristotle. After he was commissioned to decorate the papal apartments, he was quick to put his ideas into visual form. The result was four giant wall

Figure 17.38 *Raphael,* The School of Athens, *1501–1511. Fresco, 26' × 18'. Stanza della Segnatura, Vatican Palace, Rome. Photo: Scala/Art Resource.*

murals depicting the four branches of human knowledge and wisdom: Theology, Law, Poetry, and Philosophy. The last painting, the so-called *School of Athens* (figure 17.38) is itself a summary of Renaissance humanism. Grouped on the left side of the painting are the Greek philosophers who were mainly concerned with ultimate mysteries, from Plato at the top to Pythagoras writing on a slate at the lower left. Holding the *Timaeus,* Plato points to the heavens as the source of his ideas/forms. Herakleitos sits in the foreground with his elbow on a block but his face is probably that of Michelangelo. At the upper left we see Sokrates in a typical dialogue with some of his students. Aristotle holds his *Ethics* as he indicates the earth as the rightful object of all observations. Diogenes sprawls on the steps, and at the lower right, Euclid bends over a slate, but his face is that of Bramante. Continuing the portraiture, Raphael depicts himself at the extreme right. The statue of Apollo, patron of poetry, presides at the upper left, whereas Athena, goddess of wisdom, watches over the empirical philosophers and scientists. Though Plato used poetic images and Aristotle utilized rational analysis, Raphael and his circle were convinced that the philosophers agreed in substance even though they disagreed in words. Raphael has harmonized not only the schools of philosophy but the ancient and Christian worlds as well.

With the premature death of the frail Raphael, the High Renaissance in Rome came to an end. By this time the innovations of Leonardo, Michelangelo, Bramante, and Raphael were being studied and applied throughout Italy, especially in Venice, and northward into Germany, France, and the Netherlands (today's Holland and Belgium).

High and Late Renaissance and Mannerism in Sixteenth-Century Italy

Giorgione da Castelfranco, ca. 1475/77–1510

The High Renaissance style emerged very clearly in the work of a shadowy figure first known as Giorgio and later, as the famous Giorgione ("big George"; giorge-o-NAY). Very little is known about the man or even his work. He was, according to Vasari, a humanist, musician, and lover of conversation, parties, nature, and women, possibly in reverse order.

Though another hand has added some distant figures in the left landscape, Giorgione's *Adoration of the Shepherds* (figure 17.39) is a superb example of the new pastoral poetic style that

Figure 17.39 *Giorgione,* Adoration of the Shepherds, *ca. 1505. Oil on panel, 35¾" × 43½". Samuel H. Kress Collection. National Gallery of Art, Washington, D.C.*

Giorgione introduced to painting in general and to the Venetian school in particular. One of the most innovative and influential painters of the Renaissance, Giorgione used his mastery of light and color to paint magical landscapes in which human figures become part of the Arcadian mood. In fact, in figure 17.39 the landscape is so predominant that the work can be viewed as a landscape with Nativity Scene. The scene itself is depicted not in naturalistic terms, as in the works of van Eyck or Leonardo, but as nature in the raw as viewed by the eye of the poet. The figures are not drawn but rather formed of contrasting light and shadow, with the body of the child and the heads of the parents radiating a heavenly light against the gloomy recesses of the cave. The high moral tone and noble values of the Florentine/Roman High Renaissance are utterly foreign to this romantic evocation of mood and feeling.

Giorgione died at an early age of the plague, leaving a number of unfinished works. Though it is known that Titian completed some of the paintings, what may never be known is which paintings were involved and what "completed by Titian" really means. In the *Fête Champêtre* (figure 17.40) we see two opulent nudes painted in the lush Venetian manner; the one on the left

Figure 17.40 *Giorgione (and Titian?),* Fête Champêtre, *ca. 1505. Oil on canvas, 43¼" × 54¼".* **The Louvre, Paris. Cliché des Musées Nationaux, Paris.**

is gracefully emptying a crystal pitcher and the other holds a recorder while gazing dreamily into the distance. They may represent Greek muses, thus giving the painting a Neoplatonic cast. The fully clothed men are deep in conversation, but only the man casually playing the lute is fashionably dressed. Having been labeled at various times "Pastoral Symphony," "Fountain of Love," or, as here, "Country Festival," the work has even been called an allegory of poetry. In other words, the subject matter may never be known or even be important. The painting exists as an enchanting combination of forms and shapes in a poetic setting, all created by an artist who may have had in mind nothing more than that.

Michelangelo and Mannerism

The art of the remainder of the century can be considered as two basic streams of styles: Mannerism and Late Renaissance. The beauty, harmony, and proportions of the High Renaissance were seen at this time as a golden age, an era in which Leonardo, Michelangelo, and Raphael had convincingly demonstrated that there was nothing an artist could not do.

What was left for subsequent artists? Vasari used the term *maniera,* meaning style, of working "in the manner of" supreme artists such as Raphael and Michelangelo. Later artists could either adopt the techniques of the masters or use these techniques as a point of departure, to replace the serenity of the High Renaissance with a Mannerist virtuosity that delighted in twisting, confusing, and distorting human figures. Raphael and Michelangelo studied nature; the Mannerists studied Raphael and Michelangelo, especially Michelangelo.

The so-called Mannerist Crisis may also have been a reaction to the momentous events of the 1520s, some local and others international, that affected the viewpoints and lives of just about everyone. The power of Florence came to an end, as the proud city became a pawn in the hands of the Medici popes Leo X (1513–1521) and Clement VII (1523–1534). Luther's defiance of Pope Leo X led to the dissolution of unified Christianity, followed by over a century of sectarian warfare. In 1527 the political machinations of Clement VII led to the Sack of Rome by the rampaging armies of the Holy Roman Emperor Charles V of Germany. In 1529 Clement VII refused to recognize the marriage of Henry VIII of England and Anne Boleyn, leading to England's break with Rome. It was a decade of disasters. In the New World, rapidly becoming a significant factor in European culture, the decade was prefaced by Cortés's conquest of the Aztecs in Mexico (1519) and followed by Pizarro's conquest of the Incas in Peru (1533).

Artistically, the Mannerists were greatly influenced by Michelangelo's sculptures in the Medici Chapel and his *Last Judgment* fresco in the Sistine Chapel. Michelangelo's designs for the New Sacristy of the Medici Chapel were the most nearly complete of his architectural-sculptural conceptions. Signing the contract in 1519, he labored for fifteen years on a mortuary chapel for the tombs of Giuliano and Lorenzo de' Medici (son and grandson of

Figure 17.41 *Michelangelo,* Tomb of Giuliano de' Medici, *1519–1534. Marble, 20'9" × 13'10". New Sacristy, Medici Chapel, S. Lorenzo, Florence.*

Lorenzo the Magnificent). For most of its construction the project was threatened by exterior forces as indicated above, particularly the humiliation of the papacy during the 1527 Sack of Rome. By the time the poverty-stricken Clement VII had returned to his burned-out city in 1528, Florence had successfully revolted against the Medici for the third time. However, the 1530 reconquest of the Republic put a Medici governor in charge again, leading to an order for Michelangelo's assassination because he had helped the city fortify itself. Protected by the canon of the Church of San Lorenzo, Michelangelo was pardoned by the Medici pope Clement VII so he could complete the family tomb. With the installation of the pope's illegitimate son, the vicious Alessandro, Duke of Florence, Michelangelo's position was so precarious that when Clement VII died in 1534, he fled to Rome, never again to return to Florence. It is difficult to conceive of a project that was more plagued by violent events or more successful in artistic terms.

The Medici Tombs

The *Tomb of Giuliano de' Medici* (figure 17.41) is a triangular composition with the contemplative figure of Lorenzo's son, Giuliano, at the top and the figures of Night and Day reclining on either side. According to the sculptor's own explanation, Night and Day caused the Duke's death but, in death, he has conquered time. Beneath Night's shoulder a grinning mask seems to sym-

Figure 17.42 *Michelangelo,* Tomb of Lorenzo de' Medici, *1519–1534. Marble, 20'9" × 13'10". New Sacristy, Medici Chapel, S. Lorenzo, Florence.*

Figure 17.43 *Michelangelo,* The Last Judgment, *1536–1541. Fresco, 48' × 44'. Altar wall of the Sistine Chapel, Vatican, Rome. Photo: Scala/Art Resource.*

bolize earthly vanities, and the owl beneath her leg is the common symbol of night. Her heavily muscled and twisted body is complemented by the extraordinary musculature of Day, whose contorted extremities imprison the figure in an anguished tension, a characteristic of Michelangelo's second style that strongly influenced the Mannerists.

Like Giuliano, the grandson of the great Lorenzo (figure 17.42) wears Roman armor as a Prince of the Church of Rome but is flanked by a masculine Twilight and feminine Dawn. Night was portrayed as a mother, but Dawn is depicted as a virgin, just starting to sleepily stir in the faint light of the new day.

Later Works

During Michelangelo's visit to Rome to obtain Clement VII's pardon, the discussion concerned the Sistine Chapel perhaps even more than the New Sacristy that was destined to remain incomplete. The end wall of the Sistine Chapel contained the *Assumption of the Virgin* by Perugino, but Clement proposed to Michelangelo that this be replaced with a Resurrection. By the time the new pope Paul III (1534–1549) had commissioned the artist to paint the entire wall, the subject had become the Last Judgment, though how this came about is not clear. Paul III was a Counter-Reformation pope whose most significant act was the convening of the Council of Trent (1545–1564) to systematically

reform the church to counter the challenge of Protestantism. However, nepotism was rampant during Paul's reign and he, along with his sons and daughters, lived the lavish life of a Renaissance pontiff. Michelangelo, on the other hand, was deeply religious and was, moreover, sixty-one years old when he accepted the commission.

Preoccupied with the fate of humanity and that of his own soul, Michelangelo apparently began *The Last Judgment* (figure 17.43) with the conviction that the world had gone mad. (He began his project in the same year that Henry VIII defied Rome and established the Church of England.) The ideal beauty and optimism of the chapel ceiling had been superseded by a mood of terror and doom, with the gigantic figure of Christ come to judge the quick and the dead. Based on Matthew 24:30–31, everyone "will see the Son of Man coming on clouds of Heaven with power and great glory," his body twisted and his arm raised in a gesture of damnation. In an energetic clockwise motion, the figures at the bottom rise toward Christ and are either gathered in by waiting angels or pulled by demons down into Hell. The resurrected women (always clothed) and men (generally nude)

Figure 17.44 *Michelangelo,* Rondanini Pietà, *ca. 1554–1564. Marble, ht. 64". Castello Sforza, Milan. Photo: Art Resource.*

Figure 17.45 *Michelangelo,* Dome of St. Peter's *(view from the west), 1546–1564. Ht. of dome 452'. Completed by della Porta in 1590. Vatican, Rome. Photo: Art Resource.*

float into the helping arms of angels, who are unencumbered by wings or halos. The scale of the figures is from small in the region of the Damned, close to eye level, to monumental at the distant top section in the region of the Blessed. The nervous energy and the twisting, writhing, elongated figures are techniques adopted by the Mannerists. In this powerful fresco, however, they are manifestations of the unique artistic vision of a master, a natural evolution, given the subject matter, of his style for the Medici tombs in Florence.

Only a few days before his death, Michelangelo was reworking his *Rondanini Pietà* (figure 17.44), cutting the head back into the Virgin's shoulder and making the composition a slender, unified work of infinite pathos. Far removed from the High Renaissance style, the elongated figures are reminiscent of the jamb statues of the Royal Portal of Chartres Cathedral (see figure 14.34), seeming to symbolize the artist's direct appeal to God. His death in his eighty-eighth year, probably of pneumonia, left this sculpture unfinished and his major project, the dome of St. Peter's, still under construction.

Michelangelo's apse and dome of St. Peter's (figure 17.45) was not a commission but, in his words, done "solely for the love of God." Whether or not Michelangelo's late style can be described as Mannerist, still a moot point, his late architectural style is powerful and confident. The great dome is a huge sculptured shape rising above an apse, distinguished by enormous pilasters, Michelangelo's "colossal order," pilasters that are both decora-

tive and structural. The upward thrust of the pilasters is repeated and reinforced by the double columns of the drum and carried ever upward by the arching ribs to a climax in the lantern. The vertical stress of classic forms, a new Renaissance procedure, is visible proof that classicism can be as emotional and as transcendental as the High Gothic style of Chartres Cathedral (figure 14.33). Though the nave was extended far beyond Michelangelo's Greek-cross plan, the dome is still the major landmark of Rome, a fitting symbol for the art and life of Michelangelo.

Parmigianino (Francesco Mazzola), 1503–1540

Unquestionably a Mannerist, Parmigianino (par-me-dja-ah-NEE-no) painted in an elaborate, tense, elegant, and artificial style in sharp and deliberate contrast to the harmonious naturalism of the High Renaissance. His *Madonna with the Long Neck* (figure 17.46) is a marvel of decorative beauty. With a swanlike neck, exceptionally long fingers, and cold, ivory-smooth flesh, the Madonna smiles tenderly on a seemingly lifeless Christ child. The background figure of the biblical prophet is dramatically small, and the rising, uncompleted columns add to the artificiality and strange mood of unreality. Parmigianino planned a complete temple in the background but left it incomplete, further illustrating, perhaps, the perverseness of an artist known to deliberately flaunt social and artistic conventions.

Figure 17.46 *Parmigianino,* Madonna with the Long Neck, *1534–1540. Oil on panel, 7'1" × 4'4". Uffizi Gallery, Florence. Photo: Scala/ Art Resource.*

Figure 17.47 *Titian,* Venus with a Mirror, *ca. 1555. Oil on canvas, 49" × 41½". Andrew W. Mellon Collection. National Gallery of Art, Washington, D.C.*

Late Renaissance and Mannerism in Italy and Spain

Titian (Tiziano Vecelli), ca. 1488–1576

With an artistic career spanning sixty-eight years, Titian (TISH-n) was a giant of the High and Late Renaissance, excelling in every aspect of the painter's craft. After Raphael, he was the finest portrait artist of the century, courted by the nobles and royalty of Europe. Titian achieved the social status advocated by Leonardo, acquiring a towering reputation that led to many honors, the title of count, and a princely life. Repeatedly celebrating the goddess of love, his late painting, *Venus with a Mirror* (figure 17.47) is permeated with a tangible sensuality that is, however, not erotic,

expressing instead the natural loveliness of woman. The famous color tones are exceptionally rich rather than just brilliant, mellowed by layer-on-layer of glazes. Titian produced several variations on the Venus-and-mirror theme, but this painting he kept for himself and willed to his son. Perhaps more than any other Renaissance artist, Titian understood the spirit of classical art. Drawing on the Greeks, he incorporated High Renaissance techniques and some Mannerist devices in what is best described, in this work, as Late Renaissance style.

Tintoretto (Jacopo Robusti), 1518–1594

Titian's Venetian contemporary, Tintoretto (tin-toe-RET-toe), developed a more fervent style blending Mannerist devices with the drawing technique of Michelangelo. In *Christ at the Sea of Galilee* (figure 17.48) we view a turbulent sea with wave edges as sharp as a knifeblade, spottily applied white highlights, and deliberately atonal combinations that heighten the emotional content. The curved and elongated figure of Christ dominates an intensely dramatic scene in which the frightened fishermen look to the Savior for deliverance.

A comparison of Tintoretto's *The Last Supper* (figure 17.49) with that by Leonardo (see figure 17.31) dramatically illustrates the differences between the High Renaissance and the Mannerist style of the Late Renaissance. In Tintoretto's version the table is sharply angled and placed at the left. The size of the disciples diminishes from foreground to background, with Christ high-

Figure 17.48 *Tintoretto,* Christ at the Sea of Galilee, *ca. 1575–1580. Oil on canvas, 66¼″ × 46″. Samuel H. Kress Collection. National Gallery of Art, Washington, D.C.*

Figure 17.49 *Tintoretto,* The Last Supper, *1592–1594. Oil on canvas, 12′ × 18′8″. S. Giorgio Maggiore, Venice. Photo: Art Resource.*

Figure 17.50 *Palladio, Villa Rotunda, Vicenza. Begun 1550 and finished by Vencenzo Scamozzi. Photo: Art Resource.*

Figure 17.51 *Paolo Veronese,* The Finding of Moses, *ca. 1570. Oil on canvas, 22¾" × 17½". Andrew W. Mellon Collection. National Gallery of Art, Washington, D.C.*

lighted only by the brilliant glow of his halo. Almost lost in the agitation, Judas, dressed as a servant, sits on the opposite side of the table, a pathetic, isolated figure. This is the moment of the Eucharist, the transubstantiation of consecrated bread and wine into the flesh and blood of Christ. The agitated clutter of servants, hovering angels, flaming lamp, and radiant halo combine to proclaim the emotional spirit of the Counter-Reformation.

Palladio (Andrea di Pietro), 1518–1580

The intense dramatic style of Tintoretto heralds the coming age of the Baroque, but the architectural designs of Andrea Palladio (pah-LAH-djo) are clearly, lucidly classical. The only North Italian architect comparable to Brunelleschi, Alberti, Bramante, and Michelangelo, Palladio was born Andrea di Pietro but is known to posterity by a name derived from Pallas Athena, goddess of wisdom. An avid student of classical and Renaissance architecture, Palladio designed churches, public buildings, and private homes. His Villa Rotunda (figure 17.50), one of nineteen Palladian villas still in existence, was built in the countryside near Venice, much in the manner and style of Roman villas. From a central square identical porticoes thrust out from each side, each with a different view and a slightly variable climate at different hours of the day. Palladian designs became popular for English stately homes, and this particular design became a model for southern plantation homes in the American South, where outdoor living was common for much of the year. In the Villa Rotunda the proportions of length and breadth, height and width, of and between the rooms were based on the Pythagorean ratios of the Greek musical scale.

Paolo Veronese, 1528–1588

Paradoxically, only the country villas of Palladio were placed in the natural settings that the Venetian painters Giorgione, Titian, Tintoretto, and Veronese celebrated in their richly colored paintings. Venice itself, except for private gardens, was a congested city of marble, brick, stone, and waterways with few plants, flowers, or trees. The fourth of the great Venetian masters, Veronese (vair-oh-NAY-se), like his contemporaries, glorified nature in his work,

but unlike other artists he concentrated on the sumptuous material world. Pleasure-loving Venetians preferred luxurious paintings that dazzled the eye and soothed the conscience. In *The Finding of Moses* (figure 17.51) Veronese created a cheerful biblical scene redolent with the elegance and luxury that the Venetians themselves enjoyed. The Egyptian princess is richly clothed in Venetian dress, presiding benignly over the rescue of the abandoned child. The composition unwinds from the black page at the lower left up through the lady-in-waiting, who is handing Moses to the Pharaoh's daughter. On the right there is a similar unwinding upward but with a tighter rhythm. The tableau is set in a lush countryside in front of a sturdy Italian bridge and a suitably exotic and fanciful Egyptian city.

El Greco (Domenikos Theotokopoulos), 1541–1614

Veronese's style is lavishly and opulently Late Renaissance and basically secular, but that of El Greco is mystical, a fervent expression of the Counter-Reformation spirit. The last and possibly the most gifted of the Mannerists, Domenikos Theotokopoulos, known as El Greco (the Greek), was born in Crete, then a Venetian possession, and trained in Late Byzantine art and Venetian Mannerism before moving to Spain in 1576. Even before the defeat of the Spanish Armada in 1588 Spain was a fading power, artistically provincial and obsessed with the Counter-Reformation, yet it was the proper environment for an artist of El Greco's religious convictions. Combining the Byzantine tradition with his thorough knowledge of the Venetian masters, El Greco created a passionately religious art that was the embodiment of Spanish mysticism. In his *The Penitent St. Peter* (figure 17.52) the elon-

Figure 17.52 *El Greco*, The Penitent St. Peter, *ca. 1598–1600. The San Diego Museum of Art, San Diego, California.*

Figure 17.53 *El Greco*, Laokoön, *ca. 1610–1614. Oil on canvas, 54⅛" × 67⅞". Samuel H. Kress Collection. National Gallery of Art, Washington, D.C.*

gated figure with hands clasped in prayer and anguished eyes turned heavenward in repentance for having denied Christ is set against a dark and mysterious background in which a distant angel is softly illuminated. Although physically tranquil, the scene is turbulent with the emotion of spiritual forces in a triangular composition that directs our eyes to the agonized face. The oft-debated topic of El Greco's astigmatism being responsible for his elongated figures has no basis in fact; the distortions are deliberate and reflect the artist's exposure to Byzantine art and Venetian Mannerism.

Though the subject is secular, El Greco's *Laokoön* (figure 17.53) is equally tormented. Unlike the Hellenistic sculptural version (see figure 7.61), the Trojan priest and his two sons (plus three angels?) are depicted as attenuated silvery figures, fighting off slender snakes that may be venomous but certainly not capable of crushing anyone, unlike the powerful sea serpents of the sculptural group. In the background, dramatic clouds hover over the brooding city of Toledo, El Greco's version of Troy before its fall to Agamemnon and his Argive army.

A nation supercharged with religious zeal, Spain formed the spearhead of the Counter-Reformation as the birthplace of the Society of Jesus (Jesuits) and the stronghold of the merciless Inquisition. El Greco was its peerless master of religious subjects, an artist who, more than any other, made visible the spiritual content of the Catholic faith. Widely admired in his time, El Greco's reputation declined rapidly as Western Europe, but not Spain, plunged enthusiastically into the scientific and intellectual discoveries of the Enlightenment. It was not until the twentieth century that El Greco's unique and intensely personal art received proper recognition.

High and Late Renaissance in the North, ca. 1500–1600

For most of the fifteenth century, Northern artists and some Italians were influenced by the dazzling naturalism of the Flemish masters. Not until the end of the century did Italian influences begin to beguile Northern patrons with their scientific rules and especially a literary tradition that included a vocabulary of art criticism. Noble patrons were delighted with classical examples of "good" and "bad" art. Increasingly, this meant that art based on models from antiquity was good, but the rest, including the entire Flemish tradition, was "wrong" or at best "primitive." With remarkable suddenness, Italian artists were busily engaged with important projects for patrons such as Henry VII of England and the French royal family, whereas Northern artists were traveling to Italy to study the masters of the Early and High Renaissance.

During the sixteenth century it became fashionable to view Northern culture as backward and its artists as inferior, especially those who had not been blessed with Italian instruction in the rules of perspective and proportion. Speaking, in essence, for the Italian Renaissance, Michelangelo remarked to the Portuguese painter Francesco da Hollanda that Flemish landscape paintings were fit only for "young women, nuns, and certain noble persons with no sense of true harmony." "Furthermore," he observed, "their painting is of stuffs, bricks, mortar, the grass of the fields, the shadows of trees and little figures here and there. And all this," said he, "though it may appear good in some eyes, is in truth done without symmetry or proportion." Consigned to the attic of Northern art, the matchless paintings of the Flemish masters were, for over three centuries, derided as primitive or naive. It was not

Figure 17.54 *Albrecht Dürer,* Knight, Death, and the Devil, *1513. Engraving, 9¾" × 7⅝". Harvey D. Parker Fund, 68.261. Museum of Fine Arts, Boston.*

Figure 17.55 *Matthias Grünewald,* The Small Crucifixion, *ca. 1511—1520. Oil on wood, 70" × 60". Samuel H. Kress Collection. National Gallery of Art, Washington, D.C.*

until 1902 that the first international show of fifteenth-century Flemish art was opened in Bruges, and only considerably later in this century that the derogatory labels were finally dropped.

Albrecht Dürer, 1471–1528

For reasons still unknown, Italian art caught on first in Germany, where Dürer (DOO-er) became the founder of the brief but brilliant German High Renaissance. His two trips to Italy (1494–1495 and 1505–1507) exposed him to all the Italian techniques, but he was never attuned to Italian form, preferring instead the strong lines of the Northern tradition. Though he became a master painter, Dürer's most significant achievements were in the graphic arts of engraving and woodcuts, which were printed in quantity and sold throughout Germany, making the artist a wealthy man.

Northern art retained a Gothic strain, a fascination with the bizarre, the grotesque, and the supernatural, as embodied, for example, in figure 17.54. The subject of *Knight, Death, and the Devil* was apparently derived from the *Manual of the Christian Soldier* by Erasmus of Rotterdam. With death mounted on a decrepit horse in the background and a hideous devil behind him, the Christian knight rides confidently along the path of faith. Mounted on a superb horse and accompanied by his faithful dog, his unwavering gaze is fixed on his ultimate goal of the Heavenly Kingdom. The drama, control, and incredible detail of this powerful work is highly representative of the vigorous Northern Renaissance, created by an artist who had chosen to follow the faith of Martin Luther.

Dürer was deeply involved in the religious and political movements in Germany and in the Italian humanism that flourished briefly on German soil until the winds of the Reformation swept away what was essentially a Catholic point of view. The leading humanist of sixteenth-century Europe, Erasmus of Rotterdam (1466–1536), influenced many intellectuals of the period including artists such as Dürer and Hans Holbein the Younger. In the Erasmus portrait by Dürer (see figure 19.1) the scholar sits in his study surrounded by books, some presumably his own publications, as he drafts a new work. Behind him in Latin is the elaborate title of the print and the name of the artist. At the bottom is Dürer's monogram, above which is the date and above that a Greek inscription that translates as, "His writings portray him even better," meaning that his books were a more accurate measure of the man than Dürer's reverential portrait. The Northern passion for detail is, to say the least, clearly evident in this print.

Matthias Grünewald (Mathis Gothardt Neithardt), 1483?–1528

Dürer was internationally famous, but his worthy contemporary Grünewald, though widely known in his own time, was neglected until this century. A highly original artist, Grünewald, whose name was actually Mathis Gothardt Neithardt, was familiar with the work of Dürer and possibly that of Bosch, but there is no evidence of Italian classical influence, as one glance at his *Small Crucifixion* (figure 17.55) will immediately reveal. This is the brutal reality of nailing a man to a cross and leaving him there to die. His body a mass of cuts and suppurating sores, his limbs twisted, his skin gray and speckled with dried blood, Christ is depicted in relentless detail as having died for the sins of all humankind. The grief of John, Mary, and Mary Magdalene is vibrant with intense pain and sorrow. Grünewald has elevated the horror of the passion to the level of universal tragedy, producing a composition as convincing as anything in Western art.

Hans Holbein, 1497–1543

Fully conversant with all that the Italians had to teach, Holbein the Younger (hol-bine) was the last of the superb painters of the German High Renaissance and one of the finest portrait painters in the history of art. He traveled widely in France, Switzerland, and Italy, then finally settled down in London, where he became the favorite painter of Henry VIII, who furnished a special suite in St. James's Palace for "master Hans." Holbein gained access to the English court through Erasmus of Rotterdam, who provided him with a letter of recommendation to Sir Thomas More. His portrait of More (see figure 19.2) is a noble portrayal of the humanist-statesman. Depicted realistically, including a stubble of beard, More wears the luxurious clothes of his rank and the heavy chain of his office as Lord Chancellor of England. With meticulous attention to detail in the manner of van Eyck, Holbein depicts the dignity and determination of a man who will one day be executed for opposing Henry's establishment of the Church of England.

A French Chateau

The Italian influence in France is epitomized in the chain of elegant chateaux built throughout the scenic Loire River valley. Imposing and elaborate as befits the king of a prosperous nation, the Chateau of Chambord (figure 17.56) was originally a hunting lodge that was later redesigned for Francis I by an Italian architect who may have been influenced by a nearby resident named Leonardo da Vinci. The huge central block is connected by corridors leading outward to sets of apartments designed in the modern manner as self-contained units. Anchored at the four corners by large round towers, the entire complex is surrounded by a moat. The matching of horizontal and vertical features in windows and moldings is taken directly from the Italian palazzos, but the forest of dormers, chimneys, and lanterns is right out of the Gothic tradition and flamboyantly French.

Pieter Bruegel the Elder, 1525?–1569

Most of the Renaissance art of France was courtly but, as mentioned previously, there was a growing middle class of art patrons in the Netherlands, which in the sixteenth century had become a battleground of religious and political strife. Militantly Protestant, particularly in the North (today's Holland), the Netherlands fought a rigid Spanish rule that became even more brutal under the fanatical Philip II and the imported Spanish Inquisition. Nevertheless, the Netherlandish school of painting flourished and produced Bruegel (BRU-gul), the only Northern genius to appear

Figure 17.56 *Chateau of Chambord, aerial view, begun 1519.* © *Rapho/Photo Researchers, Inc.*

Figure 17.57 *Pieter Bruegel the Elder,* Landscape with the Fall of Ikaros, *ca. 1558. Oil on canvas, 44⅛″ × 29″. Musée Royaux des Beaux Arts, Brussels.*

between Dürer and Rubens. A highly educated humanist and philosopher, Bruegel studied in Italy from 1551 to 1555, returning home with a love of Italian landscapes and a profound knowledge of Italian control of form and space. In *Landscape with the Fall of Ikaros* (figure 17.57) Bruegel depicts the myth of the reckless one who ignored the advice of his father, Daidalos, and flew so near the sun that the wings fashioned by his father melted, and he plunged to his death in the sea. In the painting Bruegel emphasizes everything but Ikaros, who is just a pair of kicking legs and a splash in the sea in front of the sailing galleon. The plowman and the singing shepherd are oblivious of the fate of a foolish boy who has caused his own destruction. He dies in the sea, but the plowing, the shepherding, the world go serenely on. Bruegel viewed humankind as basically noble, but depicted men and women as faulty individuals who were easily degraded or destroyed by materialism, avarice, or, like Ikaros, just plain folly.

In *Winter (Return of the Hunters)* (figure 17.58) Bruegel demonstrates his mastery of perspective as he details what first appears to be a simple genre scene. Two moods are conveyed: the bleak coldness of nature and the warmth and activity of human beings. Our attention is drawn to the hunters and their dogs as,

Figure 17.58 *Pieter Bruegel the Elder,* Winter (Return of the Hunters), *1565. Oil on panel, 46" × 63¾". Kunsthistorisches Museum, Vienna. Photo: Art Resource.*

cold and exhausted, they return to their frosty hamlet. Before them are all sorts of activities from work to play and the promise of a warm fire in a cozy house. Bruegel has presented us with a microcosm, an image of his time and place as he saw it. But there is also the universality that masterworks have in common. This is not just 1565 in a northern clime but a sensitive portrayal of human activities in a hostile environment: working, playing, coping, surviving.

Exercises

1. Compare and contrast the *David* sculptures of Donatello, Verrocchio, and Michelangelo. Consider every detail plus the overall effect.
2. Compare and contrast the Pazzi Chapel with Sainte-Chapelle in Paris (chapter 14). Then, using the two chapels as representative of their ages, compare and contrast the Gothic era with the Renaissance.

Summary

Symbolized by Brunelleschi's dome and the dedication of Florence Cathedral in 1436, a new age came into being in fifteenth-century Florence, a city of bankers and craftsmen whose self-image was personified by the Davids of Donatello, Verrocchio, and Michelangelo. To create the new style, a fresh repertory of illusionist devices was developed by Masaccio and later used by all painters.

By the second half of the century classical designs had been fully assimilated, leading to the classically based architecture of Alberti and the mythological painting of Botticelli. Florentine innovations spread throughout Italy, promoted by Perugino and by Bellini, the founder of the Venetian school.

The Renaissance in the North took another course. Influenced by the International Style and a long tradition of brilliant craftsmanship in manuscript illuminations and stained glass, van Eyck perfected the new technique of oil painting and created matchless works of meticulous naturalism. Rogier van der Weyden and Hans Memling continued in the naturalistic style but, coinciding with the rising pessimism and fear of death and the devil, the bizarre art of Hieronymus Bosch epitomized the religious torment of a society on the brink of the Lutheran Reformation.

The High Renaissance in Italy was a time of constant warfare highlighted by the incredible achievements of Leonardo in scientific investigation, invention, and painting. Excelling in the arts of sculpture, architecture, painting, and poetry, the "divine Michelangelo" created, among other works, the *Pietà, David,* and the frescoes of the Sistine Chapel ceiling. Raphael achieved a classic balance of form and content that became the hallmark of the High Renaissance, and Bramante, in his Tempietto, designed the prototype of classical domed structures.

In sixteenth-century Venice, Giorgione was the first of the Venetian colorists, followed by the assured painting of Titian and the luxuriant style of Veronese. Michelangelo designed the Medici tombs and influenced such Mannerist painters as Parmigianino, Tintoretto, and the Spanish painter from Crete called El Greco. During the latter stages of his career Michelangelo painted the awesome *Last Judgment* and designed the apse and dome of St. Peter's. Marking the end of the Renaissance in Italy, Palladio's villas became models for eighteenth- and nineteenth-century domestic architecture in England and the United States.

In sixteenth-century Germany Albrecht Dürer, Matthias Grünewald, and Hans Holbein the Younger were the leading painters of the High Renaissance, whereas in France, Italian styles influenced French courtly art and contributed to the designs of elegant chateaux in the Loire River valley. Renaissance art in the strife-torn Netherlands culminated in the work of Pieter Bruegel the Elder.

By the end of the sixteenth century the ideals and aspirations of the Renaissance had perished in the wreckage of cultures beset by religious wars with the worst yet to come. Marking the end of an era, the Renaissance set the stage for the emergence of the modern world.

Culture and Human Values

The importance and influence of creative artists changed considerably during the Renaissance. During the Early Renaissance their role was basically a continuation of the medieval guild system that trained craftsmen, not artists. The painter's guild to which Leonardo belonged, for example, was established primarily for people who painted walls, ceilings, and staircases.

All that had changed by the High Renaissance. More than anything else, the newly acquired importance of the individual helped elevate the artist to a position comparable to his or her artistic achievements. The individual was not, however, the ultimate reality, as had been the case in ancient Greece. The analogy, rather, is with ancient Rome, in which the individual was free to act in accordance with the needs of the state. Reality in the Renaissance was the bifurcation of power into the monolithic Church of Rome and the secular authority of the many ducal states that dotted western and southern Europe. For the artists reality was the protective power of such patrons as the papacy, a dukedom, or an emerging national state.

If one had to list a single virtue in the chaos and violence marking the transition from the medieval to the modern world, that ideal quality would be *survival.* Not many artists would attain the fame and influence of Raphael or Titian; like Michelangelo, they would more often create masterpieces under the most trying and sometimes dangerous circumstances. Given all the rigors of the age, one can only marvel at the artists who survived and created, and wonder even more at the quality and quantity of the art and architecture that survived the Renaissance.

Renaissance Music: Court and Church

chapter 18

Northern Origins of the Musical Renaissance

Renaissance music dates from about 1420 to 1600, music that can be characterized, in large part, as optimistic, lively, and worldly. The once-rigid distinctions between sacred and secular music no longer applied. Sacred music was not always synonymous with devotional, noble, and edifying sounds any more than secular music was necessarily shallow, common, or folksy. The subject matter rather than the style now determined whether the work was sacred or secular. Renaissance painters used local models for their madonnas, the same models who posed as Aphrodites or nymphs. Composers used melodies where they worked best. The music for Latin poetry, for example, could also be used to accompany a portion of the Mass. Popular songs of the time were sometimes used as a basis for liturgical motets and even for entire masses.

As noted earlier, the Renaissance began around 1350 in Italy and somewhat later in the North. By the fifteenth century, humanism had spread from Italy to the North, and the work of Flemish painters Jan van Eyck and Rogier van der Weyden strongly influenced a number of Italian painters, especially their technique of oil painting. For reasons still not clearly understood, the *musical* Renaissance began in the North—in England, the Low Countries, and in northern France. The most notable of the English composers, John Dunstable (ca. 1380?–1453) was a contemporary of the early Renaissance composers on the continent and probably influenced them with what his admirers called his "sweet style." On the continent some court and church composers of northern France and the Low Countries (Flanders) formed a group known today as the Franco-Flemish school. True Renaissance artists, they were individualistic, materialistic, and boldly experimental. They had mastered the craft and art of a new style of music, and they delighted in demonstrating their compositional skills with intricate canons and musical puzzles for educated amateurs.

In their quest for new materials and fresh ideas they traveled to Italy, where the simple folk melodies and dance tunes provided further opportunities for polyphonic devices and techniques. Considering the travel hardships then, the mobility of Franco-Flemish composers in the fifteenth century was astounding. The composer Dufay, for example, was discovered at the age of nine in Cambrai in France by talent scouts seeking out precocious young musicians. Before he was twenty-six, Dufay had traveled to Italy and then studied in Paris, held a post in northern France, served the court in Bologna, and sung in the papal choir in Rome.

Franco-Flemish composers such as Dufay and others dominated Italian musical life in the courts and in the churches for over a century. St. Mark's in Venice, one of the most important musical centers in Europe, employed only Flemish composers until the latter part of the sixteenth century. When Florence dedicated its magnificent cathedral in 1436, Dufay was commissioned to write special music for the occasion.

Music was an integral part of the complex fabric of Renaissance society. A retinue of musicians became a fixture of court life, with the dukes of Burgundy setting the style. Castiglione (see chapter 19), the chief social arbiter of the Renaissance, viewed his ideal courtier as proficient in both vocal and instrumental music:

> I regard as beautiful music, to sing well by note, with ease and beautiful style; but as even far more beautiful, to sing to the accompaniment of the viol, because nearly all the sweetness lies in the solo part, and we note and observe the fine manner and the melody with much greater attention when our ears are not occupied with more than a single voice, and moreover every little fault is more clearly discerned,—which is not the case when several sing together, because each singer helps his neighbor. But above

all, singing to the viol by way of recitative seems to me most delightful, which adds to the words a charm and grace that are very admirable.

All keyed instruments also are pleasing to the ear, because they produce very perfect consonances, and upon them one can play many things that fill the mind with musical delight. And not less charming is the music of the stringed quartet, which is most sweet and exquisite. The human voice lends much ornament and grace to all these instruments, with which I would have our Courtier at least to some degree acquainted, albeit the more he excels with them, the better.[1]

The Courts of Burgundy

At different times a kingdom, a county, and a duchy, Burgundy became the most powerful and influential political entity in Europe in the first half of the fifteenth century. From Philip the Bold in 1336 through John the Fearless and Philip the Good to Charles the Bold (ruled 1467–1477), the rulers of Burgundy made the court in the capital city of Dijon one of the most magnificent in Europe (see map 18.1).

The Flemish sculptor Claus Sluter and the painter Jan van Eyck served the "court of plume and panoply" of Philip the Good at the time of its greatest splendor. The court was ostentatious and even flamboyant, but nevertheless, according to contemporary accounts, it resembled a sort of fairyland. Women wore hennins, cone-shaped headdresses with long sheer veils hanging from the pointed tops. Their gowns were opulent, frequently decorated with fur and set off by gold throat bands and necklaces. Elaborate furniture and interior designs provided a tasteful setting for the elegance of the court.

The ducal court set the styles in dress, manners, dancing, music, and the other arts. The principal court dance was the *basse dance,* which was performed with gliding steps, possibly accounting for the designation *basse* (low). The basse dance belonged to a family of related dances: the basse dance proper and the *pas de Brabant* (Italian *saltarello*). It was the custom to follow the dignified basse dance, referred to as the "imperial measure," by the quicker pas de Brabant, thus producing a contrasting pair of slow and fast dance movements, a typical procedure for Renaissance dances. Both used the same basic music; only the rhythms were changed.

Tapestries and miniatures of the period show various instrumental ensembles playing for the dancers. The standard group of instruments consisted of two shawms (early oboes) and a slide-trumpet, with the harp, lute, and flute forming the other group. The former group consisted of *hauts* (high, loud) instruments, the latter of *bas* (low, soft) instruments. The hauts instruments were used for festive occasions and were usually played from a balcony or loggia. The bas instruments were used for more intimate dancing and were placed near the dancers.

Court life at Dijon was lively and elegant. It was, in many respects, an updated version of the medieval Court of Love with music, both lively and sedate, for dancing and for songs, true French *chansons* extolling love, joy, and beauty. Secular music was in great demand for everything from the intimate rites of courtship to elaborate ceremonial music for the court. There was a remarkable development of sophisticated secular music, but not at the expense of sacred music, which incorporated the techniques and some of the melodies of secular music into a highly refined style.

The Burgundian School

Guillaume Dufay, ca. 1400–1474

Dufay (doo-FYE) was the most famous composer of the Burgundian school of the Franco-Flemish tradition and one of the greatest of French composers. Following is the beginning of a Dufay mass movement that illustrates the smoother, fuller sounds of Renaissance music. Dufay has broken down the *Kyrie Eleison* into three separate movements: *Kyrie eleison, Christe eleison,* and *Kyrie eleison.* The texture is characteristic of early Renaissance music with mixed vocal and instrumental sounds and with instruments playing the wordless portions of the Mass.

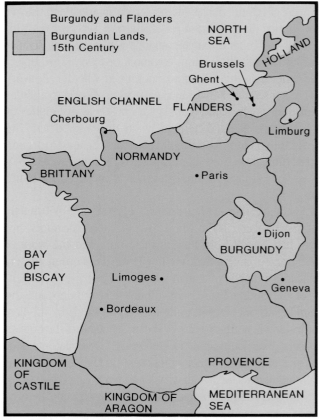

Map 18.1 *Lands of the Dukes of Burgundy.*

1. Baldassare Castiglione, *The Book of the Courtier,* trans. Leonard Eckstein Opdycke (New York: Horace Liveright, 1929).

Listening Example 13

MASS MOVEMENT

Dufay, *Missa Se la face ay pale* (15th century)[2]
Kyrie

Time: 1:40
(Complete)
Guillaume Dufay (ca. 1400–1474)

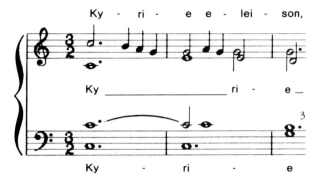

The Franco-Flemish Tradition

During the latter part of the fifteenth century the center of musical activity gradually shifted from Burgundy to northern France and the Low Countries of Flanders and the Netherlands. The fusion of French elegance, Flemish polyphonic techniques, and Italian vigor led to the cosmopolitan style of the Late Renaissance. Whatever followed from this—even the music of such giants as Palestrina and Lassus—was a continuation of northern genius suffused with Italian taste and supported by Italian patronage.

No one person was responsible for the development of the new music. It simply happened that many gifted northern composers were active at about the same time and that all, at varying times, were involved in Italian musical life. There were important composers from the Netherlands and northern France but Josquin of Flanders outshone them all.

Josquin des Près, ca. 1450–1521

Martin Luther reportedly said that "Others follow the notes; Josquin makes them do as he wishes." Josquin (JOSS–can) was known in his own time as the "prince of music." He and his Franco-Flemish contemporaries developed all the basic features of the Late Renaissance and, in so doing, established music as an international style in western European culture. Josquin was to music what Leonardo, Michelangelo, and Raphael were to the

visual arts. A master of compositional techniques, he sometimes invented and consistently refined the methods and materials of Renaissance polyphonic music.

The motet "Ave Maria" by Josquin is an example of the serene lucidity and beauty of the music of the High Renaissance. The smoothly flowing lines are woven into an elegant tapestry of luminous sound, a sound somehow comparable to the undulating arches of a Renaissance arcade. Motets are still sacred music, similar to polyphonic masses, but the text is nonscriptural. Instruments are no longer combined or alternated with the voices as in Early Renaissance music; the singing is now consistently unaccompanied (*a cappella*). The vocal texture is continuous with new phrases overlapping preceding phrases to produce an unbroken stream of simultaneous melodies. This ceaseless flow of intricately intertwined melodies is a hallmark of High and Late Renaissance vocal music.

The voices enter one at a time in *imitation;* that is, each of the four voices has essentially the same melodic line when it makes its entrance. Josquin used the text of the "Ave Maria" ("Hail Mary, full of grace . . .") and selected his basic theme from a portion of an "Ave Maria" chant:

Listening Example 14

MOTET

Josquin des Près, Motet: "Ave Maria"[4] (excerpt)

⌒ = Listening Cue   Time: 2:00

Orlando de Lassus, 1532–1594

The Flemish composer Lassus was one of the finest composers of a celebrated era, the Golden Age of Polyphony of the sixteenth century. His 1,250 compositions were literally international: Latin masses and motets; secular vocal music in French, German, and Italian; and instrumental music in different national styles. Representative of his secular music, the following Italian madrigal is a playful love song spiced with cheery nonsense syllables: "don don don diri diri don don don."

---

2. Smijers, *Algemeene Muziek Geschiedenis,* Utrecht, 1938, p. 101.

3. Musical notation is used on a modest scale throughout this book to give brief quotations from works to be studied. These are guides to listening just as literary quotations are guides to reading. Using musical quotes is a necessary, basic procedure that is in no way "technical." Performing music is technical; *reading* music is a simple procedure easily learned by anyone. Please consult the Appendix: Music Listening and Notation.

---

4. Josquin des Près, *Werke,* vol. I, Amsterdam, 1935, p. 1.

ITALIAN MADRIGAL

Orlando de Lassus, *Matona mia cara* (1550)
(excerpt)

Time: 2:00

Matona, my beloved, be bewitched by my song. I sing
beneath the window to win you for my good wife. I pray to
you, listen to my pretty singing, it will make you love me
more, like the obstinate Greek [Odysseus]. Command me to
go hunting, to hunt with the falcon, and I will bring you a
woodcock as fat as kidneys. If I were not able to speak to you
with so many good reasons, Petrarch himself would not be
able to, nor the Springs of Helicon [home of the Muses].

Developments in Italy

During the latter part of the sixteenth century, Italian genius finally surfaced in the compositions of native Italians. Italian music
had been invigorated by the presence of resident Flemish composers and by the dynamic Counter-Reformation response to Luther's revolt. Flemish composers had fled Spanish tyranny in the
Low Countries to pursue their profession in a less hostile setting.
There was, moreover, a real need to develop a new style of sacred
music because things had gotten out of hand, as Erasmus of Rotterdam cogently pointed out:

> We have introduced an artificial and theatrical music into the
> church, a bawling and agitation of various voices, such as I
> believe had never been heard in the theatres of the Greeks
> and Romans. Horns, trumpets, pipes vie and sound along
> constantly with the voices. Amorous and lascivious melodies
> are heard such as elsewhere accompany only the dances of
> courtesans and clowns.[5]

The Council of Trent (1545–1564) was convened to deal
with the abuses pointed out by Luther and other reformers. The
problem of music was only incidental to overall concerns, but
musical difficulties occupied most of the attention of the Council
for over a year. Final recommendations were negative rather than
positive. Certain practices were forbidden and particular results
were prescribed without, however, specifying the means. The
canon finally adopted by the Council in 1562 banned all seductive or impure melodies, whether vocal or instrumental, all vain
and worldly texts, all outcries and uproars, that "the House of
God may in truth be called a House of prayer."

After passing the canon against decadent musical practices,
the Council considered banning all polyphonic music, especially
polyphonic masses. This ultraconservative movement was countered by Lassus and Palestrina, who, among others, submitted
polyphonic music to a special Commission in a successful attempt to preserve their reformed style of polyphonic music. Perhaps the Commission simply recognized its inability to appraise
the quality of liturgical music, a judgment best made by the musicians themselves.

Giovanni Pierluigi da Palestrina, 1524/5–1594

Palestrina was one of the supreme exponents of Catholic polyphonic music of the Renaissance. Romanticized in the nineteenth century as a lonely and poverty-stricken artist who was
wedded to the church, Palestrina was actually a successful professional musician. He briefly considered the priesthood after the
death of his first wife, but chose instead to marry a wealthy widow.
He was paid well for the music that he wrote for the church and
even refused several more lucrative positions rather than leave
Rome.

Present-day music students study Palestrina's music for
classes in "strict counterpoint," that is, writing polyphonic music
in the manner of the sixteenth century with Palestrina as the model
composer. Though his compositions serve as a guide to correct
contrapuntal writing, Palestrina's music is anything but dogmatic.
A model it is but one of clarity, conciseness, and consistency. Using
existing plainsong melodies as a point of departure, he wrote in
a beautifully balanced style of what can be described as simultaneous plainsong.

The following plainsong, "Veni sponsa Christi," forms the
basis for a Palestrina mass:

Palestrina began with this simple melody, transforming it
into a serenely flowing melodic theme:

"Veni sponsa Christi" (named after the plainsong) is a short
composition based on this characteristic Palestrina melody. Notice
how the smoothly flowing text is fitted to graceful melodic lines.

---

5. Desiderius Erasmus, *Opera Omnia*, VI, 1705, col. 731.

Listening Example 16

MASS MOVEMENT

Palestrina, Mass: *Veni sponsa Christi*
(before 1554)[6]
Agnus Dei I

Time: 2:15
G.P. da Palestrina (1524–1594)

Italian Vocal-Instrumental Music

During the Late Renaissance instrumental music began to rival the preeminence of vocal music, assisted particularly by the musical directors of the Cathedral of St. Mark's in Venice. St. Mark's Byzantine splendor was typical of the grandiose palaces, churches, ceremonies, and even paintings of that ornate city (see figure 18.1). As a trading center and crossroads of the world, Venice deliberately (and successfully) used much pomp and pageantry to impress visitors with its magnificence. Grand productions inside the cathedral were also necessary for the desired effect, but the arrangement of the church did not lend itself to large musical groups.

St. Mark's floor plan formed a Greek cross (figure 18.2). Following the conventions of the Eastern church, the main floor was reserved for men and the smaller balcony level for women. This design was exploited by creating a new *polychoral* style of *antiphonal* singing, or a procedure whereby the ensemble (chorus with or without orchestra) was divided into several different groups singing and/or playing in *alternation*. Musical productions would include the use of the two organs in their fixed positions plus choirs and brass choirs stationed on several balconies throughout the church. The listener would be overwhelmed with vocal and instrumental music alternating between left and right, front and rear. Arrangements of choirs and brass choirs could be selected from some of the possibilities indicated in figure 18.2 (also see figure 18.3).

---

6. Ioannis Petrealoysii Praenestini, *Opera Omnia*, Leipzig, 1886, vol. 18, p. 35.

Figure 18.1 *St. Mark's Cathedral, begun 1063, Venice. With its five portals and five glittering domes, St. Mark's functioned as a sumptuous backdrop for the elaborate civic ceremonies staged in the great piazza stretched before it. Also see figure 12.25 in volume I.*

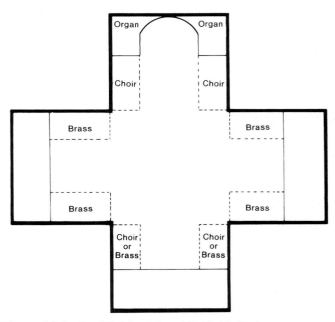

Figure 18.2 *Simplified floor plan of St. Mark's, Venice.*

Listening Example 17

MOTET

Time: 4:12
G. Gabrieli, Motet: *In Ecclesiis* (excerpt)

The complete motet consists of five verses and five alleluias and has the following overall structure of text and performing groups (which sing or play from four different locations in the church):

Figure 18.3 *Interior, St. Mark's, Venice. This view is from the west balcony where one organ is located, looking east to the small chancel with the other organ and space for a small choir. Brass choirs were placed at one or more of the four upper corners under massive arches. The conductor stood on the high podium in front of the main-floor choir.*

Verse 1.	*In ecclesiis benedicite Domino,* (Praise the Lord in the congregation)	Sopranos (Chorus I) Organ
	Alleluia	Sopranos (Chorus I) Chorus II Organ
Verse 2.	*In omnia loco . . . ,* (In every place of worship praise him)	Tenors (Chorus I) Organ
	Alleluia	Tenors (Chorus I) Chorus II Organ
Sinfonia (orchestral interlude)		
Verse 3.	*In Deo, salutari meo . . . ,* (In God, who is my salvation and glory, is my help, and my hope is in God)	Altos (Chorus I) Tenors (Chorus I) Orchestra
	Alleluia	Altos (Chorus I) Tenors (Chorus I) Chorus II Orchestra

Music Printing

Prosperous Venice was also the setting for the development of printed music. Over nine million books had been printed by the year 1500, but no one had thought of printing music on that scale. A 1457 *Psalterium* that included music had been printed at Mainz and a Roman *Missale* was printed in 1476 in Milan using, for the first time, movable type.

Ottaviano de' Petrucci (peh-TROO-tchee; 1466–1539) used movable type in his printing shop, but he was also an enterprising businessman. On 25 May 1498 he petitioned the Signoria of Venice for a twenty-year license (amounting to a monopoly) to print music to meet a growing demand for domestic music. In 1501 he produced the *Harmonice Musices Odhecaton A (One Hundred Songs of Harmonic Music),* the earliest printed collection of part-music. Rich in Franco-Flemish chansons, this anthology was followed by fifty-eight more volumes of secular and sacred music produced for music-hungry amateurs and an increasing number of professional musicians. An expanding market led, of course, to lower prices and even wider dissemination of music. By the end of the sixteenth century, music publishers were in business throughout Europe.

Figure 18.4 Lady Playing a Dulcimer *from the early sixteenth-century manuscript of the fourteenth-century poem "Les Echecs Amoreux." A few of the many Renaissance instruments are depicted here. The elegantly gowned lady is playing her dulcimer (an instrument still in use) with small hammers. A harp leans against the wall at the left, and a portable organ rests on the floor at the right. In the background are singers and players. Reading from left to right, the instruments are: recorder (still used today and ancestor of the flute), shawm (ancestor of the oboe), and bagpipes (probably of Asian origin; introduced to Europe by the Romans during the first century A.D.). Biblioteque Nazional fv. 143, Paris.*

Instrumental Music

Renaissance instrumental music continued to be primarily functional; that is, it was associated with dances, plays, masquerades, and extravaganzas of noble courts, rather than as a performance art with its own special audience (figure 18.4).

Dance and music have always been associated and rarely more effectively than in the sixteenth century, which has been called "the century of the dance." The church had long suppressed dancing as both heathenish and lascivious, but Renaissance society ignored such medieval strictures and invented social dancing. Accompanied by wind and stringed instruments, men and women of the Italian and French courts joined hands for the first time for folklike round dances and courtly pair dances such as the *danse royale.*

Because of its portability and mellow tone the lute was the preferred instrument of the age. Its chief rival was the *harpsichord*—also called cembalo, clavecin, virginal, spinet—the principal keyboard instrument of the sixteenth through the eighteenth centuries. Harpsichords have various shapes, which are generally similar in external appearance to grand, upright, and spinet pianos. The tone is produced by quills plucking the strings and is bright and sharp. Unlike the piano, harpsichords cannot vary their *dynamics* (degrees of loudness or softness) except by using two keyboards, muted strings, or different types of quills. Whole sections are played at one dynamic level; variation is achieved by changing to a louder or softer tone quality in the next section.

In England, the harpsichord was called a *virginal,* supposedly in honor of the "maiden Queen Elizabeth." English music had flourished under Henry VIII, Edward VI, and Mary, and

reached, under Elizabeth, a level rarely approached thereafter. English power and wealth, the importation of foreign talent, and increased travel all combined to make the English assimilation of the Italian Renaissance one of the outstanding periods in Western history. Tudor sacred music was superb, but the secular forms of English music—the madrigals, lute music, virginal music, and fancies for viols—had special importance in the richness of the Elizabethan Age.

English Secular Vocal Music

The English madrigal school was inspired by Italian models, but its growth and development has made the English madrigal virtually synonymous with Elizabethan England. A *madrigal,* whether English or Italian, is a secular, unaccompanied part-song, usually in four voices. English madrigals tend toward a balanced texture of polyphonic and homophonic writing, and are frequently either merry or melancholy. The outstanding characteristic, however, is the sheer delight in the sounds, rhythms, and meanings of the English language.

The madrigalists are fond of natural word rhythms. They also like to play with onomatopoeia, alliteration, metaphor, and simile and take exceptional pleasure in exploiting double meanings. Wordplay with triple meanings is even better. Word painting is another notable characteristic whereby composers manipulate the sounds of the music so that they can imitate, imply, or describe the sounds of nature and/or the meaning and sounds of words.

In the following *pastoral madrigal,* the composer quietly poses the question, "Thyrsis? Sleepest thou?" and then continues to press the question until Thyrsis is awakened with some vigorous "hollas." The cuckoo song is imitated, the music "sighs" as the shepherd "sighed as one all undone" and requests to be "let alone alas." The repetitious text of "drive him back to London" pushes the madrigal to an animated conclusion.

Listening Example 18

MADRIGAL

Bennet, Madrigal: "Thyrsis, Sleepest Thou?" (before 1625)[7]

Time: 1:40
John Bennet (ca. 1575–1625)

---

7. John Bennet, *Madrigals to Four Voices,* London, 1599, no. 8.

Summary

The environment of music experienced notable changes during the Renaissance with the inevitable result that the forms of music changed accordingly. The forces of secularization, which were set in motion during the Gothic period, began to moderate the power of the church. The expansion of the universities, the development of city centers of trade and commerce, and the rise of a mercantile middle class caused a concurrent development of secular music.

Outdoor concerts using orchestras composed of violins, shawms, trombones, and drums, and indoor concerts of recorders, viols, and harpsichord became common. Some of the outdoor performances provided music for dancing, which had changed from improvised music for one or two instruments to composed music for groups of instruments (*consorts*).

The demand for musical instruments for domestic use spurred the development and production of lutes, viols, and especially the instrument that could play both homophonic and polyphonic music, the harpsichord. An even more common household instrument was the *clavichord*.[8]

The newly awakened interest in classical culture, in humanism, and in the creative individual was reflected in the active participation in the arts by educated amateurs. Large and small social gatherings featured performances of solo songs accompanied by lute or harpsichord (or clavichord), a variety of chamber music and, particularly in England, the singing of part-songs such as madrigals and catches.

The proliferation of secular music did not provoke a decline in sacred music; rather there was a merging of techniques, instruments, and styles. Burgundian composers such as Dufay combined vocal with instrumental music in the church. Binchois specialized in secular music with particular emphasis on the special qualities of the French chanson.

Josquin des Près wrote masses and motets, Italian secular music, and French chansons. Lassus wrote 1,250 compositions in Latin, French, German, and Italian. Palestrina, serving the church in Rome, wrote much sacred music and a variety of Italian madrigals. In Venice, Gabrieli wrote antiphonal, vocal-instrumental music and considerable instrumental music.

The growth of music during the Renaissance was astounding. Within a single century, music changed from an esoteric, church-dominated art form to an international language heard in every court, noble residence, and many middle-class homes throughout Europe.

---

8. The tone of the clavichord is produced by depressing the keys so that a metal tangent on the other end of the key strikes the string. The instrument is portable and the tone light and flexible. In the eighteenth century the principle of striking a string became the hammer action of the piano.

Culture and Human Values

Musicians achieved the superior status accorded High Renaissance artists if they were composers or if they were amateur performers who had no need to make music for a living. Professional musicians, no matter how adept they were in the skillful manipulation of musical instruments, were ranked with cobblers, tailors, and other artisans. This situation reflected the medieval world's class division into the elite (aristocracy and clergy) and the rest of humankind.

Throughout the Renaissance the class structure gradually changed with the rise of a middle class. The new merchant class experienced its strongest growth in northern Europe, particularly in Burgundy and Flanders. And that was precisely where the musical Renaissance began and flourished. One can logically conclude that there is a connection between music and a middle class, but what is the connection?

In the first place, music is an art form that can entertain an audience of one (the performer) up to an audience of thousands. It is a social art whose appeal transcends all social barriers. Whether used in conjunction with dance, theatrical productions, or as a performing/listening art in its own right, music is generally perceived as the most universal of all art forms. Thus this most accessible and widespread art form found a new patron in the flourishing merchant class. Merchants and traders enthusiastically embraced music in all its forms, much as their seventeenth-century descendants commissioned portraits by Rembrandt, Hals, and other Dutch artists.

Did businessmen patronize music solely for its intrinsic value? Hardly. Heretofore, only the elite were patrons of the arts, literature, and theatre. What better way to announce your newly acquired wealth than to "buy in" to a higher social class by sponsoring music, and later, portraiture? This is not to say that every burgher was a calculating social climber. Some could credit sponsorship of the arts as good business, but others could truly enjoy participating in some of the "finer things of life."

For growing numbers of people the grim rounds of bleak survival in a feudal society had become a distant memory. Peasants still tilled the soil in overwhelming numbers but capitalism, trade, merchandising, and education began to change all that. For centuries people could only hope for a glorious afterlife that supposedly compensated for the miseries of earthly existence. Now there was hope for a better life on this earth and, increasingly, the belief that individuals could better their lives through their own efforts. Perhaps the most positive aspect of the Renaissance was the change in attitude, from mute acceptance of the old status quo to one of rising expectations. Envisioning something better can move mountains.

Exercise

What was the long-range significance of the bourgeois aspects of fifteenth-century music? How, for example, would you categorize today's popular music? Where does rock fit in? Jazz? Symphonic music?

Shadow and Substance: Literary Insights into the Renaissance

The linguistic dualism of the Renaissance had a very positive effect on the development of literature, philosophy, and science. The Latin that the Church had preserved was the common language of all intellectuals and, moreover, a direct link to the classical past. No wonder Petrarch and other humanists viewed Cicero and Virgil as contemporaries; all wrote in the same language. Developing during the Middle Ages as the spoken languages of the people, the vernaculars became the accepted languages of popular culture. Latin was still considered the proper language for scholarly work, but the vernaculars evolved into recognized national languages that became acceptable vehicles for literary expression. Latin provided a kind of intellectual unity, whereas English, French, Italian, and Spanish each reinforced a sense of national cohesion and purpose. Each nation developed its own modern literary tradition, but languages were not isolated by the rise of nationalism. Translations of every language, including Latin, flowed back and forth over national borders, making Renaissance literature as international, in its own way, as art and music.

Renaissance Authors

In a survey such as this only literary peaks can be discussed, for almost everyone of any consequence was an author of sorts, as well as an amateur painter and musician. Those selected seem to be the most important of their time, but, with equal justification, any of a dozen other writers might have been included. Most of the authors possessed the quality of *virtu*, the highest ideal of Renaissance man; they were, in some measure, universal men, active leaders in their turbulent times. Erasmus was known as the most brilliant intellect of his time, friend and adviser to popes and kings. Thomas More and Francis Bacon both served as Lord Chancellors of England (roughly equivalent to the chief justice of the Supreme Court of the United States). Petrarch was the first and among the foremost of the humanists, and both Castiglione and Machiavelli were prominent diplomats. The achievements of Michelangelo and Shakespeare were exceptional even in an age of awesome talents. Cervantes fought in the last Crusade and, a unique distinction, was captured and held prisoner by pirates. We know little about Rabelais beyond the fact that he was once a monk and priest and later a physician. He did take rakish delight in his voluntary separation from the church. The single exception among these activists was Montaigne, who retired to his study to compose his penetrating essays on Renaissance life and mores.

Miguel de Cervantes Saavedra, 1547–1616

Although he came late, in spirit it was Cervantes (sir-VAHN-teez) who tolled the death knell for medievalism. Cervantes was in a better position than most of his contemporaries to utter the words that closed the Middle Ages and opened up the Renaissance; he had been a part of the final burst of chivalry, having accompanied the fleet of Don John of Austria on the final Crusade. He fought at the Battle of Lepanto and had seen, at first hand, the last knight of Christendom.

Don Quixote is Cervantes' reaction to the medieval noble gesture. This lank, hungry, and apparently demented man rides the Spanish roads as he battles injustice. The Don's problem was his medieval point of view. His encounter with a common barber reveals a hostile knight, barmaids become noble damsels in distress, and windmills turn into giants. For Don Quixote and the medieval mind as a whole, things were never what they appeared to be. We, who are practical-minded like the people of the Renaissance, recognize that barbers are barbers and windmills are windmills, and we laugh, as did Renaissance readers, at the knight of the woeful countenance riding his flea-bitten nag. Yet the only trouble with Quixote was that he was born a hundred years too late. A century earlier, he would have been the hero of a tale of chivalry, and his windmills *would* have been giants. After Cervantes, the tale of chivalry—the most popular form of medieval literature—could no longer be taken seriously. It became as outdated as has in our time the melodrama of the beautiful daughter, the mortgage coming due, the villain with his waxed mustache, and the hero arriving in the nick of time.

Have we lost something in giving up these fond delusions and embracing stark naturalism? Chesterton raises this question in his poem "Lepanto," as he compares the real heroism of Don John with the paltry figures of other Renaissance rulers. Cervantes, too, must have experienced the same wonder, for in the second part of his book one smiles at his hero, but the smile of the reader, as of the author, is sympathetic. Cervantes was apparently disillusioned with the pragmatism of the age and longed for vanished glories. This comparison of past and present, as seen in the two parts of *Don Quixote,* brings to a focus the central problem of the Renaissance, as first discussed in chapter 16. With all the new freedoms, wealth, economic order, and a science that relegated the human soul to a secondary position below sense-apparent objects—with all these, what is man? "What a piece of work is man! . . . And yet to me what is this quintessence of dust?" Shakespeare confronts this problem in *The Tempest* and suggests a solution.

Petrarch (Francesco Petrarca), 1304–1374

Petrarch was recognized in his own time as the preeminent poet and humanist of a new age. In 1341 the Roman Senate awarded him the laurel wreath as the first poet laureate since the ancient world. Though he cherished his elaborate Latin poems he is best known today as the inventor of the Italian sonnet and creator of elegant love poetry in the vernacular. As the court poet of the papal palace at Avignon, he was continually appalled at the decadence of the French popes of the Babylonian Captivity (as discussed in chapter 16).

Erasmus of Rotterdam, 1466–1536

Italian humanism had a distinctly pagan flavor, but across the Alps the movement was entirely Christian, with Erasmus (figure 19.1), the "Prince of Humanists," in the forefront. He was a true cosmopolitan, making all Europe his home from England to Italy. Although at first well-disposed toward Luther's reforms, he could not accept Luther's denial of free will. "I laid a hen's egg," wrote Erasmus; "Luther hatched a bird of quite another species."

Erasmus was a strong supporter of overdue reforms. In his *Colloquies* he wrote that "Luther was guilty of two great crimes— he struck the Pope in his crown, and the monks in their belly." In another vein he sternly admonished his church: "By identifying the new learning with heresy you make orthodoxy synonymous with ignorance." Erasmus preferred a purified church to a divided one.

During a journey from Italy to England Erasmus conceived the idea of a satire on just about every aspect of contemporary society. Written partly during his stay with the English humanist

Figure 19.1 *Albrecht Dürer (1471–1528),* Erasmus of Rotterdam, *1526. Engraving, 9¾" × 7½". The Latin inscription states that this was a drawing from life (also see figure 17.54). Metropolitan Museum of Art, New York. Fletcher Fund, 1919.*

Sir Thomas More and dedicated to More, he called the book *Moria* (the Greek word for folly) in a punning reference to his English friend's name. Appearing in thirty-six editions in his own lifetime, the *Praise of Folly* (1509) was the most widely read book of the century after the Bible. Erasmus had brilliantly reinvented the classical paradoxical encomium in which everyone and everything unworthy of praise are ironically celebrated.

Niccolo Machiavelli, 1469–1527

If man is the measure of all things, as the humanists joyously avowed, what then is man? Machiavelli (MAK-ee-uh-VEL-li) attacked the problem with a clinical eye in *The Prince,* the most famous and influential of his many publications (see the Literary Selections). The book examines the techniques of the ruling power. As such, it is rather closely allied to both the art and the science of the Renaissance, for Machiavelli uses the scientific technique of his time to dissect the successes and failures of many rulers to see what made them tick. It is allied to art, but the art of governing successfully was not yet a conscious technique for exercising power. Machiavelli developed this difficult art form, which led to Jacob Burkhardt's later observation that a Renaissance prince manipulated the state much as an artist manipulated his art.

Machiavelli's first premise is that anything is good for a state that allows it to survive and prosper; his second premise is that any means that will work in the achievement of the goal is good. (Machiavelli did *not* write that "the end justifies the means." Rather, he used the phrase "si guarda al fine," meaning "one considers the end.") With these two premises he sweeps aside ideals and sentiment. The state, he assumes, does not exist for the happiness or well-being of people; the people exist only for the good of the state. The resulting thinking is detached, practical, and painfully accurate, though it is based on the lowest possible estimate of the worthiness of people. Its analytic method swept aside all mystery in its disregard for previous conceptions of the nature of justice and the ruling power. It was a typical, though depressing, example of the cold, clear vision of the age. Machiavelli gave the Renaissance its first candid picture of human nature with the idealism, both of medievalism and humanism, stripped away. He said simply:

> For of men it may generally be affirmed that they are thankless, fickle, false, studious to avoid danger, greedy of gain, devoted to you while you are able to confer benefits upon them, and ready, as I have said before, while danger is distant, to shed their blood, and sacrifice their property, their lives and their children for you; but in the hour of need they turn against you. . . . Love is held by the tie of obligation, which, because men are a sorry breed, is broken on every whisper of private interest.

Machiavelli's verdict was not merely the opinion of a misanthrope, soured on the world. The author was a social scientist, investigating human affairs with the detachment of a Kepler charting planetary orbits. After considering the fate of governments from that of Athens to those of his own time, he concluded that people were beasts, at best, and the successful ruler is one who treats them accordingly.

Disengagement: Michel de Montaigne, 1533–1592

Nor was Machiavelli alone in this conclusion. Montaigne (mon-TAN-y) wrote:

> The frailest and most vulnerable of all creatures is man, and at the same time the most arrogant. He sees and feels himself lodged here in the mud and filth of the world, nailed and riveted to the worst, the deadest and most stagnant part of the universe, at the lowest story of the house and the most remote from the vault of heaven, with the animals of the worst condition of the three; and he goes and sets himself in imagination above the circle of the moon, and brings heaven under his feet.

We find two disparate attitudes emerging from the new freedom of the Renaissance. The first, resulting from such opinions as those quoted above, was one of extreme pessimism and despair. Allied with that was the fear and uncertainty resulting from the loss of the security of the old faith. The second attitude is most commonly associated with the Renaissance. With all ties cut, with wealth abounding and frontiers stretching across the seas to unknown lands, people could be free. To secure freedom a person must obtain some kind of power, and the possibilities were virtually unlimited. Artists courted power through their own creativity and through the patronage of influential rulers; merchants achieved power by amassing money; rulers ruthlessly sought power in every conceivable way. The insatiable drive for power created a dog-eat-dog situation, but the rewards were immense and they were available here and now.

One reaction to a freewheeling society lusting after power was to withdraw from the rat race, a response that our own century has witnessed in many different forms. One such dropout was Montaigne, who lived long enough in the midst of the hurly-burly to realize that this was no life for him. He retired to his family home and spent the remainder of his life in quiet study and contemplation, enriching the world with the essays that are the ripe fruit of his mind.

François Rabelais, ca. 1490–1553

Symbolically this desire to retreat is revealed in the number of utopias that were written during the Renaissance. In his *Gargantua and Pantagruel* (see the Literary Selections), Rabelais (RAB-uh-lay) included a brief section on "The Abbey of Theleme" as his version of utopia. Actually, the "abbey" was a country-club version of a monastery that has been turned upside down. Instead of "Poverty, Chastity, and Obedience" the sole injunction is to "Do What Thou Wilt." The Abbey of Theleme was a quiet retreat where the "rougher element" (and at no time in Western history has that element been so rough as during the Renaissance) was excluded, and where everyone behaved with perfect manners.

Baldassare Castiglione, 1478–1529

An elegant aristocrat and skilled diplomat, Castiglione represented a viewpoint advocated by Rabelais but opposed to both Montaigne and Machiavelli. Little concerned with humankind's capacity for evil and very much a man in and of the world, Castiglione advocated urbane lives of mannered civility. His code for Renaissance patricians, *The Book of the Courtier* (see the Literary Selections), became a best-seller and remained so for over two centuries.

Thomas More, 1478–1535

Sir Thomas More (figure 19.2) quite rightly ranks as one of the heroes of the humanist movement. For his greatest work, *Utopia* (see the Literary Selections), More seized on everyone's curiosity about the newly discovered lands beyond the oceans. As a framework for his story, he relates a conversation with a sailor, Raphael Hythloday, who had sailed with Amerigo Vespucci to locate a new land named Utopia. More uses this Utopia (Gk., "no place") to severely criticize his own country and to describe his perfect government, which is a curious mixture of Plato's ideas and some of the most progressive concepts of More's time—or ours. Rather than the combination of private property and communism described by Plato, practically everything in Utopia is held in common. Most of the political officers are elected by the people in free elections, but More also provides for a monarch and for a slave class. He believes that everybody—men and women and members of all the professions including all of the clergy—should

Figure 19.2 *Hans Holbein the Younger (1497/8–1543). Sir Thomas More, ca. 1530. Holbein's superb portrait reveals a visionary and a man of conscience ("a man for all seasons"), who died at the hands of Henry VIII rather than compromise his religious convictions. © The Frick Collection, New York.*

do real work, especially manual labor. With everyone working, he imagines that all the needful chores can be accomplished in a six-hour day, so that everyone will have time for pleasant, creative recreation. He also proposes that the Utopians shall work as farmers and then move to the city to perform urban tasks. These population shifts are staggered so that the population in both country (on what we today would call collective farms) and city would remain constant.

More's *Utopia* has always been taken seriously, yet the conception of the state is naive. Actually, More seeks to return to medievalism, but at the same time he covets the advances of his own age. In the first place, More opposes the new capitalism. Time after time he speaks of the evils that result from a society in which "money is all the swing." He proposes that all property should be held in common, that all houses should be the same (except for the gardens, where he allows individual initiative), and that people should trade houses at regular intervals. Gold would be used for chamber pots and jewels serve as children's toys so citizens would not covet such things. Yet he insists that the state use gold and jewels to buy goods from neighboring countries.

Like Rabelais, More insists on equality. He proposes representative local and federal governments similar to those of Switzerland, which he knew, and little different from the future governing of the United States. His equality means that every person should work at a trade with the exception of the few selected to be priests and scholars, who are freed from the crafts to pursue their higher callings. Even with this ingenious planning, More cannot escape the fact that there is much dirty work to be done in any civilization, and he, like Plato, who was his inspiration, had slaves for labor that was unworthy of the Utopians. At this point, of course, his equality breaks down.

More was appalled by the ceaseless strife and warfare, and he insisted that his Utopians would have none of it—or little, at least. He proposes that all wars be conducted on neighboring lands and that the Utopians hire mercenary soldiers to do the fighting. Most fortunately, a neighboring nation is inhabited by a fierce and warlike people who are eager to wage war—at a price—for the Utopians. He describes these ideal mercenaries:

> They be hideous, savage and fierce, dwelling in wild woods and high mountains, where they were bred and brought up. They be of an hard nature, able to abide and sustain heat, cold and labour, abhorring from all delicate dainties, occupying no husbandry or tillage of the ground, homely and rude both in the building of their houses and in their apparel, given unto no goodness, but only to the breeding and bringing up of cattle. The most part of their living is by hunting and stealing. They be born only to war, which they diligently and earnestly seek for. And when they have gotten it, they be wonders glad thereof. They go forth of their country in great companies together, and whosoever lacketh soldiers, there they proffer their services for small wages. This is the only craft that they have to get their living by. They maintain their life by seeking their death.

The limitation of More's thinking is paradoxical, for he can extend his ideal state only to the borders of the nation. He degrades the people of other countries so that his Utopians may live well. And how like Shakespeare's Caliban the warrior group is! The good life, it would seem, must be floated on a vast sea of all that we regard as evil. When we consider the Utopians and this crude race of warriors, when we consider Prospero and Caliban, we recognize that they are as unlike as day and night, yet both seem necessary for human life. More was able to place his exploitable savages just outside the borders of his nation and our consideration; yet in everyday life, they are here and now and with us always.

Particularly abhorrent for More was the religious dissension that split the nations, and that was eventually to cause More's own death. So in *Utopia* we find complete religious freedom. Most of the people adhere to a single faith, but those of another faith or of no faith are neither chastised nor penalized. The only Utopians liable for punishment are those who insist their faith is better than any other. These people are bigots and are punished severely because they provoke dissension.

More did not write a guidebook to the perfect civilization. Practically, it won't work, and he knew this as well as Plato before him. He *is* to be taken seriously for the ideas that lay behind the practical operation of a Utopia that is a retreat for civilized people.

To make it function he must have a slave population within the borders of his state and a nation of crude ruffians outside the borders to do the dirty work. The necessity for human equality, religious tolerance, and his conviction that life should be lived for the pleasure of each individual are Renaissance ideas that foreshadow the thoughts of Rousseau, Jefferson, and others of later epochs. Indeed, they are our own best ideals, and we are still at a loss for ways of making them work, even as was Sir Thomas More.

William Shakespeare, 1564–1616

Shakespeare knew all the intricacies of the Renaissance problem, not as theory, but as one who felt the drives of the time and who experienced within himself the perplexities of the age. In each of Shakespeare's plays one finds his comment on the nature of Renaissance man, and, as Shakespeare matured and developed, the scope of his concerns becomes more and more inclusive.

In *Hamlet* the conflict is resolved with a sort of neo-Stoicism: "The readiness is all," says Hamlet at the end. In each of the great plays beyond *Hamlet,* in *Othello* and in *King Lear,* we see a growing understanding of the Renaissance world. Probably more than any other tragedy, *King Lear* fills us with the emotions of pity and fear, and purges them at the end, but the experience of the audience throughout the play leaves the soul seared. The pity, of course, is for the "good" people of the drama: Lear, his fool, Gloucester, Edgar, and perhaps Kent; the fear is for ourselves and for all humankind. This play expresses the deepest pessimism of the Renaissance but the playwright has more to say.

Beyond the pessimism of Lear we see Shakespeare reaching for the conclusion that the only salvation for humankind is love and compassion. By the time of his last complete play, *The Tempest* (1611; see the Literary Selections), Shakespeare, viewing this resolution ever more clearly, renders up his account and gives us a summation of the totality of his experience. The best of the previous plays had been tragic, but is this final play a tragedy? No, for the author has gone beyond tragedy. He places *The Tempest* in a world of imagination sufficiently removed from the workaday world to bring together all the disparate elements of the Renaissance world and resolve the conflicts. The truth-beyond-appearances that contemporary surrealist painters and writers attempt, Shakespeare achieves on Prospero's island.

What forces are here represented? Primarily there are the dark human failings that we seek to deny, but which are with us always. Among the mortals, this old evil is represented by Stephano and Trinculo, Sebastian and Antonio; among the spirits, it is symbolized by Caliban. This is the same force represented by the barbaric warrior race in More's *Utopia,* the same force found in the myths of every culture. It is Grendel and his mother in the Beowulf saga; it is the mindless drives in Freudian psychology; it is the dark creature that the Earth-Spirit and the Walpurgis-Night Scene represent in Faust. Sometimes we think of this force as lust, yet that is too limited. The Caliban thrust is all the drives that make human beings distorted and destructive, the force that Dante observed in Hell.

The opposing force is represented among the human beings by Prospero and symbolized by Ariel. This is the power of the intellect, which stands at the heart of the various utopias. Prospero is the humanist who had gone stale, as did humanism in the late Renaissance, and who realizes only now his responsibility to the world of men and women. He describes himself as being "for the liberal arts without a parallel: those being all my study." The Ariel force, then, represents the highest nature of humankind, the intellect, which in the Renaissance view made men and women akin to the angels.

Can we recognize any of the more earthly beings? Certainly we can, for Antonio has already usurped Prospero's dukedom, and he teaches his method to Sebastian when they plot to usurp yet another kingdom by eliminating Alonso, king of Naples. So Machiavellian are they that they form this plot even when they are marooned with apparently no chance of returning to Italy.

In such men as Adrian and Francisco we recognize opportunistic Renaissance courtiers, as they are despairingly described:

They'll take suggestion as a cat takes milk;
They'll tell the clock to any business that
We say befits the hour.

Finally, in Gonzalo, we recognize the wise old counselor, the one who has lived long enough to see and know much, but whose very age makes him if not foolish, at least ineffectual. He is a sort of redeemed Polonius.

Shakespeare's first purpose is to show these people as they are. He wants each one to find his true self. It is Gonzalo who sees through the plot to this first meaning when he says:

In one voyage
Did Claribel her husband find at Tunis,
And Ferdinand, her brother, found a wife
Where he himself was lost; Prospero his dukedom
In a poor isle; and all of us ourselves,
When no man was his own.

We explore the nature of evil with Caliban, who clearly recognizes his opposition to intellect when he speaks of his only profit from language as knowing how to curse, and when he admonishes Trinculo and Stephano to "burn his Book" if they would gain power over Prospero. We recognize Caliban's nature most forcibly when he celebrates his new and drunken "freedom" at the very moment when he is most in bondage, for he has lost his wits in drink and has taken as a master Stephano, who will treat him more foully than ever Prospero did. Yet Caliban is more perceptive than his mortal counterparts, for when they advance with their evil purpose of overpowering Prospero, he can distinguish between the show of power (the spangled garments hung on the line) and real power, which involves pressing on about their business. His more foolish mortal masters are tricked by the flashy garb and are routed by Prospero and Ariel. It is only after all these experiences that Caliban can say, "How fine my master is! . . . What a thrice-double ass was I, to take this drunkard for a god, And worship this dull fool!"

But there is another side to the picture. Prospero and Miranda cannot exist without Caliban. Although he is revolting in appearance and nature, so much so that Miranda says, " 'Tis a villain, sir, I do not love to look on," Prospero wisely answers,

But as 'tis
We cannot miss him: he does make our fire,
Fetch in our wood; and serves in offices
That profit us.

The Caliban nature, then, wisely used and ruled by the human will, serves a useful function in life.

But it was the state that was Shakespeare's main concern. Because the law of the Church no longer functioned to hold men in place, another type of order was necessary. This was the secular state, ruled by a king. Throughout the play, the political world was out of joint, for the right duke was not upon his seat, and evil governed in the place of good. Quite early, Shakespeare has Gonzalo propose a utopia—one not much different from that of More or of Rabelais. But the idea is ridiculous, for Gonzalo starts his speech, "Had I plantation of this isle . . . and were the king on't," but he ends the speech, saying that there would be no sovereign. In a stroke Shakespeare reveals the impossibility of the utopian dream.

We need more than this if the state is to survive and provide a sound framework for the lives of its inhabitants. Enter Ferdinand and Miranda, who are carefully schooled throughout the play in right living. Their marriage unites the man of action with the woman of spirit. One is reminded of Plato's philosopher-king, but the philosophy here is more sprightly and lighthearted. With the consummation of this marriage, and the return to Italy, we can predict an order, neither Machiavellian (as was Alonso's) nor too idealistic (as was Prospero's). This is the proper nature of the ruler.

What is Shakespeare's final conclusion? In the first place he recognizes the folly of most of the things people do. He realizes that ninety years hence it will make little difference what anyone has done or failed to do.

We are such stuff
As dreams are made on, and our little life
Is rounded with a sleep.

Perhaps our present activities will not affect the future but they are important here and now. Shakespeare's final choice is with humankind, men and women of good and evil mixed most wondrously. How else are we to interpret that little passage between Miranda and her father as she views all these mortals for the first time, people whom we have seen in all sorts of evil conspiracies and evildoing? She looks on them and says:

O Wonder!
How many goodly creatures are there here!
How beauteous mankind is! O brave new world,
That has such people in't!

And Prospero wisely answers: " 'Tis new to thee."

Is this bitter irony? Are Shakespeare and Prospero in this almost final speech venting a long-pent-up disgust with all of humanity? The brief sentence is ironic, but not bitterly so. Miranda has much to learn of the ways of these goodly creatures; that Prospero knows. But he has already forgiven them. In his eyes this motley crowd of good and evil, which is all people, is goodly, too. It is for this reason that he leaves his island, drowns the book that has given him command over the supernatural, leaves the spirits of Ariel and Caliban alike, and returns to Naples. With the good new rulers there, the combination of action and spirit, bound together by love, there will ensue a new kind of law and order in the affairs of human beings. To bring the play home, we must return from the surreal to actuality. There can be no retreat; we must commit ourselves to proper action in the precarious balance between good and evil in the real world.

Bacon and the Decline of the Renaissance

All balances must fail. This we have seen in every period that we have studied. One so delicate as that suggested in *The Tempest* cannot last for long. Sir Francis Bacon (1561–1626) proposed how the scales were to fall. Skilled in many fields, his greatest work lay in his scientific writing, in which he consistently revealed the clear-sighted realism that was the hallmark of the Renaissance. Among other things he laid bare the four idols that cause errors in human vision and thinking:

1. The Idols of the Tribe. These are the fallacies we inherit just because we are members of the human race. The greatest of these is the tendency to imagine more order in nature than actually exists there.
2. The Idols of the Cave. These are our own private prejudices that keep us from seeing things as they really are.
3. The Idols of the Marketplace. By these, Bacon was getting at the same things that modern semanticists deal with, for these are the errors into which we fall because of the imperfections of language.
4. The Idols of the Theatre. By this, Bacon referred to the errors into which people fall because they belong to "schools" of thought. As soon as one accepts the thinking of a school or a religion, one accepts it all and does not look carefully to see whether the individual and separate beliefs may be true or false, good or bad.

Bacon also wrote a utopia, which he called *The New Atlantis*. Not surprisingly, his government, Salamon's House, is composed of scientists. These are men, following the thinking of Descartes, who rule by reason alone. Reason is divorced from the spirit. It can weigh the actions of a man such as Ferdinand, judging by the results whether they are good or bad, but reason cannot measure the loveliness of a Miranda. So Bacon and those that followed him in the next period, the Age of Reason, downplayed such qualities as imagination and sentiment. They gained greatly in sureness; their way had the hard brilliance of a diamond, but who can say that clarity is worth the price of loveliness?

This, then, was the Renaissance. Its early discoverers brought to it more new big ideas than any civilization had ever faced before. At its outset the change was overwhelming, for all the basic ideas of the Middle Ages had to be adjusted in the face of a mass of new knowledge about the world. Out of this chaos of change emerged two basic attitudes. One orientation led to the glories of the Renaissance. These were the daring explorers, the superb artists, the powerful capitalists, the great monarchs. Some were as fine as Leonardo or Raphael, others as corrupt as Renaissance popes, or as ruthless as English sea dogs or Spanish conquistadores. The opposing trend of thought was one of deep pessimism. Those who felt this (Montaigne was one such) assumed that somehow people were not fine enough in their basic nature to properly use their new freedom. In their dreams of the good life, these people retreated to their utopias. Shakespeare, at the very end of his career, saw where the balance lay, in the powerful king in whose person imagination and action were joined by love. This is the pattern for the sovereignty that the enlightened despots tried to achieve. The delicacy of this balance was easily disturbed. In its decline it moved toward the emerging modern world in which science and technology would become ever more central to the culture.

Exercises

1. Describe Machiavelli's view of human nature and explain why this might contribute to the pessimism of the time. Does Machiavelli's view apply to rulers today? Consider, for example, the various governments in the Western world, the Middle East, and selected African nations.
2. Explain Bacon's "idols" in terms of his own time, and then examine contemporary life and how his idols might still apply.

Petrarch (Francesco Petrarca), 1304–1374

Though Petrarch intended his epic poem *Africa* to be his major work, his Italian sonnets have been far more influential. His love poetry was inspired by Laura, whom he first saw in the Church of St. Clara of Avignon on 6 April 1327. The following sonnet commemorates that momentous meeting while also alluding to the day on which Christ supposedly died: 6 April.

SONNET III
(Era il giorno ch'al sol si scolarara)
Petrarch (Francesco Petrarca), 1304–1374

'Twas on the morn when heaven its blessed ray
In pity to its suffering master veil'd,
First did I, lady, to your beauty yield,
Of your victorious eyes th' unguarded prey.
Ah, little reck'd I that, on such a day,
Needed against Love's arrows any shield;
And trod, securely trod, the fatal field:
Whence, with the world's, began my heart's dismay.
On every side Love found his victim bare,
And through mine eyes transfix'd my throbbing heart;
Those eyes which now with constant sorrows flow:
But poor the triumph of his boasted art,
Who thus could pierce a naked youth, nor dare
To you in armor mail'd even to display his bow!

Like Dante's Beatrice, Laura was an ideal, the object throughout Petrarch's life of an unrequited poetic passion. Unlike Beatrice, whom Dante idealized from afar, Laura accepted the poet as a friend—but no more than that. She was married and destined to be the mother of ten children. A sonnet is, by definition, a fourteen-line lyric poem that expresses a single idea or thought, in this case the poet's reaction to Laura's physical beauty.

SONNET LXIX
(Erano i capei d'oro all' aura sparsi)
Petrarch (Francesco Petrarca), 1304–1374

Her golden tresses were spread loose to air,
And by the wind in thousand tangles blown,
And a sweet light beyond all brightness shone
From those grand eyes, though now of brilliance bare;
And did that face a flush of feeling wear?
I now thought yes, then no, the truth unknown.
My heart was then for love like tinder grown,
What wonder if it flamed with sudden flare?
Not like the walk of mortals was her walk,
But as when angels glide; and seemed her talk
With other than mere human voice, to flow.
A spirit heavenly, a living sun
I saw, and if she be no longer so,
A wound heals not, because the bow's undone.

Petrarch was tormented by his passion, but he was also inspired as a poet because the one-way love affair appealed to his vanity. He was a Renaissance artist, a self-conscious man of letters seeking earthly fame, as the following sonnet clearly reveals.

SONNET XLVII
(Benedetto sia l' giorno e l' mese e l' anno)
Petrarch (Francesco Petrarca), 1304–1374

Blest be the day, and blest the month, the year,
    The spring, the hour, the very moment blest,
    The lovely scene, the spot, where first oppress'd
    I sunk, of two bright eyes the prisoner:
And blest the first soft pang, to me most dear,
    Which thrill'd my heart, when Love became its guest;
    And blest the bow, the shafts which pierced my breast.
    And even the wounds, which bosom'd thence I bear.
Blest too the strains which, pour'd through glade and grove,
    Have made the woodlands echo with her name;
    The sighs, the tears, the languishment, the love:
And blest those sonnets, sources of my fame;
    And blest that thought—Oh! never to remove!—
    Which turns to her alone, from her alone which came.

Laura died on 6 April 1348 of the Black Death, as did millions of Europeans during that ghastly summer. Petrarch was devastated, as well as transfixed by the date.

SONNET CCXCII
(Gli occhi di ch' io parlai si caldamente)
Petrarch (Francesco Petrarca), 1304–1374

Those eyes, 'neath which my passionate rapture rose,
    The arms, hands, feet, the beauty that erewhile
    Could my own soul from its own self beguile,
    And in a separate world of dreams enclose,
The hair's bright tresses, full of golden glows,
    And the soft lightning of the angelic smile
    That changed this earth to some celestial isle,—
    Are now but dust, poor dust, that nothing knows.
And yet *I* live! Myself *I* grieve and scorn,
    Left dark without the light I loved in vain,
    Adrift in tempest on a bark forlorn;
Dead is the source of all my amorous strain,
    Dry is the channel of my thoughts outworn,
    And my sad harp can sound but notes of pain.

Throughout the rest of the poet's long life, Laura remained the ideal object, becoming in death the mediator between the penitent and the Divine.

SONNET CCCXIII
(I'vo piangendo i miei passati tempi)
Petrarch (Francesco Petrarca), 1304–1374

I now am weeping, for the years passed by,
    Wasted in loving but a mortal thing,
    Though I could fly, not rising on the wing,
    To leave some work, perhaps not far from high.

My deeds unworthy, impious, from the sky,
    Thy realm, thou see'st, unseen, immortal King;
    To me, astray and feeble, succour bring,
    And with Thy grace, my soul's defect supply:
So that if tempest-tost, and oft in strife,
    I lived, I yet may die in port, at peace,
    And nobly quit, though spent in vain, my life.
Through my remaining years, so soon to cease,
    Let Thy right hand, my guide, in dying, be
    My stay; Thou know'st I have no hope but Thee.

Exercises

1. In line 11 of Sonnet III, the image of the eyes as a gateway to the heart was a poetic commonplace. Is that image still used today in poetry and songs? Give a few examples.
2. What is the meaning of the image of the "bow" in the last line of sonnets III and LXIX?

Desiderius Erasmus, 1466–1536

PRAISE OF FOLLY
Desiderius Erasmus

Erasmus uses a dramatic setting and a woman, Folly Herself, who speaks wisely and foolishly, learnedly and jokingly. The underlying issue seems to be knowledge versus ignorance, with Erasmus holding to the middle ground. Don't put too much faith in knowledge and scholars, Folly implies, and try to be tolerant and gentle with fools and with ignorance.

Folly Herself Speaks

Whatever the world says of me (for I am not ignorant of Folly's poor reputation, even among the most foolish), yet I and I alone provide joy for gods and men. I no sooner step up to speak to this full assembly than all your faces put on a kind of new and unwonted pleasantness. So suddenly have you cleared your brows, and with so pleasant and hearty a laughter given me your applause, that in truth, as many of you as I behold on every side of me, seem to me no less than Homer's gods drunk with nectar and the drug nepenthe; whereas before, you sat as lumpish and pensive as if you had come from consulting an oracle. And as it usually happens when the sun begins to show his beams, or when after a sharp winter the spring breathes afresh on the earth, all things immediately get a new face, new color, and recover as it were a certain kind of youth again: in like manner, but by beholding me, you have in an instant gotten another kind of countenance; and so what the otherwise great orators with their tedious and long-studied speeches can hardly effect, to wit, to remove the trouble of the mind, I have done it at once, with my single look.

But if you ask me why I appear before you in this strange dress, be pleased to lend me your ears, and I will tell you; not those ears, I mean, you carry to church, but abroad with you, such as you are wont to prick up to jugglers, fools, and buffoons, and such as our friend Midas once gave to Pan. For I am disposed awhile to play the sophist with you; not of their sort who nowadays cram boys' heads with certain empty notions and curious trifles, yet teach them nothing but a more than womanish obstinacy of scolding: but I'll imitate those ancients, who, that they might the better avoid that infamous appellation of *Sophi* or *Wise,* chose rather to be called "sophists." Their business was to celebrate the praises of the gods and valiant men. And the like encomium shall you hear from me, but neither of Herakles nor Solon, but mine own dear self, that is to say, Folly.

I think it high time to look down a little on the earth; wherein you'll find nothing frolicky or fortunate, that it owes not to me. So provident has that great parent of mankind, nature, been, that there should not be anything without its mixture, as it were seasoning, of Folly. For since according to the definition of the Stoics, wisdom is nothing else than to be governed by reason; and on the contrary Folly, to be given up to the will of our passions; that the life of man might not be altogether disconsolate and hard to put up with, of how much more passion than reason has Jupiter composed us? putting in, as one would say, "scarce half an ounce to the pound." Besides, he has confined reason to a narrow corner of the brain, and left all the rest of the body to our passions; as also set up, against this one, two as it were, masterless tyrants—anger that possesses the region of the heart, and consequently the very fountain of life, the heart itself; and lust, that stretches its empire everywhere. Against which double force how powerful reason is, let common experience declare, inasmuch as she, which yet is all she can do, may call out to us until she's hoarse, and tell us the rules of honesty and virtue; while they give up the reins to their governor, and make a hideous clamor, till at last being wearied, he suffer himself to be carried wherever they please to hurry him.

Is not war the very root and matter of all famed enterprise? And yet what more foolish than to undertake it for I know not what trifles, especially when both parties are sure to lose more than they get in the bargain? For of those that are slain, not a word of them; and for the rest, when both sides are close engaged "and the trumpets make an ugly noise," what use of these wise men, I pray, that are so exhausted with study that their thin cold blood has scarcely any spirits left? No, it must be those blunt fat fellows, that by how much more they excel in courage, fall short in understanding. Unless perhaps one had rather choose Demosthenes for a soldier, who, following the example of Archilochus, threw away his arms and took to his heels e'er he had scarcely seen his enemy; as ill a soldier, as happy an orator.

But good judgment, you'll say, is not of the least concern in matters of war. In a general way I grant it; but this thing of warring is no part of philosophy, but managed by parasites, pimps, thieves, assassins, peasants, sots, spendthrifts and such other dregs of mankind, not philosophers; who how inept they are in everyday conversation, let Sokrates, whom the oracle of Apollo, though not so wisely, judged "the wisest of all men living," be witness; who stepping up to speak about something, I know not what, in public, was forced to come down again well laughed at for his pains. Though yet in this he was not altogether a fool, that he refused the

appellation of wise, and returning it back to the oracle, delivered his opinion that a wise man should abstain from meddling with public business; unless perhaps he should have admonished us to beware of wisdom if we intended to be reckoned among the living, there being nothing but his wisdom that first accused and afterwards sentenced him to the drinking of his poisoned cup. For while, as you find him in Aristophanes, philosophying about clouds and ideas, measuring how far a flea could leap, and admiring that so small a creature as a fly should make so great a buzz, he meddled not with anything that concerned common life.

What should I speak of Theophrastus, who being about to make a speech, became as dumb as if he had met a wolf in his way, which yet would have put courage in a man of war? Or Isokrates, who was so fainthearted that he never tried a speech? Or Tully, that great founder of the Roman eloquence, who could never begin to speak without an odd kind of trembling, like a boy that had the hiccups; which Fabius interprets as an argument of a wise orator and one that was sensible of what he was doing; and while he says it, does he not plainly confess that wisdom is a great obstacle to the true management of business? What would become of them were they to fight it out at blows, that are so dead through fear, when the contest is only with empty words?

Even among the professions those only are in high esteem that come nearest to common sense, that is to say, Folly. Theologians are half-starved, physicists out of heart, astronomers laughed at, and logicians slighted; only the physician is worth all the rest. And among them too, the more unlearned, impudent, or unadvised he is, the more he is esteemed, even among princes. For medicine, especially as it is now practiced by most men, is nothing but a branch of flattery, no less so than rhetoric. Next to them, the second place is given to our lawyers, if not the first; whose profession, though I say it myself, most men laugh at as the ass of philosophy; yet there's scarcely any business, either great or small, but is managed by these asses. These purchase their great titles, while in the meantime the theologian, having run through the whole body of religious thought, sits gnawing a radish as he wars with lice and fleas.

Why should I bother discussing our professors of arts? Self-love is so natural to them all that they had rather part with their father's land than their foolish opinions; but especially actors, fiddlers, orators, and poets, of which the more ignorant each of them is, the more insolently he pleases himself, that is to say struts and spreads out his plumes. And like will to like; nay, the more foolish anything is, the more it is admired; the greater number being ever tickled at the worst things, because, as I said before, most men are so subject to Folly. And therefore if the more foolish a man is, the more he pleases himself and is admired by others, to what purpose should he beat his brains about true knowledge, which first will cost him dear, and next render him the more troublesome and less confident, and, lastly, please only a few?

And now that I consider it, nature has planted, not only in particular men but even in every nation, and scarcely any city is without it, a kind of common self-love. And thus it is that the English, besides other things, lay claim to beauty, music, and feasting. The Scots are proud of their nobility, blood-ties to the crown, and dialectical subtleties. The French think themselves the only well-bred men. The Parisians, excluding all others, arrogate to themselves the only knowledge of theological learning. The Italians affirm they are the only masters of good letters and eloquence, and flatter themselves on this account, that of all others they only are not barbarous. In which kind of happiness those of Rome claim the first place, still dreaming to themselves of somewhat, I know not what, of old Rome. The Venetians fancy themselves happy in the reputation of their nobility. The Greeks, as if they were the only authors of all learning, swell themselves with titles of ancient heroes. The Turks, and all that scum of the truly barbarous, claim for themselves the only true religion and laugh at Christians as superstitious. To this day the Jews confidently expect the coming of the Messiah and obstinately quarrel over their law of Moses. The Spaniards give place to none in the reputation of soldiery. The Germans pride themselves in their tallness of stature and skill in magic.

And not to list every instance, you see, I think, how much satisfaction this Self-love gives to mankind and, in this, her sister Flattery is nearly her equal.

Now if I seem to anyone to have spoken more boldly than truthfully, let us, if you please, look a little into the lives of men, and it will easily appear not only how much they owe to me, but how much they esteem me even from the highest to the lowest. And yet we will not run over the lives of everyone, for that would be too long; but only some few of the great ones, from whence we shall easily conjecture the rest.

For to what purpose is it to say anything of the common people, who without dispute are wholly mine? For they abound everywhere with so many several sorts of Folly, and are every day so busy in inventing new, that a thousand Demokritos's are too few for so general a laughter, though we need one more Demokritos to laugh at the thousand. It is almost incredible what sport and delight they daily provide for the Gods; for though the Gods set aside their sober morning hours to dispatch business and receive prayers, yet when they begin to be well soused with nectar, and cannot think of anything that's serious, they get themselves up into some part of heaven that's better for viewing, and then look down upon the actions of men. Nor is there anything that pleases them better. Good, good! What an excellent sight it is! How many varieties of fools! For I myself sometimes sit among the poetical Gods.

Here's one desperately in love with a young wench, and the more she slights him the more outrageously he loves her. Another marries a woman's money, not her self. Another's jealousy keeps more eyes on her than Argos. Another becomes a fulltime mourner, and how foolishly he carries it! Nay, hires others to bear him company, to make it more ridiculous. Another weeps over his mother-in-law's grave. Another spends all he can on his belly, to be the more hungry after it. Another thinks there is no happiness but in sleep and idleness. Another frets about other men's business, and neglects his own. Another thinks himself rich in refinancing and buying on credit, as we say borrowing from Peter to pay Paul, and in a short time becomes bankrupt. Another starves himself to enrich his heir. Another for a small and uncertain gain exposes his life to the dangers of seas and storms, which yet no money can restore. Another had rather get riches by war than live peaceably at home.

And some there are that think money easiest attained by courting childless old men with presents; and others again by making love to rich old women; both which afford the Gods most excellent pastime, to see them cheated by those persons they thought to have outwitted. But the most foolish and basest of all others are our merchants, to wit such as venture on everything be it never so dishonest, and manage it no better; who though they lie unceasingly, swear and perjure themselves, steal, deceive, and cheat, yet shuffle themselves into the first rank, and all because they have gold rings on their fingers. Nor are they without their flattering friars that admire them and give them openly the title of honorable, in hopes, no doubt, to get some small snip of it themselves.

There are also a kind of Pythagoreans, with whom all things are held in common, that if they get anything under their cloaks, they make no more scruple of carrying it away than if it were their own by inheritance. There are others too that are only rich in wishful thinking, and while they fancy to themselves pleasant dreams, conceive that enough to make them happy. Some desire to be accounted wealthy abroad, and are yet ready to starve at home. One makes what haste he can to fritter his money away, and another rakes it together by right or wrong. This man is ever laboring for public honors; and another lies sleeping in a chimney corner. A great many undertake endless lawsuits and outvie one another who shall most enrich the crooked judge or corrupt lawyer. One is all for innovations; and another for some great he-knows-not-what. Another leaves his wife and children at home, and goes to Jerusalem, Rome, or on a pilgrimage to St. James's, where he has no business.

In short, if a man like Menippus of old could look down from the moon, and behold those innumerable rufflings of mankind, he would think he saw a swarm of flies and gnats quarreling among themselves, fighting, laying traps for one another, snatching, playing, wantoning, growing up, growing old, and dying. Nor is it to be believed what stir, what commotions this little creature raises, and yet in how short a time it comes to nothing at all; while sometimes war, other times pestilence, sweeps many thousands away.

But let me be most foolish myself, and one whom Demokritos may not only laugh at but deride, if I go one foot further in the discovery of the follies and madnesses of the common people. I'll betake me to them that carry the reputation of wise men, and hunt after that "golden bough," as says the proverb. Among whom the school teachers hold the first place, a generation of men than whom nothing would be more miserable, nothing more wretched, nothing more hated of the Gods, did not I allay the troubles of that pitiful profession with a certain kind of pleasant madness. For they are not only subject to those five afflictions with which Homer begins his Iliad, but six hundred; as being ever hungry and slovenly in their schools—schools, did I say? Nay, rather prisons, sweat shops, or torture chambers—grown old among a company of boys, deaf with their noise, and wasted away in the stench and nastiness. And yet by my courtesy it is that they think themselves the most excellent of all men; so greatly do they please themselves in frightening a company of fearful boys with a thundering voice and fierce scowls; tormenting them with switches, rods, and whips; and, laying about them without fear or wit, imitate the ass in the lion's skin. In the meantime all that nastiness seems absolute spruceness, that stench a perfume, and that miserable slavery of theirs a kingdom, and such too as they would not exchange their tyranny for the empires of Phalaris or Dionysos.

Nor are they less happy in that new opinion they have taken up of being learned; for whereas most of them beat into boys' heads nothing but nonsense, yet, ye good Gods! What Palemon, what Donatus, do they not scorn in comparison with themselves? And so, I know not by what tricks, they bring it about to their boys' foolish mothers and dolt-headed fathers they pass for such as they fancy themselves.

Perhaps I had better pass over our theologians in silence and not stir this pool, or touch this fair but unsavory stinkweed; as a kind of men that are supercilious beyond comparison, and to that too, implacable; lest setting them about my ears, they attack me with proofs and force me to recant, which if I refuse, they straight away pronounce me a heretic. For this is the thunderbolt with which they frighten those whom they are resolved not to favor. And truly, though there are few others that less willingly acknowledge the kindnesses I have done for them, yet even these too are bound to me for no ordinary benefits; meanwhile being happy in their own opinion, and as if they dwelt in the third heaven, they look with haughtiness on all others as poor creeping things, and could almost find in their hearts to pity them.

And next come those that commonly call themselves "religious" and "monks"; most false in both titles, when a large part of them are farthest from religion, and no men swarm thicker in all places than themselves. Nor can I think of anything that could be more miserable, did I not support them in so many ways. For whereas all men detest them so much, that they take it for ill luck to meet one of them by chance, yet such is their happiness that they flatter themselves. For first, they reckon it one of the main points of piety if they are so illiterate that they can't so much as read. And then when they run over their Offices, which they carry about them, rather by rote than understanding, they believe the Gods more than ordinarily pleased with their braying. And some there are among them that make a great show about their pious poverty, yet roam up and down for the bread they eat; nay, there is scarcely an inn, coach, or ship into which they intrude not, to the no small damage of the common-wealth of beggars. And yet, like pleasant fellows, with all this vileness, ignorance, rudeness, and impudence, they represent to us, for so they call it, the lives of the apostles.

And as to the popes, what should I mention about them? Than most of whom though there be nothing more indebted, more servile, more witless, more contemptible, yet they would seem as they were the most excellent of all others. And yet in this only thing no men more modest, in that they are contented to wear about them gold, jewels, purple, and those other marks of virtue and wisdom, but for the study of the things themselves, they remit it to others; thinking it happiness enough for them that they can call the King Master, having learned the cringe *a la mode,* know when and where to use those titles of Your Grace, My Lord, Your Magnificence; in a word that they are past all shame and can flatter pleasantly. For these are the arts that bespeak a man truly noble and a model courtier.

But if you look into their manner of life you'll find them mere sots, as debauched as Penelope's wooers. They sleep till noon, and have their mercenary Levite come to their bedside, where he chops over his Matins before they are half up. Then to breakfast, which is scarcely done when dinner is ready for them. From thence they go to dice, tables, cards, or entertain themselves with jesters, fools, and gamblers. In the meantime they have one or two snacks and then supper, and after that a banquet, and it would be well, by Jupiter, that there be no more than one.

And in this manner do their hours, days, months, years, age slide away without the least irksomeness. Nay, I have sometimes gone away many inches fatter, to see them speak big words; while each of the ladies believes herself so much nearer the Gods, by how much the longer train she trails after her; while one cardinal edges out another, that he may get the nearer to Jupiter himself; and every one of them pleases himself the more by how much heavier is the gold chain he drapes on his shoulders, as if he meant to show his strength as well as his wealth.

But I forget myself and run beyond my bounds. Though yet, if I shall seem to have spoken anything more boldly or impertinently than I ought, be pleased to consider that not only Folly but a woman said it; remembering in the meantime that Greek proverb, "Sometimes a fool may speak a word in season," unless perhaps you'll say this concerns not women. I see you expect an Epilogue, but give me leave to tell you that you are mistaken if you think I remember anything of what I have said, having foolishly bolted out such a hodgepodge of words. It is an old proverb, "I hate one that remembers what's done over the cup." This is a new one of my own making: "I hate a man that remembers what he hears." Wherefore farewell, clap your hands, live, and drink lustily, my most excellent Disciples of Folly.

Exercises

1. Try to imagine that you are a sixteenth-century college professor. What would be your reaction to Folly's description of "professors of arts." Does her account fit any of your professors?

2. Folly makes some general statements about countries and cities, e.g., the "English lay claim to beauty, music, and feasting." Are any of these observations still valid today? Which ones?

3. Does Folly's description of "school teachers" (elementary and secondary) still have any truth today? To what extent?

4. What does the great popularity of this satire indicate about the literate public of that time? Would a twentieth-century Praise of Folly be equally popular? Why or why not?

Niccolo Machiavelli, 1469–1527

The thorough humanistic education of Niccolo Machiavelli (MAHK-iya-VEL-lee) and his own political experience helped him to reevaluate the role of the state. For medieval thinkers, the Church looked after the spiritual salvation of its flock, the State attended to their physical well-being, and all operated under Divine Law. Machiavelli observed that the Romans had encouraged civic duties and civic pride, but Christians were supposed to detach themselves from public affairs. The obvious solution was to secularize politics. Make the state preeminent and its own justification, and have it function in accordance with the observable facts of human nature. Machiavelli wrote *The Prince* as a guide for the man he and many other Italians longed to see: a ruler who would unite the squabbling city-states under a central jurisdiction (see map 16.3). This was a manual for action, the first objective analysis of how political power was obtained and kept. Machiavelli's brilliant analysis is detached, objective, and nonjudgmental. It gave the Renaissance its first candid picture of human nature with all the idealism, both of medievalism and of humanism, stripped away. Though Italy did not achieve unification until the nineteenth century, Machiavelli's theory of absolutism became a model for the rest of Europe.

Machiavelli dedicated *The Prince* to Lorenzo de' Medici, the Magnificent, Duke of Urbino (1492–1519), who should not be confused with his illustrious grandfather, Lorenzo the Magnificent (1449–1492; see figure 17.18). The Duke of Urbino never measured up to Machiavelli's estimation of his potential and is remembered today by this seminal work and by the wondrous sculpture by Michelangelo in the Medici Chapel (see figure 17.42). The translation is a modern one (1984) by Peter Bondanella and Mark Musa.

THE PRINCE
Niccolo Machiavelli

On New Principalities Acquired by One's Own Arms and Skill

No one should marvel if, in speaking of principalities that are totally new as to their prince and organization, I use the most illustrious examples; since men almost always tread the paths made by others and proceed in their affairs by imitation, although they are not completely able to stay on the path of others nor attain the skill of those they imitate, a prudent man should always enter those paths taken by great men and imitate those who have been most excellent, so that if one's own skill does not match theirs, at least it will have the smell of it; and he should proceed like those prudent archers who, aware of the strength of their bow when the target they are aiming at seems too distant, set their sights much higher than the designated target, not in order to reach to such a height with their arrow but rather to be able, with the aid of such a high aim, to strike the target.

I say, therefore, that in completely new principalities, where there is a new prince, one finds in maintaining them more or less difficulty according to the greater or lesser skill of the one who acquires them. And because this act of transition from private citizen to prince presupposes either ingenuity or fortune, it appears that either the one or the other of these two things should, in part, mitigate many of the problems; nevertheless, he who relies upon fortune less maintains his position best. Things are also facilitated when the prince, having no other dominions to govern, is constrained to come to live there in person. But to come to those who, by means of their own skill and not because of fortune, have become princes, I say that the most admirable are Moses, Cyrus, Romulus, Theseus, and the like. And although we should not discuss Moses, since he was a mere executor of things ordered by God, nevertheless he must be admired, if for nothing but that grace which made him worthy of talking with God. But let us consider Cyrus and the others who have acquired or founded kingdoms; you will find them all admirable; and if their deeds and their particular institutions are considered, they will not appear different from those of Moses, who had so great a guide. And examining their deeds and their lives, one can see that they received nothing from fortune except the opportunity, which gave them the material they could mould into whatever form they desired; and without that opportunity the strength of their spirit would have been extinguished, and without that strength the opportunity would have come in vain.

It was therefore necessary for Moses to find the people of Israel in Egypt slaves and oppressed by the Egyptians in order that they might be disposed to follow him to escape this servitude. It was necessary for Romulus not to stay in Alba and to be exposed at birth so that he might become King of Rome and founder of that nation. It was necessary for Cyrus to find the Persians discontented with the empire of the Medes, and the Medes soft and effeminate after a lengthy peace. Theseus could not have shown his skill if he had not found the Athenians scattered. These opportunities, therefore, made these men successful, and their outstanding ingenuity made that opportunity known to them, whereby their nations were ennobled and became prosperous.

Like these men, those who become princes through their skill acquire the principality with difficulty, but they hold on to it easily; and the difficulties they encounter in acquiring the principality grow, in part, out of the new institutions and methods they are obliged to introduce in order to found their state and their security. And one should bear in mind that there is nothing more difficult to execute, nor more dubious of success, nor more dangerous to administer than to introduce a new order of things; for he who introduces it has all those who profit from the old order as his enemies, and he has only lukewarm allies in all those who might profit from the new. This lukewarmness partly stems from fear of their adversaries, who have the law on their side, and partly from the scepticism of men, who do not truly believe in new things unless they have actually had personal experience of them. Therefore, it happens that whenever those who are enemies have the chance to attack, they do so enthusiastically, whereas those others defend hesitantly, so that they, together with the prince, are in danger.

It is necessary, however, if we desire to examine this subject thoroughly, to observe whether these innovators act on their own or are dependent on others: that is, if they are forced to beg or are able to use power in conducting their affairs. In the first case, they always come to a bad end and never accomplish anything; but when they depend on their own resources and can use power, then only seldom do they find themselves in peril. From this comes the fact that all armed prophets were victorious and the unarmed came to ruin. Besides what has been said, people are fickle by nature; and it is simple to convince them of something, but difficult to hold them in that conviction; and, therefore, affairs should be managed in such a way that when they no longer believe, they can be made to believe by force. Moses, Cyrus, Theseus, and Romulus could not have made their institutions long respected if they had been unarmed; as in our times happened to Brother Girolamo Savonarola, who was ruined by his new institutions when the populace began no longer to believe in them, since he had no way of holding steady those who had believed nor of making the disbelievers believe. Therefore, such men have great problems in getting ahead, and they meet all their dangers as they proceed, and they must overcome them with their skill; but once they have overcome them and have begun to be respected, having removed those who were envious of their merits, they remain powerful, secure, honoured, and happy.

On New Principalities Acquired with the Arms of Others and by Fortune

Those private citizens who become princes through fortune alone do so with little effort, but they maintain their position only with a great deal; they meet no obstacles along their way since they fly to success, but all their problems arise when they have arrived. And these are the men who are granted a state either because they have money or because they enjoy the favour of him who grants it: this occurred to many in Greece in the cities of Ionia and the Hellespont, where Darius created princes in order that he might hold these cities for his security and glory; in like manner were set up those emperors who from private citizens came to power by bribing the soldiers. Such men depend solely upon two very uncertain and unstable things: the will and the fortune of him who granted them the state; they do not know how and are not able to maintain their position. They do not know how, since if men are not of great intelligence and ingenuity, it is not reasonable that they know how to rule, having always lived as private citizens; they are not able to, since they do not have forces that are friendly and faithful. Besides, states that rise quickly, just as all the other things of nature that are born and grow rapidly, cannot have roots and ramifications; the first bad weather kills them, unless these men who have suddenly become princes, as I have noted, are of such ability that they know how to prepare themselves quickly and to preserve what fortune has put in their laps, and to construct afterwards those foundations that others have built before becoming princes.

Regarding the two methods just listed for becoming a prince, by skill or by fortune, I should like to offer two recent examples: these are Francesco Sforza and Cesare Borgia. Francesco, through the required means and with a great deal of ingenuity, became Duke of Milan from his station as a private citizen, and that which he had acquired with countless hardships he maintained with little

trouble. On the other hand, Cesare Borgia (commonly called Duke Valentino) acquired the state through the favour and help of his father, and when this no longer existed, he lost it, and this despite the fact that he did everything and used every means that a prudent and skilful man ought to use in order to root himself securely in those states that the arms and fortune of others had granted him. Because, as stated above, anyone who does not lay his foundations beforehand could do so later only with great skill, although this would be done with inconvenience to the architect and danger to the building. If, therefore, we consider all the steps taken by the Duke, we shall see that he laid sturdy foundations for his future power; and I do not judge it useless to discuss them, for I would not know of any better precepts to give to a new prince than the example of his deeds; and if he did not succeed in his plans, it was not his fault, but was instead the result of an extraordinary and extreme instance of ill fortune.

On Those Who Have Become Princes Through Wickedness

But because there are yet two more ways one can from an ordinary citizen become prince, which cannot completely be attributed to either fortune or skill, I believe they should not be left unmentioned, although one of them will be discussed at greater length in a treatise on republics. These two are: when one becomes prince through some wicked and nefarious means or when a private citizen becomes prince of his native city through the favour of his fellow citizens.

In our own days, during the reign of Alexander VI, Oliverotto of Fermo, who many years before had been left as a child without a father, was brought up by his maternal uncle, Giovanni Fogliani. While still very young he was sent to serve as a soldier under Paulo Vitelli so that, once he was versed in that skill, he might attain some outstanding military position. Then, after Paulo died, he served under his brother, Vitellozzo; and in a very brief time, because of his intelligence and his vigorous body and mind, he became the commander of his troops. But since he felt it was servile to work for others, he decided to seize Fermo with the aid of some citizens of Fermo who preferred servitude to the liberty of their native city, and with the assistance of the followers of Vitellozzo; and he wrote to Giovanni Fogliani that, having been away many years from home, he wished to come to see him and his city and to inspect his own inheritance; and since he had exerted himself for no other reason than to acquire glory, he wanted to arrive in honourable fashion, accompanied by an escort of a hundred horsemen from among his friends and servants so that his fellow citizens might see that he had not spent his time in vain; and he begged his uncle to arrange for an honourable reception from the people of Fermo, one which might bring honour not only to Giovanni but also to himself, being his pupil. Giovanni, therefore, in no way failed in his duty toward his nephew: he had him received in honourable fashion by the people of Fermo, and he gave him rooms in his own house. Oliverotto, after a few days had passed and he had secretly made the preparations necessary for his forthcoming wickedness, gave a magnificent banquet to which he invited Giovanni Fogliani and all of the first citizens of

Fermo. And when the meal and all the other entertainment customary at such banquets were completed, Oliverotto, according to plan, began to discuss serious matters, speaking of the greatness of Pope Alexander and his son, Cesare, and of their undertakings. After Giovanni and the others had replied to his comments, he suddenly rose up, announcing that these were matters to be discussed in a more secluded place; and he retired into another room, followed by Giovanni and all the other citizens. No sooner were they seated than from secret places in the room out came soldiers who killed Giovanni and all the others. After this murder, Oliverotto mounted his horse, paraded through the town, and besieged the chief officials in the government palace; so that out of fear they were forced to obey him and to constitute a government of which he made himself prince. And when all those were killed who, because they were discontented, might have harmed him, he strengthened himself by instituting new civil and military institutions; so that, in the space of the year that he held the principality, not only was he secure in the city of Fermo, but he had become feared by all its neighbours. His expulsion would have been difficult if he had not permitted himself to be tricked by Cesare Borgia, when at Sinigaglia, as was noted above, the Duke captured the Orsini and the Vitelli; there he, too, was captured, a year after he committed the parricide, and together with Vitellozzo, who had been his teacher in ingenuity and wickedness, he was strangled.

One might wonder how anyone, after so many betrayals and cruelties, could live for such a long time secure in their cities and defend themselves from outside enemies without being plotted against by their own citizens; many others, using cruel means, were unable even in peaceful times to hold on to their state, not to speak of the uncertain times of war. I believe that this depends on whether cruelty be well or badly used. Well used are those cruelties (if it is permitted to speak well of evil) that are carried out in a single stroke, done out of necessity to protect oneself, and are not continued but are instead converted into the greatest possible benefits for the subjects. Badly used are those cruelties which, although being few at the outset, grow with the passing of time instead of disappearing. Those who follow the first method can remedy their condition with God and with men, the others cannot possibly survive.

Wherefore it is to be noted that in taking a state its conqueror should weigh all the harmful things he must do and do them all at once so as not to have to repeat them every day, and in not repeating them to be able to make men feel secure and win them over with the benefits he bestows upon them. Anyone who does otherwise, either out of timidity or because of poor advice, is always obliged to keep his knife in his hand; nor can he ever count upon his subjects, who, because of their fresh and continual injuries, cannot feel secure with him. Injuries, therefore, should be inflicted all at the same time, for the less they are tasted, the less they offend; and benefits should be distributed a bit at a time in order that they may be savoured fully. And a prince should, above all, live with his subjects in such a way that no unforeseen event, either good or bad, may make him alter his course; for when emergencies arise in adverse conditions, you are not in time to resort to cruelty, and that good you do will help you little, since it be judged a forced measure and you will earn from it no thanks whatsoever.

On the Civil Principality

But coming to the second instance, when a private citizen, not through wickedness or any other intolerable violence, but with the favour of his fellow citizens, becomes prince of his native city (this can be called a civil principality, the acquisition of which neither depends completely upon skill nor upon fortune, but instead upon a mixture of shrewdness and luck), I maintain that one reaches this princedom either with the favour of the common people or with that of the nobility. For these two different humours are found in every body politic; and they arise from the fact that the people do not wish to be commanded or oppressed by the nobles, and the nobles desire to command and to oppress the people; and from these two opposed appetites there arises one of three effects: either a principality or liberty or anarchy.

A principality is brought about either by the common people or by the nobility, depending on which of the two parties has the opportunity. For when the nobles see that they cannot resist the populace, they begin to support one among them and make him prince in order to be able, under his protection, to satisfy their appetites. The common people as well, seeing that they cannot resist the nobility, give their support to one man and make him prince in order to have the protection of his authority. He who attains the principality with the aid of the nobility maintains it with more difficulty than he who becomes prince with the assistance of the common people, for he finds himself a prince amidst many who feel themselves to be his equals, and because of this he can neither govern nor manage them as he wishes. But he who attains the principality through popular favour finds himself alone and has around him either no one or very few who are not ready to obey him. Moreover, one cannot honestly satisfy the nobles without harming others, but the common people can certainly be satisfied: their desire is more just than that of the nobles—the former want not to be oppressed and the latter want to oppress. Moreover, a prince can never make himself secure when the people are his enemy because they are so many; he can make himself secure against the nobles because they are so few. The worst that a prince can expect from a hostile people is to be abandoned by them; but with a hostile nobility not only does he have to fear being abandoned but also that they will unite against him; for, being more perceptive and shrewder, they always have time to save themselves, to seek the favours of the side they believe will win. Furthermore, a prince must always live with the same common people; but he can easily do without the same nobles, having the power to create them and to destroy them from day to day and to take away and give back their prestige as he sees fit.

A Prince's Duty Concerning Military Matters

A Prince, therefore, must not have any other object nor any other thought, nor must he take anything as his profession but war, its institutions, and its disciplines; because that is the only profession which befits one who commands; and it is of such importance that not only does it maintain those who were born princes, but many times it enables men of private station to rise to that position; and, on the other hand, it is evident that when princes have given more thought to personal luxuries than to arms, they have lost their state. And the most important cause of losing it is to neglect this art; and the way to acquire it is to be well-versed in this art.

Francesco Sforza became Duke of Milan from being a private citizen because he was armed; his successors, since they avoided the inconveniences of arms, became private citizens after having been dukes. For, among the other bad effects it causes, being unarmed makes you despised; this is one of those infamies a prince should guard himself against, as will be treated below: for between an armed and an unarmed man there is no comparison whatsoever, and it is not reasonable for an armed man to obey an unarmed man willingly, nor that an unarmed man should be safe among armed servants; since, when the former is suspicious and the latter are contemptuous, it is impossible for them to work well together. And therefore, a prince who does not understand military matters, besides the other misfortunes already noted, cannot be esteemed by his own soldiers, nor can he trust them.

He should, therefore, never take his mind from this exercise of war, and in peacetime he must train himself more than in time of war; this can be done in two ways: one by action, the other by the mind. And as far as actions are concerned, besides keeping his soldiers well disciplined and trained, he must always be out hunting, and must accustom his body to hardships in this manner; and he must also learn the nature of the terrain, and know how mountains slope, how valleys open, how plains lie, and understand the nature of rivers and swamps; and he should devote much attention to such activities. Such knowledge is useful in two ways: first, one learns to know one's own country and can better understand how to defend it; second, with the knowledge and experience of the terrain, one can easily comprehend the characteristics of any other terrain that it is necessary to explore for the first time; for the hills, valleys, plains, rivers, and swamps of Tuscany, for instance, have certain similarities to those of other provinces; so that by knowing the lie of the land in one province one can easily understand it in others. And a prince who lacks this ability lacks the most important quality in a leader; because this skill teaches you to find the enemy, choose a campsite, lead troops, organize them for battle, and besiege towns to your own advantage.

On Those Things for Which Men, and Particularly Princes, Are Praised or Blamed

Now there remains to be examined what should be the methods and procedures of a prince in dealing with his subjects and friends. And because I know that many have written about this, I am afraid that by writing about it again I shall be thought of as presumptuous, since in discussing this material I depart radically from the procedures of others. But since my intention is to write something useful for anyone who understands it, it seemed more suitable to me to search after the effectual truth of the matter rather than its imagined one. And many writers have imagined for themselves republics and principalities that have never been seen nor known to exist in reality; for there is such a gap between how one lives and how one ought to live that anyone who abandons what is done for what ought to be done learns his ruin rather than his preservation: for a man who wishes to profess goodness at all times will come to ruin among so many who are not good. Hence it is necessary for a prince who wishes to maintain his position to learn how not to be good, and to use this knowledge or not to use it according to necessity.

Leaving aside, therefore, the imagined things concerning a prince, and taking into account those that are true, I say that all men, when they are spoken of, and particularly princes, since they are placed on a higher level, are judged by some of these qualities which bring them either blame or praise. And this is why one is considered generous, another miserly (to use a Tuscan word, since 'avaricious' in our language is still used to mean one who wishes to acquire by means of theft; we call 'miserly' one who excessively avoids using what he has); one is considered a giver, the other rapacious; one cruel, another merciful; one treacherous, another faithful; one effeminate and cowardly, another bold and courageous; one humane, another haughty; one lascivious, another chaste; one trustworthy, another frivolous; one religious, another unbelieving; and the like. And I know that everyone will admit that it would be a very praiseworthy thing to find in a prince, of the qualities mentioned above, those that are held to be good; but since it is neither possible to have them nor to observe them all completely, because the human condition does not permit it, a prince must be prudent enough to know how to escape the bad reputation of those vices that would lose the state for him, and must protect himself from those that will not lose it for him, if this is possible; but if he cannot, he need not concern himself unduly if he ignores these less serious vices. And, moreover, he need not worry about incurring the bad reputation of those vices without which it would be difficult to hold his state; since, carefully taking everything into account, he will discover that something which appears to be a virtue, if pursued, will end in his destruction; while some other thing which seems to be a vice, if pursued, will result in his safety and his well-being.

On Generosity and Miserliness

Beginning, therefore, with the first of the above-mentioned qualities, I say that it would be good to be considered generous; nevertheless, generosity used in such a manner as to give you a reputation for it will harm you; because if it is employed virtuously and as one should employ it, it will not be recognized and you will not avoid the reproach of its opposite. And so, if a prince wants to maintain his reputation for generosity among men, it is necessary for him not to neglect any possible means of lavish display; in so doing such a prince will always use up all his resources and he will be obliged, eventually, if he wishes to maintain his reputation for generosity, to burden the people with excessive taxes and to do everything possible to raise funds. This will begin to make him hateful to his subjects, and, becoming impoverished, he will not be much esteemed by anyone; so that, as a consequence of his generosity, having offended many and rewarded few, he will feel the effects of any slight unrest and will be ruined at the first sign of danger; recognizing this and wishing to alter his policies, he immediately runs the risk of being reproached as a miser.

A prince, therefore, being unable to use this virtue of generosity in a manner which will not harm himself, if he is known for it, should, if he is wise, not worry about being called a miser; for with time he will come to be considered more generous once it is evident that, as a result of his parsimony, his income is sufficient, he can defend himself from anyone who makes war against him, and he can undertake enterprises without overburdening his people, so that he comes to be generous with all those from whom he takes nothing, who are countless, and miserly with all those to whom he gives nothing, who are few. In our times we have not seen great deeds accomplished except by those who were considered miserly; the others were failures. Pope Julius II, although he made use of his reputation for generosity in order to gain the papacy, then decided not to maintain it in order to be able to wage war; the present King of France has waged many wars without imposing extra taxes on his subjects, only because his habitual parsimony has provided for the additional expenditures; the present King of Spain, if he had been considered generous, would not have engaged in or won so many campaigns.

Therefore, in order not to have to rob his subjects, to be able to defend himself, not to become poor and contemptible, and not to be forced to become rapacious, a prince must consider it of little importance if he incurs the reputation of being a miser, for this is one of those vices that permits him to rule. And if someone were to say: Caesar with his generosity achieved imperial power, and many others, because they were generous and known to be so, achieved very high positions; I would reply: you are either already a prince or you are on the way to becoming one; in the first instance such generosity is damaging; in the second it is very necessary to be thought generous. And Caesar was one of those who wanted to gain the principality of Rome; but if, after obtaining this, he had lived and had not moderated his expenditures, he would have destroyed his rule. And if someone were to reply: there have existed many princes who have accomplished great deeds with their armies who have been reputed to be generous; I would answer you: a prince either spends his own money and that of his subjects or that of others; in the first case he must be economical; in the second he must not restrain any part of his generosity. And for that prince who goes out with his soldiers and lives by looting, sacking, and ransoms, who controls the property of others, such generosity is necessary; otherwise he would not be followed by his troops. And with what does not belong to you or to your subjects you can be a more liberal giver, as were Cyrus, Caesar, and Alexander; for spending the wealth of others does not lessen your reputation but adds to it; only the spending of your own is what harms you. And there is nothing that uses itself up faster than generosity, for as you employ it you lose the means of employing it, and you become either poor and despised or else, in order to escape poverty, you become rapacious and hated. And above all other things a prince must guard himself against being despised and hated; and generosity leads you to both one and the other. So it is wiser to live with the reputation of a miser, which produces reproach without hatred, than to be forced to incur the reputation of rapacity, which produces reproach along with hatred, because you want to be considered generous.

On Cruelty and Mercy, and Whether It Is Better to Be Loved Than to Be Feared or the Contrary

Proceeding to the other qualities mentioned above, I say that every prince must desire to be considered merciful and not cruel; nevertheless, he must take care not to misuse this mercy. Cesare Borgia was considered cruel; none the less, his cruelty had brought order to Romagna, united it, restored it to peace and obedience. If we examine this carefully, we shall see that he was more merciful than the Florentine people who, in order to avoid being considered cruel, allowed the destruction of Pistoia. Therefore, a prince must not worry about the reproach of cruelty when it is a matter of keeping his subjects united and loyal; for with a very few examples of cruelty he will be more compassionate than those who, out of excessive mercy, permit disorders to continue, from which arise murders and plundering; for these usually harm the community at large, while the executions that come from the prince harm particular individuals. And the new prince, above all other princes, cannot escape the reputation of being called cruel, since new states are full of dangers. And Virgil, through Dido, states: 'My difficult condition and the newness of my rule make me act in such a manner, and to set guards over my land on all sides.'

Nevertheless, a prince must be cautious in believing and in acting, nor should he be afraid of his own shadow; and he should proceed in such a manner, tempered by prudence and humanity, so that too much trust may not render him imprudent nor too much distrust render him intolerable.

From this arises an argument: whether it is better to be loved than to be feared, or the contrary. I reply that one should like to be both one and the other; but since it is difficult to join them together, it is much safer to be feared than to be loved when one of the two must be lacking. For one can generally say this about men: that they are ungrateful, fickle, simulators and deceivers, avoiders of danger, greedy for gain; and while you work for their good they are completely yours, offering you their blood, their property, their lives, and their sons, as I said earlier, when danger is far away; but when it comes nearer to you they turn away. And that prince who bases his power entirely on their words, finding himself completely without other preparations, comes to ruin; for friendships that are acquired by a price and not by greatness and nobility of character are purchased but are not owned, and at the proper moment they cannot be spent. And men are less hesitant about harming someone who makes himself loved than one who makes himself feared because love is held together by a chain of obligation which, since men are wretched creatures, is broken on every occasion in which their own interests are concerned; but fear is sustained by a dread of punishment which will never abandon you.

A prince must nevertheless make himself feared in such a manner that he will avoid hatred, even if he does not acquire love; since to be feared and not to be hated can very well be combined; and this will always be so when he keeps his hands off the property and the women of his citizens and his subjects. And if he must take someone's life, he should do so when there is proper justification and manifest cause; but, above all, he should avoid seizing the property of others; for men forget more quickly the death of their father than the loss of their patrimony. Moreover, reasons for seizing their property are never lacking; and he who begins to live by stealing always finds a reason for taking what belongs to others; on the contrary, reasons for taking a life are rarer and disappear sooner.

But when the prince is with his armies and has under his command a multitude of troops, then it is absolutely necessary that he not worry about being considered cruel; for without that reputation he will never keep an army united or prepared for any combat.

I conclude, therefore, returning to the problem of being feared and loved, that since men love at their own pleasure and fear at the pleasure of the prince, a wise prince should build his foundation upon that which belongs to him, not upon that which belongs to others: he must strive only to avoid hatred, as has been said.

How a Prince Should Keep His Word

How praiseworthy it is for a prince to keep his word and to live by integrity and not by deceit everyone knows; nevertheless, one sees from the experience of our times that the princes who have accomplished great deeds are those who have cared little for keeping their promises and who have known how to manipulate the minds of men by shrewdness; and in the end they have surpassed those who laid their foundations upon loyalty.

You must, therefore, know that there are two means of fighting: one according to the laws, the other with force; the first way is proper to man, the second to beasts; but because the first, in many cases, is not sufficient, it becomes necessary to have recourse to the second. Therefore, a prince must know how to use wisely the natures of the beast and the man. This policy was taught to princes allegorically by the ancient writers, who described how Akhilleus and many other ancient princes were given to Chiron the Centaur to be raised and taught under his discipline. This can only mean that, having a half-beast and a half-man as a teacher, a prince must know how to employ the nature of the one and the other; and the one without the other cannot endure.

Since, then, a prince must know how to make good use of the nature of the beast, he should choose from among the beasts the fox and the lion; for the lion cannot defend himself from traps and the fox cannot protect itself from wolves. It is therefore necessary to be a fox in order to recognize the traps and a lion in order to frighten the wolves. Those who play only the part of the lion do not understand matters. A wise ruler, therefore, cannot and should not keep his word when such an observance of faith would be to his disadvantage and when the reasons which made him promise are removed. And if men were all good, this rule would not be good; but since men are a contemptible lot and will not keep their promises to you, you likewise need not keep yours to them. A prince never lacks legitimate reasons to break his promise. Of this one could cite an endless number of modern examples to show how many pacts, how many promises have been made null and void because of the infidelity of princes; and he who has known best how to use the fox has come to a better end. But it is necessary to know how to disguise this nature well and to be a great hypocrite and a liar: and men are so simple-minded and so controlled by their present needs that one who deceives will always find another who will allow himself to be deceived.

I do not wish to remain silent about one of these recent instances. Alexander VI did nothing else, he thought about nothing else, except to deceive men, and he always found the occasion to do this. And there never was a man who had more forcefulness in his oaths, who affirmed a thing with more promises, and who honoured his word less; nevertheless, his tricks always succeeded perfectly since he was well acquainted with this aspect of the world.

Therefore, it is not necessary for a prince to have all of the above-mentioned qualities, but it is very necessary for him to appear to have them. Furthermore, I shall be so bold as to assert this: that having them and practising them at all times is harmful; and appearing to have them is useful; for instance, to seem merciful, faithful, humane, trustworthy, religious, and to be so; but his mind should be disposed in such a way that should it become necessary not to be so, he will be able and know how to change to the contrary. And it is essential to understand this: that a prince, and especially a new prince, cannot observe all those things for which men are considered good, for in order to maintain the state he is often obliged to act against his promise, against charity, against humanity, and against religion. And, therefore, it is necessary that he have a mind ready to turn itself according to the way the winds of fortune and the changeability of affairs require him; and, as I said above, as long as it is possible, he should not stray from the good, but he should know how to enter into evil when necessity commands.

A prince, therefore, must be very careful never to let anything slip from his lips which is not full of the five qualities mentioned above: he should appear, upon seeing and hearing him, to be all mercy, all faithfulness, all integrity, all kindness, all religion. And there is nothing more necessary than to seem to possess this last quality. And men in general judge more by their eyes than their hands; for everyone can see but few can feel. Everyone sees what you seem to be, few touch upon what you are, and those few do not dare to contradict the opinion of the many who have the majesty of the state to defend them; and in the actions of all men, and especially of princes, where there is no impartial arbiter, one must consider the final result. Let a prince therefore act to conquer and to maintain the state; his methods will always be judged honourable and will be praised by all; for ordinary people are always deceived by appearances and by the outcome of a thing; and in the world there is nothing but ordinary people; and there is no room for the few, while the many have a place to lean on. A certain prince of the present day, whom I shall refrain from naming, preaches nothing but peace and faith, and to both one and the other he is entirely opposed; and both, if he had put them into practice, would have cost him many times over either his reputation or his state.

On Avoiding Being Despised and Hated

But now that I have talked about the most important of the qualities mentioned above, I would like to discuss the others briefly in this general manner: that the prince, as was noted above, should concentrate upon avoiding those things which make him hated and despised; and when he has avoided this, he will have carried out his duties and will find no danger whatsoever in other vices. As I have said, what makes him hated above all else is being rapacious and a usurper of the property and the women of his subjects; he must refrain from this; and in most cases, so long as you do not deprive them of either their property or their honour, the majority of men live happily; and you have only to deal with the ambition of a few, who can be restrained without difficulty and by many means. What makes him despised is being considered changeable, frivolous, effeminate, cowardly, irresolute; from these qualities a prince must guard himself as if from a reef, and he must strive to make everyone recognize in his actions greatness, spirit, dignity, and strength; and concerning the private affairs of his subjects, he must insist that his decision be irrevocable; and he should maintain himself in such a way that no man could imagine that he can deceive or cheat him.

That prince who projects such an opinion of himself is greatly esteemed; and it is difficult to conspire against a man with such a reputation and difficult to attack him, provided that he is understood to be of great merit and revered by his subjects. For a prince should have two fears: one, internal, concerning his subjects; the other, external, concerning foreign powers. From the latter he can defend himself by his good troops and friends; and he will always have good friends if he has good troops; and internal affairs will always be stable when external affairs are stable, provided that they are not already disturbed by a conspiracy; and even if external conditions change, if he is properly organized and lives as I have said and does not lose control of himself, he will always be able to withstand every attack. But concerning his subjects, when external affairs do not change, he has to fear that they may conspire secretly: the prince secures himself from this by avoiding being hated or despised and by keeping the people satisfied with him; this is a necessary accomplishment, as was treated above at length. And one of the most powerful remedies a prince has against conspiracies is not to be hated by the masses; for a man who plans a conspiracy always believes that he will satisfy the people by killing the prince; but when he thinks he might anger them, he cannot work up the courage to undertake such a deed; for the problems on the side of the conspirators are countless. And experience demonstrates that there have been many conspiracies but few have been concluded successfully; for anyone who conspires cannot be alone, nor can he find companions except from amongst those whom he believes to be dissatisfied; and as soon as you have revealed your intention to one malcontent, you give him the means to make himself content, since he can have everything he desires by uncovering the plot; so much is this so that, seeing a sure gain on the one hand and one doubtful and full of danger on the other, if he is to maintain faith with you he has to be either an unusually good friend or a completely determined enemy of the prince. And to treat the matter briefly, I say that on the part of the conspirator there is nothing but fear, jealousy, and the thought of punishment that terrifies him; but on the part of the prince there is the majesty of the principality, the laws, the defences of friends and the state to protect him; so that, with the good will of the people added to all these things, it is impossible for anyone to be so rash as to plot against him. For, where usually a conspirator has to be afraid before he executes his evil deed, in this case he must be afraid even after the crime is performed, having the people as an enemy, nor can he hope to find any refuge because of this.

How a Prince Should Act to Acquire Esteem

Nothing makes a prince more esteemed than great undertakings and examples of his unusual talents. In our own times we have Ferdinand of Aragon, the present King of Spain. This man can be called almost a new prince, since from being a weak ruler he became, through fame and glory, the first king of Christendom; and if you consider his accomplishments, you will find them all very grand and some even extraordinary. In the beginning of his reign he attacked Granada, and that enterprise was the basis of his state. First, he acted while things were peaceful and when he had no fear of opposition: he kept the minds of the barons of Castile busy with this, and they, concentrating on that war, did not consider changes at home. And he acquired, through that means, reputation and power over them without their noticing it; he was able to maintain armies with money from the Church and the people, and with that long war he laid a basis for his own army, which has since brought him honour. Besides this, in order to be able to undertake greater enterprises, always using religion for his own purposes, he turned to a pious cruelty, hunting down and clearing out the Moors from

his kingdom: no example could be more pathetic or more unusual than this. He attacked Africa, under the same cloak of religion; he undertook the invasion of Italy; he finally attacked France. And in such a manner, he has always done and planned great deeds which have always kept the minds of his subjects in suspense and amazed and occupied with their outcome. And one action of his would spring from another in such a way that between one and the other he would never give men enough time to be able to work calmly against him.

A prince is also respected when he is a true friend and a true enemy; that is, when he declares himself on the side of one prince against another without any reservation. Such a policy will always be more useful than that of neutrality; for if two powerful neighbours of yours come to blows, they will be of the type that, when one has emerged victorious, you will either have cause to fear the victor or you will not. In either of these two cases, it will always be more useful for you to declare yourself and to fight an open war; for, in the first case, if you do not declare your intentions, you will always be the prey of the victor to the delight and satisfaction of the vanquished, and you will have no reason why anyone would come to your assistance; because whoever wins does not want reluctant allies who would not assist him in times of adversity; and whoever loses will not give you refuge since you were unwilling to run the risk of coming to his aid.

And it will always happen that he who is not your friend will request your neutrality and he who is your friend will ask you to declare yourself by taking up your arms. And irresolute princes, in order to avoid present dangers, follow the neutral road most of the time, and most of the time they are ruined. But when the prince declares himself vigorously in favour of one side, if the one with whom you have joined wins, although he may be powerful and you may be left to his discretion, he has an obligation to you and there does exist a bond of friendship; and men are never so dishonest that they will crush you with such a show of ingratitude; and then, victories are never so clear-cut that the victor need be completely free of caution, especially when justice is concerned. But if the one with whom you join loses, you will be taken in by him; and while he is able, he will help you, and you will become the comrade of a fortune which can rise up again.

In the second case, when those who fight together are of such a kind that you need not fear the one who wins, it is even more prudent to join his side, since you go to the downfall of a prince with the aid of another prince who should have saved him if he had been wise; and in winning he is at your discretion, and it is impossible for him not to win with your aid.

A prince also should demonstrate that he is a lover of talent by giving recognition to men of ability and by honouring those who excel in a particular field. Furthermore, he should encourage his subjects to be free to pursue their trades in tranquility, whether in commerce, agriculture, or in any other trade a man may have. And he should act in such a way that a man is not afraid to increase his goods for fear that they will be taken away from him, while another will not be afraid to engage in commerce for fear of taxes; instead, he must set up rewards for those who wish to do things, and for anyone who seeks in any way to aggrandize his city or state. He should, besides this, at the appropriate times of the year, keep the populace occupied with festivals and spectacles. And because each city is divided into guilds or clans, he should take account of these groups, meet with them on occasion, offer himself as an example of humanity and munificence, always, nevertheless, maintaining firmly the dignity of his position, for this should never be lacking in any way.

Why Italian Princes Have Lost Their States

The things written above, if followed prudently, make a new prince seem well established and render him immediately safer and more established in his state than if he had been in it for some time. For a new prince is far more closely observed in his activities than is a hereditary prince; and when his deeds are recognized to be good actions they attract men much more and bind them to him more strongly than does antiquity of lineage. For men are much more taken by present concerns than by those of the past; and when they find the present satisfactory they enjoy it and seek nothing more; in fact, they will seize every measure to defend the new prince as long as he is not lacking in his other responsibilities. And thus he will have a double glory: that of having given birth to a new principality and of having adorned it and strengthened it with good laws, good arms, and good examples; as he will have double shame who, having been born a prince, loses his principality on account of his lack of prudence.

Therefore, these princes of ours who have been in their principalities for many years, and who have then lost them, must not blame fortune, but rather their own idleness; for, never having thought in peaceful times that things might change (which is a common defect in men, not to consider in good weather the possibility of a tempest), when adverse times finally arrived they thought about running away and not about defending themselves; and they hoped that the people, angered by the insolence of the victors, would eventually recall them. This policy, when others are lacking, is good; but it is indeed bad to have disregarded all other solutions for this one; for you should never wish to fall, believing that you will find someone else to pick you up; because whether this occurs or not, it does not increase your security, that method being a cowardly defence and one not dependent upon your own resources. And those methods alone are good, are certain, are lasting, that depend on yourself and your own ingenuity.

On Fortune's Role in Human Affairs and How She Can Be Dealt With

It is not unknown to me that many have held, and still hold, the opinion that the things of this world are, in a manner, controlled by fortune and by God, that men with their wisdom cannot control them, and, on the contrary, that men can have no remedy whatsoever for them; and for this reason they might judge that they need not sweat much over such matters but let them be governed by fate. This opinion has been more strongly held in our own times because of the great variation of affairs that has been observed and that is being observed every day which is beyond human conjecture. Sometimes, as I think about these things, I am inclined to their opinion to a certain extent. Nevertheless, in order that our free will be not extinguished, I judge it to be true that fortune is the arbiter of one-half of our actions, but that she still leaves the control of the other half, or almost that, to us. And I compare her to one of those ruinous rivers that, when they become enraged, flood the plains, tear down the trees and buildings, taking up earth from one spot and placing it upon another; everyone flees from them, everyone yields to their onslaught, unable to oppose them in any way. But although they are of such a nature, it does not follow that when the weather is calm we cannot take precautions with embankments and dikes, so that when they rise up again either the waters will be channelled off or their impetus will not either be unchecked or so damaging. The same things happen where fortune is concerned: she shows her force where there is no organized strength to resist her; and she directs her impact there where she knows that dikes and embankments are not constructed to hold her. And if you consider Italy, the seat of these changes and the nation which has set them in motion, you will see a country without embankments and without a single bastion: for if she were defended by the necessary forces, like Germany, Spain, and France, either this flood would not have produced the great changes that it has or it would not have come upon us at all. And this I consider enough to say about fortune in general terms.

But, limiting myself more to particulars, I say that one sees a prince prosper today and come to ruin tomorrow without having seen him change his character or any of the reasons that have been discussed at length earlier; that is, that a prince who relies completely upon fortune will come to ruin as soon as she changes; I also believe that the man who adapts his course of action to the nature of the times will succeed and, likewise, that the man who sets his course of action out of tune with the times will come to grief. For one can observe that men, in the affairs which lead them to the end that they seek—that is, glory and wealth—proceed in different ways; one by caution, another with impetuousness; one through violence, another with guile; one with patience, another with its opposite; and each one by these various means can attain his goals. And we also see in the case of two cautious men, that one reaches his goal while the other does not; and, likewise, two men equally succeed using two different means, one being cautious and the other impetuous: this arises from nothing else than the nature of the times that either suit or do not suit their course of action. From this results that which I have said, that two men, working in opposite ways, can produce the same outcome; and of two men working in the same fashion one achieves his goal and the other does not. On this also depends the variation of what is good; for, if a man governs himself with caution and patience, and the times and conditions are turning in such a way that his policy is a good one, he will prosper; but if the times and conditions change, he will be ruined because he does not change his method of procedure. Nor is there to be found a man so prudent that he knows how to adapt himself to this, both because he cannot deviate from that to which he is by nature inclined and also because he cannot be persuaded to depart from a path, having always prospered by following it. And therefore the cautious man, when it is time to act impetuously, does not know how to do so, and he is ruined; but if he had changed his conduct with the times, fortune would not have changed.

I conclude, therefore, that since fortune changes and men remain set in their ways, men will succeed when the two are in harmony and fail when they are not in accord. I am certainly convinced of this: that it is better to be impetuous than cautious, because fortune is a woman, and it is necessary, in order to keep her down, to beat her and to struggle with her. And it is seen that she more often allows herself to be taken over by men who are impetuous than by those who make cold advances; and then, being a woman, she is always a friend of young men, for they are less cautious, more aggressive, and they command her with more audacity.

An Exhortation to Liberate Italy from the Barbarians

Considering, therefore, all of the things mentioned above, and reflecting as to whether the times are suitable, at present, to honour a new prince in Italy, and if there is the material that might give a skilful and prudent prince the opportunity to introduce a form of government that would bring him honour and good to the people of Italy, it seems to me that so many circumstances are favourable to such a new prince that I know of no other time more appropriate. And if, as I said, it was necessary that the people of Israel be slaves in Egypt in order to recognize Moses' ability, and it was necessary that the Persians be oppressed by the Medes to recognize the greatness of spirit in Cyrus, and it was necessary that the Athenians be dispersed to realize the excellence of Theseus, then, likewise, at the present time, in order to recognize the ability of an Italian spirit, it was necessary that Italy be reduced to her present condition and that she be more enslaved than the Hebrews, more servile than the Persians, more scattered than the Athenians; without a leader, without organization, beaten, despoiled, ripped apart, overrun, and prey to every sort of catastrophe.

And even though before now some glimmer of light may have shown itself in a single individual, so that it was possible to believe that God had ordained him for Italy's redemption, nevertheless it was witnessed afterwards how at the height of his career he was rejected by fortune. So now Italy remains without life and awaits the man who can heal her wounds and put an end to the plundering of Lombardy, the ransoms in the Kingdom of Naples and in Tuscany, and who can cure her of those sores which have been festering for so long. Look how she now prays to God to send someone to redeem her from these barbaric cruelties and insolence; see her still ready and willing to follow a banner, provided that there be someone to raise it up. Nor is there anyone in sight, at present, in whom she can have more hope than in your illustrious house, which, with its fortune and ability, favoured by God and by the Church, of which it is now prince, could make itself the head of this redemption. This will not be very difficult if you keep before you the deeds and the lives of those named above. And although those men were out of the ordinary and marvellous, they were nevertheless men; and each of them had less opportunity than the present one; for their enterprises were no more just, nor easier, nor was God more a friend to them than to you. Here justice is great: 'Only those wars that are necessary are just, and arms are sacred when there is no hope except through arms.' Here there is a great willingness; and where there is a great willingness there cannot be great difficulty, if only you will use the institutions of those men I have proposed as your target. Besides this, we now see extraordinary, unprecedented signs brought about by God: the sea

has opened up; a cloud has shown you the path; the rock pours forth water; it has rained manna here; everything has converged for your greatness. The rest you must do yourself. God does not wish to do everything, in order not to take from us our free will and that part of the glory which is ours.

And it is no surprise if some of the Italians mentioned previously were not capable of doing what it is hoped may be done by your illustrious house, and if, during the many revolutions in Italy and the many campaigns of war, it always seems that her military ability is spent. This results from the fact that her ancient institutions were not good and that there was no one who knew how to discover new ones; and no other thing brings a new man on the rise such honour as the new laws and the new institutions discovered by him. These things, when they are well founded and have in themselves a certain greatness, make him revered and admirable. And in Italy there is no lack of material to be given a form: here there is great ability in her members, were it not for the lack of it in her leaders. Consider how in duels and skirmishes involving just a few men the Italians are superior in strength, dexterity, and cunning; but when it comes to armies they do not match others. And all this comes from the weakness of her leaders; for those who know are not followed; and with each one seeming to know, there has not been to the present day anyone who has known how to set himself above the others, either because of ingenuity or fortune, so that others might yield to him.

Therefore, if your illustrious house desires to follow these excellent men who redeemed their lands, it is necessary before all else, as a true basis for every undertaking, to provide yourself with your own native troops, for one cannot have either more faithful, more loyal, or better troops. And although each one separately may be brave, all of them united will become even braver when they find themselves commanded, honoured, and well treated by their own prince. It is necessary, therefore, to prepare yourself with such troops as these, so that with Italian strength you will be able to defend yourself from foreigners. And although Swiss and Spanish infantry may be reputed terrifying, nevertheless both have defects, so that a third army could not only oppose them but be confident of defeating them. For the Spanish cannot withstand cavalry and the Swiss have a fear of foot soldiers they meet in combat who are as brave as they are. Therefore, it has been witnessed and experience will demonstrate that the Spanish cannot withstand French cavalry and the Swiss are ruined by Spanish infantrymen. And although this last point has not been completely confirmed by experience, there was nevertheless a hint of it at the battle of Ravenna, when the Spanish infantry met the German battalions, who follow the same order as the Swiss; and the Spanish, with their agile bodies, aided by their spiked shields, entered between and underneath the Germans' long pikes and were safe, without the Germans having any recourse against them; and had it not been for the cavalry charge that broke them, the Spaniards would have slaughtered them all. Therefore, as the defects of both these kinds of troops are recognized, a new type can be instituted which can stand up to cavalry and will have no fear of foot soldiers: this will come about by creating new armies and changing battle formations. And these are among those matters that, when newly organized, give reputation and greatness to a new prince.

This opportunity, therefore, must not be permitted to pass by so that Italy, after so long a time, may behold its redeemer. Nor can I express with what love he will be received in all those provinces that have suffered through these foreign floods; with what thirst for revenge, with what obstinate loyalty, with what compassion, with what tears! What doors will be closed to him? Which people will deny him obedience? What jealousy could oppose him? What Italian would deny him homage? For everyone, this barbarian dominion stinks! Therefore, may your illustrious house take up this mission with that spirit and with that hope in which just undertakings are begun; so that under your banner this country may be ennobled and, under your guidance, those words of Petrarch may come true:

Ingenuity over rage
Will take up arms; and the battle will be short.
For ancient valour
In Italian hearts is not yet dead.

"Italia mia" 11. 93–96

Exercises

1. What does Machiavelli mean by cruelty "well used"? Give some contemporary examples of cruelty both "well used" and "badly used." Is Machiavelli correct? Have there been any twentieth-century rulers who were overthrown because of their badly used cruelties? Which ones? Regimes that are headed for destruction?

2. Is it better, according to Machiavelli, to be loved or feared? How would Hitler and Stalin have responded? Does this love or fear attitude apply also to democracies? Why or why not? Is there something between love and fear that might be more apropos?

3. Machiavelli contends that a ruler does not have to keep good faith. Why not? Under what circumstances? Have any American presidents acted like "a fox and a lion"? Name one or two.

Michelangelo Buonarroti, 1475–1564

The musicality of sonnets by Petrarch and his followers was the accepted style of the Italian Renaissance, but Michelangelo followed his own course in his poetry just as he did in sculpting, painting, and architecture. His sonnets were, as he himself said, "unprofessional, rude, and rough." Michelangelo did not consider himself a poet in Petrarchian terms, but he was praised at the time as a poet in his own right. His sonnets, like the personality of their creator, are powerful and unique, and constitute, at their best, the finest lyric Italian poetry of the Renaissance. No knowledge of Michelangelo the sculptor and painter can be complete without knowing the artist as poet. The following two poems were written for Michelangelo's close friend Tommaso de' Cavalieri.

SONNET XXX
(Veggio co' bei vostri occhi)
Michelangelo Buonarroti

With your fair eyes a charming light I see,
    For which my own blind eyes would peer in vain;
    Stayed by your feet the burden I sustain
    Which my lame feet find all too strong for me;
Wingless upon your pinions forth I fly;
    Heavenward your spirit stirreth me to strain;
    E'en as you will, I blush and blanch again,
    Freeze in the sun, burn 'neath a frosty sky.
Your will includes and is the lord of mine;
    Life to my thoughts within your heart is given;
    My words begin to breathe upon your breath:
Like to the moon am I, that cannot shine
    Alone; for lo! our eyes see nought in heaven
    Save what the living sun illumineth.

SONNET XXXII
(S'un casto amor)
Michelangelo Buonarroti

If love be chaste, if virtue conquer ill,
    If fortune bind both lovers in one bond,
    If either at the other's grief despond,
    If both be governed by one life, one will;
If in two bodies one soul triumph still,
    Raising the twain from earth to heaven beyond,
    If Love with one blow and one golden wand
    Have power both smitten breasts to pierce and thrill;
If each the other love, himself forgoing,
    With such delight, such savour, and so well,
    That both to one sole end their wills combine;
If thousands of these thoughts, all thought outgoing,
    Fail the least part of their firm love to tell:
    Say, can mere angry spite this knot untwine?

Michelangelo met Vittoria Colonna, the marquise of Pescara, while he was working on the Last Judgment (1536–1541; see figure 17.43) in the Sistine Chapel. Probably the only woman he ever loved, Vittoria was an astute judge of his work, but valued the man even above his creations. Michelangelo viewed her as "God inside a woman." Her death in 1547 was a painful loss for a seventy-two-year-old artist who was already obsessed with the fear of death and hell. In much of the poetry written for Vittoria, Michelangelo used sculpture as a theme; God had created Adam and that made him a sculptor.

SONNET LXI
(Se'l mie rozzo martello)
After the Death of Vittoria Colonna
Michelangelo Buonarroti

When my rude hammer to the stubborn stone
    Gives human shape, now that, now this, at will,
    Following his hand who wields and guides it still,
    It moves upon another's feet alone:
But that which dwells in heaven, the world doth fill
    With beauty by pure motions of its own;
    And since tools fashion tools which else were none,
    Its life makes all that lives with living skill.
Now, for that every stroke excels the more
    The higher at the forge it doth ascend,
    Her soul that fashioned mine hath sought the skies:
Wherefore unfinished I must meet my end,
    If God, the great artificer, denies
    That aid which was unique on earth before.

Exercises

1. Contrast these sonnets with those of Petrarch, granting that all are in English translation. Compare, for example, the use of verbs. Petrarch uses *shone, flamed, flow, beguile, smile,* and *rising;* Michelangelo uses *fly, stirreth, strain, bind, conquer, pierce, thrill,* and *spite.*
2. Are there similar contrasts in their adjectives and adverbs?

Baldassare Castiglione, 1478–1529

As discussed previously, Renaissance civilization reasserted "the dignity of the human race" (Cicero) and the worth of the individual. Life and human institutions could be shaped to be more efficient and more pleasant, leading to a good life that became, at its best, an art form—the art of gracious living. True ladies and gentlemen had disciplined intellects, good manners, and impeccable taste. Those who aspired to this ideal studied the countless manuals that became available, most especially *The Book of the Courtier* (1528) by Count Baldassare Castiglione (kas-teel-YO-nay; see figure 17.37). Using personalities from his own circle at the court of the Duke of Urbino, Castiglione designed a kind of Platonic dialogue to set up his utopian elite society, a model for civilized people of every age, including our own.

    As was the custom, the evening gathering of the court circle proposed various games, actually civil discourses about subjects agreeable to all. This selection begins in Book I, chapter 12, when Federico Fregoso proposes the game that will be played for four evenings.

THE BOOK OF THE COURTIER
Baldassare Castiglione

"My Lady, I would it were permitted me, as it sometimes is, to assent to another's proposal; since for my part I would readily approve any of the games proposed by these gentlemen, for I really think that all of them would be amusing. But not to break our rule, I say that anyone who wished to praise our court,—laying aside the merit of our lady Duchess, which with her divine virtue would suffice to lift from earth to heaven the meanest souls that are in the world,—might well say without suspicion of flattery, that in all Italy it would perhaps be hard to find so many cavaliers so singularly admirable and so excellent in divers other matters besides the chief concerns of chivalry, as are now to be found here: wherefore if anywhere there be men who deserve to be called good Courtiers and who are able to judge of what pertains to the perfection of Courtiership, it is reasonable to believe that they are here. So, to repress the many fools who by impudence and folly think to win the name of good Courtier, I would that this evening's game might be, that we select some one of the company and give him the task of portraying a perfect Courtier, explaining all the conditions and special qualities requisite in one who deserves this title; and as to those things that shall not appear sound, let everyone be allowed to contradict, as in the schools of the philosophers it is allowed to contradict anyone who proposes a thesis."

    Messer Federico was continuing his discourse still further, when my lady Emilia interrupted him and said:

    "This, if it pleases my lady Duchess, shall for the present be our game."

    My lady Duchess answered:

    "It does please me."

    Then nearly all those present began to say, both to my lady Duchess and among themselves, that this was the finest game that could possibly be; and without waiting for each other's answer, they entreated my lady Emilia to decide who should begin. She turned to my lady Duchess and said:

    "Command, my Lady, him who it best pleases you should have this task; for I do not wish, by selecting one rather than another, to seem to decide whom I think more competent in this matter than the rest, and so do wrong to anyone."

    My lady Duchess replied:

    "Nay, make this choice yourself, and take heed lest by not obeying you give an example to the others, so that they too prove disobedient in their turn."

    13.—At this my lady Emilia laughed and said to Count Ludovico da Canossa:

    "Then not to lose more time, you, Count, shall be the one to take this enterprise after the manner that messer Federico has described; not indeed because we account you so good a Courtier that you know what befits one, but because, if you say everything wrong as we hope you will, the game will be more lively, for everyone will then have something to answer you; while if someone else had this task who knew more than you, it would be impossible to contradict him in anything, because he would tell the truth, and so the game would be tedious."

The Count answered quickly:

"Whoever told the truth, my Lady, would run no risk of lacking contradiction, so long as you were present;" and after some laughter at this retort, he continued: "But truly I would fain escape this burden, it seeming to me too heavy, and I being conscious that what you said in jest is very true; that is, that I do not know what befits a good Courtier: and I do not seek to prove this with further argument, because, as I do not practise the rules of Courtiership, one may judge that I do not know them; and I think my blame may be the less, for sure it is worse not to wish to do well than not to know how. Yet, since it so happens that you are pleased to have me bear this burden, I neither can nor will refuse it, in order not to contravene our rule and your judgment, which I rate far higher than my own."

14.—"I wish, then, that this Courtier of ours should be nobly born and of gentle race; because it is far less unseemly for one of ignoble birth to fail in worthy deeds, than for one of noble birth, who, if he strays from the path of his predecessors, stains his family name, and not only fails to achieve but loses what has been achieved already; for noble birth is like a bright lamp that manifests and makes visible good and evil deeds, and kindles and stimulates to virtue both by fear of shame and by hope of praise. And since this splendour of nobility does not illumine the deeds of the humbly born, they lack that stimulus and fear of shame, nor do they feel any obligation to advance beyond what their predecessors have done; while to the nobly born it seems a reproach not to reach at least the goal set them by their ancestors.

"It is true that, by favour of the stars or of nature, some men are endowed at birth with such graces that they seem not to have been born, but rather as if some god had formed them with his very hands and adorned them with every excellence of mind and body. So too there are many men so foolish and rude that one cannot but think that nature brought them into the world out of contempt or mockery. Just as these can usually accomplish little even with constant diligence and good training, so with slight pains those others reach the highest summit of excellence. And to give you an instance: you see my lord Don Ippolito d'Este, Cardinal of Ferrara, who has enjoyed such fortune from his birth, that his person, his aspect, his words and all his movements are so disposed and imbued with this grace, that—although he is young—he exhibits among the most aged prelates such weight of character that he seems fitter to teach than to be taught; likewise in conversation with men and women of every rank, in games, in pleasantry and in banter, he has a certain sweetness and manners so gracious, that whoso speaks with him or even sees him, must needs remain attached to him forever.

"But to return to our subject: I say that there is a middle state between perfect grace on the one hand and senseless folly on the other; and those who are not thus perfectly endowed by nature, with study and toil can in great part polish and amend their natural defects. Besides his noble birth, then, I would have the Courtier favored in this regard also, and endowed by nature not only with talent and beauty of person and feature, but with a certain grace and (as we say) air that shall make him at first sight pleasing and agreeable to all who see him; and I would have this an ornament that should dispose and unite all his actions, and in his outward aspect give promise of whatever is worthy the society and favour of every great lord."

15.—Here, without waiting longer, my lord Gaspar Pallavicino said:

"I quite agree with what you say as to the good fortune of those endowed from birth with advantages of mind and body: but this is seen as well among the humbly born as among the nobly born, since nature has no such subtle distinctions as these; and often, as I said, the highest gifts of nature are found among the most obscure. Therefore, since this nobility of birth is won neither by talent nor by strength nor by craft, and is rather the merit of our predecessors than our own, it seems to me too extravagant to maintain that if our Courtier's parents be humbly born, all his good qualities are spoiled, and that all those other qualifications that you mentioned do not avail to raise him to the summit of perfection; I mean talent, beauty of feature, comeliness of person, and that grace which makes him always charming to everyone at first sight."

16.—Then Count Ludovico replied:

"I do not deny that the same virtues may rule the low-born and the noble: but (not to repeat what we have said already or the many other arguments that could be adduced in praise of noble birth, which is honoured always and by everyone, it being reasonable that good should beget good), since we have to form a Courtier without flaw and endowed with every praiseworthy quality, it seems to me necessary to make him nobly born, as well for many other reasons as for universal opinion, which is at once disposed in favour of noble birth. For if there be two Courtiers who have as yet given no impression of themselves by good or evil acts, as soon as the one is known to have been born a gentleman and the other not, he who is low-born will be far less esteemed by everyone than he who is high-born, and will need much effort and time to make upon men's minds that good impression which the other will have achieved in a moment and merely by being a gentleman. And how important these impressions are, everyone can easily understand: for in our own case we have seen men present themselves in this house, who, being silly and awkward in the extreme, yet had throughout Italy the reputation of very great Courtiers; and although they were detected and recognized at last, still they imposed upon us for many days, and maintained in our minds that opinion of them which they first found impressed there, although they conducted themselves after the slightness of their worth. We have seen others, held at first in small esteem, then admirably successful at the last.

17.—"But to come to some details, I am of opinion that the principal and true profession of the Courtier ought to be that of arms; which I would have him follow actively above all else, and be known among others as bold and strong, and loyal to whomsoever he serves. And he will win a reputation for these good qualities by exercising them at all times and in all places, since one may never fail in this without severest censure. And just as among women, their fair fame once sullied never recovers its first lustre, so the reputation of a gentleman who bears arms, if once it be in the least tarnished with cowardice or other disgrace, remains forever infamous before the world and full of ignominy. Therefore the more our Courtier excels in this art, the more he will be worthy of praise; and yet I do not deem essential in him that perfect knowledge of things and those other qualities that befit a commander; since this would be too wide a sea, let us be content, as we have said, with perfect loyalty and unconquered courage, and that he be always seen to possess them. For the courageous are often recognized even more in small things than in great; and frequently in perils of importance and where there are many spectators, some men are to be found, who, although their hearts be dead within them, yet, moved by shame or by the presence of others, press forward almost with their eyes shut, and do their duty God knows how. While on occasions of little moment, when they think they can avoid putting themselves in danger without being detected, they are glad to keep safe. But those who, even when they do not expect to be observed or seen or recognized by anyone, show their ardour and neglect nothing, however paltry, that may be laid to their charge,—they have that strength of mind which we seek in our Courtier.

"Therefore let the man we are seeking be very bold, stern, and always among the first, where the enemy are to be seen; and in every other place, gentle, modest, reserved, above all things avoiding ostentation and that impudent self-praise by which men ever excite hatred and disgust in all who hear them."

18.—Then my lord Gaspar replied:

"As for me, I have known few men excellent in anything whatever, who do not praise themselves; and it seems to me that this may well be permitted them; for when anyone who feels himself to be of worth, sees that he is not known to the ignorant by his works, he is offended that his worth should lie buried, and needs must in some way hold it up to view, in order that he may not be cheated of the fame that is the true reward of worthy effort. Thus among the ancient authors, whoever carries weight seldom fails to praise himself. They indeed are insufferable who do this without desert, but such we do not presume our Courtier to be."

The Count then said:

"If you heard what I said, it was impudent and indiscriminate self-praise that I censured: and as you say, we surely ought not to form a bad opinion of a brave man who praises himself modestly, nay we ought rather to regard such praise as better evidence than if it came from the mouth of others. I say, however, that he, who in praising himself runs into no error and incurs no annoyance or envy at the hands of those that hear him, is a very discreet man indeed and merits praise from others in addition to that which he bestows upon himself; because it is a very difficult matter."

Then my lord Gaspar said:

"You must teach us that."

The Count replied:

"Among the ancient authors there is no lack of those who have taught it; but to my thinking, the whole art consists in saying things in such a way that they shall not seem to be said to that end, but let fall so naturally that it was impossible not to say them, and while seeming always to avoid self-praise, yet to achieve it; but not after the manner of those boasters, who open their mouths and let the words come forth haphazard. Like one of our friends a few days ago, who, being quite run through the thigh with a spear at Pisa, said he thought it was a fly that had stung him; and another man said he kept no mirror in his room because, when angry, he became so terrible to look at, that the sight of himself would have frightened him too much."

Everyone laughed at this, but messer Cesare Gonzaga added:

"Why do you laugh? Do you not know that Alexander the Great, on hearing the opinion of a philosopher to be that there was an infinite number of worlds, began to weep, and being asked why he wept, replied, 'Because I have not yet conquered one of them;' as if he would fain have vanquished all? Does not this seem to you a greater boast than that about the fly-sting?"

19.—The Count now paused a little, and messer Bernardo Bibbiena said, laughing:

"I remember what you said earlier, that this Courtier of ours must be endowed by nature with beauty of countenance and person, and with a grace that shall make him so agreeable. Grace and beauty of countenance I think I certainly possess, and this is the reason why so many ladies are ardently in love with me, as you know; but I am rather doubtful as to the beauty of my person, especially as regards these legs of mine, which seem to me decidedly less well proportioned than I should wish: as to my bust and other members however, I am quite content. Pray, now, describe a little more in particular the sort of body that the Courtier is to have, so that I may dismiss this doubt and set my mind at rest."

After some laughter at this, the Count continued:

"Of a certainty that grace of countenance can be truly said to be yours, nor need I cite further example than this to show what manner of thing it is, for we unquestionably perceive your aspect to be most agreeable and pleasing to everyone, albeit the lineaments of it are not very delicate. Still it is of a manly cast and at the same time full of grace; and this characteristic is to be found in many different types of countenance. And of such sort I would have our Courtier's aspect; not so soft and effeminate as is sought by many, who not only curl their hair and pluck their brows, but gloss their faces with all those arts employed by the most wanton and unchaste women in the world; and in their walk, posture and every act, they seem so limp and languid that their limbs are like to fall apart; and they pronounce their words so mournfully that they appear about to expire upon the spot: and the more they find themselves with men of rank, the more they affect such tricks. Since nature has not made them women, as they seem to wish to appear and be, they should be treated not as good women but as public harlots, and driven not merely from the courts of great lords but from the society of honest men.

20.—"Then coming to the bodily frame, I say it is enough if this be neither extremely short nor tall, for both of these conditions excite a certain contemptuous surprise, and men of either sort are gazed upon in much the same way that we gaze on monsters. Yet if we must offend in one of the two extremes, it is preferable to fall a little short of the just measure of height than to exceed it, for besides often being dull of intellect, men thus huge of body are also unfit for every exercise of agility, which thing I should much wish in the Courtier.

21.—"Moreover I deem it very important to know how to wrestle, for it is a great help in the use of all kinds of weapons on foot. Then, both for his own sake and for that of his friends, he must understand the quarrels and differences that may arise, and must be quick to seize an advantage, always showing courage and prudence in all things. Nor should he be too ready to fight except when honour demands it; for besides the great danger that the uncertainty of fate entails, he who rushes into such affairs recklessly and without urgent cause, merits the severest censure even though he be successful. But when he finds himself so far engaged that he cannot withdraw without reproach, he ought to be most deliberate, both in the preliminaries to the duel and in the duel itself, and always show readiness and daring. Nor must he act like some, who fritter the affair away in disputes and controversies, and who, having the choice of weapons, select those that neither cut nor pierce, and arm themselves as if they were expecting a cannonade; and thinking it enough not to be defeated, stand ever on the defensive and retreat,—showing therein their utter cowardice.

22.—"There are also many other exercises, which although not immediately dependent upon arms, yet are closely connected therewith, and greatly foster manly sturdiness; and one of the chief among these seems to me to be the chase, because it bears a certain likeness to war: and truly it is an amusement for great lords and befitting a man at court, and furthermore it is seen to have been much cultivated among the ancients. It is fitting also to know how to swim, to leap, to run, to throw stones, for besides the use that may be made of this in war, a man often has occasion to show what he can do in such matters; whence good esteem is to be won, especially with the multitude, who must be taken into account withal. Another admirable exercise, and one very befitting a man at court, is the game of tennis, in which are well shown the disposition of the body, the quickness and suppleness of every member, and all those qualities that are seen in nearly every other exercise. Nor less highly do I esteem vaulting on horse, which although it be fatiguing and difficult, makes a man very light and dexterous more than any other thing; and besides its utility, if this lightness is accompanied by grace, it is to my thinking a finer show than any of the others. "Our Courtier having once become more than fairly expert in these exercises, I think he should leave the others on one side: such as turning summersaults, rope-walking, and the like, which savour of the mountebank and little befit a gentleman.

"But since one cannot devote himself to such fatiguing exercises continually, and since repetition becomes very tiresome and abates the admiration felt for what is rare, we must always diversify our life with various occupations. For this reason I would have our Courtier sometimes descend to quieter and more tranquil exercises, and in order to escape envy and to entertain himself agreeably with everyone, let him do whatever others do, yet never departing from praiseworthy deeds, and governing himself with that good judgment which will keep him from all folly; but let him laugh, jest, banter, frolic and dance, yet in such fashion that he shall always appear genial and discreet, and that everything he may do or say shall be stamped with grace."

Book III

Book III is devoted to the qualities of the Court Lady, who should be affable, modest, decorous, virtuous, courageous, educated, and intelligent. The following excerpt summarizes the qualities of the ideal Court Lady.

9.—"And since my lord Gaspar further asks what these many things are whereof she ought to have knowledge, and in what manner she ought to converse, and whether her virtues ought to contribute to her conversation,—I say I would have her acquainted with that which these gentlemen wished the Courtier to know. And

of the exercises that we have said do not befit her, I would have her at least possess such understanding as we may have of things that we do not practise; and this in order that she may know how to praise and value cavaliers more or less, according to their deserts.

"And to repeat in a few words part of what has been already said, I wish this Lady to have knowledge of letters, music, painting, and to know how to dance and make merry; accompanying the other precepts that have been taught the Courtier with discreet modesty and with the giving of a good impression of herself. And thus, in her talk, her laughter, her play, her jesting, in short, in everything, she will be very graceful, and will entertain appropriately, and with witticisms and pleasantries befitting her, everyone who shall come before her. And although continence, magnanimity, temperance, strength of mind, prudence, and the other virtues, seem to have little to do with entertainment, I would have her adorned with all of them, not so much for the sake of entertainment (albeit even there they can be of service), as in order that she may be full of virtue, and to the end that these virtues may render her worthy of being honoured, and that her every act may be governed by them."

10.—My lord Gaspar then said, laughing:

"Since you have given women letters and continence and magnanimity and temperance, I only marvel that you would not also have them govern cities, make laws, and lead armies, and let the men stay at home to cook or spin."

The Magnifico replied, also laughing:

"Perhaps even this would not be amiss." Then he added: "Do you not know that Plato, who certainly was no great friend to women, gave them charge over the city, and gave all other martial duties to the men? Do you not believe that there are many to be found who would know how to govern cities and armies as well as men do? But I have not laid these duties on them, because I am fashioning a Court Lady and not a Queen."

Castiglione wrote his book as a tribute to Giubaldo di Montefeltro, Duke of Urbino (1472–1509), who was a real-life courtier. Isabella d'Este, Marchioness of Mantua (1474–1539), epitomized the court lady. Praised by Castiglione and many others for her intellect and moral qualities, she used her fine literary and artistic training to create a court at Mantua that became one of the brightest centers of Italian culture. Her reputation was so widespread that she was known as the "first woman of Europe." She was also called "Machiavelli in skirts," which was probably an acknowledgment of her ability, authority, and influence.

Exercises

1. According to Castiglione, "the principal and true profession of the Courtier ought to be that of arms." What is your reaction to this statement? Why?

2. List the virtues of a Courtier. Which of these still apply in contemporary society? Which do not? How do you account for the changes in attitude?

3. Compare the virtues of a Court Lady with those of a Courtier. How might modern feminists react to these statements? Would they, for example, prefer a Queen to a Court Lady?

François Rabelais, 1494?–1553

An ebullient humanist and an outspoken rebel who detested all regimentation, Rabelais (rab-LAY) insisted that the good life was a natural consequence of freedom combined with a solid classical education. His masterwork, *Gargantua and Pantagruel,* is a long, boisterous fable about two giant-kings, father and son. In the following excerpt Gargantua writes to his son in Paris, where he was receiving, as had his father before him, the best possible education. The style of the letter is eloquent in the manner of Cicero, but the instructions are explicit, for example: "I intend, and will have it so, that thou learn the languages perfectly." This fictional letter summarizes Rabelais's view of an ideal education, an attitude in accord with what was generally expected of the intellectual elite.

GARGANTUA AND PANTAGRUEL

François Rabelais

Chapter VIII.

How Pantagruel, being at Paris, received letters from his father Gargantua, and the copy of them.

Pantagruel studied very hard, as you may well conceive, and profited accordingly; for he had an excellent understanding and notable wit, together with a capacity in memory equal to the measure of twelve oil budgets or butts of olives. And, as he was there abiding one day, he received a letter from his father in manner as followeth.

Most dear Son,—Amongst the gifts, graces, and prerogatives, with which the sovereign psalmator God Almighty hath endowed and adorned human nature at the beginning, that seems to me most singular and excellent, by which we may in a moral state attain to a kind of immortality, and in the course of this transitory life perpetuate our name and seed, which is done by a progeny issued from us in the lawful bonds of matrimony. Whereby that in some measure is restored unto us which was taken from us by the sin of our first parents, to whom it was said that, because they had not obeyed the commandment of God their Creator, they should die, and by death should be brought to nought that so stately frame and psalmature wherein the man at first had been created.

But by this means of seminal propagation there continueth in the children what was lost in the parents, and in the grandchildren that which perished in their fathers, and so successively until the day of the last judgment, when Jesus Christ shall have rendered up to God the Father his kingdom in a peaceable condition, out of all danger and contamination of sin; for then shall cease all generations and corruptions, and the elements leave off their continual transmutations, seeing the so much desired peace shall be attained unto and enjoyed, and that all things shall be brought to their end and period. And, therefore, not without just and reasonable cause do I give thanks to God my Saviour and Preserver, for that he hath enabled me to see my bald old age reflourish in thy youth; for when, at his good pleasure, who rules and governs all things, my soul shall leave this mortal habitation, I shall not account myself wholly to die, but to pass from one place unto another, considering that, in and by that, I continue in my visible image living in world, visiting and conversing with people of honour, and other my good friends, as I was wont to do.

Wherefore, if those qualities of the mind but shine in thee wherewith I am endowed, as in thee remaineth the perfect image of my body, thou wilt be esteemed by all men to be the perfect guardian and treasure of the immortality of our name. But, if otherwise, I shall truly take but small pleasure to see it, considering that the lesser part of me, which is the body, would abide in thee, and the best, to wit, that which is the soul, and by which our name continues blessed amongst men, would be degenerate and bastardized. This I do not speak out of any distrust that I have of thy virtue, which I have heretofore already tried, but to encourage thee yet more earnestly to proceed from good to better. And that which I now write unto thee is not so much that thou shouldst live in this virtuous course, as that thou shouldst rejoice in so living and having lived, and cheer up thyself with the like resolution in time to come; to the prosecution and accomplishment of which enterprise and generous undertaking thou mayst easily remember how that I have spared nothing, but have so helped thee, as if I had had no other treasure in this world, but to see thee once in my life completely well-bred and accomplished as well in virtue, honesty, and valour, as in all liberal knowledge and civility, and so to leave thee after my death, as a mirror representing the person of me thy father, and if not so excellent, and such in deed as I do wish thee, yet such is my desire.

But although my deceased father of happy memory, Grangousier, had bent his endeavors to make me profit in all perfection and political knowledge, and that my labour and study was fully correspondent to, yea, went beyond his desire, nevertheless, as thou mayst well understand, the time then was not so proper and fit for learning as it is at present, neither had I plenty of such good masters as thou hast had. For that time was darksome, obscured with clouds of ignorance, and savouring a little of the infelicity and calamity of the Goths, who had, wherever they set footing, destroyed all good literature, which in my age hath by the divine goodness been restored unto its former light and dignity, and that with such amendment and increase of the knowledge, that now hardly should I be admitted unto the first form of the little grammar-schoolboys—I say, I, who in my youthful days was, and that justly, reputed the most learned of that age.

Now is it that the minds of men are qualified with all manner of discipline, and the old sciences revived which for many ages were extinct. Now is it that the learned languages are to their pristine purity restored, viz., Greek, without which a man may be ashamed to account himself a scholar, Hebrew, Arabic, Chaldean, and Latin. Printing likewise is now in use, so elegant and so correct that better cannot be imagined, although it was found out but in my time by divine inspiration, as by a diabolical suggestion on the other side was the invention of ordnance. All the world is full of knowing men, of most learned schoolmasters, and vast libraries; and it appears to me as a truth, that neither in Plato's time, nor Cicero's, nor Papinian's, there was ever such conveniency for studying as we see at this day there is. Nor must any adventure henceforward to come in public, or present himself in company, that hath not been pretty well polished in the shop of Minerva. I see robbers, hangmen, freebooters, tapsters, ostlers, and such like, of the very rubbish of the people, more learned now than the doctors and preachers were in my time.

What shall I say? The very women and children have aspired to this praise and celestial manner of good learning. Yet so it is that, in the age I am now of, I have been constrained to learn the Greek tongue—which I contemned not like Cato, but had not the leisure in my younger years to attend the study of it—and take much delight in the reading of Plutarch's Morals, the pleasant Dialogues of Plato, the Monuments of Pausanias, and the Antiquities of Athenæus, in waiting on the hour wherein God my Creator shall call me and command me to depart from this earth and transitory pilgrimage. Wherefore, my son, I admonish thee to employ thy youth to profit as well as thou canst, both in thy studies and in virtue. Thou art at Paris, where the laudable examples of many brave men may stir up thy mind to gallant actions, and hast likewise for thy tutor and pedagogue the learned Epistemon, who by his lively and vocal documents may instruct thee in the arts and sciences.

I intend, and will have it so, that thou learn the languages perfectly; first of all, the Greek, as Quintilian will have it; secondly, the Latin; and then the Hebrew, for the Holy Scripture sake; and then the Chaldee and Arabic likewise, and that thou frame thy style in Greek in imitation of Plato, and for the Latin after Cicero. Let there be no history which thou shalt not have ready in thy memory; unto the prosecuting of which design, books of cosmography will be very conducible and help thee much. Of the liberal arts of geometry, arithmetic, and music, I gave thee some taste when thou wert yet little, and not above five or six years old. Proceed further in them, and learn the remainder if thou canst. As for astronomy, study all the rules thereof. Let pass, nevertheless, the divining and judicial astrology, and the art of Lullius, as being nothing else but plain abuses and vanities. As for the civil law, of that I would have thee to know the texts by heart, and then to confer them with philosophy.

Now, in matter of the knowledge of the works of nature, I would have thee to study that exactly, and that so there be no sea, river, nor fountain, of which thou dost not know the fishes; all the fowls of the air; all the several kinds of shrubs and trees, whether in forests or orchards; all sorts of herbs and flowers that grow upon the ground; all the various metals that are hid within the bowels of the earth; together with all the diversity of precious stones that are to be seen in the orient and south parts of the world. Let nothing of all these be hidden from thee. Then fail not most carefully to peruse the books of the Greek, Arabian, and Latin physicians, not despising the Talmudists and Cabalists; and by frequent anatomies get thee the perfect knowledge of the other world, called microcosm, which is man. And at some hours of the day apply thy mind to the study of the Holy Scriptures; first in Greek, the New Testament, with the Epistles of the Apostles; and then the old Testament in Hebrew. In brief, let me see thee an abyss and

bottomless pit of knowledge; for from hence forward as thou growest great and becomest a man, thou must part from this tranquillity and rest of study, thou must learn chivalry, warfare, and the exercises of the field, the better thereby to defend my house and our friends, and to succour and protect them at all their needs against the invasion and assaults of evildoers.

Furthermore, I will that very shortly thou try how much thou has profited, which thou canst not better do than by maintaining publicly theses and conclusions in all arts against all persons whatsoever, and by haunting the company of learned men, both at Paris and otherwhere. But because, as the wise man Solomon saith, Wisdom entereth not into a malicious mind, and that knowledge without conscience is but the ruin of the soul, it behooveth thee to serve, to love, to fear God, and on him to cast all thy thoughts and all thy hope, and by faith formed in charity to cleave unto him, so that thou mayst never be separated from him by thy sins. Suspect the abuses of the world. Set not thy heart upon vanity, for this life is transitory, but the Word of the Lord endureth for ever. Be serviceable to all thy neighbors, and love them as thyself. Reverence thy preceptors: shun the conversation of those whom thou desirest not to resemble, and receive not in vain the graces which God hath bestowed upon thee. And, when thou shalt see that thou hast attained to all the knowledge that is to be acquired in that part, return unto me, that I may see thee and give thee my blessing before I die. My son, the peace and grace of our Lord be with thee. Amen.

Thy Father Gargantua.

From Utopia the 17th day of the month of March.

These letters being received and read, Pantagruel plucked up his heart, took a fresh courage to him, and was inflamed with a desire to profit in his studies more than ever, so that if you had seen him, how he took pains, and how he advanced in learning, you would have said that the vivacity of his spirit amidst the books was like a great fire amongst dry wood, so active it was, vigorous and indefatigable.

Exercises

1. Gargantua writes about his son's education but not his vocation. Why not? What does this imply? Is education more important than what one does for a living? *Should* education be more important than a particular job?
2. Compare the education of Pantagruel with today's typical B.A. in a liberal arts discipline. What happened!? Why? Would *you* aspire to Pantagruel's college education? Why or why not?

Thomas More, 1478–1535

Gargantua wrote his letter from "Utopia," a commonly used term after the appearance of Sir Thomas More's *Utopia* (Gk., "no place"), a novel about an ideal state. Utopianism was in the air. Machiavelli's Prince was an ideal autocrat and Castiglione's Courtier functioned gracefully in an ideal society. Europeans were entranced with the hope and promise of the New World. It was in these newly discovered lands that More (figure 19.2) placed his *Utopia* (1516). See earlier in this chapter for the discussion of this philosophical romance.

UTOPIA

Sir Thomas More

The island of Utopia containeth in breadth in the middle part of it (for there it is broadest) two hundred miles. Which breadth continueth through the most part of the land, saving that by little and little it cometh in, and waxeth narrower towards both the ends. Which fetching about a circuit or compass of five hundred miles, do fashion the whole island like to the new moon. Between these two corners the sea runneth in, dividing them asunder by the distance of eleven miles or thereabouts, and there surmounteth into a large and wide sea, which by reason that the land on every side compasseth it about, and sheltereth it from the winds, is not rough, nor mounteth not with great waves, but almost floweth quietly, not much unlike a great standing pool: and maketh almost all the space within the belly of the land in manner of a haven: and to the great commodity of the inhabitants receiveth in ships towards every part of the land. The forefronts or frontiers of the two corners, what with fords and shelves, and what with rocks be very jeopardous and dangerous. In the middle distance between them both standeth up above the water a great rock, which therefore is nothing perilous because it is in sight. Upon the top of this rock is a fair and a strong tower builded, which they hold with a garrison of men. Other rocks there be that lie hid under the water, and therefore be dangerous. The channels be known only to themselves. And therefore it seldom chanceth that any stranger unless he be guided by a Utopian can come into this haven. Insomuch that they themselves could scarcely enter without jeopardy, but that their way is directed and ruled by certain landmarks standing on the shore. By turning, translating, and removing these marks into other places they may destroy their enemies' navies, be they never so many. The outside of the land is also full of havens, but the landing is so surely defenced, what by nature, and what by workmanship of man's hand, that a few defenders may drive back many armies.

There be in the island fifty-four large and fair cities, or shire towns, agreeing all together in one tongue, in like manners, institutions and laws. They be all set and situate alike, and in all points fashioned alike, as far forth as the place or plot suffereth.

Of these cities they that be nighest together be twenty-four miles asunder. Again there is none of them distant from the next above one day's journey afoot. There come yearly to Amaurote out of every city three old men wise and well experienced, there to entreat and debate, of the common matters of the land. For this city (because it standeth just in the midst of the island, and is therefore most meet for the ambassadors of all parts of the realm) is taken for the chief and head city. The precincts and bounds of the shires be so commodiously appointed out, and set forth for the cities, that never a one of them all hath of any side less than twenty miles of ground, and of some side also much more, as of that part where the cities be of farther distance asunder. None of the cities desire to enlarge the bounds and limits of their shires. For they count themselves rather the good husbands[1] than the owners of their lands. They have in the country in all parts of the shire houses or farms builded, well appointed and furnished with all sorts of instruments and tools belonging to husbandry. These houses be inhabited of the citizens, which come thither to dwell by course. No household or farm in the country hath fewer than forty persons, men and women, besides two bondmen, which be all under the rule and order of the good man, and the good wife of the house, being both very sage and discreet persons. And every thirty farms or families have one head ruler, which is called a philarch, being as it were a head bailiff. Out of every one of these families or farms cometh every year into the city twenty persons which have continued two years before in the country. In their place so many fresh be sent thither out of the city, which of them that have been there a year already, and be therefore expert and cunning in husbandry, shall be instructed and taught. And they the next year shall teach others. This order is used for fear that either scarceness of victuals, or some other like incommodity should chance, through lack of knowledge, if they should be altogether new, and fresh, and unexpert in husbandry. This manner and fashion of yearly changing and renewing the occupiers of husbandry, though it be solemn and customably used, to the intent that no man shall be constrained against his will to continue long in that hard and sharp kind of life, yet many of them have such a pleasure and delight in husbandry, that they obtain a longer space of years. These husbandmen plough and till the ground, and breed up cattle, and make ready wood, which they carry to the city either by land, or by water, as they may most conveniently. They bring up a great multitude of poultry, and that by a marvellous policy. For the hens do not sit upon the eggs; but by keeping them in a certain equal heat they bring life into them, and hatch them. The chickens, as soon as they come out of the shell, follow men and women instead of the hens. They bring up very few horses: nor none, but very fierce ones: and for none other use or purpose, but only to exercise their youth in riding and feats of arms. For oxen be put to all the labour of ploughing and drawing. Which they grant to be not so good as horses at a sudden brunt, and (as we say) at a dead lift, but yet they hold opinion that they will abide and suffer much more labour and pain than horses will. And they think that they be not in danger and subject unto so many diseases, and that they be kept and maintained with much less cost and charge: and finally that they be good for meat, when they be past labour. They sow corn only for bread. For their drink is either wine made of grapes, or else of apples, or pears, or else it is clean water. And many times mead made of honey or liquorice sodden in water, for thereof they have great store. And though they know certainly (for they know it perfectly indeed) how much victuals the city with the whole

---

1. Husbands—caretakers or farmers.

country or shire round about it doth spend: yet they sow much more corn, and breed up much more cattle, than serveth for their own use, and the over-plus they part among their borderers.[2] Whatsoever necessary things be lacking in the country, all such stuff they fetch out of the city: where without any exchange they easily obtain it of the magistrates of the city. For every month many of them go into the city on the holy day. When their harvest day draweth near and is at hand, then the philarchs, which be the head officers and bailiffs of husbandry, send word to the magistrates of the city what number of harvest men is needful to be sent to them out of the city. The which company of harvest men being there ready at the day appointed, almost in one fair day despatcheth all the harvest work.

Of the Cities, and Namely of Amaurote

As for their cities, he that knoweth one of them, knoweth them all: they be all like one to another, as farforth as the nature of the place permitteth. I will describe therefore to you one or other of them, for it skilleth[3] not greatly which: but which rather than Amaurote? Of them all this is the worthiest and of most dignity. For the residue acknowledge it for the head city, because there is the council house. Nor to me any of them all is better beloved, as wherein I lived five whole years together. The city of Amaurote standeth upon the side of a low hill in fashion almost four square. For the breadth of it beginneth a little beneath the top of the hill, and still continueth by the space of two miles, until it come to the river of Anyder. The length of it, which lieth by the river's side, is somewhat more. The river of Anyder riseth twenty-four miles above Amaurote out of a little spring. But being increased by other small floods and brooks that run into it, and among other two somewhat big ones, before the city it is half a mile broad, and farther broader. And sixty miles beyond the city it falleth into the Ocean sea. By all that space that lieth between the sea and the city, and a good sort of miles also above the city, the water ebbeth and floweth six hours together with a swift tide. When the sea floweth in, for the length of thirty miles it filleth all the Anyder with salt water, and driveth back the fresh water of the river. And somewhat further it changeth the sweetness of the fresh water with saltness. But a little beyond that the river waxeth sweet, and runneth forby the city fresh and pleasant. And when the sea ebbeth, and goeth back again, the fresh water followeth it almost even to the very fall into the sea. There goeth a bridge over the river made not of piles of timber, but of stonework with gorgeous and substantial arches at that part of the city that is farthest from the sea: to the intent that ships may go along forby all the side of the city without let.[4] They have also another river which indeed is not very great. But it runneth gently and pleasantly. For it riseth even out of the same hill that the city standeth upon, and runneth down a slope through the midst of the city into Anyder. And because it riseth a little without the city, the Amaurotians have inclosed the head spring of it with strong fences and bulwarks, and so have joined it to the city. This is done to the intent that the water should not be stopped nor turned away, or poisoned, if their enemies should chance to come upon them.

---

2. Borderers—the surrounding countries.

3. Skilleth—matters.

4. Let—hindrance.

From thence the water is derived and brought down in canals of brick divers ways into the lower parts of the city. Where that cannot be done, by reason that the place will not suffer it, there they gather the rain water in great cisterns, which doth them as good service. The city is compassed about with a high and thick wall full of turrets and bulwarks. A dry ditch, but deep, and broad, and overgrown with bushes, briers and thorns, goeth about three sides or quarters of the city. To the fourth side the river itself serveth for a ditch. The streets be appointed and set forth very commodious and handsome, both for carriage, and also against the winds. The houses be of fair and gorgeous building, and in the street side they stand joined together in a long row through the whole street without any partition or separation. The streets be twenty feet broad. On the back side of the houses through the whole length of the street, lie large gardens which be closed in round about with the back part of the streets. Every house hath two doors, one into the street, and a postern door on the back side into the garden. These doors be made with two leaves, never locked nor bolted, so easy to be opened, that they will follow the least drawing of a finger, and shut again by themselves. Every man that will, may go in, for there is nothing within the houses that is private, or any man's own. And every tenth year they change their houses by lot. They set great store by their gardens. In them they have vineyards, all manner of fruit, herbs, and flowers, so pleasant, so well furnished and so finely kept, that I never saw a thing more fruitful, nor better trimmed in any place. Their study and diligence herein cometh not only of pleasure, but also of a certain strife and contention that is between street and street, concerning the trimming, husbanding, and furnishing of their gardens: every man for his own part. And verily you shall not lightly find in all the city anything that is more commodious, either for the profit of the citizens, or for pleasure.

Of the Magistrates

Every thirty families or farms choose them yearly an officer, which is called the philarch. Every ten philarchs with all their 300 families be under an officer which is called the chief philarch. Moreover, as concerning the election of the prince, all the philarchs which be in number 200, first be sworn to choose him whom they think most meet and expedient. Then by a secret election, they name prince, one of those four whom the people before named unto them. For out of the four quarters of the city there be four chosen, out of every quarter one, to stand for the election: which be put up to the council. The prince's office continueth all his lifetime, unless he be deposed or put down for suspicion of tyranny. They choose the chief philarchs yearly, but lightly they change them not. All the other offices be but for one year. The chief philarchs every third day, and sometimes, if need be, oftener, come into the council house with the prince. Their council is concerning the commonwealth. If there be any controversies among the commoners, which be very few, they despatch and end them by-and-by. They take ever two philarchs to them in counsel, and every day a new couple. And it is provided that nothing touching the commonwealth shall be confirmed and ratified unless it have been reasoned of and debated three days in the council, before it be decreed. It is death to have any consultation for the commonwealth out of the council, or the place of the common election. This statute, they say, was made to the intent that the prince and chief philarchs might not easily conspire together to oppress the people by tyranny, and to change the state of the weal public. Therefore matters of great weight and importance be brought to the election house of the philarchs, which open the matter to their families. And afterward, when they have consulted among themselves, they show their device to the council. Sometimes the matter is brought before the council of the whole island. Furthermore this custom also the council useth, to dispute or reason of no matter the same day that it is first proposed or put forth, but to defer it to the next sitting of the council. Because that no man when he hath rashly there spoken what cometh first to his tongue's end, shall then afterwards rather study for reasons wherewith to defend and confirm his first foolish sentence, than for the commodity of the commonwealth: as one rather willing the harm or hindrance of the weal public than any loss or diminution of his own existimation. And as one that would not for shame (which is a very foolish shame) be counted anything overseen in the matter at the first. Who at the first ought to have spoken rather wisely, then hastily, or rashly.

Of Sciences, Crafts, and Occupations

Husbandry is a science common to them all in general, both men and women, wherein they be all expert and cunning. In this they be all instruct even from their youth: partly in schools with traditions and precepts, and partly in the country nigh the city, brought up as it were in playing, not only beholding the use of it, but by occasion of exercising their bodies practising it also. Besides husbandry, which (as I said) is common to them all, every one of them learneth one or other several and particular science, as his own proper craft. That is most commonly either clothworking in wool or flax, or masonry, or the smith's craft, or the carpenter's science. For there is none other occupation that any number to speak of doth use there. For their garments, which throughout all the island be of one fashion (saving that there is a difference between the man's garment and the woman's, between the married and the unmarried) and this one continueth for evermore unchanged, seemly and comely to the eye, no let to the moving and wielding of the body, also fit both for winter and summer: as for these garments (I say) every family maketh their own. But of the other foresaid crafts every man learneth one. And not only the men, but also the women. But the women, as the weaker sort, be put to the easier crafts: they work wool and flax. The other more laboursome sciences be committed to the men. For the most part every man is brought up in his father's craft. For most commonly they be naturally thereto bent and inclined. But if a man's mind stand to any other, he is by adoption put into a family of that occupation, which he doth most fantasy.[5] Whom not only his father, but also the magistrates do diligently look to, that he be put to a discreet and an honest householder. Yea, and if any person, when he hath learned one craft, be desirous to learn also another, he is likewise suffered and permitted.

When he hath learned both, he occupieth whether he will: unless the city have more need of the one, than of the other. The chief and almost the only office of the philarchs is to see and take heed that no man sit idle: but that every one apply his own craft with earnest diligence. And yet for all that, not be wearied from early in the morning, to late in the evening, with continual work, like labouring and toiling beasts.

For this is worse than the miserable and wretched condition of bondmen. Which nevertheless is almost everywhere the life of workmen and artificers, saving in Utopia. For they dividing the day and the night into twenty-four just hours, appoint and assign only six of those hours to work; three before noon, upon the which they go straight to dinner: and after dinner, when they have rested two hours, then they work three and upon that they go to supper. About eight of the clock in the evening (counting one of clock as the first hour after noon) they go to bed: eight hours they give to sleep. All the void time, that is between the hours of work, sleep, and meat, that they be suffered to bestow, every man as he liketh best himself. Not to the intent that they should misspend this time in riot or slothfulness: but being then licensed from the labour of their own occupations, to bestow the time well and thriftly upon some other good science, as shall please them. For it is a solemn custom there, to have lectures daily early in the morning, where to be present they only be constrained that be chosen and appointed to learning. Howbeit a great multitude of every sort of people, both men and women, go to hear lectures, some one and some another, as every man's nature is inclined. Yet, this notwithstanding, if any man had rather bestow this time upon his own occupation (as it chanceth in many, whose minds rise not in the contemplation of any science liberal) he is not letted, nor prohibited, but is also praised and commended, as profitable to the commonwealth. After supper they bestow one hour in play: in summer in their gardens: in winter in their common halls: where they dine and sup. There they exercise themselves in music, or else in honest and wholesome communication. But lest you be deceived, one thing you must look more narrowly upon. For seeing they bestow but six hours in work perchance you may think that the lack of some necessary things hereof may ensue. But this is nothing so. For that small time is not only enough but also too much for the store and abundance of all things that be requisite, either for the necessity, or commodity of life. The which thing you also shall perceive, if you weigh and consider with yourselves how great a part of the people in other countries liveth idle. First almost all women, which be the half of the whole number: or else if the women be anywhere occupied, there most commonly in their stead the men be idle. Beside this how great, and how idle a company is there of priests, and religious men, as they call them? Put thereto all rich men, especially all landed men, which commonly be called gentlemen, and noblemen. Take into this number also their servants: I mean all that flock of stout bragging rush-bucklers. Join to them also sturdy and valiant beggars, cloaking their idle life under the colour of some disease or sickness. And truly you shall find them much fewer than you thought, by whose labour all these things be gotten that men use and live by. Now consider with yourself, of these few that do work, how few be occupied, in necessary works. For where money beareth all the swing, there many vain and superfluous occupations must needs be used, to serve only for riotous superfluity and unhonest pleasure. For the same multitude that now is occupied in work, if they were divided into so few occupations as the necessary use of nature requireth; in so great plenty of things as then of necessity would ensue, doubtless the prices would be too little for the artificers to maintain their livings.

---

5. Fantasy—desire or choose.

But if all these, that be now busied about unprofitable occupations, with all the whole flock of them that live idly and slothfully, which consume and waste every one of them more of these things that come by other men's labour, then two of the workmen themselves do: if all these (I say) were set to profitable occupations, you easily perceive how little time would be enough, yea and too much to store us with all things that may be requisite either for necessity, or for commodity, yea or for pleasure, so that the same pleasure be true and natural. And this in Utopia the thing itself maketh manifest and plain. For there in all the city, with the whole country, or shire adjoining to it scarcely 500 persons of all the whole number of men and women, that be neither too old, nor too weak to work, be licensed from labour. Among them be the philarchs which (though they be by the laws exempt and privileged from labour) yet they exempt not themselves: to the intent they may the rather by their example provoke others to work. The same vacation from labour do they also enjoy, to whom the people persuaded by the commendation of the priests, and secret election of the philarchs, have given a perpetual license from labour to learning. But if any one of them prove not according to the expectation and hope of him conceived, he is forthwith plucked back to the company of artificers. And contrariwise, often it chanceth that a handicraftsman doth so earnestly bestow his vacant and spare hours in learning, and through diligence to profit therein, that he is taken from his handy occupation, and promoted to the company of the learned. Out of this order of the learned be chosen ambassadors, priests, chief philarchs, and finally the prince himself.

Of Warfare

Immediately after that war is once solemnly announced, they procure many proclamations signed with their own common seal to be set up privily at one time in their enemies' land, in places most frequented. In these proclamations they promise great rewards to him that will kill their enemies' prince, and somewhat less gifts, but them very great also, for every head of them, whose names be in the said proclamations contained. They be those whom they count their chief adversaries, next unto the prince. Whatsoever is prescribed unto him that killeth any of the proclaimed persons, that is doubled to him that bringeth any of the same to them alive; yea, and to the proclaimed persons themselves, if they will change their minds and come into them, taking their parts, they proffer the same great rewards with pardon and surety of their lives. Therefore it quickly cometh to pass that they have all other men in suspicion, and be unfaithful and mistrusting among themselves one to another, living in great fear, and in no less jeopardy. For it is well known, that divers times the most part of them (and specially the prince himself) hath been betrayed of them, in whom they put their most hope and trust. So that there is no manner of act nor deed that gifts and rewards do not enforce men unto. And in rewards they keep no measure. But remembering and considering into how great hazard and jeopardy they call them, endeavor themselves to recompense the greatness of the danger with like great benefits. And therefore they promise not only wonderful great abundance of gold, but also lands of great revenues lying in most places among their friends. And their promises they perform faithfully without any fraud or deceit. This custom of buying and selling adversaries among other people is disallowed, as a cruel act of a base and a cowardish mind. But they in this behalf think themselves much praiseworthy, as who like wise men by this means despatch great wars without any battle or skirmish. Yea they count it also a deed of pity and mercy, because that by the death of a few offenders the lives of a great number of innocents, as well of their own men as also of their enemies, be ransomed and saved, which in fighting should have been slain. For they do no less pity the base and common sort of their enemies' people, than they do their own; knowing that they be driven to war against their wills by the furious madness of their princes and heads. If by none of these means the matter go forward as they would have it, then they procure occasions of debate and dissension to be spread among their enemies. As by causing the prince's brother, or some of the noblemen, to hope to obtain the kingdom. If this way prevail not, then they raise up the people that be next neighbors and borderers to their enemies, and them they set in their necks under the colour of some old title of right, such as kings do never lack. To them they promise their help and aid in their war. And as for money they give them abundance. But of their own citizens they send to them few or none. Whom they make so much of and love so entirely, that they would not be willing to change any of them for their adversary's prince. But their gold and silver, because they keep it all for this only purpose, they lay it out frankly and freely; as who[6] should live even as wealthily, if they had bestowed it every penny. Yea, and besides their riches, which they keep at home, that have also an infinite treasure abroad, by reason that (as I said before) many nations be in their debt. Therefore they hire soldiers out of all countries and send them to battle, but chiefly of the Zapoletes. This people is five hundred miles from Utopia eastward. They be hideous, savage and fierce, dwelling in wild woods and high mountains, where they were bred and brought up. They be of an hard nature, able to abide and sustain heat, cold and labour, abhorring from all delicate dainties, occupying no husbandry nor tillage of the ground, homely and rude both in the building of their houses and in their apparel, given unto no goodness, but only to the breeding and bringing up of cattle. The most part of their living is by hunting and stealing. They be born only to war, which they diligently and earnestly seek for. And when they have gotten it, they be wonders glad thereof. They go forth of their country in great companies together, and whosoever lacketh soldiers, there they proffer their service for small wages. This is only the craft that they have to get their living by. They maintain their life by seeking their death. For them with whom they be in wages they fight hardily, fiercely, and faithfully. But they bind themselves for no certain time. But upon this condition they enter into bonds, that the next day they will take part with the other side for greater wages, and the next day after that, they will be ready to come back again for a little more money. There be few wars thereaway, wherein is not a great number of them in both parties. Therefore it daily chanceth that nigh kinsfolk, which were hired together on one part, and there very friendly and familiarly used themselves one with another, shortly after being separate into contrary parts, run one against another enviously and fiercely, and forgetting both kindred and friendship, thrust their swords one in another. And that for none other cause, but that they be hired of contrary princes

---

6. "As who should live," etc.: read this "as people who would live just as richly . . ."

for a little money. Which they do so highly regard and esteem, that they will easily be provoked to change parts for a halfpenny more wages by the day. So quickly they have taken a smack in covetousness. Which for all that is to them no profit. For that they get by fighting, immediately they spend unthriftily and wretchedly in riot. This people fight for the Utopians against all nations, because they give them greater wages than any other nation will. For the Utopians like as they seek good men to use well, so they seek these evil and vicious men to abuse. Whom, when need requireth, with promises of great rewards, they put forth into great jeopardies. From whence the most part of them never cometh again to ask their rewards. But to them that remain alive they pay that which they promised faithfully, that they may be more willing to put themselves in like dangers another time. Nor the Utopians pass not how many of them they bring to destruction. For they believe that they should do a very good deed for all mankind, if they could rid out of the world all that foul stinking den of that most wicked and cursed people.

Of the Religions in Utopia

There be divers kinds of religion not only in sundry parts of the island, but also in divers places of every city. Some worship for God, the sun; some, the moon; some other of the planets. There be that give worship to a man that was once of excellent virtue or of famous glory, not only as God, but also as the chiefest and highest God. But the most and the wisest part (rejecting all these) believe that there is a certain godly power unknown, everlasting, incomprehensible, inexplicable, far above the capacity and reach of man's wit, dispersed throughout all the world, not in bigness, but in virtue and power. Him they call the father of all. To him alone they attribute the beginnings, the increasings, the proceedings, the changes and the ends of all things. Neither they give divine honours to any other than to him. Yea all the other also, though they be in divers opinions, yet in this point they agree all together with the wisest sort, in believing that there is one chief and principal God, the maker and ruler of the whole world: whom they all commonly in their country language call Mithra. But after they heard us speak of the name of Christ, of his doctrine, laws, miracles, and of the no less wonderful constancy of so many martyrs, whose blood willingly shed brought a great number of nations throughout all parts of the world into their sect; you will not believe with how glad minds, they agreed unto the same: whether it were by the secret inspiration of God, or else for that they thought it next unto that opinion, which among them is counted the chiefest. Howbeit I think this was no small help and furtherance in the matter, that they heard us say, that Christ instituted among his, all things common; and that the same community doth yet remain amongst the rightest Christian companies. Verily howsoever it come to pass, many of them consented together in our religion, and were washed in the holy water of baptism. They also which do not agree to Christ's religion, fear no man from it, nor speak against any man that hath received it. Saving that one of our company in my presence was sharply punished. He as soon as he was baptised began against our wills, with more earnest affection than wisdom, to reason of Christ's religion; and began to wax so hot in his matter, that he did not only prefer our religion before all other, but also did utterly despise and condemn all other, calling them profane, and the followers of them wicked and devilish and the children of everlasting damnation. When he had thus long reasoned the matter, they laid hold on him, accused him and condemned him into exile, not as a despiser of religion, but as a seditious person and a raiser up of dissension among the people. For this is one of the ancientest laws among them; that no man shall be blamed for reasoning in the maintenance of his own religion. For King Utopus, even at the first beginning, hearing that the inhabitants of the land were, before his coming thither, at continual dissention and strife among themselves for their religions; as soon as he had gotten the victory, first of all he made a decree, that it should be lawful for every man to favour and follow what religion he would, and that he might do the best he could to bring other to this opinion, so that he did it peaceably, gently, quietly, and soberly, without haste and contentious rebuking and inveighing against other. If he could not by fair and gentle speech induce them unto his opinion yet he should use no kind of violence, and refrain from displeasant and seditious words. To him that would vehemently and fervently in this cause strive and contend was decreed banishment or bondage. This law did King Utopus make not only for the maintenance of peace, which he saw through continual contention and mortal hatred utterly extinguished; but also because he thought this decree should make for the furtherance of religion. Whereof he durst define and determine nothing unadvisedly, as doubting whether God desiring manifold and divers sorts of honour, would inspire sundry men with sundry kinds of religion. And this surely he thought a very unmeet and foolish thing, and a point of arrogant presumption, to compel all other by violence and threatenings to agree to the same that thou believest to be true. Furthermore though there be one religion which alone is true, and all other vain and superstitious, yet did he well foresee (so that the matter were handled with reason, and sober modesty) that the truth of its own power would at the last issue out and come to light. But if contention and debate in that behalf should continually be used, as the worst men be most obstinate and stubborn, and in their evil opinion most constant; he perceived that then the best and holiest religion would be trodden underfoot and destroyed by most vain superstitions, even as good corn is by thorns and weeds overgrown and choked. Therefore all this matter he left undiscussed, and gave to every man free liberty and choice to believe what he would.

Exercises

1. Try making a sketch-map or diagram of Amaurote, the Utopian capital. What considerations or specifications does More give that are unnecessary in a modern American city? Are there any specifications that might improve American cities? Such as?

2. The Zapoletes, Utopia's mercenary soldiers, must have presented some problems to their employers. What might these be? Would *you* be willing to serve as a mercenary soldier? Why or why not?

Michel de Montaigne, 1533–1592

Michel de Montaigne (mon-TAN-y), like Erasmus, remained within the Catholic church, but he was far more interested in the secular world, in the classics, and, most notably, in himself. Montaigne was a rationalist and a skeptic. He was convinced that all knowledge was necessarily incomplete and would always be less than total. Like More, he saw that absolutist beliefs of church or state led to religious strife and warfare. He deliberately withdrew from his troubled world to study Latin and Greek authors and to write, essentially for his own gratification, personal essays on a wide range of subjects that interested him. No other Renaissance writer speaks as openly, clearly, and unpretentiously as does Montaigne. In the foreword to his *Essays* he writes:

> This, reader, is a book without guile. Had I proposed to court the favor of the world, I had set myself out in borrowed beauties; but it was my wish to be seen in my simple, natural and ordinary garb without study or artifice, for it was myself I had to paint.

Elsewhere he wrote, "If the world finds fault with me for speaking too much of myself, I find fault with the world for not even thinking of itself."

Though not included in this text because of limited space, "On Cannibals" is one of the most candid and entertaining of the author's many *Essays*. The cannibals described by Montaigne also live in the New World, in Brazil, but these are real people. More used his Utopians to criticize his own society, but Montaigne is more direct. His cannibals are compared with Europeans and, cannibalism notwithstanding, judged superior:

> We may, then, well call these people barbarians in respect to the rules of reason, but not in respect to ourselves, who, in all sorts of barbarity, exceed them.

William Shakespeare, 1564–1616

Will Shakespeare was not a classical scholar, having, as he said, "little Latin and less Greek." His formal schooling was limited. His plots were mostly borrowed and his plays intended as box-office hits, which they were. Yet he is the supreme figure of Renaissance literature and the most quoted writer in the English language. How can this be? Critics have said that no human being could have written Mozart's music, and the same can be said for the plays of Shakespeare. There is no accounting for genius; we have the music and the plays, and the world is infinitely richer because of them. Shakespeare understood human nature in all its complexity and perversity and was able to translate his perceptions into dramatic speech and action. Whether borrowed, created, or actual historical figures, his characters are unforgettable: Hamlet, King Lear, Falstaff, Macbeth, Romeo, Juliet, Othello, Iago, Portia, Richard III, Cleopatra, and Julius Caesar, to name a few.

The themes in the thirty-seven plays—chronicle-plays, comedies, and tragedies—are timeless, but the flavor of the Renaissance is unmistakable. Like other Renaissance writers, Shakespeare was concerned with the active role of men and women in the lusty and prosperous Elizabethan Age: their passions, problems, and aspirations. Like Machiavelli, he saw people as they really were and the vision was, for Shakespeare if not for Machiavelli, profoundly disturbing. Nevertheless, his pessimistic view of the baser instincts of people was tempered by his belief in their ability to achieve, usually through suffering, some measure of dignity and even nobility.

THE TEMPEST
William Shakespeare

Throughout our study of the Renaissance we have stressed the fundamental contradiction between the ideal of human personality and the reality of human conduct that seemed more animal than human. The problem: how can order be established that will curb the animal aspect while freeing humanity for its nobler possibilities. Shakespeare was one artist who suggests a balance between these two aspects of the personality.

Shakespeare himself had led a turbulent life and had known all sorts of people. In the midst of the vigorous and violent life of Elizabethan England he had carved a name for himself and a fortune that enabled him to retire to his home in Stratford-on-Avon. Here he wrote *The Tempest,* the last play to come entirely from his own hand. We may consider it as a sort of final report on all his experiences, a summary of his insights and discoveries about how people lived their lives.

The play is set in a never-never land, a Mediterranean island where anything and everything can happen. Though removed from ordinary experience, this device enables Shakespeare to enlarge the scope of the play. He can order people and events as he wills them, create Prospero the wise magician, the bestial Caliban, and spritely Ariel. The play is, of course, symbolic. Caliban represents the dark side of human nature that caused so much Renaissance pessimism; Ariel is the blithe spirit that represents the higher nature of human intellect. Prospero may be Shakespeare himself or he may simply be humankind. No matter, he is the agent who must create the balance between opposing forces. He controls the rival spirits of Ariel and Caliban and through them brings balance and order to the mortals whom he brings to his fantastic kingdom. It is he who helps all of them find themselves when no one was his own man. And finally, it is Prospero who returns with them to the land of the living, with a new and higher order established, with the kingly power resting with the young couple, neither of whom had been a party to the long evil history behind them. The king is the young man of action; the queen is the young woman of spirit, educated by Prospero to assume her rightful place in the "brave new world."

CHARACTERS

Alonzo, King of Naples
Sebastian, his brother
Prospero, the right Duke of Milan
Antonio, his brother, the usurping Duke of Milan
Ferdinand, son to the King of Naples
Gonzalo, an honest old councilor
Adrian and Francisco, lords
Caliban, a savage and deformed slave
Trinculo, a jester
Stephano, a drunken butler
Master of a ship
Boatswain
Mariners
Miranda, daughter to Prospero
Ariel, an airy spirit
Iris
Nymphs
Juno } Spirits
Ceres
Reapers }

ACT 1

SCENE 1

[On a ship at sea. A tempestuous noise of thunder and lightning heard.] Enter a SHIPMASTER *and a* BOATSWAIN.

Master:
Boatswain!

Boatswain:
Here, master. What cheer?

Master:
Good,[7] speak to the mariners. Fall to't yarely,[8] or we run ourselves aground. Bestir, Bestir! *[Exit]*

[Enter MARINERS.]

Boatswain:
Heigh, my hearts! Cheerly, cheerly, my hearts! Yare, yare! Take in the topsail! Tend to the master's whistle!—Blow till thou burst thy wind, if room enough![9]

[Enter ALONZO, SEBASTIAN, ANTONIO, FERDINAND, GONZALO, and others.]

Alonzo:
Good boatswain, have care! Where's the master? Play the men!

Boatswain:
I pray now, keep below.

Antonio:
Where is the master, bos'n?

Boatswain:
Do you not hear him! You mar our labor! Keep your cabins; you do assist the storm.

Gonzalo:
Nay, good, be patient.

Boatswain:
When the sea is. Hence! What care these roarers for the name of king? To cabin! Silence! Trouble us not!

---

7. Good fellow.
8. Briskly.
9. If we have enough sea room.

Gonzalo:
Good, yet remember whom thou hast aboard.

Boatswain:
None that I more love than myself. You are a Councilor. If you can command these elements to silence and work the peace of the present, we will not hand a rope more. Use your authority. If you cannot, give thanks you have lived so long, and make yourselves ready in your cabin for the mischance of the hour if it so hap.—Cheerly, good hearts!—Out of our way, I say. *[Exit]*

Gonzalo:
I have great comfort from this fellow. Methinks he hath no drowning mark upon him; his complexion is perfect gallows. Stand fast, good Fate, to his hanging! Make the rope of his destiny our cable, for our own doth little advantage. If he be not born to be hanged, our case is miserable. *[Exeunt]*

[Re-enter BOATSWAIN.]

Boatswain:
Down with the topmast! Yare! Lower, lower! Bring her to try with maincourse! *[A cry within.]* A plague upon this howling! They are louder than the weather or our office.

[Re-enter SEBASTIAN, ANTONIO, and GONZALO.]

Yet again! What do you here? Shall we give o'er and drown? Have you a mind to sink?

Sebastian:
A pox o' your throat, you bawling, blasphemous, incharitable dog!

Boatswain:
Work you then!

Antonio:
Hang, cur, hang, you whoreson, insolent noisemaker! We are less afraid to be drowned than thou are.

Gonzalo:
I'll warrant him for drowning, though the ship were no stronger than a nutshell and as leaky as an unstanched wench.

Boatswain:
Lay her ahold, ahold! Set her two courses! Off to sea again! Lay her off!

[Enter MARINERS, wet.]

Mariners:
All lost! To prayers, to prayers! All lost!

Boatswain:
What, must our mouths be cold?

Gonzalo: *[looking within]*
The King and Prince at prayers! Let's assist them, For our case is as theirs.

Sebastian: I am out of patience.

Antonio:
We are merely cheated of our lives by drunkards. This wide-chapped rascal!—Would thou mightst lie drowning The washing of ten tides!

Gonzalo: He'll be hanged yet.
Though every drop of water swear against it
And gape at wid'st to glut him.

[A confused noise within] Mercy on us!
We split, we split! Farewell, my wife and children!
Farewell, brother! We split, we split, we split!

Antonio:

Let's all sink with the King.

Sebastian: Let's take leave of him.

[Exeunt]

Gonzalo:

Now would I give a thousand furlongs of sea for an acre of
barren ground: long heath, brown furze—anything. The wills
above be done! But I would fain die a dry death. *[Exeunt]*

SCENE 2

[The Island. Before Prospero's cell.]
[Enter PROSPERO *and* MIRANDA.*]*

Miranda:

If by your art, my dearest father, you have
Put the wild waters in this roar, allay them.
The sky, it seems, would pour down stinking pitch
But that the sea, mounting to the welkin's cheek,
Dashes the fire out. O, I have suffered
With those that I saw suffer! A brave vessel,
Who had, no doubt, some noble creature in her,
Dashed all to pieces! O, the cry did knock
Against my very heart! Poor souls, they perished!
Had I been any god of power, I would
Have sunk the sea within the earth or ere
It should the good ship so have swallowed and
The fraughting[10] souls within her.

Prospero: Be collected.

No more amazement. Tell your piteous heart
There's no harm done.

Miranda: O, Woe the day!

Prospero: No harm.

I have done nothing but in care of thee,
Of thee, my dear one, thee, my daughter, who
Art ignorant of what thou art; naught knowing
Of whence I am, nor that I am more better
Than Prospero, master of a full poor cell,
And thy no greater father.

Miranda: More to know

Did never meddle with my thoughts.

Prospero: 'Tis time

I should inform thee farther. Lend thy hand
And pluck my magic garment from me. So.
[Lays down his mantle]
Lie there, my art. Wipe thou thine eyes; have comfort.
The direful spectacle of the wreck, which touched
The very virtue of compassion in thee,
I have with such provision in mine art
So safely ordered that there is no soul—
No, not so much perdition as an hair
Betide to any creature in the vessel
Which thou heard'st cry, which thou saw'st sink. Sit down;
For thou must now know farther.

Miranda: You have often

Begun to tell me what I am, but stopped
And left me to a bootless inquisition,[11]
Concluding, "Stay! Not yet."

Prospero: The hour's now come;

The very minute bids thee ope thine ear,
Obey, and be attentive. Canst thou remember
A time before we came unto this cell?
I do not think thou canst, for then thou wast not
Out[12] three years old.

Miranda: Certainly, sir I can.

Prospero:

By what? By any other house or person?
Of any thing the image tell me, that
Hath kept with thy remembrance.

Miranda: 'Tis far off,

And rather like a dream than an assurance
That my remembrance warrants. Had I not
Four or five women once that tended me?

Prospero:

Thou hadst, and more, Miranda.
But how is it
That this lives in thy mind? What seest thou else
In the dark backward and abysm of time?
If thou rememb'rest aught ere thou cam'st here,
How thou cam'st here thou mayst.

Miranda: But that I do not.

Prospero:

Twelve year since, Miranda, twelve year since,
Thy father was the Duke of Milan and
A prince of power.

Miranda: Sir, are not you my father?

Prospero:

Thy mother was a piece of virtue, and
She said thou wast my daughter; and thy father
Was Duke of Milan, and thou his only heir.
A princess—no worse issued.

Miranda: O the heavens!

What foul play had we that we came from thence?
Or blessed was't we did?

Prospero: Both, both, my girl!

By foul play, as thou say'st, were we heaved thence,
But blessedly holp hither.

Miranda: O, my heart bleeds

To think o' the teen[13] that I have turned you to,
Which is from my remembrance! Please you farther.

Prospero:

My brother and my uncle, called Antonio—
I pray thee mark me, that a brother should
Be so perfidious!—he whom next thyself
Of all the world I loved, and to him put
The manage of my state, as at that time

---

10. Fraughting—composing the freight.

11. Useless inquiry.

12. Fully.

13. Trouble.

Through all the signories it was the first,
And Prospero the prime duke, being so reputed
In dignity, and for the liberal arts
Without a parallel. Those being all my study,
The government I cast upon my brother
And to my state grew stranger, being transported
And rapt in secret studies. The false uncle—
Dost thou attend me?

Miranda: Sir, most heedfully.

Prospero:
Being once perfected how to grant suits,
How to deny them, who to advance, and who
To trash for over-topping, new-created
The creatures that were mine, I say, or changed 'em,
Or else new-formed 'em; having both the key
Of officer and office, set all hearts i' th' state
To what tune pleased his ear, that now he was
The ivy which had hid my princely trunk
And sucked my verdure out on't. Thou attend'st not?

Miranda:
O, good sir, I do!

Prospero: I pray thee mark me.
I, thus neglecting worldly ends, all dedicated
To closeness, and the bettering of my mind
With that which but by being so retired
O'erprozed all popular rate, in my false brother
Awaked an evil nature; and my trust,
Like a good parent, did beget of him
A falsehood in its contrary as great
As my trust was, which had indeed no limit,
A confidence sans bound. He being thus lorded,
Not only with what my revenue yielded
But what my power might else exact, like one
Who having, unto truth, by telling of it,
Made such a sinner of his memory
To credit his own lie, he did believe
He was indeed the Duke, out o' the substitution
And executing the outward face of royalty
With all Perogative. Hence his ambition growing—
Dost thou hear?

Miranda:
Your tale, sir, would cure deafness.

Prospero:
To have no screen between this part he played
And him he played it for, he needs will be
Absolute Milan.[14] Me, poor man, my library
Was dukedom large enough! Of temporal royalties
He thinks me now incapable; confederates
So dry was he for sway, with King of Naples.
To give him annual tribute, do him homage,
Subject his coronet to his crown, and bend
The dukedom yet unbowed (alas poor Milan!)
To most ignoble stooping.

Miranda: O the heavens!

Prospero:
Mark his condition, and the event; then tell me
If this might be a brother.

Miranda: I should sin
To think nobly of my grandmother:
Good wombs have borne bad sons.

Prospero: Now the condition.
This King of Naples, being an enemy
To me inveterate, hearkens my brother's suit;
Which was, that he, in lieu o' the premises
Of homage and I know not how much tribute,
Should presently extirpate me and mine
Out of the dukedom and confer fair Milan,
With all the honors, on my brother. Whereon,
A treacherous army levied, one midnight
Fated to the purpose, did Antonio open
The gates of Milan; and i' the dead of darkness
The ministers for the purpose hurried thence
Me and thy crying self.

Miranda: Alack, for pity!
I, not rememb'ring how I cried out then
Will cry o'er again. It is a hint
That wrings mine eyes to't.

Prospero: Hear a little further,
And then I'll bring thee to the present business
Which now's upon 's; without the which this story
Were most impertinent.

Miranda: Wherefore did they not
That hour destroy us?

Prospero: Well demanded, wench.
My tale provokes that question. Dear, they durst not,
So dear the love my people bore me; nor set
A mark so bloody on the business; but
With colors fairer painted their foul ends.
In few, they hurried us aboard a bark,
Bore us some leagues to sea, where they prepared
A rotten carcass of a boat, not rigged,
Nor tackle, sail, nor mast; the very rats
Instinctively have quit it. There they hoist us
To cry to the sea that roared to us, to sigh
To the winds whose pity, sighing back again,
Did us but loving wrong.

Miranda: Alack, what trouble
Was I then to you!

Prospero: O, a cherubin
Thou wast that did preserve me! Thou didst smile,
Infused with a fortitude from heaven
When I have decked the sea with drops full salt,
Under my burthen groaned, which raised in me
An undergoing stomach[15] to bear up
Against what should ensue.

Miranda: How came we ashore?

Prospero:
By providence divine.

---

14. Duke of Milan.

15. Courage and strength.

Some food we had, and some fresh water, that
A noble Neapolitan, Gonzalo,
Out of his charity, being then appointed
Master of this design, did give us, with
Rich garments, linen, stuffs, and necessaries
Which since have steaded much. So, of his gentleness,
Knowing I loved my books, he furnished me
From mine own library with volumes that
I prize above my dukedom.

Miranda: Would I might
But ever see that man!

Prospero: Now I arise:
Sit still, and hear the last of our sea-sorrow.
Here in this island we arrived, and here
Have I, thy schoolmaster, made thee more profit
Than other princess can, that have more time
For vainer hours, and tutors not so careful.

Miranda:
Heavens thank you for't. And now, I pray you, sir.
For still 'tis beating in my mind, your reason
For raising this sea–storm?

Prospero: Know thus far forth.
By accident most strange, bountiful Fortune,
Now my dear lady, hath mine enemies
Brought to this shore; and by my prescience
I find my zenith[16] doth depend on
A most auspicious star, whose influence
If now I court not, but omit, my fortunes
Will ever after droop. Here cease more questions.
Thou art inclined to sleep. 'Tis a good dullness,
And give it way. I know thou canst not choose.
[Miranda sleeps.]
Come away, servant, come! I am ready now.
Approach my Ariel. Come!
[Enter ARIEL.]

Ariel:
All hail, great master! Grave sir, hail!
I come!
To answer thy best pleasure, be't to fly,
To swim, to dive into the fire, to ride
On the curled clouds. To thy strong bidding task
Ariel and all his quality.

Prospero: Hast thou, spirit,
Performed to point the tempest that I bade thee?

Ariel:
To every article.
I boarded the king's ship. Now on the beak,
Now in the waist, the deck, in every cabin,
I flamed amazement. Sometime I'd divide
And burn in many places; on the topmast,
The yards, and bowsprit, would I flame distinctly,
Then meet and join. Jove's lightnings, the precursors
O' the dreadful thunderclaps, more momentary
And sight–outrunning were not. The fire and cracks
Of sulphurous roaring the most mighty Neptune

Seem to besiege and make his bold waves tremble;
Yea, his dread trident shake.

Prospero: My brave spirit!
Who was so firm, so constant, that this coil[17]
Would not infect his reason?

Ariel: Not a soul
But felt a fever of the mad and played
Some tricks of desperation. All but mariners
Plunged in the foaming brine and quit the vessel,
Then all afire with me. The King's son, Ferdinand,
With hair upstaring, then like reeds not hair,
Was the first man that leapt; cried, 'Hell is empty,
And all the devils are here!'

Prospero: Why, that's my spirit!
But was not this nigh shore?

Ariel: Close by, my master.

Prospero:
But are they, Ariel, safe?

Ariel: Not a hair perished.
On their sustaining garments not a blemish,
But fresher than before; and as thou bad'st me,
In troops I have dispersed them 'bout the isle.
The King's son have I landed by himself,
Whom I left cooling of the air with sighs
In an odd angle[18] of the isle and sitting,
His arms in this sad knot.

Prospero: Of the king's ship
The mariners, say how thou hast disposed,
And all the rest o' the fleet.

Ariel: Safely in harbor
Is the King's ship; in the deep nook where once
Thou call'dst me up at midnight to fetch dew
From the still–vexed Bermoothes, there she's hid;
The mariners all under hatches stowed,
Who, with a charm joined to their suff'red labor,
I have left asleep; and for the rest of the fleet,
Which I dispersed, they all have met again,
And are upon the Mediterranean flote[19]
Bound sadly home for Naples,
Supposing that they saw the King's ship wrecked
And his great person perish.

Prospero: Ariel, thy charge
Exactly is performed; but there's more work.
What is the time o' the day?

Ariel: Past the mid season.

Prospero:
At least two glasses.[20] The time 'twixt six and now
Must by us both be spent preciously.

Ariel:
Is there more toil? Since thou dost give me pains,
Let me remember thee what thou hast promised,
Which is not yet performed me.

---

16. Highest fortune.

17. Turmoil.
18. An out-of-the-way corner.
19. Sea.
20. Two hourglasses. It is two o'clock.

Prospero: How Now? Moody?
What is't thou canst demand?

Ariel: My liberty.

Prospero:
Before the time be out? No more!

Ariel: I prithee,
Remember I have done thee worthy service,
Told thee no lies, make no mistakings, served
Without or grudge or grumblings. Thou didst promise
To bate me a full year.

Prospero: Dost thou forget
From what a torment I did free thee?

Ariel: No.

Prospero:
Thou dost; and think'st it much to tread the ooze
Of the salt deep,
To run upon the sharp wind of the North,
To do me business in the veins o' the earth
When it is baked with frost.

Ariel: I do not, sir.

Prospero:
Thou liest, malignant thing! Hast thou forgot
The foul witch Sycorax, who with age end envy
Was grown into a hoop? Hast thou forgot her?

Ariel:
No, sir.

Prospero:
Thou hast. Where was she born? Speak!
Tell me!

Ariel:
Sir, in Argier.[21]

Prospero: O, was she so? I must
Once in a month recount what thou hast been,
Which thou forget'st. This damned witch Sycorax,
For mischiefs manifold and sorceries terrible
To enter human hearing, from Argier,
Thou know'st was banished. For one thing she did
They would not take her life. Is not this true?

Ariel:
Ay, sir.

Prospero:
This blue-eyed hag was hither brought with child
And here was left by the sailors. Thou, my slave,
As thou report'st thyself, was then her servant;
And, for thou wast a spirit too delicate
To act her earthly and abhorred commands,
Refusing her grand hests,[22] she did confine thee,
By help of her more potent ministers
And in her most unmitigable rage,
Into a cloven pine, within which rift
Imprisoned thou didst painfully remain
A dozen years; within which space she died
And left thee there, where thou didst vent thy groans

As fast as millwheels strike. Then was this island—
Save for the son that she did litter here,
A freckled whelp, hag-born, not honored with
A human shape.

Ariel: Yes, Caliban her son.

Prospero:
Dull thing, I say so! he, that Caliban
Whom now I keep in service. Thou best know'st
What torment I did find thee in. Thy groans
Did make wolves howl and penetrate the breasts
Of ever-angry bears. It was a torment
To lay upon the damned, which Sycorax
Could not again undo. It was mine art,
When I arrived and heard thee, that made gape
The pine and let thee out.

Ariel: I thank thee, master.

Prospero:
If thou murmur'st, I will rend an oak
And peg thee in his knotty entrails till
Thou hast howled away twelve winters.

Ariel: Pardon, master.
I will be correspondent to command
And do my spiriting gently.

Prospero: Do so, and after two days
I will discharge thee.

Ariel: That's my noble master!
What shall I do? Say what! What shall I do?

Prospero:
Go make thyself like a nymph o' the sea. Be subject
To no sight but thine and mine; invisible
To every eyeball else. Go take this shape
And hither come in't. Go! Hence with diligence!
[*Exit* ARIEL.]
Awake, dear heart, awake. Thou hast slept well.
Awake!

Miranda:
The strangeness of your story put heaviness in me.

Prospero: Shake it off. Come on.
We'll visit Caliban, my slave, who never
Yields us kind answer.

Miranda: 'Tis a villain, sir
I do not love to look on.

Prospero: But, as 'tis,
We cannot miss him.[23] He does make our fire,
Fetch in our wood, and serves in offices
That profit us. What ho! Slave! Caliban!
Thou earth, thou! Speak!

Caliban:
[*within*]
There's wood enough within.

Prospero:
Come forth, I say! There's other business for thee.
Come, thou tortoise! When!
[*Re-enter* ARIEL *like a water nymph.*]

---

21. Algiers.
22. Commands.

---

23. Do without.

Fine apparition! My quaint Ariel,
Hark in thine ear.
Ariel:
My lord, it shall be done. [*Exit*]
Prospero:
Thou poisonous slave, got by the devil himself
Upon thy wicked dam, come forth!
[*Enter* CALIBAN.]
Caliban:
As wicked dew as e'er my mother brushed
With raven's feather from unwholesome fen
Drop on you both! A southwest blow on ye
And blister you all o'er.
Prospero:
For this, be sure, tonight thou shalt have cramps,
Side-stitches that shall pen thy breath up; urchins
Shall, for that vast of night that they may work,
All exercise on thee; thou shalt be pinched
As thick as honeycomb, each pinch more stinging
Than bees that made 'em.
Caliban: I must eat my dinner.
This island's mine by Sycorax my mother,
Which thou tak'st from me. When thou camest first,
Thou strokedst me and madest much of me, wouldst give me
Water with berries in't, and teach me how
To name the bigger light and how the less,
That burn by day and night; and then I loved thee
And showed thee all the qualities o' the isle,
The fresh springs, brine-pits, barren place and fertile.
Cursed be I that did so! All the charms
Of Sycorax—toads, beetles, bats, light on you!
For I am all the subjects that you have,
Which first was mine own king; and here you sty me
In this hard rock, whiles you do keep from me
The rest o' the island.
Prospero: Thou most lying slave,
Whom stripes may move, not kindness! I have used thee
Filth as thou art, with human care, and lodged thee
In mine own cell till thou didst seek to violate
The honor of my child.
Caliban:
O ho, O ho! Would't had been done!
Thou didst prevent me; I had peopled else
This isle with Calibans.
Prospero: Abhorred slave,
Which any print of goodness wilt not take,
Being capable of all ill! I pitied thee,
Took pains to make thee speak, taught thee each hour
One thing or other. When thou didst not, savage,
Know thine own meaning but wouldst gabble like
A thing most brutish, I endowed thy purposes
With words that made them known. But thy vile race,
Though thou didst learn, had that in't which good natures
Could not abide to be with; therefore wast thou
Deservedly confined into this rock, who hadst
Deserved more than a prison.

Caliban:
You taught me language, and my profit on't
Is, I know how to curse. The red plague rid[24] you
For learning me your language!
Prospero: Hag-seed, hence!
Fetch us in fuel, and be quick thou'rt best
To answer other business. Shrug'st thou, malice?
If thou neglect'st or dost unwillingly
What I command, I'll rack thee with old cramps,
Fill all thy bones with aches, make thee roar
That beasts shall tremble at thy din.
Caliban: No, pray thee.
[*Aside*] I must obey. His art is of such power,
It would control my dam's god, Setebos,
And make a vassal of him.
Prospero:
So, slave, hence! [*Exit* CALIBAN.]
[*Re-enter* ARIEL, (invisible) *playing and singing;* FERDINAND
        following.]
                            Ariel's Song
Come unto these yellow sands,
        And then take hands.
Curtsied when you have and kissed,
        The wild waves whist,
Foot it featly here and there;
And sweet sprites, the burthen bear.
        Hark, hark!
[*Burthen*[25] dispersedly.] Bow-wow
        The watchdogs bark.
        Bow-wow!
        Hark, hark! I hear
        The strain of strutting chanticleer
            Cry—
        Cock-a-diddle-dowe!
Ferdinand:
Where should this music be? I' th' air or th' earth?
It sounds no more; and, sure, it waits upon
Some god o' the island. Sitting on a bank,
Weeping again the King my father's wreck,
This music crept by me on the waters,
Allaying both their fury and my passion
With its sweet air. Thence I have followed it,
Or it hath drawn me rather; but 'tis gone—
No, it begins again.
[ARIEL *sings*]
Full fathom five thy father lies;
        Of his bones are coral made;
Those are pearls that were his eyes;
        Nothing of him that doth fade
But doth suffer a sea-change
Into something rich and strange.
Sea-nymphs hourly ring his knell—
[*Burthen*] Ding-dong!

---

24. Destroy.

25. The word *Burthen* indicates a refrain or chorus, probably sung
    by invisible spirits.

Ariel:
Hark! Now I hear them—

                                    Ding–dong bell.

Ferdinand:
The ditty does remember my drowned father.
This is no mortal business, nor no sound
That the earth owes.[26] I hear it now above me.

Prospero:
The fringed curtains of thine eye advance[27]
And say what thou seest yond.

Miranda: What, is't a spirit?
Lord, how it looks about! Believe me, sir,
It carries a brave form. But 'tis a spirit.

Prospero:
No, wench. It eats, and sleeps, and hath such senses
As we have such. This gallant which thou seest
Was in the wreck, and but he's somewhat stained
With grief, that's beauty's canker, thou mightst call him
A goodly person. He hath lost his fellows
And strays about to find 'em.

Miranda: I might call him
A thing divine; for nothing natural
I ever saw so noble.

Prospero:
[Aside]   It goes on, I see,
As my soul prompts it. Spirit, fine spirit! I'll free thee
Within two days for this.

Ferdinand: Most sure, the goddess
On whom these airs attend! Vouchsafe my pray'r
May know if you remain upon this island,
And that you will some good instruction give
How I may bear me here. My prime[28] request,
Which I do last pronounce, is, O wonder,
If you be maid or no?

Miranda: No wonder, sir,
But certainly a maid.

Ferdinand: My language! Heavens!
I am the best of them that speak this speech,
Were I but where 'tis spoken.

Prospero: How? The best?
What wert thou if the King of Naples heard thee?

Ferdinand:
A single thing, as I am now, that wonders
To hear thee speak of Naples.[29] He does hear me,
And, that he does, I weep. Myself am Naples,
Who with mine eyes, never since at ebb, beheld
The King my father wrecked.

Miranda: Alack, for mercy!

Ferdinand:
Yes, faith, and all his lords, the Duke of Milan
And his brave son being twain.

Prospero:
[Aside]   The Duke of Milan
And his more braver daughter could control thee,
If now 'twere fit to do't. At the first sight
They have changed eyes. Delicate Ariel,
I'll set thee free for this! [To FERDINAND.] A word, good sir.
I fear you have done yourself some wrong.[30]
    A word!

Miranda:
Why speaks my father so ungently? This
Is the third man that e'er I saw, the first
That e'er I sighed for. Pity move my father
To be inclined my way!

Ferdinand: O, if a virgin,
And your affection not gone forth, I'll make you
The Queen of Naples.

Prospero: Soft, sir; one word more!
[Aside] They are both in either's pow'rs.
    But this swift business
I must uneasy make, lest too light winning
Make the prize light. [To FERDINAND.] One word more!
    I charge thee
That thou attend me. Thou dost here usurp
The name thou owest not, and hast put thyself
Upon this island as a spy, to win it
From me, the lord on 't.

Ferdinand: No, as I am man!

Miranda:
There's nothing ill can dwell in such a temple.
If the ill spirit have so fair a house,
Good things will strive to dwell with 't.

Prospero: Follow me—
Speak not you for him; he's a traitor.—Come!
I'll manacle thy neck and feet together;
Sea water shalt thou drink; thy food shall be
The fresh-brook mussels, withered roots, and husks
Wherein the acorn cradled. Follow!

Ferdinand: No!
I will resist such entertainment till
Mine enemy has more power.
[He draws, and is charmed from moving.]

Miranda: O dear father,
Make not too rash a trial of him, for
He's gentle and not fearful.

Prospero: What, I say,
My foot[31] my tutor?—Put thy sword up, traitor,
Who mak'st a show but dar'st not strike, thy conscience
Is so possessed with guilt. Come from thy ward,[32]
For I can here disarm thee with this stick
And make thy weapon drop.

Miranda: Beseech you, father!

---

26. Owns.
27. Lift up.
28. First and most important.
29. The King of Naples.

30. Made a false claim about yourself.
31. My inferior.
32. Position of defense.

Prospero:
Hence! Hang not on my garments.

Miranda: Sir, have pity.
I'll be his surety.

Prospero: Silence! One word more
Shall make me chide thee, if not hate thee. What,
An advocate for an impostor? Hush!
Thou think'st there is no more such shapes as he,
Having seen but him and Caliban. Foolish wench!
To the most of men this is a Caliban,
And they to him are angels.

Miranda: My affections
Are then most humble. I have no ambition
To see a goodlier man.

Prospero:
Come on, obey!
Thy nerves are in their infancy again
And have no vigor in them.

Ferdinand:
So they are.
My spirits, as in a dream, are all bound up.
My father's loss, the weakness which I feel,
The wreck of all my friends, nor this man's threats
To whom I am subdued, are but light to me,
Might I but through my prison once a day
Behold this maid. All corners else o' the earth
Let liberty make use of. Space enough
Have I in such a prison.

Prospero: [*Aside*]
It works. [*To* FERDINAND.] Come on!
Thou hast done well, fine Ariel. [*To* FERDINAND.]
Follow me!
[*To* ARIEL.] Hark what thou else shalt do me.

Miranda:
Be of comfort.
My father's of a better nature, sir,
Than he appears by speech. This is unwonted
Which now came from him.

Prospero: [*To* ARIEL.]
Thou shalt be as free
As mountain winds; but then exactly do
All points of my command.

Ariel:
To the syllable.

Prospero:
Come, follow! [*To* MIRANDA.] Speak not for him.   [*Exeunt.*]

ACT II

SCENE 1
[*Another part of the island.*]
[*Enter* ALONSO, SEBASTIAN, ANTONIO, GONZALO,
ADRIAN, FRANCISCO *and others.*]

Gonzalo:
Beseech you, sir, be merry. You have cause—
So have we all—of joy, for our escape
Is much beyond our loss. Our hint of woe
Is common. Every day some sailor's wife,
The masters of some merchant,[33] and the merchant,
Have just our theme of woe; but for the miracle,
I mean our preservation, few in millions
Can speak like us. Then wisely, good sir, weigh
Our sorrow with our comfort.

Alonso:
Prithee peace.

Sebastian: [*Aside to Antonio*]
He receives comfort like cold porridge.

Antonio: [*Aside to Sebastian*]
The visitor will not give him o'er so.

Sebastian: [*Aside to Antonio*]
Look, he's winding up the watch of his wit: by-and-by it will strike.

Gonzalo:
Sir—

Sebastian:
One. Tell.

Gonzalo:
When every grief is entertained that offered,
Comes to the entertainer—

Sebastian:
A dollar.

Gonzalo:
Dolour comes to him, indeed. You have spoken truer than you
purposed.

Sebastian:
You have taken it wiselier than I meant you should.

Gonzalo: [*To Alonso*]
Therefore, my lord—

Antonio:
Fie, what a spendthrift is he of his tongue!

Alonso:
I prithee, spare.

Gonzalo:
Well, I have done. But yet—

Sebastian:
He will be talking.

Antonio:
Which, of he or Adrian, for a good wager, first begins to crow?

Sebastian:
The old cock.

Antonio:
The cock'rel.

Sebastian:
Done! The wager?

Antonio:
A laughter.

Sebastian:
A match!

Adrian:
Though this island seem to be desert—

Antonio:
Ha, ha ha! So. You're paid.

---

33. The owners of a merchant ship.

Adrian:
Uninhabitable and almost inaccessible—

Sebastian:
Yet—

Adrian:
Yet—

Antonio:
He could not miss 't.

Adrian:
It must needs be of subtle, tender, and delicate temperance.[34]

Antonio:
Temperance was a delicate wench.

Sebastian:
Ay, and a subtle, as he most learnedly delivered.

Adrian:
The air breathes upon us here most sweetly.

Sebastian:
As if it had lungs, and rotten ones.

Antonio:
Or as 'twere perfumed by a fen.

Gonzalo:
Here is everything advantageous to life.

Antonio:
True—save means to live.

Sebastian:
Of that there's none, or little.

Gonzalo:
How lush and lusty the grass looks! How green!

Antonio:
The ground indeed is tawny.

Sebastian:
With an eye[35] of green in't.

Antonio:
He misses not much.

Sebastian:
No, he doth but mistake the truth totally.

Gonzalo:
But the rarity of it is—which is indeed almost beyond credit—

Sebastian:
As many vouched rarities are.

Gonzalo:
That our garments, being, as they were, drenched in the sea, hold notwithstanding, their freshness and glosses, being rather new-dyed than stained with salt water.

Antonio:
If but one of his pockets would speak, would it not say he lies?

Sebastian:
Ay, or very falsely pocket up his report.

Gonzalo:
Methinks our garments are now as fresh as when we put them on first in Afric, at the marriage of the King's fair daughter Claribel to the King of Tunis.

Sebastian:
'Twas a sweet marriage, and we prosper well in our return.

---

34. Temperature.
35. Tinge.

Adrian:
Tunis was never graced before with such a paragon to their queen.

Gonzalo:
Not since widow Dido's time.

Antonio:
Widow? A pox o' that! How came that widow in? Widow Dido!

Sebastian:
What if he had said widower Aeneas too? Good Lord, how you take it!

Adrian:
Widow Dido said you? You make me study of that. She was of Carthage, not of Tunis.

Gonzalo:
This Tunis, sir, was Carthage.

Adrian:
Carthage?

Gonzalo:
I assure you, Carthage.

Antonio:
His word is more than the miraculous harp.

Sebastian:
He hath raised the wall and houses, too.

Antonio:
What impossible matter will he make easy next?

Sebastian:
I think he will carry this island home in his pocket and give it his son for an apple.

Antonio:
And sowing the kernels of it in the sea, bring forth more islands.

Gonzalo:
Ay!

Antonio:
Why, in good time.

Gonzalo: [*To Alonso*]
Sir, we were talking that our garments seem now as fresh as when we were at Tunis at the marriage of your daughter, who is now Queen.

Antonio:
And the rarest that e'er came there.

Sebastian:
Bate, I beseech you, widow Dido.

Antonio:
O, widow Dido? Ay, widow Dido!

Gonzalo:
Is not, sir, my doublet as fresh as the first day I wore it? I mean in a sort?

Antonio:
That 'sort' was well fished for.

Gonzalo:
When I wore it at your daughter's marriage.

Alonso:
You cram these words into mine ears against
The stomach of my sense. Would I had never
Married my daughter there! For, coming thence,
My son is lost; and, in my rate, she too,
Who is so far from Italy removed
I ne'er again shall see her. O, thou mine heir
Of Naples and of Milan, what strange fish
Hath made his meal on thee!

Sebastian:
Claribel.

Antonio:
She that is Queen of Tunis; she that dwells
Ten leagues beyond man's life; she that from Naples
Can have no note, unless the sun were post—
The man i' the moon's too slow—till newborn chins
Be rough and razorable; she, from whom
We all were sea-swallowed, though some cast again,
And, by that destiny, to perform an act
Whereof what's past is prologue, what to come
In yours and my discharge.

Sebastian:
What stuff is this? How say you?
'Tis true my brother's daughter's Queen of Tunis;
So is she heir of Naples, 'twixt which regions
There is some space.

Antonio:
A space whose ev'ry cubit
Seems to cry out, 'How shall that Claribel
Measure us back to Naples? Keep in Tunis
And let Sebastian wake!' Say this were death
That now hath seized them—why, they were no worse
Than now they are. There be that can rule Naples
As well as he that sleeps; lords that can prate
As amply and unnecessarily
As this Gonzalo. I myself could make
A chough of as deep chat. O, that you bore
The mind that I do! What a sleep were this
For your advancement! Do you understand me?

Sebastian:
Methinks I do.

Antonio:
And how does your content
Tender your own good fortune?

Sebastian:
I remember
You did supplant your brother Prospero.

Antonio:
True.
And look how well my garments sit upon me,
Much feater than before. My brother's servants
Were then my fellows; now they are my men.

Sebastian:
But for your conscience—

Antonio:
Ay, sir, where lies that? If 'twere a kibe,[41]
'Twould put me to my slipper; but I feel not
This deity in my bosom. Twenty consciences
That stand 'twixt me and Milan, candied be they
And melt ere they molest! Here lies your brother,
No better than the earth he lies upon,
If he were that which now he's like—that's dead;
Whom I with this obedient steel, three inches of it,

---

41. Sore heel.

Can lay to bed forever; whiles you, doing thus,
To the perpetual wink for aye might put
This ancient morsel, this Sir Prudence, who
Should not upbraid our course. For all the rest
They'll take suggestion as a cat laps milk;
They'll tell the clock to any business that
We say befits the hour.

Sebastian:
Thy case, dear friend,
Shall be my precedent. As thou got'st Milan,
I'll come by Naples. Draw thy sword. One stroke
Shall free thee from the tribute which thou payest,
And I the King shall love thee.

Antonio:
Draw together;
And when I rear my hand, do you the like,
To fall it on Gonzalo.

Sebastian:
O, but one word!

[*They talk apart.*]

[*Re-enter* ARIEL, *invisible.*]

Ariel:
My master through his art foresees the danger
That you his friend are in, and sends me forth,
For else his project dies, to keep them living.

[*Sings in* GONZALO'S *ear.*]

While you here do snoring lie,
Open-ey'd conspiracy
His time doth take.
If of life you keep a care,
Shake off slumber and beware.

Awake, awake!

Antonio:
Then let us both be sudden.

Gonzalo: [*Awakes.*]
Now, good angels, preserve the King!
[*The others awake.*]

Alonso:
Why, how now? Ho, awake!—Why are you drawn?
Wherefore this ghastly looking?

Gonzalo:
What's the matter?

Sebastian:
Whiles we stood here securing your repose,
Even now, we heard a hollow burst of bellowing
Like bulls, or rather lions. Did 't not wake you?
It struck mine ear most terribly.

Alonso:
I heard nothing.

Antonio:
O, 'twas a din to fright a monster's ear,
To make an earthquake! Sure it was the roar
Of a whole herd of lions!

Alonso:
Heard you this, Gonzalo?

Gonzalo:
Upon mine honor, sir, I heard a humming,
And that a strange one too, which did awake me.
I shaked you, sir, and cried. As mine eyes opened,

I saw their weapons drawn. There was a noise,
That's verily. 'Tis best we stand upon our guard,
Or that we quit this place. Let's draw our weapons.

Alonso:
Lead off this ground, and let's make further search
For my poor son.

Gonzalo:
Heavens keep him from these beasts!
For he is sure i' the island.

Alonso:
Lead away.

Ariel:
Prospero my lord shall know what I have done.
So, King, go safely on to seek thy son.   [*Exeunt.*]

SCENE 2
[*Another part of the island. Enter* CALIBAN *with a burden of wood. A noise of thunder heard.*]

Caliban:
All the infections that the sun sucks up
From bogs, fens, flats on Prospero fall, and make him
By inchmeal a disease! His spirits hear me,
And yet I needs must curse. But they'll nor pinch,
Fright me with urchin-shows, pitch me i' the mire,
Nor lead me, like a firebrand, in the dark
Out of my way, unless he bid 'em; but
For every trifle are they set upon me;
Sometimes like apes that mow[42] and chatter at me,
And after bite me; then like hedgehogs which
Lie tumbling in my barefoot way and mount
Their pricks at my footfall; sometime am I
All wound with adders, who with cloven tongues
Do hiss me into madness.
[*Enter* TRINCULO.]

                                                    Lo, now, lo!
Here comes a spirit of his, and to torment me
For bringing wood in slowly. I'll fall flat;
Perchance he will not mind me. [*Lies down and draws his cloak over him.*]

Trinculo:
Here's neither bush nor shrub to bear off any weather at all, and another storm brewing. I hear it sing i' the wind. Yond same black cloud, yond huge one, looks like a foul bombard[43] that would shed his liquor. If it should thunder as it did before, I know not where to hide my head. Yond same cloud cannot choose but fall by pailfuls. What have we here? A man or a fish? Dead or alive? A fish! He smells like a fish, a very ancient and fishlike smell, a kind of not-of-the-newest poor-John.[44] A strange fish! Were I in England now, as once I was, and had but this fish painted, not a holiday fool there but would give a piece of silver. There would this monster make a man.[45] Any strange beast there makes a man.

---

42. Make faces.
43. A leather wineskin.
44. Dried and salted fish of the cheapest kind.
45. Make a man's fortune.

When they will not give a doit[46] to relieve a lame beggar, they will lay out ten to see a dead Indian. Legged like a man! And his fins like arms! Warm, o' my troth! I do now let loose my opinion, hold it no longer: this is no fish, but an islander that hath lately suffered by a thunderbolt. [*Thunder*] Alas, the storm is come again! My best way is to creep under his gaberdine. There is no other shelter hereabout. Misery acquaints a man with strange bedfellows. I will here shroud till the dregs of the storm be past.
[*Enter* STEPHANO *singing, a bottle in his hand.*]

Stephano:
        I shall no more to sea, to sea;
                Here shall I die ashore.
This is a very scurvy tune to sing at a man's funeral.
Well, here's my comfort.   [*Drinks.*]
[*Sings.*]
The master, the swabber, the boatswain, and I,
        The gunner, and his mate,
Loved Mall, Meg, and Marian, and Margery,
        But none of us cared for Kate.
        For she had a tongue with a tang,
        Would cry to a sailor 'Go hang!'
She loved not the savor of tar nor of pitch,
Yet a tailor might scratch her where'er she did itch.
        Then to sea, boys, and let her go hang!
This is a scurvy tune too; but here's my comfort.   [*Drinks.*]

Caliban:
Do not torment me! O!

Stephano:
    What's the matter? Have we devils here? Do you put tricks upon 's with savages and men of Ind, ha? I have not 'scaped drowning to be afeard now of your four legs; for it hath been said, 'As proper a man as ever went on four legs cannot make him give ground'; and it shall be said so again, while Stephano breathes at nostrils.

Caliban:
    The spirit torments me. O!

Stephano:
    This is some monster of the isle, with four legs who hath got, as I take it, an ague. Where the devil should he learn our language? I will give him some relief if it be but for that. If I can recover him, and keep him tame, and get to Naples with him, he's a present for any emperor that ever trod on neat's leather.

Caliban:
    Do not torment me prithee! I'll bring my wood home faster.

Stephano:
    He's in his fit now and does not talk after the wisest. He shall taste of my bottle. If he have never drunk wine afore, it will go near to remove his fit. If I can recover him and keep him tame, I will not take too much for him; he shall pay for him that hath him, and that soundly.

Caliban:
    Thou dost me yet but little hurt. Thou wilt anon; I know it by thy trembling. Now Prospero works upon thee.

---

46. Farthing.

Stephano:

Come on your ways! Open your mouth! Here is that which will give language to you, cat. Open your mouth! This will shake your shaking, I can tell you, and that soundly. [CALIBAN *drinks*.] You cannot tell who's your friend. Open your chaps again.

Trinculo:

I should know that voice. It should be—but he is drowned, and these are devils. O, defend me!

Stephano:

Four legs and two voices! A most delicate monster! His forward voice now is to speak well of his friend; his backward voice is to utter foul speeches and to detract. If all the wine in my bottle will recover him, I will help his ague. Come! Amen! I will pour some in thy other mouth.

Trinculo:

Stephano!

Stephano:

Doth thy other mouth call me? Mercy, mercy! This is a devil, and no monster. I will leave him; I have no long spoon.

Trinculo:

Stephano! If thou beest Stephano, touch me and speak to me, for I am Trinculo. Be not afeard—thy good friend Trinculo.

Stephano:

If thou beest Trinculo, come forth. I'll pull thee by the lesser legs. If any be Trinculo's legs, these are they. Thou art very Trinculo indeed! How cam'st thou to be the siege[47] of this mooncalf; Can he vent Trinculo?

Trinculo:

I took him to be killed with a thunderstroke. But art thou not drowned, Stephano? I hope now thou art not drowned. Is the storm overblown? I hid me under the dead mooncalf's gaberdine for fear of the storm. And art thou living, Stephano? O Stephano, two Neapolitans scaped!

Stephano:

Prithee do not turn me about. My stomach is not constant.

Caliban: [*Aside*.]

These be fine things, an if they be not sprites.
That's a brave god and bears celestial liquor.
I will kneel to him.

Stephano:

How didst thou scape? How cam'st thou hither? Swear by this bottle how thou cam'st hither. I escaped upon a butt of sack[48] which the sailors heaved o'erboard, by this bottle, which I made of the bark of a tree with mine own hands since I was cast ashore.

Caliban:

I'll swear upon that bottle to be thy true subject, for the liquor is not earthly.

Stephano:

Here! Swear then how thou escap'dst.

Trinculo:

Swam ashore, man, like a duck. I can swim like a duck, I'll be sworn.

---

47. Seat.
48. A Spanish white wine.

Stephano:

Here, kiss the book.[49] Though thou canst swim like a duck, thou art made like a goose.

Trinculo:

O Stephano, hast any more of this!

Stephano:

The whole butt, man. My cellar is in a rock by the seaside, where my wine is hid. How now, mooncalf? How does thine ague?

Caliban:

Hast thou not dropped from heaven?

Stephano:

Out o' th' moon, I do assure thee. I was the Man i' the Moon when time was.

Caliban:

I have seen thee in her, and I do adore thee.
My mistress showed me thee, and thy dog, and thy bush.

Stephano:

Come, swear to that. Kiss the book. I will furnish it anon with new contents. Swear!

Trinculo:

By this good light, this is a very shallow monster! I afeard of him? A very weak monster. The Man i' the Moon? A most poor credulous monster! Well drawn, monster, in good sooth.

Caliban:

I'll show thee every fertile inch o' th' island,
And I will kiss thy foot. I prithee, be my god.

Trinculo:

By this light, a most perfidious and drunken monster!
When god's asleep, he'll rob his bottle.

Caliban:

I'll kiss thy foot. I'll swear myself thy subject.

Stephano:

Come on then. Down, and swear!

Trinculo:

I shall laugh myself to death at this puppy-headed monster. A most scurvy monster! I could find in my heart to beat him!

Stephano:

Come, kiss.

Trinculo:

But that the poor monster's in drink—An abominable monster!

Caliban:

I'll show thee the best springs; I'll pluck thee berries;
I'll fish for thee, and get thee wood enough.
A plague upon the tyrant that I serve!
I'll bear him no more sticks, but follow thee,
Thou wondrous man!

Trinculo:

A most ridiculous monster, to make a wonder of a poor drunkard!

Caliban:

I prithee, let me bring thee where crabs[50] grow;
And I with my long nails will dig thee pignuts,
Show thee a jay's nest, and instruct thee how

---

49. The book is the bottle. Imagine how they kiss the book.
50. Crab-apples.

To snare the nimble marmoset; I'll bring thee
To clust'ring filberts, and sometimes I'll get thee
Young scamels from the rock. Wilt thou go with me?

Stephano:
    I prithee now, lead the way without any more talking.
Triniculo, the King and all our company else being drowned, we
well inherit here. Here, bear my bottle. Fellow Trinculo, we'll fill
him by-and-by again.

Caliban: [*Sings drunkenly.*]
Farewell, master, farewell, farewell!

Trinculo:
A howling monster! A drunken monster!

Caliban:
No more dams I'll make for fish,
Nor fetch in firing
At requiring.
Nor scrape trenchering nor wash dish.
'Ban, 'Ban, Ca-Caliban
Has a new master. Get a new man,
Freedom, hey-day! hey-day, freedom! freedom, hey-day, freedom!

Stephano:
O brave monster! lead the way.   [*Exeunt.*]

ACT III

SCENE 1
[Before Prospero's cell. Enter FERDINAND, *bearing a log.*]

Ferdinand:
There be some sports are painful, and their labor
Delight in them sets off; some kinds of baseness
Are nobly undergone, and most poor matters
Point to rich ends. This my mean task
Would be as heavy to me as odious, but
The mistress which I serve quickens what's dead
And makes my labors pleasures. O, she is
Ten times more gentle than her father's crabbed;
And he's composed of harshness! I must remove
Some thousands of these logs and pile them up,
Upon a sore injunction. My sweet mistress
Weeps when she sees me work, and says such baseness
Had never like executor. I forget;
But these sweet thoughts do even refresh my labors,
Most busy least when I do it.

[*Enter* MIRANDA; *and* PROSPERO (*concealed*).]

Miranda:
Alas, now pray you
Work not so hard! I would the lightning had
Burnt up those logs that you are enjoined to pile!
Pray set it down and rest you. When this burns,
'Twill weep for having wearied you. My father
Is hard at study, pray now rest yourself;
He's safe for these three hours.

Ferdinand:
O most dear mistress,
The sun will set before I shall discharge
What I must strive to do.

Miranda:
If you'll sit down,
I'll bear your logs the while. Pray give me that.
I'll carry it to the pile.

Ferdinand:
No, precious creature,
I had rather crack my sinews, break my back,
Than you should such dishonor undergo
While I sit lazy by.

Miranda:
It would become me
As well as it does you; and I should do it
With much more ease, for my good will is to it
And yours it is against.

Prospero: [*Aside*]
Poor worm, thou art infected! This visitation shows it.

Miranda:
You look wearily.

Ferdinand:
No, noble mistress. 'Tis fresh morning with me
When you are by at night. I do beseech you,
Chiefly that I might set it in my prayers,
What is your name?

Miranda:
Miranda. O my father,
I have broke your hest to say so!

Ferdinand:
Admired Miranda!
Indeed the top of admiration, worth
What's dearest to the world! Full many a lady
I have eyed with best regard, and many a time
The harmony of their tongues hath into bondage
Brought my too diligent ear; for several virtues
Have I liked several women, never any
With so full soul but some defect in her
Did quarrel with the noblest grace she owed,
And put it to the foil;**51** but you, O you,
So perfect and so peerless, are created
Of every creature's best!

Miranda:
I do not know
One of my sex, no woman's face remember,
Save, from my glass, mine own; nor have I seen
More that I may call men than you, good friend,
And my dear father. How features are abroad
I am skill-less of; but, by my modesty,
The jewel in my dower, I would not wish
Any companion in the world but you;
Nor can imagination form a shape
Besides yourself to like of. But I prattle
Something too wildly, and my father's precepts
I therein do forget.

Ferdinand:
I am in my condition
A prince, Miranda—I do think a king
(I would not so!)—and would no more endure
This wooden slavery than to suffer
The flesh fly blow my mouth. Hear my soul speak!

---

51. Defeat.

The very instant that I saw you did
My heart fly to your service, there resides
To make me slave to it; and for your sake
Am I this patient log-man.

Miranda:
Do you love me?

Ferdinand:
O heaven, O earth, bear witness to this sound,
And crown what I profess with kind event
If I speak true! if hollowly, invert
What best is boded me to mischief! I,
Beyond all limit of what else i' the world,
Do love, prize, honor you.

Miranda:
I am a fool
To weep at what I am glad of.

Prospero: [*Aside*]
Fair encounter
Of two most rare affections! Heavens rain grace
On that which breeds between 'em!

Ferdinand:
Wherefore weep you?

Miranda:
At mine unworthiness, that dare not offer
What I desire to give, and much less take
What I shall die to want. But this is trifling,
And all the more it seeks to hide itself
The bigger bulk it shows. Hence, bashful cunning,
And prompt me, plain and holy innocence!
I am your wife if you will marry me,
If not I'll die your maid. To be your fellow
You may deny me, but I'll be your servant
Whether you will or no.

Ferdinand:
My mistress, dearest,
And I thus humble ever!

Miranda:
My husband then?

Ferdinand:
Ay, with a heart as willing
As bondage e'er of freedom.[52] Here's my hand.

Miranda:
And mine, with my heart in't; and now farewell
Till half an hour hence.

Ferdinand:
A thousand thousand![53]

[*Exeunt.*]

Prospero:
So glad of this as they I cannot be,
Who are surprised withal; but my rejoicing
At nothing can be more. I'll to my book;
For yet ere supper time must I perform
Much business appertaining.

[*Exit.*]

SCENE 2

[Another part of the island. Enter CALIBAN, STEPHANO, *and*
TRINCULO.]

Stephano:
Tell not me! When the butt is out, we will drink water, not a drop before. Therefore bear up and board 'em! Servant monster, drink to me.

Trinculo:
Servant monster? The folly of this island! They say there's but five upon this isle. We are three of them. If th' other two be brained like us, the state totters.

Stephano:
Drink, servant monster, when I bid thee. Thy eyes are almost set in thy head.

Trinculo:
Where should they be set else? He were a brave monster indeed if they were set in his tail.

Stephano:
My man-monster hath drowned his tongue in sack. For my part, the sea cannot drown me; I swam, ere I could recover the shore, five-and-thirty leagues off and on. By this light, thou shalt be my lieutenant, monster, or my standard.

Trinculo:
Your lieutenant, if you list; he's no standard.

Stephano:
We'll not run, Monsieur Monster.

Trinculo:
Nor go neither, but you'll lie like dogs, and yet say nothing neither.

Stephano:
Mooncalf, speak once in thy life, if thou beest a good mooncalf.

Caliban:
How does thy honor? Let me lick thy shoe. I'll not serve him; he is not valiant.

Trinculo:
Thou liest, most ignorant monster! I am in case to jostle a constable. Why, thou deboshed fish thou, was there ever man a coward that hath drunk so much sack as I today? Wilt thou tell a monstrous lie, being but half a fish and half a monster?

Caliban:
Lo, how he mocks me! Wilt thou let him, my lord?

Trinculo:
'Lord' quoth he? That a monster should be such a natural![54]

Caliban:
Lo, lo, again! Bite him to death, I prithee.

Stephano:
Trinculo, keep a good tongue in your head. If you prove a mutineer—the next tree! The poor monster's my subject, and he shall not suffer indignity.

Caliban:
I thank my noble lord. Wilt thou be pleased
To hearken once again to the suit I made to thee?

---

52. As a slave ever accepted freedom.
53. A thousand thousand farewells.

54. Idiot.

Stephano:

Marry, will I. Kneel and repeat it; I will stand, and so shall Trinculo.

[*Enter* ARIEL *invisible.*]

Caliban:

As I told thee before, I am subject to a tyrant, a sorcerer, that by his cunning hath cheated me of the island.

Ariel:

Thou liest.

Caliban: [*To* TRINCULO]

Thou liest, thou jesting monkey thou!
I would my valiant master would destroy thee.
I do not lie.

Stephano:

Trinculo, if you trouble him any more in 's tale, by this hand, I will supplant some of your teeth.

Trinculo:

Why, I said nothing.

Stephano:

Mum then, and no more.—Proceed.

Caliban:

I say by sorcery he got this isle;
From me he got it. If thy greatness will
Revenge it on him—for I know thou dar'st,
But this thing dare not—

Stephano:

That's most certain.

Caliban:

Thou shalt be lord of it, and I'll serve thee.

Stephano:

How now shall this be compassed? Canst thou bring me to the party?

Caliban:

Yea, yea, my lord! I'll yield him thee asleep. Where thou mayst knock a nail into his head.

Ariel:

Thou liest, thou canst not.

Caliban:

What a pied ninny's this! Thou scurvy patch!
I do beseech thy greatness give him blows
And take his bottle from him. When that's gone,
He shall drink naught but brine; for I'll not show him
Where the quick freshes are.

Stephano:

Trinculo, run into no further danger. Interrupt the monster one word further and, by this hand, I'll turn my mercy out o'doors and make a stockfish of thee.

Trinculo:

Why, what did I? I did nothing. I'll go farther off.

Stephano:

Didst thou not say he lied?

Ariel:

Thou liest.

Stephano:

Do I so? Take thou that! [*Beats* TRINCULO.] As you like this, give me the lie another time.

Trinculo:

I did not give thee the lie. Out o' your wits, and hearing too? A pox o' your bottle! This can sack and drinking do. A murrain on your monster, and the devil take your fingers!

Caliban:

Ha, ha, ha!

Stephano:

Now forward with your tale.—Prithee, stand further off.

Caliban:

Beat him enough. After a little time I'll beat him too.

Stephano:

Stand farther.—Come, proceed.

Caliban:

Why, as I told thee, 'tis a custom with him
I' th' afternoon to sleep. There thou mayst brain him,
Having first seized his books, or with a log
Batter his skull, or paunch him with a stake,
Or cut his weasand[55] with thy knife. Remember
First to possess his books; for without them
He's but a sot, as I am, nor hath not
One spirit to command. They all do hate him
As rootedly as I. Burn but his books.
He has brave utensils, for so he calls them,
Which, when he has a house, he'll deck withal.
And that most deeply to consider is
The beauty of his daughter; he himself
Calls her a nonpareil; I never saw a woman
But only Sycorax my dam and she,
But she as far surpasseth Sycorax
As great'st does least.

Stephano:

Is it so brave a lass?

Caliban:

Ay, lord she will become thy bed. I warrant,
And bring these forth brave brood.

Stephano:

Monster, I will kill this man. His daughter and I will be king and queen, save our Graces! and Trinculo and thyself shall be viceroys. Dost thou like the plot, Trinculo?

Trinculo:

Excellent.

Stephano:

Give me thy hand. I am sorry I beat thee; but while thou liv'st, keep a good tongue in thy head.

Caliban:

Within this half hour will he be asleep. Wilt thou destroy him then?

Stephano:

Ay, on mine honor.

Ariel:

This will I tell my master.

Caliban:

Thou mak'st me merry; I am full of pleasure.
Let us be jocund. Will you troll the catch
You taught me but whilere?[56]

---

55. Windpipe.

56. A little while ago.

Stephano:

At thy request, monster, I will do reason, any reason. Come on, Trinculo, let us sing.   [*Sings.*]
Flout 'em and scout 'em
And scout 'em and flout 'em!
Thought is free.

Caliban:

That's not the tune.
[ARIEL *plays the tune on a tabor*[57] *and pipe.*]

Stephano:

What is this same?

Trinculo:

This is the tune of our catch, played by the picture of Nobody.

Stephano:

If thou beest a man, show thyself in thy likeness. If thou beest a devil, tak't as thou list.

Trinculo:

O, forgive me my sins!

Stephano:

He that dies pays all debts. I defy thee!—Mercy upon us!

Caliban:

Art thou afeard?

Stephano:

No, monster, not I.

Caliban:

Be not afeard. The isle is full of noises,
Sounds and sweet airs that give delight and hurt not.
Sometimes a thousand twangling instruments
Will hum about mine ears; and sometime voices
That, if I then had waked after long sleep,
Will make me sleep again; and then in dreaming,
The clouds methought would open and show riches
Ready to drop upon me, that, when I waked,
I cried to dream again.

Stephano:

This will prove a brave kingdom to me, where I shall have my music for nothing.

Caliban:

When Prospero is destroyed.

Stephano:

That shall be by-and-by. I remember the story.

Trinculo:

The sound is going away. Let's follow it, and after do our work.

Stephano:

Lead, monster; we'll follow. I would I could see this taborer! He lays it on. Wilt come?

Trinculo:

I'll follow, Stephano.   [*Exeunt.*]

SCENE 3

[*Another part of the island, Enter* ALONSO, SEBASTIAN, ANTONIO, GONZALO, ADRIAN, FRANCISCO, *and others.*]

Gonzalo:

By'r Lakin, I can go no further, sir! My old bones ache. Here's a maze trod indeed. Through forthrights and meanders. By your patience
I needs must rest me.

---

57. A small drum.

Alonso:

Old lord, I cannot blame thee,
Who am myself attached with weariness
To the dulling of my spirits. Sit down and rest.
Even here I will put off my hope, and keep it
No longer for my flatterer. He is drowned
Whom thus we stray to find; and the sea
Mocks our frustrate search on land. Well, let
Him go.

Antonio: [*Aside to* SEBASTIAN]

I am right glad that he's so out of hope.
Do not, for one repulse, forgo the purpose
That you resolved to effect.

Sebastian: [*Aside to* ANTONIO]

The next advantage
Will we take thoroughly.

Antonio:

[*Aside to* SEBASTIAN]
Let it be tonight;
For, now they are oppressed with travel, they
Will not, nor cannot, use such vigilance
As when they are fresh.

Sebastian: [*Aside to* ANTONIO]

I say tonight, no more.

        [*Solemn and strange music*]

Alonso:

What harmony is this? My good friends, hark!

Gonzalo:

Marvelous sweet music?
[PROSPERO *on the top, invisible. Enter several strange Shapes, bringing in a banquet; they dance about it with gentle actions of salutation; and, inviting the King etc. to eat, they depart.*]

Alonso:

Give us kind keepers, heavens!
What were these?

Sebastian:

A living drollery. Now I will believe
That there are unicorns; that in Arabia
There is one tree, the phoenix' throne, one phoenix
At this hour reigning there.

Antonio:

I'll believe both;
And what does else want credit come to me
And I'll be sworn 'tis true. Travelers ne'er did lie,
Though fools at home condemn 'em.

Gonzalo:

If in Naples
I should report this now, would they believe
Me—If I should say I saw such islanders?
For certes these are people of the island,
Who though they are of monstrous shape, yet, note,
Their manners are more gentle-kind than of
Our human generation you shall find
Many—nay almost any.

Prospero: [*Aside*]
Honest lord,
Thou hast said well; for some of you there present
Are worse than devils.
Alonso:
I cannot too much muse
Such shapes, such gesture, and such sound, expressing,
Although they want the use of tongue, a kind
Of excellent dumb discourse.
Prospero: [*Aside*]
Praise in departing.
Francisco:
They vanished strangely.
Sebastian:
No matter, since
They have left their viands behind; for we have stomachs.
Will 't please you taste of what is here?
Alonso:
Not I.
Gonzalo:
Faith, sir, you need not fear. When we were boys,
Who would believe that there were mountaineers
Dewlapped like bulls, whose throats had hanging at 'em
Wallets of flesh? or that there were such men
Whose heads stood in their breasts? which now we find
Each putter-out of five-for-one will bring us
Good warrant of.
Alonso:
I will stand to, and feed;
Although my last, no matter, since I feel
The best is past. Brother, my lord the Duke,
Stand to, and do as we.
[*Thunder and lightning. Enter* ARIEL *like a harpy, claps his wings
upon the table, and with a quaint device the banquet
vanishes.*]
Ariel:
You are three men of sin, whom destiny—
That hath to instrument this lower world
And what is in't—the never-surfeited sea
Hath caus'd to belch up you; and on this island,
Where man doth not inhabit, you 'mongst men
Being most unfit to live, I have made you mad;
And even with such-like valor men hang and drown
Their proper selves.
[ALONSO, SEBASTIAN *etc., draw their swords.*]
                                        You fools! I and my fellows
Are ministers of Fate. The elements,
Of whom your swords are tempered, may as well
Wound the loud winds, or with bemocked-at stabs
Kill the still-closing waters, as diminish
One dowle that's in my plume. My fellow ministers
Are like invulnerable. If you could hurt,
Your swords are not too massy for your strengths
And will not be uplifted. But remember,
For that's my business to you, that you three
From Milan did supplant good Prospero;
Exposed unto the sea, which hath requit it,
Him and his innocent child; for which foul deed
The powers, delaying not forgetting, have

Incensed the seas and shores, yea all the creatures,
Against your peace. Thee of thy son, Alonso,
They have bereft; and do pronounce by me
Ling'ring perdition, worse than any death
Can be at once, shall step by step attend
You and your ways; whose wraths to guard you from,**58**
Which here is this most desolate isle else falls
Upon your heads, is nothing but heart's sorrow
And a clear life ensuing.
[*He vanishes in thunder; then to soft music enter the* SHAPES
*again, and dance with mocks and mows, and carrying out
the table.*]
Prospero:
Bravely the figure of this harpy hast thou
Performed, my Ariel; a grace it had, devouring.
Of my instruction hast thou nothing bated
In what thou hadst to say. So, with good life
And observation strange, my meaner ministers
Their several kinds have done. My high charms work,
And these, mine enemies, are all knit up
In their distractions. They now are in my pow'r;
And in these fits I leave them while I visit
Young Ferdinand, whom they suppose is drowned
And his and mine loved darling.   [*Exit.*]
Gonzalo:
I' the name of something holy, sir, why stand you
In this strange stare?
Alonso:
O, it is monstrous, monstrous!
Methought the billows spoke and told me of it;
The winds did sing it to me; and the thunder,
That deep and dreadful organ pipe, pronounced
The name of Prospero; it did bass**59** my trespass;
Therefore my son i' the ooze is bedded; and
I'll seek him deeper than e'er plummet sounded
And with him there lie mudded.   [*Exit.*]
Sebastian:
But one fiend at a time,
I'll fight their legions o'er!
Antonio:
I'll be thy second.
                              [*Exeunt* SEBASTIAN *and* ANTONIO.]
Gonzalo:
All three of them are desperate.
Their great guilt,
Like poison given to work a great time after,
Now 'gins to bite the spirits. I do beseech you
That are of suppler joints, follow them swiftly
And hinder them from what this ecstasy**60**
May now provoke them to.
Adrian:
Follow, I pray you. [*Exeunt.*]

---

58. This passage means "only repentance and a reformed life will
    deliver you from their wrath."

59. In a bass voice.

60. Madness.

ACT IV

SCENE 1

[*Before Prospero's cell. Enter* PROSPERO, FERDINAND, *and* MIRANDA.]

Prospero:
If I have too austerely punished you,
Your compensation makes amends, for I
Have given you here a third of mine own life,
Or that for which I live; who once again
I tender to thy hand. All thy vexations
Were but my trials of thy love, and thou
Hast strangely stood the test. Here, afore heaven,
I ratify this my rich gift. O Ferdinand,
Do not smile at me that I boast her of,
For thou shalt find she will outstrip all praise
And make it halt behind her.

Ferdinand:
I do believe it.
Against an oracle.

Prospero:
Then, as my gift, and thine own acquisition
Worthily purchased, take my daughter. But
If thou dost break her virgin-knot before
All sanctimonious ceremonies may
With full and holy rite be minist'red,
No sweet aspersion shall the heavens let fall
To make this contract grow; but barren hate,
Sour-eyed disdain, and discord shall bestrew
The union of your bed with weeds so loathly
That you shall hate it both. Therefore take heed,
As Hymen's lamp shall light you!

Ferdinand:
As I hope
For quiet days, fair issue, and long life,
With such love as 'tis now, the murkiest den,
The most opportune place, the strong'st suggestion
Our worser genius can, shall never melt
Mine honor into lust, to take away
The edge of that day's celebration
When I shall think or Phoebus' steeds are foundered
Or Night kept chained below.

Prospero:
Fairly spoke.
Sit then and talk with her; she is thine own.
What Ariel! My industrious servant Ariel!   [*Enter* ARIEL.]

Ariel:
What would my potent master?
Here I am.

Prospero:
Thou and thy meaner fellows your last service
Did worthily perform; and I must use you
In such another trick. Go bring the rabble,[61]
O'er whom I give thee pow'r, here to this place.
Incite them to quick motion, for I must
Bestow upon the eyes of this young couple
Some vanity of mine art. It is my promise,
And they expect it from me.

―――――――

61. Simply the crowd or group.

Ariel:
Presently?

Prospero:
Ay, with a twink.

Ariel:
Before you can say 'Come and Go,'
And breathe twice and cry 'so, so,'
Each one, tripping on his toe,
Will be here with mop and mow.
Do you love me master? No?

Prospero:
Dearly, my delicate Ariel. Do not approach
Till thou dost hear me call.

Ariel:
Well! I conceive. [*Exit.*]

Prospero:
Look thou be true. Do not give dalliance
Too much the rein. The strongest oaths are straw
To the fire i' the blood. Be more abstemious,
Or else good night your vow!

Ferdinand:
I warrant you, sir.
The white cold virgin snow upon my heart
Abates the ardor of my liver.

Prospero:
Well.
Now come, my Ariel! Bring a corollary
Rather than want a spirit. Appear, and pertly!
No tongue! All eyes! Be silent. [*Soft music.*]   [*Enter* IRIS.]

Iris:[62]
Ceres, most bounteous lady, thy rich leas
Of wheat, rye, barley, vetches, oats, and pease;
Thy turfy mountains, where live nibbling sheep,
And flat meads thatched with stover, them to keep;
Thy banks with pioned and twilled brims,
Which spongy April at thy hest betrims
To make cold nymphs chaste crowns; and thy broom groves,
Whose shadow the dismissed bachelor loves,
Being lasslorn; thy pole-clipt vineyard;
And thy sea-marge, sterile and rocky-hard,
Where thou thyself dost air, the Queen o' the Sky.
Whose wat'ry arch and messenger am I,
Bids thee leave these, and with her sovereign grace,
Here on this grass-plot, in this very place,
To come and sport. Her peacocks fly amain.
Approach, rich Ceres, her to entertain.   [*Enter* CERES.]

Ceres:
Hail, many-colored messenger, that ne'er
Dost disobey the wife of Jupiter,
Who, with thy saffron wings, upon my flow'rs
Diffusest honey drops, refreshing show'rs,
And with each end of thy blue bow dost crown
My bosky acres and my unshrubbed down,
Rich scarf to my proud earth! Why hath thy queen
Summoned me hither to this short-grassed green?

―――――――

62. We shall not attempt to render the obscure words into modern English. This whole scene is an interlude in praise of nature and fertility, all in the classical manner.

Iris:
A contract of true love to celebrate
And some donation freely to estate
On the blest lovers.
Ceres:
Tell me, heavenly bow,
If Venus or her son as thou dost know
Do now attend the Queen? Since they did plot
The means that dusky Dis my daughter got,
Her and her blind boy's scandaled company
I have forsworn.
Iris:
Of her society
Be not afraid. I met her Deity
Cutting the clouds towards Paphos, and her son
Dove-drawn with her. Here thought they to have done
Some wanton charm upon this man and maid,
Whose vows are that no bed-right shall be paid
Till Hymen's torch be lighted. But in vain,
Mars's hot minion is returned again.
Her waspish-headed son has broke his arrows,
Swears he will shoot no more, but play with sparrows
And be a boy right out.
Ceres:
Highest queen of state,
Great Juno, comes; I know her by her gait.   [*Enter* JUNO.]
Juno:
How does my bounteous sister? Go with me
To bless this twain, that they may prosperous be
And honored in their issue.
[*They sing.*]
Juno:
Honor, riches, marriage-blessing,
Long continuance, and increasing,
Hourly joys be still upon you!
Juno sings her blessings on you.
Ceres:
Earth's increase, foison plenty,
Barns and garners never empty,
Vines with clust'ring bunches growing,
Plants with goodly burthen bowing;
Spring come to you at the farthest
In the very end of harvest!
Scarcity and want shall shun you,
Ceres' blessing so is on you.
Ferdinand:
This is a most majestic vision, and
Harmonious charmingly. May I be bold
To think these spirits?
Prospero:
Spirits, which by mine art
I have from their confines called to enact
My present fancies.
Ferdinand:
Let me live here ever!
So rare a wond'red father and a wife
Makes this place Paradise.
[JUNO *and* CERES *whisper, and send* IRIS *on employment.*]

Prospero:
Sweet now, silence!
Juno and Ceres whisper seriously.
There's something else to do. Hush, and be mute,
Or else our spell is marred.
Iris:
You nymphs, called Naiads, of the winding brooks,
With your sedged crowns and ever-harmless looks,
Leave your crisp channels, and on this green land
Answer your summons, Juno does command.
Come, temperate nymphs, and help to celebrate
A contract of true love. Be not too late.
                                        [*Enter certain* NYMPHS.]
You sunburned sicklemen, of August weary,
Come hither from the furrow and be merry.
Make holiday. Your rye-straw hats put on,
And these fresh nymphs encounter every one
In country footing.
[*Enter certain* REAPERS, *properly habited. They join with the*
        NYMPHS *in a graceful dance; towards the end whereof*
        PROSPERO *starts suddenly and speaks; after which, to a*
        strange, hollow, and confused noise, they heavily vanish.]
Prospero: [*Aside*]
I had forgot that foul conspiracy
Of the beast Caliban and his confederates
Against my life. The minute of their plot
Is almost come. [*to the Spirits*] Well done!
                                        Avoid![63] No more!
Ferdinand:
This is strange. Your father's in some passion
That works him strongly.
Miranda:
Never till this day
Saw I him touched with anger so distempered.
Prospero:
You do look, my son, in a moved sort,
As if you were dismayed. Be cheerful, sir.
Our revels now are ended. These our actors,
As I foretold you, were all spirits and
Are melted into air, into thin air;
And, like the baseless fabric of this vision,
The cloud-capped towers, the gorgeous palaces,
The solemn temples, the great globe itself,
Yea, all which it inherit, shall dissolve,
And, like this insubstantial pageant faded,
Leave not a rack[64] behind. We are such stuff
As dreams are made on, and our little life
Is rounded with a sleep. Sir, I am vexed.
Bear with my weakness. My old brain is troubled.
Be not disturbed with my infirmity.
If you be pleased, retire into my cell
And there repose. A turn or two I'll walk
To still my beating mind.

---

63. Be gone.
64. Film of cloud.

Ferdinand, Miranda:
We wish your peace.   [*Exeunt.*]
Prospero:
Come with a thought! I thank thee, Ariel. Come. [*Enter* ARIEL.]
Ariel:
Thy thoughts I cleave to. What's thy pleasure?
Prospero:
Spirit,
We must prepare to meet with Caliban.
Ariel:
Ay, my commander. When I presented Ceres,
I thought to have told thee of it, but I feared
Lest I might anger thee.
Prospero:
Say again, where didst thou leave these varlets?
Ariel:
I told you, sir they were redhot with drinking;
So full of valor that they smote the air
For breathing in their faces, beat the ground
For kissing of their feet; yet always bending
Towards their project. Then I beat my tabor;
At which like unbacked colts they pricked their ears,
Advanced their eyelids, lifted up their noses
As they smelt music. So I charmed their ears
That calf-like they my lowing followed through
Toothed briers, sharp furzes, pricking goss,[65] and thorns,
Which ent'red their frail shins. At last I left them
I' the filthy mantled pool beyond your cell.
There dancing up to the chins, that the foul lake
O'erstunk their feet.
Prospero:
This was well done, my bird.
Thy shape invisible retain thou still.
The trumpery in my house, go bring it hither
For stale to catch these thieves.
Ariel:
I go, I go. [*Exit.*]
Prospero:
A devil, a born devil, on whose nature
Nurture can never stick! on whom my pains,
Humanely taken, all, all lost, quite lost!
And as with age his body uglier grows,
So his mind cankers. I will plague them all,
Even to roaring.
[*Enter* ARIEL, *loaded with glistering apparel, etc.*]
Come, hang them on this line.
[*Enter* CALIBAN, STEPHANO, *and* TRINCULO, *all wet.*
      PROSPERO *and* ARIEL *remain, invisible.*]
Caliban:
Pray you, tread softly, that the blind mole may not
Hear a foot fall. We now are near his cell.
Stephano:
    Monster, your fairy, which you say is a harmless fairy, has done
little better than played the Jack with us.

Trinculo:
    Monster, I do smell all horse-piss, at which my nose is in great
indignation.
Stephano:
    So is mine. Do you hear, monster? If I should take a
displeasure against you, look you!
Trinculo:
Thou wert but a lost monster.
Caliban:
Good my lord, give me thy favor still.
Be patient, for the prize I'll bring thee to
Shall hoodwink this mischance. Therefore speak softly.
All's hushed as midnight yet.
Trinculo:
Ay, but to lose our bottles in the pool!
Stephano:
    There is not only disgrace and dishonor in that, monster, but
an infinite loss.
Trinculo:
    That's more to me than my wetting. Yet this is your harmless
fairy, monster.
Stephano:
    I will fetch off my bottle, though I be o'er ears for my labor.
Caliban:
Prithee, my king, be quiet. Seest thou here?
This is the mouth o' the cell. No noise, and enter.
Do that good mischief which may make this island
Thine own for ever, and I, thy Caliban,
For aye thy foot-licker.
Stephano:
    Give me thy hand. I do begin to have bloody thoughts.
Trinculo:
    O King Stephano! O peer! O worthy Stephano, look what a
wardrobe here is for thee!
Caliban:
Let it alone, thou fool! It is but trash.
Trinculo:
    O, ho, monster! we know what belongs to a frippery.[66] O King
Stephano!
Stephano:
    Put off that gown, Trinculo. By this hand, I'll have that gown!
Trinculo:
Thy Grace shall have it.
Caliban:
The dropsy drown this fool! What do you mean
To dote thus on such luggage? Let 's alone,
And do the murder first. If he awake,
From toe to crown he'll fill our skins with pinches,
Make us strange stuff.
Stephano:
    Be you quiet, monster. Mistress line, is not this my jerkin? Now
is the jerkin under the line. Now, jerkin, you are like to lose your
hair and prove a bald jerkin.

---

65. Gorse.

66. Secondhand clothing store.

Trinculo:

Do, do! We steal by line and level, an 't like your Grace.

Stephano:

I thank thee for that jest. Here's a garment for't. Wit shall not go unrewarded while I am king of this country. 'Steal by line and level' is an excellent pass of pate.[67] There's another garment for't.

Trinculo:

Monster, come put some lime upon your fingers, and away with the rest!

Caliban:

I will have none on't. We shall lose our time
And all be turned to barnacles,[68] or to apes
With foreheads villainous low.

Stephano:

Monster, lay-to your fingers. Help to bear this away where my hogshead of wine is, or I'll turn you out of my kingdom! Go to, carry this.

Trinculo:

And this.

Stephano:

Ay, and this.

[*A noise of hunters heard. Enter divers* SPIRITS *in shape of dogs and hounds, hunting them about,* PROSPERO *and* ARIEL *setting them on.*]

Prospero:

Hey, Mountain, hey!

Ariel:

Silver! there it goes, Silver!

Prospero:

Fury, Fury! There, Tyrant, there! Hark, hark!
[CALIBAN, STEPHANO, *and* TRINCULO *are driven out.*]
Go, charge my goblins that they grind their joints
With dry convulsions, shorten up their sinews
With aged cramps, and more pinch-spotted make them
Than pard[69] or cat-o-'mountain.

Ariel:

Hark, they roar!

Prospero:

Let them be hunted soundly. At this hour
Lie at my mercy all mine enemies.
Shortly shall all my labors end, and thou
Shalt have the air at freedom. For a little,
Follow and do me service.   [*Exeunt.*]

ACT V

SCENE 1

[Before Prospero's cell. Enter PROSPERO *in his magic robes, and* ARIEL.]

Prospero:

Now does my project gather to a head.
My charms crack not, my spirits obey, and time
Goes upright with his carriage.[70] How's the day?

---

67. Stroke of foolishness.

68. Geese.

69. Leopard.

70. Burden.

Ariel:

On the sixth hour, at which time, my lord,
You said our work should cease.

Prospero:

I did say so
When first I raised the tempest. Say, my spirit,
How fares the King and 's followers?

Ariel:

Confined together
In the same fashion as you gave in charge,
Just as you left them; all prisoners, sir,
In thy lime-grove which weather-fends your cell.
They cannot budge till your release. The King,
His brother, and yours abide all three distracted;
And the remainder mourning over them,
Brimful of sorrow and dismay, but chiefly
Him that you termed, sir, the good old Lord Gonzalo.
His tears run down his beard like winter's drops
From eaves of reeds. Your charm so strongly works 'em
That if you now beheld them, your affections
Would become tender.

Prospero:

Dost thou think so, spirit?

Ariel:

Mine would, sir, were I human.

Prospero:

And mine shall.
Hast thou, which art but air, a touch, a feeling
Of their afflictions, and shall not myself,
One of their kind, that relish all as sharply
Passion as they, be kindlier moved than thou art?
Though with their high wrongs I am struck to the quick,
Yet with my nobler reason 'gainst my fury
Do I take part. The rarer action is
In virtue than in vengeance. They being penitent,
The sole drift of my purpose doth extend
Not a frown further. Go, release them, Ariel.
My charms I'll break, their senses I'll restore,
And they shall be themselves.

Ariel:

I'll fetch them, sir. [*Exit.*]

Prospero:

Ye elves of hills, brooks, standing lakes, and groves,
And ye that on the sands with printless foot
Do chase the ebbing Neptune, and do fly him
When he comes back; you demi-puppets that
By moonshine do the green sour ringlets make,
Whereof the ewe not bites, and you whose pastime
Is to make midnight mushrooms, that rejoice
To hear the solemn curfew; by whose aid,
Weak masters though ye be, I have bedimmed
The noontide sun, called forth the mutinous winds,
And 'twixt the green sea and the azured vault
Set roaring war. To the dread rattling thunder
Have I given fire and rifted Jove's stout oak
With his own bolt; the strong-based promontory
Have I made shake and by the spurs[71] plucked up

---

71. Roots.

The pine and cedar; graves at my command
Have waked their sleepers, oped, and let 'em forth
By my so potent art. But this rough magic
I here abjure; and when I have required
Some heavenly music which even now I do
To work mine end upon their senses that
This airy charm is for, I'll break my staff,
Bury it certain fathoms in the earth,
And deeper than did ever plummet sound
I'll drown my book.   [*Solemn music.*]
[*Here enters* ARIEL *before; then* ALONSO *with a frantic gesture,
     attended by* GONZALO; SEBASTIAN *and* ANTONIO *in like
     manner, attended by* ADRIAN *and* FRANCISCO. *They all
     enter the circle which* PROSPERO *had made, and there stand
     charmed; which* PROSPERO *observing, speaks.*]
A solemn air, and the best comforter
To an unsettled fancy, cure thy brains,
Now useless, boiled within thy skull! There stand,
For you are spell-stopped.
Holy Gonzalo, honorable man,
Mine eyes ev'n sociable[72] to show of thine
Fall fellowly drops. The charm dissolves apace.
And as the morning steals upon the night,
Melting the darkness, so their rising senses
Begin to chase the ignorant fumes that mantle
Their clearer reason. O good Gonzalo,
My true preserver and a loyal sir
To him thou follow'st, I will pay thy graces
Home both in word and deed! Most cruelly
Didst thou, Alonso, use me and my daughter;
Thy brother was a furtherer in the act.—
Thou art pinched for't now, Sebastian.—Flesh and blood,
You, brother mine, that entertained ambition,
Expelled remorse and nature, who, with Sebastian,
Whose inward pinches therefore are most strong,
Would here have killed your king, I do forgive thee
Unnatural though thou art. Their understanding
Begins to swell, and the approaching tide
Will shortly fill the reasonable[73] shore
That now lies foul and muddy. Not one of them
That yet looks on me or would know me. Ariel,
Fetch me the hat and rapier in my cell.
I will discase[74] me and myself present
As I was sometime Milan. Quickly, spirit!
Thou shalt ere long be free.
[ARIEL *sings and helps to attire him.*]

Ariel:
          Where the bee sucks, there suck I;
          In a cowslip's bell I lie;
          There I couch when owls do cry;
          On the bat's back I do fly
          After summer merrily.
     Merrily, merrily shall I live now
     Under the blossom that hangs on the bough.

---

72. In sympathy.
73. Their power of reason.
74. Take off my robe.

Prospero:
Why, that's my dainty Ariel! I shall miss thee,
But yet thou shalt have freedom. So, so, so.
To the King's ship, invisible as thou art!
There shalt thou find the mariners asleep
Under the hatches. The master and the boatswain
Being awake, enforce them to this place,
And presently, I prithee.

Ariel:
I drink the air before me, and return
Or ere your pulse twice beat.   [*Exit.*]

Gonzalo:
All torment, trouble, wonder, and amazement
Inhabits here. Some heavenly power guide us
Out of this fearful country!

Prospero:
Behold, sir King,
The wronged Duke of Milan, Prospero.
For more assurance that a living prince
Does now speak to thee, I embrace thy body,
And to thee and thy company I bid
A hearty welcome.

Alonso:
Whe'er thou be'st he or no,
Or some enchanted trifle to abuse me,
As late I have been, I not know. Thy pulse
Beats as of flesh and blood; and since I saw thee
The affliction of my mind amends, with which,
I fear, a madness held me. This must crave,
An if this be at all, a most strange story.
Thy dukedom I resign and do entreat
Thou pardon me my wrongs. But how should Prospero
Be living and be here?

Prospero:
First, noble friend,
Let me embrace thine age, whose honor cannot
Be measured or confined.

Gonzalo:
Whether this be
Or be not, I'll not swear.

Prospero:
You do yet taste
Some subtleties o' the isle, that will not let you
Believe things certain. Welcome, my friends all.
[*Aside to* SEBASTIAN *and* ANTONIO.] But you, my brace of lords,
     were I so minded,
I here could pluck His Highness' frown upon you
And justify you traitors. At this time
I will tell no tales

Sebastian: [*Aside.*]
The devil speaks in him.

Prospero:
No.
For you, most wicked sir, whom to call brother
Would even infect my mouth, I do forgive
Thy rankest fault—all of them; and require
My dukedom of thee, which perforce I know
Thou must restore.

Alonso:
If thou beest Prospero,
Give us particulars of thy preservation;
How thou hast met us here, who three hours since
Were wrecked upon this shore; where I have lost
(How sharp the point of this remembrance is!)
My dear son Ferdinand.

Prospero:
I am woe for't, sir.

Alonso:
Irreparable is the loss, and patience
Says it is past her cure.

Prospero:
I rather think
You have not sought her help, of whose soft grace
For the like loss I have her sovereign aid
And rest myself content.

Alonso:
You the like loss?

Prospero:
As great to me as late; and, supportable
To make the dear loss, have I means much weaker
Than you may call to comfort you, for I
Have lost my daughter.

Alonso:
A daughter?
O heavens, that they were living both in Naples,
The King and Queen there! That they were, I wish
Myself were mudded in that oozy bed
Where my son lies. When did you lose your daughter?

Prospero:
In this last tempest. I perceive these lords
At this encounter do so much admire[75]
That they devour their reason, and scarce think
Their eyes do offices of truth, their words
Are natural breath. But, howsoe'er you have
Been justled from your senses, know for certain
That I am Prospero, and that very duke
Which was thrust forth of Milan, who most strangely
Upon this shore, where you were wrecked, was landed
To be the lord on't. No more yet of this,
For 'tis a chronicle of day by day,
Not a relation for a breakfast, nor
Befitting this first meeting. Welcome, sir.
This cell's my court. Here have I few attendants,
And subjects none abroad. Pray you look in.
My dukedom since you have given me again,
I will requite you with as good a thing,
At least bring forth a wonder to content ye
As much as me my dukedom.

[*Here* PROSPERO *discovers* FERDINAND *and* MIRANDA *playing at chess.*]

Miranda:
Sweet lord, you play me false.

Ferdinand:
No, my dearest love,
I would not for the world.

Miranda:
Yes for a score of kingdoms you should wrangle,
And I would call it fair play.

Alonso:
If this prove
A vision of the island, one dear son
Shall I twice lose.

Sebastian:
A most high miracle!

Ferdinand:
Though the seas threaten, they are merciful.
I have cursed them without cause.   [*Kneels.*]

Alonso:
Now all the blessings
Of a glad father compass thee about!
Arise, and say how thou cam'st here.

Miranda:
O wonder!
How many goodly creatures are there here!
How beauteous mankind is! O brave new world
That has such people in't!

Prospero:
'Tis new to thee.

Alonso:
What is this maid with whom thou wast at play?
Your eld'st acquaintance cannot be three hours.
Is she the goddess that hath severed us
And brought us thus together?

Ferdinand:
Sir, she is mortal;
But by immortal providence she's mine.
I chose her when I could not ask my father
For his advice, nor thought I had one. She
Is daughter to this famous Duke of Milan,
Of whom so often I have heard renown
But never saw before; of whom I have
Received a second life; and second father
This lady makes him to me.

Alonso:
I am hers.
But, O, how oddly will it sound that I
Must ask my child forgiveness!

Prospero:
There, sir, stop.
Let us not burthen our remembrance with
A heaviness that's gone.

Gonzalo:
I have inly wept,
Or should have spoke ere this. Look down, you gods,
And on this couple drop a blessed crown!
For it is you that have chalked forth the way
Which brought us hither.

Alonso:
I say amen, Gonzalo.

---

75. Their wonder almost overcomes their reason.

Gonzalo:
Milan thrust from Milan that his issue
Should become kings of Naples? O, rejoice
Beyond a common joy, and set it down
With gold on lasting pillars: In one voyage
Did Claribel her husband find at Tunis,
And Ferdinand her brother found a wife
Where he himself was lost; Prospero his dukedom
In a poor isle; and all of us ourselves
When no man was his own.
Alonso: [*to* FERDINAND *and* MIRANDA]
Give me your hands.
Let grief and sorrow still embrace his heart
That doth not wish you joy.
Gonzalo:
Be it so! Amen!
[*Re-enter* ARIEL, *with the* MASTER *and* BOATSWAIN *amazedly
   following.*]
O, look, sir, look sir! Here is more of us!
I prophesied, if a gallows were on land,
This fellow could not drown. Now, blasphemy,
That swear'st grace o'erboard, not an oath on shore?
Hast thou no mouth by land? What is the news?
Boatswain:
The best news is that we have safely found
Our king and company; the next, our ship,
Which, but three glasses since, we gave out split,
Is tight and yare and bravely rigged as when
We first put out to sea.
Ariel: [*Aside to* PROSPERO.]
Sir, all this service
Have I done since I went.
Prospero: [*Aside to* ARIEL.]
My tricksy spirit!
Alonso:
These are not natural events; they strengthen
From strange to stranger. Say how came you hither?
Boatswain:
If I did think, sir, I were well awake,
I'd strive to tell you. We were dead of sleep
And, how we know not, all clapped under hatches;
Where, but even now with strange and several noises
Of roaring, shrieking, howling, jingling chains,
And more diversity of sounds, all horrible,
We were awaked; straightway at liberty,
Where we, in all her trim, freshly beheld
Our royal, good, and gallant ship, our master
Cap'ring to eye her. On a trice, so please you,
Even in a dream, were we divided from them
And were brought moping hither.
Ariel: [*Aside to* PROSPERO.]
Was't well done?
Prospero: [*Aside to* ARIEL.]
Bravely, my diligence; Thou shalt be free.

Alonso:
This is as strange a maze as e'er men trod,
And there is in this business more than nature
Was ever conduct of. Some oracle
Must rectify our knowledge.

Prospero:
Sir, my liege,
Do not infest your mind with beating on
The strangeness of this business. At picked leisure,
Which shall be shortly, single I'll resolve you,[76]
Which to you shall seem probable, of every
These happened accidents; till when, be cheerful
And think of each thing well. [*Aside to* ARIEL.] Come hither, spirit.
Set Caliban and his companions free.
Untie the spell. [*Exit* ARIEL.] How fares my gracious sir?
There are yet missing of your company
Some few odd lads that you remember not.
[*Re-enter* ARIEL, *driving in* CALIBAN, STEPHANO, *and*
   TRINCULO, *in their stol'n apparel.*]
Stephano:
   Every man shift for all the rest and let no man take care for
himself, for all is but fortune. Coragio, bully-monster, coragio!
Trinculo:
   If these be true spies which I wear in my head, here's a
goodly sight.
Caliban:
O Setebos, these be brave spirits indeed!
How fine my master is! I am afraid
He will chastise me.
Sebastian:
Ha, ha!
What things are these, my Lord Antonio?
Will money buy 'em?
Antonio:
Very like. One of them
Is a plain fish and no doubt marketable.
Prospero:
Mark but the badges[77] of these men, my lords,
Then say if they be true. This misshapen knave,
His mother was a witch, and one so strong
That could control the moon, make flows and ebbs,
And deal in her command without her power.
These three have robbed me, and this demi-devil
(For he's a bastard one) had plotted with them
To take my life. Two of these fellows you
Must know and own; this thing of darkness I
Acknowledge mine.
Caliban:
I shall be pinched to death.
Alonso:
Is not this Stephano, my drunken butler?
Sebastian:
He is drunk now. Where had he wine?
Alonso:
And Trinculo is reeling ripe.
Where should they
Find this grand liquor that hath gilded 'em?
How cam'st thou in this pickle?

---

76. Alone, I'll explain to you.

77. The coats-of-arms; worn on the clothes.

Trinculo:

    I have been in such a pickle, since I saw you last, that I fear me will never out of my bones. I shall not fear fly-blowing.

Sebastian:

Why, how now, Stephano?

Stephano:

O, touch me not! I am not Stephano, but a cramp.

Prospero:

You'd be king o' the isle, sirrah?

Stephano:

I should have been a sore one then.

Alonso:

This is as strange a thing as e'er I looked on.

Prospero:

He is as disproportioned in his manners
As in his shape. Go, sirrah, to my cell;
Take with you your companions. As you look
To have my pardon, trim it handsomely.

Caliban:

Ay, that I will! and I'll be wise hereafter,
And seek for grace. What a thrice-double ass
Was I to take this drunkard for a god
And worship this dull fool!

Prospero:

Go to! Away!

Alonso:

Hence, and bestow your luggage where you found it.

Sebastian:

Or stole it rather.

[*Exeunt* CALIBAN, STEPHANO, *and* TRINCULO.]

Prospero:

Sir, I invite your Highness and your train
To my poor cell, where you shall take your rest
For this one night; which, part of it, I'll waste
With such discourse as, I not doubt, shall make it
Go quick away—the story of my life
And the particular accidents gone by
Since I came to this isle. And in the morn
I'll bring you to your ship, and so to Naples,
Where I have hope to see the nuptial
Of these our dear-beloved solemnized;
And thence retire me to my Milan, where
Every third thought shall be my grave.

Alonso:

I long
To hear the story of your life, which must
Take the ear strangely.

Prospero:

I'll deliver all;
And promise you calm seas, auspicious gales,
And sail so expeditious that shall catch
Your royal fleet far off. [*Aside to* ARIEL.]   My Ariel, chick,
That is thy charge. Then to the elements
Be free, and fare thou well! Please you, draw near.   [*Exeunt.*]

EPILOGUE
[*Spoken by* PROSPERO.]

Now my charms are all o'erthrown,
And what strength I have's mine own,
Which is most faint. Now 'tis true
I must be here confined by you,
Or sent to Naples. Let me not,
Since I have my dukedom got
And pardoned the deceiver, dwell
In this bare island by your spell
But release me from my bands
With the help of your good hands.
Gentle breath of yours my sails
Must fill, or else my project fails,
Which was to please. Now I want
Spirits to enforce, art to enchant,
And my ending is despair
Unless I be relieved by prayer,
Which pierces so that it assaults
Mercy itself, and frees all faults.
As you from crimes would pardoned be,
Let your indulgence set me free.   [*Exit.*]

Finis.

Exercises

1. In reading any piece of literature, the first thing to do is to be sure that you understand the surface meaning and the story. As the first step into this, learn the names of the characters and be able to identify each of them in terms of what they do or have done.

   a. Scene 1 presents the scene of the shipwreck. In Scene 2 what do we learn about the cause of the storm and the fate of the ship and all the people on it?

   b. Also in Scene 2, what are the specific facts that we learn about Prospero's history before he came to the island?

   c. And finally, in Scene 2, what happens in the meeting between Ferdinand and Miranda? As you read this, try to imagine to whom each character is speaking, and the tone of voice in which the speech should be spoken, for the tone will indicate the feelings and emotions of the speaker and add much to the meaning of the play as a whole.

   d. In Act II, Scene 1, we get our first glimpse of the group of courtiers on the island. How would you sum up the character of each one? What evidence do you have for your belief?

   e. What is the plot that Antonio and Sebastian make? At the end of the scene, what happens to their scheme?

   f. In Act II, Scene 2, we encounter another group on the island. What did Stephano bring with him from the supposed shipwreck? And what happens when Caliban is invited to "kiss the book"? What plot does Caliban propose to Stephano and Trinculo?

   g. In Act III we have three scenes, each dealing with one of the groups of shipwrecked people. How far does each of their plots progress, and to what extent is Prospero controlling each group?

h. Act IV brings the stories of two of the groups to a temporary halt. What happens to each?

i. Finally in Act V, balance is restored, and each person in the play finds his proper place in life. What is the conclusion for each person or group of persons?

2. In the introductory chapters we have spoken about various forces and influences that shaped the Renaissance. List evidences in this play of each of the following:

a. The Machiavellian idea of the nature of the ruler, and of human nature in general.

b. Humanism.

c. The utopian ideal as we saw it in More's *Utopia.*

d. The idea of the *right* king as the only source of health and proper discipline within a state.

e. The opposite poles of the good and evil nature of men and women. In this connection, what use should be made of each, or can the evil nature of human beings be stamped out, as was suggested in the utopian ideal?

3. Considering the ideas and forces listed above, what is Shakespeare's conclusion about each one?

4. Here are some questions for discussion:

a. Consider carefully the speeches in Act I, Scene 2, dealing with the attempts to educate Caliban. What would Shakespeare have to say about compulsory universal education? To what extent is he right?

b. In the same scene, Prospero must discipline Ariel. Why, in ordinary life, as in the play, is this necessary?

c. At the end of Plato's "Allegory of the Cave" (see volume I), Sokrates states that the philosopher who has seen true being and has learned to love it must be made to return to the cave and participate in the ordinary affairs of men, even though those affairs may seem to be foolish. Do you find any suggestions of this same idea in *The Tempest?* Why is this return necessary?

Summary

The dynamic Renaissance was notable for its artistic creativity, intellectual energy, widespread violence, and almost constant warfare. Most everything was writ large because European civilization experienced drastic changes over a relatively short period of time. The Middle Ages died hard, partly because of the intransigent stance of the Church. Determined to relinquish not one iota of its vast power, the Church of Rome ultimately lost some of its authority in southern Europe and all control in northern Europe.

Critical elements of the Italian Renaissance were the rise of humanism and the revival of the Graeco-Roman heritage. Other factors included the expansion of capitalism and a steady increase in trade, industry, and banking. Northern Europe had no classical heritage, but its livelier economy, coupled with creative enterprise, produced considerable prosperity and a growing middle class.

Science made notable advances with the Copernican theory replacing the old Ptolemaic system and with Galileo's development of his laws of motion. Using his improved telescope, Galileo also helped confirm the Copernican thesis.

This was the age of exploration, with the magnetic compass, astrolabe, and tables of Henry the Navigator assisting the voyages of discovery of Columbus, Cabral, Cabot, and Magellan. The New World was explored by Cartier, Champlain, and Hudson, whereas Cortes conquered the Aztec empire in Mexico, and Pizarro captured the Inca empire in Peru.

Assisted mightily by the invention of movable type, the Reformation broke the universal power of the Church of Rome. Led by Martin Luther, John Calvin, and others, the Protestant reformers established a variety of denominations throughout northern Europe. Politically, the Renaissance saw the rise of nation-states that in many ways supplanted the controlling power of the Roman Church. The new nations of England, France, and Spain became the most powerful in Europe. After the Reformation, Henry VIII freed England from the Church of Rome, thus setting a precedent in which the State triumphed over the Church.

All of these forces contributed significantly to human freedom, but they raised the question of whether human beings were equipped to use their freedom wisely. Could selfish, greedy people rise above their animal natures to become what the Renaissance called the "noblest creatures of God" and use their God-given capacities to transform the world? That remained, for the Renaissance, an open question.

Culture and Human Values

If one were to ask what final answers were arrived at for the Renaissance problems stated here and in previous chapters, one would have to look not so much to ideas as to the lives of individuals. These were people who fulfilled the concept of "universal." This kind of person was completely free to live as he or she pleased, gaining freedom along with the ability to master knowledge and power.

The best example of such a universal person was, of course, Leonardo da Vinci, the Renaissance man *par excellence.* He, like Francis Bacon, could announce "I take all knowledge as my province," for the sum of human knowledge was still so small that one remarkable person could master it all.

What Leonardo was in life, Michelangelo symbolized in art. One cannot help admiring his *Creation of Adam* (see figure 17.34) for its concept of a human being. In the eyes of the reclining figure, one sees infinite longing, the type of yearning that will carry this man far. In the strongly muscled body, one sees the strength that will help give him the power to fulfill that longing. Representing both of the sexes, this is a person set free, with the creative vigor to conquer new worlds, to unlock the secrets of the universe, to dare and to do in a world opened up to ambition and achievement. This is the exact opposite of the retreat we saw in the life of Montaigne and in More's *Utopia.*

THE EARLY MODERN WORLD, *1600-1789*

THE EARLY MODERN WORLD

1600–1789

	People and Events	Art and Architecture	Literature and Music	Philosophy and Science
1600	**1600** English East India Company founded **1602** Dutch East India Company founded **1609** Netherlands revolt from Spain **1603–1625** James I of England **1618–1648** Thirty Years' War **1621–1665** Philip IV of Spain **1625–1649** Charles I of England **1632** Galileo condemned by Inquisition **1635** French Academy of Language and Literature established **1642–1646** English Civil War **1643–1715** Louis XIV of France **1648** French Academy of Painting and Sculpture established **1649** Charles I of England executed **1649–1659** Cromwell's Commonwealth **1660–1685** Restoration: Charles II of England **1666** Great fire of London **1669** Paris Opera established **1682–1725** Peter the Great of Russia **1685** Louis XIV revokes Edict of Nantes **1685–1688** James II of England **1687** *Principia* by Newton **1688** England's Glorious Revolution **1688–1702** William and Mary of England	**Vignola** 1507–1573 Il Gesù **Jones** 1573–1652 Queen's House **Caravaggio** 1573–1610 *Supper at Emmaus* **Rubens** 1577–1640 *The Assumption of the Virgin* **Hals** ca. 1580–1666 *Portrait of an Officer* **Gentileschi** 1593–1652 *Judith Slaying Holofernes* **Poussin** 1594–1665 *Holy Family on the Steps* **Bernini** 1598–1680 St. Peter's Piazza and Colonnade **Zurbarán** 1598–1640 *Agnus Dei* **Borromini** 1599–1644 S. Carlo alle Quatro Fontane **Velasquez** 1599–1660 *Maids of Honor* **van Dyck** 1599–1641 *Marchesa Elena Grimaldi* **Rembrandt** 1606–1669 *The Descent from the Cross* **Leyster** 1609–1660 *Self-Portrait* **Ruisdael** 1628–1682 *Wheatfields* **Vermeer** 1632–1675 *The Girl with the Red Hat* **Wren** 1632–1723 St. Paul's **Pozzo** 1642–1709 *Apotheosis of Saint Ignatius* **Mansart** 1646–1708 Palace of Versailles	**Donne** 1573–1631 *Holy Sonnets* **Milton** 1608–1674 *Paradise Lost; On His Blindness* **Molière** 1622–1673 *Tartuffe*	**Bacon** 1561–1626 *Novum Organum* **Galileo** 1564–1642 *Dialogues Concerning the Two Chief World Systems* **Kepler** 1571–1630 elliptical planetary orbits **Hobbes** 1588–1679 *Leviathan* **Descartes** 1596–1650 *Discourse on Method* **Spinoza** 1632–1677 God in nature **Locke** 1632–1704 *Two Treatises of Government*
1700	**1701–1713** Frederick I of Prussia **1702–1714** Anne of England **1713–1740** Frederick William I of Prussia **1714–1727** George I of England **1715–1774** Louis XV of France **1727–1760** George II of England **1740–1786** Frederick the Great of Prussia **1747–1772** Diderot's *Encyclopedia* **1748–** Excavations begin at Pompeii **1760–1820** George III of England **1762–1791** Catherine the Great of Russia **1774–1793** Louis XVI of France **1775** Watt's improved steam engine **1775–1783** American Revolution **1776** *Wealth of Nations* by Adam Smith **1780–1790** Joseph II Emperor of Austria	**Watteau** 1684–1721 *A Pilgrimage to Cythera* **Gibbs** 1682–1754 St. Martin's in the Fields **Chardin** 1699–1779 *The Kitchen Maid* **Boucher** 1703–1770 *Venus Consoling Love* **Falconet** 1716–1791 *Madame de Pompadour as the Venus of the Doves* **Greuze** 1725–1805 *The Village Bride* **Gainsborough** 1727–1788 *Mrs. Richard Brinsley Sheridan* **Fragonard** 1732–1806 *The Swing* **Houdon** 1741–1828 *Voltaire* **David** 1748–1825 *Death of Sokrates*	**Swift** 1667–1745 *Gulliver's Travels; A Modest Proposal* **Couperin** 1668–1733 Le Croc-en-jambe **Bach** 1685–1750 *French Suite No. 4* **Vivaldi** 1685–1743 *The Four Seasons* **Handel** 1685–1759 *The Messiah* **Pope** 1688–1744 *Essay on Man* **Montesquieu** 1689–1755 *Spirit of the Laws* **Voltaire** 1694–1778 *Candide* **Rousseau** 1712–1778 *Confessions* **Diderot** 1713–1784 *Encyclopedia* **Haydn** 1732–1809 *String Quartet in F Major*	**Newton** 1642–1727 *Principia* **Bayle** 1647–1706 *Historical and Critical Dictionary* **Halley** 1656–1742 Halley's Comet **Hume** 1711–1776 *A Treatise of Human Nature* **Smith** 1723–1790 *Wealth of Nations* **Kant** 1724–1804 *Critique of Pure Reason*
1800	**1789–1815** French Revolution	**Stuart** 1755–1828 *Mrs. Richard Yates* **Canova** 1757–1822 *Pauline Borghese as Venus* **Charpentier** 1767–1849 *Mlle. Charlotte du Val d'Ognes*	**Jefferson** 1743–1826 *Declaration of Independence* **Mozart** 1756–1791 *Symphony No. 35* **Beethoven** 1770–1827 *Symphony No. 5*	**Laplace** 1749–1827 French astronomer

Science, Reason, and Absolutism

chapter *20*

The Seventeenth Century

Europe emerged from medievalism during the tumultuous Renaissance, but not until 1648 did the passions unleashed by the Reformation and Counter-Reformation begin to subside. Initially a conflict between Catholics and Protestants, the Thirty Years' War (1618–1648) evolved into an international conflict between modern nation-states. The Peace of Westphalia of 1648 that ended the slaughter was a landmark in European history, finally laying to rest the last vestiges of medievalism. Once viable values and institutions had completely disappeared. The medieval idea of a unified Christian commonwealth was a relic of the now distant past as were the imperial and papal claims to political power. Adopting the strategies of diplomacy and alliances initiated by Italian city-states, sovereign nations staked out boundaries and competed with each other in the struggle for a new balance of power. The strongest competing powers were France, England, the Hapsburg empires of Austria and Spain, and the Ottoman Empire (map 20.1).

Rapid advances in science and technology revealed vast new horizons, and international trade opened up the whole world to European dominance and, inevitably, European exploitation. The English East Indies Company was founded in 1600, its Dutch counterpart chartered only two years later, followed by the French. The prevailing mood in northern Europe, with its growing power and wealth, was as positive as the joyful optimism voiced by Miranda in Shakespeare's *The Tempest:*

O Wonder!
How many goodly creatures are there here!
How beauteous mankind is! O brave new world,
That has such people in't!

Science and Philosophy

Francis Bacon, 1561–1626

The career of Francis Bacon spanned the late Renaissance and the emerging modern world, which is why he is discussed here and in the preceding chapter. Along with Galileo and Descartes, he ranks as one of the founders of modern science and philosophy. He formulated no new scientific hypotheses nor did he make any dramatic discoveries, but he did inquire into the function and ethics of science and scientific research in relation to human life. For Bacon, knowledge was not recognition of any given reality but a search for truth, a journey rather than a destination. Bacon knew that the old culture was being replaced by a dramatically new epoch. Inventions such as gunpowder, the printing press, the compound microscope (ca. 1590), and the telescope (ca. 1608) changed the material world, spawning new beliefs, institutions, and values. Scientific knowledge and invention, Bacon believed, should be public property to be shared democratically and to be used for the benefit of all people. In his *Novum Organum* (1620) Bacon stated the logic of scientific inquiry and the principles of the inductive method. Factual information would be collected through experiment and observation, leading to general statements based solely on observable data. For Bacon the principal task of scientific investigation was to remedy the poverty of factual data, to embark on an exhilarating voyage of scientific discovery that had been delayed for some two thousand years. There was an explosion of knowledge as seventeenth-century scientists explored a world that had been virtually unknown since the groundbreaking efforts of the Hellenistic scientists of the ancient world.

Galileo Galilei, 1564–1642

Professor of mechanics and astronomy at the University of Padua, Galileo Galilei contributed mightily to the accumulation of factual information. His was a threefold scientific method based on a Pythagorean faith in a mathematical order of nature, the practice of abstracting and intuiting mathematical laws, and most importantly, experimentation under rigidly controlled conditions. With his improved telescope he empirically proved the heliocentric theory, discovered sun spots, and viewed the moons of Jupiter. He devised two laws of motion, invented the thermometer, improved the compound microscope, investigated the principles of the lever and the pulley, measured air pressure, and studied the properties of magnetism and sound vibrations. Even more importantly, he invented the modern method of forming a theory, testing it experimentally, and adjusting the theory to conform to observable results.

It can be said, in fact, that modern science began on 24 August 1609, the date of Galileo's letter to the Doge of Venice in which he described his telescopic observations. But Galileo's was the only voice promoting examination of the heavens with his improved telescope. His fellow scientists unanimously rejected this marvelous new scientific instrument. Why was this so?

The magnifying power of a convex mirror was known to Euclid in 300 B.C., but for 1900 years no one was interested in concave mirrors nor were they concerned with the three-power spyglass that Dutch artisans had copied from a 1590 Italian model. Philosophers and scientists had learned not to trust the senses, especially visual phenomena. The problem was compounded because lenses and concave mirrors made one see figures that were contradicted by the sense of touch. Galileo's thirty-power telescope was therefore regarded as providing defective information. The Catholic cardinals who refused to view moon craters through Galileo's telescope had a very long tradition to back them up.

The startling contents of the famous letter to the Doge became common knowledge, leading to ever-growing controversy. After the publication of his *Dialogues Concerning the Two*

Map 20.1 *Europe in the 17th Century.*

Chief World Systems (1632), Galileo was charged by the Inquisition with heresy. The Holy Office (Inquisition) claimed that Galileo had agreed, in a signed statement, not to promulgate his views about the heliocentric theory. The statement was a forgery, and Galileo was not allowed to appear before the court in his own defense.[1] Nevertheless, he was judged a heretic, forced to recant, and sentenced to lifetime house arrest. The book was first sentenced to public burning but later merely prohibited.

After leaving Rome, Galileo, with the assistance of trusted friends, sent a copy of his book to Switzerland where it was published in Latin. He followed that up with *The New Sciences* (1638), the first great work on modern physics. Prince Mattia de' Medici smuggled the manuscript out of Italy, and the book was ultimately published in Holland. Galileo had thus successfully defied Rome, but his life was a shambles and Italian science was set back for generations.

René Descartes, 1596–1650

During the sixteenth century the Reformation raised the question of the reliability of religious knowledge, of whether Catholic beliefs were more or less true than Protestant or any other convictions. The rise of science extended the question to the reliability of all knowledge. Skeptics maintained that no certain knowledge was possible, that doubt was always present. Bacon argued that the inductive method, augmented by mechanical aids such as the compound microscope, provided certain knowledge about the world. Like the philosophers and scientists mentioned above, René Descartes distrusted sensory evidence. Further, based on his acquaintance with skeptics such as Montaigne and Mersenne, Descartes followed their arguments to their logical conclusion and rejected everything as false. With this process of "Cartesian doubt" he could then, in the depths of uncertainty, find truth and a criterion of truth.

In his *Discourse on Method* (1637) Descartes formulated his "natural method" to accept nothing as true except what was "clearly and distinctly" presented to his mind. It was not until his *Meditations* (1641) that Descartes responded to attacks on all knowledge. Admitting that the senses could not be trusted, Descartes proceeded to postulate an evil demon whose business it was to confuse people about the truth or falsity of anything, even whether a square had four sides. The solution is to exorcise the demon by believing in the goodness of the all-powerful God. Descartes doubts not that God exists, for if imperfect beings can envision a perfect God then the conception is based on a reality. But how does he know whether he himself exists? He finds his answer in the realization that he is a thinking person: *cogito ergo sum,* I think, therefore I am. Descartes was the founder of modern rational philosophy; along with Galileo, Bacon, and many other scientists, he was convinced of the rational power of the human mind.

Whatever is clearly and distinctly perceived by the *cogito* is true. From this point Descartes proceeded to construct a rational philosophy in which he established the reliability of the senses and proved the existence of the physical world. He knew, however, that our perception of objects could be distorted or misled. When a full moon rises, for example, we see a very large globe that appears to grow smaller as it ascends. What we are sure of is that the moon exists and we use mathematics to calculate its size.

Descartes reaffirmed the ideas first expressed by the Greek atomist Demokritos, that the whole of matter was composed of items of identical substance. All reality, for Descartes, lay in the motion of this absolute substance through space and time. For him and the many who followed him, the perfect God had created a flawless (mathematical) world; God was therefore an engineer who had built and set in motion a very complicated machine. As Randall summarizes:

> To Descartes thenceforth space or extension became the fundamental reality in the world, motion the source of all change, and mathematics the only relation between its parts. . . . He made of nature a machine and nothing but a machine; purposes and spiritual influences alike had vanished.[2]

Mathematics was "queen of the sciences" for Descartes and all that was needed to explain a mechanical universe. Applied mathematics would enable scientists to rationally study and understand an orderly cosmos that operated according to natural laws, a position with which Galileo was in complete agreement. Copernicus had proposed the heliocentric theory; Kepler had confirmed it by observation and, with mathematics, determined the three laws of planetary motion:

1. The planets move around the sun in ellipses with the sun at one focus of the ellipse.
2. We can imagine a line joining the sun and a planet. Though the planet's speed varies in its orbit around the sun, yet this imaginary line "sweeps out" equal areas in equal times.
3. The square of the time for one complete revolution of each planet is proportional to the cube of its average distance from the sun.

Bacon, Galileo, Descartes, and the early astronomers built a firm foundation for the scientific eruption that inspired Newton and that subsequently made Western culture unrivaled among the civilizations of the world.

---

1. For further information on the trial and the judicial forgery, see Giorgio de Santillana, *The Crime of Galileo* (New York: Time Incorporated, 1962).

2. J. H. Randall, Jr., *The Making of the Modern Mind.* (New York: Columbia University Press, 1976), pp. 241–242.

Absolutism

At the beginning of the century both England and France were governed by absolute monarchs who based their claims on Divine Right. The thrones of England and Scotland were united by the accession of James I (1603–1625), the son of Mary Stuart, Queen of Scots. His attempts to govern absolutely brought him into conflict with Parliament, and the absolute rule of Charles I (1625–1649) finally led to Civil War (1642–1646) between the king and Parliament. Charles I was tried and executed for treason and the Interregnum began, the Puritan era of the Commonwealth and the Protectorate (1649–1659) under what amounted to the dictatorship of Oliver Cromwell.

Beginning with the Civil War, the Social Contract theory of government became ever more prominent. Government by consent of the governed did not imply a liberal democracy, however, but that the power of the wealthy and influential class curbed kingly excesses. Apparently no one suggested that working people had any natural rights. Consent did not imply democracy unless that meant consent of *all* the people, and that was an eighteenth-century development that led to the American Revolution. The idea of a Social Contract was a strong current of political thought, but there was an important countercurrent. In 1651 Thomas Hobbes (1588–1679) published his *Leviathan* in which he revived the idea of a contract based on subjection to the sovereign power of the monarch, but not rule by Divine Right. Convinced that peace and security were prerequisites of society, Hobbes believed that certain individual freedoms had to be sacrificed for the good of the state. A state of nature was anarchy; there had to be a superior power to restore and maintain the stability of society, and that would be the unlimited power of the king. Given the Social Contract theory, the Civil War, and the execution of the king, the Hobbsian position became, of course, anathema to Cromwell and Parliament.

On the death of Cromwell in 1659, Charles II (1660–1685), son of Charles I, was invited to restore the Stuart line. Charles managed to go his own way without openly confronting Parliament, but James II (1685–1688) was not as clever and was forced to abdicate, leaving in his wake the conviction that a Catholic king was dangerous to English liberties. Mary, the daughter of James II, was Protestant and married to William of Orange, a Dutch Protestant. Providing they accepted the new Bill of Rights, William and Mary were invited to ascend the English throne. This was the bloodless Glorious Revolution that established a constitutional monarchy. Absolutism was virtually finished in England.

Absolutism in France had a far longer and more violent history. Succeeding to the throne after the assassination of Henry IV, Louis XIII reigned from 1610–1643, but royal power was gradually taken over by chief minister Cardinal Richelieu, who operated as a virtual dictator from 1624 to 1642. It was Richelieu who established the French absolutism to which Louis XIV succeeded in 1643 at the age of five under the regency of his mother. During

Figure 20.1 *French school after Gianlorenzo Bernini*, Bust of Louis XIV, *ca. 1665. Bronze, ht. 33½". Versailles was decorated and furnished in the baroque style represented by this Italian baroque bust, but the exterior is essentially neoclassical, the preferred architectural style of Louis XIV. Samuel H. Kress Collection. National Gallery of Art, Washington, D.C.*

the longest reign of any monarch, Louis XIV (1643–1715; figure 20.1) promoted the arts, built the magnificent palace at Versailles (figure 21.19), and made France the most powerful monarchy in Europe. The nation was crippled, however, by an archaic economic system with local customs barriers, tax farming, and a nobility that paid no taxes at all. Raising revenues simply increased the misery of the people. Further, the king's revocation of the Edict of Nantes that protected the Huguenots from persecution was a disaster. Over 250,000 mostly middle-class craftsmen and their families were forced to flee the country, marking the beginning of the end of Louis' greatness and ultimately, of the French monarchy itself.

The Eighteenth Century

The Enlightenment, ca. 1687–1789

"Enlightenment" and "Age of Reason" are the two terms that describe the intellectual characteristics of the eighteenth century. The Enlightenment is usually dated from the year in which Newton's epochal *Principia (Mathematical Principles of Natural Philosophy)* appeared (1687) to the beginning of the French Revolution in 1789. An alternate beginning date would be 1688, the year of the Glorious Revolution in England. No matter; the *Principia* and the Glorious Revolution were major milestones marking the advance of science, rationalism, and freedom.

The Enlightenment was a self-conscious and extremely articulate movement that was to transform all Western societies. It had its roots in France and England, but its branches extended throughout Europe and into the New World. Europe had experienced some rude shocks, what some writers called the "three

A DAY AT VERSAILLES WITH LOUIS XIV

The sun beams on the enormous palace of Versailles, with sunlight streaming into the bedchamber of the Sun King, Louis XIV. It is 10:00 A.M., and the monarch is sleepily sitting in his king-size bed with its headboard decorated by an elaborate sunburst. Richly furnished, the chamber is plated and gilded throughout with gold, including a balustrade that guards the royal bed against uninvited company. This morning, as usual, several courtiers have been accorded the privilege of witnessing the royal rising—the ritualistic *levee.* The First Physician and First Surgeon enter first to inquire about his majesty's health. As a wood-carrier lights a fire in the hearth and the time-keeper winds numerous clocks, the wig-maker adjusts the short wig the king will wear for the ceremonies.

At 10:15 the favored few are admitted to watch in awed silence as the king receives holy water and recites the office of the Holy Spirit. After a shave by the royal barber, the king receives his morning sponge bath, not in harmful water of course, but in spirits of wine. No one presumes to notice the two armed men in black velvet who empty the royal commode. As the king sips spiced wine, his royal person is gloriously adorned: silk stockings, Italian leather boots, *culottes* (knee-length trousers), ornamented vest, silk cravat, and a coat decorated with gold, jewels, and lace-trimmed cuffs. After exchanging his *"levee"* wig for an elaborately curled one, he kneels for morning prayers. All hastily kneel with him, for no one's head may be higher than that of the king, even when he is playing billiards.

After issuing orders of the day, Louis and his immediate family file into his private gallery in the sumptuous Royal Chapel designed by Mansart, his favorite architect. There the royal family and assembled court celebrate High Mass, which is highlighted by a motet by Lully, the king's court composer.

Matters of state are then discussed in the Council Room in the midst of gilded moldings, huge mirrors, crystal chandeliers, and the magnificent paintings the king has personally selected. The Foreign Secretary's report is listened to intently. The most powerful nation in Europe must keep abreast of foreign affairs, particularly in England. A minister comments on the number of gifted men produced by the rival nation—men such as Bacon, Newton, Hobbes, and Locke. The king explodes: "John Locke is a dangerous man! That sovereignty should reside in representatives of the people is an absurdity!" An alert minister quickly responds, "Everyone knows that God himself has ordained Your Majesty as the absolute ruler of this great nation." Smiling his assent, Louis leaves the room. No one left in the room dares to even think about the fate of Charles I of England or of what the English have called the Glorious Revolution of 1688.

Though many courtiers attend the luncheon the king eats in silence; eating is serious business for the gourmand. After several bowls of different soups, the king devours successive courses of partridge, pheasant, ham, and mutton. After a palate-cleaning salad, he then enjoys cheese, fruit, and pastries. (Not surprisingly, the autopsy revealed a royal stomach twice normal size.) Louis prefers eating with his fingers though forks are now in vogue. Because it is no longer proper to wipe one's hands on the tablecloth, each diner now has a linen napkin.

His official duties finished, the king decides to inspect the former hunting lodge he has transformed into the largest and most luxurious palace in Europe. The king and ten thousand resident nobles live here in style, mainly because the king refuses to live in Paris, where the Parisians are not sufficiently respectful. They would be even more hostile, he muses, if they knew how much this lodge cost to build and maintain. Not even the king knows; he has instructed Colbert, his Minister of Finance, to cover up much of the extravagant spending.

Feeling the need for vigorous exercise, the king decides to ride to hounds. The hunt ranges so far that the riders pass near some thatched-roof peasant cottages. With floors of packed earth, these crude one-room one-window dwellings contain only rough wooden furniture and a single feather bed. The peasants are returning from the fields, the men garbed in rough blouses and trousers, and the women in coarse dresses and bonnets. Those who have shoes are wearing *sabots* (wooden shoes). Their meal for tonight will be frugal—boiled millet, rye bread, and maybe a few vegetables. The king turns away from them. Peasants, he thinks, have little sense and no culture. Their prime function is to pay their taxes.

Back at the palace there is time for games of cards and billiards before adjourning to the theatre for a revival of *Tartuffe,* an old comedy by Molière. Once again Louis is reminded of how much he misses the acting of Molière and his comical plays. He mentions this to his wife Françoise d'Aubigné, Marquise de Maintenon, who reminds him that it was his deceased first wife who really knew the playwright. Louis studies his wife. She is particularly lovely tonight in her embroidered royal blue gown with its laced bodice and stylishly low neckline. He idly ponders his royal predicament (as he views it): would he have so many mistresses and concubines if he weren't so bored and if women weren't so available?

Promptly at ten o'clock the royal couple is joined by a few lucky courtiers for another lavish meal. Supper over, the king acknowledges a murmured *bon nuit* from each guest, and retires to the quarters of his legitimate family for an hour's visit.

His evening prayers finished by 1:30 A.M., the king is helped into his nightshirt and dressing gown before contentedly seating himself for his evening snack: three small loaves of bread, cold meats, and two bottles of wine. As he settles into bed he is already contemplating the meals he has ordered for the next day.

humiliations": the earth was not at the center of the universe; people were creatures of nature like other animals; and their reason was subject to passions and instincts. For the Enlightenment these new truths represented intellectual advances that enabled people to redefine their responsibilities: discover truth through science; achieve personal happiness in a viable society; explore the full meaning, and limitations, of liberty. Newton's discoveries provided convincing evidence that the world was orderly and knowable and that, by the same token, human societies could be made orderly and rational through the exercise of enlightened reason.

Montesquieu (1689–1755) was apparently among the first to extend Cartesian ideas about natural law, contending, for example, that physical *and* political phenomena were subject to general laws. The Marquis de Condorcet (1743–1794) went still further. He assumed that one could discover universally valid truths in ethics, economics, and government that were as certain as the facts of mathematics and science. The accumulation of new knowledge would guide decisions and actions and help free humankind from prejudices, superstitions, and undesirable restraints of society and government. This was the doctrine of inevitable progress that so fascinated the intellectuals of the Enlightenment. Just as the sciences progressed ever upward by discovering new facts, so would society move to an ever fuller realization of human potential. These optimistic beliefs had the force of self-fulfilling prophecies, leading to major improvements in many areas before the realization dawned that ethics, economics, society, and government had far more variables than anyone had ever dreamed.

Science and Philosophy: Newton and Locke

Isaac Newton, 1642–1727

Newton was the scientific hero of the Enlightenment. He electrified Western culture with his discovery of the universal law of gravitation, made important investigations into optics, and invented the branch of mathematics known as calculus (which was also invented independently by Baron von Leibniz; 1646–1716). As important as these discoveries were, Newton was revered by his peers for his methodology. Some of Newton's discoveries have been modified by later scientists, but his scientific method stands to this day as a model for every scientist. Willing to give credit where it was due, Newton supposedly remarked, "If I have seen a little farther than others, it is because I have stood on the shoulders of giants." There were many giants, including Copernicus, Brahe, Bruno, Kepler, and Galileo, but Newton effected the grand synthesis that explained the operation of the cosmos. First, he refined Galileo's laws of motion:

1. A body remains in a state of rest or of uniform motion in a straight line unless compelled by an external force to change that state. In other words, a body's inertia keeps it in a state

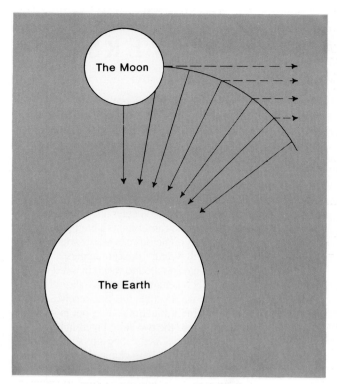

Figure 20.2 *Forces acting on the moon to determine its motion.*

of rest or its inertia keeps it moving in a straight line. External force has to be applied to move it from either its state of rest or its straight-line motion.

2. A change in momentum is proportional to the force causing the change and takes place in the direction in which the force is acting. In other words, the increase or decrease in velocity is proportional to the force.

3. To every action there is an equal and opposite reaction. We see this law in action every time a rocket roars into space.

Celestial Calculations

Galileo had demonstrated the principles of movement of bodies on earth, but not the motion of heavenly bodies. Why were their orbits curved? Newton hypothesized that all celestial bodies were mutually attracted to each other. He concentrated his studies on the moon's inertial movement in space, and then determined that its orbit was curved because it was continuously falling toward the earth (figure 20.2). Its inertia would cause it to fly out in a straight line, as shown by the dotted arrows, but the gravitational pull of the earth balances the straight-line tendency. Action and reaction are equal and the moon remains in orbit at a standard distance from the earth (just as modern satellites remain in orbit above the earth). Newton calculated the mass of the moon and its distance from the earth and determined that the gravitational pull was inversely proportional to the square of its distance from the earth. Newton also calculated the mass of the sun, the planets, and their moons and discovered that each planet would travel according to Kepler's laws only by using the same formula: the gravitational pull of the sun was inversely proportional to the square of a planet's distance from the sun. The mathematical formula was the same whether the object was a terrestrial falling body such as an apple, or the moon, a law that worked here on earth and far out in space. This was the universal law of gravitation.

Universal Principles

Newton (and Edmund Halley) demonstrated that comets obey the same universal principle. He calculated the flattening of the earth at its poles due to its rotation and proved that the size of a planet determined the length of its day. He showed the effect of latitude on the weight of an object and accounted for the tides as resulting from the combined attraction of the sun and the moon. All these examples of gravitation illustrate some of the different phenomena that can be explained with one law. No wonder Alexander Pope wrote:

Nature and nature's laws lay hid in night;
God said, "Let Newton be," and all was light.

The philosophic implications of this unification of scientific principles were astounding. Picture the universe as Newton saw it, a vast and intricate system of whirling bodies in space, a system that was orderly and predictable. Each planet, each moon, each solar system was balanced in the cosmic plan, a balance determined by mechanical forces pulling against each other. Absolute and unvarying, these forces would keep the machine in working order. What, then, was the place of God in this plan? For all practical purposes God was ruled out. Newton was an intensely religious man, however, and he yielded two functions to the Divinity. Scientists noticed that, over long periods, there were slight irregularities in the motions of the heavenly bodies in terms of Newtonian physics. One function of God was to make certain periodic readjustments. A second function was to maintain an even flow of time and space. In this world picture, then, God became a sort of celestial engineer, turning a wheel here, opening a valve there, keeping an eye on the dials. Even before the close of the eighteenth century, the French astronomer Laplace extended the mechanism of gravitation and proved that the irregularities were periodical and subject to a law that kept them within bounds. Many of those who held to the existence of God were deists who looked on him as the master designer of a perfect world-machine that needed no further tending.

In these developments we see clearly and distinctly the new reliance on intellect that characterized the Enlightenment. Human beings using the marvelous mechanisms of their minds could, in time, unlock the most hidden secrets of the universe. And what of human institutions? The cosmos was orderly, rational, and knowable; why couldn't people use their reason to design an orderly and rational society? It was precisely this optimism that inspired the American Founding Fathers to construct a democracy that would be a model and a beacon of hope for the entire world.

John Locke, 1632–1704

The founders of the American Republic had derived some political ideas from Montesquieu's *Spirit of the Laws* (1748), but they drew mainly from John Locke. Returning from exile after the Glorious Revolution, Locke wrote his *Two Treatises of Government* (1690) to justify constitutional monarchy. In the fifteenth essay from his *Second Treatise on Civil Government* Locke takes this position:

Now this power, which every man has in the state of Nature, and which he parts with to the society in all such cases where the society can secure him, is to use such means for the preserving of his own property as he thinks good and Nature allows him; and to punish the breach of the law of Nature in others; so as (according to the best of his reason) may most conduce to the preservation of himself and the rest of mankind. So that the end and measure of this power, when in every other man's hands, in the state of Nature, being the preservation of all his society, that is, all mankind in general; it can have no other end or measure, when in the hands of the magistrate, but to preserve the members of that society in their lives, liberties, and possessions.

Locke assumes a natural law that operated in the affairs of human beings much as Newton's world-machine functioned according to natural law, a position also reflected in the opening paragraph of the Declaration of Independence as composed by Thomas Jefferson:

When, in the course of human events, it becomes necessary for one people to dissolve the political bands which have connected them with another, and to assume, among the powers of the earth, the separate and equal station to which the laws of nature and of nature's God entitle them, a decent respect to the opinions of mankind requires that they should declare the causes which impel them to the separation.

According to Locke, this natural law gave people certain rights that were unalienable, and these were life, liberty, and property. Jefferson substituted for "property" a much more striking and challenging phrase:

We hold these truths to be self-evident, that all men are created equal, that they are endowed by their Creator with certain unalienable Rights, that among these are Life, Liberty, and the pursuit of Happiness. That to secure these rights, Governments are instituted among Men, deriving their just powers from the consent of the governed.

Jefferson later explained how he regarded the Declaration:

Neither aiming at originality of principles or sentiments, nor yet copied from any particular or previous writing, it was intended to be an expression of the American mind.

Locke wrote that government existed and had authority only because the people brought it into existence and gave it its authority. If the government violated its trust, the people had a right, a natural right, to set up a new government. In short, they had a right to revolt, as Jefferson later stated in the Declaration of Independence.

The Wealth of Nations: Adam Smith, 1723–1790

Exactly as Locke and Jefferson sought natural law as a guide to political affairs and Newton found such a law as the binding force of the universe, so did Adam Smith seek a unifying principle for economic affairs. His work, interestingly enough, followed the scientific method that Bacon had established in the previous epoch; his investigations of the facts of economic life were conducted in a pin factory, leading to generalizations based on his factual findings.

Smith presented his principles of capitalism in 1776 in a book that quickly became a classic: *An Inquiry into the Nature and Causes of the Wealth of Nations*. In Smith's day capitalism had taken the form called *mercantilism*, a strictly regulated system of trade controlled by the government of each nation and based on the assumption that the wealth of a nation depended on the amount of gold and silver held within the nation. To achieve a constantly increasing supply of gold and silver, each sought to maintain a favorable balance of trade; that is, each nation tried to keep the value of its yearly exports greater than the value of its yearly imports. With all nations competing for a favorable balance of trade, the system obviously will collapse—with only one way out. A colonial nation can exploit its colonies as a source for cheap raw materials and a dumping ground for more expensive manufactured goods, for example, England's policy toward its American colonies. In this way only can mercantilism work, temporarily. Sooner or later colonies will either develop their own manufacturing or be bled dry by the mother country. The system fails in either case.

Some French economists called *physiocrats* were the first to revolt against mercantilism. They claimed that a nation's wealth depended on its raw materials rather than the supply of money. They also believed that governmental regulation of trade and commerce was detrimental to economic well-being and progress. Adam Smith studied with this group while fleshing out his own theories.

Smith sought a reasonable balance in economic affairs that would insure an adequate supply of goods to meet the needs of human beings. He wanted these produced and sold at a fair price so that most people could buy the goods while the laborer earned a decent wage and the manufacturer reaped a reasonable profit. To solve this intricate problem he proposed a return to nature in economic affairs: the removal of all restrictions on wages and the manufacture and sale of goods. This is the unfettered competi-tion called *laissez-faire* that can be demonstrated by the following example.

Smith's first premise is that people are acquisitive by nature with no end to their desire for wealth. So an enterpriser (a person with capital to invest) sees that people need shoes. He builds a shoe factory and charges as much as the traffic will bear. Immediately, other capitalists are attracted to the shoe business because of the large profits. As the number of shoes increases, the price will necessarily drop if, according to the doctrine of laissez-faire, all people have equal access to raw materials and to markets with no regulation whatever. Eventually there are more shoes than buyers and prices are cut to stimulate sales, driving the least efficient manufacturers out of business. As the demand overtakes the supply the price begins to regulate itself. Finally, production is adequate for the needs of people, the price is stable, and the most efficient producers can make a fair profit. Labor, however, is still missing from this scheme.

Labor, said Smith, is a commodity that, like shoes, is for sale. Wages will be high in a new field and laborers will flock to this work. Wages will decline as labor becomes plentiful. Finally, the labor market in shoe production will become glutted, and wages will fall to less than a living wage. The least competent workers will have to seek some other employment. Eventually the price of labor, like that of shoes, will stabilize, with the most efficient workers employed at a fair wage. Those laid off will find another kind of work in which they are more efficient, and, presumably, better able to make a good living.

From these examples we can abstract the principles of Smith's laissez-faire economy. First, labor is the source of all wealth within a nation. Second, all people are acquisitive. Third, there must be unregulated access to raw materials, labor, and markets. Fourth, each person has a natural endowment of skills that should determine the kind of work to be done. Given a free choice of employment, the process should lead the worker into the most congenial job. Fifth, if all the conditions above exist, the law of supply and demand will solve the problem of sufficient goods, satisfactory price, adequate profit, and fair wages. Furthermore, each person will be doing what he or she can do best, and thus the most enjoyable kind of occupation. Q.E.D.

Or almost Q.E.D. One problem remained, which Smith recognized, and for which he produced an inadequate solution. He realized that monopolies might limit or eliminate competition and proposed that governments protect free competition by controlling monopolies; he could not, however, suggest any procedures that did not also regulate industry. Modern capitalistic nations have solved the problem with regulations and controls that still permit the operation of Smith's laws of supply and demand in a relatively free marketplace.

Smith's economic system was similar to Locke's political philosophy and to the universal law of gravitation. The first step is a return to nature, for human differences and limitations form the natural parameters. Nature will then provide a self-regulating economic mechanism. The natural forces of supply and demand, like the mutual gravitational pulls of planets and suns, like the pulls of executive and legislative branches of government, will shape the economy into a smoothly operating machine. Adam Smith contributed a principle on which an economy could be organized and operated, leading, in the fullness of time, to productive and affluent societies. Today's capitalistic economies do not function anywhere near as well as everyone would like, but there is no doubt that modern capitalism works better than anything yet devised. The catastrophic failure of central-planning economies that had neither private property nor free enterprise vividly highlights the basic validity of Smith's theories.

Philosophy and *Les Philosophes*

Locke and Educational Theory

John Locke made yet another contribution that greatly influenced education and other human institutions. He asserted that the human mind at birth was a complete blank. It was, he said, a *tabula rasa,* a blank slate. This position contradicted that of the defenders of political and religious absolutism who contended that an inclination to submit to authority was present in people's minds from the moment of birth. Not so, said Locke. The mind was a spotless tablet on which would be written all the experiences the individual had throughout life. Shaping men and women into good citizens who were honest and responsible members of society requires, therefore, positive, reinforcing experiences beginning very early in life. Beyond the family, a formal education is, according to Locke, the best way of providing the good experiences that will help form healthy and independent personalities.

The process is rational. One starts with the human mind as raw material and molds it, so to speak, with a solid education. The finished product is, at least theoretically, a good person. The process can, of course, work in the opposite direction, for bad experiences could produce a bad person. Most of our current ideas of universal education in a healthy environment are based on Locke's educational philosophy. Along with Sokrates, men and women of the Enlightenment believed that virtue was knowledge and that ignorance was vice; an educated mind was its own reward. It still is.

David Hume, 1711–1776

Locke's theories of mind and understanding revealed some inconsistencies that were later filled in by the Scottish philosopher David Hume, a sane and urbane man who epitomized the enlightened thinker. Beginning with Locke's empiricist theory of knowledge, Hume went on to prove that human reason has its limits. Anticipating a great public outcry, he published, in three volumes, *A Treatise of Human Nature being an Attempt to Introduce the Experimental Method of Reasoning into Moral Subjects (1739–1740)*. Instead, no one noticed the book at the time; as Hume sadly noted: "it fell dead-born from the press." It could

not, however, be ignored for long. In volume one Hume granted certain knowledge only to arithmetic and algebra, and to geometry providing the axioms are true. Beyond that, he said, there is only probable knowledge, thus anticipating modern scientific thought.

Hume's principal concern was with cause and effect, or causality. If we observe that a certain event A is always followed by B, then we assume that A causes B. If, for example, we hold a match to a piece of paper and see the paper burn, we connect the two events and say that the flaming match caused the paper to burn. Not so, says Hume. That paper always burns when a match is held to it is a *belief* that is developed through *custom,* that is, experience. We have seen this happen so often we assume that it *must* happen every time and therein lies the rub. Because A (the match) does not *cause* B (paper) to burn, we cannot assume that paper is *certain* to burn. It is probable but not certain. The paper, for example, could have been soaked in a chemical that no amount of flame would set afire. Further, we cannot bite into an apple with the certainty that it will taste like an apple; it could taste like roast pork. We assume that the sun will rise tomorrow, but it is impossible to establish that it must necessarily rise. Newton's law of universal gravitation is therefore probable and not necessarily universal. As space vehicles have probed ever deeper into the cosmos, scientists have watched with extreme curiosity to see if Newton's law remains valid. There have been no inconsistencies to date, but no scientist would be willing to predict what the situation might be a thousand or more light years away. As Hume says, human reason has its limits. He accepted a world based on probability rather than certainty. Through observation and reasoning we can determine, short of certainty, only *how* nature operates, but not *why.*

Hume's skepticism also applied to religion and religious beliefs and followed a long history of skeptical doubts about the truths of Judeo-Christianity. In the sixteenth century a Portuguese Jewish refugee in Holland, Uriel Da Costa, started out questioning the truth of orthodox Judaism and ended up stating that all religions were made by human beings. The French skeptic Isaac La Peyrère wrote *Man Before Adam (1656)* in which he claimed that there were people all over the world before Adam; therefore, the Bible cannot be an accurate account of human history. La Peyrère's work led two biblical scholars, Baruch de Spinoza (1632–1677) and Father Richard Simon (1638–1712), to reexamine religious knowledge. Spinoza concluded that the Bible was not divine revelation but merely a history of Jewish activities and superstitions. He proposed instead a religious pantheism in which all existence was embraced in one substance (God or Nature), a position of great appeal for the coming Romantic movement. The greatest biblical scholar of his age, Father Simon set out to prove that scholars could never find an accurate text of the Bible nor discover what it meant. Unlike Spinoza, Simon was convinced that there was a biblical message and tried, in vain, to determine what the message was.

The most famous of the French skeptics, Pierre Bayle (1647–1706), wrote his *Historical and Critical Dictionary* (1697–1702), in which he undermined the metaphysical theories of Descartes, Spinoza, Locke, and Leibniz; attacked all existing theologies; ridiculed the heroes of the Old Testament; and challenged all rational knowledge. He advocated abandoning reason in favor of blind faith, for there was little left but doubt about understanding anything at all except by describing everything in historical terms. Voltaire called Bayle's *Dictionary* the "Arsenal of the Enlightenment."

An avid reader of Bayle, Hume saw, as apparently no other Enlightenment thinker did, the plight of human beings if Bayle's skepticism could not be countered. Hume never doubted that people could be certain about the evils of murder, stealing, and the like, nor need they be unsure about Newton's laws. Uncertainty belonged in the philosopher's study. People, through a study of human history, had to recognize different kinds of knowledge and live their lives as sane and civilized human beings. Hume anticipated modern science by stating that there were no absolute truths and, further, that one should not, must not, believe anything absolutely. He was particularly concerned about religious conflicts. "Errors in religion," he wrote, "are dangerous; those in philosophy only ridiculous." He believed, in the final analysis, that people could lead their lives as he did his, exercising their natural passions and common sense as they cheerfully enjoyed the uncertainties of everyday life.

Immanual Kant, 1724–1804

The leading thinker of the German Enlightenment, Kant responded to Hume's skepticism with the famous remark that he had been "awakened from his dogmatic slumbers." In his three *Critiques (Pure Reason,* 1781; *Practical Reason,* 1788; *Judgement,* 1793) Kant laid out a complete philosophical system. He showed that knowledge *a priori* was possible because people could perceive the world of space, forms, and causality and, because of the intrinsic nature of the human mind, understand phenomena. As he said, we can know only such appearances as colors, shapes, and sounds, but never the thing-in-itself; true knowledge cannot transcend experience. But we can have reliable knowledge because all minds function the same way.

In ethics Kant stated that good actions must be performed from a sense of duty and that moral law was derived from his categorical imperative: "act only according to the maxim which you at the same time will to be a universal law." People, he said, were independent moral agents with the freedom to choose right actions. As a practical necessity Kant postulated the existence of God for those who desired (or required) a belief in divinity, so that virtue could be crowned with happiness and immortality, and the pursuit of moral perfection could continue in the afterlife.

With ethical and moral theories that appealed to the heart as opposed to Hume's dispassionate rationalism, Kant was the founder of German idealism. Subsequently, his philosophy had enormous appeal for the German Romantic movement. Kant was, however, an enlightened rather than a proto-Romantic thinker. His principle that every person had to be considered as an end in herself or himself is a form of the Enlightenment doctrine of the Rights of Man. Kant coined, moreover, the prevailing motto for the Enlightenment: "Dare to Know!"

Les Philosophes

Called *Les Philosophes* (the philosophers) or *Encyclopedistes* because most of them wrote articles for Diderot's monumental *Encyclopedia,* the philosophes were not all philosophers but included writers, poets, artists, dramatists, mathematicians, and scientists. What all had in common was the French language, which had become the international language of the Enlightenment, leading Thomas Jefferson to remark that everyone had two homelands, his own and France. One of the leading philosophes, Denis Diderot (dee-duh-RO; 1713–1784), was editor-in-chief of the *Encyclopedia* (1747–1772). Published in twenty-eight volumes but suppressed in 1759 by the government and thereafter printed clandestinely, the work was a summary of all human knowledge, a brilliant response to Kant's "Dare to Know!" Its prevailing spirit was scorn for the past and for all organized religions, and glorification of reason, the arts, the experimental sciences, and industry. The *Encyclopedia* assumed that religious toleration and freedom of thought would win out and implied throughout that the condition of the common people should be the main concern of the government. A call to arms in twenty-eight volumes, the *Encyclopedia* was probably, for the intellectuals, the key influence that led to the French Revolution.

In his *Persian Letters* (published anonymously in 1721) Montesquieu (mon-tes-KYO; 1689–1755) satirized European, especially French, society, leaving no phase of human activity untouched by its devastating wit and irony. His most influential book, *The Spirit of the Laws* (1748), was a scientific study of comparative government whose theories of checks and balances found their way into the United States Constitution.

Diderot, Voltaire, and Rousseau were the most influential of the French philosophes. Voltaire and his satirical novel *Candide* are discussed near the end of this chapter. A kind of reverse image of Voltaire the rationalist, Rousseau was a powerful influence on the Romantic movement and is considered in chapter 23.

Absolutism and the Enlightenment

Louis XIV was a despot but, with some justification, he could also be called an enlightened monarch. The same cannot be said for the next two kings. Louis XV, great grandson of Louis XIV, ruled ineptly but luxuriously from 1715–1774, and his weak and vacillating grandson, Louis XVI (1774–1793), went to the guillotine.

A rival state, the kingdom of Brandenburg-Prussia, rose to power during the decline of French power and influence. Frederick I was crowned the first king of Prussia in 1701, followed by

Frederick William I (1713–1740), who began Prussian expansion. Frederick the Great (1740–1786) excelled at waging war and made Prussia the dominant military power in Europe. Known as a "benevolent despot," he promoted social and legal reforms and established a glittering court with musical performances by Johann Sebastian Bach and by Frederick himself. But the king did remark that "my people say what they please and I do as I please." Enlightenment had a way to go.

The founder of the modern Russian state, Peter the Great (1682–1725), mercilessly "westernized" his country and savagely destroyed his enemies. He was admittedly a genius and undoubtedly more than a bit mad. To this day he has been admired as an enlightened leader and viewed with horror as a sadistic monster. Catherine the Great (1762–1791) was of German birth but she became thoroughly Russianized. Influenced by the Enlightenment, she planned vast reforms, but a peasant revolt in 1773–1775 and the French Revolution caused her to reverse course and, among other authoritarian decrees, enslave the serfs.

Only in Britain was there any real political freedom. Under the Hanoverian kings George I (1714–1727) and George II (1727–1760), Robert Walpole became, in fact if not in name, the prime minister (1721–1742). William Pitt (1757–1761) was a strong prime minister, but resigned when the next king, George III (1760–1820), decided he wanted to direct policy. Lord North was an acquiescent prime minister, and between king and prime minister they inadvertently brought a new democratic republic into being. Absolutism during the Enlightenment was anything but enlightened.

Literature, 1600–1789

John Donne, 1573–1631

Though the seventeenth century is often referred to as the Baroque era, the term is more appropriate for art and music (see chapters 21 and 22) than it generally is for literature. Donne's poetry does display some of the opulence and splendor associated with the Baroque, but Donne has, instead, been characterized as the leader of the Metaphysical school, referring, in general, to the powerful intellectual content of his work, his concentrated images, and his remarkable ability to range between the intensely personal and the cosmic. Poets such as Andrew Marvell and others were influenced by Donne, but they formed no organized school nor would they have endorsed the Metaphysical school label that John Dryden and Samuel Johnson affixed to the poetry of Donne and Marvell.

Poet, prose stylist, and preacher, John Donne was an experienced man of the world who spoke with great intellectual vigor in his love poems and in his Holy Sonnets. Neglected for three centuries after his death, he is now recognized as one of the finest poets in the English language.

In the following song Donne uses six vivid images to express the impossibility, as he saw it, of woman's constancy.

Literary Selections

SONG
John Donne

Go and catch a falling star,
    Get with child a mandrake root,
Tell me where all past years are,
    Or who cleft the devil's foot,
Teach me to hear mermaids singing,
Or to keep off envy's stinging,
      And find
      What wind
Serves to advance an honest mind.
If thou be'st born to strange sights,   10
    Things invisible to see,
Ride ten thousand days and nights,
    Till age snow white hairs on thee;
Thou, when thou return'st, wilt tell me
All strange wonders that befell thee,
      And swear,
      Nowhere
Lives a woman true and fair.
If thou find'st one, let me know;
    Such a pilgrimage were sweet;   20
Yet do not: I would not go,
    Though at next door we might meet;
Though she were true when you met her,
And last till you write your letter,
      Yet she
      Will be
False, ere I come, to two or three.

The following poem employs unique images that reflect Donne's secret marriage to his patron's niece, a happy union but one that clouded the rest of the poet's life. Only John Donne could effectively express life, love, and loving in terms of a flea.

THE FLEA
John Donne

Mark but this flea, and mark in this,
How little that which thou deniest me is;
It sucked me first, and now sucks thee,
And in this flea our two bloods mingled be;
Thou know'st that this cannot be said
A sin, nor shame, nor loss of maidenhead,
Yet this enjoys before it woo,
And pampered swells with one blood made of two,
And this, alas! is more than we would do.
Oh stay, three lives in one flea spare,   10
Where we almost, yea, more than married are.
This flea is you and I, and this
Our marriage-bed and marriage-temple is;
Though parents grudge, and you, we 're met
And cloistered in these living walls of jet.

Though use make you apt to kill me,
Let not, to that, self-murder added be,
And sacrilege, three sins in killing three.

Cruel and sudden, hast thou since
Purpled thy nail, in blood of innocence?   20
In what could this flea guilty be,
Except in that drop which it sucked from thee?
Yet thou triumph'st, and say'st that thou
Find'st not thyself, nor me the weaker now;
'Tis true, then learn how false, fears be;
Just so much honour, when thou yield'st to me,
Will waste, as this flea's death took life from thee.

Of Donne's large volume of religious poetry some, near the end of his career, reflected his obsession with the thought of death. In the following Holy Sonnet he uses intense language and images to put death in perspective.

HOLY SONNET X
John Donne

Death, be not proud, though some have callëd thee
Mighty and dreadful, for thou art not so;
For those whom thou think'st thou dost overthrow
Die not, poor Death, nor yet canst thou kill me.
From rest and sleep, which but thy pictures be,
Much pleasure, then from thee much more must flow;
And soonest our best men with thee do go,
Rest of their bones, and soul's delivery.
Thou art slave to Fate, chance, kings, and desperate men,
And dost with poison, war, and sickness dwell,
And poppy or charms can make us sleep as well
And better than thy stroke; why swell'st thou then?
One short sleep past, we wake eternally
And Death shall be no more; Death, thou shalt die.

Exercises

1. Donne's poetry has been aptly called "strong-lined" because of his powerful images and sharp changes in rhythm. Try reading his "Song" aloud, listening for the abrupt change in rhythm of *And find/What wind* plus similar changes in the second and third stanzas. How much do these contribute to "strong-lined" poetry?

2. In the "Holy Sonnet" Donne equates death with extended, restful sleep. Is his point of view convincing? Would it persuade an atheist?

Andrew Marvell (1621–1678)

Late in his career Marvell wrote stinging political satires, but he is best known today for his classically inspired lyric poetry about love and nature. "To His Coy Mistress" is a seduction poem in the tradition of Catullus and other classical writers in which the theme is the fleeting moment and the tone is urgent. We must seize the moment and make love now. Though the theme is serious, the style is both graceful and playful and, withal, sophisticated.

TO HIS COY MISTRESS
Andrew Marvell

Had we but World enough, and Time,
This coyness Lady were no crime.
We would sit down, and think which way
To walk, and pass our long Loves Day.
Thou by the *Indian Ganges* side
Should'st Rubies find: I by the Tide
Of *Humber* would complain. I would
Love you ten years before the Flood:
And you should if you please refuse
Till the Conversion of the *Jews*.   10
My vegetable Love should grow
Vaster than Empires, and more slow.
An hundred years should go to praise
Thine Eyes, and on thy Forehead Gaze.
Two hundred to adore each Breast:
But thirty thousand to the rest.
An Age at least to every part,
And the last Age should show your Heart.
For Lady you deserve this State;
Nor would I love at lower rate.   20
But at my back I alwaies hear
Times winged Charriot hurrying near:
And yonder all before us lye
Deserts of vast Eternity.
Thy Beauty shall no more be found;
Nor, in thy marble Vault, shall sound
My echoing Song: then Worms shall try
That long preserv'd Virginity:
And your quaint Honour turn to dust;
And into ashes all my Lust.   30
The Grave's a fine and private place,
But none I think do there embrace.
Now therefore, while the youthful hew
Sits on thy skin like morning dew,
And while thy willing Soul transpires
At every pore with instant Fires,
Now let us sport us while we may;
And now, like am'rous birds of prey,
Rather at once our Time devour,
Than languish in his slow-chapt pow'r.   40
Let us roll all our Strength, and all
Our sweetness, up into one Ball:
And tear our Pleasures with rough strife,
Thorough the Iron gates of Life.
Thus, though we cannot make our Sun
Stand still, yet we will make him run.

Did the Coy Mistress acquiesce? Look again at the first and last lines, at the progression from not having enough time to the illusion of time flying by.

John Milton (1608–1674)

An ardent supporter of the Puritan cause, Milton became Latin secretary in Cromwell's government and, in several important tracts, one of its principal defenders. On the Restoration of the Stuart line with Charles II (1660), Milton was fined and forcibly retired, after which he dictated his epic poems *Paradise Lost* (1667) and *Paradise Regained* (1671). One of the world's great epic poems, *Paradise Lost* relates the story of Satan's rebellion against God and the Fall of Man. Milton's intention was, as he said, to "justify the ways of God to man."

The epic poems were among the first to use blank verse (unrhymed iambic pentameter), but Milton also wrote some notable sonnets. Considered to be among his finest work in small form, the two sonnets given below are in the standard form of fourteen lines in rhymed iambic pentameter.

On Easter Sunday in 1655, in the Piedmont region of northwestern Italy, the Duke of Savoy slaughtered about 1,700 members of the Protestant Waldensian sect that dated back to 1170 (see Reformation in chapter 16). The pope celebrated the occasion with a special mass but Protestant Europe was horrified; Milton's response was a sonnet tense with low-keyed fury. The "martyred blood" refers to Tertullian's statement that "the blood of the martyrs is the seed of the Church." The "triple Tyrant" is the pope, whose tiara has three crowns, and "Babylonian woe" is a reference to Revelation 18 in which the obliteration of the city of luxury and vice is described. Along with many Protestants, especially Puritans, Milton saw the destruction of Babylon as an allegory of the ultimate fate of the Church of Rome.

ON THE LATE MASSACRE IN PIEDMONT (1655)
John Milton

Avenge, O Lord, thy slaughtered Saints, whose bones
   Lie scattered on the Alpine mountains cold;
   Even them who kept thy truth so pure of old,
When all our fathers worshiped stocks and stones,
Forget not: in thy book record their groans
   Who were thy sheep, and in their ancient fold
   Slain by the bloody Piemontese, that rolled
Mother with infant down the rocks. Their moans
The vales redoubled to the hills, and they
   To heaven. Their martyred blood and ashes sow
O'er all the Italian fields, where still doth sway
   The triple Tyrant; that from these may grow
A hundredfold, who, having learnt thy way,
   Early may fly the Babylonian woe.

Milton's eyesight, due to overwork, had become impaired as early as 1644, and by 1652 he was totally blind. The first of two sonnets about his blindness, the following poem signals the poet's submission to fate though he had not yet found his way to using, in darkness, "that one talent which is death to hide."

ON HIS BLINDNESS (1655)
John Milton

When I consider how my light is spent
   Ere half my days in this dark world and wide,
   And that one Talent which is death to hide
   Lodged with me useless, though my soul more bent
To serve therewith my Maker, and present
   My true account, lest He returning chide,
   "Doth God exact day-labour, light denied?"
   I fondly ask. But Patience, to prevent
That murmur, soon replies, "God doth not need
   Either man's work or his own gifts.
     Who best
   Bear his mild yoke, they serve him best.
     His state
Is kingly: thousands at his bidding speed,
   And post o'er land and ocean without rest;
   They also serve who only stand and wait."

Exercise

Milton seethes with indignation over the fate of the slaughtered saints in Italy, but not over the loss of his sight. What are some of the words that convey this mood of resignation? Consider, for example, such words as *spent, bent, mild,* and *murmur.*

Jean-Baptiste Poquelin Molière, 1622–1673

Milton's poetry has Baroque elements, but the arts in seventeenth-century France rarely ventured far from the classical ideals of Graeco-Roman civilization. The French seem always to view themselves as rational people living a civilized life in a sensible and orderly society. Louis XIV was regarded as the new Caesar Augustus with Paris as the New Rome or New Athens. The painter Poussin and the playwrights Racine and Molière worked in a context that combined Renaissance ideals with the less flamboyant aspects of the Counter-Reformation. France was a Roman Catholic country with a centralized government but with a definite secular orientation. It was perhaps the most restrained of Catholic countries, especially when compared with Spain, Italy, or Ireland.

Some French intellectuals believed they lived in a Christian state of grace, but numerous others perceived themselves in a state of nature in a secular society. These contrasting views led to the famous "Quarrel of the Ancients and Moderns." (The French adore intellectual disputes.) Both sides revered classical antiquity, but the Ancients believed they were only modest heirs of classical civilization. The Moderns were convinced they could

Figure 20.3 *Molière and his troupe of players. Photo: North Wind Picture Archives.*

not only emulate the Greeks and Romans but actually improve on their civilization. This notion of historical progress was, at the time, relatively new, terribly enticing, and distinctly secular. The French were convinced they had invented modern European civilization, with subsequent events only tending to confirm this sweeping supposition.

Comic playwright Molière (figure 20.3) lived and worked in this neoclassical climate. He was a rational humanist, creating characters "untouched by any thought of Christian grace," according to an early critic. People, to Molière, were products of the social order. As such, they should possess the virtues of moderation, common sense, and good taste in an urban setting that was rational and sophisticated.

Molière's comedies examine the failure of one or more individuals to measure up to these classical virtues. The title character of *Tartuffe,* for example, has none of these qualities, being a liar, cheat, rogue, and all-around scoundrel. Masquerading as a

virtuous fellow of great religiosity, he is a hypocrite; his protector, Orgon, is a foolish dupe; and Orgon's mother is an overbearing snob. In his *Devil's Dictionary* Ambrose Bierce defined a hypocrite as "one who, professing virtues that he does not respect, secures the advantage of seeming to be what he despises." So it was with Tartuffe.

To stage his play Molière had to address several petitions to Louis XIV explaining that some religious groups claimed he was attacking religious beliefs when, in fact, he was exposing a hypocrite who used his pretended religion to seduce women and cheat foolish people out of their money and property. Tartuffe represents all those who manipulate people's religious beliefs for personal gain. As Molière knew full well, there were undoubtedly Tartuffes around since the beginning of civilization; they seem to be rather numerous in our own time, particularly on television. The translation is by Richard Wilbur.

Tartuffe (1669)
Molière

CHARACTERS[3]

Madame Pernelle, Orgon's mother
Orgon, Elmire's husband
Elmire, Orgon's wife
Damis, Orgon's son, Elmire's stepson
Mariane, Orgon's daughter, Elmire's stepdaughter, in love with Valère
Valère, in love with Mariane
Cléante, Orgon's brother-in-law
Tartuffe, a hypocrite
Dorine, Mariane's lady's-maid
M. Loyal, a bailiff
A Police Officer
Flipote, Mme Pernelle's maid

The Scene *throughout: Orgon's house in Paris*

ACT 1

Scene 1. Madame Pernelle *and* Flipote, *her maid* Elmire, Mariane, Dorine, Damis, Cléante

Madame Pernelle. Come, come, Flipote; it's time I left this place.
Elmire. I can't keep up, you walk at such a pace.
Madame Pernelle. Don't trouble, child; no need to show me out.
It's not your manners I'm concerned about.
Elmire. We merely pay you the respect we owe.
But, Mother, why this hurry? Must you go? 10
Madame Pernelle. I must. This house appalls me. No one in it.
Will pay attention for a single minute.
I offer good advice, but you won't hear it.
Children, I take my leave much vexed in spirit.
You all break in and chatter on and on.
It's like a madhouse[4] with the keeper gone.
Dorine. If . . .
Madame Pernelle. Girl, you talk too much, and I'm afraid
You're far too saucy for a lady's-maid. 20
You push in everywhere and have your say.
Damis. But . . .

Madame Pernelle. You, boy, grow more foolish every day.
To think my grandson should be such a dunce!
I've said a hundred times, if I've said it once,
That if you keep the course on which you've started,
You'll leave your worthy father broken-hearted.
Mariane. I think . . .
Madame Pernelle. And you, his sister, seem so pure,
So shy, so innocent, and so demure. 30
But you know what they say about still waters.
I pity parents with secretive daughters.
Elmire. Now, Mother . . .
Madame Pernelle. And as for you, child, let me add
That your behavior is extremely bad,
And a poor example for these children, too.
Their dear, dead mother did far better than you.
You're much too free with money, and I'm distressed
To see you so elaborately dressed.
When it's one's husband that one aims to please, 40
One has no need of costly fripperies.
Cléante. Oh, Madam, really . . .
Madame Pernelle. You are her brother, Sir,
And I respect and love you; yet if I were
My son, this lady's good and pious spouse,
I wouldn't make you welcome in my house.
You're full of worldly counsels which, I fear,
Aren't suitable for decent folk to hear.
I've spoken bluntly, Sir; but it behooves us
Not to mince words when righteous fervor moves us. 50
Damis. Your man Tartuffe is full of holy speeches . . .
Madame Pernelle. And practises precisely what he preaches.
He's a fine man, and should be listened to.
I will not hear him mocked by fools like you.
Damis. Good God! Do you expect me to submit
To the tyranny of that carping hypocrite?
Must we forgo all joys and satisfactions
Because that bigot censures all our actions?
Dorine. To hear him talk—and he talks all the time—
There's nothing one can do that's not a crime. 60
He rails at everything, your dear Tartuffe.
Madame Pernelle. Whatever he reproves deserves reproof.
He's out to save your souls, and all of you
Must love him, as my son would have you do.
Damis. Ah no, Grandmother, I could never take
To such a rascal, even for my father's sake.
That's how I feel, and I shall not dissemble.
His every action makes me seethe and tremble,
With helpless anger, and I have no doubt
That he and I will shortly have it out. 70
Dorine. Surely it is a shame and a disgrace
To see this man usurp the master's place—
To see this beggar who, when first he came,
Had not a shoe or shoestring to his name,
So far forget himself that he behaves
As if the house were his, and we his slaves.
Madame Pernelle. Well, mark my words, your souls would fare far better
If you obeyed his precepts to the letter.

---

3. The name Tartuffe has been traced back to an older word associated with liar or charlatan: *truffer,* "to deceive" or "to cheat." Then there was also the Italian actor, Tartufo, physically deformed and truffle-shaped. Most of the other names are typical of this genre of court-comedy and possess rather elegant connotations of pastoral and *bergerie.* Dorine would be a *demoiselle de compagne* and not a mere maid; that is, a female companion to Mariane of roughly the same social status. This in part accounts for the liberties she takes in conversation with Orgon, Madame Pernelle, and others. Her name is short for Théodorine.

4. In the original, *la cour du roi Petaud,* the Court of King Pétaud where all are masters; a house of misrule.

Dorine. You see him as a saint. I'm far less awed;   80
In fact, I see right through him. He's a fraud.
Madame Pernelle. Nonsense!
Dorine. His man Laurent's the same, or worse;
I'd not trust either with a penny purse.
Madame Pernelle. I can't say what his servant's morals may be;
His own great goodness I can guarantee.
You all regard him with distaste and fear
Because he tells you what you're loath to hear,
Condemns your sins, points out your moral flaws,   90
And humbly strives to further Heaven's cause.
Dorine. If sin is all that bothers him, why is it
He's so upset when folk drop in to visit?
Is Heaven so outraged by a social call
That he must prophesy against us all?
I'll tell you what I think: if you ask me,
He's jealous of my mistress' company.
Madame Pernelle. Rubbish! [*To Elmire*] He's not alone, child, in complaining
Of all of your promiscuous entertaining.   100
Why, the whole neighborhood's upset, I know,
By all these carriages that come and go,
With crowds of guests parading in and out
And noisy servants loitering about.
In all of this, I'm sure there's nothing vicious;
But why give people cause to be suspicious?
Cléante. They need no cause; they'll talk in any case.
Madam, this world would be a joyless place
If, fearing what malicious tongues might say,
We locked our doors and turned our friends away.   110
And even if one did so dreary a thing,
D'you think those tongues would cease their chattering?
One can't fight slander; it's a losing battle;
Let us instead ignore their tittle-tattle.
Let's strive to live by conscience' clear decrees,
And let the gossips gossip as they please.
Dorine. If there is talk against us, I know the source:
It's Daphne and her little husband, of course.
Those who have greatest cause for guilt and shame
Are quickest to besmirch a neighbor's name.   120
When there's a chance for libel, they never miss it;
When something can be made to seem illicit
They're off at once to spread the joyous news,
Adding to fact what fantasies they choose.
By talking up their neighbor's indiscretions
They seek to camouflage their own transgressions,
Hoping that others' innocent affairs
Will lend a hue of innocence to theirs,
Or that their own black guilt will come to seem
Part of a general shady color-scheme.   130
Madame Pernelle. All this is quite irrelevant. I doubt
That anyone's more virtuous and devout
Than dear Orante; and I'm informed that she
Condemns your mode of life most vehemently.

Dorine. Oh, yes, she's strict, devout, and has no taint
Of worldliness; in short, she seems a saint.
But it was time which taught her that disguise;
So long as her attractions could enthrall,
She flounced and flirted and enjoyed it all,
But now that they're no longer what they were   140
She quits a world which fast is quitting her,
And wears a veil of virtue to conceal
Her bankrupt beauty and her lost appeal.
That's what becomes of old coquettes today:
Distressed when all their lovers fall away,
They see no recourse but to play the prude,
And so confer a style on solitude.
Thereafter, they're severe with everyone,
Condemning all our actions, pardoning none,
And claiming to be pure, austere, and zealous   150
When, if the truth were known, they're merely jealous,
And cannot bear to see another know
The pleasures time has forced them to forgo.
Madame Pernelle. [*Initially to Elmire*] That sort of talk[5] is what you like to hear;
Therefore you'd have us all keep still, my dear,
While Madam rattles on the livelong day.
Nevertheless, I mean to have my say.
I tell you that you're blest to have Tartuffe   160
Dwelling, as my son's guest, beneath this roof;
That Heaven has sent him to forestall its wrath
By leading you, once more, to the true path;
That all he reprehends is reprehensible,
And that you'd better heed him, and be sensible.
These visits, balls, and parties in which you revel
Are nothing but inventions of the Devil.
One never hears a word that's edifying:
Nothing but chaff and foolishness and lying,
As well as vicious gossip in which one's neighbor
Is cut to bits with épée, foil, and saber.   170
People of sense are driven half-insane
At such affairs, where noise and folly reign
And reputations perish thick and fast.
As a wise preacher said on Sunday last,
Parties are Towers of Babylon,[6] because
The guests all babble on with never a pause;
And then he told a story which, I think . . .
     [*To Cleante*] I heard that laugh, Sir, and I saw that wink!
Go find your silly friends and laugh some more!
Enough; I'm going; don't show me to the door.   180
I leave this household much dismayed and vexed;
I cannot say when I shall see you next.
     [*Slapping Flipote*] Wake up, don't stand there gaping into space!
I'll slap some sense into that stupid face.
Move, move, you slut.

---

5. In the original, a reference to a collection of novels about chivalry found in *La Bibliotheque bleue (The Blue Library)*, written for children.

6. i.e., Tower of Babel. Mme. Pernelle's malapropism is the cause of Cléante's laughter.

Scene 2. Cléante, Dorine

Cléante. I think I'll stay behind;
I want no further pieces of her mind.
How that old lady . . .   190
Dorine.   Oh, what wouldn't she say
If she could hear you speak of her that way!
She'd thank you for the *lady,* but I'm sure
She'd find the *old* a little premature.
Cléante. My, what a scene she made, and what a din!
And how this man Tartuffe has taken her in!
Dorine. Yes, but her son is even worse deceived;
His folly must be seen to be believed.
In the late troubles,[7] he played an able part
And served his king with wise and loyal heart,   200
But he's quite lost his senses since he fell
Beneath Tartuffe's infatuating spell.
He calls him brother, and loves him as his life,
Preferring him to mother, child, or wife.
In him and him alone will he confide;
He's made him his confessor and his guide;
He pets and pampers him with love more tender
Than any pretty maiden could engender,
Gives him the place of honor when they dine,
Delights to see him gorging like a swine,   210
Stuffs him with dainties till his guts distend,
And when he belches, cries "God bless you, friend!"
In short, he's mad; he worships him; he dotes;
His deeds he marvels at, his words, he quotes,
Thinking each act a miracle, each word
Oracular as those that Moses heard.
Tartuffe, much pleased to find so easy a victim,
Has in a hundred ways beguiled and tricked him,
Milked him of money, and with his permission
Established here a sort of Inquisition.   220
Even Laurent, his lackey, dares to give
Us arrogant advice on how to live;
He sermonizes us in thundering tones
And confiscates our ribbons and colognes.
Last week he tore a kerchief into pieces
Because he found it pressed in a *Life of Jesus:*
He said it was a sin to juxtapose
Unholy vanities and holy prose.

Scene 3. Elmire, Mariane, Damis, Cléante, Dorine

Elmire. [*To Cléante*] You did well not to follow; she stood in 230
   the door
And said *verbatim* all she'd said before.
I saw my husband coming. I think I'd best
Go upstairs now, and take a little rest.
Cléante. I'll wait and greet him here; then I must go.
I've really only time to say hello.

---

7. A series of political disturbances during the minority of Louis
   XIV. Specifically these consisted of the *Fronde* ("opposition") of
   the Parlement (1648–1649) and the *Fronde* of the Princes (1650–
   1653). Orgon is depicted as supporting Louis XIV in these
   outbreaks and their resolution.

Damis. Sound him about my sister's wedding, please.
I think Tartuffe's against it, and that he's
Been urging Father to withdraw his blessing.
As you well know, I'd find that most distressing.   240
Unless my sister and Valère can marry,
My hopes to wed *his* sister will miscarry.
And I'm determined . . .
Dorine.   He's coming.

Scene 4. Orgon, Cléante, Dorine

Orgon. Ah, Brother, good-day.
Cléante. Well, welcome back, I'm sorry I can't stay.
How was the country? Blooming, I trust, and green?
Orgon. Excuse me, Brother; just one moment.   250
   [*To Dorine*]   Dorine . . .
[*To Cléante*] To put my mind at rest, I always learn
The household news the moment I return.
[*To Dorine*] Has all been well, these two days I've been gone?
How are the family? What's been going on?
Dorine. Your wife, two days ago, had a bad fever,
And a fierce headache which refused to leave her.
Orgon. Ah. And Tartuffe?
Dorine. Tartuffe? Why, he's round and red.
Bursting with health, and excellently fed.
Orgon. Poor fellow!   260
Dorine. That night, the mistress was unable
To take a single bite at the dinner-table.
Her headache-pains, she said, were simply hellish.
Orgon. Ah. And Tartuffe?
Dorine. He ate his meal with relish,
And zealously devoured in her presence
A leg of mutton and a brace of pheasants.
Orgon. Poor fellow!
Dorine. Well, the pains continued strong,
And so she tossed and tossed the whole night long,   270
Now icy-cold, now burning like a flame.
We sat beside her bed till morning came.
Orgon. Ah. And Tartuffe?
Dorine. Why, having eaten, he rose
And sought his room, already in a doze,
Got into his warm bed, and snored away
In perfect peace until the break of day.
Orgon. Poor fellow!
Dorine. After much ado, we talked her
Into dispatching someone for the doctor.   280
He bled her, and the fever quickly fell.
Orgon. Ah. And Tartuffe?
Dorine. He bore it very well.
To keep his cheerfulness at any cost,
And make up for the blood Madame had lost,
He drank, at lunch, four beakers full of port.
Orgon. Poor fellow.
Dorine. Both are doing well, in short.
I'll go and tell Madame that you've expressed
Keen sympathy and anxious interest.   290

Scene 5. Orgon, Cléante

Cléante. That girl was laughing in your face, and though
I've no wish to offend you, even so
I'm bound to say that she had some excuse.
How can you possibly be such a goose?
Are you so dazed by this man's hocus-pocus
That all the world, save him, is out of focus?
You've given him clothing, shelter, food, and care;
Why must you also . . .
Orgon. Brother, stop right there.   300
You do not know the man of whom you speak.
Cléante. I grant you that. But my judgment's not so weak
That I can't tell, by his effect on others . . .
Orgon. Ah, when you meet him, you two will be like brothers!
There's been no loftier soul since time began.
He is a man who . . . a man who . . . an excellent man.
To keep his precepts is to be reborn,
And view this dunghill of a world with scorn.   310
Yes, thanks to him I'm a changed man indeed.
Under his tutelage my soul's been freed
From earthly loves, and every human tie:
My mother, children, brother, and wife could die,
And I'd not feel a single moment's pain.
Cléante. That's a fine sentiment, Brother; most humane.
Orgon. Oh, had you seen Tartuffe as I first knew him,
Your heart, like mine, would have surrendered to him,
He used to come into our church each day
And humbly kneel nearby, and start to pray.   320
He'd draw the eyes of everybody there
By the deep fervor of his heartfelt prayer;
He'd sigh and weep, and sometimes with a sound
Of rapture he would bend and kiss the ground;
And when I rose to go, he'd run before
To offer me holy-water at the door.
His serving-man, no less devout than he,
Informed me of his master's poverty;
I gave him gifts, but in his humbleness
He'd beg me every time to give him less.   330
"Oh, that's too much," he'd cry, "too much by twice!
I don't deserve it. The half, Sir, would suffice."
And when I wouldn't take it back, he'd share
Half of it with the poor, right then and there.
At length, Heaven prompted me to take him in
To dwell with us, and free our souls from sin.
He guides our lives, and to protect my honor
Stays by my wife, and keeps an eye upon her;
He tells me whom she sees, and all she does,
And seems more jealous than I ever was!   340
And how austere he is! Why, he can detect
A moral sin where you would least suspect;
In smallest trifles, he's extremely strict.

Last week, his conscience was severely pricked
Because, while praying, he had caught a flea
And killed it, so he felt, too wrathfully.[8]
Cléante. Good God, man! Have you lost your common sense—
Or is this all some joke at my expense?
How can you stand there and in all sobriety . . .   350
Orgon. Brother, your language savors of impiety.
Too much free-thinking's made your faith unsteady,
And as I've warned you many times already,
'Twill get you into trouble before you're through.
Cléante. So I've been told before by dupes like you:
Being blind, you'd have all others blind as well;
The clear-eyed man you call an infidel,
And he who sees through humbug and pretense
Is charged, by you, with want of reverence.
Spare me your warnings, Brother; I have no fear   360
Of speaking out, for you and Heaven to hear,
Against affected zeal and pious knavery.
There's true and false in piety, as in bravery,
And just as those whose courage shines the most
In battle, are the least inclined to boast,
So those whose hearts are truly pure and lowly
Don't make a flashy show of being holy.
There's a vast difference, so it seems to me,
Between true piety and hypocrisy:
How do you fail to see it, may I ask?   370
Is not a face quite different from a mask?
Cannot sincerity and cunning art,
Reality and semblance, be told apart?
Are scarecrows just like men, and do you hold
That a false coin is just as good as gold?
Ah, Brother, man's strangely fashioned creature
Who seldom is content to follow Nature,
But recklessly pursues his inclination
Beyond the narrow bounds of moderation,
And often, by transgressing Reason's laws,   380
Perverts a lofty aim or noble cause.
A passing observation, but it applies.
Orgon. I see, dear Brother, that you're profoundly wise;
You harbor all the insight of the age.
You are our one clear mind. Our only sage,
The era's oracle, its Cato[9] too,
And all mankind are fools compared to you.
Cléante. Brother, I don't pretend to be a sage,
Nor have I all the wisdom of the age.
There's just one insight I would dare to claim: 390
I know that true and false are not the same;

---

8. In the *Golden Legend (Legenda santorum),* a popular collection of the lives of the saints written in the thirteenth century, it is said of St. Marcarius the Elder (d. 390) that he dwelt naked in the desert for six months, a penance he felt appropriate for having killed a flea.

9. Roman statesman (95 B.C.–46 B.C.) with an enduring reputation for honesty and incorruptibility.

And just as there is nothing I more revere
Than a soul whose faith is steadfast and sincere,
Nothing that I more cherish and admire
Than honest zeal and true religious fire,
So there is nothing that I find more base
Than specious piety's dishonest face—
Than these bold mountebanks, these histrios
Whose impious mummeries and hollow shows
Exploit our love of Heaven, and make a jest   400
Of all that men think holiest and best;
These calculating souls who offer prayers
Not to their Maker, but as public wares,
And seek to buy respect and reputation
With lifted eyes and sighs of exaltation;
These charlatans, I say, whose pilgrim souls
Proceed, by way of Heaven, toward earthly goals,
Who weep and pray and swindle and extort,
Who preach the monkish life; but haunt the court,
Who make their zeal the partner of their vice—   410
Such men are vengeful, sly, and cold as ice,
And when there is an enemy to defame
They cloak their spite in fair religion's name,
Their private spleen and malice being made
To seem a high and virtuous crusade,
Until, to mankind's reverent applause,
They crucify their foe in Heaven's cause.
Such knaves are all too common; yet, for the wise,
True piety isn't hard to recognize,
And, happily, these present times provide us   420
With bright examples to instruct and guide us.
Consider Ariston and Périandre;
Look at Oronte, Alcidamas, Clitandre;[10]
Their virtue is acknowledged; who could doubt it?
But you won't hear them beat the drum about it.
They're never ostentatious, never vain,
And their religion's moderate and humane;
It's not their way to criticize and chide:
They think censoriousness a mark of pride,
And therefore, letting others preach and rave,   430
They show, by deeds, how Christians should behave.
They think no evil of their fellow man,
But judge of him as kindly as they can.
They don't intrigue and wangle and conspire;
To lead a good life is their one desire;
The sinner wakes no rancorous hate in them;
It is the sin alone which they condemn;
Nor do they try to show a fiercer zeal
For Heaven's cause than Heaven itself could feel.
These men I honor, these men I advocate   440
As models for us all to emulate.
Your man is not their sort at all, I fear:
And, while your praise of him is quite sincere,
I think that you've been dreadfully deluded.
Orgon. Now then, dear Brother, is your speech concluded?
Cléante. Why, yes.

---

10. Vaguely Greek and Roman names derived from the elegant
literature of the day; not names of actual persons.

Orgon. Your servant, Sir. [*He turns to go.*]
Cléante. No, Brother; wait.
There's one more matter. You agreed of late
That young Valère might have your daughter's hand.   450
Orgon. I did.
Cléante. And set the date, I understand.
Orgon. Quite so.
Cléante. You've now postponed it; is that true?
Orgon. No doubt.
Cléante. The match no longer pleases you?
Orgon. Who knows?
Cléante. D'you mean to go back on your word?
Orgon. I won't say that.
Cléante. Has anything occurred   460
Which might entitle you to break your pledge?
Orgon. Perhaps.
Cléante. Why must you hem, and haw, and hedge?
The boy asked me to sound you in this affair . . .
Orgon. It's been a pleasure.
Cléante. But what shall I tell Valère?
Orgon. Whatever you like.
Cléante. But what have you decided?
What are your plans?
Orgon. I plan, Sir, to be guided   470
By Heaven's will.
Cléante. Come, Brother, don't talk rot.
You've given Valère your word; will you keep it, or not?
Orgon. Good day.
Cléante. This looks like poor Valère's undoing;
I'll go and warn him that there's trouble brewing.

ACT II
Scene 1. Orgon, Mariane

Orgon. Mariane.
Mariane. Yes, Father?
Orgon. A word with you; come here.
Mariane. What are you looking for?
Orgon. [*Peering into a small closet*] Eavesdroppers, dear.
I'm making sure we shan't be overheard.
Someone in there could catch our every word.
Ah, good, we're safe. Now, Mariane, my child,
You're a sweet girl who's tractable and mild,   10
Whom I hold dear, and think most highly of.
Mariane. I'm deeply grateful, Father, for your love.
Orgon. That's well said, Daughter; and you can repay me
If, in all things, you'll cheerfully obey me.
Mariane. To please you, Sir, is what delights me best.
Orgon. Good, good. Now, what d'you think of Tartuffe, our
    guest?
Mariane. I, Sir?
Orgon. Yes. Weigh your answer; think it through.
Mariane. Oh, dear. I'll say whatever you wish me to.   20
Orgon. That's wisely said, my Daughter. Say of him, then,
That he's the very worthiest of men,
And that you're fond of him, and would rejoice
In being his wife, if that should be my choice.
Well?
Mariane. What?
Orgon. What's that?

Mariane. I . . .

Orgon. Well?

Mariane. Forgive me, pray. 30

Orgon. Did you not hear me?

Mariane. Of *whom,* Sir, must I say
That I am fond of him, and would rejoice
In being his wife, if that should be your choice?

Orgon. Why, of Tartuffe.

Mariane. But, Father, that's false, you know.
Why would you have me say what isn't so?

Orgon. Because I am resolved it shall be true.
That it's my wish should be enough for you.

Mariane. You can't mean, Father . . . 40

Orgon. Yes, Tartuffe shall be
Allied by marriage[11] to this family,
And he's to be your husband, is that clear?
It's a father's privilege . . .

Scene 2. Dorine, Orgon, Mariane

Orgon. [*To Dorine*]   What are you doing in here?
Is curiosity so fierce a passion
With you, that you must eavesdrop in this fashion?

Dorine. There's lately been a rumor going about—
Based on some hunch or chance remark, no doubt— 50
That you mean Mariane to wed Tartuffe.
I've laughed it off, of course, as just a spoof.

Orgon. You find it so incredible?

Dorine. Yes, I do.
I won't accept that story, even from you.

Orgon. Well, you'll believe it when the thing is done.

Dorine. Yes, yes, of course. Go on and have your fun.

Orgon. I've never been more serious in my life.

Dorine. Ha!

Orgon. Daughter, I mean it; you're to be his wife. 60

Dorine. No, don't believe your father; it's all a hoax.

Orgon. See here, young woman . . .

Dorine. Come Sir, no more jokes;
You can't fool us.

Orgon. How dare you talk that way?

Dorine. All right, then: we believe you, sad to say.
But how a man like you, who looks so wise
And wears a moustache of such splendid size,
Can be so foolish as to . . .

Orgon. Silence, please! 70
My girl, you take too many liberties.
I'm master here, as you must not forget.

Dorine. Do let's discuss this calmly; don't be upset.
You can't be serious, Sir, about this plan.
What should that bigot want with Mariane?

Praying and fasting ought to keep him busy.
And then, in terms of wealth and rank, what is he?
Why should a man of property like you
Pick out a beggar son-in-law?

Orgon. That will do. 80
Speak of his poverty with reverence.
His is a pure and saintly indigence
Which far transcends all worldly pride and pelf.
He lost his fortune, as he says himself,
Because he cared for Heaven alone, and so
Was careless of his interests here below.
I mean to get him out of his present straits
And help him to recover his estates—
Which, in his part of the world, have no small fame.
Poor though he is, he's a gentleman just the same. 90

Dorine. Yes, so he tells us; and, Sir, it seems to me
Such pride goes very ill with piety.
A man whose spirit spurns this dungy earth
Ought not to brag of lands and noble birth;
Such worldly arrogance will hardly square
With meek devotion and the life of prayer.
. . . But this approach, I see, has drawn a blank;
Let's speak, then, of his person, not his rank.
Doesn't it seem to you a trifle grim
To give a girl like her to a man like him? 100
When two are so ill-suited, can't you see
What the sad consequence is bound to be?
A young girl's virtue is imperilled, Sir,
When such a marriage is imposed on her;
For if one's bridegroom isn't to one's taste,
It's hardly an inducement to be chaste,
And many a man with horns upon his brow
Has made his wife the thing that she is now.
It's hard to be a faithful wife, in short,
To certain husbands of a certain sort, 110
And he who gives his daughter to a man she hates
Must answer for her sins at Heaven's gates.
Think, Sir, before you play so risky a role.

Orgon. This servant-girl presumes to save my soul!

Dorine. You would do well to ponder what I've said.

Orgon. Daughter, we'll disregard this dunderhead.
Just trust your father's judgment. Oh, I'm aware
That I once promised you to young Valère;
But now I hear he gambles, which greatly shocks me;
What's more, I've doubts about his orthodoxy. 120
His visits to church, I note, are very few.

Dorine. Would you have him go at the same hours as you,
And kneel nearby, to be sure of being seen?

Orgon. I can dispense with such remarks, Dorine.
[*To Mariane*] Tartuffe, however, is sure of Heaven's blessing.
And that's the only treasure worth possessing.
This match will bring you joys beyond all measure;
Your cup will overflow with every pleasure;
You two will interchange your faithful loves
Like two sweet cherubs, or two turtle-doves. 130
No harsh word shall be heard, no frown be seen,
And he shall make you happy as a queen.

---

11. This assertion is important and more than a mere device in the plot of the play. The second *placet* or petition insists that Tartuffe be costumed as a layman, and Orgon's plan for him to marry again asserts Tartuffe's position in the laity. In the 1664 version of the play Tartuffe had been dressed in a cassock suggestive of the priesthood, and Molière was now anxious to avoid any suggestion of this kind.

Dorine. And she'll make him a cuckold, just wait and see.
Orgon. What language!
Dorine. Oh, he's a man of destiny;
He's *made* for horns, and what the stars demand
Your daughter's virtue surely can't withstand.
Orgon. Don't interrupt me further. Why can't you learn
That certain things are none of your concern?
Dorine. It's for your own sake that I interfere.   140
    [*She repeatedly interrupts Orgon just as he is turning to
    speak to his daughter.*]
Orgon. Most kind of you. Now, hold your tongue, d'you hear?
Dorine. If I didn't love you . . .
Orgon. Spare me your affection.
Dorine. I'll love you, Sir, in spite of your objection.
Orgon. Blast!
Dorine. I can't bear, Sir, for your honor's sake,
To let you make this ludicrous mistake.
Orgon. You mean to go on talking?   150
Dorine. If I didn't protest
This sinful marriage, my conscience couldn't rest.
Orgon. If you don't hold your tongue, you little shrew . . .
Dorine. What, lost your temper? A pious man like you?
Orgon. Yes! Yes! You talk and talk. I'm maddened by it.
Once and for all, I tell you to be quiet.
Dorine. Well, I'll be quiet, but I'll be thinking hard.
Orgon. Think all you like, but you had better guard
That saucy tongue of yours, or I'll . . .
    [*Turning back to Mariane*] Now, child,   160
I've weighed this matter fully.
Dorine. [*Aside*] It drives me wild
That I can't speak.
    [*Orgon turns his head, and she is silent.*]
Orgon. Tartuffe is no young dandy,
But, still, his person . . .
Dorine. [*Aside*] Is as sweet as candy.
Orgon. Is such that, even if you shouldn't care
For his other merits . . .
    [*He turns and stands facing Dorine, arms crossed.*]   170
Dorine. [*Aside*]   They'll make a lovely pair.
If I were she, no man would marry me
Against my inclination, and go scot-free.
He'd learn, before the wedding-day was over,
How readily a wife can find a lover.
Orgon. [*To Dorine*] It seems you treat my orders as a joke.
Dorine. Why, what's the matter? 'Twas not to you I spoke.
Orgon. What *were* you doing?
Dorine. Talking to myself, that's all.
Orgon. Ah! [*Aside*] One more bit of impudence and   180
    gall,
And I shall give her a good slap in the face.
    [*He puts himself in position to slap her; Dorine, whenever
    he glances at her, stands immobile and silent.*]
Daughter, you shall accept, and with good grace,
The husband I've selected . . . Your wedding-day . . .
[*To Dorine*] Why don't you talk to yourself?
Dorine. I've nothing to say.
Orgon. Come, just one word.
Dorine. No thank you, Sir, I pass.   190

Orgon. Come, speak; I'm waiting.
Dorine. I'd not be such an ass.
Orgon. [*Turning to Mariane*] In short, dear Daughter, I mean
    to be obeyed,
And you must bow to the sound choice I've made.
Dorine. [*moving away*] I'd not wed such a monster, even in
    jest.
    [*Orgon attemps to slap her, but misses.*]
Orgon. Daughter, that maid of yours is a thorough
pest;   200
She makes me sinfully annoyed and nettled.
I can't speak further; my nerves are too unsettled.
She's so upset me by her insolent talk,
I'll calm myself by going for a walk.

Scene 3. Dorine, Mariane
Dorine. [*Returning*] Well, have you lost your tongue, girl?
Must I play
Your part, and say the lines you ought to say?
Faced with a fate so hideous and absurd,
Can you not utter one dissenting word?   210
Mariane. What good would it do? A father's power is great.
Dorine. Resist him now, or it will be too late.
Mariane. But . . .
Dorine. Tell him one cannot love at a father's whim;
That you shall marry for yourself, not him;
That since it's you who are to be the bride,
It's you, not he, who must be satisfied;
And that if his Tartuffe is so sublime,
He's free to marry him at any time.
Mariane. I've bowed so long to Father's strict control,   220
I couldn't oppose him now, to save my soul.
Dorine. Come, come, Mariane. Do listen to reason, won't
    you?
Valère has asked your hand. Do you love him, or don't you?
Mariane. Oh, how unjust of you! What can you mean
By asking such a question, dear Dorine?
You know the depth of my affection for him;
I've told you a hundred times how I adore him.
Dorine. I don't believe in everything I hear;
Who knows if your professions were sincere?   230
Mariane. They were, Dorine, and you do me wrong to doubt
    it;
Heaven knows that I've been all too frank about it.
Dorine. You love him, then?
Mariane. Oh, more than I can express.
Dorine. And he, I take it, cares for you no less?
Mariane. I think so.
Dorine. And you both, with equal fire,
Burn to be married?
Mariane.   That is our one desire.   240
Dorine. What of Tartuffe, then? What of your father's plan?
Mariane. I'll kill myself, if I'm forced to wed that man.
Dorine. I hadn't thought of that recourse. How splendid!
Just die, and all your troubles will be ended!
A fine solution. Oh, it maddens me
To hear you talk in that self-pitying key.
Mariane. Dorine, how harsh you are! It's most unfair.
You have no sympathy for my despair.

Dorine. I've none at all for people who talk drivel
And, faced with difficulties, whine and snivel.   250
Mariane. No doubt I'm timid, but it would be wrong . . .
Dorine. True love requires a heart that's firm and
    strong.
Mariane. I'm strong in my affection for Valère,
But coping with my father is his affair.
Dorine. But if your father's brain has grown so cracked
Over his dear Tartuffe that he can retract
His blessing, though your wedding-day was named,
It's surely not Valère who's to be blamed.
Mariane. If I defied my father, as you suggest,   260
Would it not seem unmaidenly, at best?
Shall I defend my love at the expense
Of brazenness and disobedience?
Shall I parade my heart's desires, and flaunt . . .
Dorine. No, I ask nothing of you. Clearly you want
To be Madame Tartuffe, and I feel bound
Not to oppose a wish so very sound.
What right have I to criticize the match?
Indeed, my dear, the man's a brilliant catch.
Monsieur Tartuffe! Now, there's a man of weight!   270
Yes, yes, Monsieur Tartuffe, I'm bound to state,
Is quite a person; that's not to be denied;
'Twill be no little thing to be his bride.
The world already rings with his renown;
He's a great noble—in his native town;
His ears are red, he has a pink complexion,
And all in all, he'll suit you to perfection.
Mariane. Dear God!
Dorine. Oh, how triumphant you will feel
At having caught a husband so ideal!   280
Mariane. Oh, do stop teasing, and use your cleverness
To get me out of this appalling mess.
Advise me, and I'll do whatever you say.
Dorine. Ah, no, a dutiful daughter must obey
Her father, even if he weds her to an ape.
You've a bright future; why struggle to escape?
Tartuffe will take you back where his family lives,
To a small town aswarm with relatives—
Uncles and cousins whom you'll be charmed
to meet.   290
You'll be received at once by the elite,
Calling upon the bailiff's wife,[12] no less—
Even, perhaps, upon the mayoress,[13]
Who'll sit you down in the *best* kitchen chair.[14]

Then, once a year, you'll dance at the village fair
To the drone of bagpipes—two of them, in fact—
And see a puppet-show, or an animal act.[15]
Your husband . . .
Mariane. Oh, you turn my blood to ice!
Stop torturing me, and give me your advice.   300
Dorine. [*Threatening to go*] Your servant, Madam.
Mariane. Dorine, I beg
of you . . .
Dorine. No, you deserve it; this marriage must go through.
Mariane. Dorine!
Dorine. No.
Mariane. Not Tartuffe! You know I think
him . . .
Dorine. Tartuffe's your cup of tea, and you shall drink him.
Mariane. I've always told you everything,   310
and relied . . .
Dorine. No. You desire to be tartuffified.
Mariane. Well, since you mock me and refuse to care,
I'll henceforth seek my solace in despair:
Despair shall be my counsellor and friend,
And help me bring my sorrows to an end. [*She starts to leave.*]
Dorine. There now, come back; my anger has
subsided.
You do deserve some pity, I've decided.
Mariane. Dorine, if Father makes me undergo   320
This dreadful martyrdom, I'll die, I know.
Dorine. Don't fret; it won't be difficult to discover
Some plan of action. . . But here's Valère,
    your lover.

Scene 4. Valère, Mariane, Dorine
Valère. Madam, I've just received some wondrous news
Regarding which I'd like to hear your views.
Mariane. What news?
Valère. You're marrying Tartuffe.
Mariane. I find   330
That Father does have such a match in mind.
Valère. Your father, Madam . . .
Mariane. . . . has just this minute said
That it's Tartuffe he wishes me to wed.
Valère. Can he be serious?
Mariane. Oh, indeed he can;
He's clearly set his heart upon the plan.
Valère. And what position do you propose to take,
Madam?
Mariane. Why—I don't know.   340
Valère. For heaven's sake—
You don't know?
Mariane. No.
Valère. Well, well!
Mariane. Advise me, do.
Valère. Marry the man. That's my advice to you.

---

12. A high-ranking official in the judiciary, not simply a sheriff's
    deputy as today.

13. The wife of a tax collector (*elu*), an important official
    controlling imports, elected by the Estates General.

14. In elegant society of Molière's day, there was a hierarchy of seats
    and the use of each was determined by rank. The seats
    descended from *fauteuils, chaises, perroquets, labourets* to
    pliants. Thus Mariane would get the lowest seat in the room.

15. In the original, *fagotin*, literally a monkey dressed up in a man's
    clothing.

Mariane. That's your advice?

Valère. Yes.

Mariane. Truly?

Valère.   Oh, absolutely.   350
You couldn't choose more wisely, more astutely.

Mariane. Thanks for this counsel; I'll follow it, of course.

Valère. Do, do; I'm sure 'twill cost you no remorse.

Mariane. To give it didn't cause your heart to break.

Valère. I gave it, Madam, only for your sake.

Mariane. And it's for your sake that I take it, Sir.

Dorine. [*Withdrawing to the rear of the stage*]
Let's see which fool will prove the stubborner.

Valère. So! I am nothing to you, and it was flat
Deception when you . . .   360

Mariane. Please, enough of that.
You've told me plainly that I should agree
To wed the man my father's chosen for me,
And since you've deigned to counsel me so wisely,
I promise, Sir, to do as you advise me.

Valère. Ah, no, 'twas not by me that you were swayed.
No, your decision was already made;
Though now, to save appearances, you protest
That you're betraying me at my behest.

Mariane. Just as you say.   370

Valère. Quite so. And I now see
That you were never truly in love with me.

Mariane. Alas, you're free to think so if you choose.

Valère. I choose to think so, and here's a bit of news:
You've spurned my hand, but I know where to turn
For kinder treatment, as you shall quickly learn.

Mariane. I'm sure you do. Your noble qualities
Inspire affection . . .

Valère. Forget my qualities, please.   380
They don't inspire you overmuch, I find.
But there's another lady I have in mind
Whose sweet and generous nature will not scorn
To compensate me for the loss I've borne.

Mariane. I'm no great loss, and I'm sure that you'll transfer
Your heart quite painlessly from me to her.

Valère. I'll do my best to take it in my stride.
The pain I feel at being cast aside
Time and forgetfulness may put an end to.
Or if I can't forget, I shall pretend to.
No self-respecting person is expected   390
To go on loving once he's been rejected.

Mariane. Now, that's a fine, high-minded sentiment.

Valère. One to which any sane man would assent.
Would you prefer it if I pined away
In hopeless passion till my dying day?
Am I to yield you to a rival's arms
And not console myself with other charms?

Mariane. Go then; console yourself; don't hesitate.
I wish you to; indeed, I cannot wait.

Valère. You wish me to?   400

Mariane. Yes.

Valère. That's the final straw.
Madam, farewell. Your wish shall be my law.
[*He starts to leave, and then returns: this repeatedly.*]

Mariane. Splendid.

Valère. [*Coming back again*] This breach, remember, is of
your making;
It's you who've driven me to the step I'm taking.

Mariane. Of course.   410

Valère. [*Coming back again*] Remember, too, that I am
merely
Following your example.

Mariane. I see that clearly.

Valère. Enough. I'll go and do your bidding, then.

Mariane. Good.

Valère. [*Coming back again*] You shall never see my face
again.

Mariane. Excellent.

Valère. [*Walking to the door, then turning about*] Yes?

Mariane. What?   420

Valère. What's that? What did you say?

Mariane. Nothing. You're dreaming.

Valère. Ah. Well, I'm on my way.
Farewell, Madame.

Mariane. Farewell.

Dorine. [*To Mariane*]   If you ask me,
Both of you are as mad as mad can be.
Do stop this nonsense, now. I've only let you
Squabble so long to see where it would get you.
Whoa there, Monsieur Valère!   430
[*She goes and seizes Valère by the arm; he makes a great
show of resistance.*]

Valère. What's this, Dorine?

Dorine. Come here.

Valère. No, no, my heart's too full of spleen.
Don't hold me back; her wish must be obeyed.

Dorine. Stop!

Valère. It's too late now; my decision's made.

Dorine. Oh, pooh!

Mariane. [*Aside*] He hates the sight of me, that's plain.   440
I'll go, and so deliver him from pain.

Dorine. [*Leaving Valère, running after Mariane*]
And now *you* run away! Come back.

Mariane. No, no
Nothing you say will keep me here. Let go!

Valère. [*Aside*] She cannot bear my presence, I perceive.
To spare her further torment, I shall leave.

Dorine. [*Leaving Mariane, running after Valère*]
Again! You'll not escape, Sir; don't you try it.
Come here, you two. Stop fussing and be quiet.   450
[*She takes Valère by the hand, then Mariane, and draws
them together.*]

Valère. [*To Dorine*] What do you want of me?

Mariane. [*To Dorine*] What is the point of this?

Dorine. We're going to have a little armistice.
[*To Valère*] Now, weren't you silly to get so overheated?

Valère. Didn't you see how badly I was treated?

Dorine. [*To Mariane*] Aren't you a simpleton, to have lost
your head?

Mariane. Didn't you hear the hateful things he said?   460

Dorine. [*To Valère*] You're both great fools. Her sole desire, Valère,
Is to be yours in marriage. To that I'll swear.
[*To Mariane*] He loves you only, and he wants no wife
But you, Mariane. On that I'll stake my life.

Mariane. [*To Valère*] Then why you advised me so, I cannot see.

Valère. [*To Mariane*] On such a question, why ask advice of me?

Dorine. Oh, you're impossible. Give me your hands, you two. 470
[*To Valère*] Yours first.

Valère. [*Giving Dorine his hand*] But why?

Dorine. [*To Mariane*] And now a hand from you.

Mariane. [*Also giving Dorine her hand*]
What are you doing?

Dorine. There: a perfect fit.
You suit each other better than you'll admit.
[*Valère and Mariane hold hands for some time without looking at each other.*] 480

Valère. [*Turning toward Mariane*]
Ah, come, don't be so haughty. Give a man
A look of kindness, won't you, Mariane?
[*Mariane turns toward Valère and smiles.*]

Dorine. I tell you, lovers are completely mad!

Valère. [*To Mariane*] Now come, confess that you were very bad
To hurt my feelings as you did just now.
I have a just complaint, you must allow.

Mariane. *You* must allow that you were most unpleasant . . . 490

Dorine. Let's table that discussion for the present;
Your father has a plan which must be stopped.

Mariane. Advise us, then; what means must we adopt?

Dorine. We'll use all manner of means, and all at once.
[*To Mariane*] Your father's addled; he's acting like a dunce.
Therefore you'd better humor the old fossil.
Pretend to yield to him, be sweet and docile,
And then postpone, as often as necessary,
The day on which you have agreed to marry.
You'll thus gain time, and time will turn the trick. 500
Sometimes, for instance, you'll be taken sick,
And that will seem good reason for delay;
Or some bad omen will make you change the day—You'll
dream of muddy water, or you'll pass
A dead man's hearse, or break a looking-glass.
If all else fails, no man can marry you
Unless you take his ring and say "I do."
But now, let's separate. If they should find
Us talking here, our plot might be divined.
[*To Valère*] Go to your friends, and tell them what's occurred, 510
And have them urge her father to keep his word.
Meanwhile, we'll stir her brother into action,
And get Elmire,[16] as well, to join our faction.
Good-bye.

---

16. Orgon's second wife.

Valère. [*To Mariane*] Though each of us will do his best,
It's your true heart on which my hopes shall rest.

Mariane. [*To Valère*] Regardless of what Father may decide,
None but Valère shall claim me as his bride.

Valère. Oh, how those words content me! Come what will . . . 520

Dorine. Oh, lovers, lovers! Their tongues are never still.
Be off, now.

Valère. [*Turning to go, then turning back.*]
One last word . . .

Dorine. No time to chat:
You leave by this door; and *you* leave by that.
[Dorine *pushes them, by the shoulders, toward opposing doors.*]

ACT III

Scene 1. Damis, Dorine

Damis. May lightning strike me even as I speak,
May all men call me cowardly and weak,
If any fear or scruple holds me back
From settling things, at once, with that great quack!

Dorine. Now, don't give way to violent emotion.
Your father's merely talked about this notion,
And words and deeds are far from being one.
Much that is talked about is never done.

Damis. No, I must stop that scoundrel's machinations; 10
I'll go and tell him off; I'm out of patience.

Dorine. Do calm down and be practical, I had rather
My mistress dealt with him—and with your father.
She has some influence with Tartuffe, I've noted.
He hangs upon her words, seems most devoted,
And may, indeed, be smitten by her charm.
Pray Heaven it's true! 'Twould do our cause no harm.
She sent for him, just now, to sound him out
On this affair you're so incensed about;
She'll find out where he stands, and tell him, too, 20
What dreadful strife and trouble will ensue
If he lends countenance to your father's plan.
I couldn't get in to see him, but his man
Says that he's almost finished with his prayers.
Go, now. I'll catch him when he comes downstairs.

Damis. I want to hear this conference, and I will.

Dorine. No, they must be alone.

Damis. Oh, I'll keep still.

Dorine. Not you. I know your temper. You'd start a brawl,
And shout and stamp your foot and spoil it all. 30
Go on.

Damis. I won't; I have a perfect right . . .

Dorine. Lord, you're a nuisance! He's coming; get out of sight.
[Damis *conceals himself in a closet at the rear of the stage.*]

Scene 2. Tartuffe, Dorine

Tartuffe. [*Observing Dorine, and calling to his manservant offstage*] Hang up my hair-shirt, put my scourge in place,
And pray, Laurent, for Heaven's perpetual grace.
I'm going to the prison now, to share 40
My last few coins with the poor wretches there.

Dorine. [*Aside*] Dear God, what affectation! What
    a fake!
Tartuffe. You wished to see me?
Dorine. Yes . . .
Tartuffe. [*Taking a handkerchief from his pocket*]
For mercy's sake,
Please take this handkerchief, before you speak.
Dorine. What?
Tartuffe. Cover that bosom,[17] girl. The flesh is weak.   50
And unclean thoughts are difficult to control.
Such sights as that can undermine the soul.
Dorine. Your soul, it seems, has very poor defenses,
And flesh makes quite an impact on your senses.
It's strange that you're so easily excited;
My own desires are not so soon ignited,
And if I saw you naked as a beast,
Not all your hide would tempt me in the least.
Tartuffe. Girl, speak more modestly; unless you do,
I shall be forced to take my leave of you.   60
Dorine. Oh, no, it's I who must be on my way;
I've just one little message to convey.
Madame is coming down, and begs you, Sir,
To wait and have a word or two with her.
Tartuffe. Gladly.
Dorine. [*Aside*] *That* had a softening effect!
I think my guess about him was correct.
Tartuffe. Will she be long?
Dorine. No: that's her step I hear.
Ah, here she is, and I shall disappear.   70

Scene 3. Elmire, Tartuffe
Tartuffe. May Heaven, whose infinite goodness we adore,
Preserve your body and soul forevermore,
And bless your days, and answer thus the plea
Of one who is its humblest votary.
Elmire. I thank you for that pious wish. But please,
Do take a chair and let's be more at ease.
    [*They sit down.*]
Tartuffe. I trust that you are once more well and strong?
Elmire. Oh, yes: the fever didn't last for long.   80
Tartuffe. My prayers are too unworthy, I am sure,
To have gained from Heaven this most gracious
cure;
But lately, Madam, my every supplication
Has had for object your recuperation.
Elmire. You shouldn't have troubled so. I don't
deserve it.
Tartuffe. Your health is priceless, Madam, and to preserve it
I'd gladly give my own, in all sincerity.
Elmire. Sir, you outdo us all in Christian charity.   90
You've been most kind. I count myself your debtor.
Tartuffe. 'Twas nothing, Madam. I long to serve you better.

---

17. The Brotherhood of the Holy Sacrament practiced almsgiving to
    prisoners and kept a careful, censorious check on female
    wearing apparel if they deemed it lascivious. Thus, Molière's
    audience would have identified Tartuffe as sympathetic—
    hypocritically—to the aims of the organization.

Elmire. There's a private matter I'm anxious to discuss.
I'm glad there's no one here to hinder us.
Tartuffe. I too am glad; it floods my heart with bliss
To find myself alone with you like this.
For just this chance I've prayed with all my power—
But prayed in vain, until this happy hour.
Elmire. This won't take long, Sir, and I hope you'll be
Entirely frank and unconstrained with me.   100
Tartuffe. Indeed, there's nothing I had rather do
Than bare my inmost heart and soul to you.
First, let me say that what remarks I've made
About the constant visits you are paid
Were prompted not by any mean emotion,
But rather by a pure and deep devotion,
A fervent zeal . . .
Elmire. No need for explanation.
Your sole concern, I'm sure, was my salvation.
Tartuffe. [*Taking Elmire's hand and pressing her fingertips*]   110
Quite so; and such great fervor do I feel . . .
Elmire. Ooh! Please! You're pinching!
Tartuffe. 'Twas from excess of zeal.
I never meant to cause you pain, I swear.
I'd rather . . .
Elmire. What can your hand be doing there?
Tartuffe. Feeling your gown: what soft, fine-woven stuff!
Elmire. Please, I'm extremely ticklish. That's enough.
    [*She draws her chair away; Tartuffe pulls his after her.*]
Tartuffe. [*Fondling the lace collar of her gown*]   120
My, my, what lovely lacework on your dress!
The workmanship's miraculous, no less.
I've not seen anything to equal it.
Elmire. Yes, quite. But let's talk business for a bit.
They say my husband means to break his word
And give his daughter to you, Sir. Had you heard?
Tartuffe. He did once mention it. But I confess
I dream of quite a different happiness.
It's elsewhere, Madam, that my eyes discern
The promise of that bliss for which I yearn.   130
Elmire. I see: you care for nothing here below.
Tartuffe. Ah, well—my heart's not made of stone, you know.
Elmire. All your desires mount heavenward, I'm sure,
In scorn of all that's earthly and impure.
Tartuffe. A love of heavenly beauty does not preclude
A proper love for earthly pulchritude,
Our senses are quite rightly captivated
By perfect works our Maker has created.
Some glory clings to all that Heaven has made;
In you, all Heaven's marvels are displayed.   140
On that fair face, such beauties have been lavished,
The eyes are dazzled and the heart is ravished;
How could I look on you, O flawless creature,
And not adore the Author of all Nature,
Feeling a love both passionate and pure
For you, his triumph of self-portraiture?

At first, I trembled lest that love should be
A subtle snare that Hell had laid for me;
I vowed to flee the sight of you, eschewing
A rapture that might prove my soul's undoing;   150
But soon, fair being, I became aware
That my deep passion could be made to square
With rectitude, and with my bounden duty,
I thereupon surrendered to your beauty.
It is, I know, presumptuous on my part
To bring you this poor offering of my heart,
And it is not my merit, Heaven knows,
But your compassion on which my hopes repose.
You are my peace, my solace, my salvation;
On you depends my bliss—or desolation;   160
I bide your judgment and, as you think best,
I shall be either miserable or blest.
Elmire. Your declaration is most gallant, Sir,
But don't you think it's out of character?
You'd have done better to restrain your passion
And think before you spoke in such a fashion.
It ill becomes a pious man like you . . .
Tartuffe. I may be pious, but I'm human too:
With your celestial charms before his eyes,
A man has not the power to be wise.   170
I know such words sound strangely, coming from me,
But I'm no angel, nor was meant to be,
And if you blame my passion, you must needs
Reproach as well the charms on which it feeds.
Your loveliness I had no sooner seen
Than you became my soul's unrivaled queen;
Before your seraph glance, divinely sweet,
My heart's defenses crumbled in defeat,
And nothing fasting, prayer, or tears might do
Could stay my spirit from adoring you.   180
My eyes, my sighs have told you in the past
What now my lips make bold to say at last,
And if, in your great goodness, you will deign
To look upon your slave, and ease his pain,—
If, in compassion for my soul's distress,
You'll stoop to comfort my unworthiness,
I'll raise to you, in thanks for that sweet manna,
An endless hymn, an infinite hosanna.
With me, of course, there need be no anxiety,
No fear of scandal or of notoriety.   190
These young court gallants, whom all the ladies fancy,
Are vain in speech, in action rash and chancy;
When they succeed in love, the world soon knows it;
No favor's granted them but they disclose it
And by the looseness of their tongues profane
The very altar where their hearts have lain.
Men of my sort, however, love discreetly,
And one may trust our reticence completely.
My keen concern for my good name insures
The absolute security of yours;   200
In short, I offer you, my dear Elmire,
Love without scandal, pleasure without fear.

Elmire. I've heard your well-turned speeches to the end,
And what you urge I clearly apprehend.
Aren't you afraid that I may take a notion
To tell my husband of your warm devotion,
And that, supposing he were duly told,
His feelings toward you might grow rather cold?
Tartuffe. I know, dear lady, that your exceeding charity
Will lead your heart to pardon my temerity;   210
That you'll excuse my violent affection
As human weakness, human imperfection;
And that—O fairest!—you will bear in mind
That I'm but flesh and blood, and am not blind.
Elmire. Some women might do otherwise, perhaps,
But I shall be discreet about your lapse;
I'll tell my husband nothing of what's occurred
If, in return, you'll give your solemn word
To advocate as forcefully as you can
The marriage of Valère and Mariane,   220
Renouncing all desire to dispossess
Another of his rightful happiness,
And . . .

Scene 4. Damis, Elmire, Tartuffe
Damis. [*Emerging from the closet where he has been hiding*]
No! We'll not hush up this vile affair;
I heard it all inside that closet there,
Where Heaven, in order to confound the pride
Of this great rascal, prompted me to hide.
Ah, now I have my long-awaited chance   230
To punish his deceit and arrogance,
And give my father clear and shocking proof
Of the black character of his dear Tartuffe.
Elmire. Ah no, Damis; I'll be content if he
Will study to deserve my leniency.
I've promised silence—don't make me break my word;
To make a scandal would be too absurd.
Good wives laugh off such trifles, and forget them;
Why should they tell their husbands, and upset them?
Damis. You have your reasons for taking such   240
a course,
And I have reasons, too, of equal force.
To spare him now would be insanely wrong.
I've swallowed my just wrath for far too long
And watched this insolent bigot bringing strife
And bitterness into our family life.
Too long he's meddled in my father's affairs,
Thwarting my marriage-hopes, and poor Valère's.
It's high time that my father was undeceived,
And now I've proof that can't be disbelieved—   250
Proof that was furnished me by Heaven above.
It's too good not to take advantage of.
This is my chance, and I deserve to lose it
If, for one moment, I hesitate to use it.
Elmire. Damis . . .

Damis. No, I must do what I think right.
Madam, my heart is bursting with delight,
And, say whatever you will, I'll not consent
To lose the sweet revenge on which I'm bent.
I'll settle matters without more ado;   260
And here, most opportunely, is my cue.[18]

Scene 5. Orgon, Damis, Tartuffe, Elmire
Damis. Father, I'm glad you've joined us. Let us advise you
Of some fresh news which doubtless will surprise you.
You've just now been repaid with interest
For all your loving-kindness to our guest.
He's proved his warm and grateful feelings
toward you;
It's with a pair of horns he would reward you.
Yes, I surprised him with your wife, and heard   270
His whole adulterous offer, every word.
She, with her all too gentle disposition,
Would not have told you of his proposition;
But I shall not make terms with brazen lechery,
And feel that not to tell you would be treachery.
Elmire. And I hold that one's husband's peace of mind
Should not be spoilt by tattle of this kind.
One's honor doesn't require it: to be proficient
In keeping men at bay is quite sufficient.
These are my sentiments, and I wish, Damis,   280
That you had heeded me and held your peace.

Scene 6. Orgon, Damis, Tartuffe
Orgon. Can it be true, this dreadful thing I hear?
Tartuffe. Yes, Brother, I'm a wicked man, I fear:
A wretched sinner, all depraved and twisted,
The greatest villain that has ever existed.
My life's one heap of crimes, which grows each minute;
There's naught but foulness and corruption in it;
And I perceive that Heaven, outraged by me,
Has chosen this occasion to mortify me.   290
Charge me with any deed you wish to name;
I'll not defend myself, but take the blame.
Believe what you are told, and drive Tartuffe
Like some base criminal from beneath your roof;
Yes, drive me hence, and with a parting curse:
I shan't protest, for I deserve far worse.
Orgon. [*To Damis*] Ah, you deceitful boy, how dare you try
To stain his purity with so foul a lie?
Damis. What! Are you taken in by such a fluff?
Did you not hear . . . ?   300
Orgon. Enough, you rogue, enough!
Tartuffe. Ah, Brother, let him speak; you're being unjust.
Believe his story; the boy deserves your trust.
Why, after all, should you have faith in me?
How can you know what I might do, or be?
Is it on my good actions that you base
Your favor? Do you trust my pious face?

Ah, no, don't be deceived by hollow shows;
I'm far, alas, from being what men suppose;
Though the world takes me for a man of worth,   310
I'm truly the most worthless man on earth.
[*To Damis*]
Yes, my dear son, speak out now: call me the chief
Of sinners, a wretch, a murderer, a thief;
Load me with all the names men most abhor;
I'll not complain; I've earned them all, and more;
I'll kneel here while you pour them on my head
As a just punishment for the life I've led.
Orgon. [*To Tartuffe*] This is too much, dear Brother.
[*To Damis*]   Have you no heart?   320
Damis. Are you so hoodwinked by this
rascal's art . . . ?
Orgon. Be still, you monster.
[*To Tartuffe*]   Brother, I pray you, rise.
[*To Damis*] Villain!
Damis. But . . .
Orgon. Silence!
Damis. Can't you realize . . . ?
Orgon. Just one word more, and I'll tear you limb from limb.
Tartuffe. In God's name, Brother, don't be harsh with him.   330
I'd rather far be tortured at the stake
Than see him bear one scratch for my poor sake.
Orgon. [*To Damis*] Ingrate!
Tartuffe. If I must beg you, on bended knee,
To pardon him . . .
Orgon. [*Falling to his knees, addressing Tartuffe*]
Such goodness cannot be!
[*To Damis*] Now, *there's* true charity!
Damis.   What, you . . . ?
Orgon. Villain,   340
be still!
I know your motives; I know you wish him ill:
Yes, all of you—wife, children, servants, all—
Conspire against him and desire his fall,
Employing every shameful trick you can
To alienate me from this saintly man.
Ah, but the more you seek to drive him away,
The more I'll do to keep him. Without delay,
I'll spite this household and confound its pride
By giving him my daughter as his bride.   350
Damis. You're going to force her to accept his hand?
Orgon. Yes, and this very night, d'you understand?
I shall defy you all, and make it clear
That I'm the one who gives the orders here.
Come, wretch, kneel down and clasp his blessed feet,
And ask his pardon for your black deceit.
Damis. I ask that swindler's pardon? Why, I'd rather . . .
Orgon. So! You insult him, and defy your father!
A stick! A stick! [*To Tartuffe*] No, no—release me, do.
[*To Damis*] Out of my house this minute! Be off with you,   360
And never dare set foot in it again.
Damis. Well, I shall go, but . . .
Orgon. Well, go quickly, then.
I disinherit you; an empty purse
Is all you'll get from me—except my curse!

---

18. In the original stage directions, Tartuffe now reads silently from
    his breviary—in the Roman Catholic church, the book
    containing the Divine Office for each day, which those in holy
    orders are required to recite.

Scene 7. Orgon, Tartuffe

Orgon. How he blasphemed your goodness! What a son!
Tartuffe. Forgive him, Lord, as I've already done.
[*To Orgon*] You can't know how it hurts when someone tries
To blacken me in my dear brother's eyes.   370
Orgon. Ahh!
Tartuffe.   The mere thought of such ingratitude
Plunges my soul into so dark a mood . . .
Such horror grips my heart . . . I gasp for breath,
And cannot speak, and feel myself near death.
Orgon. [*He runs, in tears, to the door through which he has
    just driven his son.*]
You blackguard! Why did I spare you? Why did I not
Break you in little pieces on the spot?
Compose yourself, and don't be hurt, dear friend.   380
Tartuffe. These scenes, these dreadful quarrels, have got to
    end.
I've much upset your household, and I perceive
That the best thing will be for me to leave.
Orgon. What are you saying!
Tartuffe. They're all against me here;
They'd have you think me false and insincere.
Orgon. Ah, what of that? Have I ceased believing in you?
Tartuffe. Their adverse talk will certainly continue,
And charges which you now repudiate   390
You may find credible at a later date.
Orgon. No, Brother, never.
Tartuffe. Brother, a wife can sway
Her husband's mind in many a subtle way.
Orgon. No, no.
Tartuffe. To leave at once is the solution;
Thus only can I end their persecution.
Orgon. No, no, I'll not allow it; you shall remain.
Tartuffe. Ah, well; 'twill mean much martyrdom and pain,
But if you wish it . . .   400
Orgon. Ah!
Tartuffe. Enough; so be it.
But one thing must be settled, as I see it.
For your dear honor, and for our friendship's sake,
There's one precaution I feel bound to take.
I shall avoid your wife, and keep away . . .
Orgon. No, you shall not, whatever they may say.
It pleases me to vex them, and for spite
I'd have them see you with her day and night.
What's more, I'm going to drive them to despair   410
By making you my only son and heir;
This very day, I'll give to you alone
Clear deed and title to everything I own.
A dear, good friend and son-in-law-to-be
Is more than wife, or child, or kin to me.
Will you accept my offer, dearest son?
Tartuffe. In all things, let the will of Heaven be done.
Orgon. Poor fellow! Come, we'll go draw up the deed.
Then let them burst with disappointed greed!

ACT IV

Scene 1. Cléante, Tartuffe

Cléante. Yes, all the town's discussing it, and truly,
Their comments do not flatter you unduly.
I'm glad we've met, Sir, and I'll give my view
Of this sad matter in a word or two.
As for who's guilty, that I shan't discuss;
Let's say it was Damis who caused the fuss;
Assuming, then, that you have been ill-used
By young Damis, and groundlessly accused,
Ought not a Christian to forgive, and ought   10
He not to stifle every vengeful thought?
Should you stand by and watch a father make
His only son an exile for your sake?
Again I tell you frankly, be advised:
The whole town, high and low, is scandalized;
This quarrel must be mended, and my advice is
Not to push matters to a further crisis.
No, sacrifice your wrath to God above,
And help Damis regain his father's love.
Tartuffe. Alas, for my part I should take great joy   20
In doing so. I've nothing against the boy.
I pardon all, I harbor no resentment;
To serve him would afford me much contentment.
But Heaven's interest will not have it so:
If he comes back, then I shall have to go.
After his conduct—so extreme, so vicious—
Our further intercourse would look suspicious.
God knows what people would think! Why, they'd describe
My goodness to him as a sort of bribe;
They'd say that out of guilt I made pretense   30
Of loving-kindness and benevolence—
That, fearing my accuser's tongue, I strove
To buy his silence with a show of love.
Cléante. Your reasoning is badly warped and stretched,
And these excuses, Sir, are most far-fetched.
Why put yourself in charge of Heaven's cause?
Does Heaven need our help to enforce its laws?
Leave vengeance to the Lord, Sir; while we live,
Our duty's not to punish, but forgive;
And what the Lord commands, we should obey   40
Without regard to what the world may say.
What! Shall the fear of being misunderstood
Prevent our doing what is right and good?
No, no: let's simply do what Heaven ordains,
And let no other thoughts perplex our brains.
Tartuffe. Again, Sir, let me say that I've forgiven
Damis, and thus obeyed the laws of Heaven;
But I am not commanded by the Bible
To live with one who smears my name with libel.
Cléante. Were you commanded, Sir, to indulge the whim   50
Of poor Orgon, and to encourage him
In suddenly transferring to your name
A large estate to which you have no claim?

Tartuffe. 'Twould never occur to those who know me best
To think I acted from self-interest,
The treasures of this world I quite despise;
Their specious glitter does not charm my eyes;
And if I have resigned myself to taking
The gift which my dear Brother insists on making,   60
I do so only, as he well understands,
Lest so much wealth fall into wicked hands,
Lest those to whom it might descend in time
Turn it to purposes of sin and crime,
And not, as I shall do, make use of it
For Heaven's glory and mankind's benefit.
Cléante. Forget these trumped-up fears. Your argument
Is one the rightful heir might well resent;
It *is* a moral burden to inherit
Such wealth, but give Damis a chance to bear it.   70
And would it not be worse to be accused
Of swindling, than to see that wealth misused?
I'm shocked that you allowed Orgon to broach
This matter, and that you feel no self-reproach;
Does true religion teach that lawful heirs
May freely be deprived of what is theirs?
And if the Lord has told you in your heart
That you and young Damis must dwell apart,
Would it not be the decent thing to beat
A generous and honorable retreat,   80
Rather than let the son of the house be sent,
For your convenience, into banishment?
Sir, if you wish to prove the honesty
Of your intentions . . .
Tartuffe. Sir, it is a half past three.
I've certain pious duties to attend to,
And hope my prompt departure won't offend you.
Cléante. [*Alone*] Damn.

Scene 2. Elmire, Mariane, Cléante, Dorine
Dorine. Stay, Sir, and help Mariane, for Heaven's sake!   90
She's suffering so, I fear her heart will break.
Her father's plan to marry her off tonight
Has put the poor child in a desperate plight.
I hear him coming. Let's stand together, now,
And see if we can't change his mind, somehow,
About this match we all deplore and fear.

Scene 3. Elmire, Mariane, Cléante, Dorine
Orgon. Hah! Glad to find you all assembled here.
[*To Mariane*] This contract, child, contains your happiness,
And what it says I think your heart can guess.   100
Mariane. [*Falling to her knees*]
Sir, by that Heaven which sees me here distressed,
And by whatever else can move your breast,
Do not employ a father's power, I pray you,
To crush my heart and force it to obey you,
Nor by your harsh commands oppress me so
That I'll begrudge the duty which I owe—
And do not so embitter and enslave me
That I shall hate the very life you gave me.

If my sweet hopes must perish, if you refuse   110
To give me to the one I've dared to choose,
Spare me at least—I beg you, I implore—
The pain of wedding one whom I abhor;
And do not, by a heartless use of force,
Drive me to contemplate some desperate course.
Orgon. [*Feeling himself touched by her*]
Be firm, my soul. No human weakness, now.
Mariane. I don't resent your love for him. Allow
Your heart free rein, Sir; give him your property,
And if that's not enough, take mine from me;   120
He's welcome to my money, take it, do,
But don't, I pray, include my person too.
Spare me, I beg you; and let me end the tale
Of my sad days behind a convent veil.
Orgon. A convent! Hah! When crossed in their amours,
All lovesick girls have the same thought as yours.
Get up! The more you loathe the man, and dread him,
The more ennobling it will be to wed him.
Marry Tartuffe, and mortify your flesh!
Enough; don't start that whimpering afresh.   130
Dorine. But why . . . ?
Orgon. Be still, there. Speak when you're spoken to.
Not one more bit of impudence out of you.
Cléante. If I may offer a word of counsel here . . .
Orgon. Brother, in counselling you have no peer;
All your advice is forceful, sound, and clever;
I don't propose to follow it, however.
Elmire. [*To Orgon*] I am amazed, and don't know what to say;
Your blindness simply takes my breath away.
You are indeed bewitched, to take no warning   140
From our account of what occurred this morning.
Orgon. Madam, I know a few plain facts, and one
Is that you're partial to my rascal son;
Hence, when he sought to make Tartuffe the victim
Of a base lie, you dared not contradict him.
Ah, but you underplayed your part, my pet;
You should have looked more angry, more upset.
Elmire. When men make overtures, must we reply
With righteous anger and a battle-cry?
Must we turn back their amorous advances   150
With sharp reproaches and with fiery glances?
Myself, I find such offers merely amusing,
And make no scenes and fusses in refusing;
My taste is for good-natured rectitude,
And I dislike the savage sort of prude
Who guards her virtue with her teeth and claws,
And tears men's eyes out for the slightest cause:
The Lord preserve me from such honor as that,
Which bites and scratches like an alley-cat!
I've found that a polite and cool rebuff   160
Discourages a lover quite enough.
Orgon. I know the facts, and I shall not be shaken.
Elmire. I marvel at your power to be mistaken.
Would it, I wonder, carry weight with you
If I could *show* you that our tale was true?

Orgon. Show me?
Elmire. Yes.
Orgon. Rot.
Elmire.   Come, what if I found a way
To make you see the facts as plain as day?   170
Orgon. Nonsense.
Elmire.   Do answer me; don't be absurd.
I'm not now asking you to trust our word.
Suppose that from some hiding-place in here
You learned the whole sad truth by eye and ear—
What would you say of your good friend, after that?
Orgon. Why, I'd say . . . nothing, by Jehoshaphat!
It can't be true.
Elmire.   You've been too long deceived,
I'm quite tired of being disbelieved.   180
Come now: let's put my statements to the test,
And you shall see the truth made manifest.
Orgon. I'll take that challenge. Now do your uttermost.
We'll see how you make good your empty boast.
Elmire. [*To Dorine*] Send him to me.
Dorine.   He's crafty; it may be hard
To catch the cunning scoundrel off his guard.
Elmire. No, amorous men are gullible. Their conceit
So blinds them that they're never hard to cheat.
Have him come down. [*To Cléante and Mariane*] Please leave   190
    us, for a bit.

Scene 4. Elmire, Orgon
Elmire. Pull up this table, and get under it.
Orgon. What?
Elmire. It's essential that you be well-hidden.
Orgon. Why there?
Elmire. Oh, Heavens! Just do as you are bidden.
I have my plans; we'll soon see how they fare.
Under the table, now; and once you're there,
Take care that you are neither seen nor heard.   200
Orgon. Well, I'll indulge you, since I gave my word
To see you through this infantile charade.
Elmire. Once it is over, you'll be glad we played.
    [*To her husband, who is now under the table*]
I'm going to act quite strangely, now, and you
Must not be shocked at anything I do.
Whatever I may say, you must excuse
As part of that deceit I'm forced to use.
I shall employ sweet speeches in the task
Of making that impostor drop his mask;   210
I'll give encouragement to his bold desires,
And furnish fuel to his amorous fires.
Since it's for your sake, and for his destruction,
That I shall seem to yield to his seduction,
I'll gladly stop whenever you decide.
That all your doubts are fully satisfied.
I'll count on you, as soon as you have seen
What sort of man he is, to intervene,
And not expose me to his odious lust
One moment longer than you feel you must.   220
Remember: You're to save me from my plight
Whenever . . . He's coming! Hush! Keep out of sight!

Scene 5. Tartuffe, Elmire, Orgon
Tartuffe. You wish to have a word with me, I'm told.
Elmire. Yes, I've a little secret to unfold.
Before I speak, however, it would be wise
To close that door, and look about for spies.
    [*Tartuffe goes to the door, closes it, and returns.*]
The very last thing that must happen now
Is a repetition of this morning's row.   230
I've never been so badly caught off guard.
Oh, how I feared for you! You saw how hard
I tried to make that troublesome Damis
Control his dreadful temper, and hold his peace.
In my confusion, I didn't have the sense
Simply to contradict his evidence;
But as it happened, that was for the best,
And all has worked out in our interest.
This storm has only bettered your position;
My husband doesn't have the least suspicion,   240
And now, in mockery of those who do,
He bids me be continually with you.
And that is why, quite fearless of reproof,
I now can be alone with my Tartuffe,
And why my heart—perhaps too quick to yield—
Feels free to let its passion be revealed.
Tartuffe. Madam, your words confuse me. Not long ago,
You spoke in quite a different style, you know.
Elmire. Ah, Sir, if that refusal made you smart,
It's little that you know of woman's heart,   250
Or what that heart is trying to convey
When it resists in such a feeble way!
Always, at first, our modesty prevents
The frank avowal of tender sentiments:
However high the passion which inflames us,
Still, to confess its power somehow shames us.
Thus we reluct, at first, yet in a tone
Which tells you that our heart is overthrown,
That what our lips deny, our pulse confesses,
And that, in time, all noes will turn to yesses.   260
I fear my words are all too frank and free,
And a poor proof of woman's modesty;
But since I'm started, tell me, if you will—
Would I have tried to make Damis be still,
Would I have listened, calm and unoffended,
Until your lengthy offer of love was ended,
And been so very mild in my reaction,
Had your sweet words not given me satisfaction?
And when I tried to force you to undo
The marriage-plans my husband has in view,   270
What did my urgent pleading signify
If not that I admired you, and that I
Deplored the thought that someone else might own
Part of a heart I wished for mine alone?

Tartuffe. Madam, no happiness is so complete
As when, from lips we love, come words so sweet;
Their nectar floods my every sense, and drains
In honeyed rivulets through all my veins.
To please you is my joy, my only goal;
Your love is the restorer of my soul;   280
And yet I must beg leave, now, to confess
Some lingering doubts as to my happiness.
Might this not be a trick? Might not the catch
Be that you wish me to break off the match
With Mariane, and so have feigned to love me?
I shan't quite trust your fond opinion of me
Until the feelings you've expressed so sweetly
Are demonstrated somewhat more concretely,
And you have shown, by certain kind concessions,
That I may put my faith in your professions   290
Elmire. [*She coughs, to warn her husband.*] Why be in such a
     hurry?
Must my heart
Exhaust its bounty at the very start?
To make that sweet admission cost me dear,
But you'll not be content, it would appear,
Unless my store of favors is disbursed
To the last farthing, and at the very first.
Tartuffe. The less we merit, the less we dare to hope,
And with our doubts, mere words can never cope.   300
We trust no promised bliss till we receive it;
Not till a joy is ours can we believe it.
I, who so little merit your esteem,
Can't credit this fulfillment of my dream,
And shan't believe it, Madam, until I savor
Some palpable assurance of your favor.
Elmire. My, how tyrannical your love can be,
And how it flusters and perplexes me!
How furiously you take one's heart in hand,
And make your every wish a fierce command!   310
Come, must you hound and harry me to death?
Will you not give me time to catch my breath?
Can it be right to press me with such force,
Give me no quarter, show me no remorse,
And take advantage, by your stern insistence,
Of the fond feelings which weaken my resistance?
Tartuffe. Well, if you look with favor upon my love,
Why, then, begrudge me some clear proof thereof?
Elmire. But how can I consent without offense
To Heaven, toward which you feel such reverence?   320
Tartuffe. If Heaven is all that holds you back, don't worry.
I can remove that hindrance in a hurry.
Nothing of that sort need obstruct our path.
Elmire. Must one not be afraid of Heaven's wrath?

Tartuffe. Madam, forget such fears, and be my pupil,
And I shall teach you how to conquer scruple.
Some joys, it's true, are wrong in Heaven's eyes;
Yet Heaven is not averse to compromise;
There is a science, lately formulated,
Whereby one's conscience may be liberated,[19]   330
And any wrongful act you care to mention
May be redeemed by purity of intention.
I'll teach you, Madam, the secrets of that science;
Meanwhile, just place on me your full reliance.
Assuage my keen desires, and feel no dread:
The sin, if any, shall be on my head.
     [*Elmire coughs, this time more loudly.*]
You've a bad cough.
Elmire. Yes, yes, it's bad indeed.
Tartuffe. [*Producing a little paper bag*]   340
A bit of licorice may be what you need.
Elmire. No, I've a stubborn cold, it seems. I'm sure it
Will take much more than licorice to cure it.
Tartuffe. How aggravating.
Elmire. Oh, more than I can say.
Tartuffe. If you're still troubled, think of things this way:
No one shall know our joys, save us alone,
And there's no evil till the act is known;
It's scandal, Madam, which makes it an offense,
And it's no sin to sin in confidence.   350
Elmire. [*Having coughed once more*]
Well, clearly I must do as you require,
And yield to your importunate desire.
It is apparent, now, that nothing less
Will satisfy you, and so I acquiesce.
To go so far is much against my will;
I'm vexed that it should come to this; but still,
Since you are so determined on it, since you
Will not allow mere language to convince you,
And since you ask for concrete evidence, I   360
See nothing for it, now, but to comply.
If this is sinful, if I'm wrong to do it,
So much the worse for him who drove me to it.
The fault can surely not be charged to me.
Tartuffe. Madam, the fault is mine, if fault there be,
And . . .
Elmire. Open the door a little, and peek out;
I wouldn't want my husband poking about.
Tartuffe. Why worry about the man? Each day he grows
More gullible; one can lead him by the nose.   370
To find us here would fill him with delight,
And if he saw the worst, he'd doubt his sight.
Elmire. Nevertheless, do step out for a minute
Into the hall, and see that no one's in it.

---

19. Molière appended his own footnote to this line: "It is a
    scoundrel who speaks."

Scene 6. Orgon, Elmire

Orgon. [*Coming out from under the table*]
That man's a perfect monster, I must admit!
I'm simply stunned. I can't get over it.
Elmire. What, coming out so soon? How premature!
Get back in hiding, and wait until you're sure.   380
Stay till the end, and be convinced completely;
We mustn't stop till things are proved concretely.
Orgon. Hell never harbored anything so vicious!
Elmire. Tut, don't be hasty. Try to be judicious.
Wait, and be certain that there's no mistake.
No jumping to conclusions, for Heaven's sake!
[*She places Orgon behind her, as Tartuffe re-enters.*]

Scene 7. Tartuffe, Elmire, Orgon

Tartuffe. [*Not seeing Orgon*]
Madam, all things have worked out to perfection;   390
I've given the neighboring rooms a full inspection;
No one's about; and now I may at last . . .
Orgon. [*Intercepting him*] Hold on, my passionate fellow, not
    so fast!
I should advise a little more restraint.
Well, so you thought you'd fool me, my dear saint!
How soon you wearied of the saintly life—
Wedding my daughter, and coveting my wife!
I've long suspected you, and had a feeling
That soon I'd catch you at your double-dealing.   400
Just now, you've given me evidence galore;
It's quite enough; I have no wish for more.
Elmire. [*To Tartuffe*] I'm sorry to have treated you so slyly,
But circumstances forced me to be wily.
Tartuffe. Brother, you can't think . . .
Orgon. No more talk from you;
Just leave this household, without more ado.
Tartuffe. What I intended . . .
Orgon. That seems fairly clear.
Spare me your falsehoods and get out of here.   410
Tartuffe. No, I'm the master, and you're the one to go!
This house belongs to me, I'll have you know,
And I shall show you that you can't hurt *me*
By this contemptible conspiracy,
That those who cross me know not what they do,
And that I've means to expose and punish you,
Avenge offended Heaven, and make you grieve
That ever you dared order me to leave.

Scene 8. Elmire, Orgon

Elmire. What was the point of all that angry chatter?   420
Orgon. Dear God, I'm worried. This is no laughing matter.
Elmire. How so?
Orgon. I fear I understood his drift.
I'm much disturbed about that deed of gift.
Elmire. You gave him . . . ?
Orgon. Yes, it's all been drawn and signed.
But one thing more is weighing on my mind.
Elmire. What's that?
Orgon. I'll tell you; but first let's see if there's
A certain strong-box in his room upstairs.

ACT V

Scene 1. Orgon, Cléante

Cléante. Where are you going so fast?
Orgon. God knows!
Cléante. Then wait;
Let's have a conference, and deliberate
On how this situation's to be met.
Orgon. That strong-box has me utterly upset;
This is the worst of many, many shocks.
Cléante. Is there some fearful mystery in that box?
Orgon. My poor friend Argas brought that box to me   10
With his own hands, in utmost secrecy;
'Twas on the very morning of his flight.
It's full of papers which, if they came to light,
Would ruin him—or such is my impression.
Cléante. Then why did you let it out of your possession?
Orgon. Those papers vexed my conscience, and it seemed
    best
To ask the counsel of my pious guest.
The cunning scoundrel got me to agree
To leave the strong-box in his custody,   20
So that, in case of an investigation,
I could employ a slight equivocation
And swear I didn't have it and thereby,
At no expense to conscience, tell a lie.
Cléante. It looks to me as if you're out on a limb.
Trusting him with that box, and offering him
That deed of gift, were actions of a kind
Which scarcely indicate a prudent mind.
With two such weapons, he has the upper hand,
And since you're vulnerable as matters stand,   30
You erred once more in bringing him to bay.
You should have acted in some subtler way.
Orgon. Just think of it: behind that fervent face,
A heart so wicked, and a soul so base!
I took him in, a hungry beggar, and then . . .
Enough, by God! I'm through with pious men:
Henceforth I'll hate the whole false brotherhood,
And persecute them worse than Satan could.
Cléante. Ah, there you go—extravagant as ever!
Why can you not be rational? You never   40
Manage to take the middle course, it seems,
But jump, instead, between absurd extremes.
You've recognized your recent grave mistake
In falling victim to a pious fake;
Now, to correct that error, must you embrace
An even greater error in its place,
And judge our worthy neighbors as a whole
By what you've learned of one corrupted soul?
Come, just because one rascal made you swallow
A show of zeal which turned out to be hollow,   50
Shall you conclude that all men are deceivers,
And that, today, there are no true believers?
Let atheists make that foolish inference;
Learn to distinguish virtue from pretense,
Be cautious in bestowing admiration,
And cultivate a sober moderation.

Don't humor fraud, but also don't asperse
True piety; the latter fault is worse,
And it is best to err, if err one must,
As you have done, upon the side of trust.   60

Scene 2. Damis, Orgon, Cléante

Damis. Father, I hear that scoundrel's uttered threats
Against you; that he pridefully forgets
How, in his need, he was befriended by you,
And means to use your gifts to crucify you.

Orgon. It's true, my boy. I'm too distressed for tears.

Damis. Leave it to me, Sir; let me trim his ears.
Faced with such insolence, we must not waver.
I shall rejoice in doing you the favor
Of cutting short his life, and your distress.   70

Cléante. What a display of young hotheadedness!
Do learn to moderate your fits of rage.
In this just kingdom, this enlightened age,
One does not settle things by violence.

Scene 3. Madame Pernelle, Mariane, Elmire, Dorine, Damis,
    Orgon, Cléante

Madame Pernelle. I hear strange tales of very strange events.

Orgon. Yes, strange events which these two eyes beheld.
The man's ingratitude is unparalleled.
I save a wretched pauper from starvation,   80
House him, and treat him like a blood relation,
Shower him every day with my largesse,
Give him my daughter, and all that I possess;
And meanwhile the unconscionable knave
Tries to induce my wife to misbehave;
And not content with such extreme rascality,
Now threatens me with my own liberality,
And aims, by taking base advantage of
The gifts I gave him out of Christian love,
To drive me from my house, a ruined man,   90
And make me end a pauper, as he began.

Dorine. Poor fellow!

Madame Pernelle. No, my son, I'll never bring
Myself to think him guilty of such a thing.

Orgon. How's that?

Madame Pernelle. The righteous always were maligned.

Orgon. Speak clearly, Mother. Say what's on your mind.

Madame Pernelle. I mean that I can smell a rat, my dear.
You know how everybody hates him, here.

Orgon. That has no bearing on the case at all.   100

Madame Pernelle. I told you a hundred times, when you
        were small,
That virtue in this world is hated ever;
Malicious men may die, but malice never.

Orgon. No doubt that's true, but how does it apply?

Madame Pernelle. They've turned you against him by a
        clever lie.

Orgon. I've told you, I was there and saw it done.

Madame Pernelle. Ah, slanderers will stop at nothing, Son.

Orgon. Mother, I'll lose my temper . . . For the last time, 110
I tell you I was witness to the crime.

Madame Pernelle. The tongues of spite are busy night and
        noon,
And to their venom no man is immune.

Orgon. You're talking nonsense. Can't you realize
I saw it; saw it; saw it with my eyes?
Saw, do you understand me? Must I shout it
Into your ears before you'll cease to doubt it?

Madame Pernelle. Appearances can deceive, my son. Dear
        me,   120
We cannot always judge by what we see.

Orgon. Drat! Drat!

Madame Pernelle. One often interprets things awry;
Good can seem evil to a suspicious eye.

Orgon. Was I to see his pawing at Elmire
As an act of charity?

Madame Pernelle. 'Till his guilt is clear,
A man deserves the benefit of the doubt.
You should have waited, to see how things
turned out.   130

Orgon. Great God in Heaven, what more proof did I need?
Was I to sit there, watching, until he'd . . .
You drive me to the brink of impropriety.

Madame Pernelle. No, no, a man of such surpassing piety
Could not do such a thing. You cannot shake me.
I don't believe it, and you shall not make me.

Orgon. You vex me so that, if you weren't my mother,
I'd say to you . . . some dreadful thing or other.

Dorine. It's your turn now, Sir, not to be listened to;
You'd not trust us, and now she won't trust you.   140

Cléante. My friends, we're wasting time which should be
        spent
In facing up to our predicament.
I fear that scoundrel's threats weren't made in sport.

Damis. Do you think he'd have the nerve to go to court?

Elmire. I'm sure he won't; they'd find it all too crude
A case of swindling and ingratitude.

Cléante. Don't be too sure. He won't be at a loss
To give his claims a high and righteous gloss;
And clever rogues with far less valid cause   150
Have trapped their victims in a web of laws.
I say again that to antagonize
A man so strongly armed was most unwise.

Orgon. I know it; but the man's appalling cheek
Outraged me so, I couldn't control my pique.

Cléante. I wish to Heaven that we could devise
Some truce between you, or some compromise.

Elmire. If I had known what cards he held, I'd not
Have roused his anger by my little plot.

Orgon. [*To Dorine, as M. Loyal enters*] What is that fellow 160
        looking for? Who is he?
Go talk to him—and tell him that I'm busy.

Scene 4. Monsieur Loyal, Madame Pernelle, Orgon, Damis,
    Mariane, Dorine, Elmire, Cléante

Monsieur Loyal. Good day, dear sister. Kindly let me see
Your master.

Dorine. He's involved with company,
And cannot be disturbed just now, I fear.

Monsieur Loyal. I hate to intrude; but what has brought me here 170
Will not disturb your master, in any event.
Indeed, my news will make him most content.
Dorine. Your name?
Monsieur Loyal. Just say that I bring greetings from
Monsieur Tartuffe, on whose behalf I've come.
Dorine. [*To Orgon*] Sir, he's a very gracious man, and bears
A message from Tartuffe, which, he declares,
Will make you most content.
Cléante. Upon my word,
I think this man had best be seen, and heard. 180
Orgon. Perhaps he has some settlement to suggest.
How shall I treat him? What manner would be best?
Cléante. Control your anger, and if he should mention
Some fair adjustment, give him your full attention.
Monsieur Loyal. Good health to you, good Sir. May Heaven confound
Your enemies, and may your joys abound.
Orgon. [*Aside, to Cléante*] A gentle salutation: it confirms
My guess that he is here to offer terms.
Monsieur Loyal. I've always held your family most dear; 190
I served your father, Sir, for many a year.
Orgon. Sir, I must ask your pardon; to my shame,
I cannot now recall your face or name.
Monsieur Loyal. Loyal's my name; I come from Normandy,
And I'm a bailiff, in all modesty.
For forty years, praise God, it's been my boast
To serve with honor in that vital post,
And I am here, Sir, if you will permit
The liberty, to serve you with this writ . . .
Orgon. To—*what*? 200
Monsieur Loyal. Now, please, Sir, let us have no friction:
It's nothing but an order of eviction.
You are to move your goods and family out
And make way for new occupants, without
Deferment or delay, and give the keys . . .
Orgon. I? Leave this house?
Monsieur Loyal.   Why yes, Sir, if you please.
This house, Sir, from the cellar to the roof,
Belongs now to the good Monsieur Tartuffe,
And he is lord and master of your estate 210
By virtue of a deed of present date,
Drawn in due form, with clearest legal phrasing . . .
Damis. Your insolence is utterly amazing!
Monsieur Loyal. Young man, my business here is not with you
But with your wise and temperate father, who,
Like every worthy citizen, stands in awe
Of justice, and would never obstruct the law.
Orgon. But . . .
Monsieur Loyal. Not for a million, Sir, would you rebel 220
Against authority; I know that well.
You'll not make trouble, sir, or interfere
With the execution of my duties here.
Damis. Someone may execute a smart tattoo
On that black jacket of yours, before you're through.

Monsieur Loyal. Sir, bid your son be silent. I'd much regret
Having to mention such a nasty threat
Of violence, in writing my report.
Dorine. [*Aside*] This man Loyal's a most disloyal sort!
Monsieur Loyal. I love all men of upright character, 230
And when I agreed to serve these papers, Sir,
It was your feelings that I had in mind.
I couldn't bear to see the case assigned
To someone else, who might esteem you less
And so subject you to unpleasantness.
Orgon. What's more unpleasant than telling a man to leave
His house and home?
Monsieur Loyal. You'd like a short reprieve?
If you desire it, Sir, I shall not press you,
But wait until tomorrow to dispossess you. 240
Splendid. I'll come and spend the night here, then,
Most quietly, with half a score of men.
For form's sake, you might bring me, just before
You go to bed, the keys to the front door.
My men, I promise, will be on their best
Behavior, and will not disturb your rest.
But bright and early, Sir, you must be quick
And move out all your furniture, every stick:
The men I've chosen are both young and strong,
And with their help it shouldn't take you long. 250
In short, I'll make things pleasant and convenient,
And since I'm being so extremely lenient,
Please show me, Sir, a like consideration,
And give me your entire cooperation.
Orgon. [*Aside*] I may be all but bankrupt, but I vow
I'd give a hundred louis, here and now,
Just for the pleasure of landing one good clout
Right on the end of that complacent snout.
Cléante. Careful; don't make things worse.
Damis. To give that beggar a good kick in the breeches. 260
Dorine. Monsieur Loyal, I'd love to hear the whack
Of a stout stick across your fine broad back.
Monsieur Loyal. Take care: a woman too may go to jail if
She uses threatening language to a bailiff.
Cléante. Enough, enough, Sir. This must not go on.
Give me that paper, please, and then begone.
Monsieur Loyal. Well, *au revoir*. God give you all good cheer!
Orgon. May God confound you, and him who sent you here! 270

Scene 5. Orgon, Cléante, Mariane, Elmire, Madame Pernelle, Dorine, Damis
Orgon. Now, Mother, was I right or not? This writ
Should change your notion of Tartuffe a bit.
Do you perceive his villainy at last?
Madame Pernelle. I'm thunderstruck. I'm utterly aghast.
Dorine. Oh, come, be fair. You mustn't take offense
At this new proof of his benevolence.
He's acting out of selfless love, I know.
Material things enslave the soul, and so 280
He kindly has arranged your liberation
From all that might endanger your salvation.

Orgon. Will you not ever hold your tongue, you dunce?
Cléante. Come, you must take some action, and at once.
Elmire. Go tell the world of the low trick he's tried.
The deed of gift is surely nullified.
By such behavior, and public rage will not
Permit the wretch to carry out his plot.

Scene 6. Valère, Orgon, Cléante, Elmire, Mariane, Madame
Pernelle, Damis, Dorine   290
Valère. Sir, though I hate to bring you more bad news.
Such is the danger that I cannot choose.
A friend who is extremely close to me
And knows my interest in your family
Has, for my sake, presumed to violate
The secrecy that's due to things of state,
And sends me word that you are in a plight
From which your one salvation lies in flight.
That scoundrel who's imposed upon you so
Denounced you to the King an hour ago   300
And, as supporting evidence, displayed
The strong-box of a certain renegade
Whose secret papers, so he testified,
You had disloyally agreed to hide.
I don't know just what charges may be pressed,
But there's a warrant out for your arrest;
Tartuffe has been instructed, furthermore,
To guide the arresting officer to your door.
Cléante. He's clearly done this to facilitate
His seizure of your house and your estate.   310
Orgon. That man, I must say, is a vicious beast!
Valère. You can't afford to delay, Sir, in the least.
My carriage is outside, to take you hence;
This thousand louis should cover all expense.
Let's lose no time. or you shall be undone;
The sole defense, in this case, is to run.
I shall go with you all the way, and place you
In a safe refuge to which they'll never trace you.
Orgon. Alas, dear boy, I wish that I could show you
My gratitude for everything I owe you.   320
But now is not the time; I pray the Lord
That I may live to give you your reward.
Farewell, my dears; be careful . . .
Cléante. Brother, hurry.
We shall take care of things; you needn't worry.

Scene 7. The Officer, Tartuffe, Valère, Orgon, Elmire,
Mariane, Madame Pernelle, Dorine, Cléante, Damis
Tartuffe. Gently, Sir, gently; stay right where you are.
No need for haste; your lodging isn't far.
You're off to prison, by order of the Prince.   330
Orgon. This is the crowning blow, you wretch; and since
It means my total ruin and defeat,
Your villainy is now at last complete.
Tartuffe. You needn't try to provoke me; it's no use.
Those who serve Heaven must expect abuse.
Cléante. You are indeed most patient, sweet, and blameless.
Dorine. How he exploits the name of Heaven! It's shameless.
Tartuffe. Your taunts and mockeries are all for naught;
To do my duty is my only thought.

Mariane. Your love of duty is most meritorious,   340
And what you've done is little short of glorious.
Tartuffe. All deeds are glorious, Madam, which obey
The sovereign prince who sent me here today.
Orgon. I rescued you when you were destitute;
Have you forgotten that, you thankless brute?
Tartuffe. No, no, I well remember everything;
But my first duty is to serve my King.
That obligation is so paramount
That other claims, beside it, do not count;
And for it I would sacrifice my wife,   350
My family, my friend, or my own life.
Elmire. Hypocrite!
Dorine. All that we most revere, he uses
To cloak his plots and camouflage his ruses.
Cléante. If it is true that you are animated
By pure and loyal zeal, as you have stated,
Why was this zeal not roused until you'd sought
To make Orgon a cuckold, and been caught?
Why weren't you moved to give your evidence
Until your outraged host had driven you hence?   360
I shan't say that the gift of all his treasure
Ought to have damped your zeal in any measure;
But if he is a traitor, as you declare,
How could you condescend to be his heir?
Tartuffe. [*To the Officer*] Sir, spare me all this clamor; it's
growing shrill.
Please carry out your orders, if you will.
Officer.[20] Yes, I've delayed too long, Sir. Thank you kindly.
You're just the proper person to remind me.
Come, you are off to join the other boarders   370
In the King's prison, according to his orders.
Tartuffe. Who? I, Sir?
Officer. Yes.
Tartuffe. To prison? This can't be true!
Officer. I owe an explanation, but not to you.
[*To Orgon*] Sir, all is well; rest easy, and be grateful.
We serve a Prince to whom all sham is hateful,
A Prince who sees into our inmost hearts,
And can't be fooled by any trickster's arts.
His royal soul, though generous and human,   380
Views all things with discernment and acumen;
His sovereign reason is not lightly swayed,
And all his judgments are discreetly weighed.
He honors righteous men of every kind,
And yet his zeal for virtue is not blind,
Nor does his love of piety numb his wits
And make him tolerant of hypocrites.
'Twas hardly likely that this man could cozen
A King who's foiled such liars by the dozen.
With one keen glance, the King perceived the whole   390
Perverseness and corruption of his soul,
And thus high Heaven's justice was displayed:
Betraying you, the rogue stood self-betrayed.

---

20. In the original, *un exempt.* He would actually have been a
gentleman from the king's personal bodyguard with the rank of
lieutenant-colonel or ''master of the camp.''

The King soon recognized Tartuffe as one
Notorious by another name, who'd done
So many vicious crimes that one could fill
Ten volumes with them, and be writing still.
But to be brief: our sovereign was appalled
By this man's treachery toward you, which he called
The last, worst villainy of a vile career,   400
And bade me follow the impostor here
To see how gross his impudence could be,
And force him to restore your property.
Your private papers, by the King's command,
I hereby seize and give into your hand.
The King, by royal order, invalidates
The deed which gave this rascal your estates,
And pardons, furthermore, your grave offense
In harboring an exile's documents.
By these decrees, our Prince rewards you for   410
Your loyal deeds in the late civil war,
And shows how heartfelt is his satisfaction
In recompensing any worthy action,
How much he prizes merit, and how he makes
More of men's virtues than of their mistakes.
Dorine. Heaven be praised!
Madame Pernelle. I breathe again, at last.
Elmire. We're safe.
Mariane. I can't believe the danger's past.
Orgon. [*To Tartuffe*] Well, traitor, now you see . . .   420
Cléante. Ah, brother, please,
Let's not descend to such indignities.
Leave the poor wretch to his unhappy fate,
And don't say anything to aggravate
His present woes; but rather hope that he
Will soon embrace an honest piety,
And mend his ways, and by a true repentance
Move our just King to moderate his sentence.
Meanwhile, go kneel before your sovereign's throne
And thank him for the mercies he has shown.   430
Orgon. Well said: let's go at once and, gladly kneeling,
Express the gratitude which all are feeling.
Then, when that first great duty has been done,
We'll turn with pleasure to a second one,
And give Valère, whose love has proven so true,
The wedded happiness which is his due.

Exercises

1. Imagine that you are casting *Tartuffe* for a movie production. Select the actor who, in your opinion, appears to be the best and most effective for each major role.
2. Why does Molière delay Tartuffe's entrance until Act III? Why does he have Tartuffe encounter Dorine first? Why not Orgon?
3. Describe the character traits of Orgon that make him so vulnerable to a villain like Tartuffe. Why aren't the others duped?
4. Are there any Tartuffes in contemporary American life you know of or suspect? Describe them, how they operate, and why you are suspicious of their motives.

Alexander Pope, 1688–1744

Neoclassicism became the dominant style in eighteenth-century Europe, especially in France and England. The most influential neoclassic poet in England, Alexander Pope, formulated the aesthetics of poetry in *Essay on Criticism,* emphasizing the necessity for precise language, logical order, and clear form. Pope's own poetry was didactic, witty, satiric, technically superb; it epitomized the neoclassic style of eighteenth-century England. Pope, in fact, expressed his goal in his own verse:

True wit is nature to advantage dressed,
What oft was thought, but ne'er so well expressed.

His *Essay on Man* (1733–1734) optimistically summarizes eighteenth-century views on the rational universe, reasonable behavior, and deism. Though not profound in philosophic terms, the poem is esteemed for its skillful craftsmanship and sparkling wit. Pope's optimism was rejected by the skeptical Voltaire in *Candide,* as discussed later.

ESSAY ON MAN
Alexander Pope

EPISTLE I

Awake, my St. John! leave all meaner things
To low ambition and the pride of kings.
Let us, since life can little more supply
Than just to look about us and to die,
Expatiate free o'er all this scene of man;
A mighty maze! but not without a plan;
A wild, where weeds and flowers promiscuous shoot;
Or garden, tempting with forbidden fruit.
Together let us beat this ample field,
Try what the open, what the covert yield;
The latent tracts, the giddy heights, explore,
Of all who blindly creep, or sightless soar;
Eye Nature's walks, shoot Folly as it flies,
And catch the manners living as they rise;
Laugh where we must, be candid where we can;
But vindicate the ways of God to man.

I

Say first, of God above or man below,
What can we reason but from what we know?
Of man, what see we but his station here,
From which to reason, or to which refer?
Through worlds unnumber'd though the God be known,
'Tis ours to trace him only in our own.
He, who through vast immensity can pierce,
See worlds on worlds compose one universe,
Observe how system into system runs,
What other planets circle other suns,
What varied being peoples every star,
May tell why Heav'n has made us as we are.

But of this frame, the bearings and the ties,
The strong connections, nice dependencies,
Gradations just, has thy pervading soul
Looked through, or can a part contain the whole?
Is the great chain that draws all to agree,
And drawn supports, upheld by God or thee?

II

Presumptuous man! the reason wouldst thou find,
Why form'd so weak, so little, and so blind?
First, if thou canst, the harder reason guess,
Why form'd no weaker, blinder, and no less?
Ask of thy mother earth, why oaks are made
Taller or stronger than the weeds they shade!
Or ask of yonder argent fields above
Why Jove's satellites are less than Jove!
Of systems possible, if 't is confest
That wisdom infinite must form the best,   10
Where all must full or not coherent be,
And all that rises rise in due degree,
Then, in the scale of reas'ning life, 't is plain
There must be somewhere such a rank as Man:
And all the question (wrangle e'er so long)
Is only this, if God has placed him wrong?
Respecting Man, whatever wrong we call,
May, must be right, as relative to all.
In human works, though labor'd on with pain,
A thousand movements scarce one purpose gain;   20
In God's, one single can its end produce;
Yet serves to second too some other use.
So Man, who here seems principal alone,
Perhaps acts second to some sphere unknown,
Touches some wheel, or verges to some goal;
'Tis but a part we see, and not a whole.
When the proud steed shall know why man restrains
His fiery course, or drives him o'er the plains;
When the dull ox, why now he breaks the clod,
Is now a victim, and now Egypt's god;   30
Then shall man's pride and dullness comprehend
His actions', passions', being's, use and end;
Why doing, suff'ring, check'd, impell'd; and why
This hour a slave, the next a deity.
Then say not man's imperfect, Heav'n in fault;
Say rather man's as perfect as he ought:
His knowledge measur'd to his state and place,
His time a moment, and a point his space.
If to be perfect in a certain sphere,
What matter soon or late, or here or there?   40
The blest today is as completely so,
As who began a thousand years ago.
Heav'n from all creatures hides the book of Fate,
All but the page prescrib'd, their present state:
From brutes what men, from men what spirits know:
Or who could suffer Being here below?
The lamb thy riot dooms to bleed today,
Had he thy reason, would he skip and play?
Pleas'd to the last, he crops the flow'ry food,
And licks the hand just rais'd to shed his blood.   50

Oh blindness to the future! kindly giv'n,
That each may fill the circle mark'd by Heav'n:
Who sees with equal eye, as God of all,
A hero perish, or a sparrow fall,
Atoms or systems into ruin hurl'd,
And now a bubble burst, and now a world.
Hope humbly then; with trembling pinions soar;
Wait the great teacher Death, and God adore!
What future bliss he gives not thee to know,
But gives that hope to be thy blessing now.   60
Hope springs eternal in the human breast;
Man never is, but always to be blest.
The soul, uneasy, and confin'd from home,
Rests and expatiates in a life to come.
Lo! the poor Indian, whose untutor'd mind
Sees God in clouds, or hears him in the wind;
His soul proud Science never taught to stray
Far as the solar walk or milky way;
Yet simple Nature to his hope has giv'n,
Behind the cloud-topt hill, an humbler heav'n;   70
Some safer world in depth of woods embrac'd,
Some happier island in the watery waste,
Where slaves once more their native land behold,
No fiends torment, no Christians thirst for gold!
To be, contents his natural desire;
He asks no angel's wing, no seraph's fire;
But thinks, admitted to that equal sky,
His faithful dog shall bear him company.

IV

Go, wiser thou! and in thy scale of sense,
Weigh thy opinion against Providence;
Call imperfection what thou fancy'st such,
Say, Here he gives too little, there too much!
Destroy all creatures for thy sport or gust,
Yet cry, If man's unhappy, God's unjust;
If man alone engross not Heav'n's high care,
Alone made perfect here, immortal there:
Snatch from his hand the balance and the rod,
Rejudge his justice, be the God of God!
In pride, in reas'ning pride, our error lies;
All quit their sphere and rush into the skies.
Pride still is aiming at the blest abodes,
Men would be angels, angels would be gods.
Aspiring to be gods if angels fell,
Aspiring to be angels, men rebel:
And who but wishes to invert the laws
Of order, sins against the Eternal Cause.

V

Ask for what end the heav'nly bodies shine,
Earth for whose use? Pride answers, " 'Tis for mine!
For me kind Nature wakes her genial pow'r,
Suckles each herb, and spreads out ev'ry flow'r;
Annual for me, the grape, the rose renew
The juice nectarous and the balmy dew;
For me the mine a thousand treasures brings;

For me health gushes from a thousand springs;
Seas roll to waft me, suns to light me rise;
My footstool earth, my canopy the skies." 10
But errs not Nature from this gracious end,
From burning suns when livid deaths descend,
When earthquakes swallow, or when tempests sweep
Towns to one grave, whole nations to the deep?
"No," 't is reply'd, "the first Almighty Cause
Acts not by partial but by gen'ral laws:
Th' exceptions few; some change since all began;
And what created perfect?"—Why then man?
If the great end be human happiness,
Then Nature deviates; and can man do less? 20
As much that end a constant course requires
Of show'rs and sunshine, as of man's desires:
As much eternal springs and cloudless skies,
As men forever temp'rate, calm, and wise.
If plagues or earthquakes break not Heav'n's design,
Why then a Borgia or a Catiline?
Who knows but he, whose hand the lightning forms,
Why heaves old ocean, and who wings the storms,
Pours fierce ambition in a Caesar's mind,
Or turns young Ammon loose to scourge mankind? 30
From pride, from pride our very reas'ning springs;
Account for moral, as for natural things:
Why charge we Heav'n in those, in these acquit?
In both, to reason right is to submit.
Better for us, perhaps, it might appear,
Were there all harmony, all virtue here;
That never air or ocean felt the wind;
That never passion discompos'd the mind.
But all subsists by elemental strife;
And passions are the elements of life. 40
The gen'ral order, since the whole began,
Is kept in Nature, and is kept in man.

VI

What would this man? Now upward will he soar,
And little less than angel, would be more!
Now looking downwards, just as griev'd appears
To want the strength of bulls, the fur of bears.
Made for his use all creatures if he call,
Say what their use, had he the pow'rs of all?
Nature to these, without profusion, kind,
The proper organs, proper pow'rs assign'd;
Each seeming want compensated of course,
Here with degrees of swiftness, there of force: 10
All in exact proportion to the state;
Nothing to add, and nothing to abate;
Each beast, each insect happy in its own:
Is Heav'n unkind to man, and man alone?
Shall he alone, whom rational we call,
Be pleas'd with nothing, if not bless'd with all?
The bliss of man (could pride that blessing find),
Is not to act or think beyond mankind;
No powers of body or of soul to share,
But what his nature and his state can bear. 20
Why has not man a microscopic eye?

For this plain reason, man is not a fly.
Say what the use, were finer optics giv'n,
To inspect a mite, not comprehend the heav'n?
Or touch, if tremblingly alive all o'er,
To smart and agonize at every pore?
Or quick effluvia darting through the brain,
Die of a rose in aromatic pain?
If Nature thunder'd in his opening ears,
And stunn'd him with the music of the spheres, 30
How would he wish that Heav'n had left him still
The whisp'ring zephyr and the purling rill?
Who finds not Providence all good and wise,
Alike in what it gives, and what denies?

VII

Far as creation's ample range extends,
The scale of sensual, mental powers ascends.
Mark how it mounts to man's imperial race,
From the green myriads in the peopled grass;
What modes of sight betwixt each wide extreme,
The mole's dim curtain, and the lynx's beam:
Of smell, the headlong lioness between,
And hound sagacious on the tainted green:
Of hearing, from the life that fills the flood,
To that which warbles through the vernal wood: 10
The spider's touch how exquisitely fine!
Feels at each thread, and lives along the line:
In the nice bee, what sense so subtly true
From pois'nous herbs extracts the healing dew?
How instinct varies in the grov'ling swine,
Compar'd, half-reas'ning elephant, with thine!
'Twixt that and reason, what a nice barrier;
Forever sep'rate, yet forever near!
Remembrance and reflection, how ally'd;
What thin partitions sense from thought divide; 20
And middle natures, how they long to join,
Yet never pass th' insuperable line!
Without this just gradation, could they be
Subjected, these to those, or all to thee?
The pow'rs of all subdu'd by thee alone,
Is not thy reason all these pow'rs in one?
See, through this air, this ocean, and this earth,
All matter quick, and bursting into birth.
Above, how high progressive life may go!
Around, how wide! how deep extend below! 30
Vast Chain of Being! which from God began,
Natures ethereal, human, angel, man,
Beast, bird, fish, insect, what no eye can see,
No glass can reach; from infinite to thee,
From thee to nothing. On superior pow'rs
Were we to press, inferior might on ours:
Or in the full creation leave a void,
Where, one step broken, the great scale's destroy'd:
From Nature's chain whatever link you strike,
Tenth or ten thousandth, breaks the chain alike. 40

And if each system in gradation roll
Alike essential to the amazing Whole,
The least confusion but in one, not all
That system only, but the Whole must fall.
Let earth unbalanc'd from her orbit fly,
Planets and suns run lawless through the sky;
Let ruling angels from their spheres be hurl'd,
Being on being wreck'd, and world on world;
Heav'n's whole foundations to their centre nod,
And Nature tremble to the throne of God!   50
All this dread Order break—for whom? for thee?
Vile worm!—Oh! madness! pride! impiety!

IX

What if the foot, ordain'd the dust to tread,
Or hand, to toil, aspir'd to be the head?
What if the head, the eye, or ear repin'd
To serve mere engines to the ruling Mind?
Just as absurd for any part to claim
To be another in this gen'ral frame;
Just as absurd to mourn the tasks or pains
The great directing Mind of All ordains.
All are but parts of one stupendous whole,
Whose body Nature is, and God the soul;
That, chang'd through all, and yet in all the same,
Great in the earth, as in th' ethereal frame,
Warms in the sun, refreshes in the breeze,
Glows in the stars, and blossoms in the trees,
Lives through all life, extends through all extent,
Spreads undivided, operates unspent;
Breathes in our soul, informs our mortal part,
As full, as perfect in a hair as heart;
As full, as perfect in vile man that mourns,
As the rapt seraph that adores and burns:
To him no high, no low, no great, no small;
He fills, he bounds, connects, and equals all.

X

Cease then, nor Order imperfection name:
Our proper bliss depends on what we blame.
Know thy own point: this kind, this due degree
Of blindness, weakness, Heav'n bestows on thee.
Submit: in this or any other sphere,
Secure to be as blest as thou canst bear;
Safe in the hand of one disposing Pow'r
Or in the natal, or the mortal hour.
All Nature is but art unknown to thee;
All chance, direction which thou canst not see;
All discord, harmony not understood;
All partial evil, universal good;
And, spite of pride, in erring reason's spite,
One truth is clear, *whatever is, is right.*

EPISTLE II

Know then thyself, presume not God to scan:
The proper study of mankind is Man.
Plac'd on this isthmus of a middle state,
A being darkly wise and rudely great:
With too much knowledge for the skeptic side,
With too much weakness for the Stoic's pride,
He hangs between; in doubt to act, or rest;
In doubt to deem himself a god or beast;
In doubt his mind or body to prefer;
Born but to die, and reas'ning but to err;
Alike in ignorance, his reason such,
Whether he thinks too little or too much:
Chaos of thought and passion, all confus'd;
Still by himself abus'd, or disabus'd;
Created half to rise, and half to fall;
Great lord of all things, yet a prey to all;
Sole judge of truth, in endless error hurl'd;
The glory, jest, and riddle of the world!

II

Two principles in human nature reign;
Self-love to urge, and reason to restrain;
Nor this a good, nor that a bad we call,
Each works its end to move or govern all:
And to their proper operation still
Ascribe all good; to their improper, ill.
Self-love, the spring of motion, acts the soul;
Reason's comparing balance rules the whole.
Man, but for that, no action could attend,
And, but for this, were active to no end:
Fix'd like a plant on his peculiar spot,
To draw nutrition, propagate, and rot;
Or, meteor-like, flame lawless thro' the void,
Destroying others, by himself destroyed.
Most strength the moving principle requires;
Active its task, it prompts, impels, inspires.
Sedate and quiet, the comparing lies,
Form'd but to check, deliberate, and advise.
Self-love still stronger, as its objects nigh;
Reason's at distance and in prospect lie:
That sees immediate good by present sense;
Reason, the future and the consequence.
Thicker than arguments, temptations throng,
At best more watchful this, but that more strong.
The action of the stronger to suspend,
Reason still use, to reason still attend.
Attention, habit and experience gains;
Each strengthens reason, and self-love restrains . . .

V

Vice is a monster of so frightful mien,
As to be hated needs but to be seen;
Yet seen too oft, familiar with her face,
We first endure, then pity, then embrace:
But where the extreme of vice was ne'er agreed:
Ask where's the north? at York, 'tis on the Tweed;
In Scotland, at the Orcades; and there,
At Greenland, Zembla, or the Lord knows where.
No creature owns it in the first degree,
But thinks his neighbor farther gone than he;
Even those who dwell beneath its very zone,
Or never feel the rage, or never own;
What happier natures shrink at with affright
The hard inhabitant contends is right.
Virtuous and vicious every man must be;
Few in the extreme, but all in the degree:
The rogue and fool by fits is fair and wise;
And ev'n the best, by fits, what they despise.
'T is but by parts we follow good or ill;
For, vice or virtue, self directs it still;
Each individual seeks a sev'ral goal;
But Heav'n's great view is one, and that the whole . . .

EPISTLE III

Here then we rest: "The Universal Cause
Acts to one end, but acts by various laws."
In all the madness of superfluous health,
The trim of pride, the impudence of wealth,
Let this great truth be present night and day:
But most be present, if we preach or pray.
Look round our world, behold the chain of love
Combining all below and all above.
See plastic Nature working to this end:
The single atoms each to other tend;
Attract, attracted to, the next in place
Form'd and impell'd its neighbor to embrace.
See matter next with various life endu'd,
Press to one centre still, the gen'ral good.
See dying vegetables life sustain,
See life dissolving vegetate again:
All forms that perish other forms supply,
(By turns we catch the vital breath, and die.)
Like bubbles on the sea of matter borne,
They rise, they break, and to that sea return.
Nothing is foreign; parts relate to whole;
One all-extending, all-preserving soul
Connects each being, greatest with the least;
Made beast in aid of man, and man of beast;
All serv'd, all serving: nothing stands alone;
The chain holds on, and where it ends, unknown . . .

Exercises

1. In the first section of Epistle I is Pope a "rationalist"—one who believes that the human mind can find answers to all questions? Why do you answer as you do?
2. In Epistle I:VII Pope refers to the "Vast chain of being." What does he mean by this?
3. Pope speaks of man as the *glory,* the *jest,* and the *riddle* of the world. In what sense does he use each term? Name three men or women, or one person in three different situations, that would explain Pope's meaning.
4. In your estimation, what is the point of the brief selection from Epistle III: inescapable Law; constant Change; Continuity and Interdependence; inevitable Death and Decay; the Separateness of all things; or some other idea?
5. Who would have given the more favorable review on the *Essay on Man* (if he could have read it!): Newton or Rousseau? Dante or Machiavelli? Shakespeare or Donne? Why do you think so?

Jonathan Swift, 1667–1745

Born in Ireland of English parents, Jonathan Swift (figure 20.4) is identified with Ireland and its political troubles and yet, for most of his life, he tried to break away from Ireland. His dream of becoming an English bishop failed; instead he was awarded the deanship of St. Patrick's Cathedral in Dublin. At first feeling exiled in Ireland, he later became closely identified with its pervasive poverty and political privation.

A master of language employed in a lucid and forceful style, Swift was the greatest English satirist in an age of satire, perhaps because he was more detached, critically viewing English life and customs from his vantage point in Ireland. His masterpiece, *Gulliver's Travels* (1726), savagely exposed and attacked every human weakness and vice over there in Britain. His brilliant pamphlet, "A Modest Proposal," was written in the white heat of indignation. Ireland's poverty and misery, in his own words, did "tear his heart." His proposal is all the more horrendous in its reasoned logic as he ironically suggests a practical solution to the destitution of the downtrodden Irish.

A MODEST PROPOSAL

for Preventing the Children of Poor People in Ireland from Being a Burden to Their Parents or Country, and for Making Them Beneficial to the Public.
1729
Jonathan Swift

It is a melancholy object to those who walk through this great town, or travel in the country, when they see the streets, the roads, and cabin-doors, crowded with beggars of the female sex, followed by three, four, or six children, all in rags, and importuning every passenger for an alms. These mothers, instead of being able to

Figure 20.4 *Dean Jonathan Swift. Copperplate. Photo: North Wind Picture Archives.*

work for their honest livelihood, are forced to employ all their time in strolling to beg sustenance for their helpless infants: who, as they grow up, either turn thieves for want of work, or leave their dear native country to fight for the Pretender in Spain, or sell themselves to the Barbadoes.

I think it is agreed by all parties, that this prodigious number of children in the arms, or on the backs, or at the heels of their mothers, and frequently of their fathers, is, in the present deplorable state of the kingdom, a very great additional grievance; and, therefore, whoever could find out a fair, cheap, and easy method of making these children sound, useful members of the commonwealth, would deserve so well of the public, as to have his statue set up for a preserver of the nation.

But my intention is very far from being confined to provide only for the children of professed beggars; it is of a much greater extent, and shall take in the whole number of infants at a certain age, who are born of parents in effect as little able to support them, as those who demand our charity in the streets.

As to my own part, having turned my thoughts for many years upon this important subject, and maturely weighed the several schemes of our projectors, I have always found them grossly mistaken in their computation. It is true, a child, just born, may be supported by its mother's milk for a solar year, with little other nourishment; at most, not above the value of two shillings, which the mother may certainly get, or the value in scraps, by her lawful occupation of begging; and it is exactly at one year old that I propose to provide for them in such a manner, as, instead of being a charge upon their parents, or the parish, or wanting food and raiment for the rest of their lives, they shall, on the contrary, contribute to the feeding, and partly to the clothing, of many thousands.

There is likewise another great advantage in my scheme, that it will prevent those voluntary abortions, and that horrid practice of women murdering their bastard children, alas, too frequent among us! sacrificing the poor innocent babes, I doubt more to avoid the expense than the shame, which would move tears and pity in the most savage and inhuman breast.

The number of souls in this kingdom being usually reckoned one million and a half, of these I calculate there may be about two hundred thousand couple whose wives are breeders; from which number I subtract thirty thousand couple, who are able to maintain their own children, (although I apprehend there cannot be so many, under the present distresses of the kingdom;) but this being granted, there will remain a hundred and seventy thousand breeders. I again subtract fifty thousand, for those women who miscarry, or whose children die by accident or disease within the year. There only remain a hundred and twenty thousand children of poor parents annually born. The question therefore is, How this number shall be reared and provided for? which, as I have already said, under the present situation of affairs, is utterly impossible by all the methods hitherto proposed. For we can neither employ them in handicraft or agriculture; we neither build houses (I mean in the country,) nor cultivate land: they can very seldom pick up a livelihood by stealing, till they arrive at six years old, except where they are of towardly parts; although I confess they learn the rudiments much earlier; during which time they can, however, be properly looked upon only as probationers; as I have been informed by a principal gentleman in the county of Cavan, who protested to me, that he never knew above one or two instances under the age of six, even in a part of the kingdom so renowned for the quickest proficiency in that art.

I am assured by our merchants, that a boy or a girl before twelve years old is no saleable commodity; and even when they come to this age they will not yield above three pounds or three pounds and half-a-crown at most, on the exchange; which cannot turn to account either to the parents or kingdom, the charge of nutriment and rags having been at least four times that value.

I shall now, therefore, humbly propose my own thoughts, which I hope will not be liable to the least objection.

I have been assured by a very knowing American of my acquaintance in London, that a young healthy child, well nursed, is, at a year old, a most delicious, nourishing, and wholesome food, whether stewed, roasted, baked, or boiled; and I make no doubt that it will equally serve in a fricassee or a ragout.

I do therefore humbly offer it to public consideration, that of the hundred and twenty thousand children already computed, twenty thousand may be reserved for breed, whereof only one-fourth part to be males; which is more than we allow to sheep, black-cattle, or swine; and my reason is, that these children are seldom the fruits of marriage, a circumstance not much regarded by our savages, therefore one male will be sufficient for four females. That the remaining hundred thousand may, at a year old, be offered in sale to the persons of quality and fortune through the kingdom; always advising the mother to let them suck plentifully in the last month, so as to render them plump and fat for a good table. A child will make two dishes at an entertainment for friends; and when the family dines alone, the fore or hind quarter will make a reasonable dish, and, seasoned with a little pepper or salt, will be very good boiled on the fourth day, especially in winter.

I have reckoned, upon a medium, that a child just born will weigh twelve pounds, and in a solar year, if tolerably nursed, will increase to twenty-eight pounds.

I grant this food will be somewhat dear, and therefore very proper for landlords, who, as they have already devoured most of the parents, seem to have the best title to the children.

Infants' flesh will be in season throughout the year, but more plentifully in March, and a little before and after: for we are told by a grave author, an eminent French physician, that fish being a prolific diet, there are more children born in Roman Catholic countries about nine months after Lent, than at any other season; therefore, reckoning a year after Lent, the markets will be more glutted than usual, because the number of Popish infants is at least three to one in this kingdom; and therefore it will have one other collateral advantage, by lessening the number of Papists among us.

I have already computed the charge of nursing a beggar's child (in which list I reckon all cottagers, labourers, and four-fifths of the farmers) to be about two shillings per annum, rags included; and I believe no gentleman would repine to give ten shillings for the carcass of a good fat child, which, as I have said, will make four dishes of excellent nutritive meat, when he has only some particular friend, or his own family, to dine with him. Thus the squire will learn to be a good landlord, and grow popular among his tenants; the mother will have eight shillings net profit, and be fit for work till she produces another child.

Those who are more thrifty (as I must confess the times require) may flay the carcass; the skin of which, artificially dressed, will make admirable gloves for ladies, and summer-boots for fine gentlemen. As to our city of Dublin, shambles may be appointed for this purpose in the most convenient parts of it, and butchers we may be assured will not be wanting; although I rather recommend buying the children alive, then dressing them hot from the knife, as we do roasting pigs.

A very worthy person, a true lover of his country, and whose virtues I highly esteem, was lately pleased, in discoursing on this matter, to offer a refinement upon my scheme. He said, that many gentlemen of this kingdom, having of late destroyed their deer, he conceived that the want of venison might be well supplied by the bodies of young lads and maidens, not exceeding fourteen years of age, nor under twelve; so great a number of both sexes in every country being now ready to starve for want of work and service; and these to be disposed of by their parents, if alive, or otherwise by their nearest relations. But, with due deference to so excellent a friend, and so deserving a patriot, I cannot be altogether in his sentiments; for as to the males, my American acquaintance assured me, from frequent experience, that their flesh was generally tough and lean, like that of our schoolboys, by continual exercise, and their taste disagreeable; and to fatten them would not answer the charge. Then as to the females, it would, I think, with humble submission, be a loss to the public, because they soon would become breeders themselves: and besides, it is not improbable that some scrupulous people might be apt to censure such a practice, (although indeed very unjustly,) as a little bordering upon cruelty; which, I confess, has always been with me the strongest objection against any project, how well soever intended.

But in order to justify my friend, he confessed that this expedient was put into his head by the famous Psalmanazar, a native of the island Formosa, who came from thence to London above twenty years ago; and in conversation told my friend, that in his country, when any young person happened to be put to death, the executioner sold the carcass to persons of quality as a prime dainty; and that in his time the body of a plump girl of fifteen, who was crucified for an attempt to poison the emperor, was sold to his imperial majesty's prime minister of state, and other great mandarins of the court, in joints from the gibbet, at four hundred crowns. Neither indeed can I deny, that if the same use were made of several plump young girls in this town, who, without one single groat to their fortunes, cannot stir abroad without a chair, and appear at playhouse and assemblies in foreign fineries which they never will pay for, the kingdom would not be the worse.

Some persons of a desponding spirit are in great concern about that vast number of poor people, who are aged, diseased, or maimed; and I have been desired to employ my thoughts, what course may be taken to ease the nation of so grievous an encumbrance. But I am not in the least pain upon that matter, because it is very well known, that they are every day dying, and rotting, by cold and famine, and filth and vermin, as fast as can be reasonably expected. And as to the young labourers, they are now in almost as hopeful a condition: they cannot get work, and consequently pine away for want of nourishment, to a degree, that if at any time they are accidentally hired to common labour, they have not strength to perform it; and thus the country and themselves are happily delivered from the evils to come.

I have too long digressed, and therefore shall return to my subject. I think the advantages by the proposal which I have made, are obvious and many, as well as of the highest importance.

For first, as I have already observed, it would greatly lessen the number of Papists, with whom we are yearly over-run, being the principal breeders of the nation, as well as our most dangerous enemies; and who stay at home on purpose to deliver the kingdom to the Pretender, hoping to take their advantage by the absence of so many good Protestants, who have chosen rather to leave their country, than stay at home and pay tithes against their conscience to an Episcopal curate.

Secondly, The poorer tenants will have something valuable of their own, which by law may be made liable to distress, and help to pay their landlord's rent; their corn and cattle being already seized, and money a thing unknown.

Thirdly, Whereas the maintenance of a hundred thousand children, from two years old and upward, cannot be computed at less than ten shillings a piece per annum, the nation's stock will be thereby increased fifty thousand pounds per annum, beside the profit of a new dish introduced to the tables of all gentlemen of fortune in the kingdom, who have any refinement in taste. And the money will circulate among ourselves, the goods being entirely of our own growth and manufacture.

Fourthly, The constant breeders, beside the gain of eight shillings sterling per annum by the sale of their children, will be rid of the charge of maintaining them after the first year.

Fifthly, This food would likewise bring great custom to taverns; where the vintners will certainly be so prudent as to procure the best receipts for dressing it to perfection, and, consequently, have their houses frequented by all the fine gentlemen, who justly value themselves upon their knowledge in good eating: and a skilful cook, who understands how to oblige his guests, will contrive to make it as expensive as they please.

Sixthly, This would be a great inducement to marriage, which all wise nations have either encouraged by rewards, or enforced by laws and penalties. It would increase the care and tenderness of mothers toward their children, when they were sure of a settlement for life to the poor babes, provided in some sort by the public, to their annual profit or expense. We should see an honest emulation among the married women, which of them could bring the fattest child to the market. Men would become as fond of their wives during the time of their pregnancy, as they are now of their mares in foal, their cows in calf, their sows when they are ready to farrow; nor offer to beat or kick them (as is too frequent a practice) for fear of a miscarriage.

Many other advantages might be enumerated. For instance, the addition of some thousand carcasses in our exportation of barrelled beef; the propagation of swine's flesh, and improvement in the art of making good bacon, so much wanted among us by the great destruction of pigs, too frequent at our table; which are no way comparable in taste or magnificence to a well-grown, fat, yearling child, which, roasted whole, will make a considerable figure at a lord mayor's feast, or any other public entertainment. But this, and many others, I omit, being studious of brevity.

Supposing that one thousand families in this city would be constant customers for infants' flesh, beside others who might have it at merry-meetings, particularly at weddings and christenings, I compute that Dublin would take off annually about twenty thousand carcasses; and the rest of the kingdom (where probably they will be sold somewhat cheaper) the remaining eighty thousand.

I can think of no one objection, that will possibly be raised against this proposal, unless it should be urged, that the number of people will be thereby much lessened in the kingdom. This I freely own, and it was indeed one principal design in offering it to the world. I desire the reader will observe, that I calculate my remedy for this one individual kingdom of Ireland, and for no other that ever was, is, or I think ever can be, upon earth. Therefore let no man talk to me of other expedients: of taxing our absentees at five shillings a pound: of using neither clothes, nor household-furniture, except what is our own growth and manufacture: of utterly rejecting the materials and instruments that promote foreign luxury: of curing the expensiveness of pride, vanity, idleness, and gaming in our women: of introducing a vein of parsimony, prudence, and temperance: of learning to love our country, in the want of which we differ even from LAPLANDERS, and the inhabitants of TOPINAMBOO: of quitting our animosities and factions, nor acting any longer like the Jews, who were murdering one another at the very moment their city was taken: of being a little cautious not to sell our country and conscience for nothing: of teaching landlords to have at least one degree of mercy toward their tenants: lastly, of putting a spirit of honesty, industry, and skill into our shopkeepers; who, if a resolution could now be taken to buy only our native goods, would immediately unite to cheat and exact upon us in the price, the measure, and the goodness, nor could ever yet be brought to make one fair proposal of just dealing, though often and earnestly invited to it.

Therefore I repeat, let no man talk to me of these and the like expedients, till he has at least some glimpse of hope, that there will be ever some hearty and sincere attempt to put them in practice. But, as to myself, having been wearied out for many years with offering vain, idle, visionary thoughts, and at length utterly despairing of success, I fortunately fell upon this proposal; which, as it is wholly new, so it has something solid and real, of no expense and little trouble, full in our own power, and whereby we can incur no danger in disobliging ENGLAND. For this kind of commodity will not bear exportation, the flesh being of too tender a consistence to admit a long continuance in salt, although perhaps I could name a country, which would be glad to eat up our whole nation without it.

After all, I am not so violently bent upon my own opinion as to reject any offer proposed by wise men, which shall be found equally innocent, cheap, easy, and effectual. But before something of that kind shall be advanced in contradiction to my scheme, and offering a better, I desire the author, or authors, will be pleased maturely to consider two points. First, as things now stand, how they will be able to find food and raiment for a hundred thousand useless mouths and backs. And, secondly, there being a round million of creatures in human figure throughout this kingdom, whose whole subsistence put into a common stock would leave them in debt two millions of pounds sterling, adding those who are beggars by profession, to the bulk of farmers, cottagers, and labourers, with the wives and children who are beggars in effect; I desire those politicians who dislike my overture, and may perhaps be so bold as to attempt an answer, that they will first ask the parents of these mortals, whether they would not at this day think it a great happiness to have been sold for food at a year old, in the manner I prescribe, and thereby have avoided such a perpetual scene of misfortunes, as they have since gone through, by the oppression of landlords, the impossibility of paying rent without money or trade, the want of common sustenance, with neither house nor clothes to cover them from the inclemencies of the weather, and the most inevitable prospect of entailing the like, or greater miseries, upon their breed for ever.

I profess, in the sincerity of my heart, that I have not the least personal interest in endeavouring to promote this necessary work, having no other motive than the public good of my country, by advancing our trade, providing for infants, relieving the poor, and giving some pleasure to the rich. I have no children by which I can propose to get a single penny; the youngest being nine years old, and my wife past child-bearing.

Exercise

The Irish complained that "the English are devouring the Irish." Swift turned the metaphor into "A Modest Proposal." Disregarding the actual subject matter for the moment, is this proposal rational and practical? Will it help relieve poverty by reducing the population while increasing family incomes? If you answered these questions in the affirmative, you are beginning to appreciate the intellectual nature of satire, for satire must be logical and persuasive if it is to accomplish its purpose. The proposal is made all the more horrible by Swift's dispassionate tone and flawless logic.

Voltaire (François Marie Arouet), 1694–1778

As philosopher, critic, and writer, Voltaire was the leading intellectual figure of the Enlightenment. A tireless opponent of the *ancien régime* of the Bourbon kings and of the Church of Rome, he was twice imprisoned in the Bastille (1717, 1726) and exiled in 1726. His studies in England of Newton and Locke reinforced his hatred of absolutism and heightened his admiration of English liberalism. On his return to France he published a veritable torrent of works that criticized all the existing conditions. Whereas Pope had written, "Whatever is, is right," Voltaire's motto might well have been, "Whatever is, is wrong," especially in France.

Voltaire first sought his freedom at the court of Frederick the Great, where he lived for three years, but found the German king as arrogant a despot as the French monarch. So he established himself near Geneva, where he spent most of the last quarter century of his life. One may well question Voltaire's sincerity, for he was always concerned with his personal comfort and wealth; he certainly displayed no concern for the cause of freedom when he sought the protection of Frederick.

Whatever one may say of Voltaire's personal life, his doubting and skeptical works found a wide and receptive audience. Of his incredible output *Candide* was as important as anything he ever wrote, for in it he ridiculed everything that Europe held dear.

Voltaire was the champion debunker of his time, but his problem was the dilemma of all debunkers: he has little better to offer. Everything in his world seemed futile and silly: the glories of war; the church, both Catholic and Protestant; even nature itself. All was senseless and unreasonable. The best that he can suggest is retirement to a farm, where one can at least cultivate one's garden. Though not a complete answer, it is certainly better than none. The development of one's own life and minding one's own business may be preferable to forever charging the barricades.

Voltaire's critical contribution was an unerring pen that targeted the faults of his age, a mighty pen helping spark the revolutions that doomed absolutism. Perhaps the painter Jacques Louis David best summarized Voltaire's legacy. During the ceremony of 10 July 1791, when Voltaire's body was transferred to an honored site in the Pantheon, David said, simply: "He taught us to be free."

CANDIDE

Voltaire

In a castle of Westphalia,[21] belonging to the Baron of Thunder-ten-Tronckh, lived a youth whom nature had endowed with the most gentle manners. His countenance was a true picture of his soul. He combined a true judgment with simplicity of spirit, which was the reason, I apprehend, of his being called Candide. The old servants of the family suspected him to have been the son of the Baron's sister, by a good, honest gentleman of the neighborhood, whom that young lady would never marry because he had been able to prove only seventy-one quarterings, the rest of his genealogical tree having been lost through the injuries of time.

The Baron was one of the most powerful lords in Westphalia, for his castle had not only a gate, but windows. His great hall, even, was hung with tapestry. All the dogs of his farmyards formed a pack of hounds at need; his grooms were his huntsmen; and the curate of the village was his grand almoner.[22] They called him "My Lord," and laughed at all his stories.

The Baron's lady weighed about three hundred and fifty pounds, and was therefore a person of great consideration, and she did the honors of the house with a dignity that commanded still greater respect. Her daughter Cunegonde was seventeen years of age, fresh-colored, comely, plump, and desirable. The Baron's son seemed to be in every respect worthy of his father. The Preceptor Pangloss was the oracle of the family, and little Candide heard his lessons with all the good faith of his age and character.

Pangloss was professor of metaphysicotheologico-cosmolonigology. He proved admirably that there is no effect without a cause, and that in this best of all possible worlds, the Baron's castle was the most magnificent of castles, and his lady the best of all possible Baronesses.

"It is demonstrable," said he, "that things cannot be otherwise than as they are; for all being created for an end, all is necessarily for the best end. Observe, that the nose has been formed to bear spectacles—thus we have spectacles. Legs are visibly designed for stockings—and we have stockings. Stones were made to be hewn, and to construct castles—therefore my lord has a magnificent castle; for the greatest baron in the province ought to be the best lodged. Pigs were made to be eaten—therefore we eat pork all the year round. Consequently they who assert that all is well have said a foolish thing; they should have said all is for the best."[23]

Candide listened attentively and believed innocently; for he thought Miss Cunegonde extremely beautiful, though he never had the courage to tell her so. He concluded that after the happiness of being born of the Baron of Thunder-ten-Tronckh, the second degree of happiness was to be Miss Cunegonde, the third that of seeing her every day, and the fourth that of hearing Master Pangloss, the greatest philosopher of the whole world.

One day Cunegonde, while walking near the castle, in a little wood which they called a park, . . . became quite pensive, and filled with the desire to be loved, dreamed that she might well be a *sufficient reason* for young Candide, her cousin, and he for her.

She met Candide on reaching the castle and blushed; Candide blushed also; she wished him good morrow in a faltering tone, and Candide spoke to her without knowing what he said. The next day after dinner, as they went from table, Cunegonde and Candide found themselves behind a screen; Cunegonde let fall her handkerchief, Candide picked it up, she took him innocently by

---

21. Westphalia—one of the small Prussian states of Germany.

22. Almoner—official whose duty is to distribute alms.

23. This is not far from Pope's statement, "Whatever is, is right." Actually it comes from the German philosopher, Leibniz.

the hand, the youth as innocently kissed the young lady's hand with particular vivacity, sensibility, and grace; their lips met, their eyes sparkled, their knees trembled. Baron Thunder-ten-Tronckh passed near the screen and beholding this cause and effect chased Candide from the castle with great kicks; Cunegonde fainted away; she was boxed on the ears by the Baroness, as soon as she came to herself; and all was consternation in this most magnificent and most agreeable of all possible castles.

Candide, driven from this terrestrial paradise, walked a long while without knowing where, weeping, raising his eyes to heaven, turning them often towards the most magnificent of castles which imprisoned the purest of noble young ladies. He lay down to sleep without supper, in the middle of a field between two furrows. The snow fell in large flakes. Next day Candide, all benumbed, dragged himself towards the neighboring town which was called Waldberghofftrarbkdikdorff. Having no money, dying of hunger and fatigue, he stopped sorrowfully at the door of an inn. Two men dressed in blue observed him.

"Comrade," said one, "here is a well-built young fellow, and of proper height."

They went up to Candide and very civilly invited him to dinner.

"Gentlemen," replied Candide, with a most engaging modesty, "you do me great honor, but I have not wherewithal to pay my share."

"Oh, sir," said one of the blues to him, "people of your appearance and of your merit never pay anything: are you not five feet five inches high?"

"Yes, sir, that is my height," answered he, making a low bow.

"Come, sir, seat yourself; not only will we pay your reckoning, but we will never suffer such a man as you to want money; men are only born to assist one another."

"You are right," said Candide; "this is what I was always taught by Mr. Pangloss, and I see plainly that all is for the best."

They begged of him to accept a few crowns. He took them, and wished to give them his note; they refused; they seated themselves at table.

"Love you not deeply?"

"Oh, yes," answered he; "I deeply love Miss Cunegonde."

"No," said one of the gentlemen, "we ask you if you do not deeply love the King of the Bulgarians?"

"Not at all," said he; "for I have never seen him."

"What! he is the best of kings, and we must drink his health."

"Oh! very willingly, gentlemen," and he drank.

"That is enough," they told him. "Now you are the help, the support, the defender, the hero of the Bulgarians. Your fortune is made, and your glory is assured."

Instantly they fettered him, and carried him away to the regiment. There he was made to wheel about to the right, and to the left, to draw his rammer,[24] to return his rammer, to present, to fire, to march, and they gave him thirty blows with a cudgel. The next day he did his exercise a little less badly, and he received but twenty blows. The following they gave him only ten, and he was regarded by his comrades as a prodigy.

Candide, all stupefied, could not yet very well realize how he was a hero. He resolved one fine day in spring to go for a walk, marching straight before him, believing that it was a privilege of the human as well as of the animal species to make use of their legs as they pleased. He had advanced two leagues when he was overtaken by four others, heroes of six feet, who bound him and carried him to a dungeon. He was asked which he would like the best, to be whipped six-and-thirty times through all the regiment, or to receive at once twelve balls of lead in his brain. He vainly said that human will is free, and that he chose neither the one nor the other. He was forced to make a choice; he determined, in virtue of that gift of God called liberty, to run the gauntlet six-and-thirty times. He bore this twice. The regiment was composed of two thousand men; that composed for him four thousand strokes, which laid bare all his muscles and nerves, from the nape of his neck quite down to his rump. As they were going to proceed to a third whipping, Candide, able to bear no more, begged as a favor that they would be so good as to shoot him. He obtained this favor; they bandaged his eyes and bade him kneel down. The King of the Bulgarians passed at this moment and ascertained the nature of the crime. As he had great talent, he understood from all that he learned of Candide that he was a young metaphysician, extremely ignorant of the things of this world, and he accorded him his pardon with a clemency which will bring him praise in all the journals, and throughout all ages.

An able surgeon cured Candide in three weeks by means of emollients taught by Dioscorides.[25] He had already a little skin, and was able to march when the King of the Bulgarians gave battle to the King of the Abares.

There was never anything so gallant, so spruce, so brilliant, and so well disposed as the two armies. Trumpets, fifes, hautboys,[26] drums, and cannon made music such as Hell itself had never heard. The cannons first of all laid flat about six thousand men on each side; the muskets swept away from this best of worlds nine or ten thousand ruffians who infested its surface. The bayonet was also a *sufficient reason* for the death of several thousands. The whole might amount to thirty thousand souls. Candide, who trembled like a philosopher, hid himself as well as he could during this heroic butchery.

At length, while the two kings were causing *Te Deum*[27] to be sung each in his own camp, Candide resolved to go and reason elsewhere on effects and causes. He passed over heaps of dead and dying, and first reached a neighboring village; it was in cinders; it was an Abare village which the Bulgarians had burnt according to the laws of war. Here, old men covered with wounds beheld their wives, hugging their children to their bloody breasts, massacred before their faces; there, their daughters, disemboweled and breathing their last after having satisfied the natural wants of Bulgarian heroes, while others, half burnt in the flames, begged to be dispatched. The earth was strewn with brains, arms, and legs.

Candide fled quickly to another village; it belonged to the Bulgarians; and the Abarian heroes had treated it in the same way. Candide, walking always over palpitating limbs or across ruins, arrived at last beyond the seat of war, with a few provisions in his knapsack, and Miss Cunegonde always in his heart. His provisions

---

24. Rammer—rod with which to load a muzzle-loading rifle.

25. Dioscorides—ancient Greek medical writer.

26. Hautboys—old form of the modern oboe, a musical instrument.

27. Te Deum—hymn to celebrate victory.

failed him when he arrived in Holland; but having heard that everyone was rich in that country, and that they were Christians, he did not doubt but he should meet with the same treatment from them as he had met with in the Baron's castle, before Miss Cunegonde's bright eyes were the cause of his expulsion thence.

He asked alms of several grave-looking people, who all answered him that if he continued to follow this trade they would confine him to the house of correction, where he should be taught to get a living.

The next he addressed was a man who had been haranguing a large assembly for a whole hour on the subject of charity. But the orator, looking askew, said:

"What are you doing here? Are you for the good cause?"

"There can be no effect without a cause," modestly answered Candide; "the whole is necessarily concatenated and arranged for the best. It was necessary for me to have been banished from the presence of Miss Cunegonde, to have afterwards run the gauntlet, and now it is necessary I should beg my bread until I learn to earn it; all this cannot be otherwise."

"My friend," said the orator to him, "do you believe the Pope to be Anti-Christ?"

"I have not heard it," answered Candide; "but whether he be, or whether he be not, I want bread."

"Thou dost not deserve to eat," said the other. "Begone, rogue; begone, wretch; do not come near me again."

The orator's wife, putting her head out of the window, and spying a man that doubted whether the Pope was Anti-Christ, poured over him a full bucket of slops. Oh, heavens! to what excess does religious zeal carry the ladies.

A man who had never been christened, a good Anabaptist, named James, beholding the cruel and ignominious treatment shown to one of his brethren, an unfeathered biped with a rational soul, he took him home, cleaned him, gave him bread and beer, presented him with two florins, and even wished to teach him the manufacture of Persian stuffs, which they make in Holland. Candide, almost prostrating himself before him, cried:

"Master Pangloss has well said that all is for the best in this world, for I am infinitely more touched by your extreme generosity than with the inhumanity of that gentleman in the black coat and his lady."

The next day, as he took a walk, he met a beggar all covered with scabs, his eyes diseased, the end of his nose eaten away, his mouth distorted, his teeth black, choking in his throat, tormented with a violent cough, and spitting out a tooth at each effort.

Candide, yet more moved with compassion than with horror, gave to this shocking beggar the two florins which he had received from the honest Anabaptist James. The specter looked at him very earnestly, dropped a few tears, and fell upon his neck. Candide recoiled in disgust.

"Alas!" said one wretch to the other, "do you no longer know your dear Pangloss?"

"What do I hear? You, my dear master! You in this terrible plight! What misfortune has happened to you? Why are you no longer in the most magnificent of castles? What has become of Miss Cunegonde, the pearl of girls, and nature's masterpiece?"

"I am so weak that I cannot stand," said Pangloss.

Upon which Candide carried him to the Anabaptist's stable, and gave him a crust of bread. As soon as Pangloss had refreshed himself a little:

"Well," said Candide, "Cunegonde?"

"She is dead," replied the other.

Candide fainted at this word; his friend recalled his senses with a little bad vinegar which he found by chance in the stable. Candide reopened his eyes.

"Cunegonde is dead! Ah, best of worlds, where art thou? But of what illness did she die? Was it not for grief, upon seeing her father kick me out of his magnificent castle?"

"No," said Pangloss, "she was stabbed by the Bulgarian soldiers, they broke the Baron's head for attempting to defend her; my lady, her mother, was cut in pieces; my poor pupil was served just in the same manner as his sister; and as for the castle, they have not left one stone upon another, not a bar, nor a sheep, nor a duck, nor a tree; but we have had our revenge, for the Abares have done the very same thing to a neighboring barony, which belonged to a Bulgarian lord. . . . "

"Well, this is wonderful!" said Candide, "but you must be cured."

"Alas! how can I?" said Pangloss. "I have not a farthing, my friend, and all over the globe there is no letting of blood or taking a glister[28] without paying, or somebody paying for you."

These last words determined Candide; he went and flung himself at the feet of the charitable Anabaptist James, and gave him so touching a picture of the state to which his friend was reduced that the good man did not scruple to take Dr. Pangloss into his house, and had him cured at his expense. In the cure Pangloss lost only an eye and an ear. He wrote well, and knew arithmetic perfectly. The Anabaptist James made him his bookkeeper. At the end of two months, being obliged to go by sea to Lisbon about some mercantile affairs, he took the two philosophers with him in his ship. Pangloss explained to him how everything was so constituted that it could not be better. James was not of this opinion.

"It is more likely," said he, "mankind have a little corrupted nature, for men were not born wolves, and they have become wolves; God has given them neither cannon or four-and-twenty pounders nor bayonets; and yet they have made cannon and bayonets to destroy one another. Into this account I might throw not only bankrupts, but Justice which seizes on the effects of bankrupts to cheat the creditors."

"All this was indispensable," replied the one-eyed doctor, "for private misfortunes make the general good, so that the more private misfortunes there are the greater is the general good."

While he reasoned, the sky darkened, the winds blew from the four quarters, and the ship was assailed by a most terrible tempest within sight of the port of Lisbon.

Half dead of that inconceivable anguish which the rolling of a ship produces, one half of the passengers were not even sensible of the danger. The other half shrieked and prayed. The sheets were rent, the masts broken, the vessel gaped. Work who would, no one

---

28. Glister—a medical treatment.

heard, no one commanded. The Anabaptist, being upon deck, bore a hand; then a brutish sailor struck him roughly and laid him sprawling; but with the violence of the blow he himself tumbled head foremost overboard, and struck upon a piece of the broken mast. Honest James ran to his assistance, hauled him up, and from the effort he made was precipitated into the sea in sight of the sailor, who left him to perish, without deigning to look at him. Candide drew near and saw his benefactor, who rose above the water one moment and was then swallowed up forever. He was just going to jump after him, but was prevented by the philosopher Pangloss, who demonstrated to him that the Bay of Lisbon had been made on purpose for the Anabaptist to be drowned. While he was proving this *a priori,* the ship foundered; all perished except Pangloss, Candide, and the brutal sailor who had drowned the good Anabaptist. The villain swam safely to the shore, while Pangloss and Candide were borne thither upon a plank.

As soon as they recovered themselves a little, they walked toward Lisbon. They had some money left, with which they hoped to save themselves from starving, after they had escaped drowning. Scarcely had they reached the city, lamenting the death of their benefactor, when they felt the earth tremble under their feet. The sea swelled and foamed in the harbor and beat to pieces the vessels riding at anchor. Whirlwinds of fire and ashes covered the streets and public places, houses fell, roofs were flung upon the pavements, and the pavements were scattered. Thirty thousand inhabitants of all ages and sexes were crushed under the ruins. The sailor, whistling and swearing, said booty was to be gained here.

"What can be the *sufficient reason* of this phenomenon?" said Pangloss.

"This is the Last Day!" cried Candide.

The sailor ran among the ruins, facing death to find money; finding it, he took it, and got drunk . . . .

Some falling stones had wounded Candide. He lay stretched in the street covered with rubbish.

"Alas!" said he to Pangloss, "get me a little wine and oil; I am dying."

"This concussion of the earth is no new thing," answered Pangloss. "The city of Lima, in America, experienced the same convulsions last year; the same cause, the same effects; there is certainly a train of sulphur underground from Lima to Lisbon."

"Nothing more probable," said Candide; "but for the love of God get me a little oil and wine."

"How, probable?" replied the philosopher. "I maintain that the point is capable of being demonstrated."

Candide fainted away, and Pangloss fetched him some water from a neighboring fountain. The following day they rummaged among the ruins and found provisions, with which they repaired their exhausted strength. After this they joined with others in relieving those inhabitants who had escaped death. Some, whom they had succored, gave them as good a dinner as they could in such disastrous circumstances; true, the repast was mournful, and the company moistened their bread with tears; but Pangloss consoled them, assuring them that things could not be otherwise.

"For," said he, "all that is is for the best. If there is a volcano at Lisbon it cannot be elsewhere. It is impossible that things should be other than they are; for everything is right."

[In the passage which follows, Candide is whipped and Pangloss is hanged. Candide then meets Cunegonde, who had not been killed in Westphalia. Candide kills two men and flees with Cunegonde and her maid, an old woman, to Cadiz.]

Candide, Cunegonde, and the old woman, having passed through Lucena, Chillas, and Lebrixa, arrived at length at Cadiz. A fleet was there getting ready, and troops assembling to bring to reason the reverend Jesuit Fathers of Paraguay, accused of having made one of the native tribes in the neighborhood of San Sacrament revolt against the kings of Spain and Portugal. Candide, having been in the Bulgarian service, performed the military exercise before the general of this little army with so graceful an address, with so intrepid an air, and with such agility and expedition, that he was given the command of a company of foot. Now, he was a captain! He set sail with Miss Cunegonde, the old woman, two valets, and two Andalusian horses, which had belonged to the Grand Inquisitor of Portugal.

During their voyage they reasoned a good deal on the philosophy of poor Pangloss.

"We are going into another world," said Candide; "and surely it must be there that all is for the best. For I must confess there is reason to complain a little of what passeth in our world in regard to both natural and moral philosophy."

"I love you with all my heart," said Cunegonde; "but my soul is still full of fright at that which I have seen and experienced."

"All will be well," replied Candide; "the sea of this new world is already better than our European sea; it is calmer, the winds more regular. It is certainly the New World which is the best of all possible worlds."

[After landing in Buenos Aires, Candide and his valet, Cacambo, are separated from Cunegonde. Then, Candide, in self-defense, killed an inquisitor, and the two men were forced to flee over much of South America.]

"You see," said Cacambo to Candide, as soon as they had reached the frontiers of the Oreillons, "that this hemisphere is not better than the other, take my word for it; let us go back to Europe by the shortest way."

"How go back?" said Candide, "and where shall we go? to my own country? The Bulgarians and the Abares are slaying all; to Portugal? there I shall be burnt; and if we abide here, we are every moment in danger of being spitted. But how can I resolve to quit a part of the world where my dear Cunegonde resides?"

"Let us turn towards Cayenne," said Cacambo; "there we shall find Frenchmen, who wander all over the world; they may assist us; God will perhaps have pity on us."

It was not easy to get to Cayenne; they knew vaguely in which direction to go, but rivers, precipices, robbers, savages obstructed them all the way. Their horses died of fatigue. Their provisions were consumed; they fed a whole month upon wild fruits, and found themselves at last near a little river bordered with cocoa trees, which sustained their lives and their hopes.

Cacambo, who was a good counselor, said to Candide:

"We are able to hold out no longer; we have walked enough. I see an empty canoe near the riverside; let us fill it with cocoanuts, throw ourselves into it, and go with the current; a river always leads to some inhabited spot. If we do not find pleasant things, we shall at least find new things."

"With all my heart," said Candide; "let us recommend ourselves to Providence."

They rowed a few leagues, between banks, in some places flowery, in others barren; in some parts smooth, in others rugged. The stream widened, and at length lost itself under an arch of frightful rocks which reached to the sky. The two travelers had the courage to commit themselves to the current. The river, suddenly contracting at this place, whirled them along with a dreadful noise and rapidity. At the end of four-and-twenty hours they saw daylight again, but their canoe was dashed to pieces against the rocks. For a league they had to creep from rock to rock, until at length they discovered an extensive plain, bounded by inaccessible mountains. The country was cultivated as much for pleasure as for necessity. On all sides the useful was also the beautiful. The roads were covered, or rather adorned, with carriages of a glittering form and substance, in which were men and women of surprising beauty, drawn by large red sheep which surpassed in fleetness the finest coursers of Andalusia, Tetuan, and Mequinez.

"Here, however, is a country," said Candide, "which is better than Westphalia."

He stepped out with Cacambo toward the first village which he saw. Some children dressed in tattered brocades played at quoits on the outskirts. Our travelers from the other world amused themselves by looking on. The quoits were large round pieces, yellow, red, and green, which cast a singular luster! The travelers picked a few of them off the ground; this was of gold, that of emeralds, the other of rubies—the least of them would have been the greatest ornament on the Mogul's throne.

"Without doubt," said Cacambo, "these children must be the king's sons that are playing at quoits!"

The village schoolmaster appeared at this moment and called them to school.

"There," said Candide, "is the preceptor of the royal family."

The little truants immediately quitted their game, leaving the quoits on the ground with all their other playthings. Candide gathered them up, ran to the master, and presented them to him in a most humble manner, giving him to understand by signs that their royal highnesses had forgotten their gold and jewels. The schoolmaster, smiling, flung them upon the ground; then, looking at Candide with a good deal of surprise, went about his business.

The travelers, however, took care to gather up the gold, the rubies, and the emeralds.

"Where are we?" cried Candide. "The king's children in this country must be well brought up, since they are taught to despise gold and precious stones."

Cacambo was as much surprised as Candide. At length they drew near the first house in the village. It was built like an European palace. A crowd of people pressed about the door, and there were still more in the house. They heard most agreeable music, and were aware of a delicious odor of cooking. Cacambo went up to the door and heard they were talking Peruvian; it was his mother's tongue, for it is well known that Cacambo was born in Tucuman, in a village where no other language was spoken.

"I will be your interpreter here," said he to Candide; "let us go in; it is a public house."

Immediately two waiters and two girls, dressed in cloth of gold, and their hair tied up with ribbons, invited them to sit down to table with the landlord. They served four dishes of soup, each garnished with two young parrots; a boiled condor which weighed two hundred pounds; two roasted monkeys, of excellent flavor; three hundred hummingbirds in one dish, and six hundred fly-birds in another; exquisite ragouts,[29] delicious pastries; the whole served up in dishes of a kind of rock crystal. The waiters and girls poured out several liqueurs drawn from the sugar cane.

Most of the company were chapmen[30] and wagoners, all extremely polite; they asked Cacambo a few questions with the greatest circumspection, and answered his in the most obliging manner.

As soon as dinner was over, Cacambo believed as well as Candide that they might well pay their reckoning by laying down two of those large gold pieces which they had picked up. The landlord and landlady shouted with laughter and held their sides. When the fit was over:

"Gentlemen," said the landlord, "it is plain you are strangers, and such guests we are not accustomed to see; pardon us therefore for laughing when you offered us the pebbles from our highroads in payment of your reckoning. You doubtless have not the money of the country; but it is not necessary to have any money at all to dine in this house. All hostelries established for the convenience of commerce are paid by the government. You have fared but very indifferently because this is a poor village; but everywhere else, you will be received as you deserve."

Cacambo explained this whole discourse with great astonishment to Candide, who was as greatly astonished to hear it.

"What sort of a country then is this," said they to one another; "a country unknown to all the rest of the world, and where nature is of a kind so different from ours? It is probably the country where all is well; for there absolutely must be one such place. And, whatever Master Pangloss might say, I often found that things went very ill in Westphalia."

Cacambo expressed his curiosity to the landlord, who made answer:

"I am very ignorant, but not the worse on that account. However, we have in this neighborhood an old man retired from Court who is the most learned and most communicative person in the kingdom."

At once he took Cacambo to the old man. Candide acted now only a second character, and accompanied his valet. They entered a very plain house, for the door was only of silver, and the ceilings were only of gold, but wrought in so elegant a taste as to vie with the richest. The antechamber, indeed, was only encrusted with rubies and emeralds, but the order in which everything was arranged made amends for this great simplicity.

The old man received the strangers on his sofa, which was stuffed with hummingbirds' feathers, and ordered his servants to present them with liqueurs in diamond goblets; after which he satisfied their curiosity in the following terms:

"I am now one hundred and seventy-two years old, and I learned of my late father, Master of the Horse to the King, the amazing revolutions of Peru, of which he had been an eyewitness.

---

29. Ragouts—highly seasoned stew.
30. Chapmen—peddlers; traders.

The kingdom we now inhabit is the ancient country of the Incas, who quitted it very imprudently to conquer another part of the world, and were at length destroyed by the Spaniards.

"More wise by far were the princes of their family, who remained in their native country; and they ordained, with the consent of the whole nation, that none of the inhabitants should ever be permitted to quit this little kingdom; and this has preserved our innocence and happiness. The Spaniards have had a confused notion of this country, and have called it *El Dorado;* and an Englishman, whose name was Sir Walter Raleigh, came very near it about a hundred years ago; but being surrounded by inaccessible rocks and precipices, we have hitherto been sheltered from the rapaciousness of European nations, who have an inconceivable passion for the pebbles and dirt of our land, for the sake of which they would murder us to the last man."

The conversation was long: it turned chiefly on their form of government, their manners, their women, their public entertainments, and the arts. At length Candide, having always had a taste for metaphysics, made Cacambo ask whether there was any religion in that country.

The old man reddened a little.

"How then," said he, "can you doubt it? Do you take us for ungrateful wretches?"

Cacambo humbly asked, "What is the religion in El Dorado?"

The old man reddened again, but continued.

"Can there be two religions?" said he. "We have, I believe, the religion of all the world: we worship God night and morning."

"Do you worship but one God?" said Cacambo, who still acted as interpreter in representing Candide's doubts.

"Surely," said the old man, "there are not two, nor three, nor four. I must confess the people from your side of the world ask very extraordinary questions."

Candide was not yet tired of interrogating the good old man; he wanted to know in what manner they prayed to God in El Dorado.

"We do not pray to Him," said the worthy sage; "we have nothing to ask of Him; He has given us all we need, and we return Him thanks without ceasing."

Candide, having a curiosity to see the priests, asked where they were. The good old man smiled.

"My friend," said he, "we are all priests. The King and all the heads of families sing solemn canticles of thanksgiving every morning, accompanied by five or six thousand musicians. . ."

During this whole discourse Candide was in raptures, and he said to himself:

"This is vastly different from Westphalia and the Baron's castle. Had our friend Pangloss seen El Dorado he would no longer have said that the castle of Thunder-ten-Tronckh was the finest upon earth. It is evident that one must travel."

After this long conversation the old man ordered a coach and six sheep to be got ready, and twelve of his domestics to conduct the travelers to Court.

"Excuse me," said he, "if my age deprives me of the honor of accompanying you. The King will receive you in a manner that cannot displease you; and no doubt you will make there a better entertainment."

Never was more wit shown at a table than that which fell from His Majesty. Cacambo explained the King's bon mots to Candide,

and notwithstanding they were translated they still appeared to be bon mots. Of all the things that surprised Candide this was not the least.

They spent a month in this hospitable place. Candide frequently said to Cacambo:

"I own, my friend, once more that the castle where I was born is nothing in comparison with this; but, after all, Miss Cunegonde is not here, and you have, without doubt, some mistress in Europe. If we abide here we shall only be upon a footing with the rest, whereas, if we return to our old world, only with twelve sheep laden with the pebbles of El Dorado, we shall be richer than all the kings in Europe. We shall have no more Inquisitors to fear, and we may easily recover Miss Cunegonde."

This speech was agreeable to Cacambo; mankind are so fond of roving, of making a figure in their own country, and of boasting of what they have seen in their travels that the two happy ones resolved to be no longer so, but to ask His Majesty's leave to quit the country.

"You are foolish," said the King. "I am sensible that my kingdom is but a small place, but when a person is comfortably settled in any part he should abide there. I have not the right to detain strangers. It is a tyranny which neither our manners nor our laws permit. All men are free. Go when you wish, but the going will be very difficult. It is impossible to ascend that rapid river on which you came as by a miracle, and which runs under vaulted rocks. The mountains which surround my kingdom are ten thousand feet high, and as steep as walls; they are each over ten leagues in breadth, and there is no other way to descend them than by precipices. However, since you absolutely wish to depart, I shall give orders to my engineers to construct a machine that will convey you very safely. When we have conducted you over the mountains no one can accompany you further, for my subjects have made a vow never to quit the kingdom, and they are too wise to break it. Ask me besides anything that you please."

"We desire nothing of Your Majesty," said Candide, "but a few sheep laden with provisions, pebbles, and the earth of this country."

The King laughed.

"I cannot conceive," said he, "what pleasure you Europeans find in our yellow clay, but take as much as you like, and great good may it do you!"

At once he gave directions that his engineers should construct a machine to hoist up these two extraordinary men out of the kingdom. Three thousand good mathematicians went to work; it was ready in fifteen days, and did not cost more than twenty million sterling in the specie of that country. They placed Candide and Cacambo on the machine. There were two great red sheep saddled and bridled to ride upon as soon as they were beyond the mountains, twenty pack-sheep laden with provisions, thirty with presents of the curiosities of the country, and fifty with gold, diamonds, and precious stones. The King embraced the two wanderers very tenderly.

Their departure, with the ingenious manner in which they and their sheep were hoisted over the mountains, was a splendid spectacle. The mathematicians took their leave after conveying them to a place of safety, and Candide had no other desire, no other aim, than to present his sheep to Miss Cunegonde.

"Now," said he, "we are able to pay the Governor of Buenos Aires if Miss Cunegonde can be ransomed. Let us journey towards Cayenne. Let us embark, and we will afterwards see what kingdom we shall be able to purchase."

Our travelers spent the first day very agreeably. They were delighted with possessing more treasure than all Asia, Europe, and Africa could scrape together. Candide, in his raptures, cut Cunegonde's name on the trees. The second day two of their sheep plunged into a morass, where they and their burdens were lost; two more died of fatigue a few days after; seven or eight perished with hunger in a desert; and others subsequently fell down precipices. At length, after traveling a hundred days, only two sheep remained. Said Candide to Cacambo:

"My friend, you see how perishable are the riches of this world; there is nothing solid but virtue, and the happiness of seeing Cunegonde once more."

"I grant all you say," said Cacambo, "but we have still two sheep remaining, with more treasure than the King of Spain will ever have; and I see a town which I take to be Surinam, belonging to the Dutch. We are at the end of all our troubles, and at the beginning of happiness."

As they drew near the town, they saw a Negro stretched upon the ground, with only one moiety of his clothes, that is, of his blue linen drawers; the poor man had lost his left leg and his right hand.

"Good God!" said Candide in Dutch, "what art thou doing there, friend, in that shocking condition?"

"I am waiting for my master, Mynheer Vanderdendur, the famous merchant," answered the Negro.

"Was it Mynheer Vanderdendur," said Candide, "that treated thee thus?"

"Yes, sir," said the Negro, "it is the custom. They give us a pair of linen drawers for our whole garment twice a year. When we work at the sugar canes, and the mill snatches hold of a finger, they cut off the hand; and when we attempt to run away, they cut off the leg; both cases have happened to me. This is the price at which you eat sugar in Europe. Yet when my mother sold me for ten patagons on the coast of Guinea, she said to me: 'My child, bless our fetishes adore them forever; they will make thee live happily, thou hast the honor of being the slave of our lord the whites, which is making the fortune of thy father and mother.' Alas! I know not whether I have made their fortunes; this I know, that they have not made mine. Dogs, monkeys, and parrots are a thousand times less wretched than I. The Dutch fetishes, who have converted me, declare every Sunday that we are all of us children of Adam—blacks as well as whites. I am not a genealogist, but if these preachers tell truth, we are all second cousins. Now, you must agree with me it is impossible to treat one's relations in a more barbarous manner."

"Oh, Pangloss!" cried Candide, "thou hadst not guessed at this abomination; it is the end. I must at last renounce thy optimism."

"What is this optimism?" said Cacambo.

"Alas!" said Candide, "it is the madness of maintaining that everything is right when it is wrong."

Looking at the Negro, he shed tears, and weeping, he entered Surinam.

The first thing they inquired after was whether there was a vessel in the harbour which could be sent to Buenos Aires. The person to whom they applied was a Spanish sea-captain, who offered to take them there upon reasonable terms. He appointed to meet them at a public house, whither Candide and the faithful Cacambo went with their two sheep, and awaited his coming.

Candide, who had his heart upon his lips, told the Spaniard all his adventures, and avowed that he intended to elope with Miss Cunegonde.

"Then I will take good care not to carry you to Buenos Aires," said the seaman. "I should be hanged, and so would you. The fair Cunegonde is my lord's favorite mistress!"

This was a thunderclap for Candide: he wept for a long while. At last he drew Cacambo aside.

"Here, my dear friend," said he to him, "this thou must do. We have, each of us in his pocket, five or six millions in diamonds; you are more clever than I; you must go and bring Miss Cunegonde from Buenos Aires. If the Governor makes any difficulty, give him a million; if he will not relinquish her, give him two; as you have not killed an Inquisitor, they will have no suspicion of you; I'll get another ship, and go and wait for you at Venice; that's a free country, where there is no danger either from Bulgarians, Abares, . . . or Inquisitors."

Cacambo applauded this wise resolution. He despaired at parting from so good a master, who had become his intimate friend; but the pleasure of serving him prevailed over the pain of leaving him. They embraced with tears; Candide charged him not to forget the good old woman who had aided them to escape to South America. Cacambo set out that very same day. This Cacambo was a very honest fellow.

Candide stayed some time longer in Surinam, waiting for another captain to carry him and the two remaining sheep to Italy. After he had hired domestics, and purchased everything necessary for a long voyage, Mynheer Vanderdendur, captain of a large vessel, came and offered his services.

"How much will you charge," said he to this man, "to carry me straight to Venice—me, my servants, my baggage, and these two sheep?"

The skipper asked ten thousand piastres. Candide did not hesitate.

"Oh! oh!" said the prudent Vanderdendur to himself, "this stranger gives ten thousand piastres unhesitatingly! He must be very rich."

Returning a little while after, he let him know that, upon second consideration, he could not undertake the voyage for less than twenty thousand piastres.

"Well, you shall have them," said Candide.

"Ay!" said the skipper to himself, "this man agrees to pay twenty thousand piastres with as much ease as ten."

He went back to him again, and declared that he could not carry him to Venice for less than thirty thousand piastres.

"Then you shall have thirty thousand," replied Candide.

"Oh! oh!" said the Dutch skipper once more to himself, "thirty thousand piastres are a trifle to this man; surely these sheep must be laden with an immense treasure; let us say no more about it. First of all, let him pay down the thirty thousand piastres; then we shall see."

Candide sold two small diamonds, the least of which was worth more than what the skipper asked for his freight. He paid him the money in advance.

The two sheep were put on board. Candide followed in a little boat to join the vessel in the roads. The skipper seized his opportunity, set sail, and put out to sea, the wind favoring him. Candide, dismayed and stupefied, soon lost sight of the vessel.

"Alas!" said he, "this is a trick worthy of the old world!"

[Many adventures follow this one in this best of all possible worlds. Finally Candide, Cunegonde, Pangloss (who did not die of hanging), and all the other characters of the story are reunited in Turkey, where they bought a little farm.]

In the neighborhood there lived a very famous Dervish who was esteemed the best philosopher in all Turkey, and so they went to consult him. Pangloss was the speaker.

"Master," said he, "we come to beg you to tell why so strange an animal as man was made."

"With what meddlest thou?" said the Dervish. "Is it thy business?"

"But, reverend father," said Candide, "there is horrible evil in this world."

"What signifies it," said the Dervish, "whether there be evil or good? When His Highness sends a ship to Egypt, does he trouble his head whether the mice on board are at their ease or not?"

"What, then, must we do?" said Pangloss.

"Hold your tongue," answered the Dervish.

"I was in hopes," said Pangloss, "that I should reason with you a little about causes and effects, about the best of possible worlds, the origin of evil, the nature of the soul, and the pre-established harmony."

At these words, the Dervish shut the door in their faces.

During this conversation, the news was spread that two Viziers and the Mufti had been strangled at Constantinople, and that several of their friends had been impaled. This catastrophe made a great noise for some hours. Pangloss, Candide, and Martin, returning to the little farm, saw a good old man taking the fresh air at his door under an orange bower. Pangloss, who was as inquisitive as he was argumentative, asked the old man what was the name of the strangled Mufti.

"I do not know," answered the worthy man, "and I have not known the name of any Mufti, nor of any Vizier. I am entirely ignorant of the event you mention; I presume in general that they who meddle with the administration of public affairs die sometimes miserably, and that they deserve it; but I never trouble my head about what is transacting at Constantinople; I content myself with sending there for sale the fruits of the garden which I cultivate."

Having said these words, he invited the strangers into his house; his two sons and two daughters presented them with several sorts of sherbet, which they made themselves, with Kaimak enriched with the candied peel of citrons, with oranges, lemons, pineapples, pistachio nuts, and Mocha coffee unadulterated with the bad coffee of Batavia or the American islands; after which the two daughters of the honest Mussulman perfumed the strangers' beards.

"You must have a vast and magnificent estate," said Candide to the Turk.

"I have only twenty acres," replied the old man, "I and my children cultivate them; our labor preserves us from three great evils—weariness, vice, and want."

Candide, on his way home, made profound reflections on the old man's conversation.

"This honest Turk," said he to Pangloss and Martin, "seems to be in a situation far preferable to that of the six kings with whom we had the honor of supping."

"Grandeur," said Pangloss, "is extremely dangerous, according to the testimony of philosophers . . ."

"I know also," said Candide, "that we must cultivate our garden."

"You are right," said Pangloss, "for when man was first placed in the Garden of Eden, he was put there *ut operaretur eum,* that he might cultivate it; which shows that man was not born to be idle."

"Let us work," said Martin, "without disputing; it is the only way to render life tolerable."

The whole little society entered into this laudable design, according to their different abilities. Their little plot of land produced plentiful crops. . . . They were all of some service or other. . . .

Pangloss sometimes said to Candide:

"There is a concatenation of events in this best of all possible worlds; for if you had not been kicked out of a magnificent castle for love of Miss Cunegonde; if you had not suffered misfortune in Portugal; if you had not walked over America; if you had not stabbed the Baron; if you had not lost all your sheep from the fine country of El Dorado, you would not be here eating preserved citrons and pistachio nuts."

"All that is very well," answered Candide, "but let us cultivate our garden."

Exercises

1. "El Dorado" sounds suspiciously like "Utopia," at first acquaintance; what different aspects are emphasized from those in More's account?
2. The only "answer" that Voltaire comes up with is "Let us cultivate our garden." What would Perikles say about such an answer? How good an answer is it? What are some of its defects—and virtues?
3. How important a figure is Cunegonde? Why have we not encountered such a figure earlier? In what way is she part of the "New Look" of the eighteenth century?

Thomas Jefferson, 1743–1826

The American Revolution (1775–1783) was hailed as the first significant triumph of rationalism. The causes of the uprising were certainly as much economic as ideological, yet liberal rational beliefs prevailed over the imposition of absolute authority. One of the clearest voices of the new nation was that of Thomas Jefferson, author of the Declaration of Independence, third president of the United States, and founder of the University of Virginia, the last being, for Jefferson, his most significant achievement. Jefferson's address (First Inaugural Address) on first assuming the presidency is a masterful speech that effectively summarizes the ideals of the Enlightenment.

Summary

It was not until the 1648 Peace of Westphalia that Europe was fully launched on a new age freed from medievalism. The physical world had been transformed by inventions such as gunpowder and the printing press, and the work of Bacon, Descartes, and Galileo began to change ways of thinking about the world.

At the beginning of the seventeenth century England and France had absolute monarchs, but the Glorious Revolution of 1688 saw William and Mary on the English throne as rulers of a constitutional monarchy. In France, however, Louis XIV was a divine-right king throughout the longest reign (1643–1715) of any monarch.

The publication of Newton's *Principia* in 1687 marked the dawn of the Enlightenment, an optimistic new age that relied on the intellect to design a rational society in a knowable universe. Newton had discovered the law of universal gravitation, John Locke relied on natural law as a guide to political affairs, and Adam Smith developed a similar unifying principle for economic affairs. Locke's theories of knowledge were later refined by David Hume, who granted certain knowledge only to mathematics, with all other knowledge as only probable. Immanual Kant reacted to Hume's skepticism with an idealistic philosophy that highlighted the German Enlightenment. In France, the *philosophes* Diderot, Montesquieu, Voltaire, and others wrote articles for the *Encyclopedia,* a monumental summary of all human knowledge.

Paradoxically, the Enlightenment had little influence on the absolute rulers in France, Prussia, and Russia. Only in England was there any political freedom, and even that was denied English possessions, especially the American colonies. Ironically, the most democratic nation in Europe set the forces in motion that led to the triumph of the Enlightenment in the New World.

Culture and Human Values

The Enlightenment was victorious in the United States beginning in 1776, but it failed in France only thirteen years later. How could the Enlightenment fail in its country of origin—the land of Voltaire, Diderot, and Montesquieu?

Both revolutions intended replacing an autocratic regime with a republican form of government; but there the similarity ends. A prime ingredient in the American success story was the extended and invaluable experience in the art of self-government. The British crown had long pursued a policy of benign neglect; acts of the colonial assemblies were rarely questioned, let alone vetoed by a royally appointed governor or the king himself.

There were still other advantages for the colonies. There was no titled nobility (except for some of the British overlords) and there was no state church. A solid middle class of farmers and merchants formed the backbone of colonial society, particularly in the northern colonies. Further, the Founding Fathers believed firmly in the ideals of the Enlightenment. They were convinced that human beings had the ability to govern themselves in a sane and rational manner. They not only assumed that people could find personal happiness in a viable society, but also designed a constitution and a government that could help its citizens realize life, liberty, and the pursuit of happiness.

The French revolted against a royal power that had not been challenged for centuries, a creaking monarchy that had piled up a mountain of abuses. The absolute monarchy was not the only problem, however. France was more advanced than other continental nations, but its social structure was inherited from the Middle Ages. By the eighteenth century the class structure had evolved into a First Estate (clergy), a Second Estate (nobility), and 97 percent of the population into a Third Estate (commoners). The Third Estate and some of the clergy and nobility favored reforms, but the commoners had been abused by everyone, and they longed for an end to the throne, the nobility, and the church. But, with no experience in government, there was no workable alternative to the Old Regime. To compound the problem, the idealistic slogan was coined: "Liberty, Equality, Fraternity." Subsequently, all titles were eliminated with everyone addressed as Citizen.

Hatred of the Old Regime and its abuses was such a dominant factor there was little room left for the exercise of restraint and reason. Liberty was quickly achieved, but equality proved to be an impossible dream. Within just a few years any feelings of fraternity had vanished during the unleashed passions that led to the Reign of Terror, and finally, to the dictatorship of Napoleon. The French Revolution had, at the time, failed just as completely as the American Revolution had succeeded. But it was the establishment of a New World democracy that provided hope and inspiration for a weary Old World.

In terms of the culture-epoch theory the period from 1600 to 1789 can be seen, in retrospect, as one of relative balance, preceded by the tumultuous Renaissance and followed by the French Revolution and the Napoleonic Wars. Certainly both the seventeenth and eighteenth centuries were glorious years of superb artistic achievement.

Art: Baroque, Rococo, and Neoclassic

chapter 21

The Baroque Age, ca. 1580–1700

An age of expansion following the Renaissance era of discovery, the baroque was a period of conflicts and contradictions that encompassed extremes: Louis XIV and Rembrandt; Bernini and Descartes; Milton and Bach. In architecture and the visual arts the baroque began in the last quarter of the sixteenth century and extended into the eighteenth, culminating in the music of Bach and Handel (see chapter 22).

The characteristics of baroque art are movement, intensity, tension, and energy, traits that are more often associated with music than with the more static arts of painting, sculpture, and architecture. Nevertheless, revolutionary innovations in all the arts generated a baroque style that can be extravagant, excessive, or even grotesque. At its best, baroque art is vigorous, dazzling, opulent, colorful, and frequently theatrical, all in marked contrast to the High Renaissance canon of balance, restraint, and control. Most especially, the new style proclaimed the vigorous beginning of the contentious Early Modern World.

The sometimes contradictory variations of the baroque style can be examined using three broad categories of patrons: the Counter-Reformation Church of Rome; the aristocratic courts of Louis XIV of France and the Stuarts of England; and the bourgeois merchants of Holland. Though drive, intensity, and contrast are common characteristics of all baroque art, the style will be considered here as reactions to the needs of these patrons and labeled Counter-Reformation, aristocratic, and bourgeois baroque art.

Counter-Reformation Baroque

Founded in 1534 by Ignatius of Loyola, the Society of Jesus (Jesuits) formed the spearhead of the Counter-Reformation. The mother church of the order, Il Gesù (Church of Jesus), was the first building in the new style, becoming a model for church design throughout the Catholic world, especially in Latin America (figure

Figure 21.1 *G. B. Vignola (plan) and G. C. della Porta (facade), Il Gesù, 1568–1584, Rome.*

21.1). The four pairs of pilasters on each level visually stabilize the facade and add a rhythmic punctuation that the evenly spaced columns of the classical style do not have (see figure 17.5). Baroque architecture, from its very beginning, is characterized by the strong accents of paired columns or pilasters. The dramatic effect of paired pilaster and column framing a central portal under a double cornice exemplifies the theatricality of the baroque style, making the entrance seem like an invitation to hurry into the church. The proportions of the two stories and the framing volutes are derived from Alberti's Santa Maria Novella (see figure 17.15), whereas the classical pediment is reminiscent of Palladio (see figure 17.50). Il Gesù is not a wholly new design but rather a skillful synthesis of existing elements into a new and dramatic style.

Figure 21.2 *Interior, Il Gesù. Photo: Vanni/Art Resource, N.Y.*

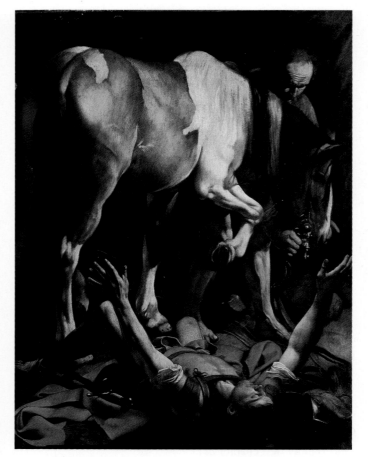

Figure 21.3 *Caravaggio,* The Conversion of St. Paul, *ca. 1601. Oil on canvas, 90" × 69". Santa Maria del Popolo, Rome. Photo: Scala/Art Resource.*

In the interior (figure 21.2), chapels recessed in the walls replace side aisles, making the richly decorated central space a theatre for the enactment of the Lord's Supper. Light pours through the dome windows and on the high altar in this architectural embodiment of the militant and mystical Society of Jesus.

Michelangelo Merisi da Caravaggio, 1573–1610
The baroque style of painting appeared abruptly in the person of the northern Italian artist called Caravaggio (ca-ra-VOD-jo), perhaps the first artist to deliberately shock not only the public but also his fellow artists. The most important Italian painter of the seventeenth century, Caravaggio was militantly opposed to such classical concepts as balance and restraint, claiming that nature would be his only teacher. Using chiaroscuro and nonrealistic dramatic lighting, his paintings had an intense psychological impact that profoundly influenced most baroque artists, including Rembrandt and Velasquez. His *The Conversion of St. Paul* (figure 21.3) must have shocked everyone who saw it, for this is

no reverent depiction of a biblical scene. This is the moment after Saul of Tarsus, while riding on the road to Damascus, experienced his vision of Christ asking why Saul persecuted him, the very instant that the Apostle Paul becomes a missionary for the new religion. The lighting is harsh and dramatic and the effect highly theatrical. The vivid contrast between light and dark (*chiaroscuro*) was a major innovation, one that first shocked and then enthralled contemporary artists. In a composition further dramatized by slashing diagonals, the realistically depicted horse towers over the recumbent Paul. Caravaggio was vividly explicit about his rejection of tradition, especially Renaissance idealism, which would hardly surprise anyone viewing this painting.

Caravaggio's life was as dramatic as his art. A man of violent passions, he killed another man in a fight and, badly wounded, fled Rome for Naples. Later thrown into prison, he violated his oath of obedience and escaped to Sicily, but subsequently returned to Naples where he was nearly fatally wounded in another fight. Destitute and ill with malaria, he died during a violent rage over a misunderstanding on the very day that his papal pardon was announced. In sharp contrast to his turbulent life, his *Supper at Emmaus* (figure 21.4) is a low-key, personal drama. As re-

Figure 21.4 *Caravaggio*, Supper at Emmaus, *ca. 1600. Oil on canvas, 69" × 55½". Brera Museum, Milan. Photo: Art Resource.*

Figure 21.5 *Artemesia Gentileschi*, Judith Slaying Holofernes, *1620. Oil on canvas. 78" × 64". Uffizi Gallery, Florence. Scala/Art Resource, New York.*

counted in Luke 24: 28–31, Christ was invited to supper by two of his disciples who, at the moment that he raised his hand to bless the food, recognized their risen Lord. The disciple on the left raises his hands in astonishment, while the other clutches the corner of the table. Unaware of the importance of the discovery, the two servants are puzzled but dutiful. Set against a dark background, the eye-level composition invites the viewer to participate, to sit at the table between the two disciples.

Artemesia Gentileschi, 1593–1652/3

A student of her father, a follower of Caravaggio, Gentileschi (jenti-LES-ki) was also strongly influenced by that artist's use of chiaroscuro and his frequently violent subject matter. Her preferred subjects were heroic women, particularly Judith, whom she portrayed many times. In this *Judith Slaying Holofernes* (figure 21.5) she selected the exact moment in which Judith beheaded the enemy general, having tricked him to gain access to his tent. The Hebrew heroine works with the cold efficiency of an executioner as she also avoids the rush of blood. The extreme chiaroscuro emphasizes the drama and horror of the scene. Criticism from some of her contemporaries because her violent images were not "feminine" deterred her not at all. Unlike most other women of her day, she had received a good education in painting solely because her father was a highly skilled artist, and she used that training to full advantage.

Gianlorenzo Bernini, 1598–1680

In his life and in his art Caravaggio was at odds with his time, but Bernini (bear-NEE-nee) was the Counter-Reformation personified. A superbly gifted sculptor/architect with a virtuosity comparable to that of Michelangelo, Bernini was regarded in his own century as not only its best artist but also its greatest man. He himself saw that his renown would decline with the waning of Counter-Reformation energy, but his emotional art has now regained some of its luster. His *David* (figure 21.6) is a young warrior tensely poised over his discarded armor and harp; every muscle strains to hurl the fatal stone at an unseen Goliath, who seems to be approaching from behind and above the level of the viewer. When compared with Michelangelo's *David* (figure 17.33), we experience the intense energy of the baroque, so much so that there is an impulse to leap out of the way of the stone missile. The bit lip is Bernini's own expression as copied from a mirror, and realism is further heightened by the grip of David's foot on the actual base of the statue. Completed just nine years before the Inquisition condemned Galileo (in 1632), the *David* epitomizes Counter-Reformation fervor.

Rome was Bernini's city and he left his stamp on it literally everywhere, but nowhere so effectively as in his enhancement of St. Peter's (figure 21.7). The oval piazza, together with the embracing arms of the colossal colonnade, form a spectacular entrance to the largest church in Christendom. The 284 massive Doric columns are 39′ high and are topped with 15′ statues of 96 saints, demarcating a piazza that can accommodate about 250,000

Figure 21.6 *Gianlorenzo Bernini,* David, *1623. Marble, life size. Borghese Gallery, Rome.*

Figure 21.7 *St. Peter's Basilica, Rome. Apse and dome by Michelangelo (1547–1564); nave and facade by Carlo Maderno (1607–1626); Colonnade and piazza by Gianlorenzo Bernini (1617–1667). Photo: Scala/Art Resource.*

Figure 21.8 *Gianlorenzo Bernini,* Baldacchino, *1624–1633. St. Peter's Basilica, Rome.*

people. Bernini used the pavement design, the Egyptian obelisk, and the two fountains to unify the piazza and give it human scale. This fifty-year project was the crowning architectural achievement of the Counter-Reformation. Ironically, it was completed one year after the Great London Fire had reduced much of that Protestant stronghold to rubble.

Once in the awesome nave of the church, the visitor is surrounded by other manifestations of Bernini's genius: monumental sculptures, the Throne of St. Peter, elegant relief carvings, even the patterned marble floor. Under Michelangelo's soaring dome stands the *Baldacchino* (ball-da-KEY-no; figure 21.8), an 85′-high canopy over the tomb of St. Peter. The title is derived

from the Italian: *baldacco* is a silk cloth draped as a canopy over important people or places. In this case, the drapery is bronze as is the entire canopy, including the intricate designs covering the four columns. The Baldacchino was commissioned by the Barberini Pope Urban VIII, who ordered the bronze plates removed

Figure 21.9 *Gianlorenzo Bernini*, Ecstasy of St. Theresa, *1645–1652. Marble and gilt, life size. Cornaro Chapel, Sta. Maria della Vittoria, Rome. Photo: Scala/Art Resource.*

Figure 21.10 *Francesco Borromini, S. Carlo alle Quattro Fontane, begun 1638. Rome.*

from the dome of the Pantheon and melted down, prompting the pope's physician to remark that, "What the barbarians didn't do the Barberini did." Bernini patterned the serpentine column design after the twisted marble columns saved from Old St. Peter's, which were thought by Constantine to have survived from King Solomon's Temple. Some critics refer to the Baldacchino as architecture and others as sculpture; in either case, it is an artistic triumph under difficult circumstances. It had to be large enough to be significant under Michelangelo's enormous dome, but not disproportionate to the size of the nave. Bernini himself called the solution one that "came out well by luck."

The appeal of Bernini's *Ecstasy of St. Theresa* (figure 21.9) is emotional, mystical, spiritual, and, withal, palpably sensual. Based on the writings of St. Theresa, the Spanish mystic, the saint is depicted in the throes of rapture as the angel is about to pierce her with the golden arrow of Divine Love. Epitomizing the Roman High Baroque, the altarpiece has become a stage for a theatrical work of intense religiosity, a visual counterpart of the *Spiritual Exercises* of Ignatius of Loyola that Bernini practiced every day.

Francesco Borromini, 1599–1644

Bernini was Pope Urban VIII's favorite, but by no means the only artist supported by the lavish building program that drained the Vatican treasury. One of Bernini's severest critics was rival architect Borromini (BOR-o-ME-nee), a brooding and introspective genius who resented Bernini's favored status and grand reputation. Rejecting Bernini's predilection for rich marbles and lavishly painted stucco, Borromini concentrated on the interplay of elaborate curves and lines. In the small monastic Church of S. Carlo alle Quattro Fontane (figure 21.10), Borromini used a series of intersecting ellipses in an undulating facade richly embellished with columns, sculpture, plaques, and scrolls, all in stone and relying for their effect on design rather than on opulent materials. The impression of restless, mystical passion must have had great appeal, for this small church was emulated throughout southern Europe.

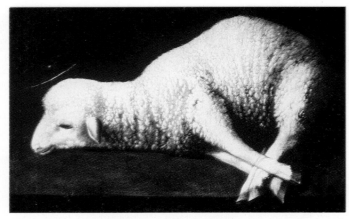

Figure 21.11 *Francisco de Zurbarán,* Agnus Dei, *1635–1640. Oil on canvas, 20½″ × 13¼″. The San Diego Museum of Art, San Diego, California. Gift of Anne R. and Amy Putman.*

Figure 21.12 *Diego Velasquez,* Maids of Honor (Las Meninas), *1656. Oil on canvas, 10′5″ × 9′. Museo del Prado, Madrid. Photo: Scala/Art Resource.*

Francisco de Zurbarán, 1598–1664

The fervent mysticism of Counter-Reformation Spain was expressed in the Mannerism of El Greco and, in the seventeenth century, in the art of Zurbarán (zoor-ba-RAHN). Influenced by Caravaggio, though he never studied in Italy, Zurbarán translates spiritual ideas into poetic visual reality. His *Agnus Dei* (figure 21.11) presents the Lamb of God as a symbol of Christ the perpetual sacrifice. With loving attention to detail he contrasts the delicate curls with the altar cloth, emphasizing the serenity of the sacrifice and the severity of the site. Reflecting the tenets of the Quietists, the most mystical of Spanish sects, the mood encompasses passivity, spiritual solitude, faith, and silence in the presence of God.

Diego Velasquez, 1599–1660

Unlike his Spanish contemporaries, Velasquez (ve-LASS-kis) was not interested in religious subjects. Allegorical figures, swirling clouds, and rhapsodic faces were never a part of a unique style that was concerned with nature and the optical effects of light. During his studies in Italy he became fascinated with the paintings of Titian and Tintoretto, but cared not at all for the style of Raphael, nor was he influenced by Rubens even though the latter was a personal friend. A court painter to King Philip IV for thirty years, Velasquez worked with the effects of light on objects and colors, producing candid portraits that never descended to the level of common courtly pictures. His *Maids of Honor* (figure 21.12) is his acknowledged masterpiece and one of the most celebrated works of the century. The painting is a symphony of deep pictorial space, light, and images of reality, from what we actually see in the room to the implied presence of the king and queen, whose images are reflected in the mirror. The painter himself looks back at us as he works on a painting that is probably the one at which we are looking. At the front of the picture plane light falls on the dog with the child's foot placed on its back, on the court dwarf, and, in the near foreground, on the Infanta Margarita and her two attendants. Standing behind a lady-in-waiting and wearing the cross of the Order of Santiago, the artist pauses with paintbrush poised; slightly deeper in the middle ground we see a couple engaged in conversation. The mirror on the back wall reveals the presence of the artist's patrons and, behind the courtier in the open doorway, space recedes to infinity. What at first looks like a genre scene in the artist's studio is actually a stunning spatial composition of five or six receding planes. As it is usually displayed in the Prado Museum, the painting faces a mirror on the opposite wall in which the spectator sees an electrifying image of receding space, an illusion that further confuses reality because the mirror includes the viewer as part of the painting. Space was a major preoccupation of the baroque, from the large interiors of baroque churches to the great piazza fronting St. Peter's, and the fascinating illusion of deep space in the *Maids of Honor.*

Figure 21.13 *Andrea Pozzo,* Apotheosis of Saint Ignatius, *1691. Fresco, nave ceiling, Sant' Ignazio, Rome. Scala/Art Resource, New York.*

Like most of the paintings of the period, the title was added in the nineteenth century when it was viewed by people other than the royal couple for whom it was originally painted. *Maids of Honor* so fascinated Pablo Picasso that he painted, in 1957, no less than forty-five different studies of all or part of this monumental creation.

Andrea Pozzo, 1642–1709

Among the most extravagant examples of Counter-Reformation power and religious rapture are the ceiling paintings found in many baroque churches. Late in the period, Pozzo (POET-zo) painted a phenomenal work on the barrel-vaulted ceiling of Sant' Ignazio, a sister church of Il Gesù (figure 21.13). Depicting the ascent of Ignatius Loyola into heaven, the illusion is dazzling, as if the ceiling has opened up to admit the saint and accompanying saints, angels, and cherubs into the heavenly kingdom. The exuberant design expresses far better than mere words the fervor and dedication of the Society of Jesus in its mission to reform and inspire the Church.

Aristocratic Baroque

Peter Paul Rubens, 1577–1640

Rubens lived during an age marked by extremes. Galileo, Kepler, and Descartes were helping shape a new vision of the world, but there was also the dark and bloody side of witchcraft trials, the brutal Inquisition, and the savage Thirty Years' War. Throughout his entire lifetime Rubens' own country, the Netherlands, was struggling to free itself from ruthless Spanish power, and yet Rubens painted works that jubilantly praised the human spirit and celebrated the beauty of the natural world. He was not indifferent to human suffering—far from it—but his temperament was wholly sunny and positive. He possessed a rare combination of robust health, good looks, common sense, a talent for business, phenomenal artistic ability, and a remarkable intellect. He was fluent in six modern languages and classical Latin and was reputed to be capable of listening to a learned lecture while painting, conversing, and dictating letters. One of the most gifted and accomplished painters who ever lived, Rubens amassed a fortune and enjoyed it all.

In only eight years of study in Italy Rubens mastered the classical style of ancient Rome plus those of the High and Late Renaissance. On completing a series of paintings for Marie de' Medici, the Dowager Queen of France, he established his reputation as the preeminent painter for kings, nobles, and princes of the church. His *The Assumption of the Virgin* (figure 21.14), though considerably smaller than his many giant paintings, is charged with the boundless energy that characterizes all his work. The diametric opposite of Caravaggio's stark realism, the figures are richly and colorfully garbed, with pink and chubby cherubs and solicitous angels effortlessly wafting the Virgin into heaven. The rich sensual quality of Rubens' work was prized by aristocratic patrons and by the church; glamour, grandeur, and glory provided favorable answers to any doubts of the faithful, assuring them that heaven and earth alike were equally splendid.

In his large-scale *Rape of the Daughters of Leucippus* (figure 21.15), Rubens depicts Castor and Pollux, the sons of Jupiter, abducting two mortal maidens with whom they have fallen in love. Using an ascending spiral design, Rubens has fashioned his colors in rich, contrasting textures: the luminous flesh of the opulent bodies; the deeply tanned, muscular gods; sparkling armor; and shimmering horseflesh. The low horizon heightens the illusion of ascension to the realm of the gods and augments the buoyancy of a composition that is explosive with energy. Only the passive cupid is isolated from the intense action. The luscious nudes are typically "Rubenesque" and designed to complement each other, adding to the balance of the composition; what is concealed in one is revealed in the other. Though Rubens was noted for his love and respect for his two wives (the first one died) and women in general, he obviously accepted the conventional masculine view of the mistreatment of women, at least in mythology.

Figure 21.14 *Peter Paul Rubens,* The Assumption of the Virgin, *ca. 1626. Oil on panel, 49⅜″ × 37⅛″. Samuel H. Kress Collection. National Gallery of Art, Washington, D.C.*

Figure 21.15 *Peter Paul Rubens,* Rape of the Daughters of Leucippus, *ca. 1618. Oil on canvas, 7′3″ × 6′10″. Alte Pinakothek, Munich. Scala/Art Resource.*

Figure 21.16 *Anthony van Dyck,* Marchesa Elena Grimaldi, *ca. 1623. Oil on canvas, 97″ × 68″. Widener Collection. National Gallery of Art, Washington, D.C.*

Anthony van Dyck, 1599–1641

No one knows how many assistants Rubens employed in his huge studio in Antwerp. As a court painter he paid no guild tax and therefore kept no records of the people who copied popular works or roughed out canvases that the master would complete and sell at a price based on the square footage and the extent of his involvement. Of the few assistants who were successful in their own right, van Dyck is by far the most notable. Unable to develop his talents in the overpowering presence of his teacher, van Dyck left to seek his fortune, which he found in abundance at the court of Charles I of England. With his aristocratic and refined style, van Dyck became the century's foremost portrait painter for court and church, producing elegant portrayals that always improved on the appearance of the model. While working in Genoa before settling down in the English court, van Dyck painted a portrait of the *Marchesa Elena Grimaldi* (figure 21.16). A model of the art of portraiture in the grand manner, van Dyck designed the angled parasol to balance the dark mass at the bottom. Contributing to the illusion of the Marchesa's regal height, the classical columns add just the right touch of aristocratic confidence and dignity. Van Dyck had a unique ability to portray his subjects as they wished to appear without, however, stepping over the line to mere sycophancy.

Figure 21.17 *Nicolas Poussin,* Holy Family the Steps, *1648. Oil on canvas, 38¼" × 27". Samuel H. Kress Collection. National Gallery o Art, Washington, D.C.*

Nicolas Poussin, 1594–1665

Throughout his mature career Poussin (poo-SAN) painted in the grand manner, but in a style entirely different from van Dyck and especially, Rubens. Emphasizing line, lucidity, and control, Poussin chose only lofty subject matter drawn from ancient history, mythology, and biblical stories. He was an elitist, an aristocrat of paint and canvas, a French classicist in an age of baroque exuberance. Religious subject matter was treated, he thought, in a base and vulgar manner in most of the works by Caravaggio and his followers. Poussin's baroque classical style attracted followers just as did the quite different baroque style of Rubens, touching off a controversy between "Rubenists" and "Poussinists" that may never be resolved. The basic disagreement was between color and line. Line and drawing were absolute values in representing things according to the Poussinists, and color was merely accidental because it depended on light. Color was, of course, what fascinated Rubens and his followers. Rubenists painted the multicolored world as they perceived it, whereas the Poussinists constructed idealized forms of the world as it should be. Actually, the conflict was not just Rubenists versus Poussinists but the eternally opposing views of artists who were, in general, inclined toward romanticism as opposed to artists who were classically oriented. Romanticism in the nineteenth century is a stylistic period and is not to be confused with romantic or classical tendencies of artists in any period. When considered in very broad terms, the Renaissance was classically oriented, whereas the baroque was inclined toward romanticism except, of course, for Poussin. Classicists emphasize objectivity, rationality, balance, and control; romanticists stress subjectivity, nonrationality, and the restless expression of emotion. Leonardo, Raphael, Poussin, Haydn, and Mozart are classicists; Tintoretto, the later Michelangelo, El Greco, Rubens, Verdi, Tchaikovsky, and Delacroix are romanticists.

In *Holy Family on the Steps* (figure 21.17) Poussin has designed an upward-angled perspective that is enforced by the steps across the bottom of the painting. Reminiscent of Raphael's style that Poussin studied so assiduously, the triangular composition is slightly off center, putting the head of Christ almost precisely in the mathematical center of the painting. From vases to temples the setting is Roman and the mode is derived, according to Poussin, from the *ethos* of the Greek musical scales which, in this case, may be the sweetly lyrical quality of the Ionic scale. Appearing at first to be starkly geometric, the drama and classical beauty of the work are apparent in the balance of solids and voids, cylinders and cubes, and in the balanced contrast of hard stone and soft foliage, drapery and coolly supple flesh. To compare this work with *The Assumption of the Virgin* (see figure 21.14) is to perceive and to understand the difference between classicism and romanticism in the broad sense in which these terms are used here.

Louis XIV and Versailles

French tastes were attuned to a rationalized version of the baroque as represented in the work of Poussin and, on a grand scale, in the enormous royal palace at Versailles. Soon after Louis XIV assumed full control of the government (ca. 1661), French classicism was deliberately used to create a "royal style" that reinforced and enhanced the absolute rule of the king of the most powerful nation in Europe. Classical architecture has, since that time, been used by banks to indicate their financial stability and by rulers and dictators from Napoleon to Hitler and Stalin to symbolize authority and power.

Originally a hunting lodge for Louis XIII, the Palace of Versailles was rebuilt and vastly enlarged for Louis XIV, the self-styled sun-king whose power was so immense that he supposedly de-

Figure 21.18 *Hyacinthe Rigaud,* Portrait of Louis XIV, *1701. Oil on canvas, 9′1½″ × 6′2⅝″. The Louvre, Paris.*

clared that *"L'état, c'est moi"* (I am the state). He certainly said, "It is legal because I wish it." The royal portrait (figure 21.18) illustrates the judgment of the English statesman Viscount Bolingbroke: "If he was not the greatest king, he was the best actor of majesty that ever filled a throne." Designed initially by Louis le Vau (luh-VO; 1612–1670) and completed by Jules Hardouin Mansart (man-SAR; 1646–1708), the palace was oriented along an east-west axis with the western front facing the extensive gardens (figure 21.19). Far too large to photograph at ground level in its entirety, the view shown is of the west wing of the three-wing Garden Front. The design is basically classical, with three floors and windows equally spaced and lined up above each other in diminishing size from ground-level French doors to the square top windows. The paired Ionic columns on the two projecting fronts are baroque and intended to enliven an exterior that would otherwise be bland and boring.

The vastness of the palace can be overpowering except when viewed as intended, as the principal structure set within the spacious formal gardens designed by André le Nôtre (lu NO-truh; 1613–1700), which are classical in every respect except for baroque scale and the vast extension of space. Every flower, shrub, hedge, and tree is set precisely in place and enlivened by reflecting pools and 1,200 fountains, a superb setting for a king who imposed his will even on nature. Because the king's minister of finance concealed expenditures, there are no reliable figures on what it cost to build and maintain Versailles, but today the French government can afford to operate the fountains during the summer tourist season and then only on Sunday evenings.

Figure 21.19 *Louis le Vau and Jules Hardouin Mansart, West wing, Palace of Versailles, 1669–1685.*

Figure 21.20 *Frans Hals,* Portrait of an Officer, *ca. 1640. Oil on linen, 33¾" × 27". Andrew W. Mellon Collection. National Gallery of Art, Washington, D.C.*

Figure 21.21 *Judith Leyster,* Self-Portrait, *ca. 1635. Oil on canvas, 29⅜" × 25⅝". Gift of Mr. and Mrs. Robert Woods Bliss. National Gallery of Art, Washington, D.C.*

Bourgeois Baroque

Dutch art flourished in an environment utterly unlike the regal splendor of France or the flamboyant baroque of the southern Catholic countries. Freed at last from the Spanish yoke, Holland became a prosperous trading nation: Protestant, hardworking, and predominantly middle class. Calvinism opposed images in churches, and there was no royal court or hereditary nobility, meaning that there were no traditional patrons of the arts. The new patrons were private collectors and there were many. Just about everyone in the nation of nearly two million inhabitants wanted paintings for their living rooms, and schools of painting at Amsterdam, Haarlem, Delft, and Utrecht labored to supply a demand somewhat comparable to the Golden Age of Greece or fifteenth-century Florence.

Frans Hals, ca. 1580–1666

The first of the great Dutch masters, Hals was one of history's most brilliant portraitists. There is no precedent for the liveliness of his canvases or the spontaneous brilliance of his brushwork. In *Portrait of an Officer* (figure 21.20), a portly gentleman with hand on hip, his head jauntily tilted, stares at the viewer. Large surfaces are treated casually but the lacework is delicately precise. Not a deep character study, this is a portrait of a passing acquaintance captured in a brief moment, but rendered as a momentary but uncompromising truth.

Judith Leyster, 1609–1660

Leyster (LIE-ster) specialized in genre paintings, especially of musicians, and was one of the few artists prior to this century who could suggest musical performance through form, line, and color. In *Self-Portrait* (figure 21.21) Leyster portrays herself in formal dress but in a relaxed and casual pose that echoes, in a lower key, the laughing violinist on her canvas, who is actually playing the instrument rather than just holding it. Influenced by the Utrecht school of Caravaggio disciples and her teacher, Frans Hals, her style is clearly her own. However, it was not until this century that "Leyster" replaced "Hals" on several paintings that she had completed during her late teens or early twenties. She was, in fact, a well-known artist at the age of eighteen. Dutch artists were proud of their craft, and this attitude is reflected in the jaunty ease and confident self-assertion of the artist. Italian artists of the High Renaissance promoted the idea of the artist as a noble creator, but in bourgeois Holland, superlative skills in the crafts were valued on their own merits.

At this point let us compare the four basic baroque styles: Bourgeois, French Classical, Aristocratic, and Counter-Reformation. The pertinent illustrations, in the same order, are figures 21.21, 21.17, 21.18, and 21.3. The radical differences in subject matter, line, color, design, and technique illustrate the extremes coexisting in this dynamic first century of the modern era.

Figure 21.22 *Rembrandt van Rijn,* The Descent from the Cross, *1655. Oil on canvas, 56¼" × 43¾". Widener Collection. National Gallery of Art, Washington, D.C.*

Rembrandt van Rijn, 1606–1669

Some Dutch artists such as Hals specialized in portraits, Leyster painted genre scenes, and others concentrated on history or landscapes. Rembrandt, however, worked with consummate ease in all areas. He is, in fact, one of a handful of supreme masters of the entire European tradition. Calvinism frowned on religious images, which may explain why sculpture was not popular, but on the other hand, the Reformed Church rejected all authority except individual conscience. This meant, in effect, that artists could study the Bible and create sacred images as they personally envisioned them, which is precisely what Rembrandt did. He could not accept the stern God of the Calvinists and he never painted a Last Judgment. He was concerned instead with the human drama of the Old Testament, the loving and forgiving God of the New Testament, and the life and passion of Christ. In *The Descent from the Cross* (figure 21.22) the two main focal points of the drama are the body of Christ and the face of his fainting mother. Eliminating all superfluous details with his characteristic dark background, the artist conveys the tenderness with which the broken body is being lowered from the cross. The composition is extremely tight, concentrating our attention on the key figures and, through the skillful use of chiaroscuro, flooding the canvas with the most profound grief. Not even Rembrandt himself surpassed the expressive combination of space and light.

Figure 21.23 *Rembrandt van Rijn,* The Apostle Bartholomew, *1657. Oil on canvas, 64¾" × 55¾". Timkin Gallery, San Diego Museum of Art, San Diego, California.*

Rembrandt's portrayal of *The Apostle Bartholomew* (figure 21.23) is a powerful study of Christ's disciple, who was flayed alive while on a preaching mission in Armenia. During the Middle Ages he was sometimes portrayed holding some of his own flesh in his hands, but Rembrandt creates instead a resurrected disciple holding the knife that symbolizes his martyrdom. That Rembrandt chose to depict this lesser-known apostle is curious and may refer to the Massacre of St. Bartholomew. The largely middle-class Huguenots (French Protestants) were opposed to both the pope and the king. On 24 August 1572 (St. Bartholomew's Day) more than 30,000 Huguenots were massacred by fanatical followers of Catherine de' Medici, the regent, and her son, King Charles IX. Pope Gregory XIII (1572–1585) celebrated the occasion by singing a *Te Deum* and having a medal struck to memorialize the event, but throughout Protestant Europe reaction to the slaughter was intensely bitter and long-lasting. A devout Protestant who followed only his own conscience, Rembrandt was opposed to the authority of Calvin, not to mention a pope or a king. His monumental study of the martyred apostle could therefore symbolize the martyrdom of the Huguenots who died on the saint's day.

Jan Vermeer, 1632–1675

Vermeer (ver-MEER) did not paint monumental subject matter with the passion of Rembrandt, but he did possess a special magic that transmuted everyday reality into eternal symbols. Fewer than forty paintings survive, and all but three are of sparsely furnished

Figure 21.24 *Jan Vermeer,* Woman Holding a Balance, *ca. 1664. Oil on canvas, 16¾" × 15". Widener Collection. National Gallery of Art, Washington, D.C.*

Figure 21.25 *Jan Vermeer,* The Girl with a Red Hat, *ca. 1665. Oil on wood, 9⅛" × 7⅛". Andrew W. Mellon Collection. National Gallery of Art, Washington, D.C.*

interiors of modest size. Vermeer has, in fact, done for ordinary rooms what High Renaissance artists did for ordinary human bodies: elevated them to the level of universals. With an eye for detail comparable to van Dyck's, Vermeer specialized in light, natural light streaming into the interior, usually from the left, filling a space punctuated by objects and figures seemingly suspended in light. In *Woman Holding a Balance* (figure 21.24) Vermeer has created an apparently simple scene of a woman, probably his wife, Catharina, in one of her eleven pregnancies, holding an empty balance. With jewelry on the table and a painting of the Last Judgment on the wall, one might assume that this is a moral analogy, a weighing of worldly possessions against a background of divine judgment. Dutch Calvinists would not have had a Last Judgment anywhere in the house, but this may be Catharina's room and she, unlike her husband, was Catholic. Nevertheless, the mood is introspective and her expression serene. Married to a painter who never sold a painting, a man of extravagant tastes with a host of creditors, this painting may represent nothing more than a woman contentedly contemplating jewelry received from a loving husband. The highest level of art may not be to encourage laughter, passion, or tears but to invoke dreams, and dreams are perhaps best left unexplained.

After his premature death, Vermeer's paintings were used to satisfy creditors who undoubtedly had no more appreciation of his worth than a society that had ignored him. Not rediscovered until the 1860s, his use of color and light was a revelation to the Impressionists, who thought themselves the first to discover that shadows were not black but also had color. In *The Girl with a Red Hat* (figure 21.25), there is a technical mastery that, in combination with Vermeer's scientific study of light, makes this one of the finest works of the artist's brief mature period. Remarkable in its own right, the painting is also a tribute to the rapidly developing science of optics, for it is all but certain that Jan Vermeer actually sought to simulate the camera obscura's effects. The principle of the camera obscura was described by Leonardo da Vinci and developed by Johannes Kepler; i.e., light passing through a small hole in the side wall of a dark room projects an image of outside objects onto an interior wall. Filling the hole with one of the new improved lenses would make the inside image as vivid as a color photograph. The artist did not copy the camera image; rather, he suggests the luminosity of such an image. Here, as if they were visualized molecules, we see floating globules of colored light. Light glints from an eye, an earring, and the lips of a young woman unexpectedly caught in a soft-focus candid "photograph." Under the spectacular hat, light and shadow are painted in subtle gradations of color emphasized by the gleaming white ruff. Never receiving a commission, Vermeer created whatever he wished, applying paint to canvas with a dexterity and charm that has never been equaled.

Figure 21.26 *Jacob van Ruisdael,* Wheatfields, *1670. Oil on canvas, 51¼″ × 39⅜″. Metropolitan Museum of Art, New York. Bequest of Benjamin Altman, 1913.*

Jacob van Ruisdael, 1628–1682

Vermeer exploited color and light, but Ruisdael (ROIS-dale) specialized in space. The finest Dutch landscape painter and one of the greatest in Western art, Ruisdael painted the immensity of space from memory and imagination. In *Wheatfields* (figure 21.26) the vast and brooding sky, forecasting a coming storm, takes up two-thirds of the canvas. Ruisdael's landscapes are frequently devoid of people, and when they are present, as here, they are inconsequential figures compared with the magnificence of nature. The atmospheric perspective encourages the illusion that we are looking into space so deep it verges on infinity.

The subject matter of the five Dutch artists illustrated here reveals the generally secular orientation of the artists, indeed of the entire nation. From the last quarter of the sixteenth century through three-quarters of the seventeenth, the tiny Dutch nation (United Provinces of the Northern Netherlands) was a great power throughout the world with colonies in Asia, Africa, and the Americas. With virtually no aristocracy, this was the first notable middle-class nation in Europe, its wealth and authority derived from vigorous international trade protected by the world's most powerful navy.

Prosperous Dutch burghers of their Golden Age are justly famed for their support of the art of painting, and Dutch museums are today filled to overflowing with "Dutch masters" and "little Dutch masters." Many painters of that illustrious era acquired wealth and fame, but for whatever reason, Rembrandt, Hals, and Vermeer, the greatest of the Dutch school, all died in poverty.

Rococo Art, ca. 1715–1789

With the death of Louis XIV in 1715 the academic classical art of the baroque had lost its chief patron. It was with immense relief that the French court abandoned the palace and the baroque, moving back to Paris and to a new way of life in their elegant townhouses, where manners and charm were far more interesting than grandeur and geometric order. This was the Age of Enlightenment and of the rococo style of art, contradictory but not mutually exclusive. In fact, the Enlightenment and the American and French revolutions cannot be fully understood without knowing what the rococo was all about. That rococo is merely baroque made small or baroque made light are bromides that do have a certain element of truth, but rococo is also a style in its own right. Royalty and nobility became obsolete during the Enlightenment, and

Figure 21.27 *Jean Antoine Watteau,* A Pilgrimage to Cythera, *1717. Oil on canvas, 51″ × 76½″. The Louvre, Paris. Cliché des Musées Nationaux, Paris.*

rococo art illustrates with astonishing accuracy the superficial values of an aristocracy whose languid days were numbered. The imposing baroque forms were reduced to depictions of the pursuit of pleasure and escape from boredom. Rococo art was not decadent but the society that it portrayed most certainly was.

France

Jean Antoine Watteau, 1684–1721

Watteau (vah-TOE), the first and greatest French rococo artist, was born of Flemish parents in Valenciennes, a city that had been French for only six years. Yet, he transformed French art from the classicism of Poussin into a new style of gaiety and tenderness, casual but elegant, that even today is recognized as Parisian in the sophisticated tradition later reinforced by artists such as Renoir and Degas. Watteau's *A Pilgrimage to Cythera* (figure 21.27), an early rococo work completed only two years after the death of Louis XIV, is also the most important. Cythera was the legendary island of Venus, whose statue at the right presides over the amorous festivities. Grouped couple by couple, the elegantly garbed party is preparing to board a fanciful boat attended by cherubs, but not without a wistful backward glance at the pleasures enjoyed on the isle of love. Characteristic of rococo design is the reverse C (Ɔ) that can be traced from the heads at the lower left, curving past the couple on the hillock, and then turning back to the left along the delicate tips of the tree branches. Though it is a large painting, the scene is remarkably intimate. Each couple is totally preoccupied with each other and form a distinct unit as they talk, smile, whisper, or touch. Beneath the frivolity and charm is a warm feeling of agreeable people and pleasant times. Watteau has transformed the amorous dalliances of an idle and privileged class into lyric poetry.

François Boucher, 1703–1770

Venus was queen of the rococo at its height in the 1750s, and Boucher (boo-SHAY) was her most talented interpreter. The protégé of Madame de Pompadour, mistress of Louis XV and arbiter of rococo style, Boucher was a master of the sensual and frequently erotic art of the period. With astounding energy and prodigious virtuosity he produced paintings, designed tapestries, decorated porcelain, and created opera and ballet settings. With his many students and widely circulated engravings, he became the most influential artist in Europe. His *Venus Consoling Love* (figure 21.28) depicts a slim and delicate beauty who would be more comfortable at the French court than on Mount Olympos. She was, in fact, at the French court, for this is one of Boucher's many portraits of Mme. de Pompadour, to whom the painting belonged. Here are the characteristic ivory, pink, blue, silver, and gold colors of the rococo, all elegantly detailed by one of the virtuosos of the painter's brush. The painting is frankly pretty, and meant to be, but its subtle design is a carefully controlled interplay of sinuous curves; nowhere is there a straight line. A study of the apparent diagonals of the goddess' body discloses a series of curves, flattering curls of supple and creamy flesh. This is an idealized version of Pompadour, totally different from other Boucher paintings that reveal the intellectual brilliance of an enlightened woman who assisted in the publication of Diderot's *Encyclopedia.* Her physician, Dr. Quesway, quoted her foreboding remark, *"Après moi le déluge!"* (After me the flood!, i.e., disaster), and Voltaire wrote, on the occasion of her death in 1764, that he would miss her because "She was one of us; she protected Letters to the best of her power."

Figure 21.28 *François Boucher,* Venus Consoling Love, *1751. Oil on canvas, 42⅛" × 33⅜". Gift of Chester Dale. National Gallery of Art, Washington, D.C.*

Figure 21.29 *Jean-Honoré Fragonard,* The Swing, *1766. Oil on canvas, 32" × 25½". Wallace Collection, London. Reproduced by permission of the Trustees of the Wallace Collection. Art Resource, N.Y.*

Jean-Honoré Fragonard, 1732–1806

The most eminent pupil of Boucher and Chardin and the last of the exceptional rococo artists, Fragonard (frah-go-NAR) lived to see the revolution destroy the rococo age and all it represented. A master of the elegantly erotic paintings that delighted his patrons, Fragonard also had a technical skill and an eye for composition that enabled him to make powerful artistic statements. *The Swing* (figure 21.29) is an apparently lightweight erotic diversion with a statue of cupid at the left and the lolling figure of a young man below, actually the aristocrat who commissioned the work. His lady friend has whimsically kicked her pump off to give him a better view up her skirt. Almost unnoticed is the key to the composition, the swing-pulling servant in the right background. Fragonard has portrayed a decadent class that neither works nor pays taxes, a frivolous aristocracy totally supported by the labors (and taxes) of 97 percent of a population symbolized by the shadowy figure of the servant. This was painted when the publication of Diderot's *Encyclopedia* was nearing completion and the Revolution itself was waiting impatiently in the wings.

Étienne Falconet, 1716–1791

The spirit of the age in three-dimensional form is represented by Falconet (fal-ca-NAY) in his harmonious sculptural group entitled *Madame de Pompadour as the Venus of the Doves* (figure 21.30). The coquettish eroticism that delighted this decadent society is clearly evident in this lighthearted work, so typical of the figures that decorated Sèvres porcelain, music boxes, snuff boxes, and other accoutrements of the opulent life of languorous luxury.

Jean-Baptiste-Simeon Chardin, 1699–1779

But there was another current, one that celebrated the sober virtues of the middle class. Chardin (shar-DAN) sought the underlying nobility that could be found in scenes of daily life. Nothing was so humble but that his brush could reveal its charm. His depiction of *The Kitchen Maid* (figure 21.31) has a natural dignity in sharp contrast to the artificiality of the courtly Rococo style. Chardin painted what he saw, which was, essentially, light falling on pleasing shapes: face, apron, basin, turnips. The result is a quietly beautiful composition by the finest still-life painter of the eighteenth century.

Figure 21.30 *Étienne Falconet,* Madame de Pompadour as the Venus of the Doves. *Samuel H. Kress Collection. National Gallery of Art, Washington, D.C.*

Figure 21.31 *Jean-Baptiste-Simeon Chardin,* The Kitchen Maid, *1738. Oil on canvas, 18⅛" × 14¾". Samuel H. Kress Collection. National Gallery of Art, Washington, D.C.*

Figure 21.32 *Thomas Gainsborough,* Mrs. Richard Brinsley Sheridan, *ca. 1783. Oil on canvas, 86½" × 60½". Andrew W. Mellon Collection. National Gallery of Art, Washington, D.C.*

England

Thomas Gainsborough, 1727–1788

The artificial elegance of the French rococo had no place in an English society that was less frivolous than the French and certainly less decadent. In both subject matter and style Gainsborough's portrait of *Mrs. Richard Brinsley Sheridan* (figure 21.32) symbolizes the dashing, worldly taste of English high society. This is the beautiful singer who married Sheridan, the wit, brilliant member of Parliament, and writer of such plays as *School for Scandal* and *The Rivals.* Here nature is synthetic, arranged as a proper background to highlight the natural beauty and unpretentious air of the sitter. In contrast to the sprightly sophistication of Boucher's women, Mrs. Sheridan is the very picture of the tasteful elegance so admired by British society.

Figure 21.33 *Dominikus Zimmermann, Wieskirche, Upper Bavaria, 1745–1754.*

Rococo Architecture

Rococo architecture is charming and beguiling in small structures and, when tastefully done, even in larger buildings. The pilgrimage church of Wieskirche (VEEZ-keer-ka; Church in the Meadow) was built in a remote rural area where the faithful believed a miracle had transpired. Pilgrims from near and far would travel to a pilgrimage church in the expectation of a miraculous cure or deliverance from some sort of evil. The interior of the church (figure 21.33) is a celestial symphony of white stucco, gold gilt, and profuse decoration set off to best advantage by the north-south orientation of the building and the large clear-glass windows. Most of the elegantly textured decorations are carved wood, and the "marble" columns are actually wood painted to look like marble. The spritely terra-cotta angels pose gracefully on stucco clouds, above which the painted vaulting soars effortlessly. Despite the multiplicity of details the rich ensemble is completely harmonious; the overwhelming impression is a mystical, deeply emotional experience.

Figure 21.34 *Inigo Jones, Queen's House, north facade, 1610–1618. Greenwich.*

Neoclassic Art

English Architecture

The visual arts of the Renaissance and the baroque made little impact on English culture. Apparently preoccupied with their justly celebrated achievements in dramatic literature, poetry, and music, the English continued to build in the Gothic and Tudor styles and to import painters such as Holbein, Rubens, and van Dyck. After a visit to Italy, Inigo Jones (1573–1652), the king's surveyor (architect), inaugurated a revolution in English architecture. Jones' middle-class British sensibilities were offended by the extravagance of Michelangelo's style, but he was profoundly impressed with Palladio's architectural designs. Jones did not copy Palladian buildings, but instead selected classical characteristics as a basis for his own architectural style. His Queen's House (figure 21.34) is the first English building designed in the neoclassic style that would become so prominent in England and North America. Chaste and clean with the poise of pure Roman classicism, the house has slight rustication on the ground floor derived from an early Renaissance style long since abandoned by the Italians (see figure 17.14). With simple window openings and matching lower and upper balustrades, the curving double stairway adds a discreet touch of dignity and grace.

English architecture was influenced by Palladian and baroque characteristics more rapidly than anyone might have anticipated. In 1666 King Charles II commissioned Christopher Wren (1632–1723) to design a new dome for the Gothic Cathedral of St. Paul's, a design that Wren planned in the "Roman manner." A professor of astronomy at Oxford and an amateur architect, Wren soon had more than he bargained for; the Great Fire of 1666 destroyed most of London, necessitating a major rebuilding program with Wren as the chief architect. Of the more than fifty churches that Wren designed, the most important project was the new St. Paul's, an eclectic design influenced by Jones, Palladio,

Figure 21.35 *Christopher Wren, St. Paul's Cathedral, 1675–1710, west facade, London. Photo: National Building Record, London.*

Figure 21.36 *James Gibbs, St. Martin-in-the-Fields, 1721–1726, Trafalgar Square, London.*

and the French and Italian baroque, and masterfully synthesized by Wren (figure 21.35). St. Paul's is one of a limited number of English buildings with baroque characteristics, but overall the design is dominated by the classical dome that is reminiscent, on a massive scale, of Bramante's Tempietto (see figure 17.35). Punctuated by paired Corinthian columns in the baroque manner, the facade is basically classical, but the ornate twin towers are similar to Borromini's curvilinear style (see figure 21.10). None of Wren's London churches is quite like any other, though most are classical; some have towers, others steeples, and a few are crowned with domes.

The Church of St. Martin-in-the-Fields (figure 21.36) was designed by James Gibbs (1682–1754) as influenced by Wren, with whom he studied. Essentially a Roman temple with a classical steeple, this is a prototype of similar churches constructed throughout the United States, especially in New England. Usually of wood frame and clapboard construction and painted white, these classical buildings became one of the most familiar church designs in nineteenth-century America.

Variations on the Palladian style spread throughout England in the designs of stately homes and their interiors, including furniture. The drawing room of Townhouse No. 1 of Crescent Circle (figure 21.37) contains an Axminster carpet, a fireplace of Italian

Figure 21.37 *Drawing Room, No. 1 Crescent Circle, Bath, England.*

Figure 21.38 *Ange-Jacques Gabriel, Petit Trianon, 1762–1768, south facade, Versailles.*

Carrara marble, Sheraton cabinettes, a Chippendale card table, and a Heppelwhite sofa and wooden chairs, all in the neoclassic style. The 1798 piano is neoclassic as are the spacious windows. The two mirrors add a rococo touch to an interior design that, with many variations, became fashionable in comparable American homes of the late eighteenth and early nineteenth centuries.

French Neoclassicism

In France the rococo style was deemed too frivolous for public buildings and the baroque style too elaborate, leaving the way open for a French version of neoclassicism. Ange-Jacques Gabriel (1698–1782), court architect for Louis XV, made his reputation with his design for the Petit Trianon on the grounds of Versailles (figure 21.38). Restrained, symmetrical, and exquisitely proportioned, the diminutive palace was constructed for Mme. de Pompadour who was, in effect, the ruler of France in place of the inept Louis XV. Clearly reflecting her classical architectural tastes, the Petit Trianon is in the austere Augustan style of Republican Rome, a style that became dominant in Paris and other French cities during the second half of the eighteenth century.

Jean-Baptiste Greuze, 1725–1805

The philosophes of the Enlightenment were, as might be expected, hostile to the rococo style. Their attitude accounts for the sudden fame of Greuze (grooz), who was praised by Diderot and other philosophes for paintings depicting bourgeois life. Diderot thought that paintings such as *The Village Bride* (figure 21.39) celebrated the virtues of the simple life and the sterling moral values of the sober and sedate middle class. Greuze's work did please, but not the middle class; rather, it appealed to the philosophes who, along with the upper middle class and aristocracy, lived a life depicted more accurately by Boucher. The charming rusticity of Greuze's painting with a gentle patriarch, blushing bride, gawky bridegroom, and chickens pecking on the floor was sentimental, as phony and romanticized as rococo paintings with their idyllic landscapes and the elite playing at being gods and goddesses. Worse yet, they were hypocritical. Greuze's rural maidens, wide-eyed in their simpering innocence, are painted with sly sensual touches and erotic undertones that make the frankly amoral paintings of Boucher and Fragonard look almost poetic and moral.

Figure 21.39 *Jean-Baptiste Greuze,* The Village Bride, *1761. Oil on canvas, 46½″ × 36″. The Louvre, Paris.*

The gap between the aristocracy and the middle class was possibly no greater than it had been for generations, but by the last quarter of the century it became far more noticeable. The philosophes expounded on the gap along with revolutionary political and economic ideas that were no longer theories but active principles in England's rebellious American colonies. When it became apparent that the art of Greuze and his imitators did not truly reflect their revolutionary fervor, the philosophes turned to neoclassic art. Excavations at Pompeii and Herculaneum, begun in 1748 under the aegis of King Charles of Bourbon, were bringing to light a new chapter from the history of ancient Rome, sparking a renewed interest in antiquity that was not confined to the arts. Political theorists who were advocating democratic equality, fervent patriotism, and the rule of reason thought they had found all this in Republican Rome.

Jacques-Louis David, 1748–1825

A far more gifted artist than Greuze, David (da-VEED) developed his neoclassic style during his studies in Rome (1775–1781). Refusing to merely copy Roman statues and paintings, to become an antiquarian, he chose instead to be a propagandist, to place his talent at the service of revolutionary ideals. David used the forms of ancient art to extol the virtues of patriotism and democracy. Painted shortly before the French Revolution, *The Death of Sokrates* (figure 21.40) became one of the most popular paintings of the century and set the tone for didactic art of the highest quality. The Greek philosopher is depicted here as the apostle of reason, the patron saint of such Roman Stoics as Epictetus and Marcus Aurelius. With the body of a young athlete and the face of a benign sage, Sokrates dominates a sharply focused composition similar to the dramatic chiaroscuro of Caravaggio. The fig-

Figure 21.40 *Jacques-Louis David,* The Death of Sokrates, *1787. Oil on canvas, 77¼″ × 51″. The Metropolitan Museum of Art, New York. Wolfe Fund, 1931.*

ures of the twelve disciples—no coincidence—are rendered as precisely as marble statues, meticulous detail being a David trademark. David's message is unmistakable: men of principle should be willing to die in defense of their ideals. Nobles and tradesmen, philosophers and priests, seemingly everyone bought engravings of the painting, including the doomed Louis XVI, who admired its noble sentiments.

David's works, with their detailed, painstaking realism and appeal to reason, were conceived and executed as cries for revolution. During the revolution itself David was a member of the Convention that sentenced Louis XVI and Marie Antoinette to death. For twenty-five years he was a virtual dictator of the arts in France. Following his dicta, rococo salons were stripped of their sensuous paintings and curvaceous furnishings, remodeled in neoclassic style, and equipped with furniture patterned after Greek vase paintings and Pompeiian murals. Fashionable men and women adopted Roman names such as Portia and Brutus, styled their hair in the antique manner, and even costumed themselves in classical togas, as illustrated in figure 21.41. This was the approved new look of the revolution as painted in the style of David by an unknown artist.

Figure 21.41 *Circle of David,* Portrait of a Lady. *San Diego Museum of Art, San Diego, California. Purchased for the museum by Anne R. and Amy Putman.*

Figure 21.42 *Constance Marie Charpentier,* Mlle. Charlotte du Val d'Ognes, *1785. Oil on canvas, 63½" × 50⅝", formerly attributed to David. The Metropolitan Museum of Art. The Mr. and Mrs. Isaac D. Fletcher Collection. Bequest of Isaac D. Fletcher, 1917.*

Figure 21.43 *Jean Antoine Houdon,* Voltaire, *ca. 1775. Chester Dale Collection. National Gallery of Art, Washington, D.C.*

Constance Marie Charpentier, 1767–1849

David was a highly successful artist with many students and, of course, numerous imitators. As with any well-known artist, paintings were sometimes attributed to him so they could command a higher price, which is what happened with the portrait of *Mlle. Charlotte du Val d'Ognes* (figure 21.42). Purchased in 1917 as a David for $200,000, the painting has since been attributed to Charpentier (shar-PEN-ty-ay), a Parisian artist who studied with David and several other noted painters. Winner of a gold medal and an exhibitor in ten salons, her work appears to be hidden away either in private collections or behind the names of more famous artists. That the painting could ever have been attributed to David is very odd. Though the style is neoclassic, the brushwork firm and lucid, and the garb elegantly classical, the mood is totally alien to David's style. Strangely haunting, there is a brooding and unreal quality about the work that prompted critics to call it a "mysterious masterpiece." André Malraux described it as "a merciless portrait of an intelligent, homely woman against the light and bathed in shadow and mystery. The colors have the subtlety and singularity of those of Vermeer. A perfect picture, unforgettable." Made while the painting bore David's name, these comments are just as appropriate for a masterpiece by Constance Marie Charpentier.

Jean Antoine Houdon, 1741–1828

Portrait sculpture, as might be expected, was a natural for the neoclassic style, but there were no sculptors comparable to David. Houdon (ooh-DON), the finest French sculptor of the age, was admired by the philosophes, many of whom he portrayed with great accuracy. His portrait of Voltaire (figure 21.43) is a realistic depiction of the aging philosopher, clearly communicating his personality with twinkling eyes and wry and cynical smile.

Antonio Canova, 1757–1822

Houdon was acquainted with other revolutionaries, including George Washington and Benjamin Franklin, and created a portrait of Franklin and two statues of Washington. Despite his revolutionary background and realistic portraits, Houdon could win only reluctant acceptance from Napoleon, who much preferred the neoclassic style of Italian sculptor Canova (ka-NO-va), whose art, like that of David, became a propaganda tool for the Empire. Canova's lovely study of *Pauline Borghese as Venus* (figure 21.44) is an idealized version of feminine charm, a very sensual portrait of Napoleon's sister and, though classical, an evocation of imperial luxury rather than the noble dignity of Republican Rome.

Figure 21.44   *Antonio Canova,* Pauline Borghese as Venus, *1805. Marble, life size. Borghese Gallery, Rome.*

Neoclassicism in the United States

Gilbert Stuart, 1755–1828

The neoclassic style found a congenial home in the new republic of the New World. The leading American painter, Stuart painted many Founding Fathers, particularly George Washington, whose portrait on the dollar bill is from a Stuart work. In his portraits Stuart displayed a mastery of flesh tones, having discovered, like the much later impressionists, that flesh coloration was a combination of colors. His portrait of *Mrs. Richard Yates* (figure 21.45) is typical of the neoclassic style in a new democracy in which neither dress nor background gives a clue to the social status of the sitter. European portraiture customarily added a proper setting and adornment indicating a regal or noble subject. In this portrait of the wife of a New York importer we see a coolly poised and confident woman. Her strongly featured face with the raised eyebrows and slightly drooping eyelids is faintly skeptical, the face of a shrewd and capable Yankee.

Figure 21.45   *Gilbert Stuart,* Mrs. Richard Yates, *1793. Oil on canvas, 30¼" × 25". Andrew W. Mellon Collection. National Gallery of Art, Washington, D.C.*

Figure 21.46 *Thomas Jefferson, State Capitol, 1785–1789, Richmond, Virginia.*

Thomas Jefferson, 1743–1826

As U.S. minister to France, Jefferson had an opportunity to study French neoclassic architecture and especially Roman architecture in France and Italy. In particular, he was fascinated by the Maison Carrée (see figure 9.8) in southern France. The first time he visited the building he studied it for seven hours, remarking afterward that he was as transfixed as a man admiring his beautiful mistress. His love affair with this temple compelled him to introduce Roman architecture into the United States. Jefferson's design of the Capitol of Virginia (figure 21.46) was patterned after the Maison Carrée, but with Ionic capitals and constructed of wood painted gleaming white. Larger than the Roman temple, the Virginia Capitol building has an aura of noble dignity precisely as intended by its designer.

Neoclassicism is popular because it is easily comprehended. Political themes and purposes aside, the classical impulse is toward physical and intellectual perfection as embodied in buildings that express the essence of poised, serene beauty. The Greeks not only invented the style but perfected it, and for twenty-five centuries the Western world has copied it.

Exercises

1. Compare and contrast the "Davids" by Donatello, Verrocchio, Michelangelo, and Bernini. Which, in your opinion, best exemplifies the shepherd boy of the Old Testament? How does the Bernini statue symbolize the baroque, particularly when compared with Michelangelo's *David*?
2. Explain the similarities and differences between baroque and rococo art. Identify current manifestations of the rococo style in modern furniture and interior design.
3. Identify buildings in your area that are basically neoclassic.

Summary

The seventeenth and eighteenth centuries witnessed diversity and conflict in virtually every field of human endeavor. In the arts, the term *baroque* embraced contradictory styles and trends, all of which had a common denominator of restless and powerful energy. The emergence of the Modern World in the seventeenth century was reflected in the development of four predominant styles in response to three categories of patronage:

1. The Counter-Reformation baroque, a dynamic, colorful, and frequently flamboyant style favored by the Counter-Reformation Church of Rome. Leading artists included Caravaggio, Bernini, Borromini, and Zurbarán.
2. The aristocratic baroque, a splendidly regal style as embodied in the work of Rubens and van Dyck, and largely supported by the court nobles of France and England.

3. The baroque classical style of Nicolas Poussin, a typically rationalistic French counterpart of the aristocratic style. Poussin emphasized line as opposed to the use of color by Rubens, setting up a confrontation between Poussinists and Rubenists, between painters who objectively controlled the lines and those who expressed themselves through color.

4. The bourgeois baroque as exemplified in the painting of Hals, Rembrandt, Leyster, Ruisdael, and Vermeer, and patronized by the bourgeois merchants of Holland. As an artistic style by and for the Protestant middle class, this contradicted the aristocratic style, and most emphatically, the Counter-Reformation baroque of the Church of Rome.

In retrospect, we can see the latter two styles as the beginning of the end of the old world, whereas the bourgeois baroque signified the coming age of world trade, free enterprise, industrial development, and democratic societies.

These multiple aspects of the baroque had in common a presentation of monumental form; an exuberance of action, expression, and idealism; and an audience that was international. To this audience baroque artists, with their outstanding accomplishments, brought Western men and women to a realization of their potential as enterprising and creative human beings. This was probably the greatest achievement of the baroque.

With the death of the "sun-king," Louis XIV, in 1715, the academic classical art of the baroque lost its chief secular patron. The French court and the aristocracy moved from Versailles, that most monumental of baroque palaces, and began a new way of life in the elegant, intimate salons of their Parisian townhouses, where manners and charm were emphasized over splendor in the grand manner. Although the eighteenth century was the Age of the Enlightenment, and science was thought to be the key to most aspects of life, in art the refinement of men, women, and nature was the overriding concept. The artists of the rococo celebrated the cult of pleasure and sentimentality, of genteel seduction and love in an enchanted land. Watteau was elegant and refined; Boucher was the flashy style-setter; Fragonard was unabashedly sensual.

By midcentury the antagonism between the aristocracy and the bourgeoisie had become blatantly apparent. The philosophes celebrated middle-class morality and the simple life as embodied in the art of Chardin and Greuze, but found their ultimate artistic exemplar in Jacques-Louis David, who had turned to classical antiquity for literary and stylistic inspiration. David placed his talent at the service of revolutionary ideals and painted to inspire honor, duty, and patriotism.

By the end of the eighteenth century all Europe was ablaze with revolutionary fervor and neoclassicism reigned supreme. The neoclassic style gave historical sanction to either liberalism or conservatism because it was so readily comprehensible. Any power structure could manipulate the style to defend and justify its existence.

Culture and Human Values

There was a critical change in art patronage during the Early Modern Age that foretold the growth of capitalism and the rise of a middle class. Churches and courts were still the main supporters of working artists, but the bourgeois baroque style was a clear sign of something new and different; nor was the middle-class sponsorship of art the only indication of a significant change in European society. The founding of the Dutch and English East India societies formed the leading edge of the coming European domination of international trade that gradually evolved into imperialism. Increased trade meant greater prosperity for a growing number of capitalists. No longer was a title or a bishop's mitre the only way to power and recognition in this world; money and power were there for the taking by a growing class of bourgeois capitalists.

The view of reality had changed again, from the Renaissance idea of individuals as the most beloved of God's creations to a materialistic view as described by Newton: a world that operated like a machine. Further, the world-machine was inhabited by societies that, according to the Enlightenment, functioned rationally—a view confirmed by the American Revolution, but denied by the French Revolution that ended the Enlightenment in Europe.

Music: Baroque, Rococo, and Classical

chapter 22

Baroque Music, 1600–1750

Modern music, music as we know it, began sometime around the year 1600 as the Renaissance waned and the new Age of Reason began to take shape. The unbroken line of development leading from early organum to the smoothly flowing symmetry of the a cappella vocal music of the Golden Age of Polyphony came to an end. The old world of *private* music for the church, the courts, and a cultural elite steadily declined in influence and importance. The modern world in which music became a *public* art was taking shape amidst the intellectual, political, and social ferment of the seventeenth century.

Stimulated by exploration, scientific discovery, the emergence of capitalism, the middle class, and the modern state, and by the continuing conflict between Reformation and Counter-Reformation, *audiences* of the common people were created. Churches could no longer take the piety of their communicants for granted; they were obliged to build structures with a maximum of floor space, structures that resembled theatres more than they did Gothic or Renaissance churches. In a setting bursting with agitated forms and twisting, curving shapes with elaborate decorative details, these audiences were preached to, firmly and fervently.

This new *baroque* style was applied to all public buildings whether they were churches, concert halls, or opera houses. Even the baroque palaces (such as Versailles) of ruling heads of state assumed a quasi-public character in their dual roles as royal residences and showcases of national prestige and power.

There was a consistent dualism in the baroque era, a sometimes precarious balance of opposing forces: church and state, aristocracy and affluent middle class. Baroque architecture achieved a sculptured effect by balancing the massiveness of its basic structure with elaborate decoration and exploitation of three-dimensional effects. Even the cylindrical columns of the facades were grouped in pairs. Baroque music displayed the same dualism with balanced vocal-instrumental groups, consistent use of two-part (binary) forms, and the reduction of the church modes to only two modes: major and minor.

The emergence of instrumental music to a position of equal importance with vocal music virtually eliminated the a cappella style. All baroque vocal music had an instrumental accompaniment whether it was a mass, motet, oratorio, passion, cantata, or opera. Purely instrumental music established new forms such as the balanced participation of small and large groups in the concerto grosso and the pieces for two solo instruments with keyboard accompaniment (called trio sonatas). Even the dynamics were dualistic, with consistent use of alternating loud and soft passages.

Keyboard Music

Harpsichord

Dance Suite

Dancing has been a fundamental activity since the dim dawn of the human race—dances to appease the gods, to exorcise evil spirits, to invoke fertility, and for the sheer exhilaration of physical and emotional release. Dancing attained a new prestige during the seventeenth-century Age of Kings, with magnificent balls in the great courts. The lords and ladies refined lusty and sometimes crude peasant dances into a social art of grace and charm.

During the early baroque period, short instrumental pieces were composed in the manner and style of various popular dances. The exotic and erotic Sarabande, for example, was transformed into a stylized and sophisticated art form that sometimes subtly implied what the original boldly proclaimed. Later on, a similar process changed the waltz from an "indecent" dance into a popular social dance, leading finally to an art form, for example, "The

Blue Danube" by Johann Strauss, Jr. Late twentieth-century composers are likely to accord similar treatment to dances of the 1980s and 1990s. During the seventeenth century these stylized dances were combined in collections of chamber music called *dance suites* and played by harpsichords, other solo instruments, and various instrumental ensembles. There are usually five or six dances (or movements) in a suite, each a different type of dance with a standard sequence: Allemande, Courante, Sarabande, Gigue. The dance suite was truly international in character; the original folk dances were, respectively, German, French, Spanish, and English (jig). Each dance suite had, however, a basic unity; that is, *each dance was in the same key.*

For the first time in history, music acquired what was considered to be a firm and rational foundation: a key. Many centuries before, the multitudinous modes of the Greeks were reduced to the eight church modes that formed the musical material of everything from plainsong through Renaissance polyphonic music. The baroque saw the emergence of two new concepts: (1) all music written in a consistent pitch relationship called a key, with a choice of either major or minor mode, and (2) a temporary disenchantment with the complexities of polyphonic music in favor of blocks of sound called chords or harmony.

By exploiting homophonic music (one sound, i.e., one block of harmony following another) and a fixed pitch relationship, composers were merely reflecting the new view of reality. The "old music" was gradually replaced by less complicated music that was considered to be lucid and rational, though of course always expressive. This is not to say that this was a conscious decision by anyone or that there was instant recognition of the drastic changes that had taken place. Rather, musicians, like all artists, reacted to the new view of reality with a combination of old and new techniques that gave a fresh sound to a new age.

This new sound, as in the music of Johann Sebastian Bach (1685–1750), can be considered the beginning of modern music. Compositions by twentieth-century composers such as Stravinsky, Prokofiev, and Bartók are more closely related to the music of Bach than Bach's work relates, in turn, to the Renaissance. Palestrina, Lassus, and other Renaissance musicians were writing for the church and for an educated aristocracy. Bach, though sometimes serving as a court composer, also performed routine services that ranged from conducting choir rehearsals to composing music for next Sunday's worship service.

The music of Bach is admired for its artistry and its superb craftsmanship. In his own day, however, Bach composed much of his music in response to specific demands. Many of his organ works were written and performed for church services and special programs. His sacred cantatas, written for particular Sundays of the liturgical year, were normally performed only once. Having served their purpose, they were consigned to storage where, many years later, a young Mozart could discover them and exclaim, "Now here is a man from whom I can learn," or words to that effect.

Figure 22.1 *Harpsichord, 1981. D. Jacques Way & Zuckermann Harpsichords.*

Much of Bach's output was intended for performance by amateur musicians and, more importantly, to be listened to by audiences composed essentially of middle-class German burghers. This middle class, of increasing affluence and influence, was becoming the primary audience not only of that period, but of all subsequent periods. Today's mass audience is a logical development of the processes that began during the eighteenth century.

The following dance suite for harpsichord is typical of solo keyboard music of the baroque. The setting for a performance could be as simple as an amateur performing in the parlor of a middle-class home or as elaborate as a professional performance at a royal court on a highly decorated harpsichord, somewhat like the modern harpsichord in figure 22.1. The suite is in six movements with only the last movement on the Listening Tape.[1]

---

1. From this point on, only a relatively small number of works could be included on the Listening Tape. Recordings of the music of all major composers since the Renaissance are readily available.

Listening Example 19

DANCE SUITE

Bach, *French Suite No. 4 in E-Flat Major*
6. Gigue (from English or Irish jig)
J. S. Bach (1685–1750)

Organ

Fugue

Intellectuals of the Enlightenment believed there was a basic explanation for the rational order of the universe—and the discoveries of Isaac Newton seemed (at that time) to support this point of view. Composers of the era mirrored this view with their consistent use of a single musical concept called, variously, *motive, theme, subject, melody,* or *tune.* They wrote *monothematic* (one theme) compositions and depended on their craftsmanship, intellectual agility, and musical sensitivity to keep their one-theme compositions from becoming exercises in monotony. Not all baroque composers succeeded and not even the best composers consistently won this game of intellectual musicianship.

The musical rules for writing monothematic dance suites, fugues, inventions, preludes, passacaglias, and so forth were well established by the eighteenth century. Superb musicians such as J. S. Bach could take a single theme and spin a web of glorious sound. Bach brought fugue writing to its highest point of artistic perfection; his *Art of Fugue,* written for a keyboard instrument, is considered the epitome of the art and the craft.

The prime instrument for the performance of fugues and other monothematic styles was the pipe organ. Baroque organs were the only solo instruments capable of filling baroque churches and concert halls with a variety and volume of sound unequaled by any other instrument. The clarity and grandeur of these magnificent instruments has never been surpassed. The proof of this statement can still be heard throughout Europe; many of the original instruments have never ceased pouring forth the unique color and brilliance of the baroque (figure 22.2).

A fugue has been called the strictest free form in music *and* the freest strict form in music. Both statements happen to be true, because the composer is limited to a theme that must occur throughout the composition in essentially its original form. However, the composition has no prescribed length nor any standard methods of achieving variety amidst the almost constant restatement of the theme in one voice or another. Writing a fugue is a thoroughly rational procedure that tests the composer's craft: making musical sense out of what is essentially a mathematical exercise. And now to the rules of the game.

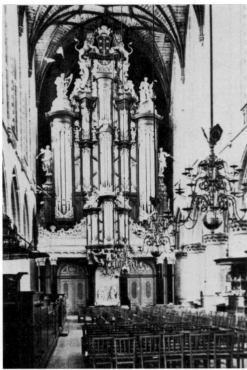

Figure 22.2 *Baroque pipe organ, dating from the fifteenth century with eighteenth-century casework, Grote Kerk, Haarlem, Holland. Organ designers were as concerned with the exterior design of the case as with the tone quality of the pipes.*

A *fugue* is an exercise in ingenuity. The composer uses a single theme (called *subject*) that is played (or sung) several times by each voice throughout a composition, for example, four voices in a four-part fugue. Fugues have staggered entries (begin with one voice, add a second voice, third voice, etc.) exactly like the imitative entries of Renaissance choral music. In fugue, however, there is only the single subject, with variety provided in part by *episodes,* or sections in which none of the voices has the subject.

After the first voice has sounded the subject, a second voice answers (starts the subject) while the first voice moves into a *counter subject,* which is a secondary theme used against (counter to) the subject. There may be two or even three counter subjects, and they may be used every time the subject appears. A typical opening fugal pattern would look like this:

1. Subject _____ Counter Subject 1

2. Subject _____

(sometimes called Answer)

Following is an organ fugue by J. S. Bach. The long subject is given in its entirety, for it is typical of Bach's strong, rhythmical themes. The fugue is referred to as "Little" because Bach wrote another, more elaborate fugue in the same key of g minor, referred to as "Great."

Organ Fugue in g Minor ("Little")

J. S. Bach
Time: 4:00

Subject

Instrumental

Trio Sonata

Baroque music was particularly notable for the widespread development of private music making by zealous performers who played or sang for the sheer joy of making their own music. Not all of them were as skilled as professionals, but self-expression was more important than technical proficiency. These multitudes of musicians whose personal pleasure was more than sufficient payment for performance were *amateurs:* true lovers of music in the best sense of the term.

Musical instruments became necessary functional furniture for a burgeoning middle class that grew ever more affluent. Baroque music was, in many respects, ready-made for amateur performances (or vice versa?), because composers never indicated the exact speed or tempo of their compositions nor did they do more than provide occasional directions regarding dynamics (relative loudness or softness). These procedures gave amateurs considerable margin for error. Moreover, specific directions as to which instruments were to be used were frequently left to the discretion (and resources) of the performers.

The ubiquitous trio sonata provided ideal material for amateurs because it was written in the conventional form of two melodic lines plus generalized directions for keyboard accompaniment. The two melodies could be performed by any two available instruments and the accompaniment by any keyboard instrument (clavichord, harpsichord, or pipe organ). The pivotal figures in trio sonatas (and large compositions) were the keyboard performers; it was assumed that they were the most competent musicians, which was usually the case. They provided the foundation for the *continuation* of the piece, which led to the adoption of the Italian word *continuo* to describe the function of the keyboard musicians. It was up to them to fill in the harmony and to cover up the blank spots whenever the less-expert performers played wrong notes, lost their place, or otherwise strayed from grace.

Baroque chamber music (but also including operatic arias) was highly improvisational because performers were expected to add their personal touches to a given melodic line. Compositions were "personalized" through available instruments, the expertise and imagination of performers and, most importantly, the musical challenge presented by the composer. Not until jazz appeared on the scene during the latter part of the nineteenth century did performers again have the individual freedom that was accorded amateur and professional musicians of the baroque period.

Concerto

The classic baroque concerto was the *concerto grosso* in which a small group of soloists *(concertino)* performed in conjunction with a full orchestra *(tutti* or *concerto grosso).* Bach, Handel, and Vivaldi did write *solo concertos* for single instruments, but baroque composers generally preferred the sonority of the concertino as it blended and contrasted with the full orchestra. An excellent example of the concerto grosso is the *Concerto for Two Trumpets* by Antonio Vivaldi.

Vivaldi wrote more than 450 concertos, the most famous of which are *The Four Seasons* for solo violin and orchestra. Each season—Spring, Summer, Autumn, Winter—has three movements that together evoke different aspects of the season. The four concertos are remarkable early examples of "program music," that is, music describing or communicating extra-musical ideas. As might be expected, the first concerto is bright and cheerful, full of allusions to nature's annual rebirth.

VIOLIN CONCERTO
Vivaldi, *Spring* from *The Four Seasons*
1. Allegro

Time: 2:20

Vocal-Instrumental

Chorale

Martin Luther translated the Bible into German because he believed that every Christian should have direct access to the text. He was also concerned about congregational participation in the service of worship because it tended to bind the congregation and the clergy together in a common endeavor. Moreover, music had, in Luther's opinion, a spiritual, transcendental quality that enriched and elevated the worship service. Unlike John Calvin, Luther, once a priest of the Church of Rome, culled the rich musical heritage of the Church, selecting and adapting plainsong to the needs and capabilities of Protestant congregations. For the first time in many centuries, common people once again took an active part in worship as they raised their voices in song. They sang what we would call hymns, though hymn tunes of the Lutheran church are called *chorales*.

The typical Lutheran service of the eighteenth century began at 7:00 A.M. and concluded at noon. In the larger churches professional musicians (such as Bach) were expected to teach school during the week, maintain the organ, train a volunteer choir, compose special instrumental and vocal music for each Sunday of the year, and play the organ and direct the choir during the Sunday service. Each Sunday occupied a special place in the liturgical year, with special emphasis on Christmas, the Epiphany, Easter, and Pentecost. The music for each Sunday of the liturgical calendar had to correspond with the special meaning of that Sunday from the opening chorale prelude through the hymns, the cantata, and the concluding postlude.

Chorale Prelude

An organ composition consisting of variations on a chorale melody is called a *chorale prelude*. The variations are to be played *before* the congregation sings the chorale, hence the term *prelude*. The intention of the organist is to set the general mood of the chorale so the congregation can sing it with more understanding.

The following chorale prelude is based on the Lutheran chorale *Sleepers Awake, A Voice Is Calling*. The opening section has a sprightly melody over a smoothly striding bass. The first part of the chorale melody becomes a third voice about halfway through the opening section, after which the entire section is repeated. In the second (concluding) section the chorale melody is interspersed throughout.

Listening Example 21

CHORALE PRELUDE

Bach, Schubler Chorale Preludes, S.645/50 (1746)
5. *Wachet auf* (Sleepers Awake)

Oratorio

An *oratorio* is a sacred or epic text set to music and performed in a church or concert hall by soloists, chorus, and orchestra; it can also be described as a concert version of a sacred opera. In the latter part of his career George Frederick Handel, the foremost composer in eighteenth-century London, turned from composing operas for an indifferent nobility to writing oratorios for the middle class. Of his twenty-one oratorios, the most celebrated is *The Messiah*. This extended composition was written in feverish haste—completed in only three weeks—leading Handel to believe it was divinely inspired. Based mainly on the New Testament, it is divided into three sections. Concluding the second section, the brilliant Hallelujah Chorus so impressed George II that he spontaneously rose to his feet, thus setting the tradition of a standing audience for this stirring chorus. The text consists primarily of "hallelujah," a Hebrew word of jubilation that has been called the college cheer of Christendom.

Opera

Opera (Italian, from Latin *opera*, work) is generally considered to be the most "baroque" of all the artistic media of the age. Opera began as a "reform" movement in the late sixteenth century as an attempt to return to what was mistakenly thought to be the proper combination of words and music used by the ancient Greeks. Text was all-important, vocal lines were sparse, and accompaniment minimal. However, within a remarkably short period opera developed into full-blown music drama with elaborate sets, costumes, and choruses. Despite various regional differences in style among Florence, Rome, Venice, Vienna, Paris, and London, opera became the most popular and spectacular art form of the period. Elaborate opera houses were built all over Europe for an art form which, in a manner of speaking, put the vitality of an era on stage for all to see and hear.

Italian operas became the favorite artistic import for most of the nations of western Europe. French nationalism, however, strongly resisted the dominance of Italian music. Critics lambasted Italian operas as being too long, monotonous, too arty, archaic in language, and with flamboyant singing that obscured the sound and the sense of the words, thus leaving no appeal to the logical French mind. Additionally, the male sopranos and altos—the *castrati*—were said to horrify the women and to cause the men to snicker.

Listening Example 22

ORATORIO CHORUS

Handel, *The Messiah* (1742)
44. Hallelujah Chorus

Time: 3:53

But the French resisted Italian opera because they valued dance over drama. Italian dramatic opera was not in the same league with the theatre of Corneille, Racine, and Molière. Dance—French ballet—was central to the French musical stage but only minimal in Italian opera.

The struggle between French and Italian music became an actual confrontation when the Italian opera composer, Cavalli, was commissioned to write a festive opera for the wedding of Louis XIV. The director of the king's music, Jean Baptiste Lully (1632–1687)—born Gianbattista Lulli in Florence—turned the occasion to his advantage. The opera was indeed performed in 1662 for the king's wedding and it was monumental, lasting some six hours. However, each act concluded with one of Lully's large-scale ballets. The French reaction to this spectacle was interesting: the production was seen, not as a music drama with interpolated dances, but as a gigantic ballet with operatic interludes. Cavalli returned to Italy, vowing never to write another opera while Lully continued his intrigues becoming, in time, as absolute a sovereign in music as Louis XIV was in affairs of state. Capping a highly successful career, Lully died with one of the greatest fortunes ever amassed by a musician.

Rococo, 1725–1775

The last stage of the baroque period is characterized by an even more ornate style called *rococo* (from the French, *rocaille,* rock, and *coquilles,* shells). The baroque principles of design were applied to surfaces rather than to outlines. The grandeur of the baroque was scaled down to an emphasis on interior design and decorative scroll and shell work, resulting in a sort of domesticated, sometimes decadent, baroque.

In music, *rococo* is the "gallant style," a highly refined art of elegant pleasantness suitable for intimate social gatherings in fashionable salons. Among the chief exponents were François Couperin and Domenico Scarlatti with rococo styles comparable to the painting of Watteau and Boucher, and the sculpture of Falconet.

The Amalienburg lodge (figure 22.3), located on the grounds of Nymphenburg Palace near Munich, represents the epitome of rococo refinement, grace, and elegance: opulence on a small scale. The central mirror reflects an outside window, indicating a room large enough for masked balls, but small enough

Figure 22.3 *François Cuvilliés, Hall of Mirrors, The Amalienburg, Nymphenburg Palace, Munich, 1734–1739.*

to be intimate. Approximately thirty couples could dance to a small chamber orchestra or listen to a harpsichord recital. The room is a compendium of rococo characteristics: white plaster ceiling with lacy silver tendrils, lavish use of mirrors, all with curvilinear frames, light blue walls with silver insets and shell-like decoration, parquet floor, elaborately carved furniture in silver with cabriole legs and, highlighting the room, an array of exquisite chandeliers.

François Couperin (1668–1733)

The foremost rococo composer was Couperin, usually referred to as "le Grand." His music crystallizes the miniature world of the rococo; it is a counterpart to the art of Cuvilliés in the Hall of Mirrors (see figure 22.3). Moreover, his work is French to the core: scintillating, elegant, refined, and witty. He wrote twenty-seven *ordres* or sets of dances for harpsichord, all with evocative titles. The name of the following composition is typically whimsical. It translates literally as "hook in leg" and means tripping someone. In this case it is the music that goes tripping along, lighthearted and saucy.

Listening Example 23

DANCE MOVEMENT FOR HARPSICHORD

Couperin, *Le Croc-en-jambe* from Ordre No. 22

Classicism in Music, 1760–1827

The classical period in music dates from about 1760, the beginning of Haydn's mature style, to about 1827, the year of Beethoven's death. Haydn, Mozart, and Beethoven were musical giants in what has been called the Golden Age of Music, an era of extraordinary musical achievements. Other eras have perhaps been as musically productive, but none has become so mutually identifiable as the classical period, the Golden Age, and the musical output of Haydn, Mozart, and Beethoven.

The basic homophonic style of classicism has many antecedents in several earlier periods of music. It is therefore appropriate to briefly review these earlier periods.

Renaissance music was primarily polyphonic and written in the old liturgical modes. Some Renaissance music, English madrigals in particular, was quite homophonic and was, moreover, tonal; that is, it was written in either a major or a minor key rather than in a liturgical mode. The music of Gabrieli in Venice was also strongly homophonic with a preference for sonorous harmonies rather than the multiple melody lines used by Renaissance composers such as Josquin, Lassus, and Palestrina.

At the beginning of the seventeenth century there was a relatively brief period of strongly homophonic music as composers attempted to re-create what they thought was the text-oriented musical style of the ancient Greeks. These experiments in words and music led to the development of the new style of music called opera. Opera, the epitome of the new baroque style, quickly became elaborate and ornate and combined homophonic and polyphonic music. The vocal-instrumental music of the age developed a new and complex style of polyphony, culminating in the music of Handel and Bach.

The rococo style used baroque ornamentation, but the style was much more homophonic, less profound, and more stylishly elegant. Some of the characteristics of the rococo, notably less complex homophonic techniques, were incorporated into a new style called *classicism, neoclassicism,* or *Viennese classicism* (Haydn, Mozart, Beethoven). Classicism is the preferred term for music of the period, whereas neoclassicism is generally applied to the sister arts.

At no time are the stylistic periods of the arts precisely synchronized. Careful study of the comparative outline given (table 22.1) will indicate that the prevailing worldviews of the periods since the Renaissance are reflected in the arts at different times. Any number of inferences can be drawn regarding the influence of an era on the arts and the arts on each other. However, the artistic production of specific individuals is of paramount concern. The uniqueness of the works of art reflects the uniqueness of the individual, the artist who creates these works.

The classical period of music might also be called the Advanced Age of the Amateur Musician. Baroque music, with its figured bass accompaniments and demands for improvisation, was partially the province of the professional but with real possibilities for gifted amateurs. On the other hand, the latter part of the eighteenth century featured modern notation, with every note written down plus indications for interpretation (tempo, dynamics, etc.), thus providing a better opportunity for music making by middle- and upper-class amateurs.

The vastly increased demand for music for all occasions resulted in a flood of mostly instrumental compositions. There were serenades for outdoor parties, chamber music for indoor gatherings, symphonies for the newly established symphony orchestras, and operas for the increasing number of private and public opera houses. The newly invented piano (ca. 1710 by Cristofori), with its ability to play soft and loud (full name, *pianoforte*) on the single keyboard, rapidly replaced harpsichord and clavichord as the standard home instrument for amateur performance. Amateur chamber music societies were organized for the presentation of programs ranging from sonatas to duets and trios for the various instruments, including the quartets for a homogeneous group of string instruments called, naturally enough, string quartets.

All of this musical activity was of little benefit to those who tried to earn a living with their music. Eighteenth-century musicians were, on the whole, accorded a lowly position on the social scale. Typically, composers such as Franz Joseph Haydn worked for a noble family like the Esterhazy, wore servant's livery, and sat at the dinner table "below the salt." Not until the latter part of

TABLE 22.1 Comparison of Stylistic Periods of the Arts

		Approximate Dates	Important Individuals
Period: The Age of Reason		1600–1700	Descartes, Galileo, Kepler, Bacon, Spinoza
Artistic Style:	Baroque		
	Architecture	1575–1740	Bernini, Wren, Mansart, Perrault, LeVau
	Music	1600–1750	Corelli, Lully, Vivaldi, Handel, Bach, Purcell
	Painting	1600–1720	Rubens, Rembrandt, Steen, Hals, Vermeer, van Dyck, Velasquez
	Sculpture	1600–1720	Bernini
Period: The Enlightenment		1687–1789	Newton, Voltaire, Diderot, Locke, Hume, Kant, Rousseau, Frederick II, Jefferson, Franklin
Artistic Style:	Rococo		
	Architecture	1715–1760	Erlach, Hildebrandt, Asam, Cuvilliés, Fischer
	Music	1725–1775	Couperin, some of Haydn and Mozart
	Painting	1720–1789	Watteau, Chardin, Boucher, Fragonard
	Sculpture	1770–1825	Clodion, Falconet
Artistic Style:	Neoclassic		
	Architecture	1750–1830	Chalgrin, Vignon, Fontaine
	Music (Classicism)	1760–1827	Haydn, Mozart, Beethoven, Gluck
	Painting	1780–1850	David, Ingres
	Sculpture	1800–1840	Canova, Thorwalden, Houdon

his life did Haydn achieve any financial independence, and he had to go to the London concert scene to do it. Ironically, the descendants of the once powerful Esterhazy family are notable today only to the extent that some of Haydn's unpublished music may still be in their possession.

Franz Joseph Haydn, 1732–1809

Haydn's professional life was typical of the vicissitudes of a musical career, yet he fared better than many of his contemporaries. In a short sketch that he contributed to a 1776 yearbook, Haydn wrote that he sang at court in Vienna and in St. Stephen's Cathedral until his services were terminated at the latter. His services were eminently satisfactory but his voice changed and he was summarily dismissed.

> When my voice finally changed I barely managed to stay alive by giving music lessons to children for about eight years. In this way many talented people are ruined: they have to earn a miserable living and have no time to study.

There were numerous musical opportunities for a musician in Vienna, and most of them paid very little. Musicians were forced to hold down a number of positions in order to survive. Haydn had as many as three jobs on a Sunday morning: playing violin at one church, the organ at another, and singing in the choir at a third. When he finally achieved full employment with the Esterhazy family, he was quite willing, at that time, to relinquish a certain amount of personal freedom.

Haydn, as the first of the composers in the classical style, led the way in establishing such basic instrumental ensembles as the symphony orchestra and the string quartet. Large enough to produce a rich, full tone but small enough to be intimate and to leave room for personal expression, the string quartet was the preferred classical musical group. Consisting of first and second violin, viola, and cello, corresponding to the SATB division of voices in choral music, the three members of the violin family can achieve a fine balance of unified tone.

Haydn's *String Quartet in F Major,* opus 3, no. 5, was composed early in his career and has both rococo and classical characteristics. The forms are classical and the melodies quite rococo in their lightness, clarity, and elegance. The first, second, and last movements use *sonata form,* an important invention of the period.

Classical composers had tired of the late baroque proclivity for ever more elaborate and sometimes ponderous polyphony. A simpler homophonic style began to emerge and to gradually replace the polyphonic manipulation of a single musical theme. By abandoning the polyphonic vocal-instrumental style, composers were faced with a dilemma: how to develop a coherent style of purely instrumental music. A certain unity was inherent in vocal music because of the text. Without a text, composers were faced with the possibility of a chaotic mass of instrumental sounds.

Sonata form[2] was an eighteenth-century solution to the problem of the design of instrumental music. In a very real sense, the invention of sonata form reflected the Enlightenment ideals of a structure that was lucid, logical, and symmetrical.

The technical term *sonata form* is a label for a procedure that uses a *dual subject* rather than the single subject of the baroque style. The first of these two subjects is usually vigorous and dynamic but the second is generally quieter and more lyrical. The two subjects should be, musically speaking, logical parts of the whole; the second subject should somehow complement and balance the first.

In the first movement of the Haydn quartet given below, *theme a* is straightforward and vigorous; *theme b* is smoother and more lyrical and with the stipulation that it be played "sweetly." The two subjects (themes) of sonata form are connected by a *bridge,* a transitional passage, which leads smoothly from *theme a* to *theme b.* Following *theme b* there is a closing section called a *codetta.* The complete unit of two themes with connecting transition and closing section contains all the thematic material which has been presented or to which the ear has been *exposed.* This unit is called an *exposition* and can be outlined as indicated below. During the classical period expositions were normally repeated, as indicated by the sets of double dots.

Exposition
||:*Theme a* Bridge *Theme b* Codetta:||

After the basic material has been presented in the exposition, the composer then proceeds to manipulate and exploit selected thematic material in the *development* section. Any and all material may be subjected to a variety of treatment.

Near the end of the development section, the composer usually introduces the *return,* a transitional section that prepares the way for a *recapitulation* of the material from the exposition. The recapitulation repeats, more or less, the material from the exposition, but there are subtle variances that help avoid monotony.

After the codetta of the recapitulation, the composer may add a final *coda* if it is felt that something is needed to bring the movement to a satisfactory conclusion.

A complete sonata form can be outlined as follows:

Exposition	Development		Recapitulation
||:*a* bridge *b* codetta:||:			return *a* bridge *b* codetta (coda):||

Wolfgang Amadeus Mozart, 1756–1791

Musical genius has been a subject of considerable interest to twentieth-century psychologists but the exact nature of the qualities that can be labeled "genius" remains tantalizingly elusive. Thus the accomplishments of Mozart, possibly the greatest musical genius who ever lived, are both awesome and inexplicable.

Mozart devoted virtually his entire life to the composition and performance of music. Like Haydn, he endured the slights of a society as yet unready and unwilling to recognize, let alone support, his incredible gifts. Unlike Haydn, he never found a noble patron. His brief, poverty-stricken life and eventual burial in an unmarked grave testify much too eloquently to the status of a musician in Vienna during the Golden Age of Music.

There are many accounts of Mozart's precocity but none more typical of his manner of composition—and life-style—than the premiere of his opera *Don Giovanni.* The opera was complete except for the overture that was, according to the composer, "finished." On the day of the premiere, Mozart was busily engaged in shooting billiards, one of his favorite occupations. In reply to urgent questioning, he reiterated that he had completed the overture. When pressed to produce a musical score, he finally admitted that the piece was indeed completed—in his head—but not yet written down. Many cups of coffee later, the complete parts, still dripping with wet ink, were rushed to the opera house where the orchestra had to sight-read the music. Characteristically, the thousands of musical notes that Mozart had mentally arranged added up to a masterpiece in operatic literature.

Symphony No. 35 was written for a festive occasion in the house of Siegmund Haffner, the *Burgermeister* (Mayor) of Salzburg. Originally a six-movement serenade, it was completed in the amazing time of only two weeks. Six months after finishing it he wrote his father that "the new Haffner symphony has quite astonished me, for I do not remember a note of it. It must be very effective." Mozart's evaluation of his new symphony is modest, for this is a joyful work of great brilliance. The example given here, the light-footed and witty fourth movement, is in sonata form.

---

2. Sonata form was not limited to sonatas, which are compositions for solo instruments plus accompaniment. The form was also used for trios, quartets, concertos, and symphonies.

Listening Example 24

SYMPHONIC MOVEMENT

Mozart, *Symphony No. 35 in D, K.385, "Haffner"*
(1782)
4. Presto

Theme a   *Time: 3:34*

Theme b

Mozart Summary

A summary of Mozart's musical compositions is given below. The list indicates at least three things: (1) the breadth of Mozart's musical interests; (2) the kinds of music required of Mozart (most of his work was commissioned); and (3) the incredible productivity of a sometimes destitute young musician who died in his thirty-sixth year.

Vocal

Secular

  57 Arias
  24 Operas and other stage works
  19 Duets and trios
  37 Songs
Many cadenzas

Sacred

   8 Cantatas
  37 Kyries and other works
   7 Litanies and vespers
  19 Masses
  17 Church sonatas (organ)
   4 Oratorio arrangements

Instrumental

Piano

  10 Piano duets
  35 Minuets and variations
  12 Trios, quartets, quintets
  33 Sonatas and fantasias
  30 Piano concertos
   9 Miscellaneous compositions
Many cadenzas

Violin, Strings, Orchestra

  40 Violin sonatas
  11 Violin concertos
   5 String duets and trios
  25 String quartets
   6 String quintets
  13 Miscellaneous chamber works
  13 Miscellaneous concertos
  52 Symphonies
 101 Serenades, divertimenti, cassations, etc.

Ludwig van Beethoven, 1770–1827

Unlike Haydn and Mozart, Beethoven forged a place for himself as an economically independent musician. He was not above selling the same composition to different publishers and did so quite often. He reasoned that the publishers had cheated composers long enough; he was merely collecting retribution for a long chain of abuses.

Beethoven's finances were generally sound though somewhat chaotic. His health was another matter. He noticed a hearing loss at an early age that gradually evolved into total deafness. This silence became, at times, almost more than a musician could bear.

That some of Beethoven's greatest music was composed while he was completely deaf is a testament to his genius and to his unconquerable spirit. He himself conducted the premiere of his Ninth Symphony, that powerful and imposing work dedicated to the exalted ideal of the Brotherhood of Man. At the conclusion of the symphony he remained facing the orchestra, solitary in his silence, and thinking that the work had failed. Finally, someone turned him about to face the thunderous applause of an audience that was both inspired and deeply moved.

Beethoven's Third Symphony, the *Eroica,* was originally dedicated to Napoleon, whom Beethoven regarded as a true Faustian man who labored to improve the lives of all the people. There were many victims of Napoleon's march to power—"while man's desires and aspirations stir, he cannot choose but err"—but it appeared that he was using his energy to make the world a better place in which people could work out their freedom. However, Napoleon declared himself emperor, and Beethoven furiously erased his name from the dedicatory page of the *Eroica,* leaving the work implicitly dedicated to the heroic impulses of a Faustian man or, simply, to an unknown hero.

Beethoven poured the very essence of classical symphonic music into his Fifth Symphony, a work that has often been cited as the perfect symphony. Though sometimes threatening to break the bounds of classical form, Beethoven, in the Fifth, channeled his titanic energy into the driving rhythms of this mighty work. The Fifth Symphony is a summary of many aspects of Beethoven's genius: the terse, surging energy of the first movement, the moving and mellow lyricism of the second movement, the exuberant vitality of the scherzo, and the sheer drive of the finale.

The orchestra as Beethoven knew it was simply not large and expressive enough for this symphony. He enlarged his tonal palette by adding instruments at both ends of the spectrum and then adding trombones in the middle to obtain the full and rich sound that he had to have. Following is the instrumentation for the enlarged orchestra needed to perform Beethoven's Fifth Symphony: piccolo, two flutes, two oboes, two clarinets, two bassoons, contra-bassoon, two French horns, two trumpets, three trombones, two timpani, sixteen violin I, fourteen violin II, ten violas, eight cellos, six basses. (The number of strings can vary; these are approximations.)

The first movement is in sonata form. The second movement is a theme and variations. The theme is stated and then followed by a series of increasingly elaborate variations. Rather than a minuet, Beethoven uses a scherzo for the third movement, which is faster and more dynamic. For the fourth movement Beethoven uses sonata form with a very long coda.

The Fifth Symphony achieves a maximum effect with the utmost economy of musical materials. Essentially, the entire symphony is built out of one musical interval and one rhythmic pattern:

Interval of 3rd plus pattern of

This *motive* is so brief that it is referred to as a *germ motive* from which the entire symphony is germinated.

Listening Example 25

SYMPHONIC MOVEMENT
Beethoven, *Symphony No. 5 in C Minor,* op. 67
(1808)
3. Scherzo

Scherzo: form is Scherzo-Trio-Scherzo (A-B-A)
Note: Scherzo is similar in form to the minuet but faster and more
vigorous.

Scherzo:
Theme a

Time: 3:38

pp low strings

violins

Theme b

Horns

ff

Trio
Theme a

f low strings (cellos, basses)

The Fifth Symphony is a prime example of the classical style: logical, direct and to the point, objective, controlled, achieving maximum effect with a minimum of means (the germ motive).

Beethoven is considered by some to be a pivotal figure in musical styles standing midway between classicism and the dawning Age of Romanticism; however, his heroic style and even his introspective later works all testify to his fundamental classical outlook, namely, his rational control of his own destiny. Beethoven's music served *him;* he was the master who, with disciplined creativity, molded (and sometimes hammered) his musical materials into the structured sounds of the classical style.

Summary

From about 1600 to 1750 the baroque style built a new kind of music on the classical foundations of the Renaissance. The flexible modal system of the past was narrowed down to a single tonal center, or *key,* with the modal possibilities reduced to two: major or minor. Compensating for the limiting of tonal materials to a single major or minor key were the new possibilities for composing in terms of contrasting keys and modulating from one key to another.

With the establishment of a tonal center, the *fugue* became one of the basic monothematic styles of the baroque. Composers could manipulate both the fugal subject and various major and minor key relations.

The ubiquitous *trio sonata* was perhaps most representative of baroque music making because of the emphasis on instrumental music with improvised accompaniment in the *continuo* part. *Concertos* were more formal because of the larger number of instrumentalists involved, but the continuo still played an important accompanying part for orchestra and soloist(s).

Following the Reformation, the German sacred songs called *chorales* assumed an important place in congregational singing and in organ literature in the form of *chorale preludes. Cantatas, oratorios,* and *operas* were the most important vocal forms of the baroque although there was still a tradition of composing masses and motets. The surface elements of the ornate baroque style assumed a primary emphasis in the style called rococo. The rococo, or "gallant style" of music (1725–1775), with its light, airy texture and elegant ornamentation, served as a bridge between the sumptuous baroque and the gracefully refined style of the classical period.

During the classical period (1760–1827), instrumental musicians, whether professional or amateur, came into their own. The improvement in musical instruments and the great interest in amateur performance encouraged the composition of chamber music (*sonatas, string quartets,* etc.) and orchestral music ranging from *serenades* for soirees to *symphonies* for the growing number of concert halls. Monothematic polyphony was replaced by a dual-subject (bithematic) structure called *sonata form* in which composers could combine two contrasting subjects into an expressive and balanced whole.

The classical period, coinciding with the height of the Age of Enlightenment, created chamber music and the symphony orchestra virtually as they are known today. Even more important, music progressed from a more or less private concern of the aristocracy or the church to a public art available to all.

Culture and Human Values

All of us are so accustomed to the ready availability of all kinds of music that we tend to forget that mass audiences for music are a relatively recent phenomenon. As late as the seventeenth century, the musical patrons were still the courts and, to a lesser extent, the Church of Rome. Protestant churches, particularly Lutheran, were far more active in commissioning music and hiring organists and choirmasters. Just as active was bourgeois Holland where both music and art were enjoyed by the good Dutch burghers. The common element in the Lutheran churches and in Holland was the growing middle class.

By the eighteenth century music had become much more of a public art. Virtually anyone with money could rent a hall and hire musicians, but few could make a living as a composer. Handel did fairly well in London, particularly with his oratorios, but Bach's reputation was based entirely on his remarkable skills as a performer. Mozart attempted to survive in Vienna as a composer without a patron but only eked out a bare living. By the end of the century, however, Beethoven had proved that music had finally become a profession in which one could make a living composing and performing. It was at this point that one can say musical art had gone public.

Exercises

1. Explain the forces that helped convert music from a private to a public art.
2. What are the pressures when music depends on an admission-paying public?

THE MIDDLE
MODERN WORLD,
1789-1914

THE MIDDLE MODERN WORLD

1789-1914

	People and Events	Art and Architecture	Literature and Music	Philosophy, Science, Invention
1800	**1760–1820** George III of England **1774–1793** Louis XVI of France **1789–1815** French Revolution **1801–1825** Alexander I of Russia **1804–1812** Napoleon Emperor of France **1814–1824** Louis XVIII of France **1815** Napoleon defeated at Waterloo **1820–1830** George IV of England **1821–1830** Greek revolt from Turks **1824–1830** Charles X of France **1825–1855** Nicholas I of Russia **1830** July Revolution in France **1830–1848** Louis Philippe of France, constitutional monarch **1830–1837** William IV of England **1837–1901** Victoria of England **1848** *Communist Manifesto* **1848–1852** Second Republic in France **1851** Crystal Palace, "Great Exhibition of the Works of All Nations" **1852–1870** Napoleon III of France **1853–1856** Crimean War **1855–1881** Alexander II of Russia **1859** *Origin of Species* by Darwin **1861–1878** Victor Emmanuel II of Italy **1870–1871** Franco-Prussian War **1871–** Third Republic in France **1871** *Descent of Man* by Darwin **1871–1888** Wilhelm I, Emperor of Germany **1878–1900** Humbert I of Italy **1881–1894** Alexander III of Russia **1888–1918** Wilhelm II, Emperor of Germany **1889** Paris Exhibition; Eiffel Tower **1894–1918** Nicholas II of Russia **1899–1902** Boer War **1900–1946** Victor Emmanuel III of Italy **1901–1910** Edward VII of England **1910–1936** George V of England	**Goya** 1746–1828 *Grand hazaña! Con muertos!* **Turner** 1775–1851 *Keelman Heaving Coals by Moonlight* **Constable** 1776–1837 *Wivenhoe Park, Essex* **Ingres** 1780–1867 *Grand Odalisque* **Géricault** 1791–1824 *The Raft of the Medusa* **Corot** 1796–1875 *Forest of Fontainbleau* **Delacroix** 1799–1863 *Arabs Skirmishing in the Mountains* **Cole** 1801–1848 *Oxbow* **Paxton** 1801–1865 The Crystal Palace **Daumier** 1808–1879 *Third-Class Carriage* **Bingham** 1811–1879 *Fur Traders Descending the Missouri* **Millet** 1814–1875 *The Sower* **Courbet** 1819–1877 *Burial at Ornans* **Manet** 1832–1883 *Olympia* **Degas** 1834–1917 *Four Dancers* **Whistler** 1834–1903 *The White Girl: Symphony in White, No. 1* **Homer** 1836–1910 *Breezing Up* **Cézanne** 1839–1906 *Le Château Noir* **Rodin** 1840–1917 *The Thinker* **Monet** 1840–1926 *Rouen Cathedral* **Renoir** 1841–1919 *Le Moulin de la Galette* **Morisot** 1841–1895 *In the Dining Room* **Eakins** 1844–1916 *Max Schmitt in a Single Scull* **Cassatt** 1844–1926 *The Bath* **Rousseau** 1844–1910 *The Equatorial Jungle* **Gauguin** 1848–1903 *Vision after the Sermon* **van Gogh** 1853–1890 *The Starry Night* **Seurat** 1859–1891 *Sunday Afternoon on the Island of La Grande Jatte* **Toulouse-Lautrec** 1864–1901 *Quadrille at the Moulin Rouge* **Munch** 1864–1944 *The Scream*	**Rousseau** 1712–1778 *Émile* **Goethe** 1749–1832 *Faust* **Schiller** 1759–1805 "Ode to Joy" **Blake** 1757–1827 "The Tiger" **Wordsworth** 1770–1850 "The World Is Too Much With Us" **Coleridge** 1772–1834 "Kubla Khan" **Byron** 1788–1824 "Prometheus" **Shelley** 1792–1822 "To a Skylark" **Mary Shelley** 1797–1851 *Frankenstein* **Keats** 1795–1821 "La Belle Dame Sans Merci" **Schubert** 1797–1828 *Gretchen am Spinnrade* **Berlioz** 1803–1869 *Symphonie Fantastique* **Emerson** 1803–1882 "Concord Hymn" **de Tocqueville** 1805–1859 *Democracy in America* **Mendelssohn** 1809–1847 *Italian Symphony* **Poe** 1809–1849 "Annabel Lee" **Tennyson** 1809–1892 "Ulysses" **Chopin** 1810–1849 *Ballade in G minor* **Liszt** 1811–1886 *Les Preludes* **Whitman** 1819–1892 "I Hear America Singing" **Melville** 1819–1891 *Moby-Dick* **Dostoevsky** 1821–1881 "The Grand Inquisitor" **Arnold** 1822–1888 "Dover Beach" **Dickinson** 1830–1886 "A Service of Song" **Brahms** 1833–1897 *Symphony No. 3* **Twain** 1835–1910 "The Notorious Jumping Frog of Calaveras County" **Hardy** 1840–1928 "Neutral Tones" **Tchaikovsky** 1840–1893 *Symphony No. 5* **Puccini** 1858–1924 *La Bohème* **Debussy** 1862–1918 *La Mer* **Strauss** 1864–1949 *Till Eulenspiegel's Merry Pranks* **Crane** 1871–1900 "War Is Kind" **Dunbar** 1872–1906 "Sympathy"	**Bentham** 1748–1832 *Utilitarianism* **Hegel** 1770–1831 *Philosophy of History* **Schopenhauer** 1788–1860 *The World as Will and Idea* **Daguerre** 1799–1851 Photography **Faraday** 1791–1867 Discovered electromagnetic induction **Morse** 1791–1872 Painting, telegraph, and Morse Code **Mill** 1806–1873 *On Liberty* **Darwin** 1809–1882 *Origin of Species* **Kierkegaard** 1813–1855 *Fear and Trembling* **Marx** 1818–1883 *Das Kapital* **Pasteur** 1822–1895 Began bacteriology **Mendel** 1822–1884 Genetics **Thomson** 1824–1907 Transatlantic cable **(1858)** **Lister** 1827–1912 Founded antiseptic surgery **James** 1842–1910 Pragmatism **Nietzsche** 1844–1900 *Thus Spake Zarathustra* **Röntgen** 1845–1913 X-rays **Edison** 1847–1931 American inventor **Bell** 1849–1922 Telephone **Friese-Greene** 1855–1921 Invented movies **Freud** 1856–1939 Psychoanalysis **Hertz** 1857–1894 First to produce wireless that led to Marconi's radio in **1895** **Planck** 1858–1947 Quantum theory **Diesel** 1858–1913 Diesel engine **Curie** 1867–1934 Radium **Wright brothers** 1867–1912; 1871–1948 Heavier than air flight **Einstein** 1879–1955 Relativity (1905)
1900				

Revolution, Romanticism, Realism

chapter 23

Revolution to Waterloo

On 14 July 1789 a Parisian mob stormed the hated prison called the Bastille only to find a handful of bewildered prisoners. When Louis XVI asked the next day if this were a riot, the response was: "No sire, a revolution." The revolt erupted only eight years after French money and troops had materially helped her American allies defeat the British. Due partly to the American effort, the national debt was enormous and getting worse because of huge defense expenditures. Failed harvests and mismanaged financial crises led to widespread shortages and skyrocketing food prices. Whatever was wrong was blamed on the government. Hunger and anger finally touched off a revolution that was long in the making. The American example had inspired, of course, much revolutionary fervor; the enemy, however, was not a distant colonial power but the French establishment itself. Nothing less than the total destruction of the *ancien régime* would suffice. In a nation at war with its own institutions, fury and violence energized the revolution from the storming of the Bastille through the guillotine and the Reign of Terror. St. Just stated the ultimate goal quite simply: "The Republic consists in the extermination of everything that opposes it." Like so many revolutions (with the notable exception of the American Revolution), the political outcome was a tyranny, its processes auto-genocide, and its economic consequences a catastrophe.

Royalty, aristocracy, and all their properties were targeted for destruction and indeed many nobles were summarily executed while howling mobs ravaged rich estates. The revolution feasted on ferocity so pervasive that 250,000 people (one-third the population) died in just one area (the Vende) of the country. Any who opposed, hindered, or even failed to strongly support the revolution could be consumed in the firestorm of savagery and death, and many thousands were.

The revolutionary battle cry of Liberty, Equality, Fraternity was a thrilling slogan that had little to do with reality. How can you have total individual liberty *and* a strong, efficient government? How can you abolish privilege and place everyone on the same social, brotherly level in a country with few teachers, lawyers, and doctors but millions of illiterate peasants? It certainly wasn't the first time that ideals clashed with the real world.

The revolution had been incredibly destructive but there were some positive results, particularly the noble "Declaration of the Rights of Man and the Citizen." Feudalism, titles, and privileges had been abolished, the monastic orders suppressed, and church properties confiscated, but the enemies of France were assaulting the borders and internal disorder was increasing. The execution of Robespierre in 1794 ended the Terror, but it took the establishment of the Directory in 1795 to temporarily stabilize the state. Composed of men of conspicuous wealth, the Directory ruled from 1795 to 1799 with the assistance of the military, most notably the Corsican general Napoleon Buonaparte (1769–1821). Under the guise of saving the revolution Napoleon seized power in a coup d'état in 1799 and declared himself First Consul. Proclaiming himself emperor in 1804, he launched a course of conquest that engulfed much of Europe and part of Africa. Waterloo (18 June 1815) was an anticlimax to the fall of a conqueror who lost his entire Grand Army of 500,000 men on the scorched steppes of Russia.

Napoleon saw himself as the enlightened, benevolent despot who had saved the revolution (figure 23.1), but he could maintain order and control only with the army and especially his secret police. He did establish the Code of Napoleon, a model of modern civil laws that buried the inequities of the *ancien régime* and set the stage for the rise of the middle class. The Napoleonic

Figure 23.1
Jacques Louis David, Napoleon in His Study, 1812. Oil on canvas, 80½" × 49¼". Wearing the Legion of Honor, Napoleon is pictured by his court painter as a conscientious ruler who has stayed up until 4:12 A.M. working for his subjects. Samuel H. Kress Collection. National Gallery of Art, Washington, D.C.

legend of the military and political genius who fostered liberalism and nationalism contains, therefore, elements of truth. The ideals of the French Revolution did, in time, inspire the spread of democracy throughout the Western world. The other side of the coin was dark and bloody; two decades of Napoleonic wars destroyed lives and property on a staggering scale (map 23.1).

Napoleon's conquerors were deep in deliberations at the Congress of Vienna when he escaped from Elba and rallied his still loyal armies for a Hundred Days campaign that ended, once and for all, on the field of Waterloo. Final banishment to the remote island of St. Helena and a heavy guard assured the allies of a peace on their terms.

Called the "peace concert of Europe," the Congress of Vienna (1814–1815) involved Austria, Prussia, Russia, and England, but its guiding spirit was Prince Clemens von Metternich (MEH-ter-NIKH; 1773–1859), the chief minister of Austria. A reactionary and arch defender of the old order, Metternich secured a balance of power that favored Austria and reinforced established monarchies at the expense of all liberal movements,

Map 23.1 *Napoleon's Empire, 1812.*

marking the period of 1815–1848 as the Age of Metternich (map 23.2). Napoleon's foreign minister, Prince Charles Maurice de Talleyrand (1754–1838), betrayed Napoleon, won easier peace terms for his country, and effected the restoration of the Bourbon kings with Louis XVIII (1814–1824), the brother of Louis XVI.

The Revolutions of 1830 and 1848

The heavy-handed, reactionary rule of Charles X (1824–1830), who succeeded Louis XVIII, led to the July Revolution of 1830 in which the workers of Paris challenged the government. When the troops and police refused to fire on the rioters, the king quickly abdicated, delighting the liberals, who saw a possibility of relieving the misery of workers oppressed by the monarchy and the factory owners. On invitation of the Chamber of Deputies, Louis Philippe (1830–1848) assumed rule of a "bourgeois monarchy," which catered to the wealthy middle class and ignored the industrial workers. The brief July Revolution sparked violence in Germany, Italy, Spain, Portugal, Poland, and Belgium, all of which

was put down by force except in Belgium which, in 1831, won its independence from Holland.

A wave of revolutions swept Europe in 1848, the year in which Marx and Engels published *The Communist Manifesto*. The suppressed forces of liberalism erupted in France, Prussia, Austria, Hungary, Bohemia, Croatia, and the Italian possessions of the Hapsburgs. Repression was even more severe than in 1830 but, as Marx and Engels had written, "The specter of Communism" was haunting Europe.

The Industrial Revolution

Between 1750 and 1850 England's economic structure changed drastically as the nation shifted from an agrarian society to modern industrialism. The transformation was astonishingly rapid because so many important factors already existed: capitalism, international trade, mercantilism, colonialism, the Protestant work ethic. England already had hand-operated domestic (cottage) industries; what was needed was power to drive the machinery, and

Map 23.2 *Europe in 1815.*

this became available when, in 1769, James Watt patented an improved version of the steam engine that Thomas Newcomen had invented in ca. 1700 to pump water out of mine shafts.[1]

Why was England the original home of the industrial revolution rather than prosperous Holland or rich and powerful France? American economic historian W. W. Rostow suggests that national pride and confidence were buoyed by a series of English military victories but, more importantly, that the mix of needed resources was best in England:

> Britain, with more basic industrial resources than the Netherlands; more nonconformists, and more ships than France; with its political, social, and religious revolution fought out by 1688—Britain alone was in a position to weave together cotton manufacture, coal and iron technology, the steam-engine and ample foreign trade to pull it off.[2]

With its head start England became the textile center of the world but, after 1850, Belgium, France, Germany, the United States, and Canada were also involved not only in industrialization but in dramatic changes in communications, agricultural chemistry, machinery, and transportation. Railroads and steamships helped turn northern Europe and North America into an energetic and highly competitive complex that, in effect, functioned like an economic community.

Development of the Western Nations

Only in France did the 1848 revolution succeed and then just briefly. The Second Republic lasted from 1848 to 1852, followed by the Second Empire of Napoleon III (1852–1870). Deliberately provoked by Bismarck, the Franco-Prussian War (1870–1871) toppled the inept emperor and humiliated the nation. The Third Republic of 1871 finally exorcised absolutism in France, but the Dreyfus Affair (1894–1906) nearly ripped the nation asunder. Falsely accused of treason, Captain Alfred Dreyfus (dry-fus; 1859–1935) was cashiered from the army and sentenced to life imprisonment on notorious Devil's Island. Generally speaking, anti-Semites, royalists, militarists, and Catholics backed the army but republicans, socialists, intellectuals, and anticlericals supported Dreyfus. Émile Zola, for example, was jailed for his inflammatory newspaper article: *"J'Accuse"* (1898). It took a civil court to ex-

onerate Dreyfus and reinstate him in the army as a major. Monarchists and Catholics were discredited, paving the way for the separation of Church and State.

Otto Fürst von Bismarck (1815–1898), the premier of Prussia (1862–1890), personally created the German Empire in 1871 when he had Wilhelm I of Prussia proclaimed emperor (1871–1888). Consolidating his gains after a series of aggressive wars, the "iron chancellor" made a unified Germany the new power in Europe. Wilhelm II (1888–1918), the grandson of Queen Victoria, had his own ideas about royal power and dismissed his chancellor in 1890. Bismarck criticized the Kaiser unceasingly as the emperor armed his nation for the conflict that erupted in 1914. Wilhelm II abdicated in 1918 after leading his nation to defeat in the catastrophic Great War.

Under the reign of Francis II (1792–1835) Austria was defeated on four different occasions by the French. Ferdinand (1835–1848) had frequent fits of insanity, which left Metternich free to govern in his name. The 1848 revolution drove Ferdinand from the throne and Metternich from power, but the monarchy continued under the ill-fated Franz Joseph (1848–1916), Emperor of Austria and King of Hungary. The emperor's brother, Maximilian I, was installed by Napoleon III as Emperor of Mexico (1864–1867) but executed by the revolutionary forces of Juarez after the French emperor withdrew his troops. Elizabeth, the wife of Franz Joseph, was assassinated in 1898 by an Italian anarchist, and his only son, Archduke Rudolf, was found dead along with his mistress Baroness Maria Vetsera at Mayerling. Thought to possibly be a double suicide, the tragedy remains a mystery. Heir-apparent to Franz Joseph, his grandnephew Archduke Franz Ferdinand (1863–1914) and his wife were assassinated on 28 June 1914 by Serbian nationalists at Sarajevo, leading to the ultimate tragedy of the Great War.

Ruled by the Turks since 1456, Greece finally began, in 1821, a rebellion that engaged the romantic imagination of the Western world. Extolling ancient Greece as the birthplace of democracy and of Western culture, Philhellenic (pro-Greek) committees in Europe and North America sent supplies and money while demanding that civilized nations intervene directly which, eventually, England, France, and Russia did. The war was ferocious, with Greek peasants slaughtering every Turk in sight and the Turks retaliating, for example, by killing or selling into slavery all 30,000 residents of the island of Chios, which inspired Delacroix's painting of *Massacre at Chios* (figure 23.2). Lord Byron could not resist the siren call of Greek independence and died there of fever in 1824. By 1832 independence had been achieved, but Greek nationalism was not fully victorious until after World War II.

---

1. Reinvented would be a more appropriate word. The ancient Greeks were apparently the first to invent the steam engine. Judging by the drawings of Heron (or Hero) of Alexandria (ca. second century A.D.), steam power was used in toy gadgets that caused birds to sing and Tritons to blow their horns. See Robert S. Brumbaugh, *Ancient Greek Gadgets and Machines* (Westport, Conn.: Greenwood Press, 1975).

2. W. W. Rostow, *The Stages of Economic Growth* (New York: Cambridge University Press, 1960), p. 33.

Figure 23.2 *Eugène Delacroix,* The Massacre at Chios, *1822–1824, 13'10" × 11'7". The Louvre, Paris. Photo: Marburg/Art Resource.*

Early in the nineteenth century Italy was temporarily unified under Napoleon, but the Congress of Vienna again reduced it to petty states. Following several abortive revolts, Giuseppe Garibaldi (1807–1882) spearheaded the Risorgimento (rie-sor-jie-MEN-toe; resurgence) which, by 1861, established Italy, under King Victor Emmanuel II (1861–1878), as the first political entity since the demise of the Roman Empire (map 23.3). By 1870 the Papal States had been incorporated into the kingdom, but not until 1929 was Vatican City established by dictator Mussolini as a separate sovereign state of 108 acres.

Plagued by Czarist repression and widespread corruption, poverty, and ignorance, Russia was the most backward country in Europe. Czar Alexander I (1801–1825) attempted some reforms but, under the influence of Metternich, he became a reactionary; his successor, Nicholas I (1825–1855), was even more rigid. The

campaign of Nicholas to dominate southeast Europe led to the Crimean War (1853–1856) in which the allied powers of Turkey, England, France, and Sardinia stopped, for a time, Russian expansionism. The main battle was the successful siege of the Russian Naval Base at Sevastopol, but the war itself was notorious for the outrageous neglect of wounded soldiers and general incompetence of command. Florence Nightingale organized field hospitals, but nothing could save the troops from tragic blunders epitomized by the futile gallantry of the Light Brigade. Tennyson's poem typifies the romantic fantasies about national honor and glory that helped plunge Europe into the Great War of 1914–1918. (This—and several subsequent selections—is included for its thematic relevance. The regular Literary Selections begin on page 234.)

Revolution, Romanticism, Realism | **227**

Map 23.3 *The Unification of Italy.*

Literary Selections

THE CHARGE OF THE LIGHT BRIGADE
Alfred, Lord Tennyson

I

Half a league, half a league,
    Half a league onward,
All in the valley of Death
    Rode the six hundred.
'Forward, the Light Brigade!
Charge for the guns!' he said:
Into the valley of Death
    Rode the six hundred.

II

'Forward, the Light Brigade!'
Was there a man dismay'd?
Not tho' the soldier knew
        Some one had blunder'd:
Their's not to make reply,
Their's not to reason why,
Their's but to do and die:
Into the valley of Death
Rode the six hundred.

III

Cannon to right of them,
Cannon to left of them,
Cannon in front of them
        Volley'd and thunder'd;
Storm'd at with shot and shell,
Boldly they rode and well,
Into the jaws of Death,
Into the mouth of Hell
        Rode the six hundred.

IV

Flash'd all their sabres bare,
Flash'd as they turn'd in air
Sabring the gunners there,
Charging an army, while
        All the world wonder'd:
Plunged in the battery-smoke
Right thro' the line they broke;
Cossack and Russian
Reel'd from the sabre-stroke
        Shatter'd and sunder'd.
Then they rode back, but not,
        Not the six hundred.

V

Cannon to right of them,
Cannon to left of them,
Cannon behind them
        Volley'd and thunder'd;
Storm'd at with shot and shell,
While horse and hero fell,
They that had fought so well
Came thro' the jaws of Death,
Back from the mouth of Hell,
All that was left of them,
        Left of six hundred.

VI

When can their glory fade?
O the wild charge they made!
        All the world wonder'd.
Honour the charge they made!
Honour the Light Brigade,
        Noble six hundred!

European Monarchs

The reign of Alexander II (1855–1881) was about as authoritarian as that of Nicholas I, but he did belatedly liberate about forty million serfs with his 1861 Emancipation Act. The assassination of Alexander II led to the brutally oppressive regime of Alexander III (1881–1894) and the inept but equally oppressive reign of Nicholas II (1894–1918), the last of the czars.

The long reign of England's George III (1760–1820) actually ended in 1811 when the king became totally insane. Functioning as Prince Regent (1811–1820) and then king, George IV (1820–1830) led a wildly profligate life that earned the hatred of his subjects. William IV (1830–1837) agreed to the Reform Bill of 1832 that extended suffrage to people who owned property but not to the large majority who did not. His niece, Victoria (1837–1901), reestablished the prestige of the crown while presiding over the enormous expansion of the British Empire, symbolized by her crowning as Empress of India in 1876. Though the English monarchy was largely decorative, Victoria determinedly took her role seriously, presiding over the conversion of the country into a political democracy with humanitarian reforms and a measure of social and economic democracy. Paradoxically, the British developed a liberal democracy at home while pursuing aggressive imperialism abroad.

Several decades before Victoria's death Victorian earnestness and sobriety had become, for many writers and artists, increasingly boring. They were as ready for a new era as Edward VII (1901–1910) was eager to rule, having been Prince of Wales for sixty years. The Edwardian Age, as flashy and flamboyant as the king himself, was a great age for those who could afford to frolic in the grand manner. The accession of George V (1910–1936) restored some measure of decorum but all that ended in 1914 with the guns of August.

America's Civil War

Inspired in part by the doctrine of Manifest Destiny, the United States tripled its size during the nineteenth century and increased its population nearly twentyfold. Even more remarkable was the fact that the nation could expand so enormously and still maintain its union. The Civil War (1861–1865) was a cruel test sufficient to destroy perhaps any other nation. Slavery was the basic issue but the conflict also stemmed from widely divergent ways of life and different economic structures. The mainly industrial North was vigorous and aggressive in the spirit of Calvinism, whereas the South was primarily agricultural, with a relaxed and cavalier life-style. Despite the four years of ferocious combat, Lee surrendered to Grant at Appomattox, the war was over, and that fact was accepted by most Southerners as the final end of a rebellion that would never again be seriously considered. Reconstruction would surely have proceeded less radically had Lincoln not been assassinated but, nevertheless, his views seemed to eventually temper vengeful northern radicals and encourage the

Figure 23.3 *Matthew Brady,* Portrait of Lincoln. *Photo © William A. Lewis.*

moderates. In his memorable Second Inaugural Address, given just five weeks before the end of the war, Lincoln set the tone of what would ultimately prove to be the sanest and wisest attitude in the aftermath of the nation's internal agony (figure 23.3).

SECOND INAUGURAL ADDRESS
March 4, 1865
Abraham Lincoln

Fellow-countrymen: At this second appearing to take the oath of the presidential office, there is less occasion for an extended address than there was at the first. Then a statement, somewhat in detail, of a course to be pursued, seemed fitting and proper. Now, at the expiration of four years, during which public declarations have been constantly called forth on every point and phase of the great contest which still absorbs the attention and engrosses the energies of the nation, little that is new could be presented. The progress of our arms, upon which all else chiefly depends, is as well known to the public as to myself; and it is, I trust, reasonably satisfactory and encouraging to all. With high hope for the future, no prediction in regard to it is ventured.

On the occasion corresponding to this four years ago, all thoughts were anxiously directed to an impending civil war. All dreaded it—all sought to avert it. While the inaugural address was being delivered from this place, devoted altogether to saving the Union without war, insurgent agents were in the city seeking to destroy it without war—seeking to dissolve the Union, and divide effects, by negotiation. Both parties deprecated war; but one of them would make war rather than let the nation survive; and the other would accept war rather than let it perish. And the war came.

One-eighth of the whole population were colored slaves, not distributed generally over the Union, but localized in the Southern part of it. These slaves constituted a peculiar and powerful interest. All knew that this interest was, somehow, the cause of the war. To strengthen, perpetuate, and extend this interest was the object for which the insurgents would rend the Union, even by war; while the government claimed no right to do more than to restrict the territorial enlargement of it.

Neither party expected for the war the magnitude or the duration which it has already attained. Neither anticipated that the cause of the conflict might cease with, or even before, the conflict itself should cease. Each looked for an easier triumph, and a result less fundamental and astounding. Both read the same Bible, and pray to the same God; and each invokes his aid against the other. It may seem strange that any men should dare to ask a just God's assistance in wringing their bread from the sweat of other men's faces; but let us judge not, that we be not judged. The prayers of both could not be answered—that of neither has been answered fully.

The Almighty has his own purposes. "Woe unto the world because of offenses! for it must needs be that offenses come; but woe to that man by whom the offense cometh." If we shall suppose that American slavery is one of those offenses which, in the providence of God, must needs come, but which, having continued through his appointed time, he now wills to remove, and that he gives to both North and South this terrible war, as the woe due to those by whom the offense came, shall we discern therein any departure from those divine attributes which the believers in a living God always ascribe to him? Fondly do we hope—fervently do we pray—that this mighty scourge of war may speedily pass away. Yet, if God wills that it continue until all the wealth piled by the bondman's two hundred and fifty years of unrequited toil shall be sunk, and until every drop of blood drawn with the lash shall be paid by another drawn with the sword, as was said three thousand years ago, so still it must be said, "The judgments of the Lord are true and righteous altogether."

With malice toward none; with charity for all; with firmness in the right, as God gives us to see the right, let us strive on to finish the work we are in; to bind up the nation's wounds; to care for him who shall have borne the battle, and for his widow, and his orphan—to do all which may achieve and cherish a just and lasting peace among ourselves, and with all nations.

The End of an Era

The industrial revolution was a major factor in the complex chain of events leading to the Great War. Germany, England, France, and Russia were competing in the quality and price of industrial products while also searching for new colonial markets that would absorb some of their booming production. In Europe, after the unification of Germany and Italy, there was very little territory "available" for annexation. There were, in other words, more predatory nations than there were suitable victims, many of which were located in Africa (map 23.4). To protect what they had and hoped to acquire, nations enlarged their armies and navies and equipped them with the latest military technology.

National identity was another crucial factor. As late as the 1860s citizens of Florence, for example, saw themselves as Florentines or Tuscans; residents of Normandy were Norman rather than French; the population of Munich was Bavarian first and German second, and so on. The physical unification of Germany and Italy stimulated a sense of national identity symbolized by the powerful image of Great Britain as a sovereign nation, with national pride fueled by feelings of national superiority. When James Thomson wrote,

The nations not so blest as thee,
Must in their turn, to tyrants fall;
Whilst thou shalt flourish great and free,
The dread and envy of them all.
Rule Britannia! Britannia rules the waves!
Britons will never be slaves.

he had no idea of sharing the waves or anything else with other nations.

The Romantic idea of the sovereign individual was enlarged to include each citizen as a critical component in the noble and heroic image of the sovereign state. There was for the Romantic no true identity separate from the homeland, as Sir Walter Scott emphasized.

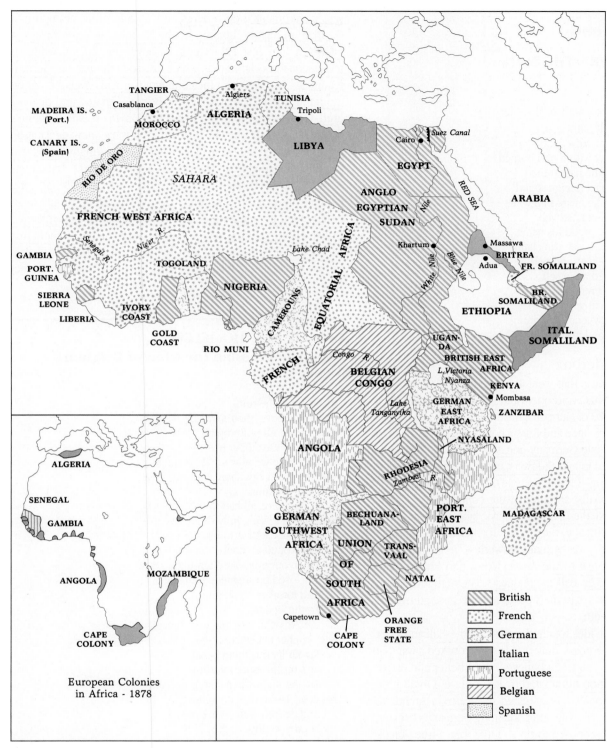

TANGIER
MADEIRA IS.
(Port.)
Casablanca
Algiers
TUNISIA
Tripoli
CANARY IS.
(Spain)
ALGERIA
MOROCCO
LIBYA
Suez Canal
Cairo
EGYPT
RIO DE ORO
SAHARA
ANGLO
EGYPTIAN
SUDAN
RED SEA
ARABIA
FRENCH WEST AFRICA
Nile
GAMBIA
Senegal R.
Niger R.
Lake Chad
Khartum
Massawa
ERITREA
FR. SOMALILAND
PORT.
GUINEA
TOGOLAND
White Nile
Blue Nile
Adua
BR.
SOMALILAND
SIERRA
LEONE
NIGERIA
EQUATORIAL AFRICA
ETHIOPIA
LIBERIA
IVORY
COAST
CAMEROUNS
ITAL.
SOMALILAND
GOLD
COAST
RIO MUNI
Congo R.
UGAN-
DA
BRITISH EAST
AFRICA
FRENCH
BELGIAN
CONGO
L. Victoria
Nyanza
KENYA
Mombasa
Lake
Tanganyika
GERMAN
EAST
AFRICA
ZANZIBAR
ANGOLA
NYASALAND
RHODESIA
Zambezi R.
MADAGASCAR
GERMAN
SOUTHWEST
AFRICA
BECHUANA-
LAND
PORT.
EAST
AFRICA
UNION
OF
SOUTH
AFRICA
TRANS-
VAAL
NATAL
Capetown
CAPE
COLONY
ORANGE
FREE
STATE

ALGERIA
SENEGAL
GAMBIA
ANGOLA
MOZAMBIQUE
CAPE
COLONY

European Colonies
in Africa - 1878

British
French
German
Italian
Portuguese
Belgian
Spanish

Map 23.4 *The Partition of Africa, 1914.*

BREATHES THERE THE MAN
Sir Walter Scott

Breathes there the man with soul so dead
Who never to himself hath said,
    This is my own, my native land!
Whose heart hath ne'er within him burned,
As home his footsteps he hath turned
    From wandering on a foreign strand!
If such there breathe, go, mark him well;
For him no minstrel raptures swell;
High though his titles, proud his name,
Boundless his wealth as wish can claim,
Despite those titles, power, and pelf,
The wretch, concentred all in self,
Living, shall forfeit fair renown,
And, doubly dying, shall go down
To the vile dust from whence he sprung,
Unwept, unhonored, and unsung.

The Balkan Tinderbox

Nations forged alliances that were supposed to maintain a balance of power and thus avoid open warfare. Bismarck effected a Triple Alliance in 1882 of Germany, Austria-Hungary, and Italy to offset French power. France and Russia countered in 1894 with a Dual Alliance that made Germany uneasy about a two-front war and, in 1907, England joined the two nations in what was called a "close understanding" (Triple Entente). The tinderbox was the Balkans where nationalist ambitions were continually clashing. Russia wanted to make the Black Sea a Slavic lake, but Britain saw a Russian thrust as a threat to the empire. By this time Turkey, the "sick man of Europe," was virtually powerless, newly independent Serbia was a threat to the Austro-Hungarian Empire, and Germany had her eye on Balkan conquests. The high level of international tension was extremely dangerous because all nations were armed to the teeth.

    Nationalist activities touched a spark to the Balkan tinder and nationalist stubbornness, duty, and honor provoked a war that many diplomats and statesmen believed was a better alternative than seeing their nation humiliated by loss of face. On 28 June 1914, a Serbian nationalist assassinated the Austrian Archduke Francis Ferdinand and his wife. After obtaining Germany's backing for whatever Austria proposed to do about Serbia, a true "blank check," Austria delivered an ultimatum that was promptly rejected. Claiming it was inconsistent with "national honor," Austria rebuffed a British offer to mediate a compromise conference and declared war on Serbia on 28 July 1914, despite German attempts to withdraw the blank check. Russia began mobilizing but backed off as Germany insisted that Austria could be made to compromise. Fearful of German might, the panic-stricken Russian government then ordered full mobilization, prompting a German ultimatum, ignored by the Kremlin, to cease or face a fight. On 1 August 1914 Germany began mobilizing while simultaneously declaring war, which says something about German readiness. Two days later the confident Germans declared war on the frantically mobilizing French. Britain dithered and delayed until Germany announced her intention to violate Belgium's neutrality as established in 1839; Britain's subsequent declaration of war prompted the German chancellor to sneeringly remark that the English had gone to war over a "scrap of paper." Actually, as pointed out by Barbara Tuchman,[3] the German Staff had long planned an invasion of helpless Belgium as the best route to an undefended French frontier. The "scrap of paper" slur inflamed British public opinion, which eagerly backed a government that had honored its treaty and thus the nation (map 23.5). The response was typified by Thomas Hardy's poem, "Cry of the Homeless."

CRY OF THE HOMELESS
After the Prussian Invasion of Belgium
Thomas Hardy

"Instigator of the ruin—
    Whichsoever thou mayst be
Of the masterful of Europe
    That contrived our misery—
Hear the wormwood-worded greeting
    From each city, shore, and lea
    Of thy victims:
    "Conqueror, all hail to thee!"
"Yea: 'All hail!' we grimly shout thee
    That wast author, fount, and head
Of these wounds, whoever proven
    When our times are thoroughly read.
'May thy loved be slighted, blighted,
    And forsaken,' be it said
    By thy victims,
    'And thy children beg their bread!'
"Nay: a richer malediction!—
    Rather let this thing befall
In time's hurling and unfurling
    On the night when comes thy call;
That compassion dew thy pillow
    And bedrench thy senses all
    For thy victims,
Till death dark thee with his pall."

                      August 1915

---

3. Barbara Tuchman, *The Guns of August* (New York: Macmillan, 1962).

World War I

Generally speaking, the war was fought with twentieth-century weapons (machine guns, tanks, poison gas, artillery) and nineteenth-century tactics (mass frontal assaults, artillery duels, use of cavalry). There were many theatres of action but the 300–mile Western Front was the main meat grinder with mass charges launched between trenches into point-blank machine gun fire. In four years sixteen nations had casualties (killed, died, wounded, missing) of about fifty million. One example can indicate the extent of the slaughter. In the center of the small French village of Sully-sur-Loire stands a war memorial designed as a tall obelisk. On one side are listed, in categories, the villagers who died in World War II. The categories themselves communicate much about the conflict with Nazi Germany: "Killed in Action," "Murdered by the Gestapo," "Died in Concentration Camp," and "Missing." Eight names are engraved on the World War II side. On the opposite side the single category is "Killed in Action." There are ninety-six names.

As some historians have noted, World War I began as the most popular war in history. Just about everyone was spoiling for a fight, a chance to demonstrate the combative spirit of their country, to prove their valor and nobility, to honor their country. Those Romantic notions died in the trenches and are buried from Flanders Fields to Verdun. Throughout Western history no event has ended an era with such finality as did the Great War (map 23.6).

MAP 23.5 *Europe in 1914.*

Romanticism

More an attitude to be explored than a term to be defined, Romanticism began around 1780 as a reaction against the Enlightenment. The Romantic Movement itself lasted from about 1780 to about 1830, but Romantic ideas and issues were present in a variety of forms right up to 1914.

In its initial stages Romanticism was mainly a German movement but it drew its inspiration from Jean Jacques Rousseau (1712–1778). Rousseau began his *Social Contract* (1762) with a ringing proclamation: "Man is born free and everywhere he is in chains." The source of the trouble, according to Rousseau, was too much education, and of the wrong kind at that. Self-forged chains could not be thrown off with more "progress"; instead, people must emulate the Noble Savage by returning to a state of innocence in nature. Civilization had corrupted us, claimed Rousseau, but a return to nature was the proper antidote. More a call to action than a coherent program, just what Rousseau meant by "back to nature" has been debated for centuries. Some idea of his attitude can be obtained from Rousseau's analysis of the "wrong kind of education":

> Astronomy was born of superstition, eloquence of ambition, hatred, falsehood, and flattery; geometry of avarice; physics of an idle curiosity; and even moral philosophy of human pride. Thus the arts and sciences owe their birth to our vices; and we should be less doubtful of their advantages, if they had sprung from our virtues.
>
> Their evil origin is, indeed, but too plainly reproduced in their objects. What would become of the arts were they not cherished by luxury? If men were not unjust, of what use were jurisprudence? What would become of history if there were no tyrants, wars, or conspiracies? In a word, who would pass his life in barren speculations if everybody, attentive only to the obligations of humanity and the necessities of nature, spent his whole life in serving his country, obliging his friends, and relieving the unhappy?

from *Discourse on the Arts and Sciences,* 1749, by Jean Jacques Rousseau

Map 23.6 *Territorial Changes following World War I.*

Territory lost

- ▥ by Germany
- ░ by Bulgaria
- ▦ by Russia
- ▥ by Austria-Hungary

Literary Selection

ÉMILE

Jean-Jacques Rousseau, 1712–1778

Rousseau presented his ideas about the proper education of children in the form of a novel. In the two brief selections given here we see first an opening essay on the nature of education, and, second, an example of the proper education of the pupil Émile.

BOOK I

Everything is good as it comes from the hand of the Author of things; everything degenerates in the hand of man. He forces a piece of ground to nourish harvests alien to it, a tree to bear fruit not its own; he mingles and confounds climates, elements, seasons; he mutilates his dog, his horse, his slave; he turns everything upside down, he disfigures everything; he loves deformity and monsters. He does not want anything to be as nature made it, not even man; it must be groomed for him, like a riding-school horse; it must conform to his whim like a tree in his garden. . . .

It is you I address, gentle and far-seeing mother, who know that you must withdraw yourself from the established highway and protect the tender sapling from the shock of human opinion! Cultivate, water the young plant before it dies; its fruits will one day be your greatest joy. Build early a protecting wall about the soul of your child; another may mark out the boundary, but you alone must erect the barrier.

Plants are formed by cultivation and men by education. If a man were born tall and strong, his height and strength would be worthless to him until he had learned to make use of them; both could be harmful to him, in keeping others from thinking he needed help; left to himself, he could die of misery before he understood his own needs. We pity the childish state; we do not see that the human race would have perished if man had not started out as a child.

We are born feeble, we need strength; we are born deprived of everything, we need help; we are born stupid, we need judgment. Everything we lack at our birth, but need when we are grown, is given by our education.

This education comes to us from nature, from men, or from things. The internal development of our faculties and organs is the education of nature; the use we learn to make of this development is the education of men; and the acquisition of our own experience from the objects which affect us is the education of things.

Each one of us, then, is fashioned by three sorts of teachers. The pupil in whom their various teachings clash is badly educated, and will never be at peace with himself; the one in whom they all emphasize the same purpose and tend towards the same ends, goes straight to his goal and lives harmoniously. Such an one is well educated.

Now, of these three different educations, that of nature is the only one that does not depend on us at all; that of things depends on man only in certain respects. That of man is the only one of which we are truly the masters: even here we are in control only theoretically; for who can hope to direct completely the discourse and actions of all those surrounding a child?

Since, then, education is an art, it is almost impossible that it should be successful, for the circumstances necessary to its success are determined by no one person. All that one can do with the greatest care is, more or less, to approach the goal, but one needs good luck to reach it.

What is this goal? It is the very same as nature's; that has just been proved. Since the combination of these educations is necessary for their perfecting, it is toward the one over which we have no control that we must direct the other two. But perhaps this word nature is too vague a term; we must try here to define it.

Nature, we are told, is only habit. What does that mean? Are there not habits which are developed only with effort, and which never stifle nature? Such is, for example, the habit of plants, the vertical direction of which is interfered with. Once the restraints are removed, the plant retains the inclination which it has been forced to take; but even so the sap has not changed its primitive direction, and, if the plant continues to thrive, its growth will return to the vertical. It is the same with the tendencies of man. As long as we stay in one situation, we keep those which are the result of custom and which are the least natural to us; but as soon as the situation changes the learned habit stops and the natural returns. Education is certainly a habit. Now are there not people who forget and lose their education and others who retain it? From whence comes this difference? If we limit the meaning of nature to the habits which conform to the natural, we may spare ourselves this nonsense.

We are born sensitive, and from our birth we are affected in diverse ways by the objects which surround us. As soon as we have, so to speak, the consciousness of our sensations, we are disposed to seek out or to flee from the objects which produce them, first according as to whether they are agreeable or displeasing to us, then according to the harmony or discord which we find between ourselves and these objects, and finally according to the judgments which we form concerning the idea of happiness and perfection which our reason gives us. These judgments are extended and strengthened in accordance with our becoming more sensitive and more enlightened; but limited by our habits, they are changed more or less by our opinions. Before this change, they are what I call nature in us.

It is to these primitive urges, then, that we must relate everything; and this could be done if our three educations were merely different; but what is to be done when they are opposed?— when, instead of educating a man for himself, we wish to educate him for others, then harmony is impossible. Forced to combat nature or social institutions, we must choose between making a man or a citizen; for one cannot do both at the same time.

All small societies, when confined and close-knit, draw away from the world at large. Every patriot is intolerant of foreigners; they are mere men, they have no worth to him. This difficulty is inevitable but it is a slight one. It is essential to be kind to the people with whom one lives. Outside, the Spartan was ambitious, miserly, unrighteous; but disinterestedness, justice, and concord reigned within his walls. Beware of those citizens of the world who study their books for dutiful acts which they disdain to carry out at home. This kind of philosopher loves the barbarian in order to be free from loving his neighbor.

The natural man is all for himself; he is a numerical unity, the absolute entity, in harmony only with himself or his equals. The civil man (the man in society) is but a fractional unit belonging to the denominator whose sole value is in relation to the whole, which is the social body. Good social institutions are those that know best how to strip man of his nature, to take from him his real existence and give him one which is only relative, and to add his personality to the common unity; to the end that each individual will no longer think of himself as one, but as a part of the whole, no longer a thinking being except in the group. A Roman citizen was neither a Caius nor a Lucius: he was a Roman. . . .

A woman of Sparta had five sons in the army and awaited news of the battle. A helot arrived and she asked for news, trembling. "Your five sons have been killed." "Ignoble slave, did I ask you that?" "We are victorious!" The mother ran to the temple and gave thank-offerings to the gods. There is your citizen.

One who, in civilized society, hopes to maintain the pre-eminence of the natural does not know what he asks. Always at odds with himself, forever vacillating between his inclinations and his duty, he will never be either man or citizen; he will be no good to himself or others. He will be one of those contemporary men, a Frenchman, an Englishman, a citizen. He will be a nonentity.

To be something, to be himself and always whole, a man must act as he speaks, he must be sure always of the road he must take, take it resolutely and follow it always. I am waiting for someone to show me such a prodigy to know if he is man or citizen, or how he undertakes to be both at the same time.

From these necessarily opposed aims come two forms of contrary institutions: the one held in common and public, the other individual and private.

If you want to get an idea of public education, read Plato's *Republic*. It is not at all a political work, as those who judge a book only by its title believe it to be: it is the finest treatise on education that anyone ever wrote.

When people want to return to a never-never land, they think of Plato's institution: if Lycurgus[4] had done no more than put his in writing, I should find it much more fanciful. Plato simply purified the heart of man: Lycurgus denaturalized it.

That public system exists no longer, and can exist no longer, because where there is no nation there can be no citizen. These two words *Nation* and *Citizen* should be removed from modern languages. I know quite well the reason for this, but I do not want to discuss it: it has nothing to do with my subject.

Those laughable institutions they call "colleges" I do not think of in connection with public education. Neither do I count the education of the world, because this education leads toward two contrary goals, and misses both of them; it is useful only to produce two-faced men, who seem always to defer to others but who are really interested only in pleasing themselves. Now this behavior, being common to all, deceives no one in particular. It is so much wasted effort.

From these contradictions arises the one which we feel constantly within ourselves. Pulled by nature and by man in opposite directions; forced to divide ourselves among these different compulsions, we make compromises which lead neither to one goal nor the other. Thus besieged and vacillating during the whole course of our life, we end it without having found peace within ourselves and without having been any good to ourselves or others.

There remains finally private education, or that of nature, but what can a man mean to others if he is educated only for himself. If perhaps the proposed double object could be resolved into one, by removing the contradictions of man we could remove a great obstacle to his happiness. To make a judgment, we must see the finished man; we must have observed his tendencies, seen his progress, followed his advance; in a word, we must know the natural man. I believe you will have taken some steps (made some progress) in our research after having read this discussion.

What must we do to fashion this rare being?—much, without doubt: that is, prevent anything from being done. When it is only a question of sailing against the wind, we tack; but if the sea is high and we want to stay in one place, we must drop anchor. Take care, young pilot, that your cable does not slip or your anchor drag, and that your vessel does not drift without your noticing it.

In the social order where every place is allocated, each one must be educated for his niche. If a man leaves the place for which he was prepared, he no longer fits anywhere. Education is useful to the extent that destiny harmonizes it with the vocation of the parents; in all other instances, it is harmful to the student, if only for the prejudices it gives him. In Egypt, where the son was obliged to step into his father's place, education at least had an assured purpose: but among us where only classes remain, and where men change from one to the other constantly, no one knows whether, in educating his son to take his place, a father may be working against the son's best interests.

In the natural order, since men are equal, their common calling is man's estate, and whoever is well educated for this, cannot fill unworthily any position which relates to it. Whether I destine my pupil for the army, the church, the bar, is of little importance. No matter what the calling of his parents, nature calls him to human life. Living is the trade I should like to teach him. Leaving my hands, he will not be, I admit, magistrate, soldier, or priest; he will be first of all a man: everything that a man should be, he will know how to be, when called on, as well as any man; and in vain will fortune change his place, for he will always be at home. . . .

*   *   *

. . . For a time we had noticed, my pupil and I, that amber, glass, wax, different substances when they were rubbed would attract straws, and that others did not attract them. By chance we discovered one which had a still stranger attribute, which was to attract from quite a distance and without being rubbed, filings and other bits of iron. How long this quality amused us without our being able to perceive anything beyond it! Finally we found that this characteristic was communicated to the iron even magnetized in a certain sense. One day we went to the fair; a juggler attracted with a piece of bread a wax duck floating on a basin of water. Very much astonished, we did not call him a sorcerer, however, for we did not know what a sorcerer was. Continually struck with effects of which we did not know the causes, we were in no hurry to make judgments, and remained quietly ignorant until we found the answer.

On returning to our lodging, as a result of talking about the duck at the fair we began to try to imitate it. We took a well-magnetized needle, covered it with white wax which we shaped like a duck as best we could, in such a way that the needle traversed the body and the eye formed the beak. We placed the duck on the water and brought near the beak a key, and we saw, with what joy you may imagine, that our duck followed the piece of bread. To observe in what direction the duck faced when left quiet on the water was something for us to do another time. As for the present, full of our plans, we asked for nothing more.

---

4. Lycurgus, the Spartan king, did not write about education; he established the actual system of training in Sparta to which Rousseau refers.

The same evening we returned to the fair with some prepared bread in our pockets and as soon as the magician performed his trick, our little savant, who could hardly contain himself, said that this trick was not difficult and that he could do as well himself. He was taken at his word and at once took from his pocket the bread containing the bit of iron. As he approached the table his heart was pounding, and, almost trembling, he held out the bread. The duck came and followed it; the child cried out and quivered with joy. As people clapped and the assembly acclaimed him, his head was completely turned and he was beside himself. The juggler, overwhelmed, came, nevertheless to embrace and congratulate him and to request the honor of his presence the next day, adding that we would take pains to assemble a still larger crowd to applaud his cleverness. My proud little naturalist wanted to make a speech, but I shut him up at once and took him away, overwhelmed with praise.

The child with evident excitement counted the minutes the next day. He invited everyone he met; he wanted the whole human race to witness his glory. He could hardly wait for the time to come, he was ready ahead of time, we flew to the meeting place; the room was already full. As he entered, his young heart swelled. Other tricks had to come first; the juggler surpassed himself and did astonishing things. The child saw nothing of all this; he was agitated, he perspired, his breathing was labored. He spent the time fingering the bread in his pocket with a hand trembling with impatience. At last it was his turn; the master announced him ceremoniously. He approached a little ashamedly, he brought out the bread. New vicissitude of human things!—the duck, so tame the day before, had become wild today. Instead of presenting its beak, it turned tail and fled; it avoided the bread and the hand which held it with the same care with which it had formerly followed them. After a thousand useless attempts, each one jeered at, the child whined, said that he was being duped, that this was another duck substituted for the first one, and defied the juggler to attract it.

The juggler, without replying, took a piece of bread and held it out to the duck; which at once followed the bread and came to the hand which held it. The child took the same piece of bread, but far from succeeding better than before, he saw the duck make fun of him and do pirouettes all around the basin; he went off at last, quite upset, and did not dare expose himself to catcalls.

Then the juggler took the bread that the child had brought and made use of it as successfully as with his own: he drew out the iron (magnet) before the people, more laughter at our expense: then with the bread thus emptied he attracted the duck as before. He did the same thing with another piece, cut by a third person, he did the same with his glove, with the end of his finger; finally he went off to the center of the room and in an emphatic tone such as show people use, declaring that the duck would obey his voice no less than his gesture, he spoke and the duck obeyed: he told it to go to the right and it turned right; to come back, and it came; to turn and it turned; the movement followed close upon the order. The redoubled applause was a still greater insult to us. We slipped out without being noticed, and shut ourselves up in our room, without going about to tell everyone of our prowess, as we had planned to do.

The next morning there was a knock at the door, I opened it; there stood the juggler. He mildly objected to our behaviour. What had he done to us that we would undertake to discredit his tricks and deprive him of a livelihood? What is so marvelous after all about drawing along a wax duck to cause us to purchase that ability at the expense of the living of an honest man? "By my faith, gentlemen, if I had some other talent by which to earn my living, I should hardly take pride in this one. You ought to know that a man who has spent his life continually practicing this miserable trade would know more about it than you who have spent only a few minutes on it. If I did not show you my finest tricks at once, it was because a man must not be in a hurry to display foolishly all he knows. I always take care to keep my best tricks for a great occasion, and beyond that I have still greater ones to halt young upstarts. Also, gentlemen, I come in goodwill to disclose the secret which embarrassed you so much, requesting that you will not make use of it to harm me, and that you will be more restrained another time."

Then he showed us his apparatus, and we saw with the utmost surprise that it was nothing but a strong, well mounted magnet which a child hidden under the table moved about without our realizing it.

The man put away his apparatus and after we had expressed our thanks and our apologies, we wanted to give him a present; he refused it. "No, gentlemen, I am not pleased enough with you to accept your gift; I leave you in my debt in spite of yourselves; this is my only revenge. Learn that there is generosity in all classes; I get paid for my tricks but not for my lessons."

Exercises

1. What are the three aspects of education according to Rousseau? What should be the aim of the two aspects that people can do anything about?

2. What distinction does Rousseau make between the *person* and the *citizen?* What is his opinion of the citizen?

3. Some of today's educators claim that vocational training is of little value because job requirements are changing so rapidly. What would Rousseau say about this problem?

4. In terms of the person and the citizen, what sort of education would Rousseau advocate, then, to accomplish his purpose?

The Romantic Movement
Germany

Johann Gottfried von Herder (1744–1803) was the leader of the precursor of Romanticism, the *sturm und drang* (SHTOORM oont DRAHNG) movement in German literature, a term derived from Klinger's novel *Der Wirrwarr; oder Sturm und Drang* ("Chaos; or storm and stress"). A passionate opponent of French rationalism of the Enlightenment, Herder emphasized the *Volksgeist* (spirit of the people) in Germany, claiming that each *volk* found its *geist* in its language, literature, and religion. This was, in effect, a cultural nationalism that became the basis of later German nationalism.

In his early writings Johann Wolfgang von Goethe (GUHR-tuh; 1749–1832) was one of the leading exponents of the movement. Written after an unhappy love affair, his *The Sorrows of Young Werther* (1774) was a morbidly sensitive tale full of sentiment and gloomy feelings that culminated in the suicide of the tragic Werther. Though Goethe was later to regret the storm and stress of his little book, it made him an instant celebrity.

The philosopher Friedrich Wilhelm Joseph von Schelling (1775–1854) contributed the theory that nature and mind were inseparable and differed only in degree rather than in kind. For Schelling the creative artist was the "ideal Romantic man," a genius who presented his work as instinctively created apart from any conscious effort. From this Nietzsche developed his idea of the creative genius as a "superman" who was "beyond good and evil."

Second only to Goethe in German literature, Friedrich von Schiller (1759–1805) was influenced by Kant and, in turn, was a major inspiration for modern German literature. An idealist who hated tyranny, Schiller envisioned the universal fellowship of all humankind. It was his poem "An die Freude" (to joy) that Beethoven used as the "Ode to Joy" in the final movement of his mighty Ninth Symphony.

Arthur Schopenhauer (1788–1860) also contributed his generally pessimistic theories to the Romantic Movement. According to Schopenhauer, reality is a blind driving force manifested in individuals as Will. Individual wills inevitably clash, causing strife and pain, from which there is no escape except by a negation of the will. Temporary escape is possible, however, through creative acts in art and science.

According to Schopenhauer and other romantics, creativity emerges from the unconscious, but there are also instinctual drives that conflict with the creative impulses. The unconscious cuts both ways and the Romantics were vividly aware of the "night-side" that could release demonic destruction, as Schopenhauer pointed out in *The World of Will and Idea* (1818). Blind human will achieves only unhappiness or, as Goya said, "The sleep of reason produces monsters." Schopenhauer concluded that reason must permit the release of creativity while simultaneously controlling the passions, but he was not optimistic about the results.

England

Romanticism was effectively expressed in nineteenth-century art and music, in historical novels, Gothic tales, and romantic stories of love and adventure. For an English-speaking audience the Romantic mood is never better expressed than in the work of the English poets.

William Blake, 1757–1827

A self-proclaimed mystic with minimal formal schooling, Blake was a fundamentalist Protestant who believed that the Bible was the sole source of religious knowledge. Very much an individualist, he detested institutionalized religion, claiming that the human imagination was the sole means of expressing the Eternal. Blake referred to people as the Divine Image, the possessors of the humane virtues of mercy, pity, peace, and love. Equally gifted as an artist, Blake illustrated all but one of his volumes of poetry plus the Book of Job, Dante, and the poems of Thomas Gray.

The collection of poems called the *Songs of Innocence*, written in 1789, coincides with the beginning of the French Revolution that, for Blake, held so much promise of a better life for all people. The following poem from that collection celebrates the joys of a Christian life and a simple pastoral existence.

Literary Selections

THE LAMB
William Blake

Little Lamb, who made thee?
　Dost thou know who made thee?
Gave thee life, and bid thee feed,
By the stream and o'er the mead;
Gave thee clothing of delight,
Softest clothing, woolly, bright;
Gave thee such a tender voice,
Making all the vales rejoice?
　Little Lamb, who made thee?
　Dost thou know who made thee?
　Little Lamb, I'll tell thee,
　Little Lamb, I'll tell thee:
He is called by thy name,
For He calls Himself a Lamb.
He is meek, and He is mild;
He became a little child.
I a child, and thou a lamb,
We are called by His name.
　Little Lamb, God bless thee!
　Little Lamb, God bless thee!

The *Songs of Experience* address the sick and corrupt world in which good and evil coexist. In "The Tiger" Blake asks the age-old question: did the good God create evil?

THE TIGER
William Blake

Tiger! Tiger! burning bright
In the forests of the night,
What immortal hand or eye
Could frame thy fearful symmetry?
In what distant deeps or skies
Burnt the fire of thine eyes?
On what wings dare he aspire?
What the hand dare seize the fire?
And what shoulder, and what art,
Could twist the sinews of thy heart?
And when thy heart began to beat,
What dread hand? and what dread feet?
What the hammer? what the chain?
In what furnace was thy brain?
What the anvil? what dread grasp
Dare its deadly terrors clasp?
When the stars threw down their spears,
And water'd heaven with their tears,
Did he smile his work to see?
Did he who made the Lamb make thee?
Tiger! Tiger! burning bright
In the forests of the night,
What immortal hand or eye,
Dare frame thy fearful symmetry?

Exercise

In his *The Marriage of Heaven and Hell* Blake wrote that "Attraction and Repulsion, Reason and Energy, Love and Hate are necessary to Human Existence." Is this attitude reflected in the poems about the lamb and the tiger? Is the tiger, in other words, wholly evil or a symbol of necessary vigor and energy?

William Wordsworth, 1770–1850
The greatest of the English nature poets, Wordsworth was influenced by Rousseau and the spirit of the French Revolution. Strongly opposed to the flowery artificiality of neoclassic poetry, Wordsworth and Samuel Taylor Coleridge published *Lyrical Ballads* (2d ed., 1800), which contained a new poetic manifesto. Wordsworth referred to his poetry as "emotion recollected in tranquility" but, as he stated in his manifesto, he deliberately chose to write in "the language of conversation in the middle and lower classes of society."

The following sonnet mourns a world so overwhelmed with materialism that it may lose its spiritual qualities. Proteus and Triton are from Greek mythology and symbolize the poet's conviction that the wonders of nature that delighted the ancients cannot, in the long run, be destroyed by the Industrial Age. Wordsworth was a Romantic optimist.

THE WORLD IS TOO MUCH WITH US
William Wordsworth

The world is too much with us; late and soon,
Getting and spending, we lay waste our powers;
Little we see in Nature that is ours;
We have given our hearts away, a sordid boon!
This Sea that bares her bosom to the moon,
The winds that will be howling at all hours,
And are up-gathered now like sleeping flowers,
For this, for everything, we are out of tune;
It moves us not.—Great God! I'd rather be
A Pagan suckled in a creed outworn;
So might I, standing on this pleasant lea,
Have glimpses that would make me less forlorn;
Have sight of Proteus rising from the sea;
Or hear old Triton blow his wreathéd horn.

Exercise

If Wordsworth were to write "The World Is Too Much with Us" today, would he be as optimistic about the survival of nature's wonders? Why or why not?

Samuel Taylor Coleridge, 1772–1834
Though he did not consider himself a Romantic poet, Coleridge did make a classic Romantic statement: "Each man is meant to represent humanity in his own way, combining its elements uniquely." Coleridge set great store on imagination over fancy, claiming that fancy was only the ability to copy or elaborate on previous examples; imagination was the ability to create new worlds. "Kubla Khan" is a notable example of an inspired vision whether or not, as Coleridge claimed, the poem was composed during an opium reverie and later written down. Coleridge and many other Romantics were fascinated with the exotic Orient. The grandson of Mongol conqueror Genghis Khan, Kubla Khan (1215?–1294) founded the Yuan dynasty of China and sponsored Marco Polo as his agent to the West.

KUBLA KHAN
Samuel Taylor Coleridge

In Xanadu did Kubla Khan
    A stately pleasure-dome decree:
Where Alph, the sacred river, ran
Through caverns measureless to man
    Down to a sunless sea.
So twice five miles of fertile ground
With walls and towers were girdled round:
And here were gardens bright with sinuous rills,
Where blossomed many an incense-bearing tree
And here were forests ancient as the hills,   10
Enfolding sunny spots of greenery.
But oh! that deep romantic chasm which slanted
Down the green hill athwart a cedarn cover!
A savage place! as holy and enchanted
As e'er beneath a waning moon was haunted
By woman wailing for her demon-lover!
And from this chasm, with ceaseless turmoil seething,
As if this earth in fast thick pants were breathing,
A mighty fountain momently was forced,
Amid whose swift half-intermitted burst   20
Huge fragments vaulted like rebounding hail,
Or chaffy grain beneath the thresher's flail:
And 'mid these dancing rocks at once and ever
It flung up momently the sacred river.
Five miles meandering with a mazy motion
Through wood and dale the sacred river ran,
Then reached the caverns measureless to man,
And sank in tumult to a lifeless ocean:
And 'mid this tumult Kubla heard from far
Ancestral voices prophesying war!   30
    The shadow of the dome of pleasure
    Floated midway on the waves;
    Where was heard the mingled measure
    From the fountain and the caves.
It was a miracle of rare device,
A sunny pleasure-dome with caves of ice!
    A damsel with a dulcimer
    In a vision once I saw:
    It was an Abyssinian maid,
    And on her dulcimer she played,   40
    Singing of Mount Abora.
    Could I revive within me
    Her symphony and song,
    To such a deep delight 'twould win me,
That with music loud and long,
I would build that dome in air,
That sunny dome! those caves of ice!
And all who heard should see them there,
And all should cry, Beware! Beware!
His flashing eyes, his floating hair!   50
Weave a circle round him thrice,
And close your eyes with holy dread,
For he on honey-dew hath fed,
And drunk the milk of Paradise.

1797

Exercise

Coleridge claimed that "Kubla Khan" appeared to him in a dream and that what he later wrote down was "a fragment." Is the poem incomplete? Could the first thirty-six lines be an exercise in creative imagination and the remainder a lament over the loss of poetic power? In these terms is the poem complete or incomplete?

George Noel Gordon, Lord Byron, 1788–1824

The most flamboyant and controversial personality of the age, Lord Byron epitomizes the Romantic hero. With his egotism and superhuman vigor he gloried in physical and mental license, learning relatively late, and only in part, the virtue of moderation. He wrote his words, he said, "as a tiger leaps" and aimed many of them at conventional social behavior, cant, and hypocrisy. Much of his poetry was prosaic when compared with the iridescent style of Shelley and Keats but, as he said, his genius was eloquent rather than poetical. His reputation was early and firmly established with *Childe Harold's Pilgrimage,* a poetic travelogue, but his masterpiece is *Don Juan,* a work full of irony and pathos of which Byron wrote in the Dedication:

I want a hero: an uncommon want,
. . .
But can't find any in the present age
Fit for my poem (that is, for my new one):
So, as I said, I'll take my friend Don Juan.

Byron was a revolutionary in spirit but his inspiration was based on classical art and its emphasis on emotion controlled by the intellect. The Greek revolt against the Turks provided Byron with the opportunity to become a revolutionary Graecophile. Several years before sailing for Greece on 14 July 1823 (Bastille Day), he wrote the following ironic lines.

WHEN A MAN HATH NO FREEDOM TO FIGHT FOR AT HOME
Lord Byron

When a man hath no freedom to fight for at home,
    Let him combat for that of his neighbours;
Let him think of the glories of Greece and of Rome,
    And get knock'd on the head for his labours.
To do good to mankind is the chivalrous plan,
    And is always as nobly requited;
Then battle for freedom wherever you can,
    And, if not shot or hang'd, you'll get knighted.

Almost to the day of his premature death Byron was torn between the heroic defiance of Prometheus and the worldly, cynical insolence of Don Juan. In the end, he tried to choose the Promethean way but died of fever during the Greek struggle for independence.

PROMETHEUS
Lord Byron

Titan! to whose immortal eyes
   The sufferings of mortality,
   Seen in their sad reality,
Were not as things that gods despise;
What was thy pity's recompense?
A silent suffering, and intense;
The rock, the vulture, and the chain,
All that the proud can feel of pain,
The agony they do not show,
The suffocating sense of woe,   10
   Which speaks but in its loneliness,
And then is jealous lest the sky
Should have a listener, nor will sigh
   Until its voice is echoless.

Titan! to thee the strife was given
   Between the suffering and the will,
   Which torture where they cannot kill;
And the inexorable Heaven,
And the deaf tyranny of Fate,
The ruling principle of Hate,   20
Which for its pleasure doth create
The things it may annihilate,
Refused thee even the boon to die:
The wretched gift eternity
Was thine—and thou hast borne it well.
All that the Thunderer wrung from thee
Was but the menace which flung back
On him the torments of thy rack;
The fate thou didst so well foresee,
But would not to appease him tell;   30
And in thy Silence was his Sentence,
And in his Soul a vain repentance,
And evil dread so ill dissembled,
That in his hand the lightnings trembled.

Thy Godlike crime was to be kind,
   To render with thy precepts less
   The sum of human wretchedness,
And strengthen Man with his own mind;
But baffled as thou wert from high,
Still in thy patient energy,   40
In the endurance, and repulse
   Of thine impenetrable Spirit,
   Which Earth and Heaven could not convulse,
   A mighty lesson we inherit:
Thou art a symbol and a sign
   To Mortals of their fate and force;
Like thee, Man is in part divine,

A troubled stream from a pure source;
And Man in portions can foresee
His own funereal destiny,   50
His wretchedness, and his resistance,
And his sad unallied existence:
To which his Spirit may oppose
Itself—and equal to all woes,
   And a firm will, and a deep sense,
Which even in torture can descry
   Its own concenter'd recompense,
Triumphant where it dares defy,
And making Death a Victory.

                         Diodati, July, 1816

    Though unable to moderate his course, Byron was fully aware of the causes of his self-destruction, as revealed in several lines from his poignant "Epistle to Augusta":

I have been cunning in mine overthrow,
   The careful pilot of my proper woe.
Mine were my faults, and mine be their reward.
   My whole life was a contest, since the day
That gave me being, gave me that which marr'd
   The gift,—a fate, or will, that walk'd astray.

Exercise

Prometheus was the Titan who stole fire from Mount Olympos and gave it to humankind. Zeus, the Thunderer in the poem, had him chained to a rock where a vulture perpetually tears out his liver. What does Prometheus symbolize for Byron? Greece under Turkish tyranny? Himself? Both?

Percy Bysshe Shelley, 1792–1822

Shelley and John Keats established romantic verse as the prime poetic tradition of the period; to this day "Shelley and Keats" and "Romantic poetry" are virtually synonymous. A lifelong heretic who was expelled from Oxford because of his pamphlet *The Necessity of Atheism,* Shelley saw all humankind as the Divine Image to whom poets spoke as the "unacknowledged legislators of the world" *(A Defense of Poetry).* His masterpiece is *Prometheus Unbound,* a lyrical drama in four acts in which he gave full expression to his "passion for reforming the world." Also composed at Leghorn, Italy, and published with *Prometheus Unbound* was "To a Skylark," the composition of which was described by Mary Wollstonecraft Shelley:

It was on a beautiful summer evening while wandering among the lanes, whose myrtle hedges were the bowers of the fireflies, that we heard the caroling of the skylark, which inspired one of the most beautiful of his poems.

TO A SKYLARK
Percy Bysshe Shelley

Hail to thee, blithe spirit!
   Bird thou never wert,
That from heaven, or near it,
   Pourest thy full heart
In profuse strains of unpremeditated art.
   Higher still and higher
      From the earth thou springest
   Like a cloud of fire;
      The blue deep thou wingest,
And singing still dost soar, and soaring ever singest.   10
   In the golden lightning
      Of the sunken sun,
   O'er which clouds are brightning,
      Thou dost float and run;
Like an unbodied joy whose race is just begun.
   The pale purple even
      Melts around thy flight;
   Like a star of heaven,
      In the broad day-light
Thou art unseen, but yet I hear thy shrill delight,   20
   Keen as are the arrows
      Of that silver sphere,
   Whose intense lamp narrows
      In the white dawn clear,
Until we hardly see, we feel that it is there.
   All the earth and air
      With thy voice is loud,
   As, when night is bare,
      From one lonely cloud
The moon rains out her beams, and heaven is overflowed.   30
   What thou art we know not;
      What is most like thee?
   From rainbow clouds there flow not
      Drops so bright to see,
As from thy presence showers a rain of melody.
   Like a poet hidden
      In the light of thought,
   Singing hymns unbidden,
      Till the world is wrought
To sympathy with hopes and fears it heeded not: 40
   Like a high-born maiden
      In a palace tower,
   Soothing her love-laden
   Soul in secret hour
With music sweet as love, which overflows her bower:
   Like a glow-worm golden
      In a dell of dew,
   Scattering unbeholden
      Its aërial hue

Among the flowers and grass, which screen it from the view: 50
   Like a rose embowered
      In its own green leaves,
   By warm winds deflowered,
      Till the scent it gives
Makes faint with too much sweet these heavy-winged thieves:
   Sound of vernal showers
      On the twinkling grass,
   Rain-awakened flowers,
      All that ever was
Joyous, and clear, and fresh, thy music doth surpass: 60
   Teach us, sprite or bird,
      What sweet thoughts are thine:
   I have never heard
      Praise of love or wine
That panted forth a flood of rapture so divine.
   Chorus Hymenaeal,
      Or triumphal chaunt,
   Matched with thine would be all
      But an empty vaunt,
A thing wherein we feel there is some hidden want.   70
   What objects are the fountains
      Of thy happy strain?
   What fields, or waves, or mountains?
      What shapes of sky or plain?
What love of thine own kind? what ignorance of pain?
   With thy clear keen joyance
      Languor cannot be:
   Shadow of annoyance
      Never came near thee:
Thou lovest; but ne'er knew love's sad satiety.   80
   Waking or asleep,
      Thou of death must deem
   Things more true and deep
      Than we mortals dream,
Or how could thy notes flow in such a crystal stream?
   We look before and after,
      And pine for what is not:
   Our sincerest laughter
      With some pain is fraught;
Our sweetest songs are those that tell of saddest thought.   90
   Yet if we could scorn
      Hate, and pride, and fear;
   If we were things born
      Not to shed a tear,
I know not how thy joy we ever should come near.
   Better than all measures
      Of delightful sound,
   Better than all treasures
      That in books are found,
Thy skill to poet were, thou scorner of the ground!   100
   Teach me half the gladness
      That thy brain must know,
   Such harmonious madness
      From my lips would flow,
The world should listen then, as I am listening now.

Exercise

How does Shelley achieve the seemingly effortless buoyancy of "To a Skylark"? Consider the rhythm and the use of words such as *blithe, springest, soar, float,* and many others.

Mary Wollstonecraft Godwin Shelley, 1797–1851

Mary Shelley deserves special mention here. She was the daughter of noted feminist Mary Wollstonecraft (1759–1797), author of *Vindication of the Rights of Woman* (1792), and the equally notable social reformer William Godwin (1756–1836), a disciple of Jeremy Bentham and a man who strongly influenced Shelley's reforming zeal. Shelley had left Harriet, his wife, for Mary and moved to the continent where he later married her. While reading ghost stories one evening, Lord Byron suggested that each should write a tale of the supernatural. Mary Shelley's contribution was *Frankenstein; or, The Modern Prometheus* (1818). Using the central themes of Faustian ambition and Promethean creativity, Mary told the story of the scientist Frankenstein who dared to create life itself. Frankenstein's creation needed love and sympathy, but was greeted instead, even by his creator, with disgust and revulsion. Symbolizing Romantic ideas of isolation and alienation, Frankenstein's creation turned from a search for love to hatred of all humankind and murderous destruction. Mary Shelley's story is even more influential today as a modern myth about the horrifying potential of such human creativity as nuclear weapons.

John Keats, 1795–1821

The poems of both Keats and Shelley have a musicality that sets their work apart from all other Romantic poetry. Trained as an apothecary with no thought of becoming a poet until he was eighteen, Keats began writing with a sense of urgency, having noted the symptoms of the tuberculosis that had already carried off his mother and his brother. Keats was the first to admit that his initial volume of poetry had many flaws but not that it was "alternately florid and arid," as one critic bitingly observed. Keats' own reaction to a barrage of criticism was quite relaxed: "About a twelvemonth since, I published a little book of verses; it was read by some dozen of my friends, who lik'd it; and some dozen whom I was unacquainted with, who did not."

Most Romantics adored what they imagined the Middle Ages to have been; none would have tolerated for a moment the reality of the medieval world. "La Belle Dame sans Merci" ("The Lovely Lady without Pity") is perhaps the finest example of Romantic medievalism. Though the title is taken from a medieval poem by Alain Chartier, the ballad is the poet's own magical version of the ageless myth of the hapless mortal who succumbed to the irresistible charms of a supernatural and pitiless seductress. The first three stanzas are addressed to the distraught knight by an unknown questioner; the balance of the poem forms his anguished reply.

LA BELLE DAME SANS MERCI
John Keats

O what can ail thee, knight-at-arms,
    Alone and palely loitering?
The sedge has withered from the lake,
    And no birds sing.

O what can ail thee, knight-at-arms,
    So haggard and so woe-begone?
The squirrel's granary is full,
    And the harvest's done.

I see a lily on thy brow,
    With anguish moist and fever dew;   10
And on thy cheek a fading rose
    Fast withereth too.

I met a lady in the meads,
    Full beautiful—a faery's child;
Her hair was long, her foot was light,
    And her eyes were wild.

I set her on my pacing steed,
    And nothing else saw all day long;
For sidelong would she bend, and sing
    A faery's song.   20

I made a garland for her head,
    And bracelets too, and fragrant zone;
She looked at me as she did love,
    And made sweet moan.

She found me roots of relish sweet,
    And honey wild, and manna-dew;
And sure in language strange she said,
    "I love thee true."

She took me to her elfin grot,
    And there she wept and sighed full sore: 30
And there I shut her wild, wild eyes
    With kisses four.

And there she lulled me asleep,
    And there I dreamed—Ah! woe betide!
The latest dream I ever dreamed,
    On the cold hill-side.

I saw pale kings and princes too,
    Pale warriors—death-pale were they all;
Who cried, "La Belle Dame Sans Merci
    Hath thee in thrall!"   40

I saw their starved lips in the gloam,
    With horrid warning gaped wide;
And I awoke, and found me here
    On the cold hill's side.

And this is why I sojourn here,
    Alone and palely loitering;
Though the sedge is withered from the lake,
    And no birds sing.

Exercise

How does Keats maintain the medieval mood in "La Belle Dame sans Merci"? Look, for example, at obvious words such as *thee*, *knight-at-arms*, and *dancing steed* and subtle words such as *meads*, *garland*, and *elfin*.

Johann Wolfgang von Goethe, 1749–1832

Goethe (GUHR-tuh), Germany's greatest writer, achieved instant fame with the publication of *The Sorrows of Young Werther* (1774), a morbid tale that captured the imagination of all Europe. Werther's hopeless longing for his best friend's wife was autobiographical, but Werther's subsequent suicide was merely in the tradition of romantic despair, emulated, tragically, by a number of young men who killed themselves while holding a copy of the novel. Calling Romanticism "a sickness," Goethe proceeded to write novels and plays in the neoclassic style. A "Renaissance man" rather than a "Romantic hero," Goethe made important contributions to botany, the theory of evolution, and physics and devoted much of the rest of his life to the retelling of the legend of Dr. Johannes Faustus (ca. 1480–1540), who supposedly sold his soul to the Devil (Mephistopheles) in exchange for youth, knowledge, and power. Goethe's *Faust* (1808–1832) became the mythic symbol for the restless search for the meaning of life, and the will to wrest the fullest possibilities from a lifetime of titanic deeds. In his relentless drive to enlarge the meaning of life the "Faustian man" is Romantic, but his will to power and knowledge was always and inevitably doomed to failure. In the final analysis, Faust's salvation lay in his heroic self-regeneration and his acceptance of his own mortality.

Late in his long career Goethe again became a romantic poet but, as usual, in his own original fashion. Long attracted to poetry of the Middle East, Goethe published his *West-Eastern Divan* (1819), his last important body of lyric poetry, in which he sought wisdom, piety, and peace through a central motif of love. Inspired by a translation of the *Divan* of Hafiz, a fourteenth-century Persian poet, Goethe wrote twelve books of mostly love poetry. This unique collection was described by noted German poet Heinrich Heine (1797–1856):

> The charm of the book is inexplicable; it is a votive nosegay sent from the West to the East, composed of the most precious and curious plants. This nosegay signifies that the West is tired of thin and icy-cold spirituality, and seeks warmth in the strong and healthy bosom of the East.

The selections given are the last two poems in the book in which the lovers are reunited after an extended separation (related by Hatem) and closing with Suleika's rhapsodic declaration of love. The idealized lovers are Goethe himself (Hatem) and Marianne von Willemer (Suleika).

VIII. BOOK OF SULEIKA

Johann Wolfgang von Goethe

THE REUNION

Can it be! of stars the star,
    Do I press thee to my heart?
In the night of distance far,
    What deep gulf, what bitter smart!
Yes, 'tis thou, indeed at last,
    Of my joys the partner dear!
Mindful, though, of sorrows past,
    I the present needs must fear.
When the still unfashioned earth
    Lay on God's eternal breast,   10
He ordained its hour of birth
    With creative joy possessed.
Then a heavy sigh arose,
    When He spake the sentence:—"Be!"
And the All, with mighty throes,
    Burst into reality.
And when thus was born the light,
    Darkness near it feared to stay,
And the elements with might
    Fled on every side away;   20
Each on some far—distant trace,
    Each with visions wild employed,
Numb, in boundless realms of space,
    Harmony and feeling—void.
Dumb was all, all still and dead,
    For the first time, God alone!
Then He formed the morning—red,
    Which soon made its kindness known:
It unraveled from the waste
    Bright and glowing harmony,   30
And once more with love was graced
    What contended formerly.
And with earnest, noble strife,
    Each its own peculiar sought;
Back to full, unbounded life,
    sight and feeling soon were brought.
Wherefore, if 'tis done, explore
    How? why give the manner, name?
Allah need create no more,
    We his world ourselves can frame.   40
So, with morning pinions bright,
    To thy mouth was I impelled;
Stamped with thousand seals by night,
    Star—clear is the bond fast held.
Paragons on earth are we
    Both of grief and joy sublime,
And a second sentence:—"Be!"
    Parts us not a second time.

SULEIKA

With what inward joy, sweet lay,
    I thy meaning have descried!
Lovingly thou seemest to say
    That I'm ever by his side;
That he ever thinks of me,
    That he to the absent gives
All his love's sweet ecstasy,
While for him alone she lives.
Yes, the mirror which reveals
    Thee, my loved one, is my breast;   10
This is the bosom, where thy seals
    Endless kisses have impressed.
Numbers sweet, unsullied truth,
    Chain me down in sympathy!
Love's embodied radiant youth,
    In the garb of Poesy!
In thousand forms mayst thou attempt surprise,
    Yet, all—belovèd one, straight know I thee;
Thou mayst with magic veils thy face disguise,
    And yet, all—present one, well I know thee!   20
Upon the cypress' purest, youthful bud,
    All—beauteous—growing one, straight know I thee;
In the canal's unsullied, living flood,
    All—captivating one, well know I thee!
When spreads the water—column, rising proud,
    All—sportive one, how gladly know I thee;
When, e'en in forming, is transformed the cloud,
    All—figure—changing one, there know I thee.
Veiled in the meadow—carpet's flowery charms,
    All—chequered starry fair one, know I thee;   30
And if a plant extend its thousand arms,
    Oh, all—embracing one, there know I thee.
When on the mount is kindled morn's sweet light,
    Straightway, all—gladdening one, salute I thee;
The arch of heaven o'er head grows pure and bright,—
    All—heart—expanding one, then breathe I thee.
That which my inward, outward sense proclaims,
    Thou all—instructing one, I know through thee;
And if I utter Allah's hundred names,
    A name with each one echoes, meant for thee.   40

Exercises

1. How did the previous relationship end? Why does the poet compare the reunion with the Creation? What are the parallels?
2. What is the cumulative effect of Suleika's repeated, similar phrases ending with "thee"?

To summarize, the Romantic Movement is perplexing if we consider only what these individual writers and philosophers advocated. What most romantics were opposed to provides a clearer picture, and the Enlightenment was their main target. Empiricism, geometric thinking, neoclassicism, all were areas subject to reason and, said the romantics, all were mechanized and dehumanized. Even the great Newton had become only a materialist and a narrow materialist at that.

Romantics emphasized individuality, the nonrational component of the personality, a sense of the infinite, and a quest for religious reality beyond sensible experience to find God in nature and within the human heart. Far from a return to orthodoxy, the impulse to re-create wonder in the world by finding God in nature was common to many romantics, except for those such as Byron and Shelley, who sought no God at all. The closest approach to a romantic consensus was the emphasis on the primacy of humane concerns, the celebration of the emotional nature of human beings, and the necessity for creative activity through the exercise of an unfettered imagination.

Perhaps more than any other period, the Romantic Era was expressed as well in literature as in music and in the visual arts. "Art," wrote Oscar Wilde, "is the most intense mode of individualism that the world has known." In no era was the creative role of the individual more consciously and effectively accomplished than in the Romantic Age. Art was, moreover, highly social, because it was the "result of a relationship between the artist and his time," (James Adams), and this was an era of extreme sensitivity to social issues. Further, the romantics, whether writers, artists, or composers, were generally attuned to certain themes that were endlessly fascinating. Figure 23.4 depicts in a single work five of the most powerful of these themes: nature, the Middle Ages, mysticism, religion, and death. The fate of this painting represents a final romantic irony.

Figure 23.4 *Kaspar David Friedrich,* Cloister Graveyard Under Snow, *1819. Oil on canvas, 47″ × 70″. Formerly Nationalgaleris, Staatliche Museen, Berlin (destroyed in 1945 during the Battle of Berlin).*

Philosophy, Science, and Social Thought

Hegel and Marx

The most important German philosopher after Kant, Georg Wilhelm Hegel (HAY-gul; 1770–1831) influenced European and American philosophers, historians, theologians, and political theorists. Described by Bertrand Russell as "the hardest to understand of all the great philosophers," the discussion of Hegel will be limited here to those doctrines that influenced Karl Marx. Hegel believed in an all-encompassing Absolute, a world Spirit that expressed itself in the historical process. Basing his logic on the "triadic dialectic," Hegel stated that for every concept or force (thesis) there was its opposite idea (antithesis). Out of the dynamic interaction between the two extremes would emerge a synthesis that, in turn, would become a new and presumably higher thesis. Absolute Being, for example, is a thesis whereas Absolute Unbeing is its antithesis. The synthesis is Absolute Becoming, meaning that the universe is eternally re-creating itself.

The notable cultures of the past were, according to Hegel, stages in the evolutionary development of the world Spirit toward perfection and freedom. Human beings and their institutions must inevitably clash because all are subject to error but, nevertheless, they must act and, through striving, find the "path of righteousness." Essentially Faustian in the conviction that perfectibility was attainable only through continuous activity and unavoidable conflict, Hegel's philosophy of history was evolutionary. Not only all humankind but the world itself was progressing ever upward, away from imperfection and toward the Absolute.

By mid-century, few could see progress of any kind, particularly for the oppressed lower class. The horrible working conditions and dismal lives of factory workers concerned social reformers throughout Europe. Many spoke out against the exploitation of the working class but none so dramatically as the Communists.

MANIFESTO OF THE COMMUNIST PARTY

Karl Marx and Friedrich Engels

A specter is haunting Europe—the specter of communism. All the powers of old Europe have entered into a holy alliance to exorcise this specter: Pope and Czar, Metternich and Guizot, French Radicals and German police spies.

Where is the party in opposition that has not been decried as communistic by its opponents in power? Where the Opposition that has not hurled back the branding reproach of communism, against the more advanced opposition parties, as well as against its reactionary adversaries?

Two things result from this fact:

I. Communism is already acknowledged by all European powers to be itself a power.

II. It is high time that Communists should openly, in the face of the whole world, publish their views, their aims, their tendencies, and meet this nursery tale of the specter of communism with a manifesto of the party itself.

To this end, Communists of various nationalities have assembled in London, and sketched the following manifesto, to be published in the English, French, German, Italian, Flemish, and Danish languages.

I

BOURGEOIS AND PROLETARIANS

The history of all hitherto existing society is the history of class struggles.

Freeman and slave, patrician and plebeian, lord and serf, guildmaster and journeyman, in a word, oppressor and oppressed, stood in constant opposition to one another, carried on an uninterrupted, now hidden, now open fight, a fight that each time ended, either in a revolutionary reconstitution of society at large, or in the common ruin of the contending classes.

In the earlier epochs of history, we find almost everywhere a complicated arrangement of society into various orders, a manifold gradation of social rank. In ancient Rome we have patricians, knights, plebeians, slaves; in the Middle Ages, feudal lords, vassals, guild-masters, journeymen, apprentices, serfs; in almost all of these classes, again, subordinate gradations.

The modern bourgeois society that has sprouted from the ruins of feudal society, has not done away with class antagonisms. It has but established new classes, new conditions of oppression, new forms of struggle in place of the old ones.

Our epoch, the epoch of the bourgeoisie, possesses, however, this distinctive feature: It has simplified the class antagonisms. Society as a whole is more and more splitting up into two great classes directly facing each other—bourgeoisie and proletariat. . . .

The Communists disdain to conceal their views and aims. They openly declare that their ends can be attained only by the forcible overthrow of all existing social conditions. Let the ruling classes tremble at a Communist revolution. The proletarians have nothing to lose but their chains. They have a world to win.

Workingmen of all countries, unite!

Because he believed in the basic goodness of human beings, Karl Marx (1818–1883), along with his collaborator Friedrich Engels (1820–1895), formulated a doctrine of inevitable progress that would lead to the perfect classless society in which private property and the profit motive would be relics of the imperfect past. From Hegel he took the dialectic, not as world Spirit but as material forces, a concept espoused by the German philosopher Ludwig Feuerbach (1804–1872). In effect, Marx turned Hegel's dialectic upside down, contending that it was not consciousness that determined human existence but the social existence of people that defined their consciousness.

For Marx, the way people made a living, their "means of production," determined their beliefs and institutions. To demonstrate the working out of dialectical materialism Marx concentrated on medieval feudal society. The thesis was the ruling class of the nobility and clergy. With the development of trade an increasingly affluent middle class, the bourgeoisie, rose as the antithesis in the class struggle. Following the American and French revolutions the bourgeois class merged with the vanquished nobility as the synthesis. Traders, bankers, and factory owners made up the ruling class of capitalists, the new thesis, whereas the oppressed workers, the proletariat, were the antithesis. The final class struggle between capitalists and workers would, according to Marx, inevitably result in victory for the proletariat, who would take over the means of production. Under the "dictatorship of the proletariat" the entire capitalist apparatus would be collectivized. With only one class remaining, the class struggle would cease. According to Marx, the state, with its laws, courts, and police served only to oppress the proletariat and would no longer be necessary; it would therefore "wither away."

It was not until late in the twentieth century that Marx was finally and decisively proven wrong, along with those who used their versions of his theories. The failure of communism is discussed in the concluding unit of this text.

Charles Darwin, 1809–1882

Anaximandros of Miletus (610–ca. 547 B.C.) postulated an elementary theory of evolution, but it was not until the nineteenth century that the theories of Erasmus Darwin, Jean-Baptiste de Lamarck, Thomas Malthus, and the detailed naturalistic observations of Charles Darwin finally led to Darwin's publication of *On the Origin of Species by Means of Natural Selection* (1859). After serving as naturalist on the surveying ship *Beagle* (1831–1836) Darwin read, in Thomas Malthus' *On Population* (1798), the thesis that population increased by geometric ratio (1, 2, 4, 16, etc.), whereas the food supply increased arithmetically (1, 3, 5, 7, 9, etc.). The limited food supply, Malthus observed, naturally checked unlimited population increases. Darwin wrote:

> It at once struck me that under the circumstances favorable variations would tend to be preserved and unfavorable ones destroyed. The result of this would be the formation of a new species. Here then I had a theory by which to work. This is the doctrine of natural selection, the result of chance enabling, in Herbert Spencer's phrase, the survival of the fittest.

Darwin proceeded from three facts to his deductions:

Fact 1. All organisms tend to increase geometrically.
Fact 2. The population of a given species remains more or less constant.
Fact 3. Within any species there is considerable variation.
Deduction 1. With more young produced than can survive there must be competition for survival.
Deduction 2. The variations within a species means that a higher percentage of those with favorable variations will survive and, conversely, a higher percentage of those with unfavorable variations will die or fail to reproduce. This is natural selection. Furthermore, the favorable variations are generally transmitted by heredity, meaning that natural selection will tend to maintain and act to improve the ability of the species to survive.

Modern evolution theory confirms Darwin's facts and deductions as outlined above, but adds some significant variations in terms of modifications, mutations, and recombinations. Modification is a variation due to external or internal factors and is not the result of inheritance. Take, for example, identical twins, one leading an active and healthy life and the other immersed in alcoholism. Barring an accident one twin will almost certainly survive the other.

The copying of genes in the process of reproduction is not always precise. A copy that differs slightly from the original is a mutation, and the mutated gene will continue to reproduce itself unless the mutation results in an unfavorable variation that increases the chances against survival. Mutations tend, on the whole, to result in unfavorable variations.

Darwin was not aware of the full implications of Gregor Mendel's (1822–1884) experiments in genetics, specifically the fact that sexual reproduction results in a recombination of existing genetic units that may produce or modify inheritable combinations. Take, for example, twelve children born of the same parents. Though there is generally a familial resemblance, each child will be distinctly different because of the different recombination of genes.

Darwin was reluctant to publish his theories until he learned that Alfred Russel Wallace (1823–1913) had independently developed a theory of evolution. Both men submitted a paper to the Linnaean Society on the theory of natural selection; both papers were read on 1 July 1858, and later published. Even when Darwin published his *Origin of Species* the following year he considered his work a brief abstract of twenty-five years of detailed studies.

Darwin's work provoked a great controversy, of course, because it denied supernatural intervention in the functioning of the universe. He rode out the theological storm, but not the attacks of naturalists who claimed a special place for *homo sapiens* separate from other species. In the introduction to his *The Descent of Man* (1871) Darwin noted that he had many notes on the origin or descent of man but that he was determined "not to publish, as I thought that I should thus only add to the prejudices against my views." Indeed, his *Origin of Species* implied "that man must be included with other organic beings in any general conclusion respecting his manner of appearance on this earth." *The Descent of Man* is therefore a response to hostile naturalists and a sequel to the *Origin of Species* in which Darwin discussed the evolution of *homo sapiens* from lower forms of life. The conclusion of this work reveals Darwin as a realist and as an optimist.

THE DESCENT OF MAN
Charles Darwin

The main conclusion arrived at in this work, namely, that man is descended from some lowly organised form, will, I regret to think, be highly distasteful to many. But there can hardly be a doubt that we are descended from barbarians. The astonishment which I felt on first seeing a party of Fuegians on a wild and broken shore will never be forgotten by me, for the reflection at once rushed into my mind—such were our ancestors. These men were absolutely naked and bedaubed with paint, their long hair was tangled, their mouths frothed with excitement, and their expression was wild, startled, and distrustful. They possessed hardly any arts, and like wild animals lived on what they could catch; they had no government, and were merciless to every one not of their own small tribe. He who has seen a savage in his native land will not feel much shame, if forced to acknowledge that the blood of some more humble creature flows in his veins. For my own part I would as soon be descended from that heroic little monkey, who braved his dreaded enemy in order to save the life of his keeper, or from that old baboon, who descending from the mountains, carried away in triumph his young comrade from a crowd of astonished dogs—as from a savage who delights to torture his enemies, offers up bloody sacrifices, practices infanticide without remorse, treats his wives like slaves, knows no decency, and is haunted by the grossest superstitions.

Man may be excused for feeling some pride at having risen, though not through his own exertions, to the very summit of the organic scale; and the fact of his having thus risen, instead of having been aboriginally placed there, may give him hope for a still higher destiny in the distant future. But we are not here concerned with hopes or fears, only with the truth as far as our reason permits us to discover it; and I have given the evidence to the best of my ability. We must, however, acknowledge, as it seems to me, that man with all his noble qualities, with sympathy which feels for the most debased, with benevolence which extends not only to other men but to the humblest living creature, with his god-like intellect which has penetrated into the movements and constitution of the solar system—with all these exalted powers—Man still bears in his bodily frame the indelible stamp of his lowly origin.

What is the status of Darwinism today? As Dennis Flanagan states it, evolution by natural selection is simply "the testing of variations in the laboratory of the environment." With the theory of evolution

. . . the trouble lies with the word "theory." The everyday meaning of "theory" is speculation but the scientific meaning of the word is a substantial body of reasoning. It is like that with the Darwinian theory of evolution. *Evolution itself is not a theory; it is an inescapable fact.* Charles Darwin did much to call attention to that fact. Modern Darwinian theory, however, is an effort to explain *how* life evolves.[5]

The difference, in science, between "law" and "theory" can be further illustrated by citing the law of gravity, which states that objects in space are attracted to each other. The *theory* of gravity, on the other hand, is the inquiry into *how* and *why* objects attract each other. As with evolution, that inquiry continues to challenge scientists.

Social Darwinism

Herbert Spencer (1820–1903) was an English philosopher and an advocate of evolution not only in nature but in human institutions as well. "Survival of the fittest," the phrase coined by Spencer, meant, claimed the Social Darwinists, that the rich were better adapted to the rigors of competitive life; they were, in short, more fit to survive than the poor. Opposed to governmental intervention in economic affairs, trade unions, and socialist ideas such as welfare, powerful capitalists such as John D. Rockefeller and Andrew Carnegie claimed that unrestrained competition had a scientific basis comparable to evolution in nature. This position was, of course, an attempt to justify laissez-faire capitalism.

On a larger scale, Social Darwinism helped reinforce the idea that some nations were more competent than rival nations and defeating an adversary in warfare would thus demonstrate that superiority. Indeed, it became almost a moral duty, in Social Darwinian terms, to conquer "inferior" people and populate their lands with fitter human beings. Late nineteenth-century imperialism had an ideal social philosophy to justify the ruthless growth of empire. British imperialist Cecil Rhodes went still further by claiming that a world of Anglo-Saxons was the best of all possible worlds, thus adding racism to the social evolution theory. In 1845 a journalist and diplomat named John Louis O'Sullivan coined the term *manifest destiny*, which, when reinforced by social evolution, provided the justification of American imperialism.

Darwinian views spread into every corner of the intellectual domain: anthropology, sociology, history, literature, art, music, legal and political institutions. Just about everything was investigated in terms of origin, development, and survival or disappearance.

There is no denying the enormous influence of evolutionary theory in all of these areas, but great care has to be taken when applying a scientific theory to nonscientific areas. "Natural

---

5. Dennis Flanagan, *Flanagan's Version: A Spectator's Guide to Science on the Eve of the Twentieth Century* (New York: Alfred A. Knopf, 1988), p. 26.

selection," for scientists, means the way things work in nature and no more than that. Social Darwinists manipulated evolutionary theory to justify individuality and unfettered competition as if the marketplace were a scientific laboratory. Scientific terminology was selected to undergird the way things were supposed to be. "Survival of the fittest" was intended to prove that the wealthy and powerful were fit and no one else. In fact, the most competent creatures in Darwin's natural world were those who left, over a period of time, the most dependents who could survive natural selection. Not necessarily the smartest, largest, or strongest; just survivors.

Furthermore, the same conservative Social Darwinists who claimed that a capitalistic economy was a struggle for existence with only the fittest surviving refused, for the most part, to compete in a free market. They wanted high tariffs to protect them from foreign competition and would tolerate no competition for improved wages and working conditions on the part of organized labor. Those who argued so persuasively for competition, such as Rockefeller and Carnegie, effectively eliminated almost all competition so they could enjoy their virtual monopolies in steel and oil. In the final analysis, Social Darwinism is a twisted play on the good name of Charles Darwin. The true social philosophy of America's Robber Barons at the height of laissez-faire capitalism can best be summed up in the callous statement attributed to William Vanderbilt: "The public be damned!"

Liberalism

Jeremy Bentham (1748–1832) was the founder of the rationalist philosophy of utilitarianism, a doctrine whose central idea is that actions are not right or wrong in themselves; they can be judged only by their consequences. Utilitarianism is based on the assumption that all human beings pursue happiness by seeking pleasure and avoiding pain. The criterion of the value of deeds is their utility, that is, whether they lead to the greatest happiness of the greatest number. Bentham's ethics are, in effect, an inversion of those of Kant. Kant calls for action as a duty and on principle; Bentham's values are based on the consequences of actions.

Bentham believed, along with classical (laissez-faire) economists, that government governs best when it governs least and that it should be relatively passive in social affairs. He was, however, an ardent reformer and his detailed studies of English institutions convinced him that the pleasure derived by some in the pursuit of self-interest caused pain for others, sometimes many, many others. He and his followers, the Philosophic Radicals, finally concluded that the state should intervene to help provide the greatest happiness for the greatest number. Their influence led to considerable administrative, legal, and economic reforms that broadened, in the twentieth century, into the concept of the welfare state that aimed to care for all its citizens "from the cradle to the grave."

John Stuart Mill, 1806–1873

James Mill was a disciple of Bentham and the director of a rigorous "educational experiment" for his son, John Stuart Mill. At the age of three, young Mill had learned Greek and, at seven, was reading Plato's dialogues. During the following year he taught Latin to his sister. By the time John Stuart Mill started college, he had what he called a twenty-five-year headstart on his classmates. There were drawbacks, however. "I grew up," Mill wrote in his celebrated *Autobiography* (1873), "in the absence of love and in the presence of fear." Referring to himself as a "reasoning machine," Mill had a breakdown at twenty from which he recovered by turning to music and the Romantic poets, especially Coleridge and Wordsworth. It was also during this period of crisis that Mill met Harriet Taylor, the wife of a London merchant. A woman of remarkable intellect comparable to that of Mill, Harriet was his intense Platonic love and intellectual companion until 1851, when her husband died and they were finally married. The belated education in music and art plus the association with Harriet, whom Mill credited with much assistance in his writing, helped make Mill the foremost humanitarian liberal of the century.

Mill adopted utilitarianism at an early age, but distinguished pleasures by qualities rather than mere quantities as Bentham had done. For Mill the greatest pleasures were intellectual, ranking far above sensual pleasures. As he said, he would "rather be Sokrates dissatisfied than a fool satisfied." Mill's position was comparable to that of the Epicureans when he said that "human beings have faculties more elevated than the animal appetites, and when once conscious of them, do not regard anything as happiness which does not include their gratification." Among the greatest pleasures for Mill were freedom of thought, speech, and action, but only up to the point where this freedom might impinge on that of another. His famous political essay *On Liberty* (1859) explores the "nature and limits of power which can be legitimately exercised over the individual." His arguments in defense of free speech in a democratic society are just as convincing today, and his repeated warning against "the tyranny of the majority" is equally apropos for our own age.

To help secure the greatest good for the greatest number, Mill was an extremely active reformer, pressing for extended suffrage, measures to protect children, and actions to improve the lot of the poor. Virtually alone among intellectuals of his time, Mill was convinced that women were the intellectual equals of men. Vigorously opposed to the inferior status of women, he wrote the *Subjection of Women* (1869), a strongly worded book that was responsible for some altered laws and a number of modifications in opinions. Though he did not reject classical economics, Mill did see that adjustments were necessary and moreover, long overdue. In the midst of self-righteous materialistic Victorians, Mill's sane and sophisticated voice was equated, by his supporters, with a generous breath of fresh air.

A DAY IN VICTORIAN LONDON

Promptly at 6:00 A.M. the foot-boy lights the fire in the servants' quarters and starts to clean sixteen pairs of boots and shoes. The spacious house, in fashionable Belgravia, comes alive with servants sweeping floors, cleaning fireplaces, filling coal scuttles, dusting with feather dusters, polishing silverware, and collecting clothes for the huge daily washing. This is a society that prizes order and cleanliness—and enough servants to do all the work.

The master and mistress, Harold and Mary Worthington, struggle awake as an upstairs maid pours hot water into a marble basin and lights a fire in the grate. Rising from their coiled-spring bed with its white, crisply ironed sheets (changed daily) and bulky comforter, they wash and then carefully select their wardrobe for the day: a minimum of two changes for him and three for her. Assisted by his valet, Harold dons a gleaming white shirt with a high stiff collar, a cravat, and the customary black outfit: tubular trousers, inner waist coat, and outer frock coat. A lady's maid assists her mistress by first brushing, combing, and coiling her long hair into a large bun. After straining to tighten the corset down to the fashionable eighteen-inch waist, she buttons madame into a full-cut floor-length, navy blue dress with long puffed sleeves, all underscored, of course, by voluminous figure-hiding petticoats. The maid smiles wryly; this dressing routine would last far longer if society ladies wore makeup like the scandalous actresses in West End theatres.

While servants noisily eat breakfast in the downstairs kitchen, the parents dine sedately upstairs with their children—Edward (visiting from boarding school), Alice, Jane, and George—attended by the house steward. After toast and muffins, eggs, bacon, and deviled kidneys, the family pauses for morning prayers. As the children are led off by the governess and nursemaid, Harold dons his tall black hat and orders the carriage brought around for his daily trip to Fleet Street.

Mary bids him goodbye and immediately assumes her role as "angel of the house," the guardian of her husband's sanctuary. A conference with the butler, instructions for Afternoon Tea, and settling the menu for the evening's dinner party take care of pressing matters. Accompanied by the sewing maid she retires to the drawing room for fine needlework and a chance to listen to some servants' gossip. Among other things, it seems that the young Mrs. Thomas was seen wearing the short skirt and loose trousers popularized by that American troublemaker Amelia Bloomer.

Mary studies her newly refurbished drawing room, wondering what may have been overlooked. The wallpaper—colorful stripes overlaid with flocked chrysanthemums—is lovely, though nearly obscured by paintings, engravings, mirrors, and mottos. Flanked by heavy drapes, the tall windows are covered with fine muslin curtains with lace fringes. The massive chairs and sofas, with carved armrests and curved legs, are comfortably springy and upholstered with horsehair. The fireplace mantle is covered with an assortment of porcelain figurines and crystal bowls flanking an ornate French clock. Embroidered cloths accent the end tables and piano, with potted plants and palms filling in the corners of the room.

Confirming the Victorian horror of vacant space, collections of wax fruit, shells, butterflies, stuffed birds, photographs, and vacation souvenirs saturate the remaining areas. The hanging tassels in the double doorways blend nicely with the Belgian carpet, Mary reflects, as she notices some dust on her Venetian glasses. That new upstairs maid obviously needs more instruction, and soon.

Meanwhile, Harold's carriage wheels majestically through streets that seem more congested every day. Harold notes the immense bulk of the new Victoria Station and farther on, the imposing mass of the Houses of Parliament. The street people are, as usual, inordinately pushy; fish vendors, flower girls, hot bun peddlers, chimney sweeps, and sandwich men add to the incredible din by loudly hawking their wares. Arriving at the London Clarion Building, Harold is vastly relieved to escape the clamor of the common people.

Begun by his grandfather, the Clarion has grown into a very prosperous family business. A sizable, literate middle class, hungry for news, helps increase circulation, and the expanding merchant class guarantees a comparable growth in advertising. The morning was busy with conferences with various editors and a meeting on coming feature stories. It is time for another laudatory article on the expanding empire, perhaps a story on India, the rich colony that the Prime Minister, Mr. Disraeli, had proudly proclaimed the "jewel in the crown" of the Queen of England.

After a hearty roast beef lunch at home, Harold accompanies his wife on a stroll to Green Park near Buckingham Palace. They discuss Harold's ambitions for Edward, the eldest child. Master Edward, age 12, is in boarding school studying Greek, Latin, mathematics, and history as part of his preparation for Cambridge. They hope the discipline is as severe as during Harold's schooldays. It is, after all, the disciplines of study and team sports (cricket and rugby) that develop the character of future empire builders. Theirs is a high calling, for they will carry the bountiful benefits of British civilization to the most remote and benighted areas of the globe.

After a tedious meeting at Town Hall about the new trade unions—would they really become a threat to management?—Harold returns home to change into formal attire for the dinner party. Soon, gentlemen of influence and ladies of society gather for an elaborate repast: soup, two kinds of fish, turkey and roast mutton, partridge and pheasant, lobster salad, and truffles and champagne. All is served family style with white-gloved servants pouring the wine and refilling platters and bowls. After dinner, as the women retire to the sitting room for tea, the men gather in the library to smoke their cigars, talk politics, and argue the merits of the new game called polo.

After seeing the last guests off, the master and mistress thankfully retire to their suite, he with a new book by Dickens and she trying to decide between Tennyson and that young poet named Thomas Hardy. Both are content, but Mary is wondering if she should tell her husband that the main topic over tea was Mr. Mill's book on the *Subjection of Women*. No, not now; maybe not ever.

Victorian Poets

By the late Victorian period England was a bustling and prosperous country. Mechanized, industrialized, and urbanized, it was also a tiny island on whose flag the sun never set, the most powerful and far-flung empire the world had ever known. Early Romantics had envisioned a new society flourishing in a golden age, but late Victorians witnessed endless colonial wars, smoke blanketing the countryside from hundreds of belching smokestacks, and miles of dreary row houses inhabited by overworked and underpaid factory workers. The industrial revolution had defiled nature but, after Darwin, there was no solace in a nature "red with tooth and claw." What, then, was the role of the poet?

Alfred, Lord Tennyson, 1809–1892

The most representative poet of the late Victorian era, Tennyson reflected the mood of the period in poetry that was contemplative, sad, quiet, melancholy, sometimes wistful, and often pessimistic. The old optimism of the early Romantics had vanished.

Tennyson wrote often about contemporary events such as "The Charge of the Light Brigade," but his best poetry is about the past, particularly the classical past. In "Ulysses" the Greek hero has returned, after twenty years, to Penelope, his "aged wife," and Telemachus, a dutiful son who is content to stay at home and "make mild a rugged people." Ulysses is always the man of action, the embodiment of the Faustian man, whose mission in life is succinctly stated in the last line of the poem.

Literary Selections

ULYSSES
Alfred, Lord Tennyson

It little profits that an idle king,
By this still hearth, among these barren crags,
Matched with an aged wife, I mete and dole
Unequal laws unto a savage race,
That hoard, and sleep, and feed, and know not me.
I cannot rest from travel: I will drink
Life to the lees: all times I have enjoyed
Greatly, have suffered greatly, both with those
That loved me, and alone; on shore, and when
Through scudding drifts the rainy Hyades   10
Vext the dim sea. I am become a name;
For always roaming with a hungry heart
Much have I seen and known: cities of men
And manners, climates, councils, governments,
Myself not least, but honored of them all,—
And drunk delight of battle with my peers,
Far on the ringing plains of windy Troy.
I am a part of all that I have met;
Yet all experience is an arch wherethrough
Gleams that untraveled world, whose margin fades   20
For ever and for ever when I move.

How dull it is to pause, to make an end,
To rust unburnished, not to shine in use!
As though to breathe were life! Life piled on life
Were all too little, and of one to me
Little remains: but every hour is saved
From that eternal silence, something more,
A bringer of new things; and vile it were
For some three suns to store and hoard myself,
And this gray spirit yearning in desire   30
To follow knowledge, like a sinking star,
Beyond the utmost bound of human thought.
This is my son, mine own Telemachus,
To whom I leave the scepter and the isle—
Well-loved of me, discerning to fulfill
This labor, by slow prudence to make mild
A rugged people, and through soft degrees
Subdue them to the useful and the good.
Most blameless is he, centered in the sphere
Of common duties, decent not to fail   40
In offices of tenderness, and pay
Meet adoration to my household gods,
When I am gone. He works his work, I mine.
There lies the port: the vessel puffs her sail:
There gloom the dark broad seas. My mariners,
Souls that have toiled, and wrought, and thought with me—
That ever with a frolic welcome took
The thunder and the sunshine, and opposed
Free hearts, free foreheads—you and I are old;
Old age hath yet his honor and his toil;   50
Death closes all: but something ere the end,
Some work of noble note, may yet be done,
Not unbecoming men that strove with Gods.
The lights begin to twinkle from the rocks:
The long day wanes: the slow moon climbs: the deep
Moans round with many voices. Come, my friends,
'Tis not too late to seek a newer world.
Push off, and sitting well in order smite
The sounding furrows; for my purpose holds
To sail beyond the sunset, and the baths   60
Of all the western stars, until I die.
It may be that the gulfs will wash us down:
It may be we shall touch the Happy Isles,
And see the great Achilles, whom we knew.
Though much is taken, much abides; and though
We are not now that strength which in old days
Moved earth and heaven, that which we are, we are,—
One equal temper of heroic hearts,
Made weak by time and fate, but strong in will
To strive, to seek, to find, and not to yield.   70

Exercise

Exercise

In Tennyson's version is Ulysses a noble hero who refuses to submit meekly to old age and death or is he an arrogant, self-centered old man with little concern for his family? Why shouldn't he be "Matched with an aged wife"? Penelope is younger than Ulysses and she did wait twenty faithful years for her husband to return from his Odyssey. Whatever your opinion, is he believable as a human being?

Matthew Arnold, 1822–1888

As a poet and literary critic, Arnold was as pessimistic about human beings and their institutions as were his colleagues, but through sheer force of will he created a cheerful demeanor and purposive character for himself. Possibly the most anti-Victorian figure in Victorian England, Arnold was an apostle of high culture and a lifelong enemy of Puritanism, the "Barbarians" (the aristocracy), and the "Philistines" (the middle class). His melancholic and despairing view of human alienation in a hostile universe is memorably expressed in "Dover Beach." When the poet says to his female companion, "Ah love, let us be true to one another!" the objective is not love but survival. Arnold was a realist, not a romantic.

DOVER BEACH
Matthew Arnold

[First published 1867.]

The sea is calm to-night,
The tide is full, the moon lies fair
Upon the Straits;—on the French coast, the light
Gleams, and is gone; the cliffs of England stand,
Glimmering and vast, out in the tranquil bay.
Come to the window, sweet is the night air!
Only, from the long line of spray
Where the ebb meets the moon-blanch'd sand,
Listen! you hear the grating roar
Of pebbles which the waves suck back, and fling,   10
At their return, up the high strand,
Begin, and cease, and then again begin,
With tremulous cadence slow, and bring
The eternal note of sadness in.

Sophokles long ago
Heard it on the Aegaean, and it brought
Into his mind the turbid ebb and flow
Of human misery; we
Find also in the sound a thought,
Hearing it by this distant northern sea.   20
The sea of faith
Was once, too, at the full, and round earth's shore
Lay like the folds of a bright girdle furl'd;
But now I only hear
Its melancholy, long, withdrawing roar,
Retreating to the breath
Of the night-wind down the vast edges drear
And naked shingles of the world.
Ah, love, let us be true
To one another! for the world, which seems   30
To lie before us like a land of dreams,
So various, so beautiful, so new,
Hath really neither joy, nor love, nor light,
Nor certitude, nor peace, nor help for pain;
And we are here as on a darkling plain
Swept with confused alarms of struggles and flight,
Where ignorant armies clash by night.

Exercises

1. Compare the liquid and nasal sounds of lines 1–8 with the much harsher sounds of lines 9–14. Notice, also, that the opening lines describe a lovely seascape, with a discordant tone entering at line 9 in both sounds and sense.
2. What was it that Sophokles heard long ago and far away?
3. What happened to the "sea of faith"? Why?
4. The verbs in lines 1–8 are positive but, in lines 30–31, the world *seems* like a land of dreams. What is the world really like?
5. What are the many implications inherent in the last line? Consider the levels of meaning in each of the key words— *ignorant, armies, clash, night*—and then reflect on the entire line. How far have we come from the opening lines?

Thomas Hardy, 1840–1928

Though he denied being a pessimist, the novels, short stories, and poems of Thomas Hardy reveal a pessimism every bit as profound as that of Matthew Arnold and Feodor Dostoevsky. Hardy claimed that human effort could make the world a better place, but his prose and poetry overflow with sadness over the waste and frustration of life. Though he outlived the Victorian era, Hardy's output typifies the late Victorian mood of ironic melancholy as, for example, in "Neutral Tones" in which the imagery is consistent and convincing.

NEUTRAL TONES
Thomas Hardy

We stood by a pond that winter day,
And the sun was white, as though chidden of God,
And a few leaves lay on the starving sod;
—They had fallen from an ash, and were gray.

Your eyes on me were as eyes that rove
Over tedious riddles of years ago;
And some words played between us to and fro
On which lost the more by our love.

The smile on your mouth was the deadest thing
Alive enough to have strength to die;
And a grin of bitterness swept thereby
Like an ominous bird a-wing. . . .

Since then, keen lessons that love deceives,
And wrings with wrong, have shaped to me
Your face, and the God-cursed sun, and a tree,
And a pond edged with grayish leaves.
1898

Written on the last day of the nineteenth century, "The Darkling Thrush" morosely defines a century that ends, for Hardy, with a whimper, and anticipates a new hundred years that seem to offer little hope of anything better.

THE DARKLING THRUSH
Thomas Hardy

I leant upon a coppice gate
    When Frost was specter-gray,
And Winter's dregs made desolate
    The weakening eye of day.
The tangled bine-stems scored the sky
    Like strings of broken lyres,
And all mankind that haunted nigh
    Had sought their household fires.
The land's sharp features seemed to be
    The Century's corpse outleant,   10
His crypt the cloudy canopy,
    The wind his death-lament.
The ancient pulse of germ and birth
    Was shrunken hard and dry,
And every spirit upon earth
    Seemed fervorless as I.
At once a voice arose among
    The bleak twigs overhead
In a fullhearted evensong
    Of joy illimited;   20

An aged thrush, frail, gaunt, and small,
    In blast-beruffled plume,
Had chosen thus to fling his soul
    Upon the growing gloom.
So little cause for carolings
    Of such ecstatic sound
Was written on terrestrial things
    Afar or nigh around,
That I could think there trembled through
    His happy good-night air   30
Some blessed Hope, whereof he knew
    And I was unaware.
1902

Materialism and Pessimism

Feodor Mikhailovich Dostoevsky, 1821–1881

One of the giants of modern literature, Dostoevsky (doss-toe-EFF-ski) was deeply scarred by his sentence to hard labor in Siberia as an enemy of the Czarist government. Darkly pessimistic about the future of European civilization, the author turned to religion as a means of redemption. This was not the organized religion of Rome or of the Russian Orthodox church, but an individual commitment to faith, action, and demonstrated compassion for all people, even the worst among them, with the expectation that all could be saved through their own individual efforts. Thus Dostoevsky can be classed with Kierkegaard and Nietzsche (see chapter 27) as an early exponent of existentialism.

In his monumental novel *The Brothers Karamazov* the author presents Ivan Karamazov as an atheist, whereas his brother, Aloysha, is spiritually whole and actively seeking Christianity in a secular society. Dostoevsky viewed his age as materialistic, spiritually bankrupt, and vulnerable to the dictates of Church and State, present or future. In this selection the author portrays the Grand Inquisitor as a symbol of everyone who rejects freedom and self-reliance and embraces power. Dostoevsky proposes the utilization of an active Christian faith to counter the totalitarian hell of a party, government, or church. His prescience immediately calls to mind the horrifying realities of fascism, communism, Hitler, Stalin, Chairman Mao, and the attendant miseries of the twentieth century.

Literary Selection

THE GRAND INQUISITOR
Feodor Mikhailovich Dostoevsky

"My story [said Ivan Karamazov to Aloysha] is laid in Spain, in Seville, in the most terrible time of the Inquisition, when fires were lighted every day to the glory of God, and

In the splendid *auto da fé*
The wicked heretics were burnt.[6]

Oh, of course, this was not the coming in which He will appear according to His promise at the end of time in all His heavenly glory, and which will be sudden 'as lightning flashing from east to west.' No, He visited His children only for a moment, and there where the flames were crackling round the heretics. In His infinite mercy He came once more among men in that human shape in which He walked among men for three years fifteen centuries ago. He came down to the 'hot pavement' of the southern town in which on the day before almost a hundred heretics had, *ad majorem gloriam Dei,*[7] been burned by the cardinal, the Grand Inquisitor, in a magnificent *auto da fé,* in the presence of the king, the court, the knights, the cardinals, the most charming ladies of the court, and the whole population of Seville.

"He came softly, unobserved, and yet, strange to say, everyone recognized Him. The people are irresistibly drawn to Him, they flock about Him, follow Him. He moves silently in their midst with a gentle smile of infinite compassion. The sun of love burns in His heart. Light, enlightenment, and power shine from His eyes, and their radiance, shed on the people, stirs their hearts with responsive love. He holds out His hands to them, blesses them, and a healing virtue comes from contact with Him, even with His garments. An old man in the crowd, blind from childhood, cries out, 'O Lord, heal me and I shall see Thee!' and, as it were, scales fall from his eyes and the blind man sees Him. The crowd weeps and kisses the earth under His feet. Children throw flowers before Him, sing, and cry 'Hosannah.' 'It is He—it is He!' all repeat. 'It must be He, it can be no one but Him!' He stops at the steps of the Seville cathedral at the moment when the weeping mourners are bringing in a little open white coffin. In it lies a child of seven, the only daughter of a prominent citizen. The dead child lies hidden in flowers. 'He will raise your child,' the crowd shouts to the weeping mother. The priest, coming to meet the coffin, looks perplexed, and frowns, but the mother of the dead child throws herself at His feet with a wail. 'If it is Thou, raise my child!' she cries, holding out her hands to Him. The procession halts, the coffin is laid on the steps at His feet. He looks with compassion, and His lips once more softly pronounce, 'Maiden arise!' and the maiden arises. The little girl sits up in the coffin and looks round, smiling with wide-open wondering eyes, holding a bunch of white roses they put in her hand.

"There are cries, sobs, confusion among the people, and at that moment the cardinal himself, the Grand Inquisitor, passes by the cathedral. He is an old man, almost ninety, tall and erect, with a withered face and sunken eyes, in which there is still a gleam of light, like a fiery spark. He is not dressed in his gorgeous cardinal's robes, as he was the day before, when he was burning the enemies of the Roman Church—at that moment he was wearing his coarse, old, monk's cassock. At a distance behind him come his gloomy assistants and slaves and the 'holy guard.' He stops at the sight of the crowd and watches it from a distance. He sees everything; he sees them set the coffin down at His feet, sees the child rise up, and his face darkens. He knits his thick gray brows and his eyes gleam with a sinister fire. He holds out his finger and bids the guards take Him. And such is his power, so completely are the people cowed into submission and trembling obedience to him, that the crowd immediately make way for the guards and in the midst of deathlike silence they lay hands on Him and lead Him away. The crowd instantly bows down to the earth, like one man, before the old inquisitor. He blesses the people in silence and passes on. The guards lead their prisoner to the close, gloomy vaulted prison in the ancient palace of the Holy Inquisition and shut Him in it. The day passes and is followed by the dark, burning 'breathless' night of Seville. The air is fragrant with laurel and lemon'.[8] In the pitch darkness the iron door of the prison is suddenly opened and the Grand Inquisitor himself comes in with a light in his hand. He is alone; the door is closed at once behind him. He stands in the doorway and for a long time, for a minute or two, gazes into His face. At last he goes up slowly, sets the light on the table and speaks.

" 'Is it Thou? Thou?' but receiving no answer, he adds at once, 'Don't answer, be silent. What canst Thou say, indeed? I know too well what Thou wouldst say. And Thou hast no right to add anything to what Thou hadst said of old. Why, then, art Thou come to hinder us? For Thou hast come to hinder us, and Thou knowest that. But dost Thou know what will be tomorrow? I know not who Thou art and care not to know whether it is Thou or only a semblance of Him, but tomorrow I shall condemn Thee and burn Thee at the stake as the worst of heretics. And the very people who have today kissed Thy feet, tomorrow at the faintest sign from me will rush to heap up the embers of Thy fire. Knowest Thou that? Yes, maybe Thou knowest it,' he added with thoughtful penetration, never for a moment taking his eyes off the Prisoner."

"I don't quite understand, Ivan. What does it mean?" Aloysha, who had been listening in silence, said with a smile. "Is it simply a wild fantasy, or a mistake on the part of the old man—some impossible *quid pro quo?* "[9]

---

6. From a poem, "Corialanus," (1834) by A. I. Polezhaev.
7. "For the greater glory of God"—motto of the Society of Jesus.

8. From Pushkin's play *The Stone Guest (Don Juan)*.
9. "One for the other," a mix–up, mistaken identity.

"Take it as the last," said Ivan, laughing, "if you are so corrupted by modern realism and can't stand anything fantastic. If you like it to be a case of *quid pro quo,* let it be so. It is true," he went on, laughing, "the old man was ninety, and he might well be crazy over his set idea. He might have been struck by the appearance of the Prisoner. It might, in fact, be simply his ravings, the delusion of an old man of ninety, approaching his death, overexcited by the *auto da fe* of a hundred heretics the day before. But does it matter to us after all whether it was a *quid pro quo* or a wild fantasy? All that matters is that the old man should speak out, should speak openly of what he has thought in silence for ninety years."

"And the Prisoner too is silent? Does He look at him and not say a word?"

"That's inevitable in any case," Ivan laughed again. "The old man has told Him He hasn't the right to add anything to what He has said of old. One may say it is the most fundamental feature of Roman Catholicism, in my opinion at least. 'All has been given by Thee to the Pope,' they say, 'and all, therefore, is still at the Pope's hands, and there is no need for Thee to come now at all. Thou must not meddle for the time, at least.' That's how they speak and write too—the Jesuits, at any rate. I have read it myself in the works of their theologians. 'Hast Thou the right to reveal to us one of the mysteries of that world from which Thou hast come?' my old man asks Him, and answers the question for Him. 'No, Thou hast not; that Thou mayest not add to what has been said of old, and mayest not take from men the freedom which Thou didst exalt when Thou wast on earth. Whatsoever Thou revealest anew will encroach on men's freedom of faith; for it will be manifest as a miracle, and the freedom of their faith was dearer to Thee than anything in those days fifteen hundred years ago. Didst Thou not often say then, "I will make you free"? But now Thou hast seen these "free" men,' the old man adds suddenly, with a pensive smile. 'Yes, we've paid dearly for it,' he goes on, looking sternly at Him, 'but at last we have completed that work in Thy name. For fifteen centuries we have been wrestling with Thy freedom, but now it is ended and over for good. Dost Thou not believe that it's over for good? Thou lookest meekly at me and deignest not even to be wroth with me. But let me tell Thee that now, today, people are more persuaded than ever that they have perfect freedom, yet they have brought their freedom to us and laid it humbly at our feet. But that has been our doing. Was this what Thou didst? Was this Thy freedom?'"

"I don't understand again," Aloysha broke in. "Is he ironical, is he jesting?"

"Not a bit of it! He claims it as a merit for himself and his Church that at last they have vanquished freedom and have done so to make men happy. 'For now' (he is speaking of the Inquisition, of course) 'for the first time it has become possible to think of the happiness of men. Man was created a rebel; and how can rebels be happy? Thou wast warned,' he says to Him. 'Thou hast had no lack of admonitions and warnings, but Thou didst not listen to those warnings; Thou didst reject the only way by which men might be made happy. But, fortunately, departing Thou didst hand on the work to us. Thou hast promised, Thou hast established by Thy word, Thou hast given to us the right to bind and unbind, and now, of course, Thou canst not think of taking it away. Why, then, hast Thou come to hinder us?'"

"And what's the meaning of 'no lack of admonitions and warnings'?" asked Aloysha.

"Why, that's the chief part of what the old man must say."

"'The wise and dread spirit, the spirit of self-destruction and nonexistence,' the old man goes on, 'the great spirit talked with Thee in the wilderness, and we are told in the books that he "tempted" Thee. Is that so? And could anything truer be said than what he revealed to Thee in three questions and what Thou didst reject, and what in the books is called "the temptation"? And yet if there has ever been on earth a real stupendous miracle, it took place on that day, on the day of the three temptations. The statement of those three questions was itself the miracle. If it were possible to imagine simply for the sake of argument that those three questions of the dread spirit had perished utterly from the books, and that we had to restore them and to invent them anew, and to do so had gathered together all the wise men of the earth—rulers, chief priests, learned men, philosophers, poets—and had set them the task to invent three questions, such as would not only fit the occasion, but express in three words, three human phrases, the whole future history of the world and of humanity—dost Thou believe that all the wisdom of the world united could have invented anything in depth and force equal to the three questions which were actually put to Thee then by the wise and mighty spirit in the wilderness? From these questions alone, from the miracle of their statement, we can see that we have here to do not with the fleeting human intelligence, but with the absolute and eternal. For in those three questions the whole subsequent history of mankind is, as it were, brought together into one whole, and foretold, and in them are united all the unsolved historical contradictions of human nature. At the time it could not be so clear, since the future was unknown; but now that fifteen hundred years have passed, we see that everything in those three questions was so justly grasped and foretold, and has been truly fulfilled, that nothing can be added to them or taken from them.

"'Judge Thyself who was right—Thou or he who questioned Thee then? Remember the first question; its meaning, though not the exact words, was this: "Thou wouldst go into the world, and art going with empty hands, with promise of freedom which men in their simplicity and their natural unruliness cannot even understand, which they fear and dread—for nothing has ever been more insupportable for a man and a human society than freedom. But seest Thou these stones in this parched and barren wilderness? Turn them into bread, and mankind will run after Thee like a flock, grateful and obedient, though forever trembling, lest Thou withdraw Thy hand and deny them Thy bread." But Thou wouldst not deprive man of freedom and didst reject the offer, thinking, what is that freedom worth, if obedience is bought with bread?

Thou didst reply that man lives not by bread alone. But dost Thou know that for the sake of that earthly bread the spirit of the earth will rise up against Thee and will strive with Thee and overcome Thee, and all will follow him, crying, "Who can compare with this beast? He has given us fire from heaven!" Dost Thou know that the ages will pass, and humanity will proclaim by the lips of their sages that there is no crime, and therefore no sin; there is only hunger? "Feed men, and then ask of them virtue!" that's what they'll write on the banner, which they will raise against Thee, and with which they will destroy Thy temple. Where Thy temple stood will rise a new building; the terrible tower of Babel will be built again, and though, like the one of old, it will not be finished, yet Thou mightest have prevented that new tower and have cut short the sufferings of men for a thousand years; for they will come back to us after a thousand years of agony with their tower. They will seek us again, hidden underground in the catacombs, for we shall again be persecuted and tortured. They will find us and cry to us, "Feed us, for those who have promised us fire from heaven haven't given it!" And then we shall finish building their tower, for he finished the building who feeds them. And we alone shall feed them in Thy name, declaring falsely that it is in Thy name. Oh, never, never can they feed themselves without us! No science will give them bread so long as they remain free. In the end they will lay their freedom at our feet and say to us, "Make us your slaves, but feed us." They will understand themselves, at last, that freedom and bread enough for all are inconceivable together, for never, never will they be able to share between them! They will be convinced, too, that they can never be free, for they are weak, vicious, worthless and rebellious. Thou didst promise them the bread of Heaven, but, I repeat again, can it compare with earthly bread in the eyes of the weak, ever sinful and ignoble race of man? And if for the sake of the bread of Heaven thousands and tens of thousands shall follow Thee, what is to become of the millions and tens of thousands of millions of creatures who will not have the strength to forego the earthly bread for the sake of the heavenly? Or dost Thou care only for the tens of thousands of the great and the strong, while the millions, numerous as the sands of the sea, who are weak but love Thee, must exist only for the sake of the great and strong? No, we care for the weak too. They are sinful and rebellious, but in the end they too will become obedient. They will marvel at us and look on us as gods, because we are ready to endure the freedom which they have found so dreadful and to rule over them—so awful it will seem to them to be free. But we shall tell them that we are Thy servants and rule them in Thy name. We shall deceive them again, for we will not let Thee come to us again. That deception will be our suffering, for we shall be forced to lie. This is the significance of the first question in the wilderness, and this is what Thou hast rejected for the sake of that freedom which Thou hast exalted above everything. Yet in this question lies hid the great secret of this world. Choosing "bread," Thou wouldst have satisfied the universal and everlasting craving of humanity individually and together as one—to find someone to worship. So long as man remains free he strives for nothing so incessantly and so painfully as to find someone to worship. But man seeks to worship what is established beyond dispute, so that all men would agree at once to worship it. For these pitiful creatures are concerned not only to find what one or the other can worship, but to find something that all would believe in and worship; what is essential is that all may be *together* in it. This craving for *community* of worship is the chief misery of every man individually and of all humanity from the beginning of time. For the sake of common worship they've slain each other with the sword. They have set up gods and challenged one another, "Put away your gods and come and worship ours, or we will kill you and your gods!" And so it will be to the end of the world, even when gods disappear from the earth; they will fall down before idols just the same. Thou didst know, Thou couldst not but have known, this fundamental secret of human nature, but Thou didst reject the one infallible banner which was offered Thee to make all men bow down to Thee alone—the banner of earthly bread; and Thou hast rejected it for the sake of freedom and the bread of Heaven. Behold what Thou didst further. And all again in the name of freedom! I tell Thee that man is tormented by no greater anxiety than to find someone quickly to whom he can hand over that gift of freedom with which the ill-fated creature is born. But only one who can appease their conscience can take over their freedom. In bread there was offered Thee an invincible banner; give bread, and man will worship Thee, for nothing is more certain than bread. But if someone else gains possession of his conscience—oh! then he will cast away Thy bread and follow after him who has ensnared his conscience. In that Thou wast right. For the secret of man's being is not only to live but to have something to live for. Without a stable conception of the object of life, man would not consent to go on living, and would rather destroy himself than remain on earth, though he had bread in abundance. That is true. But what happened? Instead of taking men's freedom from them, Thou didst make it greater than ever! Didst Thou forget that man prefers peace, and even death, to freedom of choice in the knowledge of good and evil? Nothing is more seductive for man than his freedom of conscience, but nothing is a greater cause of suffering. And behold, instead of giving a firm foundation for setting the conscience of man at rest forever, Thou didst choose all that is exceptional, vague and enigmatic; Thou didst choose what was utterly beyond the strength of men, acting as though Thou didst not love them at all—Thou who didst come to give Thy life for them! Instead of taking possession of men's freedom, Thou didst increase it, and burdened the spiritual kingdom of mankind with its sufferings forever. Thou didst desire man's free love, that he should follow Thee freely, enticed and taken captive by Thee.

In place of the rigid ancient law, man must hereafter with free heart decide for himself what is good and what is evil, having only Thy image before him as his guide. But didst Thou not know he would at last reject even Thy image and Thy truth, if he is weighed down with the fearful burden of free choice? They will cry aloud at last that the truth is not in Thee, for they could not have been left in greater confusion and suffering than Thou hast caused, laying upon them so many cares and unanswerable problems.

" 'So that, in truth, Thou didst Thyself lay the foundation for the destruction of Thy kingdom, and no one is more to blame for it. Yet what was offered Thee? There are three powers, three powers alone, able to conquer and to hold captive forever the conscience of these impotent rebels for their happiness—those forces are miracle, mystery and authority. Thou hast rejected all three and hast set the example for doing so. When the wise and dread spirit set Thee on the pinnacle of the temple and said to Thee, "If Thou wouldst know whether Thou art the Son of God then cast Thyself down, for it is written: the angels shall hold him up lest he fall and bruise himself, and Thou shalt know then whether Thou art the Son of God and shalt prove then how great is Thy faith in Thy Father." But Thou didst refuse and wouldtst not cast Thyself down. Oh! of course, Thou didst proudly and well, like God; but the weak, rebellious race of men, are they gods? Oh, Thou didst know then that in taking one step, in making one movement to cast Thyself down, Thou wouldst be tempting God and have lost all Thy faith in Him, and wouldst have been dashed to pieces against that earth which Thou didst come to save. And the wise spirit that tempted Thee would have rejoiced. But I ask again, are there many like Thee? And couldst Thou believe for one moment that men, too, could face such a temptation? Is the nature of men such, that they can reject miracle, and at the great moments of their life, the moments of their deepest, most agonizing spiritual difficulties, cling only to the free verdict of the heart? Oh, Thou didst know that Thy deed would be recorded in books, would be handed down to remote times and the utmost ends of the earth, and Thou didst hope that man, following Thee, would cling to God and not ask for a miracle. But Thou didst not know that when man rejects miracle he rejects God too; for man seeks not so much God as the miraculous. And as man cannot bear to be without the miraculous, he will create new miracles of his own for himself, and worship deeds of sorcery and witchcraft, though he might be a hundred times over a rebel, heretic and infidel. Thou didst not come down from the Cross when they shouted to Thee, mocking and reviling Thee, "Come down from the cross and we will believe that Thou art He." Thou didst not come down, for again Thou wouldst not enslave man by a miracle, and didst faith given freely, not based on miracle. Thou didst crave for free love and not the base raptures of the slave before the might that has overawed him forever. But Thou didst think too highly of men therein, for they are slaves, of course, though rebellious by nature. Look round and judge; fifteen centuries have passed, look upon them. Whom hast Thou raised up to Thyself? I swear, man is weaker and baser by nature than Thou hast believed him! Can he, can he do what Thou didst? By showing him so much respect, Thou didst, as it were, cease to feel for him,

for Thou didst ask far too much from him—Thou who hast loved him more than Thyself! Respecting him less, Thou wouldst have asked less of him. That would have been more like love, for his burden would have been lighter. He is weak and vile. What though he is everywhere now rebelling against our power, and proud of his rebellion? It is the pride of a child and a schoolboy. They are little children rioting and barring out the teacher at school. But their childish delight will end; it will cost them dear. They will cast down temples and drench the earth with blood. But they will see at last, the foolish children, that, though they are rebels, they are impotent rebels, unable to keep up their own rebellion. Bathed in their foolish tears, they will recognize at last that He who created them rebels must have meant to mock at them. They will say this in despair, and their utterance will be a blasphemy which will make them more unhappy still, for man's nature cannot bear blasphemy, and in the end always avenges it on itself. And so unrest, confusion and unhappiness—that is the present lot of man after Thou didst bear so much for their freedom! Thy great prophet tells in vision and in image, that he saw all those who took part in the first resurrection and that there were of each tribe twelve thousand.[10] But if there were so many of them, they must have been not men but gods. They had borne Thy cross, they had endured scores of years in the barren, hungry wilderness, living upon locusts and roots—and Thou mayest indeed point with pride at those children of freedom, of free love, of free and splendid sacrifice for Thy name. But remember that they were only some thousands, and gods at that; and what of the rest? And how are the other weak ones to blame, because they could not endure what the strong have endured? How is the weak soul to blame that it is unable to receive such terrible gifts? Canst Thou really have come only to the elect and for the elect? But if so, it is a mystery and we cannot understand it. And if it is a mystery, we too have a right to preach a mystery, and to teach them that it's not the free judgement of their hearts, not love that matters, but a mystery which they must follow blindly, even against their conscience. So we have done. We have corrected Thy work and have founded it upon *miracle, mystery, and authority*. And men have rejoiced that they were again led like sheep, and that the terrible gift that had brought them such suffering was, at last, lifted from their hearts. Were we right teaching them this? Speak! Did we not love mankind, so meekly acknowledging their feebleness, lovingly lightening their burden, and permitting their weak nature even sin with our sanction? Why hast Thou come now to hinder us? And why dost Thou look silently and searchingly at me with Thy mild eyes? Be angry. I don't want Thy love, for I love Thee not. And what use is it for me to hide anything from Thee? Don't I know to whom I am speaking? All that I can say is known to Thee already. I can see it in Thine eyes. And is it for me to conceal from Thee our mystery? Perhaps it is Thy will to hear it from my lips. Listen, then. We are not working with Thee, but with *him*—that is our mystery. It's long—eight

---

10. Revelation 8.

centuries—since we have been on *his* side and not on Thine. Just eight centuries ago, we took from him what Thou didst reject with scorn, that last gift he offered Thee, showing Thee all the kingdoms of the earth. We took from him Rome and the sword of Caesar, and proclaimed ourselves sole rulers of the earth, though hitherto we have not been able to complete our work.[11] But whose fault is that? Oh, the work is only beginning, but it has begun. It has long to await completion and the earth has yet much to suffer but we shall triumph and shall be Caesars, and then we shall plan the universal happiness of man. But Thou mightest have taken even then the sword of Caesar. Why didst Thou reject that last gift? Hadst Thou accepted that last counsel of the mighty spirit, Thou wouldst have accomplished all that man seeks on earth—that is, someone to worship, someone to keep his conscience, and some means of uniting all in one unanimous and harmonious anthill, for the craving of universal unity is the third and last anguish of men. Mankind as a whole has always strived to organize a universal state. There have been many great nations with great histories, but the more highly they were developed the more unhappy they were, for they felt more acutely than other people the craving for worldwide union. The great conquerors, Tamerlane[12] and Genghis Khan,[13] whirled like hurricanes over the face of the earth striving to subdue its people, and they too were but the unconscious expression of the same craving for universal unity. Hadst Thou taken the world and Caesar's purple, Thou wouldst have founded the universal and have given universal peace. For who can rule men if not he who holds their conscience and their bread in his hands? We have taken the sword of Caesar, and in taking it, of course, have rejected Thee and followed *him*. Oh, ages are yet to come of the confusion of free thought, of their science and cannibalism. For having begun to build their tower of Babel without us, they will end, of course, with cannibalism. But then the beast will crawl to us and lick our feet and spatter them with tears of blood. And we shall sit upon the beast and raise the cup, and on it will be written, "Mystery." But then, and only then, the reign of peace and happiness will come for men. Thou art proud of Thine elect, but Thou hast only the elect, those mighty ones who could become elect, have grown weary waiting for Thee, and have transferred and will transfer the powers of their spirit and the warmth of their heart to the other camp, and end by raising their *free* banner against Thee. Thou didst Thyself lift up that banner. But with us all will be happy and will no more rebel nor destroy one another as under Thy freedom. Oh, we shall persuade them that they will only become free when they renounce their freedom to us and submit to us. And shall we be right or shall we be lying? They will be convinced that we are right, for they will remember the horrors of slavery and confusion to which Thy freedom brought them. Freedom, free thought and science, will lead them into such straits and will bring them face to face with such marvels and insoluble mysteries, that some of them, the fierce and rebellious, will destroy themselves, others, rebellious

but weak, will destroy one another, while the rest, weak and unhappy, will crawl fawning to our feet, and whine to us: "Yes, you were right, you alone possess His mystery, and we come back to you, save us from ourselves!" Receiving bread from us, they will of course see clearly that we take the bread made by their hands from them, to give it to them, without any miracle. They will see that we do not change the stones to bread, but in truth they will be more thankful for taking it from our hands than for the bread itself! For they will remember only too well that in the old days, without our help, even the bread they made turned to stones in their hands, while since they have come back to us, the very stones have turned to bread in their hands. Too, too well they know the value of complete submission! And until men know that, they will be unhappy. Who is most to blame for their not knowing it, speak? Who scattered the flock and sent it astray on unknown paths? But the flock will come together again and will submit once more, and then it will be once for all. Then we shall give them the quiet humble happiness of weak creatures such as they are by nature. Oh, we shall persuade them at last not to be proud, for Thou didst lift them up and thereby taught them to be proud. We shall show them that they are weak, that they are only pitiful children, but that childlike happiness is the sweetest of all. They will become timid and will look to us and huddle close to us in fear, as chicks to the hen. They will marvel at us and will be awestricken before us, and will be proud at our being so powerful and clever, that we have been able to subdue such a turbulent flock of thousands of millions. They will tremble impotently before our wrath, their minds will grow fearful, they will be quick to shed tears like women and children, but they will be just as ready at a sign from us to pass to laughter and rejoicing, to happy mirth and childlike song. Yes, we shall set them to work, but in their leisure hours we shall make their life like a child's game, with children's songs and innocent dance. Oh, we shall allow them even sin, they are weak and helpless, and they will love us like children because we allow them to sin. We shall tell them that every sin will be expiated, if it is done with our permission, that we allow them to sin because we love them, and the punishment for these sins we take upon ourselves. And we shall take it upon ourselves, and they will adore us as their saviors who have taken on themselves their sins before God. And they will have no secrets from us. We shall allow or forbid them to live with their wives and mistresses, to have or not to have children—according to whether they have been obedient or disobedient—and they will submit to us gladly and cheerfully. The most painful secrets of their conscience, all, all they will bring to us, and we shall have an answer for all. And they will be glad to believe our answer, for it will save them from the great anxiety and terrible agony they endure at present in making a free decision for themselves. And all will be happy, all the millions of creatures except the hundred thousand who rule over them. For only we, we who guard the mystery, shall be unhappy. There will be thousands of millions of happy babes, and a hundred thousand sufferers who have taken upon themselves the curse of the knowledge of good and evil. Peacefully they will die, peacefully they will expire in Thy name, and beyond the grave they will find nothing but death. But

---

11. Pepin the Short, king of the Franks, granted Ravenna to Pope Stephen III in 756. This was the origin of the pope's temporal power (the sword of Caesar), which was strengthened when a later pope crowned Charlemagne Holy Roman Emperor on Christmas Day, A.D. 800.

12. Tamerlane (1336–1406), Tartar conqueror.

13. Genghis Khan (1155–1227), Mongolian conqueror.

we shall keep the secret, for their happiness we shall entice them with the reward of heaven and eternity. Though if there were anything in the other world, it certainly would not be for such as they. It is prophesied that Thou will come again in victory, Thou wilt come with Thy chosen, the proud and strong, but we will say that they have only saved themselves, but we have saved all. We are told that the harlot who sits upon the beast, and holds in her hands the *mystery,* shall be put to shame, that the weak will rise up again, and will rend her royal purple and will strip naked her 'loathsome' body.[14] But then I will stand up and point out to Thee the thousand millions of happy children who have known no sin. And we who have taken their sins upon us for their happiness will stand up before Thee and say: "Judge us if Thou canst and darest." Know that I fear Thee not. Know that I too have been in the wilderness, I too have lived on roots and locusts, I too prized the freedom with which Thou hast blessed men, and I too was striving to stand among Thy elect, among the strong and powerful, thirsting "to make up the number." But I awakened and would not serve madness. I turned back and joined the ranks of those *who have corrected Thy work.* I left the proud and went back to the humble, for the happiness of the humble. What I say to Thee will come to pass, and our dominion will be built up. I repeat, tomorrow Thou shalt see that obedient flock who at a sign from me will hasten to heap up the hot cinders about the pile on which I shall burn Thee for coming to hinder us. For if anyone ever deserved our fires, it is Thou. Tomorrow, I shall burn Thee. *Dixi.' "*[15]

Exercises

1. Defense lawyer Clarence Darrow claimed that he prepared his entire defense by studying the prosecutor's case. Consider the Grand Inquisitor as the prosecutor (as indeed he was) and list all the characteristics of people he considered good members of his church. Now list the human values that were prized by Dostoevsky. These will include those qualities specifically condemned plus the opposite of the human "virtues" praised by the cardinal.

2. Why do some (many?) people consider freedom of choice a kind of curse? Why, in other words, do they seek some outside authority that will tell them what is right or wrong, good or bad?

3. The Grand Inquisitor claims that he is among the few who are the unhappy ones because, among other things, they assume the sins of their congregations. Is he lying? Consider, for example, the power he has over other people's lives, especially the authority to condemn defenseless victims to death by fire. You can also consider his attitude toward Christ and toward the "wise and dread spirit." Finally, would he choose to be a Grand Inquisitor if he didn't like the job?

4. Dostoevsky warned of the danger of totalitarianism whether of a party, state, or church. Consider the Communist party in Russia prior to 1989, Nazi Germany, and the medieval Church of Rome. What do they have in common? How and in what ways do they differ? Can today's Church of Rome initiate another Inquisition? Why or why not?

Romanticism and Realism in America

For the United States the nineteenth century was the great age of expansion, from thirteen colonies to forty-five states, three territories, Alaska, Hawaii, the Philippines, Puerto Rico, Guam, and American Samoa (map 23.7). The vast physical growth and economic development was not paralleled, however, by significant developments in the fine and literary arts—not for some time. Early in the century writers were still intimidated by British letters but seeking ways to declare their literary independence. The emergence of Romanticism in England struck a responsive spark in America, and writers such as Washington Irving (1783–1859), William Cullen Bryant (1794–1878), and James Fenimore Cooper (1789–1851) produced romantic works in a new American style. Because of limited space we will begin with the next generation of writers and trace the development of American literature from Romanticism to Realism.

Edgar Allan Poe, 1809–1849

One of the few literary figures with an international reputation that the United States has produced, Poe was a brilliant literary critic, poet, and writer of highly imaginative short stories. Among the first to condemn crass American materialism, Poe devoted himself wholly to his art, becoming the first American to live his life entirely as an artist. Poe defined poetry as "the creation of beauty" and contended that all poetry should appeal equally to reason and emotion. Poe felt that all poetry should be composed in terms of beauty, restraint, and unity of effect and, indeed, his poetry is the embodiment of his theory of art. Inspired by the loss of a beautiful woman, "Annabel Lee" is a lyric masterpiece in a lilting musical style.

14. Revelation 17.
15. "I have spoken (finished)."

Literary Selections

ANNABEL LEE
Edgar Allan Poe

It was many and many a year ago,
   In a kingdom by the sea,
That a maiden there lived whom you may know
   By the name of Annabel Lee;
And this maiden she lived with no other thought
   Than to love and be loved by me.

I was a child and she was a child,
   In this kingdom by the sea,
But we loved with a love that was more than love,
   I and my Annabel Lee;   10
With a love that the wingèd seraphs of heaven
   Coveted her and me.

And this was the reason that, long ago,
   In this kingdom by the sea,
A wind blew out of a cloud, chilling
   My beautiful Annabel Lee;

So that her highborn kinsmen came
   And bore her away from me,
To shut her up in a sepulchre
   In this kingdom by the sea.   20

The angels, not half so happy in heaven,
   Went envying her and me;
Yes! that was the reason (as all men know,
   In this kingdom by the sea)
That the wind came out of the cloud by night,
   Chilling and killing my Annabel Lee.

But our love it was stronger by far than the love
   Of those who were older than we,
   Of many far wiser than we;
And neither the angels in heaven above,   30
   Nor the demons down under the sea,
Can ever dissever my soul from the soul
   Of the beautiful Annabel Lee:

For the moon never beams, without bringing me dreams
   Of the beautiful Annabel Lee;
And the stars never rise, but I feel the bright eyes
   Of the beautiful Annabel Lee;

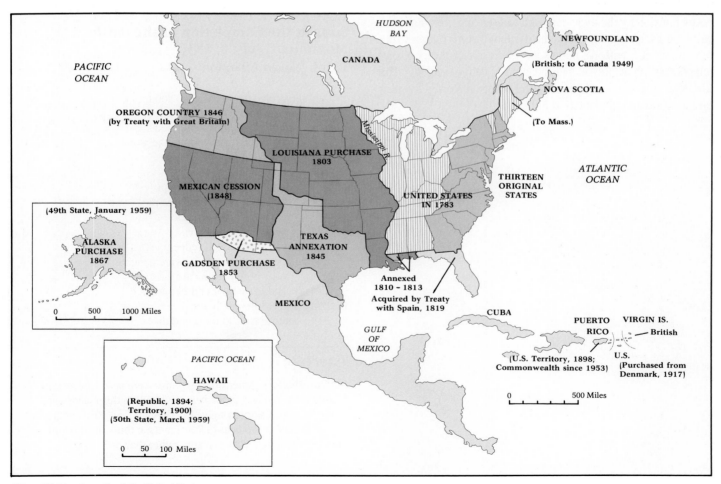

Map 23.7 *Growth of the United States.*

And so, all the night-tide, I lie down by the side
Of my darling—my darling—my life and my bride,
    In her sepulchre there by the sea,   40
    In her tomb by the sounding sea.

Exercise

This is one of the most musical of all Poe's poems. How does he achieve this effect? Consider the rhythm and the word selection, particularly the use of repeated words and phrases.

Ralph Waldo Emerson, 1803–1882

Poe was a conscious representative of a Southern tradition in literature, that of a romantic Virginia Cavalier. Just as consciously, Emerson and his colleagues were New England Romantics who reconciled romantic abstractions with the hardheaded realities of Yankee individualism. The creed of Emerson, Thoreau, Margaret Fuller, and others was transcendentalism, a belief that human beings and the universe were in perfect harmony and moving in a Hegelian manner toward perfection. High-minded and highly individualistic, transcendentalism stressed the individual's conscience as the sole judge in spiritual matters, total self-reliance in all matters, and the necessity for social reforms.

For Poe poetry was beauty, but Emerson viewed it as a necessary function for the individual who was seeking truth. Emerson wrote his essays but, in a sense, he thought that his poems wrote him. Many of Emerson's poems are the result of the poet's attempts to perceive the deeper meaning of nature, such as "The Rhodora," that was emblematic of the beauty bestowed by spirit on the world and implanted in human beings.

THE RHODORA
On Being Asked, Whence Is the Flower?
Ralph Waldo Emerson

In May, when sea-winds pierce our solitudes,
I found the fresh Rhodora in the woods,
Spreading its leafless blooms in a damp nook,
To please the desert and the sluggish brook.
The purple petals, fallen in the pool,
Made the black water with their beauty gay;
Here might the red-bird come his plumes to cool,
And court the flower that cheapens his array.
Rhodora! if the sages ask thee why
This charm is wasted on the earth and sky,
Tell them, dear, that if eyes were made for seeing,
Then Beauty is its own excuse for being:
Why thou wert there, O rival of the rose!
I never thought to ask, I never knew:
But, in my simple ignorance, suppose
The self-same Power that brought me there brought you.

Emerson's most famous poem is the "Concord Hymn" that memorialized the first battle of the Revolutionary War.

CONCORD HYMN
Sung at the Completion of the Battle Monument, July 4, 1837
Ralph Waldo Emerson

By the rude bridge that arched the flood,
    Their flag to April's breeze unfurled,
Here once the embattled farmers stood
    And fired the shot heard round the world.
The foe long since in silence slept;
    Alike the conqueror silent sleeps;
And Time the ruined bridge has swept
    Down the dark stream which seaward creeps.
On this green bank, by this soft stream,
    We set to-day a votive stone;
That memory may their deed redeem,
    When, like our sires, our sons are gone.
Spirit, that made those heroes dare
    To die, and leave their children free,
Bid Time and Nature gently spare
    The shaft we raise to them and thee.

Exercise

In "The Rhodora" Emerson says *if eyes were made for seeing,/Then beauty is its own excuse for being.* What does this mean? That beauty is as necessary as sight? In "Grecian Urn" Keats wrote that *beauty is truth, truth beauty.* Was Emerson thinking along the same lines or was he referring to nature rather than art?

Walt Whitman, 1819–1892

In his essay on "The Poet" Emerson wrote that the poet has a special mission because "the experience of each new age requires a new confession, and the world seems always waiting for its poet." It was the age of affirmation of American aspirations, and the exuberant voice of American democracy was that of Walt Whitman, which Emerson himself immediately recognized. On receiving the first edition of *Leaves of Grass* (1855), Emerson wrote Whitman that this was "the most extraordinary piece of wit and wisdom that America has yet contributed" and greeted the poet "at the beginning of a great career." Few writers, not to mention an indifferent general public, were as perceptive as Emerson, and even he later advised Whitman to go easy on the erotic poetry, advice which Whitman consistently ignored. *Leaves of Grass* was to be the poet's only book. Through nine editions (1855–1892) it grew with his life and, in effect, became his life. "This is no book," wrote Whitman, "who touches this touches a man."

A poet of many voices, Whitman rejected the genteel tradition and what he called "book-words," selecting instead the language of the common people, a unique blend of journalistic jargon, everyday speech, and a great variety of foreign words and phrases. A pantheist, mystic, and ardent patriot, Whitman advocated humanity, brotherhood, and freedom, not only in the United States, but throughout the world.

The following chantlike poem is in Whitman's "catalog style" and illustrates his lusty mode as the "bard of democracy."

I HEAR AMERICA SINGING
Walt Whitman

I hear America singing, the varied carols I hear,
Those of mechanics, each one singing his as it should be
    blithe and strong,
The carpenter singing his as he measures his plank or beam,
The mason singing his as he makes ready for work, or leaves
    off work,
The boatman singing what belongs to him in his boat, the
    deck-hand singing on the steamboat deck,
The shoemaker singing as he sits on his bench, the hatter
    singing as he stands,
The wood-cutter's song, the ploughboy's on his way in the
    morning, or at noon intermission or at sundown,
The delicious singing of the mother, or of the young wife at
    work, or of the girl sewing or washing,
Each singing what belongs to him or her and to none else,
The day what belongs to the day—at night the party of young
    fellows, robust, friendly,
Singing with open mouths their strong melodious songs.

Always an ardent supporter of the Union, Whitman was tormented by the "peculiar institution" of slavery and became an active Abolitionist. His involvement in the Civil War turned personal when he began caring for his wounded brother George in an Army hospital and stayed on to nurse others stricken by the war. The following poem is from *Drum-Taps*, which was added to *Leaves of Grass* in 1865.

BY THE BIVOUAC'S FITFUL FLAME
Walt Whitman

By the bivouac's fitful flame,
A procession winding around me, solemn and sweet and
    slow—but first I note,
The tents of the sleeping army, the fields' and woods' dim
    outline,
The darkness lit by spots of kindled fire, the silence,
Like a phantom far or near an occasional figure moving,
The shrubs and trees, (as I lift my eyes they seem to be
    stealthily watching me,)
While wind in procession thoughts, O tender and wondrous
    thoughts,
Of life and death, of home and the past and loved, and of
    those that are far away;
A solemn and slow procession there as I sit on the ground,
By the bivouac's fitful flame.

Herman Melville, 1819–1891

Born in the same year as Whitman and also influenced by Emerson, Melville had not one but two literary careers. Like Whitman, Melville was fascinated by the sea and images of the sea, but Whitman's vision was essentially positive whereas Melville's was ironic and tragic, the viewpoint of a realist as opposed to Whitman the romantic. Several years after publishing his greatest novel, *Moby-Dick* (1851), Melville turned, for reasons still unknown, to an exclusive preoccupation with poetry. (He did leave at his death the manuscript of *Billy Budd,* but with no clues as to when it was written.) Melville's ten-year career as a prose writer and thirty-year sequel as a poet were as unnoticed by the general public of the time as was the poetry of Whitman.

Deeply disturbed over the coming war, Melville followed the self-appointed mission of the Abolitionist John Brown who, in his zeal to free the slaves, had secured support from Emerson, Thoreau, and many others. Brown's capture of the U.S. Arsenal at Harper's Ferry was a major step in his campaign, but the government recaptured the Arsenal and hanged John Brown. Melville's brooding poem uses the image of the dead Abolitionist as a prologue to war.

THE PORTENT
Herman Melville

Hanging from the beam,
    Slowly swaying (such the law),
Gaunt the shadow on your green,
    Shenandoah!
The cut is on the crown
(Lo, John Brown),
And the stabs shall heal no more.
Hidden in the cap
    Is the anguish none can draw;
So your future veils its face,
    Shenandoah!
But the streaming beard is shown
(Weird John Brown),
The meteor of the war.

1859

One of the bloodiest conflicts of the Civil War, the Battle of Shiloh (6–7 April 1862) cost the lives of thousands of soldiers and forecast both the terrible battles to come and the inevitable defeat of the Confederacy. No one, not even Whitman, wrote more eloquently and sadly about the war than did Herman Melville.

SHILOH
A Requiem
(April 1862)
Herman Melville

Skimming lightly, wheeling still,
    The swallows fly low
Over the field in clouded days,
    The forest-field of Shiloh—
Over the field where April rain
Solaced the parched ones stretched in pain
Through the pause of night
That followed the Sunday fight
    Around the church of Shiloh—
The church so lone, the log-built one,
That echoed to many a parting groan
And natural prayer
    Of dying foemen mingled there—
Foemen at morn, but friends at eve—
    Fame or country least their care:
(What like a bullet can undeceive!)
    But now they lie low,
While over them the swallows skim,
    And all is hushed at Shiloh.

The naval battle between the ironclads *Merrimac* and *Monitor* (9 March 1862) symbolized for Melville the inhuman mechanization of war. He was a realist, the first poet to describe *modern* warfare for what it really was: killing people by means of advanced technology.

A UTILITARIAN VIEW OF THE MONITOR'S FIGHT
Herman Melville

Plain be the phrase, yet apt the verse,
    More ponderous than nimble;
For since grimed War here laid aside
His painted pomp, 'twould ill befit
    Overmuch to ply
    The rhyme's barbaric cymbal.
Hail to victory without the gaud
    Of glory; zeal that needs no fans
Of banners; plain mechanic power
Plied cogently in War now placed—   10
    Where War belongs—
    Among the trades and artisans.
Yet this was battle, and intense—
    Beyond the strife of fleets heroic;
Deadlier, closer, calm 'mid storm;
No passion; all went on by crank,
    Pivot, and screw,
    And calculations of caloric.
Needless to dwell; the story's known.
    The ringing of those plates on plates   20
Still ringeth round the world—
The clangor of that blacksmith's fray.
    The anvil-din
    Resounds this message from the Fates:
War shall yet be, and to the end;
    But war-paint shows the streaks of weather;
War yet shall be, but warriors
Are now but operatives; War's made
    Less grand than Peace,
    And a singe runs through lace and feather.   30

Mark Twain, 1835–1910

The second half of the century saw the emergence of realism in American literature and throughout the Western world. There was a new interest in common people and everyday facts of life. Among the new realists were Dickens, Thackeray, and George Eliot in England, Zola and Balzac in France, and William Dean Howells (1837–1921) in the United States. As editor-in-chief of the influential *Atlantic Monthly,* Howells advocated realism and supported regional writers. Mark Twain (pseudonym of Samuel Langhorne Clemens) was, however, the only major writer to emerge from what can be called the grass-roots movement.

    The first important author born west of the Mississippi, Mark Twain, more than any other writer of his time, symbolized the power and exuberance of the expansive American spirit that blossomed after the Civil War. Twain spoke and wrote in the voice of the people in celebration of the winning of the west. (The later, darker Twain will not be considered here.) His major works include *Innocents Abroad* (1869) and *Roughing It* (1872), but his masterwork can be considered as a kind of trilogy: *The Adventures of Tom Sawyer* (1876); *Life on the Mississippi* (1883); and *The Adventures of Huckleberry Finn* (1885). Perhaps his best short story, "The Notorious Jumping Frog of Calaveras County" was an oft-told tale, but it took a Mark Twain to give it form and style. The story is reprinted here but in actuality, this is only the first of a three-part exercise by the inimitable Twain. On learning that a French critic had called it a good story that, however, was not funny, Twain translated the tale into French and then translated *that* version into English. Twain concluded that the original was funny but that the French-into-English version was awkward and unfunny. The point is, of course, that Twain's American English was so idiomatic that it was untranslatable.

THE NOTORIOUS JUMPING FROG OF CALAVERAS COUNTY
Mark Twain

In compliance with the request of a friend of mine, who wrote me from the East, I called on good-natured, garrulous old Simon Wheeler, and inquired after my friend's friend, Leonidas W. Smiley, as requested to do, and I hereunto append the result. I have a lurking suspicion that *Leonidas W.* Smiley is a myth; that my friend never knew such a personage; and that he only conjectured that if I asked old Wheeler about him, it would remind him of his infamous *Jim* Smiley, and he would go to work and bore me to death with some exasperating reminiscence of him as long and as tedious as it should be useless to me. If that was the design, it succeeded.

I found Simon Wheeler dozing comfortably by the bar-room stove of the dilapidated tavern in the decayed mining camp of Angel's, and I noticed that he was fat and bald-headed, and had an expression of winning gentleness and simplicity upon his tranquil countenance. He roused up, and gave me good day. I told him that a friend of mine had commissioned me to make some inquiries about a cherished companion of his boyhood named *Leonidas W. Smiley—Rev. Leonidas W.* Smiley, a young minister of the Gospel, who he had heard was at one time a resident of Angel's Camp. I added that if Mr. Wheeler could tell me anything about this Rev. Leonidas W. Smiley, I would feel under many obligations to him.

Simon Wheeler backed me into a corner and blockaded me there with his chair, and then sat down and reeled off the monotonous narrative which follows this paragraph. He never smiled, he never frowned, he never changed his voice from the gentle-flowing key to which he tuned his initial sentence, he never betrayed the slightest suspicion of enthusiasm; but all through the interminable narrative there ran a vein of impressive earnestness and sincerity, which showed me plainly that, so far from his imagining that there was anything ridiculous or funny about his story, he regarded it as a really important matter, and admired its two heroes as men of transcendent genius in *finesse*. I let him go on in his own way, and never interrupted him once.

"Rev. Leonidas W. H'm, Reverend Le—well, there was a feller here once by the name of *Jim* Smiley, in the winter of '49—or maybe it was the spring of '50—I don't recollect exactly, somehow, though what makes me think it was one or the other is because I remember the big flume warn't finished when he first come to the camp; but anyway, he was the curiousest man about always betting on anything that turned up you ever see, if he could get anybody to bet on the other side; and if he couldn't he'd change sides. Any way that suited the other man would suit *him*—any way just so's he got a bet, *he* was satisfied. But still he was lucky, uncommon lucky; he most always come out winner. He was always ready and laying for a chance; there couldn't be no solit'ry thing mentioned but that feller'd offer to bet on it, and take ary side you please, as I was just telling you. If there was a horse-race, you'd find him flush or you'd find him busted at the end of it; if there was a dog-fight, he'd bet on it; if there was a cat-fight, he'd bet on it; if there was a chicken-fight, he'd bet on it; why, if there was two birds setting on a fence, he would bet you which one would fly first; or if there was a camp-meeting, he would be there reg'lar to bet on Parson Walker, which he judged to be the best exhorter about here, and so he was too, and a good man. If he even see a straddle-bug start to go anywheres, he would bet you how long it would take him to get to—to wherever he was going to, and if you took him up, he would foller that straddle-bug to Mexico but what he would find out where he was bound for and how long he was on the road. Lots of the boys here has seen that Smiley, and can tell you about him. Why, it never made no difference to *him*—he'd bet on *any* thing—the dangdest feller. Parson Walker's wife laid very sick once, for a good while, and it seemed as they warn't going to save her; but one morning he come in, and Smiley up and asked him how she was, and he said she was considerable better—thank the Lord for his inf'nite mercy—and coming on so smart that with the blessing of Prov'dence she'd get well yet; and Smiley, before he thought, says, 'Well, I'll resk two-and-a-half she don't anyway.'

"Thish-yer Smiley had a mare—the boys called her the fifteen-minute nag, but that was only in fun, you know, because of course she was faster than that—and he used to win money on that horse, for all she was so slow and always had the asthma, or the distemper, or the consumption, or something of that kind. They used to give her two or three hundred yards' start, and then pass her under way; but always at the fag end of the race she'd get excited and desperate like, and come cavorting and straddling up, and scattering her legs around limber, sometimes in the air, and sometimes out to one side among the fences, and kicking up m-o-r-e dust and raising m-o-r-e racket with her coughing and sneezing and blowing her nose—and *always* fetch up at the stand just about a neck ahead, as near as you could cipher it down.

"And he had a little small bull-pup, that to look at him you'd think he warn't worth a cent but to set around and look ornery and lay for a chance to steal something. But as soon as money was up on him he was a different dog; his under-jaw'd begin to stick out like the fo'castle of a steamboat, and his teeth would uncover and shine like the furnaces. And a dog might tackle him and bully-rag him, and bite him, and throw him over his shoulder two or three times, and Andrew Jackson—which was the name of the pup—Andrew Jackson would never let on but what *he* was satisfied, and hadn't expected nothing else—and the bets being doubled and doubled on the other side all the time, till the money was all up; and then all of a sudden he would grab that other dog jest by the j'int of his hind leg and freeze to it—not chaw, you understand, but only just grip and hang on till they throwed up the sponge, if it was a year. Smiley always come out winner on that pup, till he harnessed a dog once that didn't have no hind legs, because they'd been sawed off in a circular saw, and when the thing had gone along far enough, and the money was all up, and he come to make a snatch for his pet holt, he see in a minute how he'd been imposed on, and how the other dog had him in the door, so to speak, and he 'peared surprised, and then he looked sorter discouraged-like, and didn't try no more to win the fight, and so he got shucked out bad. He give Smiley a look, as much as to say his heart was broke, and it was *his* fault, for putting up a dog that hadn't no hind legs for him to take holt of, which was his main dependence in a fight, and then he limped off a piece and laid down and died. It was a good pup, was that Andrew Jackson, and would have made a name for hisself if he'd lived, for the stuff was in him and he had genius—I know it, because he hadn't no opportunities to speak of, and it don't stand to reason that a dog could make such a fight as he could under them circumstances if he hadn't no talent. It always makes me feel sorry when I think of that last fight of his'n, and the way it turned out.

"Well, thish-yer Smiley had rat-tarriers, and chicken cocks, and tomcats and all them kind of things, till you couldn't rest, and you couldn't fetch nothing for him to bet on but he'd match you. He ketched a frog one day, and took him home, and said he cal'lated to educate him; and so he never done nothing for three months but set in his back yard and learn that frog to jump. And you bet you he *did* learn him, too. He'd give him a little punch behind, and the next minute you'd see that frog whirling in the air like a doughnut—see him turn one summerset, or maybe a couple, if he got a good start, and come down flat-footed and all right, like a cat. He got him up so in the matter of ketching flies, and kep' him in practice so constant, that he'd nail a fly every time as fur as he could see him. Smiley said all a frog wanted was education, and he could do 'most anything—and I believe him. Why, I've seen him set Dan'l Webster down here on this floor—Dan'l Webster was the name of the frog—and sing out, 'Flies, Dan'l, flies!' and quicker'n you could wink he'd spring straight up and snake a fly off'n the counter there, and flop down on the floor ag'in as solid as a gob of mud, and fall to scratching the side of his head with his hind foot as indifferent as if he hadn't no idea he'd been doin' any more'n any frog might do. You never see a frog so modest and straight-for'ard as he was, for all he was so gifted. And when it come to fair and square jumping on a dead level, he could get over more ground at one straddle than any animal of his breed you ever see. Jumping on a dead level was his strong suit, you understand; and when it come to that, Smiley would ante up money on him as long as he had a red. Smiley was monstrous proud of his frog, and well he might be, for fellers that had traveled and been everywheres all said he laid over any frog that ever *they* see.

"Well, Smiley kep' the beast in a little lattice box, and he used to fetch him down-town sometimes and lay for a bet. One day a feller—a stranger in the camp, he was—come across him with his box, and says:

" 'What might it be that you've got in the box?'

"And Smiley says, sorter indifferent-like, 'It might be a parrot, or it might be a canary, maybe, but it ain't—it's only just a frog.'

"And the feller took it, and looked at it careful, and turned it round this way and that, and says, 'H'm—so 'tis. Well, what's *he* good for?'

" 'Well,' Smiley says, easy and careless, 'he's good enough for *one* thing, I should judge—he can outjump any frog in Calaveras County.'

"The feller took the box again, and took another long, particular look, and give it back to Smiley, and says, very deliberate, 'Well,' he says, 'I don't see no p'ints about that frog that's any better'n any other frog.'

" 'Maybe you don't,' Smiley says. 'Maybe you understand frogs and maybe you don't understand 'em; maybe you've had experience, and maybe you ain't only a amature, as it were. Anyways, I've got *my* opinion, and I'll resk forty dollars that he can outjump any frog in Calaveras County.'

"And the feller studied a minute, and then says, kinder sadlike, 'Well, I'm only a stranger here, and I ain't got no frog; but if I had a frog, I'd bet you.'

"And then Smiley says, 'That's all right—that's all right—if you'll hold my box a minute, I'll go and get you a frog.' And so the feller took the box, and put up his forty dollars along with Smiley's, and set down to wait.

"So he set there a good while thinking and thinking to himself, and then he got the frog out and prized his mouth open and took a teaspoon and filled him full of quail-shot—filled him pretty near up to his chin—and set him on the floor. Smiley he went to the swamp and slopped around in the mud for a long time, and finally he ketched a frog, and fetched him in, and give him to this feller, and says:

" 'Now, if you're ready, set him alongside of Dan'l, with his fore paws just even with Dan'l's, and I'll give the word.' Then he says, 'One—two—three—*git!*' and him and the feller touched up the frogs from behind, and the new frog hopped off lively, but Dan'l give a heave, and hysted up his shoulders—so—like a Frenchman, but it warn't no use—he couldn't budge; he was planted as solid as a church, and he couldn't no more stir than if he was anchored out. Smiley was a good deal surprised, and he was disgusted too, but he didn't have no idea what the matter was, of course.

"The feller took the money and started away; and when he was going out at the door, he sorter jerked his thumb over his shoulder—so—at Dan'l, and says again, very deliberate, 'Well,' he says, '*I* don't see no p'ints about that frog that's any better'n any other frog.'

"Smiley he stood scratching his head and looking down at Dan'l a long time, and at last he says, 'I do wonder what in the nation that frog throw'd off for—I wonder if there ain't something the matter with him—he 'pears to look mighty baggy, somehow.' And he ketched Dan'l by the nap of the neck, and hefted him, and says, 'Why blame my cats if he don't weigh five pound!' and turned him upside down and he belched out a double handful of shot. And then he see how it was, and he was the maddest man—he set the frog down and took out after that feller, but he never ketched him. And—"

[Here Simon Wheeler heard his name called from the front yard, and got up to see what was wanted.] And turning to me as he moved away, he said: "Just set where you are, stranger, and rest easy—I ain't going to be gone a second."

But, by your leave, I did not think that a continuation of the history of the enterprising vagabond *Jim* Smiley would be likely to afford me much information concerning the Rev. *Leonidas W.* Smiley, and so I started away.

At the door I met the sociable Wheeler returning, and he buttonholed me and recommenced:

"Well, thish-yer Smiley had a yaller one-eyed cow that didn't have no tail, only just a short stump like a bannanner, and—"

However, lacking both time and inclination, I did not wait to hear about the afflicted cow, but took my leave.

Exercise

This humorous classic is a virtual compendium of comic elements and devices. Almost immediately we are told that Simon Wheeler was an old windbag who launches right into a "monotonous narration." This is a story within a story highlighted by the comic character and folksy dialect of bald-headed Simon. The other major character, Jim Smiley, will bet on anything, even whether Parson Walker's wife will live or die. The imagery is graphic, there's lots of local color, and the "tables turned" theme provides the proper comic twist. Identify some of the images, elements of local color, and exaggerations such as the mare called the "fifteen-minute nag." Do not overlook the bull-pup named Andrew Jackson. In short, just how complex is this story?

Emily Dickinson, 1830–1886

The poetry of the "recluse of Amherst" is also realistic. Twain's universe was the exterior world; Dickinson's was the inner world of her own psyche. Published years after her death, her 1,775 poems were written as if they were entries in a diary, the private thoughts of a solitary person who took just a little from society and shut out all the rest. Her gemlike, frequently cryptic verses are unique, unlike poetry of any writer of any age.

VI: A Service of Song

Some keep the Sabbath going to church;
I keep it staying at home,
With a bobolink for a chorister,
And an orchard for a dome.
Some keep the Sabbath in surplice;
I just wear my wings,
And instead of tolling the bell for church,
Our little sexton sings.
God preaches,—a noted clergyman,—
And the sermon is never long;
So instead of getting to heaven at last,
I'm going all along!

XLVI: Dying

I heard a fly buzz when I died;
    The stillness round my form
Was like the stillness in the air
    Between the heaves of storm.
The eyes beside had wrung them dry,
    And breaths were gathering sure
For that last onset, when the king
    Be witnessed in his power.
I willed my keepsakes, signed away
    What portion of me I
Could make assignable,—and then
    There interposed a fly,
With blue, uncertain, stumbling buzz,
    Between the light and me;
And then the windows failed, and then
    I could not see to see.

XVII

I never saw a moor,
I never saw the sea;
Yet know I how the heather looks.
And what a wave must be.
I never spoke with God,
Nor visited in heaven;
Yet certain am I of the spot
As if the chart were given.

X

I died for beauty, but was scarce
Adjusted in the tomb,
When one who died for truth was lain
In an adjoining room.
He questioned softly why I failed?
"For beauty," I replied.
"And I for truth,—the two are one;
We brethren are," he said.
And so, as kinsmen met a night,
We talked between the rooms,
Until the moss had reached our lips,
And covered up our names.

XI

Much madness is divinest sense
To a discerning eye;
Much sense the starkest madness.
'T is the majority
In this, as all, prevails.
Assent, and you are sane;
Demur,—you're straightway dangerous,
And handled with a chain.

XXVII: The Chariot

Because I could not stop for Death,
He kindly stopped for me;
The carriage held but just ourselves
And Immortality.
We slowly drove, he knew no haste,
And I had put away
My labor, and my leisure too,
For his civility.
We passed the school where children played,
Their lessons scarcely done;
We passed the fields of gazing grain,
We passed the setting sun.
We paused before a house that seemed
A swelling of the ground;
The roof was scarcely visible,
The cornice but a mound.
Since then 't is centuries; but each
Feels shorter than the day
I first surmised the horses' heads
Were toward eternity.

Exercises

1. Would you call Poem VI pantheistic? Is it opposed to conventional religion or merely indifferent?
2. Is the fly in Poem XLVI metaphorical or real? Why did you answer as you did? Why did she use legal terms in stanza 3?
3. Poem XXVII contains many of the unusual metaphors for which Dickinson is famous. What are some of them? How effective are they?

Paul Laurence Dunbar, 1872–1906

Emancipation had released the slaves from bondage only to suspend African Americans somewhere between African cultures to which they could not return and an American culture that refused to admit them. The first black poet to reach a national audience, Dunbar wrote a poignant poem still frequently quoted today.

SYMPATHY
Paul Laurence Dunbar

I know what the caged bird feels, alas!
    When the sun is bright on the upland slopes;
When the wind stirs soft through the springing grass,
And the river flows like a stream of glass;
    When the first bird sings and the first bud opes,
And the faint perfume from its chalice steals—
I know what the caged bird feels!
I know why the caged bird beats his wing
    Till its blood is red on the cruel bars;
For he must fly back to his perch and cling
When he fain would be on the bough a-swing;
    And a pain still throbs in the old, old scars
And they pulse again with a keener sting—
I know why he beats his wing!
I know why the caged bird sings, ah me,
    When his wing is bruised and his bosom sore,—
When he beats his bars and he would be free;
It is not a carol of joy or glee,
    But a prayer that he sends from his heart's deep core,
But a plea, that upward to Heaven he flings—
I know why the caged bird sings!

Exercises

1. The *caged bird* is a metaphor for what? Is it a multiple metaphor? Please explain.
2. What is implied by the peaceful images in stanza 1? The violent images in stanza 2?
3. Who or what will free the caged bird?

Stephen Crane, 1871–1900

Though sometimes identified as a writer in the realistic style called naturalism, Crane was actually influenced by Monet, Renoir, and other impressionists. A journalist by profession and a war correspondent, Crane used word-painting in a manner comparable to the impressionists' use of color. His *The Red Badge of Courage* (1895) is perhaps the finest short novel in the English language, and "The Open Boat" and "The Blue Hotel" rank at the top of American short stories. Of Crane's poems, the following two seem most appropriate to conclude this survey of nineteenth-century life and literature.

TWO POEMS (UNTITLED)
Stephen Crane

Do not weep, maiden, for war is kind.
Because your lover threw wild hands toward the sky
And the affrighted steed ran on alone,
Do not weep.
War is kind.
    Hoarse, booming drums of the regiment,
    Little souls who thirst for fight
    These men were born to drill and die.
    The unexplained glory flies above them,
    Great is the battle-god, great, and his kingdom—   10
    A field where a thousand corpses lie.
Do not weep, babe, for war is kind.
Because your father tumbled in the yellow trenches,
Raged at his breast, gulped and died,
Do not weep.
War is kind.
    Swift blazing flag of the regiment,
    Eagle with crest of red and gold,
    These men were born to drill and die.
    Point for them the virtue of slaughter,   20
    Make plain to them the excellence of killing
    And a field where a thousand corpses lie.
Mother whose heart hung humble as a button
    on the bright splendid shroud of your son,
Do not weep.
War is kind.

A man said to the universe:
"Sir, I exist!"
"However," replied the universe,
"The fact has not created in me
A sense of obligation."

Summary

The revolutionary surge that began in France in 1789 was sidetracked by the imperial conquests of Napoleon and, even more effectively, by the 1815 Congress of Vienna. From 1815 to 1848, the arch conservatism of the Age of Metternich helped maintain the status quo of absolutism, disturbed only by the waves of revolution that rolled over Europe in 1830 and 1848. By midcentury the industrial revolution had helped turn northern Europe and North America into a powerful economic community, but political divisions became ever sharper with the rise of militant nationalism.

Revolution, civil war, and aggressive imperial wars became the hallmark of the last half of the so-called Romantic century. The Greek struggle for independence did spark the romantic imagination, but the Crimean and Franco-Prussian wars were, in effect, bloody preludes to the Great War of 1914–1918.

Italy finally became an independent nation in 1861 and, after the Civil War ended in 1865, the United States began to assume its place as a world power. In 1871 France became, once again, a republic; Bismarck proclaimed the German Empire; and the rival British Empire girdled the globe. Nationalism, imperialism, and militarism led, perhaps inevitably, to the conflict that ended what had been called the Age of Progress.

Culture and Human Values

The nineteenth century was noted for the prosperity stimulated by the industrial revolution, the growing middle class, and the enormous increase in manufactured products. The prevailing view of reality was more materialistic than ever; the world was a well-oiled machine bursting with machines turning out a flood of products. When these factors are combined with steady advances in science, transportation, communications, and other technologies, one can see why this has been grandly labeled as the Age of Progress.

This designation was, however, self-annointed and self-serving for the industrially advanced nations of Western Europe and North America. But not even in these industrialized countries was "progress" even remotely uniform. A large (growing ever larger) class of underpaid industrial workers, child labor, inadequate health and safety standards, and woefully substandard sanitation and housing were just some of the basic problems plaguing the working class. The poor were without power or influence in the factory, at home, and at the voting booth, while the rich got richer and more powerful.

What of the rest of the world—those nonindustrial nations of Central and South America, Africa, and Asia? Many of them became involuntary outposts of Western civilization. The monumental problem of the nineteenth century—that spilled over into the twentieth—was colonialism, and its negative aftereffects haunt us still. Whether in the colonies of England, Germany, France, Belgium, Italy, Spain, or Portugal, the locals (*natives*) had to accept whatever culture and values the foreign overlords brought with them. As arbitrary extensions or pawns of the mother country, colonies were fair game for commerce, the military, politicians, and as many industrial products as the market would bear.

In today's world these new nations exhibit a wide range of imprints (or lack of same) of the cultures of the various colonial powers. In Indonesia, for example, there is virtually no indication that these islands were ever ruled by the Dutch, let alone for four centuries. The same generally holds true for the colonies of Portugal, Spain, Italy, Germany, and Belgium, which were exploited and plundered—as was Indonesia—solely for the benefit of the mother country with little or no regard for the welfare of the subject population.

The British did attempt to create the infrastructures of modern states, but these were designed to serve the interests of the colonial masters. Their subjects did derive some indirect benefits while also acquiring other aspects of English civilization, particularly the language. In the Third World the residuals of English hegemony can be seen today in such former possessions as India, Kenya, Tanzania, Malaysia, Zimbabwe, and Fiji.

Unique among the Western powers, the French imported and educated selected colonials in the French language and culture and installed them in key positions in their colonies. The French heritage is quite apparent, for example, in Morocco, Algeria, and Indochina. Much like Alexander the Great, the French were eager to share their civilization with other nationalities. Moreover, and unlike other European nations, they were as unconcerned about racial differences as was the Macedonian conqueror.

When considering the culture-epoch theory the period is full of paradoxes. On the one hand, there was the notable increase in prosperity in the industrial nations but a status quo at best in the colonized nations. The industrial, imperialist powers enforced a certain stability as they competed to maintain a balance of power, and certainly Europe imposed its values on much of the world. But the Age of Progress of European culture was headed for a fall signaled by the onset of the Great War, the so-called war to end all wars.

Romanticism in Music

chapter 24

The ever-changing sequence of artistic styles can be seen in broad perspective as a constant back and forth movement between two extremes. In painting, these outer boundaries are represented by the Rubenists, who emphasized color, and Poussinists, who advocated line and drawing. Delacroix was a Rubenist; Ingres and David were Poussinists. These extremes are referred to, in music, as *romanticism* and *classicism*. As in painting, romantic music emphasizes color whereas the classical style stresses line and design. The two extremes can be stated as follows:

Classicism	Romanticism
intellectual	emotional
objective	subjective
rational	nonrational
tranquil	restless
simple	ornate
Apollonian	Dionysian

No artistic style can be classified as wholly classic or wholly romantic. An inclination in favor of either extreme results in a classification of the style *as* that extreme, a process that can be compared to a seesaw touching ground at one end because of a slight shift of balance. Though it is absurd to consider all of Mozart's music, for example, as intellectual but not emotional, tranquil and simple rather than ornate and restless, the fact remains that Mozart's music is essentially classic in its meticulous detail, restraint, and clarity of design.

The romantic style in music is either miniaturized or grandiose with comparatively little in between. There are intimate art songs for solo voice and piano and single-movement piano pieces at one extreme, and grandiose symphonic works at the other. The emphasis is on tone color (or sound), that fourth element of music (melody, harmony, rhythm, tone color). Symphonies have a wider range of instrumental tone color and a greater volume of sound than at any time since the invention of the symphony orchestra. The international aspects of seventeenth- and eighteenth-century music are superseded by highly individualistic styles of writing and strong nationalistic expression. The "Austrian" quality of the classical music of Haydn and Mozart is not relevant to their work. During the Romantic period, however, the "German" characteristics of Wagner, Schubert, and Schumann and the "Italian" qualities of Verdi, Rossini, and Donizetti are essential components of the stylistic picture. Along with literature and art, romantic music mirrors the rise of nationalism.

Typical of the romantic mode is the brooding, melancholy painting by Arnold Böcklin (BOEK-lin; 1827–1901), which the artist called "a picture for dreaming about" (figure 24.1). The strange and mysterious scene was enormously popular; it simply exists in its own bizarre world with no explanation necessary or even desirable, which inspired a Rachmaninoff tone poem using the same title.

Figure 24.1 *Arnold Böcklin,* Island of the Dead, *1880. Oil on wood, 29″ × 48″. The Metropolitan Museum of Art, New York, Reisinger Fund, 1926. (26.90)*

German Lieder

The Romantic movement generated a new style, the setting of preexisting poetry—almost always Romantic poetry—to music in an adroit matching of mood and meaning. Nationalism was again a salient characteristic, for the new style was a synthesis of words and music, and the language was German.

Viennese composer Franz Schubert (1797–1828) created the new artistic medium when, in 1814, he wrote music for "Gretchen am Spinnrade" from Goethe's *Faust.* Schubert invented the art song movement thereafter known as German *lieder* (Ger., "songs"). The generic term *lieder* applies to the German Romantic songs of Schubert, Schumann, Brahms, and others, though *lied* is the German word for any song.

Composers have always set poetry to music, from Sappho to the troubadours to Bach and beyond. Lieder are not just songs, however, for German composers displayed a remarkable unity of purpose—the re-creation of a poem in musical terms. Art songs (lieder) were significant miniatures in an era that indulged itself with the grandiose or doted on the diminutive. There was little middle ground, for the Romantic sought the heights and plumbed the depths with scant patience for the ordinary. Complexity was preferred and simplicity abhorred. If one art form was good then two art forms were even better. Art songs embodied the essence of romanticism for they synthesized poetry and music into a new and rarefied style.

From the poem comes the song, which attempts to capture the feelings, the mood, indeed the essence of what the poet is saying. The rhythm, inflection, sound, and meaning of the language are corroborated and heightened by the composer's own personal language of melody, harmony, rhythm, and tone color.

Following is the Schubert lied that inaugurated the German lieder movement. German art songs are always sung in German because a translation spoils the unity of words and music. The German text with English translation is provided so the listener can follow one and understand the other. There are ten verses, as indicated by the numbers in the text.

Listening Example 26

GERMAN ART SONG (*LIED*)

Franz Schubert, *Gretchen am Spinnrade*
(Gretchen at the Spinning Wheel; 1814)
Time: 3:52

Synopsis: Margaret sits in her room at the spinning wheel and sings of her love for Faust, knowing that this love will prove fatal. The scene occurs near the end of Part I of *Faust.*

1. Mei·ne Ruh' ist hin, mein Herz ist schwer;
   ich fin·de, ich fin·de sie nim·mer und nim·mer·mehr.
   (My peace is gone, My heart is sore:
   I shall find it never And never more.)

2. Wo ich ihn nicht hab', ist mir das Grab,
   die gan·ze Welt ist mir ver·gällt.
   (He has left my room An empty tomb
   He has gone and all My world is gall.)

3. Mein ar·mer Kopf ist mir ver·rückt,
   mein ar·mer Sinn ist mir zer·stückt.
   (My poor head Is all astray,
   My poor mind Fallen away.)

4. Mei·ne Ruh' ist hin, mein Herz ist schwer;
   ich fin·de, ich fin·de sie nim·mer und nim·mer·mehr.
   (My peace is gone, My heart is sore;
   I shall find it never And never more.)

5. Nach ihm nur schau' ich zum Fen·ster hin·aus,
   ('Tis he that I look through The window to see
   He that I open The door for—he!)

6. nach ihm nur geh' ich aus dem Haus.
   Sein ho·her Gang, sein' ed·le Ge·stalt,
   sei·nes Mun·des Lä·cheln, sei·ner Au·gen Ge·walt,
   (His gait, his figure, So grand, so high,
   The smile of his mouth, The power of his eye.)

7. und sei·ner Re·de Zau·ber·fluss,
   sein Hän·de·druck und ach, sein Kuss! (Piano)
   (And the magic stream Of his words—what bliss
   The clasp of his hand And, ah, his kiss!)

8. Mei·ne Ruh' ist hin, mein Herz ist schwer;
   ich fin·de, ich fin·de sie nim·mer und nim·mer·mehr.
   (My peace is gone, My heart is sore:
   I shall find it never And never more.)

9. Mein Bu·sen drängt sich nach ihm hin.
   Ach, dürft' ich fas·sen und hal·ten ihn!
   (My heart's desire Is so strong, so vast;
   Ah, could I seize him And hold him fast.)

10. und küs·sen ihn, so wie ich wollt'
    an sei·nen Küs·sen ver·ge·hen sollt',
    O köont' ich ihn küs·sen, so wie ich wollt',
    an sei·nen Küs·sen ver·ge·hen sollt',
    an sei·nen Küssen ver·ge·hen sollt'!
    Mei·ne Ruh' ist hin, mein Herz ist schwer. (Piano)
    (And kiss him forever Night and day,
    And on his kisses Pass away!)

Piano Music

The Romantic emphasis on the uniqueness of the individual was symbolized by the dominance of the piano as the single most popular musical instrument, as typical of the Romantic era as the guitar is of contemporary life. The piano was ubiquitous because it could accompany lieder, blend into a chamber music ensemble or, in a piano concerto, dominate a symphony orchestra. Its prime attraction, however, was its independence, for it is a superb solo instrument.

Eighteenth-century pianos were relatively small with a clear and delicate tone. Nineteenth-century pianos were larger, more sonorous than clear, and loud enough to fill the largest concert hall. The range of tone was representative of the Romantic propensity for extremes. Whether playing the tender "Lullaby" by Brahms or the thunderous "Revolutionary Étude" by Chopin, the pianist was a commanding figure throughout the entire Romantic period. Pianists also dominate today's concert world because of the enduring popularity of the Romantic repertoire.

Continuing a tradition from the seventeenth century, the nineteenth century was a fabulous age of virtuosos. Franz Liszt and Frédéric Chopin were spectacular performers on the piano and, equally remarkable, was Niccolo Paganini, a virtuoso of the violin. Virtuosity and showmanship were so widely admired that, for example, Paganini would conclude a concert with a razor blade hidden in his right hand. Near the end of an already sensational performance he would deftly cut the violin strings, one by one, until he could triumphantly conclude on the last remaining string.

Franz Liszt was fond of planting a female admirer in the front row of the concert hall. At the most dramatic moment the young lady, obviously enthralled by Liszt's performance, would be drawn to her feet and then ecstatically faint away. The maestro would carry her onstage and, holding her artistically draped body over one arm, triumphantly conclude the composition with one hand.

Frédéric Chopin, 1810–1849

Frédéric Chopin (sho-pan) was a superb concert pianist, but he did not confuse virtuoso performance with the circus showmanship of Paganini and Liszt. Though he was successful in the concert hall he gave fewer than seventy-five public concerts in his entire career. In terms of temperament and style, he was much more at home in the fashionable salons of Paris. He was the "poet of the keyboard," whose personal style epitomizes the Romantic spirit (figure 24.2). His musical poetry is not unlike the blending of words and music in German art songs. The formal designs of his music—sonata form, binary, and ternary forms—are traditional, but the content is unique. Some of the range of Chopin's piano style can be appreciated by considering just three compositions: a ballade, a prelude, and an étude.

The *Ballade in G minor,* op. 23 is loosely related to the medieval French verse in which the refrain comes at the end of the stanza. In this dramatic and rhapsodic composition, Chopin uses sonata form and reverses themes *a* and *b* in the recapitulation, after which he brings the work to a vigorous close with a brilliant coda. This masterwork was Chopin's personal favorite.

Chopin wrote twenty-four *preludes* in opus 28, each in a different key. The last prelude in the series is one of his most unusual and powerful compositions. As befits a prelude, which for Chopin is a short piano piece in one movement, there is only one subject. In the d-minor Prelude, the subject is limited almost entirely to a d-minor chord (d–f–a); in fact, the left hand plays the same d-minor chord for the first ten measures, and over one-third of the piece is devoted to this single chord. From the unchanging harmony of the opening section through the five statements of the theme to the final three low d's on the keyboard the cumulative effect is hypnotic.

Figure 24.2 *Eugène Delacroix,* Frédéric Chopin, *1838. Oil on canvas, 18" × 15". Delacroix (see chapter 25) seldom painted portraits on commission; instead, he depicted some of his personal friends, the victims, like himself, of what he and other artists called the "Romantic agony." The Louvre, Paris. Photo: Art Resource.*

Chopin wrote a number of studies—*études* that concentrated on various technical problems in playing the piano. Brief and brilliant, the *G-Flat Major ("Black Key") Étude* is a delightful exercise for playing on the black keys of the piano. The problem is performing at breakneck speed on narrow keys less than half the width of the white keys (3/8" to 7/8").

Prelude in d Minor, op. 28, no. 24

Form: Single Subject

Chopin
Time: 2:20

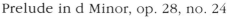

d-minor chord

Étude in G-Flat Major, op. 10, no. 5

Chopin
Time: 1:40

Vivace brillante

f legato   *p*

Listening Example 27

ÉTUDE
Chopin, *Étude in G-Flat Major,* op. 10, no. 5

The Symphony

The greatly augmented symphony orchestra with its strong brass and percussion sections and enlarged body of woodwinds provided a particularly effective medium for Romantic music. The classic orchestra had a nucleus of strings plus a small woodwind section and just a few brass and percussion instruments. Romantic composers added full sections of woodwinds and brass that could play as independent sections as well as filling in the ensemble. The comparative size of the orchestra over a period of a single century is illustrated in table 24.1.

Figure 24.3 is a seating plan observed in principle by most modern orchestras. Because of their limited volume the strings are seated in front and the woodwinds in the center; brass, bass instruments, and percussion bring up the rear (also see figure 24.4).

As might be expected, composers were highly individualistic in their approach to the symphonic tradition. The remarkable variety of orchestral music will be surveyed by considering one work by each of five composers: Felix Mendelssohn, Hector Berlioz, Franz Liszt, Richard Strauss, and Peter I. Tchaikovsky.

Felix Mendelssohn, 1809–1847

Felix Mendelssohn was the grandson of the noted Jewish philosopher Moses Mendelssohn. His father was a wealthy banker and his mother a lady of exceptional culture and taste. In addition to his superior intellect and rarefied socioeconomic environment, Mendelssohn was endowed with a wealth of musical talent (figure 24.5). He adopted classical forms but the classical spirit was acquired rather than assimilated and the classical forms were noble gestures rather than natural expressions. Because of the clarity of his writing and his control of the emotional content, Mendelssohn is best characterized as a classical Romanticist. Richard Wagner's remark that hearing Mendelssohn's music was like "staring into an abyss of superficiality" was more a reflection of Wagner's anti-Semitism than an accurate judgment of Mendelssohn's music.

The Fourth Symphony was written during an extended sojourn in Italy. The symphony is called "Italian," probably because of the sunny first theme of the opening movement and the brilliant *Saltarello,* which forms the last movement and which was probably inspired by a carnival in Rome that the composer had observed. Mendelssohn characteristically avoided anything that was overdone or in bad taste. The orchestra, therefore, was virtually the same size as that used by Mozart.

TABLE 24.1 Comparative Sizes of Orchestras

	Mozart (1788)	Beethoven (1808)	Strauss (1895)
Woodwinds	flute 2 oboes 2 clarinets 2 bassoons	piccolo 2 flutes 2 oboes 2 clarinets 2 bassoons	piccolo 3 flutes 3 oboes English horn 3 clarinets bass clarinet 3 bassoons contrabassoon
Brass	2 French horns	2 French horns 2 trumpets 3 trombones	8 French horns 6 trumpets 3 trombones tuba
Percussion		timpani	timpani, snare drum, bass drum, cymbals, triangle
Strings	violin I violin II viola cello bass	violin I violin II viola cello bass	violin I violin II viola cello bass

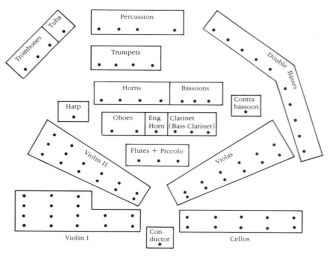

Figure 24.3 *Typical seating plan of a modern symphony orchestra.*

Figure 24.4 *A modern symphony orchestra. Photo courtesy of Columbia Artists' Management.*

Figure 24.5 *Felix Mendelssohn. Photo: Free Library of Philadelphia.*

Figure 24.6 *Hector Berlioz.*

Symphony No. 4 in A Major, op. 90 (Italian; 1833)

Felix Mendelssohn
First Movement: Sonata Form
Second Movement: Ternary Form (A__B__A)
Third Movement: Minuet—Trio—Minuet
Fourth Movement: *Saltarello* (Theme and Variations)

Hector Berlioz, 1803–1869

Hector Berlioz (bear-lee-OS; figure 24.6) was a red-headed Romantic from the south of France, a revolutionary artist whose only personal instrument was the guitar, but whose preferred instrument was the entire symphony orchestra. Despite his flamboyance—his lifetime dream was hearing ten thousand trumpets from a mountaintop—he was a solid musician and an orchestral innovator who strongly influenced Liszt, Wagner, Tchaikovsky, and Strauss.

One of his most successful and controversial works, the *Symphonie Fantastique* was completed in 1830, only three years after Beethoven's death. Berlioz had been influenced by the popular *Confessions of an English Opium Eater* (1821) by Thomas de Quincey and thought of combining an opium dream with music. He also fell madly in love with a Shakespearean actress named Harriet Smithson. It is now impossible to tell what the components were of this frenzied, desperate love affair that led to a short-lived and disastrous marriage.

Entranced by what he saw as the Romantic elements in Shakespeare's plays, Berlioz was as stagestruck by the Shakespearean women played by Miss Smithson as he was infatuated with the actress herself. In the midst of their stormy marriage Berlioz blended his conception of Shakespeare's women, his passion for Harriet, and his interest in opium into the fanciful story line (program) that created the *Symphonie Fantastique.*

Berlioz viewed classical forms as empty shells. He created, instead, an *idée fixe,* a single theme that was the common thread for each of the five movements of his daring new symphony. The idée fixe was a kind of *leit motif*—a procedure that Wagner was to exploit—that represented both the ideal of perfect love and the artist's idealized version of Harriet Smithson.

Following are the titles of the five movements plus a brief explanation of what the composer apparently had in mind when he wrote the music.

I. *Rêveries—Passions* (Daydreams—Passions). The artist, despairing of ever possessing his beloved, attempts to poison himself with opium. What follows in this and in the other movements is a series of opium-induced dreams, fantasies, and nightmares. This first movement is a frequently euphoric reverie about the artist's passion for his beloved.
II. *Un bal* (A ball). There is a fancy ball at which the beloved appears, slipping in and out of the dancers. The idée fixe, representing the beloved, is heard as she appears among the dancers.
III. *Scène aux champs* (Scene in the country). An idyllic scene of calm serenity in the bucolic countryside.
IV. *Marche au supplice* (March to the scaffold). In his delirium, the artist imagines he has killed his beloved and that he is being taken on a tumbrel to the guillotine.
V. *Songe d'une nuit de Sabbat* (Dream of a Witches' Sabbath). Following his execution the artist dreams that he is present at a gruesome Witches' Sabbath complete with a parody of the *Dies irae* (Day of Judgment) as a part of a Black Mass. The idée fixe is also parodied as his beloved appears as a debased prostitute.

Listening Example 28

SYMPHONY IN FIVE MOVEMENTS
Berlioz, *Symphonie Fantastique* (1830)
4. March to the Scaffold

Time: 4:13

Franz Liszt, 1811–1886
Franz Liszt created large orchestral works without forcing his ideas into the traditional forms of the classical period (figure 24.7). He used programs for much of his music—hence the term *program music*—but operated from a different point of view than did Berlioz. Liszt was dedicated to the Romantic ideal of uniting the various arts. He respected the uniqueness of the musical language, but he advocated the addition of extramusical concepts that would "humanize" the music and make it more meaningful to the listener.

> The musician who is inspired by nature exhales in tones nature's most tender secrets without copying them. . . . Since his language is more arbitrary and more uncertain than any other . . . and lends itself to the most varied interpretations, it is not without value . . . for the composer to give in a few lines the spiritual sketch of his work and . . . convey the idea which served as the basis for his composition. . . . This will prevent faulty elucidations, hazardous interpretations, idle quarrels with intentions the composer never had, and endless commentaries which rest on nothing.[1]

Franz Liszt was perhaps the only composer of program music to understand the real meaning of Beethoven's preface to his Sixth Symphony: "More the expression of sentiment than painting." Richard Strauss contended that a tone poem could, for example, "describe a teaspoon" so that all listeners could envision a similar image. Liszt denied the capability of music to be this literal and to be this limited. Instead, he created the symphonic poem, a new art form that followed the dictates of Beethoven. He stated broad concepts for his programs and then dissolved these concepts into the wonderfully abstract language of music.

---

1. Franz Liszt, *Gesammelte Schriften,* Leipzig, 1881–1910, p. 104.

Figure 24.7   *Franz Liszt.*

Figure 24.8   *Richard Strauss. Photo: Free Library of Philadelphia.*

Les Préludes, the most famous of Liszt's twelve symphonic poems, was inspired by a *meditation poetique* by the mystical French poet Alphonse de Lamartine. The musical score is prefaced by a quotation from Lamartine that expresses a favorite Romantic theme—humanity pitted against Fate:

> What is our life but a series of preludes to that unknown song whose first solemn note is tolled by Death? Love is the enchanted dawn of every existence, but where is the life in which the first enjoyment of bliss is not dispelled by some tempest? Yet no man is content to resign himself for long to the beneficent charms of Nature; when the trumpet sounds, he hastens to danger's post, so that in the struggle he may regain full consciousness of himself, and the possession of all his powers.

Liszt uses a germ motive that, unlike Berlioz's idée fixe, ties the work together in a process of continuous transformation. Constructed in six sections, the piece begins with the germ motive, followed by section 1 in which the motive becomes majestic. In section 2 the motive turns into a love song in a pastoral mood, followed by a new, tender love theme in section 3. The pace quickens dramatically in section 4 and then relaxes into a bucolic mood in section 5. In section 6 the two love themes are transformed into rousing battle calls and the piece concludes triumphantly in a typically romantic burst of exaltation.

Richard Strauss, 1864–1949

Richard Strauss exploited the large symphony orchestra in a manner similar to Liszt's treatment of the piano and Paganini's performances on the violin (figure 24.8). The orchestra became, in his hands, an enormous virtuoso instrument. One of the great orchestrators, Strauss expanded to an unprecedented degree the techniques of individual musicians and the capabilities of the orchestra as a whole.

The Tone Poem

The *tone poem* (or *symphonic poem*) was the favorite form of program music for the large orchestra. Originated by Franz Liszt and developed by Richard Strauss, the tone poem generally used a dramatic narrative as the basis for an extended one-movement composition. The music would attempt to describe such grandiose conceptions as *A Hero's Life, Death and Transfiguration, Don Juan,* and the adventures of a practical joker (*Till Eulenspiegel's Merry Pranks*). *Till Eulenspiegel* is one of the most successful ventures in this genre, principally because of the vivid, dramatic music and tightly knit construction. The story is by no means the only one that can be associated with the music but, nevertheless, it is the tale the composer had in mind when he wrote the tone poem.

Till Eulenspiegel was an actual fourteenth-century character who achieved considerable notoriety as a sometimes likable rogue, swindler, prankster, and scoundrel. The Strauss tone poem is built around a selection of Till's adventures, including the final adventure of being brought to justice for his many offenses.

Till Eulenspiegel's Merry Pranks (1895)
Richard Strauss
Total Time: 14:00

There are six scenes and an epilogue. There is a primary theme in each section and repeated material in the epilogue.

1. *Till in the Marketplace*
2. *Till the Priest*
3. *Till in Love*
4. *Till and the Philistines*
5. *To Be or Not to Be Himself*
6. *Till's Sad End*

Following is a brief synopsis of the events in each section:

Introduction
The two Till themes (*a* and *b*) are presented.

1. *Till in the Marketplace*
   After a pause, the 'a' theme is heard and we have a typical market scene with much bustling activity, women gossiping in their stalls and so forth. Till slips into the square, mounts a horse and careens through the square, making a shambles of it. Leaving consternation in his wake, he rides out of sight.
2. *Till the Priest*
   Till appears as a caricature of a priest, dripping unction and morality. He is not really comfortable in the role and abandons it quickly when a pretty girl walks by.
3. *Till in Love*
   A short violin solo signals this latest adventure as Till follows the girl, catches up with her, and does his best to make a good impression. His advances are repulsed and he storms off swearing vengeance on all humankind.
4. *Till and the Philistines*
   The hopping theme announces the arrival of some musty professors and doctors. Till falls in with them and amazes all and sundry with his brilliance as he propounds one ridiculous notion after another. Quickly becoming bored with such stodgy scholars, Till leaves them behind in a state of shocked amazement.
5. *To Be or Not to Be Himself*
   In the longest section of the piece Till wrestles with his conscience, such as it is. The question is whether he should continue in his erratic, exciting, and sometimes scandalous life or reform and settle down with the good burghers who have been the butt of so many of his pranks. After considerable indecision he finally decides to remain true to his real nature and continue as the scoundrel he has always been. This decision is announced by a jubilant orchestra.

6. *Till's Sad End*
   At almost the very moment he decides to be himself the snare drum roll announces that Till has been dragged off to face the stern justice of the court. The low, threatening chords hurl the charges at Till, who answers impudently the first two times (solo clarinet). The answer to the third volley of charges is an anguished squeal from the clarinet and Till is marched to the scaffold. An ominous drop in pitch (interval of a M7) portrays the dropping of the trap door. His soul takes flight to the accompaniment of fluttering clarinet and flute and the mortal Till is no more. A short pizzicato string passage leads to the Epilogue.
7. *Epilogue*
   The 'a' theme is heard for the last time. In retrospect Till becomes an amusing devil and immortal rogue, as indicated by the triumphant close for full orchestra.

Peter Ilich Tchaikovsky, 1840–1893

Peter Ilich Tchaikovsky (chy-KOF-skee) seldom succeeded in mastering musical forms, but he was remarkably skillful in his handling of the symphonic orchestra (figure 24.9). The lush sounds of Tchaikovsky's orchestra have become a kind of hallmark for the dramatic intensity and emotional extremes of the Romantic movement.

Tchaikovsky's orchestral music ranges from ponderous melodrama to vapid sentimentality and yet, at his best, he has created enormously popular works for ballet—*Swan Lake, The Nutcracker, Sleeping Beauty*—and three successful symphonies, the Fourth, the Fifth, and the Sixth.

The Nutcracker
The subject for his ballet *The Nutcracker* was drawn from stories by Dumas and E. T. A. Hoffman. It begins with children and mechanical dolls at a Christmas tree party hosted by Marie. She is fascinated by a German nutcracker fashioned in the figure of an old man with massive jaws. Some rough boys break the nutcracker, and that night Marie lies sleepless in pity for it. Getting out of bed to look after her broken darling, she watches the Christmas tree grow and the toys come to life, including the cakes, tidbits, and nutcracker. Mice attack the toys and the nutcracker challenges the king of mice to single combat, a battle being won by the mouse until Marie kills it with a well-aimed shoe. The nutcracker is immediately transformed into a handsome young prince who thanks Marie for his life as he escorts her to his enchanted kingdom.

The scene in the second act is a jam mountain in the realm of the Sugarplum Fairy. There follows a series of eight dances which comprise the suite that Tchaikovsky made from the ballet score, which is the standard available recording. The Russian Dance (Trepak) is extremely lively and is based almost entirely on the rhythmical figure in the opening measure.

Figure 24.9 *Peter Ilich Tchaikovsky. Photo: Free Library of Philadelphia.*

Figure 24.10 *Giacomo Puccini.*

Listening Example 29

DANCE

Tchaikovsky, *Suite from the Ballet "The Nutcracker,"* op. 71a (1892)
4. Russian Dance (Trepak)

Molto vivace   Time: 1:00

Opera

Opera underwent drastic changes in style and intent during the nineteenth century. Early in the century, Beethoven's *Fidelio* (1805) represented what might be called international opera. With the emergence of Romanticism there was a corresponding rise in national schools of opera with Italy dominating the European (and American) scene.

Italian opera, as typified by Verdi's *Rigoletto* (1851), was a mélange of melodramatic plots, popular-type melodies, and "ef-fective" solos and ensembles. There was more emphasis on *bel canto* (beautiful singing) than on logical development of plot and character. Later operas, Verdi's *Aïda* (1871) for example, evidenced an ever-increasing concern with dramatic values culminating, perhaps inevitably, in the complex music dramas of Richard Wagner. Wagner conceived of opera, his *Tristan und Isolde* (1859) for example, as a super art form, a viewpoint roughly comparable to Byron's conception of himself as a superhero and Nietzsche's theory of a superman.

Wagner's insistence on the musical-literary totality of his myth-based music dramas provoked strong reactions in favor of so-called realism in subject matter and a new simplicity in musical treatment. A similar reaction against academic painting led to the emergence of such Romantic realists as Millet and Corot of the Barbizon School and, especially, the realists Daumier and Courbet. A comparable movement in literature, called naturalism, was led by Émile Zola.

Giacomo Puccini, 1858–1924

Giacomo Puccini (poo-CHEE-nee; figure 24.10) was the leading Romantic realist in operatic literature. His tragic operas, *La Bohème, Madame Butterfly,* and *Tosca,* are among the most popular works in the standard repertoire of leading opera companies.

La Bohème is the opera selected for inclusion here because with it one can perhaps best persuade a neophyte that a theatrical work in which everything is sung is actually a viable means of expressive communication. The field of opera has suffered for far too long from the misguided notion that it is esoteric and "highbrow" and thus not fit for middle-class consumption.

The text of *La Bohème* was drawn from Henri Murger's *Scenes de la Vie en Bohème,* the time is 1830, and the setting is an artist's garret in the Bohemian section of the Latin Quarter of Paris. The characters in order of appearance are: Marcello, a painter, *baritone;* Rodolfo, a poet, *tenor;* Colline, a philosopher, *bass;* Schaunard, a musician, *baritone;* Benoit, a landlord, *bass;* Mimi, an embroiderer, *soprano;* Parpignol, a toy vendor, *tenor;* Musetta, a shop girl, *soprano;* Alcindoro, a councilor of state, *bass;* Customhouse sergeant, *bass;* students, working girls, citizens, shopkeepers, street vendors, soldiers, waiters, boys and girls, etc. Following is a brief summary of the plot.

La Bohème (1896)
Giacomo Puccini

ACT I
Scene: In the Attic   Time: 35:00
Four struggling young artists, Rodolfo, Marcello, Colline, and Schaunard, are living together in the garret. Mimi timidly knocks at the door and asks Rodolfo to light her candle. It is love at first sight, to coin a phrase, and they eventually exit upstage center, singing a love duet.

ACT II
Scene: In the Latin Quarter   Time: 17:00
The four artists and Mimi convene at a cafe. Musetta, Marcello's former girlfriend, appears on the arm of Alcindoro, her current admirer. Musetta uses her considerable charms to rekindle Marcello's interest in her and all march offstage behind a passing military band.

ACT III
Scene: A Toll Gate at an Entrance to Paris   Time: 24:00
Musetta and Marcello can be heard in the tavern in the background. Mimi appears and asks Marcello to help her separate from Rodolfo. As Rodolfo comes out of the tavern he exclaims that he has decided to leave Mimi. She then tells him that she must return to another lover but they cling together knowing that they must part when spring comes.

ACT IV
Scene: In the Attic   Time: 28:00
The four bachelors and Musetta are in the apartment when Mimi appears, desperately ill. The friends rush out seeking food, medicine, and a doctor, leaving Mimi and Rodolfo alone. They return in time to witness Mimi's death.

The plot of *La Bohème* is commonplace. The characterization is fixed from the outset rather than developed. The mutual attraction of the young lovers is instant and total without any attempt at verisimilitude. The stormy romance of Musetta and Marcello remains at that entry level. *La Bohème* reads, on paper, like a third-rate soap opera.

Then why has this opera been so enormously popular for almost a century? Surely it is not because of the plot, the characterization, the pathos of the tragic love affair. Perhaps it is because Rodolfo and Mimi represent some profound truths about life, suffering, love, and death? Hardly.

In the parlance of the theatre, *La Bohème* is effective when placed "on the boards" because "it plays." It is believable because it sings and sings gloriously. From the vivacious opening measures audiences willingly, even eagerly, suspend their disbelief.

Impressionism in Music

By the end of the nineteenth century the main stream of Romanticism had about run its course. The decline was marked by the appearance of what was thought to be the *new* style of *impressionism.* Just as the Renaissance had faded into mannerism and the baroque into rococo, the refined essence of Romanticism was distilled into a final stage named after the painting style of Monet, Degas, Renoir, and others.

The so-called impressionistic music of Debussy and Ravel—Debussy detested the term *impressionism*—spearheaded a French revolt against the domination of German Romanticism and particularly the overwhelming exuberance of Wagner. The competition of German and French nationalism was a major factor in the impressionist movement. Debussy cultivated an art that was subtle, delicate, and discreet, an art that was a sensuous rather than an emotional experience. For Debussy, German Romanticism was ponderous and tedious whereas French music possessed the Gallic spirit of elegance and refinement.

Many similarities exist between the painting of the impressionists and the sophisticated music of Debussy and Ravel. The impressionists tried to capture the play of color and light; favorite images included dappled sunlight through leaves and the play of light on water, fields, flowers, and buildings. The musicians dealt with an art of movement that attempted to translate this interplay of color and light into shimmering and sensual sounds.

Closely related to impressionism in painting and music was the symbolism of Mallarmé, Verlaine, and Baudelaire. They achieved an indefiniteness with words that had been the privilege of music alone. They likened their poetry to music and sought tone color in word sounds and symbolic meanings of words rather than any definite meaning. Wordplay, as with the tonal play of impressionistic music, was, according to Verlaine, "the gray song where the indefinite meets the precise."

The effects that musical impressionism achieved were the result of a number of innovations and extensions of musical resources.

Stylistic Characteristics

Modes
The old church modes came into favor again during late Romanticism and were exploited further by the impressionists. The effects they sought were counter to the clear tonality of the major-minor system. The modes, among other scales, provided a wider range of colors and the desirable vagueness of tonality.

Other Scales
The strong Asian influence was reflected in the use of the *pentatonic scale* (five-tone scale) that is the basis for the folk music of Bali, China, and other Asian cultures.

Particularly appropriate for the vague tonalities and drifting harmonies of impressionism was the *whole-tone scale*. This was a six-tone scale with a whole step between each pitch. With all tones equidistant, there was no clear tonal center. In fact, there were only two whole-tone scales possible: one starting on a white note and ending on a black note, and the other starting on a black note and ending on a white note.

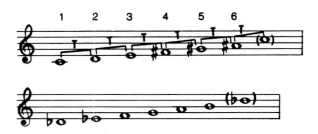

Form
Classical forms were generally abandoned in favor of the vague outlines, drifting quality, and dreamlike effects so basic to the style. This is not to say that the music is formless—there is a beginning, middle, and end—but rather that the forms are subtle and dictated by the impressions sought by the composer.

Orchestration
The massed woodwind and/or brass sounds of the orchestras of Brahms, Strauss, Wagner, and so forth, were anathema to the impressionists. They replaced the dark and ponderous sound of the Germanic orchestras with a much lighter, shimmering effect and much more individualistic use of instruments. They delighted in the exotic sounds of the English horn and the flutes and clarinets in the low register. Violins frequently played in extremely high registers and were often muted. Trumpets and horns were frequently muted. The characteristic sounds of the orchestra were supplemented by the harp, triangle, lightly brushed cymbals, and the bell tones of the small keyboard instrument called the *celeste*. The treatment of the pure sounds of the individual instruments was very much like the use of tiny brushstrokes of pure colors by the painters.

The piano remained a favorite instrument for the impressionists, but the sounds had little in common with the style, for example, of Chopin. The emphasis was on coloration, sensation, subtle harmonic effects, a great delicacy of tone. Everything was programmatic, whether a tonal description of a specific event or the evocation of a general idea, image, or sensation.

Claude Debussy, 1862–1918

Claude Debussy (deh-bes-ee; figure 24.11) used shifting harmonies and tone colors to suggest the shimmering effects of light and shade in the paintings of the impressionists. His music has a luminous quality that compares with, for example, Renoir's sun-dappled nudes. Following is a piano composition that is titled *Voiles* (*Sails*). Using the whole-tone scale and a bit of pentatonic, Debussy weaves drifting patterns of melody and harmony that encourage the listener to make any association appropriate to the music and the ambiguous one-word title.

Listening Example 30

PIANO SOLO

Debussy, *Preludes for Piano,* Book I (1913)
  2. *Voiles (Sails)*

Time: 3:05

Prelude to the Afternoon of a Faun

The delicate subtleties and discreet coloration of impressionism appear to best effect in the carefully chosen palette of the orchestra. For his *Prelude to the Afternoon of a Faun,* Debussy used the following instrumentation:

3 flutes	antique cymbals
2 oboes	(small, tuned cymbals)
English horn	violin I
2 clarinets	violin II
2 bassoons	viola
4 French horns	cello
2 harps	bass

Debussy's music was inspired by a study of the poem "Éco-logue" by Stéphane Mallarmé. All poetry is difficult to translate and that of the symbolists is impossible. The general feeling of the mood that Debussy attempted to portray can be better understood by reading the following paraphrase of Mallarmé's poem:

A faun—a simple, sensuous, passionate being—wakens in the forest at daybreak and tries to recall his experience of the previous afternoon. Was he the fortunate recipient of an actual visit from nymphs, white or golden goddesses, divinely tender and indulgent? Or is the memory he seems to retain nothing but the shadows of a vision, no more substantial than the arid rain of notes from his own flute? He cannot tell. Yet surely there was, surely there is, an animal whiteness among

Figure 24.11 *Claude Debussy. Photo: Free Library of Philadelphia.*

the brown reeds of the lake that shines out yonder? Were they, are they, swans? No! But Naiads plunging? Perhaps!

Vaguer and vaguer grows the impression of this delicious experience. He would resign his woodland godship to retain it. A garden of lilies, golden-headed, white-stalked, behind the trellis of red roses? Ah! the effort is too great for his poor brain. Perhaps if he selects one lily from the garth of lilies, one benign and beneficent yielder of her cup to thirsty lips, the memory, the ever-receding memory, may be forced back. So, when he has glutted upon a branch of grapes, he is wont to toss the empty skins into the air and blow them out in a visionary greediness. But no, the delicious hour grows vaguer; experience or dreams, he will now never know which it was. The sun is warm, the grasses yielding; and he curls himself up again, after worshipping the efficacious star of wine, that he may pursue the dubious ecstasy into the more helpful boskages of sleep.[2]

Exercise

What, exactly, is a virtuoso? Can you identify some of today's virtuosos?

---

2. Edmund Gosse, ''French Profiles,'' *The Collected Essays of Edmund Gosse* (London: William Heinemann, Ltd., 1905). Needless to say, the ''faun'' of this fantasy is in no way related to a ''fawn.''

Summary

Some of the elements of nineteenth-century Romanticism were present in the later works of Beethoven, but the lyric strains of full-blown Romanticism were paramount in the vocal and instrumental works of Franz Schubert. The characteristic style of German art songs (*lieder*) was created by the composer from Vienna and further developed by the German composers Schumann, Brahms, and Wolf. Frédéric Chopin made the piano his personal instrument with his unique style, and the very nature of Romanticism reinforced this individuality of personal expression. The music of Liszt, Strauss, Tchaikovsky, Verdi, and Richard Wagner reflected this intensely subjective approach to artistic experience. They, like Rousseau, if not better than other men, were "at least different."

The decline of absolute music in favor of a full range of miniature to grandiose program music was probably the most significant musical characteristic of the century. The abstract titles of the eighteenth century (sonata, serenade, symphony) were, to a considerable extent, abandoned for descriptive or poetic titles. In addition, there were dreamy *nocturnes,* cute *capriccios,* and dashing *rhapsodies* distinguished more by sound and fury than by strong intrinsic design. Filled with emotion for its own sake and thus unabashedly sentimental, and lacking also the disciplined energy of the pre-Napoleonic era, Romantic music provided the sounding board of the age.

The creation of the tone poem seemed to be the inevitable result of a Romantic propensity for reinforcing music with the literary arts. Two arts seemed to be better than one. By the same token, six trumpets were better than two and a hundred-piece orchestra superior to a sixty-piece orchestra. If the trend to monumental Napoleonic ideas had continued, the French Romantic, Hector Berlioz, might have eventually recruited the ten thousand trumpets playing from a mountaintop that he so ardently longed to hear.

The latter part of the century saw a gradual leveling off in the growth of the symphony orchestra. The tone poems of Strauss and the huge vocal-instrumental works of Mahler and Bruckner represented a point of no return, a stage reached after a reaction against the grandiloquence had already set in. Brahms reacted against the extravagant use of musical materials and orchestral sounds by deliberately returning to the more disciplined practices of an earlier age. Debussy, Ravel, and other impressionists also reacted negatively by sharply reducing the orchestra in order to concentrate on the pure tone colors of individual instruments. However, they did continue in the Romantic tradition of program music, carrying it to its ultimate conclusion with techniques similar to the symbolism of Mallarmé and Verlaine. The transition from nineteenth-century Romanticism to the so-called New Music of the twentieth century was accomplished in large part by the impressionists, who inaugurated many of the materials of modern music while writing the final chapter of Romantic music.

Culture and Human Values

Though we live in an era not particularly notable for romantic sentiment, nineteenth-century music still forms a large part of today's musical repertoire. Why is the Romantic style still so popular?

Some of this appeal would have to be attributed to its familiarity, for American audiences are notorious for their attachment to the tried and true compositions of the past. There is, however, an additional appeal that seems to have an enduring value—the fervent individualism of Romantic composers. The music of Chopin, for example, is totally unique, as is the music of Berlioz, Wagner, and others. Each Romantic composer was fiercely independent and even self-consciously "different."

Many of us are painfully aware of the anonymity of modern life in which people feel that they are little more than facts and figures imprisoned in the memory bank of a computer. Romantic composers, by contrast, loom large as heroic individuals from a recent past.

Romantic music is also unabashedly emotional, dramatically revealing the strains and stresses of life in all its complexity. Restraint is not a characteristic of the Romantic style. Nor can we say that our own era is particularly noted for restraint; in fact, energy, emotion, and dramatic intensity are notable components of much of modern music, with particular reference to several styles of rock.

There is, perhaps, more than a trace of nostalgia in our fondness for the Romantic style. Here is daring and derring-do. Laced with sentiment and surging emotions, Romanticism appeals to a large and faithful cross-section of today's audiences.

Nineteenth-Century Art: Conflict and Diversity

The Romantic Movement and the Neoclassic Style

The Romantic movement first manifested itself in literature and music in the poetry of Wordsworth and Coleridge and the lieder of Schubert. The visual arts were, however, in thrall to David, Napoleon's court painter, and to Napoleon's determination to confirm the legitimacy of his empire with the classical architecture of Imperial Rome. In 1806 Napoleon commissioned Jean Francois Chalgrin (shal-GREN; 1739–1811) to construct a mighty arch to honor the victories of the French fighting forces (figure 25.1). Placed in the center of twelve radiating avenues, the arch is 164′ high and 148′ wide, larger than the triumphal arch of any Caesar. It stands today at the climax of the Avenue des Champs Elysées over the tomb of the Unknown Soldier, commemorating French imperial glory and the military triumphs of an emperor who did not live to see its completion.

The Church of St. Mary Magdalen, known as *The Madeleine* (figure 25.2), was originally begun in 1764 and later razed to be replaced with a building modeled after the Pantheon in Rome. Napoleon ordered that structure replaced by a new temple, a massive building dedicated to the glory of his Grand Army. The Madeleine has fifty-two majestic Corinthian columns running completely around the building, each 66′ tall. The eight-column front and complete peristyle are reminiscent of the Parthenon (see figure 7.34), but the 23′ high podium is of Roman origin and similar to the Maison Carrée (see figure 9.8). Napoleon's Temple of Glory (also completed after his death) is a skillful synthesis of Graeco-Roman elements into a unified and imposing design.

Jean-Auguste-Dominique Ingres, 1780–1867

Only nine years old when the revolution began, Ingres (ang-r) was never an enthusiastic supporter of Napoleon's self-proclaimed revolutionary ideals. He was, however, David's most tal-

Figure 25.1 *Jean François Chalgrin (and others), Arch of Triumph, 1806–1836. Place Charles de Gaulle, Paris. Howell/Art Resource.*

Figure 25.2 *Pierre Vignon,* The Madeleine, *1806–1842, Paris. © Roger Viollet.*

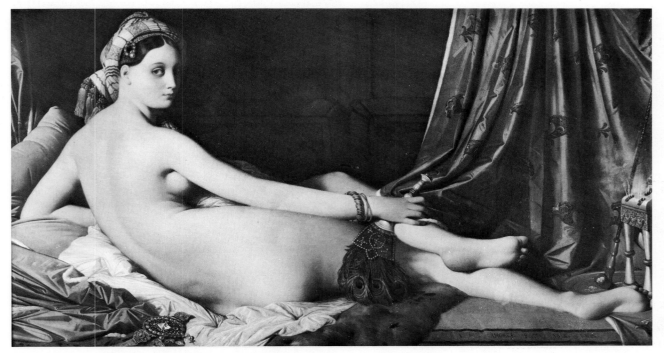

Figure 25.3 *Jean-Auguste-Dominique Ingres,* Grand Odalisque, *1814. Oil on canvas, 35¼" × 63¾". The Louvre, Paris. Photo: Art Resource.*

ented pupil and an advocate of a neoclassic style that had evolved from revolutionary art into state-endorsed dogma. Contending that David's style was too heavily incised, Ingres developed a fluid drawing technique influenced by Pompeiian frescoes and patterned after elegant linear figures of Greek vase paintings (see figure 7.27). His *Grand Odalisque* (figure 25.3) is not a classical version of feminine beauty; however, it is a superb example of the artist's unique mix of neoclassic and Romantic ideas. The reclining-nude pose can be traced to Titian and the smoothly flowing contours of the sculpturesque body are coolly classical, but the subject is an odalisque, a harem slave girl who represents an exotic concept dear to the Romantics. The small head, elongated limbs, and languid pose are very mannered in the decorative style of Parmigianino (see figure 17.46).

Francisco de Goya, 1746–1828

The first of the illustrious painters of the Romantic era, Goya (GO-ya) was unique even in a time of remarkably individualistic artists. A contemporary of David, with whom he had nothing in common, Goya was influenced by Velasquez and Rembrandt, but not at all by antiquity or the Renaissance. Excelling in both portraiture and vigorous action canvases, Goya was appointed painter to the court of Spain in 1799. In this capacity he was both a romantic and a realist with his many acutely candid studies of the incompetent royal family of Charles IV that presided over a corrupt and decadent administration. Representing his romantic bent is the portraiture in *Majas on a Balcony* (figure 25.4) which, at first glance, appears to be a lovely portrayal of two pretty, ele-

Figure 25.4 *Francisco de Goya,* Majas on a Balcony, *1810–1815. Oil on canvas, 76¾" × 49½". The Metropolitan Museum of Art, New York. Bequest of Mrs. H. O. Havemeyer, 1929. The H. O. Havemeyer Collection.*

Figure 25.5 *Francisco de Goya,* The Third of May, 1808, at Madrid: The Shootings on Principe Pío Mountain, *1814. Oil on canvas, 8'8¾" × 11'3⅞".*
Museo del Prado, Madrid. Photo: Scala/Art Resource.

gantly dressed women. But what are the shadowy figures in the background? The painting is a study in strong contrasts: light and dark; colorful foreground and drab background; beauty and menace. Goya may be making a statement but we cannot be certain of his intention. What is irrefutable, of course, is the ambiguity of Romantic art, of which this is a superb example.

Goya extended his critical appraisal of the royal family to a general view of human folly, vice, and stupidity as depicted in a series of paintings and engravings called *The Caprices*. Then, Napoleon's 1808 occupation of Spain provided the artist with a powerful new subject: the bestiality and utter futility of war. Goya and many of his countrymen had hoped for French reforms of the debased Spanish court; instead, the merciless brutality of French soldiers provoked an equally savage resistance. Among the tragic results were a series of executions of Spanish patriots. Commissioned in 1814 by a liberal government after the expulsion of the French, Goya selected the executions of the Third of May (figure 25.5) to vividly portray the underside of Napoleonic conquest. The firing squad is a faceless monster with many legs. Firing at point-blank range—the usual procedure for these exe-

cutions—the soldiers operate in a symbolic blackness of night illuminated only by a single lamp. This is probably the first of its kind, a work of art that protests the barbarism of military conquest. Later in the century, so-called social-protest works of art will become ever more common as artists attack a variety of social evils. Careful study of the painting, of the dead and those about to die, reveals a powerful universal statement about the lot of common people at the mercy of invading armies.

In a series of unforgettable etchings called *The Disasters of War,* Goya brilliantly depicted the sordid consequences of warfare. His *Grande hazaña! Con muertos!* (Great exploit! In casualties!; figure 25.6) imparts the horror of mutilation and violent death with a startling economy of means. Euripides with his *The Trojan Women* and Goya stand virtually alone in their convincing portrayals of the senselessness of warfare.

Goya's art was intensely personal and impossible to classify. He was a true Romantic, however, in his concern about placing too much faith in the primacy of reason, that goddess of an Enlightenment that ended with a bloody revolution, the Reign of Terror, and ultimately, Napoleon. Goya left Spain in 1824 during

Figure 25.6 *Francisco de Goya,* Grande hazaña! Con muertos!, *from* The Disasters of War, *ca. 1814. Etching, edition of 1863. Private collector.*

Figure 25.7 *Théodore Géricault,* The Raft of the Medusa, *1818–1819. Oil on canvas, ca. 16' × 23'. The Louvre, Paris.*

another period of repression and died in exile in France. His art was not known outside Spain until late in the Romantic movement.

Théodore Géricault, 1791–1824

The most talented French painter of early Romanticism, Géricault (ZHAY-ree-ko) won artistic immortality with his painting of *The Raft of the Medusa* (figure 25.7). Like other Romantic artists, Géricault seized on a contemporary event (in 1816), in this case a tragedy that caused a national scandal. Jammed with colonists bound for French West Africa, the *Medusa* ran aground off the African coast because of the incompetence of the ship's captain, who then filled the *Medusa's* six boats with his own party and sailed safely to shore. About 150 men and one woman were left to shift for themselves.[1] In the painting, the few remaining survivors on their makeshift raft have just sighted a rescue ship on the horizon and are frantically signaling for help. This was the *Argus,* which did not sight the raft until the following day. Géricault researched the tragedy like an investigative reporter, interviewing survivors, studying corpses in the morgue, even building a raft to scale in his studio. The result is not just a realistic reporting of the event but a drama of heroic proportions of men against the sea. The slashing diagonals and vivid chiaroscuro lead our eye to the triangle formed by the extended arms, with the waving figure at the apex; all movement is projected forward toward the distant sail. There is no movement in the left foreground, however, where an older man broods over the youthful

corpse sprawled across his lap. The dejected man seems to be mourning the inhuman price all of them had to pay, for this composition is taken from an earlier sketch depicting the cannibalism that kept the survivors alive. But, if these men had been adrift for fourteen days with almost no provisions, why do the figures look so muscular, so healthy? Simply stated, emaciated figures with shriveled flesh and horrible wounds would be pitiful, tugging too directly on our emotions. But these sturdy figures transmit such power that we are lifted past the particular to the universal. This is how you turn a catastrophe into art.

Géricault's graphic realism was characteristic of the Romantic intent to shock the sensibilities of the viewer and evoke an emotional response. Government attempts to cover up the errors of a French naval officer stirred the public to a frenzy and focused attention on the painting as a political statement, much to the artist's dismay, rather than as a compelling work of art. Géricault had hoped to avoid this reaction by first titling the painting *Scene of Shipwreck,* but to no avail. However, the *Medusa* affair has receded into history, leaving behind this vivid example of social-protest art whose timeless appeal transcends the tragedy that inspired it.

Eugène Delacroix, 1799–1863

Following Géricault's early death as a result of a riding accident, Delacroix (de-la-KWRAH), a peerless colorist, became the leading Romantic artist. The expansion of the French colonial empire into North Africa (beginning with Algeria in 1830) opened new vistas to French writers and artists. The first major French artist to visit Islamic countries, Delacroix was fascinated with the colorful vitality of Muslim cultures. In *Arabs Skirmishing in the Mountains*

---

1. For details of the century's worst French scandal prior to the Dreyfus Case, see Alexander McKee's *Death Raft: The Human Drama of the Medusa Shipwreck* (New York: Warner Books, Inc., 1977).

(figure 25.8) he demonstrates a vibrant range of intense hues and strong contrasts of light and dark. As the artist wrote in one of his journals, "the more the contrast the greater the force." His ability to capture the illusion of movement makes the dramatic impact of the pitched battle all the more convincing. Continuing the squabble between color and line (Romanticism vs. Classicism), Delacroix was the Rubenist and his rival, Ingres (see figure 25.3), the Poussinist of the nineteenth century. For a colorist such as Delacroix the perfect style, as he said, was a combination of Michelangelo and the recently discovered Goya.

Romantic painters were enamored with the sister arts: the plays of Shakespeare, medieval romances, English romantic poetry, and especially, music. Delacroix preferred, surprisingly, the classical style of Mozart to the flamboyant romanticism of his French contemporary Hector Berlioz but was a personal friend of Frédéric Chopin, whose poetic piano music had a special appeal, not only for Delacroix, but also for many writers and artists of the time. His portrait of Chopin (see figure 24.2) epitomizes the melancholy suffering of the Romantic genius.

John Constable, 1776–1837

English artists responded more to Rousseau's back-to-nature movement than to the ideological drive of the revolution and subsequent Napoleonic Wars; after all, England had its revolution in 1688. English Romantic poets—Wordsworth, Coleridge, Shelley, Keats—described the beauties of nature in highly personal terms. Landscape was prominent in their poetry but not as description for its own sake; rather, poets responded to aspects of the natural scene that stimulated their thinking, leading to meditations on nature that, as Wordsworth observed, involved the "Mind of Man." On the other hand, nature was frequently the subject matter for Romantic painters. Constable, one of the finest of all English painters, studied landscapes with a scientific objectivity. Rather than simply recording actual objects he sought the intangible qualities of atmosphere, light, and especially, the sky. The justly famed "Constable sky" is the dominating element in his poetic response to the peaceful scene at *Wivenhoe Park, Essex* (figure 25.9). Sunlight shining on the wind-driven clouds and the effect of sunshine on fields and water have a luminosity rivaling even the Dutch masters, and the entire canvas has a freshness never before achieved in painting. The lustrous sky is the crowning glory of the picture, triumphantly confirming the artist's claim that this area was the "principle instrument for expressing sentiment." After his first exposure to Constable's work, Delacroix repainted the sky of an already completed work; the impressionists were no less dazzled by the skies of Constable.

Joseph M. W. Turner, 1775–1851

The impressionists, especially Monet, were just as enthralled with the heightened, liberated colors of Turner, Constable's eminent contemporary. A Londoner by birth and preference, Turner had none of Constable's attachment to peaceful nature. Instead, he

Figure 25.8 *Eugène Delacroix,* Arabs Skirmishing in the Mountains, *1863. Oil on canvas, 36⅜" × 29⅜". Chester Dale Fund, 1966. National Gallery of Art, Washington, D.C.*

was fascinated by light, the bright southern light of Italian cities, especially Venice. His sensitivity to light enabled him to develop a subtle, colorful art of freedom and refinement. Far in advance of his time, his concentration on light and extreme effects of storms, sunsets, and fires, plus his indifference to finished details made his art wholly unique. His *Keelmen Heaving Coals by Moonlight* (figure 25.10) combines many of Turner's prized effects: moonlight, fires, and the use of color for atmospheric effects. The details are typically unclear with an overall effect that reveals Turner at his Romantic best.

Thomas Cole, 1801–1848

American Romanticism had all the characteristics of the European variety but with some distinct variations that reflected a youthful nation in a New World. George Catlin, for example, spent many years studying and painting various Indian tribes, and John James Audubon devoted twelve years to the publication of his monumental *Birds of America*. But it was the American landscape that enthralled Thomas Cole and many other artists.

Cole emigrated from England to Philadelphia at the age of seventeen and later became an influential member of a group of

Figure 25.9 *John Constable,* Wivenhoe Park, Essex, *1816. Oil on canvas, 22⅛" × 39⅞". Widener Collection. National Gallery of Art, Washington, D.C.*

artists now known as the Hudson River School. Cole and his colleagues viewed their landscape paintings as a high moral imperative in which they celebrated the beauty and purity of the American wilderness. In his *Essay on American Scenery* Cole pointed out that "the most distinctive, and perhaps the most impressive characteristic of American scenery is its wildness." He contrasted this with civilized Europe in which "the primitive features of scenery have long since been destroyed or modified." With its relatively untouched forests and mountains and newly established republic, the United States was viewed as the new Eden, the light and hope of an exhausted Old World. Cole's view of the *Oxbow* (figure 25.11) is an elaborate celebration of nature, a realistic depiction of an actual location with romantic overtones of an idealized storm that, along with the twisted tree, helps frame the river. As with most of Cole's paintings, the human figure (right foreground) is dwarfed by the majesty of nature. Currently there is a considerable revival of interest in the work of the Hudson River School occasioned, in part, by environmental concerns. Depictions of the new Eden are, after all, only about a century and a half in a past that can never be recaptured.

George Caleb Bingham, 1811–1879

Bingham pursued still another aspect of American Romanticism. Though he was born in Virginia he moved to Missouri when he was eight, there to paint the fur traders, boatmen, and politicians in what was then raw frontier country. This was also Mark Twain country, and one can find many images in the artist's work that illustrate life on the Missouri and Mississippi rivers as described in Twain's novels. *Fur Traders Descending the Missouri* (figure 25.12) communicates some of the mystery and mystique of life

Figure 25.10 *Joseph M. W. Turner,* Keelman Heaving Coals by Moonlight, *probably 1835. Oil on canvas, 36¼" × 48¼". Widener Collection, 1942. National Gallery of Art, Washington, D.C.*

on the leading edge of a developing nation. Bingham also saw these figures as exotic explorers of the American wilderness, having first titled the painting "French Trader and Half-Breed Son." His characteristic use of primary colors (red, yellow, blue) for the figures is echoed in the landscape by paler hues throughout the composition. The two figures stare out at us as they are momentarily frozen in time. Though the water is like a mirror we still

Figure 25.11 *Thomas Cole,* Oxbow (The Connecticut River near Northampton), *1846. Oil on canvas, 51½" × 76". The Metropolitan Museum of Art, New York. Gift of Mrs. Russell Sage, 1908 (08.228).*

Figure 25.12 *George Caleb Bingham,* Fur Traders Descending the Missouri, *ca. 1845. Oil on canvas, 29" × 36½". Metropolitan Museum of Art, New York. Morris K. Jesup Fund, 1933.33.61.*

Figure 25.13 *Barry and Pugin, The Houses of Parliament, London.*

have the impression of watery motion from right to left. Though clearly a Romantic work, there are classical overtones in the balanced design, luminous light, and meticulous purity of details.

Architectural Inspiration from the Past

The largest and most successful architectural recollection of the past were the Houses of Parliament, designed by Sir Charles Barry (1795–1860) with the assistance of Gothic scholar Augustus Welby Pugin (1812–1852; figure 25.13). Even more than the French or Germans, the English felt that the Gothic style was an exemplary expression of the national past, a heritage both noble and Christian. Consequently, the Parliamentary Commission decreed that the design for the new seat of government be either Gothic or Elizabethan and nothing else. Barry favored the neoclassic style, but Pugin convinced him that the English Late Gothic style was the proper glorification of the British spirit and a celebration of medieval craftsmanship in the face of mass-produced items of the Industrial Age. Actually, the body of the building is symmetrical in the Palladian manner surmounted by a Gothic fantasy of turrets, towers, and battlements.

Inspired by the design of Parliament, the Gothic Revival style of about 1855–1885 was enthusiastically adopted by English and American architects. Constructed during the height of the Revival by a timber contractor, the Victorian Gothic mansion in California (figure 25.14) is a wooden frame structure with an incredible variety of surface decoration and detail. "More is better" was a Victorian preference that is exuberantly realized in this prize example of American Gothic.

Figure 25.14 *Victorian Gothic mansion, ca. 1885, Eureka, California.*

Realism

Millet, Corot, and the Barbizon School

Countering the Romantic fantasies of their literary and artistic contemporaries, the realists concentrated on the real world as they perceived it, with an objective matter-of-factness that alienated the followers of Géricault and Delacroix. Settling near the village of Barbizon in the Forest of Fontainebleau south of Paris, painters of the Barbizon School imitated Rousseau's back-to-nature movement while simultaneously escaping the disorder and confusion of the 1848 Revolution. Rousseau's "noble savage" was interpreted by Barbizon associate François Millet (me-YAY; 1814–1875) as a heroic peasant who exemplified the dignity of working the land. In *The Sower* (figure 25.15) Millet's peasant has the monumentality of Michelangelo and an earthy quality comparable to the bourgeois Dutch tradition. Himself the son of peasants, Millet chose to live the life of a peasant, sympathetically depicting his protagonists as actors in a kind of divine drama in a style antithetic to the French academic tradition.[2]

Though he did not consider himself a member of the Barbizon School, Jean-Baptiste-Camille Corot (ko-ROW; 1796–1875) lived in the area and shared their strong commitment to direct visual experience. In the *Forest of Fontainebleau* (figure 25.16) Corot painted the full range of light and dark values, depicting visual reality at a single moment in time. Working very quickly, Corot sought the underlying rhythm of nature, composing his landscapes so that the magic moment of truth would be revealed to all. One of the finest Western landscape painters, Corot became, according to the poet Baudelaire, "the master of an entire younger generation."

Figure 25.15 *Jean François Millet,* The Sower, *ca. 1850. Oil on canvas, 101.6 × 82.6 cm (40 × 32½ in.). Gift of Quincy Adams Shaw through Quincy A. Shaw, Jr., and Mrs. Marian Shaw Haughton. Courtesy, Museum of Fine Arts, Boston.*

Figure 25.16 *Jean-Baptiste-Camille Corot,* Forest of Fontainebleau, *ca. 1830. Oil on canvas, 69⅛" × 95½". Chester Dale Collection, 1962. National Gallery of Art, Washington, D.C.*

---

2. Disdained since about 1860 as artistically inferior, French academic art has, since about 1965, experienced a rebirth. See, for example, *The Encyclopedia of World Art*, vol. XVI (New York: McGraw-Hill Book Company, 1983), pp. 230–231.

Figure 25.17 *Honoré Daumier,* Le Ventre Legislatif, *1834. Lithograph. The Arizona State University Art Collections, Arizona State University. Gift of Oliver B. James.*

Honoré Daumier, 1808–1879

Corot, Millet, and the Barbizon School can be described as Romantic realists for there is an element of escapism in their work. In Paris, however, the realities of political and social unrest before and after the 1848 Revolution were of far greater concern to a hard-bitten realist such as Daumier (doe-me-AY). Known to his contemporaries as a caricaturist, Daumier created over 4,000 lithographs[3] satirizing the major and minor foibles of the day. In his caricature of *Le Ventre Legislatif* ("The Legislative Belly"; figure 25.17) Daumier depicted the venality, pomposity, and stupidity of the collective "Legislative Belly," i.e., "Body." With devastating candor Daumier gives us a cast of characters all too well-known in the body politic of democratic societies.

Daumier was just as forceful a contemporary social critic in oils as he was in his lithographs, claiming that scenes of contemporary everyday life had to be painted because "one must be of one's own time." In *Third-Class Carriage* (figure 25.18) he used a strong chiaroscuro in the manner of Rembrandt, whom he greatly admired, to depict the isolation of each figure in the railway car; each person is utterly alone with his or her own thoughts. This painting is both Romantic and Realistic. Daumier accurately caught a stark moment in the anonymity of urban life but the painting is suffused with the emotion of an artist who has sympathetically identified with a car full of lonely strangers. It is, moreover, a third-class group without the funds to travel first-class or even second-class.

3. One of the graphic arts, lithography is a printmaking process that was widely used in the nineteenth century for newspaper and magazine illustrations. In lithography (Gk., "writing on stone") the design is drawn on stone or a metal plate with a greasy printing ink and then reproduced by the standard printing process.

Figure 25.18 *Honoré Daumier,* Third-Class Carriage, *ca. 1862. Oil on canvas, 25¾" × 35½". The Metropolitan Museum of Art, New York. Bequest of Mrs. H. O. Havemeyer, 1929. The H. O. Havemeyer Collection. (29.100.129) Photograph by Malcom Varon.*

Gustave Courbet, 1819–1877

Realism in art was given a name and a leader in the person of Courbet (koor-BAY), who even took the time to issue a "Manifesto of Realism." At the Andler Keller, one of the first Parisian beer halls, the swaggering, flamboyant Courbet held forth as the apostle of the physical world of visible objects. "Show me an angel," he once remarked, "and I will paint you an angel." Courbet found his natural subjects in the common people of his home village of Ornans in eastern France. As he said, "to paint a bit of country, one must know it. I know my country." *Burial at Ornans* (figure 25.19) depicts a rural scene on a monumental scale normally reserved for epic historical events. Much to the consternation of the critics, Courbet turned the somber reality of this simple country funeral into a noble occasion that he called "true history." Combining religious symbolism with realism, Courbet included the dog as it was depicted in the Office of the Dead in medieval manuscripts; the people were all painted from life in innumerable sittings demanded by the artist. Composed on a horizontal S-curve, the figures of clergy, pall-bearers, friends, and relatives stand in poses ranging from indifference to composed grief. The staff with the crucifix is positioned to give the illusion of Christ's actual death on Golgotha. This and other paintings were rejected by the Universal Exposition, leading to the construction of a shed, called by Courbet "The Pavilion of Realism," for the exhibition of his uncompromising works.

Winslow Homer, 1836–1910

Realism spread throughout Europe as artists were attracted to the style, but it was especially popular in the United States, where pragmatism and realism were characteristics of the American way of life. Beginning his career as an illustrator for *Harper's Weekly,*

Figure 25.19 *Gustave Courbet,* Burial at Ornans, *1849–1850. Oil on canvas, ca. 10'3" × 13'. Musée d'Orsay, Paris. Cliché des Musées Nationaux, Paris.*

Winslow Homer was influenced by Corot and Courbet, but not at the expense of his American point of view. Homer lived during the post-Civil War era that Mark Twain had called the Gilded Age, a grossly materialistic era of pretentious opulence, but his style was firmly fixed in genre paintings in the mode of American realism. In *Breezing Up* (figure 25.20) Homer celebrated his lifelong love affair with the sea in a joyous composition of wind, salt air, and sparkling sea. Fatigued but happy with the day's catch, the fisherman and boys are returning home. With the catboat placed at eye level and slanting away from the viewer, we are drawn into an illusion of movement and the feeling of a job well done. Exemplifying Homer's statement, "When I have selected a thing carefully, I paint it exactly as it appears," the details are finely drawn: wrinkled clothes, light sparkling from metal fittings, a lighthouse at the lower left, a wheeling gull at the upper right. Homer's ability to give the illusion of light emanating from his canvases paralleled the development of French impressionism across the ocean from his native New England.

Homer's career was remarkably divergent from that of his older contemporary, author Herman Melville. Both were New Englanders and fascinated by the sea, but Homer's vision was generally positive whereas Melville's was darkly ambiguous. Homer covered the Civil War as an illustrator for *Harper's Weekly;* Melville wrote two volumes of war poems that were totally unknown at the time. Homer was a highly successful and popular painter; Melville was not recognized as one of America's greatest writers until many years after his obscure death. Ironically, both were realists (see chapter 23 for some of Melville's poetry).

Figure 25.20 *Winslow Homer,* Breezing Up, *1876. Oil on canvas, 24⅛" × 38⅛". Gift of the W. L. and May T. Mellon Foundation, 1943. National Gallery of Art, Washington, D.C.*

Thomas Eakins, 1844–1916

Eakins (ay-kins) called Homer the best living American artist, but Eakins himself ranks, with Homer, as one of the very best of American artists. Like Homer, Eakins was fascinated with outdoor exercise and with the outdoors in general. In his early painting, *Max Schmitt in a Single Scull* (figure 25.21), he depicts himself in the middle distance, apparently as a kind of symbolic signature

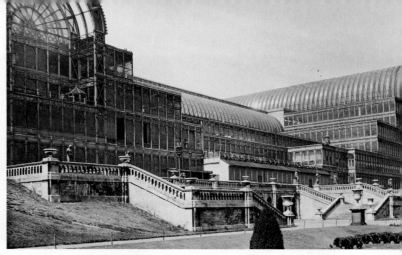

Figure 25.21 *Thomas Eakins,* Max Schmitt in a Single Scull, *1871. Metropolitan Museum of Art, New York. Purchase 1934, Alfred N. Punnett Fund and Gift of George D. Pratt.*

Figure 25.22 *Joseph Paxton, Crystal Palace, 1850–1851, London. Marburg/Art Resource, N.Y.*

of the artist's first-hand experience. As with most of the paintings of Eakins, the human figure (Max Schmitt in this case) is central, with light defining and highlighting the composition. This is an instant—now permanent—in time, from the inquiring turn of the subject's head to the distant steamboat's puff of smoke. The meticulous, balanced arrangement of diagonals reinforces the feeling of a somewhat melancholy moment.

Architecture

Realism in painting can be compared, to some extent, with the development of late nineteenth-century architecture. Abandoning copies of older styles, architects turned to modern building materials to design functional structures serving specific purposes. Epitomizing the new attitude toward utilitarian design, the Crystal Palace (figure 25.22) was constructed of 5,000 prefabricated iron columns and girders and nearly 300,000 panes of glass. A greenhouse designer by profession, Sir Joseph Paxton (1801–1865) oversaw the construction of an immense structure that covered nineteen acres in Hyde Park and contained almost a million square feet of floor space. Ironically, this first truly modern building was a response to an emergency because the Building Commission was unable to select from the more than 200 submitted designs. The Crystal Palace won by default because only Paxton's advanced technology could create a building in the time remaining.

Assembled in only thirty-nine weeks, the Crystal Palace housed London's "Great Exhibition of the Works of All Nations of 1851," a triumphant display of the miracles wrought by the industrial revolution. The theme of the exhibition was "Progress" as represented by the mechanized marvels within the glittering structure, itself a symbol of the "Age of Progress." The first of many similar buildings, the Crystal Palace was dismantled after the exhibition and reassembled south of London where, in 1936, it was destroyed by fire. Though cast-iron structures were vulnerable to fire, the Crystal Palace did establish the practicality of metal as a

Figure 25.23 *Gustave Eiffel, Eiffel Tower, 1889, Paris.*

building material. With the 1856 invention of the Bessemer process of making steel, the technology was already available for the construction of twentieth-century high-rise buildings.

The first high-rise structure in the world was designed by an engineer who had previously devised bridges and the metal framework for the Statue of Liberty. Gustave Eiffel (I-fel; 1832–1923) designed the theme tower for the Paris Exhibition of 1889, another celebration of technological advances. Rising to an imposing height of 984′, the Eiffel Tower (figure 25.23) symbolized the Age of Progress in modern France. Like a giant erector set, it was assembled on the site; 15,000 prefabricated and prepunched girders were bolted together in a masterful demonstration of precision design and production that was completed in two years, two months, and two days. The tower weighs almost 10,000 tons but it is proportionately so light that a steel scale model one foot high would weigh less than a quarter of an ounce. Though denounced from the outset by purists who objected to the violation of the Parisian skyline, the tower stands today as the enduring symbol of the City of Light.

Impressionism

In one respect impressionism was an outgrowth of realism, but in another it was a revolutionary artistic movement almost as profound in its effect as the Early Renaissance in Italy. Impressionists saw themselves as the ultimate realists whose main concern was the perception of optical sensations of light and color. Whether the impressionists were consciously aware of photographic techniques, scientific research in optics, or the physiology of the eye is not important; they painted as if the world were not matter in space but a source of sensations of light and color. Objects were perceived as agents for the absorption and reflection of light; there were no sharp edges, indeed, no lines in nature. In nature, form and space were implied by infinitely varied intensities of color and light, and shadows were not black but colored in relation to the objects casting the shadows. This is impressionist theory in essence, but the individual artists developed styles, of course, that sometimes contradicted the theories.

There was one characteristic of impressionism that differentiated the movement from all other styles; it was not limited to artists. There was a generally appealing quality that drew together not only painters and their models, but a number of writers, critics, and collectors. The general public was not part of the movement, of course, for this was a consciously avant-garde movement, a confident step into the modern world.

Édouard Manet, 1832–1883

A major innovator in Western painting, Manet (ma-NAY) was not an impressionist but his influence on the movement was critical. Realizing that modeled transitions did not exist in nature, he worked instead in planes. Also one of the first artists to paint with pure colors, eliminating dark shadows that had been used for centuries, Manet was a pioneer in the use of light as his subject; light was the actual subject matter of the painting that he submitted in 1863 to the jury of the Paris Salon. An unconventional painting with a conventional title, *Déjeuner sur l'herbe* (*Luncheon on the Grass;* figure 25.24) was refused by the jury but exhibited in a special Salon des Refusés, where it caused a storm of controversy. Though the ostensible subject matter was possibly derived from Giorgione's *Fête Champêtre* (see figure 17.40), the contemporary dress of the men in combination with the unconcerned

Figure 25.24 *Édouard Manet,* Déjeuner sur l'herbe, *1863. Oil on canvas, 6'9/⅛" × 8'10¼". Musée d'Orsay, Paris. Cliché des Musées Nationaux, Paris.*

nakedness of the woman deeply shocked the public. Even Courbet criticized the work as flat and formless. Indeed, Manet had almost totally abandoned Renaissance perspective, accepting the canvas for what it really was: a two-dimensional surface. The hue and cry over the work bewildered the artist; the subject, after all, was *light* as clustered around the nude, the background figure, the still life in the left foreground. The grouping of the dark areas further emphasized the harsh light of day, giving the painting a powerful visual impact. For Manet and the impressionists the objects and figures in their paintings were sometimes treated impersonally, as opportunities to depict light sensations. Frequently detached and nonjudgmental, Manet and the impressionists, except for Renoir, were often more entranced with optical sensations than with humanity.

The public, however, was not detached and it was very judgmental. The reaction to Manet's *Olympia* (figure 25.25), which he exhibited at the 1865 Salon, caused one of the greatest scandals in art history. Critics called Manet "a buffoon" and the nude a "female gorilla" and "yellow-bellied odalisque," and boisterous crowds flocked to see a work that another critic advised pregnant women and proper young ladies to avoid at all costs. Manet had painted his model, Victorine Meurend (who also posed for the *Déjeuner*), as an elegant and world-weary lady of the evening. With an orchid in her hair and wearing only a black ribbon around her neck, she stares disdainfully at the viewer while ignoring the bouquet proffered by her maid. Critics were no more incensed about the flagrant nakedness than with the black-on-black coloration of the maid's face against the background, not to mention the black cat at the foot of the suggestively rumpled bed, also painted against a black background. The picture became a *cause célèbre,* pitting modernists against traditionalists. In his novel *Of Human Bondage* Somerset Maugham gleefully described the Latin Quarter in which reproductions of *Olympia* were

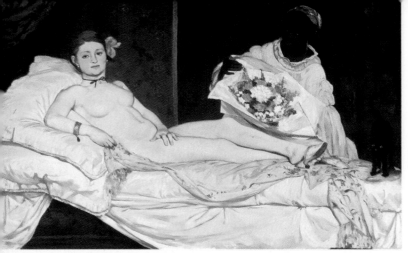

Figure 25.25 *Édouard Manet, Olympia, 1863. Oil on canvas, 51¼″ × 74¾″. Musée d'Orsay, Paris. Cliché des Musées Nationaux, Paris.*

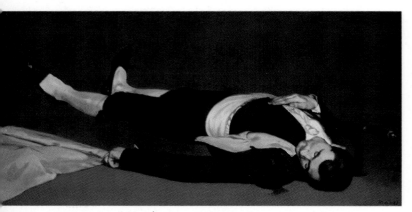

Figure 25.26 *Édouard Manet, The Dead Toreador, 1864. Oil on canvas, 29⅞″ × 60⅜″. Widener Collection. National Gallery of Art, Washington, D.C.*

prominent in virtually every student room, bistro, and café. Even today the picture is distinctly modern. Manet forces his viewers to look *at his flat picture rather than into it.* The traditional box-like space behind the frontal picture plane has been eliminated, presenting a situation that leaves much to the imagination. Further, a comparison of *Olympia* and the *Odalisque* of Ingres (figure 25.3) reveals the difference, at that time, between acceptable nudity and the disagreeable reality of a naked prostitute.

Manet was the first Western artist to reject Renaissance perspective as fraudulent, as basically contrary to the reality of an arrangement of colors and shapes on a flat surface. In *The Dead Toreador* (figure 25.26) he continued to antagonize a public that expected to see a dramatic depiction of a bullfighter fatally gored in the ring. Again, this is not a narrative but a striking arrangement of white, olive, pink, and black against a neutral background. Like many of his contemporaries, Manet was influenced by the newly popular Japanese prints (see figure 25.36) in which two-dimensionality, line, and flat color planes were basic components of the style.

Following the innovations of Manet, who went on to experiment in other directions, the impressionists developed a definite system with its own aesthetic principles. For centuries artists had been painting what they knew, but the impressionists were more interested in painting what they saw. The recent development of paint tubes and canisters liberated artists from the messy and time-consuming process of mixing pigments; more importantly, portable paints freed artists from their studios, enabling them to roam the countryside and paint *en plein air* (in open air). To see and capture the wondrous glories of nature and revel in the evanescent effects of sunlight became the new aesthetic.

Claude Monet, 1840–1926

The spokesman and chief painter of the impressionist style was Monet (mo-NAY), who throughout his long and productive career relied wholly on his visual perceptions. For him, especially, there were no objects such as trees, houses, or figures but some green here, a patch of blue there, a bit of yellow over here, and so on. Monet was "only an eye," said Paul Cézanne, "but what an eye!" The mechanics of vision were a major concern of Monet and the other impressionists. To achieve intensity of color, pigments were not combined on the palette but laid on the canvas in primary hues so that the eye could do the mixing. A dab of yellow, for example, placed next to one of blue is perceived, from a distance, as green, a brilliant green because the eye accomplishes the optical recomposition. Further, each color leaves behind a visual sensation, which is its afterimage or complementary color. The afterimage of red is blue-green and that of green is the color red. The adjacent placement of red and green reinforces each color through its afterimage, making both red and green more brilliant. Impressionists generally painted with pure pigments in the colors of the spectrum; conspicuously absent from the spectrum and thus from impressionist canvases was black, a favorite of academic painters. Monet contended that black was not a color and he was scientifically correct; black is the absence of color. This, of course, did not keep Degas and Manet *(The Dead Toreador)* from using black with dramatic effect.

Portable paints in the open sunlight and color perception were two components of impressionist technique. The third component was speed. Making natural light explode on canvas necessitated quick brushstrokes that captured a momentary impression of reflected light, a reflection that changed from minute to minute. Monet's procedure was to paint furiously for seven or eight minutes and then move quickly to another canvas to capture a different light. Should a painting require additional effort he would return to the same spot the following day at precisely the same time, a procedure he followed in his many paintings of Rouen Cathedral done at different times of day. Early in the morning the elaborate Gothic facade would appear to be quite solid but later in the day, as in *Rouen Cathedral, West Facade Sunlight* (figure 25.27), the stonework has dissolved into a luminous haze of warm colors. *Impressionism* is a term used deri-

Figure 25.27 *Claude Monet,* Rouen Cathedral, West Facade Sunlight, *1894. Oil on canvas, 39½" × 26". Chester Dale Collection, 1962. National Gallery of Art, Washington, D.C.*

Figure 25.28 *Pierre Auguste Renoir,* Le Moulin de la Galette, *1876. Oil on canvas, 51½" × 69". Musée d'Orsay, Paris.*

sively by a critic who, on seeing Monet's 1872 painting entitled *Impression, Sunrise,* remarked that it was "only an impression." That the term is generally apropos is apparent in Monet's impression of sunlight on medieval stonework. An interesting and telling sidelight is the 1872 date of this important painting. This was only a year after France had been humiliated by Germany in the Franco-Prussian War of 1870–1871. A study of French artistic output of the period points up the artists' total unconcern with politics and so-called national honor.

Auguste Renoir, 1841–1919

Monet was a magnificent "eye" whose achievements are far more appreciated today than in his own time. On the other hand, the work of his celebrated contemporary has always had great appeal, possibly because Renoir (ren-o'AR) portrayed people rather than buildings, landscapes, or lily ponds. The finest painter of luscious nudes since Rubens, Renoir had a unique ability to create the illusion of soft and glowing human flesh. He painted females of

all ages, once exclaiming that if "God had not created woman I don't know whether I would have become a painter!"

Much of the art of Millet and the realists depicts laborers at various tasks, but the impressionists viewed a world without work. An astonishing number of impressionist works portrayed people enjoying leisure activities: boating, bathing, picnicking, promenading, dancing, attending the theatre, opera, ballet, or music hall, going to the races. There is no finer representation of exuberant pleasure than Renoir's *Le Moulin de la Galette* (figure 25.28), a dazzling display of painterly virtuosity. The scene is an outdoor café with a large and crowded dance floor. The radiant color and shimmering light emphasize the fresh and youthful vigor of the celebrants, especially the women; nowhere is there a trace of black for all shadows have some degree of color. Light, air, color, and the captured moment, this is what impressionism is all about. Further, impressionism also functioned as social history, particularly of France in the latter part of the nineteenth century. People were shown enjoying leisure activities because so many more of them had the time and money to do so. The growth and rise of the middle class is right there in Renoir's painting for all to see.

Edgar Degas, 1834–1917

Degas (DAY-gah) also specialized in women, but women in their casual but graceful roles as ballet dancers. Delighting in studying forms in motion, he drew dancers and race horses and, in so doing, gained a remarkable vitality in his work. *Four Dancers* (figure 25.29) was one of his last large oil paintings, but it also shows the influence of the pastel medium that he used in most of his later works. Of all the impressionists, Degas was most interested in photography, both in taking pictures and in basing some of his

Figure 25.29 *Edgar Degas,* Four Dancers, *ca. 1899. Oil on canvas, 59½" × 71". Chester Dale Collection, 1962. National Gallery of Art, Washington, D.C.*

works on photographs. This off-stage ballet scene has the appearance of a candid snapshot of dancers limbering up and checking their costumes before going onstage. Actually, Degas posed dancers in his studio to orchestrate the illusion of spontaneity that he wanted. Degas's concern with composition and his use of black make his style less impressionistic than the style of either Monet or Renoir.

Berthe Morisot, 1841–1895

The impressionists were a cohesive group of avant-garde artists that revolved around the central personality of Manet. The regular meeting place of Manet's "school" was the Café Guerbois, where Manet, Monet, Renoir, Degas, Whistler, the photographer Nadar, Émile Zola, Baudelaire, and others congregated to argue passionately about the role of the modern artist. Morisot (more-uh-

so) was a member of the group but, as a proper young woman, she was denied the opportunity to socialize at the café with her colleagues. A student of both Corot and Manet, she earned the unusual distinction of having her work accepted by both the impressionists and the Salon. She was, in fact, one of the organizers of the first impressionist exhibition at Nadar's Gallery in 1874. In her *In the Dining Room* (figure 25.30) she depicted her maid and little white dog in a setting in which the forms are silhouetted as elements in a design literally flooded with shimmering color and light. An enthusiastic admirer of her art, the symbolist poet Stéphane Mallarmé, wrote in his catalog for an exhibition of her work: "To make poetry in the plastic arts demands that the artist portray on the surface the luminous secret of things, simply, directly, without extraneous detail."

Figure 25.30 *Berthe Morisot,* In the Dining Room, *1886. Oil on linen, 24⅛" × 19¾". Chester Dale Collection, 1962. National Gallery of Art, Washington, D.C.*

Mary Cassatt, 1844–1926

Both of the American painters who exhibited with the impressionists, Cassatt and Whistler, drew their inspiration from their techniques, but each developed a different and very personal style. Cassatt was American by birth and training and, though she lived in France for much of her life, is considered by the French to be the best artist America has yet produced. The influence of two-dimensional Japanese woodcuts (see figure 25.36) is apparent in *The Bath* (figure 25.31), but the extraordinary quality of the lines is uniquely her own. Both decorative and functional, the fluid lines enclose what seems at first to be a simple domestic scene. But this is a highly stylized composition that we look down on, an intimate and tender moment presented in a closed form that shuts out the viewer and the world. We experience the rich warmth of the scene but we are not a part of it. The frequently caustic and

Figure 25.31 *Mary Cassatt,* The Bath, *ca. 1891–1892. Oil on canvas, 39¼" × 26". The Art Institute of Chicago. Robert A. Waller Fund.*

always chauvinistic Degas remarked, after examining her work in her studio, "These are real. Most women paint pictures as though they were trimming hats, not you." For Degas, this was high praise for a great artist.

James McNeill Whistler, 1834–1903

Whistler and Henry James considered American civilization an embarrassment. Like James, Whistler became an expatriate, even denying that he was born in Lowell, Massachusetts: "I shall be born when and where I want, and I do not choose to be born in Lowell." Whistler was highly critical, naturally, of American realists such as Winslow Homer (see figure 25.20), advocating instead "art for art's sake." The impressionists were sufficiently artistic for his tastes, and he adapted some of their modern techniques to his uniquely personal style. Subject matter, he felt, was of no importance; in his *The White Girl: Symphony in White, No. 1* (figure 25.32) Whistler contended that no one could possibly be interested in the model, who happened to be the artist's

Figure 25.32 *James McNeill Whistler,* The White Girl: Symphony in White, No. 1, *1862. Oil on canvas, 84½" × 42½". Harris Whittemore Collection, 1943. National Gallery of Art, Washington, D.C.*

mistress, Joanna Heffernan. Whistler added the subtitle several years after exhibiting the painting to emphasize the aesthetic appeal of his use of rhythm and harmony in the manner of music. Some of his avant-garde colleagues recognized that art was its own subject matter, but not the art establishment. Rejected by both the Royal Academy in London and the Paris Salon, the painting became as notorious as Manet's *Déjeuner* (figure 25.24). Light was the subject of one painting and white the subject of the other.

Figure 25.33 *Auguste Rodin,* The Walking Man, *1877–1878. Gift of Mrs. John W. Simpson. National Gallery of Art, Washington, D.C.*

Auguste Rodin, 1840–1917

During the eighteenth and nineteenth centuries sculpture failed to keep pace with painting and architecture. The work of Houdon (see figure 21.43) was significant, but the sculptures of Daumier and Degas were scarcely known at the time. And then there was Rodin (ro-DAN), the greatest sculptor since Bernini, a dynamo of a man who captured the spontaneity and immediacy of impressionism in three-dimensional form. Like Renoir and Degas, Rodin was concerned with the human figure but, totally unlike any impressionist, his figures are depicted in moments of stress or tension. Intended originally as a study for *St. John the Baptist Preaching, The Walking Man* (figure 25.33) is a study in motion and motion is all that we sense. Headless and armless, there is no expression or gesture to distract our attention from the strongly striding torso moving its muscular legs in long steps. The surface shimmers with light, shaped by the artist to further heighten the illusion of motion.

Rodin's commission for *The Gates of Hell* produced a number of figures extracted from a monumental work that was never completely finished. Sitting atop the Gates and brooding over Rodin's conception of Dante's *Inferno, The Thinker* (figure 25.34) is a prodigious work of tension in repose. Similar to Michelangelo's superhuman forms that Rodin studied in detail, the figure is sunk in deep thought. What is he thinking of? Rodin said at one time that it was Dante contemplating his poem and an-

Figure 25.34 *Auguste Rodin, The Thinker, 1879–1889. Gift of Mrs. John W. Simpson. National Gallery of Art, Washington, D.C.*

Figure 25.35 *Paul Cézanne, Le Château Noir, ca. 1904. Oil on linen, 29" × 38". Gift of Eugene and Agnes E. Meyer, 1958. National Gallery of Art, Washington, D.C.*

other time that this was a dreamer and then a creator. Whether writer, dreamer, or creator, *The Thinker* remains a fascinating enigma.

Post-Impressionism

Paul Cézanne, 1839–1906

Post-impressionism is a catchall term for some highly individual artists who reacted against the purely visual emphasis of impressionism. The first and foremost of the post-impressionists, Cézanne (say-ZAN) was, in fact, one of the giants of European painting. His art lay somewhere between representation and abstraction, an intellectualized approach to applying paint to canvas. For Cézanne the whole purpose of painting was to express the emotion that the forms and colors of the natural world evoked in the artist. His landscapes look like his native Provence but not literally; everything has been clarified and concentrated. Cézanne took liberties with ordinary visual experience that challenge our perceptions and force us to view the world in a new way, in Cézanne's way. In *Le Château Noir* (figure 25.35) Cézanne gave the building a brooding air of mystery in keeping with the local legend that it was haunted by the ghost of an alchemist. In common with his other landscapes, there are no living creatures and the forms of the dense forest and the arcane building on its rocky spur are synthesized with the artist's characteristically muted blue-green and orange hues. The impressionists used color to dissolve form and space; Cézanne did precisely the opposite by using color to define form in a very tangible space. Cézanne constructed his

paintings slowly, methodically, with an intellectual control comparable to the art of Poussin. *Le Château Noir* has what he called a "durable museum quality" because Cézanne painted not just what he saw but what he knew.

Vincent van Gogh, 1853–1890

Cézanne sold some of his paintings for as little as nine dollars but the Dutch artist van Gogh (van-GO) sold only one painting during his ten-year career, depending entirely on his brother for support. Van Gogh began as an impressionist but changed his style drastically after studying Japanese prints, which he found "extremely clear, never tedious, as simple as breathing" (see figure 25.36). Though van Gogh never attained this degree of facility, he did learn to treat the picture surface as an area to be decorated in masses of flat or slightly broken color. In *La Mousmé* (figure 25.37) he painted a young girl from Provence, to which he had moved in 1888 to capture in the brilliant sunlight some of the beauty that he imagined existed in Japan. The word *mousmé* was used in a contemporary romantic novel to characterize the innocent charm of youthful Japanese teahouse attendants. Poised motionless against a neutral background and holding some oleander flowers, the thirteen-year-old peasant girl seems totally removed from everyday experience. She represents the artist's aim "to paint men and women with that quality of the eternal which used to be suggested by the halo."

Twice confined to a hospital in Arles after an apparent mental breakdown in 1889, van Gogh resumed painting and continued to produce during his subsequent year-long confinement

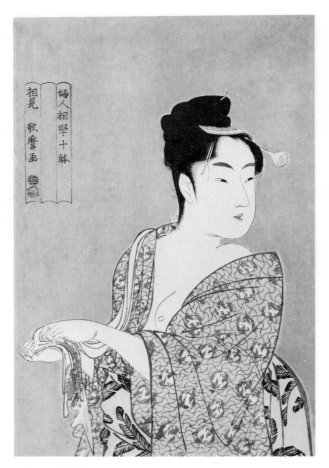

Figure 25.36 *Kitagawa Utamaro,* Uwaki, Half-Length Portrait, *from the series* Fujin Sogaku Jittai: Studies in Physiognomy; Ten Kinds of Women, *ca. 1794. Print. Color and mica on paper, 14½" × 10". Bequest of Edward L. Whittemore. Cleveland Museum of Art.*

Figure 25.37 *Vincent van Gogh,* La Mousmé, *1888. Oil on canvas, 28⅞" × 23¾". Chester Dale Collection, 1942. National Gallery of Art, Washington, D.C.*

in an asylum at St. Remy. Painted in a field near the hospital, *The Starry Night* (figure 25.38) is an ecstatic vision of the power and glory of the universe. A tall cypress flames toward the whirling and exploding stars of a cosmic drama unknown to the inhabitants of the peaceful village below. This expressive work represents the artist's reverent celebration of the wonders of nature and is not, as some have contended, symptomatic of mental problems. Moreover, recent medical research, based on a review of 796 of his letters, has determined that the artist probably suffered from a debilitating illness called Ménière's disease. Symptoms include hallucinations and a ringing in the ears.

Moving northwest of Paris to the village of Auvers-sur-Oise after his release from the asylum, van Gogh completed about sixty paintings during the last two months of his tragic life. Why he chose to commit suicide at age thirty-seven with a bullet to the abdomen (that finally killed him several agonizing days later) has never been satisfactorily explained. At his funeral his friend and physician, Dr. Paul Gachet, said, "He was an honest man and a great artist. He had only two aims: humanity and art. It was the art that . . . will insure his survival."

Paul Gauguin, 1848–1903

Van Gogh's onetime friend, Gauguin (go-GAN), has been a kind of folk hero for desk-bound romantics who dream of dropping out of the rat race to pursue their artistic muse. The reality of Gauguin's life and career is, however, not the stuff of dreams. An amateur painter for many years, Gauguin had naively assumed that he would be as successful as a full-time painter as he had been as a stockbroker. Within three years after giving up his career in 1883, everything was gone: wife, family, money; he found himself living on borrowed funds at a rundown country inn in Brittany. Fascinated by the peasant costumes and deep piety of Breton women, Gauguin painted *Vision after the Sermon (Jacob Wrestling with the Angel)* (figure 25.39) as a symbolic religious drama. The peasant women have just left the church after perhaps hearing a sermon by the priest (at the far right) about Jacob's bout with

Figure 25.38 *Vincent van Gogh,* The Starry Night, *1889. Oil on canvas, 29″ × 36¼″. Collection, The Museum of Modern Art, New York. Acquired through the Lillie P. Bliss Bequest.*

Figure 25.39 *Paul Gauguin,* Vision after the Sermon (Jacob Wrestling with the Angel), *1888. Oil on canvas, 36¼″ × 28¾″. National Galleries, Edinburgh. Courtesy National Galleries of Scotland.*

the angel, at which they are staring. Painted in flat, boldly outlined colors, the picture reveals Gauguin's keen perception of the power of belief and imagination in the almost medieval world of the Breton peasant.

A rebel at odds with conventional behavior and society in general, Gauguin was seldom bothered with self-doubt. Writing to his absent wife, he proclaimed that "I am a great artist and I know it." Probably inspired by Japanese prints, as was much of his work, his *Self-Portrait* (figure 25.40) includes a slight oriental cast to the eyes in this strikingly off-centered composition. Presenting himself with an ironic halo, his temptations are symbolized by the sharply outlined apples and the snake that he holds like a cigarette. Painted in the manner of a cloisonné enamel, the vivid colors are divided by incised lines, with everything flattened except the arrogant but sadly reflective face of a man who once wrote that he felt "like a brigand, which, for that matter, I am to many people."

Forever restless, Gauguin was drawn to the warm weather of Provence where he roomed briefly, and quarreled, with van Gogh, and then drifted to tropical climates: Panama, Martinique,

Tahiti, and the Marquesas, where he died. In Tahiti Gauguin found, he thought, an antidote to the sickness of European civilization, a "primitive life" that would nurture his style. Actually, the Society Islands were governed by the French and Gauguin had evolved his tropical style before settling down in Polynesia. Gauguin's dream of "solitude under the tropical sun" was compromised by illness, poverty, and harassment by French authorities, but his work did acquire a new vigor.

Critics of the time found Gauguin's colors bizarre and his drawing crude, but the public accepted the content of his paintings as actual illustrations of Tahitian life and customs. Though Gauguin admitted that his Tahiti was a subjective interpretation of what was "vaguest and most universal in nature," we still have a romantic image of Tahiti in Gauguin's mode. In *Where Do We Come From? What Are We? Where Are We Going?* (figure 25.41) Gauguin executed what he called his "spiritual testament," completed shortly before his abortive suicide attempt. Stating that "I will never do anything better or even like it," Gauguin painted this as a voyage of discovery, not as a statement of his rather confused ideas about birth, life, and death. The painting is a fusion of antitheses: sunlight and moonlight; night and day; the warmness of life and the coldness of death. The cycle of life can be read from childhood on the right to the old woman waiting for death at the left. Ultimately, this work attests, as Gauguin said, to "the futility of words" in any attempt to express the wonder and mystery of life. It may have been this painting that the symbolist poet Mallarmé called a "musical poem that needs no libretto."

Figure 25.40 *Paul Gauguin,* Self-Portrait, *1889. Oil on wood, 31¼"* × *20¼". Chester Dale Collection, 1962. National Gallery of Art, Washington, D.C.*

Figure 25.41 *Paul Gauguin,* Where Do We Come From? What Are We? Where Are We Going? *signed and dated 1897. Oil on canvas, 54¾"* × *147½". Tompkins Collection. Arthur Gordon Tompkins Fund. Courtesy, Museum of Fine Arts, Boston.*

Figure 25.42 *Georges Seurat,* Sunday Afternoon on the Island of La Grande Jatte, *1884–1886. Oil on canvas, 10'6" × 6'9". The Art Institute of Chicago. Helen Birch Bartlett Memorial Collection.*

Georges Seurat, 1859–1891

Causing nearly as much controversy as works by Manet and Whistler, Seurat (sue-RAH) exhibited *Sunday Afternoon on the Island of La Grande Jatte* (figure 25.42) at the eighth and final impressionist show of 1886. Critics had a field day lambasting the dots of color, the "procession of pharaohs," and a "clearance sale of Nuremberg toys." Favorable critics, and there were some, labeled the new style Neoimpressionism or Divisionism, though Paris wits chose the word "confettism." Seurat himself used the term *chromo-luminarium* to describe a method of painting with tiny dots using the colors of the spectrum. Aspiring to paint in a scientific manner based on the optical theories of Helmholtz and others, Seurat used his *petit points,* his dots, to construct a monumental composition of "museum quality," as advocated by Cézanne. The scene is a popular summer resort near Paris where middle-class city dwellers could bathe, picnic, and promenade. Though the dots of pure color were supposed to fuse in the eye this does not happen, save in the luminosity of the river. Instead, the spectator is conscious of the myriads of dots that, in a non-chromatic way, contribute as units of scale to the grandeur that Seurat achieved; his optical theories were, in practice, more artistic than scientific. In addition, he developed a control of line, proportions, and masses of light and shade that make this a classical composition in the manner of Poussin and David. In its psychological impact the work is curiously modern. People, animals, hats, and parasols are structural and decorative elements, as isolated from each other as the passengers in the *Third-Class Carriage* (figure 25.18). A typical impressionist genre scene has become a melancholic comment on alienation and isolation in late Victorian society, symbolizing the underlying pessimism of the age.

Henri de Toulouse-Lautrec, 1864–1901

The bawdy nightlife of Parisian society was vividly depicted by Toulouse-Lautrec (tu-LOSE-la-TREK), who delighted in portraying people at cabarets, theatres, the races, and brothels. He especially enjoyed the tawdry gaiety of Montmartre's most colorful music hall, the Moulin Rouge. In *Quadrille at the Moulin*

Figure 25.43 *Henri de Toulouse-Lautrec,* Quadrille at the Moulin Rouge, *1892. Gouache on cardboard, 31½″ × 23¾″. Chester Dale Collection, 1942. National Gallery of Art, Washington, D.C.*

Rouge (figure 25.43) he portrayed the earthy vitality of the dancer Gabrielle as she hikes her skirts to begin the quadrille, a dance that grew out of the high-kicking cancan. Confronted by the professional dancer is an elegant and refined patron of the establishment, who reaches obediently for her skirt to begin the dance. Far more concerned with the human comedy than most impressionists were, Toulouse-Lautrec, like Daumier, has given us, in his paintings and inimitable posters, vivid pictures of the Gilded Age.

Henri Rousseau, 1844–1910

The most influential of the post-impressionists were Cézanne and an obscure toll collector named Rousseau. An isolated and enigmatic genius who began painting late in life, Rousseau taught himself to paint "alone," as he said, "and without any master but nature." His naive ideal was what he called the "truth" of the camera; he was actually convinced that his paintings were as "realistic" as a photograph. His jungle landscapes were painted with a startling directness of vision that influenced Picasso and others,

Figure 25.44 *Henri Rousseau,* The Equatorial Jungle, *1909. Oil on canvas, 55¼″ × 51″. Chester Dale Collection, 1942. National Gallery of Art, Washington, D.C.*

Figure 25.45 *Edvard Munch,* The Scream, *1893. Oil on canvas, 36″ × 29″. Nationalgallereit, Oslo. National Gallery of Art, Washington, D.C. Rosenwald Collection (1912).*

but these were tropics of the mind produced by the magical vision of a simple man who, apparently, never left France. Nothing in *The Equatorial Jungle* (figure 25.44) is identifiable in botanical terms. What we see is a brooding and sinister jungle inhabited by a mysterious bird (a vulture?) and two strange-looking animals. There is an eerie and timeless stillness about this exotic, compelling scene that communicates the wonder that the artist must have felt as he painted his visions, images so real that, as he told his colleagues, they actually terrified the painter.

Edvard Munch, 1864–1944

Van Gogh, Gauguin, Seurat, and Rousseau were critical of the disease of civilization, but their pervasive pessimism was not limited to French urban culture. The Norwegian painter Munch (MOONK) manipulated themes of evil, terror, and death to depict the plight, as he saw it, of *fin de siècle* European civilization, themes similar to those of the poets Matthew Arnold and Thomas Hardy (see chapter 23). In *The Scream* (figure 25.45) Munch portrayed a terror-stricken person whose sexual and facial identity has been obliterated by a piercing scream that is echoed in un-

dulating lines of the landscape. Like his friend and associate, Henrik Ibsen, Munch dealt with the unbearable tensions of the modern world that led to anxiety, alienation, and, as here, terror. Though his iconography was intensely personal, Munch's pessimistic vision strongly influenced the later German Expressionist movement (see chapter 28).

A rather impromptu special event, the *banquet Rousseau* symbolically marks the end of the old era and the advent of the twentieth-century avant-garde. Held in the studio of Picasso in 1908, three years after the revolutionary show of the Fauves (see chapter 28), the guest of honor was Henri Rousseau, nearing the end of his career and still unrecognized by the public. Guests included artists Georges Braque and Marie Laurencin, writers Apollinaire, Max Jacob, Gertrude Stein, and other luminaries of the new epoch. Picasso had ordered the food for the wrong day but there was ample wine and abundant good spirits, with violin entertainment provided by the guest of honor. The only real tribute the unassuming little toll collector-cum-painter ever received prompted him to whisper confidentially to Picasso that, "after all, you and I are both great painters: I in the Modern style and you in the Egyptian." Though Picasso's "Egyptian" style was actually his African mask period, Henri Rousseau's remark turned out to be correct on both counts.

Summary

Romanticism was a reaction in all the arts against the Enlightenment. For a time, however, the visual arts in France were in the service of Napoleon and David, his court painter. The Arch of Triumph and Church of the Madeleine made significant contributions to the neoclassic face of Paris, and the paintings of Ingres established an academic style against which later artists were to rebel.

Painting in a style uniquely his own, Goya was one of the most important painters of the century. The French Romantic style was established by the dramatic work of Géricault and continued by the peerless colorist Delacroix. John Constable was the leading Romantic landscape painter in England whereas Romantic architecture was revivalist, as manifested in the Gothic Revival Houses of Parliament. The art of Turner was a Romantic style in and of itself. The Romanticism of Cole and Bingham had a distinctly American flavor.

By the second half of the century realists such as Millet, Corot, Daumier, and Courbet dominated the Parisian art scene while, in America, Winslow Homer and Thomas Eakins were leading artists in the ongoing tradition of American realism. Imaginative uses of industrial technology saw the construction of prefabricated structures such as the Crystal Palace and the Eiffel Tower.

Led by the innovations of Manet, the impressionist movement became the avant-garde of European art. Considering themselves the ultimate realists, Monet, Renoir, Degas, Morisot, Cassatt, and others helped establish impressionism as one of the most influential of all artistic styles. Whistler did his own personal version of modern art and, in Paris, Rodin produced the most dramatic and expressive sculpture since the High Renaissance.

Reacting against the visual emphasis of impressionism in very personal terms, the post-impressionists included Cézanne, who distilled on canvas the forms and colors of the natural world, and Seurat, who used a similar approach but with dots of color. Van Gogh and Gauguin employed vivid colors to create very expressive works whereas Toulouse-Lautrec portrayed the high life and low life of his age. Rousseau created works from his private dream world that were a revelation to Picasso and others of the new avant-garde. Like many artists and writers of the late Victorian era, Munch reacted against modern urban society with themes of alienation and terror. A century that began with the Arch of Triumph ended with *The Scream*.

Culture and Human Values

The facts of science, a secular worldview, and materialism were the realities of the nineteenth century. Other factors included imperialism, the rising tide of nationalism, and the sporadic violence of an almost endless procession of revolutions and wars. The optimism of the Enlightenment seemed as remote as the Middle Ages. Though pessimism was not yet endemic, there were many, especially among writers and artists, who had strong feelings of foreboding. There is no more poignant expression of the doleful end of the century than Thomas Hardy's poem "The Darkling Thrush" (see chapter 23). The entire age is brilliantly summed up by Stephen Crane's two untitled poems that end chapter 23.

Exercises

1. Explain the basic differences between nineteenth-century neoclassic and romantic art by using two works from this chapter. Then repeat this exercise using two works *not* in this book.

2. One of the purposes of art is pleasure. Explain in detail why and how you enjoy a particular work presented in this chapter. There is no need to try for a balance between subjective and objective reactions.

3. Like most reproductions, the ones in this chapter are inadequate; artworks are best appreciated when you view the real thing. You very likely have access to art in your school or community, including some of the artists discussed in this chapter. Seek these out and compare them with the works shown in this chapter. Compare the works stylistically and especially, compare the quality of the original works as opposed to book illustrations.

4. Find some paintings by the impressionists (originals or reproductions) and match them as closely as possible with the two compositions by Debussy in chapter 24.

5. What relationships can you find between the pessimistic Victorian poets in chapter 23 and some of the works discussed in this chapter? Relate all of these to some of the events of the period as outlined in the Time Chart for the Middle Modern World.

THE
TWENTIETH
CENTURY

TIME CHART FOR THE TWENTIETH CENTURY

People and Events	Literature	Art	Architecture, Music, Photography	Invention, Science, Philosophy
1905 Unsuccessful revolution in Russia Fauves in Paris **1906** San Francisco earthquake **1907** Cubism in Paris **1909** Founding of NAACP **1910–1936** George V of England **1913** Armory Show in New York Stravinsky *Rite of Spring* *Ballet Russe* in Paris **1914–1918** World War I **1916–** Beginning of Dada movement **1917** Lenin triumphs in Russia US enters WWI Beginning of International Style **1918** Worldwide flu epidemic kills 20 million **1919** Treaty of Versailles **1919–1933** Weimar Republic **1919–1939** League of Nations **1920** US women win right to vote **1920–1933** Volstead Act (prohibition) **1922** Mussolini triumphs in Italy **1924** Surrealist Manifesto in Paris **1927** Stalin dictator in Russia **1929–** Great Depression begins **1931–1945** Sino-Japanese War **1932–1934** Geneva Disarmament Conference **1933–1945** Hitler dictator of Germany **1933–1945** Roosevelt US president **1934–1938** The Great Terror: Stalin's purges **1935** Congress passes Social Security Act **1935–1936** Italy conquers Ethiopia **1935–1940** WPA Art Project **1936** Edward VIII of England **1936–1939** Spanish Civil War **1936–1952** George VI of England **1938** Germany annexes Austria Czechoslovakia dismembered **1939–1945** World War II **1941** Pearl Harbor; US enters war **1944–** Beginning of modern jazz **1945** United Nations organized Atomic bombs on Japan **1945–1990** The Cold War **1947–** Beginning of Marshall Plan **1948** Israel became independent state **1950** US advisors sent to Vietnam **1950–1953** Korean War **1952–** Elizabeth II of England **1954** School segregation disallowed **1955–** Civil Rights movement begins **1961–1989** Berlin Wall **1963** President Kennedy assassinated **1964–1975** Vietnam War **1965** M. L. King leads Selma march Beginning of protests, hippies, flower children **1968** Assassination of M. L. King, R. F. Kennedy **1969** U.S. lunar landing Race riots in Watts, Detroit, New York **1970** National Guard kills 4 students at Kent State **1974** Nixon resigns presidency **1979** American hostages seized in Iran **1980–1988** The Reagan Era **1989** Beginning worldwide collapse of Communism **1990** End of Cold War **1990s** Rapid expansion of high tech	**William Butler Yeats** 1865–1939 *The Second Coming* **Virginia Woolf** 1882–1941 *If Shakespeare Had a Sister* **Countee Cullen** 1887–1946 *Yet Do I Marvel* **Robinson Jeffers** 1887–1962 *Shine, Perishing Republic* **T. S. Eliot** 1888–1965 *The Love Song of J. Alfred Prufrock* **Wilfred Owen** 1893–1918 *Dulce et Decorum Est* **e e cummings** 1894–1962 *anyone lived in a pretty how town* **Jorge Luis Borges** 1899–1986 *The Disinterested Killer Bill Harrigan* **Langston Hughes** 1902–1967 *Harlem* **Richard Eberhart** 1904– *The Fury of Aerial Bombardment* **Jean Paul Sartre** 1905–1980 *Existentialism* **Samuel Beckett** 1906– *Waiting for Godot* **Eudora Welty** 1909– *The Worn Path* **Albert Camus** 1913–1966 *The Myth of Sisyphus* **Dylan Thomas** 1914–1953 *When All My Five and Country Senses See* **Ralph Ellison** 1914– *Invisible Man* **Henry Reed** 1914– *Naming of Parts* **John Berryman** 1914–1972 *Life, Friends, Is Boring. We Must Not Say So* **Gwendolyn Brooks** 1917– *We Real Cool* **Denise Levertov** 1923– *Tenebrae* **Nadine Gordimer** 1923– *A Soldier's Embrace* **James Dickey** 1923– *Adultery* **Joseph Heller** 1923– *Catch 22* **Adrienne Rich** 1929– *Two Songs* **Martin Luther King, Jr.** 1929–1968 *Letter from Birmingham Jail* **N. Scott Momaday** 1934– *House Made of Dawn* **Gail Godwin** 1937– *A Sorrowful Woman* **Nikki Giovanni** 1943– *Nikki-Rosa* **Susan Griffin** 1943– *I Like to Think of Harriet Tubman*	**Wassily Kandinsky** 1866–1944 *Panel 3* **Käthe Kollwitz** 1867–1945 *The Only Good Thing* **Henri Matisse** 1869–1954 *The Blue Window* **Ernst Barlach** 1870–1938 *Shivering Woman* **Georges Rouault** 1871–1958 *Christ Mocked by Soldiers* **John Sloan** 1871–1951 *Roof Gossips* **Piet Mondrian** 1872–1944 *Broadway Boogie Woogie* **Constantin Brancusi** 1876–1957 *Bird in Space* **Paul Klee** 1879–1940 *Fish Magic* **Pablo Picasso** 1881–1973 *Guernica* **Edward Hopper** 1882–1967 *House by the Railroad* **José Ôrozco** 1883–1949 *Zapatistas* **Diego Rivera** 1886–1957 *Liberation of the Peon* **Kurt Schwitters** 1887–1948 *Sichtbar* **Marcel Duchamp** 1887–1968 *The Bride Stripped Bare by Her Bachelors, Even* **Marc Chagall** 1887–1985 *I and the Village* **Georgia O'Keeffe** 1887–1986 *Jack-in-the-Pulpit, No. 5* **Giorgia de Chirico** 1888–1978 *The Nostalgia of the Infinite* **Josef Albers** 1888–1976 *Homage to the Square* **Horace Pippin** 1888–1946 *Victorian Interior* **George Grosz** 1893–1959 *I Am Glad I Came Back* **Joan Miró** 1893–1983 *Person Throwing a Stone at a Bird* **Stuart Davis** 1894–1964 *Radio Tubes* **David Siqueiros** 1896–1974 *Echo of a Scream* **René Magritte** 1898–1967 *The False Mirror* **Alexander Calder** 1898–1976 *Many Pierced Discs* **Henry Moore** 1898–1986 *Family Group* **Rufino Tamayo** 1899– *Man* **Louise Nevelson** 1900–1988 *Illumination—Dark* **Alberto Giacometti** 1901–1966 *The Palace at 4 am* **Jean Dubuffet** 1901–1985 *Portrait of Henri Michaux* **Mark Rothko** 1903–1970 *Number 10* **Willem de Kooning** 1904– *Woman I* **Salvador Dali** 1904–1989 *The Persistence of Memory* **David Smith** 1906–1965 *Cubi XV* **Francis Bacon** 1910– *Number VII from Eight Studies for a Portrait* **Jackson Pollock** 1912–1956 *Number 1* **Meret Oppenheim** 1913– *Luncheon in Fur* **Jacob Lawrence** 1917– *Daybreak-A Time to Rest* **Ronald Bladen** 1918– *X* **Roy Lichtenstein** 1923– *Drowning Girl* **Robert Rauschenberg** 1925– *Monogram* **Edward Kienholz** 1927– *State Hospital* **Tony DeLap** 1927– *Sentaro* **Helen Frankenthaler** 1928– *Interior Landscape* **Marisol** 1930– *Women and Dog* **Audrey Flack** 1931– *World War II, April 1945* **Bridget Riley** 1931– *Current* **Mark di Suvero** 1933– *Side Frames* **Christo** 1935– *Running Fence* **Fritz Scholder** 1937– *Waiting Indian No. 4* **Sylvia Mangold** 1938– *Schunnemunk Mountain* **Robert Smithson** 1938–1973 *Spiral Jetty* **Jennifer Bartlett** 1941– *Sad and Happy Tidal Wave* **Otto Duecker** 1948– *Russell, Terry, J. T.*	**Matthew Brady** 1823–1896 *Abraham Lincoln* **Antonio Gaudi** 1852–1926 Church of the Holy Family **Alfred Stieglitz** 1864–1946 *The Terminal* **Frank Lloyd Wright** 1867–1959 "Falling Water" **Arnold Schoenberg** 1874–1951 **Charles Ives** 1874–1954 Three Places in New England **Béla Bartók** 1881–1945 *Concerto for Orchestra* **Igor Stravinsky** 1882–1971 *The Rite of Spring* **Anton Webern** 1883–1945 *Three Songs* **Walter Gropius** 1883–1969 Bauhaus **Alban Berg** 1885–1935 Violin Concerto **Ludwig Mies v. der Rohe** 1886–1969 Seagram Building **Le Corbusier** 1887–1965 Notre-Dame-du-Haut **Serge Prokofiev** 1891–1953 Symphony No. 5 **Wallace Harrison** 1895–1981 Secretariat Building of the United Nations **Carl Orff** 1895–1982 *Carmina Burana* **Dorothea Lange** 1895–1965 *Migrant Mother* **Ansel Adams** 1902–1984 *Moonrise* **Margaret Bourke-White** 1904–1971 *Flood Victims* **Philip Johnson** 1906– AT&T Building **Eero Saarinen** 1910–1961 TWA Terminal **John Cage** 1912– **Milton Babbitt** 1916– *Ensemble for Synthesizer* **Joern Utzon** 1918– Sydney Opera House **W. Eugene Smith** 1918–1978 *Spanish Wake* **Michael Graves** 1937– The Portland **Philip Glass** 1937– *Einstein on the Beach*	**1900** Freud *The Interpretation of Dreams* Planck's constant; quantum theory **1901** First transatlantic radio telegraphic transmission **1902** First phonograph recordings **1903** Wright brothers' first flight **1905** Einstein Special Theory of Relativity First US motion pictures **1908** Ford introduces Model T **1909** Wireless radio **1912** Discovery of insulin **1914** Discovery of vitamins **1916** Einstein General Theory of Relativity **1922** Radar invented **1926** First TV transmission First liquid fuel rocket **1927** Heisenberg Principle of Uncertainty **1928** First sound movie **1930** Discovery of penicillin **1934** Discovery of antibiotics **1939** First commercial TV First jet engine Automatic sequence computer developed **1940** First successful plutonium fission **1942** Uranium fission, atomic reactor **1947** Jean Paul Sartre *Existentialism* (from Kierkegaard, Nietzsche) **1948** LP recordings marketed **1951** Inauguration of transcontinental TV **1952** US explodes hydrogen bomb **1956** First transatlantic telephone Inauguration of interstate highway system **1957** First earth satellite (USSR) **1958** Beginning of jet airline passenger service Laser beam invented **1961** First manned orbital flight (USSR) **1962** Rachel Carson's *Silent Spring* launches environmentalist movement **1963** Quasars discovered **1964** China detonates atom bomb **1965** Foundation of National Organization for Women (NOW) **1967** First heart transplant **1972** UN Conference on the Human Environment **1973** First orbital laboratory (Skylab) **1974** First energy crisis **1976** Genetic engineering developed **1978** First test tube baby **1981** Beginning of space shuttle flights **90s** Expansion of high tech: computers, robotics, global communications Increasing environmental concerns

chapter 26

Things Fall Apart:
The Center Cannot Hold

Historical Overview, 1914–1939

World War I can be viewed as Act 1 in a drama that began in 1871 with Bismarck's formation of the German Empire (the Prologue) and continued with World War II as Act 2 in a tragedy that engulfed most of the world. The period of 1918–1939 can be seen, in retrospect, as an entr'acte that set the stage for what may or may not be the last act.

When the Armistice between the Allies and Germany and her allies was agreed on for 11 November 1918, the stated intent was to stop the fighting and arrange for a just peace. The Treaty of Versailles that was signed on 28 June 1919 was, however, harshly punitive. Germany and her allies were forced to accept the "war guilt" clause and further, to accept *all* responsibility for causing the war. War reparations were to be paid to all thirty-two allies; Germany lost virtually her entire armed services, overseas colonies, and portions of her land area, including the critical Polish Corridor that divided Germany and gave Poland a passage to the sea. Woodrow Wilson's attempts to curb the nationalistic zeal of Britain's Lloyd George and France's Clemenceau were essentially futile. Even Wilson's prize project, the League of Nations that was part of the Peace of Versailles, ended, finally, in failure caused in part by the refusal of the United States to join this valiant, doomed attempt to civilize the conduct of nations. The League of Nations did settle a few disputes but was powerless to prevent Japan's invasion of Manchuria in 1931, Mussolini's invasion of Ethiopia in 1935, and Germany's withdrawal from the League to rearm.

The Allies had convinced the Germans that Kaiser Wilhelm II and his imperial government were primarily responsible for the war. But it was the new Weimar Republic that signed the dictated peace and it was the Republic that bore the onus of German humiliation at the conference table. Moreover, the Treaty of Versailles made no provision for the economic rehabilitation of Europe nor were there any assurances for the futures of new nations—Czechoslovakia and Yugoslavia—that had been carved out of the dismembered Austro-Hungarian empire. The Treaty of Versailles caused more discontent and unrest than even the 1815 Congress that ended the Napoleonic Wars.

The March 1917 revolution in Russia had disposed of the czar, but the new Provisional government, despite rising unrest, continued to pursue the war. V. I. Lenin (1870–1924) capitalized on new defeats at the front to seize the government and establish the All-Russian Congress of the Soviets. Concluding a separate disastrous peace with Germany, Lenin established a dictatorship of the Communist party that barely survived the ferocious Civil War of 1918–1921. Under Leon Trotsky (1877–1940) a new Red Army destroyed the rebel White armies and then helped Lenin solidify his hold on the government. Lenin established himself as the unchallenged leader by having his secret police (Cheka) murder all his political opponents and potential opponents (some 60,000 or more), conforming to the dictator's rationale: "We are exterminating the bourgeoisie as a class. This is the essence of the Red Terror."[1] The Russian aristocracy had already been eliminated and the vast body of peasants posed no threat. Therefore, eradication of the middle class would effectively head off any opposition to tyranny. Lenin contended that murdering the entire middle class (tiny as it was at that time) would stabilize his dictatorship in that it made terror a known means of governance. Following Lenin's death in 1924, a power struggle between Trotsky and Joseph Stalin (1879–1953) saw Stalin emerge, in 1927, as the absolute dictator of the Soviet Union.

---

1. Paul Johnson, *Modern Times: The World from the Twenties to the Eighties* (New York: Harper & Row, 1983), p. 71.

Figure 26.1 *Memorial Sculpture, Dachau, Germany.*

The new democracies were beset by economic difficulties in the 1920s and assaulted by Communists on the left and hard-core nationalists on the right. Benito Mussolini (1883–1945) marched on Rome in 1922 and assumed full dictatorial powers by 1926. Designed to produce a corporate totalitarian state, the doctrines of Italian fascism stressed the dominance of the state and the subordination of the individual, the desirability of war, and the Social Darwinian "right" of Italy to expand at the expense of "inferior" nations.

The initial successes of Italian fascism impressed not only the older Western democracies but also many malcontents in Germany, who bitterly resented the war guilt clause of the Treaty of Versailles. Compounding the discontent, the German military clique fostered the false belief that Germany had never been defeated on the field of battle; she had been betrayed at home, said the military, by pacifist liberals. Following the disastrous inflation of 1923, the National Socialist German Workers Party (Nazis) launched a propaganda campaign that capitalized on the supposed sellout at Versailles; coupled with the barrage was a virulent anti-Semitism that blamed the Jews for many of Germany's postwar problems while proclaiming the absolute supremacy of the Aryan master race. A spellbinding political orator, Adolf Hitler (1889–1945) mesmerized his audiences with what he called the Big Lie: "If you keep it simple, say it often, and make it burn the public will believe anything." The Nazis achieved their first significant power when, in 1933, President von Hindenburg appointed Hitler as Chancellor of the Republic. Utilizing the emergency powers of Article 48 of the constitution, Hitler eradicated all opposition with his bloody purge of 1934. He was now absolute ruler of a Third Reich that was to last for "a thousand years."

The direct road to World War II began, probably, with Japan's seizure of Manchuria in 1931, followed by her withdrawal from the League of Nations in 1933 and her invasion of China four years later. To secretly arm for war, Germany withdrew from the League in 1933, also the year in which Dachau (DAH-kow) (figure 26.1)—the first concentration camp—was opened. In defiance of the Treaty of Versailles, Hitler occupied the Rhineland in 1936, a fateful step that is now seen as the last opportunity for England and France to avert war in Europe. From then on Hitler had the might to back up his threats. Italy challenged the League of Nations by invading Ethiopia in 1935. The League's feeble response was to vote economic sanctions that failed miserably. No longer a member of the League, Germany supplied arms and supplies for her future ally.

The Spanish Civil War of 1936–1939 had the effect of polarizing world opinion between the fascists and monarchists of "loyalist" Francisco Franco (1892–1975) and rebel factions led by socialists, communists, and an assortment of liberals. Hitler backed Franco, using the opportunity to field-test his new war machines. It was German bombers that attacked the undefended Basque town of Guernica, an atrocity immortalized by Picasso in his *Guernica* (see figure 28.13).

After signing a Rome-Berlin treaty with Mussolini in 1936, Hitler launched his campaign for a union (*anschluss*) with German-speaking Austria, which he occupied in early 1938. The next target was the German-speaking Sudeten area of Czechoslovakia. After working up a full-scale crisis with his oratory, Hitler agreed to a four-power conference at Munich on 29 September 1938. Hitler, Mussolini, British Prime Minister Neville Chamberlain, and Premier Édouard Daladier of France conferred in an atmosphere of conciliation artfully orchestrated by Hitler. Chamberlain returned to England proclaiming "peace in our time" even though England and France had helped dismember hapless Czechoslovakia. Hitler acquired the Sudetenland at Munich and all of Czechoslovakia by the following spring.

The final step was Poland. Germany and Russia signed a nonaggression pact on 23 August 1939 that relieved Hitler of his concerns about waging a two-front war. The secret portion of the pact divided Poland and Eastern Europe between Germany and Russia and "awarded" the Baltic republics of Lithuania, Estonia, and Latvia to Stalin. On 1 September 1939 the German armies rolled into Poland and, two days later, England and France honored their commitment to Poland by declaring war on Germany. The Peace Treaty of Versailles that was supposed to confirm the Great War as the "war to end all wars" had lasted a scant twenty years.

The Culture-Epoch Theory and the Twentieth Century

Our distance from past ages enables us to perceive the periods when a culture was balanced, when the balance tipped into chaos, when the adjustment began that led to a new period of balance, and so on. Analyzing our own age is far more difficult, perhaps impossible, yet as thinking beings, we try to understand where we are and where we might be going. (The culture-epoch theory is explained in the Prologue.)

During the past several decades new attitudes have become increasingly important. We know through evolutionary studies, for example, that all living things are evolving—everything in the cosmos, in fact. Led by molecular biologists, the overwhelming consensus among today's scientists is that humans, chimpanzees, and gorillas evolved from a common ancestor between three million and eight million years ago. Humans, chimps, and gorillas are more closely related to each other than any of them is to other primates. The DNA sequences of hemoglobin from humans and chimps are 98.4 percent identical, and the sequences from humans and gorillas are 98.3 percent identical. Right down to the bottom of the great chain of being, all living creatures are interrelated. Therefore, Homo sapiens does not have dominion over the globe or over so-called lower forms of life. Moreover, the balance of life in our world is precarious; we know, or should know, that we cannot alter our environment without worldwide repercussions and that we cannot damage our environment without ultimately harming ourselves. It is a scientific fact that the flight of a butterfly over Tokyo can in some still unexplained way affect the weather of New York City. This is the famous "butterfly effect" that will be discussed in the section on contemporary science.

This holistic view of living things expands to include our concept of the cosmos as expressed by modern science and applies to the inner world of the human personality as probed by Freud and other psychologists. Contemporary holistic views of evolving personality, society, the environment, and the cosmos suggest a new age that may be called a planet in process, a world in which everything is in a continual stage of becoming. Goal-oriented cultures of the past may be replaced by change-oriented cultures of the future. Once people begin viewing their cultural identities as journeys rather than as destinations, the new age may have begun.

In this and the following chapters we will consider the status of modern science, the Information Age, the Global Village concept, the failure of Marxism-Leninism and the resurgence of free enterprise in democratic societies, massive damage to the environment, racism, nascent nationalism, and the reactions of artists to the chaos, adjustment, and new directions of the twentieth century.

Modern Science

Quantum Theory

The old social order was in disarray by about 1914, but the predictable world-machine described by Newtonian science was overthrown even earlier. In 1900 Max Planck (1858–1947) took a giant stride away from visible perceptions of the physical world to a theory that described the microcosmos by using mathematical abstractions. While studying the radiant energy given off by heated bodies, Planck discovered that energy radiated not in unbroken streams but in discontinuous bits or portions that he called *quanta.* In terms of both emission and absorption of atomic and subatomic particles, Planck hypothesized that the energy transfer was discontinuous and involved a unit of energy (quantum) that could be calculated: "The uncertainty in the position of a particle times the uncertainty in its velocity times its mass can never be smaller than a certain quantity," which is known as Planck's constant.[2] Roughly a decimal point followed by twenty-six zeroes and ending in 6624, this minuscule number remains one of nature's most fundamental constants.

In conjunction with quantum theory, Werner Heisenberg (1901–1976) developed, in 1927, his Principle of Uncertainty, which states that, in effect, theory can accurately predict the behavior of statistically large numbers of particles, but not the behavior of individual particles. It is impossible to simultaneously determine the position and velocity of, for example, an electron.

---

2. Stephen W. Hawking, *A Brief History of Time: From the Big Bang to Black Holes* (New York: Bantam Books, 1988), p. 55.

If the position is observed, that act of observing will alter its velocity and conversely, the more accurate the determination of its velocity the more indefinite is the position of the electron. The fundamental equation of quantum mechanics is this: there is no such thing as an electron that possesses both a precise momentum and a precise position. The old science relied on a study of cause and effect (or causality and determinism), but the Principle of Uncertainty toppled these formerly sturdy pillars. Heisenberg won the Nobel Prize in 1932 for his work in quantum mechanics, but his leadership of the German scientists who kept Hitler from developing the atomic bomb is also worthy of special mention.[3] Even now the vision of Hitler with the bomb is just too dreadful to contemplate.

Quantum theory is strange and fascinating. Niels Bohr, Heisenberg's mentor and leading physicist on the Manhattan Project that developed the bomb, cogently proclaimed that "Anyone who is not shocked by quantum theory has not understood it." What is so astonishing?

In the first place, no one knows *how* the quantum world behaves the way it does, but scientists *do know* that it does behave the way it does. "In the quantum world what you see is what you get, and nothing is real; the best you can hope for is a set of delusions that agree with one another."[4]

The *double hole experiment* is perhaps the best way to view the eerie quantum world. Picture two walls separated by several feet with a small hole in each wall, either of which can be covered up. A single electron, or a single photon, on its way through one hole in the wall, obeys the statistical laws, which are appropriate only if it "knows" whether the other hole is open.

> *This is the central mystery of the quantum world.* The electrons not only know whether or not both holes are open, they know whether or not we are watching them, and they adjust their behavior accordingly.[5]

Scientists had shown in theory, in 1970, that an atom in one energy state cannot change its energy as long as it is being observed. By 1990 scientists at the National Institute of Standards and Technology had demonstrated that the act of looking at an atom prevented it from decaying. What still remains to be proved is whether continuous observation of unstable radioactive isotopes can prevent them from disintegrating radioactively. Theoretically, if a nuclear bomb were watched intently enough, it could not explode!

All of this bizarre behavior leads one to ask if there are any practical ways to convert quantum theory into quantum mechanics.

The physics is impossible, but the math is clean and simple, familiar equations to any physicist. As long as you avoid asking what it means there are no problems. Ask why the world should be like this, however, and the reply is: 'we have no idea.'[6]

Mathematical formulas based on quantum theory are basic to the development of television, VCRs, computers, and other high-tech marvels. Further, quantum theory has opened up a whole new area of philosophic speculation. Given a fantastic world that can be used but not explained, what, then, is reality?

Einstein and Relativity

Five years after Planck discovered quanta Albert Einstein (1879–1955; figure 26.2) hammered another nail into the coffin of the Newtonian world-machine. He postulated that light photons were also quanta and developed his Special Theory of Relativity (1905). In essence, his Special Theory rests on the hypothesis that neither space nor time has an objective reality. Space is an arrangement of perceived objects and time has no independent existence apart from our measurements of a sequence of events. Our clocks are geared to our solar system. What we call an hour is actually a measurement of an arc of 15 degrees in space based on the apparent movement of the sun. A year is, therefore, the time it takes the earth to orbit the sun, which is 365¼ days. Mercury has an 88-day year and other planets have their own time frame. As Einstein said, time is subjective and based on how people remember events as a sequence of "earlier" and "later," associating a greater number with the later event, an association that is defined by means of a clock.

In particular, Einstein's Special Theory stipulates that the velocity of light is constant for all uniformly moving systems anywhere in the universe. There is neither absolute space nor absolute time, but the velocity of light is the absolute speed limit of the universe. There can be no fixed interval of time independent of the system to which it is referred nor can there be simultaneity independent of an established reference. Einstein assumes, for example, that there is an observer seated beside a railroad track who sees a bolt of lightning at the far left (bolt A) and another at the far right (bolt B). Assuming that the observer is positioned precisely between A and B, the bolts will be perceived as simultaneous because all events have the same frame of reference. Now, assume that a train is moving along the track from right to left at the brisk speed of light (186,284 miles/second) and that another observer (2) is riding on the top of the train. Assume, further, that observer 2 is exactly opposite observer 1 at the precise moment that bolts A and B strike. Observer 2 will perceive bolt A but not bolt B. The train is moving away from bolt B at the speed of light, meaning that the light waves of bolt B will never catch up with the train. Observer 2 is in a different frame of reference than is observer 1.

3. See Mark Walker, *German National Socialism and the Quest for Nuclear Power: 1939–1949* (Cambridge: Cambridge University Press, 1990).

4. John Gribbin, *In Search of Schrödinger's Cat: Quantum Physics and Reality* (New York: Bantam Books, 1984), p. 162.

5. Ibid, p. 171.

6. Ibid, p. 174.

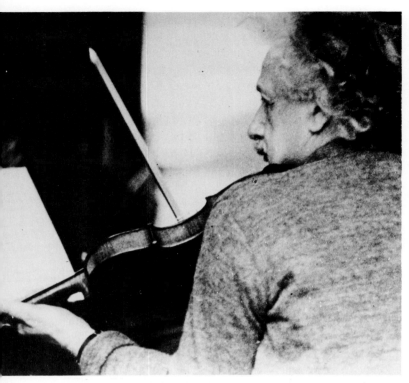

Figure 26.2 *Albert Einstein playing a violin at a chamber music rehearsal in Princeton, N.J. Photo: The Bettmann Archive.*

Based on his Special Theory, Einstein determined that with an increase in velocity, the mass of an object will also increase relative to an observer. Because motion is a form of kinetic energy, the increase in motion that leads to an increase in mass means that the mass has increased in energy. Einstein computed the value of the equivalent mass (m) in any unit of energy (e), leading to the equation that mass is equal to its energy over the square of the speed of light (c^2), or $m = e/c^2$. The remaining algebraic step results in the equation $e = mc^2$, the most famous equation of our age. As Einstein demonstrated mathematically, mass and energy were equivalent. What we normally call mass is concentrated energy that, with the proper trigger, can be released. The detonation of the first atomic device at Alamogordo, New Mexico, on 16 July 1945 demonstrated the transmutation of matter into energy in the forms of light, heat, sound, and motion.

Newton's laws still satisfactorily explain phenomena based on human experiences, but they cannot cope with modern physics. Einstein's laws of motion are based on the relativity of distance, time, and mass, what he called the "four-dimensional space-time continuum," that is, three dimensions of space and one of time. Relativity thus gives scientists the means to better describe the workings of nature.

Einstein later expanded his system into the General Theory of Relativity in which he examined what it is that guides all moving systems. His Special Theory had stated that the velocity of light was constant for all uniformly moving systems. His General Theory is broader and states that the laws of nature are the same for all

systems regardless of their states of motion. The basic premise of his Special Theory held true that all motion, uniform or non-uniform, had to be judged within some system of reference because absolute motion did not exist. He could not, however, distinguish between the motion caused by inertial forces (acceleration, centrifugal forces, etc.) and motion caused by gravitation. This led to his Principle of the Equivalence of Gravitation and Inertia, a new theory of gravitation more accurate and complete than Newton's Law of Universal Gravitation. Newton had postulated gravitation as a force or attraction, but Einstein's Law of Gravitation simply describes the behavior of objects in a gravitational field by depicting the paths they follow.

Gravitation, for Einstein, was a form of inertia, leading him to conclude that light, like any material body, was subject to gravitation when passing through a very strong gravitational field. He then proved that light travels in a predictable curve given sufficient gravitational pull. Einstein's universe has no straight lines. Euclidean geometry defines a straight line as the shortest distance between two points but, in space, there are only vast circles delineating all of space that, though it is finite, is unbounded.

It took only a few years to verify Einstein's General Theory of Relativity:

> The modern world began on 29 May 1919 when photographs of a solar eclipse, taken on the island of Principe off the coast of West Africa and at Sobral in Brazil, confirmed the truth of a new theory of the universe.[7]

As Einstein observed, relativity defined the outer limits of our knowledge and quantum theory defined the inner limits. What bothered him was that the two systems are unrelated to each other: "The idea that there are two structures of space independent of each other, the metric-gravitational and the electromagnetic is intolerable to the theoretical spirit." He went on to declare that "God does not play dice with the universe." A persistent believer in the fundamental uniformity and harmony of nature, Einstein devoted the latter part of his career to a futile search for a Unified Field Theory that would construct a bridge between relativity and quantum theory.

But Einstein was mistaken about the dice. In terms of quantum theory, physicist Stephen W. Hawking declared that "God not only plays dice, he sometimes throws the dice where they cannot be seen." Physicist Joseph Ford approached the problem from another perspective, stating that "God plays dice with the universe, but they're loaded dice. And the main objective of physics now is to find out by what rules they were loaded and how we can use them for our own ends."[8]

---

7. Johnson, op. cit., p. 1.

8. Joseph Ford as quoted in James Gleich, *Chaos; Making a New Science* (New York: Viking, 1987), p. 314.

The New Science of Chaos

Relativity eliminated the Newtonian illusion of absolute space and time; quantum theory abolished the Newtonian dream of a precise and controllable measurement process; chaos dispensed with the long held belief that random events could not be subjected to scientific analysis.

That the remarkable scientific advances of this century have led to a brand new science should not be surprising. Since about 1976 physicists, biologists, astronomers, and economists have created a new way of understanding the evolution of complexity in nature. This new science of chaos is a way of seeing order and pattern where formerly only the erratic, the random, the unpredictable—the chaotic—had been observed. According to mathematician Douglas Hofstadter, "It turns out that an eerie type of chaos can lurk just behind a facade of order—and yet, deep inside the chaos lurks an eerier kind of order."

> Where chaos begins, classical science stops. For as long as the world has physicists inquiring into the laws of nature, it has suffered a special ignorance about disorder in the atmosphere, in the turbulent sea, in the fluctuations of wildlife populations, in the oscillations of the heart and the brain.[9]

Chaos has been used to study, among other things, weather patterns to determine how to make long-range predictions. Consider, for example, the "butterfly effect." Could the flight of a butterfly over Tokyo somehow affect the weather of New York City? The surprising answer is yes, though no one knows how this happens, there being so many variables (known and unknown). The variables are, in fact, so numerous that long-range predictions (more than five days) are impossible. Chaos mathematics has identified patterns that permit short-range weather forecasts, which become increasingly inaccurate after one, two, three, and four days. Chaos has also been used to study wave motion, water turbulence, economic activity, wildlife populations, and other phenomena that were heretofore totally unpredictable, leading to the discovery that there are indeed underlying patterns that reveal "an eerier kind of order."

Chaos is a science in its infancy with no idea where its analyses of previously hidden patterns will lead. As with all science, the search is endlessly exciting because the explorers are moving ahead into what was not only unknown but, in this case, totally unexpected.

How do relativity, quantum mechanics, and chaos affect us as human beings? In the first place, human mental processes cannot be explained by existing laws of physics. The answer may come, scientists believe, with the merger of general relativity, which concerns itself with gravity, and quantum theory, which governs the submicroscopic world, a bridge that Einstein called the Unified Field Theory. The two theories are mathematically incompatible but scientists, led by Stephen Hawking, are laboring to create a quantum version of gravity. One consequence would be to establish the boundaries of quantum mechanics, which says that particles can suddenly leap from one space to another without traversing the space between. What if these properties also apply to something as large as human brain cells in the process of creative thinking?

Indeed, quantum gravity could be behind consciousness itself. Consciousness has a peculiar quality that baffles physics: all humans perceive time as moving forward rather than backward. But virtually all the laws of physics are time symmetric, working equally well either forward or backward. The speculative answer is that when quantum gravity is finally constructed it will begin with the Big Bang theory of creation and thus move only forward. Some scientists believe that human creativity and consciousness are the perceptible workings of the most basic laws of the universe, laws that are being explored using quantum theory and chaos.

The uncertainty principle applies to virtually everything in our universe with only three fundamental constants remaining: gravity, Planck's constant, and the speed of light. Given so much uncertainty, philosophers have renewed their arguments for the existence of free will. Moreover, contemporary thinkers in many fields are exploring the nature of reality given the unexplained mysteries of quantum theory and the incompatibility of the mathematics of general relativity and quantum mechanics. If physical events cannot be plotted, explained, or predicted with any certainty, then perhaps the still relatively unknown capabilities of the human intellect will be a decisive factor in the destiny of humankind.[10]

Freud and the Inner World

Though he had written his celebrated *The Interpretation of Dreams* in 1900 and *The Psychopathology of Everyday Life* in 1904, the psychological theories of Sigmund Freud (1856–1939; figure 26.3) did not become influential until after World War I. A rational social and humanitarian scientist, Freud developed cogent theories of the role of the unconscious in human actions and the irrational aspects of human behavior.

Freud evolved a theory of the tripartite personality consisting of the id, ego, and superego. There are no clear boundaries between these concepts but each can be described in isolation. Representing our biological endowment, the id (Lat., "it") resides in our unconscious as an amalgam of our drives and

---

9. Ibid, p. 3.

10. Though this chapter is primarily concerned with the 1914–1939 period, the discussion of twentieth-century science includes contemporary science because scientific knowledge and theory are continually evolving into ever more complex mosaics that encompass new discoveries and/or affirmations or denials of all past knowledge. A similar rationale also applies to the discussion of Freud and his contemporary critics.

Figure 26.3 *Sigmund Freud.*

instincts. Hunger, thirst, elimination, and sex are some of the drives that compel us to avoid pain and to seek pleasure through gratification. Either through action or wish fulfillment pent-up energy is discharged and tension relieved. Freud considered life and love as positive life forces (libido or Eros) and aggressiveness, destruction, and the death wish as negative forces.

The ego is the reality principle, the thinking, conscious self that interacts with objective reality. The well-developed ego controls the id, determining when and how instinctive drives are satisfied.

The superego is a combination of the moral code of the parents and the person, a kind of conscience that is a product of socialization and cultural traditions. Motivated by fear of punishment and desire for approval, the superego can perhaps be best described as a synthesis of the ego-ideal and conscience. The psychological rewards for the superego are feelings of pride and accomplishment; psychological punishment causes feelings of guilt and inferiority.

The well-balanced personality has a strong ego generally in control of the id and superego, restraining the id while recognizing the censorship of the superego. A neurotic person has lost some control, for whatever reason, over conscious actions, giving in to aggressive instincts from the id, or succumbing to feelings of guilt and inferiority exacted by the superego. Psychosis is a serious mental illness in which the patient has lost all touch with reality.

Freud invented what he called psychoanalysis, a systematic therapy for the treatment of neurosis. The task of the analyst was to help the patient uncover repressed matter, mainly through free association and the interpretation of dreams. Essentially, the analyst assisted the patient in understanding the reasons for abnormal behavior; once the patient uncovered the repressions that caused undesirable actions, the ego could consciously deal with the problem. Recognition of the basic problem(s) would theoretically help restore emotional balance.

Partly because he treated mostly neurotic patients, and partly because any new idea is likely to carry its originator to extremes, Freud rode his interpretations very hard in one particular direction. For him, practically all of the mental disorders that he treated were ultimately traceable to one basic frustration: the denial of the life force, the libido—that is, the sexual drive. All symbols were apparently, for him, reducible to sexual symbols. Freud's discovery that sexuality goes far back into childhood, even infancy, was a radical departure from the views of his day. It is, therefore, quite understandable that the sexual factor should loom so large in his investigations, for this human drive is hedged about with all sorts of taboos. Even in our own time, supposedly sexually liberated, there are a variety of sexual mores, both in the ways one should act and the ways in which one should not.

A number of scientists, including Adolf Grünbaum, Marshall Edelson, Frank J. Sulloway, and Nobel laureate (in biology) Peter Medawar,[11] (see the Bibliography) now claim that none of Freud's concepts or hypotheses stand up to scientific scrutiny. The basic problem was that most of his theories were not based on observation but derived from his premise that repression was the driving force of a neurosis. No one has been able to scientifically prove that this is indeed the case, thus invalidating much of his work. As demonstrated by Marx's mistaken view of history, a correct doctrine cannot be based on a false premise.

Why, then, was Freudian psychology so influential? Primarily, the time was ripe for his theories because they contributed to a new spirit of liberation. Freud's unchallenged achievement was to show that men and women were not always guided by their reason but driven to action by their impulses and passions. They did not, in other words, deliberately choose to act destructively. The liberating factor was that blame or censure need not focus on bad decisions; instead, one could consider the reasons why a person failed to control unconscious passions that produced negative results. Knowledge about these inner drives was an idea whose time had come. Sigmund Freud was the first to explore the mysterious inner world of the human personality, and for that alone he deserves a special place in the history of science.

---

11. Johnson, op. cit. According to Medawar, "psychoanalysis is akin to mesmerism and phrenology: it contains isolated nuggets of truth, but the general theory is false," p. 6.

Literary Selections

Prior to Freud, whatever illusions the nineteenth century may have preserved about the perfectibility of human behavior and human institutions perished during the four dreadful years of World War I. Much of the art and literature of the postwar period reflected a profound pessimism, a feeling that Western civilization carried the seeds of its own destruction. The following poems and essay express some of the prevailing sentiments, some of the loneliness, alienation, and despair experienced by the postwar generation. And little did anyone know that within less than a generation, the Great War was to receive a number.

THE LOVE SONG OF J. ALFRED PRUFROCK
Thomas Stearns Eliot, 1888–1965

Written in England around the beginning of World War I, *Prufrock* is a dramatic monologue of a middle-aged and frustrated social misfit who is vainly trying to adjust to a petty and superficial society. The larger perspective is that of bankrupt idealism, a decaying of nations, societies, and religious institutions. With juxtaposed images enlarged by dramatic echoes of Hesiod, Dante, and Shakespeare, Eliot builds a mood of futility and despair.

S'io credesse che mia risposta fosse
A persona che mai tornasse al mondo,
Questa fiamma staria senza piu scosse.
Ma perciocche giammai di questo fondo
Non torno vivo alcun s'i'odo il vero,
Senza tema d'infamia ti rispondo.[12]

Let us go then, you and I,
When the evening is spread out against the sky
Like a patient etherized upon a table;
Let us go, through certain half-deserted streets,   10
The muttering retreats
Of restless nights in one-night cheap hotels
And sawdust restaurants with oyster-shells:
Streets that follow like a tedious argument
Of insidious intent
To lead you to an overwhelming question . . .
Oh, do not ask, 'What is it?'
Let us go and make our visit.

In the room the women come and go
Talking of Michelangelo.   20

The yellow fog that rubs its back upon the window-panes,
The yellow smoke that rubs its muzzle on the window-panes

Licked its tongue into the corners of the evening,
Lingered upon the pools that stand in drains,
Let fall upon its back the soot that falls from chimneys,
Slipped by the terrace, made a sudden leap,
And seeing that it was a soft October night,
Curled once about the house, and fell asleep.

And indeed there will be time
For the yellow smoke that slides along the street,   30
Rubbing its back upon the window-panes;
There will be time, there will be time
To prepare a face to meet the faces that you meet;
There will be time to murder and create,
And time for all the works and days of hands[13]
That lift and drop a question on your plate;
Time for you and time for me,
And time yet for a hundred indecisions,
And for a hundred visions and revisions,
Before the taking of a toast and tea.   40

In the room the women come and go
Talking of Michelangelo.

And indeed there will be time
To wonder, 'Do I dare?' and, 'Do I dare?'
Time to turn back and descend the stair,
With a bald spot in the middle of my hair—
(They will say: 'How his hair is growing thin!')
My morning coat, my collar mounting firmly to the chin,
My necktie rich and modest, but asserted by a simple pin—
(They will say: 'But how his arms and legs are thin!')   50
Do I dare
Disturb the universe?
In a minute there is time
For decisions and revisions which a minute will reverse.

For I have known them all already, known them all:—
Have known the evenings, mornings, afternoons,
I have measured out my life with coffee spoons;
I know the voices dying with a dying fall
Beneath the music from a farther room.
So how should I presume?   60

And I have known the eyes already, known them all—
The eyes that fix you in a formulated phrase,
And when I am formulated, sprawling on a pin,
When I am pinned and wriggling on the wall,
Then how should I begin
To spit out all the butt-ends of my days and ways?
And how should I presume?

And I have known the arms already, known them all—
Arms that are braceleted and white and bare
(But in the lamplight, downed with light brown hair!)   70
Is it perfume from a dress
That makes me so digress?
Arms that lie along a table, or wrap about a shawl.
      And should I then presume?
      And how should I begin?

                . . . . . .

---

12. "If I thought I were making answer to one that might return to view the world, this flame should evermore cease shaking. But since from the abyss, if I hear true, none ever came alive, I have no fear of infamy, but give thee answer due." The speaker is Guido da Montefeltro, who was condemned to Hell as a Counselor of Fraud (Dante, *Inferno,* XXVII, 61–66). Dante had asked him why he was being punished and Guido, still fearful of what might be said about him, answers truthfully because he thinks Dante is also dead. Prufrock, like Guido, is fearful of society's judgment.

---

13. *Works and days* recalls Hesiod's poem entitled *Works and Days* (ca. 750 B.C.). Ironically contrasting with Prufrock's frivolous world, Hesiod's poem extols the virtues of hard labor on the land.

Shall I say, I have gone at dusk through narrow streets
And watched the smoke that rises from the pipes
Of lonely men in shirt-sleeves, leaning out of
windows? . . .   80
I should have been a pair of ragged claws
Scuttling across the floors of silent seas.

. . . . . .

And the afternoon, the evening, sleeps so peacefully!
Smoothed by long fingers,
Asleep . . . tired . . . or it malingers,
Stretched on the floor, here beside you and me.
Should I, after tea and cakes and ices,
Have the strength to force the moment to its crisis?
But though I have wept and fasted, wept and prayed,
Though I have seen my head (grown slightly bald) brought in   90
    upon a platter,
I am no prophet—and here's no great matter;[14]
I have seen the moment of my greatness flicker,
And I have seen the eternal Footman hold my coat, and
    snicker,
And in short, I was afraid.
And would it have been worth it, after all,
After the cups, the marmalade, the tea,
Among the porcelain, among some talk of you and me,
Would it have been worth while,   100
To have bitten off the matter with a smile,
To have squeezed the universe into a ball[15]
To roll it toward some overwhelming question,
To say: 'I am Lazarus, come from the dead,[16]
Come back to tell you all, I shall tell you all'—
If one, settling a pillow by her head,
Should say: That is not what I meant at all,
That is not it, at all.
And would it have been worth it, after all,
Would it have been worth while,   110
After the sunsets and the dooryards and the sprinkled streets,
After the novels, after the teacups, after the skirts that trail
    along the floor—
And this, and so much more?—
It is impossible to say just what I mean!
But as if a magic lantern threw the nerves in patterns on a
    screen:
Would it have been worth while
If one, settling a pillow or throwing off a shawl,
And turning toward the window, should say: 120
'That is not it at all,
That is not what I meant, at all.'

No! I am not Prince Hamlet, nor was meant to be;
Am an attendant lord, one that will do
To swell a progress, start a scene or two,
Advise the prince; no doubt, an easy tool,[17]
Deferential, glad to be of use,
Politic, cautious, and meticulous;
Full of high sentence, but a bit obtuse;
At times, indeed, almost ridiculous—   130
Almost, at times, the Fool.
I grow old . . . I grow old . . .
I shall wear the bottoms of my trousers rolled.[18]
Shall I part my hair behind? Do I dare to eat a peach?
I shall wear white flannel trousers, and walk upon the beach.
I have heard the mermaids singing, each to each.
I do not think that they will sing to me.
I have seen them riding seaward on the waves
Combing the white hair of the waves blown back
When the wind blows the water white and black.   140
We have lingered in the chambers of the sea
By sea-girls wreathed with seaweed red and brown
Till human voices wake us, and we drown.

Exercises

1. What kind of a society is implied in which "the women come
and go/Talking of Michelangelo" (19, 20)?
2. Compare Eliot's references to time in lines 32–35 with the first
line of Marvell's "To His Coy Mistress" in chapter 20. How do
the meanings differ?
3. What is implied in line 38 by "time yet for a hundred
indecisions"?
4. What kind of life has Prufrock led that can be measured "with
coffee spoons" (line 57)?
5. Describe, in your own words, Prufrock's physical appearance,
personality, and social conduct.

DULCE ET DECORUM EST
Wilfred Owen, 1893–1918

Perhaps the most promising English poet to die in the war, Wilfred
Owen, unlike most of his contemporaries, saw no honor or glory
in a conflict that he referred to as "this deflowering of Europe."
The closing quotation of this somber poem is from the poet
Horace: "It is sweet and fitting to die for one's country." Owen
apparently hoped that this "old lie" would never again lead nations to war. He was killed in action on 4 November 1918, one
week before the Armistice that ended the fighting.

---

14. *I am no prophet,* i.e., no John the Baptist, who was beheaded by
Herod and his head brought in on a tray to please Salome,
Herod's stepdaughter (Matthew 14: 3–11). Prufrock views
himself as a sacrificial victim, but he is neither saint nor martyr.

15. *Universe into a ball* recalls "Let us roll all our strength and all
our sweetness up into a ball" from the poem "To His Coy
Mistress" by Andrew Marvell (see chapter 20). Prufrock's
attempt to raise the conversation to a cosmic level with an
allusion to a love poem is doubly ironic; the imaginary lady
casually brings the discussion back to trivialities (11. 96–98).

16. *Lazarus* was raised from the grave by Christ (John 11:1–44). Can
this society be brought back from the dead?

---

17. *Advise the prince* apparently refers to Polonius, the king's
adviser in *Hamlet.* The cross-reference is to Guido da
Montefeltro, also a false counselor.

18. Cuffed (rolled) trousers were stylish at the time. Middle-aged
and socially inept, Prufrock tries to appear young and
fashionable.

Bent double, like old beggars under sacks,
Knock-kneed, coughing like hags, we cursed through sludge,
Till on the haunting flares we turned our backs
And towards our distant rest began to trudge.
Men marched asleep. Many had lost their boots
But limped on, blood-shod. All went lame; all blind;
Drunk with fatigue; deaf even to the hoots
Of tired, outstripped Five-Nines that dropped behind.
Gas! Gas! Quick, boys!—An ecstasy of fumbling,
Fitting the clumsy helmets just in time;   10
But someone still was yelling out and stumbling
And flound'ring like a man in fire or lime . . .
Dim, through the misty panes and thick green light,
As under a green sea, I saw him drowning.
In all my dreams, before my helpless sight,
He plunges at me, guttering, choking, drowning.
If in some smothering dreams you too could pace
Behind the wagon that we flung him in,
And watch the white eyes writhing in his face,
His hanging face, like a devil's sick of sin;   20
If you could hear, at every jolt, the blood
Come gargling from the froth-corrupted lungs,
Obscene as cancer, bitter as the cud
Of vile, incurable sores on innocent tongues,—
My friend, you would not tell with such high zest
To children ardent for some desperate glory,
The old Lie: Dulce et decorum est
Pro patria mori.

Exercises

1. Notice the many participles in lines 2 and 3. Is their effect active or passive?
2. Read line 6 aloud while listening to the sounds. How many weak syllables are there? Strong syllables? What is the effect?
3. Compare this poem with Tennyson's *The Charge of the Light Brigade* in chapter 23. Do they have *anything* in common? In your opinion, would Tennyson have written the same poem had he been a member of the Light Brigade?

THE SECOND COMING
William Butler Yeats, 1865–1939

Written by Yeats in 1920, the poem conveys a sense of the dissolution of civilization. His image of the cycle of history is a "gyre" (a spiral turning, pronounced with a hard g). Imagine a falconer losing control of his falcon as the bird soars in widening circles and eventually breaks away. Lines 4–8 refer to the Russian Revolution of 1917, but they can also be taken as a portent of the rise of fascism in the twenties and thirties. *Spiritus Mundi* is the soul of the universe that connects all human souls in what Yeats calls the "Great Memory," or universal subconscious.

Turning and turning in the widening gyre
The falcon cannot hear the falconer;
Things fall apart: the center cannot hold;

Mere anarchy is loosed upon the world,
The blood-dimmed tide is loosed, and everywhere
The ceremony of innocence is drowned;
The best lack all conviction, while the worst
Are full of passionate intensity.
Surely some revelation is at hand:
Surely the Second Coming is at hand.
The Second Coming! Hardly are those words out
When a vast image out of the *Spiritus Mundi*
Troubles my sight: somewhere in the sands of the desert
A shape with lion body and the head of a man,
A gaze blank and pitiless as the sun,
Is moving its slow thighs, while all about it
Reel shadows of the indignant desert birds.
The darkness drops again; but now I know
That twenty centuries of stony sleep
Were vexed to nightmare by a rocking cradle,
And what rough beast, its hour come round at last,
Slouches towards Bethlehem to be born?

Exercises

1. What does the poet mean, in lines 7 and 8, by the "best" and the "worst"?
2. There is a name for a shape with the head of a man and the body of a lion. What is it and why does Yeats evoke this image?
3. What is the implication of the "rocking cradle"?
4. Describe the feeling aroused by the last two lines of the poem.

SHINE, PERISHING REPUBLIC
Robinson Jeffers, 1887–1962

Postwar America was a world power but Jeffers saw the darker side, a crass and materialistic nation mired "in the mould of its vulgarity." The reader can determine whether the poem, written in 1924, is still apropos.

While this America settles in the mould of its vulgarity, heavily
    thickening to empire.
And protest, only a bubble in the molten mass, pops and sighs
    out, and the mass hardens.
I sadly smiling remember that the flower fades to make fruit,
    the fruit rots to make earth.
Out of the mother; and through the spring exultances,
    ripeness and decadence; and home to the mother.
You making haste haste on decay: not blameworthy; life is
    good, be it stubbornly long or suddenly
A mortal splendor: meteors are not needed less than
    mountains: shine perishing republic.
But for my children, I would have them keep their distance
    from the thickening center: corruption
Never has been compulsory, when the cities lie at the
    monster's feet there are left the mountains.

And boys, be in nothing so moderate as in love of man, a
    clever servant, insufferable master.
There is the trap that catches noblest spirits, that caught—they
    say—God, when he walked on earth.

Exercises

1. Identify the images that refer to the cycle of life and death.
2. What is implied by "meteors are not needed less than mountains"?

YET DO I MARVEL
Countee Cullen, 1887–1946

One of the leaders of a 1920s literary movement called the Harlem Renaissance, Cullen can be seen, at first glance, as a voice of moderation compared with black protests since World War II. Cullen's references are from the Western literary tradition (Greek mythology, Dante) and the form is that of a sonnet, but line 12 is derived from the last two lines of "The Tiger" by William Blake: "What immortal hand or eye/Dare frame thy fearful symmetry?" (see chapter 23). Blake asks how a good God can put evil in the world; Cullen ponders a similar question about the evil of racism. The tone is moderate but the sentiment is not.

I doubt not God is good, well-meaning, kind,
And did He stoop to quibble could tell why
The little buried mole continues blind,
Why flesh that mirrors Him must some day die,
Make plain the reason tortured Tantalus
Is baited by the fickle fruit, declare
If merely brute caprice dooms Sisyphus
To struggle up a never-ending stair.
Inscrutable His ways are, and immune
To catechism by a mind too strewn
With petty cares to slightly understand
What awful brain compels His awful hand.
Yet do I marvel at this curious thing:
To make a poet black, and bid him sing!

1924, 1925

Exercises

1. How many images are there of the way things are? Consider, for example, blind moles, Tantalus, and Sisyphus. (Tantalus was condemned by Zeus to stand up to his chin in water that receded everytime he tried to drink. Above his head hung fruit that the wind kept perpetually out of his reach. His name has given us the verb *tantalize*. The Myth of Sisyphus may be found in chapter 27.)
2. The last line implies that people who can write poetry *must* write poetry. Why is this so? Does the same compulsion hold true for painters, composers, and sculptors? Give some examples.

Summary

The nineteenth-century age of optimism and progress had established a core of belief that held people together or provided a target against which they might revolt. World War I marked the point at which the balance was finally destroyed; after that time no such center existed and people found themselves cut loose from the comforting bonds of community and shared values, alone and alienated in a frightening new world. The culture-epoch theory is reconsidered and updated at this point to highlight the chaotic nature of the period between world wars. This, in turn, provides the framework for consideration of cultural changes later in the century, as discussed in chapters 27 through 30.

Replacing the determinism of Newton's world-machine, the work of Planck, Heisenberg, and Einstein revolutionized scientific knowledge of the universe and how it operates. Also revolutionary, the theories of Sigmund Freud, though fatally flawed, helped prepare the way to new insights into the human personality.

In "The Love Song of J. Alfred Prufrock" and in "The Second Coming" Eliot and Yeats set the theme for the postwar reaction against the spiritual bankruptcy of the age. Wilfred Owen's poem "Dulce et Decorum Est" speaks for the generation of young men wasted in the trenches and, in "Shine, Perishing Republic," Jeffers depicts bankrupt idealism in a crass and vulgar nation. Harbinger of bad times, Cullen's "Yet Do I Marvel" highlights the destructive effects of racism in postwar (between the wars) America.

Culture and Human Values

Looking back some three-quarters of a century, it is difficult to fully appreciate the devastating impact the Great War had on Western culture. Bad enough were the statistics on the killed, the wounded, and the maimed for life, but there was much more. Europeans considered their civilization as the world's most advanced, with the foremost science and technology, a superb educational system, and the highest standard of living on this globe.

However, science and technology served the war machines and contributed mightily to the general death and destruction. The best-educated nation in Europe—Germany—launched a long-planned war of conquest, with victims such as neutral Belgium sacrificed to imperial goals. Germany was by no means the sole transgressor; by the end of the war most nations had contributed their own barbarous acts. In the name of duty, honor, and love of country, politicians and generals violated virtually every precept of those vaunted ideals, not to mention justice and mercy.

Ideals and empires turned out to be equally vulnerable. By the end of the war the empires of Russia, Germany, and Austria-Hungary were finished and the British Empire was simply delaying the inevitable.

Actually, the old values had been disintegrating since the latter third of the century. The pressures of workers, unions, liberals, revolutionaries, socialists, and communists had forced changes on society, but not yet on the outmoded colonial empires. It remained for the war to bring down the empires and start phasing out colonialism. The war can be seen, in retrospect, as the cataclysmic event that categorically ended the age and set the stage for the search for new values: chaos followed by a period of adjustment. The laborious process of developing new value systems is considered in the following chapters.

Ideas and Conflicts That Motivate the Twentieth Century

chapter *27*

Historical Overview, 1939–1990s

The Great Depression following the breakdown of economic systems was "cured" by the escalating production of weapons for war. England and France frantically, and belatedly, prepared for the resumption of hostilities with Germany in a war notably different from any other in humankind's interminable history of violence.

Soldiers fought in fields and pastures in the nineteenth century, in the trenches in 1914–1918, but in 1939–1945 the furious new battlefield described in the poem given below was the air itself. The bomber was the cost-efficient delivery system of World War II; targets included not only opposing armies but myriads of cities and their millions of inhabitants. Whether blasting Berlin and London, fire-bombing Dresden and Tokyo, or obliterating Hiroshima and Nagasaki, civilian casualties vastly outnumbered those of the military, and warfare was total.

Literary Selection

THE FURY OF AERIAL BOMBARDMENT[1]
Richard Eberhart, b.1904

You would think the fury of aerial bombardment
Would rouse God to relent; the infinite spaces
Are still silent. He then looks on shock-pried faces
History, even, does not know what is meant.
You would feel that after so many centuries
God would give man to repent; yet he can kill
As Cain could, but with multitudinous will,

No farther advanced than in his ancient furies.
Was man made stupid to see his own stupidity?
Is God by definition indifferent, beyond us all?
Is the eternal truth man's fighting soul
Wherein the Beast ravens in its own avidity?
Of Van Wettering I speak, and Averill,
Names on a list, whose faces I do not recall
But they are gone to early death, who late in school
Distinguished the belt feed lever from the belt holding pawl.

The Cold War, ca. 1945–1990

World War II ended on 14 August 1945 with the Japanese surrender, and the whole world expected a new era of peace and stability. The United States, with its nuclear monopoly and enormous industrial capacity, emerged as an unrivaled superpower. Having learned some bitter lessons from the League of Nations, the United Nations began to function as the first real consortium of nations; with the assistance of the Marshall Plan, war-ravaged nations launched recovery programs that frequently verged on the miraculous. However, the anticipated era of peace and stability was delayed indefinitely with Russia's postwar expansionism and the detonation of its own atomic bomb in 1949. The sharply reduced power of the Western European nations and the shambles of the old colonial order left a vacuum that was filled by the United States and Russia. Basically the confrontation was between the Western democracies led by the United States and the Eastern Bloc led by the Soviet Union under dictator Joseph Stalin.[2] Stalin

---

1. The Literary Selections in this chapter were picked for two reasons: literary merit and pertinent theme (to point up or flesh out a particular idea or conflict).

2. "If we assume the viewpoint of humanity and freedom, history does not know a despot as cynical as Stalin was. He was methodical, all-embracing, and total as a criminal. He was one of those rare terrible dogmatists capable of destroying nine tenths of the human race to 'make happy' the one tenth." Milojan Djilas, *Conversations with Stalin* (New York: Harcourt, Brace and World, 1962), p. 190.

moved quickly in 1945, creating "people's republics" in Poland, Romania, Hungary, Bulgaria, East Germany, and later, in Czechoslovakia. Soviet attempts to take over Greece and Turkey were rebuffed by the Allies but, as it had for centuries before Lenin and Stalin, Russian imperialism continued to select targets of opportunity.

Communists tried and failed to win power in the Philippines, Indonesia, and Malaysia, but they did succeed in North Korea. Russian weapons (and the permission of Stalin and Mao Zedong) encouraged the North Koreans to invade South Korea, thus launching the bitter Korean War (1950–1953) that eventually saw the People's Republic of China enter the war against United Nations troops comprised mainly of U.S. forces. The invasion ended in a stalemate near the original boundary between the two nations. Prolonged negotiations resulted in an armistice—not a peace treaty—in July 1953 that remains in effect.

The Viet Minh revolt that erupted in French Indochina after World War II ended in 1954 when the French stronghold at Dien Bien Phu surrendered to the communist insurgency led by Ho Chi Minh (1890–1969). A major power conference in Geneva subsequently recognized the independence of the former provinces of Cambodia and Laos. A Korean-style compromise divided the third province into communist North Vietnam with its capital at Hanoi and capitalist South Vietnam with Saigon as its capital.

By 1958 communist-led guerillas, supported by Ho Chi Minh and known as the Viet Cong, had disrupted and terrorized much of South Vietnam. When the North Vietnamese army joined the Viet Cong in 1966, the American response was a rapid increase in troops, from several thousand in 1965 to 500,000 in 1967. The impact of the war on the home front was enormous, this being the first war to appear every evening on American television. The mounting casualties, the known atrocities, the corrupt South Vietnamese governments, the lack of a clear-cut rationale for an Asian war, and the inability of American arms to decisively defeat a dedicated and relentless enemy led to massive antiwar protests in the United States.

Even now it is difficult to determine which came first: the antiestablishment free speech revolt of the 1960s or the violent reaction to the slaughter in Vietnam that spun off a whole decade of activism, hippies, flower children, communes, campus sit-ins and riots, and the development of a drug culture. All were manifestations of a sea change that affected every cranny of American society.

The war effectively ended the political career of President Lyndon B. Johnson and adversely affected the Nixon administration. A long-delayed cease-fire was finally arranged by January 1973, a pact that North Vietnam violated after most of the remaining American troops had left the country. Saigon fell to the North Vietnamese on 30 April 1975 as the remaining Americans frantically evacuated the American embassy on relays of helicopters. Though widely believed to be an internal war of liberation, North Vietnamese leaders later admitted that they had used the Viet Cong as pawns in a well-planned war of conquest.

Literary Selection

Tenebrae[3]
Denise Levertov, b. 1923

The war in Vietnam prompted violent home front reactions, but a large segment of the population tried to ignore American entanglement in an unpopular war. There was a feeling of not getting involved, of not thinking about distant murderous jungles, especially when—as was often the case—no friends or relatives were fighting in Asia. However, nearly 60,000 combatants died in Vietnam in the only war the United States ever lost. Written in 1967 during the protest march on the Pentagon, Levertov's poem is both an indictment and an elegy.

Heavy, heavy, heavy, hand and heart.
We are at war,
bitterly, bitterly at war.
And the buying and selling
buzzes at our heads, a swarm
of busy flies, a kind of innocence.
Gowns of gold sequins are fitted,
sharp-glinting. What harsh rustlings
of silver moiré there are,
to remind me of shrapnel splinters.   10
And weddings are held in full solemnity
not of desire but of etiquette,
the nuptial pomp of starched lace;
a grim innocence.
And picnic parties return from the beaches
burning with stored sun in the dusk;
children promised a TV show when they get home
fall asleep in the backs of a million station wagons,
sand in their hair, the sound of waves
quietly persistent at their ears.   20
They are not listening.
Their parents at night
dream and forget their dreams.
They wake in the dark
and make plans. Their sequin plans
glitter into tomorrow.
They buy, they sell.
They fill freezers with food.
Neon signs flash their intentions
into the years ahead.   30
And at their ears the sound
of the war. They are
not listening, not listening.

---

3. Tenebrae (Lat., "darkness") are church services for the last three days of Holy Week that commemorate the suffering and death of Christ. The candles that are lighted at the beginning of the service are extinguished one by one after each Psalm is sung or read, symbolizing the darkness that fell on the land at the time of the crucifixion.

Exercises

1. Compare the contrasting words and images between rampant materialism and the reality of warfare.
2. What turned *a kind of innocence* into *a grim innocence?*
3. What intentions do neon signs flash?
4. Are they *not listening* because they cannot hear, or will not hear?

Mutual assured destruction (MAD), a balance of terror, kept nuclear weapons in their silos throughout the Cold War but so-called conventional (hot) wars have abounded. If a major war is defined as one in which there are more than a thousand combatants, there have been over 100 wars since 1945. African and Asian nationalism, class conflicts in Central and South America, endless Middle East crises, including large-scale warfare—the litany of trials and tribulations of our era never ceases and yet, the world looks hopefully toward better days with the freeing of captive nations and the widespread revival of democracies.

The major event—actually series of events—of the late 1980s was the widespread failure of Marxism-Leninism. The Soviet Union and its satellites had, by that time, demonstrated that communism could not work, indeed had never achieved its goals. In *The Unperfect Society* (1969) Yugoslav author Milojan Djilas predicted the inevitable failure of communism; he identified the source of the problem by tracing the ugly roots of Stalinism back through Lenin to Marx's utopianism, ideological rigidity, and scientific pretensions. He pointed out that communist dictators assumed they had been named by a higher power—History—that awarded them the right to establish the Kingdom of Heaven (dictatorship of the proletariat) in this sinful capitalistic world. Why was History this higher power? Because Marx said so.

The flaw in Marxism was fundamental. Marx based his entire doctrine on the proclamation that began Section I of the Communist Manifesto: "The history of all hitherto existing society is the history of class struggles." If this statement is true, then history is on the side of those who would eliminate class struggles by establishing a classless society. Hegel had claimed that past cultures were stages in the evolutionary development of the world Spirit toward perfection and freedom. Marx and Engels formulated a doctrine of inevitable progress leading to the perfect classless society by twisting Hegel's philosophy from the consciousness of his world Spirit to the consciousness of societies engaged in class struggle. In fact, however, some of the most important values and issues transcend class. Family, trust, loyalty, faith, fidelity, and the many varieties of love are just a few of the values that are cherished by peasants and poets, commoners and kings. The Marxian interpretation of history was, in plain words, wrong, thus making all subsequent communist theory fatally flawed. It doesn't take a philosopher to know that any doctrine based on a false premise is fraudulent. This should not imply, however, that Marx's influence was wholly negative. He was genuinely interested in the welfare of the working class and his theories are, at least in part, responsible for the greatly improved status of the underprivileged of advanced societies.

In pragmatic terms, communism failed because not one aspect of the system worked. The classless society was never tried nor did the proletariat ever have any voice in the "dictatorship of the proletariat." Everyone had a job of some kind and there was a welfare safety net for all citizens that provided only a minimal level of existence. Production controlled by central planning failed to compete with the free-enterprise systems in capitalist countries or even come close to satisfying the domestic market. Yes, everyone was employed but no one from worker to manager had any investment in the product. As workers so often remarked: "We pretend to work and they pretend to pay us." At no time did collective farms approach the output of land farmed by their owners. Good international relations that attracted foreign investment were not possible in a country that subverted foreign relations by turmoil and revolution. Education, the sciences, and general culture that furthered only the interests of the state (and the Communist party), rather than society as a whole, highlighted the backwardness of ideologically rigid societies. Every communist country suffered under a dictatorial party whose elite class controlled the masses by coercion, fear, censorship, rewriting history (of all subjects!), and the omnipresent secret police. One of the worst—and abiding—bequests of communist inefficiency and mismanagement is the destruction of the environment. Throughout Central Europe, forests, fields, streams, lakes, and the atmosphere were destroyed or severely contaminated due to futile attempts to fulfill production quotas regardless of the consequences. The wonder of it all, as many have remarked, is not that Marxism-Leninism failed but that it took so long.

The most startling aspect of the demise of communism was how abruptly it collapsed in so many countries. The sickly Soviet economy was a critical factor, of course, but one should also consider the pivotal role of the electronic devices of the Information Age. Television, camcorders, videotapes, and VCRs played a significant role in the public's knowledge of demonstrations, repression, and rebellion. It is, in fact, no longer possible to keep a subject people in the dark about what transpires in the rest of the world, and this may be the most hopeful sign of what it means to live in a "Global Village" (discussed later in this chapter).

The decisive conclusion of the Cold War followed closely on the jubilant destruction of the Berlin Wall in 1989. Stalin had reasoned that, American power notwithstanding, a divided Germany was the key to the USSR's unrivaled dominance in Europe. Germany was unified on 2 October 1990, and the Paris Charter was signed on 21 November 1990 by the United States, Canada, and every European nation except Albania. The Paris agreement guaranteed commitment to democracy and economic well-being for all signatories, thus ending the Cold War that began after World War II but which had its roots in the attempts of both Germany and Russia to dictate the destiny of Europe. Already 1990 is viewed as one of the most important dates in the modern history of Western civilization, probably on a par with the end of the Thirty Years' War in 1648 and the termination of the Napoleonic Wars in 1815.

We can now complete the dramatic allegory described in chapter 26 in which World War I was characterized as Act I. The entr'acte of 1918–1939 connected the Great War to World War II (Act II), for the former did indeed lead to the latter. The third act was the Cold War that ended with the triumph of the Western democracies. The Western world and the European Economic Community (EEC) in particular now have a historic opportunity to secure a lasting peace. Serious problems in the Middle East (including the aftermath of the Persian Gulf War), the Far East, and Africa remain unresolved, but the United Nations, with the strong backing of the United States and the EEC may be in the best position in its history to bring some sort of stability to the entire world.

Philosophy

Probably every philosophical system ever invented has surfaced at one time or another during this troubled century. One of the most influential of these philosophies, existentialism, is more of a mood or attitude than a complete philosophical system. Formulated during World War II by French writer Jean Paul Sartre during his years with the French Resistance, existentialism had an immediate appeal for a desperate world. Actually, the roots of the movement go back to several disparate personalities of the nineteenth century, particularly Kierkegaard, a Danish anticlerical theologian, and Nietzsche, a German atheist.

Friedrich Nietzsche, 1844–1900

Nietzsche (NEE-chuh) stressed the absurdity of human existence and the inability of our reason to understand the world. Himself a passionate individualist, Nietzsche proclaimed the will to power as the only value in a meaningless world. He rejected any ideas or system that would limit the freedom of the individual, particularly Christianity, which taught, he contended, a "slave morality" of sympathy, kindness, humility, and pity, qualities beneficial only to the weak and the helpless. His "noble" man was a superman, an incarnate will to power, who would rise above the herd (the "bungled and the botched") to establish a "master morality" of the "aristocratic" qualities of strength, nobility, pride, and power. "God is dead," Nietzsche proclaimed, meaning that all absolute systems from Plato onward had died with the God of the Judeo-Christian tradition.

A fervent admirer of the culture of ancient Greece, Nietzsche evolved an influential aesthetic theory of the Apollonian and Dionysian modes. The Apollonian mode is intellectual. It draws an aesthetic veil over reality, creating an ideal world of form and beauty. The Apollonian found expression in Greek mythology, in Homer's epic poems, in sculpture, painting, architecture, and Greek vases.

The Dionysian, somewhat like Freud's id, is the dark, turgid, and formless torrent of instinct, impulse, and passion that tends to sweep aside everything in its path. Tragedy and music are typical Dionysian art forms that transmute existence into aesthetic phenomena without, however, drawing a veil over authentic existence. The Dionysian represents existence in aesthetic form and affirms this, says Nietzsche, in the human condition. True culture, for Nietzsche, was a unity of life forces, the dark Dionysian element combined with the love of form and beauty that characterizes the Apollonian. The highest product of this balanced culture is the creative genius, the superman.

Adolf Hitler drew on Nietzsche's purported work, *The Will to Power,* for key ideas about German superiority, the Master Race (Nietzsche's superman), and anti-Semitism. Scholars finally proved, by 1958, that Nietzsche did not write *The Will to Power.* After his death, Nietzsche's proto-Nazi sister combined his notebook jottings with thirty forged letters and other fabrications to publish the volume in her brother's name. Actually, Nietzsche was more anti- than pro-German, referring to Germans as "blond beasts of prey" and casting scorn on "their repulsive habit of stimulating themselves with alcohol." Far from a racist, Nietzsche saw all the races on the globe blending into a uniform color of beige and he called anti-Semites "another name for failures."

The basic theme of Nietzsche's life and thought was the antipolitical individual who sought self-perfection far from the modern world. His desire was "to live for one's education free from politics, nationality, and newspapers." For him, knowledge was power and the will to power was the use of education for the betterment of humankind. "Above all," he said, "become who you are!"

Soren Kierkegaard, 1813–1855

A melancholy and lonely Dane, Kierkegaard (KEER-kuh-gard) was almost totally unnoticed in his own time, even more so than Nietzsche. Kierkegaard's concern, like that of Nietzsche, was with the individual, whom he saw as an actor on the stage of life. For each individual there was, according to Kierkegaard, the possibility of three ascending levels of existence along life's way: aesthetic, ethical, and religious. The aesthetic level was that of the pleasure seeker, and the only goals were newer pleasant sensations. Eventually, the futile pursuit of pleasure ends in despair and life is absurd. The only way to rise above the aesthetic level is to recognize the reality of choice.

The second level is that of the ethical, which does not eliminate the aesthetic mode but rises above it. The ethical life is not, however, the same as advocating abstract ethical theories; one can know about ethical theories and still be an unethical slob. The ethical person, for Kierkegaard, is actively committed to long-range purposes, dedicated to the continuity of life, free to choose and be bound to a commitment. Choice is a necessity in the ethical life and, Kierkegaard says, the only absolutely ethical choice is between good and evil. But this is not enough. We are virtually helpless in facing the evils and injustices of everyday life; these evils can be overcome only by an outpouring of love and generosity beyond human justice and human powers. Such love and generosity is possible only if something transcending us breaks into history and works in our lives. Kierkegaard believed that the breakthrough of the eternal into history was the birth of Christ.

To recapitulate: after the vain pursuit of pleasure we feel despair; through choice we can raise ourselves to the ethical level and become committed to our responsibilities, but this eventually proves insufficient; we become a "knight of infinite resignation." At this point we can choose to leap beyond reason to the religious mode of existence using the passion called faith ("where reason ends there begins faith").

Faith, for Kierkegaard, means total commitment to the inner personality of God. We cannot cleverly argue our way to God; we either accept God completely or reject him completely. The second and final leap of faith is into the arms of Jesus. However, Kierkegaard says, this leap to the God-man of Christian history is conceptually absurd. The intensity of the leap of faith to God is vastly increased by the second venture to the level of Christianity, which is unintelligible. As Kierkegaard wrote, "In an unpermissible and unlawful way people have become *knowing* about Christ, for the only permissible way is to be *believing*."

These absolute ventures are total personal decisions taken in absolute loneliness with the utmost responsibility. The isolation of the individual in such a decision is absolute and this, says Kierkegaard, is what it means to be a human being. These leaps of faith make an existing individual. Speculative philosophy, according to Kierkegaard, plus the Christian establishment and the press had confused basic facts: "Christendom has done away with Christianity without being quite aware of it."

Values, for Kierkegaard, were not esoteric essences: "Good and evil are ways of existing and the human good is to exist authentically." Conversely, evil is an unauthentic, ungenuine existence. Authentic existence is a matter of choice, and the existing person knows the risk and feels the dread of individual responsibility. But, as Kierkegaard observed, "dread is the possibility of freedom" and "man is condemned to freedom."

Nietzsche and Kierkegaard represent the two extremes of atheistic and theistic existentialism with Feodor Dostoevsky somewhere in between. In the Grand Inquisitor section of *The Brothers Karamazov* Dostoevsky denies all authority (symbolized by the Church of Rome) in favor of the individual search for faith, spirit, and redemption.

Jean Paul Sartre, 1905–1980

Sartre (SAR-tru) was an atheistic existentialist quite unlike Nietzsche, arriving at his conclusions using logic. Sartre contended that the idea of God was self-contradictory, that the man called Christ could not be both divine and human because the terms are mutually exclusive. In other words, said Sartre, divine means nonhuman and human means that which is not divine. You cannot draw a circular square or a square circle. And, if there is no God, there are no fixed values, no absolute right or wrong or good or bad. In *The Brothers Karamazov* Dostoevsky has one of his characters say, "But you see, if there were no God, everything would be possible." And that is precisely Sartre's point, that human beings are the sole source of values and anything is possible.

Sartre's basic premise was that existence precedes essence. First, a person *is*; what he or she becomes is settled in the course of existence. For the existentialist things in the world just *are*; only human beings can create themselves. Liberty is unrestricted, our capacity for choice is absolute, and making choices is what makes us human. The only meaning that life has is in the significance of the values that we choose. Values are not waiting to be discovered; we invent values. To the question "What meaning is there in life?" the existentialist replies, "only what you put into life." But, as Sartre warns, the exercise of freedom is inseparably linked with responsibility:

Man is condemned to be free; because once thrown into the world, man is responsible for everything he does.

You can never choose anything, wrote Sartre, without realizing that this is the choice you wish all humankind to make. If you choose truth, then you want everyone to be truthful; if you choose to steal, then you are willing that everyone should be a thief. In every choice you have chosen for all humankind, a crushing responsibility, a condition that Sartre calls *anguish*.

What are the values for which the existentialist is willing to assume responsibility? The answer has a curiously old-fashioned ring: the values are those of individualism; value is *in* the individual; value *is* the individual. The supreme virtue is responsible choice, what we call integrity, and the ultimate vice is self-deception. The Greeks said that we should "know thyself" and the existentialist fervently agrees. What you choose determines what you will become but, Sartre emphasizes, you can change, you can redirect your steps. What gives meaning to life is not what *happens* to us but what we ourselves *do*. We are actors on the stage of life. As Sartre said: "Man is encompassed by his own existence and there is no exit." In 1947 Sartre wrote in *Existentialism:*

Existentialism is nothing less than an attempt to draw all the consequences of a coherent atheistic position. It isn't trying to plunge man into despair at all. But if one calls every attitude of unbelief despair, like the Christian, then the word is not being used in its original sense. Existentialism isn't so atheistic that it wears itself out showing that God doesn't exist. Rather, it declares that even if God did exist, that would change nothing. There you've got our point of view. Not that we believe that God exists, but we think the problem of his existence is not the issue. In this sense existentialism is optimistic, a doctrine of action, and it is plain dishonesty for Christians to make no distinction between their own despair and ours and then to call us despairing.

Existentialism owed its popularity in no small part to repeated failures in politics, economics, and social organizations that have scarred our century. Whatever shortcomings the movement may have, it is not just a body of philosophical speculations, but an attitude that still helps a great many people in this muddled world to pursue a personal freedom, a way of life that ranks quality over quantity.

Literary Selection

THE MYTH OF SISYPHUS
Albert Camus, 1913–1966

Both Sartre and Albert Camus were active in the French Resistance and both won the Nobel Prize for literature. Camus's brilliant novel *The Stranger* superbly delineates the existential themes of absurdity, anguish, despair, and alienation, but Camus always denied that he was an existentialist. He claimed instead that the world was so absurd that the philosopher should logically contemplate suicide. The alternative, for Camus, was to dismiss the world and lead an active, heroic life. The hero of ordinary life is the person who resolutely shoulders the responsibilities that life imposes, knowing that all is futile and meaningless, an attitude that is exemplified in the essay "The Myth of Sisyphus." In Greek mythology Sisyphus was a rogue-hero who delighted in tricking the gods. The gods were so furious that, through all eternity, they required Sisyphus to roll a huge stone up a hill only to have it plunge back down once it reached the crest. The divine plan was to keep Sisyphus too busy to plan another escape but, as Camus concludes, "One must imagine Sisyphus happy" in the act of doing.

The gods had condemned Sisyphus to ceaselessly rolling a rock to the top of a mountain, whence the stone would fall back of its own weight. They had thought with some reason that there is no more dreadful punishment than futile and hopeless labor.

If one believes Homer, Sisyphus was the wisest and most prudent of mortals. According to another tradition, however, he was disposed to practice the profession of highwayman. I see no contradiction in this. Opinions differ as to the reasons why he became the futile laborer of the underworld. To begin with, he is accused of a certain levity in regard to the gods. He stole their secrets. Ægina, the daughter of Æsopus, was carried off by Jupiter. The father was shocked by that disappearance and complained to Sisyphus. He, who knew of the abduction, offered to tell about it on condition that Æsopus would give water to the citadel of Corinth. To the celestial thunderbolts he preferred the benediction of water. He was punished for this in the underworld. Homer tells us also that Sisyphus had put Death in chains. Pluto could not endure the sight of his deserted, silent empire. He dispatched the god of war, who liberated Death from the hands of her conqueror.

It is said also that Sisyphus, being near to death, rashly wanted to test his wife's love. He ordered her to cast his unburied body into the middle of the public square. Sisyphus woke up in the underworld. And there, annoyed by an obedience so contrary to human love, he obtained from Pluto permission to return to earth in order to chastise his wife. But when he had seen again the face of this world, enjoyed water and sun, warm stones and the sea, he no longer wanted to go back to the infernal darkness. Recalls, signs of anger, warnings were of no avail. Many years more he lived facing the curve of the gulf, the sparkling sea, and the smiles of earth. A decree of the gods was necessary. Mercury came and seized the impudent man by the collar and, snatching him from his joys, led him forcibly back to the underworld, where his rock was ready for him.

You have already grasped that Sisyphus is the absurd hero. He *is,* as much through his passions as through his torture. His scorn of the gods, his hatred of death, and his passion for life won him that unspeakable penalty in which the whole being is exerted toward accomplishing nothing. This is the price that must be paid for the passions of this earth. Nothing is told us about Sisyphus in the underworld. Myths are made for the imagination to breathe life into them. As for this myth, one sees merely the whole effort of a body straining to raise the huge stone, to roll it and push it up a slope a hundred times over; one sees the face screwed up, the cheek tight against the stone, the shoulder bracing the clay-covered mass, the foot wedging it, the fresh start with arms outstretched, the wholly human security of two earth-clotted hands. At the very end of his long effort measured by skyless space and time without depth, the purpose is achieved. Then Sisyphus watches the stone rush down in a few moments toward that lower world whence he will have to push it up again toward the summit. He goes back down to the plain.

It is during that return, that pause, that Sisyphus interests me. A face that toils so close to stones is already stone itself! I see that man going back down with a heavy yet measured step toward the torment of which he will never know the end. That hour like a breathing-space which returns as surely as his suffering, that is the hour of consciousness. At each of those moments when he leaves the heights and gradually sinks toward the lairs of the gods, he is superior to his fate. He is stronger than his rock.

If this myth is tragic, that is because its hero is conscious. Where would his torture be, indeed, if at every step the hope of succeeding upheld him? The workman of today works every day in his life at the same tasks, and this fate is no less absurd. But it is tragic only at the rare moments when it becomes conscious. Sisyphus, proletarian of the gods, powerless and rebellious, knows the whole extent of his wretched condition: it is what he thinks of during his descent. The lucidity that was to constitute his torture at the same time crowns his victory. There is no fate that cannot be surmounted by scorn.

If the descent is thus sometimes performed in sorrow, it can also take place in joy. This word is not too much. Again I fancy Sisyphus returning toward his rock, and the sorrow was in the beginning. When the images of earth cling too tightly to memory, when the call of happiness becomes too insistent, it happens that melancholy rises in man's heart: this is the rock's victory, this is the rock itself. The boundless grief is too heavy to bear. These are our nights of Gethsemane. But crushing truths perish from being acknowledged. Thus, Oedipus at the outset obeys fate without knowing it. But from the moment he knows, his tragedy begins. Yet at the same moment, blind and desperate, he realizes that the only bond linking him to the world is the cool hand of a girl. Then a tremendous remark rings out: "Despite so many ordeals, my advanced age and the nobility of my soul make me conclude that all is well." Sophokles' Oedipus, like Dostoevsky's Kirilov, thus gives the recipe for the absurd victory. Ancient wisdom confirms modern heroism.

One does not discover the absurd without being tempted to write a manual of happiness. "What! by such narrow ways—?" There is but one world, however. Happiness and the absurd are two sons of the same earth. They are inseparable. It would be a mistake to say that happiness necessarily springs from the absurd discovery. It happens as well that the feeling of the absurd springs from happiness. "I conclude that all is well," says Oedipus, and that remark is sacred. It echoes in the wild and limited universe of man. It teaches that all is not, has not been, exhausted. It drives out of this world a god who had come into it with dissatisfaction and a preference for futile sufferings. It makes of fate a human matter, which must be settled among men.

All Sisyphus' silent joy is contained therein. His fate belongs to him. His rock is his thing. Likewise, the absurd man, when he contemplates his torment, silences all the idols. In the universe suddenly restored to its silence, the myriad wondering little voices of the earth rise up. Unconscious, secret calls, invitations from all the faces, they are the necessary reverse and price of victory. There is no sun without shadow, and it is essential to know the night. The absurd man says yes and his effort will henceforth be unceasing. If there is a personal fate, there is no higher destiny, or at least there is but one which he concludes is inevitable and despicable. For the rest, he knows himself to be the master of his days. At that subtle moment when man glances backward over his life, Sisyphus returning toward his rock, in that slight pivoting he contemplates that series of unrelated actions which becomes his fate, created by him, combined under his memory's eye and soon sealed by his death. Thus, convinced of the wholly human origin of all that is human, a blind man eager to see who knows that the night has no end, he is still on the go. The rock is still rolling.

I leave Sisyphus at the foot of the mountain! One always finds one's burden again. But Sisyphus teaches the higher fidelity that negates the gods and raises rocks. He too concludes that all is well. This universe henceforth without a master seems to him neither sterile nor futile. Each atom of that stone, each mineral flake of that night-filled mountain, in itself forms a world. The struggle itself toward the heights is enough to fill a man's heart. One must imagine Sisyphus happy.

Exercises

1. Imagine several children on a sandy beach busily constructing a large sand castle. A passerby maliciously stomping on a tower leads to a brief but violent confrontation. Finally the builders complete their elaborate fairy-tale structure just as the encroaching tide tentatively laps at the outer walls. The construction crew observes attentively as the noble turrets subside into the swirling water and then, losing interest, pick up their things and set off for the beach house. Why was there a fight over the mutilated tower but only calm acceptance of the watery demise of the castle? How is all of this analogous to Sisyphus and his rock?

2. Consider now the millionaire who feels that he must aim for a hundred million, then a billion, or more. How much money will be enough, or is money even the main focus? How does this relate to Sisyphus?

3. Let us say that the gods have relented and that, as Sisyphus muscles the rock into place, it teeters for a moment and then remains firmly in place. Describe Sisyphus' feelings. Have the gods indeed relented or have they devised a more fiendish form of punishment?

Existentialism: Postscript

Some existentialists, particularly the Christian existentialists, imagine that a person can become a sort of superhero when he or she infuses pointless life with meaning and thereby creates meaning in the universe. Some of the Christian existentialists believe that Christ was such a figure; and that, if the actuality for such Being exists within one individual, then it is also a potentiality for all humanity.

A large number of philosophers and Christian theologians have advanced and developed this Christian existentialist point of view. Among them are Ernst Block and the Dutch Roman Catholic theologian E. Schillebeeckx. Oversimplifying greatly, they view God as the Creative Purpose of the World; the End toward which the world is moving. Block has referred to him as "the God who is not yet"; Schillebeeckx as the God who is "wholly new." This concept is a far cry from the standard view of a God who was complete and whole from the beginning of time, and who rules the world either as loving Father or as Great Engineer. Instead, he is constantly inventing himself or being invented here on earth, exactly as the existentialist person, moment by moment, invents himself or herself.

Civil Rights

Since World War II the United States has become more democratic, but it hasn't been easy. The so-called Second Reconstruction in American history began in the late 1940s with presidential decrees that banned discrimination in federal jobs and ordered desegregation of the armed forces. The target of the first stage of the civil rights movement, segregation in public education, was struck down by the landmark Supreme Court decision of 1954. Despite sometimes violent opposition, the nation's schools were gradually integrated while, at the same time, other forms of discrimination were challenged with boycotts, sit-ins, and "freedom rides." Congress enacted, in 1957, the first civil rights legislation since 1865, followed by voting legislation in 1960, and, in 1964, by a comprehensive Civil Rights Act that banned discrimination on the basis of race, sex, nationality, or religion in public places, employment, and unions.

The most powerful moving force behind the civil rights movement was the Reverend Martin Luther King, Jr., the president of the Southern Christian Leadership Conference. He helped organize a coherent program of nonviolent resistance to networks of segregation laws, a program best described in his famous "Letter from Birmingham Jail." Written 16 April 1963 while he was confined for parading without a permit, the letter was addressed to certain Protestant ministers, Catholic priests, and a Jewish rabbi.

Literary Selections

LETTER FROM BIRMINGHAM JAIL
Martin Luther King, Jr., 1929–1968

My dear Fellow Clergymen,

While confined here in the Birmingham City Jail, I came across your recent statement calling our present activities "unwise and untimely." Seldom, if ever, do I pause to answer criticism of my work and ideas. But since I feel that you are men of genuine goodwill and your criticisms are sincerely set forth, I would like to answer your statement in what I hope will be patient and reasonable terms.

I think I should give the reason for my being in Birmingham, since you have been influenced by the argument of "outsiders coming in." Several months ago our local affiliate here in Birmingham invited us to be on call to engage in a nonviolent direct action program if such were deemed necessary. We readily consented and when the hour came we lived up to our promises. So I am here, along with several members of my staff, because we were invited here. Beyond this, I am in Birmingham because injustice is here.

Moreover, I am cognizant of the interrelatedness of all communities and states. I cannot sit idly by in Atlanta and not be concerned about what happens in Birmingham. Injustice anywhere is a threat to justice everywhere. We are caught in an inescapable network of mutuality tied in a single garment of destiny. Never again can we afford to live with the narrow, provincial "outsider agitator" idea. Anyone who lives inside the United States can never be considered an outsider anywhere in this country.

You deplore the demonstrations that are presently taking place in Birmingham. But I am sorry that your statement did not express a similar concern for the conditions that brought the demonstrations into being. I would not hesitate to say that it is unfortunate that so-called demonstrations are taking place in Birmingham at this time, but I would say in more emphatic terms that it is even more unfortunate that the white power structure of this city left the Negro community with no other alternative.

In any nonviolent campaign there are four basic steps: 1) collection of the facts to determine whether injustices are alive; 2) negotiation; 3) self-purification; and 4) direct action.

You may well ask, "Why direct action? Why sit-ins, marches, etc.? Isn't negotiation a better path?" You are exactly right in your call for negotiation. Indeed, this is the purpose of direct action. Nonviolent direct action seeks to create such a crisis and establish such creative tension that a community that has constantly refused to negotiate is forced to confront the issue. So the purpose of the direct action is to create a situation so crisis-packed that it will inevitably open the door to negotiation.

My friends, I must say to you that we have not made a single gain in civil rights without determined legal and nonviolent pressure. History is the long and tragic story of the fact that privileged groups seldom give up their privileges voluntarily. Individuals may see the moral light and voluntarily give up their unjust posture; but as Reinhold Niebuhr has reminded us, groups are more immoral than individuals.

We know through painful experience that freedom is never voluntarily given by the oppressor; it must be demanded by the oppressed. For years now I have heard the word "Wait!" It rings in the ear of every Negro with a piercing familiarity. This "wait" has almost always meant "never." We must come to see with the distinguished jurist of yesterday that "justice too long delayed is justice denied." We have waited for more than three hundred and forty years for our constitutional and God-given rights.

You express a great deal of anxiety over our willingness to break laws. This is certainly a legitimate concern. Since we so diligently urge people to obey the Supreme Court's decision of 1954 outlawing segregation in the public schools, it is rather strange and paradoxical to find us consciously breaking laws. One may well ask, "How can you advocate breaking some laws and obeying others?" The answer is found in the fact that there are two types of laws. There are *just* laws and there are *unjust* laws. One has not only a legal but a moral responsibility to obey just laws. Conversely, one has a moral responsibility to disobey unjust laws.

Now what is the difference between the two? A just law is a man-made code that squares with the moral law or the law of God. An unjust law is a code that is out of harmony with the moral law. Any law that degrades human personality is unjust. All segregation statutes are unjust because segregation distorts the soul and damages the personality. It gives the segregator a false sense of superiority and the segregated a false sense of inferiority.

Let us turn to a more concrete example of just and unjust laws. An unjust law is a code that a majority inflicts on a minority that is not binding on itself. This is *difference* made legal. On the other hand a just law is a code that a majority compels a minority to follow that is willing to follow itself. This is *sameness* made legal.

I hope you can see the distinction I am trying to point out. In no sense do I advocate evading or defying the law as the rabid segregationist would do. This would lead to anarchy. One who breaks an unjust law *openly, lovingly,* and with a willingness to accept the penalty by staying in jail to arouse the conscience of the community over its injustice, is in reality expressing the very highest respect for law.

Of course there is nothing new about this kind of civil disobedience. It was seen sublimely in the refusal of Shadrach, Meshach, and Abednego to obey the laws of Nebuchadnezzar because a higher moral law was involved. It was practiced superbly by the early Christians.

We can never forget that everything Hitler did in Germany was "legal" and everything the Hungarian freedom fighters did in Hungary was "illegal." It was "illegal" to aid and comfort a Jew in Hitler's Germany.

In your statement you asserted that our actions, even though peaceful, must be condemned because they precipitate violence. But can this assertion be logically made? Isn't this like condemning the robbed man because his possession of money precipitated the evil act of robbery? We must come to see, as federal courts have consistently affirmed, that it is immoral to urge an individual to withdraw his efforts to gain his basic constitutional rights because the quest precipitates violence. Society must protect the robbed and punish the robber.

Over the last few years I have consistently preached that nonviolence demands that the means we use must be as pure as the ends we seek. So I have tried to make it clear that it is wrong to use immoral means to gain moral ends. But now I must affirm that it is just as wrong, or even more so, to use moral means to preserve immoral ends. T. S. Eliot has said that there is no greater treason than to do the right deed for the wrong reason.

I wish you had commended the Negro sit-inners and demonstrators of Birmingham for their sublime courage, their willingness to suffer, and their amazing discipline in the midst of the most inhuman provocation. One day the South will recognize its real heroes. They will include old, oppressed, battered Negro women, symbolized in a seventy-two-year-old woman of Montgomery, Alabama, who rose up with a sense of dignity and with her people decided not to ride the segregated buses, and responded to one who inquired about her tiredness with ungrammatical profundity: "My feets is tired, but my soul is rested." One day the South will know that when these disinherited children of God sat down at the lunch counters they were in reality standing up for the best in the American dream and the most sacred values in our Judeo-Christian heritage, and thus carrying our whole nation back to great wells of democracy which were dug deep by the founding fathers in the formulation of the Constitution and the Declaration of Independence.

I hope this letter finds you strong in the faith. I also hope that circumstances will soon make it possible for me to meet each of you, not as an integrationist or a civil rights leader, but as a fellow clergyman and a Christian brother. Let us hope that the dark clouds of racial prejudice will soon pass away and the deep fog of misunderstanding will be lifted from our fear-drenched communities and in some not too distant tomorrow the radiant stars of love and brotherhood will shine over our great nation with all of their scintillating beauty.

Yours for the cause of Peace and Brotherhood
Martin Luther King, Jr.

By 1965 the attack on segregation was essentially completed and stage two of the civil rights movement had begun. The rising demand was for equal opportunity, not only for jobs but in every area in American life. Mounting dissatisfaction with ghetto life, *de facto* segregation, and deteriorating urban environments fueled frustrations that writers such as Langston Hughes early saw as unbearable. Hughes, the leading writer of the Harlem Renaissance, summed up the smoldering situation in 1951 with a prophetic eleven-line poem:

HARLEM
Langston Hughes, 1902–1967

What happens to a dream deferred?
Does it dry up
like a raisin in the sun?
Or fester like a sore—
And then run?
Does it stink like rotten meat?
Or crust and sugar over—
like a syrupy sweet?

Maybe it just sags
like a heavy load.

Or *does it explode?*

Harlem, Detroit, Watts, and other urban centers erupted in the 1960s and extreme violence did not subside until after 1969. Equal opportunity for many African Americans, Hispanics, native Americans, and other minorities remains a "dream deferred."

The Feminist Movement

A roll call of influential women in Western culture can be impressive—at first glance. Cleopatra, Eleanor of Aquitaine, Queen Elizabeth I, Queen Victoria, and Margaret Thatcher certainly made their mark. What of the rest of the feminine half of the human race? With the exception of women such as those cited above, human history has been, until recently, an uninterrupted saga of male domination of the "subordinate, inferior sex." Perhaps the first feminist to protest such treatment in print was Christine de Pizan in her *Book of the City of Ladies*,[4] published in 1405 (see chapter 13). Not surprisingly, there was no reaction from either sex. It was not until Mary Wollstonecraft (1759–1797) published *Vindication of the Rights of Woman* (1792) that there began a feminist movement, though it was barely a ripple across the broad waters of male dominance. John Stuart Mill helped change that; drawing on ideas supplied by his wife, Harriet Taylor Mill, his essay *The Subjection of Women* (1869) had considerable impact, particularly on those in England who were pressing for more and more democratic reforms. Reform moved faster in New Zealand, the first nation to give women the vote (in 1893), with the British following suit in 1918 (for some women) and 1928 (for all women).

So, as in other Western democracies, the initial target of the American feminist movement was suffrage. Reasoning that voting rights would lead to equal rights, Susan B. Anthony (1820–1906) spent most of her life campaigning for women's suffrage. Not until 1920 was that particular fight won with passage and ratification of the Nineteenth Amendment.

The right to vote changed virtually nothing for American women. Males continued their domination in government, politics, the professions, business, and unions, thus provoking increasingly militant reactions. The latest, most powerful, and most effective feminist movement began in the 1960s in the general context of a push for equal rights for all Americans regardless of race, creed, sex, age, or national origin. A key work for the movement was *The Second Sex* (1949) by Simone de Beauvoir (1908–1986), a brilliant exposition of misconceptions regarding women and their place in the world. But it was chiefly Betty Friedan's (b. 1921) *The Feminine Mystique* (1963) that sparked a wide popular reaction. Friedan analyzed social and psychological pressures on women who were supposed to remain *in the home,* and effectively attacked persistent stereotypes of feminine intellect and behavior.

By no means limited to women, the feminist movement includes many men who see the liberation of women as a necessary corollary in freeing men of traditional stereotypes as to how a "real man" should behave. In fact, the proposed Equal Rights Amendment makes no reference to either sex.

---

4. Published in English in 1982 by Persea Books of New York.

Literary Selections

I LIKE TO THINK OF HARRIET TUBMAN
Susan Griffin, b. 1943

The women's movement toward equality in all areas of American life is far from over, and some say it has only begun. In this militant poem Susan Griffin cites Harriet Tubman as a heroic symbol of activism and freedom. Tubman (ca. 1820–1913) was an Abolitionist, an escaped slave, who, before the Civil War, freed over 300 slaves through the Underground Railroad. During the Civil War she was a Union nurse, laundress, and spy.

I like to think of Harriet Tubman.
Harriet Tubman who carried a revolver,
who had a scar on her head from a rock thrown
by a slave-master (because she
talked back), and who
had a ransom on her head
of thousands of dollars and who
was never caught, and who
had no use for the law
when the law was wrong,   10
who defied the law. I like
to think of her.
I like to think of her especially
when I think of the problem of
feeding children.
The legal answer
to the problem of feeding children
is ten free lunches every month,
being equal, in the child's real life,
to eating lunch every other day.   20
Monday but not Tuesday.
I like to think of the President
eating lunch Monday, but not
Tuesday.
And when I think of the President
and the law, and the problem of
feeding children, I like to
think of Harriet Tubman
and her revolver.
And then sometimes   30
I think of the President
and other men,
men who practice the law,
who revere the law,
who make the law,
who enforce the law
who live behind
and operate through
and feed themselves
at the expense of   40
starving children
because of the law,

men who sit in paneled offices
and think about vacations
and tell women
whose care it is
to feed children
not to be hysterical
not to be hysterical as in the word
hysterikos, the Greek for   50
womb suffering,
not to suffer in their
wombs,
not to care,
not to bother the men
because they want to think
of other things
and do not want
to take the women seriously.
I want them   60
to take women seriously.
I want them to think about Harriet Tubman,
and remember,
remember she was beat by a white man
and she lived
and she lived to redress her grievances,
and she lived in swamps
and wore the clothes of a man
bringing hundreds of fugitives from
slavery, and was never caught,   70
and led an army,
and won a battle,
and defied the laws
because the laws were wrong, I want men
to take us seriously.
I am tired wanting them to think
about right and wrong.
I want them to fear.
I want them to feel fear now
as I have felt suffering in the womb, and   80
I want them
to know
that there is always a time
there is always a time to make right
what is wrong,
there is always a time
for retribution
and that time
is beginning.

Exercises

1. You will note that the poem consists mostly of one- and two-syllable words with an occasional three-syllable word. There are only three different four-syllable words in the entire poem and two of these are related. What are the words? Is this a coincidence? What does the poet seem to have in mind?
2. What does Tubman's revolver signify?
3. What does Tubman herself symbolize?

IF SHAKESPEARE HAD A SISTER
FROM *A ROOM OF ONE'S OWN* (1929)
Virginia Woolf, 1882–1941

Virginia Woolf, one of the most gifted writers of this century, often wondered why men had always had power, influence, wealth, and fame, whereas women had nothing but children. She reasoned that there would be female Shakespeares in the future provided women found the first two keys to freedom: independent incomes and rooms of their own. (The second key was a metaphor for women having access to their own private space.) When *A Room of One's Own* was first published, it was considered both radical and revolutionary. Most people—including many women—did not talk about or even think about women's liberation and certainly no one was writing about it, let alone as persuasively as Virginia Woolf. Her essay became a classic, a landmark in the movement toward equality. Even today it is hardly dated, for there are still some men (and women) who assume that men are the superior sex.

It was disappointing not to have brought back in the evening some important statement, some authentic fact. Women are poorer than men because—this or that. Perhaps now it would be better to give up seeking for the truth, and receiving on one's head an avalanche of opinion hot as lava, discoloured as dish-water. It would be better to draw the curtains; to shut out distractions; to light the lamp; to narrow the enquiry and to ask the historian, who records not opinions but facts, to describe under what conditions women lived, not throughout the ages, but in England, say in the time of Elizabeth.

For it is a perennial puzzle why no woman wrote a word of that extraordinary literature when every other man, it seemed, was capable of song or sonnet. What were the conditions in which women lived, I asked myself; for fiction, imaginative work that is, is not dropped like a pebble upon the ground, as science may be; fiction is like a spider's web, attached ever so lightly perhaps, but still attached to life at all four corners. Often the attachment is scarcely perceptible; Shakespeare's plays, for instance, seem to hang there complete by themselves. But when the web is pulled askew, hooked up at the edge, torn in the middle, one remembers that these webs are not spun in midair by incorporeal creatures, but are the work of suffering human beings, and are attached to grossly material things, like health and money and the houses we live in.

I went, therefore, to the shelf where the histories stand and took down one of the latest, Professor Trevelyan's *History of England.* Once more I looked up Women, found "position of," and turned to the pages indicated. "Wife-beating," I read, "was a recognised right of man, and was practised without shame by high as well as low. . . . Similarly," the historian goes on, "the daughter who refused to marry the gentleman of her parents' choice was liable to be locked up, beaten and flung about the room, without any shock being inflicted on public opinion. Marriage was not an affair of personal affection, but of family avarice, particularly in the 'chivalrous' upper classes. . . . Betrothal often took place while one or both of the parties was in the cradle, and marriage when they were scarcely out of the nurses' charge." That was about 1470, soon after Chaucer's time. The next reference to the position of women is some two hundred years later, in the time of the Stuarts. "It was still the exception for women of the upper and middle class to choose their own husbands, and when the husband had been assigned, he was lord and master, so far at least as law and custom could make him. Yet even so," Professor Trevelyan concludes, "neither Shakespeare's women nor those of authentic seventeenth-century memoirs, like the Verneys and the Hutchinsons, seem wanting in personality and character." Certainly, if we consider it, Cleopatra must have had a way with her; Lady Macbeth, one would suppose, had a will of her own; Rosalind, one might conclude, was an attractive girl. Professor Trevelyan is speaking no more than the truth when he remarks that Shakespeare's women do not seem wanting in personality and character. Not being a historian, one might go even further and say that women have burnt like beacons in all the works of all the poets from the beginning of time—Klytaïmnestra, Antigone, Cleopatra, Lady Macbeth, Phèdre, Cressida, Rosalind, Desdemona, the Duchess of Malfi, among the dramatists; then among the prose writers: Millamant, Clarissa, Becky Sharp, Anna Karenina, Emma Bovary, Madame de Guermantes—the names flock to mind, nor do they recall women "lacking in personality and character." Indeed, if woman had no existence save in the fiction written by men, one would imagine her a person of the utmost importance; very various; heroic and mean; splendid and sordid; infinitely beautiful and hideous in the extreme; as great as a man, some think even greater. But this is woman in fiction. In fact, as Professor Trevelyan points out, she was locked up, beaten and flung about the room.

A very queer, composite being thus emerges. Imaginatively she is of the highest importance; practically she is completely insignificant. She pervades poetry from cover to cover; she is all but absent from history. She dominates the lives of kings and conquerors in fiction; in fact she was the slave of any boy whose parents forced a ring upon her finger. Some of the most inspired words, some of the most profound thoughts in literature fall from her lips; in real life she could hardly read, could scarcely spell, and was the property of her husband.

It was certainly an odd monster that one made up by reading the historians first and the poets afterwards—a worm winged like an eagle; the spirit of life and beauty in a kitchen chopping up suet. But these monsters, however amusing to the imagination, have no existence in fact. What one must do to bring her to life was to think poetically and prosaically at one and the same moment, thus keeping in touch with fact—that she is Mrs. Martin, aged thirty-six, dressed in blue, wearing a black hat and brown shoes; but not losing sight of fiction either—that she is a vessel in which all sorts of spirits and forces are coursing and flashing perpetually. The moment, however, that one tries this method with the Elizabethan woman, one branch of illumination fails; one is held up by the scarcity of facts. One knows nothing detailed, nothing perfectly true and substantial about her. History scarcely mentions her. And I turned to Professor Trevelyan again to see what history meant to him. I found by looking at his chapter headings that it meant—

"The Manor Court and the Methods of Open-field Agriculture . . . The Cistercians and Sheep-farming . . . The Crusades . . . The University . . . The House of Commons . . . The Hundred Years' War . . . The Wars of the Roses . . . The Renaissance Scholars . . . The Dissolution of the Monasteries . . . Agrarian and Religious Strife . . . The Origin of English Sea-power . . . The Armada . . ." and so on. Occasionally an individual woman is mentioned, an Elizabeth, or a Mary; a queen or a great lady. But by no possible means could middle-class women with nothing but brains and character at their command have taken part in any one of the great movements which, brought together, constitute the historian's view of the past. Nor shall we find her in any collection of anecdotes. Aubrey hardly mentions her. She never writes her own life and scarcely keeps a diary; there are only a handful of her letters in existence. She left no plays or poems by which we can judge her. What one wants, I thought—and why does not some brilliant student at Newnham or Girton supply it?—is a mass of information; at what age did she marry; how many children had she as a rule; what was her house like; had she a room to herself; did she do the cooking; would she be likely to have a servant? All these facts lie somewhere, presumably, in parish registers and account books; the life of the average Elizabethan woman must be scattered about somewhere, could one collect it and make a book of it. It would be ambitious beyond my daring, I thought, looking about the shelves for books that were not there, to suggest to the students of those famous colleges that they should re-write history, though I own that it often seems a little queer as it is, unreal, lop-sided; but why should they not add a supplement to history? calling it, of course, by some inconspicuous name so that women might figure there without impropriety? For one often catches a glimpse of them in the lives of the great, whisking away into the background, concealing, I sometimes think, a wink, a laugh, perhaps a tear. But what I find deplorable, I continued, looking about the bookshelves again, is that nothing is known about women before the eighteenth century. I have no model in my mind to turn about this way and that. Here am I asking why women did not write poetry in the Elizabethan age, and I am not sure how they were educated; whether they were taught to write; whether they had sitting-rooms to themselves; how many women had children before they were twenty-one; what, in short, they did from eight in the morning till eight at night. They had no money evidently; according to Professor Trevelyan they were married whether they liked it or not before they were out of the nursery, at fifteen or sixteen very likely. It would have been extremely odd, even upon this showing, had one of them suddenly written the plays of Shakespeare, I concluded, and I thought of that old gentleman, who is dead now, but was a bishop, I think, who declared that it was impossible for any woman, past, present, or to come, to have the genius of Shakespeare. He wrote to the papers about it. He also told a lady who applied to him for information that cats do not as a matter of fact go to heaven, though they have, he added, souls of a sort. How much thinking those old gentlemen used to save one! How the borders of ignorance shrank back at their approach! Cats do not go to heaven. Women cannot write the plays of Shakespeare.

Be that as it may, I could not help thinking, as I looked at the works of Shakespeare on the shelf, that the bishop was right at least in this; it would have been impossible, completely and entirely, for any woman to have written the plays of Shakespeare in the age of Shakespeare. Let me imagine, since facts are so hard to come by, what would have happened had Shakespeare had a wonderfully gifted sister, called Judith, let us say. Shakespeare himself went, very probably—his mother was an heiress—to the grammar school, where he may have learnt Latin—Ovid, Virgil and Horace—and the elements of grammar and logic. He was, it is well known, a wild boy who poached rabbits, perhaps shot a deer, and had, rather sooner than he should have done, to marry a woman in the neighbourhood, who bore him a child rather quicker than was right. That escapade sent him to seek his fortune in London. He had, it seemed, a taste for the theatre; he began by holding horses at the stage door. Very soon he got work in the theatre, became a successful actor, and lived at the hub of the universe, meeting everybody, knowing everybody, practising his art on the boards, exercising his wits in the streets, and even getting access to the palace of the queen. Meanwhile his extraordinarily gifted sister, let us suppose, remained at home. She was as adventurous, as imaginative, as agog to see the world as he was. But she was not sent to school. She had no chance of learning grammar and logic, let alone of reading Horace and Virgil. She picked up a book now and then, one of her brother's perhaps, and read a few pages. But then her parents came in and told her to mend the stockings or mind the stew and not moon about with books and papers. They would have spoken sharply but kindly, for they were substantial people who knew the conditions of life for a woman and loved their daughter—indeed, more likely than not she was the apple of her father's eye. Perhaps she scribbled some pages up in an apple loft on the sly, but was careful to hide them or set fire to them. Soon, however, before she was out of her teens, she was to be betrothed to the son of a neighbouring wool-stapler. She cried out that marriage was hateful to her, and for that she was severely beaten by her father. Then he ceased to scold her. He begged her instead not to hurt him, not to shame him in this matter of her marriage. He would give her a chain of beads or a fine petticoat, he said; and there were tears in his eyes. How could she disobey him? How could she break his heart? The force of her own gift alone drove her to it. She made up a small parcel of her belongings, let herself down by a rope one summer's night and took the road to London. She was not seventeen. The birds that sang in the hedge were not more musical than she was. She had the quickest fancy, a gift like her brother's, for the tune of words. Like him, she had a taste for the theatre. She stood at the stage door; she wanted to act, she said. Men laughed in her face. The manager—a fat, loose-lipped man—guffawed. He bellowed something about poodles dancing and women acting—no woman, he said, could possibly be an actress. He hinted—you can imagine what. She could get no training in her craft. Could she even seek her dinner in a tavern or roam the streets at midnight? Yet her genius was for fiction and lusted to feed abundantly upon the lives of men and women and the study of their ways. At last—for she was very young, oddly like Shakespeare the poet in her face, with the same grey eyes and rounded brows—at last Nick Greene the actor-manager took pity on her; she found herself with child by that gentleman and so—who shall measure the heat and violence of the poet's heart when caught and tangled in a woman's body?—killed herself one winter's night and lies buried at some cross-roads where the omnibuses now stop outside the Elephant and Castle.

That, more or less, is how the story would run, I think, if a woman in Shakespeare's day had had Shakespeare's genius. But for my part, I agree with the deceased bishop, if such he was—it is unthinkable that any woman in Shakespeare's day should have had Shakespeare's genius. For genius like Shakespeare's is not born among labouring, uneducated, servile people. It was not born in England among the Saxons and the Britons. It is not born today among the working classes. How, then, could it have been born among women whose work began, according to Professor Trevelyan, almost before they were out of the nursery, who were forced to it by their parents and held to it by all the power of law and custom? Yet genius of a sort must have existed among women as it must have existed among the working classes. Now and again an Emily Brontë or a Robert Burns blazes out and proves its presence. But certainly it never got itself on to paper. When, however, one reads of a witch being ducked, of a woman possessed by devils, of a wise woman selling herbs, or even of a very remarkable man who had a mother, then I think we are on the track of a lost novelist, a suppressed poet, of some mute and inglorious Jane Austen, some Emily Brontë who dashed her brains out on the moor or mopped and mowed about the highways crazed with the torture that her gift had put her to. Indeed, I would venture to guess that Anon, who wrote so many poems without signing them, was often a woman. It was a woman Edward Fitzgerald, I think, suggested who made the ballads and the folk-songs, crooning them to her children, beguiling her spinning with them, or the length of the winter's night.

This may be true or it may be false—who can say?—but what is true in it, so it seemed to me, reviewing the story of Shakespeare's sister as I had made it, is that any woman born with a great gift in the sixteenth century would certainly have gone crazed, shot herself, or ended her days in some lonely cottage outside the village, half witch, half wizard, feared and mocked at. For it needs little skill in psychology to be sure that a highly gifted girl who had tried to use her gift for poetry would have been so thwarted and hindered by other people, so tortured and pulled asunder by her own contrary instincts, that she must have lost her health and sanity to a certainty. No girl could have walked to London and stood at a stage door and forced her way into the presence of actor-managers without doing herself a violence and suffering an anguish which may have been irrational—for chastity may be a fetish invented by certain societies for unknown reasons—but were none the less inevitable. Chastity had then, it has even now, a religious importance in a woman's life, and has so wrapped itself round with nerves and instincts that to cut it free and bring it to the light of day demands courage of the rarest. To have lived a free life in London in the sixteenth century would have meant for a woman who was poet and playwright a nervous stress and dilemma which might well have killed her. Had she survived, whatever she had written would have been twisted and deformed, issuing from a strained and morbid imagination. And undoubtedly, I thought, looking at the shelf where there are no plays by women, her work would have gone unsigned. That refuge she would have sought certainly. It was the relic of the sense of chastity that dictated anonymity to women even so late as the nineteenth century. Currer Bell, George Eliot, George Sand, all the victims of inner strife as their writings prove, sought ineffectively to veil themselves by using the name of a man. Thus they did homage to the convention, which if not implanted by the other sex was liberally encouraged by them (the chief glory of a woman is not to be talked of, said Perikles, himself a much-talked-of man), that publicity in women is detestable. Anonymity runs in their blood. The desire to be veiled still possesses them. They are not even now as concerned about the health of their fame as men are, and, speaking generally, will pass a tombstone or a signpost without feeling an irresistible desire to cut their names on it, as Alf, Bert or Chas. must do in obedience to their instinct, which murmurs if it sees a fine woman go by, or even a dog, Ce chien est à moi. And, of course, it may not be a dog, I thought, remembering Parliament Square, the Sieges Allee and other avenues; it may be a piece of land or a man with curly black hair. It is one of the great advantages of being a woman that one can pass even a very fine negress without wishing to make an Englishwoman of her.

That woman, then, who was born with a gift of poetry in the sixteenth century, was an unhappy woman, a woman at strife against herself. All the conditions of her life, all her own instincts, were hostile to the state of mind which is needed to set free whatever is in the brain. But what is the state of mind that is most propitious to the act of creation, I asked. Can one come by any notion of the state that furthers and makes possible that strange activity? Here I opened the volume containing the Tragedies of Shakespeare. What was Shakespeare's state of mind, for instance, when he wrote *Lear* and *Antony and Cleopatra?* It was certainly the state of mind most favourable to poetry that there has ever existed. But Shakespeare himself said nothing about it. We only know casually and by chance that he "never blotted a line." Nothing indeed was ever said by the artist himself about his state of mind until the eighteenth century perhaps. Rousseau perhaps began it. At any rate, by the nineteenth century self-consciousness had developed so far that it was the habit for men of letters to describe their minds in confessions and autobiographies. Their lives also were written, and their letters were printed after their deaths. Thus, though we do not know what Shakespeare went through when he wrote *Lear,* we do know what Carlyle went through when he wrote the *French Revolution;* what Flaubert went through when he wrote *Madame Bovary;* what Keats was going through when he tried to write poetry against the coming of death and the indifference of the world.

And one gathers from this enormous modern literature of confession and self-analysis that to write a work of genius is almost always a feat of prodigious difficulty. Everything is against the likelihood that it will come from the writer's mind whole and entire. Generally material circumstances are against it. Dogs will bark; people will interrupt; money must be made; health will break down. Further, accentuating all these difficulties and making them harder to bear is the world's notorious indifference. It does not ask people to write poems and novels and histories; it does not need them. It does not care whether Flaubert finds the right word or whether Carlyle scrupulously verifies this or that fact. Naturally, it will not pay for what it does not want. And so the writer, Keats, Flaubert, Carlyle, suffers, especially in the creative years of youth, every form of distraction and discouragement. A curse, a cry of agony, rises from those books of analysis and confession. "Mighty poets in their misery dead"—that is the burden of their song. If anything comes through in spite of all this, it is a miracle, and probably no book is born entire and uncrippled as it was conceived.

But for women, I thought, looking at the empty shelves, these difficulties were infinitely more formidable. In the first place, to have a room of her own, let alone a quiet room or a sound-proof room, was out of the question, unless her parents were exceptionally rich or very noble, even up to the beginning of the nineteenth century. Since her pin money, which depended on the good will of her father, as only enough to keep her clothed, she was debarred from such alleviations as came even to Keats or Tennyson or Carlyle, all poor men, from a walking tour, a little journey to France, from the separate lodging which, even if it were miserable enough, sheltered them from the claims and tyrannies of their families. Such material difficulties were formidable; but much worse were the immaterial. The indifference of the world which Keats and Flaubert and other men of genius have found so hard to bear was in her case not indifference but hostility. The world did not say to her as it said to them, Write if you choose; it makes no difference to me. The world said with a guffaw, Write? What's the good of your writing? Here the psychologists of Newnham and Girton might come to our help, I thought, looking again at the blank spaces on the shelves. For surely it is time that the effect of discouragement upon the mind of the artist should be measured, as I have seen a dairy company measure the effect of ordinary milk and Grade A milk upon the body of the rat. They set two rats in cages side by side, and of the two one was furtive, timid and small, and the other was glossy, bold and big. Now what food do we feed women as artists upon? I asked, remembering, I suppose, that dinner of prunes and custard. To answer that question I had only to open the evening paper and to read that Lord Birkenhead is of opinion—but really I am not going to trouble to copy out Lord Birkenhead's opinion upon the writing of women. What Dean Inge says I will leave in peace. The Harley Street specialist may be allowed to rouse the echoes of Harley Street with his vociferations without raising a hair on my head. I will quote, however, Mr. Oscar Browning, because Mr. Oscar Browning was a great figure in Cambridge at one time, and used to examine the students at Girton and Newnham. Mr. Oscar Browning was wont to declare "that the impression left on his mind, after looking over any set of examination papers, was that, irrespective of the marks he might give, the best woman was intellectually the inferior of the worst man." After saying that Mr. Browning went back to his rooms—and it is this sequel that endears him and makes him a human figure of some bulk and majesty—he went back to his rooms and found a stable-boy lying on the sofa—"a mere skeleton, his cheeks were cavernous and sallow, his teeth were black, and he did not appear to have the full use of his limbs. . . . 'That's Arthur' [said Mr. Browning]. 'He's a dear boy really and most high-minded.' " The two pictures always seem to me to complete each other. And happily in this age of biography the two pictures often do complete each other, so that we are able to interpret the opinions of great men not only by what they say, but by what they do.

But though this is possible now, such opinions coming from the lips of important people must have been formidable enough even fifty years ago. Let us suppose that a father from the highest motives did not wish his daughter to leave home and become writer, painter or scholar. "See what Mr. Oscar Browning says," he would say; and there was not only Mr. Oscar Browning; there was the *Saturday Review;* there was Mr. Greg—the "essentials of a woman's being," said Mr. Greg emphatically, "are that *they are supported by, and they minister to, men"*—there was an enormous body of masculine opinion to the effect that nothing could be expected of women intellectually. Even if her father did not read out loud these opinions, any girl could read them for herself; and the reading, even in the nineteenth century, must have lowered her vitality, and told profoundly upon her work. There would always have been that assertion—you cannot do this, you are incapable of doing that—to protest against, to overcome. Probably for a novelist this germ is no longer of much effect; for there have been women novelists of merit. But for painters it must still have some sting in it; and for musicians, I imagine, is even now active and poisonous in the extreme. The woman composer stands where the actress stood in the time of Shakespeare. Nick Greene, I thought, remembering the story I had made about Shakespeare's sister, said that a woman acting put him in mind of a dog dancing. Johnson repeated the phrase two hundred years later of women preaching. And here, I said, opening a book about music, we have the very words used again in this year of grace, 1928, of women who try to write music. "Of Mlle. Germaine Tailleferre one can only repeat Dr. Johnson's dictum concerning a woman preacher, transposed into terms of music. 'Sir, a woman's composing is like a dog's walking on his hind legs. It is not done well, but you are surprised to find it done at all.' " So accurately does history repeat itself.

Thus, I concluded, shutting Mr. Oscar Browning's life and pushing away the rest, it is fairly evident that even in the nineteenth century a woman was not encouraged to be an artist. On the contrary, she was snubbed, slapped, lectured and exhorted. Her mind must have been strained and her vitality lowered by the need of opposing this, of disproving that. For here again we come within range of that very interesting and obscure masculine complex which has had so much influence upon the woman's movement; that deep-seated desire, not so much that *she* shall be inferior as that *he* shall be superior, which plants him wherever one looks, not only in front of the arts, but barring the way to politics too, even when the risk to himself seems infinitesimal and the suppliant humble and devoted. Even Lady Bessborough, I remembered, with all her passion for politics, must humbly bow herself and write to Lord Granville Leveson-Gower: ". . . notwithstanding all my violence in politics and talking so much on that subject, I perfectly agree with you that no woman has any business to meddle with that or any other serious business, farther than giving her opinion (if she is ask'd)." And so she goes on to spend her enthusiasm where it meets with no obstacle whatsoever

upon that immensely important subject, Lord Granville's maiden speech in the House of Commons. The spectacle is certainly a strange one, I thought. The history of men's opposition to women's emancipation is more interesting perhaps than the story of that emancipation itself. An amusing book might be made of it if some young student at Girton or Newnham would collect examples and deduce a theory—but she would need thick gloves on her hands, and bars to protect her of solid gold.

But what is amusing now, I recollected, shutting Lady Bessborough, had to be taken in desperate earnest once. Opinions that one now pastes in a book labelled cock-a-doodle-dum and keeps for reading to select audiences on summer nights once drew tears, I can assure you. Among your grandmothers and great-grandmothers there were many that wept their eyes out. Florence Nightingale shrieked aloud in her agony. Moreover, it is all very well for you, who have got yourselves to college and enjoy sitting-rooms—or is it only bed-sitting-rooms?—of your own to say that genius should disregard such opinions; that genius should be above caring what is said of it. Unfortunately, it is precisely the men or women of genius who mind most what is said of them. Remember Keats. Remember the words he had cut on his tombstone. Think of Tennyson; think—but I need hardly multiply instances of the undeniable, if very unfortunate, fact that it is the nature of the artist to mind excessively what is said about him. Literature is strewn with the wreckage of men who have minded beyond reason the opinions of others.

And this susceptibility of theirs is doubly unfortunate, I thought, returning again to my original enquiry into what state of mind is most propitious for creative work, because the mind of an artist, in order to achieve the prodigious effort of freeing whole and entire the work that is in him, must be incandescent, like Shakespeare's mind, I conjectured, looking at the book which lay open at *Antony and Cleopatra.* There must be no obstacle in it, no foreign matter unconsumed.

For though we say that we know nothing about Shakespeare's state of mind, even as we say that, we are saying something about Shakespeare's state of mind. The reason perhaps why we know so little of Shakespeare—compared with Donne or Ben Jonson or Milton—is that his grudges and spites and antipathies are hidden from us. We are not held up by some "revelation" which reminds us of the writer. All desire to protest, to preach, to proclaim an injury, to pay off a score, to make the world the witness of some hardship or grievance was fired out of him and consumed. Therefore his poetry flows from him free and unimpeded. If ever a human being got his work expressed completely, it was Shakespeare. If ever a mind was incandescent, unimpeded, I thought, turning again to the bookcase, it was Shakespeare's mind.

Afterword

Shakespeare's sister was fictional, but Wolfgang Amadeus Mozart did have a sister: Maria Anna (called Nannerl; 1751–1829). Performing as child prodigies, she and her younger brother astonished and delighted audiences all over Europe. She "showed an early talent scarcely inferior to her brother's,"[5] and he was probably the greatest musical genius who ever lived. Though Wolfgang was extremely critical of other people's music he did approve of Nannerl's compositions; none have survived. Because women did not perform in public, her musical gifts were strictly confined to her home after she turned eighteen. For many years after her husband's death she gave piano lessons in Salzburg; she was blind, alone, and living in wretched poverty when she died.

Racism

No one needs to be reminded that racism has always been a problem for the human race. There seems to be a fairly general human failing that compels one race or nation or society to feel and act superior to another. Whether this attitude is based on ignorance or arrogance, or both, the amount of destruction inflicted on human potential and on human life itself seems to be limitless. No nation or group of people is immune to the blight of bigotry and intolerance but that does not mean that the problem can ever be ignored.

The destructive effects of racism can be seen around the globe. In the United States there has been a shift from fighting for civil rights to combating racism as such. The Civil Rights Acts of 1964 and 1965 were positive steps that eliminated racial segregation in public places and established equal access to the voting booth. The 1980s saw a shift from the quest for constitutional guarantees to a focus on changing attitudes; the effect of this thrust was to contend that the opinions, feelings, and prejudices of private individuals were legitimate targets for political action.

Many political leaders see this drive as not only inappropriate but dangerous. It is divisive because it divides humanity into "them" and "us." A member of "us" can see the self as victim; as a self-styled victim the person has endless opportunities for self-pity and self-righteous anger. This can lead to a society at war with itself because there is no constitutional *right* to be free from racism, anti-Semitism, or sexism. The legal principles of freedom and justice for all are established though certainly less than fully accomplished. The negative movement against racism can never accomplish its objective of eliminating prejudices held by individuals. What, then, is the solution to the abiding affliction of racism? This is where artists can make important contributions,

---

5. Stanley Sadie, ed., *The New Grove Dictionary of Music and Musicians,* vol. 12 (London: Macmillan Publishers Limited, 1980), p. 680.

A SOLDIER'S EMBRACE
Nadine Gordimer, b. 1923

One of the functions of art is to confront a society with its failings. In her novels and short stories South Africa's Nadine Gordimer has been primarily concerned with the movement of the black population toward freedom and justice and active participation in the government. In "A Soldier's Embrace" she describes a successful revolution in an unspecified country. But Gordimer's poignant story of the strange ambivalence of race relations has no geographical boundaries. Her setting is Africa, which still suffers from the effects of Western imperialism (map 27.1), but winning freedom from repression, whether accomplished peacefully or violently, could take place anywhere in the world. That the aftermath of the revolution has resulted in the divisiveness of "them" and "us" is what deeply troubles the white protagonists of the story.

The day the cease-fire was signed she was caught in a crowd. Peasant boys from Europe who had made up the colonial army and freedom fighters whose column had marched into town were staggering about together outside the barracks, not three blocks from her house in whose rooms, for ten years, she had heard the blurred parade-ground bellow of colonial troops being trained to kill and be killed.

The men weren't drunk. They linked and swayed across the street; because all that had come to a stop, everything *had* to come to a stop: they surrounded cars, bicycles, vans, nannies with children, women with loaves of bread or basins of mangoes on their heads, a road gang with picks and shovels, a Coca-Cola truck, an old man with a barrow who bought bottles and bones. They were grinning and laughing amazement. That it could be: there they were, bumping into each other's bodies in joy, looking into each other's rough faces, all eyes crescent-shaped, brimming greeting. The words were in languages not mutually comprehensible, but the cries were new, a whooping and crowing all understood. She was bumped and jostled and she let go, stopped trying to move in any self-determined direction. There were two soldiers in front of her, blocking her off by their clumsy embrace (how do you do it, how do you do what you've never done before) and the embrace opened like a door and took her in—a pink hand with bitten nails grasping her right arm, a black hand with a big-dialled watch and thong bracelet pulling at her left elbow. Their three heads collided gaily, musk of sweat and tang of strong sweet soap clapped a mask to her nose and mouth. They all gasped with delicious shock. They were saying things to each other. She put up an arm round each neck, the rough pile of an army haircut on one side, the soft negro hair on the other, and kissed them both on the cheek. The embrace broke. The crowd wove her away behind backs, arms, jogging heads; she was returned to and took up the will of her direction again—she was walking home from the post office, where she had just sent a telegram to relatives abroad: ALL CALM DON'T WORRY.

The lawyer came back early from his offices because the courts were not sitting although the official celebration holiday was not until next day. He described to his wife the rally before the Town Hall, which he had watched from the office-building balcony. One of the guerilla leaders (not the most important; he on whose head the biggest price had been laid would not venture so soon and deep into the territory so newly won) had spoken for two hours from the balcony of the Town Hall. 'Brilliant. Their jaws dropped. Brilliant. They've never heard anything on that level: precise, reasoned—none of them would ever have believed it possible, out of the bush. You should have seen de Poorteer's face. He'd like to be able to get up and open his mouth like that. And be listened to like that. . .' The Governor's handicap did not even bring the sympathy accorded to a stammer; he paused and gulped between words. The blacks had always used a portmanteau name for him that meant the-crane-who-is-trying-to-swallow-the-bullfrog.

One of the members of the black underground organization that could now come out in brass-band support of the freedom fighters had recognized the lawyer across from the official balcony and given him the freedom fighters' salute. The lawyer joked about it, miming, full of pride. 'You should have been there—should have seen him, up there in the official party. I told you—really—you ought to have come to town with me this morning.'

'And what did you do?' She wanted to assemble all details.

'Oh I gave the salute in return, chaps in the street saluted *me* . . . everybody was doing it. *It was marvelous*. And the police standing by; just to think, last month—only last week—you'd have been arrested.'

'Like thumbing your nose at them,' she said, smiling.

'Did anything go on around here?'

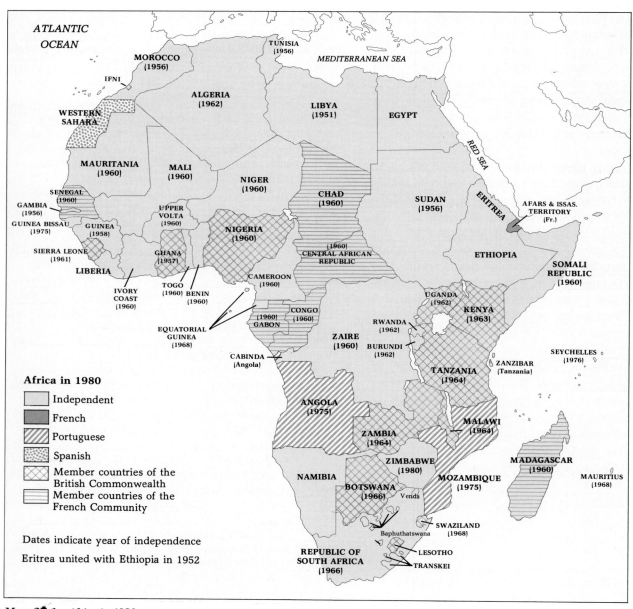

Map 27.1 *Africa in 1980.*

'Muchanga was afraid to go out all day. He wouldn't even run up to the post office for me!' Their servant had come to them many years ago, from service in the house of her father, a colonial official in the Treasury.

'But there was no excitement?'

She told him: 'The soldiers and some freedom fighters mingled outside the barracks. I got caught for a minute or two. They were dancing about; you couldn't get through. All very good-natured.— Oh, I sent the cable.'

An accolade, one side a white cheek, the other a black. The white one she kissed on the left cheek, the black one on the right cheek, as if these were two sides of one face.

That vision, version, was like a poster; the sort of thing that was soon peeling off dirty shopfronts and bus shelters while the months of wrangling talks preliminary to the takeover by the black government went by.

To begin with, the cheek was not white but pale or rather sallow, the poor boy's pallor of winter in Europe (that draft must have only just arrived and not yet seen service) with homesick pimples sliced off by the discipline of an army razor. And the cheek was not black but opaque peat-dark, waxed with sweat round the plump contours of the nostril. As if she could return to the moment again, she saw what she had not consciously noted: there had been a narrow pink strip in the darkness near the ear, the sort of tender stripe of healed flesh revealed when a scab is nicked off a little before it is ripe. The scab must have come away that morning: the young man picked at it in the troop carrier or truck (whatever it was the freedom fighters had; the colony had been told for years that they were supplied by the Chinese and Russians indiscriminately) on the way to enter the capital in triumph.

According to newspaper reports, the day would have ended for the two young soldiers in drunkenness and whoring. She was, apparently, not yet too old to belong to the soldier's embrace of all that a land mine in the bush might have exploded for ever. That was one version of the incident. Another: the opportunity taken by a woman not young enough to be clasped in the arms of the one who (same newspaper, while the war was on, expressing the fears of the colonists for their women) would be expected to rape her.

She considered this version.

She had not kissed on the mouth, she had not sought anonymous lips and tongues in the licence of festival. Yet she had kissed. Watching herself again, she knew that. She had—god knows why—kissed them on either cheek, his left, his right. It was deliberate, if a swift impulse: she had distinctly made the move.

She did not tell what happened not because her husband would suspect licence in her, but because he would see her—born and brought up in the country as the daughter of an enlightened white colonial official, married to a white liberal lawyer well known for his defence of blacks in political trials—as giving free expression to liberal principles.

She had not told, she did not know what had happened.

She thought of a time long ago when a school camp had gone to the sea and immediately on arrival everyone had run down to the beach from the train, tripping and tearing over sand dunes of wild fig, aghast with ecstatic shock at the meeting with the water.

De Poorteer was recalled and the lawyer remarked to one of their black friends, 'The crane has choked on the bullfrog. I hear that's what they're saying in the Quarter.'

The priest who came from the black slum that had always been known simply by that anonymous term did not respond with any sort of glee. His reserve implied it was easy to celebrate; there were people who 'shouted freedom too loud all of a sudden.'

The lawyer and his wife understood: Father Mulumbua was one who had shouted freedom when it was dangerous to do so, and gone to prison several times for it, while certain people, now on the Interim Council set up to run the country until the new government took over, had kept silent. He named a few, but reluctantly. Enough to confirm their own suspicions—men who perhaps had made some deal with the colonial power to place its interests first, no matter what sort of government might emerge from the new constitution? Yet when the couple plunged into discussion their friend left them talking to each other while he drank his beer and gazed, frowning as if at a headache or because the sunset light hurt his eyes behind his spectacles, round her huge-leaved tropical plants that bowered the terrace in cool humidity.

They had always been rather proud of their friendship with him, this man in a cassock who wore a clenched fist carved of local ebony as well as a silver cross round his neck. His black face was habitually stern—a high seriousness balanced by sudden splurting laughter when they used to tease him over the fist—but never inattentively ill-at-ease.

'What was the matter?' She answered herself; 'I had the feeling he didn't want to come here.' She was using a paper handkerchief dipped in gin to wipe greenfly off the back of a pale new leaf that had shaken itself from its folds like a cut-out paper lantern.

'Good lord, he's been here hundreds of times.'

'—Before, yes.'

What things were they saying?

With the shouting in the street and the swaying of the crowd, the sweet powerful presence that confused the senses so that sound, sight, stink (sweat, cheap soap) ran into one tremendous sensation, she could not make out words that came so easily.

Not even what she herself must have said.

A few wealthy white men who had been boastful in their support of the colonial war and knew they would be marked down by the blacks as arch exploiters, left at once. Good riddance, as the lawyer and his wife remarked. Many ordinary white people who had lived contentedly, without questioning its actions, under the colonial government, now expressed an enthusiastic intention to help build a nation, as the newspapers put it. The lawyer's wife's neighbourhood butcher was one. 'I don't mind blacks.' He was expansive with her, in his shop that he had occupied for twelve years on a licence available only to white people. 'Makes no difference to me who you are so long as you're honest.' Next to a chart showing a beast mapped according to the cuts of meat it provided, he had hung a picture of the most important leader of the freedom fighters, expected to be first President. People like the butcher turned out with their babies clutching pennants when the leader drove through the town from the airport.

There were incidents (newspaper euphemism again) in the Quarter. It was to be expected. Political factions, tribally based, who had not fought the war, wanted to share power with the freedom fighters' Party. Muchanga no longer went down to the Quarter on his day off. His friends came to see him and sat privately on their hunkers near the garden compost heap. The ugly mansions of the rich who had fled stood empty on the bluff above the sea, but it was said they would make money out of them yet—they would be bought as ambassadorial residences when independence came, and with it many black and yellow diplomats. Zealots who claimed they belonged to the Party burned shops and houses of the poorer whites who lived, as the lawyer said, 'in the inevitable echelon of colonial society', closest to the Quarter. A house in the lawyer's street was noticed by his wife to be accommodating what was certainly one of those families, in the outhouses; green nylon curtains had appeared at the garage window, she reported. The suburb was pleasantly overgrown and well-to-do; no one rich, just white professional people and professors from the university. The barracks was empty now, except for an old man with a stump and a police uniform stripped of insignia, a friend of Muchanga, it turned out, who sat on a beer-crate at the gates. He had lost his job as night-watchman when one of the rich people went away, and was glad to have work.

The street had been perfectly quiet; except for that first day.

The fingernails she sometimes still saw clearly were bitten down until embedded in a thin line of dirt all round, in the pink blunt fingers. The thumb and thick fingertips were turned back coarsely even while grasping her. Such hands had never been allowed to take possession. They were permanently raw, so young, from unloading coal, digging potatoes from the frozen Northern Hemisphere, washing hotel dishes. He had not been killed, and now that day of the cease-fire was over he would be delivered back across the sea to the docks, the stony farm, the scullery of the grand hotel. He would have to do anything he could get. There was unemployment in Europe where he had returned, the army didn't need all the young men any more.

A great friend of the lawyer and his wife, Chipande, was coming home from exile. They heard over the radio he was expected, accompanying the future President as confidential secretary, and they waited to hear from him.

The lawyer put up his feet on the empty chair where the priest had sat, shifting it to a comfortable position by hooking his toes, free in sandals, through the slats. 'Imagine, Chipande!' Chipande had been almost a protégé—but they didn't like the term, it smacked of patronage. Tall, cocky, casual Chipande, a boy from the slummiest part of the Quarter, was recommended by the White Fathers' Mission (was it by Father Mulumbua himself?—the lawyer thought so, his wife was not sure they remembered correctly) as a bright kid who wanted to be articled to a lawyer. That was asking a lot, in those days—nine years ago. He never finished his apprenticeship because while he and his employer were soon close friends, and the kid picked up political theories from the books in the house he made free of, he became so involved in politics that he had to skip the country one jump ahead of a detention order signed by the crane-who-was-trying-to-swallow-the-bullfrog.

After two weeks, the lawyer phoned the offices the guerilla-movement-become-Party had set up openly in the town but apparently Chipande had an office in the former colonial secretariat. There he had a secretary of his own; he wasn't easy to reach. The lawyer left a message. The lawyer and his wife saw from the newspaper pictures he hadn't changed much: he had a beard and had adopted the Muslim cap favoured by political circles in exile on the East Coast.

He did come to the house eventually. He had the distracted, insistent friendliness of one who has no time to reestablish intimacy; it must be taken as read. And it must not be displayed.

When he remarked on a shortage of accommodation for exiles now become officials, and the lawyer said the house was far too big for two people, he was welcome to move in and regard a self-contained part of it as his private living quarters, he did not answer but went on talking generalities. The lawyer's wife mentioned Father Mulumbua, whom they had not seen since just after the cease-fire. The lawyer added, 'There's obviously some sort of big struggle going on, he's fighting for his political life there in the Quarter.' 'Again,' she said, drawing them into a reminder of what had only just become their past.

But Chipande was restlessly following with his gaze the movements of old Muchanga, dragging the hose from plant to plant, careless of the spray; 'You remember who this is, Muchanga?' she had said when the visitor arrived, yet although the old man had given, in their own language, the sort of respectful greeting even an elder gives a young man whose clothes and bearing denote rank and authority, he was not in any way overwhelmed nor enthusiastic—perhaps he secretly supported one of the rival factions?

The lawyer spoke of the latest whites to leave the country—people who had got themselves quickly involved in the sort of currency swindle that draws more outrage than any other kind of crime, in a new state fearing the flight of capital: 'Let them go, let them go. Good riddance.' And he turned to talk of other things—there were so many more important questions to occupy the attention of the three old friends.

But Chipande couldn't stay. Chipande could not stay for supper; his beautiful long velvety black hands with their pale lining (as she thought of the palms) hung impatiently between his knees while he sat forward in the chair, explaining, adamant against persuasion. He should not have been there, even now; he had official business waiting, sometimes he drafted correspondence until one or two in the morning. The lawyer remarked how there hadn't been a proper chance to talk; he wanted to discuss those fellows in the Interim Council Mulumbua was so warily distrustful of—what did Chipande know?

Chipande, already on his feet, said something dismissing and very slightly disparaging, not about the Council members but of Mulumbua—a reference to his connection with the Jesuit missionaries as an influence that 'comes through'. 'But I must make a note to see him sometime.'

It seemed that even black men who presented a threat to the Party could be discussed only among black men themselves, now. Chipande put an arm round each of his friends as for the brief official moment of a photograph, left them; he who used to sprawl on the couch arguing half the night before dossing down in the lawyer's pyjamas. 'As soon as I'm settled I'll contact you. You'll be around, ay?'

'Oh, we'll be around.' The lawyer laughed, referring, for his part, to those who were no longer. 'Glad to see you're not driving a Mercedes!' he called with reassured affection at the sight of Chipande getting into a modest car. How many times, in the old days, had they agreed on the necessity for African leaders to live simply when they came to power!

On the terrace to which he turned back, Muchanga was doing something extraordinary—wetting a dirty rag with Gilbey's. It was supposed to be his day off, anyway; why was he messing about with the plants when one wanted peace to talk undisturbed?

'Is those thing again, those thing is killing the leaves.'

'For heaven's sake, he could use methylated for that! Any kind of alcohol will do! Why don't you get him some?'

There were shortages of one kind and another in the country, and gin happened to be something in short supply.

Whatever the hand had done in the bush had not coarsened it. It, too, was suede-black, and elegant. The pale lining was hidden against her own skin where the hand grasped her left elbow. Strangely, black does not show toil—she remarked this as one remarks the quality of a fabric. The hand was not as long but as distinguished by beauty as Chipande's. The watch a fine piece of equipment for a fighter. There was something next to it, in fact looped over the strap by the angle of the wrist as the hand grasped. A bit of thong with a few beads knotted where it was joined as a bracelet. Or amulet. Their babies wore such things; often their first and only garment. Grandmothers or mothers attached it as protection. It had worked; he was alive at cease-fire. Some had been too deep in the bush to know, and had been killed after the fighting was over. He had pumped his head wildly and laughingly at whatever it was she—they—had been babbling.

The lawyer had more free time than he'd ever remembered. So many of his clients had left; he was deputed to collect their rents and pay their taxes for them, in the hope that their property wasn't going to be confiscated—there had been alarmist rumours among such people since the day of the cease-fire. But without the rich whites there was little litigation over possessions, whether in the form of the children of dissolved marriages or the houses and cars claimed by divorced wives. The Africans had their own ways of resolving such redistribution of goods. And a gathering of elders under a tree was sufficient to settle a dispute over boundaries or argue for and against the guilt of a woman accused of adultery. He had had a message, in a round-about way, that he might be asked to be consultant on constitutional law to the Party, but nothing seemed to come of it. He took home with him the proposals for the draft constitution he had managed to get hold of. He spent whole afternoons in his study making notes for counter or improved proposals he thought he would send to Chipande or one of the other people he knew in high positions: every time he glanced up, there through his open windows was Muchanga's little company at the bottom of the garden. Once, when he saw they had straggled off, he wandered down himself to clear his head (he got drowsy, as he never did when he used to work twelve hours a day at the office). They ate dried shrimps, from the market: that's what they were doing! The ground was full of bitten-off heads and black eyes on stalks. His wife smiled. 'They bring them. Muchanga won't go near the market since the riot.' 'It's ridiculous. Who's going to harm him?'

There was even a suggestion that the lawyer might apply for a professorship at the university. The chair of the Faculty of Law was vacant, since the students had demanded the expulsion of certain professors engaged during the colonial regime—in particular of the fuddy-duddy (good riddance) who had gathered dust in the Law chair, and the quite decent young man (pity about him) who had had Political Science. But what professor of Political Science could expect to survive both a colonial regime and the revolutionary regime that defeated it? The lawyer and his wife decided that since he might still be appointed in some consultative capacity to the new government it would be better to keep out of the university context, where the students were shouting for Africanization, and even an appointee with his credentials as a fighter of legal battles for blacks against the colonial regime in the past might not escape their ire.

Newspapers sent by friends from over the border gave statistics for the number of what they termed 'refugees' who were entering the neighbouring country. The papers from outside also featured sensationally the inevitable mistakes and misunderstandings, in a new administration, that led to several foreign businessmen being held for investigation by the new regime. For the last fifteen years of colonial rule, Gulf had been drilling for oil in the territory, and just as inevitably it was certain that all sorts of questionable people, from the point of view of the regime's determination not to be exploited preferentially, below the open market for the highest bidder in ideological as well as economic terms, would try to gain concessions.

His wife said, 'The butcher's gone.'

He was home, reading at his desk; he could spend the day more usefully there than at the office, most of the time. She had left after breakfast with her fisherman's basket that she liked to use for shopping, she wasn't away twenty minutes. 'You mean the shop's closed?' There was nothing in the basket. She must have turned and come straight home.

'Gone. It's empty. He's cleared out over the weekend.'

She sat down suddenly on the edge of the desk; and after a moment of silence, both laughed shortly, a strange, secret, complicit laugh. 'Why, do you think?' 'Can't say. He certainly charged, if you wanted a decent cut. But meat's so hard to get, now; I thought it was worth it—justified.'

The lawyer raised his eyebrows and pulled down his mouth: 'Exactly.' They understood; the man probably knew he was marked to run into trouble for profiteering—he must have been paying through the nose for his supplies on the black market, anyway, didn't have much choice.

Shops were being looted by the unemployed and loafers (there had always been a lot of unemployed hanging around for the pickings of the town) who felt the new regime should entitle them to take what they dared not before. Radio and television shops were the most favoured objective for gangs who adopted the freedom fighters' slogans. Transistor radios were the portable luxuries of street life; the new regime issued solemn warnings, over those same radios, that looting and violence would be firmly dealt with but it was difficult for the police to be everywhere at once. Sometimes their actions became street battles, since the struggle with the looters changed character as supporters of the Party's rival political factions joined in with the thieves against the police. It was necessary to be ready to reverse direction, quickly turning down a side street in detour if one encountered such disturbances while driving around town. There were bodies sometimes; both husband and wife had been fortunate enough not to see any close up, so far. A company of the freedom fighters' army was brought down from the north and installed in the barracks to supplement the police force; they patrolled the Quarter, mainly. Muchanga's friend kept his job as gatekeeper although there were armed sentries on guard: the lawyer's wife found that a light touch to mention in letters to relatives in Europe.

'Where'll you go now?'

She slid off the desk and picked up her basket. 'Supermarket, I suppose. Or turn vegetarian.' He knew that she left the room quickly, smiling, because she didn't want him to suggest Muchanga ought to be sent to look for fish in the markets along the wharf in the Quarter. Muchanga was being allowed to indulge in all manner of eccentric refusals; for no reason, unless out of some curious sentiment about her father?

She avoided walking past the barracks because of the machine guns the young sentries had in place of rifles. Rifles pointed into the air but machine guns pointed to the street at the level of different parts of people's bodies, short and tall, the backsides of babies slung on mothers' backs, the round heads of children, her fisherman's basket—she knew she was getting like the others: what she felt was afraid. She wondered what the butcher and his wife had said to each other. Because he was at least one whom she had known. He had sold the meat she had bought that these women and their babies passing her in the street didn't have the money to buy.

It was something quite unexpected and outside their own efforts that decided it. A friend over the border telephoned and offered a place in a lawyers' firm of highest repute there, and some prestige in the world at large, since the team had defended individuals fighting for freedom of the press and militant churchmen upholding freedom of conscience on political issues. A telephone call; as simple as that. The friend said (and the lawyer did not repeat this even to his wife) they would be proud to have a man of his courage and convictions in the firm. He could be satisfied he would be able to uphold the liberal principles everyone knew he had always stood for; there were many whites, in that country still ruled by a white minority, who deplored the injustices under which their black population suffered etc. and believed you couldn't ignore the need for peaceful change etc.

His offices presented no problem; something called Africa Seabeds (Formosan Chinese who had gained a concession to ship seaweed and dried shrimps in exchange for rice) took over the lease and the typists. The senior clerks and the current articled clerk (the lawyer had always given a chance to young blacks, long before other people had come round to it—it wasn't only the secretary to the President who owed his start to him) he managed to get employed by the new Trades Union Council; he still knew a few blacks who remembered the times he had acted for black workers in disputes with the colonial government. The house would just have to stand empty, for the time being. It wasn't imposing enough to attract an embassy but maybe it would do for a Charge d'Affaires—it was left in the hands of a half-caste letting agent who was likely to stay put: only whites were allowed in, at the country over the border. Getting money out was going to be much more difficult than disposing of the house. The lawyer would have to keep coming back, so long as this remained practicable, hoping to find a loophole in exchange control regulations.

She was deputed to engage the movers. In their innocence, they had thought it as easy as that! Every large vehicle, let alone a pantechnicon, was commandeered for months ahead. She had no choice but to grease a palm, although it went against her principles, it was condoning a practice they believed a young black state must stamp out before corruption took hold. He would take his entire legal library, for a start; that was the most important possession, to him. Neither was particularly attached to furniture. She did not know what there was she felt she really could not do without. Except the plants. And that was out of the question. She could not even mention it. She did not want to leave her towering plants, mostly natives of South America and not Africa, she

supposed, whose aerial tubes pushed along the terrace brick erect tips extending hourly in the growth of the rainy season, whose great leaves turned shields to the spatter of Muchanga's hose glancing off in a shower of harmless arrows, whose two-hand-span trunks were smooth and grooved in one sculptural sweep down their length, or carved by the drop of each dead leaf-stem with concave medallions marking the place and building a pattern at once bold and exquisite. Such things would not travel; they were too big to give away.

The evening she was beginning to pack the books, the telephone rang in the study. Chipande—and he called her by her name, urgently, commandingly—'What is this all about? Is it true, what I hear? Let me just talk to him—'

'Our friend,' she said, making a long arm, receiver at the end of it, towards her husband.

'But you can't leave!' Chipande shouted down the phone. 'You can't go! I'm coming round. *Now.*'

She went on packing the legal books while Chipande and her husband were shut up together in the living-room.

'He cried. You know, he actually cried.' Her husband stood in the doorway, alone.

'I know—that's what I've always liked so much about them, whatever they do. They feel.'

The lawyer made a face: there it is, it happened; hard to believe.

'Rushing in here, after nearly a year! I said, but we haven't seen you, all this time . . . he took no notice. Suddenly he starts pressing me to take the university job, raising all sorts of objections, why not this . . . that. And then he really wept, for a moment.'

They got on with packing books like builder and mate deftly handling and catching bricks.

And the morning they were to leave it was all done; twenty-one years of life in that house gone quite easily into one pantechnicon. They were quiet with each other, perhaps out of apprehension of the tedious search of their possessions that would take place at the border; it was said that if you struck over-conscientious or officious freedom fighter patrols they would even make you unload a piano, a refrigerator or washing machine. She had bought Muchanga a hawker's licence, a hand-cart, and stocks of small commodities. Now that many small shops owned by white shopkeepers had disappeared, there was an opportunity for humble itinerant black traders. Muchanga had lost his fear of the town. He was proud of what she had done for him and she knew he saw himself as a rich merchant; this was the only sort of freedom he understood, after so many years as a servant. But she also knew, and the lawyer sitting beside her in the car knew she knew, that the shortages of the goods Muchanga could sell from his cart, the sugar and soap and matches and pomade and sunglasses, would soon put him out of business. He promised to come back to the house and look after the plants every week; and he stood waving, as he had done every year when they set off on holiday. She did not know what to call out to him as they drove away. The right words would not come again; whatever they were, she left them behind.

Exercises

1. What was symbolized by the embrace of a white European soldier, a black African freedom fighter, and a white woman? What went wrong after that? Why did it go wrong?
2. Consider the role of the black priest who did not want to come to the lawyer's home *after* freedom.
3. Muchanga, the old black servant, is a key figure in the story. At first he wasn't enthusiastic about greeting the returned black leader. Later, he stays with the lawyer and his wife but refuses to take orders from them. What happened to change his attitude? Does he represent the great mass of people who used to work for white families?
4. What was the significance of the African amulet worn next to a fine (European) watch?
5. Perhaps the most important statement was made by the lawyer's wife when she said, about Chipande, "I know—that's what I've always liked so much about them, whatever they do. They feel." What is implied?
6. What were the "right words" that were left behind?

The Information Society and the Global Village

During the several decades of civil rights and feminist activism other fundamental changes were quietly transforming American life. Once a nation of farmers, the industrial revolution made laborers the dominant work force. By the mid 1950s, however, white-collar workers outnumbered blue-collar laborers; by the early 1990s the manufacturing work force had dwindled to about 13 percent and farmers to less than 3 percent of the working population. The United States and Canada had shifted from an industrial society to an information society based on high technology; computers, communication satellites, fax machines, modems, robots, and other electronic marvels herald what has been called, variously, the Age of Information, the Computer Age, or the Communications Age. By the early 1990s over 75 percent of all jobs were involved with high tech and the products of high tech. Smokestack industries such as steel, textiles, and shipbuilding will probably continue to decline in the Western world as heavy industry expands in Third World countries that have large pools of cheap labor.

Not too many years ago children lived in a world not very different from that of their parents or grandparents. Information about the rest of the globe was confined to the printed word and technology was not even a word. The velocity of change was, metaphorically speaking, about ten miles an hour—the speed of a horse and buggy. In a society that was evolving almost imperceptibly, children tended to adopt the values, religion, and politics of their parents.

Today's world is so vastly different that comparisons boggle the mind. It has been estimated, for example, that our society has experienced more change during the past half-century than in all the preceding two or three million years. The acceleration of change appears to be the single most important influence on our lives. We can choose a philosophical, religious, or humanistic point of view (probably very different from that of our parents), but we can neither avoid nor deny the reality of a future that so insistently crowds upon the present.

During the late 1960s Alvin Toffler wrote a book whose title, *Future Shock,* became a metaphor for the frustrations and anxieties thrust on us by the onslaught of rapid and relentless change. Toffler described the understandable reluctance of people to recognize and accept the existence of what he called the "accelerative thrust." The pace of change keeps quickening, keeps confronting people with having to cope with ever faster acceleration and still more future shock. His thesis was that the shock of change can be replaced by the recognition of change as the new reality of the late twentieth century. Change can be seen as proper and necessary in an age when process is reality. It appears that children and young adults have made the transition with relative ease because rapid change is all that younger Americans have ever known. Many of those who once played 78 rpm records, placed phone calls through an operator, and listened only to radio have had their difficulties.

The magnitude of accelerating change can be comprehended by comparing the evolution of computers with the evolution of the automobile. If autos had progressed as rapidly as computers, a Rolls Royce today would

1. cost $2.75.
2. get 3 million miles per gallon.
3. have enough power to propel the Queen Elizabeth II.
4. fit six on the head of a pin.[6]

In a later book, *The Third Wave* (1980), Toffler predicted that individualized entertainment and information services would become readily available and that there would be a whole new range of social, political, psychological, and religious adaptations throughout the Western world and around the Pacific Basin: Japan, Korea, Hong Kong, Singapore, Taiwan, New Zealand, and Australia. No one is predicting any drastic changes (in the near future) for Third World countries, especially those in sub-Sahara Africa, but some countries have managed to leapfrog over older technology—such as railroads—to land in the middle of the high-tech revolution.

Developing technology tends to follow the line of least resistance. The first book printed with movable type, the Gutenberg Bible, looked like a handwritten manuscript. The first automobiles were called "horseless carriages" because they were indeed motorized carriages. Early steamships were sailing ships outfitted with paddle wheels. Much computer usage has been concerned with improving older technology: faster computations, quicker information retrieval, and improved typewriting in the form of a

---

6. Christopher Evans, *The Micro Millenium* (New York: The Viking Press, 1980), p. 4.

word processor, and so on. No one can predict the different directions computers will take except to say that inevitably, there will be startling new applications of computer technology.

Einstein gave us new conceptions of space, and the age of computers and telecommunications has forced us to recognize space as a concept connected by electronics and not just as a physical reality linked by interstate highways. International television with worldwide viewers, fax machines, modems, and other forms of rapidly evolving telecommunications have shrunk our earth to a Global Village. The mid 1990s will see a fully operational commercial telephone network that will enable subscribers to phone absolutely anywhere in the world. All of Antarctica, New Guinea, and the backwaters of the Amazon will be as immediately accessible as our next-door neighbor. Moreover, the telephone connection will enable the caller to fax or transmit computerized material throughout the world.

One important effect of electronic communications is to open all societies to the world outside despite the efforts of tyrants to control what their subjects can see and hear. In the discussion on the failure of Marxism-Leninism reference was made to the role of telecommunications in the overthrow of communist dictatorships. In Czechoslovakia, for example, videotapes of brutal government repression were duplicated and played over countless television sets throughout the country, thus reinforcing the groundswell of rebellion that brought down the government.

What will life be like in the Global Village? No one can predict what the globalization of culture will lead to, but the prognosis can be optimistic. The possibility of instantaneous close contact with people and their institutions can lead to closer human ties than at any time in human history.

Summary

The long-awaited era of peace and prosperity that was supposed to follow World War II ended abruptly in 1949 when Russia joined the United States as a nuclear superpower. The next two decades saw a Cold War between the two powers highlighted by two very hot wars. Communist aggression was successfully resisted in South Korea, but not in Vietnam. Denise Levertov's poem "Tenebrae" serves as a painful reminder of the Vietnam experience that still haunts many Americans.

The widespread and surprisingly sudden collapse of communist governments that began in 1989 was, of course, the most important series of events in the late twentieth century. Though much has already been revealed, it may take years before the extent and degree of the damage to people, societies, and the environment will be fully known. The world has yet to fully recover from the Hitler years; the Lenin legacy will undoubtedly plague civilization for decades to come.

> The central tragedy of modern world history is that both the Russian and the German republics, in turn, found in Lenin and Hitler adversaries of quite exceptional calibre, who embodied the will to power to a degree unique in our time.[7]

Existentialism as developed by Kierkegaard, Nietzsche, and Jean Paul Sartre is discussed as a significant postwar movement and illustrated, in part, with the "Myth of Sisyphus" by Albert Camus.

Martin Luther King's "Letter from Birmingham Jail" outlines the strategy of nonviolent resistance that helped make the civil rights movement so effective in overcoming some barriers to equal opportunity. The poem "Harlem" by Langston Hughes predicted the racial violence that erupted in major American cities, violence that was precipitated by the realization that equal opportunity regardless of race still had a long way to go.

Susan Griffin's poem "I Like to Think of Harriet Tubman" stresses the anger and frustration of women who deeply resent their position as the subordinate sex. Virginia Woolf creates a suicidal sister for Shakespeare to emphasize the need and the right of all women to have the freedom to be individuals in their own right, to have a "room of their own."

The South African author Nadine Gordimer moves beyond the abolishment of apartheid to a basic problem. "A Soldier's Embrace" is a melancholy look at the yawning chasm that still separates the races after oppression ends.

7. Paul Johnson, *Modern Times: The World from the Twenties to the Eighties* (New York: Harper & Row, 1983), pp. 128–129.

Culture and Human Values

The themes discussed and illustrated in this chapter were chosen to delineate some of the problems of our era. Though far from definitive, these are some of the important issues: civil rights, the feminist movement, and racism. If there were a universal, overwhelming concern for human values and human rights, these problems would not exist—and we would be living in Utopia.

Violence seems to be a fact of human existence, but there is no logical reason why a society cannot end overt discrimination and guarantee civil rights for everyone. This is no pipe dream but a goal that can be reached. Why, in the affluent world we are fortunate to inhabit, hasn't some kind of humane society come into being? Has there been enough time? Has there been enough effort?

There is another way to approach the problem. There have been three great technological revolutions in the history of humankind, all of which are still in progress:

1. Agricultural, 10,000 years ago.
2. Industrial, eighteenth and nineteenth centuries.
3. Information, late nineteenth and twentieth centuries.

New discoveries are still being made in agriculture, robotics in home and industry is in its infancy, and who knows where the knowledge explosion will lead. If virtue is knowledge and ignorance is vice, as Aristotle, Sokrates, and other Greeks contended, then perhaps the knowledge eruption can eventually lead the peoples of the world to form more rational and humane societies. Rapidly increasing scientific and technological knowledge can certainly improve our material existence; one must always consider the impact of technology on all of us.

> The universalizing imperative of technology is irresistible . . . . it will continue to shape both modern culture and the consciousness of those who inhabit that culture.[8]

Moreover, knowledge tends to lead to greater tolerance of the differences between individuals and between the varieties of cultures, an acceptance of diversity that can help offset the bane of intolerance and its spinoffs of prejudice, bigotry, sexism, and racism. More than at any time in human history, we seem to be acquiring the means to truly make this a better world for all humankind.

Peter Drucker, the noted futurist, says that we are already deep in the new and vastly different century and living in what he calls a post-business society. The business values of enterprise and profit, according to Drucker, have receded before the growth of such values as knowledge and fuller development of human potential. That we are living in a knowledge society should be apparent to everyone. We already have the technology for self-teaching that will enable everyone to learn subjects while teachers are freed to teach people. Consequently, we can expect an acceleration in the rate of change in our educational system, particularly in the light of the changes taking place in the rival trading nations in Europe and Asia.

Other authorities feel that we are living in what they call the postmodern world. In the modern movement in art, for example, artists sought originality and novelty and denied virtually the whole of the past. The postmodern movement in architecture (see chapter 28) appears to reflect a general proclivity to depart from the avant-garde tendencies of most of this century, a desire to integrate much of the recent past with contemporary Western culture and, to some extent, non-Western cultures. There is a search for human values in the context of a global civilization. This movement seems to be, in part, a reaction to the speedily evolving Information Age and the growing realization that our world is becoming a Global Village. Another factor is the recognition that a mind-set that denies the past is severely hampered when trying to confront the complexities of contemporary life. Many feel that we have lost our way in this bewildering world and that we can improve our lives by incorporating elements from the Enlightenment, the Renaissance, the Middle Ages, even the Greek and Roman worlds. The previous values of novelty and originality, of being different have little appeal when we are constantly reminded that people of any age are no different than men and women of today. The world is changing rapidly but people haven't changed at all. Progress, success, invention, and innovation may be false gods that have nothing to do with such human values as truth, justice, love, family, fidelity, integrity, and honor. *Value education* is a buzzword in public education, but one wonders how values are "taught." Values are learned from families, institutions, artists, philosophers, writers.

Finally, we should always keep in mind the profound question posed by philosopher William Barrett:

> What shall it profit a whole civilization, or culture, if it gains knowledge and power over the material world, but loses any adequate idea of the conscious mind, the human self, at the center of all that power?[9]

---

8. O. B. Hardison, Jr., *Disappearing through the Skylight: Culture and Technology in the Twentieth Century* (New York: Viking Penguin, 1989), p. 144.

9. William Barrett, *Death of the Soul: From Descartes to the Computer* (Garden City, New York: Anchor Press/Doubleday, 1986), p. 56.

Art in the Twentieth Century: Shock Waves and Reactions

chapter 28

Art is either a plagiarist or a revolutionist.

Paul Gauguin

Would you realize what Revolution is, call it Progress; and would you realize what Progress is, call it Tomorrow.

Victor Hugo

Prelude

The beginnings of modern art can be traced back to the revolutionary innovations of Édouard Manet, especially as exemplified in his *Olympia* (see figure 25.25). Manet had insisted that the actual subject matter was "light," but the new conception was even more fundamental; the artist's response to the rapidly changing world about him was visible on the canvas. *Olympia* was a naked prostitute from Manet's contemporary world. She gazed unconcernedly at a shocked public that still expected art to be an academic enterprise, art that drew its subject matter from myths and legends and instructed the viewer in the beauty of color and line. This was, however, the Age of Progress, the industrial era of cities, factories, slums, trains, Marx, Darwin, and Bismarck. The Renaissance tradition was no longer adequate or even appropriate. The impressionists did paint from nature but even Monet painted many views of a Parisian train station crowded with powerful locomotives emitting clouds of steam. Gauguin fled to Polynesia to escape a civilization that he saw as corrupt and diseased. Cézanne's sources were nature, people, and objects of the world in which he lived, not stories and myths of the past. The contemporary world was the basis for the new reality of painting. The stage was set for the advent of modernism.

Artistic Styles to 1945

Fauvism and Expressionism

Henri Matisse, 1869–1954

Modern art was in the air in 1905, especially in Collioure, a fishing port on the French Mediterranean coast a few miles from the Spanish border. Summering there with his family and a fellow artist, Matisse (ma-TEESS) saw some Tahitian paintings by Gauguin and was forcibly reminded of Gauguin's contention that color was whatever the artist perceived it to be. Still searching for a style, Matisse had become dissatisfied with copying nature as an impressionist, and he refused to even consider the dots-of-color technique of Seurat. At age thirty-six he found his style in Collioure. In the sparkling southern light he began painting in bold colors with broad and exuberant brushstrokes; he would delight in color for the rest of a long and marvelously productive career. When he displayed some of his Collioure pictures in Paris at the 1905 Salon d'Automne, critics were outraged, claiming that the "blotches of barbaric color" bore no relationship to real painting. There was, in fact, a whole room full of wildly colorful paintings by Matisse, his Collioure colleague André Derain, and other French artists. Perhaps seeking to localize the repercussions, the judges assigned all of their paintings to Room VII, leading the horrified public to believe that this was an organized school with Matisse, the eldest, as its leader. A critic's remark about a room full of fauves (foves, "wild beasts")[1] gave the group a name, and critical and public hostility helped create a movement. For a public still unfamiliar with the works of van Gogh and Gauguin, fauve paintings were shocking. Color was, after all, *true;* apples were red and trees were green. In *The Blue Window* (figure 28.1) Matisse has painted a landscape that is also a still life. The lamp-

---

1. Though commonly translated as "wild beasts," *fauves* actually means deer; the French call wild beasts *les grands fauves.*

Figure 28.1 *Henri Matisse,* The Blue Window (Summer 1913). *Oil on canvas, 51½" × 35⅜". Collection, The Museum of Modern Art, New York. Abby Aldrich Rockefeller Fund.*

Figure 28.2 *Henri Matisse,* Odalisque with Tambourine: Harmony in Blue, *1926. Oil on canvas, 36" × 25½". Courtesy of the Norton Simon Foundation, Pasadena, California.*

shade is green but the beautifully rounded trees in the background are blue. They are, nevertheless, still perceived as trees in an elegantly cool and decorative composition of curving shapes within a series of carefully proportioned rectangles. Color has been freed to become whatever the artist wants it to be.

In his *Odalisque with Tambourine: Harmony in Blue* (figure 28.2) Matisse has surrounded the harem girl with a variety of blues punctuated by spots of red and supported by a rich and colorful carpet. The color scheme in *The Blue Window* was cool and elegant but this painting is warmer and more emotional, representing the artist's reaction to an exotic African culture. (See figure 25.3 for a neoclassical reaction to similar subject matter.) Matisse expressed himself through vivid color somewhat in the manner of van Gogh and Gauguin, but he was not a tortured creator like the two lonely post-impressionists. Throughout his sixty-year career he was a hardworking and consistently cheerful painter and sculptor who seemingly paid not the slightest attention to the woes of the world, not even to the two terrible wars that his country had endured. He was neither insensitive nor indifferent; his concern was with the creation of beauty in a world that had become most unbeautiful.

Georges Rouault, 1871–1958

Rouault (roo-OH) was, on the other hand, obsessed with the plight of humankind in the twentieth century. Deeply religious,

unlike most modern artists, he was unable to accept the joyful hedonism of Matisse or the relaxed styles of other fauves. His sympathies lay with clowns and other circus performers, whom he saw as symbols for the tragic victims of society; he despised soldiers, corrupt judges, and the demimonde of prostitutes and criminals. His *Christ Mocked by Soldiers* (figure 28.3) shows a tortured Christ at the mercy of brutal soldiers, a pathetic figure who also symbolizes the victims of the ruthless modern world. At one time a worker in stained glass, Rouault uses heavy black lines similar to the lead contours that framed the pieces of stained glass. The reds, greens, and blues are themselves the standard colors of medieval stained glass. Matisse and Rouault are both French and fauves, i.e., expressionists, but there is no further similarity in their art or their lives.

German Expressionism

Ernst Barlach, 1870–1938

Beginning about the same time as fauvism, German expressionism was influenced by the French movement and by the anguished work of Edvard Munch (see figure 25.45). The leading

Figure 28.3 *Georges Rouault,* Christ Mocked by Soldiers, *1932. Oil on canvas, 36¼″ × 28½″. Collection, The Museum of Modern Art, New York. Given anonymously.*

Figure 28.4 *Ernst Barlach,* Shivering Woman. *Bronze, ht. 10″, width 6″. The University Art Collections, Arizona State University, Tempe. Gift of Oliver B. James.*

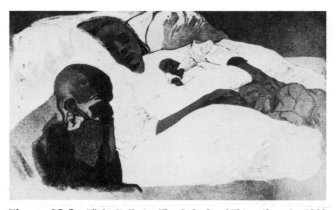

Figure 28.5 *Käthe Kollwitz,* The Only Good Thing About It, *1909. Print, 7″ × 5″. Kunstbibliothek, Berlin.*

expressionist sculptor, Barlach displays a medieval, craftsmanlike quality in his work. Even though the medium is bronze his *Shivering Woman* (figure 28.4) has the appearance of a wood carving. Monumental in mass despite its small scale, the huddled figure is a powerful study of concentrated misery. The art of the German avant-garde has an intense emotional content reminiscent of the work of Grünewald (see figure 17.55).

Käthe Kollwitz, 1867–1945

German artists were more concerned with political and social conditions before and after World War I than were the French, and none more so than Kollwitz. Both a sculptor and a graphic artist, Kollwitz became, in 1918, the first woman elected to a professorship in the Prussian Academy of Arts and later, the first female to head a department there. A socialist and a feminist, she concentrated on themes of poverty and injustice and the difficulty of being a woman and mother in militaristic Prussia. Her "Raped" from her *Peasants' War* series is an early depiction of the criminal violation from a woman's point of view. In *The Only Good Thing About It* (figure 28.5) the exhausted mother stares numbly at the viewer, her newborn baby on her chest, her other child nestled down in the bed. The baby is presumably a girl. When first published the print's caption read: "If they are not used as soldiers they at least deserve to be treated as children." Kollwitz's lifelong

campaign against German militarism began well before her personal tragedies. Her son was killed in combat in World War I and her grandson met the same fate in World War II.

George Grosz, 1893–1959

Grosz became, with his satirical drawings, a prominent spokesman for the antiwar movement in Germany during the 1920s. At first identified with the Berlin Dadaists (see Dada below), Grosz developed a pessimistic expressionist style influenced by the powerful imagery of Grünewald and Bosch (see figure 17.29). His

Figure 28.6 *George Grosz, I Am Glad I Came Back, 1943. Oil on masonite, 28" × 20". The University Art Collections, Arizona State University, Tempe. Gift of Oliver B. James.*

Figure 28.7 *Wassily Kandinsky, Panel (3) (also known as Summer), 1914. Oil on canvas, 64" × 36¼". Collection, The Museum of Modern Art, New York. Mrs. Simon Guggenheim Fund.*

opposition to the Nazis forced him to flee Germany in 1932 for the United States, where he realized his dream of becoming an American citizen. Painted during the horror of a war that he, among many, had foreseen, *I Am Glad I Came Back* (figure 28.6) depicts a grinning skeleton peering through parted draperies at the holocaust of World War II. Symbolically, the work is a vision of the rebirth of the Four Horsemen of the Apocalypse: War, Famine, Pestilence, and Death.

Wassily Kandinsky, 1866–1944

The expressive qualities of strong color also impressed some Russian artists, especially Kandinsky. Russia had a long history of robust colors derived from its Byzantine tradition, which Kandinsky realized as he studied the intense colors of richly decorated peasant clothing, furniture, and houses. Moving to Munich to study the movement, he began painting in the German expressionist style. It was not until about 1908 that he discovered, apparently accidentally, that color could operate independently of subjects. Red, for example, need not be on an apple nor green on a tree; colors could function in expressive compositions without representing specific objects. Called the first abstract expressionist as early as 1919, Kandinsky developed theories about the spiritual qualities of colors and the interrelationship of music and art. As with many of his contemporaries, Kandinsky felt that the world was headed for disaster and that there was a real need

for a spiritual rebirth in art and in life. He equated representational art with the materialism that appeared to be corrupting society and thus removed all objective references in order to return to spiritual values. In *Panel 3* (also known as *Summer;* figure 28.7) he created what can be described as "visual poetry" or "visual music," a celebration of the warmth and brightness of summer. That this work was completed in the year in which the Great War engulfed most of Europe may or may not be coincidental.

Cubism and Other Abstractions

Pablo Picasso, 1881–1973

The most famous and successful artist of this century, Picasso was a one-man art movement whose innovations throughout a long and enormously productive career make him impossible to classify or categorize. He is discussed under this heading because he,

Figure 28.8 *Pablo Picasso,* The Tragedy, *1903. Oil on wood, 41½"* × *27⅛". Chester Dale Collection, 1962. National Gallery of Art, Washington, D.C.*

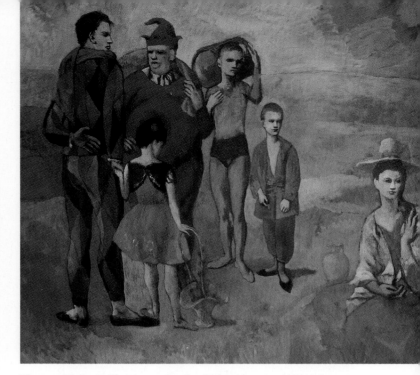

Figure 28.9 *Pablo Picasso,* Family of Saltimbanques, *1905. Oil on canvas, 90⅜"* × *83¾". Chester Dale Collection, 1962. National Gallery of Art, Washington, D.C.*

along with Georges Braque (brack; 1882–1963), invented cubism. Working in his native Spain after a discouraging first attempt at a career in Paris, Picasso painted *The Tragedy* (figure 28.8) as a somber monochromatic study, in blue, of sorrowing figures in a timeless setting by an unknown sea. There have been numerous explanations for the artist's brief Blue Period (ca. 1903–1904), but the likeliest is his prolonged melancholy at this stage of his career.

After deciding, in 1904, to live in Paris permanently, Picasso was still poverty-stricken, but his first mistress helped brighten his life and his style. The last of the circus-theme paintings of his Rose Period (ca. 1904–1905), the *Family of Saltimbanques* (figure 28.9) was his first large painting, a kind of summary that concluded the period. The Jester stands between Harlequin at the left along with two boy acrobats. Like objects in a still life, the figures are expressionless and motionless. As was his custom, Picasso has portrayed some members of his "gang," including himself as Harlequin, but there is no explanation for the isolated woman at the right.

Picasso could have painted indefinitely in the lyrical Rose Period style; his works were selling so well that he had become, next to Matisse, perhaps the best-known painter in Paris. However, having mastered the technique, he changed his style. His

studies of ancient Iberian sculptures and African masks led him to produce a painting of five nude women that astonished and horrified art dealers, and even his friends. Unlike anything ever seen in art, *Les Demoiselles d'Avignon* (figure 28.10) represented a breakthrough as epochal as Masaccio's *Tribute Money* (see figure 17.12) at the beginning of the Italian Renaissance. Masaccio established Renaissance perspective; with this painting Picasso destroyed it. Just about all the rules were broken: flat picture plane with no one-point perspective; angular and fragmented bodies; distorted faces with enormous eyes; two figures wearing grotesque African-like masks. With a remarkable economy of means Picasso created tense and massive figures whose heads and facial features are seen simultaneously in full face and profile, marking a great step forward in the evolution of cubism. A friend of the artist added the title later, a reference to a brothel on Avignon Street in Barcelona. About this painting Picasso remarked that "nature has to exist so that we may rape it!" Braque commented that it made him feel "that someone was drinking gasoline and spitting fire."

Picasso and Braque took cubism through several phases, from a faceting of three-dimensional figures to flattened images and rearranged forms. In *Still Life* (figure 28.11) Picasso uses forms from the "real" world to confuse reality and illusion. All is two-dimensional, but shadows cast by objects on the tilted tabletop further add to the confusion. What is reality here? Actually, colors and forms on canvas. Inspired in part by Cézanne's compressed forms (see figure 25.35), cubism was a refutation of our Mediterranean classical heritage as the sole criterion for creating and viewing art.

Figure 28.10 *Pablo Picasso,* Les Demoiselles d'Avignon, *(begun May, reworked July 1907). Oil on canvas, 8′ × 7′8″. Collection, The Museum of Modern Art, New York. Acquired through the Lillie P. Bliss Bequest.*

Figure 28.11 *Pablo Picasso,* Still Life, *1918. Oil on canvas, 51¼″ × 38¼″. Chester Dale Collection, 1962. National Gallery of Art, Washington, D.C.*

Inspired by a new German mistress with blond hair and high-bridged nose, Picasso painted her in a number of colorful works, but his personal favorite was *Girl Before a Mirror* (figure 28.12). Standing nude in front of a mirror, she is young and innocent, but the mirror image is older and darker, mysterious and sultry. The wide range of vivid colors set off by heavy dark lines is reminiscent of medieval stained glass, perhaps indicating that Picasso had in mind Eve the Temptress or even a modern-day version of the Madonna.

During the afternoon of 26 April 1937 the Spanish Civil War came home to the Spanish artist living in Paris. German bombers of the Condor Legion destroyed over 70 percent of the Basque town of Guernica and, twenty-five sketches and one month later, Picasso had completed his anguished protest against the brutal destruction of a defenseless city (figure 28.13). The central figure is a wounded horse that, according to the artist, represents the people, whereas the bull symbolizes the inhuman brutality of fascism. Possibly representing the threatened Light of Reason, a light bulb is superimposed on the blazing sun. Painted on an enormous scale in a stark black, white, and gray, the work is a monumental protest against the impersonal cruelty of modern warfare. At the bottom center is one small symbol of life, a fragile flower above the broken sword. Picasso decreed that the work would remain on loan to the Museum of Modern Art in New York until democracy was restored in Spain. After difficult negotiations with heirs, politicians, and two art museums, the painting was officially inaugurated in Madrid on 24 October 1981.

Figure 28.12 *Pablo Picasso,* Girl Before a Mirror, *March 1932. Oil on canvas, 64″ × 51¼″. Collection, The Museum of Modern Art, New York. Gift of Mrs. Simon Guggenheim.*

353

Figure 28.13 *Pablo Picasso,* Guernica, *1937. Oil on canvas, 25'5¾" × 11'5½". Museo del Prado. Photo: SPADEM/ARS, New York.*

American Modernists

Georgia O'Keeffe, 1887–1986

Undoubtedly reflecting her American training, O'Keeffe applied abstract concepts to American themes. She took special delight in painting organic forms found in the Southwest, to which she moved permanently after the death of her husband, the celebrated photographer Alfred Stieglitz. *Jack-in-the-Pulpit, No. 5* (figure 28.14) is from the numerous series of floral images that she painted for over forty years, steering a middle path between nature and abstraction. Her imagery is a unique combination of graceful representation and elegant geometry.

Alfred Stieglitz, 1864–1946

O'Keeffe and her husband operated the Little Gallery of the Photo-Secession that Stieglitz had earlier opened at 291 Fifth Avenue in New York. At "291," as the art world called it, the arts of photography and painting coexisted. Advocating "straight photography," Stieglitz used no gimmicks, relying instead on his eye, his camera, and his lens. Lonely in New York after nine years of study abroad, he came upon *The Terminal* (figure 28.15), capturing a moment in a world of horse-drawn streetcars, quaint streetlamps, and men in bowler hats. In this photograph we also share a personal instant in the life of the photographer.

Stieglitz was the strongest and most persuasive advocate of photography as an art form, but he was even more dedicated to the promotion of modern painting. For the first time in America his gallery showed works by Cézanne, Picasso, Toulouse-Lautrec, Rodin, Matisse, Brancusi, and Henri Rousseau.

The Armory Show

American abstract artists, like their European counterparts, had to combat the hostility of a public accustomed to representational art plus the opposition of academicians and the Ash Can school (see below). The modernists of "291" ended the internecine warfare by inducing academicians and Ash Can artists to form, in 1911, the Association of American Artists and Painters. An exhibition of contemporary American art was to be the first project, but the end result was the epochal New York Armory Show of 1913, still the most controversial exhibition ever staged in the United States.

Figure 28.14 *Georgia O'Keeffe,* Jack-in-the-Pulpit, No. 5, *1930. Oil on canvas, 48" × 30". National Gallery of Art, Washington, D.C. Alfred Stieglitz Collection, Bequest of Georgia O'Keeffe, 1987.*

Convinced that the public was ready for new ideas, the organizers included European modernists in what was officially called the International Exhibition of Modern Art. Works by Cézanne, Rousseau, Gauguin, van Gogh, Matisse, Duchamp, and Picasso astounded and infuriated artists, critics, and most of all, the public. The shocked organizers dismissed the public reaction as militant ignorance, which it was, but American modernists were dismayed to see how far behind they themselves were. The Armory Show was "the greatest single influence that I have experienced," said Stuart Davis (1894–1964) as he altered his style and, like many American artists, sailed to Paris. His cubistic *Radio Tubes* (figure 28.16) is a characteristically whimsical celebration of American technology at a time when advanced technology was naively thought to be uniquely American. Contending that the camera was the proper instrument for recording facts, Davis believed, as did most modernists, that his function was to make new state-

Figure 28.15 *Alfred Stieglitz,* The Terminal, *ca. 1890. Photograph. Alfred Stieglitz Collection. Art Institute of Chicago.*

Figure 28.17 *Piet Mondrian,* Composition in White, Black, and Red, *1936. Oil on canvas, 41" × 40¼". Collection, The Museum of Modern Art, New York. Gift of the Advisory Committee.*

Figure 28.16 *Stuart Davis,* Radio Tubes, *1940. Gouache, 22" × 14". The University Art Collections, Arizona State University, Tempe. Gift of Oliver B. James.*

ments. Though influenced by European cubism, *Radio Tubes* is, in its own way, as American as the work of Georgia O'Keeffe.

Piet Mondrian, 1872–1944

Though he was attracted to the work of the French cubists, the Dutch artist Mondrian felt that their art did not express what he called "pure reality." He sought "plastic expression" in a basic reality made up solely of colors and forms that had their own spiritual values. *Composition in White, Black, and Red* (figure 28.17) is a precisely balanced work in a style generally called geometric abstraction. No two of the sixteen rectangles are of the same size or shape nor are all the heavy black lines the same width. The poised serenity of Mondrian's "composition" is as classical as a Greek temple. Mondrian's ideas influenced many artists but they have also been popularized, in simplified and sometimes distorted versions, in fashion, interior, and advertising design.

Both Mondrian and Kandinsky produced nonrepresentational art and both believed that their paintings were analogous to music. Though this analogy may not be apparent in figure 28.17, unless in conjunction with the music of Mozart, Mondrian's *Broadway Boogie Woogie* (figure 28.18) pulses with the rhythm and vitality of New York's Great White Way. Along with European artists Marc Chagall, Max Ernst, Yves Tanguy, Thomas Mann, Bertolt Brecht, and others, Mondrian lived in New York as a refugee from Hitler's tyranny. Though he did not live to see the defeat of Nazi Germany, this work and a companion piece called *Victory Boogie Woogie* embodied the artist's admiration for his new home.

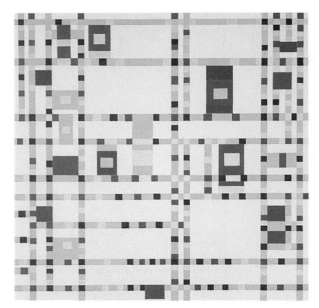

Figure 28.18 *Piet Mondrian,* Broadway Boogie Woogie, *1942–1943. Oil on canvas, 50" × 50". Collection, The Museum of Modern Art, New York. Given anonymously.*

Figure 28.19 *Constantin Brancusi,* Bird in Space, *ca. 1928. Polished bronze, unique cast, ca. 54" high. Collection, The Museum of Modern Art, New York. Given anonymously.*

Constantin Brancusi, 1876–1957

The Romanian sculptor Brancusi (bran-KOOSH) was first influenced by Rodin when studying in Paris, but developed an abstract style that influenced many artists. His *Bird in Space* (figure 28.19) conveys, in an elegantly swelling shape, the soaring spirit of flight. It is a magnificent work of transcendental beauty that epitomizes the sculptor's statement: "I bring you pure joy."

Fantasy

Marc Chagall, 1887–1985

Fantasy plays a large part in twentieth-century art, with the Russian artist Chagall (shah-GALL) a leading exponent. Chagall combines fauve color and cubist forms with a personal vision of his early life in a Russian village. In *I and the Village* (figure 28.20) cow and peasant speak to each other; a peasant marches up the street after his wife, who floats upside down; and a magic tree grows out of a hand. Chagall's paintings are meant to be enjoyed as pictorial arrangements of images that fascinated the artist and enchant the viewer.

Paul Klee, 1879–1940

The German-Swiss artist Klee (klay) was a master of fantasy. Through his teaching at the Bauhaus (see figure 28.36) and his painting, Klee was one of the most influential artists of the century. Rejecting illusionistic art as obsolete, he turned to the art of children and primitives as inspirations for his paintings. *Fish Magic* (figure 28.21) is a whimsical fantasy of disparate objects placed, with infinite care, in harmonious relationships. Nothing in this

Figure 28.20 *Marc Chagall,* I and the Village, *1911. Oil on canvas, 63⅝" × 59⅝". Collection, The Museum of Modern Art, New York. Mrs. Simon Guggenheim Fund.*

Figure 28.21 *Paul Klee,* Fish Magic, *1925. Oil and watercolor, varnished, 30⅜" × 38½". Philadelphia Museum of Art. Louise and Walter Arenberg Collection.*

work is invented. As a shrewd observer of nature and people, Klee coded his findings and arranged them on canvas. Everything is from the real world but transformed into a magical composition.

Giorgio de Chirico, 1888–1978

The fantasies of de Chirico (day KEE-re-ko) were as subjective as those of Chagall but infused with pessimism and melancholy. Like Kandinsky and other intellectuals, de Chirico perceived a sick society defiled by materialism. Born in Greece of Italian parents, de Chirico first studied in Athens but, like many artists of the time, wound up in Paris where he studied the Old Masters in the Louvre. Strongly influenced by the German philosopher Nietzsche (see chapter 27), de Chirico looked on himself as a metaphysical painter who explored the mysteries of life. In *The Nostalgia of the Infinite* (figure 28.22) he employed a distorted Renaissance perspective in a characteristic dreamlike cityscape in which everything is real, except that it isn't. Pennants are flying vigorously from a sinister and threatening tower in front of which two minuscule figures cast disproportionately long shadows. Like most of his images, this building actually exists (in Turin), but the strange juxtaposition creates another reality that is not of the waking world.

Dada

Marcel Duchamp, 1887–1968

As early as 1914 it had become obvious to some artists that World War I marked the low point of a bankrupt Western culture. In February of 1916 some exiles from the war that was consuming Europe formed, in neutral Switzerland, the Cabaret Voltaire, a loose-knit and contentious group devoted to attacking everything that Western civilization held dear. These writers, artists, musicians, and poets chose the word *Dada* to identify their iconoclastic movement, a word intended as nonsense but immediately

Figure 28.22 *Giorgio de Chirico,* The Nostalgia of the Infinite, *ca. 1913–1914, dated 1911 on the painting. Oil on canvas, 53¼" × 25½". Collection, The Museum of Modern Art, New York. Purchase.*

adopted by acclamation. Dada was an idea whose time had come, for it happened even earlier in New York with the arrival, in 1915, of Duchamp (due-SHAWM). Duchamp was the greatest exponent of the "anti-art" movement known as Dada, having already turned "found" objects into art by, for example, hanging a snow

Figure 28.23 *Marcel Duchamp,* The Bride Stripped Bare by Her Bachelors, Even, *1915–1923. Oil, lead wire and foil, and dust and varnish on plate glass (in two parts), 9′1¼″ × 5′9⅛″. Philadelphia Museum of Art. Bequest of Katherine S. Dreier.*

Figure 28.24 *Kurt Schwitters,* Sichtbar, *1923. Collage, ca. 7″ × 5″. Estate of Kurt Schwitters. Photo: Marlborough Gallery, New York.*

shovel on a gallery wall and labeling it *In Advance of a Broken Arm*. He made the first mobile in 1913 by fastening an inverted bicycle wheel to the top of a stool and presenting it as a sculpture with moving parts. Typical of his assault on the citadel of art was a reproduction of the *Mona Lisa* to which he added a mustache and a goatee and the title of *L.H.O.O.Q.,* which when pronounced letter by letter in French means "She's got a hot ass."

Duchamp found a congenial home in Stieglitz's "291" and began work on his Dada masterpiece enigmatically titled *The Bride Stripped Bare by Her Bachelors, Even,* more commonly referred to as *The Large Glass* (figure 28.23). The following analysis is based on Duchamp's notes, which given the artist's proclivity for paradox and irony, may be accepted, modified, or rejected. According to Duchamp, this is the story of a bride, located in the upper section and symbolized by an internal combustion engine with a reservoir of love gasoline and a magneto of desire. She is

lusted after by the nine bachelors in the left lower section: the reddish-brown molds resembling chessmen. Each bachelor is a stereotype of what were, at the time, masculine occupations: priest, delivery boy, policeman, warrior, gendarme, undertaker's assistant, busboy, stationmaster, and flunky. Capillary tubes carry gas from each bachelor mold to the center of the glass and to one of seven funnels, where the gas solidifies into large needles. These needles, in turn, break into spangles of frosty gas and then into liquid drops of semen that splash into the bride's domain. At the moment depicted in the glass the bride is stripped but she remains undefiled; bride and bachelors are caught between desire and possession/surrender. Duchamp intended the work to be humorous and sexual, satirizing machines, people, and social conventions. He succeeded on all counts.

Kurt Schwitters, 1887–1948

The leading German Dadaist, Schwitters collected trash from wastebaskets and gutters to compose collages of the detritus of civilization. When once asked what art was, Schwitters responded with, "What isn't?" *Sichtbar* (figure 28.24), meaning "visible," proves that an artist can arrange the unlikeliest materials into a meaningful statement. Like so many of his constructions, this work visualizes the modern city as a compressor and energizer of life, constantly changing, leaving behind the rubbish of yesterday.

Figure 28.25 *Joan Miró,* Person Throwing Stone at a Bird, *1926. Oil on canvas, 36¼" × 29". Collection, The Museum of Modern Art, New York. Purchase.*

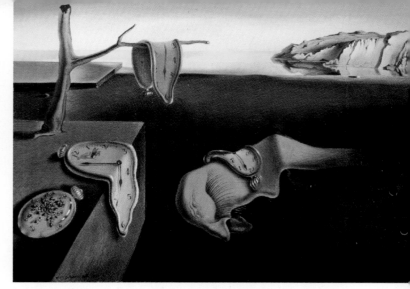

Figure 28.26 *Salvador Dali,* The Persistence of Memory, *1931. Oil on canvas, 9½" × 13". Collection, The Museum of Modern Art, New York. Given anonymously.*

Surrealism

Though Schwitters continued to collect and arrange his Dada collages, completely filling several three-story houses in the process, the movement was generally absorbed by the surrealists, who coalesced around the Manifesto of Surrealism issued in 1924 by the writer André Breton, a disciple of Sigmund Freud. Surrealism in art is, briefly stated, the theory that dreams, and those waking moments when subconscious images overwhelm our intellect, furnish us with material far more relevant to our lives than traditional subject matter. The world of psychic experience, as explored by Freud and others, was to be combined with consciousness to create a superreality called surrealism.

Joan Miró, 1893–1983

Surrealism was an organized movement in revolt against conventional art and society, but there was no single style. Artists such as Miró (ME-row) drew on their personal dream world. In *Person Throwing a Stone at a Bird* (figure 28.25) Miró does not abstract the human image but seems, instead, to humanize abstractions. In a witty and humorous style, sometimes called biomorphic abstraction, he creates an amoebic person with one huge foot, bulbous body, and orange and yellow eye. This being seems to fall back in wonder as an oblong stone falls in a delineated trajectory toward an appealing bird with a crescent torso from which a long-line neck projects to a lavender head topped by a flaming cock's comb. This is superreality. "Everything in my pictures exists," stated Miró; "there is nothing abstract in my pictures."

Salvador Dali, 1904–1989

The self-appointed spokesman of the movement, Dali (DAH-lee) stressed paradox, disease, decay, and eroticism. *The Persistence of Memory* (figure 28.26) is a tiny painting of a vast landscape in which watches hang limply and dejectedly. A strange chinless creature with protruding tongue (alive? dead?) lies in the foreground of a Renaissance perspective construction lit by an eerie

Figure 28.27 *Meret Oppenheim,* Object. *1936. Fur-covered cup, saucer, and spoon; cup, 4⅜" diameter; saucer, 9⅜" diameter; spoon, 8" long; overall ht. 2⅞". Collection, The Museum of Modern Art, New York. Purchase.*

glow. A dead tree grows out of a table (?) on which the only flat watch lies, a metal timepiece infested with sinister-looking bugs. Anything is possible in dreams.

Meret Oppenheim, 1913–1985

Startling distortions or juxtapositions are basic to surrealism as Oppenheim's surrealistic *Object* (figure 28.27) demonstrates. The absurdity of a fur-lined teacup has become a symbol of surrealism. Her now familiar but bizarre ensemble is typical of the push-pull effect of many surrealist works. Our intellect is titillated, but our senses of touch and taste are outraged.

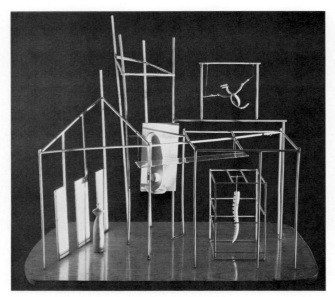

Figure 28.28 *Alberto Giacometti,* The Palace at 4 A.M., *1932–1933. Wood, glass, wire, and string, 25" × 28" × 15¾". Collection, The Museum of Modern Art, New York. Purchase.*

Figure 28.29 *René Magritte,* The False Mirror, *1928. Oil on canvas, 21¼" × 31⅞". Collection, The Museum of Modern Art, New York. Purchase.*

Figure 28.30 *John Sloan,* Roof Gossips, *ca. 1912. Oil on canvas, 24" × 20". The University Art Collections, Arizona State University, Tempe. Gift of Oliver B. James.*

Alberto Giacometti, 1901–1966

Except for one artist there has been little significant surrealist sculpture. Surrealists believed in automatism, in just letting a painting happen, and shaping solid objects is too painstaking an endeavor to be directed by the subconscious. Only Giacometti (zhak-ko-MET-ti) succeeded in creating three-dimensional equivalents of surrealist pictures. *The Palace at 4 A.M.* (figure 28.28) is an airy cage with a skeletal backbone in a smaller cage at the right and the figure of a woman on the left, the latter possibly representing the artist's mother. In the center is a spoon shape with which the artist said he identified and, at the upper right, the skeleton of a prehistoric bird that supposedly greets the dawn at 4 A.M. A dreamlike mystery is all pervasive.

René Magritte, 1898–1967

Belgian surrealist Magritte was a witty, even mischievous painter who consistently questioned the nature of reality by representing ordinary images in a strange and extraordinary manner. *The False Mirror* (figure 28.29) portrays a huge but recognizable human eye with an iris of fluffy clouds in a blue sky. Are we looking into someone's eye while viewing the world from within that other organ? Or?

Realism in America: The Ash Can School

From the early days of the Republic there has always been a strain of realism on the American scene, a tradition separate from European realists such as Courbet and Millet. While European artists were experimenting with impressionism, Americans such as Winslow Homer and Thomas Eakins (see figures 25.20 and 25.21) continued to paint reality as they perceived it.

At the beginning of this century Robert Henri (hen-RYE; 1865–1929) founded a new school of realism called The Eight. Working almost entirely in New York, the followers of Henri painted city scenes of tenement life and everyday activities, mainly of the working class. A derogatory remark by a critic gave still another new style a label. After the caustic comment that they "even painted ash cans," The Eight proudly bore the label of Ash Can school.

John Sloan, 1871–1951

Sloan painted *Roof Gossips* (figure 28.30) as if the three women on the tenement roof were the subject of a casual snapshot. Actually, the work is an artful composition of lines and forms. Reminiscent of the high viewpoint of Mary Cassatt's *The Bath* (see figure 25.31), we witness an intimate and relaxed scene but are

Figure 28.31 *Edward Hopper,* House by the Railroad, *1925. Oil on canvas, 24" × 29". Collection, The Museum of Modern Art, New York. Given anonymously.*

Figure 28.32 *Diego Rivera,* The Liberation of the Peon, *1931. Fresco, 74" × 95". The Philadelphia Museum of Art. Gift of Mr. and Mrs. Herbert Cameron Morris.*

Figure 28.33 *José Òrozco,* Zapatistas, *1931. Oil on canvas, 45" × 55". Collection, Museum of Modern Art, New York. Given anonymously.*

not a part of it. Academicians were critical of the gritty realism of Sloan and the Ash Can school but did join with them and the avant-garde of "291" to present the Armory Show the year after this work was painted.

Edward Hopper, 1882–1967

A student of Henri's in the early 1900s, Hopper was more concerned with formal design than were his Ash Can colleagues. He did not paint people in everyday life but sought such subjects as old houses and buildings along the coast of Maine. His *House by the Railroad* (figure 28.31) has a typical horizontal base (the railroad tracks in this case) from which the rising verticals and slanting diagonals outline a house "with sunlight on the side" as Hopper preferred to paint. The broad, uncluttered planes, sunlight, and shadows give the house a brooding air of loneliness and melancholy.

Mexican Social Realists

Diego Rivera, 1886–1957

Though he lived and studied in Europe for many years, Rivera disavowed modernism in his zeal to create a distinctly Mexican style in the socialist spirit of the protracted Mexican revolution (1910–1940). Rivera's statements were usually political and consistently on the side of the peons of the vast Mexican underclass. In *The Liberation of the Peon* (figure 28.32) he shows revolutionary soldiers tenderly wrapping the body of a peon who has been tortured and then murdered. The victim's bound hands are being "liberated," echoing the only liberation that a peasant could expect: death that freed him from a life of grinding poverty and ceaseless toil.

José Clemente Òrozco, 1883–1949

Òrozco was even more strongly influenced by Mexican Indian traditions than was Rivera, perhaps because he received much of his training in Mexico City. Like Rivera, his teacher and collaborator, he was deeply committed to the Revolution. His *Zapatistas* (figure 28.33) is a prime example of the painterly illusion of rhythm. Moving from right to left, the Zapatistas set up a kind of beat in a pattern of continuous movement that symbolizes the

Figure 28.34 *David Alfaro Siqueiros,* Echo of a Scream, *1937. Enamel on wood, 48" × 36". Collection, The Museum of Modern Art, New York. Gift of Edward M. M. Warburg.*

Figure 28.35 *Antonio Gaudi, Church of the Holy Family, 1883– 1926. Barcelona. SEF/Art Resource.*

ongoing Revolution. Along with Pancho Villa, Emiliano Zapata (ca. 1879–1919) was one of the leaders of the Revolution; the representation here is of some of his loyal Indian followers.

David Alfaro Siqueiros, 1896–1974

Siqueiros (see-KEER-ohs) was the most politically active artist, having served a prison term for his leftist views. Though his early painting was heavy on Marxist ideology, his later work is directed more to humanistic concerns and universal problems. His *Echo of a Scream* (figure 28.34) is a dramatic protest against the insanity of war. Set in the midst of a wasteland of debris, the enlarged head of the screaming child is the overwhelming center of attention. Forced to concentrate on the child's agonized face, we are confronted with the artist's passionate indictment of the madness called war. Edvard Munch's *The Scream* (see figure 25.45) expressed the artist's reaction to critical tensions of the modern world: alienation, desperation, terror. In his painting Siqueiros has particularized the tensions into a single issue, an antiwar statement that, ironically, appeared just two years before Hitler invaded Poland to launch World War II.

Architecture

Art Nouveau

Art nouveau was a turn-of-the-century style that grew out of an English Arts and Crafts movement to revive medieval craftsmanship. Determined to raise interior and decorative design to the eminence enjoyed by painting and sculpture, art nouveau artists and craftsmen developed an elaborate curvilinear style that assiduously avoided straight lines and right angles. Line drawings by Aubrey Beardsley (1872–1898) and multicolored lamps by Louis Comfort Tiffany (1848–1933) were art nouveau, as was the basic style of the Spanish architect Antonio Gaudi (gow-D; 1852–1926). In his Church of the Holy Family (figure 28.35) Gaudi went beyond the art nouveau style to architectural innovations never seen before or since. Working with a church already started as a Gothic revival structure, Gaudi added four bottle-shaped spires pierced by innumerable holes and topped by glittering crystal decorations. Although the enormous building is primarily of cut stone, it looks eroded and desiccated, organic rather than constructed. Much of the exterior is studded with bright ceramic decorations, with more scheduled to be added if and when the building is completed.

Figure 28.36 *Walter Gropius, Workshop of the Bauhaus, 1925–1926. Dessau, Germany. Photo: Marburg/Art Resource.*

Figure 28.37 *Le Corbusier, Villa Savoye, 1929. Poissy-sur-Seine, France. Photo: Lucien Hervé, Paris.*

The International Style

Walter Gropius, 1883–1969

Art nouveau tried, unsuccessfully, to deny the Industrial Age but the work of the design school called Bauhaus (BOUGH-house) exploited modern technology. As director of Bauhaus, Gropius promoted instruction in painting, sculpture, architecture, and the crafts, with everything oriented toward the latest in technology and industrial design. As he wrote in 1919: "The separate arts must be brought back into intimate contact, under the wings of a great architecture." The workshop (figure 28.36) is a four-story box with an interior steel skeleton enclosed by window walls of glass, the latter a Gropius invention. The design established the principles of the International Style that was to dominate architectural design into the 1970s. Expensive to heat and to cool, not to mention washing the windows, many International Style buildings appear as anomalies in the energy-conscious 1990s. For half a century, however, they were the essence of modernity.

Le Corbusier (Charles-Edouard Jeanneret), 1887–1965

The International Style was brilliantly developed by the Swiss painter-architect Le Corbusier (luh core-BOOS-iay). For Le Corbusier, houses were "machines for living," as efficient as airplanes were for flying. Totally devoid of ornament, his Villa Savoye (figure

Figure 28.38 *Frank Lloyd Wright, Kaufmann House ("Falling Water"), 1936. Bear Run, Pennsylvania. Photo: Art Resource, N.Y.*

28.37) is partially supported by the slender columns but rests mostly on a recessed unit containing service functions, servants quarters, entrance hall, and staircase to the living quarters on the second level. The living room is separated from an open interior terrace by floor-to-ceiling panes of glass, making the terrace a basic part of living arrangements.

Organic Architecture

Frank Lloyd Wright, 1867–1959

International Style buildings are, in effect, disdainful of their environment, thrusting away from the earth to create their own internal space. America's greatest architect disagreed totally with this concept. Wright's buildings are generally organic, seemingly a natural consequence of their environment. One of his most imaginative designs is the *Kaufmann House* (figure 28.38). Built on a site that would challenge any architect and that obviously inspired Wright, the house is situated on a steep and rocky hillside over a waterfall. Combining native rock construction with daring cantilevers colored beige to blend with the environment, the structure cannot even be imagined on any other site. The Villa Savoye and Falling Water represent, between them, opposite theories of modern design; subsequent developments tended to fall somewhere between the two extremes.

Artistic Styles Since 1945

Action Painting: Abstract Expressionism

Jackson Pollock, 1912–1956

The new style of abstract expressionism developed in New York, which, after World War II, replaced Paris as the artistic capital of the Western world. Once a social realist in the manner of Rivera, Pollock became the acknowledged leader of the new movement.

Figure 28.39 *Jackson Pollock,* Number 1, *1948. Oil and enamel on unprimed canvas, 68" × 8'8". Collection, The Museum of Modern Art, New York. Purchase.*

His personal style of abstract expressionism began to bloom when he quit easel painting and, instead, tacked a large, unstretched canvas to the floor. Walking all around the canvas he became completely absorbed as he dropped, dripped, poured, and spattered paint on the canvas. Though he had no preconceived ideas when he began a canvas he could, as he said, "control the flow of the paint," and he did complete works with brushstrokes as needed. His *Number 1* (figure 28.39) is an intricate and complex interplay of curvilinear lines and controlled spatters illustrating, as he remarked, "energy made visible." Pollock's energetic involvement in the act of painting led to the term *action painting* as a general descriptor of the movement.

Willem de Kooning, b. 1904
The Dutch-American artist Willem de Kooning works in violent motions using a large brush heavy with paint. His favorite theme is that of the eternal woman: earth mother and goddess of fertility. *Woman I* (figure 28.40) is a giant, earthy figure of a woman painted in slashing brushstrokes. An energetic portrayal of a goddess-cum-movie queen and sex symbol, this is one man's view of the other half of the human race.

Mark Rothko, 1903–1970
In his mature style Rothko covered large canvases with luminous, softly bleeding rectangles of color. *Number 10* (figure 28.41) is an extremely subtle combination of softly glowing colors separated by ragged, foggy edges. Compared with the dynamics of Pollock and de Kooning, this is abstract expressionism in a gentle and meditative mood in a style frequently called *color field.*

Figure 28.40 *Willem de Kooning,* Woman I, *1950–1952. Oil on canvas, 75⅞" × 58". Collection, The Museum of Modern Art, New York. Purchase.*

Reaction against Action: Pop Art
The emotional fervor of abstract expressionism burned itself out in about fifteen years, to be superseded by a Dada-type reaction. The self-confidence of America after World War II had been jolted by the Korean conflict, the Cold War, and the buildup in Vietnam. A new breed of artists was skeptical of American accomplishments and chose the banalities of American life to satirize the superficiality of American culture. First called neo-Dadaists, these artists used recognizable subject matter from American popular culture: soup cans, comic strips, road signs, and cult figures from rock music and commercial Hollywood movies.

Pop art was the label applied to what seemed to be a uniquely American reaction to the numbing vulgarity of much of popular culture. Actually, the label and the movement had surfaced in England in the mid 1950s. English images tended, however, to be romantic and sentimental commentaries on popular idols, comic strips, and American movies; American reactions were much more aggressive, perhaps because the media hype was so blatant and all-pervasive.

Figure 28.41 *Mark Rothko,* Number 10, *1950. Oil on canvas, 90⅜"* × 57⅛". *Collection, The Museum of Modern Art, New York. Gift of Philip Johnson.*

Figure 28.42 *Robert Rauschenberg,* Monogram, *1959. Construction, 48" × 72" × 72". Moderna Museet, Stockholm, Sweden. © Robert Rauschenberg/VAGA, New York, 1991. Photo: Scala/Art Resource, N.Y.*

Figure 28.43 *Roy Lichtenstein,* Drowning Girl, *1963. Oil and synthetic polymer paint on canvas, 67⅝" × 66¾". Collection, The Museum of Modern Art, New York. Philip Johnson Fund and gift of Mr. and Mrs. Bagley Wright.*

Robert Rauschenberg, b. 1925

The movement burst on the American scene in 1962, but Rauschenberg had been working his way from abstract expressionism to pop art since the mid 1950s. In his *Monogram* (figure 28.42) he combined an old tire, a stuffed Angora goat, and pieces of stenciled signs into a wry and witty commentary on American life. The goat and tire were once waste that has been recycled, so to speak. Paradoxically, they are still distasteful objects, retaining their identity and creating a tension between themselves and the total work. They should not be there but they are, undeniably there, forever and ever. Rauschenberg has stated that painting is related to art and to life and that his function is to "act in the gap between the two."

Roy Lichtenstein, b. 1923

Rauschenberg generally retains the painterly quality of abstract expressionism, but Lichtenstein adopted the mechanical techniques and imagery of comic strips, including the Benday dots used in newspaper reproductions of the comics. He also used the hard lines of comic strips but his paintings are monumental in scale. His cold and impersonal portrayal of a *Drowning Girl* (figure 28.43) is an indictment of the casual and callous attitudes of many Americans toward violence in comic strips, in the streets, in the Middle East. The technique is that of the "low art" of the comics,

but the result is a potent artistic statement. Lichtenstein, for obvious reasons, selected nothing from such comic strips as *Peanuts* or *Doonesbury.*

Edward Kienholz, b. 1927

The sculptures of Kienholz have been called pop, but his work is also expressionistic and surreal. He combines painting, sculpture, collage, and the stage to depict some of the shabbiness, stu-

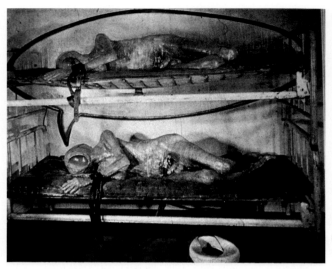

Figure 28.44 *Edward Kienholz,* The State Hospital, *1966. Mixed media, 8' × 12' × 10'. Moderna Museet, Stockholm. (© Edward Kienholz.)*

pidity, and cruelty of modern urban life. In *The State Hospital* (figure 28.44) he confronts us with an elderly patient—someone's father, someone's grandfather—who has been chained to a cot in a state facility. In the upper cot, encased in what appears to be a comic strip balloon, is the same figure, possibly representing the patient's vision of himself: chained, caged, and abandoned. Is this how life should end?

Marisol, b. 1930

Marisol's work is lighter in spirit than that of Kienholz but with oblique social commentaries that are sophisticated, witty, ironic, and often sardonic. A Venezuelan born in Paris and living in the United States, Marisol (Escobar is her unused surname) creates her own world with assemblages of wood, plaster, paint, and assorted objects. In *Women and Dog* (figure 28.45) she uses painting, drawing, stencil, relief, collage, carving, and assemblage to present this somewhat cubistic and surrealistic tableau. As is her custom, all the faces are of Marisol herself, giving the scene an introspective dimension. She has created a world without men in which the feminine gender is the self-contained reality. (We may safely assume that the dog is female.) Rather than an antimale work, this is an assemblage of self-reliant, independent females.

Color, Geometry, and Optics

Josef Albers, 1888–1976

One of the first graduates of the Bauhaus, Albers emigrated from Nazi Germany in 1933 to the United States, where his work influenced the development of abstract geometric painting and op art. His *Homage to the Square* paintings were a serialization similar to Monet's paintings of haystacks and lily ponds, a process, not a

Figure 28.45 *Marisol,* Women and Dog, *1964. Wood, plaster, synthetic polymer and miscellaneous items, 72" × 82" × 16". Courtesy Collection of the Whitney Museum of American Art. Gift of the Friends of the Whitney Museum of American Art.*

solution. Working with three or four squares of different colors, Albers explored, in hundreds of paintings, the interaction of colors and straight lines. *Homage to the Square: Star Blue* (figure 28.46) has an intensity based not on the squares themselves but on the relationship of the colors.

Helen Frankenthaler, b. 1928

Working against the currents of abstract expressionism and geometric abstraction, Frankenthaler stained the raw canvas to achieve a limpid freshness unlike the work of any other artist. In *Interior Landscape* (figure 28.47) the paint is applied in thin washes so integrated with the canvas that there is no illusion of either foreground or background. Like Pollock, she creates an open composition out of abstract shapes that she manipulates into patterns of color. In this sense she is an action painter. She begins with no preconceived idea; rather, the painting evolves as she interacts with her washes and the canvas. In another sense she is a color-field artist, in that she creates abstract landscapes of color that can be interpreted many different ways.

Louise Nevelson, 1900–1988

The assemblage of sculptures of Nevelson reflects the geometric forms of pre-Columbian sculpture, but her overriding interest in

Figure 28.46 *Josef Albers,* Homage to the Square: Star Blue, *1953. Oil on board, 29⅞" × 29⅞". Contemporary Collection of the Cleveland Museum of Art.*

working with wood can be traced to her father's career as a cabinetmaker and her involvement with the wood in his shop. *Illumination—Dark* (figure 28.48) is a large wooden wall on which the artist has arranged selected pieces of wood culled from old houses to form a three-dimensional geometric abstraction. With bronze-painted shapes against the flat black background of the wall, the piece resembles both a cupboard and a cityscape like the artist's native New York. As Nevelson has said, she "putters endlessly" with the design until she gets it right. The result here is a subtle blend of delicacy, mystery, and strength.

Bridget Riley, b. 1931

American painters such as Albers were concerned with straight lines, but British artist Riley worked with the possibilities inherent in curved lines. *Current* (figure 28.49) is a terse composition that communicates directly with the eye and the optic nerve. Though she has been called an op artist (from optical art), Riley's style goes beyond merely confusing or tricking the eye. What we have here is a new way of perceiving and experiencing motion.

Fantasy and Expressionism

Jean Dubuffet, 1901–1985

Dubuffet (due-boo-FAY), the most notable French artist since World War II, found his inspiration in strangely different areas: art of the insane, children's art, and graffiti. Dubuffet painted intuitively, somewhat like the abstract expressionists, but his subjects were fantastic figures and landscapes. He combined pigments

Figure 28.47 *Helen Frankenthaler,* Interior Landscape, *1964. Acrylic on canvas, 104⅞" × 92⅝". San Francisco Museum of Modern Art. Gift of the Women's Board.*

with different mixtures of plaster, sand, or twigs to make a thick impasto that he scratched and scored to make grotesque figures like his *Portrait of Henri Michaux* (figure 28.50). The artist referred to this style as *art brut,* which can be translated as brutal art or ugly art; both are apropos. Whatever the label, this attack on conventional artistic standards, even in the twentieth century, has a powerful primordial quality that both attracts and repels.

Francis Bacon, b. 1909

The Irish-born Bacon paints tormented visions distorted to the point of insanity. Preoccupied with deformity and disease, he selects works by Old Masters and restates them as anguished symbols of contemporary life. *Number VII from Eight Studies for a Portrait* (figure 28.51) is based on the portrait of Pope Innocent X (1644–1655) by Velasquez, who depicted the pope as a powerful, intelligent, and coolly confident pontiff. Bacon uses Renaissance perspective but places the pope in an isolation booth where his anguished screams tear his head asunder.

Figure 28.48 *Louise Nevelson,* Illumination—Dark, *1961. Wood and bronze reliefs, 10'5" × 9'4" × 5"deep. Collection of Whitney Museum of American Art, New York, Gift of the artist dedicated to the Whitney Museum of American Art.*

Figure 28.49 *Bridget Riley,* Current, *1964. Synthetic polymer paint on composition board, 58⅞" × 53⅜". Collection, The Museum of Modern Art, New York. Philip Johnson Fund.*

Figure 28.50 *Jean Dubuffet,* Portrait of Henri Michaux, *from the* More Beautiful Than They Think: Portrait Series. *1947. Oil and other substances on canvas, 51½" × 38⅜". Collection, The Museum of Modern Art, New York, The Sidney and Harriet Janis Collection.*

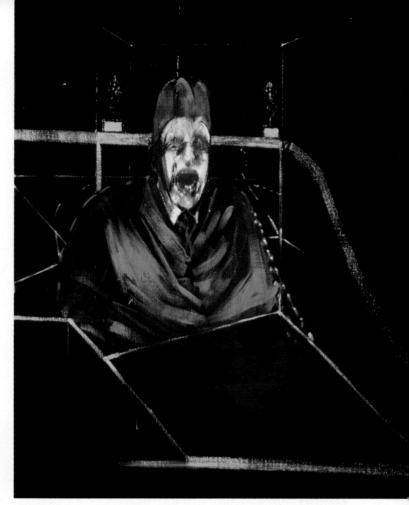

Figure 28.51 *Francis Bacon,* Number VII from Eight Studies for a Portrait, *1953. Oil on linen, 60" × 46⅛". Collection, The Museum of Modern Art, New York. Gift of Mr. and Mrs. William A. M. Burden.*

Rufino Tamayo, b. 1899

Tamayo (ta-MY-oh) follows a tradition more Mexican than Spanish in which he synthesizes Mexican primitivism with his own unique brand of sophisticated fantasy. Rejecting the revolutionary dogma of the Mexican muralists, he seeks a more personal and universal expression of his time and his country. His *Man* (figure 28.52) is a huge vision in which an angular figure representing all human-kind struggles upward toward gleaming comets and stars. Possibly representing some earthbound evil, a strange-looking dog is crouched at the lower left, eyeing a bone. The dynamic thrust of the central image suggests a powerful move away from earth to reach for the stars, possibly symbolizing human aspirations for higher values.

Fritz Scholder, b. 1937

The best-known native American artist, Scholder shows the influence of expressionism and pop art, but his subject matter sets him apart from both styles. Scholder uses serialism to portray the paradoxical position of native Americans in American life. With a poignant irony he has depicted stereotypes: a Super Chief eating an ice cream cone; a drunken Indian clutching a can of beer like a tomahawk; a Hollywood Indian and his captive Anglo maiden.

Figure 28.52 *Rufino Tamayo,* Man, *1953. Vinyl with pigment on masonite, 18' × 10'6". Dallas Museum of Art, Dallas, Texas. Dallas Art Association Commission, Neiman-Marcus Company Exposition Funds.*

Figure 28.53 *Fritz Scholder,* Waiting Indian No. 4, *1970. Oil on canvas, 70" × 64". The University Art Collections, Arizona State University, Tempe.*

Figure 28.54 *Alexander Calder,* Many Pierced Discs, *65" × 49". The University Art Collections, Arizona State University, Tempe.*

Scholder's work is satirical and searching, depicting the basic nobility and the degradation of his people. *Waiting Indian No. 4* (figure 28.53) stands majestically in a barren landscape. In his awesome dignity he refuses to accept any part of a stereotype in the Anglo world.

Alexander Calder, 1898–1976

For centuries sculptors have labored to give their works the illusion of movement. Calder invented abstract works that actually moved. Influenced by surrealism and geometric abstractions, Calder created the true mobile. *Many Pierced Discs* (figure 28.54) is a fantasy of abstract shapes wired together and delicately balanced so that it can respond to the slightest breeze. An indoor

Figure 28.55 *Mark di Suvero,* Side Frames, *1979. Steel, 24' long × 12' wide × 16' high. Courtesy of ConStruct, Chicago.*

Figure 28.56 *Henry Moore,* Family Group, *1948–1949. Bronze (cast 1950), 59¼" × 46½", at base 45" × 29⅞". Collection, The Museum of Modern Art, New York. A Conger Goodyear Fund.*

rather than an outdoor mobile that is activated by the wind, this work rests on its pedestal in an art gallery where it can gently gyrate and bow to museum visitors.

Mark di Suvero, b. 1933

Di Suvero's *Side Frames* (figure 28.55) is a giant outdoor mobile, an abstract fantasy on a grand scale. A large pendant is held, seemingly tenuously, by a cable attached to a long balanced beam. Despite the work's monumental size the pendant is completely free to sway or twist in the wind. Di Suvero's works are energy structures, metallic lyrics of action and reaction.

Henry Moore, 1898–1986

Moore was the most important English artist of his time in any medium. Like Calder, he was influenced by surrealism but went on to develop his unique abstract figural style. In *Family Group* (figure 28.56) the figures are recognizable but abstracted into curving, rather primitive shapes that emphasize the unity and stability of a family.

Minimal Art

Tony DeLap, b. 1927

Minimal art began in the 1960s as a movement to reduce art to basics: one shape or one color or one idea. Also called primary structures or primary art, the style is easier to observe than to discuss. *Sentaro* (figure 28.57) by DeLap is a sculpture/painting reduced to a basic shape and a single color. This is a beautiful hunk of a bright red rectangular box that seemingly floats within its

Figure 28.57 *Tony DeLap,* Sentaro, *1967. Aluminum, wood, plexiglass, and lacquer, 16" × 16" × 5"deep. American Art Heritage Fund. Arizona State University Art Collections, Tempe.*

Figure 28.58 *David Smith,* Cubi XV. *Steel, 10'5⅛" × 4'10½". The San Diego Museum of Art, San Diego, California.*

Figure 28.59 *Ronald Bladen,* X, *1967. Wood, 22'8" × 24'6". Fishback Gallery, New York.*

plastic case. DeLap used commercial staining and spraying techniques so that the saturated painting/sculpture is a solid color field with no trace of brushwork or other manipulation by the artist. The vitality and spontaneity of abstract expressionism has given way to a laidback restraint comparable to Cool Jazz (see chapter 29).

David Smith, 1906–1965

American sculptor Smith applied his experience of working in an automotive plant and locomotive factory to sculpting with steel which, as he said, "had little art history." His *Cubi XV* (figure 28.58) is a gravity-defying combination of simple geometric components that set up a lively interplay of forms and space. The stainless steel is highly polished, with controlled light patterns that make the metal surface as sensual as works by Brancusi (see figure 28.19) or Verrocchio (see figure 17.16).

Ronald Bladen, b. 1918

For an exhibition in Washington's Corcoran Gallery, Bladen created a giant *X* of painted wood (figure 28.59) that virtually filled a classical two-story hall. The spectator can walk not only around the sculpture but through it as well. Large-scale minimalist works such as this offer valid alternatives to representational public monuments, which, more often than not, are forgettable clichés. The understated elegance and enormous power of the Vietnam War Memorial is a case in point.

Varieties of Realism

Though never absent from the American scene, realism has again become a major factor in a variety of styles called New Realism, Magic Realism, or Photorealism. The sculptor Duane Hanson (b. 1925) makes casts of living people and paints the resulting figures to look completely lifelike, including real clothing and accessories. Richard Estes (b. 1936) projects a slide directly on canvas and makes a precise copy with an airbrush. Hanson selects such subjects as gaudily dressed tourists, junkies, and overweight shoppers, whereas Estes paints banal cityscapes totally devoid of people.

Audrey Flack, b. 1931

In their subject matter Hanson and Estes follow the orientation of pop art, but photorealism can pursue other paths in, for example, the work of Flack, the first photorealist to have a painting

Figure 28.60 *Audrey Flack,* World War II, April 1945, *1976–1977. Acrylic and oil on canvas, 8' × 8', incorporating a portion of the Margaret Bourke-White photograph "Buchenwald, 1945" copyright Time, Inc. Photograph courtesy Louis K. Meisel Gallery.*

Figure 28.61 *Otto Duecker,* Russell, Terry, J. T., and a Levi Jacket, *1979. Oil on masonite cutouts. The Elaine Horwitch Galleries, Scottsdale, Arizona.*

purchased by the Museum of Modern Art. Like others in the movement, she projects color slides onto a canvas and paints with an air brush. Her subject matter, however, is a kind of collage, a still-life arrangement that conveys a specific idea or message. *World War II, April 1945* (figure 28.60) refers to the liberation of the Nazi concentration camp at Buchenwald. Flack's painting, based on Margaret Bourke-White's famous photo, is a tribute to the survivors of the death camps and a memorial to the twelve million (including six million Jews) who perished there. The rose, burning candle, pear, watch, butterfly, and black border are all symbols of mortality or for commemorating the dead. The printed statement is a rabbinical quotation affirming belief in God and concluding: "You can take everything from me—the pillow from under my head, my house—but you cannot take God from my heart." The cakes apparently reflect the infamous remark attributed to Marie Antoinette; when told that the people had no bread her reputed response was, "Let them eat cake." The various objects are so much larger than life size that they appear not to be "real." The basic reality is, of course, the haunted faces of the survivors of Buchenwald.

Otto Duecker, b. 1948

Our society has apparently learned to accept many real/unreal mystifications of the everyday world such as, for example, twelve-foot cowboys on a giant movie screen or six-inch football players

on television. Indeed, when Duecker paints larger-than-life figures, cuts them out, and arranges them in galleries, homes, and warehouses, we are inclined to accept them as "real." In *Russell, Terry, J. T., and a Levi Jacket* (figure 28.61) we see the artist posed in front of his four cutouts and appearing, in this photograph, somehow less real than his creations.

If each generation develops its own concepts of reality, then what is real now? For the present century—sometimes called the Age of Uncertainty—it might be more accurate to say that several concepts of reality are acceptable or, possibly, tolerable, given the scientific realities of relativity, quantum theory, and the science of chaos.

Environmental Art

There are two basic kinds of environmental art: art that creates an artificial environment that one can enter and art that alters the natural or constructed environment. The latter type will be considered here in the work of two notable artists.

Robert Smithson, 1938–1973

Smithson chose Rozel Point in the Great Salt Lake for his *Spiral Jetty* (figure 28.62) because it was remote and because the water contained algae that colored it pink. The spiral design was sug-

Figure 28.62 *Robert Smithson,* Spiral Jetty, *1970. Rock, salt crystals, earth, algae, coil, 1500'. Great Salt Lake, Utah. John Weber Gallery, New York. Photograph by Gianfranco Gorgoni.*

gested, according to the artist, by the intense light radiating from the pinkish water. A dedicated environmentalist with a special interest in land reclamation, Smithson was always intent on integrating his works with their natural setting. This was particularly successful with *Spiral Jetty* because the work and the environment have indeed become accepted as one. Tragically, this was one of the artist's last works; he was killed in a plane crash while scouting a new site.

Christo (Christo Javacheff), b. 1935

The Bulgarian-American artist has wrapped sheets of plastic around everything from a woman, bicycles, and a machine to a skyscraper, a bridge in Paris, and 1,000,000 square feet of Australian coastline. Christo's most successful and best-known work is probably his *Running Fence* (figure 28.63). Laid across the rolling countryside north of San Francisco, the fence celebrated the landscape in a manner somehow comparable to the work of landscape painters. Running from a major highway down to the Pacific Ocean, the fence was in place for two weeks during September 1976. Though viewed by many, thousands more became aware of the beauty of the countryside through the movie made of the project.

Though clearly environmental art, *Running Fence* also qualifies as conceptual art for it originated in the mind of the artist, became a process as it assumed the shape of the artist's concept, and then disappeared from the site. (The movie is entirely different, of course, from the actual project.) Conceptualists claim that the final project is not as important as the idea of either the product or the process of constructing it. Not all of Christo's ideas have been as successful as *Running Fence* but maybe this was a superior idea.

Ethnic Arts

Contemporary artists of Hispanic or African heritages are just as involved with mainstream art as their colleagues; artists are, after all, contributing members of the international community of artists, more involved with breaking down national or ethnic barriers than erecting them. An overview of past and present developments by Hispanic and African-American artists is given here because American society has a history of barriers that excluded minorities from the mainstream of American life, barriers that, in effect, created a history of Hispanic and African-American art and artists. Moreover, when minority artists worked in prevailing styles, their art was frequently downgraded as "imitative." When their work expressed their ethnic heritage, it was all too often criticized because it did not conform to establishment attitudes about what art should be, a no-win situation that is finally largely in the past.

Hispanic Artists

There are no typical Hispanic (or Mexican American or Chicano) artists nor are there any styles that are clearly Hispanic. The most common attribute of Hispanic artists is that they, in general, live in the American Southwest in areas formerly belonging to Mexico. Some are influenced by the pre-Columbian past though others deny it. The European tradition that Spain brought to Mexico influences some artists and repels others. They are bilingual, their roots are in pre-Columbian times, followed by three centuries of Spanish rule and a century and a half of American culture. Their culture is complex, their tradition rich, and their search for identity as Americans is what much of their art, and culture, is all about.

The most important influences early in the century were those of Mexican muralists José Ôrozco (see figure 28.33) and

Figure 28.63 *Christo (Christo Jaracheff),* Running Fence, *1976; (left) charcoal, pastel, and pencil drawing on paper, 42" × 96"; (top) topographical map, 15" × 96"; (right) color photo, 28" × 39". Project for Sonoma and Marin Counties, California. The San Francisco Museum of Modern Art. Gift of Modern Art Council.*

Rufino Tamayo (see figure 28.52), both of whom executed major works while living in this country. Antonio García (b. 1901) and Porfirio Salinas (1912–1973) are leading artists of the first generation of Hispanic painters. Both are realists with García specializing in portraiture and Salinas in landscapes of his native Texas. In the second generation Edward Chávez (b. 1917) and Michael Ponce de León (b. 1922) have gained national prominence. Chávez is an abstractionist in the cubist mode, but de León is a printmaker who specializes in bas-relief prints. Influenced by pop art, Melesio Casas (b. 1929) has done a series of paintings based on movies and television advertising that he calls "Humanscapes." Sculptor Manuel Neri (b. 1930) is influenced by pre-Columbian art and Ôrozco and paints sculptures that he has hacked out of plaster. Ralph Ortiz (b. 1934) is a Destructive artist. For his Piano Destruction Concert, Ortiz attacks with an ax an upright piano that has plastic bags of animal blood suspended inside. The resulting mess of bloodstained keys, splinters, and strings is, according to Ortiz, an artistic realization of violence that symbolizes the violence and destruction of the real world. Luis Jimenez (b. 1940) creates polychromed sculptures made of epoxy and fiberglass. Influenced by pop art and popular culture, Jimenez's works are lusty, humorous, and charged with explosive energy, particularly works such as *Rodeo Queen* and *California Chick,* not to mention his show that he called *Texas Sweet Funk.*

African-American Artists

Joshua Johnson, 1765–1830

American artists of African ancestry have contributed to the arts in America since shortly after Jamestown was founded in 1607. Johnson was a celebrated artisan-painter, some of whose family portraits are in the National Gallery, though most have been retained by descendants of the original families. His *The Westwood Children* (figure 28.64) has a charming modern appeal with its artful asymmetrical arrangement of the children, the dog, and the tree outside. The children are dressed in identical outfits but each is distinguished by hair style, placement of the feet, and the held objects.

Robert S. Duncanson, 1817–1872

Influenced by the mysticism of the Hudson River School (see figure 25.11), Duncanson was recognized in his own time as an outstanding landscape painter. His *Blue Hole, Flood Waters, Little Miami River* (figure 28.65) is one of the finest works in the romantic style of the Hudson River tradition. Like much of Thomas Cole's work, the painting has a double scale; the fishermen have been made very tiny so that the enlarged landscape can totally dominate the composition. As stated before, Thomas Cole and others in this tradition regarded America as the new Garden of Eden with its magnificent landscapes towering over insignificant human beings.

Horace Pippin, 1888–1946

A notable artist in the manner of colonial artisan-painters, Pippin was a self-taught painter whose style can be described as modernized abstractions of folk art traditions. Unlike the French primitive Henri Rousseau, Pippin's work was acclaimed in his lifetime and acquired by major American museums. One of his most elegant works is *Victorian Interior* (figure 28.66). At first glance the painting appears closely related to simple folk art, but further study reveals a complex arrangement of strong color and selected areas of intricate linear designs. The end result is a happy medium between primitive folk art and modernism.

Figure 28.64 *Joshua Johnson,* The Westwood Children, *ca. 1807. Oil on canvas, 41⅛" × 46". Gift of Edgar William and Bernice Chrysler Garbisch, 1959. National Gallery of Art, Washington, D.C.*

Figure 28.65 *Robert S. Duncanson,* Blue Hole, Flood Waters, Little Miami River, *1851. Oil on canvas, 42¼" × 29¼". Cincinnati Art Museum.*

Jacob Lawrence, b. 1917

One of the most celebrated artists is Lawrence, who uses vigorous silhouetted patterns and narrative subject matter. Deeply committed to black history in America, Lawrence is perhaps best known for the series *The Migration of the Negro* (1940–1941) and his *Harlem* series of 1943. *Daybreak—A Time to Rest* (figure 28.67) is related, like much of his work, to the life of a black hero: Harriet Tubman, a famed conductor on the Underground Railway, in a children's book entitled *Harriet and the Promised Land,* which he illustrated. The work is balanced between a dream world and reality, an artful juxtaposition of identifiable images and abstractions. The huge feet are pointed north but even when traveling the route to freedom, there must be a time to rest and to dream of the promised land.

Other African-American Artists

Hale Woodruff's (1900–1980) most notable work is the three-panel series *The Amistad Murals* at Talladega College in Alabama. The subject is the 1839 revolt of Africans aboard the Spanish slave ship who, after seizing the ship, were captured by an American ship and tried in New Haven for mutiny. With the assistance of John Quincy Adams and other Abolitionists, the Africans were finally returned to their homeland.

Richmond Barthé (1901–1989) was one of the most prolific and successful American sculptors. Notable among his creations are the *African Dancer* and *The Blackberry Woman,* which were acquired by the Whitney Museum of American Art. Long a notable and influential art teacher at Howard University, Lois Maillol Jones (b. 1905) is an accomplished textile designer and painter of cityscapes and landscapes in the spirit of Cézanne. Particularly outstanding are her Haitian paintings and her *Africa* series of 1971.

Figure 28.66 *Horace Pippin,* Victorian Interior, *1946. Oil on canvas, 30" × 28¼". The Metropolitan Museum of Art, New York.*

Romare Bearden (1914–1988) began his career as a cartoonist. After studying with George Grosz (see figure 28.6) he developed a painting style based on cubist techniques. His mature works are powerful collages of the black experience, but genre art rather than propaganda. Juxtaposing African motifs and contemporary black figures, Bearden redefines the human image "in terms of the Negro experience I know best."

Figure 28.67 *Jacob Lawrence,* Daybreak—A Time to Rest, *1967. Tempera on masonite, 30″ × 24″. Gift of an anonymous donor, 1973. National Gallery of Art, Washington, D.C.*

377

Charles White (b. 1918), like Hale Woodruff and Jacob Lawrence, was employed during the Depression by the W.P.A. Art Project. In a style influenced by Mexican muralists Diego Rivera and David Siqueiros, White completed powerful murals such as *The Contribution of the Negro to American Democracy* (1943) at Hampton Institute. White later specialized in lithographs and charcoal and ink drawings because he felt that he could communicate better with his intended audience of African Americans.

Norma Morgan (b. 1928) divides her time between England and the United States, considering herself an artist born in America, and not necessarily a black artist. Noted for her "magic-realist" etchings and copper engravings, her *David in the Wilderness* is owned by the Museum of Modern Art. Morgan is considered a mainstream artist but there is a movement called *Blackstream* of which Benny Andrews (b. 1930) is a leading member. His *Trash* (1972) is a large and powerful work that attacks American junk culture while, at the same time, depicting Andrews' consistent theme that African-American artists are creating art as uniquely American as jazz.

Benny Andrews and other blackstream artists such as Milton Johnson, Joe Everstreet, Raymond Saunders, and Malcolm Bailey all depict the strength of black people under adverse conditions. Each of them has contributed to American art the vitality and uniqueness of the black experience, qualities that are not derived from European cultures. The current generation of black artists is, in effect, breaking down ethnic and national barriers just as an earlier generation of African Americans created jazz. First and foremost, they are artists successfully reinforcing the cultural pluralism that is the real strength of this complex nation.

Architecture: The International Style

Before World War II skyscraper designs were generally eclectic, clothing steel skeletons with older styles. The innovations of Louis Sullivan (1856–1924) and Frank Lloyd Wright were more influential in Europe than at home, and the International Style had yet to make much of an impression outside of Europe. Until the 1950s New York skyscrapers were circumscribed by the demands of clients and rigid zoning restrictions. Buildings were designed to occupy every square foot of expensive real estate but zoning ordinances required that some sunlight had to fall into manmade canyons. The result was the so-called ziggurat, a setback design with upper floors terraced back from the street.

Beginning an international Renaissance in architecture, the International Style appeared in New York with the design of the United Nations complex. Because modern buildings were so complicated most were designed by a group of architects and engineers. Wallace K. Harrison (1895–1981) headed an international team that designed the Secretariat Building (figure 28.68) in the shape of a giant slab, as suggested by Le Corbusier. Clothed on the sides in glass and on the ends in marble, the structure was the first American building to embody the Bauhaus tradition. Be-

Figure 28.68 *Wallace K. Harrison, Le Corbusier, and others, Secretariat Building of the United Nations, 1947–1950. New York. Photo: New York Conventions and Visitors Bureau.*

cause it occupied only a portion of the riverfront site, it avoided the setback restrictions that can be seen in the Empire State Building (on the left) and Chrysler Building (on the right).

Ludwig Mies van der Rohe, 1886–1969
The German architect van der Rohe was initially influenced by Gropius but developed his own minimalist version of International Style. Illustrating his motto that "less is more," his Seagram Building (figure 28.69) is a model of simplicity and elegance, a classic among glass skyscrapers.

Le Corbusier
Though he was an influential pioneer of the International Style, Le Corbusier later abandoned his boxes on stilts (see figure 28.37) for a more sculptural style. His design for the pilgrimage chapel of Notre-Dame-du-Haut (figure 28.70) was revolutionary, unlike any other building. The plan is irregular in every respect. Thick, curving white walls are topped by a heavy overhanging roof and flanked by a tall white tower on the left and a shorter tower on the right. The towers are decorative but they also transmit natural light to the two altars within. Window openings are cut through the massive walls to make tunnels of light. Randomly placed, the windows are of different sizes and cut through the walls in a variety of angles. Stained glass is used but each window has a different design and color scheme. The overall effect is intimate and magical.

Organic Architecture

Frank Lloyd Wright
Wright designed many buildings based on the circle but none as dramatic as the Solomon R. Guggenheim Museum in New York (figure 28.71). The front circle is the administrative unit with the gallery behind. The structure is essentially a cylinder rising in expanding circles. This is the antithesis, in every respect, of the

Figure 28.69 *Ludwig Mies van der Robe, Seagram Building, New York City. Photo: Ezra Stoller/Esto. Courtesy Joseph E. Seagram & Sons, Inc.*

Figure 28.70 *Le Corbusier, Notre-Dame-du-Haut, 1950–1955. Ronchamp, France. Giraudon/Art Resource.*

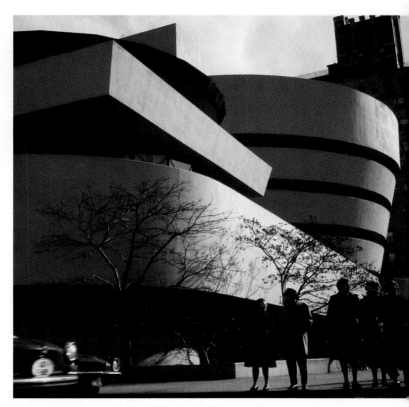

Figure 28.71 *Frank Lloyd Wright, The Solomon R. Guggenheim Museum, 1943–1959. New York. SEF/Art Resource, N.Y.*

International Style. Inside the building (figure 28.72) a circular ramp rises to the top in six complete turns around a 90′ well that climaxes in a skylight dome. Visitors are taken to the top in an elevator, permitting them to walk on a continuous downhill grade while inspecting artworks placed on the outside wall. The design necessarily limits how art is displayed, but the interior of the Guggenheim is one of Wright's boldest concepts.

Eero Saarinen, 1910–1961

New York's JFK International Airport is an uninspired collection of architectural clichés with the sole exception of the TWA Terminal (figure 28.73). Designed by Saarinen, the structure is a triumph, a curvilinear enclosure of space that actually looks like an air terminal. Built of reinforced concrete, the continuously curving surfaces symbolize flight in a manner reminiscent of Brancusi's *Bird in Space* (see figure 28.19).

Joern Utzon, b. 1918

The design competition for the new opera house in Sydney, Australia, was won by Danish architect Utzon in 1956, but it took thirteen years and several more architects to figure out how to build the unique concept (figure 28.74). A cultural center that includes

opera house, exhibition hall, theatre, and other facilities, the soaring gull-wing design faced with brilliant white ceramic tiles is a visual triumph, thanks in part to its location on one of the world's great harbors.

The Art of Photography

Anyone can take photographs, but there are few artists behind the camera. Many can master the technical aspects of photography,

Figure 28.72 *Interior, Solomon R. Guggenheim Museum. Ann Chwatsky/Art Resource, N.Y.*

Figure 28.73 *Eero Saarinen, TWA Terminal, 1956–1962. JFK International Airport, New York.*

Figure 28.74 *Utzon, Hall, Todd, and Littleton, Sydney Opera House, 1959–1972. Bennelong Point, Sydney, Australia. Photo: Australian Tourist Commission.*

but producing an artistic image is quite another matter. Unlike painting or sculpture, there is no gradual buildup to a completed work, no chance to add, delete, modify, rework. The image can be altered after the fact but the shot still begins with what the camera "sees" when the shutter is opened.

What is a good photograph? For that matter, what is a good painting? Like all art, photography is communication, a personal statement that the artist is making. Moreover, the work of a good photographer has a recognizable style just as, for example, paintings by Monet are stylistically consistent.

Portrait photographers have a special technique, an ability to reveal the nature and character of their subjects, and few were as accomplished as Matthew Brady (1823–1896). Brady took so many photographs of Abraham Lincoln that the latter is reputed to have said that his Cooper Union speech and Brady's photos put him in the White House. But it was quality, not quantity, that accounted for the fame of Brady's portraits of Lincoln. Even the calling card photo (see figure 23.3) clearly shows the strength, dignity, and nobility of the future president.[2]

Like many painters, photographers tend to concentrate on specializations such as portraiture, landscape, cityscape, sports, combat photography, and so forth. Landscape photographer Ansel

Adams (1902–1984) was one of the charter members of the photographic society named "Group f/64." This optical term was chosen because the members of the group generally set their lenses to the smallest aperture to secure the greatest depth of field: maximum sharpness from foreground to background. For most of his career Adams produced very sharp photos of the landscape of the American West. His *Moonrise* (figure 28.75) magically conveys the immensity of the landscape as it and the night sky tower over the isolation of the few inhabitants.

---

2. Brady also produced a remarkable photographic record of the Civil War.

Figure 28.75 *Photograph by Ansel Adams,* Moonrise, Hernandez, New Mexico, *1944; 15½" × 19". The Ansel Adams Publishing Rights Trust. All Rights Reserved.*

Figure 28.76 *W. Eugene Smith,* Spanish Wake, *1951. (From Spanish Village.) Photograph. Center for Creative Photography, University of Arizona. © W. Eugene Smith Estate/Black.*

Photojournalist W. Eugene Smith (1918–1978), on assignment for *Life* magazine, did a memorable photo essay on life in a Spanish village. His *Spanish Wake* (figure 28.76) from that series has characteristics comparable to a fine oil painting. The dramatic chiaroscuro and powerful composition add to the impact of the range of grief pictured here and that we, in turn, experience.

Also a photojournalist for *Life,* Margaret Bourke-White (1904–1971) photographed everything from industry and cities to natural disasters and World War II combat. It was her photo of concentration camp survivors that inspired photorealist painter Audrey Flack to create her memorial to the Holocaust (see figure 28.60). Bourke-White's *Flood Victims* (figure 28.77) is both art and social commentary on the discrepancy between the standard of living of the white middle class and that of the lowland flood victims patiently standing in a food distribution line. That the Ohio River Valley disaster took place during the Great Depression only added to the misery of the homeless who were, in many cases, also jobless.

There is no more telling image of the Great Depression than Dorothea Lange's (1895–1965) *Migrant Mother, Nipomo, California* (figure 28.78). Lange's compassion and respect for the Midwest Dust Bowl farmers who migrated to California in search of a better life are clearly revealed. This single photograph sums up the unflinching determination of thousands of homeless, rootless farmers to survive. The subject matter is comparable to John Steinbeck's novel *The Grapes of Wrath* in which the Joad family migrated from Oklahoma to California.

Figure 28.77 *Margaret Bourke-White,* Flood Victims, Louisville, Kentucky, 1937. *Life Magazine © 1937 Time Inc.*

Figure 28.78 *Dorothea Lange,* Migrant Mother, Nipomo, California, 1936. *Gelatin-silver print, 12½" × 9⅞".*

Photography's strong points include its immediacy and the ease of replication. Monday's photo of Louisville flood victims can turn up the following day in every major newspaper in the country. The earlier question about good pictures is answered by the six photographs in this volume: figures 23.3, 28.15, and 28.75–28.78. Each picture communicates more than the sum of its parts, each image is unique; and the personal communication from the artist is just as apparent in these works as in paintings by Rembrandt, Monet, or van Gogh.

Painting and Sculpture: Postmodernism

Art was self-consciously "modern" from around 1910 to about 1970. Artists viewed themselves as avant-garde creators who denied the past as they searched for new means of expression. Abstraction or a renunciation of representation, a taste for novelty that affirms originality and denies tradition (no more imitations of the world or of earlier artists) were characteristics of modernism. Beginning around 1970 or so, however, there was a general shift to a reweaving of the recent past and Western culture, a search for human values in the context of a world civilization. Representation and history were reintroduced but without reverting to graphic realism. This was, of course, a reaction to the rapidly evolving Electronic/Information Age and the idea that the world was becoming a Global Village. For want of a better term this movement is called *postmodernism.*

Postmodernism uses representation where appropriate and revives the connection with tradition by deliberately choosing between several traditions or by making explicit reference to tradition as such, which is anything but a traditional attitude. It recognizes the plurality of autonomous cultures within a world civilization. Contemporary artistic styles are therefore wildly pluralistic with no one style predominating. A renewed interest in figural painting called, for want of a better term, New Painting, seems to be significant, but some older styles persist and inno-

vations abound. One of the newer innovations is neo-expressionism, which emerged in Germany in the 1980s, much as its ancestor surfaced some seven decades earlier. This is an authentic style with a number of successful artists, especially Gerhard Richter (b. 1932). His *Vase* (figure 28.79) is a vibrant abstraction achieved by superimposing many layers of pigment with a variety of brushes, including the wide brushes used by house painters. This is a very large work that exudes vigorous emotion.

There are literally thousands of artists hard at work turning out untold numbers of artworks. In the absence, at present, of any towering figures, we have selected two artists whose work has been purchased by a major museum and who will represent the many who have yet to be recognized.

Sylvia Mangold, b. 1938

Mangold lives and works in upstate New York. Her *Schunnemunk Mountain* (figure 28.80) is a night landscape framed by larger painted rectangles and strips of applied masking tape. The country scene viewed from her studio is representational but the added rectangles, stripe, and masking tape make the illusion ambiguous; perhaps the painting is not a landscape but a commentary on how art is constructed. This is thus a poetic image that is "presented" to the viewer.

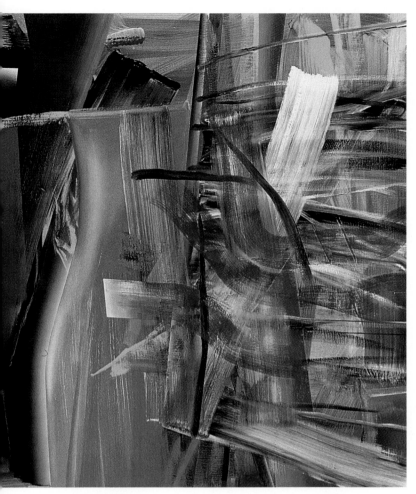

Figure 28.79 *Gerhard Richter,* Vase, *1984. Oil on canvas, 88½"* × *78¾". Museum of Fine Arts, Boston. Juliana Cheney Edward Collection.*

Figure 28.80 *Sylvia Mangold,* Schunnemunk Mountain, *1979. Oil on canvas, 59⁵⁄₁₆"* × *80⅛". General Acquisitions Fund and a gift from the 500, Inc. 1980.7. Dallas Museum of Art.*

Jennifer Bartlett, b. 1941

Contrasting sharply with the hushed image of the New York mountain, Bartlett's art is consistently cheerful and often exuberant, as in *Sad and Happy Tidal Wave* (figure 28.81). This is a dyptych with a left panel of Bartlett's distinctive painted steel tiles and the right panel a two-piece canvas. Both panels focus on the abstract figure of a swimmer composed of oval shapes. Though color and design are similar the two panels are sharply different: gleaming brilliance on the left and a softer, almost pastel quality on the right. The artist is playing not only with color, shapes, and title, but with the characteristics of different media as well.

Art in the 1990s is, in general, no longer a Bohemian activity and New York is no longer the primary center of artistic activity. Faced with a declining art market, some New York promoters seized on neo-expressionism as the new American style and then "discovered" artists who were working in the style, most of whom turned out to be Europeans. Happily discovered while working in Europe, Julian Schnabel is actually a Texan. He, along with Laurie Anderson and David Salle, is making a living out of neo-expressionism by promoting a "fast track" art market rivaling the hyped success of rock stars and soap opera personalities. The marketing of art and "art stars" has become another American enterprise with the implication that "success" is more important than aesthetics. Where this will lead is anybody's guess, but the prognosis does not favor artistic integrity. Art critic Robert Hughes has called the 1980s probably the worst decade in the history of American art, a nadir that will likely continue through the 1990s because the social conditions that fostered the era's cultural traits give no evidence of changing.

Following is a selective listing of styles, attitudes, and movements that indicate the wide range of contemporary artistic activity.

New Painting	Primitivism
Neo-Expressionism	Naives
French Nouveau Réalisme	Abstractionists
Italian Arte Povera	Nul/Zero
Pop and Post-Pop	Computer Art
Fluxus	Holographic Art
Conceptual Art	Performance Art
Minimalism	Body Art
Earth Art	Vague Art
Noise or Sound Art	Light Art
Site Sculpture	Bad Painting
Postmodern Art	

Whether any one style will predominate in the manner of impressionism or cubism is unlikely, given the rapid interactions of our Global Village in the Communications Age. Artistic influences are international but artists are individuals. They will pursue their own goals, creating artworks faster than critics can conjure up labels and this is as it should be. Works of art are always best judged on their own merits regardless of style, school, or movement.

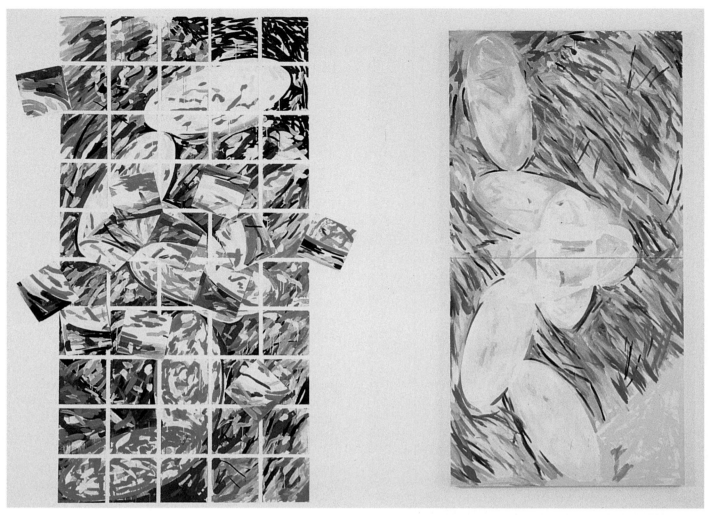

Figure 28.81 *Jennifer Bartlett,* Sad and Happy Tidal Wave, *1978. Enamel, silkscreen on steel plate (62 plates); oil on canvas (2 panels), 129½″ ×
172″. Foundation for the Arts Collection, gift of Susan and Robert K. Hoffman 1979.9.a–c.FA. Dallas Museum of Art.*

Architecture: Postmodernism

The most important architectural movement since the Bauhaus,
postmodernism has developed—since about 1970—into a worldwide phenomenon. Strictly urban in orientation, the style has appeared in New York, Paris, Hong Kong, Tokyo, Portland, Los
Angeles, and many cities in between. In fact, the rise of postmodern design has coincided with the increasing emphasis on
city-based identities as opposed to traditional national boundaries. At the same time, these urban centers, with instant worldwide communications, are clearly part of the international
community and the rapid evolution of the Global Village.

How can modernity be spoken of in the past tense? What
is meant by *post*modern? During the middle segment of this century modernism usually meant the avant-garde, unadorned geometry of the International Style. By the 1970s the stark boxes
and towers that had long dominated cityscapes were increasingly
viewed as cold and impersonal at best and, at worst, as profoundly

antihuman. Even the elegant proportions of the Seagram Building
(figure 28.69) cannot overcome the impersonal coolness of the
structure. Consciously "modern," it makes no reference to the
past and no concessions to the human beings who view it or work
within its pristine walls.

Architectural critics and historians sometimes refer to the
"coding" of a building. The Seagram Building, for example, is
immediately recognizable as an office building; its code (design)
reads "office building," but there is no other code or message, no
reference to local or historical traditions. Postmodern design, on
the other hand, is characterized by a double coding: the function
of the structure coupled with architectural references to local and/
or historical elements. Philip Johnson's (b. 1906) AT&T Building
(figure 28.82) is a hotly debated example of postmodernist dual
coding. Basically a glass and steel skyscraper, the entrance is reminiscent of Brunelleschi's Pazzi Chapel (see figure 17.5) but the
pediment resembles eighteenth-century furniture designed in

Figure 28.82 *Philip Johnson, AT&T Building, New York. AT&T Archives.*

Figure 28.83 *Michael Graves, The Portland Public Services Building, Portland, Oregon, 1980–1982. Photo: © Randy Shelton/ Architectural Images Photography, Inc.*

England by Thomas Chippendale (1718–1779). According to some detractors, this so-called Chippendale skyscraper looks very much like a grandfather clock. The design is both modern and traditional (Renaissance and neoclassic) and the overall effect, according to some, is a welcome step away from the impersonal conformity of the International Style.

The current architectural controversy is between the late modernists and the postmodernists. The former can be seen as the rear guard of modernism (mainly International Style) with a continuing commitment to advanced technology, efficiency, and austerity. The latter emphasizes the city context of each building, the needs and values of the users, and the appropriate ornamentation for each structure. Postmodernism does not, however, take a backseat to late modernism in the use of the latest technology.

The first significant competition for postmodernism took place in Portland, Oregon, where Michael Graves (b. 1937) competed against a late modernist firm. Graves won the competition (twice) and built a structure now known as *The Portland* (figure 28.83). This, the first major monument of postmodernism, has a clear three-part division: a broad green base, a buff-colored shaft, and a brown keystone resting atop brown pilasters that indicate interior elevator cores. Though still a rather heavy high-rise structure, *The Portland* has been generally accepted by the citizens as

an attractive public building that is comfortably at home in the city of Portland.

Summary

The multiplicity of styles and innumerable artists of the present century cannot be adequately covered in a chapter or even in a set of books. The discussion of most major styles and some of the important artists should be considered as a preamble to continuing studies of what today's artists are creating. Twentieth-century art is as accessible in this country as Renaissance art is in Italy and can be viewed in any good-sized American city. Most of the illustrations for this chapter, for example, were drawn from the collections of American museums and galleries from New York to the West Coast. Following is a summary in outline form, providing both a review of the chapter and a framework for personal initiative.

    I. Artistic Styles to 1945
        A. Painting and Sculpture
            1. Prelude
                a) Édouard Manet
                b) Impressionism: Monet et al.
                c) Post-Impressionism: Cézanne et al.

2. Fauvism
   a) Henri Matisse
   b) Georges Rouault
3. Expressionism
   a) Wassily Kandinsky (abstract expressionism)
   b) Ernst Barlach
   c) Käthe Kollwitz
   d) George Grosz
4. Cubism
   a) Pablo Picasso (but including Blue and Rose Periods and neoclassicism)
   b) Stuart Davis
5. Abstractionists
   a) Georgia O'Keeffe
   b) Piet Mondrian (geometric, plasticism)
   c) Constantin Brancusi
6. Fantasy
   a) Marc Chagall
   b) Paul Klee
   c) Giorgio de Chirico (metaphysical)
7. Dada
   a) Marcel Duchamp
   b) Kurt Schwitters
8. Surrealism
   a) Joan Miró
   b) Salvador Dali
   c) Meret Oppenheim
   d) Alberto Giacometti
   e) René Magritte
9. Realism in America
   a) John Sloan (Ash Can school)
   b) Edward Hopper
   c) Diego Rivera (social realism)
   d) José Clemente Orozco (social realism)
   e) David Alfaro Siqueiros (social realism)

B. Architecture
   1. Antonio Gaudi (art nouveau and expressionism)
   2. Walter Gropius (International Style)
   3. Le Corbusier (International Style)
   4. Frank Lloyd Wright (organic architecture)

II. Artistic Styles Since 1945
A. Painting and Sculpture
   1. Abstract Expressionism
      a) Jackson Pollock
      b) Willem de Kooning
      c) Mark Rothko (color field)
   2. Pop Art
      a) Robert Rauschenberg
      b) Roy Lichtenstein
      c) Edward Kienholz
      d) Marisol
   3. Color, Geometry, and Optics
      a) Josef Albers (geometric)
      b) Helen Frankenthaler (abstract color)
      c) Louise Nevelson (geometric abstraction)
      d) Bridget Riley (curved lines, optics)
   4. Fantasy and Expressionism
      a) Jean Dubuffet (*art brut*)
      b) Francis Bacon (fantasy/expressionism)
      c) Rufino Tamayo (fantasy/primitivism)
      d) Fritz Scholder (pop/expressionism)
      e) Alexander Calder (abstract fantasy/kinetic)
      f) Mark di Suvero (abstract fantasy/kinetic)
      g) Henry Moore (abstract figural)
      h) Gerhard Richter (neo-expressionism)
      i) Jennifer Bartlett (mixed media)
   5. Minimal Art
      a) Tony DeLap
      b) David Smith
      c) Ronald Bladen
      d) Sylvia Mangold
   6. Varieties of Realism
      a) Audrey Flack (photorealism)
      b) Otto Duecker (photorealism cutouts)
   7. Environmental Art
      a) Robert Smithson
      b) Christo
   8. Hispanic and African-American Artists
      a) Joshua Johnson
      b) Robert Duncanson (Hudson River tradition)
      c) Horace Pippin (naïve)
      d) Jacob Lawrence (image/abstraction)
   9. The Art of Photography
      a) Matthew Brady
      b) Alfred Stieglitz
      c) Ansel Adams
      d) W. Eugene Smith
      e) Margaret Bourke-White
      f) Dorothea Lange

B. Architecture
   1. Wallace Harrison (International Style)
   2. Ludwig Mies van der Rohe (minimalist International Style)
   3. Le Corbusier (sculptural architecture)
   4. Frank Lloyd Wright (functional/organic)
   5. Eero Saarinen (functional/expressionism)
   6. Joern Utzon (expressionism)
   7. Philip Johnson (postmodernism)
   8. Michael Graves (postmodernism)

WARNING: The above outline with artists placed neatly in pigeonholes is a generalized approximation and guide and *only* that. Artists, as stated before, are individuals and their works are unique. Treat the text and outline as points of departure, keeping in mind that artists do change their styles and that, art critics notwithstanding, we are still too close in time to many styles to make valid judgments. Mozart, for example, had no idea he was a classical composer; he was criticized in his day as an avant-garde composer.

Finally, consider art as what anyone elects to present to us as art, as evidence of human creativity. If we do not like an artwork perhaps it communicates something we already know but refuse to acknowledge. Paradoxically, a work of art that tells us something we know and understand can leave us dissatisfied. We do want the artist to challenge our emotions, our intellect, our knowledge. The more we study art the more likely we are to respond to it and to seek out challenges.

Culture and Human Values

Philosopher William Barrett wryly remarked that "Modern art tells us most, if we have but eyes to see, about the nature of the modern age which we have traversed or which has almost finished us."[3] Certainly some artistic values changed—at least in emphasis— during the century, notably the long-held beliefs that art was to communicate beauty and give pleasure. Those aspects have not been abandoned, but art as the communication of unpleasant and even terrible truths has been prominent in many artistic movements. Consider, for example, Picasso's *Les Demoiselles d'Avignon* (figure 28.10) and its portrayal of the darker aspects of human nature. His *The Tragedy* (figure 28.8) could stand for all the suffering of the working class, but *Guernica* works in even broader terms (figure 28.13). The bombs are not only destroying a defenseless Basque village, but tearing at the very fabric of civilization itself.

Barlach's *Shivering Woman* (figure 28.4) symbolizes the poor people of the world, whereas Kollwitz (figure 28.5) depicts common people at the mercy of a militaristic state. George Grosz reveals the horror of Nazi Germany and of all totalitarian states (figure 28.6).

On a smaller scale, most of the work of pop artists portrays the tacky, tawdry, and banal American materialism (figure 28.43). For a statement on the care and treatment of the elderly, Kienholz gives us *State Hospital* (figure 28.44). The Mexican social realists have pictured the plight of peasants, not just in Mexico, but in all Third World countries (figures 28.32, 33, and 34).

Consider also the sickness and terror communicated by the works of Dubuffet (figure 28.50) and Bacon (figure 28.51), and the horror depicted by Flack (figure 28.60). Whether institutionalized insanity or the madness of Nazi extermination camps, this is all part of the twentieth century.

Has modern art portrayed the twentieth century as totally violent and hopeless beyond recall? Not at all. Some of the works of Brancusi (figure 28.19), Chagall (figure 28.20), Le Corbusier (figure 28.37), Christo (figure 28.63), and Bartlett (figure 28.81) present a more positive image of a century of violent contrasts. In the final analysis, perhaps the best way to look at modern art is to recognize the truth, the beauty, the love, the faith, and the justice that artists have presented to all of us.

Exercises

1. Divide the art in this chapter into four categories:
    a. What you like
    b. What you dislike
    c. What you feel is or will become important
    d. What you feel is not or will not become important
    Draw conclusions about yourself and about twentieth-century art.

2. In the last section of this chapter, Culture and Human Values, the discussion centered on modern art as exemplifying the twentieth century in its ugliness, violence, and despair. From other sources select works that, in your opinion, communicate something of the dark side of the century, then balance this with six works that present a brighter side. Which examples were harder to find?

---

3. William Barrett, *Death of the Soul: From Descartes to the Computer* (Garden City, New York: Anchor Press/Doubleday, 1986), p. 56.

Modern Music

chapter 29

Modernism

Twentieth-century music has developed in what are essentially two phases. Phase one is a continuation and development of instruments, forms, and styles inherited from the rich tradition represented by Bach, Beethoven, and Brahms. Phase two began in the 1950s with the electronic age. Though the past is still fundamental, an exciting new world of music has burst on the scene, providing a dazzling display of electronic sounds and instruments, synthesizers, and computer composition and performance, and the innovations continue to proliferate.

Igor Stravinksy, 1882–1971

In terms of our musical heritage Stravinsky (figure 29.1) is perhaps the one modern composer whose career best summarizes the ceaseless experimentation and multiplicity of styles of this century. He exploited all the "neo" styles from neo-Gothic to neoromantic, pausing along the way to try his hand, unsuccessfully, at modern jazz. Thoroughly grounded in the music of the past—he admired the music of Bach above all—he was a superb musical craftsman as well as a bold and daring innovator. Always associated with the European avant-garde, he influenced Diaghilev, Cocteau, Picasso, and Matisse and was, in turn, influenced by all of them.

The first and perhaps strongest impetus came from Diaghilev, who commissioned several ballet scores for the Ballet Russe de Monte Carlo of which the first was *The Firebird*. Following the successful *Firebird*, Stravinsky produced the popular *Petrouchka* ballet score and then turned his attention to the ballet *The Rite of Spring*.

Success was not immediate for this daringly original work. The 1913 premiere in Paris set off a full-scale riot between Stravinsky's avant-garde partisans and his far more numerous detractors. The audience was restless before the music even began; the

Figure 29.1 *Igor Stravinsky. Photo: New York Public Library.*

two camps of "liberal artist" and "conservative establishment" had, in effect, already chosen up sides. The liberals were as determined to relish the music and the ballet as the conservatives were bent on open hostility. Conservatives viewed the work as an assault on cherished values of Western culture; liberals regarded it as a metaphor for the vulgar materialism and decadence of an age brought to a bitter end less than a year later by the Great War.

The high register bassoon solo at the very beginning of the piece provoked sneers and audible laughs from the conservative camp and the situation went downhill from there. By the time the police arrived things had gotten totally out of hand and the premiere performance was history. On a television program aired many years later Stravinsky sat in that Parisian hall in the same seat that he had occupied in 1913. When asked what he did during the riot, Stravinsky replied, "I just stood up, told all of them to go to hell and walked out."

The Rite of Spring, subtitled *Pictures of Pagan Russia,* exploits a very large symphony orchestra and uses many unique instrumental effects to portray the primitive ceremonies. Built around the spring fertility rites of ancient Russia, the scenes include the coming of spring, various spring dances, games of the rival tribes, and the selection of the sacrificial virgin. The ballet concludes with the Sacrificial Dance: frenzied convolutions by the Chosen One until she collapses and dies, after which her body is solemnly placed on the sacred mound as an offering to the fertility gods.

Listening Example 31

BALLET SUITE

Stravinsky, *The Rite of Spring*
Last scene: Sacrificial Dance
Time: 4:50

Atonality

Atonality was a musical idea whose time had come. Strictly speaking, atonality is a twentieth-century technique that arbitrarily declares the twelve different notes in an octave to be created free and equal. No one tone would predominate; there would be no tonal center, no tonic, no tonality. Curiously symptomatic of the twentieth century, the new system was associated with mathematics and, coincidentally, it stipulated the equality of black notes and white notes.

Modern science depends on highly sophisticated mathematics and, quite naturally, modern musicians developed their system of what might be called mathematical music. Atonal composers used no more than simple arithmetic, but this was quite sufficient for their manipulations of notes, rhythm, and texture. Following is a brief description of the process of change from tonal to atonal music, a development that, in retrospect, appears to have been inevitable. Also included are some games that people can play with twelve-tone arithmetic.

The tonal music that had superseded the modes during the seventeenth century was based on the idea that the seven tones of a diatonic scale belonged to a key and that the other five tones were outside the key.[1] Composers relied increasingly on the five tones outside the key to give color and variety to their music. By

---

1. In the key of C Major, for example, the white notes belong to the key and the black notes are outside the key.

Figure 29.2 *Arnold Schoenberg. Photo: New York Public Library.*

the end of the nineteenth century musicians such as Wagner and Brahms were regularly using all the tones as a twelve-tone system of tonality revolving around a central pitch called tonic, or tonal center.

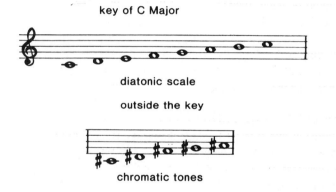

Arnold Schoenberg, 1874–1951

After World War I, Schoenberg (SHURN-burg; figure 29.2) developed a system in which all twelve tones were considered to be exactly equal and therefore with no tonal center. There would be no dissonance or consonance as such because all the pitches could be used in any combination and without reference to the predominance of any single pitch. This system of twelve equal musical pitches is called *atonality,* or the *dodecaphonic (twelve-tone) system.*

Without a tonic pitch to give the music some sort of unity, it was necessary to devise another kind of unifying system. This new device was called a *tone row,* or *basic set.* Composers invented melodic sequences of the twelve tones, using each tone only once and refraining from using any sequence of notes that would imply a key (tonality). Because it is neither necessary nor desirable to limit the twelve different tones to one octave, a basic set (tone row) could look like this:

Basically, the twelve-tone system lends itself to polyphonic rather than homophonic writing. Almost anyone can devise and use a mixture of polyphonic and homophonic techniques. Because of the infinite possibilities of manipulating the row, the problem becomes one of *selectivity,* choosing those possibilities that make musical sense.

Twelve-tone composition is not solely a musical process but partly a mathematical and/or mechanical procedure. The finished composition might be very different and original in sound (and it might not). Whether it is good music or bad music still remains the province of the composer, who makes up one or more tone rows, manipulating, selecting, and modifying until the *musical results* he or she wants have been achieved. Twelve-tone technique is neither a virtue nor a vice; it is merely a means to an end. It may assist the composer in discovering new melodic, rhythmic, and harmonic ideas and different combinations of these ideas. It will not do a thing for the finished product; that rests within the sphere of the creative individual.

Alban Berg, 1885–1935

Berg (figure 29.3) was one of the most musically creative of the twelve-tone composers. His style is also notable for clear, clean orchestral writing. For his Violin Concerto he used a small, versatile orchestra with a delicate contrapuntal texture.

Berg's tone row was not a mechanical contrivance but a point of departure for some lyrical music. He deliberately constructed a row with clear tonal implications, a mixture of *g minor, a minor,* and a portion of the whole-tone scale.

Figure 29.3 *Alban Berg. Photo: The Bettmann Archive.*

Listening Example 32

BERG, VIOLIN CONCERTO

I Andante (excerpt)

Neoclassicism, Expressionism, and Neoromanticism

The styles of twentieth-century music are many and varied, as befits a dynamic art in a rapidly changing age. The vogue of neoprimitivism *(The Rite of Spring* and other similar compositions) had its day; romanticism, whether called neoromantic or postromantic, continues to have some influence; nationalism is once again a characteristic of the works of some composers. One trend has been toward classicism, as in the works of the twelve-tone school and, among many others, the music of the Russian composer Serge Prokofiev.

Serge Prokofiev, 1891–1953

Prokofiev went through a primitive phase, and his music does have certain nationalistic characteristics. He has had exceptional success with descriptive music, as attested to by his motion-picture scores and the universally popular *Peter and the Wolf.* The bulk of his writing, however, has a classical orientation and deals mainly with the abstract forms of sonata, concerto, and symphony. His Fifth Symphony is written for the large orchestra that so delights Russian composers. The musical content is rich, expressive, and often highly dramatic. The form is lucidly classical, logical, and controlled.

Béla Bartók, 1881–1945

Bartók was one of the outstanding composers of the century. Born in Hungary, he escaped the Nazi terror and settled in New York City where he made a meager living as a piano teacher and as a concert pianist. Only after his death was there any significant recognition of the consistently high quality of his music. The shy, soft-spoken Hungarian refugee has written some powerful music characterized by great intensity and depth of feeling, music that sings and plays without becoming flippant, music that is sometimes somber and occasionally tragic in tone but that is not dejected or self-pitying. His work consistently manifests an affirmative life-force that epitomizes the man and his music.

Bartók's style was an amalgam of Hungarian folk music, great rhythmic ingenuity, and a fundamental allegiance to classical forms. He delighted in the folk music of southeastern Europe because it helped free him from the tyranny of the major-minor system; moreover, many of his rhythmic conceptions were derived from folk dances of the same area. His preoccupation with formal unity and coherence led him to a unique style of *continuous variations,* a dynamic and thoroughly modern style of relentless tension and growth.

His Concerto for Orchestra, which sounds like a contradiction in terms, is an orchestral piece in which nearly all of the instruments are treated in a soloistic manner. The virtuoso in this case is the entire orchestra. There are five movements, each very different in content, but all a part of the dynamic drive that culminates in the fifth and last movement.

Some contemporary composers have reacted against the prevailing classical concepts of the twentieth century as well as against the innovations of composers who are experimenting with computer compositions and the manipulation of electronic tapes. These modern-day neoromantics are still primarily interested in program music, major-minor tonality, tertiary harmony, and large vocal and instrumental ensembles. They have adopted some modern techniques, but have incorporated them into what is essentially a nineteenth-century framework.

Figure 29.4   *Charles Ives. Photo: © Omikron/Photo Researchers.*

Carl Orff, 1895–1982

In his cantata *Carmina Burana* (see chapter 15), Orff used the poetry of the medieval goliards to write what he called a "dramatic cantata." The wandering scholars, defrocked monks, vagabonds, minstrels, rascals, artists, and dreamers who were known as goliards rebelled against the strictures of society and protested the dominance of the aristocracy and the church.

The text of Orff's cantata was selected from the thirteenth-century collection of goliard poems that was discovered in Bavaria in the Benedictine monastery of Benediktbeuren, hence the name *Carmina Burana (Songs of Beuren).* These *cantiones profanae* (secular songs) were written in a mixture of Latin, French, and German. They sing of nature and the joys of love, the tavern, and the free life, but there is a strong undercurrent of protest against the cruel fate of these nonconformists.

Charles Ives, 1874–1954

The startling innovations of Charles Ives (figure 29.4) anticipated just about every important development of the first half century: serial and aleatory music,[2] mixed meters and tempos, blocks of sound, free forms, the possibilities of accidental or chance acoustical experiences, assemblages, collages, and even early manifestations of pop art. However, despite an impressive array of avant-garde techniques, Ives was still a traditional New Englander who wanted to maintain his philosophical relationship with the recent literary past. His important *Concord Sonata* for piano has the four movements named after the transcendentalists: Emerson, Hawthorne, the Alcotts, and Thoreau.

---

2. Aleatory (AY-lee-uh-TORE-e) or chance music.

To understand what Ives is getting at in his music one must recognize the music that he quotes, the church hymns, dance music, and military band music. These quotes are comments on life in the small towns and rural areas of America. His nostalgic *Three Places in New England,* for orchestra, is replete with quotes from Americana and illustrates a concern for his American heritage as profound as that of Walt Whitman.

Listening Example 33

IVES, *THREE PLACES IN NEW ENGLAND* (1903–1911)

II *Putnam's Camp, Redding, Connecticut* (excerpt)
Time: 3:00

Ives wrote: "Near Redding Center is a small park preserved as a Revolutionary Memorial; for here General Israel Putnam's soldiers had their winter quarters in 1778–1779. Long rows of stone camp fireplaces still remain to stir a child's imagination. The scene is a '4th of July' picnic held under the auspices of the First Church and the Village Cornet Band. The child wanders into the woods and dreams of the old soldiers, of the hardships they endured, their desire to break camp and abandon their cause, and of how they returned when Putnam came over the hills to lead them. The little boy awakes, he hears the children's songs and runs down past the monument to 'listen to the band' and join in the games and dances."

Atonality: Postscript

The twelve-tone composition of the Viennese School of Schoenberg, Berg, and Webern (VAY-burn) went into temporary decline with the growing power of fascist dictatorships in the thirties and war in the forties. Many composers fled for their lives from totalitarian states that demanded simplistic music in a national style in conformance with the military monoliths that the arts were commanded to serve. Schoenberg emigrated to the United States, Berg died in 1935, but Webern stayed on in Vienna quietly creating rigorous twelve-tone music that was to captivate postwar composers. Ironically, Webern survived tyranny and the war only to be accidentally killed by an American soldier shortly after the end of the war.

The music of Anton Webern (1883–1945; figure 29.5) is difficult to characterize apart from the sound: a kind of cubistic pointillism with meaningful breathing space. He has written some of the most beautiful rests in music—the sounds of silence. He uses few notes in a short space of time, manipulating isolated, contrasted tone colors in a space-time continuum. All is rigorous, precise, twelve-tone mathematics, but the result combines the isolation of single tones with the disassociation of sequential

Figure 29.5 *Anton Webern. Photo: The Bettmann Archive.*

events that somehow make up a total musical interrelationship. The contrasting tone colors in his *Three Songs* are soprano voice, clarinet, and guitar.

Listening Example 34

WEBERN, *THREE SONGS,* op. 18 (1925)

1. *Schatzerl klein* (little treasure)
Time: :59

Serial Technique and Electronic Music

Partly because of the presence of Schoenberg, twelve-tone composition in the United States flourished during the war and later reoccupied most of Europe, with the exception of Eastern Bloc countries, which condemned its dissonant complexities as "bourgeois decadence." The American composer Milton Babbitt (b. 1916), among others, expanded twelve-tone writing from a method into an elaborate system called *serial technique* or *serial composition*. Although the old method was never a matter of simply arranging the twelve pitches into a row, the new procedure systematized other elements of music such as rhythm, harmony, tempo, dynamics, timbre, and so forth. For example, a serial composition could contain mathematical permutations of twelve pitches, a sixteen-unit rhythmic organization, a sequence of twenty-nine chords, and fourteen timbres (tone colors). When one considers that there are approximately half a billion ways of arranging just the twelve pitches, the mathematical possibilities of serial technique systems approach infinity. Whether these combined mathematical procedures produce music worth listening to is strictly up to a composer who has to choose from an infinitely greater range of possibilities than ever confronted Stravinsky, not to mention Bach or Beethoven.

While the serialists pursue the manifold possibilities of their systems, other composers have concentrated on the exploitation of noise and timbre first introduced by the pre-World War I futurists. Traditionally, tone color has been more ornamental than essential to Western music and the incorporation of "noise" was unthinkable. But musical sounds as such are only a minuscule part of the modern world of acoustical phenomena. We are surrounded and often engulfed by noise ranging from city traffic, electrical appliances, and factory din to the "noises" of nature: sounds of the animal world, thunder, rain, hail, seasounds, windsounds, and so forth.

Previous Western cultures have tended to rank "musical" sounds (simple acoustical events with regular pitch vibrations) above "noise" (a complex mixture of regular and irregular vibrations). Some modern composers have attempted to express the sounds of nature in traditional musical terms while at the same time incorporating "noise-making" instruments of the percussion section such as drums, rattles, gourds, and cymbals. Because of the ever-growing interest in different cultures, non-Western percussion instruments were introduced in the nineteenth century and extensively used in the twentieth century. Traditionalists scorned these intruders as nonpitched and therefore antimusical, but innovative composers enthusiastically employed the possibilities of combining timbre and noise into a new musical fabric that violated virtually every precept of conventional melody and harmony.

The Electronic Revolution

Much of the experimentation with timbre and noise has been incorporated into the several varieties of electronic music. In fact, electronic music appears to be a natural consequence in the evolution of Western music. In the early predominantly vocal era, the singer was his or her own instrument. During the baroque period there was a general parity between vocal and instrumental music, after which instrumental music clearly dominated vocal music. The musician now used what amounted to a mechanical extension for music making, with varying degrees of disassociation between performer and instrument; for example, wind players are in close contact with their instruments, string players have some direct control, but keyboard instruments, especially the pipe organ, are quite mechanical. The evolution from a personal instrument (the voice) to an instrument once removed (e.g., the trumpet) has now reached a twice-removed instrument that is wholly the product of technology and that is entirely removed from direct human contact.

This instrumental evolution reflects the condition of contemporary culture in which so many activities are carried on untouched by human hands. Computers are talking to computers whereas many people find it ever more difficult to communicate with each other. One might argue that the exclusion of human beings from the production of musical sounds spells the death of art and the triumph of technology. On the other hand, there is some evidence that the new possibilities in the manipulation of sound can open up a whole new era of musical forms while simultaneously stimulating new vitality in vocal and instrumental music. If this optimistic view proves to be the correct one, it will bear out the thesis emphasized throughout this book: the ferment and rapid change in contemporary life is apparently a necessary prelude to a more humane society that may already be taking form. In any event, the work in electronic music is a reflection of the current crisis-dilemma-opportunity situation now operative in contemporary life, and electronic music, along with all our highly developed technology, is here to stay. What happens with machines is still the prerogative of those who build them.

The age of electronic music began in 1951 when Cologne Radio opened the first electronic studio. Other studios were subsequently opened in Paris, Milan, Tokyo, and at Columbia University and the Bell Laboratories in the United States—and many more are now in operation. Karlheinz Stockhausen (b. 1928) of the Cologne Studio has been a leader in a medium that has particular importance in his work: he could create new forms out of his basic idea of serial control of transformation and thus break down conventional distinctions between clarity and complexity and, most especially, between noise and pitch. Milton Babbitt began working in electronic music with the R.C.A. Electronic Sound Synthesizer. His *Ensemble for Synthesizer* uses a wide variety of tone colors and complex rhythms at tempos faster than human performers can hope to reproduce.

Listening Example 35

BABBITT, *ENSEMBLE FOR SYNTHESIZER* (EXCERPT)
Time: 1:00

Chance Music

After the mid-fifties, the nature of avant-garde music began to change, due largely to the leadership of Stockhausen. Total serialism grew into new materials based on the many ways of transforming textures, colors, and sound densities. From the earlier "controlled chance" compositions, with some options controlled by the composer and others by the performer, the movement has shifted to multiple forms of control and chance and so-called open forms with chance the major factor. Aleatory music (Lat., *alea:* "dice") is a general term describing various kinds of music in which chance, unpredictability, ambiguity, and even sheer chaos is realized in performance. If strict serial music represents a kind of Newtonian, mathematical determinism, then aleatory music represents its exact opposite: a symbolic rolling of musical dice just to see what will happen.

This conflict between calculation and chance is a musical equivalent to the current situation in science. The precision of the Newtonian world-machine has been supplanted by a modern science that is forced to settle for contingent proofs, complementary truths, and/or mathematical concepts of uncertainty. Quantum theory recognizes the element of chance, and its language has even been carried over, however ineffectively, into aesthetic theories. Strict mathematical concepts (except for "pure" mathematics), whether in science or art, can lead only to dead ends: scientific "truths" that are jarred by further gains in knowledge and strict mathematics in music that lead to the sterility of nonart. Chance music is therefore a corollary of modern science, and especially of both the profundity and absurdity of contemporary life.

John Cage, b. 1912

Cage (figure 29.6) was among the first American composers to experiment with chance music. In the late thirties he worked with a "prepared piano," which was designed to produce percussive sounds and noises that were unrelated to its traditional sound. Since the early fifties he has produced works of indeterminate length, of chance operations, of chance media (a concert of a group of radios tuned to different stations), and similar techniques. One of his most widely discussed compositions is a piano solo titled *4'33''* during which the pianist merely sits quietly at the piano for this period of time, after which he bows and leaves

Figure 29.6 *John Cage. Photo © Dorothy Norman.*

the stage. Obviously the composition "sounds" different at each performance because of the variance in noise from the audience. This composition would have to be considered the ultimate in minimal art as well as an achievement somewhat comparable in everyday life to the "non-wheat" that a farmer produces in exchange for government money. Carrying this idea to its logical conclusion would have the government paying artists for nonpoetry, nonnovels, and nonpaintings. The ultimate absurdity would seem to have been reached and Dada would reign supreme.

And Dada is related to chance music, or vice versa, just as are Cage's ideas of the Chinese chance technique of coin throwing from the *I Ching* and his fascination with Zen Buddhism. Chance music concerts may include instructions on manuscripts such as: "Start when you like and repeat as often as necessary," "Hold this note as long as you like and then go on to the next one," "Wait till the spirit moves you and then make up your own piece," and so forth. Performers are also instructed to destroy their instruments, stare at the audience, propel vehicles about the stage, blow sirens, flash lights, and perform other stimulating activities. The result might be called Aimless Theatre rather than theatre of the absurd, although there appear to be common elements. For an encore there may or may not be a full-blown Happening followed by the ultimate absurdity—leaving the concert hall to return to "real" life.

Politics and Music; Functional Music

Contemporary music contains perhaps more than its fair share of politically motivated music. Soviet composers such as Dmitri Shostakovitch (1906–1975) were expected to follow the party line and supposedly his well-known Fifth Symphony did so. In his *Memoirs* (smuggled out of Russia and published in 1979) Shostakovitch revealed some startlingly different ideas. According to him the Fifth Symphony was meant to describe Stalin's Great Terror of 1934–1938. The Seventh Symphony, called the Leningrad, was actually planned before the war; the so-called invasion theme, with its fearsomely swelling fortissimo, had nothing to do with the Nazi attack. "I was thinking," wrote Shostakovitch, "of other enemies of humanity [namely Stalin and his killers] when I composed the theme." "The majority of my symphonies are tombstones," stated Shostakovitch. "Too many of our people died and were buried in places unknown to anyone. . . . I'm willing to write a composition for each of the victims, but that's impossible, and that's why I dedicate my music to them all."

During the thirties many artists, in a quest for Utopia, moved over to the party line but most moved back again after Utopia was more clearly seen as Shostakovitch had experienced it firsthand, a brutal totalitarian empire. In the fifties the themes changed to pacifism, antiwar, and individual freedom. Britain's Benjamin Britten (1913–1979) wrote his notable *War Requiem* for the rededication of Coventry Cathedral after its destruction by German bombers during the war.

Not all contemporary music is of the avant-garde variety. Paul Hindemith (1895–1963) was a neoclassicist in his retention of tonal writing and his devotion to the style of J. S. Bach. He also advocated *Gebrauchmusik* (useful music, i.e., functional) and wrote music for all ages and degrees of musical skills and for numerous special events that called for appropriate music. One of his best works is the symphonic version of *Mathis der Maler,* a moving depiction in sound of the *Isenheim Altarpiece* by Matthias Grünewald (1483–1528). Kurt Weill (1900–1950), after he met the playwright Bertolt Brecht, deliberately rejected the complexities of modern music. In conjunction with Brecht he wrote *The Threepenny Opera* and *The Fall of the House of Mahagony.*

American Musical Theatre

Threepenny and *Mahagony* were partly responsible for the blossoming of musical theatre in America, which began with Rodgers and Hammerstein's *Oklahoma!* and continued through their *South Pacific, Carousel,* and *The Sound of Music.* Bernstein's *West Side Story,* Lerner and Loewe's *My Fair Lady* and *Camelot,* and Newley's *The Roar of the Greasepaint; The Smell of the Crowd* are notable contributions to the musical theatre. The finest talent in contemporary music theatre is unquestionably Stephen Sondheim (b. 1930), who writes both words and music. His musicals include *West Side Story* (lyrics), *A Funny Thing Happened on the Way to the Forum, A Little Night Music, Pacific Overtures, Sweeney Todd,* and, based on Seurat's painting, *Sunday in the Park with George.*

George Gershwin (1898–1937) may be one of America's best composers. Criticized by musical snobs as being "popular" and thus, for some strange reason, beyond the pale, his music has endured and much of it has become a part of the standard repertory. *Rhapsody in Blue, An American in Paris,* and the Concerto in F have all become known throughout the world as truly representative of American music. *Of Thee I Sing* is now recognized as musical theatre at its satirical best and *Porgy and Bess*— a smash hit at La Scala in Milan—is perhaps America's finest opera.

Minimalism

Philip Glass, b. 1937

Some critics claim that Glass is, after Gershwin, America's best composer. Certainly one of the most provocative of contemporary composers, Glass has developed his own unique style of minimalism. He combines Hindu rhythmic cycles and other devices of non-Western music with some rock plus Western-style intervals and harmonies that have been reduced to the barest essentials. The result—sometimes called "solid state music"—is not as austere as it sounds, for Glass is not afraid to use elements from the classical tradition. On the other hand, he is just as likely to use the synthesis of jazz and rock styles called "New Age" fusion.

One of his first major successes was *Einstein on the Beach* (1976), a 4½-hour multimedia production that has been billed as an opera, but which is actually a series of events. His first true opera was *Satyagrapha* (1980), a complex work based on the *Bhagavad Gita* and sung entirely in Sanscrit. This was followed by *Akhenaton* (1984), an opera based on the Pharaoh who introduced monotheism to ancient Egypt (see chapter 2, volume 1).

Jazz in America

Jazz is a uniquely different style of music, the result of a fusion—collision might be a better word—of certain elements of African and American musical cultures. Aside from native American music, music in the United States was of European origin and influenced by European musical styles which, of course, influenced all of North and South America. Given the European heritage and the presence of African slaves and freedmen throughout the United States, the islands of the Caribbean, Central and South America, the singular and significant fact remains that jazz originated solely in the United States. By the turn of the century, Negro spirituals, ragtime, blues, and jazz were established types or styles of music, none of which existed anywhere else in the Western Hemisphere.

The French, Spanish, Portuguese, Dutch, and even English cultures of the West Indies and Central and South America apparently provided a climate in which African arts, crafts, customs, and religious beliefs could coexist with their European counterparts: a climate in which transplanted Africans could maintain a considerable portion of their customs mixed, of course, with many elements of Western culture, Christianity in particular. For whatever reasons, and there are many, the dominant white culture of the American South was not as tolerant of African customs as were the transplanted European cultures south of the United States. There existed a strong conflict between white and black Americans in almost every area of life: religion, folklore, music, art, dance, and social and political customs.

In summary, jazz is a musical style that evolved out of a three-century history of cultural and racial conflict, a clash between an inflexible dominant culture and a powerful and persistent subculture with its own age-old beliefs and customs. Jazz continues to evolve, of course, including even a change in name. A number of jazz musicians now refer to their music as African-American classical music.

The Elements of Jazz

The elements of jazz are those of any music: melody, harmony, rhythm, and tone color. The African-American mixture makes the difference. The development of any style of music normally follows an evolutionary process *within* a single culture. Outside influences, when they appear, tend to be transformed and absorbed into the stylistic development. The Viennese waltz, for example, is a modified, speeded-up version of an old Austrian folk dance called the *ländler*. The ländler was Austrian; the changes were compatible with Austrian concepts of melody, harmony, rhythm, and tone color. The finished product was in all respects a result of Austrian culture and the musical genius of one Johann Strauss, Jr. It would be ludicrous to remove the Strauss melody and insert a Russian boat song, an Irish jig, or a Hopi rain dance. Scale, harmony, rhythm, and tone color would be all wrong because an incompatible melody was introduced into a foreign context.

In a manner of speaking, jazz sounds the way it does because it *is* a compound of several different and even opposing concepts of melody, rhythm, and tone color. In very general terms, jazz can be defined as a style of music that consists of African-European melody, European harmony, African rhythm, and African-European tone color. A built-in conflict of musical styles lies at the root of jazz and probably accounts, at least in part, for the feelings of dislocation and sometimes anguish and even pain on the part of performers and listeners.

The fundamental conflict in the materials of jazz occurs in *scale* and *tuning*. Equal temperament, with its twelve equal semitones in each octave, is the tuning standard for Western music. On the other hand, African melody was and is based on the tones present in the overtone series. The distances between pitches range from whole steps and half steps, similar to those in the tempered scale, to other intervals *between* half steps, including *quarter tones* (tones approximately midway between, say, C♯ and D♭). African harmony is quite rudimentary; melody, rhythm, and tone color are far more important.

African melodies, with their different-sized intervals, were sung in a culture that did not use such a variety of intervals, that built musical instruments in equal temperament, a culture in which African songs were often characterized as out of tune, primitive, and/or a poor imitation of "proper" singing.

Scale

The combining of African scales with the European diatonic scale produced a hybrid called the *blues scale.*[3] In terms of the equal-tempered piano the blues scale can be described as a diatonic scale plus three *blue notes:* flatted 3rd, 5th, and 7th scale degrees.

blue notes

Rhythm

Rhythm is the main ingredient in African music: highly developed, intricate, complex, as sophisticated in its own way as the harmonic system of Western culture. The African rhythms that have crossed over into jazz and into much of our modern concert music are but a relatively simple portion of a whole world of elaborate percussion music.

---

3. The blues scale is not African in itself although its origins necessarily lie in African music. Rather it is an African-American scale, and it is the elemental component out of which jazz is made.

There are two interrelated fundamental characteristics of African rhythm: *beat* and *syncopation.* Emerging from the simultaneous rhythm patterns is a *subjective beat,* a rhythmic pulsation that is not necessarily played by any one drummer but which results from the combination of the whole. The beat is implicit. This beat (whether explicit or implicit) is so much a part of jazz that it can be called its *heartbeat* or *pulse.* Jazz can thus be defined as the "beauty of the beat."

Syncopation is a displacement or shifting of accents so they disagree with natural metrical accents. It has the effect of tugging at the beat, a dynamic process that emphasizes the existence of the basic pulse by setting up a conflict with that pulse. The pull of syncopation against the ongoing beat gives a *swing* to the music, a buoyant resiliency that is a fundamental characteristic of jazz.

Tone Color

The story is told of the World War II air base in Africa that stockpiled aviation gasoline in steel drums. The drums were unloaded and stacked by native laborers, one of whom accidentally dropped a drum and noticed a booming, reverberant tone as the heavy drum hit the hard ground. His neighbor immediately dropped his drum to discover its tone color. Within a very few minutes, in their delight at discovering new tone colors, the entire crew was enthusiastically engaged in dropping, hitting, and scraping gasoline drums.

Beating on logs, sticks, bones, metal, or drums; scratching gourds; shaking rattles—all are activities designed to exploit tone colors within a rhythmic framework. African drummers can obtain several dozen different timbres as they use their thumbs, fingers, flat of the hands, or fists on various areas of a drumhead. All that is necessary for a percussion instrument is a distinctive tone color with virtually no limit to the number and variety of possible tone colors.

Distinctive tone color in jazz is not confined to the drums. It extends to the colors obtained by using mutes, hats, plungers, handkerchiefs, or anything else that will give variety to the timbre of instruments such as trumpet and trombone. Instrumentalists also use growls, slurs, slides, and so forth in an attempt to give an expressive range and personal quality to their music. The colors may be cool or hot or anything in between; in any event, jazz musicians are concerned with their sound, the distinctive coloration of their performance.

Harmony

Harmony is one of the most highly developed elements of Western culture but of only slight importance in African music. Consequently, the fusion of African and American music was essentially a combining of African melody, rhythm, and tone color with an established harmonic system. The result, as stated before, was a synthesis of conflicting stylistic elements and the beginning of a new style of music called jazz.

Pre-Jazz Styles (African-American Folk Music)

Some of the many types of African-American music date back to the arrival of the first indentured workers and slaves in the early part of the seventeenth century; other music developed in response to—or despite—the American environment. The African vocal tradition survived as it adjusted to the strange servile conditions and the new religion of Christianity. The instrumental tradition, however, was rigorously suppressed by the slaveholders who suspected, and rightly so, that African drums could communicate such terrifying possibilities as slave rebellions. The planters were also concerned about breaking up tribal units and their traditions, little suspecting that tribal histories were entirely oral and perpetuated by the drummers and the language of the drum script.[4] The banjo (African, *banjar*) did manage to survive, but European instruments were gradually taken up. Out of this melange of African and American cultures emerged a remarkably rich tradition of African-American folk music, much of which is still performed today.

Secular Music

The *work song* is closely related to an African tradition of rhythmic songs that have the effect of making hard work a bit easier. Usually unaccompanied solo songs, they sometimes use a guitar or banjo accompaniment. They are associated with manual labor that tends to a rhythmic regularity: chopping wood, rowing a boat, driving railroad spikes.

Example: "Juliana Johnson"[5]

Hollers (*field hollers*) are sung during non-rhythmic fieldwork such as picking cotton or hoeing corn. Unaccompanied and with an irregular beat, they frequently use narration mixed with singsong chants.

Example: "Old Hannah"

The *street cry* is sung by street sellers of fruit, vegetables, fish, and so forth. Unaccompanied, with constant repetition of the name of the product, the seller maintains interest with continuous changes in pitch and tone quality.

Examples: "Crab Man" and "Strawberry Woman" from Porgy and Bess (George Gershwin)

---

4. Some African languages, especially the varieties of Bantu, used different pitch levels of vowel sounds for different word meanings. Tribal historians were highly select drummers who were trained to play the *talking drum* by beating out the word rhythms while at the same time varying the pitch by means of a stretched membrane. Thus the drum script was virtually a vocal sound that could be transmitted over considerable distances with the aid of relay drummers.

5. Titles and/or performers are given rather than specific recordings, which may or may not be available given the vagaries of the recording industry.

Narrative songs with numerous verses, *ballads* were originally African heroic songs of kings, warriors, and hunters. American versions are about folk heroes such as John Henry, the steel-driving man.

Example: "John Henry"

Blues

The *blues* are the most important single influence in the development of jazz. There are two basic kinds of blues: folk (rural blues) and urban blues (true jazz blues; see p. 400). They reflect African customs and musical traditions, but they are native to America. The blues are personal, subjective, introspective, a way of protesting misfortune and identifying trouble. Singing the blues is a survival technique for counteracting bad times, loneliness, and despair.

Blues lyrics usually consist of three lines of poetry. The first line is repeated (possibly with a slight variation) followed by a third line that completes the thought. Because blues are usually improvised, the repeating of the second line gives the singer a better chance to make up the last line. There may be only one verse or there may be many verses in a narrative blues. Favorite subjects are love, traveling, and trouble, but almost anything makes a fit subject, as shown by the following blues poems.

Love:
Love is like a faucet, you can turn it off or on (twice)
But when you think you've got it, it's done turned off and gone.

Traveling:
I went to the deepot, an' looked upon de boa'd. (twice)
It say: dere's good times here, dey's better down de road.

Proverbs:
My momma tole me, my daddy tole me too: (twice)
Everybody grin in yo' face, ain't no friend to you.

Images:
Ef blues was whiskey, I'd stay drunk all de time. (twice)
Blues ain't nothin' but a po'man's heart disease.

Comedy:
Want to lay my head on de railroad line, (twice)
Let the train come along and pacify my mind.

Tragedy:
(one-line images)
Got the blues but too dam mean to cry.
Standin' here lookin' one thousand miles away.
I hate to see the evenin' sun go down.
Been down so long, Lawd, down don't worry me.

Example: "Careless Love"

Sacred Music

Most *spirituals* are derived from Protestant hymns but with significant changes in text, melody, and rhythm (usually syncopated). Frequently improvised, especially during church services and prayer meetings, they use texts that are variations on existing hymns or paraphrases of biblical verses and stories. They are notable for vividness of imagery, the relating of biblical stories with direct and telling simplicity, and a strong concern for the sounds and rhythms of words.

Example: "Swing Low, Sweet Chariot"

The *ring shout* is similar to African circle dances in form and character. Usually performed outdoors after a church service, the worshippers form a ring while singing a spiritual to start the ring slowly revolving. Accompanied by hand claps and foot stomping, the spiritual is sung over and over until the accumulative effect is hypnotic.

Example: "Come and Go with Me"

A *jubilee* is a particular kind of spiritual that sings triumphantly of the Year of Jubilee "When the Saints Go Marching In."

Gospel songs differ from hymns and spirituals mostly in the texts, which are more personal and subjective. "I," "me," "my" are the key words in songs that tend to reduce religious experience to a personal viewpoint.

Example: "My God Is Real"

The *song–sermon* is delivered from the pulpit, usually beginning with a scriptural quotation. The vocal delivery of the minister moves gradually from the spoken word to a kind of intoned chant, culminating in ringing declamation and vocalized phrases on higher and higher pitches. The African custom of responding verbally to important personages, such as a tribal chieftain, is reflected in the congregational response to the song–sermon. There are shouts of "amen," "yes sir," "hallelujah," and impromptu wordless crooning.

Example: "Dry Bones"

Voodoo (*vodun*) is the name given to the combination of African and Catholic religious rites and beliefs that was developed in Haiti by the Dahomeans of West Africa and that still exists in the West Indies and in portions of the United States, particularly Louisiana. Voodoo rites took place in Congo Square in New Orleans before being driven underground. Voodoo helped perpetuate African customs and music and made significant contributions to African-American folk music and to the development of jazz.

Example: "Drums of Haiti"

Figure 29.7 *Scott Joplin, cover of The Entertainer.*

Entertainment

Dating from about the middle of the nineteenth century, *minstrel shows* were generally sentimentalized "scenes of plantation life" performed by an all-male, all-white cast. Characteristic African-American elements were present in some of the group dances: the use of rhythmic "bones," tambourine, and banjo; the soft-shoe dances; and the cakewalk finale (see "Ragtime"). Stephen Collins Foster's songs (many of them based on African-American folk music) were a popular staple. Minstrelsy dealt with stereotypes that no longer exist, if they ever did, but it can be credited with disseminating a portion of African-American musical culture throughout the United States and Europe and preparing the way for the more authentic music of a later period.

Ragtime

Ragtime is a written-down style of music originally composed for the piano and featuring syncopated rhythmic patterns over a regular left-hand accompaniment in duple meter. The essentials of ragtime probably were in existence prior to the Civil War although Scott Joplin (figure 29.7) is formally credited as the first to write ragtime in the mid 1890s. Slaves in their segregated quarters liked to imitate the fancy balls in the plantation house by

staging a cakewalking contest. The highest-stepping couple "took the cake." The basic cakewalk patterns consisted of duple meter plus two kinds of melodic syncopations:

There is a considerable body of ragtime piano literature, most of which is too difficult for the average pianist to play. Consequently, there is much watered-down semi-ragtime popular music from the period 1900–1920. Almost any piece of music can be "ragged" by changing the meter to duple, if necessary, and converting the rhythms into ragtime patterns. In developed ragtime these syncopations would include the two patterns illustrated above plus the more difficult pattern of four-note groups in which every third note is accented:

Examples: "The Entertainer" and "Maple Leaf Rag" by Scott Joplin

The Styles of Jazz

New Orleans Style

Jazz began at one or more places in the American South sometime between the end of the Civil War and the last decade of the nineteenth century. New Orleans may or may not be the birthplace of jazz, but it certainly figured prominently in the promulgation of the new music. Jazz, New Orleans style, began in the 1890s as brass band performances of spirituals and gospel songs, and ragtime versions of standard band marches. This is the so-called *traditional jazz* which, in a more discreet version played by white musicians, became known as Dixieland jazz. The original New Orleans style, however, still exists and is normally referred to as such.

Brass bands secured many of their instruments from pawn shops where they had been deposited after the Civil War by returning military bandsmen. The instrumentation was fairly typical of marching bands: trumpets, trombones, tuba, snare drum, bass drum, and usually one clarinet. The bands played and paraded for all special functions but especially for the funeral processions. According to a long-standing tradition the bands played spirituals and dirges on the way to the cemetery and some of the same music in a jazz idiom on the way back from the cemetery.

Figure 29.8 *Louis Armstrong's Hot Five. Photo: Springer–Bettmann Film Archive.*

New Orleans jazz is ensemble jazz; everyone plays all the time. In general, the first trumpet has the melody, the clarinet a moving obbligato above the trumpet, and the trombone a contrapuntal bass below the lead trumpet. The material is normally gospel songs, spirituals, and marches, and the meter invariably duple. ("In the churches they sang the spirituals. In the bright New Orleans sun, marching down the street, they played them.") Needless to say, all the music was played by ear and everyone was free to improvise a suitable part for himself. ("You play your part and I play mine. You don't tell me what you want and I don't tell you. We will all variate on the theme.") The texture was polyphonic, a crude but dynamic grouping of musical voices improvising simultaneously on the melodic and harmonic framework of preexisting music. One word can describe New Orleans jazz: *exuberant.*

In the following Listening Example New Orleans jazz has moved indoors and added vocal and instrumental solos—plus a piano.

Listening Example 36

LIL HARDIN ARMSTRONG, *HOTTER THAN THAT* (1927)
Time: 2:59

Louis Armstrong and His Hot Five (figure 29.8)

Louis Armstrong, cornet
Johnny Dodds, clarinet
Kid Ory, trombone
Johnny St. Cyr, banjo
Lil Hardin Armstrong, piano
Vocal by Louis Armstrong

Additional Examples: Preservation Hall Jazz Band; Young Tuxedo Jazz Band; Sweet Emma Barrett and Her Dixieland Boys

Urban Blues

Urban blues are the heart of the true jazz idiom. The accompaniment has changed from the folk (or country) blues guitar to piano or jazz band. The subject matter revolves around the problems of urban (ghetto) life. The feeling is still bittersweet, and the form has crystallized into the classic twelve-bar blues accompanying the rhymed couplet in iambic pentameter. The blues may be sung or played by any instrument.

Examples: Bessie Smith; Big Bill Broonzy; Alberta Hunter; Dinah Washington; Big Joe Turner

Chicago Style

With the closing of Storyville, the legal red-light district of New Orleans (1897–1917), jazz musicians began moving north in increasing numbers. Prohibition and the resultant rise of bootlegging helped make the Roaring Twenties city of Chicago the host for unemployed musicians playing the new and exciting sounds of jazz. Briefly stated, Chicago jazz is New Orleans jazz moved indoors. The ensemble used on the march in the New Orleans sun now played in crowded speakeasies for such dances as the Fox Trot, Shimmy, Black Bottom, and Charleston.

Some of the simultaneous improvising remains, but the bands are playing many popular songs in a more homophonic but still lively and swinging style. The meter is mostly duple, but the instrumentation has changed. The piano, a newcomer to jazz, furnishes the rhythmic harmonic background: drums, guitar or banjo, tuba, or string bass, the rhythm. Varying combinations of trumpet, clarinet, trombone, and saxophone (another newcomer) play the melody and harmony. March tempos have been superseded by a range of tempos suitable for the various dances. The one word for Chicago style would be *frenetic.*

Examples—Recordings made in the 1920s (and later): Jelly Roll Morton; Bix Beiderbecke

Figure 29.9 *Duke Ellington. Photo © Bob Coyle.*

Figure 29.10 *Benny Goodman and His Orchestra. Photo: The Bettmann Archive.*

Swing

The swing era began during the Depression years, the so-called Dancing Thirties. After the repeal of Prohibition in 1933 the speakeasies closed down, leaving many jazz musicians again out of work. The musical migration turned in the direction of New York City with its radio stations, large ballrooms, and crowds of young dancers seeking evenings of economical entertainment. (The usual cost of a dancing date was 35¢—25¢ admission plus two soft drinks.)

The six- or eight-piece bands of the Chicago era were large enough for the tiny speakeasies (with minuscule dance floors) but too small for the spacious ballrooms. More musicians had to be added and stylistic changes made to accommodate them. The individuality of the New Orleans and Chicago styles was subordinated to ensemble playing mixed with improvised solo performances; Big Band jazz was born. Divided into three units of brass (two trumpets, two trombones), four saxophones, and a solid rhythm base (piano, drums, guitar, string bass), the swing band launched what is now recognized as the Classic era of jazz. Swing was by far the dominant style of the Depression years through the end of World War II.

With the advent of the rock era in the 1950s swing went into a steep decline, though a few big bands kept swinging (Count Basie, Duke Ellington (figure 29.9), Woody Herman). After the Bop Revolution that followed World War II (see below) Big Band jazz surfaced again as *progressive jazz,* a modern version of the basic swing style. By the 1970s the term was *mainstream jazz* because the Big Band sound was once again in the mainstream of American jazz.

Examples—Recordings of the 30s and 40s (Swing) and 70s and 80s (Mainstream): Count Basie; Duke Ellington; Benny Goodman (figure 29.10); Glenn Miller; Woody Herman; Stan Kenton

New Orleans Revival

The revival of swing was preceded by an even more basic revival, that of traditional New Orleans jazz. Some white San Francisco musicians took the first steps, in 1939, to save what was left of the original jazz style. First-generation jazz men and women were brought out of retirement and old records collected and studied. Some revivalists used the ragtime piano (or no piano), banjo, tuba, clarinet, trumpet, trombone, and drums in the authentic two-beat New Orleans style though others mixed New Orleans with the four-beat characteristics of swing to create Dixieland. Typical Dixieland jazz uses the "front line" of obbligato clarinet, lead trumpet, and fluid trombone (tailgate trombone) backed by drums, bass, and piano.

Listening Example 37

STEELE, *HIGH SOCIETY* (1955)

Time: 3:01

Turk Murphy and His Band

Style: New Orleans Revival

Other Examples: Preservation Hall Jazz Band; Pete Fountain; Al Hirt

The Bop Revolution

During the long musicians' recording and broadcast strike midway through World War II, an entirely new style of jazz was being developed. On the resumption of recording and broadcasting the unsuspecting public heard, in the style known as *bop* (or *rebop* or *bebop*), the startling sounds of the beginning of modern jazz. The increasingly regimented swing style had stifled most creative activity. Bop took musical control away from the arranger and returned it to the performing musician. The domination of swing was not the only issue, for the emergence of bop was much more of a revolution than most people realized at that time. The radical change in jazz was more like a first wave of the civil rights movement that began with full force in the mid 1950s. Led by black jazz musicians, the bop movement was basically opposed to the white establishment in all its aspects, with particular attention to the domination of white swing bands, who generally monopolized the commercial market of records, radio, and television.

Bop groups were small combos with six or seven instruments that played jazz for listening rather than for dancing. With fast, often frenetic tempos, highly elaborated melodic and rhythmic patterns, and the use of modern dissonant harmonies, the bop combo actually played chamber music jazz. No longer confined to maintaining the beat, the piano and guitar were played much more melodically. The beat was lighter because it was laid down by the string bass rather than the swing-style percussion of guitar, piano, and drums. The drummer was freed from the basic beat to become much more of a versatile instrumentalist.

Bop combos consistently improvised but they usually avoided the conventional pattern of paraphrasing an existing melody while "playing the changes" (improvising on the harmonies). They preferred to create new melodic lines out of existing harmonies; Dizzy Gillespie (figure 29.11) and Charlie Parker, for example, converted a popular romantic ballad named "Whispering" into an uptempo bop version called "Groovin' High."

Figure 29.11 *Dizzy Gillespie. Courtesy of Institute of Jazz Studies Collection, Rutgers University.*

Combining a new melody with the existing harmonies of a popular song had a critical extramusical function because it enabled musicians to avoid what many truly detested—audience requests for specific titles. This was the primary reason for performing "Whispering" as "Groovin' High." Technically, bewildered customer/listeners were granted their request but only on terms that the performer could accept. The problem here was not a basic antagonism between musicians and their public but different perceptions of jazz itself.

Modern Jazz

It was shortly after bop arrived on the scene (during the late 1940s) that jazz passed almost imperceptibly from a form of entertainment (dancing and listening) to an art form in its own right. Assimilated bop techniques made important contributions but the significant factor was the change in attitude: music making that had no other purpose or function than aesthetic communication between performers and their listening audience. The performance of "requests" would henceforth have about as much validity as asking the Philadelphia Orchestra to play "When the Saints Go Marching In."

The leaders of modern jazz included Dizzy Gillespie, Charlie Parker, Bud Powell, Miles Davis, and the big bands of Count Basie, Duke Ellington, Woody Herman, and Stan Kenton. It was Kenton who used the term *progressive jazz* to describe what he and some others saw as consistent advances in contemporary jazz. It is only in retrospect that we can see "progress" in jazz as the shift from mere entertainment for a dancing public to the only totally new art form this country has yet produced.

Third-Stream Jazz

Flowing between the parallel streams of classical music and jazz, third-stream jazz borrows techniques from both while attempting to remain in the jazz idiom. There had been earlier confrontations with classical music in the eras of ragtime ("ragging the classics") and swing ("swinging the classics"). Later jazz styles adopted instrumental, melodic, and harmonic techniques and musical forms from contemporary concert music. Third-stream went a step further with combinations of jazz and string quartets, and jazz combos combined with symphony orchestras. In particular, the Dave Brubeck Quartet and the Modern Jazz Quartet have made interesting third-stream recordings.

Liturgical Jazz

Liturgical jazz has met with considerably more success. Jazz has been a long-accepted practice in many African-American revivals and tent meetings but not until the 1960s did it begin to appear in the worship services of major Protestant denominations. The prime moving force was the intent to update the liturgy by using more contemporary modes of thought and expression. (The basic thrust was, of course, the youth revolt against the Establishment and the war in Vietnam.) Though liturgical jazz was generally accepted by liberal mainline churches there were those who opposed admitting a new art form to church. Some opponents confused jazz with popular music; others reasoned that music formerly associated with New Orleans bordellos, Chicago speakeasies, dance halls, and night clubs was obviously not good enough for church. The fact is, however, that much of the music presently used in churches has similar humble origins. Moreover, there is no such thing as "sacred music"; there is only music used in connection with sacred services. Duke Ellington's recordings of sacred concerts performed in church are interesting, valid modes of jazz used for religious purposes.

Crossover and Fusion

Current jazz styles range from traditional jazz in the New Orleans manner to ragtime, Dixieland, Chicago, bop, and mainstream. Added to this mélange are the eclectic styles called *crossover* and *fusion*. Crossover combines some jazz and rock with popular songs in a style that downplays the drive of both jazz and rock. Fusion is much closer to the jazz tradition; it is defined by *Downbeat*

Figure 29.12 *Chick Corea. Photo courtesy of GRP records.*

magazine as "an agreement between jazz, rock, and funk (soul)." Fusion generally uses mixtures of electronic instruments and acoustic instruments. Examples: recent recordings by Miles Davis and Chick Corea (figure 29.12).

But the latest and more authentic jazz style, called acoustic jazz or straight-ahead jazz, is successfully promoted by exceptionally talented musicians such as Wynton Marsalis (b. 1961). Trumpeter Marsalis refers to himself as a neotraditionalist, who has studied such jazz immortals as Louis Armstrong, Duke Ellington, and Charlie Parker as he forges ahead in what has become a renaissance of African-American jazz. Marsalis, like many of his colleagues, is accomplished in both classical music and jazz, having won Grammies in both types of music, from Bach to the blues. The movement is little concerned with electronic instruments, thus the occasional label of acoustic jazz.

The Listening Example is a modern cool jazz original in quintuple meter (five beats per bar) by alto saxophonist Paul Desmond.

Listening Example 38

PAUL DESMOND, *TAKE FIVE*
The Dave Brubeck Quartet

Time: 2:00

Summary

This chapter has dealt with only a few highlights selected from the bewildering complexities of modern music. Of course, twentieth-century music, like the music of any age, effectively mirrors the prevailing patterns of the age. The impending catastrophe of World War I was forecast in the primitive barbarity of Stravinsky's *The Rite of Spring.* Reflecting the rational, intellectual aspects of the Age of Analysis were the serial techniques of Alban Berg as he exploited the self-imposed discipline of the tone row to achieve the musical results of the Violin Concerto.

Prokofiev's neoclassical Fifth Symphony displayed another kind of discipline, that of casting modern tonal materials in classical forms and making the forms serve the music. Orff's *Carmina Burana* gives some indication of the persistence of the romantic tradition in a century which seems to have little time for sentiment. Charles Ives anticipated many of the innovations of avant-garde twelve-tone composers such as Schoenberg, Berg, and Webern and, after World War II, the avant-garde developed the twelve-tone method into complete serial systems.

Electronic music in various forms (*musique concrète* and synthesizers) exerted an ever-growing influence as reflected in much or all of the work of Babbitt, Messiaen, Boulez, Stockhausen, Varèse, and Cage. Aleatory music, with or without electronic assistance, is not dominating the musical scene but it is certainly making waves.

Britten and Shostakovich, among others, have used a variety of styles to convey sociopolitical viewpoints, whereas Hindemith concentrated on expanding the resources of tonal music and Weill deliberately rejected the complexities of contemporary music in favor of a synthesis of traditional styles (including jazz) which influenced the development of modern musical theatre.

The essence of much of the music of this century can be summarized in the phrase "Things fall apart: the center cannot hold." The old musical centers of clear-cut keys, major-minor tonality, and traditional musical instruments are no longer apropos. Composers have been trying to find and/or establish new centers, new ways of relating to a rapidly changing world.

The search for new musical values has utilized mathematics (twelve-tone and serial techniques), technology (electronic media), the sounds of people, and the sounds of nature. Traditional music has been bent, borrowed, violated, and ignored. The search goes on and, probably, only the next century can look back and describe where the search has led us and what twentieth-century music was all about.

The many faces of contemporary jazz and the infinite variety of the jazz-rock-pop scene seem to span the spectrum of twentieth-century life and thought.

New Orleans—basically the street band sounds of original jazz
Dixieland—a combination of New Orleans jazz and swing for an exuberant, happy sound
Cool—romantic impressionism, always keeping its cool
Mainstream—a bit of swing plus a bit more of progressive and steering down the middle of the road
Hard bop—uncompromising, blowing hard and hot
Soul—return to the roots, to unabashed emotion, to wholehearted involvement
Liturgical jazz—revitalization of the music of established churches
Crossover—some jazz with a little rock and much pop
Fusion—synthesis of jazz, rock, and funk
Straight-ahead jazz—a revival of traditional jazz combined with great technical virtuosity

Culture and Human Values

Most agree that music is the closest thing to an international language this world has. Some Western classical music has been performed around the world but classical music has not had nearly the international impact that jazz has had. As early as the 1920s, jazz was more popular in France than in its country of origin. After World War II, jazz became a worldwide phenomenon and continues to be widely popular around the globe.

The U.S. Department of State has consistently sent jazz groups as goodwill ambassadors to Africa, Asia, and Eastern Europe. Considering the lingering aftereffects of Western imperialism, and of international tensions in general, it appears that American jazz is a valuable American export and one that better exemplifies American values than, for example, the exportation of violent television programs. Whether as a very personal and direct form of communication or as a universally admired art form, jazz sounds a positive note in a world that needs all the help it can get.

Twentieth-Century Literature

chapter *30*

The analogy of the broken center certainly applies to contemporary literature. Amid the wreckage of old values today's authors search for fresh meanings, new forms, and a revitalized sense of personal identity and community.

Almost any thesis about contemporary literature can be proposed and supported with a large body of writing, for ceaseless experimentation has produced many types, moods, and themes. Following are some generalizations about twentieth-century literature leading to comments on specific literary works. The reader is free to agree or disagree with any or all comments.

Conventions and Revolts

Many writers of our century have violated most or all of the restrictions on form and idea that were characteristic of most nineteenth-century writing. There are at least two "literatures of the twentieth century," one before, the other after World War II. The two types are related because they are in revolt against both the literary tradition of the nineteenth century and the rigidity of Victorian mores. The literatures differ because early twentieth-century writers recognized a common core against which they might voice their protest; the writers since World War II are cast adrift, with little unifying force and few webs of connection, and with the urge, almost the necessity, to create anew the meanings and values of life.

The "conventional" revolt early in the century was predictable, as described by John Livingston Lowes: "The ceaseless swing of the artistic pendulum is from the convention of a former age to the revolt of a new day, which in its turn becomes a convention from which still newer artists will in their turn revolt."[1]

The poetic conventions of the nineteenth century generally favored the tight-knit structure of recognizable stanza form: blank verse or couplet, tercet or quatrain, or other nameable unit. There were exceptions, of course, but in general a poem *looked* like a poem, because that was the way poems looked! The order and pattern and design appealed to an audience that liked design, approved of pattern, and believed in order.

But, in about 1914, the Imagist poets challenged the convention with "vers libre" ("free verse")—lines unrhymed and unmetrical. Not only is the form of T. S. Eliot's poem *The Love Song of J. Alfred Prufrock,* for example (see chapter 26), different from that of the past, but the meaning of his poem represents a revolt against the predominant nineteenth-century optimism (or even the pessimism). Yet, with all the innovations of form and meaning, Eliot works within a recognizable tradition. The poem is not only to be felt and experienced, but also to be thought out as an intellectual poem within the rational legacy. Eliot expects his readers to share a common background of meanings and knowledge about, in this case, Hesiod, Dante, and Shakespeare.

At about the same time, Aldous Huxley was writing *Brave New World,* a novel that pictures a society pursuing our present value system until it has destroyed nearly everything of worth. The novel attacked entrenched and accepted values, but it followed the patterned, chronologically structured form of the plotted novel, and made certain assumptions about the common center of meanings held by both the author and the reader. Huxley assumes, for instance, a knowledge of Shakespeare, and further, he presumes the reader shares a value system that accepts Shakespeare as *good.* The great body of literature since World War II cannot make these assumptions. What has happened?

---

1. John Livingston Lowes, *Convention and Revolt in Poetry* (New York, Gordon Press, n.d.)

Because World War II involved the obvious choice between freedom or submission to inhuman systems ruled by power-mad dictators, the emotions and rituals of patriotism seemed appropriate, even noble. Yet, when the conflict ended, the world went back to its old ways, with the victors seeming to take more of a beating than the vanquished. An introspective phase, particularly in the United States, focused on our own shortcomings and the hollowness of much of our way of life. The old materialistic values, as opposed to standards involving the quality of life itself, seemed no longer appropriate. The wars in Korea and especially Vietnam challenged much of the exuberance for the "rightness" of our value system.

At the same time, the Western world was introduced to philosophies of existentialism that denied inherent intelligence and purpose in the universe or intrinsic meaning in individual life. The effect on an ever-growing number of thoughtful individuals has been to destroy the old center of certainty: to force them to peer over the brink of life and discover nothing but senseless void beyond. Thus, for many, old values have been seriously questioned or destroyed completely.

None of these literary developments are entirely new. Pessimism was not invented in the twentieth century; existentialism had its immediate source in Kierkegaard and Nietzsche in the nineteenth century and can be traced as far back as the Greek philosopher Demokritos; new forms for literature (black humor, science fiction) have antecedents. Whatever writers have done in the near and distant past appears to have all flowed together to become a rich reservoir available for literary creation.

Taboos

Previous restrictions about ethics, language, and structure have been relaxed or even swept away, profoundly affecting present-day writing.

Ethics

Social taboos about ethics in general and sexual ethics in particular are much more lax. Not too long ago it was difficult to buy Henry Miller's novels or D. H. Lawrence's *Lady Chatterly's Lover* in the United States, because they supposedly shocked the general public's idea of "proper" literature. Social restrictions have now become so relaxed that these particular books are not even very exciting in terms of raw sex. There are still restrictions, of course, on so-called hard-core pornography, but any work that has artistic value is protected by the Constitution, thus guaranteeing

society's right to know. The maturation of the public in terms of the freedom to explore the whole range of human experience has stimulated all who create and all who enjoy artworks in any medium.

There has been a change in what was once called "morality," a shift in generally accepted ideas of *good* and *bad*; in a great deal of early twentieth-century writing goodness seems to be a combination of luck and the functioning of the endocrine glands, or perhaps more simply, Not Being Caught. Examples of this—the antihero—are everywhere. Saul Bellow's fine novel, *Seize the Day*, has Tommy Wilhelm as its protagonist, certainly one of the dirtiest slobs in literature, whose one redeeming quality is a response to humanity in the midst of a cold and negative environment. Even in such popular fiction as John Le Carré's *The Spy Who Came in from the Cold*, the hero has no sense of honor or patriotism until he finally warms to the plight of a single human being in an act of personal loyalty, not in terms of such generalizations as patriotism or democracy. *Good, bad, honor, honesty, courage, loyalty, betrayal*, these and many other words no longer have clear-cut meanings. It depends entirely on the context.

The traditional hero was a knight in shining armor and the villain sneered and twirled his mustache. The modern protagonist may wear a set of rags and sport a three-day growth of beard, or she may be a bag lady moving her meager possessions around in a grocery cart, both hopeful examples of new growth and new value systems. In the two novels mentioned above, *Seize the Day* and *The Spy Who Came in from the Cold*, or McMurphy in Ken Kesey's *One Flew Over the Cuckoo's Nest*, we have protagonists whose final heroism lies in an act of faith for human life, human dignity, and human love. In these instances and many others, we see the discarding of old systems of value, but in the very rubble that they have created artists suggest new views of life and new values that promise fertility and growth both now and for the future.

More than anytime in the past there are other heroes in recent fiction, but these protagonists are heroines. In Judith Rossner's *Looking for Mr. Goodbar* schoolteacher Theresa Dunn is a tragic victim of male-oriented society. Anne Tyler's *Dinner at the Homesick Restaurant* is concerned with the pain and destruction inflicted on a family by, initially, the desertion of the father. On the other hand, Isadora Wing in Erica Jong's *Fear of Flying* has been compared with no less than the irrepressible Wife of Bath. Based on John Cleland's eighteenth-century novel *Fanny Hill*, Jong's *Fanny* is an exuberant and triumphant feminist. Gail Godwin's *A Mother and Two Daughters* is a celebration of American life in feminine terms and a solid statement of faith in human capacity for good. Included in this chapter is Godwin's "A Sorrowful Woman," a somber story of a woman victimized by enforced domesticity.

Language

"Polite" language was the norm in most nineteenth-century literature with the other words appearing in the underground erotic literature of the Victorian era. That taboo has vanished. Words found on the walls and stalls of restrooms appear regularly in our "better" magazines—in fiction, poetry, and nonfiction. This is freedom of expression as guaranteed by the Bill of Rights. Certainly by the time any boy or girl has reached junior high school age, he or she is familiar with all the four-letter words; intrinsically, the word *excrement* is neither better nor worse than its four-letter synonym. Not surprisingly, many writers, especially screenwriters, jumped on the bandwagon and used so many expletives in one form or another that the intended shock values dissipated in the murk of monotonous obscenities. People do use these words in everyday life but does art have to become a Xerox machine in the pursuit of the "real" world? Writers who feel compelled to use the short Anglo-Saxon words may find a true freedom by choosing, from the whole range of language, whatever words are best suited to the purpose of their artwork. That is, in fact, precisely what many contemporary writers are doing.

The freedom to choose from *all* of the words in the language has certainly helped recent translations of ancient, medieval, and modern foreign language literature. Generations of students have assumed that the classics of ancient Greece and Rome, for example, were written in the stilted and sanitary language adopted by earlier translators. Not so! Greek and Roman writers used the full range of their languages including as many explicit words and phrases as found in languages throughout the world. All the works of Aristophanes, Ovid, Catullus, and Juvenal, to name a few, are now available in translations closer to their lustily explicit vocabulary. These writers selected their words from the entire realm of their richly expressive languages, which helps explain their lofty rank in the world's literature.

Structure

A third restriction was the apparent necessity for rational or chronological structure in prose, for traditional "sense" in poetry. The expectation that a literary work have a beginning, a middle, and an end has vanished except for the requirements imposed by the printed page. Present-day writers need not string their words on a "plot." (Plot may be defined as the working out of a theme, usually clearly stated, which is developed in chronological order by the confrontation of two "sides" in opposition, with the ultimate victory of one side over the other.) Until the last third of a century (with notable exceptions, of course) this has been the standard structure for most fiction and drama. It is still used occasionally, especially in mass-appeal writing, but structure is not necessary, and many important writers have discarded the flow-of-time convention and the idea of opposing forces. Many playwrights have discarded logical development in an attempt to achieve immediate and direct feeling, which does not fit Aristotelian concepts of either thought or dramatic art. With the old structures no longer required, writers are free to seek truth in many different ways. Experimentalism in form, sometimes successful, sometimes merely confusing, has become a commonplace in the writers' art.

One of the most noticeable characteristics of literature in our time is its symbolic nature, for many authors use visible and tangible objects to communicate meanings that lie beyond words. The device is as old as literature but modern works abound in symbolism so challenging that readers have to become puzzle solvers. Freudian symbols were once the most frequently encountered, but now one finds color symbolism, Christian symbolism, symbols dealing with primitive fertility and initiation rites. Another sort of symbol makes a parable of the entire work. William Carlos Williams' story "The Use of Force," for example, is a seemingly simple tale of a doctor who, for diagnostic purposes, tries to force a little girl to open her mouth; this becomes a cosmic situation that reveals all the brutality and violence in the world of men and women. Modern writers employ such devices because ingenuity fascinates readers, the intellectual challenge of recognizing and following the hints and clues of the skillfully contrived tale, rather than the simple acceptance of face values. Here is one reason for abandoning the conventional plot. Many writers delight in taking a small surface incident and exploring it, probing down and down through various levels of meaning—sociological, psychological, philosophical, even mythical. Symbolism and multilevel explorations have become common procedures in much of twentieth-century fiction, some of which we will consider.

Poetry

Experiments in Form, Subject, and Language

Form, subject, and language are three aspects of poetry that are so closely united as to be inseparable in total effect. However, poetry can be analyzed by arbitrarily considering each aspect separately.

The free verse in Eliot's *The Love Song of J. Alfred Prufrock* is an excellent example of this formal innovation. Robinson Jeffers' "Shine, Perishing Republic" (chapter 27) is another instance of free verse, with his characteristic long, flowing line. The poem has rhythmic effects with phrases often indicated by punctuation; the rhythm is there but not conventional poetic meter.

A strikingly different experiment is the following poem by e e cummings. The poet delights in typographical eccentricity: lack of capitals or punctuation, frequent parentheses; the example quoted is mild in comparison with others among his poems. A notable characteristic is his use, avoidance, and distortion of rhyme: *town-down, winter-did, same-rain.* Innovation in subject matter and form almost necessarily demands a difference in language. This does not simply mean that the modern poet talks about the artifacts of our culture—computers or space travel, for example—but that he or she uses a deliberately distorted grammar, syntax, and logic. Consider "anyone lived in a pretty how town." One must untangle the phrase to find in it perhaps a sardonic amusement at a gushing cliché—"How pretty this little town is!" When this poet wishes to point out the passage of time, he does not say "time after time, as trees come out leaf by leaf"; he telescopes it to "when by now and tree by leaf," and the apparent nonsense suddenly becomes new sense.

Literary Selections

anyone lived in a pretty how town
e e cummings, 1894–1962

anyone lived in a pretty how town
(with up so floating many bells down)
spring summer autumn winter
he sang his didn't he danced his did.

Women and men (both little and small)
cared for anyone not at all
they sowed their isn't they reaped their same
sun moon stars rain

children guessed (but only a few
and down they forgot as up they grew   10
autumn winter spring summer)
that no one loved him more by more

when by now and tree by leaf
she laughed his joy she cried his grief
bird by snow and stir by still
anyone's any was all to her

someones married their everyones
laughed their cryings and did their dance
(sleep wake hope and then) they
said their nevers they slept their dream   20

stars rain sun moon
(and only the snow can begin to explain
how children are apt to forget to remember
with up so floating many bells down)

one day anyone died i guess
(and noone stooped to kiss his face)
busy folk buried them side by side
little by little and was by was

all by all and deep by deep
and more by more they dream their sleep   30
noone and anyone earth by april
wish by spirit and if by yes.

Women and men (both dong and ding)
summer autumn winter spring
reaped their sowing and went their came
sun moon stars rain

Exercises

1. Much of the poetry of cummings is very rhythmic with considerable use of what is called the "variable foot." In stanza 1, for example, the variation occurs in the third line. Try reading the poem aloud to hear how the variations set off the nimble words in the other lines.
2. Many of the phrases are dissociated from expected relationships. Try rephrasing some of these to see what happens to the rhythm. Do the conventional versions become commonplace?

WHEN ALL MY FIVE AND COUNTRY SENSES SEE

Dylan Thomas, 1914–1953

When all my five and country senses see,
The fingers will forget green thumbs and mark
How, through the halfmoon's vegetable eye,
Husk of young stars and handful zodiac,
Love in the frost is pared and wintered by.
The whispering ears will watch love drummed away
Down breeze and shell to a discordant beach,
And, lashed to syllables, the lynx tongue cry
That her fond wounds are mended bitterly,
My nostrils see her breath burn like a bush.
My one and noble heart has witnesses
In all love's countries, that will grope awake:
And when blind sleep drops on the spying senses,
The heart is sensual, though five eyes break.

The language of Dylan Thomas is so different as to seem baffling at first reading. How can *fingers* forget *green thumbs* and what is the half-moon's *vegetable eye?* Certainly the poet is not talking with simple directness; his words do not "mean" with a single, unchanging meaning, but seem to move in several directions at once. Suppose we try to paraphrase in this fashion: "If all my five natural senses could perceive clearly, see—like my eyes—then even the sense of touch, that helped love grow, would 'see' with the passage of time how love grows old and is laid by, like fruit after harvest; the sense of hearing would 'see' love finished, driven away, ending in discord; the tongue, which is both taste and talk, would 'see' love's pains reluctantly ended; the sense of smell would 'see' love consumed as in a fire. But my heart has other means of perception of love, and these will go on beyond the decaying senses, so that my heart will still know love."

Or suppose that a poet tried to deal with the same idea in a conventional fashion:

Were all my wits perceptive as my eye
Each would tell the same sad tale of waste;
That Love, to which they witness, will go by
And pass beyond them without hope or haste—
Will vanish like a leaf, a smoke, a cry,
As fleeting as a sound or smell or taste.
This I know; but more than this I know:
Still will my heart love on, tho sense be gone:
Let hand or nostril, eye, ear, tongue, all go:
In other senses will my heart love on.

Exercise

Compare the paraphrase with the original poem, with all its startling and centrifugal pulls. Here is not orderly sequence of thought, clearly conveyed; the mind leaps from "fingers" to "green thumbs" to the fertility-and-time association with "half-moon" and its "vegetable" (crescent? growing?) eye. It is not logical (neither is love!), but it is provocative and stimulating; not the mind alone, but the imagination, is stirred. One need not *like* the poem to be aware that here is something intensely alive and interesting, however unpredictable. The ambiguity is part of the effect; why is the "lynx tongue" "lashed to syllables"? Does "lashed" mean *bound, tied, confined,* or *whipped, stirred, driven?* The meanings are different to the point of contradiction, yet both may be appropriate. So, too, someone looking at the paraphrases above may exclaim, "Oh no! that's not it at all!"

Obviously these and the other poems in this chapter (and chapters 26 and 27) cannot do justice to the range and variety of contemporary poetry, but there is enough to demonstrate some of the ideas presented here.

Drama

Realistic Theatre

Modern drama is called "realistic" when its theatrical conventions generally reflect or represent the world in which we live. Actors look, act, and talk like people whom any of us might know. The sets usually give the illusion of actual rooms, lawns, or gardens. No one on stage speaks in rhymed couplets; the medium is prose, not poetry. Actors do not regularly talk to ghosts, play to the audience, or meditate in blank verse on an empty stage. The characters are, in the main, men and women in all walks of life rather than kings and queens, knights and fair ladies.

Some realistic elements appeared in theatre shortly after the Renaissance, but the main development came after the middle of the nineteenth century. Realist dramatists (and representative plays) include Henrik Ibsen (1828–1906), *Hedda Gabler*, George Bernard Shaw (1856–1950), *Pygmalion*; Anton Chekhov (1860–1904), *The Cherry Orchard*; and later, Arthur Miller (b. 1915), *Death of a Salesman*. The emergence of realistic drama paralleled a comparable development in the art of Daumier, Courbet, and Winslow Homer (see figures 25.18–25.20).

Theatre of the Absurd

The other major kind of modern theatre is generally called, for want of a better term, "unrealistic drama." Of the several varieties of "unreality" the most significant is theatre of the absurd, a movement that grew in response to existentialism as it affected, and was affected by, the status of society following World War II. Absurdist playwrights do not necessarily subscribe totally to the philosophy of existentialism, but they do share certain existential ideas: human life appears to have no meaning or purpose; we invent ourselves as we live our lives; our actions are either erratic or they respond to rules that make no sense; all we have in common with anyone else is certain death. Human existence is seen, therefore, as *absurd.*

The originator of theatre of the absurd was Samuel Beckett (1906–1989; 1969 Nobel Prize for Literature). A Protestant Irishman who once served as James Joyce's secretary (and as a spy for the French underground during World War II), Beckett preferred to live in Paris and compose his novels and plays in French. His play *Endgame* sums up human life with a blind, paralyzed protagonist who has bottled up his parents in a trash can. In *Krapp's Last Tape* a single actor sits at a tape recorder playing back a tape of a long-ago love affair. *Happy Days* stars a married couple with the wife babbling incessantly about her possessions. She is, however, buried up to the waist in the first act and up to her neck in the second act.

Beckett's first performed play, *Waiting for Godot*[2] (1953), remains one of the finest—and best known—of all absurdist dramas. Displaying most of what have become familiar qualities of absurdist theatre, the drama takes place, not in sequential time, but in a timeless present. Two main characters, who may or may not be two different aspects of the same person, are waiting for Godot, who never comes, but who may or may not already be on stage as one of the players. All is ambiguity. Such drama substitutes "tension" for the "conflict" of traditional theatre, but the tension is in the mind and emotions of the spectator. Because the tension is usually left unresolved, different from the logical endings of conventional plays, the theatre goer is left with questions that can only be resolved by each person in the audience. Theatre that, in itself, appears to be unrealistic and illogical turns out to pose the greatest intellectual questions precisely where they should be raised—in the mind of the beholder. A questioning remains rather than the catharsis of the Aristotelian definition of tragedy. Indeed, Euripides anticipated this type of drama in the choral speeches with which he completes both *The Bacchae* and *Alcestis*:

Gods manifest themselves in many forms,
Bring many matters to surprising ends;
The things we thought would happen do not happen;
The unexpected, god makes possible:
And that is what has happened here today.

Shepard, Wilson, and Wasserstein

More recently, Sam Shepard, August Wilson, and Wendy Wasserstein have emerged as leading American playwrights. Shepard (b. 1943) writes in a hyperrealistic mode comparable to the photorealism of artists such as Richard Estes and Audrey Flack (see chapter 28). But Shepard's realism is illusory; the facts are there, it seems, but where reality begins and ends borders on a fifth dimension. Like his *Buried Child* (1979 Pulitzer Prize), *Curse of the Starving Class* (1981), *Fool for Love* (1983), and *A Lie of the Mind* (1986), Shepard's dramas involve lower middle-class families contending with hate, incest, murder, and love. Shepard's symbols are derived from junk food data and rock music, movie, television, and auto mystiques that represent all that is tawdry and tacky in American life. In *True West* (1980) Shepard extols the mythic West, the Old West that is fast succumbing to bulldozers and cement mixers. In this and many more of his forty-plus plays, Shepard poses a basic question: Must this New World become like the Old World just because so much of the Old World is becoming like us?

A poet turned playwright, August Wilson (b. 1945) uses a hyperrealistic style that examines issues of primary concern to the underclass in a society in which racism is still omnipresent. In particular, he writes of individual African Americans as they seek human dignity in such plays as *Ma Rainy's Black Bottom, Joe Turner's Come and Gone, Fences* (1987 Pulitzer Prize), and *The Piano Lesson* (1990 Pulitzer Prize). Though some critics fault Wilson for limiting his subject matter, his response is confident: "I write about the Black experience in America and try to explore in terms of the life I know best those things which are common to all cultures."

Wendy Wasserstein (b. 1950) writes from the feminist perspective in *Uncommon Women and Others, Isn't It Romantic, Happy Birthday, Montpelier, Pizz-zazz,* and *The Heidi Chronicles* (1989 Pulitzer Prize). Using both absurdist and realist techniques, she displays an unerring ability to see the humorous aspects of human existence, particularly in the lives of modern women. A witty and cheery optimist, she explores the comic spheres of women who strike out for themselves and who make a real difference in the world of men and women.

---

2. The copyright holder does not allow this play to be anthologized, which explains its absence from this chapter. Reading it in its only authorized version is strongly recommended.

Modern Prose Fiction

Everything that has been said about modern literature applies also to the novel and short story. As in poetry and drama, prose writers are concerned with new forms, fresh methods of penetrating into the truths of human experience. Black humor and science fiction are two forms that writers have explored in considerable depth and with a great range of subject matter.

Black Humor

Catch-22 by Joseph Heller is perhaps the best known and one of the finest examples of black humor. Black humor *is* funny, but with a bitterness that stings. Basically it is satire, an attack on established ways of thought and action, but a satire that uses surrealistic techniques to achieve its purposes. The typical novel of this sort uses scenes that are sharply etched, with almost photographic naturalism. Yet the scenes and events exist in a bizarre juxtaposition—as in a Dali painting—so that all ordinary sense is lost, and a mind accustomed to logical relationships is utterly confounded. The reader is left with the sense of living through a comical nightmare in which time is compressed or expanded, in which space is purely relative and may change without warning. A novel such as *Catch-22* reveals a crazy world that would amuse only the insane—and then the reverse: maybe the world of the novel is sane and we, with our conventional, Aristotelian minds are the crazy ones.

A brief discussion of *Catch-22* (the novel, *not* the movie) can illustrate the nature of black humor. The central object of ridicule throughout the novel is our rational thought, which goes around in a circle until it ends in total absurdity. The novel takes place during World War II on an Air Force base off the coast of Italy and seems to satirize military life, but a closer scrutiny reveals that it is a bitter attack against much of twentieth-century society and its values. The "Catch" is first unveiled when Yossarian, a bombardier and the protagonist of the novel, objects to flying more missions and pleads insanity with the medical officer in the expectation of a medical discharge (Section 8). The doctor explains that anyone who expresses fear in a dangerous situation is obviously sane and cannot be discharged. Yossarian asks about the men who are flying missions without protest. The doctor's explanation is simple: those men are insane, but because they aren't asking to be relieved of duty he can't send them home. If they asked, they, like Yossarian, would demonstrate they were sane and be immediately returned to duty. This is "Catch-22": perfectly logical, totally absurd, allowing no hope. Repeated use of this circular logic confirms the novel's hopeless, helpless mood.

Heller satirizes other fallacies of our way of life, such as our dependency on paperwork rather than facts in making judgments. Indeed, ex-P.F.C. Wintergreen, a mail clerk, handles and scrambles messages, directing military actions more completely than the generals. Another case in point is the suicidal mission to bomb the city of Bologna, when Yossarian sneaks down to the central map at headquarters and moves the ribbon showing the Allied ground position above the city. Word flies from one level of command to the next: Bologna has been taken and the bombing mission is scrubbed. Finally, inevitably, the truth is known and the mission rescheduled.

Free enterprise and the profit system are attacked unmercifully in the person of supply officer Milo Minderbinder and his M and M Enterprises. Starting with the simple trading for supplies, he finally deals with both the enemy and his own side; at one point he directs the enemy bombing of his own airbase, at another he arranges a total battle, having charge of both sides. He reaps enormous profits of course though he constantly reminds each investor that he "has a share" in M and M Enterprises. "Having a share" is one of the great double-meanings of the book.

The first two-thirds of the book are timeless, shifting from one incident to another with no regard for chronology. For Yossarian, however, the central incident is the fate of his crewmate, Snowden. Yossarian attempts to treat the wounded gunner but, when he zips open the flak suit, Snowden's guts spill out on the floor of the plane. Yossarian suddenly realizes that the world, friend or enemy, is really divided into two groups, the killers and the victims, and that he, as bombardier, is a killer. He refuses this role and for a time goes naked (even when the general is pinning a medal on him) rather than wear the uniform. Referred to throughout the early part of the novel, the Snowden incident is not fully explained until two-thirds of the way through, at which point the story moves on in chronological time. The Snowden incident leads to the first explanation of *Catch-22* and the hopelessness of the situation.

One pilot, Yossarian's tentmate, Orr, has seemed crazier than all the others. His planes keep having engine trouble or are shot down over the sea. Orr ditches his bombers in the water from which everyone is always rescued. The last time Orr ditches his plane his crew is rescued but he is never found. It appears that he has drowned.

The novel ends with a hospital scene with Yossarian and other officers complaining that there is no hope at all. When they hear that Orr has successfully paddled his life raft to neutral Sweden (from the Mediterranean!) the mood changes. Yossarian flees to Rome, intending, somehow, to reach Sweden. The other men, bound by various obligations, will not run for it, but now there is some hope. Man may not conquer, but he can refuse to be conquered. In spite of *Catch-22,* the individual can assert himself.

Science Fiction

Science fiction is not really new, for most utopian literature shares in its fantasy and Jules Verne and H. G. Wells wrote science fiction in the past century. What is new is its reemergence as a serious genre; what had degenerated into comic-strip stuff in the 1930s is now widely accepted. The difference lies in the reasons for writing science fiction. Utopians used it to show that things could be better; Jules Verne wrote literate, highly popular adventure tales. At the present time numerous writers are jolting our minds from ordinary channels and enlarging our concepts of what is possible, or what is not impossible. As we are transported through space, time, or time warps we begin to inhabit a world in which A may not be A; in which not-A can very well be A. Writers have to really work to stay ahead of developments in science and technology; advanced technology has already generated some of the ideas and devices of earlier science fiction with more wonders certain to come.

Pessimism

Nineteenth-century writers were generally optimistic; goodness and virtue were, in the main, triumphant. Around the time of World War I that mood began to change. Many writers were convinced that society stifled the individual and turned life to tragedy or pathos or despair. Most of these novels were revolts against the materialistic goals that society had accepted, that individuals embraced, and that finally betrayed them. Theodore Dreiser's *An American Tragedy,* John Dos Passos' *Manhattan Transfer,* and even Aldous Huxley's *Brave New World* can be read as examples of this trend. More recently, Tom Wolfe's *Bonfire of the Vanities* brilliantly satirizes the gross materialism of much of urban life. Some critics have complained that Wolfe vented his spite on his city but Wolfe responds that he loves New York but hates what it has become, and thus the satire. These are pessimistic views but not totally, for they place the blame on forces external to human beings. If we could reform society, they seem to say, then the spirit of humanity could be liberated in New York and every other place. There is also the idea that the universe itself was accidental and without purpose, that the conditions supporting life on a mediocre planet resulted from a cosmic accident, and that the life or death of any person or group of people is utterly insignificant. Such a point of view, expressed early in the century in Somerset Maugham's *Of Human Bondage,* makes any human plan or purpose or striving completely pointless. All forms of society become nothing more than traps to snare the individual into a mindless conformity.

Later, American writer William Faulkner explored the depths of pessimism in his series of novels dealing with Yoknapatawpha County, Mississippi. Using symbols of violence, rape, incest, fire, and insanity, Faulkner depicts the complete degeneracy of the aristocratic or commercial white man. In his Nobel Prize acceptance speech Faulkner stated his optimistic belief that man will not only endure, he will prevail. In his works themselves, however, one can find only the expression of the lost and displaced nature of people in a universe lacking pattern or purpose.

Are today's writers as pessimistic as those discussed above? Tom Wolfe is not pessimistic nor are many of his contemporaries around the world. There are few who feel they can change the world but there are numerous artists who tackle specific issues with the expectation that their work can make a difference no matter how small—and sometimes it can. Consider, for example, the Czechoslovakian dissident, playwright Vaclav Havel, who languished in a communist prison just shortly before he was elected president of his country.

In conclusion, one observes a welter of experimentation in forms and meanings, some successful, others not. The purpose of experimentation, however, is to free our minds, to take them out of old bondages that have hampered their search for truth. New meanings demand new forms, fresh language, vigorous exploration in the realms of time, space, and consciousness.

Flourishing Literary Arts

In an age when print media are eyeing the relentless onslaught of computer technology, more books (poetry, short stories, novels, biographies, drama, essays) are being published than at any time in history. No one can reasonably predict what the coming century holds, but the literary arts are currently flourishing as perhaps never before. Momentous changes, however, are even now waiting impatiently in the wings:

> We are coming to the end of the culture of the book. Books are still produced and read in prodigious numbers, and they will continue to be as far into the future as one can imagine. However, they do not command the center of the cultural stage. Modern culture is taking shapes that are more various and more complicated than the book-centered culture it is succeeding.[3]

Many of us have difficulty facing up to the waning centrality of the printed book; it has been, after all, basic to Western civilization for five centuries. On the other hand, what is a mere five centuries in the thousands of years of human history? We must remember that the incredible pace of computer evolution is still accelerating. If, for example, "the cost of transportation had fallen as dramatically since 1950 as the cost of computing power, today's traveler would be able to buy a round-trip ticket to Mars for $12.50.[4]

---

3. O. B. Hardison, Jr., *Disappearing Through the Skylight: Culture and Technology in the Twentieth Century* (New York: Viking Penguin, 1989), p. 264.

4. Ibid., p. 270.

Literary Selections

Chapters 26, 27, and 30 include short stories, poems, and selections from essays and novels. All told, these works provide some indication of the variety of style and content of twentieth-century literature. For want of a better scheme, these selections are arranged in chronological order based on the birthdates of the writers. However, we have chosen to end with the chapter from *Catch-22*. It is perhaps the most appropriate work for our bewildering, frustrating, and challenging century.

THE DISINTERESTED KILLER BILL HARRIGAN

Jorge Luis Borges, 1899–1986

The great Argentine master of short prose forms is represented by a selection from his collection of essays called *A Universal History of Infamy* (1930s). This is a partly fictionalized story of Billy the Kid written in what Borges called "baroque," in which his writing "borders on its own parody." The style is deliberately cinematic and with an ending that becomes a playful parody on the tendency of writers to mythologize criminals and readers to venerate them—from a safe distance.

An image of the desert wilds of Arizona, first and foremost, an image of the desert wilds of Arizona and New Mexico—a country famous for its silver and gold camps, a country of breathtaking open spaces, a country of monumental mesas and soft colors, a country of bleached skeletons picked clean by buzzards. Over this whole country, another image—that of Billy the Kid, the hard rider firm on his horse, the young man with the relentless six-shooters, sending out invisible bullets which (like magic) kill at a distance.

The desert veined with precious metals, arid and blinding-bright. The near child who on dying at the age of twenty-one owed to the justice of grown men twenty-one deaths—"not counting Mexicans."

The Larval Stage

Along about 1859, the man who would become known to terror and glory as Billy the Kid was born in a cellar room of a New York City tenement. It is said that he was spawned by a tired-out Irish womb but was brought up among Negroes. In this tumult of lowly smells and wooly heads, he enjoyed a superiority that stemmed from having freckles and a mop of red hair. He took pride in being white; he was also scrawny, wild, and coarse. At the age of twelve, he fought in the gang of the Swamp Angels, that branch of divinities who operated among the neighborhood sewers. On nights redolent of burnt fog, they would clamber out of the foul-smelling labyrinth, trail some German sailor, do him in with a knock on the head, strip him to his underwear, and afterward sneak back to the filth of their starting place. Their leader was a gray-haired Negro, Gas House Jonas, who was also celebrated as a poisoner of horses.

Sometimes, from the upper window of a waterfront dive, a woman would dump a bucket of ashes upon the head of a prospective victim. As he gasped and choked, Swamp Angels would swarm him, rush him into a cellar, and plunder him.

Such were the apprentice years of Billy Harrigan, the future Billy the Kid. Nor did he scorn the offerings of Bowery playhouses, enjoying in particular (perhaps without an inkling that they were signs and symbols of his destiny) cowboy melodramas.

Go West!

If the jammed Bowery theaters (whose top-gallery riffraff shouted "Hoist that rag!" when the curtain failed to rise promptly on schedule) abounded in these blood and thunder productions, the simple explanation is that America was then experiencing the lure of the Far West. Beyond the sunset lay the goldfields of Nevada and California. Beyond the sunset were the redwoods, going down before the ax; the buffalo's huge Babylonian face; Brigham Young's beaver hat and plural bed; the red man's ceremonies and his rampages; the clear air of the deserts; endless-stretching range land; and the earth itself, whose nearness quickens the heart like the nearness of the sea. The West beckoned. A slow, steady rumor populated those years—that of thousands of Americans taking possession of the West. On that march, around 1872, was Bill Harrigan, treacherous as a bull rattler, in flight from a rectangular cell.

The Demolition of a Mexican

History (which, like certain film directors, proceeds by a series of abrupt images) now puts forward the image of a danger-filled saloon, located—as if on the high seas—out in the heart of the all-powerful desert. The time, a blustery night of the year 1873; the place, the Staked Plains of New Mexico. All around, the land is almost uncannily flat and bare, but the sky, with its storm-piled clouds and moon, is full of fissured cavities and mountains. There are a cow's skull, the howl and the eyes of coyotes in the shadows, trim horses, and from the saloon an elongated patch of light. Inside, leaning over the bar, a group of strapping but tired men drink a liquor that warms them for a fight; at the same time, they make a great show of large silver coins bearing a serpent and an eagle. A drunk croons to himself, poker-faced. Among the men are several who speak a language with many s's, which must be Spanish, for those who speak it are looked down on. Bill Harrigan, the red-topped tenement rat, stands among the drinkers. He has downed a couple of *aguardientes* and thinks of asking for one more, maybe because he hasn't a cent left. He is somewhat overwhelmed by these men of the desert. He sees them as imposing, boisterous, happy, and hatefully wise in the handling of wild cattle and big horses. All at once there is dead silence, ignored only by the voice of the drunk, singing out of tune. Someone has come in—a big, burly Mexican, with the face of an old Indian squaw. He is endowed with an immense sombrero and with a pair of six-guns at his side. In awkward English, he wishes a good evening to all the gringo sons of bitches who are drinking. Nobody takes up the challenge. Bill asks who he is, and they whisper to him, in fear, that the Dago—that is the Diego—is Belisario Villagrán, from Chihuahua. At once there is a resounding blast. Sheltered by that wall of tall men, Bill has fired at the intruder. The glass drops from Villagrán's hand; then the man himself drops. He does not need another bullet. Without deigning to glance to the showy dead man, Bill picks up his end of the conversation. "Is that so?" he drawled. "Well, I'm Billy the Kid, from New York." The drunk goes on singing unheeded.

One may easily guess the apotheosis. Bill gives out handshakes all around and accepts praises, cheers, and whiskies. Someone notices that there are no notches on the handle of his revolver and offers to cut one to stand for Villagrán's death. Billy the Kid keeps this someone's razor, though he says that "It's hardly worthwhile noting down Mexicans." This, perhaps, is not quite enough. That night, Bill lays out his blanket beside the corpse and—with great show—sleeps till daybreak.

Deaths for Deaths' Sake

Out of that lucky blast (at the age of fourteen), Billy the Kid the hero was born, and the furtive Bill Harrigan died. The boy of the sewer and the knock on the head rose to become a man of the frontier. He made a horseman of himself, learning to ride straight in the saddle—Wyoming- or Texas-style—and not with his body thrown back, the way they rode in Oregon and California. He never completely matched his legend, but he kept getting closer and closer to it. Something of the New York hooligan lived on in the cowboy; he transferred to Mexicans the hate that had previously been inspired in him by Negroes, but the last words he ever spoke were (swear) words in Spanish. He learned the art of the cowpuncher's life. He learned another, more difficult art—how to lead men. Both helped to make him a good cattle rustler. From time to time, Old Mexico's guitars and whorehouses pulled on him.

With the haunting lucidity of insomnia, he organized populous orgies that often lasted four days and four nights. In the end, glutted, he settled accounts with bullets. While his trigger finger was unfailing, he was the most feared man (and perhaps the most anonymous and most lonely) of that whole frontier. Pat Garrett, his friend, the sheriff who later killed him, once told him, "I've had a lot of practice with the rifle shooting buffalo."

"I've had plenty with the six-shooter," Billy replied modestly. "Shooting tin cans and men."

The details can never be recovered, but it is known that he was credited with up to twenty-one killings—"not counting Mexicans." For seven desperate years, he practiced the extravagance of utter recklessness.

The night of the twenty-fifth of July 1880, Billy the Kid came galloping on his piebald down the main, or only, street of Fort Sumner. The heat was oppressive and the lamps had not been lighted; Sheriff Garrett, seated on a porch in a rocking chair, drew his revolver and sent a bullet through the Kid's belly. The horse kept on; the rider tumbled into the dust of the road. Garrett got off a second shot. The townspeople (knowing the wounded man was Billy the Kid) locked their window shutters tight. The agony was long and blasphemous. In the morning, the sun by then high overhead, they began drawing near, and they disarmed him. The man was gone. They could see in his face the used-up look of the dead.

He was shaved, sheathed in ready-made clothes, and displayed to awe and ridicule in the window of Fort Sumner's biggest store. Men on horseback and in buckboards gathered for miles and miles around. On the third day, they had to use make-up on him. On the fourth day, he was buried with rejoicing.

Exercises

1. How does the meaning of "disinterested" differ from that of "uninterested"? Does the style of the writing agree with the meaning of the text? How is this accomplished?

2. Borge consistently evokes "images," which are a major factor in this cinematic style. Does the style seem less or more serious than that of a standard biography? What does this style allow him to do that more ordinary biographies cannot accomplish?

3. What did the author accomplish by fictionalizing the display and disposal of the outlaw's body?

4. As related by Borge, does this disinterested killer possess any virtues? What did he value and what was of little or no interest? Listing these items should provide a rounded picture of Billy the Kid that was accomplished by a gifted writer in a few pungent paragraphs.

THE WORN PATH

Eudora Welty, b. 1909

This is the story of an errand of love carried out. Old Phoenix laboriously makes her way into town to get some medicine for her grandson; whether he is alive or dead is beside the point. Old Phoenix will continue to make the journey on the worn path that is, quite simply, the habit of love even when it forgets its reason for being.

It was December—a bright frozen day in the early morning. Far out in the country there was an old Negro woman with her head tied in a red rag, coming along a path through the pinewoods. Her name was Phoenix Jackson. She was very old and small and she walked slowly in the dark pine shadows, moving a little from side to side in her steps, with the balanced heaviness and lightness of a pendulum in a grandfather clock. She carried a thin, small cane made from an umbrella, and with this she kept tapping the frozen earth in front of her. This made a grave and persistent noise in the still air, that seemed meditative, like the chirping of a solitary little bird.

She wore a dark striped dress reaching down to her shoetops, and an equally long apron of bleached sugar sacks, with a full pocket; all neat and tidy, but every time she took a step she might have fallen over her shoelaces, which dragged from her unlaced shoes. She looked straight ahead. Her eyes were blue with age. Her skin had a pattern all its own of numberless branching wrinkles and as though a whole little tree stood in the middle of her forehead, but a golden colour ran underneath, and the two knobs of her cheeks were illuminated by a yellow burning under the dark. Under the red rag her hair came down on her neck in the frailest of ringlets, still black, and with an odor like copper.

Now and then there was a quivering in the thicket. Old Phoenix said, "Out of my way, all you foxes, owls, beetles, jack rabbits, coons, and wild animals! . . . Keep out from under these feet, little bobwhites. . . . Keep the big wild hogs out of my path. Don't let none of those come running my direction. I got a long way." Under her small black-freckled hand her cane, limber as a buggy whip, would switch at the brush as if to rouse up any hiding things.

On she went. The woods were deep and still. The sun made the pine needles almost too bright to look at, up where the wind rocked. The cones dropped as light as feathers. Down in the hollow was the mourning dove—it was not too late for him.

The path ran up a hill. "Seem like there is chains about my feet, time I get this far," she said, in the voice of argument old people keep to use with themselves. "Something always take a hold on this hill—pleads I should stay."

After she got to the top she turned and gave a full, severe look behind her where she had come. "Up through pines," she said at length. "Now down through oaks."

Her eyes opened their widest and she stared down gently. But before she got to the bottom of the hill a bush caught her dress.

Her fingers were busy and intent, but her skirts were full and long, so that before she could pull them free in one place they were caught in another. It was not possible to allow the dress to tear. "I in the thorny bush," she said. "Thorns, you doing your appointed work. Never want to let folks pass—no sir. Old eyes thought you was a pretty little *green* bush."

Finally, trembling all over, she stood free, and after a moment dared to stoop for her cane.

"Sun so high!" she cried, leaning back and looking, while the thick tears went over her eyes. "The time getting all gone here."

At the foot of this hill was a place where a log was laid across the creek.

"Now comes the trial," said Phoenix.

Putting her right foot out, she mounted the log and shut her eyes. Lifting her skirt, levelling her cane fiercely before her, like a festival figure in some parade, she began to march across. Then she opened her eyes and she was safe on the other side.

"I wasn't as old as I thought," she said.

But she sat down to rest. She spread her skirts on the bank around her and folded her hands over her knees. Up above her was a tree in a pearly cloud of mistletoe. She did not dare to close her eyes, and when a little boy brought her a little plate with a slice of marble-cake on it she spoke to him. "That would be acceptable," she said. But when she went to take it there was just her own hand in the air.

So she left that tree, and had to go through a barbed-wire fence. There she had to creep and crawl, spreading her knees and stretching her fingers like a baby trying to climb the steps. But she talked loudly to herself: she could not let her dress be torn now, so late in the day, and she could not pay for having her arm or leg sawed off if she got caught fast where she was.

At last she was safe through the fence and risen up out in the clearing. Big dead trees, like black men with one arm, were standing in the purple stalks of the withered cotton field. There sat a buzzard.

"Who you watching?"

In the furrow she made her way along.

"Glad this not the season for bulls," she said, looking sideways, "and the good Lord made his snakes to curl up and sleep in the winter. A pleasure I don't see no two-headed snake coming around that tree, where it come once. It took a while to get by him, back in the summer."

She passed through the old cotton and went into a field of dead corn. It whispered and shook, and was taller than her head. "Through the maze now," she said, for there was no path.

Then there was something tall, black, and skinny there, moving before her.

At first she took it for a man. It could have been a man dancing in the field. But she stood still and listened, and it did not make a sound. It was as silent as a ghost.

"Ghost," she said sharply, "who be you the ghost of? For I have heard of nary death close by."

But there was no answer, only the ragged dancing in the wind.

She shut her eyes, reached out her hand, and touched a sleeve. She found a coat and inside that an emptiness, cold as ice.

"You scarecrow," she said. Her face lighted. "I ought to be shut up for good," she said with laughter. "My senses is gone. I too old. I the oldest people I ever know. Dance, old scarecrow," she said, "while I dancing with you."

She kicked her foot over the furrow, and with mouth drawn down shook her head once or twice in a little strutting way. Some husks blew down and whirled in streamers about her skirts.

Then she went on, parting her way from side to side with the cane, through the whispering field. At last she came to the end, to a wagon track, where the silver grass blew between the red ruts. The quail were walking around like pullets, seeming all dainty and unseen.

"Walk pretty," she said. "This the easy place. This the easy going."

She followed the track, swaying through the quiet bare fields, through the little strings of trees silver in their dead leaves, past cabins silver from weather, with the doors and windows boarded shut, all like old women under a spell sitting there. "I walking in their sleep," she said, nodding her head vigorously.

In a ravine she went where a spring was silently flowing through a hollow log. Old Phoenix bent and drank. "Sweetgum makes the water sweet," she said, and drank more. "Nobody knows who made this well, for it was here when I was born."

The track crossed a swampy part where the moss hung as white as lace from every limb. "Sleep on, alligators, and blow your bubbles." Then the track went into the road.

Deep, deep the road went down between the high green-coloured banks. Overhead the live-oaks met, and it was as dark as a cave.

A black dog with a lolling tongue came up out of the weeds by the ditch. She was meditating, and not ready, and when he came at her she only hit him a little with her cane. Over she went in the ditch, like a little puff of milk-weed.

Down there, her senses drifted away. A dream visited her, and she reached her hand up, but nothing reached down and gave her a pull. So she lay there and presently went to talking. "Old woman," she said to herself, "that black dog came up out of the weeds to stall you off, and now there he sitting on his fine tail, smiling at you."

A white man finally came along and found her—a hunter, a young man, with his dog on a chain.

"Well, Granny!" he laughed. "What are you doing there?"

"Lying on my back like a June-bug waiting to be turned over, mister," she said, reaching up her hand.

He lifted her up, gave her a swing in the air, and set her down. "Anything broken, Granny?"

"No, sir, them old dead weeds is springy enough," said Phoenix, when she had got her breath. "I thank you for your trouble."

"Where do you live, Granny?" he asked, while the two dogs were growling at each other.

"Away back yonder, sir, behind the ridge. You can't even see it from here."

"On your way home?"

"No, sir, I going to town."

"Why, that's too far! That's as far as I walk when I come out myself, and I get something for my trouble." He patted the stuffed bag he carried, and there hung down a little closed claw. It was one of the bobwhites, with its beak hooked bitterly to show it was dead. "Now you go on home, Granny!"

"I bound to go to town, mister," said Phoenix. "The time come around."

He gave another laugh, filling the whole landscape. "I know you colored people! Wouldn't miss going to town to see Santa Claus!"

But something held Old Phoenix very still. The deep lines in her face went into a fierce and different radiation. Without warning she had seen with her own eyes a flashing nickel fall out of the man's pocket on to the ground.

"How old are you, Granny?" he was saying.

"There's is no telling, mister," she said, "no telling."

Then she gave a little cry and clapped her hands, and said, "Git on away from here, dog! Look! Look at that dog!" She laughed as if in admiration. "He ain't scared of nobody. He is a big black dog." She whispered, "Sick him!"

"Watch me get rid of that cur," said the man. "Sick him, Pete! Sick him!"

Phoenix heard the dogs fighting and heard the man running and throwing sticks. She even heard a gunshot. But she was slowly bending forward by that time, further and further forward, the lids stretched down over her eyes, as if she were doing this in her sleep. Her chin was lowered almost to her knees. The yellow palm of her hand came out from the fold of her apron. Her fingers slid down and along the ground under the piece of money with the grace and care they would have in lifting an egg from under a sitting hen. Then she slowly straightened up, she stood erect, and the nickel was in her apron pocket. A bird flew by. Her lips moved. "God watching me the whole time. I come to stealing."

The man came back, and his own dog panted about then. "Well, I scared him off that time," he said, and then he laughed and lifted his gun and pointed it at Phoenix.

She stood straight and faced him.

"Doesn't the gun scare you?" he said, still pointing it.

"No, sir, I seen plenty go off closer by, in my day, and for less than what I done," she said, holding utterly still.

He smiled, and shouldered the gun. "Well, Granny," he said, "you must be a hundred years old, and scared of nothing. I'd give you a dime if I had any money with me. But you take my advice and stay home, and nothing will happen to you."

"I bound to go on my way, mister," said Phoenix. She inclined her head in the red rag. Then they went in different directions, but she could hear the gun shooting again and again over the hill.

She walked on. The shadows hung from the oak trees to the road like curtains. Then she smelled wood-smoke, and smelled the river, and she saw a steeple and the cabins on their steep steps. Dozens of little black children whirled around her. There ahead was Natchez shining. Bells were ringing. She walked on.

In the paved city it was Christmas time. There were red and green electric lights strung and crisscrossed everywhere, and all turned on in the daytime. Old Phoenix would have been lost if she had not distrusted her eyesight and depended on her feet to know where to take her.

She paused quietly on the sidewalk, where people were passing by. A lady came along in the crowd, carrying an armful of red-, green-, and silver-wrapped presents; she gave off perfume like the red roses in hot summer, and Phoenix stopped her.

"Please, missy, will you lace up my shoe?" She held up her foot.

"What do you want, Grandma?"

"See my shoe," said Phoenix. "Do all right for out in the country, but wouldn't look right to go in a big building."

"Stand still then, Grandma," said the lady. She put her packages down carefully on the sidewalk beside her and laced and tied both shoes tightly.

"Can't lace 'em with a cane," said Phoenix. "Thank you, missy. I doesn't mind asking a nice lady to tie up my shoe when I gets out on the street."

Moving slowly and from side to side, she went into the stone building and into a tower of steps, where she walked up and around and around until her feet knew to stop.

She entered a door, and there she saw nailed upon the wall the document that had been stamped with the gold seal and framed in the gold frame which matched the dream that was hung up in her head.

"Here I be," she said. There was a fixed and ceremonial stiffness over her body.

"A charity case, I suppose," said an attendant who sat at the desk before her.

But Phoenix only looked above her head. There was sweat on her face; the wrinkles shone like a bright net.

"Speak up, Grandma," the woman said. "What's your name? We must have your history, you know. Have you been here before? What seems to be the trouble with you?"

Old Phoenix only gave a twitch to her face as if a fly were bothering her.

"Are you deaf?" cried the attendant.

But then the nurse came in.

"Oh, that's just old Aunt Phoenix," she said. "She doesn't come for herself—she has a little grandson. She makes these trips just as regular as clockwork. She lives away back off the Old Natchez Trace." She bent down. "Well, Aunt Phoenix, why don't you just take a seat? We won't keep you standing after your long trip." She pointed.

The old woman sat down, bolt upright in the chair.

"Now, how is the boy?" asked the nurse.

Old Phoenix did not speak.

"I said, how is the boy?"

But Phoenix only waited and stared straight ahead, her face very solemn and withdrawn into rigidity.

"Is his throat any better?" asked the nurse. "Aunt Phoenix, don't you hear me? Is your grandson's throat any better since the last time you came for medicine?"

With her hand on her knees, the old woman waited, silent, erect and motionless, just as if she were in armour.

"You mustn't take up our time this way, Aunt Phoenix," the nurse said. "Tell us quickly about your grandson, and get it over. He isn't dead, is he?"

At last there came a flicker and then a flame of comprehension across her face, and she spoke.

"My grandson. It was my memory had left me. There I sat and forgot why I made my long trip."

"Forgot?" the nurse frowned. "After you came so far?"

Then Phoenix was like an old woman begging a dignified forgiveness for waking up frightened in the night. "I never did go to school—I was too old at the Surrender," she said in a soft voice. "I'm an old woman without an education. It was my memory fail me. My little grandson, he is just the same, and I forgot it in the coming."

"Throat never heals, does it?" said the nurse, speaking in a loud, sure voice to Old Phoenix. By now she had a card with something written on it, a little list. "Yes. Swallowed lye. When was it—January—two—three years ago—"

Phoenix spoke unasked now. "No, missy, he not dead, he just the same. Every little while his throat begin to close up again, and he not able to swallow. He not get his breath. He not able to help himself. So the time come around, and I go on another trip for the soothing medicine."

"All right. The doctor said as long as you came to get it you could have it," said the nurse. "But it's an obstinate case."

"My little grandson, he sit up there in the house all wrapped up, waiting by himself," Phoenix went on. "We is the only two left in the world. He suffer and it don't seem to put him back at all. He got a sweet look. He going to last. He wear a little patch quilt and peep out, holding his mouth open like a little bird. I remembers so plain now. I not going to forget him again, no, the whole enduring time. I could tell him from all the others in creation."

"All right." The nurse was trying to hush her now. She brought her a bottle of medicine. "Charity," she said, making a check mark in a book.

Old Phoenix held the bottle close to her eyes and then carefully put it into her pocket.

"I thank you," she said.

"It's Christmas time, Grandma," said the attendant. "Could I give you a few pennies out of my purse?"

"Five pennies is a nickel," said Phoenix stiffly.

"Here's a nickel," said the attendant.

Phoenix rose carefully and held out her hand. She received the nickel and then fished the other nickel out of her pocket and laid it beside the new one. She stared at her palm closely, with her head on one side.

Then she gave a tap with her cane on the floor.

"This is what come to me to do," she said. "I going to the store and buy my child a little windmill they sells, made out of paper. He going to find it hard to believe there such a thing in the world. I'll march myself back where he waiting, holding it straight in this hand."

She lifted her free hand, gave a little nod, turning round, and walked out of the doctor's office. Then her slow step began on the stairs, going down.

Exercises

1. How old was Phoenix? Did you revise your estimate upward as the story progressed? What did she mean when she said that the man's gun did not scare her? What was the "Surrender" that she said she was too old for?
2. Review everything that happened to Phoenix during her journey: her dress caught on thorns; walking the log across the creek; crawling through the barbed-wire fence; "dancing" with the scarecrow; falling on her back "like a June-bug"; encountering the hunter; and so on. Are these metaphors for the kind of life she has led? What *was* her life like?
3. Give several instances of the old lady's sense of humor.
4. What is implied when Phoenix says that "five pennies is a nickel?"
5. Why was the protagonist named Phoenix?
6. What is the connection between the last line of the story and the title?

CHAPTER 1 FROM INVISIBLE MAN
Ralph Ellison, b. 1914

A searing novel about black America and white America, Ralph Ellison's *Invisible Man,* winner of the 1952 National Book Award, is both a folk novel and a polished work in the American literary tradition. Opening with a bizarre boxing match in a white man's "smoker" and culminating in an explosive race riot, this is the epic tale of one man's voyage to self-discovery, a man who is "invisible simply because people refuse to see me." Appearing originally as a short story and then as chapter 1, the following selection gives something of the flavor of a book that should be read in its entirety.

It goes a long way back, some twenty years. All my life I had been looking for something, and everywhere I turned someone tried to tell me what it was. I accepted their answers too, though they were often in contradiction and even self-contradictory. I was naïve. I was looking for myself and asking everyone except myself questions which I, and only I, could answer. It took me a long time and much painful boomeranging of my expectations to achieve a realization everyone else appears to have been born with: That I am nobody but myself. But first I had to discover that I am an invisible man!

And yet I am no freak of nature, nor of history. I was in the cards, other things having been equal (or unequal) eighty-five years ago. I am not ashamed of my grandparents for having been slaves. I am only ashamed of myself for having at one time been ashamed. About eighty-five years ago they were told that they were free, united with others of our country in everything pertaining to the common good, and, in everything social, separate like the fingers of the hand. And they believed it. They exulted in it. They stayed in their place, worked hard, and brought up my father to do the same. But my grandfather is the one. He was an odd old guy, my grandfather, and I am told I take after him. It was he who caused the trouble. On his deathbed he called my father to him and said, "Son, after I'm gone I want you to keep up the good fight. I never told you, but our life is a war and I have been a traitor all my born days, a spy in the enemy's country ever since I give up my gun back in the Reconstruction. Live with your head in the lion's mouth. I want you to overcome 'em with yeses, undermine 'em with grins, agree 'em to death and destruction, let 'em swoller you till they vomit or bust wide open." They thought the old man had gone out of his mind. He had been the meekest of men. The younger children were rushed from the room, the shades drawn and the flame of the lamp turned so low that it sputtered on the wick like the old man's breathing. "Learn it to the younguns," he whispered fiercely; then he died.

But my folks were more alarmed over his last words than over his dying. It was as though he had not died at all, his words caused so much anxiety. I was warned emphatically to forget what he had said and, indeed, this is the first time it has been mentioned outside the family circle. It had a tremendous effect upon me, however. I could never be sure of what he meant. Grandfather had been a quiet old man who never made any trouble, yet on his deathbed he had called himself a traitor and a spy, and he had spoken of his meekness as a dangerous activity. It became a constant puzzle which lay unanswered in the back of my mind. And whenever things went well for me I remembered my grandfather and felt guilty and uncomfortable. It was as though I was carrying out his advice in spite of myself. And to make it worse, everyone loved me for it. I was praised by the most lily-white men of the town. I was considered an example of desirable conduct—just as my grandfather had been. And what puzzled me was that the old man had defined it as *treachery*. When I was praised for my conduct I felt a guilt that in some way I was doing something that was really against the wishes of the white folks, that if they had understood they would have desired me to act just the opposite, that I should have been sulky and mean, and that that really would have been what they wanted, even though they were fooled and thought they wanted me to act as I did. It made me afraid that some day they would look upon me as a traitor and I would be lost. Still I was more afraid to act any other way because they didn't like that at all. The old man's words were like a curse. On my graduation day I delivered an oration in which I showed that humility was the secret, indeed, the very essence of progress. (Not that I believed this—how could I, remembering my grandfather?—I only believed that it worked.) It was a great success. Everyone praised me and I was invited to give the speech at a gathering of the town's leading white citizens. It was a triumph for our whole community.

It was in the main ballroom of the leading hotel. When I got there I discovered that it was on the occasion of a smoker, and I was told that since I was to be there anyway I might as well take part in the battle royal to be fought by some of my schoolmates as part of the entertainment. The battle royal came first.

All of the town's big shots were there in their tuxedoes, wolfing down the buffet foods, drinking beer and whiskey and smoking black cigars. It was a large room with a high ceiling. Chairs were arranged in neat rows around three sides of a portable boxing ring. The fourth side was clear, revealing a gleaming space of polished floor. I had some misgivings over the battle royal, by the way. Not from a distaste for fighting, but because I didn't care too much for the other fellows who were to take part. They were tough guys who seemed to have no grandfather's curse worrying their minds. No one could mistake their toughness. And besides, I suspected that fighting a battle royal might detract from the dignity of my speech. In those pre-invisible days I visualized myself as a potential Booker T. Washington. But the other fellows didn't care too much for me either, and there were nine of them. I felt superior to them in my way, and I didn't like the manner in which we were all crowded together into the servants' elevator. Nor did they like my being there. In fact, as the warmly lighted floors flashed past the elevator we had words over the fact that I, by taking part in the fight, had knocked one of their friends out of a night's work.

We were led out of the elevator through a rococo hall into an anteroom and told to get into our fighting togs. Each of us was issued a pair of boxing gloves and ushered out into the big mirrored hall, which we entered looking cautiously about us and whispering, lest we might accidentally be heard above the noise of the room. It was foggy with cigar smoke. And already the whiskey was taking effect. I was shocked to see some of the most important men of the town quite tipsy. They were all there—bankers, lawyers, judges, doctors, fire chiefs, teachers, merchants. Even one of the more fashionable pastors. Something we could not see was going on up front. A clarinet was vibrating sensuously and the men were standing up and moving eagerly forward. We were a small tight group, clustered together, our bare upper bodies touching and shining with anticipatory sweat; while up front the big shots were becoming increasingly excited over something we still could not see. Suddenly I heard the school superintendent, who had told me to come, yell, "Bring up the shines, gentlemen! Bring up the little shines!"

We were rushed up to the front of the ballroom, where it smelled even more strongly of tobacco and whiskey. Then we were pushed into place. I almost wet my pants. A sea of faces, some hostile, some amused, ringed around us, and in the center, facing us, stood a magnificent blonde—stark naked. There was dead silence. I felt a blast of cold air chill me. I tried to back away, but they were behind me and around me. Some of the boys stood with lowered heads, trembling. I felt a wave of irrational guilt and fear. My teeth chattered, my skin turned to goose flesh, my knees knocked. Yet I was strongly attracted and looked in spite of myself. Had the price of looking been blindness, I would have looked. The hair was yellow like that of a circus kewpie doll, the face heavily powdered and rouged, as though to form an abstract mask, the eyes hollow and smeared a cool blue, the color of a baboon's butt. I felt a desire to spit upon her as my eyes brushed slowly over her body. Her breasts were firm and round as the domes of East Indian temples, and I stood so close as to see the fine skin texture and beads of pearly perspiration glistening like dew around the pink and erected buds of her nipples. I wanted at one and the same time to run from the room, to sink through the floor, or go to her and cover her from my eyes and the eyes of the others with my body; to feel the soft thighs, to caress her and destroy her, to love her and murder her, to hide from her, and yet to stroke where below the small American flag tattooed upon her belly her thighs formed a capital V. I had a notion that of all in the room she saw only me with her impersonal eyes.

And then she began to dance, a slow sensuous movement, the smoke of a hundred cigars clinging to her like the thinnest of veils. She seemed like a fair bird-girl girdled in veils calling to me from the angry surface of some gray and threatening sea. I was transported. Then I became aware of the clarinet playing and the big shots yelling at us. Some threatened us if we looked and others if we did not. On my right I saw one boy faint. And now a man grabbed a silver pitcher from a table and stepped close as he dashed ice water upon him and stood him up and forced two of us to support him as his head hung and moans issued from his thick bluish lips. Another boy began to plead to go home. He was the largest of the group, wearing dark red fighting trunks much too small to conceal the erection which projected from him as though in answer to the insinuating low-registered moaning of the clarinet. He tried to hide himself with his boxing gloves.

And all the while the blonde continued dancing, smiling faintly at the big shots who watched her with fascination, and faintly smiling at our fear. I noticed a certain merchant who followed her hungrily, his lips loose and drooling. He was a large man who wore diamond studs in a shirtfront which swelled with the ample paunch underneath, and each time the blonde swayed her undulating hips he ran his hand through the thin hair of his bald head and, with his arms upheld, his posture clumsy like that of an intoxicated panda, wound his belly in a slow and obscene grind. This creature was completely hypnotized. The music had quickened. As the dancer flung herself about with a detached expression on her face, the men began reaching out to touch her. I could see their beefy fingers sink into the soft flesh. Some of the others tried to stop them and she began to move around the floor in graceful circles, as they gave chase, slipping and sliding over the polished floor. It was mad. Chairs went crashing, drinks were spilt, as they ran laughing and howling after her. They caught her just as she reached a door, raised her from the floor, and tossed her as college boys are tossed at a hazing, and above her red, fixed-smiling lips I saw the terror and disgust in her eyes, almost like my own terror and that which I saw in some of the other boys. As I watched, they tossed her twice and her soft breasts seemed to flatten against the air and her legs flung wildly as she spun. Some of the more sober ones helped her to escape. And I started off the floor, heading for the anteroom with the rest of the boys.

Some were still crying and in hysteria. But as we tried to leave we were stopped and ordered to get into the ring. There was nothing to do but what we were told. All ten of us climbed under the ropes and allowed ourselves to be blindfolded with broad bands of white cloth. One of the men seemed to feel a bit sympathetic and tried to cheer us up as we stood with our backs against the ropes. Some of us tried to grin. "See that boy over there?" one of the men said. "I want you to run across at the bell and give it to him right in the belly. If you don't get him, I'm going to get you. I don't like his looks." Each of us was told the same. The blindfolds were put on. Yet even then I had been going over my speech. In my mind each word was as bright as flame. I felt the cloth pressed into place, and frowned so that it would be loosened when I relaxed.

But now I felt a sudden fit of blind terror. I was unused to darkness. It was as though I had suddenly found myself in a dark room filled with poisonous cottonmouths. I could hear the bleary voices yelling insistently for the battle royal to begin.

"Get going in there!"

"Let me at that big nigger!"

I strained to pick up the school superintendent's voice, as though to squeeze some security out of that slightly more familiar sound.

"Let me at those black sonsabitches!" someone yelled.

"No, Jackson, no!" another voice yelled. "Here, somebody, help me hold Jack."

"I want to get at that ginger-colored nigger. Tear him limb from limb," the first voice yelled.

I stood against the ropes trembling. For in those days I was what they called ginger-colored, and he sounded as though he might crunch me between his teeth like a crisp ginger cookie.

Quite a struggle was going on. Chairs were being kicked about and I could hear voices grunting as with a terrific effort. I wanted to see, to see more desperately than ever before. But the blindfold was tight as a thick skin-puckering scab and when I raised my gloved hands to push the layers of white aside a voice yelled, "Oh, no you don't, black bastard! Leave that alone!"

"Ring the bell before Jackson kills him a coon!" someone boomed in the sudden silence. And I heard the bell clang and the sound of the feet scuffling forward.

A glove smacked against my head. I pivoted, striking out stiffly as someone went past, and felt the jar ripple along the length of my arm to my shoulder. Then it seemed as though all nine of the boys had turned upon me at once. Blows pounded me from all sides while I struck out as best I could. So many blows landed upon me that I wondered if I were not the only blindfolded fighter in the ring, or if the man called Jackson hadn't succeeded in getting me after all.

Blindfolded, I could no longer control my motions. I had no dignity. I stumbled about like a baby or a drunken man. The smoke had become thicker and with each new blow it seemed to sear and further restrict my lungs. My saliva became like hot bitter glue. A glove connected with my head, filling my mouth with warm blood. It was everywhere. I could not tell if the moisture I felt upon my body was sweat or blood. A blow landed hard against the nape of my neck. I felt myself going over, my head hitting the floor. Streaks of blue light filled the black world behind the blindfold. I lay prone, pretending that I was knocked out, but felt myself seized by hands and yanked to my feet. "Get going, black boy! Mix it up!" My arms were like lead, my head smarting from blows. I managed to feel my way to the ropes and held on, trying to catch my breath. A glove landed in my mid-section and I went over again, feeling as though the smoke had become a knife jabbed into my guts. Pushed this way and that by the legs milling around me, I finally pulled erect and discovered that I could see the black, sweat-washed forms weaving in the smoky-blue atmosphere like drunken dancers weaving to the rapid drum-like thuds of blows.

Everyone fought hysterically. It was complete anarchy. Everybody fought everybody else. No group fought together for long. Two, three, four, fought one, then turned to fight each other, were themselves attacked. Blows landed below the belt and in the kidney, with the gloves open as well as closed, and with my eye partly opened now there was not so much terror. I moved carefully, avoiding blows, although not too many to attract attention, fighting from group to group. The boys groped about like blind, cautious crabs crouching to protect their mid-sections, their heads pulled in short against their shoulders, their arms stretched nervously before them, with their fists testing the smoke-filled air like the knobbed feelers of hypersensitive snails. In one corner I glimpsed a boy violently punching the air and heard him scream in pain as he smashed his hand against a ring post. For a second I saw him bent over holding his hand, then going down as a blow caught his unprotected head. I played one group against the other, slipping in and throwing a punch then stepping out of range while pushing the others into the melee to take the blows blindly aimed at me. The smoke was agonizing and there were no rounds, no bells at three minute intervals to relieve our exhaustion. The room spun round me, a swirl of lights, smoke, sweating bodies surrounded by tense white faces. I bled from both nose and mouth, the blood spattering upon my chest.

The men kept yelling, "Slug him, black boy! Knock his guts out!"

"Uppercut him! Kill him! Kill that big boy!"

Taking a fake fall, I saw a boy going down heavily beside me as though we were felled by a single blow, saw a sneaker-clad foot shoot into his groin as the two who had knocked him down stumbled upon him. I rolled out of range, feeling a twinge of nausea.

The harder we fought the more threatening the men became. And yet, I had begun to worry about my speech again. How would it go? Would they recognize my ability? What would they give me?

I was fighting automatically when suddenly I noticed that one after another of the boys was leaving the ring. I was surprised, filled with panic, as though I had been left alone with an unknown danger. Then I understood. The boys had arranged it among themselves. It was the custom for the two men left in the ring to slug it out for the winner's place. I discovered this too late. When the bell sounded two men in tuxedoes leaped into the ring and removed the blindfold. I found myself facing Tatlock, the biggest of the gang. I felt sick at my stomach. Hardly had the bell stopped ringing in my ears than it clanged again and I saw him moving swiftly toward me. Thinking of nothing else to do I hit him smash on the nose. He kept coming, bringing the rank sharp violence of stale sweat. His face was a black blank of a face, only his eyes alive—with hate of me and aglow with a feverish terror from what had happened to us all. I became anxious. I wanted to deliver my speech and he came at me as though he meant to beat it out of me. I smashed him again and again, taking his blows as they came. Then on a sudden impulse I struck him lightly and as we clinched, I whispered, "Fake like I knocked you out, you can have the prize."

"I'll break your behind," he whispered hoarsely.

"For *them*?"

"For *me*, sonofabitch!"

They were yelling for us to break it up and Tatlock spun me half around with a blow, and as a joggled camera sweeps in a reeling scene, I saw the howling red faces crouching tense beneath the cloud of blue-gray smoke. For a moment the world wavered, unraveled, flowed, then my head cleared and Tatlock bounced before me. That fluttering shadow before my eyes was his jabbing left hand. Then falling forward, my head against his damp shoulder, I whispered,

"I'll make it five dollars more."

"Go to hell!"

But his muscles relaxed a trifle beneath my pressure and I breathed, "Seven?"

"Give it to your ma," he said, ripping me beneath the heart.

And while I still held him I butted him and moved away. I felt myself bombarded with punches. I fought back with hopeless desperation. I wanted to deliver my speech more than anything else in the world, because I felt that only these men could judge truly my ability, and now this stupid clown was ruining my chances. I began fighting carefully now, moving in to punch him and out again with my greater speed. A lucky blow to his chin and I had him going too—until I heard a loud voice yell, "I got my money on the big boy."

Hearing this, I almost dropped my guard. I was confused: Should I try to win against the voice out there? Would not this go against my speech, and was not this a moment for humility, for nonresistance? A blow to my head as I danced about sent my right eye popping like a jack-in-the-box and settled my dilemma. The room went red as I fell. It was a dream fall, my body languid and fastidious as to where to land, until the floor became impatient and smashed up to meet me. A moment later I came to. An hypnotic voice said FIVE emphatically. And I lay there, hazily watching a dark red spot of my own blood shaping itself into a butterfly, glistening and soaking into the soiled gray world of the canvas.

When the voice drawled TEN I was lifted up and dragged to a chair. I sat dazed. My eye pained and swelled with each throb of my pounding heart and I wondered if now I would be allowed to speak. I was wringing wet, my mouth still bleeding. We were grouped along the wall now. The other boys ignored me as they congratulated Tatlock and speculated as to how much they would be paid. One boy whimpered over his smashed hand. Looking up front, I saw attendants in white jackets rolling the portable ring away and placing a small square rug in the vacant space surrounded by chairs. Perhaps, I thought, I will stand on the rug to deliver my speech.

Then the M.C. called us, "Come on up here boys and get your money."

We ran forward to where the men laughed and talked in their chairs, waiting. Everyone seemed friendly now.

"There it is on the rug," the man said. I saw the rug covered with coins of all dimensions and a few crumpled bills. But what excited me, scattered here and there, were the gold pieces.

"Boys, it's all yours," the man said. "You get all you grab."

"That's right, Sambo," a blond man said, winking at me confidentially.

I trembled with excitement, forgetting my pain. I would get the gold and the bills, I thought. I would use both hands. I would throw my body against the boys nearest me to block them from the gold.

"Get down around the rug now," the man commanded, "and don't anyone touch it until I give the signal."

"This ought to be good," I heard.

As told, we got around the square rug on our knees. Slowly the man raised his freckled hand as we followed it upward with our eyes.

I heard, "These niggers look like they're about to pray!"

Then, "Ready," the man said. "Go!"

I lunged for a yellow coin lying on the blue design of the carpet, touching it and sending a surprised shriek to join those rising around me. I tried frantically to remove my hand but could not let go. A hot, violent force tore through my body, shaking me like a wet rat. The rug was electrified. The hair bristled up on my head as I shook myself free. My muscles jumped, my nerves jangled, writhed. But I saw that this was not stopping the other boys. Laughing in fear and embarrassment, some were holding back and scooping up the coins knocked off by the painful contortions of the others. The men roared above us as we struggled.

"Pick it up, goddamnit, pick it up!" someone called like a bass-voiced parrot. "Go on, get it!"

I crawled rapidly around the floor, picking up the coins, trying to avoid the coppers and to get greenbacks and the gold. Ignoring the shock by laughing, as I brushed the coins off quickly, I discovered that I could contain the electricity—a contradiction, but it works. Then the men began to push us onto the rug. Laughing embarrassedly, we struggled out of their hands and kept after the coins. We were all wet and slippery and hard to hold. Suddenly I saw a boy lifted into the air, glistening with sweat like a circus seal, and dropped, his wet back landing flush upon the charged rug, heard him yell and saw him literally dance upon his back, his elbows beating a frenzied tattoo upon the floor, his muscles twitching like the flesh of a horse stung by many flies. When he finally rolled off, his face was gray and no one stopped him when he ran from the floor amid booming laughter.

"Get the money," the M.C. called. "That's good hard American cash!"

And we snatched and grabbed, snatched and grabbed. I was careful not to come too close to the rug now, and when I felt the hot whiskey breath descend upon me like a cloud of foul air I reached out and grabbed the leg of a chair. It was occupied and I held on desperately.

"Leggo, nigger! Leggo!"

The huge face wavered down to mine as he tried to push me free. But my body was slippery and he was too drunk. It was Mr. Colcord, who owned a chain of movie houses and "entertainment palaces." Each time he grabbed me I slipped out of his hands. It became a real struggle. I feared the rug more than I did the drunk, so I held on, surprising myself for a moment by trying to topple *him* upon the rug. It was such an enormous idea that I found myself actually carrying it out. I tried not to be obvious, yet when I grabbed his leg, trying to tumble him out of the chair, he raised up roaring with laughter, and, looking at me with soberness dead in the eye, kicked me viciously in the chest. The chair leg flew out of my hand and I felt myself going and rolled. It was as though I had rolled through a bed of hot coals. It seemed a whole century would pass before I would roll free, a century in which I was seared through the deepest levels of my body to the fearful breath within me and the breath seared and heated to the point of explosion. It'll all be over in a flash, I thought as I rolled clear. It'll all be over in a flash.

But not yet, the men on the other side were waiting, red faces swollen as though from apoplexy as they bent forward in their chairs. Seeing their fingers coming toward me I rolled away as a fumbled football rolls off the receiver's fingertips, back into the coals. That time I luckily sent the rug sliding out of place and heard the coins ringing against the floor and the boys scuffling to pick them up and the M.C. calling, "All right, boys, that's all. Go get dressed and get your money."

I was limp as a dish rag. My back felt as though it had been beaten with wires.

When we had dressed the M.C. came in and gave us each five dollars, except Tatlock, who got ten for being last in the ring. Then he told us to leave. I was not to get a chance to deliver my speech, I thought. I was going out into the dim alley in despair when I was stopped and told to go back. I returned to the ballroom, where the men were pushing back their chairs and gathering in groups to talk.

The M.C. knocked on a table for quiet. "Gentlemen," he said "we almost forgot an important part of the program. A most serious part, gentlemen. This boy was brought here to deliver a speech which he made at his graduation yesterday. . . ."

"Bravo!"

"I'm told that he is the smartest boy we've got out there in Greenwood. I'm told that he knows more big words than a pocket-sized dictionary."

Much applause and laughter.

"So now, gentlemen, I want you to give him your attention."

There was still laughter as I faced them, my mouth dry, my eye throbbing. I began slowly, but evidently my throat was tense, because they began shouting, "Louder! Louder!"

"We of the younger generation extol the wisdom of that great leader and educator," I shouted, "who first spoke these flaming words of wisdom: 'A ship lost at sea for many days suddenly sighted a friendly vessel. From the mast of the unfortunate vessel was seen a signal: "Water, water; we die of thirst!" The answer from the friendly vessel came back: "Cast down your bucket where you are." The captain of the distressed vessel, at last heeding the injunction, cast down his bucket, and it came up full of fresh sparkling water from the mouth of the Amazon River.' And like him I say, and in his words, 'To those of my race who depend upon bettering their condition in a foreign land, or who underestimate the importance of cultivating friendly relations with the Southern white man, who is his next-door neighbor, I would say: "Cast down your bucket where you are"—cast it down in making friends in every manly way of the people of all races by whom we are surrounded. . . .'"

I spoke automatically and with such fervor that I did not realize that the men were still talking and laughing until my dry mouth, filling up with blood from the cut, almost strangled me. I coughed, wanted to stop and go to one of the tall brass, sand-filled spittoons to relieve myself, but a few of the men, especially the superintendent, were listening and I was afraid. So I gulped it down, blood, saliva and all, and continued. (What powers of endurance I had during those days! What enthusiasm! What a belief in the rightness of things!) I spoke even louder in spite of the pain. But still they talked and still they laughed, as though deaf with cotton in dirty ears. So I spoke with greater emotional emphasis. I closed my ears and swallowed blood until I was nauseated. The speech seemed a hundred times as long as before, but I could not leave out a single word. All had to be said, each memorized nuance considered, rendered. Nor was that all. Whenever I uttered a word of three or more syllables a group of voices would yell for me to repeat it. I used the phrase "social responsibility" and they yelled:

"What's that word you say, boy?"

"Social responsibility," I said.

"What?"

"Social . . ."

"Louder."

". . . responsibility."

"More!"

"Respon—"

"Repeat!"

"—sibility."

The room filled with the uproar of laughter until, no doubt, distracted by having to gulp down my blood, I made a mistake and yelled a phrase I had often seen denounced in newspaper editorials, heard debated in private.

"Social . . ."

"What?" they yelled.

". . . equality—"

The laughter hung smokelike in the sudden stillness. I opened my eyes, puzzled. Sounds of displeasure filled the room. The M. C. rushed forward. They shouted hostile phrases at me. But I did not understand.

A small dry mustached man in the front row blared out, "Say that slowly, son!"

"What, sir?"

"What you just said!"

"Social responsibility, sir," I said.

"You weren't being smart, were you, boy?" he said, not unkindly.

"No, sir!"

"You sure that about 'equality' was a mistake?"

"Oh, yes, sir," I said. "I was swallowing blood."

"Well, you had better speak more slowly so we can understand. We mean to do right by you, but you've got to know your place at all times. All right, now, go on with your speech."

I was afraid. I wanted to leave but I wanted also to speak and I was afraid they'd snatch me down.

"Thank you, sir," I said, beginning where I had left off, and having them ignore me as before.

Yet when I finished there was a thunderous applause. I was surprised to see the superintendent come forth with a package wrapped in white tissue paper, and, gesturing for quiet, address the men.

"Gentlemen, you see that I did not overpraise this boy. He makes a good speech and some day he'll lead his people in the proper paths. And I don't have to tell you that this is important in these days and times. This is a good, smart boy, and so to encourage him in the right direction, in the name of the Board of Education I wish to present him a prize in the form of this. . . ."

He paused, removing the tissue paper and revealing a gleaming calfskin brief case.

". . . in the form of this first-class article from Shad Witmore's shop."

"Boy," he said, addressing me, "take this prize and keep it well. Consider it a badge of office. Prize it. Keep developing as you are and some day it will be filled with important papers that will help shape the destiny of your people."

I was so moved that I could hardly express my thanks. A rope of bloody saliva forming a shape like an undiscovered continent drooled upon the leather and I wiped it quickly away. I felt an importance that I had never dreamed.

"Open it and see what's inside," I was told.

My fingers a-tremble, I complied, smelling the fresh leather and finding an official-looking document inside. It was a scholarship to the state college for Negroes. My eyes filled with tears and I ran awkwardly off the floor.

I was overjoyed; I did not even mind when I discovered that the gold pieces I had scrambled for were brass pocket tokens advertising a certain make of automobile.

When I reached home everyone was excited. Next day the neighbors came to congratulate me. I even felt safe from grandfather, whose deathbed curse usually spoiled my triumphs. I stood beneath his photograph with my brief case in hand and smiled triumphantly into his stolid black peasant's face. It was a face that fascinated me. The eyes seemed to follow everywhere I went.

That night I dreamed I was at a circus with him and that he refused to laugh at the clowns no matter what they did. Then later he told me to open my brief case and read what was inside and I did, finding an official envelope stamped with the state seal; and inside the envelope I found another and another, endlessly, and I thought I would fall of weariness. "Them's years," he said. "Now open that one." And I did and in it I found an engraved document containing a short message in letters of gold. "Read it," my grandfather said. "Out loud!"

"To Whom It May Concern," I intoned. "Keep This Nigger-Boy Running."

I awoke with the old man's laughter ringing in my ears.

(It was a dream I was to remember and dream again for many years after. But at that time I had no insight into its meaning. First I had to attend college.)

Exercises

1. Why did the protagonist say that his grandfather's dying words "acted like a curse"?
2. Was the true function of the "battle royal" solely entertainment? Explain your answer.
3. What was implied in the way white males treated the naked blonde dancer? Was this at all comparable to the attitude toward blacks? In what ways?
4. The electrified rug was a metaphor for what?
5. Do you feel that the all-pervasive brutality in this story was exaggerated? If your answer was "yes" you might want to look much deeper into the history of race relations in this country and then examine your own attitude.

NAMING OF PARTS
Henry Reed, 1914–1986

It is springtime in the following poem, mating time, as soldiers name the mechanical components of a rifle. Ironically, the gun is both a destructive symbol and a phallic fertility symbol, with terminology appropriate to both war and love.

Today we have naming of parts. Yesterday,
We had daily cleaning. And tomorrow morning,
We shall have what to do after firing. But today,
Today we have naming of parts. Japonica
Glistens like coral in all of the neighboring gardens,
    And today we have naming of parts.
This is the lower sling swivel. And this
Is the upper sling swivel, whose use you will see,
When you are given your slings. And this is the pulling swivel,
Which in your case you have not got. The branches   10
Hold in the gardens their silent, eloquent gestures,
    Which in our case we have not got.
This is the safety catch, which is always released
With an easy flick of the thumb. And please do not let me
See anyone using his finger. You can do it quite easy
If you have any strength in your thumb. The blossoms
Are fragile and motionless, never letting anyone see
    Any of them using their finger.
And this you can see is the bolt. The purpose of this
Is to open the breech, as you see. We can slide it   20
Rapidly backwards and forwards: we call this
Easing the spring. And rapidly backwards and forwards
The early bees are assaulting and fumbling the flowers:
    They call it easing the Spring.
They call it easing the Spring: it is perfectly easy
If you have any strength in your thumb: like the bolt
And the breech, and the cocking piece, and the point of balance,
Which in our case we have not got; and the almond blossoms
Silent in all of the gardens and the bees going backwards and   30
    forwards,
    For today we have naming of parts.

Exercise

Some psychologists maintain that combat has a strong erotic component, that fighting and killing satisfy some kind of sexual drive. Would Freud agree? What is your own reaction?

LIFE, FRIENDS, IS BORING. WE MUST NOT SAY SO

John Berryman, 1914–1972

Berryman, like many other artists, saw the middle years of the century as a dreary procession of wars and other calamities. With his formally designed poetry he tried to relieve some of his personal anguish while making some kind of order in a disorderly world, a world that was worse than absurd; it was boring. Only three years after a critic had observed that Berryman "had come to poetic terms with the wreck of the modern world," the poet leaped to his death from a bridge in Minneapolis.

Life, friends, is boring. We must not say so.
After all, the sky flashes, the great sea yearns,
we ourselves flash and yearn,
and moreover my mother told me as a boy
(repeatedly) "Ever to confess you're bored
means you have no

Inner Resources." I conclude now I have no
inner resources, because I am heavy bored.
Peoples bore me,
literature bores me, especially great literature,
Henry bores me, with his plights & gripes
as bad as Achilles,

who loves people and valiant art, which bores me.
And the tranquil hills, & gin, look like a drag
and somehow a dog
has taken itself & its tail considerably away
into mountains or sea or sky, leaving
behind: me, wag.

Exercises

1. Describe the missing "Inner Resources."
2. Why is great literature more boring than everyday literature?
3. Why the juxtaposition of "tranquil hills" and "gin"?

THE BEAN EATERS

Gwendolyn Brooks, b. 1917

Brooks uses everyday language somewhat like Wordsworth, but her economic use of words and her vivid images mark her as one of the most effective of today's poets.

They eat beans mostly, this old yellow pair.
Dinner is a casual affair.
Plain chipware on a plain and creaking wood,
Tin flatware.

Two who are Mostly Good.
Two who have lived their day,
But keep on putting on their clothes
And putting things away.

And remembering . . .
Remembering, with twinklings and twinges,
As they lean over the beans in their rented back room that is full of
beads and receipts and dolls and cloths, tobacco crumbs, vases and
fringes.

Exercises

1. What is this couple living on and why aren't their children helping them?
2. Are they living on something special in addition to food and money? What might that be?

WE REAL COOL
The Pool Players.
Seven at the Golden Shovel.

Gwendolyn Brooks

We real cool. We
Left school. We
Lurk late. We
Strike straight. We
Sing sin. We
Thin gin. We
Jazz June. We
Die soon.

ADULTERY
James Dickey, b. 1923

Sex in all its manifestations is a basic theme in all literature. The following poem extols the mystery and excitement of an adulterous affair for, as Dickey has written, "adultery seems to me to be the most potentially beautiful and fruitful relationship between men and women, and also the most calamitous and destructive." He cites the "paradox in the relationship of men and women: the more used to each other they are, the less exciting they are to each other." He feels this is a terrible problem and things shouldn't be that way but, he concludes, "There *isn't* any justice in the world in that sense, and things *are* that way."

We have all been in rooms
We cannot die in, and they are odd places, and sad.
Often Indians are standing eagle-armed on hills

In the sunrise   open wide to the Great Spirit
Or gliding in canoes   or cattle are browsing on the walls
Far away   gazing down with the eyes of our children

Not far away   or there are men driving
The last railspike, which has turned
Gold in their hands. Gigantic forepleasure lives

Among such scenes, and we are alone with it   10
At last. There is always some weeping
Between us   and someone is always checking

A wrist watch by the bed to see how much
Longer we have left. Nothing can come
Of this   nothing can come

Of us: of me with my grim techniques
Or you who have sealed your womb
With a ring of convulsive rubber:

Although we come together,
Nothing will come of us. But we would not give   20
It up, for death is beaten

By praying Indians   by distant cows   historical
Hammers   by hazardous meetings that bridge
A continent. One could never die here

Never die   never die
While crying. My lover, my dear one
I will see you next week

When I'm in town. I will call you
If I can. Please get hold of   please don't
Oh God. Please don't any more I can't bear . . . Listen: 30

We have done it again   we are
Still living. Sit up and smile,
God bless you. Guilt is magical.

Exercises

1. Describe a room "we cannot die in."
2. Why does the poet use images of Indians "gliding in canoes" and cattle "browsing on the walls"?
3. Dickey refers to a railspike that has "turned gold" and later speaks of "historical hammers" and of bridging a continent. What actual event does he have in mind and what does this imply in the poem? Is there a double meaning here?
4. What is meant by the phrase "guilt is magical"?

TWO SONGS
Adrienne Rich, b. 1929

In the following poem, reminiscent of the enthusiastic attitude of the ancient Greeks, Adrienne Rich speaks of lust that "too is a jewel."

1
Sex, as they harshly call it,
I fell into this morning
at ten o'clock, a drizzling hour
of traffic and wet newspapers.
I thought of him who yesterday
clearly didn't
turn me to a hot field
ready for plowing,
and longing for that young man
pierced me to the roots
bathing every vein, etc.
All day he appears to me
touchingly desirable,
a prize one could wreck one's peace for.
I'd call it love if love
didn't take so many years
but lust too is a jewel
a sweet flower and what
pure happiness to know
all our high-toned questions
breed in a lively animal.

2

That "old last act"!
And yet sometimes
all seems post coitum triste
and I a mere bystander.
Somebody else is going off,
getting shot to the moon.
Or, a moon-race!
Split seconds after
my opposite number lands
I make it—
we lie fainting together
at a crater-edge
heavy as mercury in our moonsuits
till he speaks—
in a different language
yet one I've picked up
through cultural exchanges . . .
we murmur the first moonwords:
Spasibo. Thanks. O.K.

Exercises

1. Why does the poet use the phrase "as they harshly call it"?
2. Discuss the images evoked by "a drizzling hour of traffic and wet newspapers."
3. Why does line 11 end with "etc."?
4. Describe the distinction made between love and lust.
5. What are "moonwords"? Are there several levels of meaning?

Flight on the Wind
From HOUSE MADE OF DAWN
N. Scott Momaday, b. 1934

In *House Made of Dawn,* (1969 Pulitzer Prize) young Abel returns to tribal life, wondering if he can resume the ancient ways after living like an Anglo in the Army. The seemingly endless conflict of Anglo and Amerindian ways is symbolized by the excerpt given below in which the captured, shivering eagle represents an Indian view of life in America.

He had seen a strange thing, an eagle overhead with its talons closed upon a snake. It was an awful, holy sight, full of magic and meaning.

The Eagle Watchers Society was the sixth to go into the kiva at the summer and autumn rain retreats. It was an important society, and it stood apart from the others in a certain way. This difference—this superiority—had come about a long time ago. Before the middle of the last century there was received into the population of the town a small group of immigrants from the Tanoan city of Bahkyula, a distance of seventy or eighty miles to the east. These immigrants were a wretched people, for they had experienced great suffering. Their land bordered upon the Southern Plains, and for many years they had been an easy mark for marauding bands of buffalo hunters and thieves. They had endured every kind of persecution until one day they could stand no more and their spirit broke. They gave themselves up to despair and were then at the mercy of the first alien wind. But it was not a human enemy that overcame them at last; it was a plague. They were struck down by so deadly a disease that, when the epidemic abated, there were fewer than twenty survivors in all. And this remainder, too, should surely have perished among the ruins of Bahkyula had it not been for these *patrones,* these distant relatives who took them in at the certain risk of their own lives and the lives of their children and grandchildren. It is said that the cacique himself went out to welcome and escort the visitors in. The people of the town must have looked narrowly at those stricken souls who walked slowly towards them, wild in their eyes with grief and desperation. The Bahkyush immigrants brought with them little more than the clothes on their backs, but even in this moment of deep hurt and humiliation, they thought of themselves as a people. They carried three things that should serve thereafter to signal who they were: a sacred flute; the bull mask of Pecos; and the little wooden statue of their patroness *Maria de los Angeles,* whom they called Porcingula. Now, after the intervening years and generations, the ancient blood of this forgotten tribe still ran in the veins of men.

The Eagle Watchers Society was the principal ceremonial organization of the Bahkyush. Its chief, Patiestewa, and all its members were direct descendants of those old men and women who had made that journey along the edge of oblivion. There was a look about these men, even now. It was as if, conscious of having come so close to extinction, they had got a keener sense of humility than their benefactors, and paradoxically a greater sense of pride. Both attributes could be seen in such a man as old Patiestewa. He was hard, and he appeared to have seen more of life than had other men. In their uttermost peril long ago, the Bahkyush had been fashioned into seers and soothsayers. They had acquired a tragic sense, which gave to them as a race so much dignity and bearing. They were medicine men; they were rainmakers and eagle hunters.

He was not thinking of the eagles. He had been walking since daybreak down from the mountain where that year he had broken a horse for the rancher John Raymond. By the middle of the morning he was on the rim of the Valle Grande, a great volcanic crater that lay high up on the western slope of the range. It was the right eye of the earth, held open to the sun. Of all the places that he knew, this valley alone could reflect the great spatial majesty of the sky. It was scooped out of the dark peaks like the well of a great, gathering storm, deep umber and blue and smoke-colored. The view across the diameter was magnificent; it was an unbelievably great expanse. As many times as he had been there in the past, each first new sight of it always brought him up short, and he had to catch his breath. Just there, it seemed, a strange and brilliant light lay upon the world, and all the objects in the landscape were washed clean and set away in the distance. In the morning sunlight the Valle Grande was dappled with the shadows of clouds and vibrant with rolling winter grass. The clouds were always there, huge, sharply described, and shining in the pure air. But the great feature of the valley was its size. It was too great for the eye to hold, strangely beautiful and full of distance. Such vastness makes for illusion, a kind of illusion that comprehends reality, and where it exists there is always wonder and exhilaration. He looked at the facets of a boulder that lay balanced on the edge of the land, and the first thing beyond, the vague, misty field out of which it stood, was the floor of the valley itself, pale and blue-green, miles away. He shifted the focus of his gaze, and he could just make out the clusters of dots that were cattle grazing along the river in the faraway plain.

Then he saw the eagles across the distance, two of them, riding low in the depths and rising diagonally towards him. He did not know what they were at first, and he stood watching them, their far, silent flight erratic and wild in the bright morning. They rose and swung across the skyline, veering close at last, and he knelt down behind the rock, dumb with pleasure and excitement, holding on to them with his eyes.

They were golden eagles, a male and a female, in their mating flight. They were cavorting, spinning and spiralling on the cold, clear columns of air, and they were beautiful. They swooped and hovered, leaning on the air, and swung close together, feinting and screaming with delight. The female was full-grown, and the span of her broad wings was greater than any man's height. There was a fine flourish to her motion: she was deceptively, incredibly fast, and her pivots and wheels were wide and full-blown. But her great weight was streamlined, perfectly controlled. She carried a rattlesnake; it hung shining from her feet, limp and curving out in the trail of her flight. Suddenly her wings and tail fanned, catching full on the wind, and for an instant she was still, widespread and spectral in the blue, while her mate flared past and away, turning round in the distance to look for her. Then she began to beat upward at an angle from the rim until she was small in the sky, and she let go of the snake. It fell, slowly, writhing and rolling, floating out like a bit of silver thread against the wide backdrop of the land. She held still above, buoyed up on the cold current, her crop and hackles gleaming like copper in the sun. The male swerved and sailed. He was younger than she and a little more than half as large. He was quicker, tighter in his moves. He let the carrion drift by; then suddenly he gathered himself and stooped, sliding down in a blur of motion to the strike. He hit the snake in the head, with not the slightest deflection of his course or speed, cracking its long body like a whip. Then he rolled and swung upward in a great pendulum arc, riding out his momentum. At the top of his glide he let go of the snake in turn, but the female did not go for it. Instead she soared out over the plain, nearly out of sight, like a mote receding into the haze of the far mountain. The male followed, and he watched them go, straining to see, saw them veer once, dip and disappear.

Now there was the business of the society. It was getting on towards the end of November, and the eagle hunters were getting ready to set forth to the mountains. He brooded for a time, full of a strange longing; then one day he went to old Patiestewa and told him of what he had seen. "I think you had better let me go," he said. The old chief closed his eyes and thought about it for a long time. Then he answered: "Yes, I had better let you go."

The next day the Bahkyush eagle watchers started out on foot he among them, northward through the canyon and into the high timber beyond. They were gone for days, holding up here and there at the holy places where they must pray and make their offerings. Early in the morning they came out of the trees on the edge of the Valle Grande. The land fell and reached away in the early light as far as the eye could see, the hills folding together and the gray grass rolling in the plain, and they began the descent. At midmorning they came to the lower meadows in the basin. It was clear and cold, and the air was thin and sharp like a shard of glass. They needed bait, and they circled out and apart, forming a ring. When the circle was formed, they converged slowly towards the center, clapping and calling out in a high, flat voice that carried only a little way. And as they closed, rabbits began to jump up from the grass and bound. They got away at first, many of them, while the men were still a distance apart, but gradually the ring grew small and the rabbits crept to the center and hid away in the brush. Now and then one of them tried to break away, and the nearest man threw his stick after it. These weapons were small curved clubs, and they were thrown with deadly accuracy by the eagle hunters, so that when the ring was of a certain size and the men only a few feet apart, very few of the animals got away.

He bent close to the ground, his arm cocked and shaking with tension. A great jackrabbit buck bounded from the grass, straight past him. It struck the ground beyond and sprang again, nearly thirty feet through the air. He spun round and hurled the stick. It struck the jackrabbit a glancing blow just as it bounded again, and it slumped in the air and fell heavily to the ground.

The clapping and calling had stopped. He could feel his heart beating and the sweat growing cold on his skin. There was something like remorse or disappointment now that the rabbits were still and strewn about on the ground. He picked one of the dead animals from the brush—it was warm and soft, its eyes shining like porcelain, full of the dull lustre of death—then the great buck, which was not dead but only stunned and frozen with fear. He felt the warm living weight of it in his hands; it was brittle with life, taut with hard, sinewy strength.

When he had bound the bait together and placed it in the sack, he gathered bunches of tall grass and cut a number of evergreen boughs from a thicket in the plain; these he tied in a bundle and carried in a sling on his back. He went to the river and washed his head in order to purify himself. When all was ready, he waved to the others and started off alone to the cliffs. When he came to the first plateau he rested and looked across the valley. The sun was high, and all around there was a pale, dry uniformity of light, a winter glare on the clouds and peaks. He could see a crow circling low in the distance. Higher on the land, where a great slab of white rock protruded from the mountain, he saw the eagle-hunt house; he headed for it. The house was a small tower of stone, built round a pit, hollow and open at the top. Near it was a shrine, a stone shelf in which there was a slight depression. There he placed a prayer offering. He got into the house, and with boughs he made a latticework of beams across the top and covered it with grass. When it was finished there was a small opening at the center. Through it he raised the rabbits and laid them down on the boughs. He could see here and there through the screen, but his line of vision was vertical, or nearly so, and his quarry would come from the sun. He began to sing, now and then calling out, low in his throat.

The eagles soared southward, high above the Valle Grande. They were almost too high to be seen. From their vantage point the land below reached away on either side to the long, crooked tributaries of the range; down the great open corridor to the south were the wooded slopes and the canyon, the desert and the far end of the earth bending on the sky. They caught sight of the rabbits and were deflected. They veered and banked, lowering themselves into the crater, gathering speed. By the time he knew of their presence, they were low and coming fast on either side of the pit, swooping with blinding speed. The male caught hold of the air and fell off, touching upon the face of the cliff in order to flush the rabbits, while the female hurtled in to take her prey on the run. Nothing happened; the rabbits did not move. She overshot the trap and screamed. She was enraged and she hurled herself around in the air. She swung back with a great clamor of her wings and fell with fury on the bait. He saw her the instant she struck. Her foot flashed out and one of her talons laid the jackrabbit open the length of its body. It stiffened and jerked, and her other foot took hold of its skull and crushed it. In that split second when the center of her weight touched down upon the trap he reached for her. His hands closed upon her legs and he drew her down with all of his strength. For one instant only did she recoil, splashing her great wings down upon the beams and boughs—and she very nearly broke from his grasp; but then she was down in the darkness of the well, hooded, and she was still.

At dusk he met with the other hunters in the plain. San Juanito, too, had got an eagle, but it was an aged male and poor by comparison. They gathered round the old eagle and spoke to it, bidding it return with their good will and sorrow to the eagles of the crags. They fixed a prayer plume to its leg and let it go. He watched it back away and crouch on the ground, glaring, full of fear and suspicion. Then it took leave of the ground and beat upward, clattering through the still shadows of the valley. It gathered speed, driving higher and higher until it reached the shafts of reddish-gold final light that lay like bars across the crater. The light caught it up and set a dark blaze upon it. It levelled off and sailed. Then it was gone from sight, but he looked after it for a time. He could see it still in the mind's eye and hear in his memory the awful whisper of its flight on the wind. He felt the great weight of the bird which he held in the sack. The dusk was fading quickly into night, and the others could not see that his eyes were filled with tears.

That night, while the others ate by the fire, he stole away to look at the great bird. He drew the sack open; the bird shivered, he thought, and drew itself up. Bound and helpless, his eagle seemed drab and shapeless in the moonlight, too large and ungainly for flight. The sight of it filled him with shame and disgust. He took hold of its throat in the darkness and cut off its breath.

Exercises

1. What is symbolized by the image of an eagle holding a snake?
2. Consider the first full paragraph. Could this be a capsule history of what happened to Native Americans?
3. What kinds of feelings are invoked by the descriptions of the land? Can cities be described in this general manner?
4. Consider the mating flight of the two eagles and what this symbolizes.
5. Why was the old eagle freed? Why was the female killed?

A SORROWFUL WOMAN
Gail Godwin, b. 1937

The following short story is a study of the gradual disintegration of a human personality. In keeping with the "once upon a time" lead, the style is similar to a fairy tale but no one lives "happily ever after." The reader should consider the monotonously repetitive tasks taken over by the husband and later shared with the live-in girl, and compare these with the various responsibilities of men in their jobs at the office or wherever. Then, decide how all of this relates to the final "legacy" of food, laundry, and most importantly, sonnets.

Once upon a time there was a wife and mother one too many times

One winter evening she looked at them: the husband durable, receptive, gentle; the child a tender golden three. The sight of them made her so sad and sick she did not want to see them ever again.

She told the husband these thoughts. He was attuned to her; he understood such things. He said he understood. What would she like him to do? "If you could put the boy to bed and read him the story about the monkey who ate too many bananas, I would be grateful." "Of course," he said. "Why, that's a pleasure." And he sent her off to bed.

The next night it happened again. Putting the warm dishes away in the cupboard, she turned and saw the child's grey eyes approving her movements. In the next room was the man, his chin sunk in the open collar of his favorite wool shirt. He was dozing after her good supper. The shirt was the grey of the child's trusting gaze. She began yelping without tears, retching in between. The man woke in alarm and carried her in his arms to bed. The boy followed them up the stairs, saying, "It's all right, Mommy," but this made her scream. "Mommy is sick," the father said, "go and wait for me in your room."

The husband undressed her, abandoning her only long enough to root beneath the eiderdown for her flannel gown. She stood naked except for her bra, which hung by one strap down the side of her body; she had not the impetus to shrug it off. She looked down at the right nipple, shriveled with chill, and thought, How absurd, a vertical bra. "If only there were instant sleep," she said, hiccuping, and the husband bundled her into the gown and went out and came back with a sleeping draught guaranteed swift. She was to drink a little glass of cognac followed by a big glass of dark liquid and afterwards there was just time to say Thank you and could you get him a clean pair of pajamas out of the laundry, it came back today.

The next day was Sunday and the husband brought her breakfast in bed and let her sleep until it grew dark again. He took the child for a walk, and when they returned, red-cheeked and boisterous, the father made supper. She heard them laughing in the kitchen. He brought her up a tray of buttered toast, celery sticks and black bean soup. "I am the luckiest woman," she said, crying real tears. "Nonsense," he said. "You need a rest from us," and went to prepare the sleeping draught, find the child's pajamas, select the story for the night.

She got up on Monday and moved about the house till noon. The boy, delighted to have her back, pretended he was a vicious tiger and followed her from room to room, growling and scratching. Whenever she came close, he would growl and scratch at her. One of his sharp little claws ripped her flesh, just above the wrist, and together they paused to watch a thin red line materialize on the inside of her pale arm and spill over in little beads. "Go away," she said. She got herself upstairs and locked the door. She called the husband's office and said, "I've locked myself away from him. I'm afraid." The husband told her in his richest voice to lie down, take it easy, and he was already on the phone to call one of the baby-sitters they often employed. Shortly after, she heard the girl let herself in, heard the girl coaxing the frightened child to come and play.

After supper several nights later, she hit the child. She had known she was going to do it when the father would see. "I'm sorry," she said, collapsing on the floor. The weeping child had run to hide. "What has happened to me, I'm not myself anymore." The man picked her tenderly from the floor and looked at her with much concern. "Would it help if we got, you know, a girl in? We could fix the room downstairs. I want you to feel freer," he said, understanding these things. "We have the money for a girl. I want you to think about it."

And now the sleeping draught was a nightly thing, she did not have to ask. He went down to the kitchen to mix it, he set it nightly beside her bed. The little glass and the big one, amber and deep rich brown, the flannel gown and the eiderdown.

The man put out the word and found the perfect girl. She was young, dynamic and not pretty. "Don't bother with the room, I'll fix it up myself." Laughing, she employed her thousand energies. She painted the room white, fed the child lunch, read edifying books, raced the boy to the mailbox, hung her own watercolors on the fresh-painted walls, made spinach soufflé, cleaned a spot from the mother's coat, made them all laugh, danced in stocking feet to music in the white room after reading the child to sleep. She knitted dresses for herself and played chess with the husband. She washed and set the mother's soft ash-blonde hair and gave her neck rubs, offered to.

The woman now spent her winter afternoons in the big bedroom. She made a fire in the hearth and put on slacks and an old sweater she had loved at school, and sat in the big chair and stared out the window at snow-ridden branches, or went away into long novels about other people moving through other winters.

The girl brought the child in twice a day, once in the later afternoon when he would tell of his day, all of it tumbling out quickly because there was not much time, and before he went to bed. Often now, the man took his wife to dinner. He made a courtship ceremony of it, inviting her beforehand so she could get used to the idea. They dressed and were beautiful together again and went out into the frosty night. Over candlelight he would say, "I think you are better, you know." "Perhaps I am," she would murmur. "You look . . . like a cloistered queen," he said once, his voice breaking curiously.

One afternoon the girl brought the child into the bedroom. "We've been out playing in the park. He found something he wants to give you, a surprise." The little boy approached her, smiling mysteriously. He placed his cupped hands in hers and left a live dry thing that spat brown juice in her palm and leapt away. She screamed and wrung her hands to be rid of the brown juice. "Oh, it was only a grasshopper," said the girl. Nimbly she crept to the edge of a curtain, did a quick knee bend and reclaimed the creature, led the boy competently from the room.

So the husband came alone. "I have explained to the boy," he said. "And we are doing fine. We are managing." He squeezed his wife's pale arm and put the two glasses on her table. After he had gone, she sat looking at the arm.

"I'm afraid it's come to that," she said. "Just push the notes under the door; I'll read them. And don't forget to leave the draught outside."

The man sat for a long time with his head in his hands. Then he rose and went away from her. She heard him in the kitchen where he mixed the draught in batches now to last a week at a time, storing it in a corner of the cupboard. She heard him come back, leave the big glass and the little one outside on the floor.

Outside her window the snow was melting from the branches, there were more people on the streets. She brushed her hair a lot and seldom read anymore. She sat in her window and brushed her hair for hours, and saw a boy fall off his new bicycle again and again, a dog chasing a squirrel, an old woman peek slyly over her shoulder and then extract a parcel from a garbage can.

In the evening she read the notes they slipped under her door. The child could not write, so he drew and sometimes painted his. The notes were painstaking at first; the man and boy offering the final strength of their day to her. But sometimes, when they seemed to have had a bad day, there were only hurried scrawls.

One night, when the husband's note had been extremely short, loving but short, and there had been nothing from the boy, she stole out of her room as she often did to get more supplies, but crept upstairs instead and stood outside their doors, listening to the regular breathing of the man and boy asleep. She hurried back to her room and drank the draught.

She woke earlier now. It was spring, there were birds. She listened for sounds of the man and the boy eating breakfast; she listened for the roar of the motor when they drove away. One beautiful noon, she went out to look at her kitchen in the daylight. Things were changed. He had bought some new dish towels. Had the old ones worn out? The canisters seemed closer to the sink. She inspected the cupboard and saw new things among the old. She got out flour, baking powder, salt, milk (he bought a different brand of butter), and baked a loaf of bread and left it cooling on the table.

The force of the two joyful notes slipped under her door that evening pressed her into the corner of the little room; she had hardly space to breathe. As soon as possible, she drank the draught.

Now the days were too short. She was always busy. She woke with the first bird. Worked till the sun set. No time for hair brushing. Her fingers raced the hours.

Finally, in the nick of time, it was finished one late afternoon. Her veins pumped and her forehead sparkled. She went to the cupboard, took what was hers, closed herself into the little white room and brushed her hair for a while.

"The girl upsets me," said the woman to her husband. He sat frowning on the side of the bed he had not entered for so long. "I'm sorry, but there it is." The husband stroked his creased brow and said he was sorry too. He really did not know what they would do without that treasure of a girl. "Why don't you stay here with me in bed," the woman said.

Next morning she fired the girl who cried and said, "I loved the little boy, what will become of him now?" But the mother turned away her face and the girl took down the watercolors from the walls, sheathed the records she had danced to and went away.

"I don't know what we'll do. It's all my fault, I know. I'm such a burden, I know that."

"Let me think. I'll think of something." (Still understanding these things.)

"I know you will. You always do," she said.

With great care he rearranged his life. He got up hours early, did the shopping, cooked the breakfast, took the boy to nursery school. "We will manage," he said, "until you're better, however long that is." He did his work, collected the boy from the school, came home and made the supper, washed the dishes, got the child to bed. He managed everything. One evening, just as she was on the verge of swallowing her draught, there was a timid knock on her door. The little boy came in wearing his pajamas. "Daddy has fallen asleep on my bed and I can't get in. There's not room."

Very sedately she left her bed and went to the child's room. Things were much changed. Books were rearranged, toys. He'd done some new drawings. She came as a visitor to her son's room, wakened the father and helped him to bed. "Ah, he shouldn't have bothered you," said the man, leaning on his wife. "I've told him not to." He dropped into his own bed and fell asleep with a moan. Meticulously she undressed him. She folded and hung his clothes. She covered his body with the bedclothes. She flicked off the light that shone in his face.

The next day she moved her things into the girl's white room. She put her hairbrush on the dresser; she put a note pad and pen beside the bed. She stocked the little room with cigarettes, books, bread and cheese. She didn't need much.

At first the husband was dismayed. But he was receptive to her needs. He understood these things. "Perhaps the best thing is for you to follow it through," he said. "I want to be big enough to contain whatever you must do."

All day long she stayed in the white room. She was a young queen, a virgin in a tower; she was the previous inhabitant, the girl with all the energies. She tried these personalities on like costumes, then discarded them. The room had a new view of streets she'd never seen that way before. The sun hit the room in late afternoon and she took to brushing her hair in the sun. One day she decided to write a poem. "Perhaps a sonnet." She took up her pen and pad and began working from words that had lately lain in her mind. She had choices for the sonnet, ABAB or ABBA for a start. She pondered these possibilities until she tottered into a larger choice: she did not have to write a sonnet. Her poem could be six, eight, ten, thirteen lines, it could be any number of lines, and it did not even have to rhyme.

She put down the pen on top of the pad.

In the evenings, very briefly, she saw the two of them. They knocked on her door, a big knock and a little, and she would call Come in, and the husband would smile though he looked a bit tired, yet somehow this tiredness suited him. He would put her sleeping draught on the bedside table and say, "The boy and I have done all right today," and the child would kiss her. One night she tasted for the first time the power of his baby spit.

"I don't think I can see him anymore," she whispered sadly to the man. And the husband turned away, but recovered admirably and said, "Of course, I see."

The man and boy came home and found: five loaves of warm bread, a roast stuffed turkey, a glazed ham, three pies of different fillings, eight molds of the boy's favorite custard, two weeks' supply of fresh-laundered sheets and shirts and towels, two hand-knitted sweaters (both of the same grey color), a sheath of marvelous watercolor beasts accompanied by mad and fanciful stories nobody could ever make up again, and a tablet full of love sonnets addressed to the man. The house smelled redolently of renewal and spring. The man ran to the little room, could not contain himself to knock, flung back the door.

"Look, Mommy is sleeping," said the boy. "She's tired from doing all our things again." He dawdled in a stream of the last sun for that day and watched his father roll tenderly back her eyelids, lay his ear softly to her breast, test the delicate bones of her wrist. The father put down his face into her fresh-washed hair.

"Can we eat the turkey for supper?" the boy asked.

Exercises

1. Itemize the steps in the "abnormal" behavior of the wife from the opening paragraph on. Does this progression appear to be inevitable? What might the husband have done to stop this deterioration?

2. Consider the husband's solution of a live-in girl. What does this tell us about the husband and about his attitude toward his wife?

3. What is the significance of each of the gifts that the wife left for her son and her husband?

4. Why was it necessary for the child to be a boy? Why not a girl? Consider the implications of the final sentence.

NIKKI-ROSA
Nikki Giovanni, b. 1943

The following poem is autobiographical and the poet did indeed become "famous or something." Written in 1968 during the latter days of violent social protests, this is a proud, clear statement of identity. Woodlawn, in the poem, was a black suburb of Cincinnati, Ohio.

childhood remembrances are always a drag
if you're Black
you always remember things like living in Woodlawn
with no inside toilet
and if you become famous or something
they never talk about how happy you were to have your
     mother
all to your self and
how good the water felt when you got your bath from one of
     those   10
big tubs that folk in chicago barbecue in
and somehow when you talk about home
it never gets across how much you
understood their feelings
as the whole family attended meetings about Hollydale
and even though you remember
your biographers never understand
your father's pain as he sells his stock
and another dream goes
and though you're poor it isn't poverty that   20
concerns you
and though they fought a lot
it isn't your father's drinking that makes any difference
but only that everybody is together and you
and your sister have happy birthdays and very good
     christmasses
and I really hope no white person ever has cause to write
     about me
because they never understand Black love is Black wealth and
     they'll   30
probably talk about my hard childhood and never understand
     that
all the while I was quite happy.

Exercise

Are childhood remembrances "always a drag" if you are poor, white, and live in a slum, even if the slum is not a ghetto? How does black love differ from white love? In other words, is this a poem about racism or is it more about a loving family that produced a very fine American poet?

Chapter 39, The Eternal City, From CATCH-22

Joseph Heller, b. 1923

Before starting this excerpt the reader should review the discussion of *Catch-22* given earlier in this chapter.

By the end of chapter 38, Nately, one of Yossarian's companions, has been killed, and Nately's girl friend, named only "Nately's whore," is pursuing Yossarian relentlessly in an effort to kill him. (Can she represent The Furies?) Yossarian has simply refused to fly any more missions, but for various reasons he cannot be court-martialed. His commanding officers simply do not know what to do with him. If he can get away with it, the other men will refuse to fly, too.

Chapter 39 is written in a surrealistic style with the added ironies of black humor: the MPs do not arrest Aarfy, the super-conformist, although he has just raped and killed a woman; when Yossarian is returned to the airbase he discovers that his commanding officers have decided to send him home.

This chapter, however, represents much more than technique in writing. The title has a double meaning. Rome has always been called "the eternal city," but in this chapter it seems to represent Hell on earth, its eternity a bitter comment on life in general. The events within the chapter deal with a descent into the underworld in the classic pattern of Virgil's and Dante's descent. Another interesting parallel can be drawn. Milo Minderbinder, who represents the profit motive in society, can here be compared to Mephistopheles in Goethe's *Faust*. As Faust makes his journey into the classical underworld he is accompanied by Mephistopheles until they encounter the "evil Phorkyads." At that point Mephistopheles deserts Faust exactly as Milo deserts Yossarian to pursue his profits.

After the journey to Rome, the scene starts in the comparative innocence of the brothel, now destroyed by the military police, and continues through the depths of human misery and cruelty, finally ending at the apartment reserved for officers-on-leave, and ends with the return to the airbase.

Yossarian was going absent without official leave with Milo, who, as the plane cruised toward Rome, shook his head reproachfully and, with pious lips pursed, informed Yossarian in ecclesiastical tones that he was ashamed of him. Yossarian nodded. Yossarian was making an uncouth spectacle of himself by walking around backward with his gun on his hip and refusing to fly more combat missions, Milo said. Yossarian nodded. It was disloyal to his squadron and embarrassing to his superiors. He was placing Milo in a very uncomfortable position, too. Yossarian nodded again. The men were starting to grumble. It was not fair for Yossarian to think only of his own safety while men like Milo, Colonel Cathcart,

Colonel Korn and ex-P.F.C. Wintergreen were willing to do everything they could to win the war. The men with seventy missions were starting to grumble because they had to fly eighty, and there was a danger some of them might put on guns and begin walking around backward, too. Morale was deteriorating and it was all Yossarian's fault. The country was in peril; he was jeopardizing his traditional rights of freedom and independence by daring to exercise them.

Yossarian kept nodding in the co-pilot's seat and tried not to listen as Milo prattled on. Nately's whore was on his mind, as were Kraft and Orr and Nately and Dunbar, and Kid Sampson and McWatt, and all the poor and stupid and diseased people he had seen in Italy, Egypt and North Africa and knew about in other areas of the world, and Snowden and Nately's whore's kid sister were on his conscience, too. Yossarian thought he knew why Nately's whore held him responsible for Nately's death and wanted to kill him. Why the hell shouldn't she? It was a man's world, and she and everyone younger had every right to blame him and everyone older for every unnatural tragedy that befell them; just as she, even in her grief, was to blame for every man-made misery that landed on her kid sister and on all other children behind her. Someone had to do something sometime. Every victim was a culprit, every culprit a victim, and somebody had to stand up sometime to try to break the lousy chain of inherited habit that was imperiling them all. In parts of Africa little boys were still stolen away by adult slave traders and sold for money to men who disemboweled them and ate them. Yossarian marveled that children could suffer such barbaric sacrifice without evincing the slightest hint of fear or pain. He took it for granted that they did submit so stoically. If not, he reasoned, the custom would certainly have died, for no craving for wealth or immortality could be so great, he felt, as to subsist on the sorrow of children.

He was rocking the boat, Milo said, and Yossarian nodded once more. He was not a good member of the team, Milo said. Yossarian nodded and listened to Milo tell him that the decent thing to do if he did not like the way Colonel Cathcart and Colonel Korn were running the group was go to Russia, instead of stirring up trouble. Yossarian refrained from pointing out that Colonel Cathcart, Colonel Korn and Milo could all go to Russia if they did not like the way he was stirring up trouble. Colonel Cathcart and Colonel Korn had both been very good to Yossarian, Milo said; hadn't they given him a medal after the last mission to Ferrara and promoted him to captain? Yossarian nodded. Didn't they feed him and give him his pay every month? Yossarian nodded again. Milo was sure they would be charitable if he went to them to apologize and recant and promised to fly eighty missions. Yossarian said he would think it over, and held his breath and prayed for a safe landing as Milo dropped his wheels and glided in toward the runway. It was funny how he had really come to detest flying.

Rome was in ruins, he saw, when the plane was down. The airdrome had been bombed eight months before, and knobby slabs of white stone rubble had been bulldozed into flat-topped heaps on both sides of the entrance through the wire fence surrounding the field. The Colosseum was a dilapidated shell, and the Arch of Constantine had fallen. Nately's whore's apartment was a shambles. The girls were gone, and the only one there was the old woman. The windows in the apartment had been smashed. She was bundled up in sweaters and skirts and wore a dark shawl about her head. She sat on a wooden chair near an electric hot plate, her arms folded, boiling water in a battered aluminum pot. She was talking aloud to herself when Yossarian entered and began moaning as soon as she saw him.

"Gone," she moaned before he could even inquire. Holding her elbows, she rocked back and forth mournfully on her creaking chair. "Gone."

"Who?"

"All. All the poor young girls."

"Where?"

"Away. Chased away into the street. All of them gone. All the poor young girls."

"Chased away by who? Who did it?"

"The mean tall soldiers with the hard white hats and clubs. And by our *carabinieri*. They came with their clubs and chased them away. They would not even let them take their coats. The poor things. They just chased them away into the cold."

"Did they arrest them?"

"They chased them away. They just chased them away."

"Then why did they do it if they didn't arrest them?"

"I don't know," sobbed the old woman. "I don't know. Who will take care of me? Who will take care of me now that the poor young girls are gone? Who will take care of me?"

"There must have been a reason," Yossarian persisted, pounding his fist into his hand. "They couldn't just barge in here and chase everyone out."

"No reason," wailed the old woman. "No reason."

"What right did they have?"

"Catch-22."

"What?" Yossarian froze in his tracks with fear and alarm and felt his whole body begin to tingle. *"What* did you say?"

"Catch-22," the old woman repeated, rocking her head up and down. "Catch-22. Catch-22 says they have a right to do anything we can't stop them from doing."

"What the hell are you talking about?" Yossarian shouted at her in bewildered, furious protest. "How did you know it was Catch-22? Who the hell told you it was Catch-22?"

"The soldiers with the hard white hats and clubs. The girls were crying. 'Did we do anything wrong?' they said. The men said no and pushed them away out the door with the ends of their clubs. 'Then why are you chasing us out?' the girls said. 'Catch-22,' the men said. 'What right do you have?' the girls said. 'Catch-22,' the men said. All they kept saying was 'Catch-22, Catch-22.' What does it mean, Catch-22? What is Catch-22?"

"Didn't they show it to you?" Yossarian demanded, stamping about in anger and distress. "Didn't you even make them read it?"

"They don't have to show us Catch-22," the old woman answered. "The law says they don't have to."

"What law says they don't have to?"

"Catch-22."

"Oh, God damn!" Yossarian exclaimed bitterly. "I bet it wasn't even really there." He stopped walking and glanced about the room disconsolately. "Where's the old man?"

"Gone," mourned the old woman.

"Gone?"

"Dead," the old woman told him, nodding in emphatic lament, pointing to her head with the flat of her hand. "Something broke in here. One minute he was living, one minute he was dead."

"But he can't be dead!" Yossarian cried, ready to argue insistently. But of course he knew it was true, knew it was logical and true: once again the old man had marched along with the majority.

Yossarian turned away and trudged through the apartment with a gloomy scowl, peering with pessimistic curiosity into all the rooms. Everything made of glass had been smashed by the men with the clubs. Torn drapes and bedding lay dumped on the floor. Chairs, tables and dressers had been overturned. Everything breakable had been broken. The destruction was total. No wild vandals could have been more thorough. Every window was smashed, and darkness poured like inky clouds into each room through the shattered panes. Yossarian could imagine the heavy, crashing footfalls of the tall M.P.s in the hard white hats. He could picture the fiery and malicious exhilaration with which they had made their wreckage, and their sanctimonious, ruthless sense of right and dedication. All the poor young girls were gone. Everyone was gone but the weeping old woman in the bulky brown and gray sweaters and black head shawl, and soon she too would be gone.

"Gone," she grieved, when he walked back in, before he could even speak. "Who will take care of me now?"

Yossarian ignored the question. "Nately's girlfriend—did anyone hear from her?" he asked.

"Gone."

"I know she's gone. But did anyone hear from her? Does anyone know where she is?"

"Gone."

"The little sister. What happened to her?"

"Gone." The old woman's tone had not changed.

"Do you know what I'm talking about?" Yossarian asked sharply, staring into her eyes to see if she were not speaking to him from a coma. He raised his voice. "What happened to the kid sister, to the little girl?"

"Gone, gone," the old woman replied with a crabby shrug, irritated by his persistence, her low wail growing louder. "Chased away with the rest, chased away into the street. They would not even let her take her coat."

"Where did she go?"

"I don't know. I don't know."

"Who will take care of her?"

"Who will take care of me?"

"She doesn't know anybody else, does she?"

"Who will take care of me?"

Yossarian left money in the old woman's lap—it was odd how many wrongs leaving money seemed to right—and strode out of the apartment, cursing Catch-22 vehemently as he descended the stairs, even though he knew there was no such thing. Catch-22 did not exist, he was positive of that, but it made no difference. What did matter was that everyone thought it existed, and that was much worse, for there was no object or text to ridicule or refute, to accuse, criticize, attack, amend, hate, revile, spit at, rip to shreds, trample upon or burn up.

It was cold outside, and dark, and a leaky, insipid mist lay swollen in the air and trickled down the large, unpolished stone blocks of the houses and the pedestals of monuments. Yossarian hurried back to Milo and recanted. He said he was sorry and, knowing he was lying, promised to fly as many more missions as Colonel Cathcart wanted if Milo would only use all his influence in Rome to help him locate Nately's whore's kid sister.

"She's just a twelve-year-old virgin, Milo," he explained anxiously, "and I want to find her before it's too late."

Milo responded to his request with a benign smile. "I've got just the twelve-year-old virgin you're looking for," he announced jubilantly. "This twelve-year-old virgin is really only thirty-four, but she was brought up on a low-protein diet by very strict parents and didn't start sleeping with men until—"

"Milo, I'm talking about a little girl!" Yossarian interrupted him with desperate impatience. "Don't you understand? I don't want to sleep with her. I want to help her. You've got daughters. She's just a little kid, and she's all alone in this city with no one to take care of her. I want to protect her from harm. Don't you know what I'm talking about?"

Milo did understand and was deeply touched. "Yossarian, I'm proud of you," he exclaimed with profound emotion. "I really am. You don't know how glad I am to see that everything isn't always just sex with you. You've got principles. Certainly I've got daughters, and I know exactly what you're talking about. We'll find that girl. Don't you worry. You come with me and we'll find that girl if we have to turn this whole city upside down. Come along."

Yossarian went along in Milo Minderbinder's speeding M & M staff car to police headquarters to meet a swarthy, untidy police commissioner with a narrow black mustache and unbuttoned tunic who was fiddling with a stout woman with warts and two chins when they entered his office and who greeted Milo with warm surprise and bowed and scraped in obscene servility as though Milo were some elegant marquis.

"Ah, Marchese Milo," he declared with effusive pleasure, pushing the fat, disgruntled woman out the door without even looking toward her. "Why didn't you tell me you were coming? I would have a big party for you. Come in, come in, Marchese. You almost never visit us any more."

Milo knew that there was not one moment to waste. "Hello, Luigi," he said, nodding so briskly that he almost seemed rude. "Luigi, I need your help. My friend here wants to find a girl."

"A girl, Marchese?" said Luigi, scratching his face pensively. "There are lots of girls in Rome. For an American officer, a girl should not be too difficult."

"No, Luigi, you don't understand. This is a twelve-year-old virgin that he has to find right away."

"Ah, yes, now I understand," Luigi said sagaciously. "A virgin might take a little time. But if he waits at the bus terminal where the young farm girls looking for work arrive, I—"

"Luigi, you still don't understand," Milo snapped with such brusque impatience that the police commissioner's face flushed and he jumped to attention and began buttoning his uniform in confusion. "This girl is a friend, an old friend of the family, and we want to help her. She's only a child. She's all alone in this city somewhere, and we have to find her before somebody harms her. Now do you understand? Luigi, this is very important to me. I have a daughter the same age as that little girl, and nothing in the world means more to me right now than saving that poor child before it's too late. Will you help us?"

"Si, Marchese, now I understand," said Luigi. "And I will do everything in my power to find her. But tonight I have almost no men. Tonight all my men are busy trying to break up the traffic in illegal tobacco."

"Illegal tobacco?" asked Milo.

"Milo," Yossarian bleated faintly with a sinking heart, sensing at once that all was lost.

"Si, Marchese," said Luigi. "The profit in illegal tobacco is so high that the smuggling is almost impossible to control."

"Is there really that much profit in illegal tobacco?" Milo inquired with keen interest, his rust-colored eyebrows arching avidly and his nostrils sniffing.

"Milo," Yossarian called to him. "Pay attention to *me,* will you?"

"Si, Marchese," Luigi answered. "The profit in illegal tobacco is very high. The smuggling is a national scandal, Marchese, truly a national disgrace."

"Is that a fact?" Milo observed with a preoccupied smile and started toward the door as though in a spell.

"Milo!" Yossarian yelled, and bounded forward impulsively to intercept him. "Milo, you've got to help me."

"Illegal tobacco," Milo explained to him with a look of epileptic lust, struggling doggedly to get by. "Let me go. I've got to smuggle illegal tobacco."

"Stay here and help me find her," pleaded Yossarian. "You can smuggle illegal tobacco tomorrow."

But Milo was deaf and kept pushing forward, nonviolently but irresistibly, sweating, his eyes, as though he were in the grip of a blind fixation, burning feverishly, and his twitching mouth slavering. He moaned calmly as though in remote, instinctive distress and kept repeating, "Illegal tobacco, illegal tobacco." Yossarian stepped out of the way with resignation finally when he saw it was hopeless to try to reason with him. Milo was gone like a shot. The commissioner of police unbuttoned his tunic again and looked at Yossarian with contempt.

"What do you want here?" he asked coldly. "Do you want me to arrest you?"

Yossarian walked out of the office and down the stairs into the dark, tomblike street, passing in the hall the stout woman with warts and two chins, who was already on her way back in. There was no sign of Milo outside. There were no lights in any of the windows. The deserted sidewalk rose steeply and continuously for several blocks. He could see the glare of a broad avenue at the top of the long cobblestone incline. The police station was almost at the bottom: the yellow bulbs at the entrance sizzled in the dampness like wet torches. A frigid, fine rain was falling. He began walking slowly, pushing uphill. Soon he came to a quiet, cozy, inviting restaurant with red velvet drapes in the windows and a blue neon sign near the door that said: TONY'S RESTAURANT. FINE FOOD AND DRINK. KEEP OUT. The words on the blue neon sign surprised him mildly for only an instant. Nothing warped seemed bizarre any more in his strange, distorted surroundings. The tops of the sheer buildings slanted in weird, surrealistic perspective, and the street seemed tilted. He raised the collar of his warm woolen coat and hugged it around him. The night was raw. A boy in a thin shirt and thin tattered trousers walked out of the darkness on bare feet. The boy had black hair and needed a haircut and shoes and socks. His sickly face was pale and sad. His feet made grisly, soft, sucking sounds in the rain puddles on the wet pavement as he passed, and Yossarian was moved by such intense pity for his poverty that he wanted to smash his pale, sad, sickly face with his fist and knock him out of existence because he brought to mind *all* the pale, sad, sickly children in Italy that same night who needed haircuts and needed shoes and socks. He made Yossarian think of cripples and of cold and hungry men and women, and of all the dumb, passive, devout mothers with catatonic eyes nursing infants outdoors that same night with chilled animal udders bared insensibly to that same raw rain. Cows. Almost on cue, a nursing mother padded past holding an infant in black rags, and Yossarian wanted to smash her too, because she reminded him of the barefoot boy in the thin shirt and thin, tattered trousers and of all the shivering, stupefying misery in a world that never yet had provided enough heat and food and justice for all but an ingenious and unscrupulous handful. What a lousy earth! He wondered how many people were destitute that same night even in his own prosperous country, how many homes were shanties, how many husbands were drunk and wives socked, and how many children were bullied, abused or abandoned. How many families hungered for food they could not afford to buy? How many hearts were broken? How many suicides would take place that same night, how many people would go insane? How many cockroaches and landlords would triumph? How many winners were losers, successes failures, rich men poor men? How many wise guys were stupid? How many happy endings were unhappy endings? How many honest men were liars, brave men cowards, loyal men traitors, how many sainted men were corrupt, how many people in positions of trust had sold their souls to blackguards for petty cash, how many had never had souls? How many straight-and-narrow paths were crooked paths? How many best families were worst families and how many good people were bad people? When you added them all up and then subtracted, you might be left with only the children, and perhaps with Albert Einstein and an old violinist or sculptor somewhere. Yossarian walked in lonely torture,

feeling estranged, and could not wipe from his mind the excruciating image of the barefoot boy with sickly cheeks until he turned the corner into the avenue finally and came upon an Allied soldier having convulsions on the ground, a young lieutenant with a small, pale, boyish face. Six other soldiers from different countries wrestled with different parts of him, striving to help him and hold him still. He yelped and groaned unintelligibly through clenched teeth, his eyes rolling up into his head. "Don't let him bite his tongue off," a short sergeant near Yossarian advised shrewdly, and a seventh man threw himself into the fray to wrestle with the ill lieutenant's face. All at once the wrestlers won and turned to each other undecidedly, for now that they held the young lieutenant rigid they did not know what to do with him. A quiver of moronic panic spread from one straining brute face to another. "Why don't you lift him and put him on the hood of that car?" a corporal standing in back of Yossarian drawled. That seemed to make sense, so the seven men lifted the young lieutenant up and stretched him out carefully on the hood of a parked car, still pinning each struggling part of him down. Once they had him stretched out on the hood of the parked car, they stared at each other uneasily again, for they had no idea what to do with him next. "Why don't you lift him up off the hood of that car and lay him down on the ground?" drawled the same corporal behind Yossarian. That seemed like a good idea, too, and they began to move him back to the sidewalk, but before they could finish, a jeep raced up with a flashing red spotlight at the side and two military policemen in the front seat.

"What's going on?" the driver yelled.

"He's having convulsions," one of the men grappling with one of the young lieutenant's limbs answered. "We're holding him still."

"That's good. He's under arrest."

"What should we do with him?"

"Keep him under arrest!" the M.P. shouted, doubling over with raucous laughter at his jest, and sped away in his jeep.

Yossarian recalled that he had no leave papers and moved prudently past the strange group toward the sound of muffled voices emanating from a distance inside the murky darkness ahead. The broad, rain-blotched boulevard was illuminated every half-block by short, curling lampposts with eerie, shimmering glares surrounded by smoky brown mist. From a window overhead he heard an unhappy female voice pleading, "Please don't. Please don't." A despondent young woman in a black raincoat with much black hair on her face passed with her eyes lowered. At the Ministry of Public Affairs on the next block, a drunken lady was backed up against one of the fluted Corinthian columns by a drunken young soldier, while three drunken comrades in arms sat watching nearby on the steps with wine bottles standing between their legs. "Pleeshe don't," begged the drunken lady. "I want to go home now. Pleeshe don't." One of the three sitting men cursed pugnaciously and hurled a wine bottle down at Yossarian when he turned to look up. The bottle shattered harmlessly far away with a brief and muted noise. Yossarian continued walking away at the same listless, unhurried pace, hands buried in his pockets. "Come on, baby," he heard the drunken soldier urge determinedly. "It's my turn now." "Pleeshe don't," begged the drunken lady. "Pleeshe don't." At the very next corner, deep inside the dense impenetrable shadows of a narrow, winding side street, he heard the mysterious, unmistakable sound of someone shoveling snow. The measured, labored, evocative scrape of iron shovel against concrete made his flesh crawl with terror as he stepped from the curb to cross the ominous alley and hurried onward until the haunting, incongruous noise had been left behind. Now he knew where he was; soon, if he continued without turning, he would come to the dry fountain in the middle of the boulevard, then to the officers' apartment seven blocks beyond. He heard snarling, inhuman voices cutting through the ghostly blackness in front suddenly. The bulb on the corner lamppost had died, spilling gloom over half the street, throwing everything visible off balance. On the other side of the intersection, a man was beating a dog with a stick like the man who was beating the horse with a whip in Raskolnikov's dream. Yossarian strained helplessly not to see or hear. The dog whimpered and squealed in brute, dumbfounded hysteria at the end of an old Manila rope and groveled and crawled on its belly without resisting, but the man beat it and beat it anyway with his heavy, flat stick. A small crowd watched. A squat woman stepped out and asked him please to stop. "Mind your own business," the man barked gruffly, lifting his stick as though he might beat her too, and the woman retreated sheepishly with an abject and humiliated air. Yossarian quickened his pace to get away, almost ran. The night was filled with horrors, and he thought he knew how Christ must have felt as he walked through the world, like a psychiatrist through a ward full of nuts, like a victim through a prison full of thieves. What a welcome sight a leper must have been! At the next corner a man was beating a small boy brutally in the midst of an immobile crowd of adult spectators who made no effort to intervene. Yossarian recoiled with sickening recognition. He was certain he had witnessed that same horrible scene sometime before. *Déjavu?* The sinister coincidence shook him and filled him with doubt and dread. It was the same scene he had witnessed a block before, although everything in it seemed quite different. What in the world was happening? Would a squat woman step out and ask the man to please stop? Would he raise his hand to strike her and would she retreat? Nobody moved. The child cried steadily as though in drugged misery. The man kept knocking him down with hard, resounding open-palm blows to the head, then jerking him up to his feet in order to knock him down again. No one in the sullen, cowering crowd seemed to care enough about the stunned and beaten boy to interfere. The child was no more than nine. One drab woman was weeping silently into a dirty dish towel. The boy was emaciated and needed a haircut. Bright-red blood was streaming from both ears. Yossarian crossed quickly to the other side of the immense avenue to escape the nauseating sight and found himself walking on human teeth lying on the drenched, glistening pavement near splotches of blood kept sticky by the pelting raindrops poking each one like sharp fingernails. Molars and broken incisors lay scattered everywhere. He circled on tiptoe the grotesque debris and came near a doorway containing a crying soldier holding a saturated handkerchief to his mouth, supported as he sagged by two other soldiers waiting in grave impatience for the military ambulance that finally came clanging up with amber fog lights on and passed them by for an altercation on the next block between a single civilian Italian with books and a slew of civilian policemen with armlocks and clubs. The screaming, struggling civilian was a dark man with a face white as flour from fear. His eyes were pulsating in hectic desperation, flapping like bat's wings, as the many tall policemen seized him by arms and legs and lifted him up. His books were spilled on the ground. "Help!" he shrieked shrilly in a voice strangling in its own emotion as the policemen carried him to the open doors in the rear of the ambulance and threw him inside. "Police! Help! Police!" the doors were shut and bolted, and the ambulance raced away. There was a humorless irony in the ludicrous panic of the man screaming for help to the police while policemen were all around him. Yossarian smiled wryly at the futile and ridiculous cry for aid, then saw with a start that the words were ambiguous, realized with alarm that they were not, perhaps, intended as a call for police but as a heroic warning from the grave by a doomed friend to everyone who was *not* a policeman with a club and a gun and a mob of other policemen with clubs and guns to back him up. "Help! Police!" the man had cried, and he could have been shouting of danger. Yossarian responded to the thought by slipping away stealthily from the police and almost tripped over the feet of a burly woman of forty hastening across the intersection guiltily, darting furtive, vindictive glances behind her toward a woman of eighty with thick, bandaged ankles doddering after her in a losing pursuit. The old woman was gasping for breath as she minced along and muttering to herself in distracted agitation. There was no mistaking the nature of the scene; it was a chase. The triumphant first woman was halfway across the wide avenue before the second woman reached the curb. The nasty, small, gloating smile with which she glanced back at the laboring old woman was both wicked and apprehensive. Yossarian knew he could help the troubled old woman if she would only cry out, knew he could spring forward and capture the sturdy first woman and hold her for the mob of policemen nearby if the second woman would only give him license with a shriek of distress. But the old woman passed by without even seeing him, mumbling in terrible, tragic vexation, and soon the first woman had vanished into the deepening layers of darkness and the old woman was left standing helplessly in the center of the thoroughfare, dazed, uncertain which way to proceed, alone. Yossarian tore his eyes from her and hurried away in shame because he had done nothing to assist her. He darted furtive, guilty glances back as he fled in defeat, afraid the old woman might now start following him, and he welcomed the concealing shelter of the drizzling, drifting, lightless, nearly opaque gloom. Mobs . . . mobs of policemen—everything but England was in the hands of mobs, mobs, mobs. Mobs with clubs were in control everywhere.

The surface of the collar and shoulders of Yossarian's coat was soaked. His socks were wet and cold. The light on the next lamppost was out, too, the glass globe broken. Buildings and featureless shapes flowed by him noiselessly as though borne past immutably on the surface of some rank and timeless tide. A tall monk passed, his face buried entirely inside a coarse gray cowl, even the eyes hidden. Footsteps sloshed toward him steadily through a puddle, and he feared it would be another barefoot child. He brushed by a gaunt, cadaverous, tristful man in a black raincoat with a star-shaped scar in his cheek and a glossy mutilated depression the size of an egg in one temple. On squishing straw sandals, a young woman materialized with her whole face disfigured by a God-awful pink and piebald burn that started on her neck and stretched in a raw, corrugated mass up both cheeks past her eyes! Yossarian could not bear to look, and shuddered. No one would ever love her. His spirit was sick; he longed to lie down with some girl he could love who would soothe and excite him and put him to sleep. A mob with a club was waiting for him in Pianosa. The girls were all gone. The countess and her daughter-in-law were no longer good enough; he had grown too old for fun, he no longer had the time. Luciana was gone, dead, probably; if not yet then soon enough. Aarfy's buxom trollop had vanished with her smutty cameo ring, and Nurse Duckett was ashamed of him because he had refused to fly more combat missions and would cause a scandal. The only girl he knew nearby was the plain maid in the officers' apartment, whom none of the men had ever slept with. Her name was Michaela, but the men called her filthy things in dulcet, ingratiating voices, and she giggled with childish joy because she understood no English and thought they were flattering her and making harmless jokes. Everything wild she watched them do filled her with enchanted delight. She was a happy, simple-minded, hard-working girl who could not read and was barely able to write her name. Her straight hair was the color of rotting straw. She had sallow skin and myopic eyes, and none of the men had ever slept with her because none of the men had ever wanted to, none but Aarfy, who had raped her once that same evening and had then held her prisoner in a clothes closet for almost two hours with his hand over her mouth until the civilian curfew sirens sounded and it was unlawful for her to be outside.

Then he threw her out the window. Her dead body was still lying on the pavement when Yossarian arrived and pushed his way politely through the circle of solemn neighbors with dim lanterns, who glared with venom as they shrank away from him and pointed up bitterly toward the second-floor windows in their private, grim, accusing conversations. Yossarian's heart pounded with fright and horror at the pitiful, ominous, gory spectacle of the broken corpse. He ducked into the hallway and bolted up the stairs into the apartment, where he found Aarfy pacing about uneasily with a pompous, slightly uncomfortable smile. Aarfy seemed a bit unsettled as he fidgeted with his pipe and assured Yossarian that everything was going to be all right. There was nothing to worry about.

"I only raped her once," he explained.

Yossarian was aghast. "But you killed her, Aarfy! You killed her!"

"Oh, I had to do that after I raped her," Aarfy replied in his most condescending manner. "I couldn't very well let her go around saying bad things about us, could I?"

"But why did you have to touch her at all, you dumb bastard?" Yossarian shouted, "Why couldn't you get yourself a girl off the street if you wanted one? This city is full of prostitutes."

"Oh, no, not me," Aarfy bragged. "I never paid for it in my life."

"Aarfy, are you insane?" Yossarian was almost speechless. "You *killed* a girl. They're going to put you in jail!"

"Oh, no," Aarfy answered with a forced smile. "Not me. They aren't going to put good old Aarfy in jail. Not for killing *her*."

"But you threw her out the window. She's lying there dead in the street."

"She has no right to be there," Aarfy answered. "It's after curfew."

"Stupid! Don't you realize what you've done?" Yossarian wanted to grab Aarfy by his well-fed, caterpillar-soft shoulders and shake some sense into him. "You've murdered a human being. They *are* going to put you in jail. They might even *hang* you!"

"Oh, I hardly think they'll do that," Aarfy replied with a jovial chuckle, although his symptoms of nervousness increased. He spilled tobacco crumbs unconsciously as his short fingers fumbled with the bowl of his pipe. "No, sirree. Not to good old Aarfy." He chortled again. "She was only a servant girl. I hardly think they're going to make too much of a fuss over one poor Italian servant girl when so many thousands of lives are being lost every day. Do you?"

"Listen!" Yossarian cried, almost in joy. He pricked up his ears and watched the blood drain from Aarfy's face as sirens mourned far away, police sirens, and then ascended almost instantaneously to a howling, strident, onrushing cacophony of overwhelming sound that seemed to crash into the room around them from every side. "Aarfy, they're coming for you," he said in a flood of compassion, shouting to be heard above the noise. "They're coming to arrest you. Aarfy, don't you understand? You can't take the life of another human being and get away with it, even if she is just a poor servant girl. Don't you see? Can't you understand?"

"Oh, no," Aarfy insisted with a lame laugh and a weak smile. "They're not coming to arrest me. Not good old Aarfy."

All at once he looked sick. He sank down on a chair in a trembling stupor, his stumpy, lax hands quaking in his lap. Cars skidded to a stop outside. Spotlights hit the windows immediately. Car doors slammed and police whistles screeched. Voices rose harshly. Aarfy was green. He kept shaking his head mechanically with a queer, numb smile and repeating in a weak, hollow monotone that they were not coming for him, not for good old Aarfy, no sirree, striving to convince himself that this was so even as heavy footsteps raced up the stairs and pounded across the landing, even as fists beat on the door four times with a deafening, inexorable force. Then the door to the apartment flew open, and two large, tough, brawny M.P.s with icy eyes and firm, sinewy, unsmiling jaws entered quickly, strode across the room, and arrested Yossarian.

They arrested Yossarian for being in Rome without a pass.

They apologized to Aarfy for intruding and led Yossarian away between them, gripping him under each arm with fingers as hard as steel manacles. They said nothing at all to him on the way down. Two more tall M.P.s with clubs and hard white helmets were waiting outside at a closed car. They marched Yossarian into the back seat, and the car roared away and weaved through the rain and muddy fog to a police station. The M.P.s locked him up for the night in a cell with four stone walls. At dawn they gave him a pail for a latrine and drove him to the airport, where two more giant M.P.s with clubs and white helmets were waiting at a transport plane whose engines were already warming up when they arrived, the cylindrical green cowlings oozing quivering beads of condensation. None of the M.P.s said anything to each other either. They did not even nod. Yossarian had never seen such granite faces. The plane flew to Pianosa. Two more silent M.P.s were waiting at the landing strip. There were now eight, and they filed with precise, wordless discipline into two cars and sped on humming tires past the four squadron areas to the Group Headquarters building, where still two more M.P.s were waiting at the parking area. All ten tall, strong, purposeful, silent men towered around him as they turned toward the entrance. Their footsteps crunched in loud unison on the cindered ground. He had an impression of accelerating haste. He was terrified. Every one of the ten M.P.s seemed powerful enough to bash him to death with a single blow. They had only to press their massive, toughened, boulderous shoulders against him to crush all life from his body. There was nothing he could do to save himself. He could not even see which two were gripping him under the arms as they marched him rapidly between the two tight single-file columns they had formed. Their pace quickened, and he felt as though he were flying along with his feet off the ground as they trotted in resolute cadence up the wide marble staircase to the upper landing, where still two more inscrutable military policemen with hard faces were waiting to lead them all at an even faster pace down the long, cantilevered balcony overhanging the immense lobby. Their marching footsteps on the dull tile floor thundered like an awesome, quickening drum roll through the vacant center of the building as they moved with even greater speed and precision toward Colonel Cathcart's office, and violent winds of panic began blowing in Yossarian's ears when they turned him toward his doom inside the office, where Colonel Korn, his rump spreading comfortably on a corner of Colonel Cathcart's desk, sat waiting to greet him with a genial smile and said,

"We're sending you home."

Exercises

1. What, exactly, is Catch-22? Why is this so absurd?
2. Why did MPs smash *everything* in the whorehouse?
3. What is symbolized by "Nately's whore's kid sister" and the search for her?
4. Assuming that all of the events that Yossarian observes on his nighttime stroll are metaphors for the war, select several events and discuss what they represent.
5. How much of what happens in this chapter can be considered rational and reasonable? Irrational and unreasonable? Give some examples.

Summary

The Time Chart for the Twentieth Century at the beginning of this unit provides an overview of our bewildering century of violence and invention. The century has been one of interminable warfare, including the two most destructive wars in human history, but there have also been remarkable technological developments. Consider transportation, for example. The Wright brothers flew the first heavier-than-air flying machine in 1903. Thirty-one years later the jet engine was invented and, eighteen years after that, commercial jets were making the world much smaller. Goddard invented the liquid fuel rocket in 1926, the Russians put Sputnik into orbit thirty-one years later and, twelve years after that, an American astronaut walked on the moon, just sixty-six years after the Wright brothers' flying machine.

Communications technology also developed in a rush. Twelve years after the beginning of commercial television transcontinental television became a reality; a decade later communication satellites were starting to beam television to the entire world. We do indeed live in a Global Community with the possibility, no matter how faint, of evolving into a peaceful community in which human values will be more important than material possessions and national rivalries. High-tech makes this possible, but only human beings can make it a reality.

Culture and Human Values

Does literature really matter? Further, are those who read and write morally or ethically superior to those who neither read nor write?

Literature has been manifestly important in every literate culture known to humankind; but whether or not literature makes anyone superior in any way seems to be an arbitrary, even artificial issue. Nonliterate societies are not necessarily morally or ethically inferior to any other culture regardless of the literacy rate.

If literature does not make us better human beings, then what does it do? Does it, as so often stated, conserve the past? The literature of past cultures is, of course, our heritage; but, as is amply demonstrated in this chapter, literature consumes the past as it seeks its own ways to expose and confront the foibles, vanities, and shenanigans of humankind.

The plays of Shakespeare, for example, were subversive; in effect they were dangerous to every aspect of English civilization that had a formal existence: government, religion, societal conventions, and so on. *Waiting for Godot,* in turn, is clearly hostile to the formal existence of every Shakespearean dramatic convention: chronology, character development, and logical plot construction. *Godot* is absurd because it violates all accepted dramatic conventions and, most importantly, because it directly confronts the absurdities seemingly inherent in the human condition.

The novel *Catch-22* attacks traditional attitudes about the necessity of warfare. Those who see war as insane can logically refuse to become involved. Anyone, however, who recognizes the insanity of war can still be ordered to fight because he is sane enough to know that warfare is madness—and *that* is *Catch-22.* Joseph Heller's novel is subversive literature; it challenges the whole concept of war as a necessary and proper instrument of national policy.

Similarly, literature such as Ellison's *Invisible Man* confronts a basic problem in American society. This and other selections in this unit attack the sickness of racism, whereas works such as Virginia Woolf's "If Shakespeare Had a Sister" are directed at chauvinism and a male-dominated society.

Most of the literary selections in this unit have targeted war, bigotry, and chauvinism, but what of the rest? Consider again the remarks at the end of chapter 29 about modern art reflecting the twentieth century. The same statement can be made about modern literature, and to one extent or another, about all the arts.

Artists seem to be more sensitive and articulate (in their medium) than the average person and, one way or another, their era is reflected in their creative output. Though all art is concerned with truth as perceived by the artist, that truth is not always nor necessarily the ugliness of bigotry or war. Literature—and the other arts—can be concerned with such themes as beauty, love, faith, and justice. Eudora Welty's "The Worn Path," for example, is a quiet story about faith, hope, and love. Marquez's *One Hundred Years of Solitude* presents all of these themes in a novel that is fantastic and realistic, simple and profound. Our society may be neither better nor worse than a nonliterate culture, but our literature certainly helps make it more articulate and much more interesting.

Suggested Reading and Viewing

Rather than giving a definitive list of the "most important" literary works of this century we are providing a basic list of titles and authors, who have, in some way, contributed to the cultural tenor of our time. By using this bibliography as a basis for study and exploration, students can select those authors or works that are of particular interest and thus create their personalized adventures in twentieth-century literature. Most of these titles are available in school and public libraries and most are published in paperback editions.

Fiction

Bellow, Saul. *Humboldt's Gift,* 1975.
Borges, Jorge Luis. *Labyrinths,* 1961.
Bowen, Elizabeth. *Death of the Heart,* 1939.
Camus, Albert. *The Stranger,* 1942; *The Fall,* 1957.
Celine, Louis-Ferdinand. *Death on the Installment Plan,* 1938.
Conrad, Joseph. *Heart of Darkness,* 1902.
Didion, Joan. *Play It as It Lays,* 1970.
Dos Passos, John. *U. S. A.,* 1937.
Dreiser, Theodore. *Sister Carrie,* 1900.
Farrell, James T. *Studs Lonigan,* 1935.
Faulkner, William. *The Sound and the Fury,* 1929.
Fitzgerald, F. Scott. *The Great Gatsby,* 1925.
Foley, Martha, editor. *Fifty Best American Short Stories, 1915–1965,* 1966.
Forster, E. M. *A Passage to India,* 1924.
Gide, André. *The Counterfeiters,* 1926.
Golding, William. *Lord of the Flies,* 1954.
Grass, Günter. *The Tin Drum,* 1962.
Greene, Graham. *The Power and the Glory,* 1946.
Heller, Joseph. *Catch-22,* 1961.
Hemingway, Ernest. *For Whom the Bell Tolls,* 1940.
Huxley, Aldous. *Brave New World,* 1932.
James, Henry. *The Golden Bowl,* 1904.
Jones, James. *From Here to Eternity,* 1951.
Joyce, James. *Ulysses,* 1922.
Kafka, Franz. *The Trial,* 1937.
Kazantzakis, Nikos. *Zorba the Greek,* 1946.
Kerouac, John. *On the Road,* 1957.
Kesey, Ken. *One Flew Over the Cuckoo's Nest,* 1962.
Koestler, Arthur. *Darkness at Noon,* 1941.
Lawrence, D. H. *Sons and Lovers,* 1913.
Lessing, Doris. *The Golden Notebook,* 1962.
Lewis, Sinclair. *Babbitt,* 1922.

Mailer, Norman. *The Naked and the Dead,* 1948.

Malamud, Bernard. *The Fixer,* 1966.

Malraux, André. *Man's Fate,* 1934.

Mann, Thomas. *Buddenbrooks,* 1901.

Maugham, Somerset. *Of Human Bondage,* 1915.

McCullers, Carson. *The Heart Is a Lonely Hunter,* 1940.

Miller, Henry. *Tropic of Cancer,* 1934.

Mishima, Yukio. *The Decay of the Angel,* 1975.

Moravia, Alberto. *The Woman of Rome,* 1949.

Nabakov, Vladimir. *Lolita,* 1955.

Oates, Joyce Carol. *Then,* 1969.

O'Conner, Flannery. *Everything that Rises Must Converge,* 1965.

Orwell, George. *Nineteen Eighty-four,* 1949.

Pasternak, Boris. *Dr. Zhivago,* 1957.

Paton, Alan. *Cry the Beloved Country,* 1948.

Proust, Marcel. *Remembrance of Things Past,* 1934.

Pynchon, Thomas. *V,* 1963.

Remarque, Erich Maria. *All Quiet on the Western Front,* 1929.

Renault, Mary. *The King Must Die,* 1958.

Richter, Conrad. *The Trees,* 1940.

Rolland, Romain. *Jean-Christophe,* 1912.

Roth, Philip. *Goodbye Columbus,* 1959.

Salinger, Jerome D. *Catcher in the Rye,* 1951.

Sartre, Jean-Paul. *Nausea,* 1949.

Sholokhov, Mikhail. *And Quiet Flows the Don,* 1934.

Solzhenitsyn, Aleksandr. *One Day in the Life of Ivan Denisovich,* 1963.

Steinbeck, John. *The Grapes of Wrath,* 1939.

Thurber, James. *The Thurber Carnival,* 1945.

Vidal, Gore. *Burr: A Novel,* 1973.

Vonnegut, Kurt. *Slaughterhouse Five,* 1969.

Warren, Robert Penn. *All the King's Men,* 1946.

Wolfe, Thomas. *You Can't Go Home Again,* 1940.

Woolf, Virginia. *To the Lighthouse,* 1927.

Wright, Richard. *Native Son,* 1940.

Drama

Albee, Edward. *Who's Afraid of Virginia Woolf,* 1962.

Anderson, Maxwell. *Winterset,* 1935.

Anouilh, Jean. *Becket,* 1960.

Baldwin, James. *Blues for Mr. Charlie,* 1965.

Beckett, Samuel. *Waiting for Godot,* 1952.

Brecht, Bertolt. *Mother Courage and Her Children,* 1949.

Frisch, Max. *The Firebugs,* 1958.

Genet, Jean. *The Balcony,* 1956.

Ionesco, Eugene. *Exit the King,* 1961.

Maeterlinck, Maurice. *The Bluebird,* 1908.

Miller, Arthur. *Death of a Salesman,* 1949.

Odets, Clifford. *Awake and Sing,* 1935.

O'Neill, Eugene. *Long Day's Journey into Night,* 1956.

Osborne, John. *Look Back in Anger,* 1956.

Pinter, Harold. *The Homecoming,* 1967.

Pirandello, Luigi. *Six Characters in Search of an Author,* 1921.

Shaw, George Bernard. *Pygmalion,* 1912.

Synge, John. *Playboy of the Western World,* 1907.

Weiss, Peter. *Marat/Sade,* 1965.

Wilder, Thornton. *Our Town,* 1938.

Williams, Tennessee. *The Glass Menagerie,* 1945.

Poetry

Auden, W.H.

cummings, e e

Eliot, T.S.

Ferlinghetti, Lawrence

Frost, Robert

Housman, A.E.

Hughes, Langston

Jeffers, Robinson

Plath, Sylvia

Pound, Ezra

Rich, Adrienne

Rilke, Rainer Maria

Robinson, Edwin Arlington

Roethke, Theodore

Sandburg, Carl

Sitwell, Edith

Stevens, Wallace

Thomas, Dylan

Yeats, William Butler

Yevtushenko, Yevgeny

The Literature of Moving Images

Film can and should be studied as an art form, but it is a medium that must be experienced, preferably in a theatre with an audience. With very few exceptions movies are made to make money in public showings before a mass audience. "Motion picture industry" is the term generally used to describe corporate enterprises that use a large number of highly skilled people: screenwriter, director, actors, cinematographer, film editor, film scorer, set and costume designers, and many others. Unlike a novel, say, by Albert Camus, a film cannot be credited to a single creator. Critics tend to lavish credit on the director as the person in charge but this is only a convention that tends to slight everyone else. One cannot, for example, think of director Elia Kazan's *On the Waterfront* without recalling Marlon Brando's masterful performance. In the final analysis no film is better than its literary base, the screenplay itself, for this is where virtually all movies begin.

Movies are a prime mass entertainment medium the world over and, as commercial enterprises, about 99 percent of them are eminently forgettable. But from the beginning of motion pictures, there have been exceptions, movies that have made an artistic impact and that have withstood the test of time. Usually referred to as film classics, these are masterpieces that have effectively synthesized the efforts of many creators. Following is a list of movies that are generally regarded as true classics. Some, perhaps, are not to everyone's taste, but all are notable works of art and all should be seen, preferably more than once. They are among the best of a new literature that began in this century. Following the standard procedure, credit for the movies is assigned to the directors but, in every case, the viewer should give due credit to all participants, both on and off camera.

Antonioni, Michelangelo. *L'Avventura.* Italy, 1959.
Bergman, Ingmar. *The Seventh Seal.* Sweden, 1956.
———. *Wild Strawberries.* Sweden, 1957.
———. *Fanny and Alexander.* Sweden, 1985.
Buñuel, Luis. *Belle de Jour.* France, 1968.
Chaplin, Charles. *The Gold Rush.* U.S., 1925.
Cocteau, Jean. *Beauty and the Beast.* France, 1947.
DeSica, Vittorio. *The Bicycle Thief.* Italy, 1948.
Eisenstein, Serge. *Potemkin.* Russia, 1925.
Fellini, Federico. *La Strada.* Italy, 1954.
———. *La Dolce Vita.* Italy, 1959.
Gance, Abel. *Napoleon.* France, 1925, 1982.
Griffith, David W. *Intolerance.* U.S., 1916.
Hitchcock, Alfred. *Vertigo.* U.S., 1958.
Kazan, Elia. *On the Waterfront.* U.S., 1954.
Kurosawa, Akira. *Roshomon.* Japan, 1950.
———. *Ikiru.* Japan, 1952.
———. *Seven Samurai.* Japan, 1954.
———. *Ran.* Japan, 1986.
Lang, Fritz. *M.* Germany, 1931.
Penn, Arthur. *Bonnie and Clyde.* U.S., 1967.
Renoir, Jean. *La Grande Illusion.* France, 1938.
———. *Rules of the Game.* France, 1939, 1965.
Truffaut, Francois. *The 400 Blows.* France, 1959.
———. *Jules and Jim.* France, 1961.
Welles, Orson. *Citizen Kane.* U.S., 1941.
Wiene, Robert. *The Cabinet of Dr. Caligari.* Germany, 1919.
Wilder, Billy. *Some Like It Hot.* U.S., 1959.

Music Listening and Notation

appendix

Music listening is always enriched by a knowledge of basic facts such as those outlined herein. This appendix should, ideally, be studied for content and used, along with the glossary, as often as necessary in conjunction with the material on music.

Characteristics of Musical Sounds

Musical tones are sounds of definite pitch and duration, as distinct from noises and other less definite sounds. Musical tones have the four characteristics of *pitch, intensity, tone color,* and *duration,* which may be described as follows:

Pitch   The location of musical sound from low to high or high to low.

Intensity   Relative degree of softness or loudness.

Tone Color   The quality of a sound that distinguishes it from other musical sounds of the same pitch and intensity; for example, the different tone quality of a flute as contrasted with a clarinet. Also called *timbre.*

Duration   The length of time a tone is audible.

The Four Elements of Music

Rhythm, melody, harmony, and *tone color* are the essential elements of music. Composers and performers are concerned with each, whereas the listener experiences as a web of sound that makes it difficult to single out any one element. Each can, however, be considered in isolation as a guide to understanding.

Rhythm

Though little is known about prehistoric music, the earliest music was probably the beating out of rhythms long before the existence of either melody or speech. There is rhythm in the universe: our heartbeat, alternating day and night, the progression of the seasons, waves crashing on a beach. Manufactured rhythm can be heard in train wheels clicking on rails, a Ping-Pong game, or the clacking castanets of a Spanish dancer.

Essentially, rhythm is the organization of musical time, that is, everything that takes place in terms of sound and silence, accent and nonaccent, tension and relaxation. Rhythm can also be defined as the "melody of a monotone"; music can be recognized just by hearing its rhythm. For example, tapping out the rhythmic patterns of "Dixie" can bring that familiar melody to mind.

Rhythm is the name of the whole and is not to be confused with *beat,* which results from a certain regularity of the rhythmic patterns. Beat, or pulse, can be compared with the heartbeat or the pulse rate. The beat will usually be steady but it may temporarily speed up or slow down. It may be *explicit* (the uniform thump of a bass drum in a marching band) or *implicit* (resulting from combinations of rhythmic patterns). As soon as one duration follows another, there will be rhythm but not necessarily beat. Certain types of music (such as Gregorian chant) do not produce the regular pulsation called beat.

When beats are produced by the music in a repeating pattern of accents, the result is *meter. Metered* music is *measured* music, with groupings of two, three, or four beats (or combinations of these) in each *measure,* or *bar.*

Time Signatures

When there is a regular pattern of accented and unaccented beats, it is customary to use a *time signature* in which the upper figure indicates the number of beats in a measure and the lower figure (though not in every case), the unit of beat; that is, the note value the composer has selected to symbolize one beat. For example:

2 = two beats per measure (duple meter)
4 = ♩ unit of beat (quarter note receives one beat)
3 = three beats per measure (triple meter)
8 = ♪ unit of beat (eighth note receives one beat)

Melody and Harmony

A melody is a horizontal organization of pitches or, simply, a succession of musical tones. Harmony is a vertical organization of pitches in which two or more tones are sounded together. The following example illustrates melody on the upper staff and harmony on the lower staff.

Old Folks at Home

Tone Color

Sometimes called timbre (TAM-ber), tone color is to music what color is to the painter. It is tone color that enables us to distinguish between a flute, a clarinet, and an oboe. A soprano voice is higher in pitch than a bass voice, but the tone color is also different. Through experience, everyone has learned to recognize the unique colors of many instruments. Further study leads to finer discriminations between similar instruments such as violin and viola, oboe and English horn, and so on. Composers select instruments for expressive purposes based largely on their coloration, whether singly or in combination. The full sound of a Beethoven symphony differs from a work by Richard Strauss, for example, because Strauss uses a wider range of instrumental colors.

Musical Literacy

The most abstract of the arts, music is sound moving in time. Factual information about music certainly helps the listener, but all the facts in the world can only assist the listening process; information about music can never replace the sound of music. One extremely useful method of instruction is to present major themes and ideas in musical notation, a practice common to virtually all books on music listening.

A practical approach to intelligent listening must include some instruction in musical literacy sufficient to read a single line of music. This is a simple process that can be quickly learned by young children and can be taught to an adult in a few minutes. The strangely prevalent folklore about musical notation being "too hard" or "too technical" has no foundation in fact, and probably refers to reading music as a performer, which is a very different matter that need not concern us here. As basic to music as the ABCs of written language but easier to understand, musical notation is an indispensable guide for music listeners. Learning to read music well enough to figure out a single line of music and to plunk it out on a piano is simply basic musical literacy.

Educated listeners quickly learn to enjoy picking out musical themes. This turns abstract sounds into tangible tunes, thus giving the listener an opportunity to preview the themes so that they can be anticipated in the music. Equally valuable is the repetition of themes after the listening experience. To summarize, picking out melodies is an aid to understanding, a helpful preview of music to be listened to, and a reminder of music already heard.

Approach the following material not with apprehension but with anticipation. Master the principles of musical notation with the positive attitude that this will not only materially assist in a better understanding of the music in this text but also lead, in time, to a lifetime of pleasurable listening.

Musical Notation

Pitch

The essential elements of our notational system were devised some ten centuries ago and subsequently altered and augmented to become a reasonably efficient means of communicating the composer's intentions to listener and performer. The system is based on the first seven letters of the alphabet and can best be illustrated by using a segment of the piano keyboard. The pitches range from low to high, from A through G in a repeating A–G pattern.

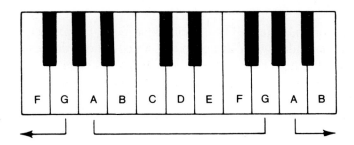

To know which of the eight As available on the piano is the intended note, the following is necessary:

1. Use a musical *staff* of five lines and four spaces.

2. Use a symbol for a musical pitch, 𝅝 i.e., *note*.
3. Place the notes on the lines or in the spaces of the staff.

4. Indicate by means of a *clef sign* the *names* of the notes.

Clef (French, *key*) implies that the key to precise placement of the notes is the establishment of the letter name of *one* of the lines or spaces of the staff. There are two clefs in common use. Both are ornamental symbols derived from the letters G and F. The solid lines are the present clef signs and the dotted lines their original form:

The clefs are placed on the staff to indicate the location of the letters they represent. The lower portion of the G clef curls around the second line to fix the location of G; the two dots of the F clef are placed above and below the fourth line to show that this is the F line.

Once the five-line staff has received its pitch designation of G or F, the *staff* is subsequently identified as a *treble* or a *bass staff*.

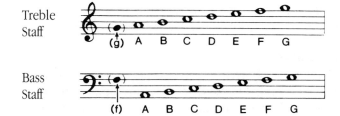

Not all melodies are composed so that they can be played on the white notes only of the piano. Sometimes another *key*, or different set of pitches, is used as demonstrated in the following examples:

In the second version the *key signature* indicates that all the Fs and Cs have been raised a half step to the next closest note. A symbol called a sharp (♯) indicates raised notes. Key signatures can include up to seven sharps or flats.

The other common symbol that changes a note is the *flat* (♭), which lowers a note a half step to the next closest note. Following is the same melody written in the key of B♭. As indicated by the key signature, all the Bs and Es have been lowered to B♭ and E♭.

You will note that the staff given above has an added short line, a *ledger line,* used to accommodate the last two notes.

A piano keyboard has *white* keys and *black* keys, with the black keys grouped in alternating sets of two and three. The white note, or key, immediately to the left of the two black keys is always C. There are eight Cs; the C closest to the center is *middle C.* It is from this C that you can locate the notes of the themes.

Middle C   Middle C

See the guide to the *chromatic scale,* which is all of the black and white keys in one octave.

Chromatic Scale

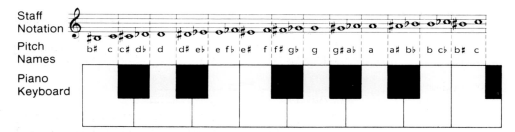

Duration

The notation of the length of time of musical sounds (and silences) was developed in conjunction, more or less, with the notation of pitch. The modern *note-value* system consists of fractional parts of a whole unit, or *whole note* (𝅝), expressed in mathematical terms as 1/1. A *half note* (𝅗𝅥) is one-half the whole unit, or 1/2; a *quarter note* (♩) is one-quarter the unit, or 1/4; and so forth.

The *name* of the note value indicates the *number* of notes in the whole-note unit. There are four quarter notes (4 × 1/4 = 1/1), eight eighth notes (8 × 1/8 = 1/1), etc.

With note values smaller than the whole note, the relationships remain constant. There are two quarter notes in a half note (2 × 1/4 = 1/2), two eighth notes in a quarter note (2 × 1/8 = 1/4), etc.

Rhythmic notation is both relative and fixed. The duration of a whole note is dependent on the tempo (speed) and notation of music. It may have a duration of one second, eight seconds, or something in between. The interior relationships, however, never vary.

A whole note has the same duration as two half notes, four quarter notes, and so forth. The mathematical relationship is fixed and precise. See table A.1 below for an outline of the system.

TABLE A.1 Note and Rest Values	
Note Value	**Symbol**
Whole note (basic unit)	𝅝
Half note	𝅗𝅥
Quarter note	♩
Eighth note	♪
Sixteenth note	𝅘𝅥𝅯
Rest Value	**Symbol**
Whole (note) rest	▬
Half rest	▬
Quarter rest	𝄽
Eighth rest	𝄾
Sixteenth rest	𝄿

Voices and Instruments

Choral ensembles are usually divided into four voice parts ranging from high to low: soprano and alto (women) and tenor and bass (men).

Instruments of the symphony orchestra and other ensembles are grouped by family, from highest pitch to lowest:

Strings	Woodwinds	Brass	Percussion
violin	piccolo	trumpet (and	snare drum
viola	flute	cornet)	timpani
cello	oboe	French horn	bass drum
bass	clarinet	trombone	cymbals
	bassoon	tuba	many others

Keyboard instruments include piano, harpsichord, and organ. The piano, originally called pianoforte, is based on the principle of hammers striking the strings; the harpsichord has a mechanism that plucks the strings. Built with two or more keyboards called manuals, organs either use forced air to activate the pipes or some version of an electronic reproduction of sound.

Musical Texture

The words for the three kinds of musical texture are derived from Greek and are virtually self-explanatory:

Monophonic (one sound)
Homophonic (same sound)
Polyphonic (many sounds)

Monophonic music has a single unaccompanied melody line. Much of the world's music is monophonic, including Chinese and Hindu music and, in Western civilization, Gregorian chant and troubadour songs. Homophonic music has a principal melodic line accompanied by harmony, sometimes referred to as chordal accompaniment. Although it is relatively unknown outside Western culture, homophonic music comprises the bulk of our music including nearly all popular music. Polyphonic music has two or more melodies sounding simultaneously. Familiar rounds such as "Three Blind Mice" and "Row, Row, Row Your Boat" are polyphonic, as is most Renaissance music. The music of Baroque composers such as Bach, Handel, and many others is basically polyphonic.

Musical Form

Briefly stated, form in music is a balance of unity and variety. Too much unity becomes boring, whereas excessive variety leads to fragmentation and even chaos. Understanding form in music is a high priority for educated listeners. As Robert Schumann remarked, "Only when the form is quite clear to you will the spirit become clear to you."

The smallest unit of form is the *motive,* which to be intelligible must have at least two notes plus an identifiable rhythmic pattern. The principle motive in the first movement of Beethoven's Fifth Symphony has two different pitches in a four-note rhythmic pattern:

A musical phrase is a coherent group of notes roughly comparable to a literary phrase and having about the same function. Two related phrases form a *period,* in the manner of a literary sentence. In the period illustrated below, the first phrase has a transitional ending called a *half cadence,* and the second phrase ends solidly with a *full cadence.* Note the extreme unity; the first three measures of both phrases are identical.

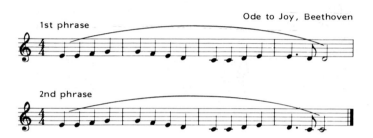

In large works the musical periods are used in various combinations to expand the material into sections comparable to paragraphs, and these are then combined to make still larger units.

Musical structure can be comprehended only *after* the music has arrived at wherever the composer intends it to go. Look again at "Ode to Joy." You can "see" its form only because the music is notated, which is why learning some notation is so important. When the music is played, your ear follows the line to the half cadence, which is then heard as a statement that demands completion. As the second phrase begins, there is aural recognition of its relationship to the first phrase. When the second phrase concludes with a gratifying full cadence, there is a kind of flashback to the memory of the first phrase. In other words, the conclusion of the second phrase is satisfying because it completes the thought of the still-remembered first phrase. The music conforms to its own inner logic; that is, the second phrase is a logical consequence of the first.

As a general rule, most music is constructed around two different but logically related (inner logic) musical ideas. We can call one idea A and the other B. One common musical form is two-part (binary), or simply A–B. An even more common form is three-part (ternary), or A–B–A. In two-part form the composer makes a musical statement (A), which is followed by a new section (B), which is sufficiently different to provide variety but not so different as to destroy the balance. The following hymn tune is a complete composition in two-part form, with two phrases in each section. Section B has the same rhythm as Section A, but the melody is a kind of inversion of the melody in A. The inner logic is maintained through the similarities.

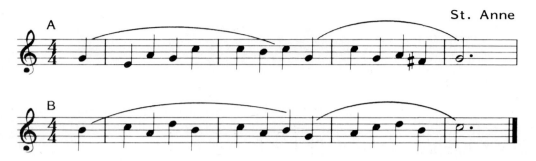

St. Anne

The following complete hymn tune has a form related to two-part form: A–A'–B, called A, A prime, B. Part A is followed by another A that is varied going into the cadence. Part B is properly different but related to A and A' by the similarity of measures 2, 6, and 10. In terms of measures, the structure of the piece can be diagrammed as:

A	A'	B
2 + 2	2 + 2	2 + 2

Regent Square

Three-part form operates on the principle of closing with the melody that began the piece, a rounding off of the material: A–B–A. The following example can be analyzed as A–A'–B–A' and diagrammed as:

A	A'	B	A'
4 + 4	4 + 4	4 + 4	4 + 4.

This is the thirty-two-measure form most commonly used for popular songs.

In the Gloaming

There are, of course, other variants of AB and ABA forms as well as several other structures. However, the examples given illustrate the principle of a balance between unity and variety, of which unity is paramount. Perhaps because it is rather amorphous, music, more than any other art, emphasizes repetition, restating the material again and again, but mixing with enough variety to maintain interest. The forms illustrated can also be heard in the larger context of longer compositions. For example, "In the Gloaming" has 32 measures in a basic ABA form; a large symphonic work could have, say, 200 measures and be diagrammed as follows:

A	B	A	or	A	B	A′	or	A	B	A′
aba	aba	aba		aba′	aba	aba′		aa′ba	aba	aa′ba′

The Listening Experience

Listening to music begins with the question, What do you hear? This is an objective question that has nothing whatever to do with a story you may imagine the music is telling, random associations the music happens to trigger, or any meaning that may be attributed to the music. For the educated listener the procedure is to objectively identify the sounds to determine how the sounds are produced, and to try to determine how the sounds are organized.

Composers do not pour out notes as if emptying a glass of water on a tabletop. They arrange their sounds in a sort of container in a manner that molds the receptacle to the material it holds. Learning to comprehend the musical structure leads inevitably to the ability to *anticipate* the next melody, cadence, section, or whatever. Being able to anticipate what is to happen next means that you are tuned in to the web of sound, listening along with the pace of the music. Almost everyone has already acquired the ability to follow the progress of popular music and to anticipate what comes next in favorite recordings. As stated before, the larger world of classical music is only a step beyond the listening expertise of most individuals. It is an inspiring and enriching stride into Western culture's unique contribution to the world's music.

Glossary

Pronunciation: Approximations are given where necessary. The syllables are to be read as English words and with the capital letters accented.

Abbreviations: Lat., Latin; F., French; G., German; Gk., Greek; I., Italian; v., Vide (see).

Asterisks: An asterisk preceding a word or phrase indicates that a definition and/or illustration can be found under that heading.

A

Abacus   The flat slab on top of a *capital.

Abstract art   Term covers many kinds of nonrepresentational art, e.g., action painting, works by Kandinsky. All art is abstracted to some degree.

Academy   Originally derived from the *Akademeia,* the grove in which Plato taught his seminars.

Acanthus   A plant whose thick leaves are reproduced in stylized form on *Corinthian capitals. (See figure 9.9.)

A cappella   (ah ka-PELL-ah; Lat.) Originally unaccompanied music sung "in the chapel." Term now applies to choral music without instrumental accompaniment.

Acoustics   The science of sound. Important in architectural design and city planning as well as music.

Aerial perspective   *See* Perspective.

Aesthetic   Concerned with a sensitivity to the pleasurable and the beautiful; the opposite of anaesthetic.

Aesthetics   The study or philosophy of beauty; theory of the fine arts and human responses.

Agnosticism   (Gk., *agnostos,* unknowing) The impossibility of obtaining knowledge of certain subjects; assertion that people cannot obtain knowledge of God.

Agora   In ancient Greece, a marketplace/public square.

Allegory   A literary mode with a literal level of meanings plus a set of meanings above and beyond themselves. This second level may be religious, social, political, or philosophical, e.g., *The Faerie Queen* by Spenser is an allegory about Christian virtues.

Alleluia   Latinization for the Hebrew *Halleluyah* ("praise ye the Lord"). Third item of the *Proper of the *Mass.

Altarpiece   A painted (or sculptured) panel placed over or behind an altar.

Ambulatory   A passageway around the *apse of a church. (See figure 14.32.)

Amphora   Greek vase, usually quite large, with two handles and used to store food staples. (See figure 7.8.)

Apocalypse   Prophetic revelation; the Book of Revelation in the New Testament.

A posteriori   (a-pos-TEER-e-or-e; Lat., following after) Reasoning from observed facts to conclusions; inductive; empirical.

A priori   (a-pree-OAR-e) Reasoning from general propositions to particular conclusions; deductive; nonempirical.

Apse   A recess, usually semicircular, in the east wall of a Christian church or, in a Roman *basilica, at the wall opposite to the general entrance way.

Arabesque   Literally Arab-like. Elaborate designs of intertwined flowers, foliage, and geometric patterns used in Islamic architecture.

Arcade   A series of connected *arches resting on columns. (See figure 9.10.)

Arch   A curved structure (semicircular or pointed) spanning a space, usually made of wedge-shaped blocks. Known to the Greeks, who preferred a *post and lintel system, but exploited by the Romans.

Archetype   (Gk., *arche,* first: *typos,* form) The original pattern of forms of which things in this world are copies.

Architrave The lowest part of an *entablature, a horizontal beam or *lintel directly above the *capital. (See figure 7.31.)

Aria (I., AHR-yah; F., air) Solo song (sometimes duet) in *operas, *oratorios, *cantatas.

Ars antiqua (Lat., old art) Music of the late twelfth and thirteenth centuries.

Ars nova (Lat., new art) Music of the fourteenth century. Outstanding composers were Machaut (France) and Landini (Italy).

Art Nouveau A style of architecture, crafts, and design of the 1890s and a bit later characterized by curvilinear patterns. Examples include Tiffany lamps and the work of Beardsley and Klimt.

Art song Song intending an artistic combination of words and music, as distinct from popular song or folk song.

Atheism (G., *a,* no; *theos,* god) The belief that there is no God; also means "not theistic" when applied to those who do not believe in a personal God.

Atonal Music that has no tonal center, in which all notes are of relatively equal importance. In a composition in C Major, on the other hand, C is the most important note. Almost all popular music is written in keys such as C Major, D Major, and so on. Most compositions by Schoenberg are atonal.

Atrium The court of a Roman house, roofless, and near the entrance. (See figure 9.6.) Also the open, colonnaded court attached to the front of early Christian churches.

Aulos (OW-los) A shrill sounding oboelike instrument associated with the Dionysian rites of the ancient Greeks. Double-reed instrument normally played in pairs by one performer. (See figure 7.63.)

Avant-guard (a-vahn-GARD) A French term meaning, literally, advanced guard, and used to designate innovators and experimentalists in the various arts.

B

Babylonian Captivity The Church of Rome in Avignon rather than in Rome, 1309–1377.

Baldachino (ball-da-KEEN-o) A canopy over a tomb or altar of which the most famous is that over the tomb of St. Peter in St. Peter's in Rome; designed by Bernini.

Ballad (Lat., *ballare,* to dance) Originally a dancing song. A narrative song, usually folk song but term also applied to popular songs.

Ballade Medieval *trouvère song. In the nineteenth and twentieth centuries dramatic piano pieces, frequently inspired by romantic poetry.

Balustrade A railing plus a supporting row of posts.

Banjo *Guitar family instrument, probably introduced into Africa by Arab traders and brought to America on the slave ships. The body consists of a shallow, hollow metal drum with a drumhead on top and open at the bottom. It has four or more strings and is played with fingers or plectrum.

Baptistery Originally a separate building, later a part of the church containing the baptismal font.

Barrel vault v. Vault.

Basilica In Roman architecture, a rectangular public building used for business or as a tribunal. Christian churches that use a *cruciform plan are patterned after Roman basilicas. (See figure 11.10.) Though basilica is an architectural style, the Church of Rome designates a church a basilica if it contains the bones of a saint.

Bay In Romanesque and Gothic churches the area between the columns. (See figure 14.32.)

Behaviorism School of psychology that restricts both animal and human psychology to the study of behavior; stresses the role of the environment and conditioned responses to exterior stimuli.

Blank verse Unrhymed *iambic pentameter* (v. meter) in the English language, much used in Elizabethan drama.

Bourgeoisie The middle class; in Marxist theory the capitalist class, which is opposed to the proletariat, the lower or industrial working class.

Buttress Exterior support used to counter the lateral thrust of an *arch or *vault. A *pier buttress* is a solid mass of masonry added to the wall; a *flying buttress* is typically a pier standing away from the wall and from which an arch "flies" from the pier to connect with the wall at the point of outward thrust. (See figure 14.31.)

C

Cadence Term in music applied to the concluding portion of a phrase (temporary cadence) or composition (permanent cadence).

Campanile Italian for bell tower, usually freestanding. The Leaning Tower of Pisa is a campanile. (See figure 14.23.)

Canon (Gk., law, rule) 1. A body of principles, rules, standards, or norms. 2. In art and architecture, a criterion for establishing proportion, measure, or scale. 3. In music, in which a melody is imitated strictly and in its entirety by another voice. Canons that have no specified way to end but keep going around are called "rounds," for example, "Three Blind Mice."

Cantata (I., *cantare,* to sing) A "sung" piece as opposed to a "sound" (instrumental) piece, for example, sonata. The term is now generally used for secular or sacred choral works with orchestral accompaniment, which are on a smaller scale than *oratorios.

Cantilever A self-supporting projection that needs no exterior bracing; e.g., a balcony or porch can be cantilevered.

Cantus firmus (Lat., fixed song) A preexisting melody used as the foundation for a *polyphonic composition. *Plainsong melodies were used for this purpose, but other sources included secular songs, Lutheran *chorales, and *scales. Any preexisting melody may serve as a cantus firmus.

Capital The top or crown of a column. (See figure 7.31.)

Cartoon A full-size preliminary drawing for a pictorial work, usually a large work such as a *mural, *fresco, or tapestry. Also a humorous drawing.

Caryatid (care-ee-AHT-id) A female figure that functions as a supporting *column; male figures that function in a like manner are called *atlantes* (at-LAN-tees; plural of Atlas). (See figure 7.43.)

Catharsis (Gk., *katharsis,* purge, purify) Purification, purging of emotions effected by tragedy (Aristotle).

Cella The enclosed chamber in a classical temple that contained the cult statue of the god or goddess after whom the temple was named.

Chamber music Term now restricted to instrumental music written for a limited number of players in which there is only one player to each part, as opposed to orchestral music, which has two or more players to some parts, for example, sixteen players on the first violin part. True chamber music emphasizes ensemble rather than solo playing.

Chanson (F., song) A major part of the *troubadour-*trouvère tradition, dating from the eleventh through the fourteenth centuries. Generic term for the general song production to a French text.

Chevet (sheh-VAY; F., pillow) The eastern end of a church, including *choir, *ambulatory, and *apse.

Chiaroscuro (kee-AR-oh-SKOOR-oh; I., light-dark) In the visual arts the use of gradations of light and dark to represent natural light and shadows.

Chinoiserie (she-nwaz-eh-REE; F.) Chinese motifs as decorative elements for craft objects, screens, wallpaper, and furniture; prominent in eighteenth-century rococo style.

Choir That part of the church where the singers and clergy are normally accommodated; usually between the *transept and the *apse; also called chancel. (See figure 14.32.)

Chorale A *hymn tune of the German Protestant (Lutheran) church.

Chord In music the simultaneous sounding of three or more tones.

Chromatic (Gk., *chroma,* color) The use of notes that are foreign to the musical *scale and have to be indicated by a sharp, flat, natural, etc. The *chromatic* scale is involved in these alterations. It consists of twelve tones to an octave, each a semitone apart.

Cire perdue (seer pair-DUE; F., lost wax) A metal casting method in which the original figure is modeled in wax and encased in a mold; as the mold is baked the wax melts and runs out, after which the molten metal is poured into the mold.

Clavichord The earliest type of stringed keyboard instrument (twelfth century). Probably developed from the *monochord. It is a 2′ × 4′ oblong box with a keyboard of about three octaves. The strings run parallel to the keyboard, as opposed to harpsichords and pianos, in which the strings run at right angles to the keyboard. The keys are struck from below by metal tangents fastened to the opposite ends of elongated keys. The tone is light and delicate but very expressive because the performer can control the loudness of each note. It was sometimes called a "table *clavier" because it was portable.

Clavier Generic term for any instrument of the stringed keyboard family: clavichord, harpsichord, and piano.

Clef (F., key) In music a symbol placed on the staff to indicate the pitches of the lines and spaces. There are three clefs in use today: G, F, and C. The G clef is used to indicate that the note on the second line is G (treble clef). The F clef is usually used to indicate that F is on the fourth line (bass clef).

Treble Clef   **Bass Clef**

Clerestory (Clearstory) In a *basilica or church, the section of an interior wall that rises above the roof of the side aisles and which has numerous windows.

Cloister An inner court bounded by covered walks; a standard feature of monastery architecture.

Collage (F., pasting) Paper and other materials pasted on a two-dimensional surface.

Colonnade A series of spaced *columns, usually connected by *lintels. (See figure 11.11.)

Column A vertical support, usually circular, which has a base (except in *Doric style), shaft, and *capital. (See figure 7.31.)

Comedy A play or other literary work in which all ends well, properly, or happily. Opposite of *tragedy.

Concerto (con-CHAIR-toe; I.) A musical work for one or two solo instruments with orchestral accompaniment.

Concerto grosso A musical work for a small group of instruments (usually three or four) with orchestral accompaniment.

Corinthian The most ornate style of Greek architecture, little used by the Greeks but preferred by the Romans; tall, slender, channeled *columns topped by an elaborate *capital decorated with stylized *acanthus leaves. (See figure 9.9.)

Cornice The horizontal, projecting member crowning an *entablature.

Cosmology Philosophic study of the origin and nature of the universe.

Couplet In poetry two successive rhymed lines in the same meter.

Crocket In Gothic architecture an ornamental device shaped like a curling leaf and placed on the outer angles of *gables and pinnacles. (See figure 14.60.)

Crossing In a church, the space formed by the interception of the *nave and the *transepts.

Cruciform The floor plan of a church in the shape of a *Latin cross. (See figure 14.32.)

Cuneiform A writing system of ancient Mesopotamia consisting of wedge shapes.

Cupola A rounded roof or ceiling; a small *dome.

D

Daguerrotype   After L. J. M. Daguerre (1789–1851) the inventor. Photograph made on a silver-coated glass plate.

Determinism   (Lat., *de* + *terminus,* end) The doctrine that all events are conditioned by their causes and that people are mechanical expressions of heredity and environment; in short, we are at the mercy of blind, unknowing natural laws in an indifferent universe.

Deus ex machina   (DAY-oos ex ma-KEE-na; Lat.) In Greek and Roman drama a deity who was brought in by stage machinery to resolve a difficult situation; any unexpected or bizarre device or event introduced to untangle a plot.

Dialectic   Associated with Plato as the art of debate by question and answer. Also dialectical reasoning using *syllogisms (Aristotle) or, according to Hegel, the distinctive characteristic of speculative thought.

Didactic   Intended to instruct or teach.

Dome   A hemispherical vault; may be viewed as an *arch rotated on its vertical axis.

Doric   The oldest of Greek temple styles, characterized by sturdy *columns with no base and an unornamented cushionlike *capital. (See figure 7.31.)

Drum   The circular sections that make up the shaft of a *column; also the circular wall on which a *dome is placed.

Drums   Percussion musical instruments having a skin stretched over one or both ends of a frame.

Dualism   In *metaphysics, a theory that admits two independent substances, e.g., Plato's dualism of the sensible and intelligible worlds, Cartesian dualism of thinking and extended subjects, Kant's dualism of the noumenal and the phenomenal.

E

Elegy   A meditative poem dealing with the idea of death.

Elevation   The vertical arrangements of the elements of an architectural design; a vertical projection.

Empiricism   A proposition that the sole source of knowledge is experience, that no knowledge is possible independent of experience.

Engaged column   A nonfunctional form projecting from the surface of a wall; used for visual articulation. (See figure 9.8.)

Engraving   The process of using a sharp instrument to cut a design into a metal plate, usually copper; also the print that is made from the plate after ink has been added.

Entablature   The part of a building of *post and lintel construction between the *capitals and the roof. In classical architecture this includes the *architrave, *frieze, and *cornice. (See figure 7.31.)

Entasis   (EN-ta-sis) A slight convex swelling in the shaft of a *column.

Epic   A lengthy narrative poem dealing with protagonists of heroic proportions and issues of universal significance, e.g., Homer's *Iliad.*

Epicurean   One who believes that pleasure, especially that of the mind, is the highest good.

Epistemology   A branch of philosophy that studies the origin, validity, and processes of knowledge.

Eschatology   (Gk., *ta eschata,* death) That part of theology dealing with last things: death, judgment, heaven, hell.

Estampie   (es-TAHM-pea) A dance form popular during the twelfth to fourteenth centuries. Consists of a series of repeated sections, for example, aa, bb, cc, etc.

Etching   A kind of *engraving in which the design is incised into a wax-covered metal plate, after which the exposed metal is etched by a corrosive acid; the print made from the plate is also called an etching.

Ethos   In ancient Greek music the "ethical" character attributed to the various modes. The Dorian was considered strong and manly; the Phrygian, ecstatic and passionate; the Lydian, feminine, decadent, and lascivious; the Mixolydian, mournful and gloomy. See under Plato in chapter 6.

Euphemism   An innocuous term substituted for one considered to be offensive or socially unacceptable, e.g., "passing away" for "dying."

F

Facade   One of the exterior walls of a building, usually the one containing the main entrance.

Fenestration   The arrangement of windows or other openings in the walls of a building.

Fiddle   Colloquialism for the violin. Also used to designate the bowed ancestors of the violin, particularly the medieval instrument used to accompany dances.

Finial   In Gothic architecture an ornament fitted to the peak of an *arch; any ornamental terminating point, such as the screw-top of a lamp. (See figure 14.60.)

Flamboyant   Late Gothic architecture of the fifteenth or sixteenth centuries, which featured wavy lines and flamelike forms.

Flèche   (flesh; F., arrow) In architecture a slender spire above the intersection of the *nave and *transepts. (See figure 14.31.)

Flute   A woodwind instrument made of wood (originally), silver, gold, or preferably platinum. It is essentially a straight pipe with keys, which is held horizontally and played by blowing across a mouthpiece.

Fluting   The vertical grooves, usually semicircular, in the shaft of a *column or *pilaster.

Foot   A metrical unit in poetry such as the iamb ⌣ -. Also see meter.

Foreshortening   Creating the illusion in painting or drawing that the subject is projecting out of or into the frontal plane of a two-dimensional surface.

Free Verse   Verse that uses parallelism and sound effects rather than *meter and rhyme.

Fresco   (I., fresh) Painting on plaster, usually wet plaster on which the colors are painted, sinking in as the plaster dries and the fresco becomes part of the wall.

Frieze   In architecture, a decorated horizontal band, often embellished with carved figures and molding; the portion of an *entablature between the *architrave and the *cornice above. (See figure 7.31.)

Fugue   *Polyphonic musical composition in which a single theme is developed by the different musical voices in succession. A favorite style of Baroque composers such as Bach and Handel.

G

Gable   In architecture the triangular section at the end of a pitched roof, frequently with a window below.

Genre   (ZHAN-re) In the pictorial arts, a depiction of scenes of everyday life. In literature, the type of work—epic, novel, and so on.

Gnosticism   The doctrines of certain early Christian cults (particularly in Egypt) that valued inquiry into spiritual truth above faith.

Goliards   Wandering scholars of the tenth through the thirteenth centuries: students, young ecclesiastics, dreamers, and the disenchanted.

Gospels   In the Bible, New Testament accounts (Matthew, Mark, Luke, and John) of the life and teachings of Christ.

Gouache   (gwAHSH; F.) Watercolor made opaque by adding zinc white.

Graphic arts   Visual arts that are linear in character: drawing, engraving, printing, printmaking, typographic, and advertising design.

Great Schism   Rival popes of the Church of Rome in Rome, Avignon, and Pisa, 1378–1417.

Greek cross   A cross in which the four arms are of equal length.

Gregorian chant   v. Plainsong.

Groin   In architecture the edge (groin) formed by the intersection of two *vaults. (See figure 14.18.)

Guitar   A plucked string instrument with a flat body and six strings (modern guitar). Brought into Europe during the Middle Ages by the Moorish conquest of Spain.

H

Harpsichord   Actually a harp turned on its side and played by means of quills or leather tongues operated by a keyboard. It was the most common keyboard instrument of the sixteenth to eighteenth centuries and is again being built today in increasing numbers.

Hatching   A series of closely spaced parallel lines in a drawing or print giving the effect of shading.

Hedonism   The doctrine that pleasure or pleasant consciousness are intrinsically good; that pleasure is the proper—and the actual—motive for every choice.

Heroic couplet   Two successive lines of rhymed iambic pentameter, e.g., Pope's *Essay on Man.*

Hieratic   (HYE-uh-RAT-ik) Of or used by priests; priestly.

Hieroglyphics   Symbols or pictures standing for a word, syllable, or sound; writing system of ancient Egyptians.

Homophonic   (Gk., same sound) Music in which a single melodic line is supported by chords or other subordinate material (percussion instruments).

Hubris   (HU-bris) *Tragic flaw,* i.e., excessive pride or arrogance that harms other people and brings about the downfall of the person with the flaw.

Hue   The name of a color. The chief colors of the spectrum are: red, yellow, blue (primary); green, orange, violet (secondary).

Humanism   That "Man is the measure of all things" (Protagoras) and "Many are the wonders of the world, and none so wonderful as man" (Sophokles) give the essence of humanism. The Greeks conceived their gods as perfect human beings, free from infirmities and immortal, but subject to human passions and ambitions. The Renaissance conception of man as the potential master of all things arose out of the awakening to the glories of Greece and Rome.

Hydraulis   Ancient Greek pipe organ, probably invented in the Middle East 300–200 B.C. Air for the pipes was provided by hydraulic pressure and the pipes activated by a keyboard. Originally the tone was delicate and clear, but the Romans converted it into a noisy outdoor instrument by a large increase in air pressure.

Hymn   A poem of praise. Usually, but not necessarily, sacred. The music accompanying a hymn is called the hymn tune.

I

Icon   (EYE-kon; Gk., image) Two-dimensional representation of a holy person; in the Greek church a panel painting of a sacred personage. (See figure 11.27.)

Iconoclast   Originally one who destroys religious images; one who attacks established ideas or beliefs.

Iconography   Visual imagery used to convey concepts in the visual arts; the study of symbolic meanings in the pictorial arts.

Illumination   Decorative illustrations or designs, associated primarily with medieval illuminated manuscripts. (See figure 14.53.)

Impasto   (I., paste) A painting style in which the pigment is laid on thickly, as in many of van Gogh's paintings.

Inductive method   The process of arriving at a general conclusion from a set of particular facts.

Intaglio   (in-TAL-yo) A graphic technique in which the design is incised; used on seals, gems, and dies for coins and also for the kinds of printing and printmaking that have a depressed ink-bearing surface.

Ionic   A style of Greek classical architecture using slender, *fluted *columns and *capitals decorated with scrolls and *volutes. (See figure 7.31.)

Isocepholy   (I-so-SEPH-uh-ly) In the visual arts a convention that arranges figures so that the heads are at the same height. (See figure 7.26.)

J

Jamb figure Sculpted figure flanking the portal of a Gothic church. (See figure 14.20.)

Jihad Muslim holy war; a Muslim crusade against unbelievers.

Jongleur (zhon-GLEUR) French professional musicians (minstrels) of the twelfth and thirteenth centuries who served the *troubadours and *trouvères.

K

Keystone The central wedge-shaped stone in an *arch; the last stone put in place and which makes the arch stable.

Kibla The point toward which Muslims turn when praying, toward Mecca.

Kithara (KITH-a-ra) The principal stringed instrument of the ancient Greeks. Essentially a larger version of the *lyre, it has a U-shaped form and usually seven to eleven strings running vertically from the cross arm down to the sound box at the base of the instrument. The legendary instrument of Apollo. (See figure 7.67.)

Kore Archaic Greek sculpture of a standing, clothed female figure. (See figure 7.10.)

Kouros Archaic Greek sculpture of a standing, usually nude, male figure. (See figure 7.12.)

L

Lantern In architecture a small decorative structure that crowns a *dome or roof.

Latin cross A cross in which the vertical member is longer than the horizontal arm it bisects.

Libretto (I., little book) The text or words of an *opera, *oratorio, or other extended choral work.

Lied, Lieder (leet, LEE-der; G., song, songs). Term usually applied to the German romantic *art songs of Schubert, Schumann, Brahms, Wolf, and others.

Lintel In architecture a horizontal crosspiece over an open space, which carries the weight of some of the superstructure. (See figure 7.28.)

Lithography A printmaking process that uses a polished stone (or metal plate) on which the design is drawn with a crayon or greasy ink. Ink is chemically attracted only to the lines of the drawing, with a print made by applying paper to the inked stone.

Liturgical Pertaining to public worship, specifically to the organized worship patterns of the Christian churches.

Liturgical drama Twelfth- and thirteenth-century enactments of biblical stories, frequently with music. Developed into the "mystery plays" of the fourteenth through sixteenth centuries.

Lituus (Lat.) Bronze trumpet used by the Roman armies. Shaped like the letter J.

Lost wax process v. *cire perdue.*

Lute Plucked stringed instrument with a pear-shaped body and a fingerboard with frets. It had eleven strings tuned to six notes (five sets of double strings plus a single string for the highest note). It was the most popular instrument of the sixteenth century and was used into the eighteenth century. Lutes are again being made, mainly for present-day performances of Renaissance music.

Lyre (or Lyra) Ancient Greek instrument, a simpler form of the *kithara. The sound box was often made of a tortoise shell. Used mainly by amateurs. The larger kithara was used by professional musicians. (See figure 7.62.)

Lyric Poetry sung to the accompaniment of a *lyre (Greek); *troubadour and *trouvère poetry intended to be sung; short poems with musical elements. (See figure 7.62.)

M

Madrigal Name of uncertain origin that refers to fourteenth-century vocal music or, usually, to the popular sixteenth-century type. Renaissance madrigals were free-form vocal pieces (usually set to love lyrics) in a *polyphonic style with intermixed *homophonic sections. Flemish, Italian, and English composers brought the madrigal to a high level of expressiveness in word painting and imagery. Madrigals were sometimes accompanied but mostly *a cappella.

Mass The central service of public worship of some Christian churches, principally the Church of Rome. The musical portions are indicated below.

Ordinary (Same Text)	*Proper (Text Varies by the Liturgical Calendar)*
Kyrie Eleison	Introit
Gloria in Excelsis Deo	Gradual
Credo in Unum Deum	Alleluia
Sanctus	Offertory
Agnus Dei	Communion

Materialism The doctrine that the only reality is matter; that the universe is not governed by intelligence or purpose but only by mechanical cause and effect.

Melisma A melodic unit sung to one syllable; *plainsong has frequent *melismatic* passages.

Metaphor A form of figurative language that compares dissimilar objects (e.g., publicity is a two-edged sword).

Metaphysics Philosophic inquiry into the ultimate and fundamental reality; "the science of being as such."

Meter In music a grouping of beats into patterns of two, three, or four beats or combinations thereof; in English poetry the basic rhythmic pattern of stressed (−) and unstressed (⌣) syllables. Metrical patterns include: *iambic* (⌣ −), *trochaic* (− ⌣), *anapestic* (⌣ ⌣ −), and *dactylic* (− ⌣ ⌣).

Metope (MET-o-pay) In classical architecture the panel between two *triglyphs in a *Doric *frieze; may be plain or carved. The Parthenon metopes are all carved. (See figure 7.31.)

Minaret A tall, slender tower attached to a Muslim mosque from which a muezzin calls the faithful to prayer. (See figure 11.23.)

Modes, rhythmic A thirteenth-century system of music rhythmic notation based on the patterns of poetic meter. Rhythmic modes give the characteristic flavor to thirteenth-century *organum and *motets because of the constant repetition of the same rhythmic patterns. All modes were performed in so-called perfect meter, that is, triple.

Monism (Gk., *mones,* single) The philosophical position that there is but one fundamental reality. The classical advocate of extreme monism was Parmenides of Elea; Spinoza is a modern exponent.

Monochord A device consisting of a single string stretched over a soundboard with a movable bridge. Used to demonstrate the laws of acoustics, especially the relationships between intervals and string lengths and the tuning of *scales. (See figure 15.2.)

Monophonic (Gk., one sound) A single line of music without accompaniment or additional parts, as in *plainsong, *troubadour-trouvère songs, and some folk songs, hollers, street cries, and blues.

Montage (moan-TAHZH) A composition made of existing photographs, paintings, or drawings; in cinematography the effects achieved by superimposing images or using rapid sequences.

Mosaic The technique of embedding bits of stone, colored glass, or marble in wet concrete to make designs or pictures for walls or floors. To achieve a complex interplay of light and shadows, the bits are set in the holding material with minute differences in the angles, as in the mosaics of San Vitale in Ravenna. (See figures 11.20 and 11.21.)

Motet (from F., *mot,* word) The most important form of early *polyphonic music (ca. thirteenth to seventeenth centuries). 1. *Medieval motet* (thirteenth–fourteenth centuries). Usually three parts (triplum, motetus, tenor). The tenor "holds" to a *cantus firmus and the upper two voices sing different texts (sacred and/or secular). 2. *Renaissance motet* (fifteenth–sixteenth centuries). A four- or five-part composition, *a cappella, generally *polyphonic, with a single Latin text. A serious vocal piece intended for use in sacred services.

There are also Baroque motets (by J. S. Bach) for mixed chorus and orchestra (German text) and some Romantic motets (Brahms), again in the *a cappella style.

Mullion A vertical member that divides a window into sections; also used to support the glass in stained-glass windows.

Mural A painting on a wall; a *fresco is a type of mural.

Myth Stories explaining natural phenomena, customs, institutions, religious beliefs, and so forth of a people. Usually concerned with the supernatural, gods, goddesses, heroic exploits, and the like.

N

Narthex A porch or vestibule of a church through which one passes to enter the *nave.

Naturalism The view that the universe requires no supernatural cause or government, that it is self-existent, self-explanatory, self-operating, and self-directing, that the universe is purposeless, deterministic, and only incidentally productive of humankind. In relation to literature sometimes defined as "realism on all fours." The dominant traits of literary naturalism are biological determinism (people are what they must be because of their genes) and environmental determinism (people are what they are because of where they were nurtured).

Nave The main central space of a church running from the entrance to the *crossing of the *transepts; typically flanked by one or two side aisles. Name derived from *naval* because the barrel *vault ceiling has the appearance of the inside hull of a ship.

Notre Dame school The composers of the twelfth- and thirteenth-century cathedral school at Notre Dame de Paris, most notably Leonin and Perotin. The Notre Dame school invented rhythmic notation for *polyphonic music.

O

Oboe (from F., "high wind," that is, high-pitched instrument) A double-reed, soprano-range instrument with a conical bore (slightly expanding diameter from reed to bell). It has a nasal but mellow and poignant tone.

Odalisque (oh-de-LISK) French word for a harem slave or concubine but used more broadly to refer to a reclining female figure, a favorite subject of such painters as Ingres and Matisse.

Ode A formal lyric on a usually dignified theme, in exalted language, e.g., works by Horace.

Office hours In the Church of Rome the services (usually observed only in monastic churches) that take place eight times a day (every three hours): Matins, Lauds, Prime, Terce, Sext, None, Vespers, and Compline. Musically the important services are Matins, Vespers, and Compline.

Ontology (Gk., *on,* being + *logos,* logic) Philosophic inquiry into the ultimate nature of things, what it means to be.

Opera (from I., *opera in musica,* work in music) A play in which the text is generally sung throughout to the accompaniment of an orchestra. Modern opera had its beginnings in Florence in the late sixteenth century when some musicians, poets, and scholars attempted a revival of Greek drama, which they assumed to have been sung throughout.

Oratorio A musical setting of a religious or epic theme for performance by soloists, chorus, and orchestra in a church or concert hall. Originally (early seventeenth century) they were similar to operas (sacred operas) with staging, costumes, and scenery. They are now usually presented in concert form, for example, *The Messiah,* by G. F. Handel.

Orchestra (from Gk., *orcheisthai,* to dance) In ancient Greek theatres the circular or semicircular space in front of the stage used by the chorus; group of instrumentalists performing ensemble music, e.g., symphony orchestra.

Ordinary of the Mass v. Mass.

Organ, Pipe organ An instrument (see Hydraulis) of ancient origin consisting of from two to seven keyboards (manuals) and a set of pedals (usually thirty-two notes) for the feet.

Organum (OR-ga-num; Lat.) The name given to the earliest types of *polyphonic music. Beginning with about the ninth century, organum was first strict, then parallel, free (contrary motion), and *melismatic. See (in the text) the section on medieval music for description and illustrations of the stages of organum.

P

Pantheism (Gk., *pan,* all, + *theos,* god) As a religious concept, the doctrine that God is immanent in all things.

Pediment In classic architecture a triangular space at the end of a building framed by the *cornice and the ends of the sloping roof (*raking cornices). (See figure 7.30.)

Pendentive In architecture a concave triangular piece of masonry, four of which form a transition from a square base to support the circular rim of a *dome. (See figure 11.19.)

Percussion Instruments that are played by striking, shaking, scraping, etc.

Peristyle A series of *columns that surround the exterior of a building or the interior of a court, e.g., the Parthenon has a peristyle. (See figure 7.34.)

Perspective The illusion of a three-dimensional world on a two-dimensional surface. *Linear perspective* uses lines of projection converging on a vanishing point and with objects appearing smaller the further from the viewer. *Aerial (atmospheric) perspective* uses diminished color intensity and blurred contours for objects apparently deeper in space.

Pier A mass of masonry, usually large, used to support *arches or *lintels; more massive than a *column and with a shape other than circular. (See figure 14.35.)

Pietà (pyay-TA; I., pity, compassion) Representations of the Virgin mourning the body of her Son.

Pilaster A flat vertical column projecting from the wall of a building; usually furnished with a base and *capital in the manner of an *engaged column, which is rounded rather than rectangular like the pilaster.

Plainsong The term generally used for the large body of nonmetrical, *monophonic, *liturgical music of the Church of Rome. Also called Gregorian chant.

Polyphony (po-LIF-o-nee) *Polyphonic* (pol-ly-PHON-ik) "Many-voiced" music, that is, melodic interest in two or more simultaneous melodic lines. Examples of polyphonic music would be *canons and *rounds.

Positivism Philosophic inquiry limited to problems open to scientific investigation. Traditional subjects such as *aesthetics and *metaphysics are dismissed as "meaningless" because their content cannot be subjected to verification.

Post and lintel A structural system in which vertical supports or columns support horizontal beams. The lintel can span only a relatively short space because the weight of the superstructure centers on the midpoint of the horizontal beam. In a structural system using *arches the thrust is distributed to the *columns supporting the bases of the arches, thus allowing for a greater span. The lintel is also called an *architrave. (See figure 7.28.)

Pragmatism (Gk., *pragma,* things done) Philosophic doctrine that the meaning of a proposition or course of action lies in its observable consequences and that its meaning is the sum of its consequences. In everyday life the favoring of practical means over theory; if something works, it's good; if not, it's bad.

Primary colors The *hues of red, yellow, and blue with which the colors of the spectrum can be produced. Primary colors cannot be produced by mixing.

Program music Music intended to depict ideas, scenes, or other extramusical concepts.

Proper of the Mass v. Mass.

Proscenium (Gk., *pro,* before; *skene,* stage) In traditional theatres the framework of the stage opening.

Psalm A sacred song, poem, or *hymn; the songs in the Old Testament book of Psalms.

Psalter Vernacular name for the book of Psalms.

Psaltery Ancient or medieval instrument consisting of a flat soundboard over which a number of strings are stretched. A psaltery is plucked with the fingers. A similar instrument, the dulcimer, is played by striking the strings with hammers. The *harpsichord is a keyed psaltery. (See figure 13.1.)

Putto (I., plural *putti,* boy) The cherubs in Italian Renaissance painting and in rococo painting of the eighteenth century.

Q

Quatrain A stanza of four lines, either rhymed or unrhymed.

R

Raking cornice The end (*cornice) on the sloping sides of a triangular *pediment.

Rebec A small bowed medieval string instrument adapted from the Arabian *rebab.* One of the instruments from which the violin developed during the sixteenth century. (See figure 15.3.)

Recorder A straight, end-blown *flute, as distinct from the modern side-blown (transverse) flute. It was used from the Middle Ages until the eighteenth century and has been revived in the twentieth century.

Refrain   Recurring section of text (and usually music), e.g., verse-refrain.

Relief   In sculpture, carvings projecting from a background that is a part of the whole. Reliefs may be high (almost disengaged from the background) or low (*bas-relief,* slightly raised above the background).

Reliquary   (F., remains) A receptacle for storing or displaying holy relics. (See figure 14.21.)

Round   In music a commonly used name for a circle *canon. At the conclusion of a melody the singer returns to the beginning, repeating the melody as often as desired. Examples: "Brother James," "Dona Nobis Pacem," and "Row, Row, Row Your Boat."

S

Sanctuary   A sacred or holy place set aside for the worship of a god or gods; a place of refuge or protection.

Sarcophagus   A stone coffin.

Satire   An indictment of human foibles using humor as a weapon, e.g., the relatively mild satires of Horace and the bitter ones of Juvenal and Jonathan Swift.

Scale   (Lat., ladder) The tonal material of music arranged in a series of rising or falling pitches. Because of the variety in the world's music there are many different scales. The basic scale of European music is the diatonic scale (C-D-E-F-G-A-B-C), i.e., the white keys of the piano. This arrangement of tones is also called a major scale or, more properly, a C major scale.

Scholasticism   The philosophy and method of medieval theologians in which speculation was separated from observation and practice, revelation was regarded as both the norm and an aid to reason, reason respected authority, and scientific inquiry was controlled by theology.

Secondary colors   Those *hues located between the *primary colors on a traditional color wheel: orange, green, and violet.

Sequence   A type of chant developed in the early Middle Ages in which a freely poetic text was added to the long *melisma at the end of the *Alleluias. Subsequently separated from the Alleluias, the sequences became independent syllabic chants. The composition of many original sequences finally led to the banning of all but five sequences by the Council of Trent (1545–1563).

Sfumato   (sfoo-MAH-toe) A hazy, smoky blending of color tones in a painting to create ambiguities of line and shape, as in Leonardo's *Mona Lisa.*

Silk screen   Stencil process. Closely woven silk is tacked tightly over a frame; areas on silk not to be printed are "stopped out;" then paint is squeezed through the silk mesh onto cloth or paper underneath.

Simile   A comparison between two quite different things, usually using "like" or "as."

Sonata   (I., *sonare,* to sound.) A musical composition, usually in three or four movements (sections) for a piano or organ or a solo instrument (violin, trumpet, etc.) with keyboard accompaniment.

Sonnet   A fourteen-line poem in iambic pentameter. Petrarch, the fourteenth-century Italian poet, used a rhyming scheme of *abbaabba* followed by *cde cde* or variants thereof. Shakespeare used a rhyming scheme of *abab cdcd efef gg,* or four *quatrains followed by a rhymed couplet.

Squinch   In architecture a device to effect a transition from a polygonal base to a circular *dome. (See figure 11.19 and accompanying explanation.)

Stele   (STEE-lee) A carved slab of stone or pillar used especially by the Greeks as a grave marker. (See figure 7.26.)

Still life   In pictorial arts inanimate objects used as subject matter.

Stylobate   The third of three steps of a Greek temple on which the *columns rest; essentially the platform on which the *cella and *peristyle are erected. (See figure 7.35.)

Syllogism   A form of deductive reasoning consisting of a major premise, minor premise, and a conclusion. Example: all men are mortal; Sokrates is a man; therefore Sokrates is mortal.

T

Teleology   (Gk., *telos,* end, completion) The theory of purpose, ends, goals, final cause; opposite of materialism.

Tempera   A painting technique using pigment suspended in egg yolk.

Tenor   (Lat., *tenere,* to hold) (1) Originally the part that "held" the melody on which early sacred *polyphonic music was based. (2) The highest male voice (S A T B). (3) Prefix to the name of an instrument, for example, tenor saxophone.

Terra-cotta   (I., baked earth) A baked clay used in ceramics and sculptures; a reddish color.

Tesserae   (TESS-er-ee) Bits of stone and colored glass used in *mosaics.

Thrust   The outward force caused by the weight and design of an *arch or *vault, a thrust that must be countered by a *buttress. (See figure 14.31.)

Tragedy   A serious play or other literary work with an unhappy or disastrous ending caused, in Greek drama, by *hubris on the part of the protagonist.

Transcendental   Beyond the realm of the senses; rising above common thought or ideas; exalted.

Transept   That part of a *cruciform-plan church whose axis intersects at right angles the long axis of the cross running from the entrance through the *nave to the *apse; the cross-arm of the cross.

Triforium   In a Gothic cathedral, the gallery between the *nave arcades and the *clerestory; the triforium gallery opens on the nave with an *arcade. (See figure 14.37.)

Triglyph   Projecting block with vertical channels that alternates with *metopes in a *Dorian *frieze of a Greek temple. The ends of the marble beams are stylized versions of the wooden beams used in early temples.

Trompe-l'oeil (trohmp LUH-yuh; F.) Illusionistic painting designed to convince the observer that what is seen is an actual three-dimensional object rather than a two-dimensional surface; literally, "eye fooling."

Trope Additional text and/or music added to a preexisting *plainsong. The earliest tropes were *sequences. Troping became so widespread that it was banned by the Council of Trent. *Liturgical drama was a direct outgrowth of the trope.

Troubadour Poet-musicians, mostly men and women of aristocratic birth, of southern France (Provence) who, during the period ca. 1100–1300, cultivated the arts of poetry and music in chivalrous service to romantic love. Their music was *monophonic in style and popular in flavor but exerted considerable influence on the development of *polyphonic music.

Trouvère Poet-musicians of central and northern France from ca. 1150–1300. Their music developed from the *troubadours and showed the same general characteristics except for the change in language from that of the south (Provençal) to the medieval forerunner of modern French.

Trumeau A pillar or column placed in the center of a portal to help support the *lintel. (See figure 14.20.)

Tympanum The space, usually elaborately carved, enclosed by the *lintel and *arch of a doorway; also, the space within the horizontal and *raking cornices of a *pediment. (See figure 14.17.)

V

Vanishing point In linear *perspective the point at which parallel lines converge on the horizon.

Vault A masonry ceiling constructed on the principle of the *arch. A *barrel vault* is an uninterrupted series of arches amounting to a very deep arch. (See figure 14.7.)

Virginal A *harpsichord used mainly in England and supposedly played by young ladies. The shape was frequently rectangular.

Volute The spiral scrolls of an *Ionian *capital.

Voussoir (voo-SWAHR; F.) The wedge-shaped blocks of stone used to construct *arches and *vaults.

W

Woodcut A wood block that has been carved so that the design stands out slightly from the block, comparable to printing type.

Z

Ziggurat A temple tower of the ancient Mesopotamians. (See figure 1.1.)

Annotated Bibliography

The bibliographies were selected as particularly useful and interesting with a range from popular to scholarly works.

Prologue

Bennett, William J. *To Reclaim a Legacy: A Report on the Humanities in Higher Education.* Washington, DC: Government Printing Office, 1984. Bennett bewails the current lack of emphasis on our past cultural creations and argues for their centrality in education and for understanding our own civilization.

Boorstein, Daniel J. *The Discoverers: A History of Man's Search to Know His World and Himself.* New York: Random House, 1983. An exciting introduction to cultural and intellectual history. Very highly recommended.

Hassan, Ihab, and Sally Hassan, eds. *Innovation/Renovation: New Perspectives on the Humanities.* Madison: University of Wisconsin Press, 1982. Innovative approaches to furthering our understanding of the humanities.

Munro, Thomas. *The Arts—Their Interrelations.* Western Reserve University Press, 1967. An unusual and fascinating approach to comparative aesthetics by a man who is both a professor of philosophy and professor of art.

Post, Gaines, Jr. *The Humanities in American Life.* Berkeley: University of California Press, 1980. Supported by the Rockefeller Foundation, this report of a special commission notes deficiencies in current education and recommends a better integration of the humanities into the curriculum.

Rader, Melvin, and Bertram Jessup. *Art and Human Values.* Englewood Cliffs, NJ: Prentice-Hall, 1976. The role of art in formulating and communicating values.

Read, Herbert. *Education Through Art.* New York: Pantheon Books, 1974. The author bases his approach to aesthetic education on Plato's thesis that art should be the basis of education.

Toynbee, Arnold. *A Study of History.* In several editions (preferably the one-volume abridgement). This classic study articulates and documents one of the most impressive culture-epoch theories of the rise and fall of civilizations.

16

Bainton, Roland H. *Here I Stand: A Life of Martin Luther.* Nashville: Abingdon Press, 1978. Acclaimed as the best introductory biography in English.

Women of the Reformation: In Germany and Italy. Minneapolis: Augsburg Publishing House, 1971. Explores a dimension too often neglected.

Burckhardt, Jacob C. *The Civilization of the Renaissance in Italy.* In any edition. The nineteenth-century classic that formulated, in part, the modern view of a golden age. An important source that totally ignored, however, the northern Renaissance.

Dickens, A. G. *The Counter-Reformation.* New York: W. W. Norton, 1969. The Catholic response to the Reformation.

Gilmore, Myron P. *The World of Humanism, 1453–1517.* New York: Greenwood, 1983. A well-written survey.

Grimm, Harold J. *The Reformation Era: 1500–1650.* New York: Macmillan, 1973. Fine overview.

Hale, John R. *Renaissance Exploration.* New York: W. W. Norton, 1972. Splendid introduction.

Morison, Samuel E. *Christopher Columbus, Mariner.* New York: New American Library, 1983. A fine shorter version of this master storyteller's definitive *Admiral of the Open Sea.*

Rachum, Ilan. *The Renaissance: An Illustrated Encyclopedia.* New York: W. H. Smith Publishers, 1980. Exceptionally useful.

Simon, Edith. *The Reformation.* Alexandria, VA: Time-Life Books, 1966. Another excellent work in the Great Ages of Man Series.

Weber, Max. *The Protestant Ethic and the Spirit of Capitalism.* New York: Charles Scribner's Sons, 1977. The classic study arguing that Calvinism led to the triumph of capitalism.

17

Ackerman, James S. *Palladio.* New York: Penguin, 1977. Fine study of a very influential architect.

Andres, Glenn, and others. *The Art of Florence,* 2 vols. New York: Abbeville Press, 1989. Florence from 1200 to 1600 is given a social and historical context in an excellent new study.

Berenson, Bernard. *The Italian Painters of the Renaissance.* Ithaca: Cornell University Press, 1980. A classic study, still influential.

Civilisation: A Personal View. New York: Harper & Row, 1970. Excellent chapters on the Renaissance in a work that was the basis for a notable television series.

Clark, Kenneth. *The Art of Humanism.* New York: Harper & Row, 1983. An urbane art historian presents his sophisticated analysis of Renaissance works.

Coulas, Ivan. *The Borgias.* New York: Franklin Watts, 1989. A readable scholarly study of an infamous but fascinating family.

De Tolnay, Charles. *Michelangelo: Sculptor, Painter, Architect.* Princeton: Princeton University Press, 1982. A condensation of the author's magisterial six-volume study.

Fine, Elsa Honig. *Women and Art; A History of Women Painters and Sculptors from the Renaissance to the 20th Century.* Montclair/London: Allanheld & Schram/Prior, 1978.

Fuller, Edmund, ed. *Vasari's Lives of the Painters, Sculptors, and Architects.* New York: Dell Publishing Company, 1963. The most pertinent selections from the Renaissance classic.

Hale, John R. *Renaissance.* Great Ages of Man Series. Alexandria, VA: Time-Life Books, 1965. More superb coverage.

MacCurdy, Edward, trans. *The Notebooks of Leonardo da Vinci.* Two volumes. London: Chatto Bodley Jonathan, 1978. Only in the notebooks can one begin to appreciate the range and richness of one of the greatest minds in history.

Martineau, Jane, and Charles Hope, eds. *The Genius of Venice.* New York: Abrams, 1984. Art in the unique city.

Panofsky, Erwin. *The Life and Art of Albrecht Durer.* Princeton: Princeton University Press, 1955. Probably the finest single work in English on the German genius.

Simon, Edith. *The Reformation.* Great Ages of Man Series. Alexandria, VA: Time-Life Books, 1966. Excellent coverage.

Snyder, James. *Northern Renaissance Art.* New York: Abrams, 1985. Excellent coverage.

18

Dolmetsch, Mabel. *Dances of England and France from 1450–1600: With Their Music and Authentic Manner of Performance.* New York: Da Capo Press, 1975.

Lincoln, Harry B., ed. *Madrigal Collection L'amorosa Ero* (Brescia, 1588). Albany, NY: State University of New York Press, 1968.

Scott, Charles K., ed. *Madrigal Singing.* Westport, CT: Greenwood Press, n.d.

Thomson, James C. *Music through the Renaissance.* Dubuque, IA: Wm. C. Brown Publishers, 1965. A brief survey of music from primitive times. Condensed and simplified for the nonmusician.

19

Chute, Marchette. *Shakespeare of London.* New York: E. P. Dutton & Co., 1950. One of the best popular biographies.

Montaigne, Michel de. *Essays.* J. M. Cohen, trans. New York: Penguin Books, 1959. Recommended translation of fascinating essays by the inventor of the form.

More, Thomas. *UTOPIA and Other Writings.* James Green and John Dolan, eds. New York: The New American Library, 1984. Excellent edition.

Phillips, Margaret M. *Erasmus and the Northern Renaissance.* New York: Rowman, 1981. Explores the central role of Erasmus.

Rabelais, Francois. *Gargantua and Pantagruel.* John M. Cohen, trans. New York: Penguin Books, 1955. Excellent translation of the ribald classic.

Ross, James Bruce, and Mary Martin McLaughlin, eds. *The Portable Renaissance Reader.* New York: The Viking Press, 1968. Excellent collection of writings of acknowledged masters.

20

Historical Background

Blitzer, Charles. *Age of Kings.* Great Ages of Man Series. New York: Time, Inc. 1967. Every volume in the series is interesting and informative.

Lefebvre, Georges. *The French Revolution: Vol. I From Its Origins to 1793.* John H. Stewart, trans. New York: Columbia University Press, 1962. By the greatest modern scholar of the French revolt.

Stone, Laurence. *The Causes of the English Revolution, 1529–1642.* New York: Harper & Row, 1972. How clashes between Puritans and monarchs led to the Cromwell commonwealth experiment.

Cultural Developments

Bennet, Jonathan. *Locke, Berkeley, Hume: Central Themes.* New York: Oxford University Press, 1971. Three of the most influential thinkers of the time.

Burke, Peter. *Popular Culture in Early Modern Europe.* New York: New York University Press, 1978. A fascinating account of the period 1500–1800.

Gay, Peter. *The Enlightenment: An Interpretation.* Two volumes. New York: W. W. Norton, 1977. A remarkable work by a noted authority.

Hall, A. Rupert. *The Revolution in Science: 1500–1750.* New York: Longman, 1983. From Copernicus and Galileo to Newton and the foundation of the modern scientific outlook.

Original Materials

Brady, Frank, ed. *Boswell's Life of Samuel Johnson.* New York: The New American Library, Inc., 1981. An abridged version of this mammoth biographical masterpiece.

Montesquieu, Charles de. *The Spirit of the Laws*. Ed. David W. Carrithers. Berkeley: University of California Press, 1978. Also influential in several revolutions.

Peterson, Merrill D., ed. *The Portable Thomas Jefferson*. New York: Penguin Books, Inc., 1979. Ample collection of writings by the Yankee genius, including correspondence with prominent people.

21

The Baroque: Principles, Styles, Modes, Themes. New York: W. W. Norton, 1978. A comprehensive analysis of general features.

Bazin, Germain. *Baroque and Rococo Art*. New York: Oxford University Press, 1964. Good survey by a noted authority.

Brown, Dale. *The World of Velasquez, 1599–1660*. Library of Art Series. New York: Time-Life Books, Inc., 1969. A thorough study in a very fine series. This series is valuable and rewarding for critics and laypeople alike. One wonders why the former have not given them the time and appraisal they so clearly deserve. No matter—don't miss any volume in this extensive series.

Clark, Kenneth. *An Introduction to Rembrandt*. New York: Harper & Row, 1978. A fine art historian on one of the most famous painters.

Schneider, Pierre. *The World of Watteau, 1684–1721*. Library of Art Series. New York: Time-Life Books, Inc., 1967. A delightful volume, as charming as the artists, works, and society it presents.

Wallace, Robert. *The World of Bernini, 1598–1680*. Library of Art Series. New York: Time-Life Books, Inc., 1970. Superb, as usual, for the series.

Wright, Christopher. *The Dutch Painters: One Hundred Seventeenth Century Masters*. Woodbury, New York: Barron, 1978.

22

Pauly, Reinhard. *Music in the Classic Period*. Englewood Cliffs, NJ: Prentice-Hall, 1965. Survey of the style with a minimum of technical obstacles.

Rosen, Charles. *The Classical Style: Haydn, Mozart, Beethoven*. New York: W. W. Norton, 1972. Winner of the 1972 National Book Award for Arts and Letters.

23

Historical Background

Arendt, Hannah. *On Revolution*. New York: Penguin Books, Inc., 1977. A noted political analyst examines what the American and French revolutions mean to people living today.

Burchell, Samuel C. *The Age of Progress*. Great Ages of Man Series. New York: Time-Life Books, 1966. Excellent.

Fieldhouse, D. K. *Colonialism, 1870–1945: An Introduction*. New York: St. Martin's Press, 1981. Today's world, especially the Third World, cannot be fully understood without constant reference to colonialism and its aftermath.

Schama, Simon. *Citizens: A Chronicle of the French Revolution*. New York: Alfred A. Knopf, 1989. A revisionist theory claiming that the *ancien régime* was itself the catalyst of the political and social changes. Historians have attacked the theory as irresponsible nonsense.

Tuchman, Barbara. *The Guns of August*. New York: Macmillan, 1962. A vivid account of the Great War's outbreak. Her *The Proud Tower* is an equally riveting study of the two decades leading into the war.

Cultural Developments

Eiseley, Loren C. *Darwin's Century: Evolution and the Men Who Discovered It*. Garden City, NY: Doubleday & Co., Inc., 1958. A beautifully written account.

The Immense Journey. New York: Random House, 1957. A classic account of evolution and the story of humankind.

Literature and Criticism

Bloom, Harold, and Lionel Trilling, eds. *Romantic Prose and Poetry*. New York: Oxford University Press, 1973. An excellent anthology.

Rozanov, Vasily. *Dostoevsky and the Legend of the Grand Inquisitor*. Ithaka, NY: Cornell University Press, 1972. The origins of Dostoevsky's ideas.

Sandor, Ellis. *Political Apocalypse: A Study of Dostoevsky's Grand Inquisitor*. Baton Rouge: Louisiana State University Press, 1971.

Trilling, Lionel, and Harold Bloom, eds. *Victorian Prose and Poetry*. New York: Oxford University Press, 1973. A fine companion volume to their anthology of Romantic works.

24

Dannreuther, E. *The Romantic Period*. New York: Cooper Square Publishers, 1973. Quite a thorough exposition of the varieties of Romantic expression.

Holoman, D. Kern. *Berlioz: A Musical Biography of the Creative Genius of the Romantic Era*. Cambridge: Harvard University Press, 1990. By far the most intellectual of the great composers, Berlioz is also honored in French literature as a writer and a critic.

Plantinga, Leon. *Romantic Music*. New York: W. W. Norton, 1982. Introductory text.

25

Herbert, Robert L. *Impressionism*. New Haven: Yale University Press, 1988. A major new interpretation of the style in its social/cultural context. Strongly recommended.

Prather, Marla, and Charles F. Stuckey, eds. *Gauguin: A Retrospective*. New York: Hugh Lauter Levin Associates, 1987. Outstanding text and illustrations.

Prideaux, Tom et al. *The World of Delacroix*. Library of Art. New York: Time-Life Books, 1966. The focus is on Delacroix, but his important contemporaries are also included.

Post-Impressionism: From van Gogh to Gauguin. New York: New York Graphic Society Books, 1979.

Rewald, John. *The History of Impressionism.* New York: New York Graphic Society Books, 1980. Any book by Rewald on impressionism or post-impressionism is highly recommended.

Schneider, Pierre. *The World of Manet, 1832–1883.* Library of Art. New York: Time-Life Books, 1968. Scholarly, clear, concise, and beautiful.

Shapiro, Meyer. *Van Gogh.* New York: Harry N. Abrams, 1984. One of the few objective studies. Highly recommended.

Simpson, Marc and others. *Winslow Homer: Paintings of the Civil War.* Fine Arts Museum of San Francisco and Bedford Arts Publications, 1988. A unique visual overview of the conflict. Poignant.

Wallace, Robert, et al. *The World of van Gogh, 1853–1890.* New York: Time-Life Books, 1969. Concise biographies of van Gogh and other artists who have been romanticized in literature and in the movies.

The World of Whistler, 1834–1903. Library of Art. New York: Time-Life Books, 1970. Still more in a fine series.

26

Historical Background

Galbraith, John Kenneth. *The Great Crash,1929.* Boston: Houghton Mifflin, 1979. The celebrated economist on the catastrophe that ushered in the Great Depression.

Mitchell, Broadus. *Depression Decade: From New Era through New Deal, 1929–1941.* Arnmonk, NY: M. E. Sharpe, 1977.

Our Twentieth-Century World, 1903–1969. Vol. IV in the Milestones of History Series. New York: Newsweek Books, 1970. Fine review of significant developments.

Taylor, A. J. *The Origins of the Second World War.* New York: Atheneum Publishers, 1983. A respected historian reviews the evidence.

This Fabulous Century: Sixty Years of American Life. New York: Time-Life Books, 1969–1970. From 1870 to 1970 in eight volumes. A vivid overview.

Cultural Developments

Calder, Nigel. *Einstein's Universe.* New York: Greenwich House, 1982. Einstein explained for the general reader.

Dawkins, Richard. *The Blind Watchmaker; Why the Evidence of Evolution Reveals a Universe Without Design.* New York: W. W. Norton, 1986. The author's thesis is that the Darwinian world view could, in principle, help solve the mystery of our existence.

Edelson, Marshall. *Hypothesis and Evidence in Psychoanalysis.* Chicago: University of Chicago Press, 1984.

Grünbaum, Adolf. *The Foundations of Psychoanalysis: A Philosophical Critique.* Berkeley: University of California Press, 1984.

Hitler, Adolf. *Meinkampf.* Boston: Houghton Mifflin, 1962. Hitler's self-serving autobiography of 1925 with his version of history and vision of the future.

Noakes, Jeremy, and Geoffrey Pridham, eds. *Documents on Nazism, 1919–1945.* New York: The Viking Press, 1975. A revealing collection, to say the least.

Pipes, Richard. *The Russian Revolution.* New York: Alfred A. Knopf, 1990. The thesis that the February Revolution was a military rebellion (not a workers' revolt) and the Bolshevik takeover in October a coup d'état. Further, that when Stalin came to power in 1924 Lenin had all the totalitarian controls firmly in place.

Historical Fiction

Pasternak, Boris. *Dr. Zhivago.* New York: Ballantine Books, 1981. The Nobel Laureate's portrait of the Russian Revolution and its aftermath as seen from the inside.

Steinbeck, John. *The Grapes of Wrath.* New York: Penguin Books, 1977. An indelible picture of the Great Depression as experienced by the Joad family from Oklahoma.

27

Historical Background

Capute, Philip. *A Rumor of War.* New York: Ballantine Books, 1978. Acclaimed the best memoir of the American experience in Vietnam.

Hilberg, Raul. *The Destruction of European Jews.* New York: Harper & Row, 1979. Another study of Nazi genocide.

Johnson, Paul. *Modern Times: The World from the Twenties to the Eighties.* New York: Harper & Row, 1983. Highly recommended.

Lerner, Gerda. *Women and History. Volume One: The Creation of Patrimony.* New York: Oxford University Press, 1986. Excellent.

Wiesel, Elie. *Night.* Stella Rodway, trans. New York: Bantam Books, 1982. The celebrated writer and Nobel Laureate describes his experiences in Hitler's death camps.

Cultural Developments

Baruch, Grace, Rosalind Barnett, and Caryl Rivers. *Life Prints: New Patterns of Love and Work for Today's Women.* New York: McGraw-Hill, 1983. Important study and strongly recommended.

Blashfield, Jean F. *Hellraisers, Heroines, and Holy Women: Women's Most Remarkable Contributions to History.* New York: St. Martin's Press, 1981. Just about everything from the "Astronomer to Classify the Most Stars" (Annie Jump Cannon) to the "First Woman to be Kicked Out of Harvard" (Harriet Hunt, 1859).

Bullock, Alan, and R. B. Woodings, eds. *Modern Culture: A Biographical Companion.* New York: Harper & Row, 1984. Articles on key figures in twentieth century culture.

Greer, Germaine. *Sex and Destiny: The Politics of Human Fertility.* New York: Harper & Row, 1984. An analysis of gender relations in contemporary society.

Herbert, Nick. *Quantum Reality: Beyond the New Physics.* Garden City, NY: Anchor Press/Doubleday, 1985. A popular exposition of six emergent models of the ultimate nature of atomic reality based on post-Einsteinian physics.

Littwin, Susan. *The Postponed Generation: Why American Youth Are Growing Up Later.* New York: William Morrow and Company, 1986. An intriguing analysis of diminished expectations.

Mosse, George L. *Nazi Culture.* New York: Schocken Books, 1981. A noted historian analyzes the vulgarity of Hitler's Germany.

28

An exhaustive bibliography would be nearly endless and therefore, pointless. Rather, the following list is highly selective, but with a wide range of interesting and useful books.

Arnason, H. Hovard. *History of Modern Art: Painting, Sculpture, and Architecture.* New York: Harry N. Abrams, Inc., 1986. Excellent general study with an exhaustive bibliography.

Bearden, Romare, and Harry Henderson. *Six Black Masters of American Art.* New York: Doubleday & Company, 1972. Includes Johnson, Duncanson, Pippin, and Lawrence.

Billington, David P. *The Tower and the Bridge: The New Art of Structural Engineering.* New York: Basic Books, Inc., Publishers, 1983. The efficiency, economy, and elegance of structural engineering.

Broude, Norma, and Mary D. Garrard, eds. *Feminism and Art History: Questioning the Litany.* New York: Harper & Row, 1982. Essays toward revising the history of art.

Chipp, Herschel. *Picasso's Guernica: History, Transformations, Meanings.* Berkeley: University of California Press, 1988.

Connor, Steven. *Postmodernist Culture: An Introduction to Theories of the Contemporary.* New York: Blackwell, 1990.

Fine, Elsa Honig. *The Afro-American Artist: A Search for Identity.* Reprint. New York: Hacker, 1982. Twenty important artists.

Goodman, Cynthia. *Digital Visions: Computers and Art.* New York: Harry N. Abrams, 1987. Computer-generated art.

Huffington, Arianna Stassinopoulos. "Picasso: Creator and Destroyer." *The Atlantic* 261:6 (June 1988): 37–78. Controversial and highly critical biography of Picasso the man.

Hughes, Robert. *The Shock of the New: Art and the Century of Change.* New York: Alfred A. Knopf, 2d ed., 1990. This fascinating work grew out of the television series for BBC and later, PBS.

Hutcheon, Linda. *A Poetics of Postmodernism: History, Theory, Fiction.* New York: Routledge, 1990. Primary focus on literature.

Jencks, Charles. *Architecture Today.* New York: Abrams, 1988. Significant trends in late-modern and postmodern architecture.

Newhall, Beaumont. *The History of Photography: From 1839 to the Present.* Completely Revised and Enlarged Edition. New York: The Museum of Modern Art, 1982. Hailed as a classic work on the subject.

Normand-Romain, Antoinette Le. *Sculpture: The Adventure of Modern Sculpture in the Nineteenth and Twentieth Centuries.* New York: Rizzoli International Publications, 1986. Fine overview and beautifully illustrated.

Parker, Rozsica, and Griselda Pollock. *Old Mistresses: Women, Art, and Ideology.* New York: Pantheon, 1982. A reexamination not merely of women artists, but of art history in general.

Quirarte, Jacinto. *Mexican American Artists.* Austin: University of Texas Press, 1973. A good overview with an extensive bibliography.

Rosen, Randy, and Catherine Brewer. *Making Their Mark: Women Artists Move into the Mainstream.* New York: Abbeville Press, 1989. The prominent role of women: 1970–1985.

Rubinstein, Charlotte Streifer. *American Women Artists: From Early Indian Times to the Present.* Boston: G. K. Hall & Co., 1982. The first comprehensive survey of American women artists.

Russell, John. *The Meaning of Modern Art.* New York: Harper & Row, 1981. Outstanding interpretation. Invaluable.

Slatkin, Wendy. *Women Artists in History: From Antiquity to the 20th Century.* Englewood Cliffs, NJ: Prentice-Hall, Inc., 1985. Good overview. Recorded names of women artists dating back to the third century B.C.

Tomkins, Calvin et al. *The World of Marcel Duchamp.* Library of Art. New York: Time-Life Books, 1966. One of the most informative and enjoyable (at times hilarious) studies in art literature.

Toulmin, Stephen. *Cosmopolis: The Hidden Agenda of Modernity.* New York: Free Press, 1990. Primary focus on philosophy.

29

Classical Music

Hamm, Charles. *Music in the New World.* New York: W. W. Norton, 1983. Good overview of American music.

Morgan, Robert P. *Twentieth-Century Music.* New York: W. W. Norton, 1987. From the Norton Introduction to Music Series.

Zaimont, Judith Lang, and Karen Famera, eds. and comps. *Contemporary Concert Music by Women: A Directory of the Composers and Their Works.* Westport, CT: Greenwood Press, 1981.

Jazz

Berendt, Joachim. *The Jazz Book: From Ragtime to Fusion and Beyond.* Westport, CT: Hill, Lawrence and Co., 1982. Excellent work by a recognized authority.

Booth, Mark W. *American Popular Music: A Reference Guide.* Westport, CT: Greenwood Press, 1983. Valuable resource for ragtime, jazz, Tin Pan Alley, Broadway, Hollywood, Nashville, and so on.

Oliver, Paul. *The Meaning of the Blues.* New York: Macmillan, 1963. Probably the best single book on the blues.

Placksin, Sally. *American Women in Jazz: 1900 to the Present.* New York: Seaview Books, 1982. Overdue recognition of some fine jazz musicians.

Tanner, Paul et al. *Jazz.* 6th ed. Dubuque, IA: Wm. C. Brown Publishers, 1988. Good general text.

Credits

Chapter 19

Page 76: © Peter Bondanella and Mark Musa 1979. Reprinted from *The Prince* by Niccolo Machiavelli translated by Peter Bondanella and Mark Musa (1984) by permission of Oxford University Press.

Page 90: "Second Book, Chapter Eight" from *The Works of Francois Rabelais,* Volume I by Alfred J. Nock, C. R. Wilson, translated by Urguhart-Lemontteux, copyright 1931 by Harcourt Brace Jovanovich, Inc. and renewed 1959 by Catherine Rose Wilson and S. Nock, reprinted by permission of the publisher.

Chapter 20

Page 143: *Tartuffe* by Moliere, translated by Richard Wilbur, copyright © 1963, 1962, 1961 by Richard Wilbur, reprinted by permission of Harcourt Brace Jovanovich, Inc.

Chapter 23

Page 155: "The Grand Inquisitor" by Dostoevsky is reprinted from *The Brothers Karamazov,* translated by Ralph E. Matlaw. Copyright © 1976 by W. W. Norton & Company, Inc.

Chapter 26

Page 320: "The Love Song of J. Alfred Prufrock" from *Collected Poems 1909–1962,* copyright 1936 by Harcourt Brace Jovanovich, Inc., copyright © 1964, 1963 by T. S. Eliot, reprinted by permission of Harcourt Brace Jovanovich, Inc., and Faber and Faber Limited, London.

Page 321: "Dulce et Decorum Est" from *Complete Poems and Fragments of Wilfred Owen,* edited by Jon Stallworthy, © Chatto & Windus. Reprinted by permission of the estate of Wilfred Owen, and Chatto and Windus, Ltd; and Wilfred Owen: *Collected Poems of Wilfred Owen.* Copyright © 1963 by Chatto & Windus, Ltd. Reprinted by permission of New Directions Publishing Corporation.

Page 322: "The Second Coming" reprinted with permission of Macmillan Publishing Company from *The Poems of W. B. Yeats: A New Edition,* edited by Richard J. Finneran. Copyright © 1924 by Macmillan Publishing Company, renewed 1952 by Bertha Georgie Yeats.

Page 322: From the *Selected Poetry of Robinson Jeffers* by Robinson Jeffers. Copyright © 1925 and renewed 1953 by Robinson Jeffers. Reprinted by permission of Random House, Inc.

Page 323: Reprinted by permission of GRM Associates, Inc., Agents for the Estate of Ida M. Cullen, from the book *On These I Stand* by Countee Cullen. Copyright © 1925 by Harper & Brothers; copyright renewed 1953 by Ida M. Cullen.

Chapter 27

Page 324: From *Collected Poems 1930–1976* by Richard Eberhart. Copyright © 1976 by Richard Eberhart. Reprinted by permission of Oxford University Press, Inc.

Page 325: Denise Levertov: *Poems 1968–1972.* Copyright © 1968 by Denise Levertov Goodman. Reprinted by permission of New Directions Publishing Corporation.

Page 329: From *The Myth of Sisyphus and Other Essays* by Albert Camus, translated by J. O'Brien. Copyright © 1955 by Alfred A. Knopf, Inc. Reprinted by permission of Alfred A. Knopf, Inc., New York, NY, and Hamish Hamilton Ltd., London.

Page 331: "Letter From Birmingham Jail" from *Why We Can't Wait* by Martin Luther King, Jr. Copyright © 1963, 1964 by Martin Luther King, Jr. Reprinted by permission of HarperCollins Publishers.

Page 332: From *The Panther and the Lash* by Langston Hughes. Copyright © 1951 by Langston Hughes. Reprinted by permission of Alfred A. Knopf, Inc. and Harold Ober Associates Incorporated.

Page 333: "I Like to Think of Harriet Tubman" from *Like the Iris of an Eye* by Susan Griffin. Copyright Susan Griffin. Reprinted by permission.

Page 334: "If Shakespeare Had A Sister" from *A Room of One's Own* by Virginia Woolf, copyright 1929 by Harcourt Brace Jovanovich, Inc. and renewed 1957 by Leonard Woolf, reprinted by permission of the publisher, the estate of Virginia Woolf, and Hogarth Press.

Page 339: "A Soldier's Embrace," copyright © 1975 by Nadine Gordimer, from *A Soldier's Embrace* by Nadine Gordimer. Used by permission of Viking Penguin, a division of Penguin Books USA Inc., and Jonathan Cape Ltd., London.

Chapter 30

Page 408: "anyone lived in a pretty how town" is reprinted from *Complete Poems, 1913–1962,* by E. E. Cummings, by permission of Liveright Publishing Corporation, and McGibbon and Kee, an imprint of HarperCollins Publishers Ltd. Copyright © 1923, 1925, 1931, 1935, 1938, 1939, 1940, 1944, 1945, 1946, 1947, 1948, 1949, 1950, 1951, 1952, 1953, 1954, 1955, 1956, 1957, 1958, 1959, 1960, 1961, 1962 by the Trustees for the E. E. Cummings Trust. Copyright © 1961, 1963, 1968 by Marion Morehouse Cummings.

Page 409: "When All My Five and Country Senses See" from Dylan Thomas, *The Poems,* copyright © J. M. Dent and Sons Ltd. Reprinted by permission of David Higham Associates, London; and Dylan Thomas: *Collected Poems of Dylan Thomas,* Copyright © 1939 by New Directions Publishing Corporation. First printed in *Poetry.* Reprinted by permission of New Directions Publishing Corporation.

Page 413: "The Disinterested Killer Bill Harrigan," from *A Universal History of Infamy* by Jorge Luis Borges, translated by Norman Thomas di Giovanni, Translation copyright © 1970, 1971, 1972 by Emece Editores, S.A. and Norman Thomas di Giovanni. Used by permission of the publisher, Dutton, an imprint of New American Library, a division of Penguin Books USA Inc., and Penguin Books Ltd., London.

Page 415: "A Worn Path" from *A Curtain of Green and Other Stories,* copyright © 1969 by Eudora Welty, reprinted by permission of Harcourt Brace Jovanovich, Inc.; and Russell & Volkening Inc. as agents for the author. Copyright © 1941 by Eudora Welty, renewed in 1969 by Eudora Welty.

Page 418: From *Invisible Man* by Ralph Ellison. Copyright © 1948 by Ralph Ellison. Reprinted by permission of Random House, Inc.

Page 424: Henry Reed, "Naming of Parts," from *A Map of Verona.* Copyright © Jonathan Cape Ltd. Reprinted by permission of the Peters Fraser & Dunlop Group Ltd.

Page 425: Dream Song #14 from *The Dream Songs* by John Berryman. Copyright © 1969 by John Berryman. Reprinted by permission of Farrar, Straus and Giroux, Inc. and Faber & Faber Limited.

Page 425: "The Bean Eaters" and "We Real Cool" from *Blacks,* by Gwendolyn Brooks, The David Company, P.O. Box 19355, Chicago, Illinois 60619. Reprinted by permission.

Page 426: "Adultery" Reprinted from *Poems, 1957–1967.* © 1967 by James Dickey. Wesleyan University Press. Reprinted by permission of University Press of New England.

Page 426: "Two Songs" is reprinted from *The Fact of a Doorframe,* Poems Selected and New, 1950–1984, by Adrienne Rich, by permission of W. W. Norton & Company, Inc. Copyright © 1984 by Adrienne Rich. Copyright © 1975, 1978 by W. W. Norton & Company, Inc. Copyright © 1981 by Adrienne Rich.

Page 427: "Flight on the Wind" from *House Made of Dawn* by N. Scott Momaday. Copyright © 1966, 1967, 1968 by N. Scott Momaday. Reprinted by permission of HarperCollins Publishers.

Page 430: From *Dream Children* by Gail Godwin. Copyright © 1976 by Gail Godwin. Reprinted by permission of Alfred A. Knopf, Inc.

Page 432: From Nikki Giovanni, "Nikki-Rosa," in *Black Judgment.* Copyright © 1968 by Nikki Giovanni. Reprinted by permission of Broadside Press, Detroit, MI.

Page 433: From *Catch-22* by Joseph Heller. Copyright © 1955, 1961, 1989 by Joseph Heller. Reprinted by permission of Simon & Schuster, Inc.

Index

All B.C. dates are specified. Titles of works are set in *italics* with the artist/creator's name (or name of style) in parentheses. Page numbers of illustrations are in **boldface** type. See the Glossary for definitions of technical terms.

A

"Abbey of Theleme, The" (Rabelais), 67
Absolutism, 132, 138–39, 172
Abstract art, 356, 363–64, 366
Abstract expressionism, 351, 365, 367, 372
Act of Supremacy (Henry VIII), 14, 16
Adams, Ansel, American photographer (1902–1984), 380, 381
Adams, James, American historian (1878–1949), 5 (quote), 245
Adoration of the Shepherds (Giorgione), 45–**46**
Adultery (Dickey), 426 (text)
Adventures of Huckleberry Finn, The (Twain), 265
Adventures of Tom Sawyer, The (Twain), 265
Africa, The Partition of, 1914 (map), 231
Africa (Petrarch), 71
Africa in 1980 (map), 340
African-American art, 374, 375–78
African-American classical music, 396
African-American folk music
    ballad, 398
    blues, 398
    gospel song, 398, 399, 400
    holler, 397
    jubilee, 398
    minstrel show, 399
    ragtime, 396, 399, 401, 403
    ring shout, 398
    song sermon, 398
    spirituals, 396, 398, 399, 400
    street cry, 397
    voodoo, 398
    work song, 397
Agamemnon, King of Mycenae (ca. 1200 B.C.), 53

Age of
    Chivalry, 28
    Enlightenment, 194. *See also* Enlightenment
    Progress, 296, 297, 348
    Reason, 71, 132, 207
Agnus Dei (Zurbarán), **186**
Aiskhylos, Greek dramatist (525–456 B.C.), 9
Akhenaton (Glass), 395
Alba Madonna, The (Raphael), **44**
Albers, Joseph, American artist (1888–1976), 366
Alberti, Leonbattista, Florentine architect (1404–1472), 29–30, 181
Alexander I, Czar of Russia (1777–1825), 227
Alexander II, Czar of Russia (1818–1881), 229
Alexander III, Czar of Russia (1854–1894), 229
Alexander VI, Borgia Pope (1492–1503), 39, 41, 43
Amalienburg Lodge, Munich (Cuvilliés), 213
American Revolution (1775–1783), 132, 179, 194, 223, 247
Anaximandros of Miletus, Greek philosopher (ca. 610–547 B.C.), 248
Anderson, Laurie, American artist (b. 1947), 383
Andrews, Benny, American artist (b. 1930), 378
Annabel Lee (Poe), 260, 261–62 (text)
Annunciation (Van Eyck), 35, **36**
Anouilh, Jean, French playwright (b. 1910–1987), 5 (quote)
Anthony, Susan B., American feminist (1820–1906), 333
anyone lived in a pretty how town (cummings), 408 (text)
Apollinaire, Guillaume, French poet (1880–1918), 309

Apollonian mode (Nietzsche), 327
Apostle Bartholomew, The (Rembrandt), **192**
Apotheosis of Saint Ignatius (Pozzo), **187**
Arabs Skirmishing in the Mountains (Delacroix), 289-**90**
Architecture
    Art nouveau, 362
    Baroque, 181–82, 184–85, 189–90, 207
    gothic, 24, 25, 30, 49, 55, 292
    International style, 363, 378, 379, 384, 385
    late nineteenth-century, 292–93, 296–97
    Neoclassic, 198–200, 205, 286, 385
    Neogothic, 292–93
    Organic, 363, 378–79
    Post-Modern, 384–85
    Renaissance, 23–25, 29–30, 43, 49, 52, 55, 129, 385
    Rococo, 198, 213
    twentieth-century, 362–63, 378–79, 384–85
    Victorian, 292, 293
Arch of Triumph (Chalgrin), **286**
Arete "diligence in the pursuit of excellence" (Greek), 11n
Aristophanes, Athenian dramatist (Old Comedy; ca. 448–380 B.C.), 9, 407
Aristotle, Greek philosopher (384–322 B.C.), 3, 5 (quote), 44
Arkhimedes, Greek mathematician, physicist, inventor (287–212 B.C.), 12
Armory Show, New York (1913), 354
Armstrong, Louis, American jazz musician (1900–1971), 400, 403
Armstrong's Hot Five, Louis, **400**
Arnold, Matthew, English poet (1822–1888), 253, 309

Art
    Abstract, 356, 363–64, 366
    Abstract Expressionism, 351, 363–64
    Action painting, 363–64
    African-American, 374, 375–78
    Art nouveau, 362, 363
    Ash Can School, 354, 360–61
    Barbizon School, 293, 294
    Baroque, 182–94
        Aristocratic, 187–90, 191
        Bourgeois, 191–94
        Counter-Reformation, 52, 53,
            181–87, 191
    Blackstream, 378
    Byzantine, 52, 53
    Conceptual, 374
    Cubism, 352–53
    Dada, 357–58, 359, 394
    Environmental, 373–74
    Expressionism, 349–51, 367–70
    Fantasy, 356–57, 367, 369, 370
    Fauvism, 348–49
    Flemish, 33–39, 53–54
    Geometric Abstraction, 355
    Hispanic, 374–75
    Impressionism, 295, 297–303
    Mannerism, 49–53
    Minimal, 371–72
    Mobile, 370–71
    Neoclassic, 198–205, 286–87
    Neo-Expressionism, 382, 383
    nineteenth-century, 286–309 (chap. 25)
    Op, 367, 369
    photography, 299, 354, 379–82
    Photorealism, 372–73
    pop, 364–66
    Post-Impressionism, 303–9
    Postmodernism, 382–83
    Realism, 293–95, 360–61, 372–73
    Renaissance, 23–56 (chap. 17)
        Early, 23–39
        High, 39–48
        Late, 45–56
    Rococo, 194–97
    Romanticism, 287–92
    Social Realism, 361–62, 363
    Surrealism, 359–60
    twentieth-century, 348–85 (chap. 28)
Art Nouveau, 362, 363
Arts, Comparison of Stylistic Periods of (table),
    215
Ash Can School, in art, 354, 360–61
Assumption of the Virgin (Rubens), **187,** 189
Astrolabe, 12
AT&T Building (Johnson), 384–**85**
Athens, Golden Age of, 4
Atomic device, 317
Audubon, John James, American ornithologist
    (ca. 1780/85–1851), 290

Augustine, St., Bishop of Hippo (354–430), 5,
    14
Autobiography (Mill), 250
Ave Maria (Josquin), music (Listening
    Example 15), 59

B

Babbitt, Milton, American composer (b. 1916),
    392, 393–94
Babylonian Captivity, 66
Bach, Johann Sebastian, German composer
    (1685–1750), 139, 181, 208–10, 214, 273,
    388, 393, 403
Bacon, Francis, English scientist and
    philosopher (1561–1626), 65, 70, 71, 129,
    131, 136
Bacon, Francis, Irish painter (b. 1909), 367,
    369
Balboa, Vasco Nunez de, Portuguese explorer
    (1475–1517), 13
Baldacchino, St. Peter's (Bernini), **184**
Ballade in g minor, op. 23 (Chopin), 275
Ballet, 213, 388–89
Ballet Russe de Monte Carlo, 388
Balzac, Honoré de, French writer (1799–1850),
    265
Banquet Rousseau, 309
Baptistery of S. Giovanni of Florence Cathedral
    (Ghiberti), **26**
Baptists, 16
Barbizon School, in art, 293
Barlach, Ernst, German sculptor (1870–1930),
    349–50
Baroque style
    in architecture, 181–82, 184–85, 189–90
    in art, 182–94
    in music, 207–13
Barry, Sir Charles, English architect (1795–
    1860), 292
Barthé, Richmond, American sculptor (1901–
    1989), 376
Bartlett, Jennifer, American artist (b. 1941),
    383, 384
Bartók, Bela, Hungarian composer (1881–
    1945), 208, 391
Basie, William (Count), American jazz
    musician (1904–1986), 401, 403
Bath, The (Cassatt), **301,** 360
Battle of San Romano (Uccello), 28, **29**
Baudelaire, Charles, French poet (1821–1867),
    283, 293, 300
Bauhaus, 356, 363, 366, 378, 384
Bauhaus, Workshop for the (Gropius), **363**
Bayle, Pierre, French skeptic (1647–1706), 138
Bean Eaters, The (Brooks), 425 (text)
Bearden, Romare, American artist (1914–
    1988), 376

Beardsley, Aubrey, English artist (1872–1898),
    362
Beauvoir, Simone de, French writer (1908–
    1986), 333
Beckett, Samuel, English playwright (1906–
    1989), 410
Beethoven, Ludwig van, German composer
    (1770–1827), 2, 5, 214, 218–19, 238, 276
    (table), 278, 281, 388, 393
Bellow, Saul, American writer (b. 1915), 406
Bennet, John, English madrigal composer (ca.
    1575–1625), 63
Bentham, Jeremy, English political
    philosopher (1748–1832), 243, 250
Berg, Alban, Austrian composer (1885–1935),
    390, 392
Berlioz, Hector, French composer (1803–
    1869), 276, **277–78**
Bernini, Gianlorenzo, Italian architect and
    sculptor (1592–1688), 181, 183–85, 302
Berryman, John, American poet (1914–1972),
    425
Bible, 14, 16, 66, 137, 192, 211, 238
Big Bang theory, 318
Bill of Rights, 407
Billy Budd (Melville), 264
Bingham, George Caleb, American artist
    (1811–1879), 291–92
Bird in Space (Brancusi), **356,** 379
Birth of Venus (Botticelli), 31, **32,** 39, 41
Bismarck, Otto von, German statesman (1815–
    1898), 226, 232, 348
Black Death (Bubonic Plague), 23, 72
Black humor, 411
Bladen, Ronald, American sculptor (b. 1918),
    372
Blake, William, English artist, poet and mystic
    (1757–1827), 238–39
Block, Ernst, Christian existentialist, 330
Blue Hole, Flood Waters, Little Miami River
    (Duncanson), 375, **376**
Blue Window, The (Matisse), 348–**49**
Boccaccio, Giovanni, Italian writer and
    humanist (1313–1375), 9, 10
Böcklin, Arnold, German artist (1827–1901),
    272, 273
Bohème, La (Puccini), 281, 282
Book of Suleika (Goethe), 244–45 (text)
Book of the City of Ladies (Christine de Pizan),
    333
Book of the Courtier, The (Castiglione), 44,
    86–89 (text)
Borges, Jorge Luis, Argentine writer (1899–
    1986), 413–14
Borgia, Rodrigo (Pope Alexander VI) (1431?–
    1503), 39, 41, 43
Borromini, Francisco, Italian architect (1599–
    1667), 185, 199

Bosch, Hieronymus, Flemish painter (ca. 1450–1516), 37–39, 350

Botticelli, Sandro, Florentine painter (1444–1510), 31, 41

Boucher, François, French painter (1703–1770), 195, 196, 197, 200, 213

Bourke-White, Margaret, American photojournalist (1904–1971), 373, 381, 382

Brady, Matthew, American photographer (1823–1896), 229, 380

Brahe, Tycho, Danish astronomer (1546–1601), 134

Brahms, Johannes, German composer (1833–1897), 273, 274, 283, 388, 389

Bramante, Donato d'Agnolo, Milanese architect (1444–1514), 30, 39, 42, 43, 44, 45, 199

Brancusi, Constantin, Romanian sculptor (1876–1957), 354, 356, 372

Braque, Georges, French painter (1882–1963), 309, 352

Brave New World (Huxley), 405

Breathes There the Man (Scott), 232 (text)

Brecht, Bertolt, German playwright (1898–1956), 355, 395

Breezing Up (Homer), **295**

Breton, André, French writer (1896–1966), 359

Bride Stripped Bare by Her Bachelors, Even, The (Duchamp), **358**

Britten, Benjamin, English composer (1913–1979), 395

Broadway Boogie Woogie (Mondrian), 355, **356**

Brooks, Gwendolyn, American poet (b. 1917), 425

Brothers Karamazov, The (Dostoevsky), 254, 328

Brown, John, Abolitionist (1800–1859), 264

Brubeck, Dave, American jazz musician (b. 1920), 403

Bruegel the Elder, Pieter, Flemish painter (1525–1569), 55–56

Brunelleschi, Filippo, Florentine architect (1377–1446), 23–25, 28, 29, 30

Bruno, Giordano, Italian philosopher (1548–1600), 134

Bryant, William Cullen, American writer (1794–1878), 260

Bull, ceiling painting (Lascaux), **1**

Buonarroti. *See* Michelangelo

Burgundy, Dukes of, 57, 58

Burial at Ornans (Courbet), 294, **295**

Byron, George Gordon, Lord, English poet (1788–1824), 226, 240, 241, 243, 245, 281

By the Bivouac's Fitful Flame (Whitman), 263 (text)

Byzantine, 52, 53, 61

C

Cabaret Voltaire (Dada), 357

Cabot, John, English mariner (1450–1498), 13

Cabral, Pedro Alvarez, Portuguese sailor (ca. 1460–1526), 13

Cage, John, American composer (b. 1912), **394**

Calder, Alexander, American sculptor (1898–1976), 370–71

Calvin, John, Protestant reformer (1509–1564), 16, 192, 211

Calvinism, 192, 229

Camera obscura, 193

Campanile (Giotto), 24, 26

Camus, Albert, French novelist and essayist (1913–1960), 329–30

Candide (Voltaire), 138, 164, 172–79 (text)

Canova, Antonio, Italian sculptor (1757–1822), 203, 204

Capitalism, 18–19, 20, 136–37, 225, 249, 250

Caprices, The (Goya), 288

Caravaggio (Michelangelo Merisi), Milanese painter (1573–1610), 182–83, 186, 187, 189, 191, 201

Carmina Burana (Orff), 391

Carnegie, Andrew, American industrialist (1835–1919), 249, 250

Carolingian Renaissance, 9

Cartier, Jacques, French mariner, (1494–1553), 13

Casas, Melesio, American artist (b. 1929), 375

Cassatt, Mary, American artist (1844–1926), 301

Castiglione, Baldassare, Count, Italian writer (1478–1529), **44,** 57–58 (quote), 65, 67, 86–89 (text), 92

Catch-22 (Heller), 411, 433

Categorical Imperative (Kant), 138

Catherine the Great, Queen of Russia (1729–1796), 139

Catlin, George, American artist (1796–1872), 290

Catullus, Gaius Valerius, Latin poet (84–54 B.C.), 140, 407

Cervantes Saavedra, Miguel de, Spanish writer (1547–1616), 65–66

Cézanne, Paul, French painter (1839–1906), 298, 303, 307, 348, 352, 354, 376

Chagall, Marc, Russian-French painter (1887–1985), 355, 356, 357

Chalgrin, Jean Francis, French architect (1739–1811), 286

Chamberlain, Neville, English statesman (1869–1940), 314, 315

Chambord, Chateau of, **55**

Champlain, Samuel de, French explorer (1567–1635), 13

Chaos, science of, 318

Chardin, Jean-Baptiste, French painter (1699–1779), 196, 197

Charge of the Light Brigade, The (Tennyson), 228 (text), 252

Chariot, The (Dickinson), 268 (text)

Charles I, King of England (1600–1649), 132, 188

Charles II, King of England (1630–1685), 132, 141, 198

Charles V, Holy Roman Emperor (1500–1558), 14, 19, 47

Charles VII, King of France (1403–1461), 35

Charles VIII, King of France (1470–1498), 37, 39

Charles the Bold, Duke of Burgundy (1433–1477), 58

Charpentier, Constance Marie, French artist (1767–1849), 203

Chartres Cathedral, 5, 9, 24, **25,** 49

Chateau Noir, Le (Cézanne), **303**

Chávez, Edward, American artist (b. 1917), 375

Chekhov, Anton, Russian playwright (1864–1904), 5, 409

Cherry Orchard, The (Chekhov), 409

Childe Harold's Pilgrimage (Byron), 240

China, 12

Chippendale, Thomas, English furniture designer (1718–1779), 385

"Chippendale" skyscraper (Johnson), 384–**85**

Chirico, Giorgio de, Italian painter (1888–1980), 357

Chopin, Frédéric, Franco-Polish pianist and composer (1810–1849), 274, **275**–76, 283, 290

Chorale prelude: *Wachet auf* (Bach), 211–12

Christ, Jesus, founder of Christianity (ca. 4 B.C.–A.D. 29), 182, 186, 192, 328, 330
  in art, 25, 28, 32, 40, 41, 44, 48, 50, 51, 54–55, 182, 189, 349

Christ at the Sea of Galilee (Tintoretto), 50, **51**

Christ Mocked by Soldiers (Rouault), **349**

Christine de Pizan, Italian writer (ca. 1364–ca. 1431), 333

Christo (Christo Javacheff), Bulgarian-American artist (b. 1935), 374, 375

Church of England, 16, 48, 55

Church of Rome, 4, 10, 12, 14, 48, 141, 172, 181, 211, 328

Church of S. Carlo alle Quattro Fontane (Borromini), **185**

Church of St. Mary Magdalen (The Madeleine), 286

Church of the Holy Family (Gaudi), Barcelona, **362**

Cicero (Marcus Tullius Cicero), Roman statesman and orator (106–43 B.C.), 3, 9 (quote), 10, 65, 86 (quote), 90

Civil rights, 331–32, 339, 345

Civil War
      American, 229, 263, 264, 265, 295, 333, 380n, 399
      English, 132
      Russian, 313
      Spanish, 314, 353
Cleland, John, English writer (1709–1789), 406
Clemenceau, Georges, French premier (1841–1925), 313
Clemens, Samuel Langhorne. *See* Mark Twain
Clement VII, Medici Pope (ca. 1475–1534), 47, 48
Cleopatra VII, Queen of Egypt (63–30 B.C.), 333
Cloister Graveyard Under Snow (Friedrich), **246**
Cocteau, Jean, French poet, novelist, and playwright (1891–1963), 5, 388
Cold War, 324, 326, 327, 364
Cole, Thomas, American artist of Hudson River School (1801–1848), 290–91, 292, 375
Coleridge, Samuel Taylor, English poet (1772–1834), 239, 240, 250, 286, 290
Colloquies (Erasmus), 66 (quote)
Colosseum, Rome, 29
Columbus, Christopher, Italian explorer (1451–1506), 12, 39
Communism, 225, 247, 325, 326
Communist Manifesto, The (Marx and Engels), 225, 247 (text)
Compass, magnetic, 12
Composition in White, Black and Red (Mondrian), **355**
Concerto for Orchestra (Bartók), 391
Concord Hymn (Emerson), 262 (text)
Condorcet, Marquis de, 134
Confessions of an English Opium Eater (de Quincey), 278
Congress of Vienna, 224, 227
Constable, John, English painter (1776–1836), 290
Constantine I, the Great, Roman emperor (288?–337), 10, 27, 185
Conversion of St. Paul, The (Caravaggio), **182**
Cooper, James Fenimore, American writer (1789–1851), 260
Copernicus, Nicholas, Polish astronomer and mathematician (1473–1543), 12, 131, 134
Corbusier, Le (Charles-Edouard Jeanneret), Swiss architect (1886–1965), 363, 378
Corea, Chick, American jazz musician (b. 1941), **403**
Corinthian architectural order, 25, 29
Corneille, Pierre, French playwright (1606–1684), 213
Corot, Jean Baptiste Camille, French landscape painter (1796–1875), 281, 293, 294, 295, 300

Cortés, Hernando, Spanish explorer (1485–1547), 13, 47
Costa, Uriel de, Portuguese-Jewish theologian (ca. 1591–1647), 137
Council of Trent (1545–1563), 48, 60
Counter-Reformation, 16, 48, 52, 53, 60, 129, 141, 207
Couperin, François, French composer (1668–1733), 213, 214
Courbet, Gustave, French painter (1819–1877), 281, 294, 295, 297, 360, 409
Cranach the Younger, Lucas, German painter (1515–1586), 15
Crane, Stephen, American writer (1871–1900), 269
Creation of Adam, Sistine Chapel (Michelangelo), **42**–43
Crimean War (1853–1856), 227
Croc-en-jambe, le (Couperin), music (Listening Example 24), 213, 214
Cromwell, Oliver, Puritan leader and Lord Protector of the Commonwealth (1599–1658), 132
Crucifixion with the Virgin, Saint Jerome, and Saint Mary Magdalene (Perugino), 32, **33**
Cry of the Homeless (Hardy), 232 (text)
Crystal Palace, London (Paxton), **296**
Cubi XV (Smith), **372**
Cubism, in art, 352–53
Cullen, Countee, American poet (1887–1946), 323
Culture-Epoch Theory, 3–4, 315
cummings, e e, American poet, (1894–1962), 408
Current (Riley), 367, **369**
Cuvilliés, François de, French architect (1731–1777), 213

D

Dachau, Germany, Nazi concentration camp, 314
Dadaism, in art, 357–58
Daladier, Edouard, French premier (1884–1940), 314
Dali, Salvador, Spanish artist (1904–1989), 359, 411
Dance, 63, 207–8, 213
Dante Alighieri, Florentine poet (1265–1321), 3, 5, 69, 71, 238, 302, 320, 323, 405, 433
Darkling Thrush, The (Hardy), 253 (text)
Darwin, Charles, English naturalist (1809–1892), 248–49, 252, 348
Darwin, Erasmus, physician and grandfather of Charles Darwin (1731–1802), 248
Daumier, Honoré, French artist (1808–1879), 281, 294, 302, 409

David
      (Bernini), **184**
      (Donatello), **27**, 41, 42
      (Michelangelo), 5, **41**–42, 183
      (Verrocchio), **30**, 41, 42
David, Jacques-Louis, French painter (1738–1825), 172, 201–2, 203, 272, 286, 287, 307
Davis, Stuart, American artist (1894–1964), 354–55
Day, A (chronological order)
      in Renaissance Florence, 17
      at Versailles with Louis XIV, 133
      in Victorian London, 251
Daybreak—A Time to Rest (Lawrence), 376, **377**
Dead Toreador, The (Manet), **298**
Death of a Salesman (Miller), 409
Death of Sokrates, The (David), 201–2
Debussy, Claude, **284**
Debussy, Claude, French composer (1863–1918), 282, 284
de Chirico. *See* Chirico
Declaration of Independence (Jefferson), 135 (quote), 136, 179
Degas, (Hilaire-Germain-) Edgar, French artist (1834–1917), 195, 282, 298, 299–300, 301, 302
Déjeuner sur l'herbe (Manet), **297,** 302
de Kooning, Willem, Dutch-American painter (b. 1904), 364
Delacroix, Eugène, French painter (1798–1863), 189, 226, 227, 272, 275, 289–90, 293
DeLap, Tony, American painter (b. 1927), 371–72
Democracy, 3, 132, 224, 226, 229, 263, 353
Demoiselles d'Avignon, Les (Picasso), 352, **353**
Demokritos, Greek atomist philosopher (ca. 460–ca. 362 B.C.), 131, 406
deQuincy, Thomas, English essayist (1785–1859), 278
Derain, André, French painter (1880–1954), 348
Descartes, René, French philosopher and mathematician (1596–1650), 70, 129, 131, 138, 181, 187
Descent from the Cross, The (Rembrandt), **192**
Descent of Man, The (Darwin), 248, 249 (text)
Diaghilev, Serge Pavlovich, Russian ballet producer (1872–1929), 388
Dialogues Concerning the Two Chief World Systems (Galileo), 130–31
Dickens, Charles, English novelist (1812–1870), 265
Dickey, James, American poet (b. 1923), 426
Dickinson, Emily, American poet (1830–1886), 268
Diderot, Denis, French philosopher and encyclopedist (1713–1784), 138, 195, 196, 200

Dionysian mode (Nietzsche), 327
Disasters of War, The (Goya), 288
Discourse on Method (Descartes), 131
Discourses on the Arts and Sciences
    (Rousseau), 234 (quote)
Disinterested Killer Bill Harrigan, The
    (Borges), 413
Dixieland jazz, 399, 401
Donatello (Donato di Niccolò di Betto Bardi),
    Florentine sculptor (1386–1466), 24,
    26–27, 29, 30, 41
Donation of Constantine, 10
Donizetti, Gaetano, Italian opera composer
    (1797–1848), 272
Don Juan (Byron), 240 (quote)
Donne, John, English poet (1572–1631),
    139–40 (text)
Do Not Weep, Maiden, for War Is Kind
    (Crane), 269 (text)
Don Quixote (Cervantes), 65–66
Doric architectural order, 43, 183
Dos Passos, John, American novelist (1896–
    1970), 412
Dostoevsky, Feodor Mikhailovich, Russian
    novelist (1821–1881), 253, 254–60, 328
Dover Beach (Arnold), 253 (text)
Drama
    Tartuffe (Molière), 143–64 (text)
    Tempest, The (Shakespeare), 66, 97–124
        (text)
    twentieth-century, 409–10
Dreiser, Theodore, American novelist (1871–
    1945), 412
Dreyfus, Alfred, French officer (1859–1935),
    226
Dreyfus Affair (1894–1906), 226
Drowning Girl (Lichtenstein), **365**
Dubuffet, Jean, French painter (1901–1985),
    367
Duchamp, Marcel, French-American artist
    (1887–1968), 354, 357–58
Duecker, Otto, American artist (b. 1948), 373
Dufay, Guillaume, Burgundian composer
    (1400–1474), 24, 57, 58
Dulce et Decorum Est (Owen), 321–22 (text)
Dunbar, Paul Lawrence, American poet (1872–
    1906), 269
Duncanson, Robert J., American artist (1817–
    1872), 375, 376
Dunstable, John, English composer (ca.
    1380?–1453), 57
Dürer, Albrecht, German painter and engraver
    (1471–1528), 54, 55
Dying (Dickinson), 268 (text)

E

Eakins, Thomas, American artist (1844–1916),
    295, 360
East Indies Company, 129

Eberhart, Richard, American poet (b. 1904),
    324
Echo of a Scream (Siqueiros), **362**
Ecologue (Mallarmé), 284
Economics. *See also* Capitalism
        Enlightenment, 136–37
        Social Darwinism, 249–50
Ecstasy of St. Theresa, The (Bernini), **185**
Edict of Nantes, 132
Edward VI, King of England (1537–1553), 63
Edward VII, King of England (1841–1910), 229
Egyptians, 2
Eiffel, Gustave, French engineer (1832–1923),
    296
Eiffel Tower (Eiffel), **296**–97
Einstein, Albert, German-American physicist
    (1879–1965), 3 (quote), 4, 5, 316–17, 346
Einstein on the Beach (Glass), 395
Einstein Playing a Violin, Albert, **317**
Eleanor of Aquitaine, Queen of France and
    then of England (1122–1204), 9, 333
Electronic music, 388, 393–94
Eliot, George (Marian Evans), English novelist
    (1819–1880), 265
Eliot, Thomas Stearns, American poet and
    playwright (1888–1965), 320, 408
Elizabeth I, Queen of England (1533–1603),
    19, 63, 333
Elizabethan Age, 97
Ellington, Edward Kennedy (Duke), American
    jazz musician and composer (1899–1974),
    401, 403
Ellison, Ralph, American writer (b. 1914),
    418–23
Emerson, Ralph Waldo, American essayist,
    philosopher, and poet (1803–1882), 5
    (quote), 262, 263, 264, 391
Émile (Rousseau), 234–37 (text)
Encyclopedia (Diderot), 138, 195, 196
Encyclopedistes. *See Philosophes*
Engels, Friedrich, German socialist writer
    (1820–1895), 225, 326
Enlightenment, 53, 132–39, 209, 238, 245
Ensemble for Synthesizer (Babbit), music
    (Listening Example 36), 394
Environmental art, 373–74
Epictetus, Stoic philosopher (60–110), 201
Equal Rights Amendment, 333
Equatorial Jungle, The (Rousseau), **307**
*Equestrian Monument of Bartolommea
    Colleoni* (Verrocchio), 30, **31**
Equestrian Monument of Gattamelata
    (Donatello), **27,** 30
Equestrian Statue of Marcus Aurelius
    (Roman), 27
Erasmus, Desiderius (of Rotterdam), Dutch
    humanist (ca. 1466–1536), 54, 55, 60
    (quote), 65, 66, 72, 97
Erasmus of Rotterdam (Dürer), 54, **66**
Ernst, Max, German-American painter (1891–
    1976), 355

Essay on Man (Pope), 164–68 (text)
Essays (Montaigne), 97 (quote)
Este, Isabella d', Italian patron of the arts
    (1474–1539), 89
Estes, Richard, American photorealist artist (b.
    1936), 372, 410
Eternal City, The, Catch-22 (Heller) 433–39
    (text)
Ethos (Greek music), 189
Étude in G-Flat Major, op. 10, no. 5 (Chopin),
    music (Listening Example 28), 275, 276
Euclid, Greek mathematician (fl. ca. 300 B.C.),
    130
Eugene IV, Pope (1383–1447), 24
Euripides, Greek tragic dramatist (480–406
    B.C.), 9, 288, 410
Europe in the 17th Century (map), 130
Europe in 1815 (map), 225
Europe in 1914 (map), 233
Evolution, 248–49
Existentialism, 254, 327–30, 406, 410
Existentialism (Sartre), 328–29 (quote)
Exploration, 12–13
Expressionism, in art, 349–51, 367–70

F

Falconet, Étienne, French sculptor (1716–
    1791), 196, 197, 213
Falling Water, Kaufmann House (Wright), **363**
False Mirror, The (Magritte), **360**
Family Group, (Moore), **371**
Family of Saltimbanques (Picasso), **352**
Fascism, 314, 322
Faulkner, William, American novelist (1897–
    1962), 412
Faust (Goethe), 69, 244, 273, 274 (text), 433
Faustian man, 244, 252
Fauvism, 348–49
February, Très Riches Heures du Duc de Berry
    (Limbourg brothers), 33–**34**
Feminine Mystique, The (Friedan), 333
Feminist Movement, 333–39
Ferdinand, Francis, Archduke of Austria
    (1863–1914), 226, 232
Ferdinand V, King of Spain (1452–1516), 19
Fête Champêtre (Giorgione), **46**–47, 297
Feuerbach, Ludwig, German philosopher
    (1804–1872), 247
Ficino, Marsilio, Florentine humanist (1433–
    1499), 10, 31, 42
Finding of Moses, The (Veronese), **52**
First Inaugural Address (Jefferson), 179
Fish Magic (Klee), 356–**57**
Flack, Audrey, American artist (b. 1931),
    372–73, 410
Flea, The (Donne), 139–40 (text)
Flemish art, 33–39, 53–54
Flight on the Wind, House Made of Dawn
    (Momaday) 427–29 (text)

Flood Victims (Bourke-White), 381, **382**
Florence Cathedral, **24,** 41
Forest of Fontainebleau (Corot), **293**
Foster, Stephen Collins, American composer (1826–1864), 399
Four Dancers (Degas), 299–**300**
Four Horsemen of the Apocalypse, 351
4' 33" (Cage), 394
Fragonard, Jean-Honoré, French painter (1732–1806), 196, 200
Francis I, King of France (1494–1547), 19, 55
Franco, Francisco, general and dictator of Spain (1892–1975), 314
Franco-Flemish School, music, 57, 59–60
Franco-Prussian War (1870–1871), 226, 299
Frankenstein (Shelley), 243
Frankenthaler, Helen, American artist (b. 1928), 366, 367
Franklin, Benjamin, American statesman, scientist, and writer (1706–1790), 203
Frederick I, King of Prussia (1657–1713), 138
Frederick II, the Great, King of Prussia (1712–1786), 139, 172
Frederick William I, King of Prussia (1688–1740), 139
French Revolution (1789–1815), 132, 138, 139, 194, 201, 223–24, 238, 239, 247
French Suite No. 4 in E-Flat Major (Bach), music, (Listening Example 20), 209
Freud, Sigmund, Austrian physician (1856–1939), 315, 318–**19,** 320, 327, 359
Friedan, Betty, American feminist and writer (b. 1921), 333
Friedrich, Kaspar David, German painter (1774–1840), 246
Friends (Quakers), 16
Fugger
    Anton, German textile merchant (1348–1409), 18
    Jacob I, German merchant (d. 1469), 18
    Jacob II, German merchant prince (1459–1525), 18
Fugue in G Minor (Bach), music, 210
Fuller, Margaret, American writer and lecturer (1810–1850), 262
Fur Traders Descending the Missouri (Bingham), 291–**92**
Fury of Aerial Bombardment, The (Eberhart), 324 (text)
Future Shock (Toffler), 345

G

Gabriel, Ange-Jacques, French architect (ca. 1698–1782), 200
Gabrieli, Giovanni, Italian composer (ca. 1554/57–1612), 61–62, 214
Gachet, Dr. Paul, friend of Vincent van Gogh, 304 (quote)
Gainsborough, Thomas, English painter (1727–1788), 197

Galen, Greek physician (ca. 130–ca. 200), 12
Galileo (Galileo Galilei), Italian scientist (1564–1642), 129, 130–31, 134, 183, 187
Gama, Vasco da, Portuguese explorer (ca. 1469–1524), 12
Garcia, Antonio, American artist (b. 1901), 375
Garden of Delights (Bosch), **38**
Gargantua and Pantagruel (Rabelais), 67, 90–91 (text)
Garibaldi, Giuseppe, Italian patriot and soldier (1807–1882), 227
Gates of Hell, The (Rodin), 302
Gates of Paradise (Ghiberti), 25, **26**
Gattamelata, Equestrian Monument of (Donatello), **27**
Gaudi, Antonio, Spanish architect (1852–1926), 362
Gauguin, Paul, French painter (1848–1903), 304–6, 309, 348 (quote), 349, 354
Geneva Conventions, 20
Gentileschi, Artemesia, Italian artist (1593–1652/3), 183
Geometric abstraction, in art, 355
George I, King of England (1660–1727), 139
George II, King of England (1683–1760), 139, 212
George III, King of England (1738–1820), 139, 229
George IV, King of England (1762–1830), 229
George V, King of England (1865–1936), 229
Géricault, Théodore, French painter (1791–1824), 289, 293
Gershwin, George, American composer (1898–1937), 395
Gesù, Il (da Vignola and della Porta), **181–82,** 187
Ghent Altarpiece (van Eyck), **34–35**
Ghiberti, Lorenzo, Florentine sculptor (ca. 1378–1455), 24, 25, 26
Ghirlandaio, Domenico, Florentine painter (1449–1494), 31, 37, 39, 41
Giacometti, Alberto, Italian sculptor (1901–1966), 360
Gibbs, James, English architect (1682–1754), 199
Gilded Age, 295, 308
Gillespie, Dizzy (John Birks), American jazz musician (b. 1917), **402,** 403
Ginevra de'Benci (Leonardo), **39**
Giorgione da Castelfranco, Venetian painter (1478–1510), 45–47, 52
Giotto de Bondone, Florentine painter (1266–1337), 24, 26
Giovanni, Nikki, American poet (b. 1943), 432
Giovanni Arnolfini and His Bride (van Eyck), **36**
Girl Before a Mirror (Picasso), **353**
Girl with a Red Hat, The (Vermeer), **193**
Glass, Philip, American composer (b. 1937), 395
Global Village, 315, 326, 345, 346, 382, 383, 384

Glorious Revolution (England), 132, 135
Godwin, Gail, American writer (b. 1937), 406, 430–32
Godwin, William, English political philosopher (1756–1836), 243
Goethe, Johann Wolfgang von, German poet and dramatist (1749–1832), 238, 244–45, 273, 274, 433
Goodman, Benny, American jazz musician (1909–1986), **401**
Gordimer, Nadine, South African writer (b. 1923), 339–44
Gothic, 24, 25, 30, 34, 49, 54, 55, 198
Goya y Lucientes, Francisco José de, Spanish painter (1746–1828), 238, 287–89, 290
Graeco-Roman civilization, 4, 9, 141
Grande hazana! Con muertos! (Goya), 288, **289**
Grand Inquisitor, The (Dostoevsky), 254, 255–60 (text), 328
Grand Odalisque (Ingres), 287, **287,** 298
Grapes of Wrath, The (Steinbeck), 381
Graves, Michael, American architect (b. 1934), 385
Gravitation, universal law of, 134, 135, 136, 137, 317
Gray, Thomas, English poet (1716–1771), 238
Great Depression, 324, 381
Great Exhibition of the Works of All Nations, London, 296
Great War, The, 226, 227, 229, 233, 320, 327, 351, 388. *See also* World War I
Greco, El (Kyriakos Theotokopoulos), Greek painter (1541–1614), 52–53, 186, 189
Greece, Golden Age of, 191
Greek(s), 2, 3, 23, 26, 43, 47, 50, 142, 202, 205, 208, 212, 214, 240, 287, 327, 328, 355, 426
Gretchen am Spinnrade (Schubert), 273, 274 (text), (Listening Example 27), 274
Greuze, Jean-Baptiste, French painter (1725–1805), 200, 201
Griffin, Susan, American poet (b. 1943), 333–34
Gropius, Walter, German-American architect (1883–1969), 363
Grosz, George, German-American artist (1893–1959), 350–51, 376
Grotius, Hugo, Dutch jurist (1583–1645), 20
Grünewald, Matthias (Mathis Gothart Nithart), German painter (1455–1528), 54–55, 350, 395
Guernica, Spain, 314, 353
Guernica (Picasso), 314, 353, **354**
Guggenheim Museum, New York (Wright), 378–**79,** 380
Guilds, 18, 19
Gulliver's Travels (Swift), 168
Gunpowder, 12, 129
Gutenberg Bible, 345

H

Hagia Sophia, Istanbul, 25
Hallelujah Chorus, The Messiah (Handel), music (Listening Example 23), 212
Halley, Edmund, English astronomer (1656–1742), 135
Hall of Mirrors, The Amalienburg, Nymphenburg Palace, Munich (Cuvilliés), **213**
Hals, Frans, Dutch painter (1580–1666), 37, 191, 194
Hamlet (Shakespeare), 5 (quote), 19 (quote), 68 (quote)
Handel, George Frederick, German composer (1685–1759), 5, 181, 210, 212, 214
Hanson, Duane, American artist (b. 1925), 372
Hapsburgs, 19, 20
Hardy, Thomas, English novelist and poet (1840–1928), 232, 253–54, 309
Harlem (Hughes), 332 (text)
Harlem Renaissance, 323, 332
Harmonice Musices Odhecation A (de Petrucci), 62
Harpsichord, 207–9
Harrison, Wallace K., American architect (1895–1981), 378
Hawking, Stephen, British theoretical physicist (b. 1942), 317 (quote), 318
Hawthorne, Nathaniel, American novelist (1804–1864), 391
Haydn, Franz Joseph, Austrian composer (1732–1809), 189, 214, 215–16, 218, 272
Hegel, Georg Wilhelm Friedrich, German philosopher (1770–1831), 246, 326
Heine, Heinrich, German poet (1797–1856), 244 (quote)
Heisenberg, Werner, German physicist (1901–1976), 315, 316
Heller, Joseph, American novelist (b. 1923), 411, 433–39
Helmholtz, Hermann Ludwig Ferdinand von, German scientist in optics, acoustics, and energy (1821–1894), 307
Henri, Robert, American artist (1865–1929), 360, 361
Henry IV (Henry of Navarre), King of France (1553–1610), 19, 132
Henry V, King of England (1387–1422), 34
Henry VII, King of England (1457–1509), 53
Henry VIII, King of England (1491–1547), 14, 16, 19, 47, 48, 55
Henry the Navigator, Prince of Portugal (1394–1460), 12
Herculaneum, 201
Herder, Johann Gottfried von, German philosopher and poet (1744–1803), 238

Herman, Woody (Woodrow Charles), American jazz musician (1913–1987), 401, 403
Hermes (Praxiteles), 27
Herodotos, Greek historian (ca. 484–425 B.C.), 9, 10
Hesiod, Greek poet (ca. 8th c. B.C.), 320, 405
Highet, Gilbert, American theologian and philosopher (1906–1978), 2 (quote)
High Society (Steele), music, (Listening Example 38), 402
Hindemith, Paul, German-American composer (1895–1963), 395
Hippokrates, Greek physician (ca. 460–ca. 370 B.C.), 12
Hispanic art, 374–75
Historical and Critical Dictionary (Bayle), 138
Hitler, Adolf, Dictator of Nazi Germany (1889–1945), 189, 254, 314, 315, 316, 327, 355, 362
Hobbes, Thomas, English philosopher (1588–1679), 132
Holbein, Hans, the Younger, German painter (1497–1543), 54, 55, 68, 198
Holy Family, Church of the, Barcelona (Gaudi), 362
Holy Family on the Steps (Poussin), **189**
Holy Sonnet X (Donne), 140 (text)
Homage to the Square: Star Blue (Albers), 366, **367**
Homer, Greek epic poet-musician (fl. 8th c. B.C.), 9, 327
Homer, Winslow, American painter (1836–1910), 294–95, 301, 360, 409
Hopper, Edward, American painter (1882–1967), 361
Horace (Quintus Horatius Flaccus) Latin poet (65–8 B.C.), 321
Hotter than That (Armstrong), music (Listening Example 37), 400
Houdon, Jean Antoine, French sculptor (1741–1828), 203, 302
House by the Railroad (Hopper), **361**
House Made of Dawn (Momaday), 427
Houses of Parliament, London (Barry and Pugin), **292**
Howells, William Dean, American journalist and critic (1837–1921), 265
Hudson, Henry, English explorer in Dutch service (fl. 1607–1611), 13
Hudson River School (artists), 291
Hudson River tradition, 375
Hughes, Langston, American poet (1902–1967), 332
Hugo, Victor Marie, French writer and critic (1802–1885), 348 (quote)
Huguenots (French Protestants), 19, 132, 192

Human Bondage, Of (Maugham), 297, 412
Humanism, 4, 9, 45, 54, 57, 66
Hume, David, Scottish philosopher (1711–1774), 137, 138
Hundred Years' War (1337–1453), 12, 35
Hus, Jan, Czechoslovakian religious reformer and martyr (ca. 1369–1415), 14
Huxley, Aldous Leonard, English novelist (1894–1963), 405, 412

I

I Am Glad I Came Back (Grosz), **351**
I and the Village (Chagall), **356**
Ibsen, Henrik, Norwegian dramatist (1828–1906), 309, 409
I Died for Beauty (Dickinson), 268 (text)
If Shakespeare Had a Sister (Woolf), 334–38 (text)
Ignatius of Loyola, Spanish founder of the Jesuits (1491–1556), 16, 181, 185, 187
I Hear America Singing (Whitman), 263 (text)
I Like to Think of Harriet Tubman (Griffin), 333–34 (text)
Illumination-Dark (Nevelson), 367, **368**
Impression, Sunrise (Monet), 299
Impressionism
    in art, 295, 297–303
    in music, 282–84
Impressionists, 193, 348
In Advance of a Broken Arm (Duchamp), 358
I Never Saw a Moor (Dickinson), 268 (text)
In the Dining Room (Morisot), 300, **301**
Indulgences, sale of, 14
Industrial Revolution, 225–26, 230, 345
In Ecclesiis (Gabrieli), music (Listening Example 18), 61–62
Inferno (Dante), 302
Information Age/Society, 345, 382
Ingres, Jean-Auguste-Dominique, French painter (1780–1867), 272, 286, 287, 290
Innocent VIII, Pope (1432–1492), 38
Inquiry into the Nature and Causes of the Wealth of Nations, An (Smith), 136
Inquisition, 16, 19, 53, 55, 131, 183, 187, 255
Institutes of the Christian Religion, The (Calvin), 16
Instruments, musical
    Baroque, 207–12
    Classical, 215
    electronic, 393–94
    Impressionism, 283–84
    in jazz, 397, 399–403
    Renaissance, 58, 63
    Rococo, 213–14
    Romantic, 274, 276–77

Interior Landscape (Frankenthaler), 366, **367**
International Style (Late Gothic), 25, 33, 34
Invisible Man (Ellison), 418–24 (text)
Ionic architectural order, 190, 205
Irving, Washington, American author (1783–1859), 260
Island of the Dead (Böcklin), **273**
Isabella I, Queen of Spain (1451–1504), 19
Italy, The Unification of (map), 228
Ives, Charles, American composer (1874–1954), **391**–92

J

Jack-in-the-Pulpit, No. 5 (O'Keeffe), **354**
Jacob, Max, French writer and painter (1876–1944), 309
James, Henry, American novelist (1843–1916), 301
James I, King of England (1566–1625), 132
James II, King of England (1633–1701), 132
Japanese prints, 298, 303, 305
Jazz, 210, 372, 378, 396–403
    elements of, 396–97
    origins, 396
    pre-jazz styles, 397–99
    styles of, 399–403
        Blues, 396, 398, 400, 403
        Bop, 401, 402, 403
        Chicago, 400, 401, 403
        Cool, 372, 403
        Crossover, 403
        Dixieland, 399, 401, 403
        Fusion, 403
        Liturgical, 403
        Mainstream, 401, 403
        Modern, 402–3
        New Orleans, 399–400, 401, 403
        New Orleans Revival, 401
        Straight-ahead, 403
        Swing (Big Band), 401, 402
        Third-Stream, 403
Jeffers, Robinson, American poet (1887–1962), 322–23, 408
Jefferson, Thomas, American statesman and president (1743–1826), 3, 69, 135, 136, 138, 179, 205
Jesuit order (Society of Jesus), 16, 53, 181, 182
Jimenez, Luis, American artist (b. 1940), 375
Joan of Arc, French heroine (ca. 1412–1431), 35
Job, Book of (Bible), 238
Johnson, Joshua, American artist (1765–1830), 375, 376
Johnson, Philip, American architect (b. 1906), 384–85
Jones, Inigo, English architect (1573–1652), 198

Jones, Lois Maillol, American artist (b. 1905), 376
Jong, Erica, American writer (b. 1942), 406
Joplin, Scott, American composer (1868–1917), **399**
Josquin des Prez, French composer (1450–1521), 59, 214
Judaism, 137
Judith Slaying Holofernes (Gentileschi), **183**
Julius II (Giuliano della Rovere), Pope (1443–1513), 42, 43
Juvenal (Decimus Junius Juvenalis), Latin satiric poet (60–140), 407

K

Kandinsky, Wassily, Russian painter (1886–1949), 351, 355, 357
Kant, Immanual, German philosopher (1724–1804), 138, 246, 250
Kaufmann House (*Falling Water;* Wright), **363**
Keats, John, English poet (1795–1821), 240, 241, 243, 290
Keelmen Heaving Coals by Moonlight (Turner), 290, **291**
Kenton, Stan, American jazz musician (1912–1980), 401, 403
Kepler, Johannes, German astronomer (1571–1620), 10, 67, 131, 134, 135, 187, 193
Kesey, Ken, American writer (b. 1935), 406
Kienholz, Edward, American sculptor (b. 1927), 365–66
Kierkegaard, Soren Aabye, Danish philosopher (1813–1855), 254, 327–28, 406
King, Martin Luther, Jr., American civil rights leader (1929–1968), 3, 331–32
King Lear (Shakespeare), 69
Kitchen Maid, The (Chardin), 196, **197**
Klee, Paul, Swiss painter (1879–1940), 356–57
Knight, Death, and the Devil (Dürer), **54**
Knox, John, Scottish founder of the Presbyterian church (ca. 1505–1572), 16
Kollwitz, Käthe, German artist (1867–1945), 350
Korean War, 325, 364, 406
Kubla Khan (Coleridge), 239, 240 (text)
Kyrie, Missa Se La Face Ay Pale (Dufay) music, (Listening Example 14), 59

L

L.H.O.O.Q. (Duchamp), 358
La Belle Dame Sans Merci (Keats), 243 (text)
Lady Chatterley's Lover (Lawrence), 406
Lady Playing a Dulcimer, **63**
Laissez-faire, 136, 249, 250

Lamarck, Jean-Baptiste de, French naturalist (1744–1829), 248
Lamb, The (Blake), 238 (text)
Landscape with the Fall of Ikaros (Bruegel), **55**
Lange, Dorothea, American photographer (1895–1965), 381, 382
Laokoön (El Greco), **53**
Laplace, Pierre Simon, Marquis de, French astronomer (1749–1827), 135
Large Glass, The (The Bride Stripped Bare by Her Bachelors, Even) (Duchamp), 358
Lascaux, caves of, 1
Lassus, Orlando de, Flemish composer (1532–1594), 59–60, 208, 214
Last Judgement, The (Michelangelo), **48**–49, 85
Last Supper, The (Leonardo), **40**
Last Supper, The (Tintoretto), 50–52, **51**
Laurencin, Marie, French painter (1885–1956), 309
Law of War and Peace (Grotius), 20
Lawrence, D(avid) H(erbert), English author (1885–1930), 406
Lawrence, Jacob, American painter (b. 1917), 376, 377, 378
League of Nations, 313, 314, 324
Leaves of Grass (Whitman), 263 (text)
Le Carré, John (David John Moore Cornwall), English novelist (b. 1931), 406
Le Corbusier. *See* Corbusier
Leibniz, Gottfried Wilhelm, Baron von, German philosopher (1646–1716), 134, 138
Lenin, Vladimir Ilyich, Russian revolutionary (1870–1924), 313, 325, 326
Le Nôtre, André, French landscape designer (1613–1700), 190
León, Michael Ponce de, American artist (b. 1922), 375
Leonardo da Vinci, Florentine artist (1452–1519), 11, 20, 26, 27, 30, 31, 39, 41, 43, 45, 46, 47, 50, 55, 59, 71, 189, 193
Leo X, Medici pope (1475–1521), 14, 47
Letter from Birmingham Jail (King), 331–32 (text)
LeVau, Louis, French architect (1612–1670), 190
Levertov, Denise, American poet (b. 1923), 325
Leviathan (Hobbes), 132
Leyster, Judith, Dutch painter (1609–1660), 191
Liberation of the Peon, The (Rivera), **361**
Lichtenstein, Roy, American artist (b. 1923), 365
Lieder, German, 273–74
Life, Friends, Is Boring. We Must Not Say So (Berryman), 425 (text)
Life magazine, 381, 382

Life on the Mississippi (Twain), 265
Limbourg brothers, Pol, Jan, and Herman, Flemish painters (fl. 1380–1416), 33–34
Lincoln, Abraham, 16th President of the United States (1809–1865), **229**, 380
Liszt, Franz, Hungarian composer and pianist (1811–1886), 274, 275, 276, 278, **279**
Literary selections (in chronological order)
    Renaissance, 10–11, 43, 71–124
      seventeenth-century, 142–64
      eighteenth-century, 164–79
      nineteenth-century, 228, 229, 230, 232, 234–45, 247, 249, 252–69
      twentieth-century, 320–23, 324, 329–30, 331–44, 408–9, 413–39
Literature of Moving Images, The, 442
Little Gallery of the Photo-Secession ("291") (Stieglitz), 354, 358
Lives of the Most Excellent Italian Architects, Painters, and Sculptors from Cimabue to Our Own Times (Vasari), 10
Lloyd George, David, British statesman (1863–1945), 313
Locke, John, English political philosopher (1633–1704), 3, 135–36, 137, 138, 172
Lorenzo de' Medici (the Magnificent), Florentine banker (1449–1492), 20, 28, 30, 31, 39, 47, 76
Lorenzo de' Medici, Duke of Urbino (1492–1519), 76
Lorenzo de' Medici (Verrocchio), 30, **31**
Louis XIII, King of France (1601–1643), 132, 189
Louis XIV (Sun King), King of France (1639–1715), 19, 132, 138, 141, 142, 181, 189, 194, 195, 213
Louis XIV, Bust of (French school after Bernini), **132**
Louis XIV, Portrait of (Rigaud), **190**
Louis XV, King of France (1710–1774), 138, 195, 200
Louis XVI, King of France (1754–1793), 138, 202, 223, 225
Louis XVIII, King of France (1755–1824), 225
Louis Philippe, King of France (1773–1850), 225
Love Song of J. Alfred Prufrock, The (Eliot), 320–21 (text), 405, 408
Lowes, John Livingston, American scholar (1867–1945), 405 (quote)
Loyola. *See* Ignatius of Loyola
Lully, Jean Baptiste, Italian composer in France (1632–1687), 213
Luncheon on the Grass (Manet), **297**
Luther, Martin, German leader of the Reformation (1483–1546), 12, 14–15, 16, 39, 47, 54, 59, 60, 66, 211

Lutheran church, 15–16
Lyrical Ballads (Wordsworth and Coleridge), 239

M

Machiavelli, Niccolo, Florentine diplomat, novelist and political philosopher (1469–1527), 65, 66–67, 76, 92
Madame de Pompadour as the Venus of the Doves (Falconet), 196, **197**
Madeleine, The (Vignon), **286**
Madonna with the Long Neck (Parmigianino), 49, **50**
Magellan, Ferdinand (Fernas de Magalhaes), Portuguese explorer (1480–1521), 13
Magritte, René, French artist (1898–1967), 360
Maids of Honor (Velasquez), **186**–87
Maison Carrée, France, 205, 286
Majas on a Balcony (Goya), **287**–88
Mallarmé, Stéphane, French poet (1842–1898), 284, 300, 306
Malraux, André, French writer, (1901–1976), 1 (quote), 5 (quote), 203 (quote)
Malthus, Thomas R., English economist (1766–1834), 248
Man (Tamayo), 369, **370**
Manet, Edouard, French painter (1832–1883), 297–98, 300, 307, 348
Mangold, Sylvia, American artist (b. 1938), 382, 383
Manifest Destiny, 229, 249
Manifesto of
    the Communist Party (Marx and Engels), 247 (text)
      Realism (Courbet), 294
      Surrealism (Breton), 359
Mann, Thomas, German writer (1875–1955), 355
Mannerism, in art, 49–53
Man Said to the Universe, A (Crane), 269 (text)
Mansart, Jules Hardouin, French architect (1598–1666), 190
Many Pierced Discs (Calder), **370**, 371
Maps
    Africa, The Partition of, 1914, 231
    Africa in 1980, 340
    Burgundy, Lands of the Dukes of, 58
    Europe about 1520, 15
    Europe in the 17th Century, 130
    Europe in 1815, 225
    Europe in 1914, 233
    Italy, The Unification of, 228
    Napoleon's Empire, 1812, 224
    Renaissance Italy, 20

    United States, Growth of the, 261
    World Exploration 1271–1295; 1486–1611, 13
Marchesa Elena Grimaldi (van Dyck), **188**
Marco Polo, Venetian traveler (1254?–1324?), 12, 239
Marcus Aurelius (Marcus Aelius Aurelius Antoninus), Roman emperor and philosopher (121–180), 4, 201
Marie Antoinette, Queen of France (1755–1793), 202, 373 (quote)
Marisol (Escobar), Venezuelan-American artist (b. 1930), 366
Marsalis, Wynton, jazz/classical musician (b. 1961), 403
Marshall Plan, 324
Martin Luther and the Wittenberg Reformers (Cranach the Younger), **15**
Marvell, Andrew, English poet (1621–1678), 139, 140 (text)
Marx, Karl, German writer on economics and socialism (1818–1883), 225, 246, 319, 326, 348
Marxism-Leninism, 315, 326, 346
Masaccio (Guidi de San Giovanni) Tommaso, Italian painter (1401–1428), 27–28, 39
Massacre at Chios (Delacroix), 226, **227**
Massacre of St. Bartholomew, 192
Mathematics, 130, 131, 134, 315, 316, 318
Mathis der Maler (Hindemith), 395
Matisse, Henri, French artist (1869–1954), 348–49, 352, 354, 388
Matona Mia Cara (Lassus), music (Listening Example 16), 59–60
Matsys (Massys), Quentin, Flemish painter (ca. 1465–1530), 18
Maugham, William Somerset, English novelist and playwright (1874–1965), 297, 412
Max Schmitt in a Single Scull (Eakins), 295–**96**
Medici, Cosimo de', Florentine banker (1389–1464), 10
Medici, Lorenzo de', Florentine banker (1449–1492), 20, 28, 30, 31, 39, 47, 76
Medici, Marie de', Queen of France (1573–1642), 187
Medici Chapel, 47–48, 76
Medici(s), 37, 40, 41
Meditations (Descartes), 131
Melville, Herman, American novelist and poet (1819–1891), 264–65, 295
Memling, Hans, Flemish painter (ca. 1430–1494), 32, 37
Memorial Sculpture, Dachau, Germany, **314**
Mendel, Gregor, Austrian geneticist (1822–1884), 248
Mendelssohn, Felix, German composer (1809–1847), 276, **277**

Messiah, The (Handel), 212

Methodist church, 16

Metternich, Clemens, Fürst von, Austrian statesman (1773–1859), 224, 226, 227

Mexican Revolution (1910–1940), 361, 362

Michelangelo Buonarroti, Italian artist (1475–1564), 5, 20, 25, 26, 27, 30, 39, 40, 41–43, 44, 45, 47–49, 53, 59, 65, 76, 85–86, 183, 184, 185, 189, 198, 290, 293, 302

Microscope, 129, 130, 131

Middle Ages, 9, 10, 14, 18, 19, 65, 71, 192, 243, 245

Mies van der Rohe, Ludwig, German architect (1886–1969), 378, 379

Migrant Mother, Nipomo, California (Lange), 381, **382**

Mill, James, British philosopher (1773–1836), 250

Mill, John Stuart, British philosopher (1806–1873), 250, 333

Miller, Arthur, American playwright (b. 1915), 409

Miller, Henry, American novelist (1891–1980), 1 (quote), 5 (quote), 406

Millet, Jean François, French painter (1814–1875), 281, 293, 294, 299, 360

Milton, John, English poet (1608–1674), 141 (text), 181

Minimal art, 371–72

Mirandola. *See* Pico

Miró, Joan, Spanish painter (1893–1983), 359

Mlle. de Val d'Ognes (Charpentier), **203**

Moby-Dick (Melville), 264

Modest Proposal, A (Swift), 168–71 (text)

Molière and his troupe of players, **142**

Molière (Jean Baptiste Poquelin), French actor and playwright (1622–1673), 141–64, 213

Momaday, N. Scott, American writer (b. 1934), 427–29

Mona Lisa (Leonardo), 5, 39

Mondrian, Piet, Dutch painter (1872–1944), 355, 356

Monet, Claude, French artist (1840–1926), 282, 290, 298–99, 300, 348, 366, 382

Moneylender and His Wife, The (Matsys), 18

Monogram (Rauschenberg), **365**

Montaigne, Michel de, French essayist and philosopher (1533–1592), 65, 67, 71, 97, 131

Montesquieu, Charles Louis de Secondat, baron de la Brède et de, French jurist and political philosopher (1689–1755), 134, 135, 138

Moonrise. Hernandez, New Mexico (Adams), 380, **381**

Moore, Henry, English sculptor (1898–1986), 371

Moravian church, 14

More, Sir Thomas, English statesman and author (1478–1535), 13, 55, 65, 66, 67–69, 92–96, 97

Morgan, Norma, American artist (b. 1928), 378

Morisot, Berthe, French painter (1841–1895), 300, 301

Motion, laws of, 130, 134

Motion pictures, 442

Moulin de la Galette, Le (Renoir), **299**

Mousmé, La (van Gogh), 303, **304**

Mozart, Maria Anna, Austrian composer (1751–1829), 339

Mozart, Wolfgang Amadeus, Austrian composer (1756–1791), 97, 189, 208, 214, 216–17, 218, 272, 276, 276 (table), 290, 339, 355

Mrs. Richard Brinsley Sheridan (Gainsborough), **197**

Mrs. Richard Yates (Stuart), **204**

Much Madness is Divinest Sense (Dickinson), 268 (text)

Munch, Edvard, Norwegian painter (1864–1944), 309, 349

Murphy, Turk (Melvin E.), American jazz musician (b. 1915), 402

Music
    aleatory, 391, 394
    atonal, 389–90, 392
    Baroque, 207–13
    Burgundian School, 58
    Classical period, 215–19
    electronic, 388, 393–94
    English madrigals, 63, 214
    Franco-Flemish, 59–60
    Impressionism, 282–84
    jazz, 372, 388, 396–403
    modern, 388–403 (chap. 29)
    musical theatre, 395
    Neoclassic, 390–91
    Neo-Romantic, 388, 390, 391
    opera, 212–13, 214, 216, 281–82
    oratorio, 212
    printing of, 62
    Renaissance, 57–64 (chap. 19), 141, 208, 214
    Rococo period, 213–14
    Romanticism, 219, 272–85 (chap. 24)
    Serial composition, 391, 392–93

Music, African-American folk. *See* African-American folk music

Mussolini, Benito, Italian dictator (1883–1945), 227, 314

Myth of Sisyphus, The (Camus), 329–30 (text)

N

Nadar, French photographer (1820–1910), 300

Naming of Parts (Reed), 424 (text)

Napoleon Buonaparte, general and Emperor of France (1769–1821), 40, 189, 203, 218, 223–25, 227, 286, 288

Napoleon III (Louis Napoleon Buonaparte), Emperor of the French (1808–1873), 226

Napoleon in His Study (David), **224**

Napoleon's Empire, 1812 (map), 224

Natural selection, 248, 249

Nazi(s), 314, 351, 355, 366, 373, 391, 395

Neo-Expressionism, in art, 383

Neoplatonism, 31, 42, 47

Neri, Manuel, American sculptor (b. 1930), 375

Neutral Tones (Hardy), 253, 254 (text)

Nevelson, Louise, American sculptor (1900–1988), 366–67, 368

New Atlantis, The (Bacon), 70

New Sciences, The (Galileo), 131

Newton, Sir Isaac, English scientist and mathematician (1642–1727), 131, 132, 134–35, 136, 137, 138, 172, 209, 245, 317

New World, 12, 13, 39, 92, 97, 132, 204, 290, 410

Nicholas I, Czar of Russia (1796–1855), 227, 229

Nicholas II, Czar of Russia (1868–1917), 229

Nietzsche, Friedrich, German philosopher (1844–1900), 238, 254, 281, 327, 328, 357, 406

Nikki-Rosa (Giovanni), 432 (text)

Nobel Prize (literature), 329, 410, 412

Nostalgia of the Infinite, The (de Chirico), **357**

Notorious Jumping Frog of Calaveras County (Twain), 265–67 (text)

Notre-Dame-du-Haut (le Corbusier), 378, **379**

Novum Organum (Bacon), 129

Number 1 (Pollock), **364**

No. 1 Crescent Circle, Bath, England, **199**–200

Number VII from Eight Studies For a Portrait (Bacon), 367, **369**

Number 10 (Rothko), 364, **365**

Nutcracker Suite, The (Tchaikovsky), music (Listening Example 30), 280, 281

O

Object (Oppenheim), **359**

Odalisque with Tambourine: Harmony in Blue (Matisse), **349**

O'Keeffe, Georgia, American painter (1887–1986), 354, 355

Old Man with a Child (Ghirlandaio), 31, **32**

Olympia (Manet), 297–**98**, 348

On Cannibals, Essays (Montaigne), 97

On His Blindness (Milton), 141 (text)

On Liberty (Mill), 250

Only Good Thing About It, The (Kollwitz), **350**

On Population (Malthus), 248

On the Late Massacre in Piedmont (Milton), 141 (text)

On the Origin of Species by Means of Natural Selection (Darwin), 248

On the Painting of the Sistine Chapel (Michelangelo), 43 (text)

Op art, 367, 369
Opera, 212–13, 214, 216
Oppenheim, Meret, American artist (1913–1985), 359
Oration on the Dignity of Man (Pico), 10–11 (text)
Orchestras, Comparative Sizes of, 276 (table)
Orff, Carl, German composer (1895–1982), 391
Organ, pipe, 209–10
Orozco, Jose, Mexican painter (1883–1949), 361–62, 374
Ortiz, Ralph, American artist (b. 1934), 375
Othello (Shakespeare), 69
Ovid (Publius Ovidius Naso), Latin poet (43 B.C.–A.D. 18), 407
Owen, Wilfred, English poet (1893–1918), 321–22
Oxbow (Cole), 291, **292**

P

Paganini, Niccolo, Italianviolinist and composer (1782–1840), 274, 275
Painting
    Baroque, 182–83, 186–94
        Aristocratic, 187–90
        Bourgeois, 191–94
        Counter Reformation, 52–53, 182–83, 186–87
    Flemish, 33–39, 53–54
    Impressionism, 297–303
    Neoclassicism, 200–203, 286–87
    Post-Impressionism, 303–9
    Realism, 293–96
    Renaissance, 18, 28–29, 32–40, 42, 44–47, 48, 50–56
    Rococo, 195–97
    Romanticism, 287–92
    twentieth-century, 348–57, 359–65, 366, 372–73, 374–78, 382–83
Palace at 4 A.M., The (Giacometti), **360**
Palazzo Rucellai (Alberti), **29**
Palestrina, Giovanni Pierluigi da, Italian composer (1525–1594), 60–61, 208, 214
Palladio, Andrea di Pietro, Italian architect (1518–1580), 30, 52, 181, 198
Panel 3 (Kandinsky), **351**
Pantheon
    Paris, 172
    Rome, 24, 185, 286
Paradise Lost (Milton), 141
Paris Exhibition of 1880, 296
Parker, Charlie "Bird," jazz musician (1920–1955), 403
Parker, Dorothy, American writer (1893–1967), 5
Parliament, Houses of (Barry and Pugin), **292**

Parmigianino (Francesco Mazzuoli), Italian painter, 49, 50, 287
Parthenon, Athens, 4, 5, 286
Paul, Apostle (d. 67?), 182
Paul III, pope (1468–1549), 16, 48
Pauline Borghese as Venus (Canova), **203**
Paxton, Sir Joseph, English architect (1801–1865), 296
Pazzi Chapel (Brunelleschi), Santa Croce, Florence, 21, 24–**25**, 384
Peace of Westphalia, 129
Penitent St. Peter, The (El Greco), 52–**53**
Persian Gulf War, 327
Persian Letters (1721; Montesquieu), 138
Persistence of Memory, The (Dali), **359**
Person Throwing Stone at a Bird (Miró), **359**
Perugino (Pietro Vannucci), Italian painter (1455–1523), 32, 39, 41, 44, 48
Peter the Great, Czar of Russia (1672–1725), 139
Petit Trianon, Versailles (Gabriel), **200**
Petrarch, Francesco, Florentine humanist and poet (1304–1374), 9, 65, 66, 71–72, 85
Petrucci, Ottaviano de', Venetian music printer (1466–1539), 62
Pheidias, Greek sculptor (ca. 500–ca. 432 B.C.), 5
Philip II, King of Spain (1527–1598), 55
Philip IV, King of Spain (1605–1665), 186
Philip the Bold, Duke of Burgundy (1336–1397), 33, 58
Philip the Good, Duke of Burgundy (1419–1467), 34, 37, 58
Philosophes, Les, 200, 201, 203
Philosophy, 246
    Absolutism (Hobbes), 132
    Cartesian, 131
    Christian existentialism, 330
    Enlightenment, 135, 137–38
    existentialism, 254, 327–30, 406
    Greek, 4
    liberalism, 250
    reality, concepts of, 3–4, 9
    Renaissance, 10
    transcendentalism, 262
    utilitarianism, 250
Photography, 299, 354, 379–82
Photorealism, in art, 372–73
Picasso, Pablo, Spanish artist (1881–1973), 187, 308, 314, 351–54, 388
    Blue period, 352
    Cubism, 352–53
    Rose period, 352
Pico della Mirandola, Giovanni, humanist writer (1463–1494), 10
Pietà (Michelangelo), **41**
Pilgrimage to Cythera, A (Watteau), **195**
Pippin, Horace, American artist (1888–1946), 375, 376

Pitt, William, British statesman (1708–1778), 139
Pizarro, Francisco, Spanish explorer (1471–1541), 13, 47
Planck, Max, German physicist (1858–1947), 315, 316
Planck's constant, 315, 318
Plato, Greek philosopher (427–347 B.C.), 3, 9, 10, 44, 67, 68, 250, 327
Platonic Academy, Florence, 10, 31, 42
Platonic love, 10
Plotinus, Hellenistic philosopher, founder of Neoplatonism, 10
Poe, Edgar Allen, American writer (1809–1849), 260–62
Poems (Dickinson), 268
    VI *A Service of Song,* 268
    XLVI *Dying,* 268
    XVII *I Never Saw a Moor,* 268
    X *I Died for Beauty,* 268
    XI *Much Madness is Divinest Sense,* 268
    XXVII *The Chariot,* 268
Poetry
    Neoclassic, 164–68
    realism, 264–65, 268–69
    Renaissance, 71–72, 85–86
    Romantic, 238–45, 273, 274
    seventeenth-century, 139–41
    twentieth-century, 320–23, 324, 332–34, 408–9
    Victorian, 252–54
Pollock, Jackson, American painter (1912–1956), 363–64, 366
Polo, Marco, Venetian traveler (1254–1324), 12
Pompadour, Jeanne Antoinette Poisson, Marquise (Madame) de, mistress of Louis XV (1721–1764), 195, 200
Pompeii, 201, 202
Pop art, 364–66
Pope, Alexander, English poet (1688–1744), 135, 164–68 (text), 172
Popes. *See names of individual popes*
Porgy and Bess (Gershwin), 395
Portent, The (Melville), 264 (text)
Portland Public Services Building (Graves), **385**
Portrait of a Lady (circle of David), **202**
Portrait of a Lady (van der Weyden), **37**
Portrait of an Officer (Hals), **191**
Portrait of Henri Michaux (Dubuffet), 367, **369**
Portrait of Lincoln (Brady), **229**
Post-Impressionism, in art, 303–9
Poussin, Nicholas, French painter (1593–1665), 141, 189, 195, 303, 307
Poussinist(s), 189, 272, 290
Pozzo, Andrea, Italian artist (1642–1709), 187
Praise of Folly, (Erasmus), 66, 72–75 (text)
Praxiteles, Greek sculptor (fl. 370–330 B.C.), 27

Predestination, 16

Prelude in d minor, op. 28, no. 24 (Chopin), music, 275

Preludes, Les (Liszt), 279

Prelude to the Afternoon of a Faun (Debussy), 284

Presentation in the Temple, The (Memling), 37

Prince, The (Machiavelli), 66, 76–85 (text)

Principia (Mathematical Principles of Natural Philosophy) (Newton), 132

Principle of Uncertainty (Heisenberg), 315, 316

Printing, 12

Printing press, 12, 129

Prokofiev, Sergei, Russian composer (1891–1953), 208, 390, 391

Prometheus (Byron), 241 (text)

Prometheus Unbound (Byron), 241

Prophet ("Zuccone"; Donatello), **26**

Protestantism, 16, 17, 19, 48, 55

Protestant work ethic, 17, 225

Ptolemy (Claudius Ptolemaeus), Graeco-Egyptian mathematician and astronomer (fl. 2nd c.), 11

Puccini, Giacomo, Italian opera composer (1858–1924), 281–82

Pugin, Augustus Welby, Gothic revivalist architect (1812–1852), 292

Puritan(s), 132, 141

Q

Quadrille at the Moulin Rouge (Toulouse-Lautrec), 307–**8**

Quantum theory, 315–16, 318

Queen's House, Greenwich, (Jones), **198**

R

Rabelais, François, French writer (1494–1553), 10, 65, 67, 68, 90–91 (text)

Rachmaninoff, Sergei, Russian-American composer (1873–1943), 272

Racine, Jean Baptiste, French dramatic poet (1639–1699), 141, 213

Racism, 339–45

Radio Tubes (Davis), 354–**55**

Raft of the Medusa, The (Géricault), 289

Ragtime, 399, 401, 403

Randall, John Herman, Jr., American philosopher (1899–1980), 131 (quote)

Rape of the Daughters of Leucippus (Rubens), **187**

Raphael (Raffaello Sanzio), Italian artist (1483–1520), 5, 20, 26, 39, 43, 44–45, 47, 50, 59, 71, 186, 189

Rauschenberg, Robert, American artist (b. 1925), 365

Ravel, Maurice, French composer (1875–1937), 282

Realism, in art, 293–95, 360–61, 372–73

Reality, concepts of, 3–4, 9

Red Badge of Courage (Crane), 269

Reed, Henry, American poet (1914–1986), 424

Reformation, 4, 12, 14–16, 37, 39, 43, 54, 129, 131, 207

Reign of Terror (France), 223, 288

Relativity, theory of, 316–17, 318

Rembrandt van Rijn, Dutch painter (1606–1669), 2, 37, 181, 182, 192, 194, 287, 294, 382

Renaissance, 3, 4, 8–125 (unit 6), 187, 189, 191, 193, 198, 207, 297, 352, 409

Renaissance Italy (map), 20

Renoir, Pierre Auguste, French painter (1841–1919), 195, 282, 297, 299, 300, 302

Revolution

American (1775–1783), 132, 179, 194, 223, 247

French (1789–1815), 132, 138, 139, 194, 201, 223–24, 238, 239, 247

Mexican (1910–1940), 361

Russian (1917), 322

Rhodes, Cecil John, British imperialist (1853–1902), 249

Rhodora, The (Emerson), 262 (text)

Rich, Adrienne, American poet (b. 1929), 426–27

Richelieu, Cardinal, chief minister of Louis XIII (1585–1642), 132

Richter, Gerhard, German artist (b. 1932), 382, 383

Rigaud, Hyacinthe, French artist (1659–1743), 190

Riley, Bridget, English artist (b. 1931), 367, 369

Rite of Spring, The (Stravinsky) music, (Listening Example 32), 388–89

Rivera, Diego, Mexican artist (1886–1957), 361, 363, 378

Robespierre, Maximilian Marie Isidore, leader in French Revolution (1758–1794), 223

Rockefeller, John D., American industrialist (1839–1937), 249, 250

Rococo style

in architecture, 198

in art, 194–97

in music, 213–14, 215

Rodin, Auguste, French sculptor (1840–1917), 302–3, 354, 356

Roman(s), 23, 76, 142, 199, 205

Romanticism, 189, 234–45, 260–63

Romantic Movement, 137, 138, 234, 238–45

Rome, 24, 183, 187, 200, 201, 203

Rondanini Pietà (Michelangelo), **49**

Roof Gossips (Sloan), **360**–61

Room of One's Own, A (Woolf), 334

Rorem, Ned, American composer (b. 1923), 2 (quote)

Rossini, Gioachino, Italian opera composer (1792–1868), 272

Rossner, Judith, American writer (b. 1935), 406

Rostow, Walt Whitman, American economist (b. 1916), 226 (quote)

Rothko, Mark, Russian-American artist (1903–1970), 364–65

Rouault, Georges, French painter (1871–1958), 349, 350

Rouen Cathedral, West Facade, Sunlight (Monet), 298–**99**

Rousseau, Henri, French artist (1844–1910), 308–9, 354, 375

Rousseau, Jean-Jacques, French philosopher (1712–1778), 69, 138, 234, 239, 290, 293

Rubenist(s), 189, 272, 290

Rubens, Peter Paul, Flemish painter and statesman (1577–1640), 55, 186, 187, 188, 189, 198, 299

Ruisdael, Jacob van, Dutch artist (ca. 1628–1682), 194

Running Fence (Christo), **374**

Russell, Bertrand, British philosopher and mathematician (1872–1970), 246

Russell, Terry; J. T., and a Levi Jacket (Duecker), **373**

Russian Revolution (1917), 322

S

Saarinen, Eero, Finnish-American architect (1910–1961), 379, 380

Sad and Happy Tidal Wave (Bartlett), 383, **384**

St. Mark's Cathedral, Venice, 57, **61–62**

St. Martin-in-the-Fields, London, (Gibbs), **199**

St. Mary Magdalen Church. *See* Madeleine, The

St. Paul's Cathedral (Wren), 198–**99**

St. Peter's, Old, Rome, 43, 185

St. Peter's Basilica, Rome, 14, 43, 49, 183–**84,** 186

Salinas, Porfirio, American artist (1912–1973), 375

Salle, David, American painter (b. 1952), 383

San Carlo alle Quattro Fontane, Rome (Borromini), **185**

Santa Croce, Church of, Florence, 24

Santa Maria del Fiore, Florence, **23–24**

Santa Maria Novella, Florence (Alberti), 24, **30**, 181

Sant' Ignazio, Rome, 187

Sappho of Lesbos, Greek poet-musician (fl. 6th c. B.C.), 273

Sartre, Jean Paul, French novelist and philosopher (1905–1980), 327, 328–29

Savonarola, Girolamo, Italian religious reformer (1452–1498), 41

Scarlatti, Domenico, Italian composer (1687–1757), 213

Schelling, Friedrich Wilhelm Joseph von, German philosopher (15–1854), 238

Schillebeeckx, Edward, Dutch Roman Catholic theologian (b. 1914), 330

Schiller, Friedrich von, German dramatist, poet, and historian (1759–1805), 238

Schnabel, Julian, American artist (b. 1951), 383

Schoenberg, Arnold, Austrian composer (1874–1951), **389**, 392

Scholder, Fritz, American painter (b. 1937), 369–70

School of Athens, The (Raphael), **45**

Schopenhauer, Arthur, German philosopher (1788–1860), 238

Schubert, Franz Peter, Austrian composer (1797–1828), 272, 273–74, 286

Schumann, Robert, German composer (1810–1856), 272, 273

Schunnemunk Mountain (Mangold), 382, **383**

Schwitters, Kurt, German artist (1887–1948), 358, 359

Science
    Age of Reason, 132, 134–35
    Greek, 4
    Hellenistic, 129
    nineteenth-century, 248, 249
    Renaissance, 11–12
    seventeenth-century, 129–31, 132
    twentieth-century, 2, 315–18, 412

Science fiction, 412

Scientific method, 3, 129, 130, 136

Scott, Sir Walter, Scottish poet and novelist (1771–1832), 230, 232

Scream, The (Munch), **309**, 362

Sculpture
    Baroque, 183–85
    Impressionism (19th c.), 302–3
    Neoclassic, 203, 204
    Renaissance, 26–27, 30–31, 41–42, 47–48, 49
    Rococo, 196, 197
    twentieth-century, 314, 356, 359–60, 365–67, 370–72, 383, 384

Seagram Building, New York (Mies van der Rohe), 378, **379**, 384

Second Coming, The (Yeats), 322 (text)

Second Inaugural Address (Lincoln), 229 (text)

Second Sex, The (de Beauvoir), 333

Second Treatise on Civil Government (Locke), 135 (quote)

Secretariat Building, United Nations (Harrison, Le Corbusier, et al.), **378**

Self-Portrait (Gauguin), 305, **306**

Self-Portrait (Leyster), **191**

Seligman, Edwin R., American economist (1861–1939), 18 (quote)

Sentaro (DeLap), **371**–72

Service of Song, A (Dickinson), 268 (text)

Seurat, Georges, French painter (1859–1891), 307, 309, 348, 395

Sforza, Ludovico, Duke of Milan (1451–1508), 40

Shakespeare, William, English playwright (1564–1616), 2 (quote), 5, 19 (quote), 65, 66 (quote), 68, 69–70, 97–124 (text), 129 (quote), 278, 290, 320, 334, 339, 405

Shaw, George Bernard, Irish writer, (1856–1950), 409

Shelley, Mary Wollstonecraft, English writer (1797–1851), 241, 242

Shelley, Percy Bysshe, English poet (1792–1822), 240, 241–42, 243, 245, 290

Shepard, Sam, American playwright and actor (b. 1943), 410

Shiloh (Melville), 264 (text)

Shine Perishing Republic (Jeffers), 322–23 (text), 408

Shivering Woman (Barlach), **350**

Shostakovitch, Dmitri, Russian composer (1906–1975), 395

Sichtbar (Schwitters), **358**

Side Frames (di Suvero), **371**

Simon, Father Richard, Biblical scholar (1638–1712), 137

Siqueiros, David Alfaro, Mexican artist (1898–1974), 362, 378

Sir Thomas More (Holbein the Younger), 55, **68**

Sistine Chapel, 42, 47, 48, 85

Sixtus IV, Pope (1414–1484), 14, 39

Sleepers Awake, A Voice is Calling (Bach), music, (Listening Example 22), 211, 212

Sloan, John, American painter (1871–1952), 360–61

Small Crucifixion (Grünewald), **54**–55

Smith, Adam, Scottish economist (1723–1790), 136–37

Smith, David, American sculptor (1906–1965), 372

Smith, W. Eugene, American photographer (1918–1978), 381

Smithson, Robert, American artist (1938–1973), 373–74

Social Contract, The (Rousseau), 234

Social Darwinism, 249, 250

Social Realism, in art, 361–62, 363

Society of Jesus (Jesuit order), 16, 53, 181, 182, 187

Sokrates, Greek philosopher (469–399 B.C.), 2 (quote), 137, 201, 250

Soldier's Embrace, A (Gordimer), 339–44 (text)

Solomon, Temple of, 185

Solon, Athenian lawgiver (ca. 640–558 B.C.), 3

Sonata form, 215–16, 218

Sondheim, Stephen, American composer and lyricist (b. 1930), 395

Song (Donne), 139 (text)

Songs of Experience (Blake), 238

Songs of Innocence (Blake), 238

Sonnets (Michelangelo), 85–86

Sonnets (Petrarch), 71–72

Sophokles, Greek dramatist (ca. 496–406 B.C.), 9

Sorrowful Woman, A (Godwin), 430–32 (text)

Sorrows of Young Werther, The (Goethe), 238, 245

Sower, The (Millet), **293**

Spanish Armada, 19, 52

Spanish Wake (Smith), **381**

Spencer, Herbert, English philosopher (1820–1903), 249

Spinoza, Baruch de, German philosopher (1632–1677), 137, 138

Spiral Jetty (Smithson), 373-**74**

Spirit of the Laws, The (Montesquieu), 135, 138

Spiritual Exercises (Ignatius of Loyola), 185

Spirituals, 396, 398, 399, 400

Spring, Four Seasons (Vivaldi), music, (Listening Example 21), 210, 211

Stalin, Joseph, Soviet dictator (1879–1953), 189, 254, 313, 315, 324, 325, 395

Starry Night (van Gogh), 304, **305**

State Hospital, The (Kienholz), **366**

Stein, Gertrude, American author (1874–1946), 309

Steinbeck, John, American novelist (1902–1968), 381

Stieglitz, Alfred, American photographer (1864–1946), 354

Still Life (Picasso), 352, **353**

Stockhausen, Karlheinz, Swedish composer (b. 1928), 393, 394

Story of Adam and Eve (Ghiberti), 25, **26**

Storyville, New Orleans, 400

Stranger, The (Camus), 329

Strauss, Johann, Jr., Austrian composer (1825–1899), 396

Strauss, Richard, Austrian composer (1864–1949), 276, 278, **279**–80, 283

Stravinsky, Igor, Russian-American composer (1882–1971), 208, **388**, 393

String Quartet in F Major, op. 3, no. 5 (Haydn), 215–16

Stuart, Gilbert, American painter (1755–1828), 204

Subjection of Women, The (Mill), 250, 333
Sullivan, Louis, American architect (1856–1924), 378
Summer (Kandinsky), **351**
Sunday Afternoon on the Island of La Grande Jatte (Seurat), **307,** 395
Supper at Emmaus (Caravaggio), 182–**83**
Surrealism, in art, 359–60
Suvero, Mark di, American artist (b. 1933), 371
Swift, Jonathan, English satirist (1667–1745), 168–71
Swing, The (Fragonard), **196**
Sydney Opera House (Utzon), 379, **380**
Sympathy (Dunbar), 269 (text)
Symphonie Fantastique (Berlioz), music, (Listening Example 29), 278
Symphony No. 3 in E-flat Major, op. 55 (*Eroica*) (Beethoven), 218
Symphony No. 4 in A Major, op. 90 (Mendelssohn), 276, 277
Symphony No. 5 (Shostakovitch), 395
Symphony No. 5 in B-flat Major, op. 100 (Prokofiev), 391
Symphony No. 5 in C minor, op. 67 (Beethoven), music, (Listening Example 26), 218–19
Symphony No. 7 (Leningrad; Shostakovitch), 395
Symphony No. 9 in d minor (Beethoven), 218, 238
Symphony No. 35 in D (Haffner; Mozart), music, (Listening Example 25), 216, 217

T

Take Five (Desmond), music, (Listening Example 39), 403
Talleyrand, Charles Maurice de, French statesman (1754–1838), 225
Tamayo, Rufino, Mexican artist (b. 1899), 369, 370, 375
Tanguy, Ives, French-American painter (1900–1955), 355
Tartuffe, 142
Tartuffe (Molière), 143–64 (text)
Tchaikovsky, Peter Ilich, Russian composer (1840–1893), 189, 276, 277, 280, **281**
Technology, 11, 129, 345, 354, 363, 385, 393, 412
Telescope, 129, 130
Tempest, The (Shakespeare), 69–70, 97–124 (text)
Tempietto Chapel, San Pietro in Montorio, Rome (Bramante), **43,** 199
Tenebrae (Levertov), 325 (text)
Tennyson, Alfred Lord, English poet (1809–1892), 227, 228, 252
Terminal, The (Stieglitz), 354, **355**

Tetzel, Johann, Dominican monk (1465–1519), 14
Thackeray, William Makepeace, English novelist (1811–1863), 265
Thatcher, Margaret, former English Prime Minister (b. 1925), 333
Theatre of the Absurd, 410
Thinker, The (Rodin), 302–**3**
Third-Class Carriage (Daumier), **294,** 307
Third of May, The (Goya), **288**
Third Wave, The (Toffler), 345
Thirty Years' War (1618–1648), 20, 129, 187, 327
Thomas, Dylan, Welsh poet (1914–1953), 409
Thoreau, Henry David, American author and naturalist (1817–1862), 2 (quote), 262, 264, 391
Threepenny Opera (Brecht and Weill), 395
Three Places in New England (Ives), music, (Listening Example 34), 392
Three Songs (Webern), music, (Listening Example 35), 392
Throne of St. Peter (Bernini), 184
Thucydides, Athenian historian (471–399 B.C.), 9, 10
Thyrsis, Sleepest Thou? (Bennet), music, (Listening Example 19), 63
Tiffany, Louis Comfort, American designer of stained glass (1848–1933), 362
Tiger, The (Blake), 238, 239 (text), 323
Till Eulenspiegel's Merry Pranks (Strauss), 279–80
Time Charts
    Early Modern World, 128
    Middle Modern World, 222
    Renaissance, 8
    Twentieth Century, 312
Tintoretto (Jacopo Robusti), Venetian painter (1518–1594), 50–52, 186, 189
Titian (Tiziano Vecellio), Venetian painter (ca. 1488–1576), 46, 50, 52, 186, 287
To a Skylark (Shelley), 241, 242 (text)
Toffler, Alvin, American futurist writer (b. 1928), 345
To His Coy Mistress (Marvell), 140 (text)
Tomb of
    Giuliano de' Medici (Michelangelo), **47**–48
    Lorenzo de' Medici (Michelangelo), **48**
Tone poem, in music, 279–80
Toulouse-Lautrec, Henri de, French artist (1864–1901), 307–8, 354
Townhouse No. 1 of Cresent Circle, Bath, 199–200
Tragedy, The (Picasso), **352**
Trajan's Column, 28
Transcendentalism, 262
Treatise on Human Nature Being an Attempt to Introduce the Experimental Method of

Reasoning into Moral Subjects, A (Hume), 137
Treaty of Versailles, 313, 314, 315
Tribute Money, The (Masaccio), 27–**28,** 352
Trojan Women, The (Euripides), 288
Trotsky, Leon, Russian revolutionary (1879–1940), 313
Tubman, Harriet, American abolitionist (ca. 1820–1913), 333, 376
Tuchman, Barbara, American historian (1912–1989), 232
Turner, Joseph M. W., English painter (1775–1851), 290, 291
Twain, Mark (pseud. of Samuel Langhorne Clemens), American writer (1835–1910), 265–67, 268, 291, 295
TWA Terminal, New York (Saarinen), 379, **380**
Two Songs (Rich), 426–27 (text)
Tyler, Anne, American novelist (b. 1941), 406

U

Uccello, Paolo, Florentine painter (1397–1475), 28
Ulysses (Tennyson), 252 (text)
Unhorsing of Bernardino della Carda, The Battle of San Romano (Uccello), **28**
Unitarian church, 16
United Nations, 324, 325, 327, 378
United States, Growth of the (map), 261
Utamaro, Kitagawa, Japanese print maker (fl. 18th century), (Figure 25.36), 304
Utilitarianism, 250
Utilitarian View of the Monitor's Fight, A (Melville), 265 (text)
Utopia, 67, 70, 92, 395
Utopia (More), 13, 67–69, 92–96 (text)
Utzon, Joern, Danish architect (b. 1918), 379, 380
Uwaki. Half-Length Portrait (Utamaro), 304

V

Valla, Lorenzo, Renaissance scholar (ca. 1407–1457), 10
Vanderbilt, William, American railroad magnate (1821–1885), 250
van der Weyden, Rogier, Flemish painter (1400–1464), 36–37, 57
van Dyck, Anthony, Flemish painter (1599–1641), 188, 189, 193, 198
van Eyck, Jan, Flemish painter (1390–1441), 28, 34–36, 37, 46, 55, 57, 58
van Gogh, Vincent, Dutch painter (1853–1890), 303–4, 306, 309, 348, 349, 354, 382
Vasari, Giorgio, Italian art historian (1511–1574), 10, 32, 34, 40, 45, 47

Vase (Richter), 382, **383**
Vatican City, 227
Velasquez, Diego, Spanish painter (1599–1660), 182, 287, 367
Veni Sponsa Christi (Palestrina), music, (Listening Example 17), 60–61
Ventre Legislatif, Le (Daumier), **294**
Venus Consoling Love (Boucher), 195, **196**
Venus with a Mirror (Titian), **50**
Verdi, Giuseppe, Italian opera composer (1813–1901), 189, 272, 281
Verlaine, Paul, French poet (1844–1896), 284
Vermeer, Jan, Dutch painter (1632–1675), 192–93, 194, 203
Verne, Jules, English novelist (1828–1905), 412
Veronese, Paolo, Venetian painter (1528–1588), 52
Verrocchio, Andrea di Cioni, Florentine sculptor (1435–1488), 30, 39, 372
Versailles, Palace of (le Vau and Mansart), 189–**90**, 207
Versailles, Treaty of, 313, 314, 315
Victor Emmanuel II, King of Italy (1820–1878), 227
Victoria Alexandrina, Queen of England (1819–1901), 226, 229, 333
Victorian Gothic mansion, **292**
Victorian Interior (Pippin), 375, **376**
Vietnam War, 325, 364, 403, 406
Vietnam War Memorial, Washington, D.C., 372
Vignola, Giacomo da, Italian architect (1507–1573), 181–82
Vignon, Pierre, French architect (1762–1828), 286
Viking(s), 12
Village Bride, The (Greuze), 200, **201**
Villa Rotunda (Palladio), **52**
Villa Savoye (Corbusier), **363**
Vindication of the Rights of Woman (Wollstonecraft), 243, 333
Violin Concerto (Berg), music, (Listening Example 33), 390
Virgil (Publius Vergilius Maro), Latin poet (70–19 B.C.), 9, 65, 433
Virginia State Capital (Jefferson), **205**
Virtu, "excellence as a person" (Renaissance), 11, 28
Vision After the Sermon (Jacob Wrestling with the Angel) (Gauguin), 304–**5**
Vitruvius Pollio Marcus, Roman architect and engineer (1st c. B.C.), 29
Vivaldi, Antonio, Italian composer (1685–1743), 210, 211

Voiles (Sails) (Debussy), music, (Listening Example 31), 284
Voltaire (François Marie Arouet), French writer and political philosopher (1694–1778), 3, 138, 164, 172–79, 195, **203**

W

Wagner, Richard, German composer (1813–1883), 272, 276, 278, 281, 282, 283, 389
Waiting for Godot (Beckett), 410
Waiting Indian No. 4 (Scholder), **370**
Waldo, Peter, French religious reformer (d. 1217), 14
Walking Man, The (Rodin), **302**
Wallace, Alfred Russel, English naturalist (1823–1913), 248
War
 Cold, 324, 326, 327
 Crimean, 227
 Franco-Prussian, 226
 Korean, 325, 364, 406
 Persian Gulf, 327
 Vietnam, 325, 364, 403, 406
 World War I (Great), 233, 313, 318, 320, 327, 350, 357, 389, 393, 412
 World War II, 40, 226, 233, 313, 314, 323, 324, 325, 326, 327, 331, 350, 351, 362, 363, 364, 367, 378, 397, 401, 402, 405, 406, 410, 411
Washington, George, American general and first president (1732–1799), 203, 204
Wasserstein, Wendy, American playwright (b. 1950), 410
Waterloo, 223, 224
Watt, James, Scottish scientist and inventor (1736–1819), 226
Watteau, Antoine, French painter (1684–1721), 195, 213
Webern, Anton, Austrian composer (1883–1945), **392**
Weill, Kurt, German-American composer (1900–1950), 395
Wells, H(erbert), G(eorge), English writer (1866–1946), 412
Welty, Eudora, American novelist (b. 1909), 415–18
We Real Cool (Brooks), 425 (text)
Wesley, John, founder of Methodist church (1703–1791), 16
Western civilization, 2–3, 131, 320, 327, 412
West-Eastern Divan (Goethe), 244 (text)

Westwood Children, The (Johnson), 375, **376**
Wheatfields (van Ruisdael), **194**
When All My Five and Country Senses (Thomas), 409 (text)
When a Man Hath No Freedom to Fight for at Home (Byron), 240 (text)
Where Do We Come From? What Are We? Where Are We Going? (Gauguin), **306**
Whistler, James McNeil, American painter (1834–1903), 300, 301–2, 307
White, Charles, American artist (b. 1918), 378
White Girl: Symphony in White, No. 1, The (Whistler), 301–**2**
Whitman, Walt, American poet (1819–1892), 263, 264, 392
Wiclif (or Wycliffe), John, English religious reformer (1320–1389), 14
Wieskirche, Upper Bavaria (Zimmermann), **198**
Wilde, Oscar, English author (1854–1900), 5 (quote), 245
Wilhelm I, Emperor of Prussia (1871–1888), 226
Wilhelm II, Emperor of Germany (1888–1918), 226, 313
William III of Orange and Mary II, King and Queen of England (1650–1702), 132
William IV, King of England (1765–1837), 229
Williams, William Carlos, American physician and author (1883–1963), 407
Will to Power, The (Nietzsche), 327
Wilson, August, American playwright (b. 1945), 410
Wilson, Woodrow, American 27th president (1856–1924), 313
Winter (Return of the Hunters), 55–**56**
Witches Hammer, The, 38
Wivenhoe Park, Essex (Constable), 290, **291**
Wolfe, Tom, American writer and journalist (b. 1931), 412
Wollstonecraft, Mary, English feminist and writer (1759–1797), 243, 333
Woman Holding a Balance (Vermeer), **193**
Woman I (de Kooning), 364
Women and Dog (Marisol), **366**
Woodruff, Hale, American artist (1900–1980), 376, 378
Woolf, Virginia, English author (1882–1941), 334–38
Wordsworth, William, English poet (1770–1850), 239, 250, 286, 290, 425
World Exploration 1271–1295; 1486–1611 (map), 13

World Is Too Much With Us, The (Wordsworth), 239 (text)
World of Will and Idea, The (Schopenhauer), 238
World War I, 234, 313, 318, 320, 327, 350, 357, 389, 393, 412
World War I, Territorial Changes following (map), 234
World War II, 226, 313, 314, 323, 324, 325, 326, 327, 331, 350, 351, 362, 363, 364, 367, 378, 397, 401, 402, 405, 406, 410, 411
World War II, April 1945 (Flack), **373**
Worn Path, The (Welty), 415–18 (text)
Wren, Sir Christopher, English architect (1632–1723), 198–99
Wright, Frank Lloyd, American architect (1869–1959), 363, 378–79

X

X (Bladen), **372**

Y

Yeats, William Butler, Irish poet (1865–1939), 322
Yet Do I Marvel (Cullen), 323 (text)

Z

Zapata, Emiliano, Mexican revolutionary leader (ca. 1879–1919), 362
Zapatistas (Orozco), **361**–62
Zimmermann, Dominikus, German architect (1685–1766), 198
Zola, Émile, French novelist (1840–1902), 226, 265, 281, 300
Zuccone (Donatello), **26**
Zurbarán, Francisco de, Spanish painter (1598–1664), 186
Zwingli, Ulrich, Swiss leader of the Reformation (1484–1531), 16

VOLUME II

THE HUMANITIES IN WESTERN CULTURE

EDITION IX

 WCB Brown & Benchmark

ISBN 0-697-10667-5

90000

9 780697 106674

LAMM CROSS